Reference Guides in Literature

Ronald Gottesman, *Editor*
Joseph Katz, *Consulting Editor*

Mark Twain:
A Reference Guide

Thomas Asa Tenney

Foreword by Hamlin Hill

G. K. HALL & CO., 70 LINCOLN STREET, BOSTON MASS.

Library of Congress Cataloging in Publication Data

Tenney, Thomas
    Mark Twain: a reference guide.

    (Reference guides in literature)
    Includes index.
    1.   Clemens, Samuel Langhorne, 1835 - 1910—Bibliography.
I.   Title.
Z8176.T45 (PS1331)   016.818′4′09   76-41752
ISBN 0-8186-7966-2

This publication is printed on permanent/durable acid-free paper
MANUFACTURED IN THE UNITED STATES OF AMERICA

to
Margaret, Bob, Charles, and Will
with love and gratitude

Contents

Foreword

"It is not worth the while," Thoreau observed, "to go round the world to count the cats in Zanzibar." But if Professor Tenney has had some stray felines to deal with among his 4900 entries, he also has the advantage of knowing that his Reference Guide to Mark Twain scholarship and criticism has a more vital significance than the census that Thoreau imagined.

Mark Twain has enjoyed a dual reputation (curiously harmonious with his dual personality) for over half a century. Highbrowed critics and harmless scholars have produced every conceivable "reading" of his works, from imaginative interpretations to definitive texts. They have explicated a single word and they have used Mark Twain to make grand syntheses of American thought and character. They have created, blindly followed, and sometimes vigorously attacked the "trends" in Mark Twain scholarship--trends which themselves have been both provocative and ultimately stultifying. The very quantity of academic research and publication about Mark Twain does much to bring into question the notion of an Establishment which, like eunuchs, protects its one-man harem from unauthorized violation. If such an arrangement does exist, it is the largest collection of eunuchs since Sollermun kept what Jim calls in Huckleberry Finn his "bo'd'n-house."

While academia has been fussing with Mark Twain's respectable image, his popular reputation has never suffered from fluctuations of any sort. Celebrities begin interviews with, "As Mark Twain once said..." He is the American touchstone for comparison with practically anything--the Mississippi, the Far West, post-Civil War New England, the debasement of the Protestant work ethic, even (in the recent Indo-China fiasco) as a rival to Thoreau on disobedience to law. Two idolatrous publications--The Twainian and the Mark Twain Journal--are devoted almost exclusively to him; and it will not surprise anyone if, before long, the Reader's Digest begins printing direct quotations from him in red ink. At least ten documentary educational movies about Mark Twain were produced between 1946 and 1969 to carry the Sacred Relic down to junior-high-school level for Adoration by the next generation.

This is not the place to raise questions about what this dual reputation has done to Mark Twain--about the accuracy of either interpretation, or the conflict between the two images, or the wisdom of attempting to deflate the folk-hero concept of his life and literary career. But this volume is the foundation and starting-place for dozens of such investigations. Though Henry Adams was being facetious about plotting the curve of history into the future, it is possible with this bibliography at least to plot backward from 1974 the curves of Mark Twain's reputation.

If it is one of the most paradoxical literary reputations in our culture, it is also one of the most fundamental to try to comprehend. And the very elusiveness of the man heightens the challenge of attempting to find his essential qualities. That search must begin here.

If the editors of the Literary History of the United States were correct back in 1948 that "each generation must define the past in its own terms," maybe it will be possible to use Professor Tenney's scrupulous checklist to discern areas which are not yet examined and methods which have not yet been exhausted. This bibliography would be a Godsend if it only underscored those subjects of scholarly investigation which have been explored, mapped, meted and bounded, and subdivided to the point of contemptuous familiarity.

What can be said without the need of prophecy is that the flood will continue. However the next generation defines Mark Twain, it will find him as irrestible as earlier generations have; perhaps, with this survey of secondary materials before it, it can find not only more to say but also some important things which have not been said before. Scholarship should build upon its earlier insights, refining rather than merely repeating them. Here is the survey of what scholarship has done so far; and here, by implication at least, is the challenge to move ahead.

Hamlin Hill
University of New Mexico

Introduction

This <u>Reference Guide</u> collects in a single volume all listings of books, reviews, and articles concerning Mark Twain in the major bibliographies through 1974. Except where indicated by an asterisk, the material for each entry has been personally examined; there are descriptive annotations, where possible noting any reprintings or abstracts published elsewhere. The index lists authors, topics, and works by Mark Twain, and also includes sections for the several hundred articles which contain his letters or photographs and drawings of him. The work here begun will be corrected, expanded, and kept up to date in an annual supplement in <u>American Literary Realism</u>.

In the compilation I have tried to be objective and complete within the scope of coverage. The annotations are descriptions rather than abstracts, and as an aid to evaluation I have often quoted directly so authors might describe their own work; cross-references or the index will lead the reader to reviews of books listed and to replies in critical controversies. I have made no attempt to limit coverage to what I personally consider important: if a book or article appears in another bibliography the reader should be able to decide from my annotation whether he would find it useful. Some books and articles do not fulfill the promise of their titles (<u>See</u> 1949.B45 and 1964.B27, for example), and time need not be wasted on them again. I have excluded only dissertations (which ought to be treated in a volume of their own), ordinary editions of Mark Twain's works without significant editing or introductions, and appreciative poems by persons who did not know him. Finally, I have listed few newspaper interviews of Mark Twain, because Louis J. Budd has compiled a very full list, with summaries (scheduled for publication in January, 1977).

This <u>Reference Guide</u> includes and extends the coverage of the major bibliographies. The original finding-list followed the Modern Humanities Research Association's <u>Annual Bibliography of English Language and Literature</u>, Roger Asselineau's <u>The Literary Reputation of Mark Twain</u> (1954.A2), Beebe and Feaster's checklist in <u>Modern Fiction Studies</u> (1968.B6), Lewis Leary's first two volumes of <u>Articles on American Literature</u> (1954.B35 and 1970.B51), and the bibliographies in Henderson (1911.A3) and the early issues of <u>The Twainian</u> (1939.B12, 1940.B10, and 1943.B3); there were also useful leads in the dissertations of Robert Rodney (1945.A2) and Webster L. Smalley (1948.A3). A full search of the abstracts in <u>Abstracts of English Studies</u>, <u>American Literature Abstracts</u>, and <u>MLA Abstracts</u> (all of which are cited in the annotations in this <u>Reference Guide</u>) revealed more articles. Finally, while waiting for printer's proofs I had time to check my text against the <u>MLA Bibliography</u> from the first volume, and the installments of "Articles on American Literature" in <u>American Literature</u> from 1951-1974; a few more items turned up, have been checked where possible, and are listed in the Addenda beginning on p. 397. The reader looking for material I might have missed should consult the "Bibliographies" heading in my index.

INTRODUCTION

The intended value of this guide to writings about Mark Twain has been twofold: not only to record the history of his popular and critical reputation, but also to codify a substantial body of factual data which would otherwise be difficult to trace. The major studies of Mark Twain are all listed here, but there are also many brief notes on sources and analogues, family history, and reminiscences by people who knew or met him; taken collectively, they add detail and insight to the picture of an important and complicated figure in our national literature.

In the beginning of my work I was sometimes impatient with the human limitations of my predecessors, but experience has bred respect for their accuracy and thoroughness in a task which only the foolhardy would attempt to expand. I am particularly grateful for the early work of Roger Asselineau, a remarkable achievement under pressure of time and one which proved to be so useful that it was later reprinted in this country; Professor Asselineau pointed the way to many items I should otherwise have missed.

A Reference Guide such as this could not have been produced without the facilities of numerous libraries and the skilled, patient help of their staffs. I am indebted to the libraries of Columbia University, Harvard University, the University of Pennsylvania, Bryn Mawr College, the University of North Carolina, and Duke University, and to the Boston, New York, Philadelphia, Chicago, San Francisco, and Oakland public libraries, and the Library Society of Charleston. I am particularly grateful for the hospitality and help I received in three summers in McLennan Library at McGill University; the time spent there was productive and thoroughly pleasant. In Montreal I also found useful material and kind treatment at Sir George Williams University.

No student of Mark Twain should overlook the Mark Twain Papers in The Bancroft Library at the University of California, Berkeley. In addition to the wealth of manuscripts, letters, photographs, scrap-books, newspaper clippings, early editions of Mark Twain's works, and books containing his marginal notations, there are extensive holdings in secondary materials; among the latter are books, offprints of articles, and a number of master's essays and doctoral dissertations. Unfortunately, I was able to spend only a week there, but the fine collection and the generous help of Frederick Anderson made it the most enjoyable week in the long period of compilation. The collection at Berkeley is still growing, and it should be the first thought for any person who has Mark Twain material of any sort and wishes to make it more accessible to scholars.

I would like to thank my colleague Robert Geraldi for his help with a number of articles in Italian, and Susan and Joanne Bogdanowicz for their accurate work in numbering the entries and typing the mass of index material. I also owe thanks to my sons Bob, Charles, and Will for their careful work on the finding list and the preliminary sorting of the 15,000 index slips.

My debt to the fraternity of Mark Twain scholars is incalculable, both for the material they have provided and the insights they have shared; working with their published writing has been a continuing pleasure, and I have tried to repay them with as comprehensive and accurate a summary of their work as I could achieve. The task should be continued, and I earnestly solicit corrections and additions from those who use this guide.

List of Abbreviations

AES   Abstracts of English Studies (the statement "reprinted in Twainian" after the listing of an AES citation indicates a reprinting of the abstract, not the article abstracted)

ALA   American Literature Abstracts

CY   A Connecticut Yankee in King Arthur's Court (1889)

FE   Following the Equator (1897)

GA   The Gilded Age (1874)

"Hadleyburg"   "The Man that Corrupted Hadleyburg"; also, the book, The Man that Corrupted Hadleyburg, and Other Stories and Essays (1900)

HF   Adventures of Huckleberry Finn (1885)

IA   The Innocents Abroad (1869)

JA   Personal Recollections of Joan of Arc (1896); this should not be confused with the article, "Saint Joan of Arc" (1904)

LOM   Life on the Mississippi (1883)

MT   Mark Twain; this abbreviation is also used for Samuel Langhorne Clemens, who created Mark Twain. The purpose here is to provide an easily recognizable abbreviation for a bibliography, with no attempt to resolve the obvious absurdity of referring to MT's boyhood, and MT's mother, sister and brothers, and so on.

MS   The Mysterious Stranger (1916)

P&P   The Prince and the Pauper (1882)

PW   The Tragedy of Pudd'nhead Wilson and the Comedy of Those Extraordinary Twins (1894)

RI   Roughing It (1872)

TA   A Tramp Abroad (1880)

TS   The Adventures of Tom Sawyer (1876); also used as part of
                            the titles of Tom Sawyer Abroad (1894) and Tom Sawyer,
                            Detective (1896)

Note: Where a journal lists a winter issue as for two years connected by a hy-
        phen (as: Winter 1972-1973) it has been my practice to list entries
        from that issue for the earlier year.

Writings about Mark Twain, 1858-1975

A1 ANON. Mark Twain: Biography-Reminiscence
[undated scrap-book in Chicago Public Libra-
ry].
Magazine articles and mounted newspaper
clippings (mainly portraits and obituaries);
much is familiar material, but the present
bibliography lists this as the source of
items from the Hannibal Morning Journal for
April 22, 24, 26, 1910; from the St. Louis
Times for April 22, 1910; from the Politikens Kronik (n.p.) for April 23, 1910; and
for the 1914 Catalogue of First and Other
Editions of the Writings of "Mark Twain,"
Samuel Langhorne Clemens, and of Lafcadio
Hearn.

A2 ANON. Mark Twain Region of Missouri. Jefferson City, Missouri: Missouri State Division
of Resources and Development.
A pamphlet of photographs of the region,
some showing MT's birthplace and the MT
State Park, monuments, etc., but providing
no new information.

A3 *DUNCAN, CAPTAIN CHARLES. [Manuscript log of
the Quaker City trip; in the Patten Free Library, Bath, Maine.]
[Source: Charles Shain, in "The Journal
of the Quaker City Captain" (1955) and in
Ganzel (1968), p. xiii and passim.] Provides the captain's perspective on the tour
on which IA is based.

A4 LAUTREC, GABRIEL DE. Contes Choisis par Mark
Twain Traduits de l'anglais par Gabriel de
Lautrec et précédés d'une étude sur l'humour. Paris: Nelson, Editeurs [Londres,
Edimbourg et New-York]. "Introduction:
Mark Twain et l'Humour," pp. 9-20.
MT is the best representative of American
humor in France because his pleasantries
are of more general interest than those of
such countrymen as Artemus Ward, but like
all great writers he has become universal
while remaining national; he has painted a
society and a period. Much of the essay is
given over to general discussion of humor.
[Year of publ. not given, but Lautrec mentions MT's death in 1910]

B1 ANDERSON, CARL L. "Strindberg's Translations
of American Humor," Americana Norvegica,
pp. 152-94.
[Source: undated photocopy in Mark Twain
Papers; a preceding article cites sources as
recent as 1964.] August Strindberg translated two volumes of sketches and stories by
MT, Artemus Ward, and others, published in
Stockholm in 1878 and 1879; "perhaps the actual work of translation had not been his at
all, but that of his wife, a writer of ver-
satile talents." The MT works translated
were "Alonzo Fitz Clarence' och Rosannah
Etheltons Kälekshistoria," "Berättelser om
ädla handlingar," and "About Magnanimous-
Incident Literature." "The Swedish translation is, in fact, quite uneven; some parts
are fairly literal and accurate, but most
have been treated cavalierly."

B2 COVENEY, PETER. Poor Monkey.
[Source: Winfield Townley Scott, "Mark
Twain Revisited" (1961).] Contains a chapter on MT, reflecting the Brooks thesis and
attributing the despair and frustration of
MT's later years to his dichotomy between
rebellion and conformity.

B1 *ANON. "A Sad Meeting," St. Louis News and In-
telligencer, June 19, reprinted from Memphis
Eagle and Inquirer.
[Source: Reprinted in Twainian, IX
(January-February, 1950), 2.] On SLC's
grief at seeing his brother Henry, fatally
scalded in the explosion of the steamboat
Pennsylvania.

B1 *WRIGHT, WILLIAM [pseud. DAN DEQUILLE]. "Reporter in California," California Monthly,
IV, 170.

1862 - Shorter Writings

(*WRIGHT, WILLIAM [pseud. Dan DeQuille])
[Source: Edwin A. Ford, A Bibliography
of Literary Journalism in America. Minneapolis: Burgess Publishing Company, 1937.]

1866 A BOOKS - NONE

1866 B SHORTER WRITINGS

B1 *HARTE, BRET [signed F. B. H.] [Estimate of
Mark Twain's October 2, 1866 lecture on the
Sandwich Islands.] Springfield (Mass.)
Daily Republican, (November 10).
[Source: Quoted in Stewart (1941).]

1867 A BOOKS - NONE

1867 B SHORTER WRITINGS

B1 [Announcement of the Quaker City excursion.]
American Agriculturalist, XXVI (March), 86.
Mostly straightforward description of the
projected itinerary. Captain Duncan is described as "the captain who has been eighteen years at sea, about half the time as
master of large ships--who never swore an
oath--never drank a glass of liquor, and
though he has crossed the Atlantic fifty-
eight times, never suffered a shipwreck,
nor lost a man by accident. The company is
to be select--every applicant's name is
submitted to a committee."

B2 *[Reports of Mark Twain's Sandwich Islands
lecture at St. Louis.] Missouri Republican
(St. Louis), March 24, 26, 28.
[Source: Quoted in Lorch (1947),
pp. 299-307.] Includes text of speech
(March 28) and a letter to the editor by
MT (March 24).

B3 WEBB, CHARLES HENRY. "Advertisement," in
MT's The Celebrated Jumping Frog of Calaveras County, and Other Sketches (New York:
C. H. Webb).
MT is known not only as a humorist, but
also as a moralist, "and it is not unlikely
that as such he will go down to posterity,"
although the present volume consists of
humorous writings. "Mark Twain never resorts to tricks of spelling nor rhetorical
buffoonery for the purpose of provoking a
laugh...there are few who can resist the
quaint similies, keen satire, and hard good
sense which form the staple of his writings." Reprinted in Scott (1955), p. 12;
(1967), p. 12.

1868 A BOOKS - NONE

1868 B SHORTER WRITINGS

B1 [HARTE, BRET.] [Review: John Franklin Swift,
Going to Jericho; or, Sketches of Travel in
Spain and the East.] Overland Monthly, I
(July), 101-103.

This book "is in legitimate literary succession to Howell's [sic] Venetian Life,
Ross Browne's multifarious voyages, and Mark
Twain's Holy Land letters. It is somewhat
notable that three of these writers are Cal-
ifornians, and all from the west." Comments
on MT's use of "brickbats on stained glass
windows with damaging effect" and his "lawless humor and lyric fire." [Note that this
precedes the 1869 book publication of MT's
newspaper letters in IA.]

1869 A BOOKS - NONE

1869 B SHORTER WRITINGS

B1 *ANON. [Review: Innocents Abroad.] Buffalo
Express, October 16.
[Source: Reprinted in Anderson (1971),
pp. 25-26.] MT was a part owner of the Express when this review appeared; it is com-
mendatory.

B2 ANON. [Review: Innocents Abroad.] Nation
(New York), IX (September 2), 194-95.
Some of this imitates other writing in the
genre and it is padded for sale by subscription, "but if some of the book is needless,
none of it is really poor, and much of it
very good." It is of some value as description, and fresh and well-told. Reprinted in
Anderson (1971), pp. 21-22.

B3 *ANON. [Review: Innocents Abroad.] Packard's
Monthly, II (October), 318-19.
[Source: Reprinted in Anderson (1971),
pp. 23-24.] Places MT "first among American
humorists. It is, indeed, doubtful if he
has ever had an equal; he certainly has not
had in his line--that of dry, self-contained,
unobtrusive and pervading fun."

B4 *CLEMENS, SAMUEL L. [Letter, satirizing a snob-
bish American family just returned from Europe.] Boston Transcript (December 29),
p. 1.
[Source: Quoted by Arthur L. Vogelback
(1948), p. 111, n. 1.]

B5 *"FOLIO, TOM." [Review: Innocents Abroad.]
Boston Evening Transcript (December 15),
p. 1.
[Source: Reprinted in Anderson (1971),
pp. 31-32.] Praises MT's humor and keen observation.

B6 [HOWELLS, WILLIAM DEAN.] [Review: Innocents
Abroad.] Atlantic Monthly, XXIV (December),
764-66.
The humor is "droll," "good-natured,"
"not always delicate," but reflecting human
nature. The book will give MT a reputation
as more than a newspaper humorist. Reprinted in his My Mark Twain (1910), pp. 107-12;
also in Anderson (1971), pp. 27-30.

1870 A BOOKS - NONE

1870 B SHORTER WRITINGS

B1   *ANON. [Brief biography of MT.] Frank Les-
     lie's Illustrated Newspaper, July 16.
        [Source: Twainian, II (February, 1940),
     7.]

B2   ANON. [Review: Innocents Abroad.] Athe-
     naeum, No. 2239 (September 24), 394-95.
        Recognizes MT's satire as encompassing
     not only the sights and experiences of his
     trip, but also the limitations of his fel-
     low-tourists. Reprinted in Anderson (1971),
     pp. 36-38.

B3   ANON. [Review: Innocents Abroad.] Saturday
     Review (London), XXX (October 8), 467-68.
        Compares MT and his companions to the
     Cook's tourist type of traveler, although
     MT is frank and original in his remarks.
     "In short, his pages may be turned over
     with amusement, as exhibiting more or less
     consciously a very lively portrait of the
     uncultivated American tourist, who may be
     more obtrusive, but not quite so stupidly un-
     observing as our native product. We should
     not choose either of them for our compan-
     ions on a visit to a church or a picture-
     gallery, but we should expect most amuse-
     ment from the Yankee as long as we could
     stand him." Reprinted in Scott (1967),
     pp. 17-21; in Anderson (1971), pp. 36-43.

B4   *BIERCE, AMBROSE. "Town Crier" page, San
     Francisco News-Letter, February 19.
        "Mark Twain, who, whenever he has been
     long enough sober to permit an estimate,
     has been uniformly found to bear a spotless
     character, has got married. It was not the
     act of a desperate man--it was not committed
     while laboring under temporary insanity;
     his insanity is not of that type, nor does
     he ever labor--it was the cool, methodical,
     cumulative, culmination of human nature
     working in the heart of an orphan hankering
     for some one with a fortune to love--some
     one with a bank account to caress. For
     years he has felt this matrimony coming on.
     Ever since he left California there has
     been an undertone of despair running
     through all his letters like the subdued
     wail of a pig in a wash-tub." [Source:
     Quoted by Carey McWilliams in Ambrose
     Bierce: A Biography (1929), p. 88.]

B5   *CABLE, GEORGE WASHINGTON. "Drop Shot," New
     Orleans Picayune, July 17.
        [Source: Reprinted in Turner (1960),
     pp. 4-5.] A regular column, here comparing
     MT and Josh Billings (Henry Wheeler Shaw):
     MT may have "the superior weight of mind,"
     although Cable is more drawn to Josh, "such
     a blessed old fool."

B6   *EGGLESTON, EDWARD. "The November Magazines,"
     The Independent, October 27.
        Eggleston said he was amused by an MT
     sketch in the Galaxy, but was more impressed
     by a poem by Helen Hunt in the same issue.
     [Source: William Peirce Randel, Edward Eg-
     gleston (1947), p. 109.]

B7   [HARTE, BRET.] [Review: Innocents
     Abroad.] Overland Monthly, IV (January),
     100-101.
        Note's MT's fresh vision, although he
     "seems to have followed his guide and guide-
     books with a simple, unconscious fidelity."
     He shows a "serious eloquence," though lack-
     ing "that balance of pathos which we deem
     essential to complete humor." Reprinted in
     Scott (1955), pp. 13-16; (1967), pp. 13-16;
     Cardwell (1963), pp. 1-4; Anderson (1971),
     pp. 32-35.

B8   *HINGSTON, EDWARD P. [Introduction.] The In-
     nocents Abroad. London: John Camden Hotten.
        [Source: Henderson (1911), p. 215;
     Asselineau (1954), No. 1.]

B9   *WARD, WILLIAM. "American Humorists," Macon
     (Mississippi) Beacon (May 14), p. 2.
        [Source: Reprinted in Anderson (1971),
     pp. 44-45.] "But, since Irving, no humor-
     ist in prose has laid the foundation of a
     permanent fame, except it be Mark Twain,
     and this, as in the case of Irving, because
     he is a pure writer. Aside from the subtle
     mirth that lurks through his compositions,
     the grace and finish of his more didactic
     and descriptive sentences indicate more than
     mediocrity, though much of his writing has
     a dash of Bulwer in it."

1871 A BOOKS

A1   *GRISWOLD, MRS. STEPHEN. A Woman's Pilgrimage
     to the Holy Land; or, Pleasant Days Abroad.
     Hartford: J. B. Burr & Hyde.
        [Source: Ganzel (1968), p. xiii and
     passim.] Reminiscences by a fellow-traveler
     on the Quaker City tour on which IA was
     based. See 1907.B21.

1871 B SHORTER WRITINGS

B1   ANON. "American Humour," Graphic (London)
     III (April 1), 295.
        MT, "who does not equal either 'Josh Bil-
     lings' or 'Orpheus C. Kerr,' has rather a
     forced sense of humour"; the writer likes
     MT "best when he is serious, and he can be
     both earnest and poetical," though he lacks
     the genius of Bret Harte.

B2   ANON. "The Literature of the United States in
     1870," Athenaeum, No. 2254 (January 7),
     p. 15.
        Briefly mentions IA, which shows "real
     travels in the East, as they impressed one
     of the drollest of voyagers. But the palm

1871 - Shorter Writings

(ANON.)
must this year be awarded to Mr. Bret
Harte, author of The Luck of Roaring Camp,
and Other Sketches..."

B3 ANON. "Mark Twain," Leisure Hour (London),
No. 1039 (November 25), 752.
 Reprints from the River Column of the St.
Louis Republican (n.d.) an account of MT's
writing a sketch of Captain Sellers, steamboat pilot. "After he had written the article, he inquired of John Morris, now
steward of the Belle Memphis, what name he
should sign to it," and at that moment
heard a leadsman sing out "Mark Twain."
"This sketch...was subsequently placed in
the hand of Mr. T. E. Garrett, who was at
that time River editor of this journal, and
it found a place in the River department of
the Republican. It proved to be a decided
hit, and was extensively copied by Western
journals." [MT's real name is given as
"Clements."]

B4 *CLEMENS, SAMUEL L. [Letter on Ruloff murder
case.] New York Tribune, April 29.
 [Source: Cited in Vogelback (1948),
p. 112, n. 2, and by Paine in Mark Twain,
I, 436-37; text appears ibid., III, as Appendix K, 1628-29. Signed "Samuel Langhorne."]

1872 A BOOKS

A1 WARNER, CHARLES DUDLEY. Backlog Studies.
Boston: James R. Osgood and Company (Re-
printed Boston and New York: Houghton,
Mifflin and Company, 1899).
 Conversations in the Nook Farm community
in Hartford; MT is "Our Next Door," Joseph
Twichell is "The Parson," etc.

1872 B SHORTER WRITINGS

B1 ANON. "Literary Notes," Book Section, The
Academy, III (August 1), 283.
 Item in full: "M. [sic] Th. Bentzon begins a series of sketches of American humorists with an account of Mark Twain in the
Revue des Deux Mondes (July 15). His criticisms are quite unexceptionable, but he
seems to have been misled by the advertisements of a certain type of publisher, so
that he exaggerates the popularity of his
author, while expressing surprise at its
extent."

B2 *ANON. "Mark Twain's Pipe," San Francisco
Chronicle, n.d.; reprinted in Cleveland
Herald Supplement, November 2.
 [Source: Quoted in Fatout (1964),
pp. 36-37.] On a small, convivial group
who first called themselves the "Companions
of the Jug," and later "The Visigoths."

B3 ANON. "Uncivilised America," Manchester
Guardian (March 6), p. 7.
 Includes a review of Roughing It; largely
descriptive, setting MT's humor below that
of Artemus Ward: "Mark Twain, too, often
falls into the slang of transatlantic journalism, and displays also its characteristic
inability to distinguish between the picturesque and the grotesque." Reprinted in Anderson (1971), pp. 46-47.

B4 ANON. [Review: Roughing It.] Overland
Monthly, VIII (June), 580-81.
 The rollicking humor is "genuine, and
thoroughly enjoyable," but there are also
"fresh descriptions of natural scenery" and
"impressive narrative." Reprinted in Anderson (1971), pp. 49-51.

B5 ANON. [Review: Screamers, an unauthorized
edition of short pieces by MT (some signed
"Carl Byng"). London: John Camden Hotten.]
Spectator, XLV (May 18), 633-34.
 Places MT below Bret Harte, John Hay, and
Artemus Ward in subtlety; "yet Mark Twain
ranks high, and is much more certain to be
understood and appreciated by a general
public, especially in countries where the
politics, manners, customs, and tone of
thought of Americans are comparatively little known." "The book is rather a hotch-
potch, and of very unequal merit. The tales
are not all 'screamers.' Some even have a
distinctly serious purpose, though put humorously."

B6 BENTZON, TH[ÉRÈSE] (MME. MARIE-THÉRÈSE BLANC).
"Les Humoristes Américains: I. Mark Twain,"
Revue des Deux Mondes, C (July 15), 313-35.
 An introduction of MT to French readers,
including a translation of "The Jumping
Frog" (pp. 314-319) and discussions of IA
and RI. Concludes by expressing the hope
that although Bret Harte and MT are still
strong fare for the French, "bientôt nous
serons accoutumés à une langue américaine
dont la verdeur savoureuse n'est pas à
dédaigner, en attendant les qualités plus
délicates et plus relevées que le temps lui
apportera sans doute."

B7 [Caricature of MT.] Once-A-Week (London),
XXVII (December 14), 519, 521.
 MT is depicted astride his jumping frog on
p. 519, and there is a brief, descriptive
appreciation of him on p. 521 (one of a series of caricatures of public figures).

B8 CLEMENS, SAMUEL L. "Mark Twain and His English Editor," Spectator, XLV (September 21),
1201-1202.
 A letter to the editor, accusing John
Camden Hotten of having produced a pirated
edition of his work as Screamers, with the
addition of material attributed to "Carl
Byng"--a nom de plume MT disavows. [See
Hotten's reply, 1872.B12.]

B9 *____. [Letter, describing a rescue at sea by the crew of the Batavia, together with commentary by the editors.] Boston Transcript (November 26), p. 1.
   The account also appeared in the New York Tribune (Nov. 27), p. 1, and there is further MT correspondence on the topic and editorial commentary there in 1873 (January 27, p. 4; April 11, p. 5).
   [Source: Discussed and quoted by Arthur L. Vogelback in "Mark Twain: Newspaper Contributor," AL, XX (May), 114-17.]

B10 *____. [Letter.] Spectator (London), September 20.
   On Routledge as his authorized English publisher. [Source: Reprinted in Grenander, (1975), p. 2; p. 4, n. 8 adds: "Reprinted in Charles Meeker Kozlay, The Lectures of Bret Harte (Brooklyn--New York: Charles Meeker Kozlay, 1909), p. 51. This letter was picked up and commented on by The Nation, 15 (October 10, 1872), 234-35."]

B11 *EGGLESTON, EDWARD. "H.G.," Hearth and Home, (February 24).
   On Horace Greeley. Eggleston had joined Bret Harte, John Hay, and MT in celebrating his sixty-fifth birthday. [Source: Cited by William Peirce Randel in Edward Eggleston: Author of "The Hoosier School-Master" (1946), p. 131.]

B12 HOTTEN, JOHN CAMDEN. "'Mark Twain' and His English Editor," Spectator, XLV (September 28), 1237.
   A letter to the editor, defending himself against MT's charges a week before (1872-B8). Attributing the "Carl Byng" material to MT simply follows the prevalent belief that it is his work. Hotten denies that he is a pirate: the material he has taken has no copyright protection in England, if it succeeds anybody can bring out a cheaper edition; moreover, three letters to MT (one offering payment) have gone unanswered.

B13 [HOWELLS, WILLIAM DEAN.] [Unsigned Review: Roughing It.] Atlantic Monthly, XXIX (June), 48-49.
   Descriptive and appreciative. Reprinted in his My Mark Twain (1910), pp. 113-14. and in Anderson (1971), pp. 48-49.

1873 A BOOKS - NONE

1873 B SHORTER WRITINGS

B1 ANON. "Cracking Jokes," Once-A-Week (London), n.s. XII (November 8), 402-405.
   A review of MT's Hanover Square lectures ("Our Fellow Savages of the Sandwich Islands"); chiefly descriptive, followed by quotations from his books, "brimming over with fun."

B2 ANON. "Mark Twain," Every Saturday (Boston), IV (November 15), 555-56.
   On MT's lecture on the Sandwich Islands and on the nature of his humor, which is lesser than that of Artemus Ward but may bring him even greater popularity. [Reprinted from London Spectator, according to Twainian, II (February, 1940), 6.]

B3 ANON. "The Sandwich Islands," Saturday Review (London), XXXVI (October 18), 503-504.
   Chiefly on the interest of the history of the islands, with passing reference to MT's current lecture on the subject.

B4 ANON. "Twain Can Do't," Punch, LXV (December 20), 248.
   Various plays on MT's name, regret that his stay in London will be brief; readers are urged to go hear him lecture.

B4a *ANON. [Account of MT's "Our Fellow Savages of the Sandwich Islands" lecture.] The Brooklyn Eagle, February 8.
   [Source: Listed in Lorch (1958), p. 54, n. 12.]

B5 ANON. [Advertisement of MT's lecture on "Our Fellow Savages of the Sandwich Islands."] Graphic (London), VIII (October 11), 335.

B6 ANON. [Review of MT's lecture on "Our Fellow Savages of the Sandwich Islands."] Graphic (London), VIII (December 6), 539.
   A brief account of a successful evening, marked by MT's "quaint humour" and "curious anecdotes and bits of sly satire...The peroration...was a splendid piece of word-painting."

B7 ANON. [Brief comment on MT's new London lecture on the "Silver Frontier."] Graphic (London), VIII (December 13), 534.
   It would be "a hopeless task" to give a condensation of the lecture, since "his quaint conceits follow each other with so little intermission that one has scarcely time to straighten one's features ere they are puckered o'er by some fresh jest or tall story."

B8 *ANON. [Reports on MT's arrangements for London publication of GA.] New York Daily Graphic, November 5, p. 29; November 8, p. 54.
   [Source: Grenander (1975), p. 4, n. 10.]

B9 *CLEMENS, SAMUEL L. [Letters, praising the crew of the Batavia for a rescue at sea he witnessed and urging the establishment in America of a Humane Society like England's; also, editorial commentary.] New York Tribune, January 27, p. 4; April 11, p. 5.
   MT's eyewitness account of the rescue appeared in the Boston Transcript (November 26, 1872), p. 1, and New York Tribune (November 27, 1872), p. 1. [Source: Vogelback (1948), pp. 114-17.]

1873 - Shorter Writings

B10 *[Commentary supporting MT's proposal that
ships be equipped with life-rafts instead
of life-boats.] Chicago Tribune, April 26,
p. 4.
[Source: Quoted in Vogelback (1948),
p. 119. Also see New York Tribune for this
period, as discussed by Vogelback.]

B11 *[Discussions of Foster murder case in New York
Tribune.] Editorial (March 6, p. 6); MT
letter to editor (March 10, p. 5); letter
by "H.K." criticizing MT's "ghastly flippancy" (March 11, p. 5).
[Source: Quoted in Vogelback (1948),
pp. 112-13.]

B12 HART, JOHN S. A Manual of American Literature: A Text-Book for Schools and Colleges.
Philadelphia: Eldredge & Brothers,
pp. 437-42. (Reprinted New York, London:
Johnson Reprint Corporation, 1969.)
In a section on American humorists, presents a purely uncritical biographical summary, followed by excerpts from IA.

B13 *[HOTTEN, JOHN CAMDEN.] [Introduction.] The
Choice Humorous Tales of Mark Twain. Lon-
don: John Camden Hotten.
[Source: Henderson (1911), p. 215.]

B14 *[Sandwich Islands annexation debated in New
York Tribune.]
MT describes the Islands (January 6, p. 4);
editorial on the annexation question
(January 9, pp. 4, 5); MT letter on Prince
Lunalilo and the native drinking habits, and
a scathing portrait of Harris, one of the
"Royal Ministers" (ibid., pp. 4, 5); further
Tribune comment on the issue and MT's in-
volvement (January 10, p. 4; January 22,
p. 4; February 5, p. 4; February 8, p. 4).
[Source: Discussed and quoted by Arthur L.
Vogelback (1948), pp. 119-25. Vogelback
takes issue with the treatment of the MT
letters of January 6 and 9 by Paine and
Frear (p. 123, n. 24).]

1874 A BOOKS - NONE

1874 B SHORTER WRITINGS

B1 ANON. "American Literature," Saturday Review
(London), XXXVII (January 24), 125-28.
A review-article, with brief notice on
p. 128: "The name of Mark Twain will be a
sufficient recommendation of The Gilded
Age, a three-volume novel of the English
form, purporting to be jointly written by
him and Mr. C. D. Warner."

B2 *ANON. "Mark Twain Toasts the Scotch," Lafay-
ette (Indiana) Daily Courier, January 14.
[Source: Reprinted in Twainian, XVI
(November-December, 1957), 4 (1957.B2).]

B3 *ANON. "Mark Twain's Trails in London," New
York Daily Graphic, January 15, p. 499.
[Source: Cited in Grenander (1975),
p. 4.] On MT's lectures; reprints a humorous MT letter to the London Post.

B4 ANON. [Review: The Gilded Age.] Athenaeum,
No. 2411 (January 10), 53.
"We think it is just possible that the
authors, one or both, may have it in them to
produce a story which we may read without
fatigue, and without constant jars to our
taste, while it shall have no lack of humour;
but we cannot say that in The Gilded Age
they have reached this desirable consumma-
tion."

B5 ANON. [Review: The Gilded Age.] Graphic
(London), IX (February 28), 199.
"If any Englishman had ventured on a picture of American manners and institutions
half as highly coloured, he would at once
have been loudly accused of the most rancor-
ous spite and the grossest misrepresentation." As a novel, the book is occasionally
clever, but a failure because of poor construction; "The best character is decidedly
the speculative 'Colonel' Eschol Sellers."

B6 ANON. [Review: The Gilded Age.] Old and New
(Boston), IX (March), 386-88.
"There is great power in the book, and of
an uncommon kind. It is a determined and
bitter satire," but "without comment and
moral explanation." The review barely mentions Colonel Sellers and describes the
portrayal of Senator Dilworthy as crude and
over-close, but "For two men situated as the
authors of The Gilded Age are situated, it
is a remarkably well-executed work; and
without any relative or qualifying expression, it is a book of real and high purpose,
much graphic and portrait power, much knowledge of men and things, and uncommon swift-
ness and force of action."

B7 *[BURLINGAME, EDWARD.] [Review: The Gilded
Age.] Appleton's Journal, XI (January 10),
59.
[Source: Identified by John W. Crowley in
"A Note on the Gilded Age," 1972.]

B8 FERRIS, GEORGE T. "Mark Twain," Appleton's
Journal, XII (July 4), 15-18.
A popular account, with portrait, largely
biographical. MT's humor is "so genial, so
charged with rich and unctuous [sic] humor,
that we forget the lack of finesse and delicacy in its breadth and strength." Reprinted in Scott (1955), pp. 17-22; (1967),
pp. 22-27.

B9 *LIKENS, MRS. J. W. Six Years Experience as a
Book Agent in California. San Francisco:
Women's Union Book and Job Printing Office.
Mrs. Likens found GA sold very well.
[Source: Cited by Bryant Morey French in
Mark Twain and "The Gilded Age" (1965),
pp. 6, 9.]

1875 A BOOKS - NONE

1875 B SHORTER WRITINGS

B1 BENTZON, TH[ÉRÈSE] (MME. MARIE-THÉRÈSE BLANC).
    "L'Age Doré en Amérique," Revue des Deux
    Mondes, VIII (March 15), 319-43.
    A review of GA (1874), which, as the work
    of MT and Charles Dudley Warner ("talent
    plus sage et moins original"), is difficult
    to read, with "une exubérante confusion, un
    mélange de bon sens et de folie" attribut-
    able to MT's audacious humor.

B2 *CLEMENS, SAMUEL L. "Mark Twain on Spelling,"
    Saint Louis Republican, May 23.
    [Source: Reprinted without comment in
    Missouri Historical Review, XXV (April),
    532-33.] Text of an introductory speech
    by MT before a spelling match at the Asylum
    Hill Congregational Church, Hartford, Con-
    necticut.

B3 *_____. [Letter, urging American support for
    a Shakespeare theater at Stratford-on-Avon
    (reprinted by several papers around the
    country), and editorial comments.] New York
    Times, April 29, p. 6; Boston Transcript,
    May 1, p. 6; Chicago Tribune, May 7, p. 4
    (editorial).
    [Source: Discussed and quoted in Vogel-
    back (1948), pp. 124-25.]

B4 *HOWELLS, WILLIAM DEAN. [Review: Sketches,
    New and Old.] Atlantic, XXXVI (December).
    749-51.
    [Source: Reprinted in his My Mark Twain
    (1910), pp. 120-24; also in Anderson
    (1971), pp. 52-55.] Notes MT's growing se-
    riousness in this book, especially in "A
    True Story," in which "the rugged truth of
    the sketch leaves all other stories of
    slave life infinitely far behind, and re-
    veals a gift in the author for the simple
    dramatic report of reality which we have
    seen equaled in no other American writer."

1876 A BOOKS - NONE

1876 B SHORTER WRITINGS

B1 ANON. "American Literature," Saturday Review
    (London), XLI (January 29), 154.
    A review of Sketches, New and Old (1875).
    The sketches "are nearly all capital, and
    all of them worthy of the author; short and
    lively, for the most part free from vulgar-
    ity and offence, raising a smile more often
    than provoking a roar of laughter, but al-
    ways amusing."

B2 ANON. [Review: Tom Sawyer.] Athenaeum,
    No. 2539 (June 24), p. 851.
    MT is already known in England as a popu-
    lar comic like Artemus Ward, but in this
    new book "The humour is not always uproar-
    ious, but it is always genuine and sometimes
    almost pathetic, and it is only now and then
    that the heartiness of a laugh is spoilt by
    one of those pieces of self-consciousness
    which are such common blots on Mark Twain's
    other works. The Adventures of Tom Sawyer
    is an attempt in a new direction. It is
    consecutive, and much longer than the former
    books," though not strictly a novel or "even
    a story, for that presupposes a climax and a
    finish; nor is it a mere boys' book of ad-
    ventures." Reprinted in Anderson (1971),
    pp. 64-65.

B3 ANON. [Review: Tom Sawyer.] British Quarter-
    ly Review, LXIII (October), 264.
    "The book is full of roaring fun, inter-
    spersed with true pathos.... It might...
    have given more emphasis to truth and
    straightforwardness. But it is irresistible;
    fully up to the mark of the 'Innocents
    Abroad.'"

B4 *ANON. [Review: Tom Sawyer.] Times (London),
    August 28, p. 4.
    Praises the humor in this story of a boy
    whose "eventful career exhibits an unprece-
    dented precocity." [Source: Reprinted in
    Anderson (1971), pp. 66-68.]

B5 *[CONWAY, MONCURE D.] [Review: Tom Sawyer.]
    Examiner (London), June 17, pp. 687-88.
    [Source: Reprinted in Anderson (1971),
    pp. 62-64, noting another Conway review of
    TS June 26, in the Cincinnati Commercial.]
    Praises MT's humor and vivid, apt descrip-
    tion; regrets the book is not longer.

B6 *HOWELLS, WILLIAM DEAN. [Review: Tom Sawyer.]
    Atlantic, XXXVII (May), 621-22.
    [Source: Reprinted in his My Mark Twain
    (1910), pp. 125-28, giving original Atlantic
    publication as December, 1875; also reprint-
    ed in Cardwell (1963), pp. 4-5, and in An-
    derson (1971), pp. 59-61.] Praises the por-
    trait of boy-nature.

B7 LITTLEDALE, RICHARD F. "New Novels," Academy,
    IX (June 24), 604-605.
    On p. 605, a brief description of TS, end-
    ing: "The book is designed primarily for
    boys, but older people will also find it
    worth looking through."

B8 *TURNER, MATTHEW FREKE. "Artemus Ward and the
    Humourists of America," New Quarterly Maga-
    zine, No. 11 (April), pp. 208-12.
    [Source: Reprinted in Anderson (1971),
    pp. 55-58.] Probably based on Eye Openers
    (1875). Only MT and Bret Harte deserve "any
    kind of public criticism," and MT's is a low
    humor, ridiculing sacred things, forced,
    long-winded, tedious in his parodies. "It
    will be seen that Mark Twain is, by no means,
    a genial, kindly humourist, like his prede-
    cessor, Artemus Ward; that, though he hits
    the same blots, his mode of attack is alto-
    gether different. Mark Twain is a jester,

1876 - Shorter Writings

(TURNER, MATTHEW FREKE)
and very little more. When he is not on the
trail of some joke, he is apt to be insuf-
ferably tedious."

B9   WHIPPLE, EDWIN P. "The First Century of the
Republic (Seventeenth Paper)," Harper's
Monthly, LII (March), 514-23.
     Describes popular humorists such as Arte-
mus Ward and John Phoenix, pp. 525-26.
"Mark Twain, the most widely popular of
this class of humorists, is a man of wide
experience, keen intellect, and literary
culture. The serious portions of his writings indicate that he could win a reputation
in literature even if he had not been blessed with a humorous faculty inexhaustible in
resource."

1877 A BOOKS - NONE

1877 B SHORTER WRITINGS

B1   *ANON. "The Ship-Owners and Mr. Duncan," New
York Times (date not available).
     On the accusations against Captain Duncan
of the Quaker City, involving misuse of
funds. [Source: Reprinted in Twainian, XI
(July-August, 1952), 3-4.]

B2   ANON. "Twain and Harte's New Play: Its First
Production in Washington," Argonaut (San
Francisco), I (May 19), 5.
     A long, descriptive review of the play Ah
Sin. "The plot of the play and cast of
characters is decidedly Californian, so
much so as to suggest that it is but a re-
vamping of 'The Two Men of Sandy Bar,'
written by Bret Harte and brought to grief
by the same unkind means that brought Anna
Dickinson low--dramatically speaking."

B3   *ANON. [Review: Tom Sawyer (1876).] New York
Times, January 13, p. 3.
     [Source: Reprinted in Anderson (1971),
pp. 69-72.] Praises MT's humor and accurate
portrayal of Tom's world (although he is
somewhat precocious), but finds the violence
rather strong for young readers.

B4   *CASSIDY, GEORGE W. [Statement that the pseudonym "Mark Twain" was derived from
S. L. C.'s custom of asking a Virginia City
bartender to chalk up drinks for himself and
a friend.] Eureka, Nevada Sentinel, May 8.
     [Source: Quoted in Fatout (1964),
pp. 35-36.]

B5   *CLEMENS, SAMUEL L. "Mark Twain on His Muscle.
Emulating MacBeth, He Kills Duncan Over
Again. The 'Innocent' at Home Tells the
Story of His Crimes Abroad," New York World,
February 18.
     Letter to the editor, criticizing the cap-
tain of the Quaker City. [Source: Reprint-
ed in Twainian, XI (July-August, 1952), 3-4.]

B6   [JOHNSON, ROBERT UNDERWOOD.] "A New Book by
Mark Twain," Scribner's Monthly, XIII
(April), 874-75.
     A tongue-in-cheek review of Mark Twain's
Adhesive Scrap-Book (1873). Reprinted in
Twainian, VII (July-August, 1948) attribut-
ing the review to Johnson on the basis of a
statement in his Remembered Yesterdays
(1923).

B7   *[Sketch, by or of MT.] World (London),
December 20.
     [Source: Dixon Wecter, "Frank Finlay; or,
The Thameside Tenderfoot in the Wooly West,"
Twainian, VI (July-August, 1947), 1-4. A
letter from Finlay of that date refers to
"a well-meant but imperfect sketch of one
Mark Twain in the World of today."]

1878 A BOOKS - NONE

1878 B SHORTER WRITINGS

B1   ANON. "Mark Twain at Home," Leisure Hour,
No. 1389 (August 10), 510-11.
     Briefly describing an interview with MT,
notes "the excellency of his literary taste"
and calls him not a "professional humorist,"
but "a constitutional humorist," in his
point of view toward any subject.

B2   *ANON. [Description of MT's Hartford house.]
English World, January, 1878.
     [Source: Quoted in Blair (1960), p. 16.]

B3   WAKEMAN, CAPTAIN EDGAR. The Log of an Ancient
Mariner. Being the Life and Adventures of
Captain Edgar Wakeman. Written by Himself,
and Edited by His Daughter [Minnie Wakeman-
Curtis.] San Francisco: A. L. Bancroft &
Co., Printers.
     Wakeman was the "Ned Blakely" of RI, and
appeared elsewhere under various names, in-
cluding "Hurricane Jones" and "Captain
Stormfield."

1879 A BOOKS - NONE

1879 B SHORTER WRITINGS

B1   ANON. "Table Talk." Gentleman's Magazine,
CCXLVI (April), 505.
     Brief mention of an MT story.

B2   *ANON. [Interview.] Hartford Courant, May 14,
p. 1, col. 8.
     MT comments that what can be satirized in
England can also be found nearer home.
[Source: Quoted in Baetzhold (1970),
pp. 76-77.]

B3   *CLEMENS, SAMUEL L. Letters to Hartford Courant, concerning new postal order requiring
more complete addresses on letters; as reprinted by the Boston Transcript
(November 28, p. 3; December 11, p. 4;

(*CLEMENS, SAMUEL L.)
December 12, p. 4) and the Chicago Tribune
(November 29, p. 13). Also, a reply to MT
by the private secretary to the Postmaster-
General (Boston Transcript, December 11,
p. 4).
[Source: Discussed and quoted in Vogelback (1948), pp. 126-27. The private secretary to the Postmaster-General mentioned
having read MT's letter in the Cincinnati
Inquirer (date not given).]

B4   *YATES, EDMUND. "Mark Twain at Hartford," in
his Celebrities at Home, n.p. Reprinted
from The World (London). Third Series.
[Source: Henderson (1911), p. 216.]

1880 A BOOKS - NONE

1880 B SHORTER WRITINGS

B1   ANON. "Mark Twain and Dan De Quille," Argonaut (San Francisco), VI (January 31), 6.
An apocryphal story, reprinted from the
Carson Appeal, of an attempt by Dan De
Quille (William Wright) and MT to start a
paper in Mendocino County; on their way
there they were attacked by Indians and
used up their type as shot in defending
themselves--so they went on to Virginia
City and took jobs on the Enterprise.

B2   ANON. "Mark Twain on Plagiarism," Leisure
Hour, No. 1482 (May 15), p. 320.
Quotes MT's account of having unconscious-
ly borrowed a dedication to a book from
Oliver Wendell Holmes; provides no new in-
formation or perspective.

B3   ANON. [Review: A Tramp Abroad.] British
Quarterly Review, LXXII (July), 228-29.
"Mr. Mark Twain is a lively companion.
He indulges in the kind of facetiae which
luckily, to a great degree, please the cultured and uncultured alike," but "he is
apt...to practice his trick too often; so
that it is not advisable to read too much
of him all at once.... But Mr. Mark Twain
is delightful. No more pleasant and airy
pages, or fuller of sudden and playful anti-
theses, have recently been given to the
public."

B4   ANON. [Review: A Tramp Abroad.] Graphic
(London), XXI (May 1), 451.
"Writing pleasantly about well-known
things...Mark Twain's charm is that he puts
things so unexpectedly--says the very thing
which nobody would ever think of saying";
some of his topics are briefly listed.

B5   ANON. [Review: A Tramp Abroad.] Saturday
Review (London), XLIX (April 17), 514-15.
The book contains some good things, among
them Jim Baker's story about the blue-jay
and the "Tale of the Fishwife and Its Sad
Fate," but as a whole is too long, often

dull, and carelessly put together; it should
be read in snatches, with judicious skip-
ping, and will then "furnish a good deal of
genuine amusement." Reprinted in Anderson
(1971), pp. 76-80.

B6   [HENLEY, WILLIAM ERNEST.] [Unsigned Review:
A Tramp Abroad.] Athenaeum, No. 2739
(April 24), pp. 529-30.
"He has a keen, sure sense of character
and uncommon skill in presenting it dramatically; and he is also an admirable story-
teller, with the anecdotic instinct and habit in perfection." Reprinted in Anderson
(1971), pp. 73-76, with attribution to Henley.

B7   [HOWELLS, WILLIAM DEAN]. [Review: A Tramp
Abroad.] Atlantic Monthly, XLV (May),
686-88.
Attempts by others to imitate MT have
failed, and this new book is enlightening
and delightful. Reprinted in his My Mark
Twain (1910), pp. 129-33, and in Anderson
(1971), pp. 81-84.

1881 A BOOKS - NONE

1881 B SHORTER WRITINGS

B1   ANON. Facts. By a Woman. Oakland, California: Pacific Press Publishing House.
On her experiences in selling TS by subscription in the area of Oroville, California, pp. 34-53.

B2   ANON. "Personating Mark Twain," The Californian: A Western Monthly Magazine, IV (July),
97-98.
From an exchange copy of another journal
(not named), an anecdote of the Honorable
DeShane Hornet, a temperance lecturer who
was asked to substitute when MT could not
keep a lecturer engagement in Gloucester;
not realizing a change had been made, the
audience greeted Hornet's every remark with
laughter and he angrily walked out.

B3   ANON. [Brief Review: The Prince and the
Pauper.] Athenaeum, No. 2826 (December 24),
p. 849.
"A heavy disappointment...some four hundred pages of careful tediousness, mitigated
by occasional flashes of unintentional and
unconscious fun...if to convert a brilliant
and engaging humourist into a dull and painful romancer be necessarily a function of
the study of history, it cannot be too
steadily discouraged." Reprinted in Anderson (1971), pp. 91-92 (quoting what MT later
said about the reviewer).

B4   ANON. [Review: The Prince and the Pauper.]
Critic, I (December 31), 368.
This is not a complete change of direction:
"What has made Mark Twain's extravagant hu-
mour so effective has been (apart from its

1881 - Shorter Writings

(ANON.)
more glaring qualities) the skillfully painted background of more subdued and often delicate description."

B5 *[BOYESON, H. H.] "Mark Twain's New Departure," Atlantic, XLVIII (December), 843-45. [Source: Reprinted in Anderson (1971), pp. 85-89).] A review of P&P; praises MT in his new role "as the author of a tale ingenious in conception, pure and humane in purpose, artistic in method, and, with barely a flaw, refined in execution."

B6 *HOWE, E. W. [On MT.] Atchinson (Kansas) Globe, December 31, p. 3.
"Mark Twain's career is nearly at an end. The paragraphists have commenced to pelt him, and they will finish him before they get through. His wit has been watered until it is without flavor." [Source: Quoted by S. J. Sackett in his E. W. Howe (New York: Twayne Publishers, Inc., 1972), p. 74.]

B7 PURCELL, E. [Review: The Prince and the Pauper.] Academy (London), XX (December 24), 469.
"A ponderous fantasia on English history," in which "a few smart sayings relieve the monotony of a prolix work singularly deficient in literary merit." Reprinted in Anderson (1971), pp. 90-91.

1882 A BOOKS - NONE

1882 SHORTER WRITINGS

B1 *ANON. "California Writers: Mark Twain," The Occident (Berkeley, California) November 10.
[Source: Twainian, II (April, 1943).]

B2 ANON. "Mark Twain Tries to Pull Wool Over the Marines, But Doesn't," Vicksburg Daily Herald, April 26.
[Possibly reprinted from the Memphis Ledger.] On MT's attempt to revisit his old haunts incognito while gathering material for the expanded LOM: he registered at the Peabody Hotel as "C. L. Samuels." Also tells apocryphal stories about MT as cub pilot on the old Aleck Scott, under Captain Bart Bowen: "he used to play pranks on the celebrated Captain Isaiah Sellers, the pilot on the other watch, who was hard to awaken." [Transcript provided by William Van S. Carhart.]

B3 ANON. "Mark Twain Visits the Historic City and Takes Some Views of Things as They Exist in These Parts. How He Looked to a Casual Observer," Vicksburg Daily Herald, April 27.
General description. MT "looked yesterday, like a man who had just escaped from a lunatic asylum, whose only sense was in the perfect realization of that fact, and whose every energy was concentrated in an effort to dodge its keeper." [Transcript provided by William Van S. Carhart.]

B4 ANON. [Review: Innocents Abroad.] British Quarterly Review, LXXV (January), 101.
This book is too well-known to need lengthy description. MT "always avoids irreverence" in his description of Palestine and skillfully balances between exaggeration and subtlety. "It consititutes a type; and the wisdom is as much as the wit, the serious meaning as the outrageous extravagance."

B5 ANON. [Review: The Prince and the Pauper.] British Quarterly Review, LXXV (January), 118.
MT "has written a story which gives a vivid idea of a historical period, but which outrages history at every point in the most daring and barefaced manner.... We do not think that this sort of writing in ordinary hands would be advisable for the young of any age...but Mr. Mark Twain's fun and satiric chaff, his mingled humour and pathos, his fine perception of human nature, and his nimble fancy make him an exception," as has been shown by the experience of young readers.

B6 *ANON. [Review: The Prince and the Pauper.] Century, XXIII (March), 783-84.
[Source: Reprinted in Anderson (1971), pp. 92-94, with the suggestion that it may be a response to the 1881 Boyeson review.] "So far as it was the author's purpose to produce a work of art after the old models, and to prove that the humorous story-teller and ingenious homely philosopher, Mark Twain, can be a literary purist, a scholar, and an antiquary, we do not think his 'new departure' is a conspicuous success."

B7 ANON. [Review: The Prince and the Pauper.] Graphic (London), XXV (March 25), 306.
"This delightful story" is for all ages, with its "subtle plot, marked by the crisp incisiveness of a clever, though not quite faultless, style, and...the quaint and shadowed mystery--perhaps, too, the barbaric horror--of medieval times. Its humour is delicate; its fun joyously real; and its pathos tender and deep."

B8 ANON. [Brief Review: The Prince and the Pauper.] Spectator, No. 2795 (January 21), p. 95.
"An ingenious idea, which has been well worked out"; the new lives of the two boys "make a contrast both humorous and pathetic, and consequently very effective."

B9 ANON. [Review: The Prince and the Pauper.] Westminster Review, n.s. LXI (April), 576.
"The story has its merits, though it is a little long, and at times threatens to be tedious. On the whole, Mr. Mark Twain is more at home in his earlier efforts."

B10 ANON. [Brief Review: The Stolen White Elephant.] Athenaeum, No. 2852 (June 24), p. 795.
  The title story "is really good work. With 'The Invalid's Story' it is enough to make the book a success, and to compensate for the pompous dulness and the wooden morality of The Prince and the Pauper."

B11 ANON. [Brief Review: The Stolen White Elephant.] British Quarterly Review, LXXVI (October), 247.
  Of these short stories, "some are satirical, others grotesque, a few merely fanciful and touched by sentiment.... Mark Twain is always ingenious, funny, and dashing, but sometimes in satire he overdoes it, and is too much on the 'broad grin.'"

B12 ANON. [Brief note on The Stolen White Elephant.] Critic, II (June 17), 163.
  Among "Minor Notices"; primarily descriptive.

B13 ANON. [Review: The Stolen White Elephant.] Graphic (London), XXVI (July 15), 62.
  "A sad falling-off from the works which have made Mr. Clemens' reputation in two continents" this book has as its "funniest story, 'The Recent Carnival of Crime in Connecticut'...but what slight humour there may be in 'The Invalid's Story' is quite lost in the inherent repulsiveness of the incident."

B14 ANON. [Brief Review: The Stolen White Elephant.] Nation (New York), XXXV (August 10), 119.

B15 ANON. [Review: The Stolen White Elephant.] Westminster Review, n.s. LXII (October), 576-77.
  "It is difficult to choose where all is good, but perhaps the 'Gossip about old Captain Hurricane Jones of the South Pacific' and 'The Invalid's Story,' are the most irresistibly funny of all." "The American Language" is discussed at length by the reviewer.

B16 ARNOLD, MATTHEW. "A Word about America," Nineteenth Century, XI (May), 680-96.
  "The Quinionian humour of Mr. Mark Twain, so attractive to the Philistine of the more gay and light type both here and in America, another French critic fixes upon as literature exactly expressing a people of this type, and no higher. 'In spite of all its primary education,' he says, 'America is still, from an intellectual point of view, a very rude and primitive soil, only to be cultivated by violent methods. These childish and half-savage minds are not moved except by very elementary narratives composed without art, in which burlesque and melodrama, vulgarity and eccentricity, are combined in strong doses'" (pp. 689-90).

B17 *BENTZON, THÉRÈSE (MME. MARIE-THÉRÈSE BLANC). Littérature et Moeurs Étrangères: Études. Paris: G. Lévy, 2 vols.
  Reprints her essays on MT from Revue des Deux Mondes, 1872, 1875 (II, pp. 1-38, 231-71). [Source: Asselineau (1954), No. 4.]

B18 HAWEIS, H. R. "Mark Twain," in his American Humorists: Lectures Delivered at the Royal Institution. (London: Chatto & Windus), pp. 163-96. (Source: Third Edition, 1890.)
  Praises MT's vivid observation, ability not to bore his readers, noting that he is not very profound. "In freshness and fertility Twain resembles poor ARTEMUS, and rises above BRET HARTE, though he is less intense and pathetic than the latter." Reprinted in Scott (1955), pp. 29-33 and (1967), pp. 34-38.

B19 HOWELLS, WILLIAM DEAN. "Mark Twain," Century Magazine, XXIV (September), 780-83.
  A general study of his life and works, noting the autobiographical quality of his writing, which is at once American and universal. He is a gifted story-teller and painter of character; it is his artistry that will make his humor last. Frontispiece sketch of MT. Reprinted in his My Mark Twain (1910), pp. 134-44, and abridged in Anderson (1971), pp. 98-103 and Kesterson (1973), p. 13.

B20 NAST, THOMAS. [Cartoon of MT.] Harper's Weekly, XXVI (January 21), 37.
  Shows MT in Canada to arrange for copyright of his books. Also, Anon., "Canadian Copyright," a brief comment on the cartoon and on MT's problem with foreign copyright. Cartoon reprinted in Meltzer, 1960, p. 153, and on front cover of Mark Twain Journal, XVI (Winter, 1971).

B21 NICHOL, JOHN. American Literature: An Historical Sketch 1620-1880. Edinburgh: Adam and Charles Black, pp. 426-32.
  "It is probable that, to the lower class of British Philistines, American prose is, at this day, represented not so much by Irving, Emerson, or Hawthorne, as by 'Mark Twain,' who has done perhaps more than any other living writer to lower the literary tone of the English-speaking people." In LOM, a beautiful book, he spoke of the loss in freshness of vision suffered by a pilot or doctor as he learns to turn a professional eye toward his subject, and to them must be added "the professional humorist, who has lost the power of seeing the beauty of the universe, because he has come to regard it as a mere text-book for his sadly incessant and ultimately wearisome jests." Reprinted in Anderson (1971), pp. 94-97; in Scott (1955), pp. 23-28 and (1967), pp. 28-33. Excerpted in Kesterson (1973), pp. 15-16. In 1902

1882 - Shorter Writings

(NICHOL, JOHN)
Nichol dismissed MT with an oblique reference in his Encyclopaedia Britannica article (1902.B21).

B22 NOBEL, JAMES ASHCROFT. [Brief Review: The
Stolen White Elephant.] Academy (London),
XXII (July 1), 6.
This resembles MT's other works, and will
be popular with those who like them. "Several of the sketches are quite amusing...
the volume as a whole is quite up to its
author's average."

1883 A BOOKS - NONE

1883 B SHORTER WRITINGS

B1 ANON. [Review: Life on the Mississippi.]
Athenaeum, No. 2901 (June 2), pp. 694-95.
"Mr. Clemens's new book is a disappointment." Much of it is derived from books,
except for the chapters recalling actual
experience, where "we come in contact with
Mark Twain at his best." Reprinted in Anderson (1971), pp. 113-16.

B2 ANON. [Review: Life on the Mississippi.]
Atlantic Monthly, LII (September), 406-408.
Descriptive and appreciative; gives no
indication of a falling-off in the second
half.

B3 ANON. [Review: Life on the Mississippi.]
British Quarterly Review, LXXXVIII (July),
123-24.
Discusses the book in terms of its humor,
which is not of the highest order.

B4 ANON. [Review: Life on the Mississippi.]
Congregationalist (British), XIII (August),
702-705.
"There are passages in this book which
are equal to anything he has ever written,
if, indeed, they are not superior. For if
the humour is less condensed in its character, being spread over a larger surface, it
has lost nothing of its old richness of
flavour; while the purely descriptive parts
of his narrative are marked by even more
than his customary sprightliness and spirit."

B5 ANON. [Review: Life on the Mississippi.]
Graphic, XXVIII (September 1), 231.
MT's earlier chapters contain "an admirable specimen of his powers as a serious
writer of history," but he "soon slips into
his accustomed style," moving from "the
graphic to the grotesque." This will probably not be as popular as some of his other
works; "nevertheless, it is well worth
reading." Reprinted in Anderson (1971),
pp. 118-19.

B6 ANON. [Review: Life on the Mississippi.]
Nation, XXXVII (August 30), 192.

A minor review: The book is important as
the record of a period, and MT should not
be burdened with the title of professional
humorist.

B7 BROWN, ROBERT. [Review: Life on the Mississippi.] Academy (London), XXIV (July 28),
58.
"The fun in Mr. Clemens' Tramps Abroad is
frequently forced, and sometimes quite un-
suited to the subject in hand. His American
experiences have rarely this fault; the
writer seems to feel the ground he is tread-
ing more secure.... The book is indeed the
best account of social life on the Mississippi with which we are acquainted," and
also gives a valuable account of the river.
Reprinted in Anderson (1971), pp. 116-18.

B8 *[Counterfeit MT letter.] Discussed in Arkansaw [sic] Traveler (August 4), p. 4.
[Source: Quoted by Vogelback (1948),
pp. 127-28.]
On a bet, an 1859 MT letter was concocted
and published, "and was immediately reproduced by many of the leading newspapers in
the country."

B9 *HAWEIS, H. R. "Mark Twain," Elzevir Library,
March 12.
[Source: Twainian, II (February, 1940).]

B10 *HEARN, LAFCADIO. [Review: Life on the Mississippi.] New Orleans Times-Democrat
(May 30), p. 4; Hearn, Essays on American
Literature, ed. Sanki Ichikawa (Tokyo, 1929),
pp. 127-33.
[Source: Parsons (1969), 10-11. "In
some respects...the most solid book that
Mark Twain has written."] Reprinted in Anderson (1971), pp. 109-12.

B11 *MILLER, "JOAQUIN" (CINCINNATUS HINER MILLER).
[His description of a dinner in his honor,
attended by MT.] Somerville (New Jersey)
Unionist, reprinted in Hartford Courant,
January 9.
[Source: Anon. "Mark Twain and Anthony
Trollope, Equestrians," (1951), 14-15.]

B12 *PERRY, THOMAS SERGEANT. "An American on American Humour," St. James's Gazette, VII
(July 5), 5-6.
[Source: Reprinted in Anderson (1971),
pp. 103-108.] Sees MT's humor as representative of a democratic, serious, ironic quality in the American national character, reacting against Europe, though not independently and perhaps not in hostility.

B13 READE, A. ARTHUR. Study and Stimulants; or,
The Use of Intoxicants and Narcotics in Relation to Intellectual Life, as Illustrated
by Personal Communications on the Subject,
from Men of Letters and of Science. Philadelphia: J. B. Lippincott and Co.,
pp. 120-22.
Contains a letter from MT beginning, "I

(READE, A. ARTHUR)
have not had a large experience in the matter of alcoholic drinks." MT goes on to
say that two glasses of champagne stimulate
the tongue and go well before an after-dinner speech, but "wine is a clog to the pen,
not an inspiration." The greater part of
the letter concerns his immoderate smoking,
his conviction that it does not injure his
health, and one or two occasions when he
stopped.

1884 A BOOKS

A1   *GAUTHIER-VILLARS, HENRY (WILLY). Mark Twain.
Paris: Gauthier-Villars.
[Source: Asselineau (1954), No. 5.]

1884 B SHORTER WRITINGS

B1   ANON. "Mark Twain," Leisure Hour (London),
p. 510.
Retells MT's own account of the origin
of his pen-name; adds no commentary or new
information.

B2   ANON. "Mark Twain in Bronze," Critic, n.s.
II (October 18), 184-85.
About the bust of MT by Karl Gerhardt.
Includes a description of it by Charles
Dudley Warner in the Hartford Courant (date
not given).

B3   *ANON. "Mark Twain in a Dilema [sic]--A Victim of a Joke He Thinks the Most Unkindest
Cut of All," New York World (November 27),
p. 1.
An illustration in the first edition of
Huckleberry Finn was rendered obscene by
somebody in the electrotyper's office.
[Source: Major portion of text reprinted
in Vogelback (1939), pp. 262-63.]

B4   *ANON. "Mark Twain's Altered Book," New York
Herald, November 29.
On the mutilated cut on p. 283 of HF;
gives the caption as "What [sic] do you
reckon it is?" [Source: Reprinted in
Twainian, V (March-April, 1946), 2.]

B5   ANON. "Tampering with Mark Twain's Book,"
New York Tribune, November 29, p. 3.
[Source: Reprinted in Twainian, V
(March-April, 1946), 2; cited in Vogelback
(1939), 263, n., indicating that this is a
modified reprinting from the New York World,
November 27, p. 1.] On the mutilation of
the cut on p. 283 to render it obscene.

B6   *ANON. [Story of the mutilation of a plate in
first edition of HF to produce an obscene
effect.] Boston Transcript, December 2,
p. 6.
[Source: Cited by Vogelback (1939),
p. 263, n. Vogelback indicates this is a
reprinting, possibly with variations, of an
account in the New York World (November 27),
p. 1.]

B7   *ANON. [Story of the mutilation of a plate in
first edition of HF to produce an obscene
effect.] Chicago Tribune, November 30,
p. 23.
[Source: Cited by Vogelback (1939),
p. 263, n. Vogelback indicates this is a
reprinting, perhaps with variations, from
the New York World, November 27, p. 1.]

B8   ANON. [Brief item: 150 "people of distinction in literature and the arts" sent requests for MT's autograph, timed to reach
him April 1st.] Critic (New York), IV
(April 5), 163.

B9   *ANON. [The rambling narrative style of Twain,
Riley, and Artemus Ward is the pose of "innocence victimized by the world, flesh, and
devil."] Washington Post, November 25.
[Source: Quoted by Henry Nash Smith,
introduction to HF, Riverside edition (1959),
p. xviii.]

B10   ANON. [Brief Review: The Adventures of Huckleberry Finn.] Athenaeum, No. 2983
(December 27), p. 855.
Laudatory and descriptive. "For some time
Mr. Clemens has been carried away by the am-
bition of seriousness and fine writing. In
Huckleberry Finn he returns to his right
mind and is again the Mark Twain of old
time.... Jim and Huckleberry are real creations, and the worthy peers of the illustrious Tom Sawyer." Reprinted in Anderson
(1971), pp. 120-21, with a suggestion that
the reviewer may be William Ernest Henley.

B11   PEASE, THOMAS H. [Letter to the editor of the
Palladium, from New Haven, April 23; here
reprinted.] Literary Era (Philadelphia),
II (July), 207.
Describes the book, The Enemy Conquered;
or, Love Triumphant, subject of the Hartford
Courant article (here attributed to Joseph
Twichell); the dealer's remaining copies of
the book were eventually sold for scrap.

B12   *SHIRLEY, JAMES. "Some Verses by Mark Twain,"
The Wasp (San Francisco), January 19.
[Source: Reprinted in Twainian, V
(July-August, 1946), 4.]

B13   STEPHENS, H. B. "Mark Twain's 'Dorg,'" Every
Other Saturday (Boston), I (December 20),
457-58.
On MT's dog "Burns," with an MT letter to
Stephens containing an obituary poem to the
dog. Article reprinted in Twainian, XII
(July-August, 1953), 3.

B14   [TWICHELL, JOSEPH.] "Mark Twain's Quest. The
Efforts of a Humorist to Secure a Rare Book--
A Long Search," Literary Era (Philadelphia),
II (June), 185-86.
Reprints an article from the Hartford Cour-
ant on the attempts by MT and Twichell to lo-
cate a copy of The Enemy Conquered; or, Love
Triumphant; for further comment see letter by

1884 - Shorter Writings

([TWICHELL, JOSEPH])
Thomas H. Pease reprinted in July issue (1884.B11), where this article is attributed to Twichell.

1885 A BOOKS - NONE

1885 B SHORTER WRITINGS

B1   ANON. "The American Humorists," Critic, VII (December 5), 274 ("From the London Daily News").
    Mostly about MT: "His gravity in narrating the most preposterous tale, his sympathy with every one of his absurdest characters, his microscopic imagination, his vein of seriousness, his contrasts of pathos, his bursts of indignant plain speaking about certain national errors, make Mark Twain an author of the highest merit, and far remote from the mere buffoon."

B2   ANON. "Modern Comic Literature," Saturday Review (London), LIX (March 7), 301-302.
    A reply to Mr. Cowle's intemperate attack on Modern Comic Literature in the Melbourne Review, this includes a lengthy defense of MT, and of Huckleberry Finn in particular. Reprinted in Anderson (1971), pp. 127-28; notes the conjecture of Brander Matthews "that it is the work of...Mr. Andrew Lang."

B3   *ANON. [Banning of HF by the Concord Public Library.] Boston Transcript, March 17.
    [Source: Long passage reprinted in Marks (1959), p. xi.] The committee do not call the book actually immoral, but it "contains but little humor, and that of a very coarse type"; it is "the veriest trash...rough, coarse and inelegant, dealing with a series of experiences not elevating, the whole book being more suited to the slums than to intelligent, respectable people." Also excerpted in Gerber (1971), p. 8, and Kesterson (1973), p. 17.

B4   *ANON. [Banning of HF by Concord Public Library.] Springfield (Massachusetts) Republican, as quoted in The Critic, VI (March 28), 155.
    [Source: Reprinted in Gerber (1971), pp. 8-9.] "Mr. Clemens is a genuine and powerful humorist, with a bitter vein of satire on the weaknesses of humanity which is sometimes wholesome, sometimes only grotesque, but in certain of his works degenerates into a grotesque trifling with every fine feeling. The trouble with Mr. Clemens is that he has no reliable sense of propriety. His notorious speech at an Atlantic dinner, marshalling Longfellow and Emerson and Whittier in vulgar parodies in a Western miner's cabin, illustrated this, but not in much more relief than the Adventures of Tom Sawyer did, or these Huckleberry Finn stories, do..."

B5   *ANON. ["A discursive and ill-argued attack on the vulgarity of 'modern' humour."] Melbourne Review, X (January), 94-100.
    [Source: Headnote to Item No. 37 in Anderson (1971), p. 127.]

B6   NO ENTRY

B7   ANON. [Interview with Jane Clemens, MT's mother.] Critic (New York), VII (December 12), 276.
    The boy avoided school, though he enjoyed reading history (clipping from an undisclosed source).

B8   *ANON. [MT's lectures in Keokuk, Iowa, and greetings to his mother.] Keokuk Daily Gate City, January 15, Weekly Gate City, January 22.
    [Source: Reprinted in Twainian, XXIV (November-December, 1965), 2-3.]

B9   ANON. [Notice, which follows in full.] Graphic, XXXI (May 23), 530.
    "Humourists will delight in 'The Mark Twain Birthday Book,' edited by 'E. O. S.' (Remington), which contains excerpts from Mr. Clemens' writings. Each day is allotted several sentences, presumably summarising the character of the person who writes his name on the opposite page, such as 'A Meddling Old Clam,' or 'She was attractively attired in her new and beautiful false teeth.'"

B10   *ANON. [Recitation by MT and Cable in Paris, Kentucky, New Year's night.] Paris Kentuckian, January 3.
    Praises their performance, describes the visit, but says nothing new about topics or performance. [Source: Reprinted in Twainian, XXIV (November-December, 1965), 1-2.]

B11   ANON. [Reprinted item from The Summary, "A weekly journal published in the interests of the New York State Reformatory"], Critic, VI (May 30), 264.
    "The Reformatory Library also procured Huckleberry Finn," was impressed with it as irreligious, as the Concord (Massachusetts) library had been, "and the fact came under the notice of Professor Sanborn, who was visiting us." He wrote the Superintendent: "I have read 'Huckleberry Finn,' and I do not see any reason why it should not go into your Reference Library, at least, and form the subject of a debate in your Practical Morality Class. I am serious in this." Reprinted in Gerber (1971), pp. 9-10.

B12   ANON. [Review: Huckleberry Finn.] British Quarterly Review, LXXXI (January-April), 465-66.

(ANON.)
Although MT "is sometimes a little coarse, sometimes a little irreverent, and inclined to poke fun at the Old Testament," his humor redeems him and "Huckleberry Finn's adventures are told with a prevailing dryness and sense of reality which do much to compensate for offences against taste." The book is discussed as a successful sequel to Tom Sawyer, with no reference to the events after Huck escaped from his father's cabin.

B13 *ANON. [Review: Huckleberry Finn.] Boston Transcript, March 19.
[Source: Quoted by Blair (1960), p. 2: the book is "so flat, as well as coarse, that nobody wants to read it after a taste of it."]

B14 ANON. [Review: Huckleberry Finn.] Westminster Review, n.s. LXVII (April), 596.
"'The Adventures of Huckleberry Finn' are good even for Mark Twain.... There is abundance of American humour of the best sort; plenty of incident, sometimes thrilling, at others, extravagantly burlesque; charming descriptions of scenery, and admirable sketches of character."

B15 *[BRIDGES, ROBERT.] "Mark Twain's Blood-Curdling Humor," Life, V (February 26), 119.
A hostile review of Huckleberry Finn. [Source: Reprinted in Durant da Ponte (1959); Anderson (1971), pp. 126-27; Lettis (1962), p. 275; and Gerber (1971), pp. 7-8.]

B16 CLARK, CHARLES H. "Authors at Home, V. Mark Twain at 'Nook Farm' (Hartford) and Elmira," Critic, VI (January 17), 25-26.
A general account of his homes and his current activities, among them bicycling, billiards, the Monday Evening Club, and smoking cigars. [Reprinted in J. L. Gilder and J. B. Gilder, eds., Authors At Home (New York: Cassell Publishing Company), according to Henderson (1911), p. 217.]

B17 *CLEMENS, SAMUEL L. [Letter.] Critic, VI (April 11), 180.
To Concord (Massachusetts) Free-Trade Club, on being elected an honorary member. "A committee of the public library of your town have condemned and excommunicated my last book [HF]--and doubled its sale"; also criticizes a decision by a Boston judge allowing sale of an unauthorized edition of his work. [Source: Reprinted in Gerber (1971), p. 9.]

B18 "Mark Twain's Semi-Centennial," Critic, VII (November 28), 253.
Consists of a poem by Oliver Wendell Holmes ("To Mark Twain [On His Fiftieth Birthday]"); a note from Frank R. Stockton (congratulating him on his first half-century: "May you repeat the whole performance and 'mark twain!'"); a note from Charles Dudley Warner; and a letter to the editor from Joel Chandler Harris, praising MT and singling out Huckleberry Finn: "There is not in our fictive literature a more wholesome book." Harris letter reprinted in Gerber (1971), pp. 12-13; excerpted in Kesterson (1973), p.118. Holmes poem reprinted in Scott (1955), pp. 34-35; (1967), pp. 39-40; Kesterson (1973), pp. 19-20.

B19 [MATTHEWS, BRANDER.] [Review: Huckleberry Finn.] Saturday Review (London), LIX (January 31), 153-54.
Superior to Tom Sawyer, because of the skill and self-restraint with which MT tells the story through Huck, this is the work of "a literary artist of a very high order." (Unsigned, the review is attributed to Matthews by Walter Blair in Mark Twain and Huck Finn (1960), p. 5, and by Anderson and Sanderson in Critical Heritage (1971), where it is reprinted as Item 35, pp. 121-25.) Also reprinted in Bradley, et al. (1962), pp. 275-79, and in Gerber (1971), pp. 2-7.

B20 PERRY, THOMAS SERGEANT. "Mark Twain," Century, XXX (May), 171-72.
A review of Huckleberry Finn. The use of Huck as narrator lends unity and truthfulness; the ending seems contrived. Considers in terms of humor questions now taken somewhat differently, as in Huck's "mixed feelings about rescuing Jim, the negro, from slavery. His perverted views about the unholiness of his actions are most instructive and amusing." Reprinted in Lettis (1962), pp. 276-77; in Anderson (1971), pp. 128-30; in Gerber (1971), pp. 10-12.

1886 A BOOKS - NONE

1886 B SHORTER WRITINGS

B1 *ANON. [Account of the "Sir Robert Smith of Camelot" reading at Governors Island, November 11, 1886.] Hartford Courant, November 13, p. 1.
MT describes the early stages of his Connecticut Yankee. Reprinted from the New York Sun of November 12. [Source: Quoted by Baetzhold, (1970), pp. 104-107; also see his "The Autobiography of Sir Robert Smith of Camelot: Mark Twain's Original Plan for A Connecticut Yankee," (1961), 456-61. Also noted in Mark Twain's Fable of Progress (1964) by Henry Nash Smith (p. 111, n. 11), who says this Sun and Courant version uses the name "Sir Robert Smith," but the New York Herald report of November 12 used the name "Sir Bob Smith.']

B2 *ANON. [Account of the "Sir Robert Smith of Camelot" reading at Governors Island, November 11, 1886.] New York Herald, November 12, p. 10.
Another account of the reading reported in

1886 - Shorter Writings

(*ANON.)
the Hartford Courant for November 13; the
Courant entry gives details mentioned by
Baetzhold (1961, 1970) and Henry Nash
Smith (1964).

B3 FORGUES, EUGÈNE. "Les Caravanes d'un Humoriste," Revue des Deux Mondes, LXXIII
(February 15), 879-918.
A review of Life on the Mississippi,
which is summarized and quoted at length,
together with a discussion of MT as a writer and a defense against accusations of
mere poor taste and vulgarity: "Mark Twain
n'est pas uniquement un amuseur incorrigible
et perpétuel.... C'est un observateur
sagace et pénétrant, qui voit bien et
raconte juste." Most of his writing has
concerned travel, by land and sea, with
the exception of "son exquise idylle," Tom
Sawyer. Unfortunately, his works have not
been successful in France.

B4 *LANG, ANDREW. "For Mark Twain," Longman's
Magazine, VII (February), 445-46.
[Source: Anderson (1971), pp. 146-47).]
A conventional ode honoring MT on his 50th
birthday.

B5 RICHARDSON, CHARLES F. American Literature
1607-1885. New York: G. P. Putnam's Sons.
2 vols. I, 521, 523-24.
Brief mention. "The reigning favorites
of the day are Frank R. Stockton, Joel
Chandler Harris, the various newspaper
jokers, and 'Mark Twain.' But the creators
of Pomona and Rudder Grange, of Uncle Remus
and his Folklore Stories, and of Innocents
Abroad, clever as they are, must make hay
while the sun shines. Twenty years hence,
unless they chance to enshrine their wit in
some higher literary achievement their unknown successors will be the privileged
comedians of the republic. Humor alone
never gives its masters a place in literature; it must coexist with literary qualities, and must usually be joined with such
pathos as one finds in Lamb, Hood, Irving,
or Holmes." Artemus Ward, like MT, made
his lampoons "either for the sake of fun
alone, or for the ridicule of solemn pretence and hypocrisy." Bret Harte is
praised passim in both volumes.

1887 A BOOKS - NONE

1887 B SHORTER WRITINGS

B1 *BARNES, GEORGE E. "Mark Twain," San Francisco Morning Call, April 17.
Barnes was the editor who asked Clemens
to resign from the Call in 1866. Fatout
quotes this article in Mark Twain in Virginia City (1964), concerning MT's investments in mining stock (p. 21), his unpopu-
larity in Nevada (p. 46), and his (and Artemus Ward's) dullness in conversation
(p. 126).

B2 *BOLTON, SARAH H. "Mark Twain," in her Famous
American Authors (New York: Thomas Y.
Crowell.)
[Source: Henderson (1911), p. 216.]

B3 *HAWEIS, HUGH REGINALD. [Introduction.] Inno-
cents Abroad (abridged ed.). London:
Routledge's World Library.
[Source: Asselineau (1954), No. 7.]

1888 A BOOKS - NONE

1888 B SHORTER WRITINGS

B1 ALLEN, GRANT. "Genius and Talent." Fortnightly Review, n.s. CCLX (August 1),
240-55.
Brief reference to MT as a leader among
the western American humorists, approached
only by Artemus Ward, Josh Billings, and
Orpheus C. Kerr. Quoted in Anderson (1971),
p. 12.

B2 ANON. "The Great American Language," Corn-
hill, n.s. XI (October), 363-77.
Briefly mentions MT, passim.

B3 *ANON. [MT accepts honorary M.A. from Yale and
defends American humorists against the attacks of Matthew Arnold.] Hartford Courant,
June 22.
[Source: Quoted in Baetzhold (1970),
pp. 120, 342, n. 33.]

B4 ARNOLD, MATTHEW. "A Word about America," in
his Civilization in the United States:
First and Last Impressions of America.
(Boston: Cupples and Hurd), pp. 92-93.
"The Quinionian humour of Mr. Mark Twain,
so attractive to the Philistine of the more
gay and light type, both here and in America," reflects an elementary taste in literature. "But now it seems doubtful whether
America is not suffering from the predomi-
nance of Murdstone and Quinion herself--of
Quinion at any rate." [Quinion was the
warehouse manager of Murdstone and Grinby in
David Copperfield.]

B5 GRIPENBERG, BARONESS ALEXANDRA. "Mark Twain,"
in her A Half Year in the New World: Mis-
cellaneous Sketches of Travel in the United
States (Source: Trans. and ed. by Ernest
J. Moyne, Newark: University of Delaware
Press, 1954), pp. 67-72.
Describes a visit to MT's Hartford home.
For further details see Moyne (1973).

B6 LANG, ANDREW. "International Girlishness,"
Murray's Magazine (London), IV (October),
433-41.
On MT, briefly comments that not all Americans appreciate Lang's praise of him "as
one of the greatest of living geniuses
(perhaps it is not saying much) who now use
the English language." Some Americans "are
not as proud of Mark Twain as one could
wish."

B7   MATTHEWS, BRANDER, and CLEMENS, SAMUEL L.
     "American Authors and British Pirates,"
     New Princeton Review (London), V (January),
     46-65.
         In "A Private Letter and a Public Post-
     script" (pp. 46-54) MT tells Matthews that
     American law gives foreigners less protec-
     tion than British law does, and Americans
     are as guilty as anybody of literary theft.
     In the following "An Open Letter to Close a
     Correspondence," Matthews argues that pro-
     tection for a foreigner's books under Brit-
     ish law is less easy to obtain than MT rep-
     resents. This correspondence led to an es-
     trangement described by Matthews in his
     "Memories of Mark Twain" (1920).

1889 A BOOKS - NONE

1889 B SHORTER WRITINGS

B1   *ANON. [Interview.] New York Times,
     December 10, p. 5.
         MT praises Dan Beard's illustrations for
     A Connecticut Yankee. [Source: Cited in
     Mark Twain's Fable of Progress (1964) by
     Smith, who adds that MT "complicated the
     task of future critics by unqualified
     praise of the illustrations as a whole"
     (pp. 81, 115, n. 23).]

B2   *[BAXTER, SYLVANUS.] [Review: Connecticut
     Yankee.] Boston Sunday Herald,
     December 15, p. 17.
         [Source: Reprinted in Anderson (1971),
     pp. 148-52.] "Of all the extraordinary
     conceits that have germinated in his fruit-
     ful imagination, nothing more delicious has
     ever occurred to Mark Twain."

B3   GOULD, E. W. Fifty Years on the Mississippi;
     or, Gould's History of River Navigation.
     St. Louis: Nixon-Jones Printing Co.
         Generally praises LOM and its recognizable
     portraits of individuals, but says MT ex-
     aggerated the authority of pilots and their
     independence of the captains (pp. 489-96).
     A section of biographies of old steamboat-
     men includes a discussion of Captain John
     Klinfelter of the Pennsylvania (pp. 612-17)
     and of the explosion in which Henry Clemens
     died. Both accounts are heavily padded
     with extracts from LOM.

B4   LANG, ANDREW. "American Humour," in his Lost
     Leaders. (New York: Longmans, Green and
     Co.), pp. 70-77.
         Finds Bret Harte's humor "more humane, on
     the whole, than the laughable and amazing
     paradoxes of Mark Twain, or the naïvetés of
     Artemus Ward" and notes MT's exaggerations
     and dry delivery, his turning his material
     to comic account, but also his healthy out-
     spokenness. The copy of the book examined
     is a second edition with no indication of
     the original date, and there was earlier
     publication in the Daily News (London).

B5   *"TWARK MAIN," "Archimedes," Australian Stan-
     dard, VI (July), 2-3.
         On the power of land monopoly. [Source:
     Reprinted in Twainian, XII (November-
     December, 1953), 2-3.]

1890 A BOOKS - NONE

1890 B SHORTER WRITINGS

B1   *ANON. "Didactic Humorists," Speaker, I
     (January 11), 49-50.
         [Source: Reprinted in Anderson (1971),
     pp. 158-59.] Includes a review of Connecti-
     cut Yankee: "Mr. Clemens is not only dull
     when he is offensive; he is perhaps even
     more dull when he is didactic." The illus-
     trations are badly done and ill-placed:
     "We hope--we may even believe--that we have
     seen the artist at his worst; we certainly
     have not seen the author at his best."

B2   ANON. "Mark Twain's Camelot," Spectator,
     LXIV (April 5), 484.
         Deplores its portrayal in CY: "Is it not
     written in this coarse and clumsy burlesque,
     of which America in general, and Mark Twain
     in particular, ought to be heartily ashamed?
     Mr. Howells, however, is in raptures over
     this sorry performance."

B3   *ANON. "Mark Twain's New Book. A Crusher for
     Royalty." Sydney (Australia) Bulletin,
     March 8.
         "The one most favorable British review"
     of CY, according to Baetzhold (1970),
     pp. 353-54, n. 2.

B4   *ANON. "Modern Men: Mark Twain," Scots Ob-
     server, IV (September 20), 454-55.
         [Source: Smalley thesis (1948), pp. 41,
     61, 70.]

B5   ANON. "The Way Mark Twain Impressed England,"
     Critic, n.s. XIV (November 29), 286-7.
         From The Scots Observer (date not given).
     On MT's incomparable humor.

B6   *ANON. [Excerpt from Connecticut Yankee, with
     comment.] Nationalist, February 2, p. 116.
         [Source: Reprinted in American Literary
     Realism, 1870-1910, V (Winter, 1972),
     87-88.] Praises MT's emphasis on "loyalty
     to one's country, not to its institutions
     or its office-holders," and his appeal for
     human equality.

B7   ANON. [Review: Connecticut Yankee.] Athena-
     eum, No. 3251 (February 15), p. 211.
         This "rather laborious piece of fun with
     a sort of purpose in it" is mechanical and
     too long, but harmless: "Sir Thomas Malory
     and Lord Tennyson will survive." Reprinted
     in Anderson (1971), pp. 170-71.

1890 - Shorter Writings

B8   ANON. [Review: <u>Connecticut Yankee.</u>] <u>Critic</u>,
       n.s. XIII (February 22), 90.
          "We do not at all approve of Mark's per-
       formance; it is very naughty indeed: but--
       and that is all he and his publishers want--
       we cannot help laughing at it."

B9   *ANON. [Review: <u>Connecticut Yankee.</u>] <u>Daily</u>
       <u>Telegraph</u> (London), January 13.
          [Source: Reprinted in Anderson (1971),
       pp. 160-63.] "It is quite possible that a
       serious purpose underlies what otherwise
       seems a vulgar travesty," but there was an
       idealism in Arthurian legend as there is
       today; and today there are still oppressors:
       "Which, then, is to be the most admired--
       the supremacy of the knight or the success
       of the financier? Under which King will
       the American serve--the ideal or the real?
       Will they own allegiance to King ARTHUR or
       JAY GOULD?"

B10   *ANON. [Review: <u>Connecticut Yankee.</u>] <u>Liter-</u>
       <u>ary World</u> (Boston), XXI (February 15),
       52-53.
          [Source: Anderson (1971), pp. 172-72.]
       We can laugh at MT's exaggerations in <u>LOM</u>,
       "When he prostitutes his humorous gift to
       the base uses of historical injustice,
       democratic bigotry, Protestant intolerance,
       and nineteenth-century vainglory, we must
       express the very sincere animosity we feel
       at such a performance. If anything could
       be less of a credit to our literature than
       the matter of this book, it certainly is
       the illustrations which disfigure it."

B11   *ANON. [Review: <u>Connecticut Yankee.</u>] Quincy
       (California) <u>Plumas National</u> (July 5),
       p. 2.
          [Source: Reprinted in Anderson (1971),
       pp. 174-76.] Praises <u>CY</u> as "one long sat-
       ire on modern England and Englishmen, under
       the clever guise of an attempt to picture
       the England of the sixth century and of
       Arthurian legend."

B12   *ANON. [Review: <u>Connecticut Yankee.</u>] <u>Scots</u>
       <u>Observer</u>, January 18.
          [Source: Reprinted in Anderson (1971),
       pp. 164-66.] "As for Mark Twain, he has
       turned didactic, and being ignorant is also
       misleading and offensive."

B13   *ANON. [Review: <u>Connecticut Yankee.</u>] New
       York <u>Standard</u>, VII (January 1), 10.
          [Source: Smith (1964), pp. 80, 115,
       n. 20.] Smith quotes the reviewer in Henry
       George's journal as commenting that MT sup-
       plied the feeling for democracy in general,
       and the Dan Beard illustrations pointed out
       fundamental causes and cures for wrongs;
       Smith observes that in some instances Beard
       went beyond the text, as in advocating his
       own single-tax doctrine.

B14   ANON. [Review: <u>The Prince and the Pauper</u>
       (play).] <u>Critic</u> (New York), XIII
       (January 25), 43.
          Mrs. Richardson, who prepared the play
       for the stage, "has done her part of the
       work as well, perhaps, as could be expected;
       but the piece, as it stands, has no real
       value, and would have but a poor chance of
       success without a public favorite like Elsie
       Leslie to play the two principal charac-
       ters.... The improbabilities, not to say
       absurdities, of all this are much more ap-
       parent in a play than in the original story
       .... The best act, artistically, is the
       last, in which a good deal of the original
       dialogue is preserved, including some happy
       examples of Mark Twain's peculiar humor."

B15   AUSTIN, L. F. [Review: <u>Connecticut Yankee.</u>]
       <u>New Review</u> (London), II (February), 187-88.
          Treats the book as a joke, along with the
       praise of it by Howells in his <u>Harper's</u> re-
       view.

B16   BAINTON, GEORGE, comp. and ed. <u>The Art of</u>
       <u>Authorship: Literary Reminiscences, Methods</u>
       <u>of Work, and Advice to Young Beginners, Per-</u>
       <u>sonally Contributed by Leading Authors of</u>
       <u>the Day.</u> New York: D. Appleton and Company.
          On pp. 85-88, quotes an undated letter
       from MT, who describes an author's method
       of composition as the unconscious accumula-
       tion of sentences that please him, as mod-
       els, collected for "the building, brick by
       brick, of the eventual edifice which we call
       our style." Reprinted in <u>Twainian</u>, IX
       (March-April, 1950), 1-2.

B17   HOWELLS, WILLIAM DEAN. [Review: <u>Connecticut</u>
       <u>Yankee.</u>] <u>Harper's Monthly</u>, LXXX (January),
       319-21.
          Praises MT's social satire and Dan Beard's
       illustrations, which reflect "the wrath and
       the pathos as well as the fun of the thing."
       Reprinted in his <u>My Mark Twain</u> (1910),
       pp. 145-49, and (with some material not in
       <u>My Mark Twain</u>) in Anderson (1971),
       pp. 152-56. Abridged in Cardwell (1963),
       pp. 6-8.

B18   *KIPLING, RUDYARD. [MT Interview.] New York
       <u>Herald</u>, August 17.
          "Kipling had included a paragraph of
       shocked disbelief that Mark Twain had writ-
       ten such a book as <u>A Connecticut Yankee</u>.
       But the glittering encomiums of the rest of
       the account evidently offset its ending,"
       according to Baetzhold in <u>Mark Twain and</u>
       <u>John Bull</u> (1970), p. 188; he adds that the
       interview was published in two Allahbad,
       India papers, <u>The Pioneer</u> (March 18) and
       <u>The Pioneer Mail</u> (March 19) before it ap-
       peared in the <u>Herald</u>. According to Baetz-
       hold, the interview is reprinted in Kip-
       ling's <u>From Sea to Sea</u> (1899) without the
       last paragraph, with its comments on <u>CY</u>
       (p. 358, n. 18).

B19 *KRIEGER, G. [Introduction: <u>Tom Sawyer</u>.]
     Leipzig: G. Freytag.
     [Source: Henderson (1911), p. 217.]

B20 NOBLE, JAMES ASHCROFT. [Brief review: <u>Con-
     necticut Yankee</u>.] <u>Academy</u> (London),
     XXXVII (February 22), 130.
       MT's "new book is utterly unworthy of
     him. Though burlesque is the cheapest kind
     of humour which can be produced by men
     whose humorous facility is of the slender-
     est sort," it has a proper field. Arthuri-
     an legend is not this field, and "if we
     laugh at the new book we are ashamed of
     ourselves."

B21 *O'BRIEN, DESMOND. [Review: <u>Connecticut
     Yankee</u>.] <u>Truth</u>, XXVII (January 2), 25.
       [Source: Reprinted in Anderson (1971),
     pp. 157-58.] "<u>A Yankee at the Court of
     King Arthur</u> is a bizarre book, full of all
     kinds of laughable and delightful incon-
     gruities--the most striking of its incon-
     gruities, however, being unconscious, grim,
     and disenchanting.... His fooling is ad-
     mirable, and his preaching is admirable,
     but they are mutually destructive."

B22 [STEAD, WILLIAM T.] "Mark Twain's New Book;
     A Satirical Attack on English Institutions,"
     <u>Review of Reviews</u> (London), I (February),
     144-56.
       Selects <u>CY</u> as the Novel of the Month:
     for all its many faults, "to those who en-
     deavour to understand what the mass of men
     who speak English are thinking, as opposed
     to those who merely care about what they
     ought to be thinking, this book of Mark
     Twain's is one of the most significant of
     our time." MT attacks the present as well
     as the past, and America as well as Eng-
     land; <u>CY</u> "is the latest among the volumes
     whereby Americans are revolutionising the
     old country," together with Henry George's
     books and Edward Bellamy's <u>Looking Back-
     ward</u>. Reprinted in Anderson (1971),
     pp. 167-70 (without the extensive quotation
     from <u>CY</u>, identification of the author as
     Stead is by Anderson).

1891 A BOOKS - NONE

1891 B SHORTER WRITINGS

B1   ANON. "American Fiction," <u>Edinburgh Review</u>,
     CLXXIII (January), 31-65.
       Mentions MT's name in a list of humor-
     ists, observing that "the humorous drama
     with a single character in different situ-
     ations is one which American humourists
     have made peculiarly their own"; the crit-
     ic's own preference is for Lowell.

B2   ANON. "The Luck of Arthur Scoresby: One of
     Mark Twain's Stories," <u>Review of Reviews</u>
     (London), IV (August), 153.

       Summarizes and extensively quotes MT's
     story, "Luck," from the August <u>Harper's</u>.

B3   ANON. "Mark Twain Among the Prophets," <u>Re-
     view of Reviews</u> (London), IV (December),
     590.
       Summarizes and extensively quotes MT's
     article on "Mental Telegraphy" in the
     December <u>Harper's</u>.

B4   ANON. "To an Old Humorist," <u>Bookman</u> (London),
     I (November), 61-62.
       Passing references: MT is grouped with
     Rabelais, Swift, Sterne, Dickens, and
     Holmes, but "If Mark Twain had to be judged
     summarily by his <u>Connecticut Yankee at the
     Court of King Arthur</u>, he would have but an
     indifferent reputation with at least half
     the English-speaking race."

B5   BEERS, HENRY A. <u>Initial Studies in American
     Letters</u>. New York: Chautauqua Press.
       The material touching on MT is virtually
     the same as in Beer's earlier <u>An Outline
     Sketch of American Literature</u> (New York:
     Phillips and Hunt, 1887). In 1891 Beers
     still groups MT with Artemus Ward and the
     other popular humorists of the age (pp. 188-
     89), though conceding that "his humor has a
     more satirical side than Ward's, sometimes
     passing into downright denunciation. He de-
     lights particularly in ridiculing sentiment-
     al humbug and moralizing cant" (p. 194).

B6   *CLEMENS, WILL. M. "Life of Mark Twain, 1,"
     <u>Library and Studio</u>, July-December.
       [Source: <u>Twainian</u>, II (November, 1940),
     4.]

B7   COFFIN, WILLIAM A. "J. Carroll Beckwith,"
     <u>Harper's Weekly</u>, XXXV (September 26), 734.
       On Beckwith's life and paintings; his
     portrait of MT is reproduced as a woodcut
     frontispiece, p. 717.

B8   GOODMAN, ARTHUR JULE. [Full-page portrait of
     MT]. <u>Illustrated American</u>, VII (July 11),
     facing 352.
       Half-tone reproduction of sepia sketch;
     no text.

B9   HAWTHORNE, JULIAN, and LEONARD LEMMON. "Mark
     Twain," in their <u>American Literature: An
     Elementary Text-Book for Use in High Schools
     and Academies</u>. (Boston: D. C. Heath & Co.,
     Publishers), pp. 313-15.
       He has keen eyes and describes both scene
     and character vividly. "Whether in jest or
     in earnest, [MT] is always and instinctively
     an artist; it is a necessity of his nature
     to perfect his work."

B10 LANDON, MELVILLE D. ("ELI PERKINS"). <u>Eli
     Perkins: Thirty Years of Wit and Reminis-
     cences of Witty, Wise and Eloquent Men</u>.
     New York: Cassell Publishing Company.
       MT said he liked <u>HF</u> best of all his books
     "because it has the truest dialect" (p. 76);
     Landon describes MT as "both a humorist and
     a wit" (p. 81).

1891 - Shorter Writings

B11 LANG, ANDREW. "The Art of Mark Twain," Illus-
     trated London News, XCVIII (February 14),
     222.
          A general defense of MT as a serious writ-
     er in addition to being a gifted humorist.
     "I have abstained from reading his work on
     an American at the Court of King Arthur,
     because here Mark Twain is not, and cannot
     be, at the proper point of view. He has
     not the knowledge which would enable him to
     be a sound critic of the Middle Ages." But
     in TS and HF he reveals himself as "one
     among the greatest contemporary makers of
     fiction" and HF is "a masterpiece." Re-
     printed in The Critic (London), XVIII
     (March 7), 130; XIX (July 25), 45-46 (as
     "Mr. Lang on the Art of Mark Twain," mis-
     takenly attributed to Illustrated News of
     the World). Reprinted in Anderson (1971),
     pp. 131-35 ("This article is apparently
     Lang's response to Clemens' request for
     support in the face of adverse criticism.")
     Also reprinted in Scott (1955), pp. 36-40;
     (1967), pp. 41-45.

1892 A BOOKS

A1   CLEMENS, WILL M. Mark Twain: His Life and
     Work, A Biographical Sketch. San Francis-
     co: The Clemens Publishing Company. Also
     Chicago, New York: F. Tennyson Neely,
     Publisher.
          A note by Isobel Lyon, MT's secretary,
     indicates that this contains facts not in
     the Paine biography (Note in New York Pub-
     lic Library; photocopy in Mark Twain Pa-
     pers, Berkeley).

1892 B SHORTER WRITINGS

B1   ANON. [Review: The American Claimant.]
     Bookman (London), III (November), 60.
          Brief, noting the humor, "But there are
     dull patches, and misplaced serious patches,
     and indeed Mulberry Sellers has carried
     away his biographer to regions where extra-
     vagance and exaggeration are no longer
     wholesome farce, but wearisome and fatuous,
     occasionally something worse."

B2   ANON. [Brief Review: The American Claim-
     ant.] Review of Reviews (London), VI
     (October), 399-400.
          A bare reference: those who have enjoyed
     MT will like this, and this time "he has
     refrained from hurting the feelings of
     those who were distressed by the travesty
     of the Arthurian legend."

B3   ANON. [Review: The American Claimant.]
     Spectator (Supplement), No. 3360
     (November 19), p. 714.
          Chiefly descriptive and only moderately
     enthusiastic, noting that "There is some
     satire in this book, good humoured and
     reasonably effective, and there is plenty

of fun, the quality of which is beyond all
question." The elaborate scheme of Colonel
Sellers "is one of the most characteristic
pieces of the American humour of extravagance that we have ever seen."

B4   ANON. [Brief reference.] Review of Reviews
     (London), V (February), 188.
          Mark Twain is a valuable asset to the new
     Idler.

B5   *CLEMENS, WILL M. "Life of Mark Twain, II,"
     Library and Studio, January-June.
          [Source: Twainian, II (November, 1940),
     4.]

B6   FAIRBANKS, MARY MASON. "The Cruise of the
     Quaker City. With Chance Recollections of
     Mark Twain," Chautauquan, XIV (January),
     429-32.
          The author was a traveling companion on
     the tour on which IA was based, and a life-
     long friend and confidante. The trip was
     more successful than MT represented; she
     appreciates his account and speaks warmly
     but judiciously of MT and his works. Quotes
     a lengthy "extract from a letter written by
     him to a young friend on the occasion of
     her début" on the change from childhood and
     the building of a mature life, and quoting
     from Thomas Fuller, whose pithy "pemmican
     sentences" he admires. Lengthy excerpt re-
     printed in Review of Reviews (London), V
     (January), 43.

B7   *GOODMAN, JOSEPH T. "Artemus Ward," San Fran-
     cisco Chronicle, January 10.
          Describes Ward's famous visit to Virginia
     City. [Source: Quoted by Fatout (1964),
     pp. 123, 129, 131, 133.]

B8   RANKIN, SCOTT. "People I Have Never Met:
     Mark Twain," Idler, II (October), 339.
          A cartoon of MT, dressed as a sailor, on
     the bridge of a ship; a life-ring reads
     "Quaker City."

B9   SHARP, LUKE. "Mark Twain: A Conglomerate In-
     terview, Personally Conducted by Luke
     Sharp," Idler, I (February), 79-92.
          Contains "Good Stories of Mark Twain in
     London" by Bruce Hatton; an account of his
     smoking; an excerpt from the interview Kip-
     ling published in his From Sea to Sea (1899)
     and MT's recollections of Kipling; a refer-
     ence to a passage in MT's "Mental Telegra-
     phy" as foundation for his The American
     Claimant [beginning as a serial in this is-
     sue of Idler]; and a reprinting of the poem
     to MT on his fiftieth birthday, by Oliver
     Wendell Holmes. There is also an extract
     from an interview in which MT expressed his
     admiration for Thomas Bailey Aldrich. The
     article is illustrated by eight snapshots
     of MT taken on board the French liner, La
     Gascogne as it neared Havre, and the issue
     has a sketch of MT as frontispiece.

B10 SLADEN, DOUGLAS. "New York as a Literary
     Centre," English Illustrated Magazine, X
     (October), 136-44.
         Brief and superficial description of MT
     as seen by the (N.Y.?) World; portrait
     (pp. 142-43).

B11 *STUART, J. "Mark Twain," Literary Opinion,
     July.
         [Source: Twainian, II (December, 1940),
     6.]

B12 TOWNER, AUSBURN. "Langdon, Jervis," in his
     Our County and Its People: A History of
     the Valley and County of Chemung (Syracuse,
     New York: D. Mason & Co., Publishers),
     pp. 609-17.
         On MT's father-in-law, noting his concern
     for his business, home, and religion, and
     describing his benefactions. The volume
     also describes other prominent citizens.

B13 WALLACE, WILLIAM. [Brief review: The Ameri-
     can Claimant.] Academy (London), XLII
     (October 29), 386.
         "Quite up to its author's usual standard.
     It is well balanced and well written,"
     though somewhat monotonous in its humor.

1893 A BOOKS - NONE

1893 B SHORTER WRITINGS

B1   *ANON. "Mark Twain at the Lotos," Critic,
     November 18.
         [Source: Henderson (1911), p. 217.]

B2   ANON. "Stockton on Mark Twain," Critic,
     n.s. XX (August 12), 111.
         Summary of Stockton's "Mark Twain and his
     Recent Work" in the August Forum.

B3   ANON. [Brief Review: The American Claimant.]
     Athenaeum, No. 3407 (February 11), p. 184.
         "Only rather amusing."

B4   ANON. [Brief Review: The £1,000,000 Bank-
     Note, and Other Stories.] Athenaeum,
     No. 3432 (August 5), p. 191.
         Faintly praises the title story and
     "Playing Courier"; "Petition to the Queen
     of England" is in the fading tradition of
     Artemus Ward.

B5   ANON. [Brief Review: The £1,000,000 Bank-
     Note, and Other Stories.] Bookman (London),
     IV (June), 91.
         "There is one good thing in this volume
     ["The Enemy Conquered; Or, Love Trium-
     phant"], and that apparently is not Mark
     Twain's. What of the remainder is passable
     is Mark Twain's commentary on the good
     thing." The rest of the book is disap-
     pointing.

B6   *ANON. [Sketch of MT at banquet honoring Henry
     Irving.] Once-A-Week (London), December 2.
         [Source: Twainian, n.s. II (April, 1943),
     6.]

B7   *DAGGETT, ROLLIN M. "Daggett's Recollections,"
     San Francisco Examiner, January 22.
         Description of MT's appearance on first
     arrival in Virginia City. [Source: Quoted
     by Fatout (1964), pp. 7-8.]

B8   *"DE QUILLE, DAN" [WILLIAM WRIGHT.] "Artemus
     Ward in Nevada." The Californian, IV
     (August), 403-406.
         [Source: Quoted by Fatout (1964), pp.
     pp. 128-29.] For MT's version see his
     "First Interview with Artemus Ward" in
     Sketches New and Old. Twainian, I (Decem-
     ber, 1939), 6, erroneously gives the name
     as "Dan Quille."

B9   *_____. "Reporting with Mark Twain," Califor-
     nia Illustrated, July, 170-78.
         [Source: Quoted by Fatout (1964), pp. 31,
     114, 117, 173, 174. Twainian, I (December,
     1939), 6, lists this as having appeared in
     The Californian for July, 1893.]

B10 *_____. "Salad Days of Mark Twain," San Fran-
     cisco Examiner, March 19.
         [Source: Quoted by Fatout (1964), p. 166.]

B11 *McEWEN, ARTHUR. "In the Heroic Days," San
     Francisco Examiner, January 22.
         [Source: Quoted by Fatout (1964),
     pp. 17-18.] Quotes MT's complaint that "to
     write a burlesque so wild that its pretended
     facts will not be accepted in perfect good
     faith by somebody, is very nearly an impos-
     sible thing to do." Describes the imagina-
     tive reporting of MT and Dan De Quille, who
     "often did the better work."

B12 MIGHELS, ELLA STERLING (CUMMINS). The Story
     of the Files: A Review of California Writ-
     ers and Literature. San Francisco: World's
     Fair Commission of California, Columbian
     Exposition, pp. 103, 123-25.
         Derived chiefly from RI and other MT
     works, and the Will Clemens biography, and
     generally superficial. "He is not particu-
     larly amiable nor generous personally, but
     he is endowed with a sense of justice, and
     he knows exactly what he is about." There
     are chapters on the Californian, Sacramento
     Union, and other periodicals for which MT
     wrote.

B13 SAINTSBURY, GEORGE. [Brief Review: The
     £1,000,000 Bank-Note, and Other Stories.]
     Academy (London), XLIV (July 8), 28.
         A dull book. "If there is fun in this
     volume of Mark Twain's (except a certain
     faint and overwrought strain of it in the
     mock romance of 'The Enemy Conquered') this
     reviewer avows himself a conquered enemy."

1893 - Shorter Writings

B14   STOCKTON, FRANK R. "Mark Twain and His Recent
       Works," Forum, XV (August), 673-79.
           Largely on MT's humor, praising his
       "courage"--the audacity of his conceptions
       and expression; also praises him as a story-
       teller, "a man of broad sympathies," while
       recognizing that "the figure with the trag-
       ic mask stalks through much of Mark Twain's
       work." Reprinted in Scott (1955),
       pp. 41-48; (1967), pp. 46-53.

B15   *VEDDER, HENRY C. [Article in series on "Liv-
       ing American Writers."] New York Examiner,
       April 6.
           [Source: Anderson (1971), pp. 176-81.]
       A conventional view, noting MT's serious
       purpose, and integrity, praising his his-
       torical novels, and, still more, those
       about the Mississippi Valley. Unfortunate-
       ly, MT is insufficiently understood and
       appreciated, especially in England. See
       also Vedder's American Writers of To-Day
       (1894.B10).

1894 A BOOKS - NONE

1894 B SHORTER WRITINGS

B1   [ALDEN, WILLIAM LIVINGSTONE.] "The Book
       Hunter," Idler, VI (August), 213-24.
           Contains a brief review of PW (pp. 222-23)
       as primarily a novel, containing "a care-
       fully painted picture of life in a Missis-
       sippi town in the days of slavery," although
       the twins "are as little like Italians as
       they are like Apaches." The extracts from
       "Pudd'nhead Wilson's Almanac" leave the
       reader wanting more. Reprinted in Anderson
       (1971), pp. 182-83.

B2   ANON. "Test Readings of Mark Twain's Hands,"
       Borderland (London), I (October), 558-60.
           In the previous issue, experts in palmis-
       try were invited to read the character of
       an unidentified person from pictures of his
       hands. Readings by "Miss Ross," "J. E.,"
       "Lucis," and "E. L. C." are given, showing
       partial success in describing the subject,
       now revealed as MT, who had been debating
       with friends over whether palmistry was a
       superstition not to be taken seriously even
       in fiction. "In our next Number I hope to
       be able to publish his opinion upon the ac-
       curacy or otherwise with which strangers
       have hit off his distinguishing character-
       istics." [The September and November issues
       were not available in the libraries where
       this bibliography was compiled, but MT's
       comments are in the January, 1895 issue
       (1895.B2).] There are clear photographs of
       the front and back of MT's right hand.
       [Henderson (1911), p. 218 lists an article
       by this title for January, 1894; I have not
       checked it--T.A.T.]

B3   ANON. [Brief Review: Tom Sawyer Abroad.]
       Athenaeum, No. 3474 (May 26), p. 676.
           A dull book, and "a grievous disappoint-
       ment to admirers of The Adventures of Tom
       Sawyer and of his friend Huckleberry Finn...
       it is a pity that [MT] should squander him-
       self on such a book as this."

B4   ANON. [Review: Tom Sawyer Abroad.] Bookman
       (London), VI (June), 89-90.
           "Tom was a promising boy in the old days.
       He is mostly conceited and sententious now.
       He says a shrewd thing or two, but all his
       adventures with balloons, and lions, and
       tigers, and dervishes, and the incongruity
       of American new humour meeting African bar-
       barism and strangeness, hardly do more than
       provoke a wearied smile."

B5   ANON. [Review: Tom Sawyer Abroad.] Saturday
       Review (London), LXXVII (May 19), 535-36.
           "The humour is genuine and characteristic,
       but it is thin." Chiefly a summary, con-
       demns the ending: "anything more flat and
       unprofitable or more shabby to the reader
       was never devised."

B6   CHAMBERS, E. K. [Brief Review: Tom Sawyer
       Abroad.] Academy (London), XLVI (July 14),
       p. 27.
           This is not offensive, as was CY: "It is
       more decent to parody Jules Verne than Sir
       Thomas Malory, and Mark Twain may therefore
       be said to have returned in his latest
       flight of humour to the limits of legitimate
       burlesque." Unfortunately, this is not a
       very funny book.

B7   CLEMENS, SAMUEL L. "Private History of the
       'Jumping Frog' Story," North American Re-
       view, CLVIII (April), 446-53; briefly sum-
       marized and quoted in "Mark Twain as Pla-
       giarist," Critic, XXIV (March 31), 221.
           Begins by telling of the stir created a
       few years ago when "a lady from Finland"
       [Baroness Alexandra Gripenberg] mistakenly
       attributed to him a story by Hopkinson
       Smith, using a plot previously used by
       Boccaccio; and now a version of the "Jumping
       Frog" story has turned up in Sidgwick's
       Greek Prose Translation. [The passage later
       turned out to have been adapted by Sidgwick
       from MT's story--T.A.T.]

B8   *FREEMAN, WILLIAM H. The Press Club of Chica-
       go: A History, with Sketches of Other
       Prominent Press Clubs of the United States.
       Chicago: The Press Club of Chicago.
           [Source: Material on MT (including a note
       by him) is quoted by George Hiram Brownell
       in "Mark Twain Lauched the Chicago Press
       Club of which George Ade Later Became a
       Member," Twainian, IV (March, 1945), 1-2.]

B9 *WILLIAMS, MARTHA McCULLOCH. "In Re 'Pudd'n-
head Wilson,'" Southern Magazine
(February), pp. 99-102.
[Source: Quoted in Rowlette (1971),
p. vii.] Describes the book (as serialized
in the Century) as "tremendously stupid,"
and malicious and misleading."

B10 VEDDER, HENRY C. American Writers of To-Day.
New York, Boston, Chicago: Silver, Burdett
and Company, pp. 94, 124-40.
Vedder's article in the New York Examiner
for April 6, 1893, here titled "Mark Twain"
and augmented by a sketchy biographical introduction (pp. 124-29) and a conclusion
praising MT's business sagacity, ending
with a comment on reports that his best is
reserved for private conversation: "Pity
it is, if this be true, that there is not a
chiel amang them to take notes and prent
'em" (pp. 139-40). Scott reprints the article without the added material in Selected Criticism (1955, pp. 49-54 and 1967,
pp. 54-59).
Also see Vedder's "Charles Dudley Warner"
(pp. 87-103): "Mr. Samuel L. Clemens has
published certain books in serious literature, without in the least persuading the
public to take him seriously. Many read
The Prince and the Pauper through with mis-
giving, lest a huge jest might after all be
concealed beneath the apparently sober
tale. They failed to enjoy the story, because they were continually and nervously
looking for some hidden snare. It is only
when, as 'Mark Twain,' he writes some such
trash as The Adventures of Huckleberry Finn
that this really capable writer can make
sure of an appreciative hearing" (p. 94).

B11 ZANGWILL, I. [Review: Tom Sawyer Abroad.]
Pall Mall Magazine, IV (November), 524-25.
Chiefly descriptive. "There are no so
many good things" as in TS and HF, "but
there are not a few memorable passages."

1895 A BOOKS - NONE

1895 B SHORTER WRITINGS

B1 ALDEN, W. L. "The Book Hunter," Idler, VII
(May), 565-76.
On p. 575 Alden comments on Personal Recollections of Joan of Arc, which has begun
serial publication in the April Harper's
Magazine as the work of the Sieur Louis De
Conte, translated by Jean François Alden:
"Every student of French literature knows
that the 'Personal Recollections' in question were written by the Sieur Uquel Berri-
Finn, and that they were originally translated into English by M. Marc Touêne.
Nothing that the Sieur Uquel Berri-Finn has
written is more characteristic of that
charming author than are the opening chapters of this new romance."

B2 ANON. "Character Reading by Palmistry and
Otherwise: The Story of the Tell-Tale Hands
of Mark Twain," Borderland (London) II
(January), 60-64.
Contains poorly reproduced photographs of
the front and back of MT's left hand, a letter to the editor by MT commenting on the
accuracy of the readings in the October,
1894 Borderland (1894.B2), and a reproduction
of the envelope in which the letter was
mailed. In turn, there are character readings by graphologists, using his handwriting
on the envelope: "The result will probably
convince Mark Twain that he had better be
judged by palmistry than by graphology."

B3 ANON. "A Frenchman on Mark Twain and His
Criticisms of Bourget," Literary Digest, X
(March 2), 10-11.
A translated portion of an article by M.
Labadie-Lagrave in Le Figaro (Paris,
February 2), defending Paul Bourget, whom
MT had recently attacked in North American
Review, and comparing their approaches to a
topic. MT "begins by choosing a thesis,
and he then invents a series of adventures,
generally very interesting, which are built
up so as to throw into full light a truth
that he has previously formulated in his
mind."

B4 ANON. "Mark Twain's Serious Stories," Review
of Reviews (London), XII (September), 231.
Briefly summarizes MT's "Mental Telegraphy" article in the September Harper's.

B5 *ANON. [Interview.] Cleveland Daily Leader,
July 16.
[Source: Quoted by Fatout (1964),
p. 215.]

B6 *ANON. [Interview.] Portland Oregonian,
August 11; reprinted there February 8, 1925.
Contains MT's comments in favor of govern-
mental monopolies, on travel, and on his
characters (and their names), not created,
but recollected as combinations of people
he had known. [Source: Reprinted in Twainian, XXIV (January-February, 1965), 1-2.]
This, together with a review in the New
Whatcom, Washington Reveille (1895.B13),
is incorrectly listed by the 1965 MHRA Annual Bibliography as "FATOUT, PAUL. Mark
Twain on the Lecture Circuit: Newspaper Accounts Concerning Mark Twain's Lectures...";
in fact these are reprintings of articles
cited by Fatout in his 1960 book.

B7 *ANON. [Interview.] Sydney Morning Herald
(September 17).
MT describes Lewis Carroll as "a true and
subtle humorist" and comments on The Mikado.
[Source: Quoted by Baetzhold (1970),
pp. 36, 115-16, with notes on pp. 328, n. 9
and 341, n. 26.]

1895 - Shorter Writings

B8   *ANON. [Interviews in which MT praises Kip-
         ling.] Adelaide South Australia Register
         and Advertiser (October 14); Minneapolis
         Penny Press (July 23), and Times (July 24);
         Sydney Morning Herald and Daily Telegraph
         (September 17); Bombay Times of India
         (January 24, 1896).
            Baetzhold (1970, p. 358, n. 21) lists
         these as clippings in the Mark Twain Pa-
         pers.

B9   ANON. [Review: The Prince and the Pauper.]
         London Quarterly Review, LXXXVIII (July),
         388.
            Brief and descriptive. "The adventures
         of the two boys in their new worlds keep
         one amused and interested throughout."

B10   ANON. [Brief Review: Pudd'nhead Wilson.]
         Athenaeum, No. 3508 (January 19),
         pp. 83-84.
            "The story in itself is not much credit
         to Mark Twain's skill as a novelist," and
         few of the characters are striking, but
         "If the preface [with its tasteless humor]
         be skipped, the book well repays reading
         just for the really excellent picture of
         Roxana." Reprinted in Anderson (1971),
         p. 183.

B11   ANON. [Review: Pudd'nhead Wilson.] Book-
         man (London), VII (January, 1895), 122.
            Brief and descriptive: MT's use of the
         fingerprint device is "ingenious," and by
         the long confusion of the children "the end
         is prevented from being a very cheerful
         one."

B12   ANON. [Review: Pudd'nhead Wilson and Those
         Extraordinary Twins.] Critic, XXVI
         (May 11), 338-39.
            Among the American humorists, "the one
         accomplished artist...is Lowell, whose
         university traditions were very strong and
         controlled his bubbling humor. The others
         are pure 'naturalists'--men of instinctive
         genius who have relied on their own con-
         scious strength to produce delight in the
         reader, irrespective of classicity of
         form, literary grace or any other of the
         beloved conventions on which literature as
         literature has hitherto depended." PW is
         "admirable in atmosphere, local color and
         dialect, a drama in its way, full of power-
         ful situations, thrilling even; but it can-
         not be called in any sense literature."
         Reprinted in Anderson (1971), pp. 184-85.

B13   *ANON. [Review: MT lecture.] New Whatcom
         (Washington) Reveille, August 16.
            Notes his bad cold, solemn, severe man-
         ner; the same issue carries what is appar-
         ently a reprint from a Portland newspaper,
         noting his blend of humor and pathos;
         there was a large audience. [Source: Re-
         printed in Twainian, XXIV (January-February,
         1965), 2-3.]

B14   ELDERKIN, JOHN. A Brief History of the Lotos
         Club. New York: Lotos Club, pp. 112-18.
            On the 1893 dinner honoring MT.

B15   HANNIGAN, D. F. "Mark Twain as a Critic,"
         Free Review [later The University Magazine
         and Free Review], V (October), 39-43.
            In response to MT's "The Literary Offenses
         of Fenimore Cooper" in the July North Ameri-
         can Review, defends Cooper but concedes that
         "Mark Twain possesses a gift which Cooper
         lacked."

B16   KIMBALL, ARTHUR REED. "Hartford's Literary
         Corner," Outlook (New York), LI (June 1),
         903-906.
            A popular account, with pictures of MT,
         Charles Dudley Warner, Harriet Beecher
         Stowe, and their homes, and also a picture
         of Richard Burton; notes that MT is consid-
         erably more than a mere jester.

B17   MATTHEWS, BRANDER. "Of Mark Twain's Best Sto-
         ry," in his Books and Play-Books: Essays
         on Literature and the Drama (London: Os-
         good, McIlvaine & Co.), pp. 184-92.
            On the truth and vitality of HF. On
         pp. 160-61, writing of Robert Louis Steven-
         son, he recalls Stevenson's "hearty praise
         of Mark Twain's Huckleberry Finn, and his
         cordial belief that it was a great book,
         riper in art and ethically richer than the
         Tom Sawyer of which it is the sequel."

B18   O'RELL, MAX. "Mark Twain and Paul Bourget,"
         North American Review, CLX (March), 302-10.
            A reply to MT's "What Paul Bourget Thinks
         of Us," which appeared in the January issue,
         attacking the picture of America in Bour-
         get's Outre-Mer. O'Rell concedes that Bour-
         get's main appeal is stylistic, and lost in
         the English translation MT read; he adds a
         spirited defense of French morality.

1896 A BOOKS - NONE

1896 B SHORTER WRITINGS

B1   ANON. "Mark Twain Up-to-Date," Idler, IX
         (July), 901-906.
            A brief, general discussion containing no
         new information, but with fourteen photo-
         graphs of MT at different ages and an excel-
         lent photograph of his birthplace at Flori-
         da, Missouri before restoration.

B2   ANON. "Portraits of Mark Twain." McClure's,
         VII (June), 73-78.
            Fifteen halftone portraits and a picture
         of MT's Florida, Missouri birthplace; also,
         a brief, conventional biographical sketch.

B3   *ANON. [Interview.] The Englishman (Febru-
         ary 8).
            [Source: Baetzhold (1970), p. 184.] MT
         "told a Calcutta reporter that on the basis
         of progress in industry, education, securi-
         ty, and prosperity one must inevitably judge
         British rule to be best for India.

B4   ANON. [Review: Joan of Arc.] Bookman (London), X (July), 124.
"It is all very fresh, and much finer in texture than, we confess, we had expected from its writer," and there is only one serious flaw: "Joan was argumentative, it is true; but he makes her arguments into long-winded discourses."

B5   *ANON. [Review: Mark Twains humoristische Schriften.] Beilage z. Allgemeinen Zeitung (May 6).
[Source: Henderson (1911), p. 218.]

B6   B., R. C. "Mark Twain on the Platform" (Reprinted from The Sketch), Critic (New York), XXVIII (April 25), 286.
On MT's world lecture-tour, with a description of his choice of material and of his platform appearance and manner. Followed by an excerpt from the Tribune, quoting an MT letter of February 16 to Charles Henry Webb, and by brief comment on Twichell's sketch of MT in the May Harper's.

B7   *CABLE, GEORGE WASHINGTON. "Samuel L. Clemens, 'Mark Twain,'" The Letter (a publication of the Home Culture Clubs of Northampton, Massachusetts), (February 1).
[Source: Reprinted in Turner (1960), pp. 122-24.] Praises the entertaining quality of MT's humor, and the way it bears rereading.

B8   HOWELLS, WILLIAM DEAN. [Review: Joan of Arc.] Harper's Weekly, XLI (May 30), 535-36.
MT was more restricted by historical facts here than in CY, and his attempts to portray language and attitudes of the age are less successful than passages in which he forgets and writes in his own idiom: "I am not at all troubled when he comes out with a good, strong, downright American feeling; my suffering begins when he does the supposed medieval thing." Reprinted in his My Mark Twain (1910), pp. 129-35.

B9   LE GALLIENNE, RICHARD. [Review: Personal Recollections of Joan of Arc.] Idler, X (August), 112-14.
Compares the historical approach to that of Carlyle's French Revolution, adding: "The man who has inaugurated a great epoch in the history of humour--and the whole of modern humour is the invention of Mark Twain--must have a great imagination, as he must also have a great heart. We have not waited for Joan of Arc to find these important gifts in Mark Twain, but certainly they are here once more, with even more than their ancient vitality." [Much of the review consists of long quoted passages.]

B10   MATTHEWS, BRANDER. "The Penalty of Humor," Harper's Monthly, XCII (May), 897-900.
MT's writing is uneven, but the best of it is very good; critics do an injustice if they dismiss him as merely a humorist. Reprinted in Twainian, XXX (March-April, 1971), 1-4.

B11   "ROUNDABOUT, ROBERT" (pseud.), "Roundabout Readings," Punch, CX (January 4), 4.
High praise for HF. Extensively quoted in Linneman (1965).

B12   TRENT, WILLIAM PETERFIELD. "Mark Twain as an Historical Novelist," Bookman (New York), III (May), 207-10.
Chiefly on JA. MT has failed in his effort, and Joan and the other characters (with the exception of the narrator) are not truly brought to life. Fortunately, MT has made his contribution elsewhere, as in TS, and "is something far more than a mere man of letters, even a great one; he is something more than a mere humorist, even a thoroughly genial and whole-souled one--he is a great writer." Reprinted in Anderson (1971), pp. 186-90.

B13   TWICHELL, JOSEPH H. "Mark Twain," Harper's Monthly, XCII (May), 817-26.
A survey of MT's career and works, with personal recollections, by MT's Hartford minister and friend of many years. There is a frontispiece portrait of MT, "Engraved by Florian from a photograph by Falk and Company, Sydney, October, 1895." Text extensively quoted by Chester L. Davis in Twainian, XXIX (September-October, 1970), 1-4; (November-December), 1-3. A summary, with quotations, may be found in Anon., "Mark Twain: A Character Sketch by a Friend," Review of Reviews (London), XIII (May, 1896), 442.

1897 A BOOKS - NONE

1897 B SHORTER WRITINGS

B1   ANON. "Facts versus Fun," Academy (London), LII (December 11), 519-20.
A review of More Tramps Abroad (Following the Equator), "a good-humoured, instructive, entertaining, careless, ill-considered, and rather disappointing book." Reprinted in Anderson (1971), pp. 207-209.

B2   ANON. "Mark Twain," in Charles Dudley Warner, ed., Library of the World's Best Literature (New York: R. S. Peale and J. A. Hill), VII, 3787-89.
An introduction to excerpts from LOM, CY, and P&P, emphasizing MT as an important writer as well as "the first of living humorists." The passages are selected to support the claim for his place as a writer who, "if the fashion of humor changes...will remain for other qualities--certain primordial qualities such as are exhibited in his work on the Mississippi--a force to be reckoned with in the literature of this century."

1897 - Shorter Writings

B3   ANON. "Mark Twain, Benefactor," _Academy_, LI
      (June 26), 653-55.
         Before Kipling, MT was "the ideal of mas-
      culine writers" in his direct approach to
      his subject, but "in the early eighties....
      He abandoned his zest in lawless life and
      the records of his personal impressions in
      the serious places of the earth, and he
      turned to satire and romance"; Kipling "is
      a finer artist than Mark Twain, his sympa-
      thies are wider, his genius is more compre-
      hensive, and yet, when all be said, the
      fact remains that Mark Twain is his literary
      progenitor." Reprinted in Anderson (1971),
      pp. 195-98.

B4   ANON. "Mark Twain's Home in the Temple of
      Fame," _Literary Digest_, XIV (April 10),
      701-701.
         Summarizes the estimate of MT by Charles
      Miner Thompson in the April _Atlantic_
      (1897.B28).

B5   ANON. "Mr. Stead on Mark Twain," _Academy
      Fiction Supplement_ (London), LII
      (August 28), 58-59.
         An excerpt from the sketch of MT (here
      attributed to William T. Stead) in the _Re-
      view of Reviews_, 1897.B27.

B6   *ANON. [Review: _Mark Twains humoristische
      Schriften_.] _Illustrierte Zeitung_,
      Nr. 2843.
         [Source: Henderson (1911), p. 219.]

B7   ANON. [Summary of reviews of _More Tramps
      Abroad (Following the Equator)_.] _Academy_
      (London), LII (December 25), 580.

B8   ANON. [Review: _More Tramps Abroad (Follow-
      ing the Equator)_.] _Athenaeum_, No. 3661
      (December 25), pp. 883-84.
         "It is too long, and there are passages in
      it that are too diffuse; but none of his
      works would stand better for a sample of all
      his wares--humour, good sense, good nature,
      genuine good fun, shrewd observation, and
      bits of description which would be hard to
      equal in the writings of the most serious
      travelers."

B9   *ANON. [Review: _More Tramps Abroad (Follow-
      ing the Equator)_.] _Speaker_, XVI
      (December 11), 671.
         [Source: Reprinted in Anderson (1971),
      pp. 209-10.] A disappointing book, though
      "distinctly worth reading," it contains
      prosy and labored sections as well as some
      good specimens of MT's humor and some "quick-
      witted and caustic social judgments."

B10   ANON. [Brief review: _Tom Sawyer, Detective;
      and Other Tales_.] _Academy_ (London), LI
      (January 2), 18.
         "On the whole, this is a bright, readable
      book, with nothing of that detestable tend-
      ency to parody the wrong things which we
      have occasionally regretted in the author."

B11   ANON. [Review: _Tom Sawyer, Detective_.]
      Bookman (London), XI (February), 151-52.
         "We have liked Tom Sawyer and Huck Finn
      better in other circumstances," but there
      are "much feebler things" in the book: "In
      'Adam's Diary' Mark Twain is at his feeblest
      and vulgarest; he fell no lower in 'A Yankee
      at the Court of King Arthur.'"

B12   ANON. [Review: _Tom Sawyer, Detective, and
      Other Tales_.] _Athenaeum_, No. 3617
      (February 20), p. 244.
         The title story is a disappointment, "How
      to Tell a Story" does not make its case, and
      the chapters on Paul Bourget "hardly seem
      worth reprinting."

B13   ANON. [Editorial comment.] _Academy_, LI
      (June 26), 652.
         On the mistaken rumor that MT was in ill
      health in London, and on the subscription
      established by the New York _Herald_ to re-
      lieve his financial distress.

B14   ANON. [Several brief items.] _Critic_ (New
      York), XXXI (November 20), 307.
         On MT in Vienna, his speech before the
      Concordia literary association in broken
      German, narrowly escaping being photographed
      while inspecting the royal box at the new
      Burgtheater, and his plans to remain in
      Vienna for approximately eight months.

B15   BIGELOW, POULTENEY. "Foreign Notes," _Harper's
      Weekly_, XLI (May 8), 463.
         MT finished his new book (_FE_) last night;
      he and his family are well and happy in Lon-
      don, the daughters enjoying their bicycles.

B16   CLEMENS, SAMUEL L. "Mark Twain on Empire-
      Building. A Philosophy of Clothes-Lines,"
      Review of Reviews (London), XVI (November),
      468.
         Excerpts from a portion of _FE_ in _McClure's_,
      November.

B17   ELLIS, ALFRED. [Photograph of MT in London.]
      McClure's, X (November), 2.
         Precedes "From India to South Africa," an
      excerpt from _FE_.

B18   *ENGEL, E. "Die Humoristen," in _Geschichte der
      nordamerikanischen Literatur_. Leipzig: J.
      Baedaker.
         [Source: Henderson (1911), p. 219.]

B19   FLAGG, CHARLES NOËL. [Full-page (frontis-
      piece) portrait of MT, from portrait by
      Flagg.] _McClure's_, VIII (March).
         This is the painting commissioned by Mrs.
      Clemens in 1891, and hung in the house in
      Hartford.

B20   *HAMMOND, MRS. JOHN HAYS. _A Woman's Part in a
      Revolution_. New York and Bombay: Longmans,
      Green and Company.

(*HAMMOND, MRS. JOHN HAYS)
On p. 152, describes MT's visit to the prisoners at Pretoria. [Source: Twainian, XVII (January-February, 1958), 1-3.]

B21 MARTIN, E. S. "This Busy World," Harper's Weekly, XLI (May 8), 462.
A brief note describes MT's original plan to dedicate JA to his wife Olivia as a silver-wedding present; through oversight the dedication was omitted from the first copies sold, but it will be on an inserted slip in copies sold in the future.

B22 ____. "This Busy World," Harper's Weekly, XLI (November 20), 1146.
A brief note on MT cites a newspaper story on a banquet in his honor in Vienna and quotes a Times (London, n.d.) story on his attendance at a stormy all-night session of the Austrian parliament.

B23 MASTERS, DAVID. "Mark Twain's Place in Literature," Chautauquan, XXV (September), 610-14.
MT has worked to overcome the handicap of his early reputation as a comic writer, and has done significant serious work. "While not a master of literary technique," he surpasses his contemporaries in the directness, clarity, and vividness of his prose. Reprinted in Anderson (1971), pp. 199-204.

B24 *MATTHEWS, BRANDER. "Mark Twain--His Work," Book Buyer, n.s. XIII (January), 977-79.
[Source: Reprinted in Anderson (1971), pp. 191-94.] A general estimate of MT, whose true worth has yet to be recognized by a public that still thinks of his early humor--which, good though it is, has been far surpassed by his later work.

B25 *____. [Review: The Gilded Age play.] Scribner's (July).
[Source: George B. Odell, Annals of the New York Stage, IX (1870-1875), New York: Columbia University Press, 1937, p. 556.] This review could not be found in examination of Scribner's at several libraries. Scribner's reviews at the beginning and ends of issues were sometimes cut out by binders, and it is possible that the Odell listing is correct. (T.A.T.)

B26 MURRAY, DAVID CHRISTIE. "My Contemporaries in Fiction. XII.--The Americans," Canadian Magazine, IX (October), 497-98.
MT is distinctively American, as Henry James and Mary Wilkins Freeman are not. Although he can be eloquent, "the medium he employs is the simplest and plainest American English." His creed is "manly, and clean, and wholesome." MT shows his limitations in CY: "Apart from its ethics, the book is a mistake, for a jest which could have been elaborated to tedium in a score of pages is stretched to spread

through a bulky volume, and snaps to pieces under that tension." Excerpted in Anderson (1971), pp. 205-206.

B27 [STEAD, WILLIAM T.] "Character Sketch: Mark Twain," Review of Reviews (London), XVI (August), 122-33.
[Unsigned; attributed to Stead (an editor of Review of Reviews) in Anon., "Mr. Stead on Mark Twain," Academy Fiction Supplement, 1897.B5.] Praises MT's works, and describes the man in part on the basis of meetings with him at which MT spoke of his books, Mississippi River water, clothing, bicycling, the type-setting machine, and the effect on employment of introducing new industrial processes. Includes several photographs of MT, including one "taken in 1890 by Peter Mapes Dodge" [Apparently at Onteora, New York--T.A.T.] Also appeared in Review of Reviews, Australasian ed., in September, according to Henderson (1911), p. 219.

B28 THOMPSON, CHARLES MINER. "Mark Twain as an Interpreter of American Character," Atlantic Monthly, LXXIX (April), 443-50.
"He is not a great or a skillful writer," and lacks the taste of an Oliver Wendell Holmes. His character Tom Sawyer is inferior to the Bad Boy of Thomas Bailey Aldrich, but the character Huck rises above the conventional vagabond in "his essential honesty, his strong and struggling moral nature." Despite the artistic flaws in MT's work the reflection of his life is appealing: "If a man can thoroughly express the individuality of a nation, he may fairly be called great." Reprinted in Scott (1955), pp. 55-64; (1967), pp. 60-69.

1898 A BOOKS - NONE

1898 B SHORTER WRITINGS

B1 *ANON. "The Anecdotal Side of Mark Twain," contributed by friends of Mark Twain. Ladies Home Journal, October.
[Source: Twainian, II (November, 1940), 4.]

B2 ANON. "Facts About Mark Twain," Review of Reviews (London), XVIII (September), 254.
Summarizes Carlyle Smythe's "The Real Mark Twain" (1898.B27) and quotes passages on "His Literary Tastes" (MT once told Smythe, "I have no really literary taste, and never had"), and "His Love of Children."

B3 ANON. "Following the Equator in Zigzag," Overland Monthly, XXXI (April), 378-80.
A review, using abundant quotation to illustrate an estimate of Following the Equator as "a happy and interesting jumble...a traveler's miscellany."

B4 *ANON. "Lettres Anglaises," Mercure de France, February.

1898 - Shorter Writings

(*ANON.)
Contains a review of More Tramps Abroad
(Following the Equator). [Source: Henderson (1911), p. 219.]

B5   ANON. "Mark Twain as a Globe-Trotter," Literary Digest (New York), XVI (January 22), 115-16.
A review of Following the Equator; consists largely of excerpts showing MT's observation and humor, but little on his social commentary.

B6   *ANON. "Mark Twains Lebengeschichte," an unauthorized and offensive biography in a six-volume edition of MT's works published in Stuttgart by Robert Lutz.
[Source: Discussed in Twainian, VI (March-April, 1947), 1.] Also listed for 1899 (1899.B9).

B7   *ANON. [Review: Following the Equator.] Critic, XXXII (February 5), 89-90.
[Source: Reprinted in Anderson (1971), pp. 212-14.] Praises the description, social commentary, and humor: "One reads as if traveling with a shrewd, kindly, sincere, and humorous man of the world who has kept only illusions enough to make life really living.... With less of broad farce, this latest book has more wit, and more literary value, than any other volume of the author's work."

B8   ANON. [Review: More Tramps Abroad (Following the Equator).] Bookman (London), XIII (February), 164.
Brief and descriptive: MT's manner has been often imitated and this will not be as popular as his earlier travel books. The reader will find MT "an agreeable fellow-tramp, observant, thirsty for information, unprejudiced, and unconventional, often flippant in the wrong place, but not obtrusively playing the funny man."

B9   ANON. [Review: More Tramps Abroad (Following the Equator).] Review of Reviews (London), XVII (January), 79-82.
Chiefly summary and extensive quotation of "a first-class book of travel, entertaining, interesting, up-to-date, genial, full of Mark Twain's descriptive charm, and richly spiced with his extravagant nonsense."

B10   ANON. [Review: More Tramps Abroad (Following the Equator)]. Saturday Review (London), LXXXV (January 29), 153.
At his best, MT is "the Great American Spirit, tongue in cheek, strolling irresponsibly around the universe. And, between its wads of padding, 'More Tramps Abroad' does afford us this spectacle," but too often it is merely labored and contrived. Reprinted in Anderson (1971), pp. 210-11.

B11   ANON. [Brief item, praising the industry with which MT repaid the debts from his business failure.] Academy (London), LIII (March 5), 259.

B12   ANON. [Brief reply to Carlyle Smythe's "The Real Mark Twain" in the September Pall Mall Magazine.] Academy (London), LIV (August 27), 197.
Smythe belabors that point that MT is more than a humorist: "Who, it may be asked, doubted it?"

B13   ANON. [Brief item.] Literary Digest (New York), XVI (February 5), 163.
Quotes a Westminster Gazette citation of correspondence in the (British) Methodist Times recommending MT's New Pilgrim's Progress [the British title of IA], but only for "the reader who understands the difference between American humor and lying"; he will find beneath the joking "the mind of a 'cute, observant, and--yes--reverent traveller in the Holy Land.'"

B14   ANON. [Brief item, noting the unanimous praise by the British press for MT's paying off the last of the Webster and Company debts.] Literary Digest, XVI (April 16), 463.

B15   BARR, ROBERT. "Samuel L. Clemens: Mark Twain; A Character Sketch." McClure's X (January), 246-51.
Also in Idler (1898.B16).

B16   ____. "Samuel L. Clemens, 'Mark Twain.'" A Character Sketch by Robert Barr. With a Reproduction of Mark Twain's Latest Portrait," Idler (London), XIII (February), 23-29.
MT is a greater man than the label of popular humorist would suggest: "I am convinced that in Samuel L. Clemens America has lost one of its greatest statesmen; one of its most notable Presidents." Among MT's works, "The Prince and the Pauper is certainly one of the very best historical novels that ever was [sic] written, and if it had not appeared, some popular books which might be mentioned would not now be in existence. Joan of Arc has been hailed by several of the most distinguished critics of Europe as a distinct gain to the serious literature of this country. In A Connecticut Yankee at the Court of King Arthur the author ran counter, not only to his own label, but to a labelled section of history. The age of Arthur has been labelled 'sentimental,' and the iconoclast who stirred it up with the inflexible crowbar of fact, and showed under what hard and revolting conditions the ordinary man then existed, naturally brought upon himself the censure of the Slaves of the Label. But these are three books which, aside from their intrinsic interest, cause a man to think; and I hope

(BARR, ROBERT)
that some day Mr. Clemens will turn his attention to American history and give us a
volume or two which will be illuminating."

B17   BENTON, JOEL. "Reminiscences of Eminent Lecturers," Harper's Monthly, XCVI (March),
603-14.
Contains a rather conventional description
of MT's manner on the lecture platform,
pp. 610-11.

B18   BESANT, SIR WALTER. "My Favorite Novelist
and His Best Book," Munsey's Magazine,
XVIII (February), 659-64.
Praises HF for the pleasure it gives a
reader, as an adventure story and for a picture of its time and place, "because, you
see, there is no moral in this book; and no
motive; and no plot." Reprinted in Anderson
(1971), pp. 136-45.

B19   BROOKS, NOAH. "Early Days of the Overland,"
Overland Monthly, XXXII (July), 3-11.
Contains passing reference to MT, pp. 7-9,
as one of the contributors to the Overland
Monthly.

B20   _____. "Mark Twain in California," Century,
LVII (November), 97-99.
Repeats the familiar history of MT's early days in California; interesting only for
the weight lent by the fact that Brooks was
managing editor of the Sacramento Alta California, which sent MT on the Quaker City
tour. (P. 96 is an engraving by T. Johnson
from a photograph by Sarony).

B21   DE LAGUNA, THEODORE. "Mark Twain as a Pros-
pective Classic," Overland Monthly, XXXI
(April), 364-67.
Praises MT as story-teller rather than
novelist, his style "historically...of in-
finite import. Aesthetically, it has been
seriously undervalued. Quite unpretentious,
it is none the less admirably adapted to
its content." Summarized in "Mark Twain
as a Word-Painter," Literary Digest (New
York), XVI (May 28), 642. Reprinted in
Anderson (1971), pp. 216-20.

B22   HILLIER, ALFRED P. [Passage from his "newly
published Raid and Reform."] Academy (London), LIII (January 22), 96.
An extract from his diary, describing
MT's visit to the prison camp in Pretoria
during his world lecture tour. MT told
the prisoners that prison life provides
valuable leisure, and promised to ask the
president to extend their sentences.

B23   PANCOAST, HENRY S. An Introduction to American Literature. New York: Henry Holt and
Company.
Briefly discusses MT in a section on American humorists (pp. 328-30), criticizing
the "cynical levity" of IA; concedes in a
footnote: "It is but just to remind the

student that Mark Twain has done some excellent work of a quite different character.
He is here alluded to simply as a humorist."

B24   *POTTER-FRISSELL, E. "Americans in Vienna:
Mark Twain," Musical Courier, December 7.
[Source: Twainian, II (February, 1943),
6.]

B25   *SCHLIECH, K. L. "Psychophysik des Humors,"
Zukunft, XXV, pp. 374-93.
[Source: Henderson (1911), p. 219.]

B26   SCOLIK, CH. "Mark Twain Sitting for His Portrait, March, 1898." McClure's, XI (May),
2.
Photograph by Ch. Scolik, Vienna: MT
sitting for a bust by Miss Theresa Feodorowna Ries.

B27   SMYTHE, CARLYLE. "The Real Mark Twain," Pall
Mall Magazine, XVI (September), 28-36.
A general discussion of the man and his
works, noting that his reputation as humorist sometimes proved burdensome; includes
personal reminiscences of MT in India, and
three photographs of him. An extensive excerpt appears under the same title in Literary Digest (New York), XVII (September 24),
372-73. Summarized in "Facts About Mark
Twain" (1898.B2).

B28   *STANLEY, HIRAM M. [Review: Following the
Equator.] Dial, XXIV (March 16), 186-87.
[Source: Reprinted in Anderson (1971),
pp. 214-15.] "A first-rate specimen of
that eminently sagacious mixture of sense
and nonsense which is so characteristic of
him."

B29   *STEUART, JOHN A. "American Fiction in England," Outlook, I (June 25), 658-59.
[Source: Rodney dissertation [1945],
p. 281).

B30   *T., S. "Mark Twain," Monatblätter für
deutsche Literatur, III, pp. 33-35.
[Source: Henderson (1911), p. 219.]

1899 A BOOKS – NONE

1899 B SHORTER WRITINGS

B1   *ANON. "Lettres Anglaises," Mercure de France,
December.
A review of Mark Twain's Collected Works.
[Source: Henderson (1911), p. 220.]

B2   *ANON. "Mark Twain as a Cub Pilot," Saturday
Evening Post (December 16).
[Source: Twainian, n.s., II (June, 1943),
6.]

B3   ANON. [Brief comment on the reminiscences
which MT says he has been writing.] Academy
(London), LVI (May 27), 572.

1899 - Shorter Writings

B4   ANON. [Brief comment on MT's graceful, natu-
      ral way of accepting the praise given him
      and his works.] Academy (London), LVI
      (June 17), 648.

B5   ANON. [Brief comment on the forthcoming
      Author's Edition of MT's works, and on his
      "Concerning the Jews."] Academy (London)
      LVII (September 9), 243.

B6   ANON. [Brief quotation from MT on topic of
      Christian Science, in the current Cosmo-
      politan.] Academy (London), LVII
      (October 21), 445.

B7   ANON. [Quotations from More Tramps Abroad
      (Following the Equator).] Academy (London),
      LVII (November 18), 560.
            Editorial comment notes MT's scant sympa-
      thy for the Boers.

B8   *ANON. [Article identifying the original of
      Colonel Sellers (in The Gilded Age) as
      James W. Wardner.] Utica (N.Y.) Saturday
      Globe, February 11.
            [Source: letter to Chester L. Davis from
      George H. Town in Twainian, XVI (January-
      February, 1957), 4.]

B9   *ANON. [Introduction: Mark Twains humoris-
      tische Schriften.] Stuttgart: Lutz.
            [Source: Henderson (1911), p. 220.]
      Also listed for 1898 (1898.B6).

B10   ARCHER, WILLIAM. America Today: Observa-
      tions and Reflections. New York: Charles
      Scribner's Sons.
            On MT, pp. 212-13: "If any work of in-
      contestable genius, and plainly predestined
      to immortality, has been issued in the Eng-
      lish language in the past quarter century,
      it is that brilliant romance of the Great
      Rivers, The Adventures of Huckleberry Finn.
      Intensely American though he be, 'Mark
      Twain' is one of the greatest living mas-
      ters of the English language." [Apparently
      this may have appeared previously in Pall
      Mall Gazette or Pall Mall Magazine, accord-
      ing to a note on p. vii.]

B11   BROOKS, NOAH. "Noah Brooks on Mark Twain,"
      Overland Monthly, XXXIII (April), 379-80.
            An excerpt from Brooks's recent article
      in The Century, on MT's connection with the
      Overland in its early days.

B12   *DOTEN, ALF. "Early Journalism in Nevada,"
      The Nevada Magazine, (Winnemucca, Nevada), I
      (October), 182-84.
            Includes the account of a joke Steve Gil-
      lis played, presenting MT with an imitation
      Meerschaum pipe. [Source: Benson (1938),
      pp. 88, 90, 162.]

B13   DOUMIC, RÉNÉ. "Revue Littéraire: Nos Humor-
      istes," Revue des Deux Mondes, CLV
      (October 15), 924-25.

Brief mention of MT (p. 932), citing The
Stolen White Elephant as an example of his
works famous in the English- and German-
speaking countries: "Cela est puéril et
long. On a l'impression d'une farce pour
grands enfans qui aiment à être secoués d'un
gros rire. L'impression n'est pas juste,
évidemment; et il est clair que, pour avoir
conquis une si grande réputation, Mark
Twain doit être un fantaisiste éminent.
Mais de cette fantaisie rien ne passe dans
la traduction."

B14   FIELDER, ELIZABETH DAVIS. "Familiar Haunts of
      Mark Twain," Harper's Weekly, XLIII
      (December 16), 10-11.
            A description of Hannibal, Missouri, with
      several photographs, including "Laura Hawk-
      ins as a girl" and the "The Hannibal of Fif-
      ty Years Ago."

B15   *HARLAND, HENRY. "Mark Twain," London Daily
      Chronicle, December 11.
            [Source: Reprinted in Anderson (1971),
      pp. 227-31.] Primarily on IA, which typi-
      fies MT's work: "The qualities and defects
      of The Innocents Abroad are the qualities
      and defects of Mark Twain's temperament, and
      they are present in varying proportions in
      all his books: vulgarity, naturalness, ir-
      reverence, freshness of vision, honesty,
      good-humor, wholesomeness." RI, TS, and HF
      are better books.

B16   HIGGINSON, THOMAS WENTWORTH. Cheerful Yester-
      days. Boston, New York: Houghton, Mifflin
      and Company, pp. 284-85.
            Visiting Darwin, in 1872, learned of his
      "hearty enjoyment of Mark Twain, who had
      then hardly begun to be regarded as above
      the Josh Billings grade of humorist; but
      Darwin was amazed that I had not read 'The
      Jumping Frog,' and said that he always kept
      it by his bedside for midnight amusement."

B17   *HUNEKER, J. G. [Mention of MT.] Musical
      Courier, XXXVIII (June 28), 23.
            [Source: Quoted by Robert Falk in The
      Victorian Mode in American Fiction, 1865-
      1885 (1965), p. 165.] "Mr. Clemens is one
      of the most original writers America has
      produced and more of an artist than is gen-
      erally believed. Being a humorous soul the
      public was slow to recognize his power in
      other fields. I pin my faith on Huckleberry
      Finn. For me it is the great American novel,
      even if it is written for boys."

B18   *KEELING, ANNE E. "American Humour: Mark
      Twain," London Quarterly Review [Not the
      same as Quarterly Review], XCII (July),
      147-62.
            [Source: Asselineau (1954), No. 18; re-
      printed in Anderson (1971), pp. 221-27.]
      Discusses the joking in IA, the irreverence
      in CY, the indictment of slavery in PW and
      FE, calling MT "this sturdy foe of oppression

(*KEELING, ANNE E.)
and injustice, this lover of the heroic and
the magnanimous...who still continues to
provide clean, wholesome food for laughter,
under the familiar style of Mark Twain."

B19   KIPLING, RUDYARD. "An Interview with Mark
       Twain," in his From Sea to Sea: Letters of
       Travel. New York: Doubleday & McClure
       Company and Toronto: George N. Morang &
       Co., Ltd. II, pp. 167-81.
          [Originally published in The Pioneer
       (Allahbad), March 18, 1890 and The Pioneer
       Mail, March 19, 1890, according to Asseli-
       neau (1954), No. 8. In his "Preface" to
       Vol. I, Kipling says the material in the
       two volumes "was written by me for the Civ-
       il and Military Gazette and the Pioneer
       between 1887-1889" (p. v.)]. After pages
       on his reverence for MT and the difficulty
       of finding his Elmira home, quotes him on
       copyright, and on a possible sequel to TS:
       "Suppose we took the next four and twenty
       years of Tom Sawyer's life and gave a lit-
       tle joggle to the circumstances that con-
       trolled him. He would, logically and ac-
       cording to the joggle, turn out a rip or an
       angel" (p. 175). Also gives MT's views on
       the impossibility of candid autobiography,
       the nuisance of conscience, his lack of in-
       terest in current novels, and his distinc-
       tion between public and private opinions.
       Describes MT's grey hair and corncob pipe.

B20   LEVY, M. S. "A Rabbi's Reply to Mark Twain,"
       Overland Monthly, XXXIV (October), 364-367.
          An answer to MT's "Concerning the Jews"
       in the September Harper's, lists Jewish
       patriots and their contributions to American
       freedom, and points to brave Jewish soldiers
       in American and other armies.

B21   LIVINGSTONE, LUTHER S. "The First Books of
       Some American Authors: V.--Mark Twain,
       Bret Harte, and Artemus Ward," Bookman (New
       York), VIII (February), 563-67.
          On The Celebrated Jumping Frog of Cala-
       veras County, and Other Sketches (1867), re-
       producing the title page and with comments
       by MT on the book (pp. 563-64).

B22   MOFFETT, SAMUEL E. "Mark Twain: A Biograph-
       ical Sketch," McClure's, XIII (October),
       523-29.
          "Editor's Note.--Owing to the number of
       unauthorized and largely apocryphal ac-
       counts of his life that have appeared in
       various countries, Mark Twain asked his
       nephew, Mr. Samuel E. Moffett, to write a
       sketch of him that should be authentic.
       The result was the present article, of
       which Mark wrote, when it was submitted for
       his opinion, 'this biographical sketch suits
       me entirely--in simplicity, directness, dig-
       nity, lucidity--in all ways.' It so com-
       pletely satisfied him that he has chosen it
       to appear in the collected subscription
       edition." In the Authorized Edition (New

York: Harper & Brothers, 1925) it appears
at the end of In Defense of Harriet Shelley
(XVI, 387-96).

1900 A BOOKS

A1   *LAUTREC, GABRIEL DE. Contes Choisis de Mark
      Twain, traduits par G. de Lautrec et pré-
      cedés d'une étude sur l'humour. Paris:
      Mercure de France, 2e éd.
         [Source: Asselineau (1954), No. 20:
      "First dated edition of Twain's Sketches in
      French translation, preceded only by a se-
      lection published by Nelson."]

1900 B SHORTER WRITINGS

B1   ANON. "General Gossip of Authors and Writ-
      ers," Current Literature, XXIX (December),
      708-10.
         On pp. 708-709, summarizes "a tribute in
      the New York Times" by Major J. B. Pond,
      who describes MT's world lecture tour and
      praises his personal traits.

B2   ANON. "The Lounger," Critic (New York),
      XXXVII (November), 398.
         Includes brief comment on MT's return from
      London, where he told a reporter he had
      "done more regular, systematic work here
      than in any other city."

B3   ANON. "Mark's New Way," Academy (London),
      LIX (September 29), 258-59.
         A review of The Man that Corrupted Hadley-
      burg. "The new Mark Twain--the Mark Twain
      of this book in particular--is not a whit
      less readable than the old, and he is more
      provocative of thought."

B4   ANON. "Mark Twain, American," Harper's Week-
      ly, XLIV (December 15), 1204.
         A short editorial praising MT "for his hu-
      mor, for his integrity, for the glorious ex-
      ample he has set, for his philosophy, his
      kindness of heart, and his gentleness of
      manners, but, above all...the incarnation of
      all the virtues of civic life."

B5   ANON. "Mark Twain, American Citizen," Na-
      tion, LXXI (November 29), 419-20.
         Praises MT's attacks on American corrup-
      tion at home, policy in Philippines and
      China.

B6   ANON. "Mark Twain's Aftermath," Outlook
      (London), VI (September 29), 280.
         A review of The Man that Corrupted Hadley-
      burg. There are a few good parts, but "most
      of this volume reads like a third-rate imita-
      tion of the Mark Twain whom we knew and
      loved of old."

B7   ANON. "Mr. Kipling and Mark Twain," Academy
      (London), LVIII (March 17), 237.
         On Kipling's interview with MT, as re-
      printed in his From Sea to Sea. Here quoted

1900 - Shorter Writings

(ANON.)
extensively, it "is in some respects the
best interview that we have ever read," revealing Kipling's profound admiration for
MT.

B8   ANON. [Brief Review: The Man that Corrupted
Hadleyburg.] Athenaeum, No. 3805
(September 29), p. 410.
This collection includes some good things,
but "diffuseness...spoils most of the matter in this book." The title story is not
mentioned.

B9   ANON. [Review: The Man that Corrupted Hadleyburg.] Blackwood's, CLXVIII (November),
733-34.
Nothing on the title story, and the other
stories and sketches in the volume are dismissed as "nothing very great," but TS, HF,
LOM "form as conspicuous and valuable a
contribution to the literature of the United
States as has been made since the days of
Poe" and "Mark Twain at his best is as good,
in his own line, as any living writer of
English prose." At times he is "too fond of
being didactic, of pointing morals, of
teaching the old world how to conduct its
affairs," and he "is conspicuously defective
in the historical sense." See 1900.B11.

B10   ANON. [Brief notice: The Man that Corrupted
Hadleyburg.] Critic (New York), XXXVII
(November), 468.

B11   ANON. [Review: The Man that Corrupted Hadleyburg.] Living Age, Seventh Series, IX
(from beginning, CCXXVII; December 15), 695.
After TS, HF, and LOM it would be wrong
to reproach MT for this new book. There are
glimpses of his old humor, but now "He is
too fond of being didactic, of pointing
morals, of teaching the old world how to conduct its affairs." His sense of history is
weak. See 1900.B9.

B12   ANON. [Review: The Man that Corrupted Had-
leyburg.] Review of Reviews (London),
XXII (September), 398.
Mostly extracts.

B13   *ANON. [Review: Gabriel de Lautrec, trans.,
Contes Choisis de Mark Twain.] Mercure de
France (September).
[Source: Henderson (1911), p. 221.]

B14   ANON. [Brief summary and quotation of J. E.
Hodder Williams's illustrated article on
MT in the current Bookman (London).] Acad-
emy, LIX (September 8), 184.

B15   ANON. [Brief Notice: Vols. VI-XII of the
Chatto collected edition.] Bookman (London), XVIII (April), 30.
Comments on the pleasure in looking again
on RI, TS, GA, and LOM.

B16   ARCHER, WILLIAM. "'The Man that Corrupted Hadleyburg'--A New Parable." Critic (New York),
XXXVII (November), 413-15.
"A parable pure and simple...were we to
take it as a story, as a representation of
life, its cynicism would be intolerable."
MT has given us moral lessons "translated
into modern terms of almost Swiftian stern-
ness." (More a discussion of this one tale
than a review of the book.)

B17   BEACH, E. E. [Review: The Man that Corrupted
Hadleyburg.] Harper's Weekly, XLIV
(August 25), 806.
A general and largely uncritical descrip-
tion of several stories in the new book.

B18   *BELEZZA, PAOLO. Humour. Strenna a Beneficio
del Pio Instituto dei Rachitici. Milan:
P. Agnelli.
[Source: Reviewed by Howells in "A Modern
Italian View of Mark Twain" (1901.B18),
also Asselineau (1954), No. 21.]

B19   BIGELOW, POULTENEY. "God Speed Mark Twain!"
Independent, LII (October 25), 248-50.
On MT's return to New York from his
world lecture tour, and on his kindness to
other authors. Sketch of MT by Bigelow.

B20   *BRIDGMAN, L. J. "To Mark Twain," Harper's
Weekly (December 8).
[Source: Listed in Twainian, II
(March, 1940), 3 as "poem illustrated by
author"; a search of this issue was unsuccessful, and the citation appears to be incorrect.]

B21   BRONSON, WALTER C. [Discussion of MT] in his
A Short History of American Literature, Designed Primarily for Use in Schools and Colleges. (Boston: D. C. Heath & Co., Publishers), pp. 286-87.
Calls MT "the greatest writer of the West,"
noting both his vigor in books dealing with
the Mississippi, and in another group of "his
better works...an historical imagination and
a finish of manner hardly to be expected in
the author of the rougher books.... Time
will winnow much chaff from his pages, but
much of great merit will remain."

B22   BURTON. "Aldine Club Dinner to Mark Twain,
December 4, 1900," Harper's Weekly, XLIV
(December 15), 1203.
A photograph of MT and other guests at the
dinner, with identifications but no other
text.

B23   CLEMENS, WILL M. "Mark Twain on the Lecture
Platform: The story of an unwilling orator,
with extracts and unpublished letters written
by the famous humorist," Ainslee's Magazine
(New York), VI (August), 25-32.
Contains a number of MT letters to James
Redpath, and reprints the reactions of Joel
Benton and H. R. Haweis to his lectures;

(CLEMENS, WILL M.)
tells of the time when the Hon. Demshain
[De Shane?] Hornet gave a temperance lecture
when MT failed to arrive, but left in disgust when the audience mistook him for MT
and laughed at every word he said. Frontispiece photograph of MT by Sarony, p. 2.

B24 *D. "Mark Twain," Alte und Neue Welt, XXXIV,
p. 700.
A review of his Ausgewählte humorist.
Schriften. [Source: Henderson (1911),
p. 221.]

B25 *FORD, JAMES L. "An American Humorist," Collier's Weekly (November 3).
[Source: Twainian, I (December, 1939),
6.]

B26 H., W. J. [Quotations from letter.] Critic
(New York), XXXVII (November), 398-400.
Extensive quotations from a letter from
W. J. H. on possible bombshells in MT autobiography to be published a hundred years
after his death--but "how slender is the
possibility" that his reputation will endure.

B27 HAWLEY, B. F., M.D. "A Further Glimpse of
Mark Twain's Hero," Century, LX (May),
157-58.
A letter to the editor, occasioned by
MT's "My Debut as a Literary Person" in
the November Century; describes an 1876
sea-trip on which Captain Josiah Mitchell
was Hawley's fellow-passenger, with a cabin
across the corridor. Although Mitchell was
weakened by the ordeal MT described, and
now terminally ill, by will-power he remained alive long enough to reach New York
and see his wife a day before he died.

B28 HOLLISTER, WILFRED R., and HARRY NORMAN.
Five Famous Missourians. Kansas City,
Missouri: Hudson-Kimberley Publishing
Company.
On MT, pp. 7-85; basically biographical.
"The data relating to the subjects has been
furnished the authors almost entirely by
members of the families and personal friends
of the subjects, and has been authenticated
by reference to them, in order that apocryphal matter might not be used" (Preface,
p. 3). Contains anecdotes of MT's early
years, some of which may be useful; refers
to Pamela Clemens as "Parmelia" (pp. 13, 29).

B29 HOWELLS, W[ILLIAM] D[EAN]. "The Surprise Party to Mark Twain," Harper's Weekly, XLIV
(December 15), 1205.
Howells' imaginary conversation with a
number of the characters created by MT,
who plan a party in his honor; Howells,
asked to help in the festivities, remembers
and liberally quotes his tribute to MT at
a Lotos Club dinner as a text which might be
used again.

B30 LANS, MATTHEW IRVING. "Biographical Sketch,"
in English as She Is Taught, by Mark Twain.
(Boston: Mutual Book Company) [pp. iii-v.]
A brief review of the salient events in
MT's life as they were generally known at
the time.

B31 NICHOLSON, WILLIAM [Color sketch of MT.]
Harper's Weekly, XLIV (December 15), 1201.
Front-cover portrait, without text.

B32 *POND, JAMES B. "Across the Continent with
Mark Twain," Saturday Evening Post
(September 29), p. 6.
[Source: Twainian, n.s., II (June, 1943),
6; Harnsberger (1960), p. 281, n. 4.]

B33 _____. Eccentricities of Genius: Memories of
Famous Men and Women of the Platform and
Stage. New York: G. W. Dillingham Company,
197-233 (preceded by portrait), and passim.
Extensive account of MT on lecture tours,
but very little on his actual lecturing.
The page numbers given in the index are not
entirely accurate. Contains MT letters.

B34 REGAN, W. A. "A Surprise Party to Mark Twain
by His Characters," Harper's Weekly, XLIV
(December 15), 1215-16.
A two-page drawing of MT and his characters; there is a brief description in Anon.,
"Mark Twain and His Characters," p. 1219,
also noting MT's enjoyment of the dramatization of P&P.

B35 SHINN, EVERETT. [Portrait.] Critic (New York),
XXXVI (March), facing p. 193.
Full-length, "from a pastel drawing by
Everett Shinn." Also, brief note on p. 193:
MT will return to America in April; where he
will live is uncertain.

B36 WASHINGTON, BOOKER T. Up from Slavery: An
Autobiography. [The copy examined was Garden
City, New York: Doubleday, Doran & Company,
1938, with a 1900 copyright notice], p. 284.
Reports that his first meeting with MT was
in London in 1899, at a reception given by
Ambassador Choate; he does not elaborate.

B37 WHITING, LILIAN. Kate Field: A Record. Boston: Little, Brown and Company.
Contains text of an MT letter of March 8,
1886 in which he agrees with her hostility
toward the Mormon religion: "I would like to
see it extirpated, but always by fair means,
not these Congressional rascalities. If you
can destroy it with a book,--by arguments
and facts, not brute force,--you will do a
good and wholesome work." MT would be willing to publish such a book, if his publishing
company were not already committed by
contracts for the next few years.

B38 WILLIAMS, J. E. HODDER. "Mark Twain," Bookman
(London), XVIII (September), 169-74.
A very general sketch of MT's life and

1900 - Shorter Writings

(WILLIAMS, J. E. HODDER)
works, providing no new information and
very little critical comment.

1901 A BOOKS - NONE

1901 SHORTER WRITINGS

B1　ANON. "Mark Twain and the Missionaries: The
Parable of the Watermelons," Review of Re-
views (London), XXIII (February), 467.
Extract from MT's reply to Dr. Ament in
North American Review, February. No signi-
ficant commentary.

B2　ANON. "Mark Twain on M'Kinley," Nation,
LXXII (February 7), 104-105.
Editorial on "To the Person Sitting in
Darkness" in the February North American
Review: "delicious though biting satire."

B3　*ANON. "Mark Twain--The World's Greatest Hu-
morist. Twenty Reasons Why We Say So.
From a Personal Examination," Phrenologic-
al Journal and Science of Health, CXI
(April), 103-106.
[Source: Reprinted in Madeline B. Stern,
"Mark Twain Had His Head Examined" (1969).]

B4　ANON. "A Sketch of Mark Twain. The Veteran
Author Returns to America," Review of Reviews (New York), XXIII (January), 37-41.
A popular account of MT's life, travels,
and works; laudatory and largely descriptive, illustrated with photographs of MT and
his Hannibal and Hartford homes.

B5　ANON. "To a Person Sitting in Darkness,"
Outlook (New York), LXVII (February 16),
386-87.
MT's article in the North American Review
"will have no effect on the opinion of the
fairly informed, unprejudiced, and independently thoughtful student of current affairs.... Most Americans will think that
American soldiers and Christian missionaries are as much entitled as Satan not to
be condemned without a hearing."

B6　ANON. [Anecdote concerning an MT lecture introduced by a local minister's lengthy
prayer.] Book Buyer, XXII (April), 179.
Includes photograph of MT, facing p. 179.

B7　ANON. [Portrait of MT in Harper's Magazine
advertisement.] Harper's Weekly, XLV
(November 16), verso of front cover.
[Mistakenly reported as a full-page
portrait in Twainian, II (March, 1940),
4.]

B8　ANON. [Selections from Extracts from Adam's
Diary in April Harper's Magazine.] Review
of Reviews (London), XXIII (April), 378-89.
Commentary says it is amusing.

B9　ANON. [Summary of "To the Person Sitting in
Darkness" in North American Review,
February.] Review of Reviews (London),
XXIII (February), 254-56.
A few words of praise are given, but no
significant analysis.

B10　DOUMIC, RENÉ. Études sur la Littérature Française, Quatrième Série. Paris: Perrin &
Cie., p. 257.
In a chapter titled "Nos Humoristes," says
the Anglo-Saxon humor does not readily trans-
late into French because of different customs and attitudes. An example is MT, with
his le Vol de l'Éléphant blanc: "Cela est
puéril et long."

B11　ELDERKIN, JOHN, CHESTER S. LORD, and HORATIO
N. FRASER, eds. After Dinner Speeches at
the Lotos Club. New York: Privately Printed.
Contains the text of MT's speech at the
dinner in his honor, November 10, 1900
(pp. 374-79); without editorial comment,
but with group photograph facing p. 374.

B12　"EPHE, UNCLE." "To Mark Twain: A Southern
Tribute," Harper's Weekly, XLV (March 16),
301.
An affectionate poem in Negro dialect.

B13　FRANCE, CLEMENS J. "Mark Twain as Educator,"
Education, XXI (January) 265-74.
Sympathy, insight into human nature, and
freedom from prejudice qualify MT to speak
as an educator, and his works embody "a
common sense philosophy of life." TS shows
how a real boy can mature through experience
if allowed to do so, and has the further
value of reminding adult readers of the importance of boyhood.

B14　HALSTEAD, MURAT. "Happenings to Humorists:
Tales of Three of the Old Masters," Criterion, II (August), 15-18.
Anecdotes of Artemus Ward, Ned Sothern,
and MT.

B15　HARKINS, E. F. "Mark Twain," in his Famous
Authors (Men). (Boston: L. C. Page &
Company), pp. 43-57.
An admiring but superficial biography
for the general reader.

B16　*HEIM, H. "Mitteilungen a. d. gesammten
Gebiete d. engl. Sprache u. Literatur,"
Beibl. z. Anglia, pp. 28-31.
(Contains a review of TS, in gekürzten
Fassg.; W. K. Krüger, Leipzig: Freitag,
1900.)
[Source: Henderson (1911), p. 222, also
listing another review "by J. Ellinger.
Same journal, s. 148."]

B17 HOWELLS, WILLIAM DEAN. "Mark Twain: An Inquiry," North American Review, CLXXII
(February), 306-21; also CXCI (June, 1910),
836-50.
A general discussion of his career and
works, noting their seriousness and importance but also the delight and entertainment
they bring readers. Discusses MT's deliberate avoidance of purely logical structure
in his writing: "He would take whatever
offered itself to his hand out of that
mystical chaos, that divine ragbag, which
we call the mind." His language is straightforward, with words used in their common acceptance and without regard for derivation.
"The result is the English in which the
most vital works of English literature are
cast, rather than the English of Milton and
Thackeray and Mr. Henry James." Reprinted
in his My Mark Twain (1910), pp. 165-85,
and (almost in full) in Scott (1955)
pp. 65-78; (1967), pp. 70-83; excerpted in
Simpson (1968), pp. 103-105.

B18 _____. "A Modern Italian View of Humor
(Second Paper)," North American Review,
CLXXIII (November), 709-20; on MT,
pp. 710-11, 714-17, 720.
A review of Paolo Bellezza, Humour (Stren-
na a Beneficio del Pio Instituto dei
Rachitici, 1900). Generally agrees with
Bellezza's general discussion of humor, es-
pecially in calling MT the greatest living
humorist. Reprinted in Howells' My Mark
Twain (1910), pp. 157-64.

B19 *HUBBARD, ELBERT. "Heart to Heart Talks with
Philistines by the Pastor of His Flock,"
The Philistine, XII (April), 146-49.
[Source: reprint of an anecdote in Abe
C. Ravit and Norris Yates, "Mark Twain,
Cable, and The Philistine," Mark Twain Jour-
nal, X (Summer, 1955), 14, 23.]

B20 LEUPP, FRANCIS E. "Mark Twain as Inventor,"
Harper's Weekly, XLV (September 7), 903.
Describes patents assigned to MT for a
buckle strap, self-pasting scrap-book, and
history game.

B21 LUTHER, MARK LEE. "Mark Twain and the First
Nevada Legislature," Land of Sunshine [later
became Out West: A Magazine of the Old
Pacific and the New], XV (August-September),
144-49.
Describes a copy of the Territorial Enterprise, quotes extensively from RI, defends
the Legislature against "the implication of
selfish incompetence," comparing Nevada
legislative records with MT's account, but
gives little other new information.

B22 McARTHUR, JAMES. "Notes of a Bookman," Harper's Weekly, XLV (October 19), 1058.
Briefly notes Paul Kester's dramatization
of Tom Sawyer, now in the hands of Charles
Frohman. "Mr. Kester has taken his own time

in making the play, and the result will, I
believe, be highly satisfactory."

B23 *MANN, MAX. [Biographical Introduction to A
Tramp Abroad (selected chapters for use in
the schools).] Leipzig: Freytag.
[Source: Henderson (1911), p. 222.]

B24 NEWCOMER, ALPHONSO G. American Literature.
Chicago: Scott, Forasman and Company,
277-79, and passim.
Praises MT as storyteller, satirist, moral-
ist, and for his portrayal of character.
[A textbook.]

B25 [PECK, HARRY THURSTON.] "As to Mark Twain,"
Bookman (New York), XII (January), 441-42.
[Incorrectly listed as "Mark Twain: A
Humorist Only," in Twainian, I (November,
1939), 3.] Takes issue with the lavish
praise given him: "Mark Twain is first and
last and all the time, so far as he is anything, a humourist and nothing more." Photograph of MT, p. 440. Reprinted in Anderson
(1971), pp. 231-34, with the attribution to
Peck. Anderson adds that the Washington
Times answered Peck in "A Little Man and a
Great Subject" (January 31).

B26 PHILLIPS, R. E. "Mark Twain: More than Humorist," Book Buyer, XXII (April), 196-201.
Praises his keen observation and his dedication to "justice, absolute democracy and
humanity" in a discussion of MT as a serious
writer. Reprinted in Anderson (1971),
pp. 234-42.

B27 *RAMSAY, W. "Mark Twain: A Biographical
Sketch," Great Thoughts (December).
[Source: Twainian, II (February, 1940),
7.]

B28 TRENT, W. P. "A Retrospect of American Humor,"
Century Illustrated Monthly Magazine, LXIII
(n.s. XLI; November), 45-64.
A very general discussion of a number of
humorists, including MT; includes drawing
and photograph of MT.

B29 *WAGNER, PH. [Review: The Adventures of Tom
Sawyer. In gekürzten Fassg. (W. G. Krüger,
Leipzig: Freytag, 1900).] Englische Studi-
en, p. 164.
[Source: Henderson (1911), p. 222.]

B30 WENDELL, BARRETT. A Literary History of America. New York: Charles Scribner's Sons, and
London: T. Fisher Unwin.
Comparatively little on MT, but only because the book emphasizes authors no longer
living. Compares MT to Franklin and Irving,
despite lesser grace, for his sober confusion of fact and nonsense (pp. 101, 173,
508), and says that his power "would have
been exceptional anywhere" (p. 513). HF,
with its dialect, is a "masterpiece, that
amazing Odyssey of the Mississippi," the

1901 - Shorter Writings

(WENDELL, BARRETT)
product of "an artistic conscience as stren-
uous as Irving's, or Poe's, or Hawthorne's"
(p. 477); it is "a book which in certain
moods one is disposed for all its eccentricity to call the most admirable work of literary art as yet produced on this continent"
(p. 503).

1902 A BOOKS - NONE

1902 B SHORTER WRITINGS

B1   ABERNETHY, JULIAN W. American Literature.
New York: Charles E. Merrill Co. [A text-
book; Source: 1908 Reprinting.] On MT,
pp. 469-72.
      Sees MT as essentially a humorist and de-
cries his supposed vulgarity, though praising his clear vision and "clean-cut, effective expression." TS and HF are "astonishingly clever studies of the American bad
boy," and LOM is his "best autobiographical
narrative."

B2   ANON. "American Booksellers Entertained by
Harper & Brothers," Harper's Weekly, XLVI
(June 28), 814.
      A group photograph of authors and other
guests at the American Booksellers' Convention; MT appears prominently in the left
foreground.

B3   ANON. "A Banquet of Sensations" [Review of
A Double-Barrelled Detective Story], Outlook (London), IX (July 5), 717.
      "Starting with an idea sombre enough to
satisfy a tragic dramatist of ancient
Greece, he suddenly becomes farcical and
fizzles...not only does the inventor of
tragic 'situations' destroy their dignity,
but the humorist...turns giggler" in his
Sherlock Holmes burlesque.

B4   ANON. "In Honor of Mark Twain: Verses at a
Dinner Celebrating His Sixty-Seventh Birthday," Harper's Weekly, XLVI (December 13),
1943-44.
      Includes William Dean Howells, "A Double-
Barreled Sonnet to Mark Twain (Written to
be Heard, Not Read)"; John Kendrick Bangs,
"Mark Twain (A Post-Prandial Obituary)"
[with passing mention of the "Gyascutus,"
which has been compared to the "Royal Nonesuch" in HF]; Henry Van Dyke, "A Toast to
Mark Twain!" All are comic, laudatory, and
affectionate. Also, on p. 1927, F. M. Ashe,
"In Honor of Mark Twain's Sixty-Seventh
Birthday," a full-page drawing of the group
at the Metropolitan Club, November 28.

B5   ANON. The "Man in the Street" Stories. From
"The New York Times." Containing Over Six
Hundred Humorous After-Dinner Stories about
Prominent Persons. New York: J. S. Ogilvie
Publishing Company.
      Anecdotes Nos. 1, 87, 203, 208, 263, 344,
419, 492, and 596 concern MT.

B6   ANON. "Mark Twain and His Career," Review of
Reviews (London), XXVL (July), 54.
      Summarizes and quotes W. B. Northrop's "A
Day with Mark Twain" in the July Cassell's,
(1902.B22).

B7   ANON. "Mark Twain on Christian Science,"
Harper's Weekly, XLVI (December 27), 2022.
      An editorial on MT's article in the Decem-
ber North American Review; chiefly descriptive, but suggests that MT exaggerates the
likelihood of Christian Science becoming a
new religion: it is merely another new
sect.

B8   ANON. "Mark Twain Unveils a Tablet to Eugene
Field," Harper's Weekly, XLVI (July 5), 851.
      Describes MT's unveiling of a tablet at
Field's birthplace in ceremonies on June 7;
MT had come to receive an honorary LLD from
the University of Missouri. Includes two
photographs of MT at the unveiling, and his
brief remarks.

B9   *ANON. "The Sixty-Seventh Birthday of Mark
Twain," The Critic, November 30.
      [Source: Twainian, II (January, 1940),
5. The article is not in the November, 1902
issue of The Critic: An Illustrated Monthly
Review of Literature Art and Life (G. P.
Putnam's Sons).]

B10   ANON. "Was Mark Twain Tom Sawyer?" Review of
Reviews (London), XXVI (September), 272.
      A summary of Henry M. Wharton, "The Boy-
hood Home of Mark Twain," (1902.B26).

B11   ANON. [Review: A Double-Barrelled Detective
Story.] Academy, LXIII (June 26), 14.
      A short review, briefly describes the be-
ginning; then: "The story thus launched is
of breathless interest, and it is short."

B12   ANON. [Review: A Double-Barrelled Detective
Story.] Athenaeum, No. 3901 (August 2), p. 152.
      "The hand of the master is not easy to
recognize.

B13   ANON. [Brief Review: A Double-Barrelled Detective Story.] Saturday Review (London),
XCIV (August 2), 147.
      The book is "hopeless...an odd jumble:
there is very nearly a serious plot, arising
out of a very disgusting incident, and then
the story tails off into a feeble burlesque
of detective fiction."

B14   *ELLINGER, J. "Altertümliche Sprache in d.
Roman: The Prince and the Pauper."
      [Source: Henderson (1911), p. 223, list-
ing with 1903 entries, but with facts of
publication thus: "Beiträge zur neuer.
Philogie J. Schipper z. 19 Juli 1902,
ss. 88-107."]

B15   *ANON. "Mitteilungen a. d. gesamten Gebiete d.
engl. Sprache u. Literatur," Beibl. z. Anglia, p. 149.

(ANON.)
A review of A Tramp Abroad, edited by M. Mann (Leipzig: Freytag, 1901). [Source: Henderson (1911), p. 223.]

B16 FARMER, A. O., and ALICE G. HOWLAND. "Obituaries of Mark Twain," Harper's Weekly, XLVI (November 29), 1791.
Letters to the editor, offering humorous obituaries in response to MT's request in "Amended Obituaries" in the November 15 issue, p. 1704.

B17 HALSEY, FRANCIS W. "Some Books to Read this Summer," Review of Reviews (New York), XXV (June), 700-707.
Portrait of MT and brief mention of A Double-Barreled Detective Story (p. 707), without critical comment.

B18 *HOWE, E. W. [Apparently on MT's Autobiography, appearing serially in Harper's.] Atchinson (Kansas) Globe (June 2).
[Source: Quoted by Calder M. Pickett in his Ed Howe: Country Town Philosopher (Lawrence and London: The University Press of Kansas, 1968, p. 123).] MT, "scraping the moss of his memory," would find turning backward brings "only a great shaking up of stiff limbs and illusions."

B19 HOWELLS, WILLIAM DEAN. "Mr. Howell's [sic] Literary Appreciation of Mark Twain," Connecticut Magazine, No. III-IV (December), pp. 409-12.
A condensation of his "Mark Twain: An Inquiry" (1901.B17), with only minimal editorial comment added.

B20 MATTHEWS, BRANDER. "The Penalty of Humor," in his Aspects of Fiction, and Other Ventures in Criticism. (New York: Charles Scribner's Sons), Third ed., enlarged, pp. 43-56; pp. 54-56 on MT.
Franklin, Lincoln, Canning, and Disraeli were taken less seriously than they deserved, and the same fate has befallen MT. Praises parts of TS, HF, PW, and MT's storytelling and mastery of English prose in the highest terms. He is uneven, to be sure, and has written some poor things, but it is chiefly because of his humor that he is not ranked at his true value.

B21 NICHOL, JOHN. "American Literature," Encyclopaedia Britannica (Akron, Ohio: Werner Company), I, 718-35.
Under "Travels," p. 727, mentions Nathaniel Parker Willis as holding "a respectable place" among the numerous American authors who have published their impressions of the Old World, with every variety of good and bad taste, from Old Home to the Innocents Abroad." Discussing humor (pp. 727-28), shows moderate approval for Bret Harte and Artemus Ward, but apparently includes MT with the worst of Ward's imitators, who "have caught the trick of his phrase and

who are unrestrained by his good feeling and good sense, an easy descent to the lowest level of light literature--that which panders to the vice of moral scepticism and thrives on the buffoonery of making great and noble things appear mean or ridiculous. The names of those who habitually feed on mental garbage should be left to sink into the oblivion from which they have unfortunately emerged." There is no other mention here of MT, whom Nichol attacked in his 1882 book, American Literature, (1882.B21).

B22 NORTHROP, W. B. "A Day with Mark Twain," Cassell's Magazine, XXXIV (July), 115-21.
On a visit to MT at Saranac Lake, New York; consists largely of familiar biographical data, with five photographs. Summarized in Anon., "Mark Twain and His Career," (1902.B6).

B23 PATTEE, FRED LEWIS. "American Literature," Encyclopaedia Britannica, New American Supplement. Akron, Ohio: The Werner Company, XXV, 168-69. (Copyrighted 1896; a note refers to the "earlier account of this subject" by John Nichol in Vol. I [1882.B21])
"His descriptions, sometimes even approaching the realms of poetry, his accurate characterizations, his powers of minute observation and of narration, his facility and his sense of proportion, give [his books] their truest value." His humor, from IA on, "has ever been leveled against sham and hypocrisy." "His later works have been growing more and more serious, and it is more than probable that the critics of the future will rank him as a strong and intensely original writer who was incidentally a humorist."

B24 PERRY, BLISS. A Study of Prose Fiction. Boston: Houghton Mifflin Company (Source: 1920 reprint with only minimal alterations.)
On pp. 338-39, cites Fenimore Cooper, Poe, and Hawthorne as "American fiction-writers who have won a secure place in the world's literature." One might also consider "Bret Harte...Mark Twain, Howells, Aldrich, Stockton, James, Cable, Crawford, and many another living writer of admirable craftsmanship and honorable rank. But I suppose that there are few critics who would deliberately select among these later men a fourth to be placed in equality of universal recognition with that great trio who more than a century ago were in the fullness of their power."

B25 PHILLIPS, ROLAND. "Mark Twain and the Chat Noir," Book Buyer, XXIV (June), 379-82.
Concerns a joke played on M. Salis, cabaret-owner, friend of poets, and admirer of MT; contains nothing bearing directly on MT.

B26 WHARTON, HENRY M. "The Home of Mark Twain," Century, XLIV (September), 674-77.
A popular description of Hannibal, with five photographs; briefly summarized in Anon., "Was Mark Twain Tom Sawyer?" (1902.B10)

1902 - Shorter Writings

B27 *[WHITELOCK, WILLIAM WALLACE.] "The Literary
Guillotine," The Reader, issues of late
1902 and early 1903.
[Source: Twainian, II (May, 1943), 6,
identifying Whitelock as "presumed author."]

1903 A BOOKS

A1 ANON. Mark Twain's Birthday. A Report of the
Celebration of the Sixty-Seventh Thereof at
the Metropolitan Club, New York,
November 28th, 1902. N.p., Copyright by
George Harvey, 1903.

1903 B SHORTER WRITINGS

B1 *ANON. "Fiftieth [sic] Birthday of Mark
Twain," Critic (January).
[Source: Henderson (1911), p. 223.]

B2 ANON. "Mark Twain's Audiences," Harper's
Weekly, XLVII (December 19), 2071.
A brief, undocumented anecdote of MT's reply to a question of what audiences make the
most responsive and sympathetic listeners:
"college men and convicts." Also, p. 2030,
photograph of MT, without comment, in "A
Group of Our Harper Authors and Artists."

B3 ANON. "More from Mark Twain about Christian
Science," Harper's Weekly, XLVII
(January 24), 145.
Summarizes from the current North Ameri-
can Review the second installment of MT's
writing on Christian Science.

B4 ANON. "Will Christian Science Rule the
World?" and "The Future of Christian Sci-
ence," Review of Reviews (London), XXVII
(January), 35-36; (March), 280.
Summaries of articles by MT in North Amer-
ican Review, December, 1902 and March, 1903.

B5 ANON. [Two caricatures of MT, who "has announced his intention of leaving America
and making his permanent home in Italy."]
Bookman (New York), XVII (July), 449.

B6 *CATANI, UGO. [Portrait of Mark Twain, from
the miniature of Ugo Catani.] Studio,
(September 15).
[Source: Henderson (1911), p. 223.]

B7 CHESTERTON, G. K. "Bret Harte," in his Varied
Types. (New York: Dodd, Mead and Company),
pp. 179-95.
Chesterton regards American humor as
based on exaggeration. Passing references
to MT as lacking Harte's subtlety and reverence, pp. 182-84.

B8 *DIEDRICH, B. "Mark Twain u.d. amerikanische
Humor," Der Türmer (Stuttgart), July,
pp. 434-45.
[Source: Henderson (1911), p. 223.]

B9 *FITCH, THOMAS. "Recollections and Reflections
of Thomas Fitch." San Francisco Sunday Call,
October 4, 1903.
[Source: Quoted by Fatout (1964, pp
pp. 173-75) concerning a continued novel in
the Occidental (cf. RI, Vol. II, Ch. X).]

B10 *HAMMERTON, J. A., ed. Stevensoniana. London,
pp. 88, 293-94.
Stevenson's praise of MT's books. [Source:
Quoted by Baetzhold (1970), pp. 204-205,
361, n. 17.]

B11 HIGGINSON, THOMAS WENTWORTH, and HENRY WALCOTT
BOYNTON. A Reader's History of American
Literature. Boston, New York, Chicago:
Houghton, Mifflin Company, pp. 246-48.
Sees MT as primarily a humorist, but rec-
ognizes a somewhat different achievement in
HF.

B12 KELLER, HELEN. The Story of My Life by Helen
Keller. With Her Letters (1887-1901) and A
Supplementary Account of Her Education, In-
cluding Passages from the Reports and Letters
of Her Teacher, Anne Mansfield Sullivan by
John Albert Macy. New York: Doubleday,
Page & Company, passim.
Recollections of MT are affectionate but
not illuminating. There were several meet-
ings, one of them March 31, 1895 when she
was fourteen (pp. 227-28). Photograph of
Helen Keller with MT facing p. 138.

B13 LEVERING, ALBERT. "The Man Who Corrupted Eddy-
ville. Being Some Account of the Troubles
which Beset Mark Twain During His Quest for
Mrs. Eddy's Book," Harper's Weekly, XLVII
(February 7), 215.
A cartoon sequence in which several Christian Scientist booksellers and Mary Baker
Eddy herself refuse to sell or give a copy
of Science and Health to MT, who appears disguised as various characters from his books.

B14 MABIE, HAMILTON W[RIGHT.] "The Best-Known
American Humorist," Ladies' Home Journal, XX
(March), 17.
Brief item, noting the lasting importance
of his works; with photograph of "Mark Twain,
with his Wife and Daughter."

B15 STODDARD, CHARLES WARREN. "A Humorist Abroad,"
in his Exits and Entrances: A Book of Essays and Sketches (Boston: Lothrop Publishing Company), pp. 61-74.
On MT when he was lecturing in London,
1873-74, and they shared rooms.

B16 *SWOBODA, WILHELM. [Review: A Tramp Abroad,
edited by M. Mann (Leipzig: Freytag, 1900).]
Die neueren Sprachen, (July), pp. 223-35.
[Source: Henderson (1911), p. 223.]

B17   WOODBERRY, GEORGE EDWARD.   America in Litera-
      ture. New York and London: Harper & Broth-
      ers. Republished Upper Saddle River, N.J.:
      Literature House/Gregg Press, 1970,
      pp. 159-61.
          [According to a note facing the verso of
      the t.p., "The papers in this volume origi-
      nally appeared in Harper's Magazine and
      Harper's Weekly."]
          MT was the climax of Western humor, "al-
      though, fun for fun's sake being his rule,
      he often goes sprawling, for fun seldom
      stands alone; for long life it has to mate
      with something, to blend with other ele-
      ments, as in the great humorists." The
      picturesqueness of the West called for the
      artist, and "the artist came in Bret Harte."

1904 A BOOKS - NONE

1904 B SHORTER WRITINGS

B1   ALDEN, W. L. "Mark Twain; Samuel L. Clemens,"
      English Illustrated Magazine, n.s., XXXII
      (November), 182-84, 188.
          "Mark Twain is essentially an enthusiast,
      and his enthusiasm is always for the things
      that are noble, and heroic, and right."
      Photo of MT by Walter Barnett, and bibliog-
      raphy of his works and secondary material
      concerning him.

B2   ANON. "Mark Twain's Latest," Spectator, XCII
      (June 11), 925-26.
          A review of Extracts from Adam's Diary.
      "Not only is this little book to be acquit-
      ted of the charge of any real irreverence,
      but...its audacity is so tempered by deli-
      cacy, and even tenderness, of feeling that
      no broad-minded reader can arise from its
      perusal without enhanced admiration for the
      great and kindly humourist who, since Dick-
      ens's death, has done more than any other
      writer to promote the gaiety of the two
      great branches of the Anglo-Saxon race."

B3   *ANON. [Interview with MT in Florence.]
      [Source: Reprinted in James McArthur,
      "Books and Bookmen," Harper's Weekly,
      XLVIII (May 14), 753.]
          Describes MT's appearance and quotes his
      views on copyright and Christian Science;
      photograph: "Mark Twain in the Garden of
      the Villa di Quarto, near Florence." Fol-
      lowed by James McArthur's brief, uncritical
      description of Adam's Diary.

B4   ANON. [Portrait of MT, "From a photograph
      recently taken in Italy."] Review of Re-
      views (New York), XXX (July), 122.

B5   *BURTON, RICHARD. Literary Leaders of America.
      New York: Charles Scribner's Sons.
      [Source: Andrews (1950), p. 273.]

B6   "A CONSTANT READER." "The God of Battles,"
      Harper's Weekly, XLVIII (November 26), 1814.
          Incorrectly ascribes to MT a letter in the
      previous issue. Also, p. 1820, a brief MT
      anecdote on an occasion when the missed his
      steamboat and made no excuse in his report:
      "My boat left at 7.20. I arrived at the
      wharf at 7.35 and could not catch it."

B7   CONWAY, MONCURE DANIEL. Autobiography: Memo-
      ries and Experiences. Boston and New York:
      Houghton, Mifflin and Company. 2 vols. II,
      142-45.
          Describes an 1872 MT lecture in St.
      George's Hall (London), MT at a Savage Club
      dinner, where he praised the Albert Memorial
      "which will stand in all its beauty when the
      name it bears has crumbled into dust." De-
      scribes a visit to the Hartford home in
      1876, and MT as master of ceremonies in an
      entertainment for Harriet Beecher Stowe.
      It was Conway who took the MS of Tom Sawyer
      to England. Also, describes MT and Olivia
      visiting Stratford-on-Avon, MT's amusement
      in London when shown a mechanical "leaping
      frog," which he followed around the room on
      hands and knees. Describes MT reading aloud
      from the MS of A Tramp Abroad in Paris in
      1879, "and the tact and insight displayed by
      his wife in her comments were admirable."
      Much of this is reprinted in Twainian, XII
      (September-October, November-December, 1953);
      XIII (January-February, 1954).

B8   *FIELDS, MRS. JAMES T. Charles Dudley Warner.
      New York: McClure, Phillips & Co.
          [Source: Bryant Morey French, ed., The
      Gilded Age (1972), "Selected Readings,"
      p. xli: "A contemporary memoir of Warner by
      the wife of the publisher of the Atlantic
      Monthly."]

B9   GELLI, E. "A New Portrait of Mark Twain,
      Painted by the Italian Artist E. Gelli, to
      be Exhibited at the World's Fair at St.
      Louis," Harper's Weekly, XLVIII (September 3),
      1347.
          The portrait is reproduced, full-page,
      without further comment.

B10   GILDER, RICHARD WATSON. "Mark Twain: A Glance
      at His Spoken and Written Art," Outlook (New
      York), LXXVIII (December 3), 842-44.
          The two forms of his art overlap; both are
      marked by strong convictions and a dramatic
      presentation. On p. 843, a full-page por-
      trait of MT, "Drawn from life for The Out-
      look by Kate Rogers Nowell."

B11   *M'ARTHUR, J. [Interview with Mark Twain.]
      Harper's Weekly (May 14).
          [Source: Henderson (1911), p. 223.]

B12   *MORRIS, CLARA. "An Interview with Mark Twain,"
      Metropolitan Magazine (March).
          [Source: Twainian, II (February, 1943),
      6.]

1904 - Shorter Writings

B13 PARROTT, T. M. "Mark Twain: Made In America," Booklovers' Magazine (February),
pp. 145-54.
[Source: Scrapbook, Mark Twain: Biography-Reminiscence in Chicago Public Library; also, listed in Twainian, I
(November, 1939), 3.] An extensive, general discussion of MT's writing, which is
characterized by a sweet sunniness, across
which no shadow of impurity ever falls."
Reprinted in Anderson (1971), pp. 243-53.

B14 *[PECK, HARRY THURSTON.] "Mark Twain at Ebb
Tide," Bookman (New York), XIX (May),
235-36.
A review of Extracts from Adam's Diary as
showing "just how far a man who was once a
great humorist can fall. We thought when
we read A Double-Barrelled Detective Story
that Mark Twain could do no worse. But we
were wrong." [Source: Reprinted in Anderson (1971), p. 254, with attribution as
"quite probably" by Peck.]

B15 SIMBOLI, RAFFAELE. "Mark Twain from an Italian Point of View," Critic, XLIV (June),
518-24.
Primarily on MT at the Villa di Quarto in
Florence, with photographs of the Villa,
two photographs of MT, and one of Jean
Clemens on her horse. There is only brief
comment on MT, as a writer whose humor is
not much understood in Italy although JA
"met with considerable success."

B16 THOMAS, FREDERICK MOY. Fifty Years of Fleet
Street. Being the Life and Recollections of
Sir John R. Robinson. London and New York:
Macmillan, pp. 157-58.
Far from joking all the time, "As a matter
of fact he is, or was some ten years ago, a
sad, slow, somewhat ponderous man. He
spoke with a deliberation that was almost
irritating. He was greatly interested in
labour questions, and would tell in a deliberate, matter-of-fact way the story of
the Knights of Labour and similar organiza-
tions in the United States. Of humour there
was none in his conversation.... His hair
some years ago was wild and bushy, his eyes
had a kindly but plaintive expression."
When MT dined at a London club, all the
waiters found pretexts to come to his table
and he recognized one of them and chatted
with him.

B17 TRENT, WILLIAM P. "Mark Twain," in his A
Brief History of American Literature. (New
York: D. Appleton and Company), pp. 235-36.
TS raised MT to a place "as one of the
greatest living writers of the fiction of
blended humour, adventure, and realistic
description of characters and places....
So thoroughly American a career and two
such masterpieces as Tom Sawyer and Huckleberry Finn seem to assure [MT]...an abiding
reputation not surpassed by that of any of
his fellow writers of the modern period."

B18 *WURM, A. "Mark Twain als Mensch u. Humorist,"
Alte und neue Welt (Einsiedeln), p. 718.
[Source: Henderson (1911), p. 224.]

1905 A BOOKS - NONE

1905 B SHORTER WRITINGS

B1 ANON. "If Emperors Were All Stripped Naked,"
Review of Reviews (London), XXXI (April),
375.
Summary of "The Czar's Soliloquy," which
appeared in North American Review in March.

B2 ANON. "Mark Twain at Seventy," Outlook (New
York), LXXXI (December 2), 808.
Notes the uneven quality of MT's work:
"some of it is distinctly slovenly and lacking in spontaneity, with grave defects not
only of conventional but of fundamental
taste; but much of it is fresh, vivid, original, and of a quality not yet fully appreciated by cultivated Americans." Life on
the Mississippi, Tom Sawyer, Huckleberry
Finn "are likely to be kept with the real
books from American hands two or three centuries hence, when a whole world of well-
bred, scholarly, and cultivated writing will
have passed into that oblivion which awaits
everything except life expressed in terms of
beauty, freedom, humor, and power."

B3 ANON. "Mark Twain on Copyright," Review of
Reviews (New York), XXXI (February), 213-14.
A summary of his article in the January
North American Review.

B4 ANON. "Mark Twain on Copyright," Review of
Reviews (London), XXXI (February), 165.
Summarizes and quotes his article in the
January North American Review.

B5 *ANON. "Mark Twain u. d. amerik. Humor,"
Beilage zur Allgemeinen Zeitung (München),
Nr. 77.
[Source: Henderson (1911), p. 224.]

B6 *ANON. "Mark Twain's Autobiography, 1872,"
Connecticut Magazine (April).
[Source: Henderson (1911), p. 224.]

B7 ANON. "Mark Twain's 70th Birthday. Souvenir
of Its Celebration," Supplement to Harper's
Weekly, XLIV (December 23), 1883-1914.
An extensive record of the dinner in MT's
honor at Delmonico's, December 5, with the
guest list (p. 1884), and with full-page
photographs of those seated at each table
(pp. 1894-1914); gives texts of speeches,
poems, and messages honoring MT by Theodore
Roosevelt, William Dean Howells, Brander
Matthews, John Kendrick Bangs, Kate Douglas
Riggs [Wiggin], Richard Watson Gilder, An-
drew Carnegie, George Washington Cable,
Amelia E. Barr, Weir Mitchell, Virginia
Frazer Boyle, Joel Chandler Harris, Wilbur
D. Nesbit, Louise Morgan Sill, Hamilton W.

(ANON.)
Mabie, Agnes Repplier, Irving Bacheller, Rex E. Beach, Hopkinson Smith, Carolyn Wells, and Henry Van Dyke, and a list of signers of a telegram of birthday greetings from Europe. The text of MT's speech appears on pp. 1885-86.

B8 *BRUNI, LIVIA. "1'Umorismo americano, Mark Twain," Nuova Antologia (Rome), ser. IV, CXV (CXCIX), 697-709.
[Source: facts of publication are from Asselineau (No. 27, 1954); summarized in Review of Reviews (New York), XXXI (June), 743-44, with long quotations (and the author's name rendered as "Livia Pruni").] The article contains Italian translations of several short stories; the only major work already available in translation was The Prince and the Pauper. There is a discussion of the nature of humor and the loss in translation. MT's humor has none of the obscenity all too common in Italy and France. His harsh words for Italy in the early travel books were justified, and he now is in sympathy with the new government.

B9 CLEMENS, SAMUEL. "Mark Twain for Jerome," Harper's Weekly, XLIX (August 26), 1238.
A brief letter to the editor, concluding: "Out of respect for him, his morals, and his principles, I mean to vote for him only once on election-day, but if I were free from this restraint I would make it a hundred."

B10 CRILLY, DANIEL. "The After-Dinner Oratory of America," Nineteenth Century, LVII (May), 853-68.
References to MT, passim, but purely derivative.

B11 *DE LEON, DANIEL. "An Irrepressible Humorist," Daily People (New York), September 7.
[Source: Foner (1958), p. 329.]

B12 *DIEDERICH, B. "Mark Twain," Tägl. Rundschau (Leipzig), Nr. 280.
[Source: Henderson (1911), p. 224.]

B13 EATON, CHARLOTTE. "Mark Twain on Copyright," Harper's Weekly, XLIX (February 11), 214.
A letter to the editor, supporting MT's article on copyright in the current North American Review.

B14 *HUENDGREN. [Review: A Tramp Abroad, edited by M. Mann. Leipzig: Freytag, 1901.] Gymnasium (Paderborn), p. 49.
[Source: Henderson (1911), p. 224.]

B15 HUTTON, LAURENCE. Talks in a Library with Laurence Hutton. Recorded by Isabel Moore. New York and London: G. P. Putnam's Sons, passim.
Contains silhouette of MT by Alice I. Bunner (facing p. 6); MT a dinner guest (pp. 22, 326); MT and Helen Keller's first meeting: "He was peculiarly tender and lovely with her--even for Mr. Clemens--and she kissed him when he said good-by" (pp. 390-91). On the night when the death of Bret Harte became known, "he was discussed in a most feeling way in a monologue talk of an hour or two by Mark Twain," who referred to him as "Frank" Harte, thereby losing his audience, who did not realize he was talking about Bret Harte (p. 407); also, tells of Harte's hearing the "Jumping Frog" story and urging MT to publish it (p. 409). MT's introduction of Cable to a Hartford audience, anecdotes about Jean Clemens and Harriet Beecher Stowe, and two MT notes (pp. 419-21).

B16 JOHNSON, CLIFTON. "Mark Twain's Country," Outing Magazine, XLV (January), 433-40.
On a visit to Hannibal and Florida, Missouri; illustrated with several photographs, including one of the front of the home of Tom Blankenship ("when he left home, it was to go to the penitentiary"). One old acquaintance called MT "the most overrated man in America.... As a boy, Sam was just like other boys, except he might have been a little slower. He was considered blamed dull, to tell you the truth." Another acquaintance remembered him as solitary, not interested in hunting and fishing with the other boys, although fond of exploring the cave. Both remembered his slow, drawling speech.

B17 *KELLNER, L. "Mark Twain (zum siebzigsten Geburtstag)," Neue Freie Presse (Literaturblatt), December 3, pp. 31-32.
[Source: Henderson (1911), p. 224.]

B18 [LAMONT, HAMMOND.] "Mark Twain at Seventy," Nation (New York), LXXXI (December 14), 478-79.
MT has won respect as a writer, here and in England, although he does not belong to the coteries of Boston and New York. "He knows America and knows it whole," writing with power rather than fine academic distinctions. He is "a humorist of the first rank," to be sure, but also a humanist. Reprinted in Anderson (1971), pp. 255-57, with attribution to Lamont.

B19 *SALOMON, LUDWIG. "Mark Twain (zu seinem siebzigsten Geburtstage)," with portrait. Illustrierte Zeitung (Leipzig), November 30.
[Source: Henderson (1911), p. 224.]

1906 A BOOKS - NONE

1906 SHORTER WRITINGS

B1 ANON. "Further Anecdotes of Mark Twain," Harper's Weekly, L (March 24), 421.
Chiefly on MT in Hartford, with texts of some brief MT notes.

1906 - Shorter Writings

B2   ANON. "Mark Twain's Life of Samuel L. Clemens," Current Literature (October).
[Source: Henderson (1911), p. 225.]

B3   *ANON. "A Playmate of Mark Twain's," Human
Life (May).
[Dixon Wecter (1952), pp. 52-53, 282-83,
reports that this contains "a garbled interview with [MT's] cousin Tabitha Quarles
Greening," with a variant account of the
incident in which little Sam was almost
left behind when the family moved from
Florida, Missouri to Hannibal.]

B4   ANON. "Writing His Autobiography," Harper's
Weekly, L (December 22), 1845.
A full-page cartoon, showing MT, in furs,
writing and leaning against a mile-post
reading "71 Years Young"; nearby is an
overturned automobile on which the front
license plate reads "Serious Life."

B5   ANON. [Comment on MT's Autobiography.] Putnam's Monthly, I (November), 217-20.
Spurred by current publication of MT's
reminiscences in the North American Review, describes and quotes his 1871 burlesque autobiography and reprints a long
portion of his discussion of simplified
spelling. There is almost no editorial
comment.

B6   ANON. [Full-page drawing of MT receiving a
laurel wreath from a girl dressed as Joan
of Arc, at a dinner of the Society of
American Illustrators.] Harper's Weekly,
L (January 6).

B7   BARNES, L. CALL. "Fresh Light on the Dark
Continent," American Journal of Theology,
X (January), 192-99.
A review-article, discussing a number of
books about Africa. On p. 198: "Several
succinct statements of the case against
the Congo State are available in this country. But the brochure which is likely to
do the most popular execution is King Leopold's Soliloquy, by Mark Twain. The
great humorist never wielded his pen more
pointedly in behalf of honesty and humanity. It is significant, too, that he puts
added emphasis in his second edition, issued since the publication of the report of
the king's commission."

B8   *DIEDERICH. B. "Mark Twain: Neues v. Alt,"
Der Türmer (May), pp. 173-78.
[Source: Henderson (1911), p. 225.]

B9   GODDARD, HENRY P. "Anecdotes of Mark Twain,"
Harper's Weekly, L (February 24), 280-81.
Recollections by Goddard, who knew MT in
the 1870's. Notes MT's generosity in sign-
ing over a lecture fee to Colonel Richard
Malcolm Johnston; describes MT's comments
on lecturing and his gradual reduction of
lecture notes to a few marks on his finger-
nails.

B10   KING, FREDERICK A. "The Story of Mark
Twain's Debts," Bookman (New York), XX
(January), 519-22.
Reprinted in issue of June (1910.B101).

B11   MERRILL, W. H. "When Mark Twain Lectured,"
Harper's Weekly, L (February 10), 199, 209.
Describes an MT lecture "in the early
seventies...in a thriving village in western New York."

B12   ORR, CHARLES. "An Unpublished Masterpiece,"
Putnam's Monthly, I (November), 250-51.
Three letters, dated June 21, June 24,
and July 7, 1880, from John Hay to Alexander Gunn, concerning MT's 1601; there is no
clue as to the topic, although its racy nature is vaguely suggested.

B13   SIDGWICK, ARTHUR, and ELEANOR MILDRED SIDG-
WICK. Henry Sidgwick: A Memoir by A. S.
and E. M. S. London and New York: Mac-
Millan, p. 406.
Quotes the Cambridge professor's journal
(March 29, 1885), praising HF: "Huck Finn
is a kind of boyish, semi-savage Gil Blas,
of low--the lowest--Transatlantic life,
living by his wits on the Mississippi. The
novelty of the scene heightens the romantic
imprévu of his adventures: and the comic
imprévu of his reflections is--about once
every three times--irresistably laughable."

B14   STOKER, BRAM. Personal Reminiscences of
Henry Irving. London: William Heinemann.
2 vols.; I, 166; II, 324.
MT was a guest at a supper with Sarah
Bernhardt one night in 1899 when she was
playing Hamlet at the Adelphi; F. P. Dunne
was also present (I, 166). Among those
listed as having dined with Irving are
"S. L. Clemens ('Mark Twain')" and "Mrs.
and Misses S. L. Clemens" (II, 324).

1907 - A BOOKS - NONE

1907 B SHORTER WRITINGS

B1   ANON. "Are We Standing at the Birth of a
Great Religion?" Current Literature, XLII
(March), 321-24.
In part a descriptive review of MT's
Christian Science, but chiefly devoted to
a broader treatment of the topic, giving
background on Mary Baker Eddy and newspaper
discussion of her work.

B2   ANON. "The Innocents Abroad and How Mark
Twain Came to Write It," Review of Reviews
XXXVI [?] (London), 167.
Summarizes MT's own account in the in-
stallment of his autobiography in the July
North American Review; also summarizes
William Lyon Phelps, "Mark Twain" in the
same issue, and includes comments on what
MT could do at his best and most serious

(ANON.)
from the unsigned "Musings without Method" [by Charles Whibley] in the August Blackwood's.

B3   ANON. "Mark Twain," Living Age, Seventh Series, XXXVI (from beginning, CCLIV; July 6), 60-62.
General praise: "Mark Twain will always be remembered first and foremost as a humorist; but it is only because his claims as a humorist are overwhelming that he had not been acclaimed as a serious student of character, a novelist, and a charming writer of whimsical historical romance." Praises many of MT's books, even CY as "an extremely clever and imaginative tour de force." (Reprinted from Spectator, n.d.; Henderson [1911], p. 225 gives Spectator printing as May 25). See 1907.B4.

B4   *ANON. "Mark Twain," Spectator, XCVIII (May 25), 825-26.
[Source: Reprinted in Anderson (1971), pp. 258-61.] An enthusiastic but rather superficial survey of MT's life and works for English readers when MT came to England to receive an honorary doctoral degree from Oxford. See 1907.B3.

B5   ANON. "Mark Twain, Doctor of Letters," Harper's Weekly, LI (July 13), 1010.
Editorial comment on MT's honorary Oxford degree, awarded not just because he is a celebrity, but because he is an able and recognized author.

B6   ANON. "Mark Twain, En Route for Oxford to Receive the Degree of Doctor of Letters, Besieged by Reporters on His Steamship in England," Harper's Weekly, LI (July 13), 1034.
Photograph, without commentary.

B7   ANON. "Mark Twain's Publicity R. I. P.," Bookman (New York), XXVI (September), 9-10.
"'Mark Twain's work,' said one British writer when British applause was at its loudest, 'has absolutely no connection with literature,' and some of it 'has for sheer concentrated vulgarity never been beaten'; and it was a pity, said another, that Oxford did not honor Henry James instead." The American press reported only England's praise when MT visited. The trouble with these journalistic orgies of praise is that they "always look the week after like public funerals of common sense."

B8   ANON. "Social and Anecdotal" page. Illustrated London News, CXXXI (July 6), 10.
Describes MT's friendly meeting with a porter.

B9   ANON.. "To a Master of His Art" (Cartoon). Punch, CXXXII (June 26), 453.

MT with cigar, Mr. Punch offering him glass from "The Punch Bowl." Text (in full): "Mr. Punch (to Mark Twain): 'Sir, I honor myself in drinking to your health. Long life to you--and happiness-and perpetual youth!'"

B10   ANON. [Review: Christian Science.] Athenaeum, No. 4147 (April 20), pp. 466-68.
Mostly summary; favorable, calls MT "one of the sanest, least prejudiced of men."

B11   ANON. [Review: King Leopold's Soliloquy.] Athenaeum, No. 4153 (June 1), p. 664.
Very brief review. Declares that "Mark Twain is a serious writer of considerable courage as well as a humorist," and his pamphlet is "a trenchant satire."

B12   ANON. [Review: King Leopold's Soliloquy.] Bookman (London), XXXII (July), 150.
Brief, notes that "There has not in our time been a fiercer satire or a finer instance of the value of humour as an instrument of reform."

B13   ANON. [Comment on King Leopold's Soliloquy.] Punch, CXXXII (June 19), 439.
Text in full: "We are glad to see MARK TWAIN taking part in the campaign against the owner of the Congo Free State. Mark II is ammunition which has done good service in the past."

B14   ANON. [Comment on King Leopold's Soliloquy.] Punch, CXXXII (June 26), 451.
Text in full: "It is rumored that MARK TWAIN has received a communication from the King of the BELGIANS offering to defray the entire expense of the obsequies referred to by the American humorist upon his arrival in this country. The only provision that His MAJESTY makes is that the funeral shall take place at once."

B15   ANON. [Account of MT at the Royal Garden Party.] Illustrated London News, CXXX (June 29), 983, 985.
At a party for 8,000, MT was "prominent among the distinguished guests." Illustrated.

B16   ANON. [Portrait of MT in Oxford gown.] Burr McIntosh Monthly (New York), XIV (September), [47].
No significant text.

B17   BLAND, HENRY MEADE. "Mark Twain," Overland Monthly, XLIX (January), 22-27.
Praises MT's tenderness and his "sternly philosophical side," notes his friendship with Charles Warren Stoddard; a popular account providing no new information or unusual critical perception. Illustration (p. 22): "Mark Twain, drawn by Alice Resor from latest copyrighted portrait by Rockwood, N.Y."

1907 - Shorter Writings

B18   BROOKS, SYDNEY. "England's Ovation to Mark
       Twain," Harper's Weekly, LI (July 27),
       1086-89.
           On MT's cordial reception when he received
       an honorary degree from Oxford, with an ac-
       count of his speech at a Pilgrims' Club
       banquet. Includes sketch of MT chatting
       with King Edward at Windsor, and photograph
       of MT in the procession at Oxford just af-
       ter the degree was awarded.

B19   ____. "Mark Twain in England," Harper's
       Weekly, LI (July 20), 1053-55.
           On MT's popularity, and his reception
       when he was there to receive his Oxford
       degree. Cartoons of MT from London Daily
       Chronicle by David Wilson (p. 1053) and
       P. Richards (p. 1054), and photograph of
       MT after receiving his degree (p. 1055).

B20   *GOULD, STUART. "Samuel L. Clemens," Broadway
       Magazine (later Hampton's Broadway Maga-
       zine) (February).
           [Source: Twainian, I (December, 1939),
       6.]

B21   GRISWOLD, STEPHEN. "Quaker City Excursion,"
       in his Sixty Years with Plymouth Church
       (New York: Fleming H. Revell Company),
       pp. 153-66.
           Describes the tour on which IA was based;
       briefly mentions MT. Quotes at length
       (pp. 156-64) the account of the visit to
       the Czar at Yalta in Mrs. Griswold's A
       Woman's Pilgrimage to the Holy Land (1871).

B22   KIMBALL, EDWARD A. "Mark Twain, Mrs. Eddy,
       and Christian Science," Cosmopolitan,
       XLIII (May), 35-41.
           A reply to MT's Christian Science by "a
       prominent Christian Science author."

B23   LANG, ANDREW. "At the Sign of St. Paul's"
       [literature page]. Illustrated London News,
       CXXX (May 25), 798.
           Brief note (in full): "The great Ameri-
       can humorist, who has just passed his sev-
       entieth birthday, comes to Oxford this sum-
       mer to receive the degree of D.C.L."
       Portrait.

B24   ____. "Mark Twain," Albany Review (London),
       L (April), 35-43.
           A general account of MT's works, which
       Lang first encountered while riding on a
       train with his friend and tutor Benjamin
       Jowett (later Master of Balliol); Lang
       "shrieked and exploded with laughter" over
       "The Celebrated Jumping Frog," then handed
       it over to his companion. "He read through
       it with perfect solemnity combined with
       disapproval, and returned it to me without
       a word." Of MT's works, TS is the Iliad,
       HF "the Odyssey, of life, not of boy's life
       only," but "I have never read, and never
       will read," CY.

B25   MABIE, HAMILTON W. "Mark Twain the Humorist,"
       Outlook (New York), LXXXVII (November 23),
       648-53.
           A general, admiring discussion of the man
       and his works, generally uncritical though
       noting the ephemeral quality of some of his
       writing. On p. 648, full-page photograph
       of MT.

B26   MATTHEWS, BRANDER. "Mark Twain," in his In-
       quiries and Opinions. (New York: Charles
       Scribner's Sons, 1907), pp. 137-66.
           A biographical and critical account by one
       of MT's early advocates in the academic
       world. This was written as the introduction
       to a complete edition of MT's works, and
       appears in Innocents Abroad in the Author's
       National Edition. Asselineau (1954), No.
       28 gives a cross-reference to Matthews's
       "Mark Twain--His Work," Book-Buyer, XIII
       (January, 1897), 977-79.

B27   MOFFETT, SAMUEL E. "Mark Twain, Doctor of
       Letters," Review of Reviews (New York),
       XXXVI (August), 167-68.
           General praise of MT on the occasion of
       his receiving an honorary degree from Ox-
       ford; no new information. Includes photo-
       graph of MT.

B28   PEARSON, E[DMUND] L[ESTER]. "The Children's
       Librarian versus Huckleberry Finn: A Brief
       for the Defense," Library Journal, XXXII
       (July), 312-14.
           "Extreme Respectability" in the children's
       departments of public libraries is excluding
       TS and HF, which Pearson defends for honest
       portrayal: "Not Henty's wooden heroes, nor
       golden-curled, lace-collared Fauntleroys;
       but real boys." Reprinted in his The Libra-
       ry and the Librarian (1910.B114).

B29   PHELPS, WILLIAM LYON. "Mark Twain," North
       American Review, CLXXXV (July 5), 540-48.
           Discusses the growth of MT's standing and
       declares him now "our foremost living Ameri-
       can writer," not only for his humor, but for
       his literary art in the creation of charact-
       ers and in his dramatic power. Reprinted in
       his Essays on American Novelists (New York,
       1910), pp. 99-114; in Anderson (1971),
       pp. 262-70; in Scott (1955), pp. 79-88, and
       (1967), pp. 84-93.

B30   SEAMAN, OWEN. "To Mark Twain," Punch, CXXXII
       (June 27), 463.
           A poem honoring MT, guest of the Pilgrims
       Club, June 25th.

B31   SIMBOLI, RAFFAELE. "Mark Twain and His Dou-
       ble," Ladies' Home Journal, XXIV (May), 59.
           While living in Florence MT was often mis-
       taken for Professor Borzi [later director
       of the Botanical Gardens at Palermo]. In
       turn, when Borzi visited Sweden and Norway
       in 1899 he was widely mistaken for MT and
       "even Ibsen fell into the error and came to
       call on me," said Borzi.

B32 *TEICHMANN, E. [Review: The $30,000 Bequest and other Stories.] Neue Philologische Rundschau, p. 503.
[Source: Henderson (1911), p. 225.]

B33 THOMPSON, VANCE. "The Yarns of a Traveler," Outing Magazine, LI (October), 16-22.
Stories about murder told by a group of men on an ocean liner; MT suggested the topic, but told no story and made no significant comments.

B34 *WATSON, AARON. "Artemus Ward and Mark Twain," and "Mark Twain's Own Account," in his The Savage Club (London: T. Fisher Unwin), pp. 119-35.
[Source: Henderson (1911), p. 226.]

B35 [WHIBLEY, CHARLES.] "Musings without Method: The Hilarity of London--Mark Twain's Message of Mirth--The Limitations of Humour--an Obvious Incongruity--The Example of the Eighteenth Century--Cotton and Bridges--Life on the Mississippi--The Talent of Mark Twain--The Sin of Exaggeration..." Blackwood's Edinburgh Magazine, CLXXXII (August), 279-86.
A generally unsympathetic response to the adulation MT was receiving on his last visit to England; praises the beauty of LOM, but condemns CY as "such a masterpiece of vulgarity as the world has never seen. His book gives you the same sort of impression which you might receive from a beautiful picture over which a poisonous slug had crawled." Reprinted in Scott (1955), pp. 89-97; (1967), pp. 94-102, with a note: "Authorship revealed in note from Wm. Blackwood & Sons, Ltd., October 12, 1953." Also reprinted in Anderson (1971), pp. 271-76.

B36 WILBUR, SIBYL. The Life of Mary Baker Eddy. New York and London: Concord Publishing Company, pp. 216-18.
Cites MT's charges in Christian Science that Mary Baker Eddy's Science and Health is absurd, unoriginal, and not her work; gently disagrees.

1908 A BOOKS - NONE

1908 B SHORTER WRITINGS

B1 ANON. "Four Distinguished Americans. From a Photograph Taken at Lakewood, N.J., Where a Luncheon Was Given to Mr. Howells to Bid Him Godspeed on His Journey to Europe," Harper's Weekly, LII (January 18), 13.
Full-page photograph of Howells, MT, Henry M. Alden, and Mayo W. Hazeltine.

B2 ANON. "Mark Twain's New Home at Redding," Harper's Weekly, LII (July 4), 24, 29.
On the purchase of the land, building of the house, and the neighbors. Illustrated with photographs of the house, local scenes, and MT playing billiards with Albert

Bigelow Paine. Attributed to Paine in Henderson (1911), p. 226.

B3 *ANON. "Mark Twain's Pastor: Some Stories of Samuel L. Clemens," Daily Graphic (London), July 11.
[Source: Leah A. Strong (1966), p. 178.]

B4 ANON. [Portrait of MT and daughter Clara.] Burr McIntosh Monthly (New York), XV (March), [57-58].
Accompanying text states that MT had approximately $50,000 on deposit at the Knickerbocker Trust Company in New York at the time of the crash; he opposed establishing a permanent receivership on the grounds that it would be as expensive to maintain as a harem: "Anybody who has had experience in this line will endorse my statement."

B5 ABERNETHY, JULIAN W. "American Humor," in American Literature. New York: Charles E. Merrill Co. [copyright 1902 by Maynard, Merrill & Co.], pp. 465-72.
The book is a broad survey, intended for use in the schools, and the treatment of MT is superficial, though laudatory (except for regretting his frequent coarseness). TS and HF are "astonishingly clever studies of the American bad boy, and LOM is "his best autobiographic narrative," a product of the river which inspired him. Abernethy appears to be guided primarily by Brander Matthews and H. R. Haweis, both of whom he quotes in praise of MT (the attributions are unclear, but the sources seem to be Aspects of Fiction, Harper, 1892, and American Humorists, Funk, 1883, respectively).

B6 BRERETON, AUSTIN. The Life of Henry Irving. London: Longmans, Green, and Co., 2 vols.; II, 37, 42. 68.
MT a guest at a dinner given in Irving's honor at the Somerset Club by Charles Fairchild and James R. Osgood; Howells and Aldrich were also present, 1884 (p. 37); Irving a guest at MT's home in Hartford, 1884 (p. 42). MT's name was among over a hundred signatures on a letter dated 14th March, 1885, inviting Irving to a banquet in his honor at Delmonico's, April 6 (p. 68).

B7 GREENSLET, FERRIS. The Life of Thomas Bailey Aldrich. Boston and New York: Houghton Mifflin Company.
Includes the correspondence with MT that followed Aldrich's attribution in Every Saturday of the "Carl Byng" and "Hy Slocum" sketches in the Buffalo Express to him, with MT's tribute to Harte's influence as literary mentor, although their friendship had ended (pp. 94-99); correspondence in which MT deluged Aldrich with photographs in response to a request for one (pp. 112-17, including a self-portrait sketch, facing p. 114); anecdote on their comparative popularity in France (p. 117); quotes MT declaring "that if he was a fool, he was at least God's fool, and entitled to some

1908 - Shorter Writings

(GREENSLET, FERRIS)
respect" (p. 192); on MT as so well known
that "little donkey-boys on the Nile...will
tell you that they were 'Mark Twain's' don-
key boys" (p. 220).

B8   *MATTHEWS, BRANDER. "American Humor," Saturday Evening Post (November 21).
[Source: Twainian, II (June, 1943), 6.]
Reprinted in his The American of the Future,
and Other Essays (1910, B105).

B9   *PEMBERTON, T. EDGAR. Life of Bret Harte.
London: C. Arthur Pearson.
[Source: Henderson (1911), p. 226.]

B10   SEDGWICK, HENRY DWIGHT. "Mark Twain," in his
The New American Type, and Other Essays
(Boston, New York: Houghton, Mifflin and
Company), pp. 281-313.
On MT as the embodiment of a democratic,
American spirit in literature.

B11   STEWART, WILLIAM M. Reminiscences of Senator
William M. Stewart of Nevada, ed. George
Rothwell Brown. New York and Washington:
The Neale Publishing Company.
"Chapter XXIII. Mark Twain becomes my
secretary--Back from the Holy Land, and he
looks it--The landlady terrorized--I inter-
fere with a humorist's pleasures and get a
black patch--Revenge!--Clemens the hero of
a Nevada hold-up" (pp. 219-24). An unsympathetic portrayal of MT, who briefly was
Stewart's secretary in Washington. Concludes: "Clemens remained with me for some
time. He wrote his book in my room, and
named it The Innocents Abroad. I was so
confident that he would come to no good
end, but I have heard of him from time to
time since then and I understand that he
has settled down since then and become respectable.

B12   *____. "A Senator of the Sixties," Saturday
Evening Post (February 15).
[Source: Twainian, II (June, 1943), 6.]

B13   STODDARD, CHARLES WARREN. "In Old Bohemia,
II, The Overland and the Overlanders,"
Pacific Monthly, XIX (March), 261-73.
Contains anecdotes of MT in California
and recollections of sharing rooms with
him in London in the winter of 1873-74.
Includes photograph of MT.

B14   WHIBLEY, CHARLES. "American Literature,"
Blackwood's, CLXXXIII (March), 414-22.
On MT, pp. 419-20: "There is but one
author who represents with any clarity the
spirit of his country, and that author is
Mark Twain. Not Mark Twain the humourist,
the favourite of the reporters, the facile
contemner of things which are noble and of
good report, but Mark Twain, the pilot of
the Mississippi, the creator of Huck Finn
and Tom Sawyer. He, indeed, is national as
Fielding is national. Future ages will

look upon Huck Finn as we look upon Tom
Jones,--as an embodiment of national virtue."

1909 A BOOKS - NONE

1909 B SHORTER WRITINGS

B1   ANGERT, EUGENE H. "Is Mark Twain Dead?"
North American Review, CXC (September),
319-29.
A spoof, purporting to demonstrate that
MT died in 1906 in Europe and his subsequent
public appearances are those of an impostor,
and works bearing his name are those of a
person lacking humor: he could not have
written either the scholarly Is Shakespeare
Dead? or Christian Science, and even if he
could have written the latter, he would not
have chosen to. Significantly, he did not
sign the articles of incorporation of the
Mark Twain Company. Angert proposes Elbert
Hubbard as the author of works attributed to
MT in recent years.

B2   *ANON. "Horace Ezra Bixby, Mark Twain's Boss,"
Broadway Magazine (later Hampton's Broadway
Magazine), January.
[Source: Twainian, I (December, 1939),
6.]

B3   ANON. "The Lounger," Putnam's Magazine, VII
(December), 369-70.
Brief comment on Clara's wedding to Ossip
Gabrilowitsch, quoting MT's answer when
asked whether the marriage pleased him:
"Yes, fully as much as any marriage could
please me or perhaps any other father.
There are two or three tragically solemn
things in this life, and a happy marriage
is one of them, for the terrors of life are
all to come. A funeral is a solemn office,
but I go to them with a spiritual uplift,
thankful that the dead friend has been set
free. That which follows is to me tragic
and awful--the burial. I am glad of this
marriage, and Mrs. Clemens would be glad,
for she always had a warm affection for
Gabrilowitsch, but all the same it is a
tragedy, since it is a happy marriage with
its future before it, loaded to the Plim-
soll line with uncertainties." Also contains comments by MT at a musicale in Redding (Sept. 21). The writer mentions having
"spoken of Mr. Clemens's country home more
than once in these pages."

B4   *ANON. "Mark Twain from a New Angle," Current
Literature (August).
[Source: Henderson (1911), p. 227.]

B5   *ANON. "Mark Twain's House at Redding, Connec-
ticut," American Architect & Building News,
(February 10).
[Source: Twainian, I (October, 1939), 4.]

B6   ANON. "Mark Twain's New Book and a Commenta-
     tor," Bookman (New York), XXIX (June).
        MT's Is Shakespeare Dead? is a comic
     piece which "can be read through cheerfully
     in an hour"--yet a writer for the Boston
     Evening Transcript finds "depth and subtle-
     ty" in it!

B7   ANON. "Stormfield, Mark Twain's New Country
     Home. How the Humorist Built a House With-
     out Seeing It--An Italian Villa in the
     Connecticut Hills--The Second in a Series
     of Articles on Country Homes of Notable
     Americans." Photographs by A. Radclyffe
     Dugmore. Country Life in America, XV
     (April), 607-11, 650-51.
        A description of the house at Redding,
     Connecticut, illustrated by pictures of the
     house and MT at his ease there, and a fac-
     simile of his "Notice. To the next Bur-
     glar" warning that hung in the billiard-
     room.

B8   BAILEY, ELMER JAMES. "The Essayists and the
     Humourists," in Theodore Stanton, ed.,
     A Manual of American Literature (New York:
     G. P. Putnam's Sons), pp. 321-59; on MT,
     pp. 357-59.
        Regrets that MT was burdened by his repu-
     tation as a humorist and predicts that
     "future critics may come to regard The
     Prince and the Pauper (1882) and Personal
     Recollections of Joan of Arc (1896), two
     serious and dignified pieces of writing, as
     Mr. Clemens's best work." The Oxford de-
     gree awarded him, though a surprise to
     many, was evidence that "humour at last
     seems to be coming into its own."

B9   *FISCHER, M. "Mark Twain on Christian Sci-
     ence," Die Neueren Sprachen, pp. 206-28.
        [Source: Henderson (1911), p. 227.]

B10 GILMAN, ARTHUR. "Atlantic Dinners and Di-
     ners," Atlantic Monthly, C (November),
     646-57, on MT, pp. 651-53.
        A brief account of his Whittier Birthday-
     Dinner speech, with no indication that it
     gave offense.

B11 HENDERSON, ARCHIBALD. "Mark Twain," Harper's
     Monthly, CXVIII (May), 948-55.
        Praises MT's robustly national qualities,
     although "he is America's greatest cosmo-
     politan." "But, after all, Mark Twain's
     supremest title to distinction as a great
     writer inheres in his mastery in that
     greatest sphere of thought, embracing re-
     ligion, philosophy, morality, and even
     humor, which we call sociology." Reprinted
     in Scott (1955), pp. 98-106, and (1967),
     pp. 103-11. This appears to be the "Philos-
     opher, Moralist, Sociologist" chapter in
     Henderson's 1911 book (1911.A3) and trans-
     lated into German in Deutsche Revue
     (1911.B9).

B12 *____. "Mark Twain--Wie Er Ist. Eine Skizze
     nach dem Leben," Deutsche Revue, XXXIV
     (November), 195-205.
        [Source: Henderson (1911), p. 227;
     Leary (1954), p. 49.

B13 *____. "The Real Mark Twain. The Man and His
     Work," Charlotte (North Carolina) Observer,
     Sunday, May 16.
        [Source: Henderson (1911), p. 226.]

B14 HOWELLS, WILLIAM DEAN. "The Editor's Easy
     Chair," Harper's Monthly, CXIX (July),
     313-16.
        On the debate over the authorship of
     Shakespeare's plays; praises MT's knowledge
     of the details, and his Is Shakespeare Dead?
     as "his humorous exposition of the mock
     combat," in which "the controversy is for-
     ever destroyed, and only the miracle of
     Shakespeare remains."

B15 LUCY, HENRY W. "Mark Twain," in his Sixty
     Years in the Wilderness: Some Passages by
     the Way. (London: Smith, Elder & Co.),
     pp. 220-29, (364).
        Reminiscences of MT at a dinner in his
     honor at the Punch offices, and a scheme
     MT and Lucy had jokingly concocted to
     blackmail wealthy persons with scurrilous
     obituaries supposedly to be published on
     their death; also, two letters from MT to
     Lucy and an MT letter to the editor to be
     sent out to newspapers, offering to pay a
     good price for "access to my standing obit-
     uaries, with the privilege...of editing,
     not their facts, but their verdicts"
     (p. 226). Also, tells the story of MT at
     a dinner given in his honor by the American
     Ambassador, Whitelaw Reid; MT had prepared
     a speech, but was not called on to give one,
     and later confided to Lucy that he had sold
     it for two hundred dollars (p. 228).

B16 *LUX, JACQUES. "Mark Twain," L'Indépendence
     Belge, July 16.
        [Source: Henderson (1911), p. 227.]

B17 *MENCKEN, H. L. [Review: Is Shakespeare
     Dead?] Smart Set, XXVIII (August), 157.
        [Source: Conclusion reprinted in Anderson
     (1971), p. 277.] An inaccurate, unsuccess-
     ful book by "the most noble figure America
     has ever given to English literature. Hav-
     ing him, we may hold up our heads when
     Spaniards boast of Cervantes and Frenchmen
     of Molière." He has given us HF, "But since
     Following the Equator, his decline has been
     almost pathetic."

B18 NORTHRUP, CLARK SUTHERLAND. "The Novelists,"
     in Theodore Stanton, ed., A Manual of Amer-
     ican Literature (New York: G. P. Putnam's
     Sons), pp. 115-240; on MT, pp. 187-88.
        "Artistically defective his work is in-
     deed, but it cannot be denied the qualities
     of eloquence, naturalness, and sincerity.
     The work, like the man, is genuine."

1909 - Shorter Writings

B19   PAINE, ALBERT BIGELOW. "Mark Twain at Storm-
       field: The House of Many Beatitudes,"
       Harper's Monthly, CXVIII (May), 955-59.
          On MT's home at Redding, Connecticut, and
       his life there.

B20   PENN, PETER. "Some American Humour," English
       Illustrated Magazine, XLI (June), 299-301.
          Contains passing and superficial refer-
       ences to MT; praises his "variety."

B21   THOMPSON, PAUL. "A Day with Mark Twain,"
       Burr McIntosh Monthly (New York), XVII
       (March) [22-24].
          Superficial description of a visit to MT
       at his "Stormfield" home in Redding, Con-
       necticut; illustrated with two photographs
       of MT and two of the house.

1910 A BOOKS

A1   CHUBB, PERCIVAL, ed. Travels at Home. New
       York and London: Harper & Brothers.
          Selections from MT's works for school
       use in 6th, 7th, and 8th grades. The in-
       troduction is conventionally laudatory and
       biographical, and contains no new informa-
       tion or significant criticism.

A2   EPUY, MICHEL. Le legs de 30.000 Dollars et
       autres contes, traduits et préfacés d'une
       étude sur l'auteur par Michel Epuy. Paris:
       Marcure de France.
          [Source: Asselineau (1954), No. 41.]

A3   HOWELLS, WILLIAM DEAN. My Mark Twain: Rem-
       iniscences and Criticisms. New York and
       London: Harper & Brothers Publishers.
          A collection of Howells' writings on MT
       and reviews of his books, with minor re-
       visions or none at all. The first section
       is the material which appeared as "My Memo-
       ries of Mark Twain" in Harper's Monthly
       (August-October), with the change of an
       occasional word or paragraph division, and
       the second part consists of reviews of MT's
       books and some more general discussions,
       "allowed to follow here in the order of
       their original publication, with no sort of
       correction or effort to reconcile them with
       one another." Reprinted 1967, ed. Marilyn
       Austin Baldwin, with introduction, notes,
       and index. See 1967.A3.

A4   *HYATT, EDWARD (Superintendent of Public In-
       struction). A Calaveras Evening with Mark
       Twain and Bret Harte, a diversion for the
       English class. Sacramento: W. W. Shannon,
       Supt. State Printing.
          [8-page pamphlet. Source: Asselineau
       (1954), No. 34.]

A5   *JOHNSON, MERLE. A Bibliography of the Works
       of Mark Twain. New York and London: Harp-
       er & Brothers.

          [Source: Asselineau (1954), No. 29.]
       Now superceded by Revised and Enlarged edi-
       tion, 1935 (A12), reprinted 1972, Westport,
       Connecticut: Greenwood Press, Publishers.

A6   KENDALL, C. N. Travels in History. New York
       and London: Harper & Brothers.
          Extracts from P&P, CY, and JA for school
       use in 6th, 7th, and 8th grades. Introduc-
       tion (pp. vii-ix) notes the importance of
       "authors who interpret life with vitality
       and reality" for young readers and (follow-
       ing Howells) points out the "national spir-
       it" in MT. P&P is "largely imaginative,"
       with "variety, pathos, and abundant humor."
       In CY "The ignorance and savagery beneath
       the ancient pomp and glitter are well con-
       trasted with the resourcefulness and human-
       itarianism of to-day." "The tone of Joan of
       Arc is devout, the humor subdued, and the
       treatment dignified and elevated."

A7   *LIVINGSTON, LUTHER S. The Works of Mark
       Twain. The description of a set of first
       editions of his books in the library of a
       New York collector (R. F. Pick). With Fac-
       similes.
          [Source: Asselineau (1954), No. 30; he
       adds: "only 75 copies were printed accord-
       ing to Wilfred Partington (cf. Bookman,
       March 1933)."]

A8   PAINE, ALBERT BIGELOW. The Ship-Dwellers: A
       Story of a Happy Cruise. New York and Lon-
       don: Harper & Brothers Publishers.
          Paines's account of his own trip forty-
       two years after the cruise of the Quaker
       City and covering much the same itinerary.
       In some respects this is an admiring
       (though pale) imitation of IA, to which
       there are frequent references. On
       pp. 51-53 Paine describes a meeting at
       Gibraltar with Michael Benueñes, who said
       he had been the local guide for MT's party.

1910 SHORTER WRITINGS

B1   ADE, GEORGE. "Mark Twain and the Old Time
       Subscription Book," Review of Reviews (New
       York), XLI (June), 703-704.
          Reminiscence of the bulk and appearance
       of the books; unlike most of the others,
       MT's were a delight for a boy to read.
       Reprinted in Anderson (1971), 337-39.

B2   _____. "Mark Twain as our Emissary," Century,
       LXXXI (December), 204-206.
          A popular appreciation of MT's popularity
       at home and abroad.

B3   ALDEN, HENRY M. "Mark Twain--An Appreciation,"
       Bookman (New York), XXXI (July), 366-69.
          A general and popular appreciation, noting
       MT's imagination and sensitivity. Photo-
       graph: "Mark Twain at Oxford."

B4   ____. "Mark Twain: Personal Impressions,"
Book News Monthly, XXVIII (April), 579-82.
On the autobiographical element in MT's
work, and his "openly dramatized personality." Praises "the profound spiritual implications of some of his short stories,
like The Man Who Corrupted Hadleyburg and
"Was It Heaven or Hell?" All these show
the finest lines of his art, of his humor,
of his large but delicately sensitive personality." Photograph of MT as frontispiece to issue (facing p. 573).

B5   ANON. "Chesterton on Mark Twain," New York
Times, May 7, "Saturday Review of Books and
Art," p. 262.
Summarizes and quotes G. K. Chesterton's
assessment of MT in T. P.'s Weekly
(1910.B77).

B6   ANON. "Comment," Harper's Weekly, LIV
(April 30), 4.
MT was probably the world's greatest
living writer; irreverent toward shams but
of the highest honor and integrity. (Photographs of MT, front cover, p. 3).

B7   ANON. "A Correspondent Writes," Athenaeum,
No. 4305 (April 30), p. 527.
Note from a reader who wrote MT in 1900:
"Who is your favorite novelist, and what is
your favorite novel?" MT's reply: "Q. My
favorite novel? A. 'Huckleberry Finn.'
Very truly yours, Mark Twain."

B8   ANON. "The Death of Mark Twain," Chautauquan,
LIX (June), 9-10.
Obituary praise for his humanity and wis-
dom.

B9   ANON. "Fashions in Humor," Emporia (Kansas)
Gazette, April 28, p. 1.
Quotes Franklin P. Adams in the New York
Evening Mail (n.d.), predicting that HF
and "The Jumping Frog" will last, but much
of MT's other work will not; because of
changing tastes; the writer uses this as a
point of departure for a general discussion
of this change in taste.

B10   ANON. "French Sneer at Mark Twain," New York
Times, April 24, p. 3.
Reports that the French press generally
has expressed sympathetic notice of MT's
death, reflecting "an extraordinarily
widespread knowledge of the subtleties of
the English language among Frenchmen. A
surprising exception is to be found in Ernest Charles, a critic much in the public
view, who in a short article on Mark Twain
seems determined to convince every reader
possessing any degree of penetration that
the views which he expresses are the product
of ignorance and anti-Americanism combined.
This article is published in Gil Blas...
Mr. Charles says in effect that Mark Twain
did well to die, and that it was not his
fault if while he was all his life the most

laborious humorist, he was totally lacking
in wit. 'Mark Twain's humor,' M. Charles
adds, was painful, his fantasies dense and
difficult to follow. By them one may estimate the exact distance which separates the
Yankee country from the civilized world."
[The New York Times is the best single
source for American and foreign tributes
during the period following MT's death.]

B11   ANON. "The Frontiersmen," T. P.'s Weekly
(London), XV (June 24), 793.
Summarizes the unsigned article by Frank
Jewett Mather in The Nation (N.Y., April 28,
1910.B104) on MT and Henry James. Questions
Mather's suggestion that the prospects of
survival as a major author are good for MT
but uncertain for James.

B12   ANON. "His Career as Soldier: Captain Grimes
Tells of First Battle--It Was with a Mule,"
St. Louis Times, April 22.
[Source: Scrapbook, Mark Twain: Biography-Reminiscence, n.d., in Chicago Public
Library.] Reminiscences by Captain Horace
Ezra Bixby and Captain A. C. Grimes ("former proprietor of Grimes' Clubhouse, King's
Lake, Lincoln County"). The brief account
by Crimes adds nothing to MT's own "Private
History of a Campaign that Failed." Bixby
said that "Clemens was a good pilot, in
spite of what the rest of the profession
said about him. I soon saw that he was a
smart fellow, and it was his brains that
made the other pilots jealous and led them
to say that he did not know the river, that
he was just an inspired loafer, or something of that sort. He was a good pilot,
and he learned it from me...Mark never was
jolly exactly, always serious, but he
showed the gift of humor, even at that time.
He was not entirely popular with his fellows,
as I have said, and maybe his tongue had
something to do with that." Bixby interview
reprinted (as "Special to the World") in New
York World, April 24, p. 3.

B13   ANON. "In the Interpretor's House" [A regular
section of the magazine], American Magazine,
LXX (July), 428-32.
Presented as a discussion between the Observer and the Poet of MT's originality,
integrity, kindliness, contempt for sham.
Gives considerable space to the familiar
biographical details, and says little specifically about MT's works.

B14   ANON. "A Land of No Laughter?" The British
Weekly, XLVIII (April 28), 81-82.
Title is taken from the first lines of
James Rhoades's 1867 poem on the death of
Artemus Ward: "Is he gone to a land of no
laughter,/ This man that made mirth for us
all?" Reprinting the entire poem, the article takes up the question of whether there
can be a place for laughter in heaven, and
is primarily devoted to a discussion of humor and religion. The occasion is the death

1910 - Shorter Writings

(ANON.)
of Mark Twain, who had won a place in the world's heart. "Mark Twain was certainly much more than a mere jester. He had an intensely serious side."

B15   ANON. "Last Honors to Mark Twain. Scenes at the Services Held over the Body of the Dead Author at the 'Brick Church,' Fifth Avenue and Thirty-Seventh Street, New York," Harper's Weekly, LIV (May 7), 11.
Five photographs.

B16   *ANON. "The Late Mark Twain (Samuel L. Clemens)," Phrenological Journal and Science of Health, CXXIII (June), 190.
[Source: Reprinted in Madeleine B. Stern, "Mark Twain Had His Head Examined" (1969).]

B17   ANON. "Learned River for $500," St. Louis Republic, April 22, p. 3.
Interview with Captain Horace Bixby, who taught MT to be a river pilot. "While he was with me on the boats he was writing all his spare time. He wrote for some of the magazines, but I don't know which ones."

B18   ANON. "Mark Twain," Athenaeum, No. 4305 (April 30), pp. 524-25.
In the past twenty years he has built a reputation as a fearless spokesman on public affairs. "He was one of the most serious-minded of men, though his serious writing was not effective. But his humour had wholesome teaching behind, and keen, though kindly criticism of human foibles and weaknesses."

B19   ANON. "Mark Twain," Century, LXXXI (June), 315.
"Chivalrous as he was in his championship of causes in his more serious work, he had no false shame about writing pure fun, with no other purpose but to amuse."

B20   ANON. "Mark Twain," Collier's XLV (April 30), 9.
Short editorial, praising the writer and man.

B21   ANON. "Mark Twain," Dial, XLVIII (May 1), 305-307.
His best works are TS, HF, RI, and others in which he draws on western experience, and his next best are the travel books, which reveal an increasing sophistication and corresponding decline in naturalness. By transplanting himself in the East he cut off his sources. "Over some of his later flounderings in the alien elements of literary criticism, history, and metaphysics, it were best discreetly to draw a veil" (p. 306). Reprinted in Anderson (1971), pp. 281-84.

B22   ANON. "Mark Twain," Independent, LXVIII (April 28), 934-35.
A general discussion, much of it bio-

graphical; declines to predict whether his fame will endure.

B23   ANON. "Mark Twain," Outlook, XCIV (April 30), 971-72.
A general and somewhat derivative obituary account.

B24   ANON. "Mark Twain," The Public (Chicago), XIII (April 29), 385-86.
An editorial praising MT's democracy. "The death of this man at his age calls for no tears of grief. He passes out of his life normally, after doing a life's work so well that it will be a wholesome influence with many a generation yet to come." Gives the text of a brief note thanking the editor of The Public for sending him a book, "which I prize for its lucidity, its sanity & its moderation, & because I believe its gospel" (from Villa di Quarto, Firenze, January 7, 1904). The issue of May 13 contains a letter to the editor from Daniel Kiefer praising MT for speaking out against the wrongs committed by his own country in the Philippines, as well as the wrongs of other nations (pp. 439-40).

B25   ANON. "Mark Twain," Punch, CXXXVIII (April 27), 306.
Short farewell poem, unsigned.

B26   ANON. "Mark Twain," Spectator, CIV (April 30), 720-21.
On MT's dry humor, gentle satire, portrayal of life and character. TS and HF "will live always in the first rank of American literature. They are great because they are simple."

B27   ANON. "Mark Twain," (London) Times Literary Supplement, April 28, p. 153.
Much of the obituary is biographical and general, with the usual praise for TS and HF for their portrayal of boy-nature. "A Yankee at King Arthur's Court is a book which we have sedulously avoided as we would avoid a book on Sir Lancelot at the Court of Mr. Taft," but "his heart was in the right place" in JA. Reprinted in Living Age, CCLXV (May 28), 564-67.

B28   ANON. "Mark Twain: An American Pioneer in Man's Oldest Art, Whose Death Is Mourned by the World at Large," Collier's XLV (April 30), 10-11.
A general discussion, intelligent but not original. Photograph p. 11.

B29   ANON. "Mark Twain and Christian Science," The British Weekly, XLVIII (May 12).
A brief note, concerning an article on MT in "The New York Christian Advocate--a most reputable journal," which praised his attack on Christian Science. This note is followed by "Mark Twain's minister," on the death of the wife of Joseph Twichell.

B30 ANON. "Mark Twain as a Serious Force in Literature," Current Literature, XLVIII (June), 663-67.
Summarizes and extensively quotes recent discussions of MT as a serious writer by Archibald Henderson, William Dean Howells, William Lyon Phelps, Henry M. Alden, and by anonymous writers in the New York Times and the San Francisco Argonaut; all but the Argonaut article are listed in this bibliography, and the article adds nothing to them. Includes photograph, copyright by Gessford.

B31 ANON. "Mark Twain Commemorated," Outlook, XCVI (December 10), 801-802.
Brief account of a meeting held in Carnegie Hall the previous week; the account in Harper's Weekly (December 17) is considerably more extensive.

B32 ANON. "Mark Twain in Memoriam. Interesting Passages from the Tributes Paid to the Great Humorist at the Memorial Meeting in Carnegie Hall, New York," Harper's Weekly, LIV (December 17), 8-10.
Includes list of a number of the distinguished guests, a large photograph, and texts of the remarks of several, among them Howells, Twichell, Joseph G. Cannon, Champ Clark, George Washington Cable, and Henry Van Dyke (who wrote a poem to MT for the occasion, 1910.B134).

B33 ANON. "Mark Twain Moraliste," La Revue (Paris, old Revue des Revues), LXXXVI (15 Mai), 278.
Brief summary of Régis Michaud, "L'Envers d'un Humoriste: Mark Twain" (Revue du Mois, 10 April, 1910.B108).

B34 ANON. "Mark Twain's Estate," Bookman (New York), XXXI (June), 339.

B35 ANON. "Mark Twain's Gold and Dross," Literary Digest, XL (June 11), 177.
Summarizes and quotes Harry Thurston Peck's "Mark Twain a Century Hence" (Bookman, N.Y., June); briefly quotes William Lyon Phelps (Review of Reviews, June), who places RI above IA.

B36 ANON. "Mark Twain's Investments," Collier's, XLVI (November 12), 32.
A list of the securities in his estate.

B37 ANON. "Mark Twain's Mysterious Book," T. P.'s Weekly (London), XV (May 27), 675.
On What is Man? Consists almost entirely of summary and quotation, and contains no critical estimate.

B38 ANON. "Mark Twain's Pessimistic Philosophy," Current Literature, XLVIII (June), 643-47.
On What is Man? Almost entirely description of the book and quotation from it. Includes a photograph of MT in bed (copyright by Van der Weyde) and one of him looking out a window at Redding (copyright by Paul Thompson).

B39 ANON. "Mark Twain's Religious Book," Literary Digest, XL (May 7), 920.
A description of What is Man? with extensive quotation and no added interpretation; based on an account in the New York Tribune, it concludes with a quotation from The Outlook on MT's serious purpose and broad popularity (dates not given). Includes photograph of MT by Paul Thompson, copyright 1909.

B40 ANON. "Mark Twain's Secret Book Gives Startling Views," New York Times, May 1, Magazine Section, p. 2.
Summary and extensive quotation of What Is Man?

B41 ANON. "More About Twain," Bookman (New York), XXXI (July), 458-59.
Anecdotes about a letter addressed "Mark Twain, God Knows Where" which reached him, and MT's comment that the Ah Sin play (written in collaboration with Bret Harte) "had a run of one consecutive week."

B42 ANON. "Mr. Twichell's Praise," Hartford Times, April 22, p. 11.
An interview with MT's friend of many years' standing, providing a number of stories and insights, not all of which may be available elsewhere; mentions MT's lack of relish for Dickens and enthusiastic readings from Browning, and visits to the Farmington Avenue house by Henry Irving, Bret Harte, Charles Kingsley, and [Joe] Jefferson. When his coachman Patrick [McAleer] died, MT wired, "explaining that he wished to be a bearer, but the coachman's family, while appreciating the sympathy, decided that this service was out of place. The author attended the funeral and was, outside of the family, the principal mourner." The Hartford Times, like the Courant, reported MT's death and his career at length, making full use of local and wire-service material.

B43 ANON. "News for Bibliophiles," Nation (New York), XCI (September 22), 260.
Describes the bibliography of MT's published works being compiled by Merle Johnson, to be published shortly by Harper's.

B44 ANON. "News Notes," Bookman (London), XXXVIII (May), 53.
"Whatever may be the ultimate fate of his other books, there is no doubt that in Tom Sawyer and in Huckleberry Finn he has done work that will endure."

B45 ANON. "Obituary Notes: Mark Twain," Publishers' Weekly, LXXVII (April 30), 1796-97.
Chiefly biographical, but contains a statement by Albert Bigelow Paine on MT's connection with Charles L. Webster & Company and one by Colonel George Harvey, president

1910 - Shorter Writings

(ANON.)
of Harper & Brothers, on the offer MT accepted from that firm: "It was proposed to take over all his books, guarantee him an income from royalties of not less than $25,000 per annum, and pay him 30 cents a word for all he should write, whether published or not for five years."

B46   ANON. "One of Twain's Final Letters Sent to Ambitious Little Girl," New York American, April 27, p. 5.
Quotes part of a letter from MT in Bermuda to Sulamith Ish-Kishor, then a girl of thirteen (and later a writer herself), who had written him of a dream she had after reading P&P.

B47   ANON. "The Originals of Some of Mark Twain's Characters," Review of Reviews (N.Y.), XLII (August), 228-30.
A summary, with quotations, of Homer Croy's "The Originals of Mark Twain's Characters" in Bellman (1910.B81).

B48   ANON. "Portland Woman Bitter at Twain," Portland Oregonian, April 22, p. 4.
An interview with Nina Larowe, who was on the Quaker City tour and has nothing good to say for the young MT: "he drank and he swore...Twain was mean and he had no idea of what that trip meant--that it was a trip of influence. But then he was a nobody then and could not understand such things." In a letter to the editor on April 23 (p. 5), Mrs. Larowe says that in a hurried interview "the reporter extracted apparently all the bitter and none of the sweet, making me seem very narrow and unable to appreciate genius." She summarizes the trip and describes some of the passengers, speaking more charitably of MT than she had according to the earlier news story. The interview angered Harriet Oxer, whose letter to the editor (April 25, p. 6) condemns Nina Larrowe's lack of Christian charity and argues that the cruise would have attracted little attention if MT had not immortalized it in IA.

B49   ANON. "Quelques Anecdotes sur Mark Twain," La Revue (Paris, old Revue des Revues), LXXXVI (1 Juin), 423.
Only a few anecdotes, which originally appeared in Alexander McD. Stoddart's "Twainiana," Independent, May 5 (1910.B127).

B50   ANON. "Real and Unreal Propriety," Chicago Tribune, April 24 (Drama-Editorial Section), p. 4.
Quotes from President Taft's tribute to MT, disseminated through the wire services: "He never wrote a line that a father could not read to a daughter" and uses this as a point of departure: "As applied to Mark Twain the comment was without value, but as explanation of American literature it could not be excelled." The attitudes behind such statements as Taft's reflect a national cultural immaturity.

B51   ANON. "Recollections of His Life Here," San Francisco Examiner, April 22, p. 2.
Includes those of Alf Doten, apparently recorded indirectly, observing that MT had a few close friends but did not seek wide popularity. Retells the story of the pretended holdup of MT at Gold Hill, and also gives an unusual version of the origin of the "Mark Twain" pseudonym: "Doten delighted in pretending to their new acquaintances that it originated from Clemens using the expression in the booming days of Virginia City on such occasions as he found it convenient to 'stand off' a friendly bartender for drinks for Doten and himself." Other reminisicences reflect (and may be derived from) MT's own accounts of his western years. The whole issue of the Examiner is rich in tributes to MT, most of them from the wire services.

B52   *ANON. ["Some very good pictures," apparently relating to MT.] Portland Sunday Oregonian, July 3.
[Source: Letter from S. L. Severance to Albert Bigelow Paine, March 13, 1912, printed in Twainian, XXVI (March-April, 1967), 3.]

B53   *ANON. "The Spirit of American Humor," The Nation (London?), VII (April 30), 149.
[Source: Smalley thesis (1948), pp. 63, 70.]

B54   ANON. "Topics of the Day: Mark Twain," Literary Digest, XL (April 30), 857-58.
Summary of press comments on MT.

B55   ANON. "Tributes to Mark Twain," Harper's Weekly, LIV (May 14), 35.
In Harper & Brothers advertisement for the Author's National Edition of MT's works, tributes by President Taft, Theodore Roosevelt, President Woodrow Wilson [of Princeton University], Dr. Van Dyke, Mrs. Julia Ward Howe, James Whitcomb Riley, Booth Tarkington. All of these tributes may be found elsewhere, distributed by the newspaper wire servies (the Boston Globe printed most of them).

B56   ANON. "Twain Nearly 80, Says Goodwin," Sacramento Union (April 23), p. 4.
Reminiscences by C. C. Goodwin, who joined the Territorial Enterprise after MT's departure, and heard a number of MT stories. He based his estimate of MT's age on a book of biographies erroneously giving his year of birth as 1830. This interview with Goodwin, distributed by the press services and widely reprinted, is anecdotal and contains no new or valuable information. Surprisingly, the coverage of MT's death in the Union is rather thin, with nothing of value concerning his former connection with that paper.

B57 ANON. "A Western Word on Mark Twain," New York Times (May 7), "Saturday Review of Books," p. 253.
Briefly summarizes his eulogy in the San Francisco Argonaut.

B58 ANON. [Brief obituary notice.] Spectator, CIV (April 23), 655.
More than a humorist, a great humanist. "Though not a man of learning, he had in him the spirit of letters.... The mass of his literary work was very great, but he never wrote a line that he had cause to be ashamed of."

B59 ANON. [Obituary.] Illustrated London News, CXXXVI (April 30), 640, 643.
Brief commentary, praises MT and compares him to Dickens for sympathy and sense of fun, and for a "reforming and philanthropic spirit" which, however, was more prominent in the works of Dickens. Portrait, p. 643.

B60 ANON. [Obituary Notice.] Saturday Review (London), CIX (April 23), 516. MT was
MT was comic on a lower level, "first among the comic men of America--a country which can never become seriously minded or reflective enough to produce a humourist." Despite his crudity, he forced his readers to laugh. "With his faults he had the supreme excuse that condones many of the artistic blemishes in Shakespeare's early farces-- he was vital." Reprinted in Anderson (1971), p. 278.

B61 ANON. [Untitled brief biographical summary.] Nation (N.Y.), XC (April 28), 440.

B62 ANON. [Untitled notice.] Literary World, LXXVI (May 15), 131-32.
Brief, biographical and anecdotal; treats MT primarily as a humorist.

B63 ANON. [Photographs of MT.] The World's Work, XX (June), 12976-77.
MT at the billiard table, in bed (reading The World's Work), and sitting in a large wicker chair.

B64 ANON. [Review: Captain Stormfield's Visit to Heaven.] Book News Monthly, XXVIII (May), 717.
"No better demonstration of the untruth of dead liberalism exists. No better hit at the weakness of narrowness and ultra-conservatism has appeared.... Yet there is nothing in it which ought to offend the most orthodox fair mind."

B65 *ANON. [Review: Captain Stormfield's Visit to Heaven.] Harper's Weekly (January 22).
[Source: Twainian, II (March, 1940), 4.]

B66 ANON. [Brief Review: Captain Stormfield's Visit to Heaven.] Literary Digest, XL (January 1), 33.
"Mark Twain treats his subject in a good-natured, liberal, and rollicking manner and with a daring extravagance, somewhat machine-made, and always banal, which is absolutely lacking in humor, but he does not make any moral or political point." There is nothing offensive, but also nothing interesting in the picture of Stormfield's destination.

B67 ANON. [Review: Mark Twain's Speeches.] Athenaeum, No. 4322 (August 27), pp. 229-30.
Criticizes the editing.

B68 *ANON. [Review: Merle Johnson, A Bibliography of the Works of Mark Twain.] Nation, XCI (December 22), 601.
[Source: Twainian, II (March, 1943), 5; Asselineau (1954), No. 32.]

B69 BEARD, DAN. "Mark Twain as a Neighbor," Review of Reviews (New York), XLI (June), 705-709.
Reminiscences of MT at his "Stormfield" home, with an account of his first arrival there and his greeting. Photographs of MT, and of the house and grounds.

B70 _____. "Mark Twain, the Man, as Dan Beard Knew," San Francisco Examiner, April 25, p. 16.
At this time Dan Beard was living near MT's "Stormfield" home at Redding, Connecticut; years before, he had illustrated CY, and here he quotes MT's description of the hero: "Now, Mr. Beard, you know the character of the Yankee. He is a common, uneducated man. He's a good telegraph operator; he can make a Colt's revolver or a Remington gun--but he's a perfect ignoramus. He's a good foreman for a manufacturer, can survey land and run a locomotive; in other words he has neither the refinement nor the weakness of a college education. In conclusion I want to say that I have endeavored to put in all the coarseness and vulgarity into the Yankee in King Arthur's Court that is necessary and rely upon you for all the refinement and delicacy of humor your facile pen can depict." [There is an unconfirmed report that a shorter version of this feature story by Beard may be extant in a copy of the New York American of about this period either in the New York Public Library or at the Library of Congress, but that not all editions of the American carried the story.] Paine (1912.A3) gives an abbreviated account of these words (II, 887-89), but does not cite a source.

B71 "BRITANNICUS" [BROOKS, SYDNEY.] "England and Mark Twain," North American Review, CXCI (June), 822-26.
England has had no national author since the death of Dickens (Tennyson was not as generally beloved), and "we have perforce claimed Mark Twain as the representative 'racial' author of his day and have felt for him only a little less admiration, gratitude

1910 - Shorter Writings

("BRITANNICUS" [BROOKS, SYDNEY.])
and affection than his own countrymen."
Reprinted in Anderson (1971), 286-90, where
"Britannicus" is identified as Brooks (also
so identified in Asselineau [1954], No. 52).

B72 BROADLEY, A. M. Chats on Autographs. London: T. Fisher Unwin, pp. 229, 341.
Contains the conclusion of a letter in
which MT says that the Atlantic notice of
RI is entirely satisfactory, "and I am as
uplifted and reassured by it as a mother
who has given birth to a white baby when
she was awfully afraid it was going to be
a mulatto" (p. 229). Autograph letters by
MT are listed as having sold for $150 and
$100 (p. 341).

B73 [BURTON, RICHARD.] "Mark Twain--R.I.P.,"
Bellman (Minneapolis), VIII (April 30),
541.
Vague and general praise. Unsigned:
identified from cover list of contents.

B74 CARMAN, BLISS. "The Last Day at Stormfield,"
Collier's, XLV (May 7), 9.
A poem on the death in springtime of the
weary humorist; "haply...In Avalon, Isle of
Dreams," Chaucer, Shakespeare, Molière, and
Cervantes are enjoying his humor. (With
full-page half-tone portrait of MT.)

B75 CARNEGIE, ANDREW, et al. "Tributes to Mark
Twain," North American Review, CXCI (June),
827-35.
Carnegie, Andrew. Says MT credited him
with the inspiration for CY through his
Triumphant Democracy and with the authorship of a chapter heading in PW. Praises
his business integrity (pp. 827-28).
Paine, Albert Bigelow. Compares MT to
Halley's Comet (p. 828).
Washington, Booker T. Saw MT several
times at his Hartford and New York homes,
and at the Lotos Club. Praises MT's sympathetic portrayal of Jim in HF and his
work for Congo reform, and "the flavor of
the South" in his works (pp. 828-30).
Tarkington, Booth. MT was "the American
Spirit.... Everything seemed safer because
he was with us" (pp. 830-31).
Gompers, Samuel. "He was a deep student
of men and events, a philosopher" (p. 831).
Nesbit, Wilbur D. "He is Cervantes and
Carlyle and Hugo and Dickens all in one"
(pp. 831-32).
Ade, George. MT knew better than to publish too much, or too much of the same
thing, and so he never lost public favor
(pp. 832-33).
Garland, Hamlin. On MT as a westerner
and "a great fictionist and a rough-hewn
stylist uttering himself in his own way,
which was a large, direct and forceful
way" (pp. 833-34).
Bangs, John Kendrick. "I sometimes wonder if he were not quite the most command-
ing literary personality of this period"
(p. 834).

Matthews, Brander. Much of MT's work may
be forgotten, but much is great and will
survive: TS, HF, RI, LOM, TA, "Hadleyburg."
"Mark Twain was great...as a humorist, as a
story-teller, as a stylist, and as a moralist" (pp. 834-35).

B76 CASTELLANOS, JESÚS. "Mark Twain," Reprinted
in his Los Optimistas: Lecturas y Opiniones
Críticas de Arte. Collección Póstuma Publi-
cada por la Academia Nacional de Artes y
Letras. (Habana: Talleres Tipográficos del
"Avisador Comercial," 1914), pp. 169-73.
An obituary summary, dated "Abril 1910"
at the end but without facts of original
publication. "La obra de Mark Twain se
comparaba en vida suya con la de Cervantes
y Molière" (p. 173). Asselineau (1954),
No. 199 cites a 1918 Madrid ed. of Los
Optimistas, pp. 115-20.

B77 CHESTERTON, G. K. "Mark Twain," T. P.'s
Weekly (London), XV (April 29), 535-36.
In part, this is more interesting as an
example of Chestertonian paradoxes than as
a discussion of MT, although it contains
his views of the American culture and MT's
relation to it. On CY says MT failed to
understand what Arthur stood for: "But all
these limitations of his only re-emphasize
the ultimate fact: he never laughed at a
thing unless he thought it laughable. He
was an American; that is to say, an unfath-
omably solemn man." Reprinted in Scott
(1967), pp. 112-17.

B78 "CLAUDIUS CLEAR" [SIR ROBERTSON NICOLL.]
"Mark Twain," The British Weekly, XLVIII
(April 28), 93.
In part a conventional tribute, this
notes MT's tenderness toward his wife and
daughters, and grief at their loss. Praises
him as a writer: "Perhaps the criticisms
that have appeared, excellent as some are,
have scarcely done justice to Mark Twain's
exceeding care in his style. He was a most
precise and painstaking writer, and attached
the greatest importance to the music of
words and the harmonious ordering of claus-
es"; MT's strictures on Fenimore Cooper are
quoted to illustrate his concern for language. The account is entirely sympathetic,
more so than required by courtesy toward
the dead, and contrasts with the words of
"Claudius Clear" in 1912.B21. [Attributed
to Sir Robertson Nicoll by The Literary
Digest (November 30, 1912).]

B79 CLEMENS, SAMUEL L. "Mark Twain's Address
Before Hannibal High School Class of 1902.
Delivered in the Park Theatre Friday Even-
ing, May 30, 1902--He Presented Diplomas to
Members of the Class," Hannibal Morning
Journal, April 23 (copy in scrapbook: Mark
Twain: Biography-Reminiscence in Chicago
Public Library).
Consists largely of MT's remarks, with
very brief description of the event.

B80 COLBY, F. M. "Mark Twain's Illuminating Blunder," Bookman (New York), XXXII (December),
354-58.
Defends MT's Whittier Birthday Dinner
Speech, and condemns the cold audience:
"Reading the speech nowadays we can think
only of the inhumanity of that awful group
of diners toward Mark Twain. No other motive than the desire to amuse them is dis-
cernible in a single line of it.... Whether Mark Twain's joke was good or bad it was
at least vivacious and therein lay its
blasphemy. Suddenly and without warning he
burst out talking in a group of deeply dyed
New Englanders as if among men."

B81 CROY, HOMER. "The Originals of Mark Twain's
Characters," Bellman (Minneapolis), VIII
(June 25), 804-805.
Superficial discussions of several
friends, acquaintances, and relatives of
MT's; provides no new information. The
identification of Laura Fraser as Becky
Thatcher and B. C. M. ("Barney") Farthing
as Huckleberry Finn was common in the
April, 1910 newspapers, although Farthing's
claims have since been passed over in favor
of Tom Blankenship (identified by MT).
Summarized and extensively quoted in Review
of Reviews (N.Y.), August (1910.B47).

B82 DE QUILLE, DAN [WILLIAM WRIGHT.] "His Life in
Virginia City as Reported Was Full of Wild
Pranks and Merriment. Active in Stirring
Days of Old Mining Camp," Rocky Mountain
News (Denver), April 22, p. 3.
Somewhat conventional reminiscences of
rooming with MT at the Daggett & Meyers
building, and of the practical jokes played
on them; also, describes MT as a fencing
enthusiast: "Twain became quite an expert
with the foils. In attack he was fiery and
particularly dangerous, for the reason that
one could not watch his eyes, which he
habitually wears about half closed. In defence he was not so good, and would nearly
always give ground when hotly pressed."

B83 DICKIE, J. F. "Mark Twain," in his In the
Kaiser's Capital (New York: Dodd, Mead
and Co.), pp. 182-90.
On his acquaintance with MT in New York
and Berlin; anecdotal.

B84 DREDD, FIRMIN. "Mark Twain's Biographer,"
Bookman (N.Y.), XXXI (June), 363-65.
On Albert Bigelow Paine and his association with MT. In preparation for the monumental biography, "No trouble or expense
has been spared. For example, a year or
two ago Mr. Paine made a long pilgrimage,
following step by step the Innocents Abroad"
(p. 365; cf. Paine, The Ship-Dwellers,
1910.A8). Two photographs of Paine, one
showing him playing billiards with MT at
Stormfield.

B85 EGGLESTON, GEORGE CARY. Recollections of a
Varied Life. New York: Henry Holt and
Company.
Contains personal recollections of MT,
mostly at public meetings; indexed.

B86 *EPUY, MICHEL. Antholgie des humoristes anglais et américains. Paris: Delagrave
[Source: Asselineau (1954), No. 40: "On
Mark Twain, pp. 422-423; extracts
pp. 423-481."]

B87 _____. "Mark Twain (Samuel Clemens)," Grande
Revue, LXI (10 Mai), 66-75.
Largely biographical, but notes his fine
character, and the serious tone in some of
his books. Was he a heavy-handed buffoon,
lacking art, as some of the recent notices
of his death have charged? Yes, he was that
at the beginning of his career, but he was
capable of pity and tenderness, as in "A
Dog's Tale" or "Was It Heaven or Hell?" and
in "Eve's Diary" "il a atteint la perfection
d'un Homère ou d'un La Fontaine."

B88 GAINES, CLARENCE H. "Mark Twain the Humorist,"
Book News Monthly, XXVIII (April), 583-88.
Humor gave MT perspective. "While Samuel
Clemens has jested more tremendously than
any of his contemporaries, he is perhaps the
sincerest writer in America. So that, on
the whole, one does him the greatest injustice ever to call him (merely) a humorist."
Illustrations: photographs of "Stormfield"
home, and of MT and a bust of MT.

B89 *GRISWOLD, STEPHEN. [Letter or interview, in
which he apparently criticized MT. Griswold
had been a shipmate on the Quaker City tour
on which IA was based.] Brooklyn Eagle,
June 5.
[Source: Ganzel (1968), pp. 260n, 266n.]

B90 Hannibal Morning Journal. [Source: Scrap-
book, Mark Twain: Biography-Reminiscence in
Chicago Public Library, n.d.],
April 22.
RoBards, John L. "Tribute to Mark Twain."
Affectionate, general. "Mark Twain's Last
Visit to Hannibal." Reprints of news sto-
ries in the Journal, May 29-June 3, 1902:
MT honored by schools, local dignitaries.
April 24.
"Prophetic Words of Hon. George A. Mahan,
Uttered October 24, 1906." Someday there
will be a monument to MT in Hannibal.
"Characteristic Mark Twain Letters." In
1903 Mr. T. F. Gatts requested permission to
set a "Mark Twain Day" at the St. Louis
World's Fair; MT replied in part: "I hope
that no society will be named for me while
I am still alive, for I might at some time
or another do something which could cause
its members to regret having done me that
honor." In reply to further urging he repeated his thanks, but "I am a Missourian
and so I shrink from distinctions which have
to be arranged before hand and with my

(Hannibal Morning Journal)
privity, for I then become a party to my
own exalting."
April 26.
"Hannibal's Tribute to Samuel L. Clemens,
'Mark Twain.'" Describes the meeting at
the Presbyterian Church the previous afternoon, quoting tributes by local dignitaries,
among them MT's boyhood friend John L. Ro-
Bards; like the rest he was laudatory but
general.

B91 HENDERSON, ARCHIBALD. "The International
Fame of Mark Twain," North American Review,
CXCII (December), 805-15.
Surveys some of the more significant
critical commentary on MT in France, Ger-
many, Italy, and elsewhere. Reprinted in
Anderson (1971), 302-12; revised as "The
World-Famed Genius" in Henderson's Mark
Twain (London, 1911), pp. 127-76.

B92 HERON, HERBERT. "Mark Twain," Harper's Weekly, LIV (June 11), 24.
On the laughter MT gave the world, and
the falsehoods he exposed; he will be
mourned.

B93 HOWELLS, WILLIAM DEAN. "A Critical Comment
on Mark Twain's Work," Harper's Weekly,
LIV (April 30), 10, 27.
Excerpts from his "Mark Twain: an Inquiry" (North American Review, 1901; reprinted there 1910 and in Howells, My Mark
Twain).

B94 _____. "Mark Twain: An Inquiry," North
American Review, CXCI (June), 836-50.
Reprinted from North American Review,
February, 1901; also reprinted in his My
Mark Twain (1910.A3). Photograph of MT,
p. 720.

B95 _____. "My Memories of Mark Twain," Harper's
Monthly, CXXI (July), 165-78; (August),
340-48; (September), 512-29.
Admiring discussion of author and man by
a professional colleague and close personal
friend of more than forty years; reprinted
with only minor changes in his My Mark
Twain, pp. 1-100 (1910.A3). Summarized,
with excerpts, as "Mark Twain as William
Dean Howells Saw Him," Current Literature,
XLIX (October), 445-47.

B96 _____. [Introduction: Mark Twain's Speeches.] New York and London: Harper & Brothers Publishers.
A rather general, two-page introduction
without new information. "I never heard
Clemens speak when I thought he quite
failed," but he was at his best when he
carefully prepared his apparently spontaneous performances. [This edition differs
significantly from that of 1923 in the
selection of speeches.]

B97 JAMES, GEORGE WHARTON. "Mark Twain and the
Pacific Coast," Pacific Monthly, XXIV
(August), 115-32.
On MT in Nevada and California, with recollections by acquaintances, some from
published works and some apparently from
conversations. Repeats a story that MT was
twice captured in the Civil War, the second
time escaping and fleeing to Nevada to escape punishment for violating parole after
the first capture. Also quotes accounts by
Ella Sterling Cummings, and, at length, from
recollections (some apparently given orally)
by Charles Warren Stoddard, on MT's lack of
self-confidence while lecturing in London
in 1873. Quotes at length an interview of
Nina Larowe and her letter to the editor
(1910.B48) on MT as she saw him on the Quaker City tour. Includes photograph of MT by
Major J. B. Pond on the world lecture tour,
and four photographs by A. F. Bradley.

B98 JENSEN, JOHANNES V. "Mark Twain," Politikens
Kronik (n.p.), (April 23).
[Source: Scrap book, Mark Twain: Biogra-
phy-Reminiscence in Chicago Public Library.]
A memorial tribute, in Norwegian.

B99 JEROME, JEROME K., et al. "Mark Twain. Some
Personal Recollections and Opinions," Bookman (London), XXXVIII (June), 116-19. Portrait and Cartoon.
"Jerome's First Meeting with Him." After
MT had dined with him in London, Jerome was
struck by the fact "that neither of us had
made a single joke or told a funny story."
Struck by MT's "deep feeling and broad sympathies" (p. 116).
"E. V. Lucas and Twain at a 'Punch Dinner.'" Praises TS and HF; describes MT as
"visibly touched, almost melted" by the reception (pp. 116-17).
"Walter Emanuel's Opinion of Mark Twain's
Humour." An original, an example to other
humorists; his best work will endure
(p. 117).
"J. J. Bell and a Twain Joke." Bell never
met MT, but appreciated his joke about Noah
(pp. 117-18).
"Leonard Henslowe on Interviewing Mark
Twain." "Mark Twain was always kind to the
interviewer, and showed tact even in putting
him off." A holograph note from MT is reproduced in facsimile (p. 118).
"Arnold Bennett Considers Twain Was a Divine Amateur." Never met MT. Best work in
first half of LOM. "Episodically, both
Huckleberry Finn and Tom Sawyer are magnificent, but as complete works of art they are
of quite inferior quality.... He had no
notion of construction, and very little
power of self-criticism. He was great in
the subordinate business of decoration....
The praise poured out on his novels seems
to me exceedingly exaggerated" (p. 118).
[Reprinted in Anderson (1971), p. 285.]

(JEROME, JEROME K., et al.)
"Owen Seaman's Welcome to Mark Twain in 1907." A reprint of the "To Mark Twain" poem in Punch (1907.B30), without added commentary (p. 118).
"Mr. Pett Ridge on the Charm of Mark Twain." After a busybody introduced him to MT as the MT of London, Ridge told MT: "What he intended to say was that you were the Pett Ridge of America!" MT replied, "Ah, now I can see we shall get along well together" (p. 118).
"F. Anstey in Praise of Mark Twain." No personal recollections; likes HF (p. 119).

B100   JERROLD, WALTER, "Mark Twain, the Man and the Jester," Bookman (London), XXXVIII (June), 111-16.
On the deep feeling behind MT's humor, and the distinctively American quality of his writing. Quotes Bret Harte's account of his first meeting with MT. Includes portraits of MT by George Hutchinson and by Spiridon.

B101   KING, FREDERICK A. "The Story of Mark Twain's Debts," Bookman (New York), XXXI (June), 394-96.
A superficial popular account, somewhat inaccurate ("His popularity with Englishmen had never been great, owing to the liberties he had taken with that nation's people in Innocents Abroad"); chiefly descriptive and based on secondary sources. ["Reprinted from THE BOOKMAN for January, 1906."]

B102   *LANCASTER, CHARLES. "Mark Twain," Liverpool Daily Post and Mercury, May 5.
[Source: Cited in letter by W. E. Benjamin to Albert Bigelow Paine in Twainian, XXVI (November-December, 1967), 4.]

B103   [Mark Twain Number.] Bookman (London), XXXVIII (June).
Cover photograph of MT by E. H. Mills.

B104   [MATHER, FRANK JEWETT.] "Two Frontiersmen," Nation (New York) XC (April 28), 422-23.
MT and Henry James are both frontiersmen with fidelity to their vision; MT's reputation will probably endure, "while the fate of Mr. James's delicate art seems to be involved in the hesitancy that afflicts his own heroes." Also appeared in New York Evening Post, April 23, p. 6. Reprinted in Anderson (1971), where this unsigned article is attributed to Mather (pp. 279-81).

B105   MATTHEWS, BRANDER. "American Humor," in his The American of the Future, and Other Essays (New York: Charles Scribner's Sons), passim.
MT, here described as a great humorist, is in a class with Cervantes and Molière. There is a strong implication that MT is more than simply amusing, but the article does not lend itself to exploration of other aspects of his writing. Reprint of 1908.B8.

B106   MAURICE, ARTHUR BARTLETT. "Best Sellers of Yesterday. II--Mark Twain's The Innocents Abroad," Bookman (New York), XXXI (June), 374-79.
Second in a series on such best-sellers by various authors; chiefly descriptive, based on secondary sources, with extensive quotation and illustrations from IA. Praises MT's "keen observation, clear perception and a remarkable freshness of the point of view"; the book remains a best Seller of To-day."

B107   *MENCKEN, H. L. [On his admiration for HF.] Smart Set, XXXI (June), 153-54.]
[Source: Cited in Anderson (1971), p. 277.]

B108   MICHAUD, RÉGIS. "L'Envers d'un Humoriste: Mark Twain," Revue du Mois, IX (April 10), 430-44.
Notes the serious element in MT's work, his literary art, concluding: "Au point de vue artistique, Mark Twain est, après Dickens, un des plus grands caricaturistes des lettres anglaises. Ainsi que l'auteur de Gargantua et celui de Don Quichotte, il a plus de fois donné à satire la forme d'une épopée.... Mark Twain en est l'Homère, plus sérieux qu'on ne pensait, sous son travesti d'humoriste."

B109   MILLARD, BAILEY. "Mark Twain in San Francisco," Bookman (New York), XXXI (June), 369-73.
Superficial, dependent on secondary sources, and not wholly accurate. Reports that MT worked for a time for the San Francisco Morning Call before three months of pocket-mining for gold in Calaveras County, and quotes a conversation between Noah Brooks and MT [who was in New York at the time], in which MT won reluctant approval for the Quaker City tour at the expense of the San Francisco Alta California.

B110   MURRAY, ADA FOSTER. "To Mark Twain," Harper's Weekly, LIV (May 7), 27.
A short poem on the enchantment in MT's humor, and his "exquisite and true" touch for "the deeper things" as well.

B111   NESBIT, WILBUR D. "Samuel Langhorne Clemens, 1835-1910," Harper's Weekly, LIV (May 7), 30.
Reprints a poem which appeared "at the time of Mark Twain's death" in the Chicago Evening Post. His monument will be "a boy who hugs a well-thumbed book,/ Wherein dwell the companions of his heart."

B112   PAIN, BARRY. "The Humour of Mark Twain," Bookman (London), XXXVIII (June), 107-11.
Largely hostile, by an acquaintance of Bret Harte. "Mark Twain's humorous writing at its best does bear some resemblance to Bret Harte's, but Bret Harte made far fewer inartistic blunders." Much of MT's humor

1910 - Shorter Writings

(PAIN, BARRY)
is now dated; and "if we make this allow-
ance, it may be said that when Mark Twain's
humour fails, it is because his taste fails.
It was his misfortune to hate all that was
old and established.... I do not allude
only to that dismal failure, his Yankee at
the Court of King Arthur. Many instances
of this dullness of perception may be found
in his travel books." Even HF is marred
by MT's inability to maintain a consistent
esthetic distance from his material. Pain
agrees, however, with MT's condemnation of
The Vicar of Wakefield as insincere.

B113   PAINE, ALBERT BIGELOW. "Mark Twain: A Biographical Summary," Harper's Weekly, LIV
(April 30), 6-10.
A useful brief biography, but superseded
by Paine's extensive 1912 life of MT
(1912.A3).

B114   PEARSON, EDMUND LESTER. "The Children's Librarian versus Huckleberry Finn: A Brief
for the Defense," in his The Library and
the Librarian. (Woodstock, Vermont: The
Elm Tree Press), pp. 26-32.
Reprinted from Library Journal
(1907.B28).

B115   PECK, HARRY THURSTON. "Mark Twain a Century
Hence," Bookman (New York), XXXI (June),
382-93.
"I should say that the first two books--
The Jumping Frog (1867) and The Innocents
Abroad (1869) are never likely to go out of
print or out of favour. Roughing It (1872)
will be valued both for its humour and for
its history for many years. The Adventures
of Tom Sawyer (1876) and Huckleberry Finn
(1885) will remain for perhaps two decades.
All the rest of Mr. Clemens's books may
perhaps be sold by subscription agents among
his 'complete works' for a certain time,
but they will not be read." Includes several photographs of MT, and one of Theresa
Feodorowna Ries working on a bust of him.
Reprinted in Anderson (1971), pp. 291-95.

B116   PHELPS, WILLIAM LYON. "Mark Twain," in his
Essays on Modern Novelists (New York: Mac-
Millan), pp. 99-114.
Originally in North American Review,
1907.B29.

B117   _____. "Mark Twain, Artist," Review of Reviews (New York), XLI (June), 702-703.
"Mark Twain was a greater artist than he
was humorist; a greater humorist than he
was philosopher; a greater philosopher than
he was thinker. Goethe's well-known remark
about Byron, 'The moment he thinks, he is a
child,' would in some respects be applicable
to Mark Twain,'" but MT "was a profoundly
serious artist." Reprinted in Anderson
(1971), pp. 296-98.

B118   _____. "Some Notes on Mark Twain. With Some
Unpublished Letters," Independent, LXVIII
(May 5), 956-60.
"Some Rambling Notes of an Idle Excursion"
parallels Sir Thomas Browne's Religio Medici
in suggesting that Elijah kindled a fire on
a wet altar because he soaked it in petroleum rather than water; an MT letter on the
subject to Phelps (April 24, 1901) is here
printed, together with one to Bret Harte
(May 1, 1867) on the recent publication of
the Jumping Frog book, Also includes miscellaneous comments on MT's hesitating agreement
that HF is his best work, his support for the
Japanese side in the war with Russia, his
visible distress over the final illness of
his wife, and his popularity among German
readers; cites an unnamed French journal
which in 1907 ranked him at the head of the
day's leading authors. Sketch of MT by
Poulteney Bigelow. Reprinted with minor revisions in Phelps's Essays on Books (1914).

B119   RIDEING, WILLIAM H. "Mark Twain in Clubland,"
Bookman (New York), XXXI (June), 379-82.
Anecdotes of MT when he stayed for a few
months at the Players Club in New York; describes his manner of speaking, when at ease
or angry, and his reaction on being shown a
Greek version of his "Jumping Frog" story
(which later turned out to be a translation
for classroom use by Henry Sidgwick).

B120   RILEY, JAMES WHITCOMB, et al. "Indiana School
of Authors, in Deep Grief, Drops Tender
Praise at Bier of the Humorist," Indianapolis
Star, April 22, p. 7.
Somewhat conventional appreciations, without added editorial comment, by Riley, George
Ade, Meredith Nicholson, Charles Major, and
Newton Booth Tarkington. The general tenor
of the remarks is that MT was lovable, sane,
and distinctively American; although this
appears to be the first and fullest publication, these authors' remarks were widely
quoted through the wire services.

B121   _____. "Tribute of America's 'Funny Men' to
the King of Them Who Has Passed Away," Boston Post, April 23, p. 7.
"Yesterday the Post wired the leading humorists of the country, asking for express
sions upon the death of the dean and most
famous of the corps, Mark Twain. The love
and admiration in which Mr. Clemens was held
is told in the following tributes," by James
Whitcomb Riley, Frank L. Stanton, George
Ade, Sewell Ford, R. F. Outcault, C. B. Lewis (M. Quad), Paul West, S. E. Kiser, Newton
Newkirk, Walt Mason, Wilbur D. Nesbit, Wallace Irwin, Samuel G. Blythe, and Franklin
P. Adams. The Boston Post also contained a
rich sampling of tributes by public figures
as reported by the wire services.

B122 SHERMAN, STUART P. "Literary News and Reviews: The Humor of Mark Twain," New York Evening Post, May 14.
[Source: clippings in Mark Twain--Biography-Reminiscence scrapbook in Chicago Public Library.] Extensive, biographical, and laudatory, noting the American quality of his works. "Handicapped by uproarious laughter, he produced two or three pieces of fiction which deserved serious attention; but his leonine head had grown gray before he lived down his record as a 'platform humorist.'"

B123 _____. "Mark Twain," Nation (New York), XC (May 12), 477-80.
On MT as a big-hearted, unsubtle, robust American, and on his humor. Reprinted in Cardwell (1963), 9-14; Scott (1955), 107-16; Scott (1967), 118-27. Asselineau (1954), No. 169 reports a reprinting in Gustav Pollak, ed., Fifty Years of American Idealism (Boston, 1915, pp. 388-400); revised and expanded as "The Democracy of Mark Twain" in Sherman's On Contemporary Literature (New York: Henry Holt, 1917, pp. 18-49); Asselineau (1954), No. 519 reports reprinting of the book in 1931, and (No. 330) of the essay in Kenneth Allan Robinson, et al., Essays Towards Truth (New York: Henry Holt, 1924, pp. 368-95). The revision also discusses the Paine biography as "a part of the prose Odyssey of the American people," which "will continue to be read when many of Mark Twain's writings are forgotten" and concludes with a postscript on MS, which a boy of nine can read "with delight and without undesirable stimulation," despite the irony and atheism in "a book written at his elders."

B124 SMITH, H. B. [Review: Mark Twain's Speeches.] Bookman (N.Y.), XXXII (September), 78-79.
A descriptive review, mostly summary and quotation.

B125 STEDMAN, LUCY, and GEORGE M. GOULD. Life and Letters of Edmund Clarence Stedman. New York: Moffat, Yard & Co. 2 vols.
Contains partial text of Stedman's letter to MT (July 7, 1889), praising CY but with a number of criticisms of details, by page-number (II, 370-72).

B126 STERN, CAROLINE. "Mark Twain (A Nocturne of the Mississippi)," Harper's Weekly, LIV (July 2), 32.
A poem on MT and the river.

B127 STODDART, ALEXANDER McD. "Twainiana," Independent, LXVIII (May 5), 960-63.
Anecdotes, most of them not apocryphal but also not new; one, apparently not printed elsewhere, describes MT's participation in charades, as told by T. Max Smith, music critic of the New York Press.

B128 [STRUNSKY, SIMEON]. "Serious Humorists," Nation (New York), XC (June 30), 645-46.
Through the "certain paradoxical habit we have fallen into when passing judgment on the illustrious dead," we praise their less salient qualities: MT had a serious side, but this is not what made him a great humorist and "There was no fundamental pessimism in Mark Twain." Reprinted in Anderson (1971), pp. 299-301, with attribution of this unsigned article to Strunsky.

B129 TAFT, WILLIAM HOWARD, et al. "Honor His Memory," Boston Globe (April 22), pp. 1-2.
A number of brief and generally conventional tributes, of which those by Taft, Hamlin Garland, and William Dean Howells appeared in many or most American newspapers; also includes tributes by Thomas Wentworth Higginson, Julia Ward Howe, Thomas Nelson Page, Henry Cabot Lodge, Sam Walter Foss, Woodrow Wilson, William Lyon Phelps, and Charles Follen Adams.

B130 THOMPSON, JAMES WESTFALL. "Mark Twain," Harper's Weekly, LIV (May 14), 34.
A poem, evoking the great Mississippi River and mourning MT's death.

B131 TORREY, CHARLES L. "Mark Twain, Sir Thomas Browne, and the Old Testament," Nation, XC (June 2), 553-54.
A letter, commenting on William Lyon Phelps, "Some Notes on Mark Twain" (Independent, May 5, 956-60); begins by drawing a parallel between Sir Thomas Browne's Religio Medici and MT's Captain Ned Wakeman suggesting naphtha as the source of the altar fire which discomfited the prophets of Baal. Torrey points to a still older parallel in II Maccabees, i, 19 ff., in which "Nehemiah watered the grand altar with petroleum."

B132 TWICHELL, JOSEPH H. "Mark Twain: Mr. Twichell's Tribute to His Old and Very Dear Friend," Hartford Courant, April 23, p. 8.
A letter to the editor which notes his "big, warm and tender heart," and, beneath his "exterior roughnesses...exquisite refinements of taste and sentiment." "He was quickly responsive to any appeal to his sympathy, especially to his pity. I have seldom known a person so easily moved to tears. He could sometimes be of an unsparingly hostile temper toward a fellow man, but he could never bear to see an animal in pain." Leah A. Strong reproduces the entire text of this letter in Joseph Hopkins Twichell: Mark Twain's Friend and Pastor (1966.A11), pp. 68, 89-90.

B133 VALE, CHARLES. "Mark Twain as an Orator," Forum, XLIV (July), 1-13.
Chiefly obituary praise of the man and works, of which "Huckleberry Finn is his supreme and incontestable masterpiece." Describes MT's speech at a 1907 dinner

1910 - Shorter Writings

(VALE, CHARLES)
given in his honor by the Lord Mayor of London, presided over by T. P. O'Connor, and his presence years earlier at a party at which the guests included Wagner, Liszt, Turgenev, Browning, Rosetti, Sir Frederick Leighton, Burne-Jones, William Morris, Bret Harte, and Joaquin Miller. Quotes the last part of Augustine Birrell's speech in his honor at a Pilgrims' dinner given for MT, and concludes with a reprinting of Owen Seaman's poem to him in Punch. "Acknowledgments are especially due to Mr. William Archer and Mr. T. P. O'Connor, M. P., for valued assistance."

B134 VAN DYKE, HENRY. "We Knew You Well, Dear Yorick of the West" [poem], American Academy and the National Institute of Arts and Letters, Public Meeting, Held at Carnegie Hall, November 30, 1910, in Memory of Samuel Langhorne Clemens (New York, 1922).
[This attribution by Scott, who reprints in (1955), p. 117, and (1967), p. 128]; poem also in "Mark Twain Commemorated," Outlook, XCVI (December 10), 802, and "Mark Twain in Memoriam..." Harper's Weekly, LIV (December 17), 10.

B135 WATTERSON, HENRY. "Mark Twain--An Intimate Memory," American Magazine LXX (July), 372-75.
MT originally meant the part of Colonel Sellers in the GA play for Edwin Booth, and resented the purely comic interpretation of the part by John T. Raymond; describes but does not reprint an MT letter on the original of Sellers, described in some detail, and Raymond's reaction to reading a letter from him to Watterson: "'Do you know,' said he, 'it makes me want to cry. That is not the man I am trying to impersonate at all.' Be sure it was not; for there was nothing funny about the spiritual being of Mark Twain's own Mulberry Sellers; he was as brave as a lion and as stern and upright as a covenanter." Describes a joke he and MT played on Murat Halstead by giving a cub reporter an interview in his name, repudiating his well-known principles.

B136 WHITE, FRANK MARSHALL. "Mark Twain as a Newspaper Reporter," Outlook, XCVI (December), 961-67.
White was responsible for engaging MT to write an account of the 1897 Diamond Jubilee for the New York World. It was at this time that a reporter called, having heard that he had died; MT sent him this note (here reproduced in facsimile): "James Ross Clemens, a cousin of mine, was seriously ill two or three weeks ago in London, but is well now. The report of my illness grew out of his illness; the report of my death was an exaggeration." Also publishes the texts of several MT notes to White. Includes photograph of MT.

B137 WILLIAMS, C. "Mark Twain," Harper's Weekly, LIV (August 20), 21.
A poem on the death of MT: he was kind, wholesome and wise in his humor. [Reprinted from Sunset (San Francisco), XXV (July), 58, according to Asselineau (1954), No. 82.]

B138 WOOLF, S. J. "Painting the Portrait of Mark Twain. The Humorist's Character as It Became Unfolded to the Artist," Collier's, XLV (May 14), 42-44.
Includes quotations from MT (from memory?) and sensitive observation of his character, based on meetings and sittings in February, 1906.

1911 A BOOKS

A1 *ANDERSON AUCTION COMPANY. Catalogue of the Library and Manuscripts of Samuel L. Clemens...to be Sold Feb. 7 & 8, 1911. New York: The Anderson Auction Co.
[Source: Asselineau (1954), No. 104.]

A2 *ANON. Mark Twain: Autograph Manuscripts and First Editions Offered by Dodd & Livingston. New York.
[Source: Asselineau (1954), No. 103.]

A3 HENDERSON, ARCHIBALD. Mark Twain. London: Duckworth & Co. [Also New York: Frederick A. Stokes Company, 1912, and reprinted Folcroft, Pa.: The Folcroft Press, Inc., 1969.]
A major study of man and works, reflecting some personal acquaintance. The chapter titled "The World-Famed Genius" appeared in somewhat different form as "The International Fame of Mark Twain" (North American Review, December [1910.B91]), and "Philosopher, Moralist, Sociologist" appeared as "Mark Twain als Philosoph, Moralist und Soziologe" (Deutsche Revue, 1911.B9). Contains an extensive bibliography of articles and reviews concerning MT (pp. 215-30), incorporated in the present bibliography. Illustrated.

1911 B SHORTER WRITINGS

B1 ADAMS, JOHN. "Mark Twain As Psychologist," Bookman (London), XXXIX (March), 270-72.
A review of What Is Man? as a depressing work, and one ill-suited to MT's literary style. MT fails to observe the dualism he creates in distinguishing between the part of man that does things and the inner force that impels him to do them, and his purely mechanistic view of man disregards the undeniable existence of remorse.

B2 ANON. "Mark Twain as the Embodiment of American Romance," Current Literature, LI (November), 566-68.
A review of Archibald Henderson's Mark Twain. Summarizes parts and quotes freely,

(ANON.)
but does not make a critical estimate.
Full-page photograph of MT, p. 566.

B3   ANON. "Mark Twain's European Fame," Bookman
(New York), XXXIII (June), 347-50.
Summarizes the chapter in Archibald Henderson's Mark Twain on European translations
and estimates of MT: he is not greatly appreciated in France and Italy, but very
popular in the Scandinavian countries and
in Germany, where the two American authors
most widely read are MT and Emerson.

B4   ANON. [Review: Archibald Henderson, Mark
Twain.] Bookman (London), XL (April),
37-38.
MT indeed "belongs among the immortals of
his generation," although Henderson tends
to over-state the case because he was personally charmed by an acquaintance with
him; hence his criticism is "unreliable";
nonetheless, he vividly shows "the breadth,
the height, the depth, and the ingrained
humanity" of MT's character.

B5   C., M. B. "Mark Twain as a Reader," Harper's
Weekly, LV (January 7), 6.
A letter written to William Dean Howells
from one of the women who used to meet in
MT's home in Hartford to listen to him read
from Browning.

B6   CAMPBELL, KILLIS. "From Aesop to Mark
Twain," Sewanee Review, XIX (January),
43-49.
"A Dog's Tale" follows ancient tradition
in its account of a dog wrongly punished
after saving the master's child.

B7   *FROHMAN, DANIEL. Memories of a Manager. New
York: Doubleday, Page & Co., p. 50.
Comments on the play, Colonel Sellers as
a Scientist, written in collaboration with
William Dean Howells. [Source: Quoted by
W. J. Meserve in The Complete Plays of
William Dean Howells (1960), p. 208.]

B8   HALLECK, REUBEN POST. History of American
Literature. New York: American Book Company.
On MT, pp. 355-64 and passim. Recognizes
HF as "Mark Twain's masterpiece." MT will
survive because of his artistry; his humor
is "a preservative salt, but salt is valuable only to preserve substantial things."

B9   HENDERSON, ARCHIBALD. "Mark Twain als Philosoph, Moralist un Soziologe," Deutsche Revue (Stuttgart und Leipzig), XXXVI, Erster
Band (Januar bis März), 189-205.
A German translation of the concluding
chapter of his Mark Twain [1910.A3].

B10   *_____. "Mark Twain Seen in Three Aspects,"
NCR, II (March 5), 6-7, 10.
[Source: Leary (1954), p. 49.]

B11   *HERTS, ALICE MINNIE [HENIGER]. The Children's
Educational Theatre, with an introduction
by Charles W. Eliot. New York and London:
Harper & Brothers.
[Source: Asselineau (1954), No. 106,
noting that it "contains a few pages on The
Prince and the Pauper"; a copy of this book
is listed in the card catalogue of the Oakland (California) Public Library, but not
on the shelf.]

B12   *HOWELLS, WILLIAM DEAN. "In Memory of Mark
Twain," American Academy Proceedings, I
(November 1), 5-6.
[Source: Leary (1954), p. 50.] This may
be the same as the item listed for 1913.B8.

B13   JAMES, GEORGE WHARTON. "How Mark Twain Was
Made," National Magazine (Boston), XXXIII
(February), 525-37.
An enthusiastic popular account of MT's
early years as a writer, molded by California and the great West. Based primarily on
familiar published accounts, but the source
of the story of MT and his imitation meer-
schaum pipe is given as Dan de Quille in
private conversation. MT in London in 1873
with Charles Warren Stoddard is described
as homesick, and, when in his cups, lachry-
mose, pessimistic, and convinced that he
will die in the poorhouse. James contends
that his account of MT reading to Stoddard
from the book of Ruth is more complete and
less expurgated than Stoddard's in the
chapter "A Humorist Abroad" in his Exits
and Entrances.

B14   MATTHEWS, BRANDER. "'Mark Twain' (Samuel L.
Clemens)," in An Introduction to American
Literature revised ed. (New York: American
Book Company), pp. 220-31.
This is a text-book, with questions for
students at the ends of chapters. Matthews
remains essentially unchanged in his estimate of MT, though more frankly acknowledging his willingness to satisfy the public
demand for humor, even at the expense of
art.

B15   PAINE, ALBERT BIGELOW. "Mark Twain: Some
Chapters from an Extraordinary Life,"
Harper's Monthly, CXXIII (November),
813-28; CXXIV (December), 42-53.
The first of thirteen installments of
Paine's biography of MT, which appeared as
a book in 1912; includes illustrations not
used in the book.

B16   SMALLEY, GEORGE W. Anglo-American Memories.
New York and London: G. P. Putnam's Sons.
On MT dining with Edward, Prince of Wales
(afterward Edward VII) at Bad Nauheim; MT
"did not care to adapt himself to the circumstances; considering, perhaps, that the
circumstances ought to adapt themselves to
him. The meeting was not a success, and,
so far as I know, was never repeated. Socially speaking, the Mississippi Pilot was

1911 - Shorter Writings

(SMALLEY, GEORGE W.)
an <u>intransigeant</u> at times, and this was one
of the times. He could not, I suppose,
overcome his drawling manner of speech nor
reduce his interminable stories to dinner-
table limits. He had the air of usurping
more than his share of the conversation and
of the time, which he certainly did not
mean to" (pp. 412-15).

1912 A BOOKS

A1 ANON. <u>Saturday Morning Club of Hartford</u>.
Hartford: The Case, Lockwood & Brainard
Co.
A pamphlet, including a list of 15 lec-
tures there by MT, 1876-1907.

A2 *CLEMENS, SAMUEL L. <u>Cuentos Escogidos</u>:
traducíon directa y esmerada de A. Barrado,
precedidos de un prólogo de Angel Guerra.
Madrid: Noticiero-guía de Madrid.
[Source: Asselineau (1954), No. 114.]

A3 PAINE, ALBERT BIGELOW. <u>Mark Twain: A Biography, The Personal and Literary Life of
Samuel Langhorne Clemens</u>. New York and
London: Harper & Brothers Publishers.
3 vol. (Part of this biography appeared
in <u>Harper's</u>, 1911-1912; the texts are not
identical).
The authorized biography. Paine met MT
in late 1901, and in January, 1906 made
arrangements to become his official biographer. His account of the later years is
based on personal observation and information supplied by acquaintances of MT, and
on documentation provided by MT and his
friends and family. He took pains to obtain material from surviving individuals
who had known MT, and but for his efforts
much of value might have been lost. Paine
was more dependent on MT's own recollections for the earlier period, but often
heard different versions of the same incident and conceded that MT's accounts ought
to be confirmed from other sources whenever possible.
Paine has justly been criticized for suppression of factual material and for a
somewhat casual attitude toward papers in
his charge and toward the responsibilities
of an editor. In his behalf it may be
argued that some information was withheld
out of concern for Clara Clemens, and that
as MT's literary executor he was interested in maintaining the value of MT's literary name as an asset which continued to
provide her support. As biographer and
editor Paine assembled and organized a
large amount of material, laying a substantial foundation for MT scholarship.
His great work is being supplemented and
corrected, but will never be entirely replaced.

1912 B SHORTER WRITINGS

B1 *ANON. "Busy Life of the Rev. Joseph H. Twich-
ell, Mark Twain's Friend," New York <u>Sun</u>,
February 4, p. 7.
[Source: Listed by Leah A. Strong in
<u>Joseph Hopkins Twichell</u> (1966), p. 176.]

B2 ANON. "The 'Cub' Days of Mark Twain," <u>Liter-
ary Digest</u>, XLIV (February), 305-307.
A popular account of MT on the "Orion
Enterprise" (<u>sic</u>) in Nevada; based on an
extract from Paine's biography serialized
in <u>Harper's</u>.

B3 ANON. "How 'The Players' Was Formed," <u>Liter-
ary Digest</u>, XLV (October 12), 621.
Excerpts from the Paine biography on MT's
part in the founding of the New York club.

B4 ANON. "Mark Twain," <u>Athenaeum</u>, No. 4433
(October 12), pp. 403-404.
A review of the Paine biography: it is
too long and English critics will question
the estimates of some of MT's works.

B5 ANON. "Mark Twain's Failures," <u>Literary Di-
gest</u>, XLV (July 27), 150.
On works MT abandoned, sometimes on the
urging of Olivia Clemens--whose voice was
simply that of good judgment. Summary of
an installment of the Paine biography in
<u>Harper's Monthly</u> (July), with the greater
part of the text consisting of quotations
from it, adds no information or judgment.

B6 ANON. "Mark Twain's Lucky Failure," <u>Literary
Digest</u>, XLIV (February 24), 391-92.
A summary of part of the fourth install-
ment of the Paine biography in <u>Harper's</u>, on
MT's failure as a miner.

B7 ANON. "Mark Twain's Portrait," <u>Outlook</u> (New
York), CII (November 9), 528-29.
A general discussion, occasioned by the
three-volume Paine biography, which "is
much too long; but it presents the apology
of being interesting from cover to cover."

B8 ANON. "Mark Twain's Private Girls' Club,"
<u>Ladies' Home Journal</u>, XXIX (February), 23,
54.
A series of letters from MT to a little
girl in France, 1902-1909, and "Constitu-
tion and Laws of the Juggernaut Club."
Photograph: "Mark Twain Trying to Make the
Life of Joan of Arc Intelligible to a Young
Girl Friend."

B9 ANON. "Napoleon III in America," <u>Bookman</u>
(New York), XXXVI (November), 238.
Briefly notes MT's comment on Napoleon III
in <u>IA</u>; erroneously reported in Asselineau
(1954, No. 134) as dealing with MT's "con-
sultation of Cheiro, a famous chiromancer."

B10   ANON. "One Who Didn't Like Mark Twain," Lit-
        erary Digest, XLV (November 30), 1014-15.
           Sir Robertson Nicoll, writing as "Claudi-
        us Clear" in The British Weekly (1912.B21)
        criticized MT's hostility toward Christian-
        ity and his "habitual, incessant, and dis-
        gusting profanity"; Nicoll questioned MT's
        stature as a humorist and called him "a
        man absolutely destitute of culture, and
        incapable of consecutive thought....
        There are signs that Mark Twain was occa-
        sionally very kind to people who needed
        help, but not many signs."

B11   ANON. "The Origin of Pudd'nhead Wilson,"
        Literary Digest, XLV (October 26), 740-41.
           An extract from the Memoirs of the palm-
        ist "Cheiro," recently published by Lippin-
        cott; he read the palm of MT, who was in a
        serious mood at the time. MT examined
        Cheiro's collection of hand-prints, and was
        especially impressed by the similar prints
        of a mother and daughter, whose lives were
        also similar; claims this suggested the
        theme for PW.

B12   ANON. "Punch, Brothers," Bookman (New York),
        XXXVI (November), 236-37.
           Excerpts the background of MT's "A Liter-
        ary Nightmare" from the new Paine Biography,
        and ends with a French version of the jin-
        gle said to be by Swinburne.

B13   *ANON. "Spiritual Tragedy of Mark Twain,"
        Current Literature, LIII (November),
        582-84.
           [Source: Asselineau (1954), No. 136:
        MT's sense of failure grew out of public
        expectation of humor, not serious writing.]

B14   ANON. "The Story of Grant's Memoirs," Liter-
        ary Digest, XLIV (September 7), 373-75
           Summarizes part of the September install-
        ment of the Paine biography in Harper's.

B15   ANON. "A Typical American," Nation, XCV
        (November 14), 475-59.
           Reviews the Paine biography as "The
        prose Odyssey of the American people...it
        will continue to be read when half of Mark
        Twain's writings are forgotten."

B16   ANON. [Review: Paine, Mark Twain.] Spec-
        tator, CIX (October 12), 557-58.
           Paine wrote the last volume "on a differ-
        ent scale from the others"; the reader will
        enjoy this biography despite its length.

B17   BACHELLER, IRVING. "Mr. Paine's Biography
        of Mark Twain," Literary Digest, XLV
        (November 16), 909.
           "Mark Twain was one of seven men who in
        the last sixty years have reconstructed
        America and voiced its spirit. [The others
        were Lincoln, Vanderbilt, Edison, Greeley,
        Whitman, and Howells.] This is less a re-
        view of Paine's biography, than Bacheller's
        own tribute to MT: "He found the East

still in the bondage of Puritanism. Lincoln
freed the negro. Mark Twain freed the white
man."

B18   BICKNELL, PERCY F. "Mark Twain," The Dial,
        LIII (October 16), 290-92.
           A review of the Paine biography, mostly
        summary. "The authoritative life of the
        great humorist has been written."

B19   *BODINE, T. V. "Birthplace of Mark Twain.
        The Story of the Great Humorist and Philo-
        sopher and his Equally Whimsical Uncle--
        Judge John S. Quarles," Kansas City Star
        Magazine, May 19.
           Draws heavily on published accounts by
        MT, but informed by familiarity with the
        region. [Source: Reprinted in Twainian,
        XVII (March-April, 1958), 1-4; Asselineau
        (1954), No. 125.]

B20   CAIRNS, WILLIAM B. A History of American
        Literature. New York: Oxford University
        Press.
           [Source: Asselineau (1954), No. 486.]
        Examined: 1930 revised edition, apparently
        unchanged in the portion on MT (pp. 444-52).
        Describes his life and work, arguing that
        his writing matured but that the serious
        writing of the later years has been over-
        rated. "He has left, however, a consider-
        able amount of truly genuine work in which
        the humor is more than cleverness and the
        seriousness is without affectation; and it
        will be strange if American readers willing-
        ly let this die."

B21   "CLAUDIUS CLEAR" [SIR ROBERTSON NICOLL.]
        "Mark Twain," The British Weekly LIII
        (October 24), 109.
           Begins with a hostile discussion of MT,
        most of which is excerpted in The Literary
        Digest, November 30 (1912.B10), but the
        article is primarily a conventional discus-
        sion of the man and his works, occasioned
        by the recent publication of the three-vol-
        ume Paine biography. The attribution to
        Nicoll is made by The Literary Digest. The
        British Weekly's subtitle of "A Journal of
        Social and Christian Progess" may help ex-
        plain the vehement exception taken to MT's
        irreligion.

B22   ____. "Mark Twain in Adversity and Prosperi-
        ty," The British Weekly, LIII (October 31),
        141.
           A conventional biographical account
        which adds nothing to the Paine biography.
        The identification of "Claudius Clear" as
        Sir Robertson Nicoll is by The Literary Di-
        gest, November 30 (1912.B10), which, how-
        ever, does not mention this account.

B23   KYNE, PETER B. "The Great Mono Miracle: An
        Echo of Mark Twain," Sunset: The Pacific
        Monthly, XXIX (July), 37-49.
           A work of fiction with MT as a character.

1912 - Shorter Writings

B24   MARKHAM, EDWIN. [Review: Paine, Mark Twain.]
       Hearst's Magazine, XXII (December), 135-38.
          Summarizes MT's life and comments that
       Paine reports the facts more carefully than
       MT did.

B25   PAINE, ALBERT BIGELOW. "Mark Twain: Some
       Chapters from an Extraordinary Life," Harp-
       er's Monthly, CXXIV (January), 215-28;
       (February), 419-33; (March), 583-97;
       (April), 737-51; (May), 934-47; CXXV
       (June), 104-19; (July), 249-63; (August),
       405-17; (September), 593-605; (October),
       767-80; (November), 923-35.
          Concluding installments of Paine's biogra-
       phy of MT, which began in November, 1911;
       includes illustrations not used in the book.

B26   PERRY, BLISS. "Humor and Satire," in his The
       American Mind. Boston and New York: Hough-
       ton Mifflin Company, pp. 166-208; on MT,
       pp. 197-202.
          Asselineau (1954), No. 146, reports a
       1913 edition, London: Constable.
          MT embodies American extravagance and ir-
       reverence, but draws the line short of what
       the American mind reveres. His "hatred of
       pretence and injustice, his scorn at senti-
       mentality coupled with his insistence upon
       the rights of sentiment, in a word his
       persistent idealism, make Mark Twain one of
       the most representative of American writers.
       Largeness, freedom, human sympathy, are re-
       vealed upon every page," although perhaps
       his "extraordinary fantasies" are no more
       successful than "the delicate humor of
       Charles Lamb." [From the E. T. Earle Lec-
       tures delivered at the Pacific Theological
       School, Berkeley, in 1912, and later at the
       Lowell Institute, Boston, the Brooklyn In-
       stitute, and elsewhere, as "American Traits
       in American Literature."]

B27   RICHARDS, P. "Mark Twain," in his Zeichner
       und "Gezeichnete" aus den Erinnerungen eines
       amerikanischen Zeichners und Journalisten
       (Berlin: Reflektor-Verlag), pp. 9-20.
          Describes MT's trip to England on the
       S. S. Minneapolis in 1907, and his receiv-
       ing an honorary degree from Oxford; in-
       cludes sketches of MT by Richards, several
       photographs (one on front cover), and
       facsimile reproductions of a letter from
       R. W. Ashcroft informing Richards of MT's
       death and a note by MT that "Taking the
       pledge will not make bad liquor good, but
       it will improve it."

B28   RIDEING, WILLIAM HENRY. "Mark Twain and E.
       C. Stedman," in his Many Celebrities and a
       Few Others: A Bundle of Reminiscences
       (Garden City, New York: Doubleday, Page &
       Company, and London: Eveleigh Nash),
       pp. 153-72.
          On MT at the Players Club, describing the
       genesis of "The Jumping Frog," and on the
       difficulties in dealing with his contribu-
       tions to The Century. Notes that in an

evening of speech-making MT preferred to
speak late, in order to pick up cues from
those preceding him.

B29   *ROBERTSON, J. M. "The Positions of Mark
       Twain," in The Baconian Heresy: A Confuta-
       tion (n.p.), Chapter II.
          On MT's influence in favor of the thesis
       that Bacon wrote Shakespeare's plays: "He
       is apt to win the laughers--a thing not be-
       fore to be apprehended from Baconian propa-
       ganda." Apparently regards MT's Is Shakes-
       peare Dead? as moderately important.
       [Source: quoted by Henry M. Partridge in
       "Did Mark Twain Perpetrate Literary Hoaxes?"
       (1934.B22).]

B30   *SMITH, ALPHONSO. "Mark Twain und die ameri-
       kanische Humor," in his Die amerikanische
       Literatur (Verlesungen, geh. am. d. Kgl.
       Friedrich-Wilhelms-Universität zu Berlin).
       Berlin: Wiedmannsche Buchh. [Bibliothek
       der amerikanischen Kulturgeschichte]),
       pp. 312-37.
          [Source: Asselineau (1954), No. 118.]

B31   TRENT, W. P., and JOHN ERSKINE. "Mark Twain
       and Bret Harte," in their Great Writers of
       America. (Home University Library of Mod-
       ern Knowledge). Pp. 232-50; on MT
       pp. 243-50.
          Harte has greater delicacy, but MT has
       greater force; MT's honor led him to a lec-
       ture tour to repay his debts, while Harte
       "disappointed his countrymen"; also notes
       "the tragic decline of Bret Harte's char-
       acter." MT's humor may be forgotten as
       tastes change, but TS revealed him as "a
       novelist of the first rank." There is a
       "tragic contrast between the boy's simple
       point of view and the things he saw but did
       not understand"; in HF "this note of ele-
       mental tragedy is increased until certain
       passages...would be hard to overmatch in
       any literature."

1913 A BOOKS

A1   WALLACE, ELIZABETH. Mark Twain and the Happy
       Island. Chicago: A. C. McClurg & Co.
       Prefatory note by Albert Bigelow Paine.
          An adult's recollections of her friendship
       with MT, whom she met in Bermuda and later
       visited at Stormfield. Includes photographs
       and letters.

1913 B SHORTER WRITINGS

B1   ABBOTT, KEENE. "Tom Sawyer's Town," Harper's
       Weekly, LVII (August 9), 16-17.
          A popular account of Hannibal, Missouri,
       with reminiscences by local people. Photo-
       graphs include one of Laura Frazer at nine-
       teen; she says that for a time another wom-
       an (who moved to Hannibal after Sam Clemens
       had left) had claimed to be the original of
       Becky Thatcher.

B2   ANON. "Mark Twain as Publisher," Bookman,
        XXXVI (January), 489-94.
          On MT's ultimately unsuccesful connection
        with the Webster Company; there are several
        anecdotes but no significant new informa-
        tion.

B3   ANON. [Review: Paine, Mark Twain (1912).]
        North American Review, CXCVII (January),
        136-38.
          The book is important not only as the
        life of a man, but as a picture of his
        time.

B4   *CARUS, PAUL. "Mark Twain's Philosophy," in
        his The Mechanistic Principle and the Non-
        Mechanical. An Inquiry into Fundamentals
        with Representatives from Either Side
        (Chicago: The Open Court Publishing Com-
        pany), pp. 54-97.
          [Source: Asselineau (1954), No. 140;
        describes this as a reprint of his article
        in The Monist (1913.B5), consisting largely
        of quotations from What Is Man?]

B5   _____. "Mark Twain's Philosophy," Monist,
        XXIII (April 13), 181-223.
          Lengthy quotations from What Is Man?
        with occasional brief comments by the edi-
        tor.

B6   *GOODWIN, C. C. As I Remember Them. Salt
        Lake City: Published by a Special Commit-
        tee of the Salt Lake Commercial Club.
          [Source: Asselineau (1954), No. 141;
        notes: "Charles Carroll Goodwin was a
        friend of Mark Twain's during the latter's
        stay in Nevada. Cf. DeVoto's Mark Twain's
        America, p. 135, n. 2."]

B7   [HOWELLS, WILLIAM DEAN.] "Editor's Easy
        Chair," Harper's Monthly, CXXVI (January),
        310-12.
          Favorably reviewing the 1912 Paine bio-
        graphy, this is chiefly a description of
        MT's life as described by Paine and as
        known to Howells.

B8   *_____. "In Memory of Mark Twain," in Pro-
        ceedings of the American Academy of Arts
        and Letters and the National Institute of
        Arts and Letters. Vol. I: 1909-1913.
        New York.
          [Source: Asselineau (1954), No. 147.]
        This may be the same as the item listed
        for 1911.B12.

B9   *KELLNER, LEON. Geschichte der Nordamerikan-
        ischen Literatur. Berlin: G. J. Göschen.
        2 vols.
          [Source: Asselineau (1954), No. 142.]

B10   LONG, WILLIAM J. American Literature: A
        Study of the Men and the Books that in the
        Earlier and Later Times Reflect the Ameri-
        can Spirit. Boston, New York: Ginn and
        Company.
          Criticizes MT's crudity in IA, CY, but

also in TS, with its "dime-novel sensation-
alism," its emphasis on "the lawless, barbarous side of boy-life...its self-assertion
without its instinctive respect for authority" (pp. 466-67). HF "ends not with a
moral climax," but in Jim's rescue "by the
most approved dime-novel methods. The portrayal of all these astonishing scenes is
vivid and intensely dramatic; one needs
hardly to add that it is a portrayal, not
of the great onward current of American
life, but only of its flotsam and jetsam."
Still, MT portrayed character and scene
vividly, and "was at heart a reformer"
(pp. 467-68). Some critics believe his
"more dignified works," such as P&P and JA,
will last longest (p. 466).

B11   MACY, JOHN. "Mark Twain," in his The Spirit
        of American Literature (Garden City, New
        York: Doubleday, Page & Company),
        pp. 248-77, and passim.
          Laudatory, following Paine, Howells, Mat-
        thews, and Phelps. Attacks the critics who
        libeled MT with words about his "kindly wit
        and humor which never hurt any one."
        Notes his "lofty idealism" as in JA, "an
        eloquent book," its tone "sustainedly per-
        fect" (p. 269); also notes the sentimental-
        ism of "A Dog's Tale" (p. 252, n). Elsewhere
        in the book Macy cites MT's comments in his
        discussions of Cooper (pp. 39, 41, 44) and
        Howells (pp. 290-91). On William James,
        says only MT reaches "his stature and ori-
        ginality.... Even the fine novelists,
        Mr. Howells and Mr. Henry James, are not
        the human equals of those two" (pp. 297-98);
        the chapter ends by confessing that associa-
        tion was made partly to shock some people,
        but chiefly because it is just. Reprinted
        in Scott (1965), pp. 118-28; (1967),
        pp. 129-39; in Anderson (1971), pp. 313-26.

B12   *MENCKEN, H. L. "The Burden of Humor," Smart
        Set, XXXVIII (February), pp. 151-54.
          [Source: Reprinted in Anderson (1971),
        pp. 327-31.] Calls HF "one of the great
        masterpieces of the world," and praises
        MT's language and vision. HF, LOM, CY,
        and Captain Stormfield's Visit to Heaven
        "are alone worth more, as works of art and
        as criticisms of life, than the whole out-
        put of Cooper, Irving, Holmes, Mitchell,
        Stedman, Whittier and Bryant.... I believe
        that he was the true father of our national
        literature, the first genuinely American
        artist of the blood royal." Reprinted in
        A Mencken Chrestomathy, Edited and Annotated
        by the Author (New York: Alfred A. Knopf,
        1967), p. 485; also reprinted in Gerber
        (1971), pp. 15-19 (giving volume number as
        XXXIX, but with the same month, year, and
        pagination as reported by Anderson).

B13   MILLARD, BAILEY. "When They Were Twenty-One,"
        Bookman (New York), XXXVII (May), 296-304.
          On "California authors in their salad
        days"; describes MT writing for the Golden

1913 - Shorter Writings

(MILLARD, BAILEY)
Era and traveling in Europe with Charles
Warren Stoddard (p. 298).

B14   O'CONNOR, MRS. T. P. "Sir Walter Scott and
the Civil War," in her My Beloved South
(New York and London: G. P. Putnam's
Sons).
    Defends Scott against MT's accusations in
LOM: "Mark Twain ought to have been a
Southerner, but he was born with a too
practical soul. His hardness made him understand the North, and he did it more
than justice; his want of romance made him
misunderstand the South, and he did it less
than justice."

B15   PHELPS, WILLIAM LYON. [Review: Paine, Mark
Twain (1912).] Independent, LXXXIV
(March 6), 531-33.
    "This is assuredly a great biography,
probably the best ever written in America."
Chiefly descriptive, noting Paine's tact,
patience, and devotion in MT's last years.
The book's only flaw is careless proof-
reading.

B16   RICHARDSON, CHARLES F. [Review: Paine,
Mark Twain (1912).] Yale Review, n.s. II
(Spring), 563-67.
    A good book because of the author's en-
thusiasm, and MT's role as a representative
man may justify the length; but MT does
not belong in a class with Poe and Hawthorne.

B17   *TWICHELL, JOSEPH H. "Mark Twain," in Dudley
Payne Lewis, ed., History of the Class of
1903, Yale College (New Haven), n.p.
    [Source: Asselineau (1954), No. 143.]

B18   *URBAN, WILBUR MARSHALL. "Mark Twain, Pure
Fooling," Neale's Monthly, May.
    [Source: Twainian, II (March, 1943), 5.]

1914 A BOOKS

A1   Catalogue of First and Other Editions of the
Writings of "Mark Twain," Samuel Langhorne
Clemens, and of Lafcadio Hearn. The Prop-
erty of The Tomlinson-Humes Company (In
Bankruptcy) and of Mr. Merle Johnson. To
Be Sold at Unrestricted Public Sale on
January Twentieth, 1914 Under the Manage-
ment of the American Art Association,
American Art Galleries, Madison Square
South, New York. Contains Foreword by
Merle Johnson, dated December 29, 1913.
    [Source: Bound in scrapbook, Mark
Twain: Biography-Reminiscence, Chicago
Public Library, n.d.]

1914 - B SHORTER WRITINGS

B1   *BURTON, RICHARD. Little Essays in Literature
and Life (New York: The Century Company),

pp. 201-208.
    [Source: Asselineau (1954), No. 158:
"A chapter on Twain, insists on his seriousness and even sadness."]

B2   COLBRON, GRACE ISABEL. "The American Novel
in Germany," Bookman (New York), XXXIX
(March), 45-48.
    MT was a close second to Bret Harte in
popularity, as measured by sales of the
Tauchnitz editions; TS and HF were his most
popular.

B3   FULTON, ROBERT. "Glimpses of the Mother Lode,"
Bookman (New York), XXXIX (March), 49-57.
    On a visit in 1912 to the region made fam-
ous by MT and Bret Harte; with several photographs.

B4   HAWTHORNE, HILDEGARDE. "Mark Twain and the
Immortal Tom," St. Nicholas, XLII
(December), 164-66.
    Very briefly describes meeting MT at his
"Stormfield" Home in Redding, Connecticut,
and summarizes his life and works for young
readers.

B5   HIGGINSON, MARY THACHER. Thomas Wentworth
Higginson: The Story of His Life. As reissued Port Washington, N.Y. and London:
Kennikat Press, 1971.
    Higginson first saw MT at a farewell din-
ner to Wilkie Collins in 1874; thought him
"something of a buffoon, though with earnestness underneath; and when afterwards at
his own house in Hartford, I heard him say
grace at table, it was like asking a blessing over Ethiopian minstrels. But he had
no wine at his table and that seemed to
make the grace a genuine thing." The two
later became good friends (pp. 259-60).
Describes MT writing in bed in later years
(pp. 373-74).

B6   HOWE, J. OWEN. "Twichell, Chum of Mark
Twain," Boston Evening Transcript (April 4),
Part III, p. 5.
    A half-page account of Joseph Hopkins
Twichell, with biography and a portrait;
describes his friendship with MT.

B7   *MURET, MAURICE. Les Contemporains étrangers.
Lausanne: Payot, 2 vols.
    [Source: Asselineau (1954), No. 159:
"On Mark Twain, vol. 2, pp. 133-189."]

B8   PHELPS, WILLIAM LYON. "Notes on Mark Twain,"
in his Essays on Books (New York: The Macmillan Company), pp. 211-22.
    Reprinted with minor revisions from Inde-
pendent (1910.B118).

B9   *RICHARDS, P. Mark Twain Anekdoten, gesammelt
und mit einem Vorwort von P. Richards, mit
neun Bild-beigaben. Berlin: Reflektor-
Verlag.
    [Source: Asselineau (1954), No. 157.]

B10   STREET, JULIAN. "Hannibal and Mark Twain,"
      in his Abroad at Home: American Ramblings,
      Observations, and Adventures (New York:
      The Century Company), pp. 237-52. Also in
      Collier's, LIII (August 29), 18-19, 31-34.
         An impressionistic and somewhat unsympa-
      thetic account of a visit to Hannibal. In-
      cludes five lines of verse MT wrote in the
      autograph book of his friend Ann Virginia
      Ruffner.

B11   TICKNOR, CAROLINE. "Mark Twain's Missing
      Chapter," Bookman (New York), XXXIX (May),
      298-309.
         On MT's writing of LOM, with extensive
      quotation of his marginalia in Mrs. Trol-
      lope's Domestic Manners of the Americans.
      The original Chapter XLVIII of LOM (here
      reproduced, pp. 306-309) was suppressed
      out of fear that unfavorable comparison of
      the South to the North would cost Southern
      sales; also here reproduced are the can-
      celled cuts from p. 356 showing a shrouded
      body and from p. 441 showing MT surrounded
      by flames.

B12   *UNDERWOOD, JOHN C. "Democracy and Mark
      Twain," in his Literature and Insurgency
      (New York: Mitchell Kennerley), pp. 1-40.
         [Source: Asselineau (1954), No. 161;
      Underwood compares MT to Grant and Lincoln
      as a democratic hero.]

1915 A BOOKS

A1   *WHITE, IDA BELLE. Spirits Do Return. Kansas
      City, Missouri: The White Publishing Com-
      pany.
         [Source: Asselineau (1954), No. 170;
      quotes: "This book was written through
      the inspirational spirit of the well-known
      writer, Samuel L. Clemens, Mark Twain."]

1915 B SHORTER WRITINGS

B1   *ANON. "Captain Horace E. Bixby; Who Taught
      Mark Twain How to Pilot," New England Maga-
      zine, n.s., LII (April), 281-83.
         [Source: Asselineau (1954), No. 173.]

B2   ANON. "Mark Twain's War Map," North American
      Review, CCI, (June), 827-29.
         MT's map of Paris (1870) and his accom-
      panying text, with a 40-word introductory
      note added.

B3   BALL, SIR ROBERT. Reminiscences and Letters
      of Sir Robert Ball, Edited by His Son, W.
      Valentine Ball. London, New York, Toronto
      and Melbourne: Cassell and Company, Ltd.
         Sir Robert Ball was Astronomer Royal of
      Ireland, 1874-1892. He mentions meeting
      MT in New York at a lecture by Mr. Seton-
      Thompson (January 1, 1902): "He is a most
      striking-looking man, and we had a nice
      little talk. I told him how fond we were
      of 'Mr. Bixby'" (p. 348; the editor mentions
      Sir Robert's enjoyment of LOM on p. 126).

B4   COREY, WILLIAM ALFRED. "Memories of Mark
      Twain," Overland Monthly, LXVI (September),
      263-65.
         "Herewith are set down some hitherto un-
      published incidents culled from the recol-
      lections of Mr. W. W. Barnes of Oakland,
      concerning Samuel L. Clemens while the
      great humorist was 'Roughing It' in Virginia
      City, Nevada." This is the Barnes of the
      rival newspaper, the Union, and he here re-
      lates several incidents from Roughing It,
      adding a few details; he applied the term
      "yellow journalism" to MT's "Massacre at
      Empire City" story [described in "My Bloody
      Massacre" in Sketches New and Old]. Ac-
      cording to Barnes, MT stole the "Jumping
      Frog" story, which "before Clemens ever
      heard of it, was written by Samuel Seabough,
      and was published in the San Andreas Inde-
      pendent, the leading newspaper of Calaveras
      County. Seabough...editor of the Independ-
      ent...got the story of the Jumping Frog
      from a man named Parker who was afterwards
      a member of the legislature from Mono
      County.... Clemens simply warmed it over,
      dished it up as his own, and got all the
      credit." Finally, Corey tells of Artemus
      Ward's visit to Virginia City on a speaking
      tour: "It was hardly fair in Clemens, with
      the lecture hour drawing near, to get Ward
      hopelessly drunk, black his face with burnt
      cork and then thrust him out before his
      waiting audience. In fact it was, as Mr.
      Barnes tersely characterized it, 'a damned
      dirty trick'" but typical of this stage in
      MT's and Artemus Ward's lives, and the audi-
      ence "probably regarded the matter as a
      great joke, and alone worth the price of
      admission."

B5   HOPKINS, R. THURSTON. Rudyard Kipling: A
      Literary Appreciation. New York: Frederick
      A. Stokes Company, n.d. (Preface dated
      November, 1915).
         Anecdotes involving MT, pp. 50-54; quotes
      an 1895 MT letter to Kipling on the possi-
      bility of a meeting in India: "I shall
      come riding my ayah with his tusks adorned
      with silver bells and ribbons, and escorted
      by a troop of native howdahs richly clad
      and mounted upon a herd of wild bungalows;
      and you must be on hand with a few bottles
      of ghee, for I shall be thirsty."

B6   JAMES, GEORGE WHARTON. "Mark Twain at Lake
      Tahoe" and "Mark Twain and the Forest
      Rangers," in his The Lake of the Sky: Lake
      Tahoe (Pasadena, California: G. W. James;
      reprinted with same pagination, Chicago:
      The Charles T. Powner Co., 1956),
      pp. 359-62, 363-65.
         These are two appendices, the first an ex-
      cerpt from RI and the second from "a quar-
      terly magazine published solely for the
      Rangers of the Tahoe Reserve," describing
      MT's accidental burning of a forest as he
      told it in RI and as the incident would
      have taken place in 1912: rangers would

1915 - Shorter Writings

(JAMES, GEORGE WHARTON)
put out the fire and a court would fine
him for carelessness.

B7   KELLNER, LEON. American Literature, translated from the German by Julia Franklin.
Garden City, New York: Doubleday, Page &
Company. Pp. 200-11.
MT's humor involves exaggeration, but its
essence is "the human...delight in the
weakness, perversity, folly, of a beloved
fellow-creature" (p. 207); the Germans appreciate his portrayal of character. "Our
American, in his fine humanity, in his
idealism, in his gentleness, is almost an
old-fashioned gentleman" (p. 210).

B8   PAINE, ALBERT BIGELOW. "A Boys' Life of Mark
Twain," St. Nicholas, XLIII (November),
2-11; (December), 146-47.
Begins the serialization of Paine's
1916 book; illustrated with drawings and
photographs.

B9   PATTEE, FRED LEWIS. "Mark Twain," in his A
History of American Literature since 1870
(New York: The Century Co.), pp. 45-62 and
passim (indexed).
"With Mark Twain, American literature became for the first time really national."
He is a droll comedian, social critic, and
author of romance, and his fame will endure
in this last capacity, in which his masterpieces are LOM and RI; in these, as in GA
("a few chapters of it"), TS, HF, and PW,
"he has done work that can never be done
again." "To turn from Mark Twain to Bret
Harte is like turning from a great river on
a summer night, fragrant and star-lit, to
the glamour and unreality of the city theater" (p. 65). Pp. 58-61 reprinted in
Kesterson (1973), pp. 54-56.

B10   WARD, LESLIE. Forty Years of "Spy." London:
Chatto & Windus.
On p. 129, describes drawing MT's portrait
for Vanity Fair: "The whole time I watched
him he paced the room like a caged animal,
smoking a large calabash pipe." MT wanted
to wear his Oxford academic gown, but Ward
preferred to depict him in the more familiar
white suit. "He struck me as being a very
sensitive man, whose nervous pacings during
my interview were the result of a highly
strung temperament."

B11   YOUNG, JOHN P. Journalism in California.
San Francisco: Chronicle Publishing Co.,
pp. 66, 71, 131.
Bare mention of MT, and no new information.

1916 A BOOKS

A1   PAINE, ALBERT BIGELOW. The Boys' Life of
Mark Twain: The Story of a Man Who Made
the World Laugh and Love Him. New York and
London: Harper & Brothers Publishers.
A revision for young readers of Paine's
1912 three-volume biography; serialized in
St. Nicholas, 1915-16.

1916 B SHORTER WRITINGS

B1   ANON. "Capitalizing Mark Twain," Literary
Digest, LIII (October 14), 959-60.
Undated excerpts from the St. Louis Post-
Standard on the exploitation of MT's name
by Hannibal, Missouri, and from the Newark
Star-Eagle on a spiritualist attempt to
communicate with MT, and on the "Jap Herron"
novel he supposedly dictated.

B2   BOWEN, EDWIN W. "Mark Twain," South Atlantic
Quarterly, XV (July), 250-68 [also listed,
incorrectly, under "Henderson, Archibald"
in several bibliographies].
A general discussion of MT as a great humorist and self-made man, with a summary of
his career and uncritical listing of his
works. "Certainly he has produced books
that will make his name live in American
literature because they themselves are genuine literature."

B3   *FITCH, GEORGE HAMLIN. "Mark Twain--Our Greatest Humorist," in his Great Spiritual Writers of America (San Francisco: P. Elder &
Co.), pp. 111-18.
[Source: Asselineau (1954), No. 176,
noting that Fitch "insists most unspiritually
on the success story."]

B4   GILDER, RICHARD WATSON. Letters of Richard
Watson Gilder. Edited by his Daughter,
Rosamond Gilder. Boston & New York: Houghton Mifflin Company, The Riverside Press,
passim on MT (indexed).
On MT's winning the Grant Memoirs from the
Century, pp. 124-25; at a reading for international copyright, introduction to the
President, pp. 195-96; on MT as next-door
neighbor, Summer 1904, pp. 361-62. Defends
MT against charge by "a superintendent of
schools in a distant part of the West" that
his works are "destitute of a single redeeming quality"; however, Gilder concedes (in
copy of letter he sent MT) that "Mr. Clemens
has great faults; at times he is inartistic-
ally and indefensibly coarse" (pp. 398-99).

B5   *JONES, DR. J. T. "The House Mark Twain's
Father Built," in his Prose and Poems, Col-
umbia, Kentucky, n.p.
[Source: Wecter (1952), p. 320.]

B6 McCLELLAND, CLARENCE PAUL "Mark Twain and Bret Harte," Methodist Review, XCVIII (Fifth Series, XXXII; January-February), 75-85.

Chiefly descriptive. Although Harte gives a graphic view of the West in stories "perfect in form and yet melodramatic and sentimental, still it is Mark Twain who will give us purer enjoyment, and, above all, a better insight into human nature."

B7 PAINE, ALBERT BIGELOW. "A Boys' Life of Mark Twain," St. Nicholas, XLIII (January), 210-19; (February), 328-36; (March), 408-14; (April), 498-505; (May), 598-606; (June), 696-704; (July), 801-809; (August), 881-90; (September), 998-1006; (October), 1078-88.

Completes the serialization, begun in 1915, of Paine's 1916 book. Illustrated with drawings and photographs.

B8 ROSEWATER, VICTOR. "How a Boy Secured a Unique Autograph of Mark Twain," St. Nicholas, XLIII (March), 415.

As a sixteen-year-old Senate page in 1888, Rosewater got "Mark Twain" written in his album; then, on request, MT wrote "S. L. Clemens" diagonally across the first autograph. (Reproduced in facsimile.)

B9 YARMOLINSKY, ABRAHAM. "The Russian View of American Literature," Bookman (New York), XLIV (September), 44-48.

MT is very popular, and has been translated into both Russian and Ukranian. "The Prince and the Pauper was the first to appear, and it has to this very day remained the standard juvenile, more popular with Russian readers than The Adventures of Tom Sawyer or his Huckleberry Finn." His purely humorous works are widely available, both in conventional volumes and in cheap paper-covered "brochures." Quotes an interview in Vienna by a Russian journalist; MT comments on the failure to pay him royalties, and observes that the Russian press is becoming Americanized.

1917 A BOOKS

A1 *BARRIE, JAMES M. Who Was Sarah Findlay? by Mark Twain with a suggested solution of the mystery by J. M. Barrie. London: Privately Printed by Clement Shorter. [11-page pamphlet. Source: Asselineau (1954), No. 183.]

A2 CLEMENS, SAMUEL L. Mark Twain's Letters, Arranged with Comment by Albert Bigelow Paine. New York and London: Harper & Brothers, 2 vols.

Paine has been criticized for his editing. These letters are only a small selection from those left by MT, and they are not reprinted in their entirety nor are omissions always clearly indicated. Other parts of some of the letters may be found in Paine's 1912 Biography.

A3 HUTCHINGS, EMILY GRANT. [Introduction.] Jap Herron: A Novel Written from the Ouija Board. New York: Mitchell Kennerley.

A novel attributed to the spirit of MT.

1917 B SHORTER WRITINGS

B1 ANON. "Editing Mark Twain," Literary Digest, XLIV (January 20), 127-28.

Summarizes New York Times article on R. W. Gilder's experience with MT as a Century contributor; reproduces text of a Gilder letter to a western school superintendent, also quoted in 1916.B4.

B2 ANON. "Mark Twain's Pen Picture of His All-Too-Human Brother," Current Opinion, LXII (May), 351-52.

Quotes MT's letters to Howells (concerning Orion Clemens) recently published in Harper's; only brief commentary added.

B3 ANON. "The Saving of Mark Twain," Literary Digest, LV (November 24), 54-59.

About Henry H. Rogers, who straightened out MT's financial affairs; a summary of MT letters currently appearing in Harper's.

B4 ANON. "Three Stories a Year Are Enough for a Writer. Ring W. Lardner, Humorist, Who Makes Fiction Out of Life of Baseball Players, Thinks Fewer and Better Short Stories Needed," New York Times Magazine (March 25), p. 14.

Speaking of authors, Lardner ranks George Ade above MT and prefers Booth Tarkington's "Penrod" books to HF. "No, I certainly don't believe that Mark Twain is our greatest American humorist. Some of his fun is spontaneous, but a great deal of it is not."

B5 ANON. "When Twain Conquered Grant," Literary Digest, LV (July 21), 57-60.

Summarizes and quotes part of the July installment of MT's letters in Harper's.

B6 *AYRES, J. W. "Recollections of Hannibal," Palmyra Spectator, August 22.

Discusses Tom Blankenship (the original of Huck), who, rather than Sam Clemens, led the boys. [Source: Cited by Walter Blair (1960), p. 55.]

B7 CLEMENS, MILDRED LEO. "Trailing Mark Twain Through Hawaii. 'Roughing It' in the Islands, Fifty Years After," Sunset: The Pacific Monthly, XXXVIII (May), 7-9, 95-98.

About a recent trip to the Islands, illustrated with recent photographs and enlivened with references to MT's descriptions in RI.

B8 [HYSLOP, JAMES H.]. "The Return of Mark Twain," Journal of the American Society for Psychical Research, XI (July), 361-65.

On Jap Herron, recently published by Mitchell Kennerly and said to have been dictated by MT's spirit and recorded by Mrs. Emily Grant Hutchings, of St. Louis.

1917 - Shorter Writings

([HYSLOP, JAMES H.])
  As confirmation, MT was consulted again, through other mediums, revealing "unmistakable evidence in the experiments with Mrs. Chenoweth that Mark Twain colored the facts quite as much as the psychic." [This journal is indexed, and several volumes contain numerous references to "Clemens," "Mark Twain," and "Twain, Mark" not listed in the present bibliography.]

B9 LINDSAY, VACHEL. "Mark Twain and Joan of Arc" and "The Raft," in his The Chinese Nightingale and Other Poems. (New York: The Macmillan Company), pp. 47, 71-74.
  On Joan of Arc, shows MT's glorious portrait but mourns "at bloodshed caused by angels, saints, and men." "The Raft" is a more extensive tribute to MT, not limited to HF. "When the Mississippi Flowed to Indiana" appeared in his The Golden Whales of California (New York: Macmillan, 1920), on the world of Tom Sawyer and Becky Thatcher. These are now grouped as "Three Poems about Mark Twain," and may be found in Selected Poems of Vachel Lindsay, ed. Mark Harris (New York: Macmillan and London: Collier Macmillan, 1963), pp. 16-21.

B10 PAINE, ALBERT BIGELOW, ed. "Mark Twain's Letters" (title varies), Harper's, CXXXIV (May), 781-94; CXXXV (July), 177-86; (August), 378-88; (September), 569-77; (October), 638-47; (November), 812-19.
  Includes photographs, and facsimile reproductions of some of the letters.

B11 SHUSTER, GEORGE NAUMAN. "The Tragedy of Mark Twain," Catholic World, CIV (March), 731-37.
  About MT's pessimism as reflected in MS and elsewhere.

B12 WHITE, EDGAR. "Mark Twain's Printer Days," Overland Monthly, LXX (December), 573-76.
  Contains recollections of MT in Hannibal by Jimmy Tisdale, Major Frank Daulton, and Alex Lacey, but adds no new information and appears to be indebted to MT's own published recollections. There are photographs of MT (by Paine), Hannibal, and Major Daulton, but nothing new or significant.

B13 WIER, JEANNE ELIZABETH. "Mark Twain's Relation to Nevada and to the West," Nevada Historical Society Papers, I (1913-1916). Carson City: State Printing Office, 99-104.
  A general, popular account of MT's Nevada days, illustrated with photographs of cabins in which he lived in Aurora and Unionville, and of his sister-in-law, "Mrs. Orion Clemens, 1866." Facing this article (p. 98) is a picture of the flag-raising on Mt. Davidson described in RI (II, Chapter XIV), part of an article with contemporary accounts. On pp. 89-90 are a description and photo-

graph of "Mark Twain Relics": part of a pistol and a more serviceable pipe.

B14 WOODBRIDGE, H. E. "Mark Twain's Fatalism," Nation, CV (October 11), 399.
  MT's view of life as a chain of events, in which a small change can have profound effects.

B15 WYATT, EDITH. "An Inspired Critic," North American Review, CCV (April), 603-15.
  MT as philosopher and critic of his time.

1918 A BOOKS - NONE

1918 B SHORTER WRITINGS

B1 ANON. "Literature and Life Mirrored in Mark Twain's Letters," Current Opinion, LXIV (January), 50-51.
  A review of Mark Twain's Letters (1917). Mostly extracts. Cites a New York Evening Post review (n.d.) that calls them a welcome change from "Maeterlinck, Wilde, Strindberg, Ibsen, and the Russian gloom artists."

B2 ANON. "Mark Twain's Childhood Sweetheart Recalls their Romance," Literary Digest, LVI (March 23), 70-75.
  Summarizes, with lengthy excerpts, an interview of Laura [Hawkins] Frazer, the original of Becky Thatcher; from Kansas City Star (n.d.).

B3 ANON. "Mark Twain's Unedited and Unpublished Satire: 3,000 Years among the Microbes," Current Opinion, LXV (July), 48-49.
  Summarizes and extensively quotes a review in New York Evening Mail (n.d.) by Edna Kenton, who considered MT a great satirist but a martyr to editing.

B4 BELDEN, H. M. "Scyld Scefing and Huck Finn," Modern Language Notes, XXXIII (May), 315.
  Seeking a body with a floating loaf of bread was anticipated in "divination by shield, sheaf, and candle."

B5 *CASTELLANOS, JESÚS. Los Optimistas. Madrid: Editorial América, Biblioteca Andrés Bello. [Source: Asselineau (1954), No. 199: "On Mark Twain, pp. 115-120. Ranks Twain with Cervantes and Molière."]

B6 D[ANZIGER], S[AMUEL]. "Democracy of Mark Twain," Public (New York), XXI (February 23), 242-43.
  On CY as "a textbook of democracy, economic as well as political," and on the economic implications of the magic tree in MS. [Signed with initials "S.D."; the name "Samuel Danziger" appears on the masthead.]

B7 HARRIS, JULIA COLLIER. The Life and Letters of Joel Chandler Harris. Boston and New York: Houghton Mifflin Company.

Contains letters revealing MT's interest in folk-tales of the slaves and in the manner of story-telling, mentioning "The Golden Arm" (pp. 167-70), and thanking Harris for praising HF in an interview in the Atlanta Journal (p. 566). Efforts to persuade Harris to give readings could not overcome his diffidence; letters show the two men planning to meet in New Orleans and for Harris to visit in Hartford, but there are no new details (pp. 170-72, 190-92).

B8 HENDERSON, ARCHIBALD. "A Laughing Philosopher," Bookman (New York), XLVI (January), 583-84.

A review of Paine's edition of Mark Twain's Letters (1917), with praise for "the entirely natural picture it presents of an almost miraculous development"; the influence of Olivia Clemens and Howells was beneficial.

B9 HOWELLS, W. D. "The Editor's Easy Chair," Harper's, CXXXVI (March), 602-604.

"Mr. Albert Bigelow Paine has ended his very faithful and intelligent labors on the biography of a man nearer and dearer to his generation than any other, in two volumes of Mark Twain's Letters. Unless more material should unexpectedly offer itself, these letters will tell us the last we shall ever be told of one who can never be told enough of, and who tells himself in them more explicitly and directly than in all his other work."

B10 HYSLOP, JAMES H. "The Return of Mark Twain," Journal of the American Society for Psychical Research, XII (January), 4-38.

Further discussion of the 1916 Jap Herron book and communications with the spirit of MT. Mrs. Emily Grant Hutchings, of St. Louis, was unfamiliar with MT's work at the beginning of the project, and Mrs. Hays, the psychic, was said to have read "a great deal of Mark Twain's work" but the statement was challenged by Mrs. Hutchings in the next issue (p. 74). (A sequel to "The Return of Mark Twain," 1917.B8.)

B11 *MATTHEWS, BRANDER. [Introduction.] The Adventures of Huckleberry Finn. New York & London: Harper & Brothers.
[Source: Asselineau (1954), No. 198.]

B12 MENCKEN, H. L. A Book of Prefaces. New York: Alfred A. Knopf (revised ed.), pp. 131-32, 203-34.

Cites William Lyon Phelps's Essays on Modern Novelists on the slow academic recognition of MT; praises MT as an artist but regrets his Philistine smugness and Puritan distrust of new ideas and beautiful things (as in IA).

B13 *MICHAUD, RÉGIS. "L'épopée humoristique de Mark Twain," in his Mystiques et Réalistes Anglo-Saxons, d'Emerson à Bernard Shaw (Paris: A. Colin), pp. 133-66.
[Source: Asselineau (1954), No. 200; describes this as "good second-hand criticism."]

B14 PERRY, BLISS. The American Spirit in Literature: A Chronicle of Great Interpreters. New Haven: Yale University Press; Toronto: Glasgow, Brook & Co.; London: Humphrey Milford, Oxford University Press. (The Chronicles of America Series, Vol. XXXIV), pp. 237-40.

RI, LOM, GA, TS, and HF are "books that make our American Odyssey, rich in the spirit of romance," and in the public eye "It is clear that Mark Twain the writer of romance is gaining upon Mark Twain the humorist." Notes his literary integrity, hatred of evil, and his pessimism as in Hadleyburg and MS.

B15 *SHOEMAKER, FLOYD CALVIN. "Samuel L. Clemens, Mark Twain, America's Greatest Humorist," in his Missouri's Hall of Fame: Lives of Eminent Missourians (Columbia: Missouri Book Co.), pp. 3-18.
[Source: Asselineau (1954), No. 202.]

B16 WHEELER, CANDACE. "Mark Twain," in her Yesterdays in a Busy Life (New York: Harper & Brothers), pp. 324-38.

On the Clemens family in Hartford and visiting the Wheelers in Onteora, N.Y., with one photograph of MT and one of his family, and two MT letters [August 30, 1885?] and October 31, 1890. There are also brief references to MT on pp. 307, 310-11 (not indexed).

B17 *WINKLER, EUNICE. "The Return of Mark Twain," Azoth (January).
[Source: Twainian, I (October, 1939), 5.] Apparently this is a spiritualist publication.

1919 A BOOKS - NONE

1919 B SHORTER WRITINGS

B1 ANON. "American Humour: Poor Samples," Saturday Review (London), CXXVII (September 27), 294.

A review-article, dismissing The Curious Republic of Gondour, and Other Whimsical Sketches as material MT himself had not considered worth reprinting. "Altogether we are quite content with the ample range of Mark Twain's works published in the uniform edition."

B2 ANON. "Mark Twain," Athenaeum, No. 4675 (December 5), pp. 1288-89.

A review of What Is Man? And Other Essays

1919 - Shorter Writings

(ANON.)
as less daring than MT thought: "It is difficult to understand what all the excitement is about."

B3   ANON. "When Mark Twain Petrified the Brahmins," Literary Digest, LXII (July 12), 28-29.
Summarizes an article by E. B. Osborn in the London Morning Post (n.d.) about the speech given by MT at the Whittier Birthday Dinner. Osborne took MT's part, describing those who criticized the speech as "a dreadful set of hard-shell prigs."

B4   ANON. "Belaboring the Brahmins Again," Literary Digest, LXIII (October 4), 31.
E. B. Osborn attacked the Boston literati a second time in the London Morning Post (n.d.) for their chilly reception of MT's Whittier Birthday Dinner Speech. American newspapers commented on Osborn's articles and individuals wrote him letters generally approving his stand.

B5   ANON. [Review: What is Man? And Other Essays.] Athenaeum, No. 4673 (November 21), p. 1241.
Descriptive and very brief.

B6   *BOSC, R. "Mark Twain et l'humour américain," Revue de Synthèse Historique, XXIX, 181-87.
[Source: Asselineau (1954), No. 215: "A discussion of Régis Michaud's chapter on Twain in Les Mystiques et Réalistes Anglo-Saxons."]

B7   BOYNTON, PERCY H. "The West and Mark Twain," in his A History of American Literature (Boston, New York: Ginn and Company), pp. 380-95.
For undergraduates. Begins with discussion of Bret Harte, who "seems like a trinket shop at the foot of Pike's Peak as Mark Twain looms above him (p. 381)." Praises MT as decent and serious, and notes the humor in JA; IA is not irreverent toward what deserves respect. There is a discussion of MT as a thinker on religion (with a quotation from What Is Man?), but nothing on his major works.

B8   *BRIDGES, HORACE J. "The Pessimism of Mark Twain," The Standard (Cooperstown, N.Y.), July.
[Source: Twainian, II (July, 1943).]

B9   *CLEMENS, SAMUEL L. [Facsimile of letter from MT, June 24, 1874, about appropriating his pseudonym from Captain Isaiah Sellers.] The Eighteenth Year Book 1919. Boston: The Bibliophile Society, 1919, p. 124.
[Source: Quoted in Fatout (1964), p. 34.]

B10   ELLSWORTH, WILLIAM W. "Mark Twain--The Grant Memoirs--Nicolay and Hay's Lincoln," in his A Golden Age of Authors: A Publisher's Recollection (Boston and New York: Houghton Mifflin Company), pp. 221-42.
On MT in amateur dramatics (he tended to go on talking after having spoken another actor's cue lines), his part in founding the Saturday Morning Club, the restraining influence of Olivia Clemens, MT on lecture tour, his practical joke on Thomas B. Reed and Richard Watson Gilder, and the advantage to the Grant family of having the Memoirs published by the Webster Company rather than the less-experienced Century Company. Includes facsimile of MT letter to Ellsworth (January 13, 1893) praising the advertising for The Million Pound Bank-Note.

B11   *FITCH, TOM. [Quotes MT on his brief military service in Missouri.] San Francisco Examiner, March 30.
[Source: Quoted in Fatout (1964), pp. 66-67.]

B12   *FRANK, WALDO. "The Land of the Pioneer," in his Our America (New York: Boni & Liveright), pp. 37-44.
[Source: Reprinted in Scott (1955), pp. 129-33; (1967), pp. 140-44.] "Out of the bitter wreckage of his long life one great work emerges by whose contrasting fire we can observe the darkness. This work is Huckleberry Finn. It must go down in history, not as the expression of a rich natural culture like the books of Chaucer, Rabelais, Cervantes, but as the voice of American chaos, the voice of a pre-cultural epoch.... Huckleberry Finn is the American epic hero. Greece had Ulysses. America must be content with an illiterate lad. He expresses our germinal past. He expresses the movement of the American soul through all the sultry climaxes of the Nineteenth Century." Frank describes MT as "a man of genius.... The soul of Mark Twain was great," but he anticipates Van Wyck Brooks (1920.B12) in arguing that the frontier life followed by Eastern respectability destroyed the artist MT might have been: apart from HF, "the balance of his literary life, before and after, went mostly to the wastage of half-baked, half-believed, half-clownish labor." What Is Man? is the work of MT's last years, "the profane utterance of a defeated soul bent upon degrading the world to the low level where it was forced to live."

B13   *HYSLOP, JAMES HERVEY (formerly professor of logic and ethics at Columbia University). Contact with the Other World; the latest evidence as to communication with the dead. New York: The Century Company.
[Source: Asselineau (1954), No. 213.] Chapter XVI (pp. 249-81) concerns communication with MT's spirit, which claimed to have spoken freely and without suppression in his lifetime. [Several university libraries which do not have this book do have a number of other books by Hyslop on psychic matters--T.A.T.]

B14 _____. "Mark Twain Returns?" Unpartizan Review ("Originally The Unpopular Review"), XII (October-December), 397-409.
On psychic experiments involving Mrs. Emily Grant Hutchings and Mrs. Lola Hays of St. Louis, a Mrs. Chenoweth of Boston, and a Miss Burton of Toledo. There was apparent contact with MT's spirit, to which the books Jap Herron and Brent Roberts are attributed. Hyslop approaches his material cautiously but not skeptically.

B15 *JAMES, G. W. "Mark Twain: An Appreciation of His Pioneer Writing on Fasting and Health," Physical Culture (May).
[Source: Asselineau (1954), No. 217.] According to Twainian, II (May, 1943), 6, the issue also includes a front-cover portrait and other portraits of MT by Bradley.

B16 MARCOSSON, ISAAC F. Adventures in Interviewing. London and New York: John Lane, pp. 216, 244-47.
On MT's friendship with Henry H. Rogers. Includes facsimile of an anecdote about Rogers that MT wrote out for Marcosson to incorporate in an article on Rogers (it could not be signed by MT, because of an agreement with his publishers for exclusive rights to material bearing his name); also photograph of MT.

B17 *MENCKEN, H. L. "The Man Within," Smart Set, (October) pp. 139-43.
[Source: Reprinted in A Mencken Chrestomathy, Edited and Annotated by the Author (1967), pp. 488-89.] On MT's combination of moral arrogance and hesitation to offend public opinion. Praises the honesty and excellence of What Is Man? but deplores MT's witholding it from print for many years. MT's timidity in speaking his mind has lessened his contribution to American letters--but there remains HF, with "something that vastly transcends the merit of all ordinary books."

B18 MILBANK, ELIZABETH PALMER. "In Mark-Twain Land," St. Nicholas, XLVI (August), 934.
Briefly describes Florida, Missouri for young readers. Includes photographs of MT monument and his birthplace.

B19 SCHÖNEMANN, FRIEDRICH. "Mark Twain and Adolph Wilbrandt," Modern Language Notes, XXXIV (June), 372-74.
Finds MT's response to the Meister von Palmyra and "the ethical lesson of it in complete harmony" with his pessimism. "It is possible that this 'majestic drama of depth and seriousness' set his mind to work," resulting in What Is Man? and MS.

B20 _____. [Note.] Modern Language Notes, XXXIV (February), 128.
Comment on Mark Twain's Letters (1917) and what it shows of "Mr. Clemens' relation to the land and people of Germany." See his longer article in Modern Language Notes, XXXIV (June), 372-4, citing as his own this note which was signed "F.S."

B21 SEITZ, DON C. Artemus Ward (Charles Farrar Browne). New York and London: Harper & Brothers Publishers, pp. 141-50.
Describes Ward's visit to Virginia City, his friendship with MT, and MT's lecture on him; the sources of information seem to include nothing not already familiar to students of MT (MT's own accounts are evident). His letter to MT from Austin (January 1, 1864), is included, with regrets at having become so drunk one night (pp. 144-45). The book is unindexed, but includes an extensive bibliography.

B22 WATTERSON, HENRY. "Mark Twain--The Original of Colonel Mulberry Sellers--The 'Earl of Durham'--Some Noctes Ambrosianae--A Joke on Murat Halstead," in his "Marse Henry": An Autobiography (New York: George H. Doran Company), I, 119-33.
Watterson and MT were distantly related by marriage. This account describes several of their joint relatives, among them James Lampton, who, for all his folly, "was as brave as a lion and as upright as Sam Clemens himself" (p. 123). Tells of receiving a long, amusing letter from MT; "Two or three hours later came a telegram. 'Burn letter. Blot it from your memory. Susie is dead'" (p. 127). Concludes with the story of a joke on a New York World reporter: MT introduced his friend as Murat Halstead, and Watterson "lined out to him a column or more of very hot stuff, reversing Halstead in every opinion" (pp. 130-32).

B23 WOODBRIDGE, H. E. "Mark Twain and the 'Gesta Romanorum,'" Nation, CVIII (March 22), 424-25.
Shows parallels to MS in story of an angel changing human destinies.

1920 A BOOKS

A1 BROOKS, VAN WYCK. The Ordeal of Mark Twain. New York: E. P. Dutton & Co.
One of the seminal works on MT, considering him as a victim of his environment: the sterility of the frontier and the genteel influence of Eastern respectability (particularly through Olivia Clemens and William Dean Howells) had a devastating influence on MT as a writer. This book established one pole of MT criticism, and led to a reply by Bernard DeVoto in Mark Twain's America (1932); Brooks slightly revised his own book (1933) in the light of DeVoto's criticisms, but left his argument basically intact. The 1920 version of the book is excerpted briefly or at some length, either to catch the flavor of Brooks's thesis or his discussion

1920 - Books

(BROOKS, VAN WYCK)
of MT's humor or of specific works, in
Marks (1959), pp. 1-18; Scott (1955),
pp. 134-47, (1967), pp. 145-58; Bradley
(1962), pp. 283-88; Leary (1962), pp. 35-61;
Lettis (1962), pp. 284-96; Cardwell (1963),
pp. 15-25; Smith (1963), pp. 13-28; Simpson
(1968), pp. 106-107; Gerber (1971),
pp. 19-29; Kesterson (1973), p. 29.

A2 *PAINE, ALBERT BIGELOW, ed. The Letters of
Mark Twain. London: Chatto & Windus.
[Source: Asselineau (1954), No. 226;
also, several British reviews. The present
bibliography will use throughout the title
of the 1917 American edition, Mark Twain's
Letters--T.A.T.]

A3 _____, ed. Moments with Mark Twain. New
York and London: Harper & Brothers Publishers.
Selections in chronological order, taken
from MT's published work and introduced
briefly by Paine, who says his intent was
to show that MT "was something more than a
mere fun-maker" (p. vi). Contains no new
information or judgment.

A4 *_____. A Short Life of Mark Twain. New York
London: Harper & Brothers.
[Source: Asselineau (1954), No. 223.]

1920 B SHORTER WRITINGS

B1 ALDRICH, MRS. THOMAS BAILEY. Crowding Memories. Boston and New York: Houghton
Mifflin Company.
References passim to MT--who revealed in
his Autobiography and elsewhere that he detested Mrs. Aldrich. Gives a different
perspective to several stories involving
MT and the Aldriches, including the one
about MT's asking them, while visiting in
Hartford, not to make noise upstairs because it disturbed Livy, who had a headache.
According to Mrs. Aldrich, Livy told them
the next morning that she had no headache
and that their bedroom was in another wing
of the house (pp. 146-48.)

B2 ANON. "Business versus Genius," Freeman, I
(July 14), 412-13.
Van Wyck Brooks's The Ordeal of Mark
Twain has been misinterpreted as blaming
the failure of MT's later years on the
earlier ones and on his wife and mother;
rather, Brooks shows MT more broadly (and
successfully) as a product of his time,
the get-rich-quick epoch after the Civil
War.

B3 ANON. "Mark Twain," New Statesman, XV
(October 2), 707-10.
A review of Mark Twain's Letters (1917),
which reveal "his modesty, his quiet reserve of strength"; MT is more himself
here than in Paine's biography, which was
"written from the Boston angle." MT

"needed education; he needed 'showing'--but
he was shown the wrong things" by his wife
and Howells, who "wanted to help." Fortunately, MT "let culture go," and gave the
world IA, RI, TA, LOM, and HF.

B4 ANON. "Mark Twain's First Sweetheart, Becky
Thatcher, Tells of Their Childhood Court-
ship," in Willard Grosvenor Bleyer, How to
Write Special Feature Articles (Boston, New
York: Houghton Mifflin Company), pp. 299-
305.
The text of an interview in the Kansas
City Star (n.d.) with Mrs. Laura Hawkins
Frazer, with her recollections of Sam Clem-
ens in childhood.

B5 ANON. "Taming Mark Twain," Literary Digest,
LXVII (November 13), 34-35.
On Van Wyck Brooks's The Ordeal of Mark
Twain and on The New Statesman reviews
(liberally quoted) of the Paine biography
and edition of MT's letters.

B6 ANON. "Two Literary Shrines Menaced," Literary Digest, LXV (May 29), 36-37.
On plans to convert the MT house in Hartford into apartments (the other shrine was
the house of John Keats in London).

B7 ANON. [Review: Van Wyck Brooks, The Ordeal
of Mark Twain.] Weekly Review (New York),
III (August 4), 108-109.
"Mr. Brooks's bias is strong, but not
literary, and it appears to be the corrective or curative of the normal literary bias.
His theory obliges him to look for both
great abilities and for great disabilities
in Mark Twain, and this guides him unerring-
ly to the perfectly sound conclusion that
Mark Twain's force was far beyond his capacity." Brooks "owns a thesis which attracts
to its defense a large number of crisp facts
and observations. His book will interest
and serve even the unbeliever."

B8 ANON. [Review: Paine, ed., Mark Twain's
Letters.] Living Age, Eighth Series, XX
(from beginning, CCCVIII: November 27),
555-57.
(Reprinted from The Nation). Notes the
humanity and sincerity revealed in the letters; presumably, Paine has witheld "the
most unconventional of his musings."

B9 ANON. [Review: Paine, ed., Mark Twain's
Letters.] Times Literary Supplement,
September 23, p. 615.
MT is revealed as "a deeper, more complex
character than any he created...the most
laborious of writers, throwing into the fire
twice what he publishes." The reviewer
finds "this most generous man a prey to
money troubles that were the appropriate
punishment of something very like greed."

B10 *BOYNTON, PERCY. [Introduction.] The Adventures of Tom Sawyer. New York and London: Harper & Brothers. (Harper's Modern Classics, ed. for educational use by Prof. W. T. Brewster).
[Source: Asselineau (1954), No. 228.]

B11 BRADFORD, GAMALIEL. "Mark Twain," Atlantic Monthly CXXV (April), 462-73.
Using biographical data and basic interpretations from Paine, this appreciation sets MT outside of and above "the ordinary standards of mere literary men." Notes MT's melancholy and lack of religious faith. Reprinted in Scott (1955), pp. 163-74, and (1967), pp. 174-85.

B12 BROOKS, VAN WYCK. "The Genesis of Huck Finn," Freeman, I (March 31), 59-63.
HF succeeds because MT through Huck "was licensed to let himself go.... Huck's illiteracy, Huck's disreputableness and general outrageousness are so many shields behind which Mark Twain can let all the cats out of the bag with impunity." Eastern respectability had controlled MT but not changed his instincts: "You see what happens with Mark Twain when the lion-tamer turns his back."

B13 ____. "A Lost Prophet," Freeman, I (March 24), 46-47.
Chiefly on Horace Traubel and on his study of Walt Whitman; notes that MT's and Whitman's comments on each other were few and inconsequential.

B14 ____. "Mark Twain's Humour," Dial, LXVIII (March), 275-91.
Chapter VIII of The Ordeal of Mark Twain, abridged.

B15 ____. "Mark Twain's Satire," Dial, LXVIII (April), 424-43.
Chapter X of The Ordeal of Mark Twain, abridged.

B16 CARNEGIE, ANDREW. Autobiography of Andrew Carnegie. Boston: Houghton Mifflin, pp. 282-85.
Contains text of MT's letter requesting a dollar and a half to buy a hymn-book, and pays tribute to his warmth and integrity. Of first visit to MT after the death of Olivia: "I fortunately found him alone and while my hand was still in his, and before one word had been spoken by either, there came from his, with a stronger pressure of my hand, these words: 'A ruined home, a ruined home'" (pp. 284-85).

B17 *FARRAN I MAYORAL. Lletres a una Amiga Estrangera, Barcelona. [Critical study of MT, p. 84.] Reviewed in La Revista.
[Source: MHRA Annual Bibliography (1920), No. 197; other facts of publication on the book and the review in La Revista not available.]

B18 HEWLETT, MAURICE. [Review: Mark Twain's Letters.] London Mercury, III (December), 230-32.
An intelligent but minor review; praises MT as author and man, though not one of the great letter writers.

B19 *HOLT, HENRY. [Recollection of MT.] Unpartizan Review (October).
[Source: Reprinted in his Garrulities of an Octogenerian Editor (1923.B15).]

B20 JAMES, WILLIAM. The Letters of William James, Edited by His Son Henry James. Boston: The Atlantic Monthly Press. 2 vols. I: 333, 341-42; II: 264.
In a letter to Josiah Royce from Florence (December 18, 1892), described MT as "a fine, soft-fibred little fellow...I should think that one might grow very fond of him, and wish he'd come and live in Cambridge" (I, 333); to Francis Boot from Florence (January 30, 1893) mentions MT dining with him the night before, calls him "a dear man" (pp. 341-42). In a letter to his brother Henry and son William James, Jr. (Feb. 14, 1907) describes the aged MT at dinner as "good only for monologue, in his old age, or for dialogue at best, but he's a dear little genius all the same" (II, 264).

B21 JOHNSON, ALVIN. "The Tragedy of Mark Twain," New Republic, XXIII (July 14), 201-04.
In answer to Van Wyck Brooks, concedes that "Mark Twain yielded himself to his environment, to the prejudice of his best work"; but "Mark Twain was not in revolt against American institutions," and so could not be a satirist. He "was essentially a pioneer, with his character formed under pioneer discipline or indiscipline," and his pessimism was largely that of his generation.

B22 MATTHEWS, BRANDER. "Mark Twain and the Art of Writing," Harper's CXLI (October), 635-43.
Praises the directness and colloquial ease of MT's style, but his limitations as a critic. Reprinted in Scott (1955), pp. 148-62; (1967), pp. 159-73.

B23 ____. "Memories of Mark Twain," Saturday Evening Post, CXCII (March 6), 14-15, 77-81.
A friend's reminiscences for a general audience; notes that his "An Open Letter to Close a Correspondence" in New Princeton Review (1888) temporarily cooled their friendship. Illustrated with pictures of MT, including photograph taken on a porch at Onteora, New York, with Matthews, Lawrence Hutton, and Carroll Beckwith.

B24 MENCKEN, H. L. Prejudices, Second Series. New York: Alfred A. Knopf. On MT, p. 98.
Brief mention of MT, alternately striving for English approval and clowning for the public, "shrinking poltroonishly from his own ideas, obscenely eager to give no

1920 - Shorter Writings

(MENCKEN, H. L.)
offense," a greater artist than Poe or Whitman but less of a man.

B25 O'DAY, CLARENCE. "Stories from the Files: Famous Writers Who Contributed to the Overland Monthly Fifty Years Ago," Overland Monthly, LXXV (April), 326-28; (May), 407-409; (June), 517-519, 551.
Reprints material MT wrote for the Overland and later used in Innocents Abroad, the brief editorial comment by O'Day merely provides necessary background for readers of a later time.

B26 PECKHAM, H. HOUSTON. "The Literary Status of Mark Twain, 1877-1890," South Atlantic Quarterly, XIX (October), 332-40.
A brief survey, drawing chiefly on Paine and several reviews of MT's works in the Atlantic, Academy, Athenaeum, Critic, etc. "In the realm of pure literature perhaps the most representative American author of the eighties was Mark Twain."

B27 PHILLIPS, MICHAEL J. "Mark Twain's Partner," Saturday Evening Post, CXCIII (September 11), 22-23, 69-74.
On recollections left in manuscript by Calvin H. Higbie, the friend to whom MT dedicated RI; the manuscript is extensively quoted, and there are photographs of Higbie, MT's cabin in Aurora, Nevada, and of Aurora as it was in 1920.

B28 *QUINN, ARTHUR HOBSON. [Introduction.] The Prince and the Pauper. New York and London: Harper & Brothers (Harper's Modern Classics, ed. for educational use by Prof. W. T. Brewster).
[Source: Asselineau (1954), No. 227.]

B29 R., V. "Humorist and Moralist," Athenaeum, No. 4719 (October 8), p. 470.
A review of Paine, ed., Mark Twain's Letters. More about MT, the man and author, than about the letters; favorable.

B30 *RICHEPIN, JEAN. "Les Humoristes--Marck Twain," in his L'Âme Américaine (Paris: Flammarion), pp. 155-74.
[Source: Asselineau (1954), No. 234; notes that the article is made up largely of quotations, and Richepin misspells MT's name and is unsure whether he is still living.]

B31 *SCHÖNEMANN, FRIEDRICH. "Amerikanischer Humor," Germanistisch-Romanistisch Monatsschrift, VIII, 152-54, 216-27.
[Source: Asselineau (1954), No. 250.]

B32 TEN EYCK, ANDREW. "Uncle Sam's Tin Halo: Something about Mark Twain, Europe, and the Poor American Diplomat," Outlook (New York), CXXVI (December 22), 724-27.

On America's poorly paid and inexperienced ambassadors; dramatizes the point with a passing reference to MT's words on the subject. Includes photograph of MT.

B33 VAN DOREN, CARL. "The Fruits of the Frontier," Nation, CXI (August 14), 189.
[Source: Reprinted in Leary (1962), pp. 65-68.] A review of Van Wyck Brooks, The Ordeal of Mark Twain. It "is so brilliant a book and comes so near the truth in its general outlines that it seems almost an excess of seriousness to point out certain excesses of seriousness into which Mr. Brooks has been carried by his ardor for the dignity of the literary profession.... If only Mr. Brooks were willing to lay a little more stress upon the tragedy and a little less upon the guilt of his offending author and nation!"

1921 A BOOKS - NONE

1921 B SHORTER WRITINGS

B1 ANON. "A Scotch Tilt against Mark Twain," Literary Digest, LXVIII (January 8), 35.
Robert Blatchford, editor of The Clarion, an English laborite paper, took issue there with MT's comments on Scott; as excerpted in Literary Digest it appears that Blatchford was defending Scott, rather than attacking MT.

B2 ANON. "Tom, Mark, and Huck," English Journal, X (September), 403-404.
Superficial description and praise of TS and HF. "If the report that one of these stories is soon to be available in a school edition is correct, teachers should not be slow to transfer it from 'home reading' to class study."

B3 BOK, EDWARD W. The Americanization of Edward Bok: The Autobiography of a Dutch Boy Fifty Years After. New York: Charles Scribner's Sons.
In his distinguished career as editor and publisher Bok is probably best known as editor of the Ladies' Home Journal. There are several references in his book to MT, and two letters--one in response to a request from Bok in his youth for an autograph and one in response to a request for permission to print an interview (pp. 205-207).

B4 BURTON, RICHARD. "The Mystery of Personality," Bookman (New York), LII, No. 5 (January), 333-37.
A review of Van Wyck Brooks, The Ordeal of Mark Twain (1920). "The conclusion is unsound," because "He has succumbed to the danger which always confronts the thesis-maker who has to subdue data so they may buttress his belief." [The pagination in

(BURTON, RICHARD)
the volume LII of Bookman examined was confused, but No. 5 (January) includes this
article on pp. 333-37.] Reprinted in Leary
(1962), pp. 69-75.

B5   CORTISSOZ, ROYAL. The Life of Whitelaw Reid.
New York: Charles Scribner's Sons. 2 vols.
I, 157, 248, 272-75; II, 380-81.
Reid was editor of the New York Tribune,
and, later, Ambassador to England. Vol. I
includes notes to him from MT (pp. 157, 248,
273-75) and from Charles Dudley Warner
(p. 273--about plans for GA). In Vol. II
there is a brief description of an MT
speech and the letter from Lord Curzon inviting Reid to receive an honorary Oxford
degree, and asking him to cable the same
invitation to MT and Thomas Edison (who declined with thanks, citing the pressure of
his work).

B6   HAM, GEORGE H. "Mark Twain, the Great Humorist," in Reminiscences of a Raconteur, Between the '40s and the '20s (Toronto: The
Musson Book Company, Limited), pp. 142-47.
Anecdotal. Ham speaks of frequent meetings with MT, and friendship with his former business manager, Ralph W. Ashcroft,
and Mrs. Ashcroft (formerly Miss Lyon, MT's
secretary); he notes that they "could give
the world a more realistic insight of the
dead author than has ever yet been presented," but gives no details and does not hint
at the acrimonious parting of the two from
the Clemens employment (pp. 142-43). Unreliable: describes MT as "a very shrewd
investor," who would put his money from a
book or lecture tour "into some sound enterprise" and "developed what is now the linotype, the first type-setting machine"
(pp. 145-46).

B7   *HARRIS, FRANK. "Memoirs of Mark Twain,"
Pearson's Magazine (November).
[Source: Twainian, II (May, 1943), 6.]

B8   HEWLETT, MAURICE. "Mark Twain and Sir Walter
Scott," Sewanee Review, XXIX (April),
130-33.
Defends Scott, though conceding his books
are "occasionally absurd."

B8   *HOLT, HENRY. [Brief mention of MT.] Unpartizan Review (January).
[Source: Reprinted in his Garrulities of
an Octogenerian Editor (1923.B15).]

B10 *MATTHEWS, BRANDER. "Mark Twain and the Art of
Writing," in his Essays on English (New
York: Charles Scribner's Sons), pp. 243-68.
[Source: Asselineau (1954), No. 255; de-
scribes this as a reprinting from Harper's,
(1920.B22).]

B11 MORRISSEY, FRANK R. "The Ancestor of the
'Jumping Frog,'" Bookman (New York), LIII
(April), 143-45.
An improbable analogue: suggests that
MT's story may derive from a similar compe-
tition in Virginia City, involving chloro-
formed grasshoppers.

B12 O'HIGGINS, HARVEY, and EDWARD H. REEDE, M.D.
"Mark Twain as Exhibit A," McClure's , LIII
(April), 12-13, 42-44.
A psychological interpretation of MT as
having developed his literary art to compensate for feelings of inadequacy which may
be traced to his childhood, beginning with
the weakness resulting from premature birth;
doubting his literary powers, "he compromised
on humor. He attacked only what it was safe
for him to attack: the injustices of the
feudal system...Christian Science in its in-
fancy, Tammany Hall in an election campaign...." Uses Paine extensively, but makes
no mention of Van Wyck Brooks.

B13 PAINE, ALBERT BIGELOW. "The Lost Napoleon,"
in his The Car that Went Abroad: Motoring
through the Golden Age (New York and London: Harper & Brothers Publishers),
pp. 72-78.
Following by car the course of MT's excursion down the Rhône, Paine rediscovered the
formation described in an MT sketch.

B14 RINAKER, CLARISSA. [Bibliography of MT.]
Cambridge History of American Literature.
Cambridge: Cambridge University Press, and
New York: The MacMillan Company [from 1931
reissue], IV, 635-39.
Uneven and incomplete; the bibliography in
the 1931 reissue lists nothing later than
1920.

B15 SCHÖNEMANN, FRIEDRICH. "Mark Twains Weltan-
shauung," Englische Studien, LV (January),
53-84.
Despite his reputation as a jester MT had
a serious outlook on life, as is reflected
in his letters and in such works as MS,
What Is Man?, JA, and CY. "Mark Twain,
'Gottes Narr,' ist um den Ausgang seines
Lebens nie besorgt gewesen, und ebensowenig
um Schluss und Ende seiner Philosophie."

B16 SHERMAN, STUART P. "Mark Twain's Place in
American Literature," in Cambridge History
of American Literature. (Cambridge: Cambridge University Press, and New York: The
Macmillan Company [from 1931 reissue]), III,
1-20.
Somewhat unsympathetic and superficial,
devoting considerable space to biography and
plot-summaries, and drawing on William Dean
Howells and Brander Matthews for a positive
view of MT as a writer.

1921 - Shorter Writings

B17 *STEARNS, HAROLD. "Van Wyck Brooks: Critic and Creator," in his America and the Young Intellectual (New York: George H. Doran Company), pp. 24-33.
[Source: Reprinted in Leary (1962), pp. 76-80.] The Ordeal of Mark Twain (1920) is a serious and provocative work, though somewhat vacillating because Brooks lacks a clear central philosophy of life, writing at some times like a believer in free will, at others like a determinist.

B18 VAN DOREN, CARL. "Mark Twain," in his The American Novel. (New York: The Macmillan Company), pp. 157-87; passim.
A "Revised and Enlarged Edition" appeared in 1940, but the changes in the treatment of MT are comparatively minor: Van Doren drops the charge that MT's failure to become a national satirist stems "partly from excess of patriotism, partly from a lack of the literary seriousness which might have enabled him to hold out against the influence of his wife and his new environment" (p. 167; cf. p. 145 in the 1940 ed., where these words do not appear). Considers MT as a major author, though flawed, with HF his great work, in a class with The Scarlet Letter (pp. 170-75). Pp. 137-38, 160-62 of the 1940 revised edition are reprinted in Kesterson (1973), pp. 57-59.

1922 A BOOKS

A1 *ANON. Public Meeting under the Auspices of the American Academy and the National Institute of Arts and Letters Held at Carnegie Hall, New York, November 30, 1910 in Memory of Samuel Langhorne Clemens (Mark Twain). New York: American Academy of Arts and Letters.
[Source: Asselineau (1954), No. 266; See 1910 entries for details-T.A.T.]

A2 FISHER, HENRY W. Abroad with Mark Twain and Eugene Field: Tales They Told to a Fellow Correspondent. New York: Nicholas L. Brown.
"Editor's Note" by Merle Johnson vouches for the substantial accuracy in "substance and manner, if not always the exact language" in these recollections of MT and Field in Berlin, Vienna, London, and Paris; some are recorded from memory, but Fisher also had diaries and notebooks to follow (pp. vii-x). Fisher's "Preface" begins: "To begin with, of course, I don't claim that all these stories are absolutely first hand. I sometimes jotted down what I heard Mark say, or stored his talk in some compartment of memory, only to hear him repeat the yarn, after a space, in quite different fashion" (p. xv).

A3 *LAUTREC, GABRIEL DE, trans. Mark Twain, Contes Choisis, traduits par Gabriel de Lautrec et précédés d'une étude sur l'humour. Paris: Nelson.
[Source: Asselineau (1954), No. 268.]

1922 B SHORTER WRITINGS

B1 ADE, GEORGE. Single Blessedness and Other Observations, Garden City, New York: Doubleday, Page & Co.
Reprints his 1910 essay, "Mark Twain as Our Emissary" without significant revisions, pp. 203-210.

B2 ANON. "Alas Poor Yorick!" Times Literary Supplement, October 26, p. 678.
A review, chiefly descriptive, of Van Wyck Brooks, The Ordeal of Mark Twain. [The British edition appeared in 1922, according to Asselineau (1954), No. 264.]

B3 ANON. "On the Trail of Mark Twain," New York Times Book Review and Magazine (October 8), p. 7.
On a tour of the Sierra Nevadas by Nicholas Murray Butler, described at length and enlivened by MT's description of Mono Lake, quoted from RI. Includes photographs of Butler's party and of the King River Canyon.

B4 *ANON. "Tells of Mark Twain's Brief Soldiery in 1861," Hannibal (Missouri) Courier-Post, September 2.
[Source: Asselineau (1954), No. 289.]

B5 ANON. [Review: Henry W. Fisher, Abroad with Mark Twain and Eugene Field.] Boston Transcript, April 8, p. 10.
Descriptive; includes picture of MT.

B6 ANON. [Review: Henry W. Fisher, Abroad with Mark Twain and Eugene Field.] Dial, LXXIII (August), 235.
Makes short work of the book; concludes: "Mr. Fisher appears to have been assiduous without great success; his contribution to the bulk of Mark Twain's wit is hardly commensurate with the size of his book."

B7 ANON. [Review: Henry W. Fisher, Abroad with Mark Twain and Eugene Field.] The Literary Review ("Published by the New York Evening Post"), II (April 1), 550.
MT would not be grateful for the editing, which makes this book "all droll waggishness," and therefore of a type that ultimately tires a reader. Fisher honestly concedes that the tales may not be exactly as he heard them from MT. "A remark of this kind was in order, for some of the things said about the ex-Kaiser, his troops, his U-boats, and his big guns, leave the impression that they were edited after, not before, the World War. The few pages devoted to Eugene Field are less amusing but more informative."

B8   AYERS, COL. JAMES. "'Mark Twain' Doing the Islands--How He Discharged Himself from the Call--Mark as a Joker--Could Give But Could Not Take----His Intended Father-in-Law Makes an Awkward Proposition--He Disposes of It Handsomely," in his Gold and Sunshine: Reminiscences of Early California (Boston: Richard G. Badger), pp. 223-26.

    Ayers writes from personal acquaintance and says MT resigned from the San Francisco Call because of a tactful suggestion that he do so.

B9   B., L. [Review: Henry W. Fisher, Abroad with Mark Twain and Eugene Field.] Freeman, V (July 12), 429.

    "The record of many incidents, scraps of conversation, and bits of reminiscence; all lined up with their heels together and their eyes to the front, without a twinkle in them."

B10   BRADFORD, GAMALIEL. "Mark Twain," in his American Portraits. (Boston and New York: Houghton Mifflin Co.), pp. 1-28.

    "Somehow in Mark Twain the humor and the pathos are not essentially blended." Because of a "lack of depth in thinking and feeling," Bradford is "reluctant to class Mark with the greatest comic writers of the world. His thought was bitter because it was shallow." Nonetheless, "He did more than make men laugh, he made them think, on practical, moral questions.... My final, total impression is desolating": MT's influence in many ways is harmful, although "he was a big man and he had a big heart."

B11   "BURGLAR, A." "The Mark Twain Burglary," in his In the Clutch of Circumstance--My Own Story (New York, London: D. Appleton Company), pp. 168-82.

    On the burglary of MT's "Stormfield" home in Redding, Connecticut. He believes that MT was influential in having the charges against him reduced, so that the sentence was ten years rather than thirty.

B12   CLEMENS, SAMUEL L. "Unpublished Chapters from the Autobiography of Mark Twain," Harper's, CXLIV (February), 273-80; (March), 455-60; CXLV (June), 310-15.

    Each installment begins with a brief headnote by Albert Bigelow Paine, addressed to the general reader.

B13   *CLEMENS, WILL M. "The Genesis of Mark Twain," The Biblio (Pompton Lakes, New Jersey). In eight parts, August 1922 to March 1923. [Source: Twainian, I (November, 1939), 3.]

B14   *_____. "The Genesis of Mark Twain," Genealogy Magazine (Pompton Lakes, New Jersey), October, 1922; January, April, 1923. [Source: Twainian, II (May, 1943), 6, with a note that this is probably the same text as that appearing in The Biblio.]

B15   DICKEY, MARCUS. The Maturity of James Whitcomb Riley. Indianapolis: The Bobbs-Merrill Company, Publishers.

    On p. 165, text of address on an envelope written by MT in Vienna to "Mr. James Whitcomb Riley/Poet & a dern capable one, too,/ Indianapolis, Indiana,/ U.S. of America." On p. 231, text of MT letter (October 3, 1888) to "Mr. W. D. Foulke and Others," regretfully declining an invitation to a dinner honoring Riley, because "I am finishing a book begun three years ago. I see land ahead; if I stick to the oar without intermission I shall be at anchor in thirty days; if I stop to moisten my hands I am gone." Briefly mentions MT, passim (indexed).

B16   DREW, JOHN. My Years on the Stage. New York: E. P. Dutton & Company.

    Contains recollections of MT and the theater passim (indexed).

B17   HOLMES, RALPH. "Mark Twain and Music," Century, CIV (October), 844-50.

    Following the Paine biography for factual data, discusses MT's early distaste for opera, his love for Negro spirituals, fascination with a music box, painful sensitivity to some sounds (such as ticking clocks and barking dogs), and his eventual solace in the music played on an orchestrelle in the New York home of his later years. In Vienna, according to Clara Clemens, "my father was always ill at ease among the musical people, for they were concerned with a form of art that left him wholly unmoved, and sometimes actually uncomfortable."

B18   HOWE, M. A. DEWOLFE. Memories of a Hostess: A Chronicle of Eminent Friendships Drawn Chiefly from the Diaries of Mrs. James T. Fields. Boston: The Atlantic Monthly Press.

    Describes visits to the Clemens home in Hartford. MT verses (a parody of Poe's "The Bells") and a letter from him to James T. Fields are reproduced in facsimile (pp. 248-49).

B19   _____. "Bret Harte and Mark Twain in the 'Seventies: Passages from the Diaries of Mrs. James T. Fields," Atlantic Monthly, CXXX (September), 341-48.

    Entries for April and May, 1876 in the diary of the wife of the former Atlantic Monthly editor (pp. 344-48) describe MT's love for reading, dissatisfaction with American government, support for women's suffrage, apology for having spoken too quickly before Olivia. This is "part of a book to be published October 1," according to "The Contributors' Column," p. 428.

B20   HUNEKER, JAMES GIBBONS. [Brief mention of MT.] Steeplejack. New York: Charles Scribner's Sons, 2 vols, in 1; I, 100.

    Calls MT "our most American of writers, one who would outlive the pallid philosophy

1922 - Shorter Writings

(HUNEKER, JAMES GIBBONS)
of Emerson, the swaggering humbuggery of
Walt Whitman, or the sonorous platitudes of
Longfellow."

B21   *KWEST, DR. FRANZ. [Introduction.] Die Abenteuer Tom Sawyers und Huckleberry Finns.
Berlin: Mitteldeutsche verlangstalt, Leh-
mann und Fink.
[Source: Asselineau (1954), No. 267.]

B22   LUCY, SIR HENRY. The Diary of a Journalist:
Later Entries. London: John Murray,
pp. 231, 290, 315-16.
Briefly mentions MT, but provides no new
information beyond what he gave in his Sixty
Years in the Wilderness: Some Passages by
the Way (1909).

B23   MATTHEWS, BRANDER. "Memories of Mark Twain,"
in his The Tocsin of Revolt and Other Essays.
(New York: Charles Scribner's Sons),
pp. 253-94.
Personal recollections, including those of
a summer with MT at Onteora, N.Y. in 1890;
notes a temporary falling-out over copyright
laws and also comments on occasional failures as a speaker. Takes MT's word that
his primary resource for inspiration is
memory, and notes his life-long quality of
boyishness. The date "(1919)" appears at
the end, and this may well be a mere reprint
of the Saturday Evening Post article of the
same title (1920.B23).

B24   McCUTCHEON, GEORGE BARR. "When Mark Twain
Was a 'New' Writer," Literary Digest International Book Review, I (December), 16-17.
Portrait. An appreciative review of the
35-volume Gabriel Wells Definitive Edition,
noting that there is included "an appreciation written especially for each of the
main titles," by E. V. Lucas, Hamlin Garland, Mary E. Wilkins Freeman, Booth Tarkington, Hugh Walpole, Kate Douglas Wiggin,
Meredith Nicholson, William Allen White,
Stephen Leacock, G. K. Chesterton, Brander
Matthews, and William Dean Howells.

B25   MOORE, OLIN HARRIS. "Mark Twain and Don
Quixote," Publications of the Modern Language Association, XXXVII (June), 324-46.
"The purpose of this paper is to trace the
influence of Cervantes upon Mark Twain, with
particular attention to th supposedly autobiographical tales Huckleberry Finn and Tom
Sawyer." The humor of both authors "lies
to a great extent in the contrast between
imaginative and unimaginative characters,"
and MT, more widely read than is generally
recognized, parodied literary sources and
created characters misled by their reading.

B26   PEARSON, EDMUND LESTER. [Review: Fisher,
Abroad with Mark Twain and Eugene Field.]
Independent, CVIII (April 8), 353.3
"I suspect that there is more of Mr. Fisher than of Mark Twain" in this book, with
its "continual use of slang phrases which
were unknown until after Mark Twain's death
('hard-boiled,' for instance)."

B27   SCHÖNEMANN, F. "Amerikanische Mark Twain-
Literatur 1910-1920," Englische Studien,
LXVI (January), 148-53.
A survey of writing by and about MT pub-
lished since his death; essentially an an-
notated bibliography.

B28   _____. [Review: Bümmel durch Europa (A Tramp
Abroad.] Das literarische Echo: Halbmonat-
schrift fur Literaturfreunde (Stuttgart;
after Vol. XXV became a monthly, Die Literatur), XXII (November 1), 177.
Brief review, noting that a high point of
the book is the description of a journey in
the Black Forest [In German].

B29   TICKNOR, CAROLINE. "Mark Twain's 'Life on the
Mississippi,'" in her Glimpses of Authors.
Boston and New York: Houghton Mifflin Company (also London: T. Werner Laurie Ltd.--
but printed by The Riverside Press), 132-51
and passim on MT. Reprinted 1972: Free-
port, New York: Books for Libraries Press
(Essay Index Reprint Series).
Caroline Ticknor was the daughter of the
publisher Benjamin Holt Ticknor and her
reminiscences are at first-hand. In addition to giving a few details about the publication of LOM (and quoting MT's correspondence with the publisher), she describes
MT's seventieth birthday dinner, and the
train trip with him to the Thomas Bailey Aldrich home in Portsmouth. Elsewhere in the
book she notes MT's interest in Edward Bellamy's Looking Backward (p. 117), and a
tribute Howells at his own seventy-fifth
birthday dinner paid to the memory of his
friend (pp. 177-78).

B30   *WADE, MRS. MAY HAZLETON BLANCHARD. "Mark
Twain, Giver of Mirth," in her Real Americans (Boston: Little, Brown & Co.),
pp. 192-241.
[Source: Asselineau (1954), No. 276:
"merely a sentimental biographical sketch."]

1923 A BOOKS

A1   CLEMENS, SAMUEL L. Europe and Elsewhere, with
an appreciation by Brander Matthews and an
introduction by Albert Bigelow Paine. New
York: Harper & Brothers.
The first is a "'Biographical Criticism'...
prepared by Prof. Brander Matthews, as an
introduction to the Uniform Edition of Mark
Twain's Works, published in 1899." Paine's
introduction discusses MT's unpublished
writings and gives background on the materials published here.

A2 _____. Mark Twain's Speeches, with an Introduction by Albert Bigelow Paine and an Appreciation by William Dean Howells. New
York and London: Harper & Brothers.
   The Paine introduction is a biographical
summary, emphasizing MT's career as a
speaker; the Howells appreciation is reprinted from the 1910 edition of the Speeches (1910.B96), in which the selection of
speeches is somewhat different.

1923 B SHORTER WRITINGS

B1 ANON. "Miscellaneous Twain," Springfield
(Massachusetts) Daily Republican
October 26, p. 16.
   A review of the "lesser writings" in Eu-
rope and Elsewhere; descriptive and largely
indebted to the introductory "Biographical
Criticism" by Brander Matthews.

B2 ANON. "Missouri Honors the Prince of Humorists," Literary Digest, LXVIII (August 11),
30.
   Excerpts (n.d.) from the St. Louis Globe-
Democrat and the Quincy (Missouri) Whig
Journal on Florida, Missouri, on the house
there where MT was born, and on the proposed
state park.

B3 *ANON. [Review: Mark Twain's Speeches.] New
York World, May 27, p. 7.
   [Source: Asselineau (1954), No. 309.]

B4 ANON. [Review: Mark Twain's Speeches.] Outlook (New York), CXXXV (June 27), 287-88.
   "A great deal of the sparkle of the humor
is lost in the stolid printed page. Yet
there is good browsing in the book, and
there is what Mark Twain loved to call
'horse sense' as well as fun."

B5 ANON. [Review: Mark Twain's Speeches.]
Springfield (Massachusetts) Daily Republican, June 22, p. 16.
   Descriptive and based primarily on the
introduction.

B6 BERGENGREN, RALPH. "Mark Twain in Europe and
Elsewhere. The Great American Humorist Discourses on Many Things that Touch the Heart
of Humanity," Boston Evening Transcript
October 13, Book Section, p. 2.
   A review: "Europe and Elsewhere, opened
here and there, usually provides something
that catches the attention and interests
the reader though the timeliness of the
topic has gone past." Illustration: "Mark
Twain (From a Drawing by S. J. Woolf...)"

B7 *BRIDGES, HORACE JAMES. "The Pessimism of
Mark Twain," in his As I Was Saying--A Sheaf
of Essays and Discourses (Boston: Marshall
Jones Co.), pp. 35-51.
   [Source: Asselineau (1954), No. 295;
Bridges argues that pessimism is a product
of satire.]

B8 CANBY, HENRY SEIDEL. "Mark Twain," The Literary Review ("Published by the New York Evening Post"), IV (November 3), 201-202.
   Occasioned by the publication of the Gabriel Wells "Definitive Edition" of MT's works;
takes issue with Van Wyck Brooks: "Most
artists are suppressed in one way or another,
and not only in America. Yet it is arguable,
nevertheless, that Clemens was the kind of
spirit that needed a certain amount of suppression, without which he would have fizzed
his way through life like an uncapped soda
spring." Reprinted in Canby's Definitions:
Essays in Contemporary Criticism (Second Series). New York: Harcourt, Brace & Co.,
1924, pp. 157-65 (Reprinted Port Washington,
N.Y.: Kennikat Press, 1967).

B9 CLEMENS, CLARA. "How I Got Rid of Nervousness
in Public," Étude, XLI (May), 295-96.
   On her way of achieving mental serenity
before concerts; followed by extensive excerpts from Ralph Holmes, "Mark Twain and
Music" (1922).

B10 COOK, SHERWIN LAWRENCE. "Mark Twain as a Mak-
er of Speeches," Boston Evening Transcript,
June 16, Book Section, p. 3.
   A review of Mark Twain's Speeches, noting
MT's development: "It is not often that a
literary man's ability to speak keeps step
with his progress as a writer," as did MT's.
On the Whittier Birthday Dinner speech,
cites contemporary newspaper accounts indicating that "certain of the diners must
have been amused." Portrait: "Mark Twain.
(From an Etching by Otto Schneider...)"

B11 *DUNN, HARRY H. "To Revive Pony Express to
Honor Mark Twain," Dearborn Independent,
July 14.
   [Source: Twainian, II (January, 1940),
5.]

B12 FISHER, SAMUEL J. "Mark Twain," Spectator,
CXXX (June 2), 922.
   A letter to the editor, from Pittsburgh,
Pennsylvania. Answers the charges in Kreym-
borg's favorable review of The Ordeal of
Mark Twain (p. 701), in particular noting
that MT was financially independent to write
as he pleased, and in their last years both
MT and his wife lacked religious convictions.

B13 *FITZGERALD, F. SCOTT. "10 Best Books I Have
Read," Jersey City Journal (April 24), p. 9.
Syndicated by the North American Newspaper
Alliance.
   [Source: reprinted in Fitzgerald/Heming-
way Annual (1972), 67-68.] Fitzgerald's
complete statement on MT: "'The Mysterious
Stranger.' (Mark Twain). Mark Twain in his
most sincere mood. A book and a startling
revelation."

B14 HARRIS, FRANK. "Memories of Mark Twain," in his Contemporary Portraits, Fourth Series, (New York: Brentano's), pp. 162-73.
     Attacks MT for his hostility toward Bret Harte, calls JA "a dreadful book" that "makes a Puritan maiden of the great French-woman," and objects to his essay on Howells "in which that tedious person is praised as if he were one of the great writers."

B15 HOLT, HENRY. Garrulities of an Octogenerian Editor. Boston and New York: Houghton Mifflin Company. On MT, pp. 99-102, 129 (originally appeared in the Unpartizan Review, October, 1920 and January, 1921).
     On meetings with MT, the last one at a dinner in the Times Tower honoring the editor of the London Times. "If Mark said anything funny it was bitterly funny. His wife was dead. The burden of his talk was that he was growing old, that the future was dark, and that the heart was gone out of him." Holt was distressed that MT was not interested in Psychical Research, despite published evidence of psychical experiences in the family (pp. 100-101).

B16 HUTCHISON, PERCY A. "Dinner-Talk by Mark Twain," New York Times Book Review (June 10), p. 8.
     A review of Paine's new edition of Mark Twain's Speeches; they give little evidence of the pessimism attributed to MT by recent critics [such as Van Wyck Brooks].

B17 JOHNSON, ROBERT UNDERWOOD. Remembered Yesterdays. Boston: Little, Brown and Company.
     On the loss of Grant's Memoirs by the Century Company to MT's publishing company, not quite suggesting unethical practice by MT (pp. 217-19); MT's lobbying for a stronger copyright law (pp. 267-69); a probing examination of his personality, noting both his tenderness and his hard hitting and hard hating: "His violence was almost unexampled among literary men" (pp. 319-25). Two photographs: "Mark Twain at Onteora" and "Mark Twain in Tesla's Laboratory. Photographed by phosphorescent light" (facing p. 324).

B18 JORDAN-SMITH, PAUL. "Mark Twain," in his On Strange Altars: A Book of Enthusiasms. (London: Brentano's, Ltd.), pp. 136-45.
     A superficial over-view of several of MT's works, largely plot-summary. Praises MT's social satire and argues that humor saved him from bitterness.

B19 KREYMBORG, ALFRED. [Review: Brooks, The Ordeal of Mark Twain.] Spectator, CXXX (April 28), 701.
     Praises Brooks for his "intellectual honesty and integrity of utterance," and shares his view of MT as having shrunk from the heights he might have achieved as a satirist to become a mere clown—but he created "at least one masterpiece: Huck Finn."

B20 MATTHEWS, BRANDER. "Mark Twain," in An Introduction to the Study of American Literature (Revised). (New York, Cincinnati, Chicago, Boston, Atlanta: American Book Company), pp. 215-26.
     A policy of not including living authors kept MT out of the first edition of this school survey (1896); the essay in this late edition is primarily biographical and descriptive, and adds little to his judgments published in the earlier period when Matthews was among the first in the academic community to recognize the importance of MT.

B21 _____. "Mark Twain and the Theater," in his Playwrights on Playmaking, and Other Studies of the Stage. (New York, London: Charles Scribner's Sons), pp. 159-83.
     On MT's appreciation of the theatre, and his efforts as a playwright. His dramatization of GA apparently owes something to Gilbert S. Densmore's plotting in a version that was suppressed after a cash settlement by MT. MT failed as a dramatist because for all his dramatic genius in creating characters, he lacked the constructive skill the stage requires.

B22 _____. "Mark Twain Stands and Delivers," Literary Digest International Book Review, I (August), 57.
     A review of Mark Twain's Speeches, but including Matthews's own discussion of MT as a skilled speaker who prepared carefully and knew his audience—but Matthews cites two failures. This new edition of the speeches supercedes the carelessly edited 1910 version.

B23 MAVOR, JAMES. My Windows on the Street of the World. London and Toronto: J. M. Dent & Sons Ltd; New York: E. P. Dutton & Co., I, 197; II, 183.
     William Morris read aloud from HF until past two in the morning, then stayed up until five to finish it (I, 197). Quotes a comic poem MT wrote in an album about Laurence Housman (II, 183).

B24 O'BRIEN, EDWARD J. "Bret Harte and Mark Twain," in his The Advance of the American Short Story. (New York: Dodd, Mead and Company), pp. 98-116; on MT, pp. 112-16, (entry based on 1931 revised ed., apparently unchanged in content and pagination).
     Charges Harte with personal irresponsibility; his writings portray the vanished West, but they are shallow and sentimental and his tales of life in Europe are "rubbish." On MT, discusses only the short stories and leaves the general discussion of MT to "Van Wyck Brooks, who ranks with T. S. Eliot as the most intellectually mature of contemporary American critics."

B25 PHELPS, WILLIAM LYON. "The American Humorist: Mark Twain," in his Some Makers of American Literature (Boston: Marshall Jones Company), pp. 163-87.
On MT as careful literary artist, interpreter of life, and "the incarnate spirit of America."

B26 _____. "Mark Twain, the American Humorist," Ladies' Home Journal, XL (May), 18, 208-11.
A lengthy discussion of the man and his works, praising his artistry and a humor that kept him from being conceited.

B27 *RANKIN, J. W. [Introduction.] Life on the Mississippi. New York and London: Harper & Brothers (Modern Classics).
[Source: Asselineau (1954), No. 291.]

B28 *ROBERTS, CARL ERIC BECHHOFER. The Literary Renaissance in America. London: William Heinemann, Ltd.
On pp. 2-7, follows Brooks in accounting for MT's pessimism. [Source: Asselineau (1954), No. 294; family name "Roberts," according to card files at Duke University Library and Oakland Public Library.]

B29 SCHÖNEMANN, FRIEDRICH. "Mr. Samuel Langhorne Clemens," Archiv für das Studium der neueren Sprachen und Literaturen, CXLV (August), 184-213.
On MT as revealed in the 1917 edition of his letters; notes the problem even in America of distinguishing between Clemens and the "Mark Twain" he created. [In German.]

B30 _____. [Review: MT's Tolle Geschichten.] Die Literatur (Stuttgart), XXVI (December), 179.
Brief review, comments, "Mit solch einem tieferen Blick in Mark Twains Seele entdeckten wir auch ein Amerikanertum, zu dem uns die 'Tollen Geschichten,' so ergösslich und Mark Twainisch sie sein mögen, nicht führen können, was bei unserer recht magelhaften Einsicht in das Wesen der amerikanischen Kultur sehr zu bedauern ist."

B31 TASSIN ALGERNON, and ARTHUR BARTLETT MAURICE. "Mark Twain, Idol-Smasher," in The Story of American Literature. (New York: The Macmillan Company), pp. 318-27.
Laudatory and rather superficial, intended for younger readers. A "Foreword" notes that the papers in this book originally appeared weekly, in serial form, but does not indicate where they were published.

B32 VAN DOREN, CARL. "The Lion and the Uniform," in his The Roving Critic, New York: Alfred A. Knopf [as reprinted Port Washington, N.Y.: Kennikat Press, 1950], pp. 45-55.
On Van Wyck Brooks's The Ordeal of Mark Twain (1920), which in its arraignment of MT's times "exhibits instances of special pleading and a definite animus [that] must be admitted even by those who, like myself, agree that the picture here drawn of our greatest humorist is substantially accurate as well as brilliant."

B33 WIGGIN, KATE DOUGLAS. My Garden of Memory: An Autobiography. Boston and New York: Houghton Mifflin Company.
Passim on public functions at which MT was present (indexed). Describes a serious and not wholly successful MT reading (pp. 240-41) and MT receiving his honorary degree from Oxford (pp. 304-307).

1924 A BOOKS

A1 CLEMENS, SAMUEL LANGHORNE. Mark Twain's Autobiography, edited and with introduction by Albert Bigelow Paine. New York and London: Harper & Brothers Publishers, 2 vols.
The text of reminiscences written and dictated by MT and selected by Paine. "Perhaps it is proper to assure the reader that positive mistakes of dates and occurrence have been corrected, while, for the rest, the matter of mere detail is of less importance than that the charm of the telling should remain undisturbed." By MT's request, the order is that of composition, rather than chronology of events. Much is not included here, either because of Paine's judgment or because of MT's injunction that certain items not be published for a number of years after his death, but this version of MT's autobiographical material has not been replaced by DeVoto's edition of Mark Twain in Eruption (1940) and Neider's The Autobiography of Mark Twain (1959). MT's "Chapters from My Autobiography" had appeared in North American Review, 1906-1907; since they appeared before his death and he had approved the texts for publication they have a greater authority than this version by Paine, with several silent expurgations.

A2 *GILLIS, WILLIAM R. Memories of Mark Twain and Steve Gillis: A Record of Mining Experiences. Sonora, California: Printed by The Banner.
[Source: Asselineau (1954), No. 321.]

A3 FINGER, CHARLES J. Mark Twain, the Philosopher Who Laughed at The World. Girard, Kansas: Haldeman-Julius Company.
[Source: Asselineau (1954), No. 320: "Pays homage to Mark Twain's condemnation of mob-rule and anti-Semitism."]

1924 B SHORTER WRITINGS

B1 ANON. "Conrad Pays Tribute to Mark Twain," Mentor, XII (May), 45.
From a Mentor interview. "'Mark Twain was a good pilot,' said Conrad. 'He must have been. No man who had not done the actual work could write of steamboat life as he did.'" The descriptions of life in America are what count. "'They have life--American life. They are authentic.'" "'Often,' says

1924 - Shorter Writings

(ANON.)
Conrad musingly, 'I thought of "The Missis-sippi Pilot" and of Twain while I was in command of a steamer in the Congo and stood straining in the night looking for snags. Very often I thought of him. He understood all that sort of job.'"

B2   ANON. "Gleams of Mark Twain Humor. Selected Incidents and Anecdotes Reflecting the Unique Character and Whimsical Quality of the Humorist," Mentor, XII (May), 56-58.
A few anecdotes apparently not reported elsewhere; also, three cartoon representa-tions of his 1907 visit to England and photograph of MT in Harper & Brothers office, New York.

B3   ANON. "Mark Twain," New Statesman, XXIV (November 8), "Additional Pages," x, xii, xiv.
A review of Mark Twain's Autobiography, which its random arrangement makes "a scrapbook...but this lack of order and pro-gression cannot spoil its chief charm, which is the companionship of Mark Twain himself; his fun and his honest angers, his tender affections...there is an exhilarating air of freedom blowing through these pages."

B4   ANON. "Mark Twain and General Grant," Mentor, XII (May), 46-47.
Anecdotes and the account of MT's involve-ment in publication of Grant's Memoirs; pro-vides no new information.

B5   ANON. "Mark Twain Memorial Park," Mentor, XII (May), 54-55.
The history of the park in Florida, Missouri.

B6   ANON. "Mark Twain--Radical," Saturday Review of Literature, I (November 1), 241.
MT spoke more freely on social issues than recent critics would admit, but "knew much more of America than his more scornful successors. Perhaps that is why he liked his country in spite of the deeds of his countrymen."

B7   ANON. "One Love of a Lifetime," Mentor, XII (May), 50.
On Olivia; adds little to the Paine bio-graphy.

B8   ANON. "Self-Revelation of our Greatest Humor-ist," Current Opinion, LXXVII (November), 578-80.
A review of Mark Twain's Autobiography. "His greatest tragedy lay in his inability to resist the moods which robbed him of faith and of happiness," but his writings brought "unmeasured delight to millions of readers."

B9   ANON. [Review: Mark Twain's Autobiography.] Times Literary Supplement, November 6, p. 701.
An evaluation of MT as he emerges in his book. Despite hatred for the human race, he was warm in his personal affections. He was a conscious literary craftsman, and it was his art rather than money-making that could charm his depressions away: "His most successful calculation must have been the miscalculation that led to his bankruptcy. In paying off his debts he was at his happiest." The book's deliberate absence of formal organization "gives the impulsive man, and when it has illumined President and coachman with an equal light abruptly shut off, they have fulfilled their function of reflecting Mark Twain."

B10   NO ENTRY

B11   BOYNTON, PERCY H. "Biography and the Personal Equation," in his Some Contemporary Ameri-cans: The Personal Equation in Literature. Chicago: The University of Chicago Press (Reprinted New York: Biblo and Tannen, 1967), pp. 242-64; on MT, pp. 244-57.
Discusses several interpretations of MT. The Paine biography contains an abundance of data, and Paine was aware of MT's creative memory, but inclined to hero-worship and "as keen about Twain's billiards as he was about his books" (p. 245). Howells' My Mark Twain "was by title and nature a per-sonal tribute which is only half read if Mr. Howells is not interpreted into every page" (p. 250). Brooks's The Ordeal of Mark Twain is written to a thesis, pompously sol-emn, and prone to regard opposing opinions as wrong because they are generally accepted. Boynton regards Gamaliel Bradford's portrait of MT as "bafflingly indeterminate" as to whether it praises or condemns. This essay is one of a group incorporating material which previously appeared in the Dial, the Freeman, the Independent, and the New Repub-lic (p. vii).

B12   CLEMENT, MRS. N. E. "Clement, Clements, Clem-ans. With a Notice of Mark Twain's Ances-try," Virginia Magazine of History and Bio-graphy [title also appears as Virginia His-torical Magazine], XXXII (292-98).
"In the Genealogy Magazine edited by Wm. M. Clemens, of Pompton Lakes, New Jersey, there appears an article beginning in Vol. X, No. 9, called 'The Genesis of Mark Twain,' in which the author treats of the Virginia ancestry of the distinguished American humor-ist and author." Numerous statements of fact in that article are here challenged in a detailed account.

B13 *FINGER, CHARLES J. "Mark Twain, the Philosopher Who Laughed at the World," Life and Letters, (April [Mark Twain Number]).
[Source: Twainian, II (November, 1940), 4; this is not the British Life and Letters—T.A.T.]

B14 GABRILOWITSCH, CLARA CLEMENS. "My Father," Mentor, XII (May), 21-3.
Clara was somewhat overawed by her famous and sometimes rather reserved father; tells the story of his keeping the secret of her destructive pet squirrels.

B15 LAROM, WALTER H. "Mark Twain in the Adirondacks," Bookman (New York), LVIII (January), 536-38.
Recollections of a visit to MT's bungalow on Saranac Lake; includes texts of two MT letters to Mr. and Mrs. George V. W. Duryee (June 14, September 19, 1901).

B16 LEISY, ERNEST ERWIN. "Mark Twain," in his American Literature: An Interpretive Survey. (New York: Thomas Y. Crowell Company), pp. 170-78.
Biographical, broadly appreciative. Notes his serious thought, pessimism. "Mark Twain's reputation, however, does not rest on his philosophy but on his portrayal of life in mid-nineteenth-century America, ... He is the incarnation of democratic America, best fulfilling Whitman's conception of the promise of American life.... He spoke the national idiom."

B17 LITTELL, ROBERT. [Review: Mark Twain's Autobiography.] New Republic, XL (October 29), 230.
"What we learn about Mark Twain from himself is pleasant, or touching, or tedious, or explicit, or narrative, but not very illuminating." The recollections of his youth are the best, most vivid parts.

B18 "Mark Twain Number—Articles by His Biographer and Close Friends," Mentor, XII (May).
Articles are listed individually in this section. Illustrated with photographs and drawings.

B19 MARSHALL, ARCHIBALD. "Last Century's Literary Favorites: I, Huckleberry Finn," Literary Digest International Book Review, II (January), 104, 106.
Appreciative: a masterpiece, though the ending is weak.

B20 MATTHEWS, BRANDER. "Mark Twain as Speech-Maker and Story-Teller," Mentor, XII (May), 24-28.
Insists on MT's artistry and careful preparation; tells the anecdote of MT mistaking a guest for a book agent.

B21 _____. "The Truth about Mark Twain," Literary Digest International Book Review, II (November), 845-48.
An extended (and favorable) review of Mark Twain's Autobiography by an old friend and advocate. Includes a drawing of MT by Carroll Beckwith in Onteora, N.Y., 1890, and a photograph of MT, Matthews, and friends, also Onteora, 1890.

B22 MIEROW, HERBERT EDWARD. "Cicero and Mark Twain," Classical Journal, XX (December), 167-69.
On the first Tusculan Disputation and "The Death of Jean": "Each suffered the loss of a daughter, and each sought refuge in writing. Some of the sentiments we find in Cicero reappear in Mark Twain."

B23 *MITCHELL, EDWARD PAGE. Memoirs of an Editor. New York: Charles Scribner's Sons.
[Source: Asselineau (1954), No. 328: passim on MT.]

B24 *NELSON, W. H. "Mark Twain Out West," Methodist Quarterly Review, LXXIII (January), 65-83.
[Source: Asselineau (1954), No. 346; Methodist Review, LXXIII (1891) and CVII (1924) checked at Duke University without success—T.A.T.]

B25 *O'HIGGINS, HARVEY, and EDWARD H. REEDE, M.D. The American Mind in Action New York and London: Harper & Brothers.
[Sources: Asselineau (1954), No. 329 ("A Chapter on Twain, pp. 26-49, takes up again Brooks's thesis: Mark Twain 'was as profound a biological failure as America has produced.'"). Also discussed in Claudia C. Morrison, Freud and the Critic: The Early Use of Depth Psychology in Literary Criticism (1968), pp. 112-13 (the discussions of Margaret Fuller and of MT "represent in some respects more rounded treatments of their subjects than the full-length Freudian biographies of them written at the same time."]

B26 PAINE, ALBERT BIGELOW. "Mark Twain—Boy and Man. The Story of His Life," Mentor, XII (May), 3-20.
Condensed biography, illustrated; contains no new information.

B27 PEARSON, EDMUND LESTER. "Huckleberry and Sherlock," Outlook (New York), CXXXVIII (October 15), 256-57.
A review-article on Arthur Conan Doyle's Memories and Adventures and Mark Twain's Autobiography; the latter is "a great and grievous disappointment...the book consists of a great deal that was printed years ago in the North American Review, together with other pages which are superfluous after Mr. Paine's magnificent biography."

1924 - Shorter Writings

B28 RAYMOND, E. T. "The Victorian Humorist,"
     London Mercury, X (August), 374-86.
          On MT, pp. 378-79: "Mark Twain offers per-
     haps the supreme illustration of this nine-
     teenth-century complacency" in his views
     concerning language, morals, philosophy--
     and foreigners.

B29 RICE, CLARENCE C., M.D. "Mark Twain as His
     Physician Knew Him," Mentor, XII (May),
     48-49.
          Chiefly anecdotal, on cigars, billiards,
     shirts, spelling, etc. As a speaker, "He
     had two voices, two styles of speech and
     delivery: the humorous, slow-spoken drawl,
     and, on rare occasions, the loud and sonor-
     ous voice of the eloquent orator." Notes
     MT's love for the word "gaudy."

B30 RODGERS, CLEVELAND. "The Many-Sided Mark
     Twain," Mentor, XII (May), 29-44.
          A rather general discussion and a number
     of photographs of MT, his homes, and Missou-
     ri scenes.

B31 ROGERS, CAMERON. "In Which Mark Twain Reveals
     Himself," World's Work, XLVIII (October),
     679-81.
          A review of Mark Twain's Autobiography:
     appreciative, uncritical; concerned with
     content rather than form.

B32 *ROSENFELD, PAUL. [Essay on Van Wyck Brooks;
     speculates on his blind spot concerning MT.]
     Port of New York.
          [Source: Cited in James R. Vitelli,
     Van Wyck Brooks (1969), p. 113.]

B33 SEABRIGHT, J. M. "A Shrine to the Prince of
     Humorists," Literary Digest International
     Book Review, II (November), 848-49.
          On the Mark Twain Memorial Park at Flori-
     da, Missouri.

B34 SEITZ, DON C. "Mark Twain's Autobiography,"
     Bookman (New York), LX (December), 446-48.
          A review. Chiefly descriptive; enjoys the
     rambling. "It sometimes seems in reading
     Mark Twain that he was far too contemptu-
     ous of himself, and this fact the 'auto-
     biography' emphasizes."

B35 SHAW, BERNARD. Saint Joan: a Chronicle Play
     in Six Scenes and an Epilogue. New York:
     Brentano's.
          In "Preface," pp. xxv-xli, argues that
     MT's JA fails to put Joan in the context of
     her time: his portrait "makes her creator
     ridiculous, and yet, being the work of a
     man of genius, remains a credible human
     goodygoody in spite of her creator's infatu-
     ation"; moreover, MT misunderstands Joan's
     judges.

B36 *SPRINGFIELD, LINCOLN. Some Piquant People.
     London: T. Fisher Unwin.
          Contains two MT anecdotes, one concerning
     Darwin. [Source: Starrett (1945), p. 1.]

B37 STANTON, THEODORE. "Mark Twain's 'Lost Napole-
     on,'" Stratford Monthly (Boston), VII
     (April), 36-41.
          On the rock formation to be seen from the
     Rhône, resembling Napoleon, and described
     in "The Lost Napoleon" in Europe and Else-
     where. Stanton was unsuccessful in a search
     for the formation, undertaken at MT's re-
     quest; Albert Bigelow Paine described his
     own successful search in a chapter in his
     book, The Car that Went Abroad, 1921.B13,
     and later wrote that he had seen the forma-
     tion several times. Stanton quotes from a
     conversation with MT on the subject, and
     from an MT letter of October, 1901.

B38 STEINDORFF, ULRICH. "Mark Twain's Broad Ger-
     man Grin. New Translations Have Helped to
     Restore a Lost Sense of Humor," New York
     Times Book Review (July 13), p. 6.
          On the growth of MT's reputation in Ger-
     many; he is an important writer.

B39 *STEUART, JOHN A. Robert Louis Stevenson: A
     Critical Biography. Boston, II, 135.
          MT's description of RLS, after a meeting
     in New York in April, 1888. [Source: Quot-
     ed by Baetzhold (1970), pp. 203-204.]

B40 STRATE, JESSIE B. "Mark Twain and Geography,"
     Journal of Geography, XXIII (March), 81-92.
          She finds MT's work filled with passages
     she can read to her high-school classes in
     geology and commercial geography to give
     them a sense of a place, people, geographi-
     cal features, or the passage of time.

B41 VAN DOREN, CARL. "Posthumous Thunder," Satur-
     day Review of Literature, I (October 25),
     225.
          A review of Mark Twain's Autobiography,
     which "bears witness on many pages that Mark
     Twain was, for all his rough power, a man
     imperfectly schooled in any kind of knowl-
     edge or any kind of logic." Although the
     book contains no explosions "it crackles
     constantly, and now and then it stuns. The
     question remains: Is there more of it some-
     where?"

B42 VAN DOREN, MARK. [Review: Mark Twain's Auto-
     biography.] Nation, CXIX (November 12),
     524.
          No order, no stirring disclosures of MT's
     private opinions, but "first-rate writing,"
     or, rather, "first-rate talk."

B43 WHITE, EDGAR. "The Old Home Town," Mentor,
     XII (May), 51-53.
          Description of Hannibal, with anecdotes.

B44 WILSON, FRANCIS. Francis Wilson's Life of
     Himself. Boston and New York: Houghton
     Mifflin Company.
          On MT at the Players Club in New York, and
     several anecdotes, pp. 298-301; includes MT
     photograph.

B45 WOOLF, LEONARD. "Mark Twain," Nation & Athenaeum, XXXVI (November 8), 217.
A review of Mark Twain's Autobiography, interesting for its "trenchant outspokenness," though "not quite so unreserved as one might be led to expect from the Preface." Praises MT's "literary craftsmanship.... But behind the clarity and exactness of style was something more--a very good brain. Mark Twain's humour is often very much on the surface; it covers an intense seriousness and a highly intellectual interest in things and ideas."

1925 A BOOKS

A1 *CLEMENS, SAMUEL L. Mark Twain, 1601, or Conversation at the Social Fireside as It Was in the Time of the Tudors, introduction by Charles Erskine Wood, and other letters by Mark Twain. New York: Grabhorn Press.
[Source: Asselineau (1954), No. 363.]

A2 LAWTON, MARY. A Lifetime with Mark Twain. The Memories of Katy Leary, for Thirty Years His Faithful and Devoted Servant. Written by Mary Lawton. New York: Harcourt, Brace and Company.
A servant's view, as told to Mary Lawton, of persons and incidents in MT's life; useful for extending the perspective furnished by Paine and others. Illustrated.

A3 SCHÖNEMANN, FRIEDRICH. Mark Twain als Literarische Persönlichkeit. Jenaer Germanistische Forschungen, Heft 8. Jena: Verlag der Frommannschen Buchhandlung (Walter Biedermann).
Reveals the impressive breadth of MT's reading. Summed up, with the reviews it received, in Hemminghaus, Mark Twain in Germany (1939).

1925 B SHORTER WRITINGS

B1 ANDERSON, SHERWOOD. Dark Laughter. New York: Boni & Liveright, pp. 14-18, 100, 168.
A work of fiction. Anderson's John Stockton (alias "Bruce Dudley") thinks about MT in Hartford, on the river, piloting, writing HF; regrets that MT didn't describe the less glamorous things he had seen on the river, and when he returned to finish LOM, why didn't he write an epic of what had been destroyed, instead of filling the book with statistics and old jokes? (pp. 14-18). On "a kind of big continental poetry" of the river that "Mark Twain had almost got and didn't dare try to quite get" (p. 100). The character Aline remembers IA, which her father had loved but which "had really been nothing but a kind of small boy's rather nasty disdain of things he couldn't understand" (p. 168).

B2 ANON. "Mark Twain as a Billard Fan," Literary Digest, LXXXVI (July 25), 55.
Anecdotes and an MT note (to Mrs. Henry Rogers, thanking her for her husband's gift of a billiard-table), excerpted from Willie Hoppe's book, Thirty Years of Billiards.

B3 ANON. [Review: Mark Twain's Autobiography.] Edinburgh Review, CCXLI (January), 203.
"He has let imagination have as free a reign as memory. The result is a series of descriptions--humorous, satirical, or pathetic--in which the reader sees not so much the subject as the personality of the author developing from his sympathies or full-blooded hatreds."

B4 ANON. [Review: Mary Lawton, A Lifetime with Mark Twain.] Saturday Review of Literature, II (December 26), 452.
The book chiefly concerns minor domestic details, although it casts light on MT's view of the incident involving Maxim Gorki; it also shows that "native kindliness and unselfishness characterized both master and servant. Malice simply did not exist in either."

B5 BARRUS, CLARA. The Life and Letters of John Burroughs. Boston and New York: Houghton Mifflin; reissued New York: Russell & Russell, 1968. 2 vols. II, 87-88, 221-22.
Journal entry of November 8, 1905 says MT was "very diverting, as he always is" at the first dinner of the American Academy of Arts and Letters (p. 87); at the MT seventieth birday dinner in December, Burroughs sat by Mrs. Henry Rogers; "Her husband sat at Mark Twain's table.... How Mark Twain can accept favors from him is a mystery." MT's speech was amusing, but only because of the delivery (p. 88). When sitting for a bust by Pietro in 1915, Burroughs was kept still by friends reading to him from MT's Joan of Arc (pp. 221-22).

B6 BEERS, HENRY A. "Among the New Books," Yale Review, n.s. XV (Autumn), 162-65.
Includes a review of Mark Twain's Autobiography (1924): "The charm of the book is its informality."

B7 BIGELOW, POULTNEY. Seventy Summers. New York: Longmans, Green & Co.; London: Edward Arnold & Co., II, 156-165-68.
Describes MT in Johannesburg (1896), in poor health but courteous toward individuals who claimed to have known him in the West; but afterward: "I never thought there could be so many G--d d----d liars in any one town! They were not even intelligent liars-- they gave dates when I was not even in America and they named places that I never heard of before--the blank-blank damned liars!" (pp. 166-67). Also tells of MT in London (1899), tricked into attending a large dinner at the Goerz residence with the promise that it was to be a "family" party of four (p. 168).

1925 - Shorter Writings

B8   BIRON, CHARTRES. [Review: Mark Twain's Autobiography (1924).] London Mercury, XI
(January), 325-26.
"A mere scrap-book of detached and incoherent incidents"; "Yet to read the passages
in this book about his wife and children is
to realize how exquisitely he could write on
occasion."

B9   *BRAGMAN, LOUIS J. "The Medical Wisdom of
Mark Twain," Annals of Medical History, VII,
425-39.
[Source: Asselineau (1954), No. 382:
"Made up of extracts from his works."]

B10   BRANDL, ALOIS. [Review: Friedrich Schönemann, Mark Twain als literarische Persönlichkeit.] Die Literatur (Stuttgart),
XXVII, No. 10, 627-28.
Chiefly descriptive [In German].

B11   *[BROWNELL, GEORGE HIRAM (?)] "Sam Slick,
The Connecticut Clockmaker, Original of
Uncle Sam and Source of Inspiration for
Dickens, Mark Twain and Other Humorists,"
Dearborn Independent (The Ford Internation-
al Weekly), XXV (October 10).
[Source: Reprinted in Twainian, XVI
(March-April, 1957), 3-4; (May-June), 4.]
Contains very little on MT, except for argu-
ing that CY and IA follow the example of
Thomas Chandler Haliburton's "Sam Slick" in
the Yankee's irreverent view of the glories
of the old world. (Article somewhat vague-
ly attributed to Brownell by Chester L.
Davis in Twainian.]

B12   CATHER, KATHERINE DUNLAP. "The Boy Who Went
Back," in her The Younger Days of Famous
Writers (New York and London: The Century
Company), pp. 185-204.
A children's account of MT's boyhood, pro-
viding no new information.

B13   COLLINS, JOSEPH. "Litterateurs: American
Writers," in his The Doctor Looks at Biography: Psychological Studies of Life and
Letters (New York: George H. Doran Company), pp. 63-97; pp. 73-79 on MT's Autobiography.
Appreciative; praises his warmth, humanity, and tenderness. "His was the antithesis
of the Messianic complex. He had a simple
heart, and an intricate soul."

B14   ELLINGER, JOH. [Review: Friedrich Schönemann, Mark Twain als literarische Persönlichkeit.] Anglia Beiblatt, XXXVI
(December), 372-74.
Notes that Schönemann has revealed MT as
better read and more influenced by his reading than generally realized; warmly recom-
mends the book. [In German.]

B15   *FEDERICO, P. J. "Mark Twain as an Inventor,"
Journal of the Patent Office Society, VIII,
75-79.
[Source: Asselineau (1954), No. 383.]

B16   GARBETT, A. S. "When Mark Twain Sang Spiritu-
als," in his department, "The Musical Scrap-
Book," Etude, XLII (December), 854.
An excerpt from Mary Lawton's transcription of Katy Leary's recollections in Pictorial Review (now more readily available in
her A Lifetime with Mark Twain, 1925.B24),
with only a very brief headnote.

B17   GESSFORD, J. G. [Photograph of Mark Twain.]
Bookman (New York), LXI (March), facing
p. 31.

B18   GILLIS, JAMES M. "Mark Twain," in his False
Prophets (New York: The Macmillan Company),
pp. 125-45.
MT's early works are crude, and appeal,
as Henry James says, to "rudimentary minds."
His final despair is the product of life-long
scoffing at sacred things: "If ever a man
sowed what he reaped, it was Mark Twain."

B19   GOLDBERG, ISAAC. The Man Mencken: A Biographical and Critical Survey. New York: Simon
and Schuster, passim.
The many references to MT in the index
lead to statements of his influence on
Mencken, who read HF at the age of seven,
and comparisons of Mencken to MT.

B20   HARWOOD, H. C. "Mark Twain," Spectator,
CXXXV (December 19), 1146, 1148.
A review of the Florida Edition of The
Works of Mark Twain. Ranks MT low as a humorist and satirist, who "only succeeded in
satirizing what he did not understand" and
lacked the courage of a Voltaire or a Swift.
"He need not, by the way, have been afraid
of the effect on religion of his doubts; at
his shrewdest, he would only have become the
William Jennings Bryan of agnosticism. But
it was not timidity that makes the mass of
Mark Twain's work a desert of dullness. It
was stupidity. He lacked any kind of philosophy." TS and HF, however, "deserve every
one of the superlative praises lavished upon
them. They are bright with the magic that
only memories of boyhood can cast, and informed with the sympathies that could only
be given by one who ever remained a child at
heart as, alas! he did in mental development."

B21   HIGGINS, AILEEN CLEVELAND. "She Was Mark
Twain's Sweetheart," Collier's, LXXV
(June 27), 32.
On Mrs. Laura Hawkins Frazer, in 1925 a
cheerful, elderly lady; she had long been
superintendent of Hannibal's "Home for the
Friendless."

B22   HOPPE, WILLY. "Mark Twain, a Great Old Bil-
liard Fan," in his Thirty Years of Billiards,
(New York: G. P. Putnam's Sons), pp. 190-14.
[Source: 1975 Dover Publications reprint.]
MT attended Hoppe's 1906 match with George
Butler Sutton; pressed to address the crowd,

(HOPPE, WILLY)
he told of losing a game to a Nevada shark who played him left-handed--and conceded afterward that he was a left-handed man. MT attended a number of championship matches.

B23 INGLIS, REWEY BELLE. "A Lesson on Mark Twain," English Journal, XIV (March), 221-32.
This lesson "was part of a three-months' course in American literature given to juniors in the University High School.... The students were not told that a stenographic record was being made, lest the spontaneity of the lesson be spoiled." Text of class discussion.

B24 LAWTON, MARY. [Excerpts from her A Lifetime with Mark Twain, as Told by Katy Leary to Mary Lawton.] Literary Digest, LXXXV (April 25: "A Maid's-Eye View of Mark Twain"), 36, 38, 40; LXXXVI (August 22: "Mark Twain's 'Glory Halleluiah!'"), 38, 40.
Reprinted from Pictorial Review, XXVI [(April-September, according to Asselineau (1954), No. 361.)]

B25 LUDEKE, HENRY. [Review: Van Wyck Brooks, The Ordeal of Mark Twain (1922) and Friedrich Schönemann, Mark Twain als Literarische Persönlichkeit (1925).] Deutsche Literaturzeitung für Kritik der internationalen Wissenschaft, XLVI:2 (12 September), 1802-1814.
Summarizes Brooks's thesis, but expresses some reservations; argues that Schönemann ought to have made more of MT's western backgrounds. [In German.]

B26 PAINE, ALBERT BIGELOW. "Innocents at Home: How Mark Twain Dictated His Life Story to Him in 'Cowboy' Billiard Games or Lying Comfortably in Bed, Told by His Biographer," Collier's, LXXV (January 3), 5-6, 45.
A popular account, with an amusing description of MT at the billiard table.

B27 _____. Joan of Arc: Maid of France. New York: The Macmillan Company, 2 vols., passim.
There are a few quotations from MT in the two volumes, and a tribute to his JA in the introduction, but nothing significant.

B28 *_____. "Who Wrote 1601?" Two Worlds, December.
[Source: Twainian, II (June, 1943), 6; describes this as an excerpt from his Biography, "also slightly-censored version of Twain's '1601.'"]

B29 RANDALL, A. W. G. [Review: Friedrich Schönemann, Mark Twain als Literärische Persönlicheit.] Saturday Review of Literature, II (September 5), 108.
"A very thorough, and yet very lively and challenging piece of criticism," which

should help correct the European misconception of MT as unliterary, a mere fun-maker.

B30 *SCHÖNEMANN, F. "Mark Twains Autobiographie," Hannoverscher Kurier, August 5; also in Magdeburger Zeitung, October 4.
[Source: Asselineau (1954), No. 387.]

B31 SINCLAIR, UPTON. "The Uncrowned King," in his Mammonart: An Essay in Economic Interpretation (Pasadena, California: Published by the Author), pp. 326-33.
"Mark Twain had in him the making of one of the world's great satirists.... But he was not allowed to express himself as an artist; he must emulate his father-in-law, the Elmira coal-dealer." Briefly describes a meeting with MT in Bermuda: "I saw that he was kind, warm-hearted, and also full of rebellion against capitalist greed and knavery; but he was an old man, and a sick man, and I did not try to probe the mystery of his life." Also passim on MT; indexed.

B32 TANDY, JENNETTE. Crackerbox Philosophers in American Humor and Satire. New York: Columbia University Press, passim.
A published doctoral dissertation, this also appears in a variant form without thesis note. The few brief references to MT are based on familiar sources and there is little critical discussion, but Miss Tandy anticipated later scholarship in her passing remark that "Mark Twain's indebtedness to Southwestern humor has never been fully acknowledged" (p. 94).

B33 VAN DOREN, CARL. "Mark Twain and Bernard Shaw," Century, CIX (n.s. LXXXVII; March), 705-10.
A comparison: Shaw is the more interested in pure ideas, MT in rounded characters; in their treatments of Joan of Arc Shaw portrays a clash of individual and institution, while for MT innocence ultimately loses to evil. Reprinted in Scott (1955), pp. 175-82.

B34 _____. "Two in One," Century, CIX (January), 429-30.
A review of Paine's two-volume edition of Mark Twain's Autobiography (1924) as "a work which with admirable flexibility fits itself to his strong, rich, casual nature."

B35 _____, and MARK VAN DOREN. American and British Literature since 1890. London and New York: The Century Company, p. 44.
Calls MT's last years "that fascinating chapter of his life which was to reveal him as a man of bitter thought as well as a humorist, a commentator upon the times in unstinted language, a kind of prophet who was to be listened to with more respect after his death than before it." Other references to MT in this school manual are minor.

1925 - Shorter Writings

B36 *WATKINS, LOUISE W. Four Short Stories and a
     Play. Los Angeles, California: Privately
     Printed.
        [Source: Asselineau (1954), No. 371:
     "Contains a short essay on Twain."]

B37 WATSON, AARON. A Newspaper Man's Memories.
     London: Hutchinson & Co., pp. 281-83.
        On MT's election to honorary membership
     in the Savage Club in London, in 1899; al-
     though he had been making jokes about being
     accused of stealing the Ascot Cup he ap-
     parently was not pleased at being presented
     with a large replica. Says MT contributed
     a chapter to Watson's book about the Savage
     Club.

B38 WEBSTER, DORIS, and CHARLES WEBSTER. "White-
     washing Jane Clemens," Bookman (New York),
     LXI (July), 531-35.
        A portrait of MT's mother as a lively,
     independent person with a good sense of
     humor; she was not a Puritan (or any other
     sort of Yankee), and certainly not the
     blighting influence on her son that Van
     Wyck Brooks and Harvey O'Higgins have de-
     picted.

B39 WHITE, EDGAR. "Tom Sawyer and Huckleberry
     Finn Memorial Statue. The Immortal Boys
     Will Stand in Bronze in Mark Twain's Own
     Home Town," Mentor, XIII (October), 54-55.

B40 WINTER, WILLIAM. The Life of David Belasco.
     (As reissued, New York: Benjamin Blom,
     Inc., 1972). 2 vols. I, 64-68, 365-67.
     ["Third Edition, First Published in New
     York, 1925. Reissued 1972 by Benjamin
     Blom, Inc. New York, N.Y."]
        On the play of The Gilded Age, including
     the text of a letter by John T. Raymond
     (who played Colonel Sellers) to the New York
     Sun, December 2, 1874, and a lengthy quota-
     tion from "W.W." in "The Wallet of Time," on
     the contribution of Raymond to the success
     of the play (pp. 64-68). On the dramatiza-
     tion of The Prince and the Pauper, suggested
     by Elsie Leslie, who played both Tom Canty
     and Prince Edward, and on Belasco's impa-
     tience with the cast (pp. 365-67). Margaret
     Duckett lists a 1918 publication for this
     book (New York: Moffett, Yard and Company)
     in her Mark Twain and Bret Harte (Norman,
     1964), p. 351.

B41 WOOLF, LEONARD. "Mark Twain," Nation & Athena-
     eum, XXXVI (September 26), 765.
        A review of The Florida Edition of Mark
     Twain (Chatto & Windus), with estimates of
     TA ("first-rate journalism"), P&P (betrays
     "a commonness and tawdriness, a lack of
     sensitiveness, which do not matter to the
     impetuous appetite of youth, but which can-
     not be ignored by the more discriminating
     and exacting taste of middle-age"), and HF;
     this, "in humour as in everything else, is
     far the best thing Mark Twain wrote. Its
     freshness, gusto, exuberant vitality are

astonishing," especially under the influence
of the river; there is a falling-off after
the King and Duke come aboard. Woolf feels
that MT's humor is losing its old charm,
and ranks it below that of "Mr. Dooley"
[Finley Peter Dunne].

1926 A BOOKS

A1   *CLEMENS, SAMUEL L. Rapporto della visita di
     Capitan Tempesta in Paradiso, translated by
     Laura Balini, preface by Conrado Alvaro.
     Aquila: Vecchioni.
        [Source: Asselineau (1954), No. 393.]

A2   _____, and BRET HARTE; ed. John Howell.
     Sketches of the Sixties. Being Forgotten
     Material Now Collected for the First Time
     from "The Californian," 1864-67. San Fran-
     cisco: John Howell.
        Now superceded by the 1927 revised edi-
     tion, (1927.A1).

A3   MAYFIELD, JOHN S. Mark Twain vs. The Street
     Railway Co. Introduction by Charles Finger.
     N.p.: Privately Printed.
        A pamphlet containing two MT letters
     (May 5, 13, 1906; reproduced in facsimile),
     together with affidavits and correspondence
     from the Metropolitan Street Railway Com-
     pany involving MT's complaint that his
     daughter Clara had been short-changed by a
     conductor; he received a twenty-cent refund.

1926 B SHORTER WRITINGS

B1   ANON. "Sam Clemens in 'Sideburns' to 'Dear
     Friend Annie,'" Literary Digest, LXXXIX
     (May 8), 36, 38, 42, 44, 46.
        On the discovery of five letters from MT
     to Annie Elizabeth Taylor in May-June, 1857
     when she was a girl of seventeen. Three of
     these letters have since been lost; those of
     May 25 and June 1 are printed here, together
     with background material and photographs of
     MT and Annie Elizabeth Taylor. [From Kansas
     City Star Magazine, n.d.]

B2   BACHELLER, IRVING. Opinions of a Cheerful
     Yankee. Indianapolis: The Bobbs-Merrill Co.
        Recollections of visits to MT at his homes
     in Hartford and on Fifth Avenue, and a lunch-
     eon with him "at a little Bohemian club or-
     ganized by myself and Stephen Crane and Ed-
     ward Marshall and Willis Hawkins, all edi-
     tors or special writers on the metropolitan
     press," pp. 6-11.

B3   *CESTRE, CHARLES, and B. GAGNOT. Anthologie de
     la Littérature Américaine. Paris: Delagrave.
        [Source: Asselineau (1954), No. 394.]

B4   CHILDS, MARQUIS W. "The Home of Mark Twain,"
     American Mercury, IX (September), 101-105.
        Describes Hannibal, Missouri of the later
     day as ugly, commercial, and taken over by
     the Rotary Club. Near Bird Street (with its

(CHILDS, MARQUIS W.)
three bordellos) is the Mark Twain Home. "Within is a hodge-podge of relics of the great man. Every citizen of Hannibal has gone to his attic and brought forth a chair on which Mark once sat, or a glass from which he once drank. The front room, into which one steps directly from the street, has about it an air of mouldering decay, filled as it is with a conglomerate array of junk. Albert Bigelow Paine has contributed many of the pieces."

B5 DONOVAN, M. M. "Custodian of a Famous Cabin," Sunset: The Pacific Monthly, LVII (September), 47.
Photograph of "William R. Gillis, Custodian of the Mark Twain Cabin on Jackass Hill," with reminiscences.

B6 FISCHER, WALTHER. [Review: Friedrich Schönemann, Mark Twain als literarische Persönlichkeit (1925).] Englische Studien, LXI (December), 135-39.
This review is itself a thoughtful investigation of MT's thinking, taking into account a number of his published works; notes the romantic element in MT, and suggests that his pessimism was personal rather than a result of literary influences.

B7 GARNETT, DAVID. "Mark Twain: 1835-1910," in Walter James Turner, ed., Great Names; Being an Anthology of English and American Literature from Chaucer to Francis Thompson (New York: The Dial Press), pp. 261-62.
A brief introduction to selections from IA and RI; follows the interpretation of MT by Van Wyck Brooks.

B8 GOURMONT, RÉMY DE. "Études de Littérature Américaine: II.--L'Humour et les Humoristes," Promenades Littéraires, 6e Serie, pp. 87-138.
Notes MT's rare power of observation and gift for language, and his understanding of Negro speech and psychology. He could have been an Aristophanes, but with the encouragement of the public he chose to play the buffoon.

B9 GRIMES, ABSALOM. "Campaigning with Mark Twain," in his Confederate Mail Runner, Edited from Captain Grimes' Own Story by M. M. Quaife. (New Haven: Yale University Press; London: Humphrey Milford, Oxford University Press), pp. 1-19.
Grimes claims to have been associated with MT as a pilot and in the Confederate irregular unit described by MT in "The Private History of a Campaign that Failed." Quaife's introduction describes the book, written in 1910-1911, as "an old-age narration," with many possibilities for error (p. xi). Asselineau (1954), No. 724 also lists a 1926 edition of this book.

B10 *HALDEMAN-JULIUS, EMANUEL. Iconoclastic Literary Reactions. Kansas City, Kansas: Big Blue Book, No. B-16.
[Source: Asselineau (1954), No. 399: "Contains three articles on Mark Twain."]

B11 HOUSE, EDWARD M. The Intimate Papers of Colonel House, Arranged as a Narrative by Charles Seymour. Boston and New York: Houghton Mifflin Company, I, 21.
Paine took Captain Bill McDonald of the Texas Rangers to dinner at MT's home on Fifth Avenue; House came later, to see McDonald shooting billiards awkwardly, sighting his cue "just as if it were a rifle.... It entertained Mr. Clemens immensely. When we went upstairs Clemens ran and Bill ran after, as if to catch him, but did not do so."

B12 HULBERT, MARY ALLEN. "Other Celebrities," Liberty, II (March 6), 12-14.
On pp. 13-14, recollections of MT and Henry Rogers in Bermuda. MT's secretary, Miss Lyon, always referred to MT as "The King"--a sobriquet Mrs. Hulbert took to be a reference to the disreputable character in HF. On p. 12, photograph: "Mrs. Hulbert, at extreme left, and party of her guests, with Mark Twain and H. H. Rogers in the foreground."

B13 *JANTZEN, H. [Review: Friedrich Schönemann, Mark Twain als literarische Persönlichkeit (1925).] Zeitschrift für französischen und englischen Unterricht, XXV, 368-69.
[Source: Asselineau (1954), No. 406.]

B14 JONES, HOWARD MUMFORD. [Review: Friedrich Schönemann, Mark Twain als literarische Persönlichkeit (1925).] Journal of English and Germanic Philology, XXV (January), 130-31.
"The sole defects of the monograph" are a European's occasional "misreadings of Twain and the United States" and "a tendency to mistake parallelism for indebtedness, or at least to leave this impression with the reader." With only these reservations, "no summary or extract can do justice to the brilliance and breadth of this monograph.... All future interpretations are bound to be influenced by these essays."

B15 LAW, FREDERICK HOUK. "Samuel Langhorne Clemens (Mark Twain): Humorist," in his Modern Great Americans: Short Biographies of Twenty Great Americans of Modern Times Who Won Wide Recognition for Achievements in Various Types of Activity (Students' Edition). (New York, London: The Century Company), pp. 77-91.
Provides no new information and is marred by factual errors: states that the Clemens house in Hannibal was made of brick, that "mark twain" means "up to the mark of two feet," that he briefly owned the Comstock Lode, prospected for gold with Bret Harte,

1926 - Shorter Writings

(LAW, FREDERICK HOUK)
and made a profit of $100,000 from his
patented scrap-book.

B16   MUMFORD, LEWIS. The Golden Day: A Study in
American Experience and Culture. New York:
Boni and Liveright Publishers. Reprinted
by W. W. Norton & Company in 1934; in paperback, Boston: Beacon Press, 1957 (with different pagination).
    Chapter IV, "The Pragmatic Acquiescence,"
treats MT on pp. 170-79. MT felt contempt
for mankind as a result of the cheapening of
values in the miserable struggle for existence in Missouri and Nevada, took the com-
forts of his century and the society that
produced them too much to heart, and "did
not see that his Yankee mechanic was as absurd as Arthur himself." "In a different
fashion from Howells, Mark Twain was afraid
of his imagination," and turned to burlesque
his impulses toward poetry or beauty. His
despair was the result of accepting the values around him although he realized that
they were not central human values. Reprinted in Scott (1955), pp. 183-87; excerpt in
Leary (1962), pp. 81-82.

B17   ORCUTT, WILLIAM DANA. "Friends through the
Pen," in his In Quest of the Perfect Book
(Boston: Little, Brown & Co.), pp. 171-77.
    On a visit to MT at the Villa di Quarto
(Florence) three days before the death of
Olivia Clemens, and on MT moved to tears at
his seventieth birthday dinner in New York.

B18   PHELPS, WILLIAM LYON. As I Like It, Third
Series. New York, London: Charles Scribner's Sons.
    "This book contains selections from the
articles of the same name printed in Scribner's Magazine from September, 1924 to
January, 1926, inclusive." Indexed by
Dr. Frederick Pottle, passim on MT.

B19   *SHERWOOD, ROBERT EDMUND. "Regarding Tom Sawyer and Others," in his Here We Are Again:
Recollections of an Old Circus Clown (Indianapolis: The Bobbs-Merrill Co.),
pp. 213-18.
    [Source: Asselineau (1954), No. 403.]

1927 A BOOKS

A1   CLEMENS, SAMUEL L., and BRET HARTE, edited by
John Howell. Sketches of the Sixties, by
Bret Harte and Mark Twain. Being Forgotten
Material Collected for the First Time from
"The Californian," 1864-1867. San Francisco: John Howell.
    A revision of the 1926 edition (1926.A2).
The introduction by Howell gives background
of San Francisco in the 1860's, and of The
Californian and MT's and Harte's association
with it. There is also a list of all their
articles in The Californian, with dates of
publication. This 1927 revision includes
material not in the 1926 edition.

1927 B SHORTER WRITINGS

B1   BENNETT, JAMES O'DONNELL. Much Loved Books:
Best Sellers of Yesterday. New York: Liveright Publishing Company, pp. 210-22, 459.
    Chapter XXX, "Mark Twain's 'Adventures of
Huckleberry Finn,'" consists of quotations
from the book and appreciative words by Bennett (pp. 210-16). Chapter XXXI, "How Huckleberry Finn Was Written" includes information from the Paine biography and quotes
familiar praise of the book by several critics. Provides no new information or original
judgment (pp. 217-22). There is a brief
bibliography of secondary material on p. 459;
most of it is well known and all is included
in the present bibliography. The material on
HF was reprinted in Bennett's paperback Much
Loved Books (Greenwich, Connecticut: Faw-
cett Publications, Inc., 1959), pp. 128-40.

B2   BUSBEY, L. WHITE. "A Distinguished Lobbyist,"
in his Uncle Joe Cannon: The Story of a
Pioneer American as told to L. White Busbey,
for 20 years his private secretary (New York:
Henry Holt and Company), pp. 270-81.
    On pp. 270-75, describes MT's efforts in
behalf of stronger copyright legislation.

B3   BUXBAUM, KATHERINE. "Mark Twain and American
Dialect," American Speech, II (February),
233-36.
    In HF "The inconsistencies of Huck's
speech can hardly be attributed to anything
but carelessness," although it may have its
counterpart in the alternation between correct and incorrect usage by actual persons.
Nonetheless, MT's "admirable use of phonetic
spelling" is superior to that of Lowell and
others, and even his inconsistency adds to
the book's unstudied charm.

B4   ERSKINE, JOHN. "The First and Best Story of
Main Street: John Erskine Tells Why Huckleberry Finn has won a place among the Immortals," Delineator, CX (February), 10, 94,
97.
    TS is "built up with anecdotes, each one
complete in itself, and none developed beyond the point of the joke"; in MT's better-
constructed book, Huck "tells us far more
than he knows; through his naive confessions
we see the panorama of his world and become
sophisticated. We are really studying ourselves." Reprinted in Erskine's The Delight
of Great Books (1928), pp. 263-74; also reprinted in Lettis (1962), pp. 297-304.

B5   ESPENSHADE, A. H. "Tom Sawyer's Fiftieth
Birthday: A Brief Sketch of Mark Twain's
Life," St. Nicholas, LIV (August), 808-809.
    Biography for young readers, containing no
unusual information.

B6   GRIMES, ABSALOM. "Campaigning with Mark Twain
Twain," Missouri Historical Review, XXI
(January), 188-201.

(GRIMES, ABSALOM)
An excerpt from his Absalom Grimes, Confederate Mail Runner (1926), describing Civil War service with MT.

B7 *HARBECK, HANS. "Amerikanische Humor," Der Kreis: Zeitschrift für künstliche Kultur, IV, 276-84.
[Source: Asselineau (1954), No. 427.]

B8 HAZARD, LUCY LOCKWOOD. "Mark Twain: 'Wild West Humorist of the Pacific Slope,'" "The Psychic Frontier," and "Mark Twain: Son and Satirist of the Gilded Age," in her The Frontier in American Literature (New York: Thomas Y. Crowell Company), pp. 198-200, 200-201, 220-30.
"If the frontier of Bret Harte is melodrama, the frontier of Mark Twain is farce" (p. 198). Criticizes Brooks for lacking humor (p. 201), and notes the freedom from convention on the frontier (p. 201). On MT's "compassion for failure," and therefore less worship of success than Brooks suggests (pp. 222-23); notes MT's affection for Colonel Sellers and contempt for Senator Dilworthy (p. 227).

B9 *LESSING, O. E. Brücken über den Atlantik-- Beiträge zum amerikanischen und deutschen Geistesleben. Stuttgart: Deutsche Verlags-Anstalt.
[Source: Asselineau (1954), No. 419.]

B10 MEYER, HAROLD. "Mark Twain on the Comstock," Southwest Review, XII (April), 197-207.
A general account of MT in Nevada, adding nothing significant to Paine's 1912 biography. Not documented.

B11 NEVINS, ALLAN. The Emergence of Modern America, 1865-1878. Vol. VIII in A History of American Life, ed. Arthur M. Schlesinger and Dixon Ryan Fox (New York: The Macmillan Company), pp. 247-51 and passim.
Nevins is interested in MT's "rapid conquest of a half-reluctant national public and his success in presenting the remote frontier as well as the Mississippi Valley to the reading world" (p. 249), but his account is essentially a repetition of material from Paine and Howells and elsewhere his treatment is chiefly one of using MT's works to illustrate his own discussion of the age. There is no new information on MT and very little interpretation.

B12 QUINN, ARTHUR HOBSON. A History of the American Drama from the Civil War to the Present Day. New York and London: Harper & Brothers Publishers, 2 vols., passim.
On Ah Sin and the plays from The Gilded Age and The American Claimant, I, 110-16, with place and date of first performances, II, 299, 304, 332; also, brief note of other attempts at the drama by MT, and dramatizations of his works by others, I, 110-16. Briefly describes Augustin Daly's

Roughing It play, not a dramatization of the novel, but burlesquing the West of MT and Bret Harte in Act III (I, 20). Quotes a long paragraph from MT's curtain speech at the first night in New York of Ah Sin (I, 111-12).

B13 SADLEIR, MICHAEL. Trollope: A Commentary. London: Constable & Co., Ltd.
On p. 285, quotes a Trollope letter of July, 1873: he will dine with MT and Joaquin Miller the following week, at his club.

B14 SHERMAN, STUART. "Mark Twain's Last Phase," in his The Main Stream (New York, London: Charles Scribner's Sons), pp. 80-88.
A review of Mark Twain's Autobiography, originally in "Books," the literary supplement of the New York Herald Tribune, 1924 or 1925 (p. ix). Bad autobiography, but an "interesting hodgepodge.... As far as I can make out, he grew in sympathy, insight, bitterness, courage and passion to the end. At seventy he was a clear-eyed youth, pushing steadily forward toward a fresh conception of reality." MT had broken many of his chains, and is still "dangerous--like all free spirits."

B15 SPEAKMAN, HAROLD. "Becky and Ignition," in his Mostly Mississippi (New York: Dodd, Mead and Company), pp. 173-90.
Describes a visit to Hannibal, where one local citizen told him MT had been a poor steamboat pilot. Speakman visited Laura Hawkins Frazer (sketch of her, p. 178); she told him she and MT had never been lost in a cave, as described in TS.

B16 WOOD, CHARLES ERSKINE SCOTT. Heavenly Discourse. New York: The Vanguard Press, passim.
A series of satiric conversations in the next world, originally written for the Masses; only a few appeared before the demise of that journal. The cast includes God, Jesus, St. Peter, Socrates, Buddha, Socrates, and others, and MT participates in a number of conversations on such topics as "Freedom," "Censorship," "God on Catholicism and the K.K.K.," "God Advises Peter as to the Church," and "Satan Recovers His Reason."

1928 A BOOKS

A1 CLEMENS, SAMUEL L. The Adventures of Thomas Jefferson Snodgrass. Edited by Charles Honce, with a Foreword by Vincent Starrett, and a Note on "A Celebrated Village Idiot" by James O'Donnell Bennett. Chicago: Pascal Covici, Publisher, Inc.
Three travel letters in the Keokuk (Iowa) Post, November 1, 29, 1856; April 10, 1857. Bennett's "A Celebrated Village Idiot" is an anecdotal account of Orion Clemens, reprinted from the Chicago Tribune (n.d.)

A2 *CLEMENS, SAMUEL L. Selections, with notes by
Vincenzo Grasso. Palermo: R. Gino.
[Source: Asselineau (1954), No. 431.]

1928 B SHORTER WRITINGS

B1 ANON. "Mark Twain's Masonic Record," Grand
Lodge Bulletin, Grand Lodge of Iowa, A. F.
& A. M., XXIX (May), 575-76.
Describes a painting of MT at age 21,
"presented by Mrs. Orion Clemens some years
ago," and "now on display at the Iowa State
Insurance Company's office at Keokuk, Iowa."
[Reproduced on front cover, p. 561.] "Bro.
Ray V. Denslow, Grand Secretary, Grand
Council R. & S. M. of Missouri, gave an account of Mark Twain's Masonic record in
Scottish Rite Progress a few years ago,
from which the following extract is taken."
The lengthy extract tells of MT's election
to Polar Star Lodge No. 79; he received his
third degree in Masonry on July 10 [1861],
but was out of touch with his lodge when he
went to Nevada and "he allowed himself to
be temporarily suspended. He was reinstated
in April, 1867" before traveling on the
Quaker City to Europe and the Holy Land,
and while in the Holy Land he cut wood from
a cedar in the Forest of Lebanon and had it
made into a gavel for Polar Star Lodge No.
79. After his marriage he appears to have
ceased affiliation, although he and friends
played billiards at the old Masonic Club in
Elmira, New York. [Source: photocopy provided by courtesy of Charles T. Jackson,
Grand Secretary, Grand Lodge of Iowa, Iowa
Masonic Library, Cedar Rapids.]

B2 *BARTON, SIR DUNBAR PLUNKET. Links Between
Shakespeare and the Law. London: Faber &
Gwyer Ltd.
[Source: Asselineau (1954), No. 432;
notes comments on MT's Is Shakespeare Dead?]

B3 BECK, WARREN. "Huckleberry Finn versus The
Cash Boy," Education, XLIX (September),
1-13.
Compares HF to the turgid, shallow boy
stories of Horatio Alger, Jr.: Huck is
notable for his warmth, integrity, and wisdom, and he could grow with a college education as the Alger hero could not.

B4 BIKLE, LUCY LEFFINGWELL (CABLE). "Readings
with Mark Twain: Dr. Sevier (1884)," and
"More Readings with Mark Twain: Home in
Northampton (1885-1887)," in her George W.
Cable: His Life and Letters (New York:
Charles Scribner's Sons), pp. 114-36,
137-53.
Includes letters describing their joint
lecture tours, and on visits to the Clemens
home, with descriptions of the family.
[Also, reissued New York: Russell & Rus-
sell, 1967, with same pagination.]

B5 CHAPMAN, HELEN POST. My Hartford of the Nineteenth Century. Hartford: Edwin Valentine
Mitchell.
Mentions Joseph Twichell teaching MT to
ride a bicycle (p. 43), and MT presenting
Tiffany pins to the Saturday Morning Club
(p. 61).

B6 *COWPER, FREDERICK A. G. "The Hermit Story, as
Used by Voltaire and Mark Twain," in Papers,
Essays, and Stories by His Former Students,
in Honor of the Ninetieth Birthday of Charles
Frederick Johnson, ed. Odell Shepard and
Arthur Adams (Hartford, Connecticut: Trini-
ty College), pp. 313-37.
[Source: MHRA Annual Bibliography (1929),
No. 172; Asselineau (1954), No. 433; William
M. Gibson, ed., Mark Twain's Mysterious
Stranger Manuscripts (1969), p. 2.] Sug-
gests that sources for MS may include Chap-
ter XX ("L'hermite") of Voltaire's Zadig,
and Goethe's Faust.

B7 CRAVEN, THOMAS. "A Cure for Critics: Painting Defended from Both the Cynical and the
Rapturous," Bookman (New York), LXVIII
(October), 163-64.
In IA MT ought to have attacked the professional critics, rather than the old masters, about which both he and the critics
knew "precisely nothing."

B8 ERSKINE, JOHN. "Huckleberry Finn," in his
The Delight of Great Books. Indianapolis:
The Bobbs-Merrill Company, pp. 263-74.
A reprint of his 1927 article in Delinea-
tor (1927.B4).

B9 FRENCH, MRS. DANIEL CHESTER. [Anecdotes.]
Memories of a Sculptor's Wife (Boston and
New York: Houghton Mifflin Company),
pp. 159-61.
Describes MT at the Richard Watson Gilders'
in New York and repeats two stories he told
on himself: of being introduced to a poet
and telling her how funny her poems were
(only to discover she was not the poet he
had thought), and of sitting across the
aisle on the elevated train from a man who
stared, and finally told him he looked just
like Mark Twain.

B10 HOPE, ANTHONY. Memories and Notes. London:
Hutchinson & Co., pp. 172-73.
[Also listed in Asselineau (1954), No.
435 as Garden City: Doubleday, Doran &
Co.] Describes a heated debate between MT
and Lord Kelvin over whether any nation has
the right to deny others freedom to travel
or trade in its territory. Hope considers
MT's slow, drawling speech a disadvantage.
"At his best he is a great writer, but his
worst is terribly far below his best"; it
is a failing in humorists, as also in
Sterne.

B11   HOWELLS, WILLIAM DEAN. Life in Letters of William Dean Howells. Ed. by Mildred Howells. New York: Doubleday, Doran & Company. 2 vols. passim.
The MT-Howells correspondence is now available in a well-edited two-volume edition (1960), but there is still much of interest in what Howells wrote about MT to others, as in his letter to Charles Eliot Norton about "that hideous mistake of poor Clemens's" in his disastrous speech at the Whittier dinner (letter of December 19, 1877, I, 243).

B12   *JAN, EDUARD VON. "Das literarische Bild der Jeanne d'Arc," Beihefte zur Zeitschrift für Romanische Philologie, Heft 76.
On MT's JA, pp. 139-43. [Source: Asselineau (1954), No. 441; MHRA Annual Bibliography (1928), No. 646.]

B13   *MICHAUD, RÉGIS. Panorama de la Littérature Contemporaine. Paris: Kra.
[Source: Asselineau (1954), No. 437: "On Mark Twain, pp. 78-79, 99-102."]

B14   PAINE, ALBERT BIGELOW. "The Prince and the Pauper. How Mark Twain Came to Write the Story in Which He Himself Took Such Keen Delight," Mentor, XVI (December), 8-10.
The inspiration came from The Prince and the Page, by Charlotte M. Yonge.

B15   PATTEE, FRED LEWIS. "On the Rating of Mark Twain," American Mercury, XIV (June), 183-91.
"Mark Twain must be rated as a thwarted creator like Melville, one ham-strung by his times and his temperament." He produced "glorious fragments," not "rounded masterpieces," but "he will endure long."

B16   ROSENBERGER, EDWARD G. "An Agnostic Hagiographer," Catholic World, CXXVII (September), 717-23.
MT's usual literary crudity and hostility toward conventional religious belief make the "reverential enthusiasm" of his JA a welcome surprise. "The depth of Joan's sanctity as described by this blustering agnostic is a most tender and beautiful thing," and one may hope and predict that JA will outlast TS, HF, and the rest of MT's works.

B17   YORK, ALVIN C. "The Diary of Sergeant York, Part One," Liberty, V (July 14), 7-10.
Says his great-grandfather hunted with MT's father, "and his famous Tennesse Land Grant is where I live."

1929 A BOOKS

A1   *CLEMENS, CYRIL. A Letter of Mark Twain to His Publishers, Chatto & Windus of London, calling their attention to certain indiscretions of the proof-readers of Messrs. Spottiswoode & Co., printed for the first time from the letter in the collection of James Hart, with an introduction by Cyril Clemens and a portrait by Valenti Angelo. San Francisco: The Penguin Press. [4-page pamphlet.]
[Source: Asselineau (1954), No. 448.]

A2   _____, ed. Mark Twain Anecdotes: Tributes to Mark Twain by G. K. Chesterton & John Galsworthy, Members of the Society. Webster Groves, Missouri: Mark Twain Society.
Contains two very brief "Tributes to Mark Twain" by Galsworthy and Chesterton, followed by a number of miscellaneous jokes "submitted in the Second Annual Contest of the Mark Twain Society."

A3   PAINE, ALBERT BIGELOW. The Boy's Life of Mark Twain. Ed. Walter Barnes. New York and London: Harper & Brothers Publishers. Harper's Modern Classics.
Walter Barnes has added a very brief "Preface" and a two-page "To the Student" at the beginning, and an outline, questions, a biography of Paine, and "To the Teacher" at the end; his suggestion is that as far as possible the book should stand on its own merits [sensible advice, since Paine's is at least as good as most biographies for younger readers that have appeared since--T.A.T.].

1929 B SHORTER WRITINGS

B1   ANON. "Albert Bigelow Paine's Biography of Mark Twain," Overland Monthly, LXXXVII (June), 190.
A review of the revised edition: laudatory and descriptive, with no mention of any specific revisions.

B2   ANON. "In School with Becky Thatcher and Tom Sawyer," Literary Digest, C (March 9), 60-64.
On the occasion of the death of Laura Frazer, the original Becky; summarizes and excerpts an interview of some years earlier from the Kansas City Star, a portion of Tom Sawyer dealing with Tom and Becky, and stories from the New York Herald Tribune and New York World.

B3   *ANON. "Tom Sawyer and Huckleberry Finn: Erronotts," World Review, VIII (May 6), 201-203.
[Source: Asselineau (1954), No. 478.]

B4   BAY, J. CHRISTIAN. "Tom Sawyer, Detective: The Origin of the Plot," in William Warner Bishop and Andrew Keogh, eds., Essays Offered to Herbert Putnam by His Colleagues and Friends on his Thirtieth Anniversary as Librarian of Congress, 5 April 1929 (New Haven: Yale University Press), pp. 80-88.
MT's source was The Minister of Veilby (1829) by the Danish poet, Steen Steensen Blicher, and based on events of 1607-26 involving the execution of a man whose alleged

(BAY, J. CHRISTIAN)
"victim" had disappeared. Bay traces the steps by which MT could have become familiar with the account and notes that he had been periodically accused in Denmark of carelessness with his sources. MT's footnote in the original Harper's Magazine publication in 1896 gave his source as "an old-time Swedish criminal trial" (pp. 85-86).

B5   BRASHEAR, MINNIE M. "An Early Mark Twain Letter," Modern Language Notes, XLIV (April), 256-59.
Reprints from the Hannibal Daily Journal of September 10, 1853 a letter dated "New York, Aug. 31, 1853"; about his job as a printer in New York, and impressions of the city.

B6   [BRIGGS, JOHN ELY.] "Comment by the Editor," Palimpsest, X (October), 387-88.
On the General Directory of the Citizens of Keokuk, Iowa, compiled and published by Orion Clemens in 1856, followed by a Business Mirror in 1857.

B7   CLEMENS, CYRIL. "Becky Thatcher--Personal Reminiscences," Overland Monthly, LXXXVII (May), 142, 157.
On a visit to Hannibal and meeting with Laura Frazer, the original of Becky Thatcher; she said some incidents involving her in TS and in the Paine biography represented literary license.

B8   _____. "Map, drawn by Cyril Clemens, President Mark Twain Society, showing places associated with Mark Twain's first sojourn in the West," Overland Monthly, LXXXVII (April), 100.

B9   _____. "Mark Twain: 1835-1910," Overland Monthly, LXXXVII (April), 103-104.
A popular biographical account, appropriate to this special MT issue of the Overland Monthly but containing no new material.

B10   _____. The True Character of Mark Twain's Wife," Missouri Historical Review, XXIV (October), 40-49.
Beginning with the story of MT's "exaggerated" death and an excerpt from Mary Lawton's A Lifetime with Mark Twain, prints the texts of several letters from MT and Olivia Clemens to Cyril Clemens' parents in order to demonstrate "the happy family life of the Clemenses," and thereby show that Olivia Clemens had better sense than Van Wyck Brooks attributed to her.

B11   _____. "A Visit to Mark Twain's Country," Overland Monthly, LXXXVII (April), 116-117, 127; (May), 145-146, 158.
Describes Angel's Camp and Jackass Hill, local sights, a jumping-frog contest, etc. Two illustrations: "William Gillis in front of Mark Twain Cabin on Jackass Hill" (p. 116), and "Cyril Clemens, President Mark Twain Society" (p. 117).

B12   CLEMENS, J. R. [DR. JAMES ROSS CLEMENS.] "Some Recollections of Mark Twain," Overland Monthly, LXXXVII (April), 105, 125.
Anecdotes, including one about MT with Thomas Hardy, and a story by MT about experimenting with ants and little paper churches (they went to the one with honey in it). Makes the claim (justified) that "I was the innocent cause of Mr. Clemens' famous cablegram: 'The report of my death is greatly exaggerated.'"

B13   CLEMENS, SAMUEL L. "Some Unpublished Letters by Mark Twain," Overland Monthly, LXXXVII (April), 115, 122, 124.
"The following heretofore unpublished letters were written to Dr. and Mrs. James Ross Clemens, parents of Cyril Clemens through whose courtesy they are here printed for the first time." Fourteen postcards and letters, 1897-1910, chiefly on matters personal but not intimate.

B14   DEVOTO, BERNARD. "Brave Days in Washoe," American Mercury, XVII (June), 228-37.
Chiefly about Virginia City in its heyday; about MT pp. 236-37.

B15   ESKEW, GARNETT LAIDLAW. "Steamboats Come Back Despite Mark Twain," in his The Pageant of the Packets: A Book of American Steamboating (New York: Henry Holt and Company), pp. 161-74.
Only passing mention of MT, providing no new information or interpretation.

B16   "Excerpts of Letters written by Thomas A. Edison and G. Bernard Shaw, to be used in Cyril Clemens' forthcoming Biography of Mark Twain," Overland Monthly, LXXXVII (April), 102.
Edison tells of a visit by MT to his laboratory, where he was recorded telling several stories; the recordings were lost in a fire several years later. Shaw describes MT's "complete gift of intimacy which enabled us to treat one another as if we had known one another all our lives, as indeed I had known him through his early books, which I had known and reveled in before I was twelve years old."

B17   FEE, HARRY T. "Jackass Hill," Overland Monthly, LXXXVII (May), 146.
A poem about his thoughts on visiting a place made famous by MT and Bret Harte.

B18   GAITHER, RICE. "Steamboatin' Days on Our Rivers," New York Times Magazine (November 10), pp. 4-5, 20.
Almost entirely devoted to steamboats of the past and present, with only passing mention of MT (listed in several standard bibliographies).

B19   GORDON, GILBERT. "To Mark Twain's Shrine," Sunset Magazine: The Pacific Monthly, LXII (June), 16-17.

(GORDON, GILBERT)
On MT in Nevada and California, with brief description of a projected shrine, which "is not as yet completed. It will be located in Angel's Camp, Calaveras County." Photograph: "Twain's old shack at Virginia City, now preserved at Reno."

B20   HAWTHORNE, JULIAN. "Mark Twain As I Knew Him," Overland Monthly, LXXXVII (April), 111, 128.
Adding little information to what appears in MT's published works, expresses personal admiration. "He would never have been widely known but for his humor, and yet it was his humor that made him stop short of greatness. One felt in contact with him a largeness of nature which he failed to put into literary form. There was a 'kink' in his grain that gave him fortune, but denied him immortality.... His popularity kept him in a groove which, otherwise, he might have escaped from." Ends with credit-line: "(Courtesy of the Pasadena Star-News)."

B21   JAMES, OLIVER CLEMENS (FLORENCE CLEMENS). "The Everlasting Author," Overland Monthly, LXXXVII (April), 106.
Praises MT for his humor, tenderness, strength, and general sanity.

B22   JUDD, IDA BENFEY. "The Mark Twain Association," Overland Monthly, LXXXVII (April), 126, 128.
On the formation of the Association, which conducts a "yearly Prize Contest for the ten best quotations from Mark Twain's books"; William Lyon Phelps of Yale is chairman of the judges. Plans are being made for "the establishment of a Mark Twain Professorship of Humor and the Comic Spirit at one of our universities in 1935, which will be the hundredth anniversary of his birth."

B23   KELLER, HELEN. "Mark Twain, as Revealed by Himself to Helen Keller," American Magazine, CVIII (July), 50-51, 80, 82.
An excerpt from her Midstream: My Later Life (1929.B24). Photograph of MT.

B24   _____. "Our Mark Twain," in her Midstream: My Later Life. Garden City, N.Y.: Doubleday, Doran & Company, Inc., pp. 47-69 and passim.
A sensitive account of their meetings at Stormfield and elsewhere. Quotes MT on his loneliness after the death of Olivia (pp. 50-51). Also, tells of MT speaking at Princeton on the Phillipine situation, the killing of six hundred Moros, and Funston's capture of Aguinaldo by a stratagem. Woodrow Wilson, who was present, looked out the window during the talk and afterward commented to the effect that "much heroism does not always keep military men from committing follies" (pp. 48-49, 103-104). Helen Keller

concedes the difficulty of quoting MT exactly, but says she made notes after their conversations (p. 68).

B25   KENNEDY, KATHERINE. "Mark Twain," Overland Monthly, LXXXVII (April), 111.
A short poem about the success of the "Man of Mark."

B26   *LEISY, ERNEST ERWIN. American Literature: An Interpretive Survey. New York: Thomas Y. Crowell.
[Source: Asselineau (1954), No. 454: "pp. 170-179 on Mark Twain--very superficial."]

B27   LORCH, FRED W. "Adrift for Heresy," Palimpsest, X (October), 372-80.
On the expulsion of Orion Clemens from the local Presbyterian Church for heretical views expressed in a public lecture and reiterated in an examination before the minister and several members of the congregation; includes text of a letter from Orion to his mother (August 10, 1876) on his religious views (pp. 373-76) and a photograph: "Orion and Molly Clemens at Home" (facing p. 378).

B28   _____. "The Closing Years," Palimpsest, X (October), 381-86.
On the passing of Orion Clemens, and the affection in which he was held by his neighbors; includes a poem, "The Keokuk Pilgrim," probably by Orion Clemens.

B29   _____. "Lecture Trips and Visits of Mark Twain in Iowa," Iowa Journal of History and Politics, XXVII (October), 507-47.
On lecture trips in the 1860's and 1880's, his 1882 trip to gather material for LOM, and his last visit, in 1890, shortly before his mother's death. Includes MT's letter to his sister-in-law, Molly, on his brother Orion's death, and says that most of the correspondence to Orion and Molly was burned by the administrator after Molly's death in 1904.

B30   _____. "Literary Apprenticeship," Palimpsest, X (October), 364-71.
On the efforts by Orion Clemens as an author, and the gossip suggesting that he helped MT write some of his books.

B31   _____. "Mark Twain in Iowa," Iowa Journal of History and Politics, XXVII (July), 408-56.
On MT at Muscatine and Keokuk in the 1850's, with correspondence to his brother Orion's paper from Philadelphia and elsewhere, " "Thomas Jefferson Snodgrass" correspondence to the Keokuk Post, and a letter to his mother from Nevada, published in the Keokuk Gate City.

B32   _____. "Molly Clemens's Note Book," Palimpsest, X (October), 357-63.
Family history, including the death of MT's brother Henry, and the 1861 move to Nevada.

1929 - Shorter Writings

(LORCH, FRED W.)
"It is unfortunate that the note book consists so largely of mere chronology." Photograph of Orion Clemens (facing p. 362).

B33 _____. "The Tradition," Palimpsest, X (October), 353-56.
On the lasting popularity of MT's brother Orion, who was "witty, absent-minded, and often humorously inconsistent," but not ridiculous.

B34 McKAY, DONALD. "On the Vanishing Trail of Tom Sawyer," New York Times Magazine, (October 27), pp. 8-9.
Describes Hannibal, Missouri, as McKay saw it on a visit while he was working on illustrations for a new edition of TS.

B35 McWILLIAMS, CAREY. Ambrose Bierce: A Biography. New York: Albert & Charles Boni, pp. 87-88, 99-100.
Bierce's first meeting with MT, and text of his comment in the San Francisco Newsletter in 1890 (quoted in 1870.B4) on MT's marriage to a rich woman (pp. 87-88); also, Bierce, MT, and Joaquin Miller as dinner guests at the White Friars' Club, London, in the winter of 1873 (pp. 99-100).

B36 OLDER, FREMONT. "The Famous Jumping Frog Story. William Gillis, one-time associate of Mark Twain, tells Fremont Older the true story of the Jumping Frog. Told by William Gillis," Overland Monthly, LXXXVII (April), 101-102.
Older says Gillis heard the story from "an old man from Arkansas. The Arkansas man heard the story from old Dan Rice, the famous circus clown who owned a circus in the early sixties, and who used to tell the story in his circus work.... Samuel Sebaugh, a brilliant writer on the San Andreas Independent, hearing this story wrote it as a local happening, and the new version of it became very popular along the Mother Lode." There follows a version of the story, here told in dialect as by an elderly Negro, with frogs named Jim Polk and Henry Clay.

B37 *_____. "Russell K. Colcord," San Francisco Call-Bulletin, September 12.
Reminiscence by Colcord, who remembered MT in Aurora as "cold, selfish, and unsocial"--though conceding they had only a nodding acquaintance. [Source: Quoted by Fatout (1964), p. 45.]

B38 OVERTON, GRANT. "Howells: Twain," in his An Hour of the American Novel. (Philadelphia and London: J. B. Lippincott Company), pp. 37-43.
A popular account, describing the two men and their principal works. Compares MT, Melville in "their vitality and early adventurousness; they had minds of the same order. Success, world-wide popularity and

the restraints of Howells and Mrs. Clemens soothed and distracted Twain through most of his lifetime. But well before the end of it he put on paper a misanthropic bitterness that Melville probably suffered, too, but left unwritten" (pp. 39-40). In MS, MT's "moral nihilism finds frankest expression. His view of the cosmic spectacle is a good deal like that of Thomas Hardy in 'The Dynasts,' but without Hardy's dignity and courage." MT's best works are HF and "The Man that Corrupted Hadleyburg," but his Autobiography "is uninteresting in a few spots and trivial in many." Brooks's The Ordeal of Mark Twain "cannot be overlooked...but its argument must be received cautiously; it probably infers too much on too slender evidence" (p. 42).

B39 PHILPOTTS, EDEN. "On Mark Twain's Visit to England," Overland Monthly, LXXXVII (April), 106.
A poem praising MT and welcoming him to England (apparently on the occasion of his visit in 1907).

B40 [QUAIFE, M. M.] [Discussion of the unpublished autobiography of Orion Clemens.] Mississippi Valley Historical Review, XVI (December), 438-39.
The author of "Mark Twain in Iowa" [Fred W. Lorch, 1929] sought permission from Albert Bigelow Paine to examine Orion Clemens's autobiographical papers, but "It was not granted, and in this connection the information was vouchsafed that most of them have already been burned, while permission to examine any that may have escaped destruction is 'quite out of the question'"; legally, this may be proper, but Quaife condemns the action as wholly irresponsible. [Author identified as Quaife in Twainian, II (February, 1943), 6.] On p. 443 there is an unsigned note that Cyril Clemens has lent the Historical Society of St. Louis "a collection of Clemens family letters, most of which passed between Mark Twain and wife and the donor's parents in the years 1881-1908."

B41 RICHARDS, P. "Mark Twain als Wildwest-Journalist," Westermanns Monatshefte, CXLVII (October), 158-60.
A popular account of MT's frontier journalism, based principally on RI.

B42 SOSEY, FRANK H. "Palmyra and Its Historical Environment," Missouri Historical Review, XXIII (April), 361-79.
"In 1914 a great eastern magazine published a story purporting to have been written by Mark Twain in which he told of a thrilling incident of slavery days in Marion City," here retold and followed by a more complete and accurate account.

B43 VAN DOREN, MARK. _An Autobiography of America_. New York: Albert & Charles Boni.
Contains passages from _LOM_ (pp. 353-67) and _RI_ (pp. 432-45, 454-61), with very brief headnotes; listed elsewhere (incorrectly) as containing "several chapters devoted to Mark Twain."

B44 VAN DYKE, HENRY. "Mark Twain--A Memorial Poem Given at Carnegie Hall, New York City, November 30, 1910," _Overland Monthly_, LXXXVIII (April), 104.
A reprinting of the poem originally published in 1910, in "Mark Twain in Memoriam," _Harper's Weekly_, LIV (December 17), 10.

B45 ____, et al. "Tributes to Mark Twain, Written for this Number of the _Overland_ by Members of the Mark Twain Society," _Overland Monthly_, LXXXVII (April), 107-108, 123.
Tributes by Henry Van Dyke, Hamlin Garland, H. M. Tomlinson, Rupert Hughes, E. F. Benson, Sir Esme Howard (British Ambassador to the United States), Ida Tarbell, G. M. Trevelyan, Concha Espina, W. W. Jacobs, Temple Bailey, E. V. Lucas, [Lord] Dunsany, Knut Hamsun, Stephen Leacock, William J. Locke, Arthur Pinero, Walter de la Mare, and Anthony Hope Hopkins.

B46 WINTERICH, JOHN T. "Mark Twain and _The Innocents Abroad_," in his _Books and the Man_. (New York: Greenberg: Publisher), pp. 170-92.
About the publication and sale of _IA_, based primarily on such familiar accounts as MT's autobiography and Paine; gives interesting information on the illustrations and a few first-edition points. "Acknowledgements" (p. vii) says the papers in this volume originally appeared in _Publishers' Weekly_, but does not give specific issues.

1930 A BOOKS

A1 EDWARDS, FRANCES M., ed. and introduction. _Twainiana Notes from the Annotations of Walter Bliss_. Hartford: The Hobby Shop, Publishers.
Annotations by Bliss in his copy of the 1910 bibliography of MT's works compiled by Merle Johnson.

A2 GILLIS, WILLIAM R. _Gold Rush Days with Mark Twain_. Introduction by Cyril Clemens. New York: Albert & Charles Boni.
Anecdotes, some of which concern MT, by a friend and mining partner.

A3 MARTIN, ALMA BORTH. _A Vocabulary Study of "The Gilded Age."_ With an Introduction by Robert L. Ramsay and a Foreword by Hamlin Garland. Webster Groves, Missouri: Mark Twain Society.
Lists 142 words not in the _Oxford English Dictionary_ ("either altogether or in the meaning used by Mark Twain"--p. 26) and 71

words for which _The Gilded Age_ provides earlier citations. In the foreword titled "Mark Twain's Freshness of Diction" Garland concludes: "With all his coarseness he was essentially wholesome, and his vocabulary was as wide and as varied as his almost unparalleled experience" (p. 3).

A4 *_Tributes to Mark Twain by Members of the Society_. Paris [Kentucky?]: Printed for the Mark Twain Society by H. Clarke.
[Source: Asselineau (1954), No. 483.] Conventional tributes by Galsworthy, Chesterton, Hamlin Garland, W. W. Jacobs, E. V. Lucas, Dunsany, Knut Hamsun, W. De la Mare, Pinero, G. M. Trevelyan, A. E. Housman, and others. [13-page pamphlet.]

A5 WEST, VICTOR ROYCE. _Folklore in the Works of Mark Twain_. Lincoln: University of Nebraska Studies in Language, Literature, and Criticism, No. 10.
There are chapters on "Ghostlore," "Demonology," "Witchcraft," "Luck and Unluck," "Signs, Portents, Omens," "Proverbs," and "Sundry Superstitions" in MT's works, but this is basically a series of organized lists. There is no attempt made to place the material in a broader folklore perspective and the references are only to works by MT and to the Paine biography.

1930 B SHORTER WRITINGS

B1 ARMSTRONG, C. J. "Mark Twain's Early Writings Discovered," _Missouri Historical Review_, XXIV (July), 485-501.
On the contributions to Hannibal newspapers by young Samuel Clemens (among them "Love Concealed. To Miss Katy of H--l," the "Rambler" and "Grumbler" correspondence, and "'Local' Resolves to Commit Suicide," illustrated by a clumsy woodcut by Sam).

B2 BLAIR, WALTER. "Burlesques in Nineteenth-Century American Humor," _American Literature_, II (November), 236-47.
MT is among the authors treated. This article is reprinted as part of Blair's _Two Phases of American Humor_, an excerpt from his doctoral dissertation at the University of Chicago (Private Edition, Distributed by the University of Chicago Libraries, n.d. The copy at McGill University is stamped as having been received May 21, 1932); this reprint has the pagination of the _American Literature_ printing).

B3 BRASHEAR, MINNIE M. "Mark Twain Juvenilia," _American Literature_, II (March), 25-53.
Includes texts of Hannibal newspaper sketches by young SLC. "These early writings will not suggest the need of any new rating of Mark Twain."

B4   *BROWN, GEORGE ROTHWELL. Washington, A Not
       Too Serious History. Baltimore: Norman
       Publishing Company.
          On pp. 417-18, says MT was a customer at
       James Guild's bookshop whenever he was in
       Washington. [Source: French (1965),
       pp. 36; 291, n. 30.]

B5   CHURCHILL, WINSTON S. A Roving Commission:
       My Early Life. New York: Charles Scrib-
       ner's Sons.
          On p. 360, very briefly describes a meet-
       ing with MT, who introduced him at his
       first public lecture in New York. MT auto-
       graphed a set of his books for Churchill
       and conversed pleasantly with him, but was
       unsympathetic toward England's position in
       the Boer War.

B6   CLEMENS, CLARA. "Recollections of Mark
       Twain. Part I--Her Childhood Memories,"
       North American Review, CCXXX (November),
       522-29; "Part II--Love Letters of the Humor-
       ist" (December), 652-59.
          Extracts from her forthcoming My Father,
       Mark Twain (1931); three-part series ends
       January, 1931.

B7   CLEMENS, CYRIL. "Mark Twain's Favorite
       Book," Overland Monthly, LXXXVIII (May),
       157.
          Years of research and painstaking compo-
       sition made MT prefer his JA for a time,
       but his real favorite, although the writing
       had been burdensome, was HF.

B8   GARLAND, HAMLIN. Roadside Meetings. New
       York: The Macmillan Company.
          On MT traveling and lecturing with the
       "gentle, religious, and rather effeminate"
       George Washington Cable (pp. 104-105). De-
       scribes interviewing MT in London for
       McClure's (on the Grant Memoirs, and the
       failure of the Webster Company); Mrs. Clem-
       ens asked that the interview not be pub-
       lished (pp. 449-53). The latter part ap-
       pears in Garland's "Roadside Meetings of a
       Literary Nomad" in Bookman (New York), LXXI
       (July), 425-27, and the comparatively brief
       comment on MT and Cable may have been in an
       earlier issue.

B9   HAPGOOD, NORMAN. "Mark Twain," in his The
       Changing Years: Reminiscences of Norman
       Hapgood (New York: Farrar & Rinehart, In-
       corporated), pp. 202-11.
          On acquaintance with MT, with anecdotes
       showing his "almost Quixotic" concern for
       the feelings of other people. Quotes MT
       in his late years: "I was happy in the ear-
       ly part of my life. I am happy now; but
       there was a stretch of years in the middle
       of my life when I was not happy...and that
       middle period was the only part that was
       worth anything."

B10   JOSEPHSON, MATTHEW. "Those Who Stayed," in
       his Portrait of the Artist as American (New
       York: Harcourt, Brace and Company),
       pp. 154-61.
          MT lacked the seriousness of a Whitman or
       of a Henry James (whom "he despised, and
       nicknamed 'Henrietta-Maria'"). Josephson
       rejects Brooks's notion that MT was sup-
       pressed: he liked the life he had chosen.
       Nonetheless, Brooks is correct about MT's
       dual nature, which reflects a duality in the
       national character. Reprinted (in part;
       pp. 158-61) in Leary (1962), pp. 83-84.

B11   KEMBLE, E. W. "Illustrating Huck Finn," Colo-
       phon, Part I (February; pages not numbered .
          Kemble was 23 when he illustrated HF, and
       was paid $2,000 for the job. He used one
       model, a boy named Cort Morris, for all the
       characters--including Huck, Jim, and all the
       men and women. When HF was filmed, the di-
       rector, William Desmond Taylor, made the
       characters fit the drawings.

B12   LORCH, FRED W. "A Mark Twain Letter," Iowa
       Journal of History and Politics, XXVIII
       (April), 268-76.
          A letter published in the Keokuk Gate City
       (June 25, 1862) to his mother, from Carson
       City, Nevada Territory, dated March 20, 1862;
       it does not appear in Paine's edition of MT's
       letters.

B13   MABBOTT, T. O. "Mark Twain's Artillery: A
       Mark Twain Legend," Missouri Historical Re-
       view, XXV (October), 23-29.
          Reprints from the Silver Cliff Daily Pros-
       pect (March 16, 1860, "printed from a photo-
       static copy without intentional emendations")
       an apocryphal tale there credited to the
       Carson Appeal: "Mark Twain's Artillery.
       How He Defeated a Band of Redskins in the
       Days of '49. Type as Grape Shot." By this
       account, MT and his friend "Dan de Quille"
       (William Wright) attempted to start a paper
       in Menocina County and after using up their
       type as shot, joined the Territorial Enter-
       prise together.

B14   MORRIS, HARRISON S. Confessions in Art. New
       York: Sears Publishing Company, Inc.,
       pp. 202-203.
          Describes MT at a dinner in his honor in
       New York, given by the illustrators when
       his Joan of Arc had just appeared. A girl
       dressed as Joan and accompanied by pages
       and trumpeters presented him with a crown.
       He was exuberant. Includes illustration:
       "Menu for a Dinner to Mark Twain," showing
       Pudd'nhead Wilson and bearing the date
       December 21, 1905.

B15   PARRINGTON, VERNON LEWIS. "The Backwash of
       the Frontier: Mark Twain," in his The Be-
       ginnings of Critical Realism in America
       1860-1920, Vol. III is his Main Currents in
       American Thought (New York: Harcourt,
       Brace and Company), pp. 86-101 and passim.

(PARRINGTON, VERNON LEWIS)

Completed only to 1900, due to Parrington's death in 1929. Sees MT as the irreverent frontier adolescent taken in hand by the East--but he remained boyish and clung to his integrity. His life is important as a reflection of his time, to which he only surrendered in part (p. 88). Agrees with Brooks that the later bitterness may be attributed in part to this surrender, but "a humane and generous spirit cannot long watch with indifference the motley human caravan hastening to eternity--cannot find food for laughter alone in the incredible meanness and folly of men cheating and quarreling in a wilderness of graves" (p. 89). Parrington notes MT's intellectual isolation: "If he had known Henry Adams as intimately as he knew Henry H. Rogers, very likely his eyes would have been opened to many things that would have done him good" (p. 90). HF shows MT's rebellion against the laws of society (pp. 94-95), and CY is an attack, not so much on chivalry, as on centuries of oppression (pp. 95, 97-98). Reprinted in Scott (1955), pp. 188-99; (1967), pp. 186-97; Leary (1962), pp. 87-98; brief excerpt in Lettis (1962), pp. 305-307.

B16 PATTEE, FRED LEWIS. The New American Literature 1890-1930. New York, London: The Century Co., p. 89 and passim.

Most of the brief references to MT are not illuminating, but on p. 89 Pattee quotes W. P. Trent's dismissal of JA as "a large piece of mosaic work," alternating history and fiction without a fusing process.

B17 POWELL, LYMAN P. Mary Baker Eddy: A Life Size Portrait. New York: The Macmillan Company, passim.

Several references to MT, with an attempt to show him as less hostile to Christian Science: "Mark Twain's final reversal of his previous judgment may come as news to many: 'Christian Science is humanity's boon. Mother Eddy deserves a place in the Trinity as much as any member of it,'" for her healing principle (p. 40, with a footnote on p. 81 giving the source as the 1912 Paine biography, III, 1271).

B18 *READ, OPIE. "Mark Twain and the Pilot," in his I Remember (New York: R. R. Smith, Inc.), pp. 155-65.

On a meeting with MT on a steamboat. [Source: Asselineau (1954), No. 491.]

B19 RILEY, JAMES WHITCOM. Letters of James Whitcom Riley, ed. William Lyon Phelps. Indianapolis: The Bobbs-Merrill Company. Passim on MT (indexed).

Texts of MT letters to W. D. Foulke, October 3, 1888, and to Riley, February 2, 1891 (pp. 329-30; MT praises Riley as more accomplished than most poets at reading his own poems aloud).

B20 VAN DOREN, MARK. "Clemens, Samuel Langhorne," in Allen Johnson and Dumas Malone, eds., Dictionary of American Biography (New York: Charles Scribner's Sons), IV, 192-98.

[Source: 1958 reprint, II, Part II, with the same pagination.] MT's best works are HF and the first part of LOM. Van Doren notes MT's limitations as a thinker, the uneven quality of his writing, and "the violence which frequently led him into burlesque so fantastic as to be dull"; but Howells and Olivia Clemens helped "to keep Mark Twain's genius within decorous bounds."

B21 WINTERICH, JOHN T. "The Life and Works of Bloodgood H. Cutter," Colophon, Part II (May), 8 pp. (not numbered).

Cutter wanted to be known as a humorous poet, did not mind the way he was depicted as the "Poet Lariat" in IA, and did not realize that he was himself portrayed as a comic object. Comparatively little on MT.

1931 A BOOKS

A1 *ANON. The Movie Story of Tom Sawyer. Racine, Wisconsin: Whitman Publishing Company.

"(Shortened to The Story of Tom Sawyer on the front cover but with the first wording on the title page). The book contains 24 pages, including pastedowns. Illustrations were color photographs taken from the Paramount motion picture starring Jackie Coogan as Huck." [Source: Asselineau (1954), No. 535; additional details quoted from letter (April 15, 1974) from William H. Larson, Senior Editor, Western Publishing Company, Inc. (Whitman/Golden Press), Racine, Wisconsin.]

A2 *ANON. The Story of the Paramount Picture "Huckleberry Finn." N.p.: Lubin Press, circa 1931.

[Source: Asselineau (1954), No. 534. Asselineau attributes this to a typewritten bibliography in Widener Library at Harvard University. The title suggests that this may have been a publicity release on the filming, or--more probably--a version of MT's book released at a time to cash in on the new film--T.A.T.]

A3 CLEMENS, CLARA. My Father, Mark Twain. Illustrated from Family Photographs with Hitherto Unpublished Letters of Mark Twain. New York and London: Harper & Brothers Publishers.

Contains reminiscences and useful primary materials; unindexed.

A4 *LEWIS, OSCAR. The Origin of the Celebrated Jumping Frog of Calaveras County. San Francisco: The Book Club of California.

[Source: Asselineau (1954), No. 505: "Gives the different versions of the tale."]

1931 - Books

A5 *WALL, BERNHARDT. In Mark Twain's Missouri, etched and published by Bernhardt Wall, Lime Rock, Connecticut.
[4 pp. pamphlet. Source: Asselineau (1954), No. 506.]

1931 B SHORTER WRITINGS

B1 ANON. [Review: Clara Clemens, My Father, Mark Twain.] Times Literary Supplement, November 26, p. 937.
Long, but primarily descriptive.

B2 ARMSTRONG, C. J. "John L. RoBards--A Boyhood Friend of Mark Twain," Missouri Historical Review, XXV (April), 493-98.
Includes the text of several MT letters (and one by Jane Clemens) to RoBards, chiefly on transferring the remains of MT's father and his brother Henry to one lot in Mt. Olivet Cemetery in Hannibal. In one letter from Hartford (April 17 [1876]), MT urged simplicity: "I enclose check for $100. If Henry and my father feel as I would feel under the circumstances, they want no prominent or expensive lot, or luxurious entertainment in the new cemetery. As for a monument--well, if you remember my father, you are aware that he would rise up & demolish it the first night. He was a modest man & would not be able to sleep under a monument."

B3 * ____. "Sam Clemens Considered Becoming a Preacher," The Christian (June 13).
[Source: Reprinted under this title in Twainian, IV (May, 1945), 1; other facts of publication and information about The Christian not given.] The Reverend Mr. Armstrong was scheduled to retire May 31, 1945 as pastor of the First Christian Church in Hannibal.

B4 ASHTON, J. W. [Review: Victor Royce West, Folklore in the Works of Mark Twain (1930).] Philological Quarterly, X (October), 416.
MT's interest "seems to differ very slightly, if at all, from that of the ordinary intelligent person," and West errs in trying to show more; he also reads too much into such conventional locutions as "poor devil" and "luck," which probably had little folk significance. "The chapter on Signs, Portents, Omens is perhaps the best since it presents actual situations rather than casual references."

B5 BALDWIN, CHARLES C. Stanford White. New York: Dodd, Mead & Company.
An eccentric book, with references to MT passim. He is described in the Index (p. 397) as "potentially the greatest of American writers, but (alas) cowed and beaten by the prejudices and conclusions of his contemporaries in society and the arts-- best remembered for Huckleberry Finn and for the anecdotes attributed to him." This

description is not followed up in the text, which says little about MT with relation to White but does tell of his visiting White and St. Gaudens in Paris; they counted the black cigars he smoked.

B6 BLAIR, WALTER. "The Popularity of Nineteenth-Century American Humorists," American Literature, III (May), 175-94.
Contains relatively little on MT.

B7 BLANKENSHIP, RUSSELL. "Lost in the Gilded Age," in his American Literature as an Expression of the National Mind (New York: Henry Holt and Company), pp. 457-76.
Discusses MT jointly with Henry Adams. In "Mark Twain" (pp. 458-70) describes the man, his works, and his inner conflicts.

B8 BURPEE, CHARLES W. A Century in Hartford. Being the History of the Hartford County Mutual Fire Insurance Company. Hartford: The Hartford County Mutual Fire Insurance Company.
On p. 81, quotes MT's reaction in 1878 when asked if he would have his house connected to the telephone system: "No! I want something to keep voices further away-- not bring them nearer."

B9 CESTRE, C. [Review: Alma Borth Martin, A Vocabulary Study of Mark Twain's "The Gilded Age" (1930).] Revue Anglo-Américaine, VIII (June), 458-59.
Brief and descriptive. [In French.]

B10 CHAPIN, ADÈLE LE BOURGEOIS [MRS. R. W. CHAPIN.] "Their Trackless Way": A Book of Memories, ed. by Christina Chapin. London: Constable & Co. Ltd. Passim on MT (indexed).
On dining with MT in South Africa (pp. 119-23) and in London (pp. 140-41); on his meeting James McNeill Whistler in London (pp. 180-82); on lunching with MT at the Yale Bicentennial (pp. 211-12); quotes a letter from Lord Gray, discussing patriotism and citing a statement to him by MT that America had left England's government rather than England itself, and it would now be an honor to be a colony (p. 220).

B11 CLEMENS, CLARA. "Recollections of Mark Twain: Last Years of the Humorist," North American Review, CCXXXI (January), 50-57.
Extracts from her My Father, Mark Twain, concluding a three-part series begun in 1930.

B12 DAVIS, ARTHUR KYLE. [Review: Victor Royce West, Folklore in the Works of Mark Twain (1930).] Modern Language Notes, XLVI (May), 350.
"A commendable piece of extracting and... interesting if essentially uncritical."

B13 DEVOTO, BERNARD, '18. "Mark Twain and the Genteel Tradition," Harvard Graduates' Magazine, XL (December), 155-63.

MT "was a humorist. He had had no formal education. His life had been spent in activity, away from what are known as aesthetic pursuits.... He came East and he accepted tuition," especially from Howells, and "accepted, to the small extent of which he was capable, without any awareness of surrender, the dominant criteria of his age." Richard Watson Gilder purified the language of HF for serialization in The Century, but MT accepted a similar service for PW, and kept Gilder's changes for the book publication. "This damage was purely verbal. The tradition may have wrought a greater damage by turning him from Pudd'nhead Wilsons and Huck Finns to knights, kings, and armored virgins," but such questions are conjectural.

B14 _____. "The Matrix of Mark Twain's Humor," Bookman (New York), LXXIV (October), 172-78.

Frontier humor in the newspapers gave MT a style, form, and themes.

B15 _____. "The Real Frontier: A Preface to Mark Twain," Harper's, CLXIII (June), 60-71.

Only tangentially on MT, this article defends the frontier against charges by Van Wyck Brooks and others that it was merely a region of violence, spiritual repression, and intellectual vacuity.

B16 DRAKE, ERIC. [Review: Alma Borth Martin, A Vocabulary Study of Mark Twain's "The Gilded Age" (1930).] Anglia Beiblatt, XLII (December), 364-67.

The thesis cannot be taken seriously, despite the interest of many of the words and phrases: a) the categories are too simple, and vaguely defined by inadequate criteria; b) "There is a naive assumption of the accuracy of the New English Dictionary"; c) Mrs. Martin is "confused between syntax and vocabulary" in treatment of some word-combinations as though they were single words, as with gawky-looking, canvas-covered, Bible class; d) "The running commentary is curiously child-like"; e) for about 120 Americanisms, century of origin is not given. "It is...surprising to find a study based on these rather naive and uncritical methods sponsored by a university professor. Surely the evident good will and sincerity of the author could have been turned to better account." [In English.]

B17 GARLAND, HAMLIN. "Mark Twain, Carnegie, and Roosevelt," in his Companions on the Trail: A Literary Chronicle (New York: Macmillan), pp. 192-207.

Describes a dinner with the Clemens family in 1903 at their home in Riverdale, New York; quotes MT's spoken remarks on Christian Science.

B18 GILBERT, ARIADNE. "Mark Twain: Sam, Sinner and Saint," in her Over Famous Thresholds (New York, London: The Century Company), pp. 230-62.

A biographical sketch, apparently based largely on Paine.

B19 GOODPASTURE, A. V. "Mark Twain, Southerner," Tennessee Historical Magazine, Series II, I (July), 253-60.

After a lengthy family history (pp. 253-56), argues that "every drop of Mark Twain's blood was Southern." "While in the East he wrote his stories of Southern and Western life, but he never wrote a story of Eastern life.... The fact is, he never understood nor appreciated the New England culture." MT's reason for leaving the Confederate military service was probably the appointment of his brother Orion as Secretary of the Territory of Nevada.

B20 GRATTAN, C. HARTLEY. "Mark Twain," in John Macy, ed., American Writers on American Literature, by Thirty-Seven Contemporary Writers (New York: Horace Liveright, Inc.) pp. 274-84; also, Hamlin Garland quotes MT on Howells, p. 289.

Notes MT's volatile temperament, uneven writing, emotional ambivalence: "His ordeal was an ordeal by temperament as much as by anything else," and his pursuit of wealth shows that he "was incapable of defying his age" (p. 277). Notes MT's clear, direct style (p. 283), his satire, his final pessimism, and concludes by contrasting him with Henry James, although "it is those two who are fast becoming the great figures in our literature for the period 1870-1900" (p. 284).

B21 *HAMON, LOUIS ("CHEIRO"). Fate in the Making. Revelations of a Lifetime. New York & London: Harper & Brothers.

[Source: Asselineau (1954), No. 513; notes that "Cheiro" once examined MT's hand but makes no specific comment on this book.]

B22 HARRIS, JOEL CHANDLER. Joel Chandler Harris, Editor and Essayist: Miscellaneous Literary, Political, and Social Writings, ed. by Julia Collier Harris. Chapel Hill: The University of North Carolina Press, pp. 253-54, 375.

Takes issue with MT's criticism of the The Vicar of Wakefield, but praises him as "not only our greatest humorist, but our greatest writer of fiction." [Originally in Uncle Remus's Magazine, February, 1908.]

B23 HEINEMAN, DAVID E. [Letter to the Editor.] Michigan History Magazine, XV (Winter), 136-42.

On "a receipt book...each page of which has the caption 'Young Men's Society, of Lansing.'" The entry for December 24, 1864 lists MT's lecture, "An American Vandal Abroad," at one hundred dollars (p. 137);

1931 - Shorter Writings

(HEINEMAN, DAVID E.)
his "Out West" lecture of December 15, 1871 brought one hundred twenty-five dollars (p. 139).

B24 HICKS, GRANVILLE. "Mark Twain's Pessimism," Nation, CXXXIII (October 28), 463-64.
A review of Clara Clemens, My Father, Mark Twain. "Certainly his daughter, though she prints a number of new letters, presents no information that will involve a new conception of his character."

B25 HUGHES, ROBERT M. "A Deserter's Tale," Virginia Magazine of History and Biography, XXXIX (January), 21-28.
A defense of "Governor John B. Floyd, of Virginia, Secretary of War in Buchanan's Cabinet. My mother was his adopted daughter, and one of her last requests of me was to defend his memory from the vile slanders against him," as in MT's "The Case of George Fisher." The actual case is here discussed in detail, with Hughes expressing sorrow that a Southerner should join Floyd's detractors--but MT's Confederate service was brief and undistinguished.

B26 LORCH, FRED W. "A Source for Mark Twain's 'The Dandy Frightening the Squatter,'" American Literature, III (November), 390-13.
With parallel columns, shows strong similarity to "A Scene on the Ohio" in the Bloomington (now Muscatine, Iowa) Herald of February 13, 1849.

B27 MASON, LAURENS D. "Real People in Mark Twain's Stories," Overland Monthly LXXXIX (January), 12-13, 27.
Attributes living originals to MT's characters, chiefly on the basis of what he wrote about them in his Autobiography and elsewhere.

B28 RAOUL, MARGARET LENTE. "Debunking a Famous Story," Bookman (New York), LXXIII (August), 607-608.
Reproduces in facsimile, with commentary, MT's note in which he stated that "the report of my death was an exaggeration." The story was also told by Mrs. Raoul's father, Frank Marshall White (1910.B136), and on several occasions by Cyril Clemens.

B29 ROURKE, CONSTANCE. Native American Humor. New York: Harcourt, Brace and Company, pp. 209-21, and passim (indexed).
MT was a story-teller with "a pioneer talent," a social critic only in the "instinctive and incomplete" way of the American comic tradition. "He was never the conscious artist, always the improviser." These pages on MT reprinted in Scott (1955), pp. 200-206; (1967), pp. 198-204; in Leary (1962), pp. 99-106; in Cardwell (1963), pp. 26-30; some reprintings are partial.

B30 STEWART, GEORGE R. Bret Harte: Argonaut and Exile. Boston and New York: Houghton Mifflin Company, passim.
The frequent references to MT are based on material already known in MT scholarship.

B31 UNDERHILL, IRVING S. "An Inquiry into Mark Twain's Latest Book! The Adventures of Huckelberry [sic] Finn," Colophon, Part 6, 10 pp. (including facsimiles; pages not numbered).
About the copies of the first edition of HF shipped to California, and there altered to replace the offensive cut on p. 283. See Underhill's "The Haunted Book" (1935.B75).

B32 WINSTEN, ARCHER. "The Intimate Twain," Scribner's, XC (November), 16, 18 (specially numbered section at beginning of issue).
A brief review of Clara Clemens, My Father, Mark Twain as a book which makes almost no attempt at interpretation, adds very little to the Paine biography, and supports rather than refutes Brooks's "penetrating study of Mark Twain."

1932 A BOOKS

A1 CLEMENS, CYRIL, ed. Mark Twain the Letter Writer. Boston: Meador Publishing Company.
Letters by MT, some of them reproduced in facsimile, together with biographical details and anecdotes.

A2 DEVOTO, BERNARD. Mark Twain's America. Boston: Little, Brown and Company.
One of the central critical works on MT, brilliant but pugnacious; DeVoto calls this reply to Van Wyck Brooks's The Ordeal of Mark Twain (1920) an "essay in the correction of ideas" (p. v, dedication). DeVoto made a broad study of the frontier and frontier humor, and insists on their salutory influence in developing MT and shaping him as a writer. Reprinted Chautauqua, New York: Chautauqua Institution, and often reprinted thereafter. Excerpts reprinted in Bradley (1962), pp. 288-97; Leary (1962), pp. 109-23; Lettis (1962), pp. 307-15; Cardwell (1963), pp. 31-35; Simpson (1968), pp. 7-15; Gerber (1971), pp. 32-41.

A3 LEACOCK, STEPHEN. Mark Twain. London: Peter Davies (Also New York: D. Appleton and Company, 1933).
A popular biography by a fellow-humorist; more enthusiastic than penetrating.

A4 POTTER, JOHN K. Samuel L. Clemens: First Editions and Values. Chicago: The Black Archer Press.
Gives prices as an approximation, based on auction records, booksellers' listings, etc., and lists points distinguishing first editions; superseded in the latter by Merle Johnson and Jacob Blanck.

1932 B SHORTER WRITINGS

B1   ANON. "Copyright in the Days of Mark Twain," <u>Publishers' Weekly</u>, CXXI (February 27), 949.
Describes and quotes a letter from MT to Kate Douglas Wiggin (date not given) about his attempts to lobby for an improved copyright bill.

B2   ANON. "Mark and His Temper," <u>Quarterly Journal of the University of North Dakota</u> (now <u>North Dakota Quarterly</u>), XXII (Spring), 277-78.
A brief, descriptive review of Clara Clemens, <u>My Father, Mark Twain</u>.

B3   ANON. [Review: Stephen Leacock, <u>Mark Twain</u>.] <u>Times Literary Supplement</u>, November 24, p. 886.
"A clear and well-proportioned sketch," primarily concerned with MT as an artist; English readers will assent to Leacock's praise of <u>HF</u>, but not his praise of <u>CY</u>: "He does not seem to be aware that in this book more than in any other Mark Twain exhibited his insensitivity to the ideal."

B4   ARVIN, NEWTON. "Mark Twain Simplified," <u>New Republic</u>, LXXII (October 5), 211-12.
A review of Bernard DeVoto, <u>Mark Twain's America</u>, which distorts and misrepresents "what is perhaps the most remarkable piece of interpretive biography in our literature, <u>The Ordeal of Mark Twain</u>," by Van Wyck Brooks. "Mr. DeVoto, in one chapter, has pointed out several details in which Brooks is fairly open to attack. But he has nowhere grappled with a serious interpretation on its own merits, and by disposing not only of Brooks, but of such writers as Waldo Frank and Lewis Mumford, as romantic ignoramuses, he prejudices his own theory (for he distinctly has one) in the eyes of every fair-minded bystander." Reprinted in <u>American Pantheon</u>, ed. Daniel Aaron and Sylvan Schendler (New York: Delacorte Press, 1966), pp. 135-41.

B5   BENNETT, ARNOLD. <u>The Journals of Arnold Bennett, 1896-1910</u>, ed. by Newman Flower. London, Toronto, Melbourne and Sydney: Cassell and Company, Ltd. [MT is not listed in the indexes of other volumes of Bennett's journals examined.]
Robert Barr says MT once told him his average expenses were $35,000 per year; Pond once offered MT $50,000 for a lecture series, and Hearst offered him $52,000 for 52 weekly articles in the <u>Journal</u> (p. 188); in 1905 Bennett was enjoying <u>LOM</u> (p. 206).

B6   BOYNTON,, PERCY H. "Mr. Clemens' Family," <u>New Republic</u>, LXIX (January 27), 302-303.
A review of Clara Clemens' <u>My Father, Mark Twain</u> (1931). "The book of reminiscences does not attempt character analysis or aesthetic criticism, but as an obviously honest and candid piece of work it

provides data on which to modify or confirm the abundant literature of this sort."

B7   BROWNELL, GEORGE HIRAM. "Mark Twain and the Hannibal Journal," <u>American Book Collector</u>, II (August-September), 173-76; (October), 202-204.
An "extract from a longer essay, by Mr. Brownell, entitled 'Mark Twain in Magazines and Newspapers'" (facts of publication not given). Extends and corrects MT's own accounts of his work on his brother Orion's newspaper. Sources include Minnie M. Brashear, "Mark Twain Juvenilia" (1930), articles by the Reverend C. J. Armstrong in <u>Missouri Historical Review</u> and <u>Hannibal Courier-Post</u> (dates not given), and "an extensive correspondence with Rev. Armstrong."

B8   *BUCKBEE, EDNA BRYAN. "Mark Twain's Treasure Pile," in her <u>Pioneer Days of Angel's Camp</u> (Angel's Camp, California: Published by Calaveras Californian), pp. 21-35.
On the Origin of "The Jumping Frog." [Source: Asselineau (1954), No. 544.]

B9   CALVERTON, V. F. <u>The Liberation of American Literature</u>. New York: Charles Scribner's Sons, passim.
The "liberation" is first from European models and later it is what is implied by Calverton's avowedly Marxist views. With the rise of America to world power came a change in psychology, so "that Whitman and Twain came to be looked upon as native geniuses instead of as isolated eccentrics" (pp. 31-32). "Products of the frontier force," they were "the first American poet" and "the first American prose writer of any importance." The two Mark Twains were the youthful frontier optimist and an older pessimist, disappointed in his dreams for America. Had he lived in our time he might have been a communist; as it was, he remained among the petty bourgeoisie, condemning American imperialism because it infringed on the property rights of smaller nations (pp. 319-28, 338). Reprinted in Scott (1955), pp. 207-14; (1967), pp. 205-12.

B10   CANBY, HENRY SEIDEL. "Mark Twain Himself," <u>Saturday Review of Literature</u>, IX (October 29), 201-202.
A review of Bernard DeVoto's <u>Mark Twain's America</u>, a useful corrective to Van Wyck Brooks, who appeared "more concerned with the ills of America than with the truth about Mark Twain"; however, "I wish that Mr. DeVoto had thrown his stones in a pamphlet and written his book afterward."

B11   CARPENTER, FREDERICK I. "Anent American Humor," <u>Saturday Review of Literature</u>, VIII (March 12), 590.
A letter to the editor, arguing the immaturity of earlier American humor, such as

(CARPENTER, FREDERICK I.)
MT's: Neither Tom [Sawyer] nor Mark ever
grew up. American humor remained a childish evasion."

B12   CHAPMAN, JOHN W. "The Germ of a Book: A
Footnote on Mark Twain," Atlantic Monthly,
CL (December), 720-21.
Text of two letters by MT (Hartford,
1887) to the Reverend Mr. Chapman, a charity hospital chaplain who had written him on
behalf of a dying patient named Jesse Leathers. MT said he had sent only a small
amount of money, having been warned that
Leathers, a distant relative, was "inordi-
nately selfish and self-seeking, and not
very scrupulous," and that aid would do him
little good. Chapman notes that in The
American Claimant (1892) the claimant next
before Mulberry Sellers was Simon Lathers.

B13   *CLEMENS, CYRIL. "The Ancestry and Birth of
Mark Twain," in Susan Louise Marsh and
Charles Garrett Vannest, eds., Missouri An-
thology (Boston: The Christopher Publishing
House), pp. 91-96.
[Source: Asselineau (1954), No. 542.]

B14   COOPER, LANE. "Mark Twain's Lilacs and Labur-
nums," Modern Language Notes, XLVII
(February), 85-87.
The passage beginning Chapter IV of A
Double-Barreled Detective Story parodies
Walter Besant and James Rice's The Seamy
Side, a Story (1880), pp. 168, 297.

B15   DEVOTO, BERNARD. "In re Mark Twain," Saturday Review of Literature, VIII (April 2),
640.
A letter to the editor, in reply to one
by Frederick I. Carpenter, March 12·
(1932.B11). Carpenter's assertion that repression by his wife kept MT's humor from
maturing is unsupported, and "only a repetition of the ideas of Mr. Van Wyck Brooks,
which are a compound of frivolous and superficial psycho-analysis and a theory about
the obligation of the artist based on the
sentimental politics and economics of pre-
war 'Liberalism.' In common with everyone
else who has written about Mark Twain since
the publication of The Ordeal of Mark Twain,
except Mr. Macy, Mr. C. Hartley Grattan, and
Mr. Carl Van Doren, Mr. Carpenter has let
Mr. Brooks's notions substitute in his
thinking for an examination of what Mark
Twain actually wrote."

B16   _____. "Tom, Huck, and America," Saturday
Review of Literature, IX (August 13), 37-39.
"The following article will constitute
part of a chapter to appear in Mr. DeVoto's
Mark Twain's America."

B17   _____. [Review: Clara Clemens, My Father,
Mark Twain (1931).] New England Quarterly,
V (January), 169-71.
Chiefly an attack on Albert Bigelow Paine
for his refusal to allow scholars access to

MT's unpublished manuscripts and letters:
"About four years ago a writer who contem-
plated a critical discussion of Mark Twain
was informed by Mr. Paine that no further
book about him was necessary. The canon was
established: whatever of Mark Twain's writing it was proper for the public to see was
in print." Rumor has it that Paine is planning another book exploiting the materials,
and now Clara has one of her own; but "she
had all that precious stuff to dip into and
she chose to publish some love-letters from
Mark Twain to his wife.... Miss Clemens's
taste is really dreadful. Katie Leary, the
parlor maid, wrote a far more valuable, and
far more understanding book about Mark
Twain." [For Paine's reply, see Anon.,
"Mark Twain's Biographer Denies He Had a
Shady Side" (1933.B2).]

B18   HENDRICK, BURTON J. The Life of Andrew Carnegie. Garden City, N.Y.: Doubleday, Doran &
Company, Inc. II, 271, 277.
Anecdote of MT asking Carnegie for a dollar and a half to buy a hymn book (no new
details in the familiar story) and brief
mention of MT as a dinner guest; portrait of
MT facing p. 278.

B19   KING, GRACE. Memories of a Southern Woman of
Letters. New York: The Macmillan Company.
On MT and his family in Hartford
(pp. 75-78, 82-88, 92-96) and in Florence
(pp. 168-79), and on the deaths of Jean and
Olivia Clemens (pp. 201-203). Grace King
was close to the Clemens daughters and
writes well about them. Includes the text
of an MT letter. For further details, see
Robert Bush article in American Literature
(1972.B24).

B20   KNIGHT, GRANT C. "Mark Twain," in his American Literature and Culture (New York: Ray
Long and Richard R. Smith, Inc.)
pp. 358-67.
MT is important as an American voice for
independence from Europe and for recording
social history, as in TS, HF, and LOM. MT
is remembered as humorist, rather than as
novelist or essayist. Knight praises CY as
"a masterpiece in irony," which exposes
evils of the past and shows the advantages
of living in a later time. HF "does not
strike the bottom of human experience. All
its events are seen through immature eyes,"
and it is not outstanding in dignity, humor,
tragedy, or weight and power.

B21   LEWISOHN, LUDWIG. "Demos Speaks," in his Expression in America (New York and London:
Harper & Brothers, Publishers),
pp. 194-232; pp. 212-32 concern MT.
Views MT as folk-artist, "Huck Finn grown
up," and not spoiled by false sophistication. "I gravely doubt whether he underwent
any ordeal," although he may have chafed at
some of Olivia Clemens's restrictions (some
of which were needed); and some of the words
and passages she removed were inserted in

(LEWISOHN, LUDWIG)
the manuscript for that purpose (pp. 217-18).
[Asselineau (1954, No. 548) reports that
"this book was later republished as The Story of American Literature."] Reprinted in
Leary (1962), pp. 127-31.

B22 LODGE, SIR OLIVER. [Anecdote.] Past Years:
An Autobiography. New York: Charles Scribner's Sons, pp. 219-20.
At a dinner in London, Andrew Lang was introduced to Mr. and Mrs. Clemens but misunderstood the name as "Cummins" and paid no
attention to them until Lodge told him afterward and Lang hastened to make amends.
MT was displeased.

B23 *MARKOVITCH, M. "Servantes i Mark Tven," Venaz
[The Crown, Belgrade], XVIII, No. 1.
[Source: Asselineau (1954), No. 564*.]

B24 OLDS, NATHANIEL S. "A Mark Twain Retort,"
Saturday Review of Literature, VII (May 7),
722.
Reviewing A Double-Barreled Detective
Story (in "the Post Express, in Rochester,
N.Y., then a highly respectable afternoon
daily and now owned by Mr. Hearst"), Olds
questioned the plausibility of the incident
in which a pregnant woman is tied to a post
and dogs are set on her; in a letter here
published MT tells Olds that the fictional
account is based on a real event.

B25 PHELPS, WILLIAM LYON. "As I See It," Scribner's Magazine, XCI (January), 54-55.
Contains a descriptive and laudatory review of Clara Clemens' My Father, Mark
Twain, "a book that should have an enormous
circulation.... These pages are worth reams
of serious criticism or heavy-handed attempts at psycho-analysis by those who never
knew him and are devoid of a sense of humor."

B26 RASCOE, BURTON. "Mark Twain: The First American," in his Titans of Literature from
Homer to the Present (New York, London:
G. P. Putnam's Sons), pp. 421-29.
The writing of HF, the first use of the
native idiom in "an unquestioned work of
genius," is "the most important single event
in American literature." In later years MT
gave way to pessimism couched in conventional literary language, worn out by his years
of struggle against propriety. Accepts the
view of Brooks that Mrs. Clemens was MT's
censor--but says the autobiography gives no
indication that he objected and some of MT's
outbursts needed restraint.

B27 *SELDES, GILBERT. "American Humor," in his
America as Americans See It (New York:
Harcourt, Brace and Company, Inc.)
[Source: Reprinted in James Dow McCallum,
ed., The College Omnibus (New York: Harcourt, Brace and Company, Inc., 1934),
pp. 272-81.] MT was too ready to accept the

"humorous habits of his time," and too dependent upon exaggeration. In Europe he defended America by belittling what he saw,
but on the river and in the West he was more
at ease, "neither defending the common man
nor afraid of the superior man."

B28 SIEGEL, ELI. [Review: Bernard DeVoto, Mark
Twain's America.] Scribner's, XCII
(November), 5-6 (specially numbered at front
of issue).
DeVoto "goes, at times, critically wild
and is unfair" to Brooks, Frank, and Mumford;
our critical outlook ought to consider more
than one sort of great American literature.

B29 SMITH, REED. [Review: Russell Blankenship's
American Literature as an Expression of the
National Mind (1931).] American Literature,
IV (March), 78-82.
The part on the treatment of MT merely
paraphrases Blankenship.

B30 UNDERHILL, IRVING S. "A Dog's Tale," American Book Collector, I (January), 14-18.
On his experience in obtaining several
hundred copies of the pamphlet first edition
of this work, and his inability to dispose
of them all profitably without destroying
the market for them as a rarity.

B31 _____. "Two Interesting Letters Pertaining to
Huckleberry Finn," American Book Collector,
II (November), 282-89.
A short letter from William Gannon, New
York book seller (September 15, 1932), inquiring about bibliographical points of HF,
and a lengthy reply by Underhill
(pp. 382-89), in the course of which he
states that the English edition of TS preceded the American one, and gives his opinion that the first English edition of HF
was set from a complete copy of the American
edition.

B32 VAN DOREN, CARL. "Toward a New Canon," Nation
(New York), CXXXIV (April 13), 429-30.
Brief mention: "Mark Twain seems a great
man of letters as well as a great man."

B33 VAN DOREN, MARK. "DeVoto's America," Nation,
CXXXV (October 19), 370-71.
A review of Mark Twain's America. "Mr.
DeVoto thinks he is meeting a theory with
facts, but as usual in such situations he
only gets tangled in a profusion of data."
To put matters in perspective will require
"someone less cantankerous" than DeVoto.

B34 WARD, A. C. "Three Voices," in his American
Literature 1880-1930. London: Methuen
[also New York: Lincoln McVeagh, The Dial
Press, according to Asselineau (1954), No.
550)], pp. 33-62; on MT pp. 52-62 and
passim.
The other two with independent vision and
freedom from conventional habits of thinking were Whitman and Emily Dickinson

(WARD, A. C.)
(pp. 61-62). MT suffers from his tendency toward horse-play and a strain of the Philistine. Eve's Diary and JA show his "insight and a comprehensive sense of pity" (p. 57), but he ended in the despair of Hadleyburg. CY was one of MT's "aesthetic indecencies" of which he was guilty only because the public demanded them (p. 30), and the English feel about it "very much as a cathedral custodian would if a boisterous holiday-maker vomited over an exquisite medieval carving" (p. 56). Links TS and HF as reflecting MT's "impatience with conventional uses" (p. 58). On the insights of Brooks and defects of the Paine biography, brief mention on p. 253.

1933 A BOOKS

A1   BROOKS, VAN WYCK. The Ordeal of Mark Twain. New York: E. P. Dutton.
A new edition of his 1920 book, with revisions in the light of DeVoto's Mark Twain's America (1932) but with the basic argument unchanged.

A2   *CLEMENS, CYRIL. The International Mark Twain Society: Its History and Members. Webster Groves, Missouri: International Mark Twain Society.
[Source: Asselineau (1954), No. 572.]

A3   PARTRIDGE, H. M., and D. C. PARTRIDGE. The Most Remarkable Echo in the World. New York: Privately Printed.
An elaborate spoof purporting to demonstrate that MT wrote works attributed to Poe, Hawthorne, and Lewis Carroll.

1933 B SHORTER WRITINGS

B1   *ANON. "Excerpt from a letter dated March 1, 1899," Autograph Album, I (December), 44.
[Source: Leary (1954), p. 43.]

B2   ANON. "Mark Twain's Biographer Denies He Had a Shady Side," Literary Digest, CXVI (July 29), 23.
In an excerpt from an interview in the New York Herald Tribune Albert Bigelow Paine says that while there is much left behind by MT that remains unpublished, there is no indecent writing being suppressed; rather, much of the material is of inferior quality, and MT himself asked that some things not be published until a hundred years after his death. "Because the trustees of the estate and Clara Clemens and I, who are the literary executors, have not given all these papers to the public we have been severely criticized. A young man in an excellent book stated I had written him that I thought any further books about Mark Twain were unnecessary. Of course, I never said anything of the kind. The more books written about Mark Twain the

better I am satisfied." [For one version of DeVoto's accusation against Paine, see annotation to his review (New England Quarterly, 1932.B17) of Clara Clemens's My Father: Mark Twain.]

B3   ANON. "Mark Twain's New Deal," Saturday Review of Literature, X (December 16), 352.
Reports that Franklin D. Roosevelt took the phrase from CY, and discusses the similarities of the two New Deals.

B4   ANON. "Two Etymologies," Word Study (G. & C. Merriam Co.), IX (November), 5-7.
Winston Churchill's novel The Crisis suggested that a stateroom on a river boat is so called because the first ones were named for states, and the texas, after the annexation of Texas, as a structure annexed to the staterooms; the publishers of the Merriam-Webster Dictionaries wrote MT for confirmation, and he called the theory far-fetched in a letter from Ampersand, N.Y. (July 26 [1901], here reproduced, partly in facsimile). The other etymology concerns Hervey Allen.

B5   ANON. [Review: Cyril Clemens, ed., Mark Twain, the Letter Writer (1932).] Times Literary Supplement, January 19, p. 38.
"These letters add nothing significant to what is already known" about MT.

B6   ARVIN, NEWTON. "The Friend of Caesar," New Republic, LXXIV (March 29), 191.
A review of Van Wyck Brooks, The Ordeal of Mark Twain (New and Revised Edition: valuable, but to be more profound would require "a genuinely dialectical history of the development of American society") and Stephen Leacock, Mark Twain, which "rather surprisingly...shows that he has not read The Ordeal of Mark Twain to no effect." Review reprinted in Arvin, American Pantheon (1966), 141-44.

B7   BLAIR, WALTER. [Review: Bernard DeVoto, Mark Twain's America (1932) and Cyril Clemens, Mark Twain the Letter Writer (1932).] American Literature, IV (January), 399-404.
Blair says DeVoto's book is "splendid" on Clemens and his frontier background, but in writing about the critics "his judgment is as unsound as his judgment concerning Mark Twain and his predecessors is sound." Cyril Clemens's book is anecdotal, filled out with "newspaper stories about Mark Twain and letters to and from the humorist. There does not seem to be much system in the arrangement of the material."

B8   BOYNTON, PERCY H. [Review: Bernard DeVoto, Mark Twain's America (1932).] New England Quarterly, VI (March), 184-87.
"The virtue of Mr. DeVoto's book is that it is definite and that it so concretely relates the shaggy realist, humorist, satirist to a western way of life and a western

(BOYNTON, PERCY H.)
manner of expression," but DeVoto's attacks
on Brooks and others are a distraction:
"It is too bad that so otherwise clear,
rational, and convincing an account should
be thus becluttered."

B9   *BRADFORD, GAMALIEL. "Mark Twain," in his Portraits and Personalities (Boston and New
York: Houghton Mifflin Co.), pp. 213-35;
also on MT, pp. 265-66.
[Source: Asselineau (1954), No. 571.]

B10   BROWNELL, GEORGE HIRAM. "Kipling's Meeting
with Mark Twain," American Book Collector,
IV (September-October), 191-92.
On the publication of Kipling's interview
of MT in the New York Herald, August 17,
1890.

B11   _____. "Mark Twainiana," American Book Collector, III (March), 172-77; (April),
207-12.
On MT's early writings in Missouri and
Iowa, in Nevada and California, and elsewhere, with credit to Willard S. Morse for
his part in uncovering much of the West
Coast material.

B12   _____. "Mark Twain's First Published Literary Effort," American Book Collector, III
(February), 92-95.
On Franklin J. Meine's discovery of "The
Dandy Frightening the Squatter," and, briefly, on MT's writings on the West Coast, and
in the Buffalo Express and the Galaxy.

B13   _____. "Mark Twain's Speech at the Whittier
Banquet," American Book Collector, IV
(August), 73-75.
A popular account, adding little or nothing to Paine's, about MT's unsuccessful
speech; notes that the holograph manuscript
of the speech is in the collection of Willard S. Morse.

B14   CHASE, MARY ELLEN. "Mississippi America,"
Commonweal, XVII (January 11), 303-304.
A review of DeVoto, Mark Twain's America
(1932); criticizes the style and controversial tone, but finds "the virtues of Mr.
DeVoto's book far over-balance its shortcomings. It is far more than a criticism,
an interpretation of Mark Twain...it is a
text-book of social history...a study in
anthropology...a revelation in frontier
religion; it is physiology, sociology,
physiography, all in one."

B15   CLEMENS, CYRIL. "Mark Twain and Jane Austen:
An Imaginary Conversation on a Transatlantic Steamer," Overland Monthly, XCI
(January), 21.
An amusing fictionalized dialogue consisting of a heated exchange, chiefly about
vivid characterization.

B16   CLEMENS, J[AMES] R[OSS.] "Mark Twain and the
Ants," Atlantic Monthly, CLI (June), 34-36.
[sic: end of issue].
"Dr. Jim" Clemens (Cyril's father) describes an MT story, from the unpublished
papers, of experiments with ants. MT said
he made them little paper churches, labeled
for the different congregations, but they
always went to the one with honey in it.
Later, he put an ant family in a little paper cottage and made the eldest son drunk
three nights; they accepted him twice, then
threw him out, thus demonstrating more than
human wisdom.

B17   DEVOTO, BERNARD. [Letter to the Editor.]
Saturday Review of Literature, X (July 22),
4.
Answering Van Wyck Brooks's The Ordeal of
Mark Twain, the Lewis Mumford review of it
(May, pp. 573-75, 1933.B25) and a brief editorial comment in Saturday Review (July 8,
p. 688), says that the Mississippi steamboating world was indeed materialistic, but
"my melancholy quarrel with Messrs. Brooks,
Frank, and Mumford proceeds from their insistence that pioneer life was somehow more
'materialistic' than life anywhere else in
America, and that this same 'materialism,'
somehow as a result of the frontier, suf-
fused American life. My book expressed my
dissent from that beautiful simplicity."
In the preceding column appears "The Pipe of
Peace," an unsigned editorial statement ac-
quiescing in DeVoto's position but arguing
that the frontier provided both temptation
and opportunity for materialists.

B18   FENN, WILLIAM PURVIANCE. Ah Sin and His
Brethren in American Literature. Peking:
College of Chinese Studies, Co-operating
with California College in China.
Briefly describes what MT wrote about the
Chinese in America (pp. 33-35 and passim),
making no attempt to go beyond the familiar
sources.

B19   GARY, LORENA M. "Oh, Youth! Mark Twain: Boy
and Philosopher," Overland Monthly, XCI
(November), 154-55.
Biographical summary, apparently based on
the Paine Biography and William Dean Howells' My Mark Twain (1910).

B20   *HICKS, GRANVILLE. "A Banjo on My Knee," in
his The Great Tradition (New York: The Macmillan Co.), pp. 38-49.
[Source: Reprinted in Scott (1955),
pp. 215-22; (1967), pp. 213-20; Leary (1962),
pp. 132-40. Leary quotes a request by Hicks
that he indicate "that it does not fully
represent my present opinion. The chief
difference is that I should make more today
of what Mark Twain did accomplish, though I
have much the same feeling about what he
didn't and why." Also see Hicks, 1935.B43
entry.] "Because there was so little in his

(HICKS, GRANVILLE)
own preparation, and so little in the intellectual life of his time, to guide him, Mark Twain could never satisfy himself that a literary career adequately expressed the powers that he felt within him." TS, HF, PW, LOM, CY, and JA are "his chief contribution to American literature...it is doubtful if he ever achieved all that he had given promise of doing or really deserved the high rank that was so readily accorded him."

B21 LEISY, ERNEST E., and JAY B. HUBBELL. "Doctoral Dissertations in American Literature," American Literature, IV (January), 419-65.
On p. 438, lists five completed dissertations on MT, and on p. 460 lists two dissertations in progress [later completed]. Supplemented by Leary (1948).

B22 LORCH, FRED W. [Review: Van Wyck Brooks, The Ordeal of Mark Twain.] American Literature, V (May), 185-7.
In this revision of the 1920 edition Brooks has not abandoned his thesis that MT's creative life was blocked by the influence of time and place, and of those near him. "In matters of detail, however, Mr. Brooks has made a number of changes, though few of these seem important enough to have warranted the labor of bringing out a revised edition." A few intemperate assertions have been dropped, but "the additions to the present volume are meager and on the whole unimpressive." Sides with DeVoto, and does not view restraint as necessarily harmful to MT's creative life.

B23 LOVEMAN, AMY. "The Clearing House," Saturday Review of Literature, X (September 16), 120.
"A Study of Mark Twain" notes a request by Edward Wagenknecht for pertinent information he might use in the book he is writing on MT.

B24 MATTHIESSEN, F. O. "Mark Twain and the Jameses," Yale Review, n.s. XXII (Spring), 605-609; on DeVoto's Mark Twain's America, pp. 605-607.
Brooks's Ordeal was "brilliant and challenging," but "too rigidly intellectualized"; DeVoto's Mark Twain's America is angry, often inaccurate, prone to oversimplify: "It furnishes a mass of not too well-organized material that is useful for interpreting him, but it is not the trenchant essay in social and intellectual history that was needed." [A review article; also discusses books on Henry James.]

B25 MUMFORD, LEWIS. "Prophet, Pedant and Pioneer," Saturday Review of Literature, IX (May), 573-75.
A review of Van Wyck Brooks, The Ordeal of Mark Twain, defending it against Bernard DeVoto, whose book "in itself generously contains enough data to support every item in Mr. Brook's characterization." To Mumford, "not merely as a writer but as a man Mark Twain seems a small, spoiled effigy of the person he might have been."

B26 PARKS, EDD WINFIELD. "Mark Twain Misconstrued." American Review, I (June), 363-67.
A review of Stephen Leacock's Mark Twain: "Mr. Leacock has relied almost entirely upon the compendious but uncritical biography by Albert Bigelow Paine, and the interesting but highly imaginative 'psychograph' by Van Wyck Brooks, The Ordeal of Mark Twain." What Leacock lacks is familiarity with American frontier life, as revealed by DeVoto.

B27 PARTINGTON, WILFRED. "Mark Twain--in Love, in Anger, and in Bibliography," Bookman, (New York), LXXVI (March), 313-14, iii-iv [sic].
A rambling account of the collector's interest and problems with MT first editions and letters; quotes MT's letters of November 28, December 2, 1868, on his engagement to Olivia Langdon.

B28 PHELPS, WILLIAM LYON. "The Real Mark Twain," Scribner's Magazine, XCIII (March), 182-83.
A review of Bernard DeVoto's Mark Twain's America (1932): "I think Mr. DeVoto overestimates the importance of Mr. Brooks's work The Ordeal of Mark Twain (1920)." DeVoto knows his material and has a sense of humor.

B29 RICHARDS, P. "Reminiscences of Mark Twain," Library Review, No. 25 (Spring), pp. 19-22.
Richards, who "drew hundreds of caricatures of the great humorist," here records MT's comments on teasing James McNeill Whistler, what President Eliot of Harvard told MT about Darwin's use of his books as bedtime reading, on speaking in London before the Authors' Club and the Savage Club, on his preference for short words (especially when he was paid by the word), and on a humorist's difficulty in being taken seriously. "This article will serve to introduce Mark Twain by Stephen Leacock."

B30 RUSSELL, FRANCES THERESA. [Review: Bernard DeVoto, Mark Twain's America (1932).] University of California Chronicle, XXXV (January), 157-61.
"Both as much needed counter propaganda and as a mine of information displayed with skillful artistry...a valuable addition to the national garner."

B31 *TARKINGTON, BOOTH. [Introduction.] The Adventures of Huckleberry Finn. New York: The Limited Editions Club.
[Source: Asselineau (1954), No. 569: "Attacks Brooks without naming him."]

B32 UNDERHILL, IRVING S. "Diamonds in the Rough, Being the Story of Another Book that Mark Twain Never Wrote," Colophon, Part 13 (February), 8 pp. (not numbered).
Contains the text of an MT letter to J. H. Riley, proposing a business arrangement to send him to the South African diamond fields to collect information and impressions for another travel book like IA and RI.

B33 _____. "'Tempest in a Teapot' or 'Notes on Huckleberry Finn': Announcement of a New Book," American Book Collector, IV (September-October), 153-56.
A rambling discussion of the first printing of HF, and of the mutilated cut on p. 283. "These notes will be a summary, with many additions and a few amendments, of articles that have appeared in The Colophon, Number Six, and The American Book Collector, November, 1932." [Apparently, Underhill's book never appeared--T.A.T.]

B34 *VAN DOREN, CARL. American Literature: An Introduction. Los Angeles: U. S. Library Association. On MT, pp. 58-62.
[Source: Asselineau (1954), No. 576.]

1934 A BOOKS

A1 BRASHEAR, MINNIE M. Mark Twain: Son of Missouri. Chapel Hill: University of North Carolina Press.
"This book is an attempt to verify an impression, formed from personal observation, that commentaries on Mark Twain which have pointed to his Middle West up-bringing as unfortunate, even tragic in its suppressions, are not true accounts." Includes chapters on MT's reading and the influence on him of eighteenth-century Europe, and a 21-page bibliography (not systematically incorporated in the present bibliography). [Also, reprinted: New York: Russell & Russell, Inc., 1964.]

A2 *CLEMENS, CYRIL. Mark Twain and Mussolini. Webster Groves, Missouri: International Mark Twain Society.
[Source: Asselineau (1954), No. 607: "The author recounts interviews with Mussolini, Shaw, Galsworthy, Maurois, Chesterton, Drinkwater, and F. D. Roosevelt, on the subject of Mark Twain's importance."]

A3 DECASSERES, BENJAMIN. When Huck Finn Went Highbrow. New York: Thomas F. Madigan, Inc.
A pamphlet containing an MT letter to Mary Hallock Foote (December 2, 1887, reproduced in facsimile) on his readings from Browning.

A4 *VYGODSKAYA, EMMA OSIPOVNA. Marka Twena piedzivojumi [The Adventures of Mark Twain.] Riga, Latvia.
[Source: Asselineau (1954), No. 604.]

1934 B SHORTER WRITINGS

B1 ADAMS, SIR JOHN. "Mark Twain, Psychologist," Dalhousie Review, XIII (January), 417-26.
A discussion of What Is Man? and the light cast on MT's thinking by a letter to Adams (December 5, 1898) on his new book, The Herbartian Theory Applied to Education. The letter is reproduced in full in Lawrence Clark Powell, "An Unpublished Mark Twain Letter" (1942).

B2 ALTROCCHI, JULIA COOLEY. "Along the Mother Lode," Yale Review, n.s. XXIV (Autumn), 131-45.
Description of California gold fields and their history; MT is mentioned only in passing. This marginal item probably attracted the attention of previous bibliographers because it follows Stephen Leacock's essay on MT and Dickens (1934.B14).

B3 ANON. "Mark Twain Anticipates Roosevelt," Word Study (G. & C. Merriam Co.), IX (April), 4.
Reprints a brief news item from the St. Louis Post-Dispatch (n.d.): Cyril Clemens presented the gold medal of the International Mark Twain Society to the President, who credited CY as his source of the term, "the New Deal."

B4 ANON. [Review: Van Wyck Brooks, The Ordeal of Mark Twain (revised edition, 1932).] Times Literary Supplement, June 28, p. 456.
"Still the most striking study of the inner reality of its subject that has yet been published," but revised very little for the new edition. Regrettably, in his more recent critical works Brooks has not fulfilled his early high promise.

B5 ANON. [Brief, minor review: Minnie M. Brashear, Mark Twain, Son of Missouri.] Nation (New York), CXXXVIII (April 4), 395.

B6 ARVIN, NEWTON. [Brief Review: Minnie M. Brashear, Mark Twain: Son of Missouri.] New Republic, LXXVII (March 28), 194.
"Miss Brashear is less shrewish than De-Voto and more concrete," but her idyllic picture of life in Hannibal must be taken with some reservation.

B7 BROWNELL, GEORGE HIRAM. "Mark Twainiana," American Book Collector, V (April), 124-26.
On the first publication of "The Jumping Frog," and on other early publications of MT's writings in the Sunday Mercury and Saturday Press.

B8 CLEMENS, CYRIL. "Mark Twain's Religion," Commonweal, XXI (December 28), 254-55.
MT has been accused of irreverence and atheism by critics who cite Captain Stormfield's Visit to Heaven and Eve's Diary to support their argument. These critics misrepresent MT's views, as is made clear in a

(CLEMENS, CYRIL)
letter from Dr. Henry Van Dyke (here published for the first time), who says that "No one who heard him speak of the simple faith of his dearly beloved wife (as he often spoke to me) could think of him as being indifferent to religion."

B9   COMPTON, CHARLES HERRICK. "Who Reads Mark Twain?" American Mercury, XXXI (April), 465-71; expanded in his Who Reads What? Essays on the Readers of Mark Twain, Hardy, Sandburg, Shaw, William James, and the Greek Classics (New York: The H. W. Wilson Co.), pp. 11-34.
Records of book-borrowing at the St. Louis Public Library, if typical of national patterns, suggest that "Mark Twain is the most widely read American author, living or dead"; Compton tabulates the popularity of individual works, and adds comments by "a seamstress," "an unemployed telegraph operator," "a chemical engineer," "a contractor," and "a musician" in response to a questionnaire he sent out.

B10   *DOUGLAS, GILBERT. "Behind that Door," New York World Telegram (August 15), p. 21. Contains an unpublished MT letter from Hamilton, Bermuda, January 26, 1910.
[Source: MHRA Annual Bibliography (1934), No. 3853.]

B11   GRINSTEAD, FRANCES. "Mark Twain Biography," Southwest Review, XIX (Winter), 12-13.
A review of Minnie M. Brashear, Mark Twain, Son of Missouri. Chiefly descriptive. "The author has unearthed a number of facts which will be valuable to every Mark Twain student of the future; but perhaps the most striking part of her book is her contention that [MT]...was a product of eighteenth-century ideals."

B12   *HARPER, JOSEPH HENRY. I Remember. New York and London: Harper & Brothers.
Contains reminiscences of MT, pp. 134-49.
[Source: Asselineau (1954), No. 609.]

B13   HOWELLS, WILLIAM DEAN. "When Mark Twain Missed Fire," Golden Book, XX (July), 97-98.
On MT's disastrous speech at the Whittier Birthday Dinner; excerpted from his "My Memories of Mark Twain," Harper's, CXXI (August, 1910), 512-13 and his My Mark Twain (1910), pp. 58-61.

B14   LEACOCK, STEPHEN. "Two Humorists: Charles Dickens and Mark Twain," Yale Review, n.s. XXIV (Autumn), 118-29.
Both authors show a kind of "divine retrospect" that blends humor and pathos.

B15   *LE BRETON, MAURICE. "Mark Twain: An Appreciation," Revue Anglo-Américaine, XII (October), 401-18.
[Source: Reprinted in Smith (1963), pp. 29-39; translated by Myra Jehlen. Note

that "Un Centenaire: Mark Twain" attributed to Le Breton is listed for 1935, but the article could not be found; my source of bibliographical data may have been in error.] Emphasizes MT's original, realistic, Western quality, his feeling for "the deeper reality beneath appearances." His feeling for the beautiful "in no way implies conformity to rules or canons. It is purely the emotion of an imaginative man who, dissatisfied with the commonplace, takes refuge in the unique. It is a moment of happiness, not the goal of a patient and rational search."

B16   _____. [Review: Minnie M. Brashear, Mark Twain: Son of Missouri.] Revue Anglo-Américaine, XII (October), 81-83.
Summarizes Miss Brashear's thesis that Missouri was particularly important in shaping MT, and that there was a strong influence of European literature, and especially of the eighteenth century. This would require a reshaping of conventional thinking on MT and the question remains open. Miss Brashear's research is especially useful and original in the first part of her book. [In French.]

B17   LYMAN, GEORGE D. The Saga of the Comstock Lode: Boom Days in Virginia City. New York, London: Charles Scribner's Sons. On MT, pp. 202-15, 246-304.
Provides a vivid popular account of MT's Washoe days, supported by copious notes (pp. 380-95 on MT). Although Lyman is writing for a general audience and stresses the more lively aspects of his material, he has turned up a wealth of evidence which merits further investigation; his sources have not been systematically traced for the present bibliography.

B17A MARQUIS, DON. Chapters for the Orthodox. Garden City, New York: Doubleday, Doran & Co., Inc.
[Source: Quoted by Christopher Morley in "Hunting Mark Twain's Remainders" (1935.B63); year and facts of publication are from National Union Catalogue.] God told a reporter he had given MT a river of his own in Heaven, and tolerated the "gorgeous lyric" of his profanity. MT was ready to accept Satan's offer to run the river in Hell for a while, but "his wife and William Dean Howells wouldn't let him."

B18   MILLER, JAMES MacDONALD. An Outline of American Literature. New York: Farrar & Rinehart, pp. 208-209, 234-35, and passim.
The greater part of this book is given over to biographical outlines, lists of works, and discussions of literary movements. Contrasts MT to the local colorists in that he dug deeper, as Hardy did (pp. 208-209). He is "the essential American, the complete verbal expression of his age," and Whitman prepared the way for him. Despite his artistic disorder and extravagance, his

(MILLER, JAMES MacDONALD)
irreligion, and the faults of his age, "he was generous and sympathetic and gentle... straightforward and passionately honest and altogether lovable."

B19   MILNE, JAMES.   The Memoirs of a Bookman.   London: John Murray.
Describes MT as being touched on hearing of John Bright's account of a Quaker funeral in London, and MT having conducted Charles Kingsley around Boston (pp. 59-60).   Describes MT as representing the bond between England and America: "He had a curious old-worldism in his nature as well as the fresh, alert, untrammelled mentality of the country whose child he was to the end" (p. 121).   Also, on his serious attitude toward writing, and his concern over copyright laws (pp. 122-24).

B20   O'FAOLÁIN, SEÁN.   "The Slavery of Mark Twain," Spectator, CLIII, 137.
A review of the revised edition of Brooks's The Ordeal of Mark Twain (1933), which O'Faoláin summarizes and praises. "And yet there is Huckleberry Finn and at least half of Life on the Mississippi--all lovely and all real.   One should read The Ordeal of Mark Twain if only to see how it was possible, by the grace of God, for these pure pearls to be saved from the corrosive of a cynic born without a will."

B21   OLDER, FREMONT.   "Mark Twain and Jackass Hill," Overland Monthly, XCII (July), 118.
First appeared as an editorial in the San Francisco Call-Bulletin under this title; discusses the competition of various places where MT lived to establish an official shrine to him, with Hartford as a leading contender, ready to guarantee $500,000 for the purpose.   Jackass Hill can make no such offer, but it was there that he wrote "The Jumping Frog."

B22   PARTRIDGE, HENRY M.   "Did Mark Twain Perpetrate Literary Hoaxes?"   American Book Collector, V (December), 351-57.
A literary spoof, attributing George Horatio Derby's Phoenixiana and Squibob Papers to MT.   Also, cites his contribution to the debate over the authorship of Shakespeare's plays, as discussed by J. M. Robertson in The Baconian Heresy: A Confutation (1912.B29).   "(To be concluded in next issue.)"

B23   PHELPS, WILLIAM LYON.   "As I like It," Scribner's Magazine, XCV (June), 432-35.
Contains anecdotes of MT giving his own introduction at a lecture in Newark, New Jersey (described himself as "a tall, sparse man"), and of Joseph Twichell reproving MT for swearing, only to be told, "Oh, Joe, you and I use exactly the same words, you in your prayers and I in my conversation; but we don't either of us mean anything by it."

B24   *SMITH, ANNELLA.   "Mark Twain--Occultist," Rosicrucian Magazine, XXVI, 65-68.
[Source: Asselineau (1954), No. 628.]

B25   TINKER, EDWARD LAROQUE.   "Cable and the Creoles," American Literature, V (January), 313-26.
Contains comments on the strained relationship of Cable and MT on their lecture tour; quotes an MT letter in possession of Major Pond's son describing Cable as "a Christ-besprinkled, psalm-singing Presbyterian."

B26   WARFEL, HARRY R.   "George W. Cable Amends a Mark Twain Plot," American Literature, VI (November), 328-31.
Consists of half-page introduction by Warfel and text of a letter from Cable to Richard Watson Gilder (May 9, 1884) concerning a scheme for a literary joke.   "The charm lies in reading a story whose salient events are already known, & reading it told over & over in 1/2 doz ways."   Involved, according to Warfel, were MT, Cable, Gilder, "and probably Howells and Aldrich."

B27   WEISS, H. B.   "Mark Twain's Hidden Autography," American Book Collector, V (October), 289-93.
Summarizes the argument in D. C. Partridge and H. M. Partridge's The Most Remarkable Echo in the World (1933) that internal ciphers reveal MT's authorship of the works attributed to Poe, Hawthorne, and Lewis Carroll; a letter from Irving S. Underhill suggests a hoax may be involved, and George S. Frisbee writes in to agree with the Partridges, adding passages from Alice's Adventures Under Ground and elsewhere, in support of the thesis.

1935 A BOOKS

A1   *ANON.   In Commemoration of the 100th Anniversary of the Birth of Samuel Langhorne Clemens, Famed as Mark Twain, this book is affectionately dedicated by the citizens of his boyhood home, Hannibal, Missouri.   Hannibal: Lithographed by the Standard Printing Co.
[24-page pamphlet.   Source: Asselineau (1954), No. 651.]

A2   CLEMENS, CYRIL.   Mark Twain's Religion, with a foreword by Russell Wilbur.   Webster Groves, Missouri: International Mark Twain Society.
"This monograph originally appeared in the Commonweal for December 28, 1934" (1934.B8).

A3   _____, ed.   Mark Twain Wit and Wisdom.   New York: Frederick A. Stokes Company.
Consists of Mark Twain anecdotes from various sources (not listed).   There is a rather conventional preface by Stephen Leacock, who concludes: "Of one or two stories in the present volume I have heard it said by the pedantic that they are as old as the

(CLEMENS, CYRIL)
Greeks. To which I can only reply that in that case the Greeks stole them from Mark Twain" (p. viii).

A4   CLEMENS, SAMUEL L. The Family Mark Twain. New York and London: Harper & Brothers Publishers.
A generous anthology of 1462 pages, containing four complete novels (LOM, TS, HF, CY) and many popular tales and sketches. Contains Albert Bigelow Paine's "Mark Twain: A Biographical Summary," a condensed version of an appreciative account which first appeared in Harper's Weekly, LIV (April 30, 1910), 6-10, and Owen Wister's "In Homage to Mark Twain," which also appeared in Harper's Monthly, CLXXI (October, 1935), 547-556. This would have been a fine gift book in the centennial year of MT's birth, but it contains nothing of special importance to the scholar.

A5   *____. Mark Twain's Notebook, prepared for publication with comments by Albert Bigelow Paine. New York and London: Harper & Brothers.
[Source: Asselineau (1954), No. 641; also in Authorized Edition.]
A selection of materials from MT's unpublished notebooks, from his days as a river pilot until 1906. Paine's brief introduction denies that there has been any deliberate suppression of racy material in MT's unpublished manuscripts: "Mark Twain had his say; as much as any author could have it, thirty, forty, fifty years ago. When restricted at all it was chiefly through his own expressed wish to observe the conventions and convictions of that more orthodox, more timid and delicate (possibly more immaculate) day."

A6   *____, (translator). Slovenly Peter; or, Happy Tales and Funny Pictures, freely translated by Mark Twain, with Dr. Heinrich Hoffmann's illustrations, adapted from the rare first edition by Fritz Kredel. New York and London: Harper & Brothers; also, "now printed for the first time for members of the Limited Editions Club," New York: The Marchbanks Press.
[Source: Asselineau (1954), Nos. 643, 644.]

A7   *CROSS, WILBUR L. A Statement [Regarding] the Centenary of Mark Twain. Hartford, Connecticut.
[Source: Asselineau (1954), No. 652.] A broadside: a proposal by the Governor of Connecticut to designate November 1 as Mark Twain Day.

A8   EMBERSON, FRANCES GUTHRIE. Mark Twain's Vocabulary: A General Survey. University of Missouri Studies, X (July 1), 1-53.
Includes a Preface by Robert L. Ramsay. Treats the development of MT's vocabulary,

and special aspects of it such as Americanisms, possible coinages, adoptions, revivals, and a miscellaneous category. The "major parts" were reprinted in Twainian, XI (November-December, 1952), 1-4; XII (January-February, 1953), 1-4; (March-April), 1-4; (May-June), 3.

A9   *HELLER, OTTO. The Seriousness of Mark Twain. Address at the Annual Dinner of the State Historical Society at Hannibal, Missouri, May 9, 1935. Hannibal: Hannibal Chamber of Commerce.
[Source: Asselineau (1954), No. 635; described as a 14-page pamphlet, "A protest against Brooks's thesis in the name of local patriotism."]

A10   HERZBERG, MAX J., ed. The Mark Twain Omnibus Drawn from the Works of Mark Twain and Edited by Max J. Herzberg. New York, London: Harper & Brothers.
Consists of PW, a number of stories, sketches, and letters, introductory material, and exercises, with a bibliography of secondary material (not annotated and apparently not selected according to a plan). A school anthology.

A11   HÜPPY, AUGUST. Mark Twain und die Schweiz. Dem Grossen Freund und Bewunderer unseres Landes zum 100. Geburtstag. Zurich: Reutimann & Co.
Concerned with MT's visits to Switzerland, rather than with Swiss interest in his works. Contains a discussion of A Tramp Abroad on pp. 52-60.

A12   JOHNSON, MERLE. A Bibliography of the Works of Mark Twain, Samuel Langhorne Clemens. A List of First Editions in Book Form and of First Printings in Periodicals and Occasional Publications of His Varied Literary Activities. Revised and Enlarged. New York and London: Harper & Brothers.
This has only been superseded in part by Jacob Blanck's Bibliography of American Literature (Vol. II [1957], 173-254) and is still extremely valuable. In addition to th the material listed in the descriptive title there is a wealth of notes, commentary, and information on material about MT. Of particular interest are "Books Containing Mark Twain Letters," discussion of MT's plays and of dramatizations of his work, discussion of newspaper interviews, "General Notes and Comment" (a miscellany of brief items which do not fit in elsewhere), "Several Items by Mark Twain" ("a selection of juvenilia and specimens of the later writings as a professional newspaperman"). There is an extensive and detailed index. [Reprinted Westport, Connecticut: Greenwood Press, Publishers, 1972.]

A13   *LANGDON, JERVIS. Mark Twain and Elmira, Mark Twain Centennial Committee of New York.

(*LANGDON, JERVIS)
[Source: Asselineau (1954), No. 635, which describes it as a 6-leaf pamphlet by a nephew of MT.]

A14 PATTEE, FRED LEWIS, ed. Mark Twain: Representative Selections. New York: American Book Company.

"Luckily he had a sensible wife. Carefully was he directed into the literary areas where lay his great power. Assisted by Twichell and Howells he was led to the writing of Old Times on the Mississippi, a marvellous classic. He was directed by Warner into the wonder area of The Gilded Age, he was induced to add to it his Tom Sawyer and best of all his Huckleberry Finn" (p. xxxvi). Pattee also notes MT's power as a satirist, but "What results from Mark Twain's furious assaults upon his times? Archibald Henderson has classed the man as 'the greatest sociologist in letters.' Just why? He accomplished nothing"--people read GA for amusement (pp. xlii-xliii).

A15 TAYLOR, COLEY B. Mark Twain's Margins on Thackerary's "Swift." New York: Gotham House.

Contains text of MT's pencilled comments in the section on Swift in Thackeray's English Humorists ("the Harper edition of 1868"-- p. 29). This is nominally a 55-page booklet, in which the first 27 pages are given over to the half-title, title-page, and a very general preface on MT in Redding by a neighbor who did not know him well; the latter part of the book is valuable and has frequently been cited by students of MT.

A16 WAGENKNECHT, EDWARD. Mark Twain: The Man and His Work. New Haven: Yale University Press.

Reflects thorough familiarity with the MT scholarship of the time, and includes a ten-page bibliography. A completely revised edition appeared in 1961. Pp. 57-80 excerpted in Scott (1955), pp. 223-30.

1935 B SHORTER WRITINGS

B1 ALTICK, RICHARD D. "Mark Twain's Despair: An Explanation in Terms of His Humanity," South Atlantic Quarterly, XXXIV (October), 359-67.

"He was not a psychological wreck all his life, tormented by a sense of guilt at having betrayed his artistic instincts. On the contrary, he was more than ordinarily happy during his best years," and, by his own standards, a success; but he became a pessimist and a cynic because of his growing materialism at the expense of "his idealistic-intellectual-artistic side.... Mark Twain remained all his life immature, socially, intellectually, or emotionally; and thus when old age came he was totally unprepared for it."

B2 ANON. "Ever this Twain Is Met. World-Wide Tributes Paid on Centenary of Writer's Birth; Hannibal, Missouri to Be Shrine; Mussolini Heads Movement," Literary Digest, CXX (November 30), 19.

Contains no specific references, except to an editorial in the Hannibal Courier-Post urging the establishment of a memorial shrine to MT in that city; includes pictures of sculptures by Walter Russell of MT and Tom and Huck for the memorial, and comments on the oddity of Mussolini's part in sending a $200 contribution and his selection to be Honorary President of the fund for a memorial in St. Louis.

B3 ANON. "A Garland for Mark Twain's Centennial," New York Times Book Review (August 4), p. 5.

A review of Cyril Clemens, ed., Mark Twain: Wit and Wisdom, which brings MT "freshly and vividly into the reader's consciousness... it is a delightful book for casual reading."

B4 ANON. "Mark Twain," Saturday Review of Literature, XIII (November 16), 8.

On MT's warm, kindly side, as exemplified in the two letters on the following page (1935.B25, as "Two Letters of Mark Twain, Hitherto Unpublished").

B5 ANON. "Mark Twain," Times Literary Supplement, November 30, pp. 779-80.

A review-article and general discussion of MT, who was no novelist, but a humorist and, still more, "a poet, even in his humor"; his lasting works are TS, HF, LOM, RI, and parts of GA and PW. "All that Mark Twain was and was not [was] inherent in his frontier origin." There is comparatively brief discussion of Albert Bigelow Paine, ed., Mark Twain's Notebook (Contains "no surprises...it is in fact incomplete and textually unreliable in addition to being inadequately edited"); Edward Wagenknecht, Mark Twain: The Man and His Work ("Sums up the outstanding facts and critical views, stands so squarely in the centre of the field as to suggest little need of further discussion"); Minnie M. Brashear, Mark Twain: Son of Missouri (1934; "Seeks to prove the existence on the frontier of an 'authentic' culture, but shows it as little more than 'an interest in the safe and reliable classics'--which is not culture but its simulacrum, too partial and provincial to fulfill the true function of culture"); Fred Lewis Pattee, ed., Mark Twain: Representative Selections (Briefly noted).

B6 ANON. "Mark Twain Centennial. Commemorations Will Be Held Throughout Nation this Year," Literary Digest, CXIX (April 20), 31.

On the Mark Twain Centennial Committee, quoting a note to Nicholas Murray Butler, the chairman, from Rudyard Kipling: "To my mind he was the largest man of his time, both in the direct outcome of his work, and, more important still, as an indirect force

(ANON.)
in an age of iron Philistinism. Later generations don't know their debt, of course,
and they would be quite surprized if they
did." Other commemorative groups are also
mentioned, and there is a photo of MT (copyrighted by Paul Thompson).

B7   ANON. "Mark Twain Centennial to be Widely
Celebrated," Publishers' Weekly, CXXVII
(February 9), 697.
A survey of plans: Nicholas Murray Butler
is chairman of a centennial committee, and
there will be formal dinners in the larger
cities, radio programs, films, a special
stamp issue, articles in national magazines,
and interviews with people who knew MT.
There are also plans for celebration of the
centennial in England, and there will be
showings of an early film showing him, as
well as a commemorative medal and a special
edition of his works.

B8   ANON. "The Mark Twain Commemoration," Columbia University Quarterly, XXVII (December),
357-78.
Nicholas Murray Butler presided over the
ceremonies, held October 31, 1935. The addresses were by James Campbell on "The Case
of Clemens vs. Twain" (pp. 358-69) and
Christopher Morley on "The Return of Huckleberry Finn" (pp. 369-78). Butler praised
MT's "many-sided and truly rich personality"
and told several anecdotes. Campbell discussed the changes in MT's critical reputation and discussed the question of whether
a great artist was stifled in him, concluding that he was the man our national literature needed to provide a regeneration, to
blow the masses of stale air out, although
his philosophy was mechanical and works such
as MS were marred by a failure to keep psychic distance; his great achievement was
"the perfect expression of the culture of
western America" in such products of his
personal experience as TS and HF. Christopher Morley commented on the dated quality
of some of MT's humor and the way his minor
works are being forgotten. The debunking
by Brooks and others, though humorless and
often mistaken, is a healthy preventive to
adulation of MT. MT's great works are TS
and HF, which, for all their flaws, contain
"writing admirable and perfect for its purpose." [Morley covers much the same ground
in his "Hunting Mark Twain's Remainders" in
the Saturday Review of Literature,
November 2 (1935.B63), and Campbell's speech
is reprinted as "Twain Versus Clemens"
[(1936.B8).]

B9   ANON. "Our Mark Twain," Scholastic, XXVII
(November 23), 3.
An editorial, discussing MT's fame, critical views of him, and the importance of
his work. Introduces a Mark Twain Number,
containing the following, in addition to
articles listed in the present bibliography:

a reprinting of Owen Wister's "In Homage to
Mark Twain," (pp. 6-7, 21); "Mark Twain Digs
for Gold," a Radio Play by Gladys Schmidt
(pp. 9-10); "Chronology of the Life of Mark
Twain" (p. 16, "From Mark Twain, by Stephen
Leacock"); "Mark Twain Bibliography" (p. 17,
selected from Wagenknecht's bibliography in
Mark Twain: The Man and His Work); "Twain
Poster Contest" (p. 35); and pictures of the
Arthur W. Woelfle portrait of MT, Walter
Russell's model of the center portion of a
sculpture group for the Mark Twain Memorial,
and a number of photographs of scenes in
Hannibal, Missouri.

B10   *ANON. "Princes de l'humour: Alphonse Allais,
Mark Twain," Annales Politiques et Littér-
aires, CLX (September 25), 316-17.
[Source: Asselineau (1954), No. 715.]

B11   ANON. "Scattered Letters of Mark Twain, Together with Eulogistic Contributions for His
Centennial" ("Published through the courtesy
of Mr. Cyril Clemens"), Missouri Historical
Society Glimpses of the Past (now Missouri
Historical Society Bulletin), II (October),
123-32.
Includes an MT letter of April 14 (1868?)
asking a person named Williams to "see that
no reports or synopses (even the most meagre
ones) are made of my lecture"; to P. D. Pel-
tier (October 14 [1879]) on a lecture welcoming Georgia veterans to Hartford ("Personal contact & communion of Northerners &
Southerners over the friendly board will do
more toward obliterating sectional lines and
restoring mutual respect and esteem than any
other thing that can be devised"); to Sig-
mund Schlesinger (Vienna, February 2, 1898
about a play on which they had planned to
collaborate); also several MT letters to
James Ross Clemens. Tributes to MT from
Lord Dunsany, Eugene O'Neill, Irvin S. Cobb,
Carl Sandberg, David Warfield, and Hendrik
Willem Van Loon.

B12   *ANON. [Interview with Mrs. W. E. Ireland.]
Hannibal Courier-Post, March 6.
MT renamed Holliday's Hill for Cardiff,
South Wales because it reminded him of a
similar hill there. [Source: Wecter (1952),
pp. 157, 300.]

B13   ANON. [Review: Slovenly Peter, translated by
MT from Dr. Heinrich Hoffman's Struwelpet-
er.] Saturday Review of Literature, XIII
(November 16), 26.
"Mark's translation has the gay insouci-
ance one would expect."

B14   ANON. [Brief, descriptive review: Slovenly
Peter, translated from Dr. Heinrich Hoffman's Struwelpeter.] Times Literary Supplement, November 30, p. 780.

B15   ARVIN, NEWTON. "Mark Twain: 1835-1935," New Republic, LXXXIII (June 12), 125-27.
      MT won a great and lasting readership, but writing for such a large and uncritical audience was harmful to him as artist and critic of his time; nonetheless, for works such as his attacks on American imperialism, "and despite the vast wastage of his career, Mark Twain may well survive as a writer and in the affections of later generations and of a class to which he did not directly address himself." He will survive, "but surely far less as a writer, at the best, than as a folk-hero, a grand half-legendary personality." Reprinted in Scott (1955), pp. 231-35, and in Leary (1962), pp. 141-44.

B16   BECKER, MAY LAMBERTON. "Books: A Reading Menu for the Week," Scholastic, XXVII (November 23), 17.
      A review of LOM as a "truly American" book some critics say will outlive all MT's books except TS and HF, and of DeVoto's Mark Twain's America (1932), which "can hardly be surpassed" as introduction to MT and "as a preface to the understanding of American literature and its differences from English literature."

B17   *BINGHAM, ROBERT WARWICK. "Buffalo's Mark Twain," Museum Notes, Buffalo Historical Society, II, No. 4-6.
      [Source: Asselineau (1954), No. 672.]

B18   BORGES, JORGE LUIS. "Una Vindicación de Mark Twain," Sur, V (Noviembre), 40-46.
      Supports DeVoto's view of MT as vigorously American, in opposition to "la depresiva tesis de Brooks." "Mark Twain (importa repetirlo) ha escrito Huckleberry Finn, libro que hasta pura la gloria. Libro ni burlesco ni trágico, libro solamente feliz."

B19   CANBY, HENRY SEIDEL. "Mark Twain: Anti-Victorian," Saturday Review of Literature, XII (October 12), 3-4, 14.
      A review of Mark Twain's Notebook and Edward Wagenknecht, Mark Twain: The Man and His Work, which, "if it contributes nothing really new, is a sane and accurate discussion of a man hard to analyze, and very difficult to estimate without exaggeration either of his tragic pessimism or his boisterous humor. This writer's sensible handling of the wife-suppression theory is excellent, and indeed his volume is the most useful, if not the most brilliant or penetrating, short book on Mark Twain." The Notebook provides no startling evidence, and "the novelty is in a change in emphasis," stressing MT's "inmost thoughts." He was not suppressed, and managed to express radical ideas in his lifetime, as in HF and CY. Picture of MT and Olivia Clemens on front cover.

B20   _____. [Brief review: Mark Twain's Notebook.] Book of the Month Club News, November, p. 15.
      The book refutes the Brooks view of suppressed genius but provides no starling revelations.

B21   CHARPENTIER, JOHN. "Humour Anglais et Humour Américain, À Propos du Centenaire de Mark Twain," Mercure de France, CCLXIV (15 Décembre), 475-500.
      Consists of two somewhat distinct essays; the first ends (p. 488): "Nous allons voir, maintenant, en prenant pour exemple Mark Twain, comment l'humour révolutionnaire est devenu matérialiste de l'autre côte de l'océan." On the basis of photographs in the Paine biography and in Clara Clemens's My Father, Mark Twain Charpentier asks, "Mark Twain avait-il des origines juives, comme on l'a hasardé?" (p. 490).

B22   CLEMENS, CYRIL. "The First Book on Mark Twain," Commonweal, XXII (Ocober 11), 591.
      A review of Fred Lewis Pattee's Mark Twain: Representative Selections, which are well chosen and come with "a scholarly and fascinating introduction." Pattee, as a college professor, errs in denying MT a place "among our few great literary masters."

B23   _____. "Mark Twain's Joan of Arc," Commonweal, XXII (July 26), 323-24.
      A discussion for the general reader of JA and MT's admiration of Joan. (See letter by Walsh, August 23, p. 408, 1935.B80.)

B24   *CLEMENS, SAMUEL L. "Letter to the Hon. Secretary of the Treasury," dated October 13, 1902. Book News (American Book Company), Autumn.
      [Source: MHRA Annual Bibliography (1935), No. 3744.]

B25   _____. "Two Letters of Mark Twain, Hitherto Unpublished," Saturday Review of Literature, XIII (November 16), 9, 29.
      To twelve-year-old Margaret Blackmer (September 18, October 6, 1908), mentioning visits from several of his "Angel-Fishes," listing JA, P&P, HF, and TS as his favorite books, commenting on the recent burglary of his Redding, Connecticut home, and mentioning an expected visit from his childhood sweetheart [Laura Hawkins Frazer].

B26   COLUM, MARY M. "The Misunderstood Jester," Forum, XCIV (November), 277-78.
      A review of Edward Wagenknecht's Mark Twain: The Man and His Work, which here receives little critical attention; instead, the reviewer praises MT as "a folk writer," in a picaresque tradition with which he was familiar, and a writer of genius although he had "from his intellectual side, an uninteresting mind." MT "had an immense audience, to which he was devoted, and which he did not wish to disturb in any of its convictions." There is passing mention of

1935 - Shorter Writings

(COLUM, MARY M.)
"that brilliant book of Van Wyck Brooks',
The Ordeal of Mark Twain."

B27 DAVIDSON, LOUIS B. "He Fell in Love with a
Picture," Liberty, XII (November 30), 48-50.
A popular account of MT's love for his
wife Olivia, adding nothing to the details
given by Paine and in other familiar sources.

B28 DEANE, THE REV. CANON ANTHONY. "Mark Twain,"
in The Right Hon. Earl of Lytton, ed.,
Essays by Divers Hands, Being the Transactions of the Royal Society of Literature of
the United Kingdom. n.s., XIV (London:
Humphrey Milford, Oxford University Press),
pp. 99-110. [Read March 7, 1935.]
Praises MT's courage in meeting his af-
flictions, and puts HF first among his
books. Despite occasionally forced humor
and uncertain taste, his work "caused a
vast amount of wholesome and hearty laughter" (pp. 109-10).

B29 DEVOTO, BERNARD. "The Greatness of Mark
Twain. A New Biography that Silences the
Frustration Theory--And His Notebook,"
New York Times Book Review, October 27,
pp. 1, 22.
A review of Edward Wagenknecht, Mark
Twain: The Man and His Work and Albert
Bigelow Paine, ed., Mark Twain's Notebook.
Wagenknecht's "sane, sound and tolerant
book" provides little new evidence, apart
from the Fairbanks correspondence, but
gives a useful survey of MT criticism--
rendering verdicts which are just but sometimes less scornful than the targets deserve. He rightly shows the careful artist
but errs in calling MT a thinker. The notebooks are good to have, but Paine is incorrect in saying that they are complete "and
he accompanies them with notes in his familiar piety."

B30 _____. [Review: Fred Lewis Pattee, ed.,
Mark Twain: Representative Selections.]
New England Quarterly, VIII (September),
427-30.
As an anthology it is flawed by the absence of anything written after 1877 (as a
result of copyright restrictions), and the
introduction, despite its "sound judgment"
and "critical sanity," overestimates the
beneficial influence of the East while suggesting that almost nothing written under
that influence will endure. Pattee misunderstands the influences of the popular
humor of the time; for example, in fact
"the influence of Artemus Ward on Mark
Twain was the influence of a man who finds
a publisher for a young writer and no more."

B31 DICKINSON, ASA DON. "Huckleberry Finn is Fifty Years Old--Yes; But Is He Respectable?"
Wilson Bulletin for Librarians, X (November),
180-85.
A general discussion of HF, followed by an
account of the difficulty of getting the
book into the children's section at the
Brooklyn Public Library. Dickinson wrote
MT, whose reply (December 21, 1905) is reproduced in facsimile; there is also a page
of photographs showing MT's grave, and several homes, including the one on Fifth Avenue, New York City.

B32 DREISER, THEODORE. "Mark the Double Twain,"
English Journal, XXIV (October), 615-27.
"From his grave he fairly yells: 'I was
restrained. I was defeated. I hate the
lying, cowardly world that circumvented me.
Man is not good. He is not honest. Life is
a lie! Life is a lie!' Read What Is Man?
Read The Mysterious Stranger. The truth is,
as you see, that Twain was not two people,
but one--a gifted but partially dissuaded
Genius who, in time, and by degrees changed
into his natural self." Reprinted in Leary
(1962), pp. 145-58.

B33 _____. "Mark Twain: Three Contacts. Revealing a Writer's Curiosity about the Sentiments
Another Writer Leaves Out of His Books," Es-
quire, IV (October), 22, 162-162B.
Dreiser twice met MT and tried unsuccessfully to interview him; the second attempt
almost succeeded after Dreiser mentioned
W. D. Howells (whom he regarded less highly:
"I was interested to see whether Twain...
was still overawed by this polished minor
realist, who had insinuated himself into
the sanctuary of eastern literary punditry.")
Finally, in 1907 or 1908, Dreiser achieved
a meeting in the back room of a New York
saloon with MT, who was "thanks to the magi-
cal release of a little alcohol--voicing
things never said in his published works or
public addresses," setting forth his pessimistic philosophy. Commenting on a breach
of promise suit then prominent in the papers,
MT commented [quoted from memory, and only
"approximately"] "that all men love their
wives, and are faithful to them, particularly if they're in the public eye; that you're
supposed to love your wife and be sexually
faithful.... Just the same, after the first
few years of marriage, men·don't love their
wives, and they are not strictly faithful....
The passion that brings about courtship,
marriage and the honeymoon is one thing, and
ends with the honeymoon, or a year or two
later. The sex desire is an unmanageable
thing, and can be aroused in any real man by
any young and attractive and sensuous girl."

B34 DUNSMOOR, KATHRYN. "Land of Tom and Huck,"
Scholastic, XXVII (November 23), 11-12.
Describes Hannibal, Missouri as it appeared in 1935 (based on the Hannibal Courier-Post of March 6 and on MT's Autobiography).

B35 ESKEW, GARNETT LAIDLAW. "Steamboating Again on Mark Twain's River," Rotarian, XLVII (November), 25-28, 50.
On a recent steamboat trip, a popular account apparently drawing on Paine and LOM; includes photographs of steamboats and of MT's pilot's certificate.

B36 *FEDERICO, P. J. [Article on MT Centennial.] Journal of the Patent Office Society.
[Source: Twainian, XVI (November-December, 1957), 1-4.]

B37 FISCHER, WALTHER. "Mark Twain (Zu seinem 100 Geburtstage am 30. November 1935)," Neueren Sprachen, XLIII, Heft 11, 471-80.
A survey of his works on the hundredth anniversary of his birth.

B38 FOOTE, E. B. "A Mark Twain Problem: The Mysterious Paragraph," Saturday Review of Literature, XII (October 26), 9.
Letter to the editor, quoting a paragraph attributed to MS by "a San Francisco evening paper nearly twenty years ago" but not to be found in the book; can a reader provide information? [For further comment see Wagenknecht, 1935.B79.]

B39 FROHMAN, DANIEL. Daniel Frohman Presents: An Autobiography. New York: Claude Kendall & Willoughby Sharp.
On the P&P play and on litigation with MT ("During the day we sued each other in court. At night we played billiards together at the Players' Club"), pp. 141-44; also, brief references to MT, passim (indexed).

B40 HAIGHT, GORDON S. [Review: Edward Wagenknecht, Mark Twain: The Man and His Work.] Yale Review, XXV (Autumn), 212-13.
Praises Wagenknecht's thoroughness but regrets "his lack of critical perspective."

B41 *Hannibal (Missouri) Courier-Post, Mark Twain Centennial Edition, March 6.
[Source: Ferguson (1943), p. 334.]

B42 HEMINGWAY, ERNEST. Green Hills of Africa. New York: Charles Scribner's Sons. On MT, pp. 22-23.
"All modern American literature comes from one book by Mark Twain called Huckleberry Finn. If you read it you must stop where Nigger Jim is stolen from the boys. That is the real end. The rest is just cheating. But it's the best book we've had. There was nothing before. There has been nothing as good since." MT and Henry James "both lived to be old men but they did not get any wiser as they got older. You see we make our writers into something very strange." Hemingway cites pressures that include the demands of an expensive standard of living, and the effect of the critics on an author who heeds them.

B43 HICKS, GRANVILLE. The Great Tradition: An Interpretation of American Literature since the Civil War. Rev. ed. New York: Macmillan (Reprinted New York: Biblo and Tannen, 1967), pp. 38-49, 68-72.
The frontier as it influenced MT was vital, but it was also provincial, and this accounts for the virtues and defects of IA (pp. 39-42). MT lacked discipline, and none of his books fulfills the promise of its early chapters (pp. 43-44). MT's concern with making money is typical of the age, but his books look back to a simpler, more innocent time; unfortunately, he was an entertainer, not a realist, and a recognition of his lack of independence and his status as a writer helps account for his later pessimism (pp. 45-48). On GA as it reflected the times, pp. 68-72. [See also 1933.B20.]

B44 HUGHES, RUPERT. "I Heard Mark Twain Laugh," Good Housekeeping, CI (November), 44-45, 184-93.
Hughes, who grew up in Missouri and in Keokuk, Iowa, later became a newspaper reporter in New York. He recalls the Lotos Club dinner honoring MT, and the fulsome tributes in a succession broken by Richard Watson Gilder, who said: "I think I may claim to be one of Mark Twain's most sincere admirers. I doubt that any one else has bought more of his work or paid as much for it. But I must say that I can not approve of all he writes. I regret to find a tendency to coarseness, flippancy, irreverence, in much of his writing. I am often compelled to delete a great deal of what he submits to us. Still, when he is at his best, he is a charming writer whom I am most happy to publish." MT broke the tension by asserting that he put in some passages just to shock Gilder--and was paid for them even though they were deleted. Hughes also attended MT's seventieth birthday dinner, but his account is limited to recollections of the speech, which is in print elsewhere. From Mary Lawton he heard the story (not in her 1925 book), of MT's disappointment in finding that his newly purchased house in New York faced so that the sun did not shine in his room: "Livy would have thought of that. Livy always thought of everything." (Includes several photographs of MT.)

B45 *KIPLING, RUDYARD. [Preface.] Tom Sawyer à travers le monde, traduction d'Albert Savine. Paris: Albin Michel.
[Source: Asselineau (1954), No. 642: "A translation of Tom Sawyer Abroad."]

B46 LACOSSITT, HENRY. "Hail to Hannibal, Honoring Mark Twain," New York Times Magazine (December 1), pp. 11, 16.
A conventional portrait of the Missouri town where MT grew up, and briefly describing his visit there in 1902.

1935 - Shorter Writings

B47 LAUTREC, GABRIEL DE. "Mark Twain," Mercure de France, CCLXIV (15 Novembre), 69-83.
   A superficial account, apparently based on secondary material; emphasizes biography, comments briefly on some of MT's minor work, and makes the remarkable statement that MT avoided racial questions: "Chose étrange, Mark Twain ne fait jamais allusion aux nègres. On ne sait s'il partage ou non les préventions absurdes et féroces de ses contemporains. Pour un Étatsunisien pur, encore aujourd'hui, un nègre n'est pas un homme.... Mark Twain a évité prudemment de donner son opinion, qui, s'il l'avait exprimée, lui aurait fait perdre d'un coup toute sa popularité" (p. 79).

B48 LEACOCK, STEPHEN. "Mark Twain and Canada," Queen's Quarterly (Queen's University, Kingston), XLII (Spring), 68-81.
   On MT's visits, made out of concern for copyright rather than any particular interest in Canada; based in part on information provided by "my friend Cyril Clemens of St. Louis, who knows more about Mark Twain than even Sam Clemens did." Includes "the main part" of an interview in the Montreal Gazette (November 29, 1881) and the text of a speech at a public dinner (Montreal Gazette, circa December 7-8, 1881). Two years later, according to Cyril Clemens, MT attended a meeting of the Royal Society. "It remains for some research scholar to open the dusty folios of that august body and see if their proceedings were enlivened by any remarks of their illustrious visitor." (Also see W., A. L. O., "More of Mark Twain in Canada," 1935.B78.)

B49 *LE BRETON, MAURICE. "Un Centenaire: Mark Twain," Revue Anglo-Américaine, XIII (June), 401-19.
   On MT's limited popularity in France, his Americanism and nostalgia for his youth, accounting for the different schools of criticism. [Source: Asselineau (1954), No. 690, with a lengthy abstract; the article could not be found in a check of this issue at Duke University. It may be the same as the article listed as "Mark Twain: An Appreciation" for 1934.B15.]

B50 *LEMONNIER, LÉON. "L'Enfance de Mark Twain," Revue de France, XV (November), 130-58.
   [Source: Asselineau (1954), No. 693.]

B51 ____. "Les Débuts d'un Humoriste," Grande Revue, CXLIX (November), 76-88.
   Chiefly biographical; sees MT less as a man of action than as an amused witness of the adventurous life.

B52 * ____. "Les débuts d'un humoriste," Revue Anglo-Américaine, XIII (June), 401-19.
   [Source: Asselineau (1954), No. 691: "Insists on the duality of Mark Twain's genius." The article could not be found in a check of this issue at Duke University-- T.A.T.]

B53 LORCH, FRED W. [Review: Minnie M. Brashear, Mark Twain: Son of Missouri (1934).] American Literature, VI (January), 460-63.
   "The title of this book does not adequately suggest the serious, scholarly purpose which motivated the study. Miss Brashear does not attempt, primarily, to reclaim Mark Twain for the state of Missouri, but to deal with the more significant question, 'How is Mark Twain to be accounted for?'" This is a major study which brings MT's background into perspective.

B54 ____. [Review: Cyril Clemens, ed., Mark Twain: Wit and Wisdom.] American Literature, VII (November), 351.
   Because the occasions have passed, "Many of the anecdotes appear to be nearly pointless. In some of them it is obvious that the narrator is attempting to capitalize a very slight acquaintance with Mark Twain and is hard pushed to give his slender substance the semblance of importance."

B55 ____. [Review: Fred Lewis Pattee, Mark Twain: Representative Selections.] American Literature, VII (November), 350-1.
   Pattee wastes time in refuting Brooks and arguing the favorable influence of the East: "It had been better for general purposes had he developed in a more systematic way Mark Twain's social, political, and literary theories..."

B56 LOVETT, ROBERT MORSS. "Mark Twain the American," New Republic, LXXXV (November 20), 50-51.
   A review article, briefly noting Cyril Clemens, ed., Mark Twain Wit and Wisdom and Albert Bigelow Paine, ed., Mark Twain's Notebook, and describing at greater length Wagenknecht's Mark Twain: The Man and His Work.

B57 M., A. N. [Review: Albert Bigelow Paine, ed., Mark Twain's Notebook.] Manchester Guardian, December 19, p. 5.
   Chiefly descriptive. This is a book to be dipped into, not read straight through.

B58 MASTERS, EDGAR LEE. "Mark Twain: Son of the Frontier," American Mercury, XXXVI (September), 67-74.
   MT was shaped by "the uncontaminated America of the West," and attempts by Livy to refine him were unsuccessful. Only brief discussions of specific works, except for a page on MS.

B59 ____. Vachel Lindsay: A Poet in America. New York and London: Charles Scribner's Sons, passim.
   Lindsay read Adam's Diary, TS, and HF. Masters ranks Lindsay's "Three Poems about Mark Twain" below his best, although it might be put with them.

B60   MEIGS, CORNELIA. "Mark Twain," St. Nicholas,
       LXIII (November), 14-16, 50-51.
           A story for children of an escapade by
       young Sam Clemens; no source is cited.

B61   METZ, J. J. "Mark Twain Centennial," Indus-
       trial Arts and Vocational Education, XXIV
       (December), 364-65.
           Primarily biographical. "His versatility
       is truly astounding, but what is of more
       importance, Mark Twain was strictly honest.
       This characteristic should be pointed out
       specially to the shop students. The best
       craftsman, unless he be honest, cannot be
       held up as a model for the student. What
       dishonesty has done to the world is only
       too well illustrated by present-day condi-
       tions." There is an account of MT's pay-
       ment of the Webster debts: "It is this
       type of sterling honesty which is found so
       seldom, and which is, nevertheless, so
       desperately needed to cure the evils of
       the times. It is well, therefore, to em-
       phasize this admirable trait, not only in
       the school auditorium, at a formal Mark
       Twain centennial celebration, but also in
       the classroom and in the school shop."

B62   MONROE, HARRIET. "On the Great River,"
       Poetry, XLVI (August), 268-74.
           By steamboat to Hannibal; the little on
       MT is impressionistic.

B63   MORLEY, CHRISTOPHER. "Hunting Mark Twain's
       Remainders," Saturday Review of Litera-
       ture, XIII (November 2), 15-16.
           Praises HF for its humor and beauty,
       and suggests that except for this book and
       TS "the other books are fast fading out."
       Takes issue with MT's more solemn critics,
       and quotes with satisfaction a chapter
       from Don Marquis's Chapters for the Ortho-
       dox in which God tells a reporter that MT
       has been given his own river in Heaven and
       once ran a steamboat race through Hell.
       Satan once asked to borrow MT and his riv-
       er, and MT was willing, but "his wife and
       William Dean Howells wouldn't let him."

B64   PAINE, ALBERT BIGELOW, ed. "Unpublished
       Diaries of Mark Twain," Hearst's Inter-
       national, XCIX (August), 24-27, 134-36;
       (September), 48-51, 111-12.
           Excerpts from MT's notebooks, with very
       brief editorial comment by Paine.

B65   PARTRIDGE, HENRY M. "Did Mark Twain Perpe-
       trate Literary Hoaxes?" American Book
       Collector, VI (January), 20-23;
       (February), 50-53.
           Concludes a series begun in 1934, pre-
       tending to demonstrate his authorship of
       Lewis Carroll's works; includes illustra-
       tions of "The Mark Twain Club Badge" and
       the suppressed cut from LOM showing MT in
       the next world, in flames (pp. 52-53.)

B66   PAULLIN, CHARLES O. "Mark Twain's Virginia
       Kin," William and Mary College Quarterly,
       XV (July), 294-98.
           Notes errors by W. M. Clemens in Genealogy
       Magazine, XI (1923), 17-19, 65, and suggests
       that some descriptions of relatives in MT's
       Autobiography are "not to be taken serious-
       ly." Photograph: "Birthplace of Mark
       Twain's grandmother, Pamela Goggin Clemens,
       in Bedford County, Virginia."

B67   PHELPS, WILLIAM LYON. "Mark Twain," Yale Re-
       view, XXV (December), 291-310.
           He never escaped the evangelical piety of
       his time until he revolted, and "the only
       tradition or convention that he definitely
       abandoned was religious faith." Despite
       his boisterous profanity he had "a chival-
       rous reverence for the chastity of women,"
       and "in his own writings his frequent bad
       taste was equalled only by his prudishness."
       "He was not a profound thinker, but rather
       a shrewd observer.... He was a greater ar-
       tist than humorist, a greater humorist than
       philosopher." Includes the text of a let-
       ter to Mrs. Mary Hallock Foote (December 2,
       1887) about readings from Browning, and
       discusses in some detail, reproducing MT's
       schedule for an evening's reading.

B68   QUICK, DOROTHY. "A Little Girl's Mark Twain,"
       North American Review, CCXL (September),
       342-48.
           For a fuller account of MT by one of the
       "Angel Fishes," see her Enchantment
       (1961.A14).

B69   R., V. "Walter Scott and the Southern States
       of America," Notes and Queries (London),
       CLXIX (November 9), 328-30.
           Refutes MT's charges in LOM that the ro-
       manticism of Scott lay behind the Southern
       romanticism MT blames for the Civil War;
       there was an earlier attack on Scott's ro-
       mantic influence in 1851, in George Bor-
       row's Lavengro; in any case, MT should not
       be taken "seriously as a literary critic,
       while his anti-King and anti-feudal bias
       makes him suspect when he turns to social
       comment," as in his "cheap and crude" CY.

B70   ROBBINS, L. H. "Mark Twain's Fame Goes
       Marching On: His Century Which Closes this
       Year Finds Him Still the Best-Loved and
       Most Widely Read of American Authors," New
       York Times Magazine (April 21), pp. 4, 16.
           A sound but conventional account of MT's
       life and his enduring reputation.

B71   ROBERTS, R. ELLIS. "Mark Twain," Fortnightly
       Review, CXLIV (November), 583-92.
           A general discussion of the man, who put
       much of himself into the character of Huck
       Finn. Although it has been argued with
       some justice that MT "was essentially non-
       adult," the same might be said of his crit-
       ics, and "perhaps no artist ever completely
       grows up." Ellis finds MT intellectually

1935 - Shorter Writings

(ROBERTS, R. ELLIS)
beneath Ibsen, and "none of the American author's works can rank with the greatest of Dickens."

B72 *SCHÖNEMANN, FRIEDRICH. "Mark Twain--ein Freund Deutschlands," Deutsche Allgemeine Zeitung, November 24.
[Source: Asselineau (1954), No. 706.]

B73 SMITH, BERNARD. Forces in American Criticism: A Study in the History of American Literary Thought. New York: Harcourt, Brace and Company. Pp. 184, 235-37, and passim on MT.
On MT's Western truthfulness, love for the common language, but also his cynicism (p. 184); takes DeVoto's side in the controversy with Brooks (pp. 235-37).

B74 STEWART, HERBERT L. "Mark Twain on the Jewish Problem," Dalhousie Review, XIV (January), 455-58.
About "Concerning the Jews."

B75 UNDERHILL, IRVING S. "The Haunted Book: A Further Explanation Concerning Huckleberry Finn," Colophon, n.s. I (Autumn), 281-91.
On the copies of HF shipped to Californa and there altered to replace the offensive cut on p. 283; contains text of "Mark Twain's Altered Book" from New York Herald of November 29, 1884, on the Charles L. Webster offer of $500 for the apprehension and conviction of the person who mutilated the plate for p. 283. See Underhill's "An Inquiry into Mark Twain's Latest Book!" (1931.B31).

B76 VAN DOREN, MARK. "A Century of Mark Twain," Nation (New York), CXLI (October 23), 472-74.
On MT's growing reputation in the years since his death.

B77 VAN DYKE, TERTIUS. Henry Van Dyke: A Biography by His Son. New York and London: Harper & Brothers Publishers.
On p. 218, quotes an MT letter on the difficulty in finding the right plan for a short story that will tell itself; he usually succeeded only after several failures. On p. 259, Henry Van Dyke said MT's white suit was "all right, but I wore one long before he did."

B78 W., A. L. O. "More of Mark Twain in Canada: 1895," Queen's Quarterly (Queen's University, Kingston), XLII (Summer), 272-74.
Personal impressions of MT, whom the author met in Winnepeg. [An addendum to Stephen Leacock's "Mark Twain and Canada" in the Spring issue.]

B79 WAGENKNECHT, EDWARD. "The Mysterious Paragraph: A Reply," Saturday Review of Literature, XIII (November 16), 29.
A brief note: in his query of October 26, E. B. Foote erroneously says that MS was not published until 1922; in fact it was serialized in Harper's and then published as a book. The passage about which he inquires is not to be found there.

B80 WALSH, JAMES J. "Mark Twain and Joan of Arc," Commonweal, XXII (August 23), 408.
A letter to the editor, occasioned by the Cyril Clemens article (July 26, pp. 323-24, 1935.B23). Mentions an appreciative letter from MT to Rose Hawthorne, daughter of Nathaniel Hawthorne; also describes a conversation in which MT "told me that the Bishop of Orleans had assured him that Saint Joan had assured him that anyone who wrote so beautifully about her would get into heaven.... He seemed to be very much interested in the prospect of a hereafter that would place him near the Maid, and the good Archbishop reiterated his assurance on that prospect."

B81 WISTER, OWEN. "In Homage to Mark Twain," Harper's, CLXXI (November), 547-56.
Includes an account of a meeting with MT, and a discussion of him as thinker and critic, noting the interest he shared with Hawthorne in the problem of evil. [Reprinted frequently - see index.]

1936 A BOOKS

A1 ADE, GEORGE. Revived Remarks on Mark Twain. Also the Address of John T. McCutcheon Commemorating the Centenary of Mark Twain's Birth. Compiled by George Hiram Brownell. Chicago: Privately Printed.
Consists of reprinted tributes to MT: Oliver Wendell Holmes, "To Mark Twain on His Fiftieth Birthday"; George Ade, "Tribute to Mark Twain" (from North American Review, June, 1910); "Mark Twain and the Old-Time Subscription Book" (Review of Reviews (New York), June, 1910); "Mark Twain as Our Emissary" (Century, December, 1910); "On the Death of Mark Twain" (comment in Chicago Tribune, April 21, 1910); John T. McCutcheon, "Mark Twain's Seventieth Birthday" (an address in Chicago in honor of MT's Centennial birthday, November 30, 1935); George Hiram Brownell, "Compiler's Commentary." Also, caricatures of MT by John T. McCutcheon and others.

A2 *BENSON, IVAN. Mark Twain in the West. Sacramento: California State Printing Office.
[37-page pamphlet. Source: Asselineau (1954), No. 723.]

A3 *CLEMENS, SAMUEL L. 1601; or, Conversation by the Social Fireside as It Was in the Time of the Tudors, with Notes on Mark Twain's 1601 and a checklist of various editions and

(CLEMENS, SAMUEL L.)
reprints compiled by Irvin Haas. Chicago:
Black Cat Press.
[Source: Asselineau (1954), No. 728.]

A4 *O'CONNOR, LAUREL. Drinking with Mark Twain:
Recollections of Mark Twain and His Cronies
as Told to Me. New York: Riemsdyk Book-
service.
[Source: MHRA Annual Bibliography (1936),
No. 3599.]

1936 B SHORTER WRITINGS

B1 ANON. "He Kept His Nerve," Saturday Review of
Literature, XIII (January 11), 8.
TS, HF, PW, and LOM show as much of the
"human weakness, vice, degradation, prejudice, and superstition" as is found in
Faulkner, Caldwell, and others of the "new
school of the Mississippi valley," but MT
"did not give up humanity" or call for revolution.

B2 ANON. "Mark Twain's Favorite Music," Étude,
LIV (October), 661.
A list, sent to Mrs. Georgia Chew by MT's
daughter Clara: "I'm Awearin' Awa', Jean";
"Flow Gently, Sweet Afton"; "Annie Laurie";
"Banks and Braes of Bonnie Doon"; "Go Chain
the Lion Down"; "Swing Low, Sweet Chariot";
"Ever Lighter Grows My Slumber" (Brahms);
"Lullaby" (Brahms); "Serenade" (Schubert);
"Ave Maria" (Schubert); "Almighty Jehovah"
(Schubert).

B3 ANON. [Review: Mark Twain's Notebook
(1935).] Nation, CXLII (February 26), 258.
"The 'heresies' are rare and mild," and
the writing is often very good.

B4 BENSON, ADOLPH B. "Mark Twain in Småland,"
American Swedish Monthly, XXX (September),
4 6, 37.
MT took his daughter Jean to Sweden in
the summer of 1899 for treatment by Dr.
Heinrick Kellgren. A popular account,
based largely or entirely on such familiar
sources as Paine's 1912 Biography and 1917
edition of the Letters, and Mary Lawton's
A Lifetime with Mark Twain (1925).

B5 BRASHEAR, M[INNIE] M. "Mark Twain in Perspective," Virginia Quarterly Review, XII
(January), 127-30.
A review article, Edward Wagenknecht's
Mark Twain: The Man and His Work (1935) is
the most successful of the MT centennial
books in demonstrating the "broad human
significance in his life and writings."
MT's translation of Dr. Heinrich Hoffman's
Struwelpeter as Slovenly Peter (with an introduction by his daughter Clara), "with
its quaint illustrations...adds something
to our impression of the irrepressible
gaiety of its author."

B6 BURGESS, GELETT. "A Famous Author Tells about
His Meeting with Mark Twain," Mark Twain
Quarterly, I (Fall), 13.
Burgess met MT on a park bench in Washington Square forty years ago. MT consoled
Burgess about his name being forever linked
with his Purple Cow: "I wouldn't worry
about that, son. There's a lot of writers
trying to be humorous who are so poor they
can't keep a cow."

B7 BURKE, W. J. "Mark Twain: An Exhibition,"
Bulletin of the New York Public Library,
XL (June), 499-501.
On the centenary exhibit, which opened
November, 1935; this account is partly bio-
graphical, and lists various MT memorabilia
and manuscripts which were on exhibit. Not
illustrated.

B8 CAMPBELL, OSCAR JAMES. "Twain Versus Clemens,"
in Erich A. Walter, ed., Essay Annual (New
York: Scott, Foresman), pp. 151-68.
A reprinting of his address originally in
Anon., "The Mark Twain Commemoration"
(1935.B8).

B9 CARPENTER, C. E. "Mark Twain, 1898," Mark
Twain Quarterly, I (Fall), 4-5.
Memories of MT in Vienna: his language
was vigorous, and when Carpenter showed MT
an interview of him he had written for the
New York World MT cut out the adjectives.

B10 CHUBB, PERCIVAL. "The Two Mark Twains," The
Standard ("Issued by the American Ethical
Union"), XXII (January), 97-98.
On the darker, tragic side of MT, here attributed to his largeness and headlong impatience: "There was so much of him that he
never organized himself into any sort of
harmony or unity."

B11 CLARKE, EDWARD J. "Cynic and Humorist," Commonweal, XXIII (February 7), 415-16.
A review of Albert Bigelow Paine, ed.,
Mark Twain's Notebook (1935). Praises
Paine's "illuminating comments and efficient
editorial work," but criticizes the bad
taste, "salacity, and blasphemy" of MT, as
here revealed and in 1601 and his Stomach
Club address.

B12 CLEMENS, CYRIL. "Mark Twain's Reading," Commonweal, XXIV (August 7), 363-64.
On the authors and books MT liked--and
some he disliked. A useful summary for the
beginning student, but undocumented and
presenting familiar information.

B13 DAVIDSON, LOUIS B. "He Fell in Love with a
Picture," Reader's Digest, XXVIII (January),
9-12, "Condensed from Liberty" [November 30,
1935].
On MT's love for his wife, Olivia, from
the time her brother showed him her picture
on the Quaker City cruise; a popular account, based chiefly on Paine.

1936 - Shorter Writings

B14   DEVOTO, BERNARD. "Mark Twain and the Limits
      of Criticism," in his Forays and Rebuttals
      (New York: Little, Brown and Company),
      pp. 373-403.
         "Read before the American Literature Sec-
      tion of the Modern Language Association at
      Cincinnati, January 1, 1936." "The purpose
      of this essay is to examine some of the
      critical judgments that have been made
      about the books of Mark Twain and to deter-
      mine how far their results are acceptable."
      DeVoto argues that vocabulary studies,
      textual criticism, and the study of possible
      influences are of secondary importance at
      the most. "Theoretical, systematic criti-
      cism" is the most ambitious, although it
      may distort the work it examines.

B15   _____. "Mark Twain: The Ink of History,"
      in his Forays and Rebuttals (Boston: Lit-
      tle, Brown and Company), pp. 348-72.
         "An Address delivered at Columbia, Mis-
      souri December 6, 1935, as part of the con-
      cluding exercises of Mark Twain Week at the
      University of Missouri," insisting on MT's
      conscious artistry--which the literary es-
      tablishment of his time had been reluctant
      to see.

B16   _____. [Review: Edward Wagenknecht, Mark
      Twain: The Man and His Work (1935).]
      New England Quarterly, IX (June), 332-38.
         "Independence and exhaustiveness are...Mr.
      Wagenknecht's principal virtues: he pre-
      sents little new material and does not say
      much that has not been said before," but
      he "examines all the known evidence on his
      own behalf. The result is a new and origi-
      nal study of Mark Twain--and a complete
      vindication of the criticism of the last
      few years."

B17   DRURY, WELLS. "Mark Twain, while 'Roughing
      It,'" in his An Editor on the Comstock Lode
      (New York: Farrar & Rinehart, Incorporat-
      ed), pp. 220-31.
         Contains anecdotes of MT told by Steve
      Gillis; there is also a chapter on "Dan de
      Quille" (William Wright).

B18   FARMER, A.-J. [Review: Fred Lewis Pattee,
      Mark Twain: Representative Selections
      (1935).] Revue Anglo-Américaine, XIII
      (December), 367-68.
         Brief and laudatory: a good selection
      meriting the attention of those who are
      familiar with MT and of those who are not.
      [In French.]

B19   FERGUSON, DELANCEY. "Mark Twain and the
      Cleveland Herald," American Literature,
      VIII (November), 304-305.
         In June, 1869 MT had written his mother:
      "I am offered an interest in a Cleveland
      paper.... The salary is fair enough, but
      the interest is not large enough, and so I
      must look a little further." According to
      letters from MT to Mary Mason Fairbanks,
      wife of the publisher, the paper was the
      Cleveland Herald.

B20   _____. "The Uncollected Portions of Mark
      Twain's Autobiography," American Literature,
      VIII (March), 37-46.
         Portions of Mark Twain's Autobiography
      published serially in the North American Re-
      view in 1906 and 1907, and in Harper's Maga-
      zine in 1922 do not appear in the two-volume
      edition of 1924. Collation shows scope of
      the omissions, and Ferguson points to a num-
      ber of "alterations which show the work of
      another hand, and not a skilful one."

B21   FLANAGAN, JOHN T. "Mark Twain on the Upper
      Mississippi," Minnesota History, XVII
      (December), 369-84.
         On MT's trip in 1882 to collect additional
      materials for LOM; also about visits to
      Minnesota in 1886 and 1895 (quotes Duluth,
      Minneapolis, and St. Paul papers for July,
      1895).

B22   *HAMADA, MASAJIRO. "Mark Twain's Conception of
      Social Justice," Studies in English Litera-
      ture (Japan), XVI (October), 593-616.
         [Source: Asselineau (1954), No. 753:
      "Naïve and superficial."]

B23   *[HAMON, LOUIS.] Cheiro's Language of the Hand.
      Los Angeles, n.p., pp. 169-70.
         Claims to have interested MT in finger-
      printing and thus to have inspired PW.
      [Source: Wigger (1957), p. 518, n. 1.]

B24   LAWRENCE, D. H. Preface to E. D. Dekker's
      Max Havelaar; reprinted in Edward D. McDon-
      ald, ed., Phoenix: The Posthumous Papers of
      D. H. Lawrence. London: William Heinemann
      Ltd. (Repr. 1961), pp. 236-39; on MT, p. 238.
         Mentions Dekker's "bitter, almost mad-dog
      aversion to humanity," which also appears
      in Jean Paul Richter, "as it appears in the
      later Mark Twain."

B25   LEACOCK, STEPHEN. The Greatest Pages of Amer-
      ican Humour: A Study of the Rise and Dev-
      elopment of Humorous Writings in America
      with Selections from the Most Notable of the
      Humorists. London: Methuen & Co., Ltd.,
      pp. 123-54.
         Leacock's discussion notes MT's unevenness,
      prolixity, and elementary theology and his-
      tory. "The book he treasured most among his
      works, his Joan of Arc, is worthless as his-
      tory, practically without humour, utterly
      false in its picture of the times," but TS,
      RI, IA, LOM, CY, and HF "are among the
      world's great books" (p. 124). Selections
      from IA, HF, and RI on pp. 128-54. Asseli-
      neau (1954), No. 732, lists an American edi-
      tion for the same year (Garden City: Dou-
      bleday, Doran & Co.).

B26   LORCH, FRED W. "Mark Twain's Orphanage Lec-
      ture," American Literature, VII (January),
      453-5.
         MT delivered "The American Vandal Abroad"
      January 22, 1869 for benefit of an orphanage
      of which Mrs. Fairbanks was a trustee.

(LORCH, FRED W.)
Contains text of his letter accepting the invitation to lecture and his closing words in behalf of the orphanage (reprinted from Cleveland Daily Leader).

B27   LOWE, ORTON. Our Land and Its Literature. New York, London: Harper & Brothers Publishers, passim on MT.
A high-school anthology, this includes "The Jumping Frog," two MT letters, and passages from RI, LOM, and HF. Critical judgments are derivative and not penetrating; ranks HF with The Scarlet Letter as "two really important novels of the American scene" in the century between Cooper and Dreiser (p. 93).

B28   [McCOLE, CAMILLE.] [Review: Edward G. Wagenknecht, Mark Twain: The Man and His Work (1935); Fred Lewis Pattee, ed., Mark Twain: Representative Selections (1935); and Albert Bigelow Paine, ed., Mark Twain's Notebook (1935).] Catholic World, CXLII (January), 499-500.
Wagenknecht has written "the sanest life of Twain that has yet come to my notice," fair to MT and to the various critical positions taken toward him. Pattee's anthology contains a few items that might better have been left out, but the choice is generally judicious and the background material is good. The notebooks add little to what we know from the Paine biography and MT's letters, but they do add roundness to our picture of him; notes Paine's "somewhat over fervent commentary" and a tendency to play down "crude banalities, vaudeville jokes, inconsistencies, and attitude toward the whole 'damned human race.'" [Reviewer identified as Camille McCole in the "Index to Reviewers," p. 511.]

B29   MacMANUS, SEUMAS. "What a Famous Irishman Thinks of Twain," Mark Twain Quarterly, I (Fall), 16.
Brief comment on MT's contribution to the world's merriment.

B30   MASON, WALT. "Mark Twain the Healer," Mark Twain Quarterly, I (Fall), 3.
A poem: MT brings cheer when patent medicines fail.

B31   MASTERS, EDGAR LEE. "The House where Mark Twain Was Born," Mark Twain Quarterly, I (Fall), 5.
A poem describing Florida, Missouri and the house.

B32   *MONTENEGRO, ERNESTO. "Doble Personalidad de Mark Twain," Ateneo (Chile), October, 47-69.
[Source: Asselineau (1954), No. 756: "A summary of Brooks's theory."]

B33   *NEUBAUER, HEINZ. Amerikanische Goldgräber-literatur (Bret Harte, Mark Twain, Jack London). Grossenheim i. Sa.: H. Plasnick.
[Source: Asselineau (1954), No. 735.]

B34   ODELL, GEORGE C. D. Annals of the New York Stage. New York: Columbia University Press. Vol. VIII (1865-1870), passim.
MT gave his "Sandwich Islands" lecture at Irving Hall on May 15, 1866 (pp. 227-28), at the Athenaeum, May 10, 1866 (p. 253), and at the Bedford Avenue Reformed Church, Brooklyn on December 1, 1869 (p. 686). He gave "The American Vandals Abroad" lecture before the Newtown Y.M.C.A., Long Island City, on March 16, 1869 (p. 553).

B35   PELIKAN, HARRY R., JR. "Mark Twain and the Ozarks," Mark Twain Quarterly, I (Fall), 14.
Both will live on; let us hope the Ozarks will not be despoiled.

B36   "Poems to Mark Twain," Mark Twain Quarterly, I (Fall), 4-5.
Tributes in verse by Wm. Robert Woodburn, Robert P. Tristram Coffin, Thomas Caldecott Chubb, Wittner Bynner, Arthur Guiterman, Margaret Fishback, and Ernest Rhys.

B37   QUINN, ARTHUR HOBSON. "Mark Twain and the Romance of Youth," in his American Fiction: An Historical and Critical Survey. New York: Appleton-Century Co. (Reprinted New York: Appleton-Century Crofts, Inc., 1964), pp. 243-56.
A general survey, providing a good summary but no new information.

B38   RANDALL, DAVID A. [Review: Merle DeVore Johnson, A Bibliography of the Works of Mark Twain (1935).] Publishers' Weekly, CXXIX (February 22), 917-18.
"The work, in short, is excellent."

B39   *RATCLIFFE, S. K. [Introduction.] What Is Man? London: Watts & Co.
[Source: Asselineau (1954), No. 729.]

B40   ROLLINS, CARL PURINGTON. "A Mark Twain Item," Saturday Review of Literature, XIII (January 25), 20.
A review of MT's translation of Dr. Heinrich Hoffman's Der Struwelpeter (New York: Limited Editions Club). "The verses are not electrifying, but it is a Mark Twain 'item,' and worth perpetuating. The pictures are by far the better portion."

B41   SAKHAROV, W. [Librarian, Culture Library, Leningrad.] "Twain Exhibit in Russia," Library Journal, LXI (February 15), 157.
Describes an exhibit of MT's books and other materials collected under some difficulty in order to be ready with an exhibit by November 30; the response was good.

B42 SALLS, HELEN HARRIET. "Joan of Arc in English and American Literature," South Atlantic Quarterly, XXXV (April), 167–84.
Passim on MT's JA, noting a "sense of the ludicrous [that] at times overlaps bounds" but is generally amusing, and his sentiment, reverence, and his charming portrait of Joan: "Sentimentalized as she is--a figure dainty as a Dresden statuette, and debonair as a princess--she appeals to us as an impulsive, lovable, very human little fighting saint after all. To Clemens, as to Michelet, her essential charm lay in her womanliness--her sensibility and her pity."

B43 *SCHÖNEMANN, FRIEDRICH. "Mark Twain und Deutschland," Hochschule und Ausland, XIV (January), 37-43; reprinted in Auslese (February).
[Source: Asselineau (1954), No. 758: "Summary of a commemorative speech delivered in Berlin in 1935"; MHRA Annual Bibliography (1936), No. 3603.]

B44 _____. "Neue Mark-Twain-Studien," Neueren Sprachen, XLIV, Heft 6, 260-72.
A survey of recent MT studies, chiefly descriptive, but criticizing Wagenknecht for "einem geschmacklosen Ausfall gegen unseren Führer und Reichskanzler."

B45 SCHULTZ, JOHN RICHIE. "New Letters of Mark Twain," American Literature, VIII (March), 47-51.
Five letters MT wrote to Bayard Taylor in 1878, interesting chiefly for showing comic exasperation with the German language.

B46 SEAMAN, OWEN. "To Mark Twain," Saturday Review of Literature, XIII (February 29), 13.
Reprints a poem which originally appeared in Punch.

B47 SMITH, BERNARD. "Van Wyck Brooks," New Republic, LXXXVIII (August 26), 69-72.
Takes the side of Bernard DeVoto in a brief discussion of his quarrel with Brooks, who "exaggerated" MT's "potentialities."

B48 SPILLER, ROBERT E. [Review: Edward Wagenknecht, Mark Twain: The Man and His Work (1935).] American Literature, VIII (March), 96-98.
"Mr. Wagenknecht is loath to take sides" when critics disagree. "Such lack of prejudice is honorable in the peacemaker, but even common sense seems to demand of the critic more firmness of judgment." Nonetheless, "the book is among the most useful we have on the subject" because of Wagenknecht's "humane sympathy" toward MT, and it will serve as a good introduction.

B49 TARKINGTON, BOOTH. "Mark Twain and Boys," Mark Twain Quarterly, I (Fall), 6-7.
HF is secure as an American classic, and Tom Sawyer's character is based on the boy Mark Twain. Quotes appreciative statements by Robert Louis Stevenson and Arnold Bennett.

B50 TAYLOR, WALTER FULLER. "'Mark Twain' (Samuel Langhorne Clemens, 1835-1910)," in his A History of American Letters (Boston, New York: American Book Company), pp. 262-74.
A general study in a survey for the undergraduate, noting MT's regionalism, weak construction, humanity and the perspective of a satirist, and his final pessimism.

B51 WALKER, FRANKLIN. "An Influence from San Francisco on Mark Twain's The Gilded Age," American Literature, VIII (March), 63-66.
On November 3, 1870 Laura D. Fair (whom MT may have known in Virginia City) shot her married lover on the ferry from Oakland to San Francisco. She was tried, convicted of murder, and then retried and acquitted on the ground of "emotional insanity." The case attracted national attention at the time MT and Charles Dudley Warner were writing GA, and parallels the story of Laura Hawkins in that book.

B52 WINTERICH, JOHN T. "Mark Twain's Only Son," Saturday Review of Literature, XIV (October 3), 20.
Reproduces, with brief comment, "the only known photographic print of Mark Twain's only son, Langdon Clemens," inscribed with MT's "warm regards" to Bret Harte.

B53 *_____. [Introduction.] The Adventures of Tom Sawyer, illustrated by Norman Rockwell. New York: The Heritage Press; London: The Nonesuch Press.
[Source: Asselineau (1954), No. 727.]

1937 A BOOKS

A1 CLEMENS, SAMUEL L. Letters from the Sandwich Islands Written for the Sacramento "Union" by Mark Twain, ed. G. Ezra Dane. San Francisco: The Grabhorn Press.
Correspondence in 1866, MT's first full-scale travel-writing. Some of these letters were later revised and incorporated in RI. This 1937 edition was limited, but there was a 1938 reprinting by Stanford University Press (by photolith, according to Ivan Benson in Mark Twain's Western Years [1938], p. 162).

A2 *LEMONNIER, LÉON. La Jeunesse aventureuse de Mark Twain. Paris: Desclée de Brouwer.
[Source: MHRA Bibliography (1937), No. 4211, and review by M. Le Breton (1937.B22); both give year of publication as 1937. Asselineau (1954, No. 725) lists it for 1936; he describes it as "a lively and entertaining book, which, however, contains no new information on Mark Twain."]

1937 B SHORTER WRITINGS

B1 BABLER, OTTO F. "Mark Twain: An Aphorism," Notes and Queries (London), CLXXIII (July 17), 45.

(BABLER, OTTO F.)
MT's aphorism "It is not always easy to bear prosperity. Another man's, I mean" appears in autograph facsimile in a Paris bookseller's catalogue.

B2 BACON, LEONARD. "Our Golden Mark," Mark Twain Quarterly, I (Spring), 17.
A poem on MT's humor, compassion, imagination, and portrayal of his time.

B3 BALICER, HERMAN C. "Szczepanik's 'Portrait' of Mark Twain," Publishers' Weekly, CXXXI (February 20), 968-69.
On a portrait of MT (here reproduced) woven in silk on a machine designed and demonstrated by the inventor of whom MT wrote in "The Austrian Edison Keeping School Again" and "From the London Times of 1904."

B4 BENSON, ADOLPH B. "Mark Twain's Contacts with Scandinavia," Scandinavian Studies and Notes (now Scandinavian Studies), XIV (August), 159-67.
A general, but substantial and meticulously documented summary of MT's admittedly limited travel in the Scandinavian countries, reading in the literature, and acquaintance with individuals. [Not all of Benson's sources are included in the present bibliography.]

B5 BLAIR, WALTER. "Mark Twain," in his Native American Humor (1800-1900) (New York: American Book Company), pp. 147-62 [Source: 1960 paperback reprinting, San Francisco: Chandler Publishing Company, Inc., with the same pagination].
Shows MT's indebtedness to the popular humor of his formative years; for example, his portrait of his mother (so tenderhearted that before drowning kittens she warmed the water) and of Tom Sawyer's Aunt Polly may be traced to Benjamin P. Shillaber's "Mrs. Partington." "American humor, then, gave Mark Twain his materials, his methods, and his inspiration. His success was merely the working out of its attempted achievements on the level of genius." Reprinted in part in Scott (1955), pp. 236-48; (1967), pp. 221-33; in Marks (1959), pp. 19-27.

B6 BLANCK, JACOB. "Mark Twain's Sketches Old and New," Publishers' Weekly, CXXXII (October 30), 1740-41.
On the accidental inclusion of a paragraph from Jane Stuart Woolsey's Hospital Days in the first state of the first edition of Sketches New and Old; moreover, MT unconsciously borrowed from the same book phrasing (from a description of an ice-storm) which later appeared in his speech on the weather and eventually in FE.

B7 *BROWN, STERLING. The Negro in American Fiction, Washington, D.C., p. 68.
[Source: Quoted in Haslam (1967), pp. 190-91: "Sterling Brown of Howard University, himself an Afro-American and one of the first scholars in this country to study the treatment of Negro characters in our literature, claimed that 'Jim is the best example in nineteenth-century fiction...he is completely believable.' Brown was particularly moved by the 'great tenderness and truth of this portrayal.'"]

B8 *BROWNELL, EUGENE [GEORGE?] HIRAM. "Twainiana Notes," Reading and Collecting, I (June), 9-10.
[Source: MHRA Annual Bibliography (1937), No. 4205.]

B9 BURTON, RICHARD. "Mark Twain in the Hartford Days," Mark Twain Quarterly, I (Summer), 5.
MT criticized Burton's early writing and helped him get it published in The Century Magazine and elsewhere. When Burton was seeing to the publication of the Yale Lectures on Preaching delivered by his father (who had been pastor of the Park Congregational Church in Hartford), MT persuaded him to let the Charles L. Webster company handle it; the royalties were generous.

B10 CLEMENS, CYRIL. "Mark Twain's Gold Hill Holdup," Rotarian, LI (November), 38-39.
On the joke played on MT in 1866, as described to Cyril Clemens by William R. Gillis and James W. Thompson, and described by MT in the Territorial Enterprise (November 11, 1866) and the San Francisco Bulletin (December 6, 1866); also cites an account in the Sacramento Union (November 15, 1866). Includes 1866 photographs of MT and Virginia City.

B11 COLUM, PADRAIC. "Homage to Mark Twain," Mark Twain Quarterly, I (Spring), 17.
Poem in tribute, with comments on the cave and playing pirates.

B12 CORYELL, IRVING. "Josh, of the Territorial Enterprise," North American Review, CCXLIII (Summer), 287-95.
A lively, popular account of the Territorial Enterprise and MT's connection with it; based on generally sound material (including RI), but undocumented.

B13 [DEVOTO, BERNARD.] "At the Cannon's Mouth," Saturday Review of Literature, XV (April 3), 8.
Takes issue with the comparative ranking of American authors by Dumas Malone in the current Harper's; placing MT at the head of the list is a personal choice, however.

1937 - Shorter Writings

B14 DOUGLAS, LLOYD C. "Potatoes for Mark Twain," Mark Twain Quarterly, II (Fall), 20.
His father, a country parson, had little to spend on books but "always found a few bushels of potatoes that could be spared for another volume of Mark Twain."

B15 FERGUSON, DELANCEY. "The Petrified Truth," Colophon, n.s., II (Winter), 189-96.
Ferguson's search of The Lancet, Cleveland Plain Dealer, Cleveland Herald, Harper's, and Leslie's Weekly turned up no evidence to support MT's claim that many were taken in by his Nevada "petrified man" hoax.

B16 FROHMAN, DANIEL. "Mark Twain," in his Encore (New York: Lee Furman, Inc.), pp. 107-108.
Quotes The Theatre Magazine for May 31, 1866 on the wisdom of withdrawing The American Claimant from the stage; also notes the play was written for the humorous lecturer A. E. Burback; Frohman was successful with a play based on P&P.

B17 HAGEDORN, HERMANN. Brookings: A Biography. New York: The Macmillan Company, p. 178.
Brief mention: "Men and women who counted sat at his table--Mark Twain, languid and casual..."

B18 HAPGOOD, NORMAN. "My Feeling about Mark Twain," Mark Twain Quarterly, II (Winter), 15.
Brief comments on having found MT appreciated everywhere. "Some years ago, I was having a private chat with Sir James Barrie, and in the course of it I spoke of Hawthorne with The Scarlet Letter and The House of the Seven Gables, and Mark Twain, with Tom Sawyer and Huckleberry Finn, as at the top of American fiction. The author of Peter Pan agreed, but added that also those books are up near the top of English fiction."

B19 HERRICK, ROBERT. "Mark Twain and the American Tradition," Mark Twain Quarterly, II (Winter), 8-11, 24.
"There have always been two American traditions,--the imported and the indigenous, the native. Brooks tried to judge MT by the wrong standards, applying a criticism "born of European nostalgia and spurious psychology."

B20 JOHNSON, BURGES. "When Mark Twain Cursed Me," Mark Twain Quarterly, II (Fall), 8-9, 24.
For a fuller version of this article see Johnson's "A Ghost for Mark Twain" (1952).

B21 L. "Mark Twain Gleanings," Southwest Review, XXII (Winter), 212.
A review of Cyril Clemens, ed., Mark Twain Wit and Wisdom (1935). "So many stories he never fathered have been attributed to Mark Twain that it is a pleasure

to find the names of contributors attached to the anecdotes in this volume to vouch for their authenticity." Some of the 150 stories were in the Paine biography, but most are previously unpublished.

B22 LE BRETON, M. [Review: Léon Lemonnier, La Jeunesse aventureuse de Mark Twain.] Études Anglaises, I (September), 465.
A lively account, although there was also a quiet melancholy in the adventure. [In French.]

B23 LEISY, ERNEST E. "Mark Twain's Part in The Gilded Age," American Literature, VIII (January), 445-47.
On the collaboration of MT with Charles Dudley Warner, showing how their contributions were interwoven; uses MT's copy of GA.

B24 L[OVEMAN], A[MY.] "Mark Twain on the Screen," Saturday Review of Literature, XVI (June 12), 10.
"The Prince and the Pauper must be called the poorest of Mark Twain's novels," yet "by leaving out a good deal that Mark put into the book and adding a good deal that he did not, the movies have made an excellent picture of it.... It was possible to lift the events of The Prince and the Pauper out of the book because the events were the whole of the book." Though better novels, TS and HF can hardly be filmed without distortion, HF because "the events as they have meaning for us are inseparable from their impact on the mind and sympathies of Huck Finn."

B25 MALONE, DUMAS. "Who Are the American Immortals?" Harper's, CLXXIV (April), 544-48.
Only brief mention of MT, ranking him third among American writers, after Emerson and Hawthorne and ahead of Whitman. "Mark Twain and Whitman [seem] to be gaining." Melville is not mentioned. See DeVoto, "At the Cannon's Mouth," above.

B26 MARCOSSON, ISAAC F. "Mark Twain as Collaborator," Mark Twain Quarterly, II (Winter), 7, 24.
MT wrote out a reminiscence of Henry H. Rogers for Marcosson to incorporate in an article he was writing on Rogers in 1904 for The World's Work; credit could not be given to MT because of his contract with Harper's.

B27 MORLEY, CHRISTOPHER. "George Ade on Mark Twain," Saturday Review of Literature, XV (March 20), 12.
Briefly describes and quotes Ade's Revived Remarks on Mark Twain (1936). Reproduces a sketch of MT in the book "from a drawing in Life (1898) by an unknown artist."

B28 N., H. "Knowing Mark Twain," The Standard ("Issued by the American Ethical Union"), XXIII (May), 217.
A brief review of Mark Twain's Notebook, which should silence the charges that MT

(N., H.)
was censored by his wife and William Dean
Howells; "Still better the Notes bring the
man himself before us again."

B29   ODELL, GEORGE C. D. Annals of the New York
Stage. New York: Columbia University
Press, Vol. IX (1870–75), passim.
"Little Mac" appeared as MT's Jumping
Frog with Bryant's Minstrels, December,
1870 (p. 76). On MT with The Man Who
Laughs, Steinway Hall, January 24, 1872
(p. 207). MT was going to speak on "Recol-
lections of Some Un-Commonplace Characters
I Have Met" at the Plymouth Church, Brook-
lyn, November 21, 1871; he spoke on Artemus
Ward instead, apparently (p. 231). MT gave
his Sandwich Islands lecture at Steinway
Hall, February 5 and 10, 1873 (p. 335) and
at the Academy of Music, Brooklyn,
February 7, 1873 (p. 352). On the play
from The Gilded Age (with a photograph of
J. T. Raymond as Colonel Sellers),
pp. 556–57.

B30   PABODY, E. F. "Mark Twain's Ghost Story,"
Minnesota History, XVIII (March), 28–35.
About MT's lecture with Cable in Minnea-
polis, January 24, 1885.

B31   *PRAZ, MARIO. ["A stimulating essay on
Twain,"] Studi e Svaghi inglesi. Firenze:
Sansoni, pp. 157–63.
[Source: Asselineau (1954), No. 772;
also MHRA Annual Bibliography (1937),
No. 1540, 4216.]

B32   ROBERTSON, STUART. "Mark Twain in German,"
Mark Twain Quarterly, II (Fall), 10–12.
On a copy of Huckleberry Finn in Robert-
son's possession, badly translated into
German by H. Koch (Leipzig: Hess u. Becker
Verlag, n.d.).

B33   ROWE, IDA. "Mark Twain's Interest in Nature," Mark Twain Quarterly, I (Summer), 7,
9–10, 14.
On MT's interest in animals, streams,
landscapes, with examples drawn from works,
biography, and published reminiscences of
friends.

B34   *SWAIN, LOUIS H. "Mark Twain as a Music Crit-
ic: A Case Study in Esthetic Growth,"
Furman Bulletin, XIX (April), 48–53.
[Source: MHRA Annual Bibliography (1937),
No. 4219.]

B35   *VERDAGUER, MARIO. "Humorismo inglés y ironía
yanqui," La Razón (Panama), V (July 3), 2.
[Source: "Articles on American Literature Appearing in Current Periodicals,"
American Literature, IX (January, 1938),
473: "Biographical sketch, stressing Mark
Twain's triumph in England."]

B36   WAGGONER, HYATT HOWE. "Science in the Thought
of Mark Twain," American Literature, VIII
(January), 357–70.
MT had a broad and enthusiastic acquaintance with science, and a "philosophically
sound, if not scientifically detailed,
knowledge of the main outline of anthropology.... was ... one of the principal bulwarks
of his deterministic philosophy" (p. 359).

B37   WILSON, HARRY LEON. "Mark Twain a Negligible
Item," Mark Twain Quarterly, II (Winter),
13, 24.
When a boy Wilson read TS despite parental
disapproval, and later discovered RI. Finally, at a testimonial dinner to Brander
Matthews he saw MT and found the man, like
his books, "too good to be true."

B38   WOOD, GRANT. "My Debt to Mark Twain," Mark
Twain Quarterly, II (Fall), 6, 14, 24.
TS and HF were boyhood favorites he re-
read until they were tattered; Wood liked
the adventure and the sense of fairness.
"My favorite was Huckleberry Finn; probably,
I realize now, because of its richness in
sense impressions of the type that made my
own boyhood so vivid."

B39   YEATS, WILLIAM BUTLER. "W. B. Yeats Receives
the Mark Twain Medal," Mark Twain Quarterly,
I (Summer), 21.
Includes three brief notes by Yeats, sending thanks for the medal and recalling that
"Lady Gregory and I dined with him many
years ago, and I remember vividly his talk
and his stories, always admirable in matter
and manner."

1938 A BOOKS

A1   BENSON, IVAN. Mark Twain's Western Years.
Together with Hitherto Unreprinted Clemens
Western Items. Stanford University, California: Stanford University Press, and London: Humphrey Milford, Oxford University
Press.
"During his Western period he became an
accomplished social satirist, and with a
gradually broadening scope he wrote artistically, with a variety of effects, from the
coarsest burlesque to fine descriptive and
informational articles" (p. vii). Includes
an extensive bibliography of MT's published
writing for this period (pp. 165–74), and
a generous sampling of his writings in Nevada and California papers (pp. 175–213).

A2   CLEMENS, SAMUEL L., ed G. Ezra Dane. Letters
from the Sandwich Islands Written for the
Sacramento "Union" by Mark Twain. Stanford
University, California: Stanford University
Press, and London: Humphrey Milford, Oxford
University Press.
A reprint of the limited 1937 edition pub-
lished by the Grabhorn Press.

1938 - Books

A3 CLEMENS, SAMUEL L. Mark Twain's Letter to William Bowen, Buffalo, February Sixth, 1870. Prefatory Note by Clara Clemens Gabrilowitsch; Foreword by Albert W. Gunnison. San Francisco: The Book Club of California.

Clara's note is descriptive and affectionate, and Gunnison's brief forward comments on William Bowen and reprints a note Bowen sent with a copy of the letter.

A4 _____, ed. Franklin Walker. The Washoe Giant in San Francisco. Being Heretofore Uncollected Sketches by Mark Twain Published in the Golden Era in the Sixties Including Those Blasted Children, The Lick House Ball, The Kearny Street Ghost Story, Fitz Smythe's Horse, and Thirty-Four More Items by the Wild Humorist of the Pacific Slope. San Francisco: George Fields.

Contains text of MT material, helpful introduction and headnotes, a list of MT material published in the Golden Era (1863-66), and a "Bibliographical Note" indicating the few reprintings of this material (p. 143).

A5 *LANGDON, JERVIS. Samuel L. Clemens, Some Reminiscences and Some Excerpts from Letters and Unpublished Manuscripts. n.p., n.d. (dedication dated October 7, 1938). (Pamphlet.)

[Source: Cited in Baetzhold (1970), p. 49 and p. 330, n. 6. Baetzhold refers to notes by MT criticizing Sir Walter Scott for weakening his writing by vagueness and verbosity.]

A6 *LEE, ALFRED PYLE. First and Other Editions of Samuel L. Clemens, collected by the well-known bibliographer, Dr. Albert P. Lee of Philadelphia, with a few additions. New York: F. C. Duschenes.

[31-page pamphlet. Source: Asselineau (1954), No. 795.]

A7 MASTERS, EDGAR LEE. Mark Twain: A Portrait. New York and London: Charles Scribner's Sons.

A lively biographical account, shaped by Masters' view that MT failed in his duty as a satirist; for example, he says MT was dabbling in trivial matters while "Ibsen was writing An Enemy of the People and Pillars of Society in which he attacked the whole fabric of modern society, its corruption and its hypocrisy. We needed just this surgery here in America, and the regret is that Twain did not administer it for us. The love of money and fear of the crowd kept him from doing it" (p. 174). See reviews.

A8 RAMSAY, ROBERT L., and FRANCES GUTHRIE EMBERSON. A Mark Twain Lexicon. University of Missouri Studies, XIII (January), cxix, 278 pp.

Based on master's theses by Margaret Sellars Edwards, Ernestine Ernst, True Gaines, Amelia Madera, Alma B. Martin, Florence Potter Stedman, Avera Leolin Taylor, Donald C. Thompson, Georgia House Watson, Everette M. Webber, and Emma C. Woods, each of whom worked with a single volume (1929-35). "The Lexicon makes no attempt to include the whole of Mark Twain's extraordinarily large vocabulary. Merely those elements of it have here been brought together that seemed best to illustrate the man and his many-sided genius...and the English language to whose development in America he significantly contributed" (p. v). "A total of nearly eight thousand words, combinations, and meanings have been selected...with four aims in mind": to collect his Americanisms, his new words and usages, his archaisms, and "without aiming at completeness, certain miscellaneous groups of words which seemed to be significant or interesting for various reasons" (p. vii).

A9 SEVERANCE, EMILY A. Journal Letters of Emily A. Severance, "Quaker City," 1867. Ed. Julia Severance Millikan. Cleveland: The Gates Press.

Another perspective on the tour that produced IA; cited (repeatedly) in Ganzel (1968).

1938 B SHORTER WRITINGS

B1 A., E. L. "A Guest of Mark Twain," More Books: The Bulletin of the Boston Public Library, Sixth Series, XIII (November), 430.

Contains the text of an MT letter (February 14, 1881, just acquired by the Boston Public Library) to Edward House, who visited the Clemenses and spent several months in Hartford, working on a dramatization of P&P; the project ended in acrimony and a lawsuit.

B2 ADAMS, HENRY. Letters of Henry Adams (1892-1918), ed. by Worthington Chauncey Ford. Boston and New York: Houghton Mifflin Company, pp. 326-27.

Of Adam's Diary: "There are one or two good jokes in it, but of these I am not an expert judge. What charms my historical soul is the point of view, which is unconsciously the same as that of the twelfth-century mystery and of Milton, and they were all unconscious. Is it not curious that the man should always have represented himself as a fool and a tool in contact with the woman? Mark Twain's Adam is really a very interesting person. His affectation of science is keenly true,--no one knows more about that than I do. The Eve is not studied, of course; the paper is a study of Adam alone; and it is marvelous true; in fact, to own up, it is me myself; a portrait by Boldini." (Letter of April 8, 1901 to Elizabeth Cameron.)

B3 BEEKMAN, JUDGE DOW. "Mark Twain and the Watering Troughs," Mark Twain Quarterly, II (Summer-Fall), 5, 24.

An anecdote told by Governor David B. Hill of New York: on the birth of each child,

(BEEKMAN, JUDGE DOW)
MT had a stone watering trough set up beside the road, with the child's name on it.

B4   BLAIR, WALTER. "Mark Twain's Way with Words," University Review (Kansas City), V (Autumn), 60–62.
A joyous discussion of MT's vocabulary as part of a review of the Ramsay and Emberson Mark Twain Lexicon, which Blair considers sound.

B5   BLODGETT, HAROLD. "A Note on Mark Twain's Library of Humor," American Literature, X (March), 78–80.
The 1888 edition was compiled by Howells and his assistant, Charles Hopkins Clark; the 1906 edition, compiled at the Harper's offices, consists mostly of materials from other sources.

B6   BUCHNER, THOS. A. "Twain's House-Buying," Mark Twain Quarterly, III (Winter), 23.
An anecdote, vaguely recalled, of MT's purchase of a home after he decided to leave Riverdale-on-Hudson, New York.

B7   CLEMENS, CLARA. My Husband Gabrilowitsch. New York: Harper & Brothers.
Passim on MT, chiefly in passing references and comparisons of his temperament to that of Gabrilowitsch [indexed]. Declares she and her sister Jean "knew more German than our genius father" (p. 1), discusses MT's attitude toward the Jews (p. 6, in connection with her love for, and later marriage to the great pianist Ossip Gabrilowitsch, who was Jewish), and his condemnation of lynching and comment on Negroes and further comment on the Jews (pp. 12–16); texts of two letters from MT to his daughter Clara appear pp. 46–47 and 115–16.

B8   CLEMENS, KATHARINE. "My Husband and Mark Twain," in her Gardens and Books: The Autobiography of Katharine Clemens. With Foreword by Cyril Clemens [her son]. (Webster Groves, Missouri: International Mark Twain Society), pp. 205–16 and passim (indexed).
Provides family history, and describes MT in London in 1899. On p. 166, notes that Kaiser Wilhelm's memoirs mention a meeting with MT at the home of General Maximilian von Versen. Photograph of MT, p. 212.

B9   DEVOTO, BERNARD. "Mark Twain: A Caricature," Saturday Review of Literature, XVII (March 19), 5.
A review of Edgar Lee Masters, Mark Twain: A Portrait: "The worst book yet written about Mark Twain, the most inaccurate, the most wildly incomprehensible, and the stupidest.... A bad book, a false book, sometimes a vicious book, and the silliest of the now numerous books that waste time savagely assailing Mark Twain for not having been what he did not want to be, what he

could not possibly have been, what no intelligent person supposes it to have been possible for him to have been."

B10 _____. "The Mark Twain Papers," Saturday Review of Literature, XIX (December 10), 3–4, 14–15.
A description of the papers for which DeVoto has just assumed editorial responsibility, succeeding Albert Bigelow Paine. In a letter to the editor (p. 9) he says that he "cannot answer questions about the content of the papers" because of the pressure of his work and because "the terms of the agreement under which I am working forbid me to give out any information until the books on which I am working are ready."

B11 EASTMAN, MAX. "Mark Twain's Elmira," Harper's, CLXXVI (May), 620–32.
Eastman's family moved to Elmira in 1894, when he was eleven, and he describes the town and the Langdon family as he learned of them. The town was not intellectually stagnant, as Van Wyck Brooks and others suggest, and Jervis Langdon, MT's father-in-law, "was one of the most "un-coal-dealer-and-mine-owner-like characters that ever got ahead in business," generous, unaffected by his wealth, and an ardent abolitionist. [Reprinted in Eastman's Heroes I Have Known: Twelve Who Lived Great Lives (New York: Simon and Schuster, 1942,) pp. 105–42, according to MHRA Annual Bibliography (1942). No. 2137.]

B12 FERGUSON, DELANCEY. "Huck Finn Aborning," Colophon, n.s., III (Spring), 171–80.
Textual changes in the manuscript of HF show, not submission to censorship, but improvements in tone, language more suitable for Huck, and clarification of details. Reprinted in Bradley (1962), pp. 297–305; in Scott (1955), pp. 249–58; Scott (1967), pp. 234–43.

B13 H., H. W. "On Mark Twain," Manchester Guardian (April 29), p. 7.
A review of Edgar Lee Masters, Mark Twain: A Portrait, an unconvincing book. "After hearing Edgar Lee Masters on Mark Twain one cannot help regretting that it is impossible to hear Mark Twain on Edgar Lee Masters."

B14 HIBBARD, FREDERICK C. "Mark Twain From a Sculptor's Viewpoint," Mark Twain Quarterly, III (Winter), 1–3, 24.
An appreciation of MT by the sculptor who made the Hannibal group of Tom Sawyer and Huck Finn; he never met MT.

B15 JACOBS, W. W. "An Englishman's Opinion of Mark Twain," Mark Twain Quarterly, II (Summer-Fall), 1–2.
An impressionistic discussion of MT as distinctively American, a great writer, humorist, and a great personality.

B16   JORDAN, ELIZABETH. "A Silent Celebrity," Christian Science Monitor, XXX (November 4), 9.

At a dinner she seated MT beside May Sinclair in the hope that he could draw her into conversation; the attempt failed. [An excerpt from Elizabeth Jordan's Three Rousing Cheers (New York: Appleton-Century).]

B17   KANTOR, McKINLAY. "The Boy in the Dark: A Fantasy of the Mark Twain Country," Scholastic, XXXIII (September 17), 6, 35.

On his nephew, Benny Fuller, who was lost in the cave at Hannibal and was shown unknown parts of the cave by a mysterious boy named Sammy--who then led him back to the tourist area and could not afterward be found. "Reprinted from the Mark Twain Quarterly, by permission of Mr. Cyril Clemens, editor."

B18   LORCH, FRED W. "Mark Twain's Trip to Humboldt in 1861," American Literature, X (November), 343-49.

Includes text of an MT letter to his mother (January 30, 1862), interesting as one of his early literary treatments of the region.

B19   _____. [Review: August Hüppy, Mark Twain und die Schweiz (1935).] American Literature, IX (January), 488-89.

Concerns visits to Switzerland by MT in 1878, 1891, 1897. Appreciative, based on material already well known, but gives Swiss readers "the vigor, freshness, and charm" of MT.

B20   _____. [Review: Edgar Lee Masters, Mark Twain: A Portrait.] American Literature, X (November), 373-76.

Masters distorts his portrait through proletarian bias; the book "has at least three serious faults: inaccurate reporting, unwarranted assumptions, and a confused philosophy."

B21   MABBOTT, THOMAS OLLIVE. [Brief review: Ivan Benson, Mark Twain's Western Years.] Commonweal, XXVIII (July 8), 302.

"Well written and entertaining reading for all the solidity of its scholarship."

B22   _____. [Review: G. Ezra Dane, ed., Letters from the Sandwich Islands, Written for the Sacramento Union by Mark Twain.] Commonweal, XXVIII (September 2), 480.

"The editing is competent," but unfortunately four letters were omitted.

B23   MacALISTER, SIR IAN. "Mark Twain, Some Personal Reminiscences," Landmark, XX (March), 141-47.

"Extracts from a speech made recently at Dartmouth House." Comments on MT's gloom of the 1890's and the attempts of MacAlister's father "to get him out of this kind of neurosis" with a visit to the Savage Club--successfully, since no demands were made on him. Also describes a visit to MT in New York in 1903, and seeing him at Oxford in 1907. "My father had in his possession hundreds of pages of manuscript" blue-penciled by Olivia Clemens.

B24   MOORE, JOHN BASSETT. "Mark Twain and Copyright," Mark Twain Quarterly, III (Winter), 3.

Appreciative. As "Third Assistant Secretary of State," Moore met MT at a reception given by Grover Cleveland in honor of authors who had come to Washington to speak in favor of international copyright law; Moore later saw MT "on several occasions and was always deeply impressed."

B25   MORRIS, COURTLAND P. "The Model for Huck Finn," Mark Twain Quarterly, II (Summer-Fall), 22-23.

Boyhood memories by the boy who posed for the HF illustrations by E. W. Kemble, from May 1-October 1, 1884; he was paid four dollars per week.

B26   MOTT, HOWARD S., JR. "The Origin of Aunt Polly," Publishers' Weekly, CXXXIV (November 19), 1821-23.

Benjamin P. Shillaber's character, Mrs. Partington, anticipates Tom Sawyer's aunt in circumstances, personality, and an incident in which she figures, and (as MT later described his mother) she kindly warmed the water before drowning the kittens. The frontispiece of The Life and Sayings of Mrs. Partington (1854) bears a strong resemblance to the picture of Aunt Polly on the last page of the first edition of TS (1876).

B27   NYE, RUSSEL B. "Mark Twain in Oberlin," Ohio State Archaeological and Historical Quarterly [now Ohio History], XLVII (January), 69-73.

On the MT-George Washington Cable reading there (February 11, 1885). Local press accounts ranked Cable above MT; according to local belief, the cold reception led MT to use Oberlin as his model for Hadleyburg, but there is only the internal evidence of a general similarity between the description of Hadleyburg and the pious town of Oberlin, founded some three generations earlier. (See Cardwell [1951].)

B28   ODELL, GEORGE C. D. Annals of the New York Stage. New York: Columbia University Press, Vol. X (1875-1879), passim.

Mentions MT giving his "Roughing It in the Land of the Big Bonanza" lecture at Chickering Hall, March 28, 29, and 31, 1876 (p. 105), and at the Academy of Music, Brooklyn, March 30, afternoon (p. 136). MT appeared at the Academy of Music as part of a program that included Emma Thursby and the Young Apollo Club November 13, 1876 (p. 322). On the misfortunes of MT and Bret Harte's Ah Sin (pp. 370-71); it also ran for a week

(ODELL, GEORGE C. D.)
at the Grand Opera House, September 24-30, 1877 (p. 391), and at the Bowery Theatre, October 29 to early November (p. 407).

B29 PADEREWSKI, IGNACE, and MARY LAWTON. "America," Chapter IX in The Paderewski Memoirs (New York: Charles Scribner's Sons).
On p. 205, describes meeting MT at the home of Richard Watson Gilder: "The beautiful impression he made upon me abides with me still. He was a purely American product, some one that only America could have produced, in the quality of his mind, his humor and character. I think he remains an undimmed figure in your history. The years will not diminish his towering qualities and virtues."

B30 *PARKS, EDD WINFIELD. "Mark Twain as Southerner," in his Segments of Southern Thought (Athens: University of Georgia Press.)
[Source: Asselineau (1954), No. 803.]

B31 PUTNAM, SAMUEL. "The Americanism of Mark Twain," Mark Twain Quarterly, II (Fall), 13, 34.
MT was more than a humorist; he depicted his time and country for a world audience.

B32 QUICK, DOROTHY. "My Author's League with Mark Twain," North American Review, CCXLV (Summer), 315-29.
Young Dorothy was a budding writer; see her Enchantment (1961) for details of her friendship with MT.

B33 QUINN, ARTHUR HOBSON. [Review: Ivan Benson, Mark Twain's Western Years.] Pacific Historical Review, VII (September), 282-83.
Notes the book's readability, and the value of its bibliography of MT's Nevada and California writings, 1861-1865, with reprintings of some of them; agrees with Benson on the beneficial influence of Mrs. Clemens, Howells, Aldrich, "who toned Mark Twain down, and kept him from some of the banalities quoted by Mr. Benson."

B34 REYNOLDS, HORACE. "Mark Twain's Literary Beginnings," Christian Science Monitor, XXX, June 15, Magazine Section, 10.
A descriptive, uncritical review of Franklin Walker, ed., The Washoe Giant in San Francisco.

B35 ROADES, SISTER MARY TERESA. "Don Quixote and A Connecticut Yankee in King Arthur's Court," Mark Twain Quarterly, II (Summer-Fall), 8-9.
Draws a number of parallels, among them the contrast of "the modern with the antique" and the attack on books of chivalry; but "the character of Don Quixote is in marked contrast with that of the Boss."

B36 SULLIVAN, MARK. The Education of an American. New York: Doubleday, Doran & Co., pp. 230-33.
On MT in New York, Norman Hapgood's humorless description of MT in his autobiography, and Robert Collier's participation in the elaborate scheme to persuade MT that he was being sent an elephant for Christmas, to keep him company at Stormfield.

B37 TAYLOR, WALTER FULLER. "Mark Twain and the Machine Age," South Atlantic Quarterly, XXXVII (October), 384-96.
The portrayal of industrialism in GA and CY follows "a fairly simple, coherent philosophy of acquisition, control of obvious abuses, and concern for the interests of the whole people. Within him, satirist, capitalist, and democrat worked toward the same object--that of enjoying the uses of the machine, and lessening the abuses." [Reprinted in Fifty Years of the South Atlantic Quarterly (1952), according to Asselineau (1954), No. 831.]

B38 WAGENKNECHT, EDWARD. "Crucial Years for Mark Twain," New York Times Book Review (June 19), p. 2.
A review of Ivan Benson, Mark Twain's Western Years, which reflects "a very careful, judicial and exhaustive study of all the factors which influenced Mark Twain during these crucial years."

B39 _____. "Mr. Masters on Mark Twain," New York Times Book Review (May 8), p. 10.
A review of Mark Twain: A Portrait. "Masters's book is nothing more than a crude restatement of the Van Wyck Brooks theory of 1920.... What Mr. Brooks could not do with a scalpel, Mr. Masters is hardly likely to achieve with a bludgeon."

B40 WHITELEY, MRS. RICHARD P. "Interview with Mark Twain," Mark Twain Quarterly, II (Summer-Fall), 9, 24.
A headnote explains that this is about a dream her father, Robert Fitch Shepard, had about interviewing MT.

1939 A BOOKS

A1 ADE, GEORGE. One Afternoon with Mark Twain. Chicago: The Mark Twain Society of Chicago.
Describes visit to MT in "the late summer or early autumn of 1902, as nearly as I can fix the date" (p. 5). Contains no new information or critical judgment. A letter from MT to Howells (July 22, 1908), praising Ade, is reproduced in facsimile between pp. 8 and 9. "Editorial Notes" by George Hiram Brownell at end (pp. 14-15). Reprinted in Twainian, XXV (July-August, 1966), 1-4. Abstract in AES, XI (1968), 1735; reprinted in Twainian, XXVIII (January-February, 1969), 3.

A2 *BLANCK, JACOB. A Supplement to "A Bibliography of Mark Twain." New York: Privately Printed (4-page pamphlet discussing the defaced first issue of HF).
[Source: Blair (1950), p. 385 and Twainian, I (May, 1939), 4.]

A3 CLEMENS, CYRIL. My Cousin Mark Twain. With an Introduction by Booth Tarkington. Emmaus, Pa.: Rodale Press.
The first half of the book is biographical, seasoned with anecdotes; much of this will be familiar to readers acquainted with MT's works, although sources are not very fully documented. The second part, also highly anecdotal and sometimes drawn from MT's work, consists of "Mark Twain as a Dramatist," "Some Friends of Mark Twain," "Mark Twain and Smoking," "Did Mark Twain Say It?" (on quotations attributed to him), "With Mark Twain in Europe," and "The Mark Twain Medal" (a history of the granting of the medal "to show recognition for outstanding achievement in various fields of human endeavor"; the first recipient, in 1930, was Benito Mussolini (p. 205). There are stories here of interest for the general reader, although academic studies of MT have tended to ignore this book.

A4 *CLEMENS, SAMUEL L. Conversation As It Was at the Fireside of the Tudors [1601]. Embellished with an illuminating introduction, facetious notes and a bibliography by Franklin J. Meine. Chicago: Privately Printed for the Mark Twain Society of Chicago.
[Source: Asselineau (1954), No. 840.]

A5 _____. Letters from Honolulu, Written for the Sacramento "Union" by Mark Twain. Introduction by John W. Vandercook. Honolulu: Thomas Nickerson.
Letters dated June 25, September 10, April, and March, 1866, "Excerpts from the Diaries of Captain Mitchell and the Ferguson Brothers," and "Mark Twain's Concluding Remarks Reprinted from Harper's New Monthly Magazine, December, 1866." "The letters are printed exactly as they appeared in the SACRAMENTO UNION, typographical and editorial errors included." Vandercook's introduction is general and descriptive, and the material in this book is now more readily available from other sources such as A. Grove Day's 1966 edition of the letters from Hawaii.

A6 *_____. The Prince and the Pauper, ridotto e annotato da G. Tacconis. Turin: Società ed. internazionale (Scrittori inglesi e americani commentati per le scuole).
[Source: Asselineau (1954), No. 843.]

A7 *_____. Tom Sawyer, with an introduction by Bernard DeVoto, including as a prologue the "Boy's Manuscript," here first printed. Cambridge, Massachusetts: Printed for the

Members of the Limited Editions Club at the University Press.
[Source: Asselineau (1954), No. 839; the introduction and "Boy's Manuscript" were incorporated in DeVoto's Mark Twain at Work (1942).]

A8 *HELLMAN, FLORENCE S. List of Writings by Mark Twain Translated into Certain Foreign Languages. Washington: Library of Congress, Division of Bibliography (Selected list of references, No. 1450; 14 pp., typewritten).
[Source: Asselineau (1954), No. 834.]

A9 HEMMINGHAUS, EDGAR H. Mark Twain in Germany. New York: Columbia University Press [Reprinted New York: AMS Press, Inc., 1966].
A survey of German interest in MT, and scholarly work on him, from 1874-1937, with appendixes listing German publication of his works in English, in German translations, and in school editions, followed by an extensive bibliography of German scholarship. Because of the scope and quality of this work, there has been no attempt to incorporate this material in the present bibliography; the Hemminghaus book should be considered the first reference for the period through 1937.

A10 MENDELSON, M. Mark Tven. Fskblksm Molodaja Gvardija.
[Source: Asselineau (1954), No. 838; confirmed by Clarence A. Manning review (1948.B42).

A11 *WALKER, FRANKLIN. San Francisco's Literary Frontier. New York: Alfred A. Knopf.
[Source: 1969 reissue, 1969.A9. A general study, passim on MT.]

1939 B SHORTER WRITINGS

B1 ANON. "Mark Twain in His Proper and Profane Moments," New York Times Book Review (February 5), p. 3.
A review of Cyril Clemens, ed., My Cousin, Mark Twain, which is neither distinguished nor valuable, "but it is lively and pleasantly familiar, and thus becomes (in spite of some careless editing) a real addition to the Mark Twain library."

B2 ANON. "Mark Twain's First Lecture Tour. Based on the Original Newspaper Accounts," Mark Twain Quarterly, III (Summer-Fall), 3-6, 24.
On MT's tour in October-December, 1866, quoting newspapers of the time.

B3 ANON. "Time and the Joke: Mark Twain Today," Times Literary Supplement, October 14, p. 587.
A review of Cyril Clemens, [My Cousin,] Mark Twain. Primarily descriptive, calling the book "a commentary on what is presumed to be common knowledge rather than a full-length portrait."

B4 *ANON. [Interview with Captain Horace Bixby, 1914.] Memphis (Tennessee) Commercial Appeal, June 23, p. 4A.
[Source: Quoted by Elmo Howell in "Mark Twain and the Civil War" (1972), p. 54, n. 4.] MT knew the river but lacked confidence: "Being a coward, he was a failure as a pilot."

B5 BEARD, DAN. "Mark Twain," in his Hardly a Man Is Now Alive: The Autobiography of Dan Beard (New York: Doubleday, Doran & Company, Inc.), pp. 334-50.
Affectionate reminiscences by the illustrator of CY, and later, neighbor at Redding, Connecticut.

B6 BLAIR, WALTER. "Mark Twain, New York Correspondent," American Literature, XI (November), 247-59.
About MT's correspondence for the San Francisco Alta California in New York in 1867, before he sailed on the tour that produced IA. For text of these Alta letters see Franklin Walker and G. Ezra Dane, Mark Twain's Travels with Mr. Brown (1940; reprinted New York: Russell & Russell, 1971).

B7 _____. "On the Structure of Tom Sawyer," Modern Philology, XXXVII (August), 75-88.
MT was writing at a time of general rebellion against the model boy of earlier juvenile literature, and he produced a boy who "could play pranks at the same time he was developing qualities which would make him a normal adult." The book is well structured toward this end, with four themes: "the story of Tom and Becky, the story of Tom and Muff Potter, the Jackson's Island episode, and the series of happenings (which might be called the Injun Joe story) leading to the discovery of the treasure." Each episode begins with a boyish action and concludes with an opposing action of maturity. Reprinted in Cardwell (1963), pp. 36-45.

B8 BLAISE, BUNKER. "The Mark Twain Society," Saturday Review of Literature, XX (July 15), 11-12.
Describes the Society, which "has only one active member--President [Cyril] Clemens. But its roster of nominal associates is more imposing than that of any organization since the Sons and Daughters of I Will Arise." Among those listed on the letterhead is the Honorary President, Benito Mussolini, a fact that has led to rejection of honorary membership by some to whom it was offered; thus, Robert Graves wrote: "My admiration for Mark Twain prevents me from accepting a vice-president to Mussolini, the enemy to all Huck Finns," and Bertrand Russell declared "Mussolini is a man I hold in utmost abhorrence!" Don Marquis rejected the offer of a vice-presidency because "It's a matter of principle not to

let a foreigner like Mussolini have a higher office than mine even if he is funnier than I am." There is a description of Cyril Clemens's lecturing and of the books published by the Society.

B9 BLEARSIDES, OLIVER. [Review: Dan Beard, Hardly a Man is Now Alive.] Mark Twain Quarterly, III (Summer-Fall), 22.
Contains a brief account of Beard and his part in founding the Boy Scouts of America; quotes an MT note praising his Connecticut Yankee illustrations, and quotes Beard's description of MT at home.

B10 BOSTWICK, ARTHUR E. A Life with Men and Books. New York: The H. W. Wilson Company, p. 156.
Reports that Harper & Brothers were obliged to seek an injunction against the sale of a book supposedly by the spirit of MT, but gives no further details.

B11 BRASHEAR, M[INNIE] M. [Review: Cyril Clemens, My Cousin Mark Twain.] American Literature, XI (May), 231-32.
A "humorless retelling" of two hundred anecdotes from various sources, including earlier biographies, this is "a fairly readable book" for the uncritical. The significant parts are a frontispiece portrait of Sam Clemens at twenty-one, previously unpublished, and accounts of him in London and Vienna.

B12 [BROWNELL, GEORGE HIRAM.] "About Twain in Periodicals," Twainian, I (October), 4-5; (November), 3-4; (December), 6.
A bibliography of secondary material, in installments that continued to the demise of the old Twainian in 1940 and was resumed in the new series beginning in 1942 and carried to completion. The installments are in alphabetical order by the names of the journals covered; the 1939 installments include Academy Magazine (London) through Collier's Weekly. This material has been incorporated in the present bibliography.

B13 _____. "Californiana," Twainian, I (December), 3-5.
On the search by Walter Francis Frear for material in Nevada and California pertaining to MT. Among his discoveries were a number of reviews of MT lectures in 1866, with a hostile account in the Petaluma Journal and Argus and a defence in the Sonoma Democrat. There is bibliographical data on a dodger advertising his July 2, 1868 lecture on Venice, and a listing of sketches in the Overland Monthly which later appeared in IA.

B14 _____. "Concerning Cyril," Twainian, I (March), 2.
Sarcastic reference to Cyril Clemens, prefatory to a reprinting of "The Mark Twain Tradition" from the Chicago Daily News (December 5, 1938) on The International Mark Twain Society.

1939 - Shorter Writings

B15   [BROWNELL, GEORGE HIRAM.] "Mr. Howe's 'Modest' Collection," Twainian, I (November), 4-5.

The large book collection of W. T. H. Howe, assembled by him at a cost of between two and three million dollars, is to be sold on the open market and dispersed, by his expressed wish, rather than being transferred intact to a library; the MT material alone cost almost one hundred thousand dollars. A note in Twainian, II (November, 1940), 1, reports that the collection will be transferred intact to the New York Public Library.

B16   _____. "The Real Jane Clemens," Twainian, I (October), 2-4.

On the article, "Whitewashing Jane Clemens," by Doris and Samuel Webster (1925), and the Van Wyck Brooks view of MT's mother.

B17   _____. "A Tale of 'A Dog's Tale,'" Twainian, I (June), 2, 5-6.

Irving S. Underhill acquired the 223 mint copies of the pamphlet from Foyle's in London; realizing he could not sell them without depressing the market, he placed them in trust at Williams College, to be sold at a rate of two per year, but the whole lot is now on sale at $15.00 per copy.

B18   _____. "Tale of Two Twain (?) Tales," Twainian, I (April), 2-3.

On Rodman Gilder's attempts to find first printings of "The Revised Catechism" and "The Last Stamp," attributed to MT in clippings from unknown newspapers; they appear to come from the late 1860's. "The Revised Catechism" is Twainian in style.

B19   _____. "Twain's 'Weather' Witticism," Twainian, I (April), 3-4.

Robert Underwood Johnson's Remembered Yesterdays (Little, Brown, 1923, p. 322) quotes MT's remark in a form Brownell finds authentic: "'We all grumble about the weather, but' (dramatic pause) '--but--nothing is done about it.'"

B20   _____. [Brief item.] Twainian, I (February), 3.

Opie Read has a series of "Mark Twain and I" anecdotes in the Chicago Daily News: they read well, but often place MT "at a time and place where the facts show that Mark just wasn't."

B21   _____. [Brief discussions of MT's original pilot license.] Twainian, I (November), 1-3, 6; (December), 1-2; also see "License Mystery Nears Solution," Twainian, II (January, 1940), 2-3.

B22   _____. [Item on influence of Artemus Ward on MT, and MT's sketch, "First Interview with Artemus Ward."] Twainian, I (March), 1-2.
Lists a number of printings.

B23   BUTLER, NICHOLAS MURRAY. Across the Busy Years: Reflections and Reflections. New York and London: Charles Scribner's Sons. I, 8-9; II, passim.

Reference in Vol. I merely notes long acquaintance with MT, and there is no new information in Vol. II.

B24   CAMPBELL, OSCAR JAMES. [Review: G. Ezra Dane, ed., Letters from the Sandwich Islands (1938).] American Speech, XIV (February), 47-49.

Extensive passages of the speech of sea-captains and the wife of one of them illustrate MT's "unfailing interest in all the phenomena of living speech," as an amateur and artist rather than a linguistic scientist.

B25   _____. [Review: Robert L. Ramsay and Frances G. Emberson's A Mark Twain Lexicon (1938).] American Speech, XIV (April), 132-33.

"A meticulously accurate and revealing study of the way in which the American language develops its peculiar and distinctive vocabulary and idioms. No happier choice than the works of Mark Twain could have been made for such an investigation."

B26   *CHASE, ROY. [Article on MT, title unknown; contains anecdotes.] Australian National Review, May.
[Source: Quoted by George Mackaness (1962), pp. 6-10.]

B27   CLEMENS, CYRIL. "Mark Twain's View of '1601,'" Saturday Review of Literature, XX (September 30), 9.

A letter to the editor, extending his "heartfelt congratulations on Mr. Basil Davenport's scholarly and discriminating review of '1601'" a book which does not deserve publication. MT "would turn in his grave if he knew that this ephemera [sic] was embalmed with footnotes and critical comment. He never meant it for publication at all."

B28   _____. "My Cousin, Mark Twain," Saturday Review of Literature, XIX (April 8), 9.

A reply to Bernard DeVoto's hostile review of his book by that title (March 11). Cyril Clemens says the similarities of his book to the Paine biography stem from their having talked to the same acquaintances of MT; he does not comment on DeVoto's statement describing "the degree of cousinship involved."

B29   _____. "A Reply to Miss Brashear," American Literature, XI (November), 296-97.

Takes issue with her review of his My Cousin Mark Twain in the May issue; in detail Cyril Clemens argues the significance of the material in the book and describes his efforts to confirm his anecdotes.

B30   CLEMENS, SAMUEL L. "Mark Twain and John Smith," Twainian, I (May), 2-4.

(CLEMENS, SAMUEL L.)

Fred W. Lorch has found correspondence between MT and a "John Smith" in the Quincy (Illinois) Herald, publicizing a lecture to be given there on April 9, 1867. The text of the letters is reproduced.

B31 _____. "More Cemeterial Ghastliness," Mark Twain Quarterly, III (Spring), 23.

Reprinted from Territorial Enterprise, February 3, 1866. MT's satirical account of a local undertaking firm owning large shares in both the Lone Mountain Cemetery and in the toll road leading to it: in funeral processions, the toll is charged even for the corpse.

B32 COWIE, ALEXANDER. "Mark Twain Controls Himself," American Literature, X (January), 488-91.

A reply to DeLancey Ferguson (Huck Finn Aborning," 1938): MT "did like to write a more robust style than was agreeable to his late Victorian public," but tempered what he said. "Whether Olivia or Howells or Mark Twain was the censor does not much matter."

B33 *CURTIS, JOE [Article on MT as a pilot.] Memphis Commercial Appeal, June 23.

Article quotes Captain Horace Bixby, who said MT knew the river but lacked the self-confidence needed to be a good pilot. [Source: Quoted in Hutcherson (1940), pp. 353-55.]

B34 DAVENPORT, BASIL. "1601 and All That," Saturday Review of Literature, XX (July 1), 19.

MT's book, recently published by the Mark Twain Society of Chicago, is merely tedious filth, and historically inaccurate to boot: "One need only cite the courtier who went into exile for seven years for the same breach of decorum which is the beginning of the merriment in 1601."

B35 DEVOTO, BERNARD. "Mark Twain About the Jews," Jewish Frontier, VI (May), 7-9.

"Under the title of '"Jewish Persecution" A Business Passion--Mark Twain' a leaflet is being circulated, ostensibly by one Robert Edward Edmonson... It is based on excerpts from an essay by Mark Twain called 'Concerning the Jews.' A vile and dishonest misrepresentation of that essay, it is as vicious a piece of propaganda as I have ever seen." DeVoto sets the record straight, partly with references to the "Edmonson" leaflet but chiefly through a summary of MT's essay and the known biographical details a general reader would need.

B36 _____. "An Unpublished Chapter of Mark Twain's Autobiography," Saturday Review of Literature, XX (October 14), 11.

A letter to the editor, taking exception to the strictures of Cyril Clemens and Basil Davenport against the publication of MT's bawdy 1601, which "people enjoy" reading. MT himself "took a naive pleasure and even a solemn pride in having written it... he thought of it not as an ephemeron but as one of his lasting and most important books," as is shown in MT's own words, here published for the first time.

B37 _____. [Review: Cyril Clemens, My Cousin, Mark Twain.] Saturday Review of Literature, XIX (March 11), 16.

Begins by describing "the degree of cousinship involved: Mr. Clemens's great-grandfather was, I believe, a cousin of Mark Twain's father." In the book Cyril Clemens is careless in attributing credit. Part I is so dependent upon Paine and so similar in phraseology that two hundred passages ought to be placed in quotation marks. "Part II has no close relationship with the first part but harmonizes with it in being dull"; it is a poor lot of anecdotes "told to Mr. Clemens by people who either did or did not know Mark Twain," and vapid tributes to MT "which Mr. Clemens has obtained from various celebrities who either did or did not know what they were talking about."

B38 DOS PASSOS, JOHN, and ALAN TATE. "The Situation in American Writing," Partisan Review, VI (Summer), 26-92.

Dos Passos and Tate were among those answering a questionnaire question concerning figures in a "usable past." Dos Passos says "the best immediate ancestor (in Auden's sense) for today's American writing is a dark star somewhere in the constellation containing Mark Twain, Melville, Thoreau and Whitman." Tate: "I place Mark Twain nearer to Augustus Longstreet than to Walt Whitman; he was a regional writer in Huckleberry Finn, and he mastered a subtly modulated style; compare this with the vulgarity of The Gilded Age, written when Mark Twain had accepted the nationalist myth. At his best Twain was regional and universal; toward the end of his life he became national and parochial."

B39 *FEDERICO, P. J. "The Facts in the Case of Mark Twain's Vest Strap," Journal of the Patent Office Society, March.

On MT's patent applications and litigation. [Source: Reprinted in Twainian, XVI (November-December, 1957), 1-4.]

B40 FERGUSON, DELANCEY. "The Case for Mark Twain's Wife," University of Toronto Quarterly, IX (October), 9-21.

Livy's judgment was sometimes better than MT's and she steered him away from several literary blunders. What she found objectionable is not his best work, and despite her censorship he spoke more freely than did most of his contemporaries. Moreover, he loved her and respected her opinions. Reprinted in Leary (1962), pp. 159-73.

B41 FERGUSON, DELANCEY. "A Letter to the Editors of American Literature," American Literature, XI (May), 218-19.
A reply to Alexander Cowie's "Mark Twain Controls Himself" in the January issue. Cowie concedes that MT was intellectually lazy, but errs in company with Brooks when he argues that MT was censored by his wife and Howells. MT was not a frustrated satirist, and would have fought for any points he really cared about.

B42 FISCHER, W. [Review: Ramsay and Emberson, A Mark Twain Lexicon (1938).] Anglia Beiblatt, L (March), 91-94.
A lengthy summary. [Incorrectly attributed to F. Holthausen in Asselineau (1954), No. 857.]

B43 FULLER, MURIEL. "'Mark Twain and the Middle Ages' with reply by Basil Davenport," Saturday Review of Literature, XIX (January 28), 9.
Muriel Fuller takes issue with a statement in Basil Davenport's review of T. H. White's The Sword in the Stone that MT "hated the middle ages, knowing nothing about them." In his reply to Muriel Fuller, Davenport gives detailed reasons for saying that MT "was lacking in the historic sense"; CY states "the nineteenth-century dogma of progress...in its most naive absurdity."

B44 GATES, WILLIAM BRYAN. "Mark Twain to his English Publishers," American Literature, XI (March), 78-80.
Four autograph letters to Chatto and Windus, dated Oct. 7, 1881, Sept. 1, 1883, Sept. 17, 1888, and Jan. 27, 1892--all on mundane business matters.

B45 GORDON, CHARLES W. (RALPH CONNOR). "Meeting Mark Twain," Mark Twain Quarterly, III (Spring), 17, 22.
In his youth Gordon enjoyed IA, TS, and HF; years later, he was introduced to MT by George Doran, the publisher, and was pleased to find him serious-minded and sympathetic.

B46 GREET, CABELL. [Review: Robert L. Ramsay and Frances Guthrie Emberson, A Mark Twain Lexicon (1938).] American Literature, XI (May), 233.
The excellence of this study should not surprise those familiar with the work of Ramsay and his students, but their success in transmitting Mark Twain's language is an unexpected pleasure. This is an important contribution to the study of the English language in America, with "4,342 entries for which Mark Twain gives the earliest recorded literary evidence."

B47 HAPGOOD, HUTCHINS. A Victorian in the Modern World. New York: Harcourt, Brace and Company, p. 146.
The Hapgoods were friends of the Clemens family. Notes the secret love of Josiah Flynt for Clara Clemens, whose picture he carried everywhere he went (p. 146).

B48 HORGAN, PAUL. "News of Mark Twain," Yale Review, XXVIII (Summer), 846-49.
A review of Ivan Benson, Mark Twain's Western Years (1938; "A...useful arrangement of much known information," with a bibliography and an appendix "which in itself makes this an important book"), and MT's Letters from the Sandwich Islands, ed. G. Ezra Dane (1938; they reveal why MT won a reputation with his combination of humor and clarity; it is unfortunate that this is not the entire series MT wrote).

B49 HULBERT, J. R. [Review: Robert L. Ramsay and Frances G. Emberson, A Mark Twain Lexicon (1938).] Journal of English and Germanic Philology, XXXVIII (April), 313-14.
A lexicon devoted to a single author tends to suggest that he "introduced far more words and meanings of words into written literature than he really did," and "on pages x and following there is repeated evidence of the idea that by Twain's usage, regardless of other evidence, it can be determined whether an expression is an Americanism or not."

B50 LEMONNIER, LÉON. [Review: Robert L. Ramsay and Frances Guthrię Emberson, A Mark Twain Lexicon (1938).] Études Anglaises, III (January-March), 105.
Brief and descriptive. "Un bon et solide travail, qui fait honneur à l'Université de Missouri."

B51 LORCH, FRED W. "Mark Twain's Early Nevada Letters," American Literature, X (January), 486-88.
Corrects the sequence in Paine's edition of Mark Twain's Letters (New York, 1917) of MT's letters to his mother and sister, Sept. (?) 1861-April 2, 1862, "from which point on the sequence...seems correct."

B52 _____. [Review: G. Ezra Dane, ed. Mark Twain's Letters from the Sandwich Islands (1938).] American Literature, X (January), 511-13.
Approves Dane's chronological arrangement of the letters, and the omission of three on commercial topics and the account of the burning of the clipper ship Hornet. Agrees on the importance of the letters as a transition from earlier crudities to the comparative polish of Innocents Abroad.

B53 OXENHAM, JOHN. "Mark Twain and The Idler," Mark Twain Quarterly, III (Spring), 8.
Oxenham never met MT. He and Robert Barr, while planning their journal, The Idler, had hoped to get MT as editor; "Unfortunately, however, his idea of the proper division of profits left absolutely nothing for anyone else."

B54 PHELPS, WILLIAM LYON. Autobiography with Letters. New York, London, Toronto: Oxford University Press.

Contains numerous recollections of MT, including one of the time when Phelps in his youth mistook the great man's ducks for wild ones and killed five of them (pp. 61-63). Most of the later references to MT are incidental, and reveal only Phelps's respect for him; they add nothing to what he has said of MT elsewhere. Contains a letter from MT to a Mrs. Foote about reading from Browning (December 2, 1887, pp. 65-66) and one to Bret Harte about the Jumping Frog book (May 1, 1867, p. 492); both of these letters have been printed elsewhere.

B55 _____. "Mark Twain's White Ducks," Mark Twain Quarterly, III (Spring), 4.

As a boy in Hartford, Phelps shot some white ducks, not knowing they were domesticated and the property of MT; he never dared confess. [Phelps also tells the story in his Autobiography, 1940.B54.]

B56 ROBERTS, KENNETH. "The Necessity of Humor," Mark Twain Quarterly, III (Spring), 21.

"It is fashionable nowadays to award rich prizes to grim, gripping novels of the soil--dull books...Mark Twain, fortunately for the world, knew better."

B57 ROERICH, NICHOLAS. "Mark Twain in Russia," Mark Twain Quarterly, III (Spring), 7.

As a boy in Russia, Roerich found happiness in many things, among them reading P&P; MT was a popular author in Russia.

B58 SKINNER, OTIS. "Mark Twain in Hartford," Mark Twain Quarterly, III (Spring), 8.

As a boy, Skinner saw MT on Hartford streets; in later years, he enjoyed hearing him tell stories to friends at the Players' Club in New York.

B59 SMITH, GRANT H. [Review: Franklin Walker, ed., The Washoe Giant in San Francisco (1938).] American Literature, X (January), 513-18.

Smith emphasizes the crudity of these contributions to the Golden Era and other journals in 1863 and 1864: "their only value lies in the fact that they were written by a man who became famous."

B60 THOMSON, O. R. "How Important Is Mark Twain?" Saturday Review of Literature, XIX (January 7), 9.

A letter to the editor from a Williamsport, Pennsylvania librarian. TS and HF "will always be read," and there is "fine indignation" in FE, but MT's other books are fading. MT's humor was often "primitive" and "sadistic," and he was cautious on matters of religion and politics. "Never was a man so given to foreign stupidities; never one so silent on our own idiocies."

B61 VOGELBACK, ARTHUR LAWRENCE. "The Publication and Reception of Huckleberry Finn in America," American Literature, XI (November), 260-72.

Chiefly on the chorus of complaint that the book was "vulgar," "coarse," and "inelegant"; also tells of the mutilated cut in the first state.

1940 A BOOKS

A1 CLEMENS, SAMUEL L. Mark Twain in Eruption: Hitherto Unpublished Pages about Men and Events, ed. Bernard DeVoto. New York and London: Harper & Brothers Publishers.

In the 1924 edition of Mark Twain's Autobiography, Paine "used something less than half of the typescript in which everything Mark Twain wanted in his memoirs had been brought together. This book uses about half of the remainder. It has been selected, rearranged, and to some extent edited."

A2 _____. Mark Twain's Travels with Mr. Brown. Being Heretofore Uncollected Sketches Written by Mark Twain for the San Francisco "Alta California" in 1866 & 1867, Describing the Adventures of the Author and His Irrepressible Companion in Nicaragua, Hannibal, New York, and Other Spots on Their Way to Europe. Franklin Walker and G. Ezra Dane, eds. New York: Alfred A. Knopf.

These letters cover the period before the sailing of the Quaker City; McKeithan has collected the letters for the next period in Traveling with the Innocents Abroad (1958). MT later drew on parts of Letters XXIV ("A Curious Book," pp. 251-54) and XXVI for Innocents Abroad. Indexed and annotated.

A3 *_____. Tom Sawyer Story Book, retold in 96 pp. by Bennett Kline; illustrated by Henry E. Vallely. Racine, Wisconsin: Whitman Publishing Company.

[Source: Asselineau (1954), No. 887.] A letter received from William H. Larson, Senior Editor, Whitman Golden Press (April 15, 1974) cites a 1940 catalogue giving the title listed above but noting that "The cover and title page wording sometimes varied in books of this era. It has 96 pages, counting pastedowns." Apparently it is an abridgement for younger readers.

A4 *MÖHLE, DR. GUNTER. Das Europabild Mark Twains (Neue Deutsche Forschungen, Abt. Amerikanische Literatur- und Kulturgeschichte, Band VII). Berlin: Junker und Dünnhaupt.

[Source: MHRA Annual Bibliography (1940), No. 4108.]

A5 PROUDFIT, ISABEL. River-Boy: The Story of Mark Twain. New York: Julian Messner, Inc.

A biography for younger readers.

1940 - Books

A6   READ, OPIE. Mark Twain and I. Chicago:
     Reilly & Lee.
          A collection of MT anecdotes, with circum-
     stances only vaguely given.

A7   *TAYLOR, HOWARD P. Mark Twain and the Old
     "Enterprise" Gang; reminiscences of Howard
     P. Taylor and Steve Gillis. Holiday Greet-
     ings from the Watsons. San Francisco:
     The Grabhorn Press.
          [9-page pamphlet. Source: Asselineau
     (1954), No. 885: "Letters written to Joseph
     T. Goodman on the occasion of Mark Twain's
     death, edited by Douglas S. Watson."]

1940 B SHORTER WRITINGS

B1   ABRAHAMS, ROBERT D. "At Hannibal, Missouri,"
     Saturday Evening Post, CCXIII (November 30),
     66.
          A poem: Sam Clemens was a boy like other
     boys, and he and his friends live on in
     MT's books.

B2   ANON. "Hannibal Crosses Mr. Farley," Common-
     weal, XXXI (February 16), 355.
          Editorial commentary on the attack on
     MT's Civil War record by Representative
     Shannon (Missouri) when Congress was con-
     sidering the issuing of a stamp honoring
     him. [James Aloysius Farley was Postmas-
     ter-General--T.A.T.]

B3   ANON. "Mark Twain Stories," New York Times
     Book Review (April 7), p. 28.
          A descriptive review of Opie Read's Mark
     Twain and I.

B4   ANON. "Mark Twain to Young Writers" [From the
     New York Times, n.d.], Word Study (G. & C.
     Merriam Co.), XV (March), 2-4.
          MT recommends simplicity in prose, and a
     minimum of adjectives, in a letter of
     March 20, 1880 to D. W. Bowser, whose re-
     cent death is noted.

B5   ANON. "Tired Volcano," Time, XXXVI
     (December 2), 80.
          A descriptive review of Bernard DeVoto,
     ed., Mark Twain in Eruption, a weakened
     sampling from MT's late years when "he
     was utterly lonely. For most of his life
     Twain remained, as he still is, the last
     major U.S. literary voice."

B6   ANON. [Reply to the charge by Representative
     Shannon of Missouri that MT had deserted
     the Confederate Army.] New York Times
     February 7, p. 20.

B7   ANON. [Review: Edgar H. Hemminghaus, Mark
     Twain in Germany (1939).] Notes and Quer-
     ies (London), CLXXIX (July 6), 17.
          The critical estimates of MT by Germans,
     as surveyed by Hemminghaus, are often
     "plainly futile, led off to conclusions
     which are far-fetched and wholly unjusti-
     fied to anyone who has a competent

knowledge of Mark Twain's life and ways."
MT's popularity is now declining both in
Germany and in England.

B8   BLANCK, JACOB. "'The Gilded Age': A Colla-
     tion," Publishers' Weekly, CXXXVIII
     (July 20), 186-88.
          Describes variant imprints bearing 1873,
     1874, and 1875 dates.

B9   BROOKS, VAN WYCK. New England: Indian Summer.
     New York: E. P. Dutton.
          Makes no new critical comment on MT, though
     mentioning his name passim.

B10 [BROWNELL, GEORGE HIRAM.] "About Twain in
     Periodicals," Twainian, II (January), 4-5;
     (February), 6-7; (March), 3-4; (November),
     3-4; (December), 6.
          A continuation of a bibliography of sec-
     ondary material, in installments that began
     in Twainian, I (1939) and was carried to
     completion in the new series which began in
     1942. The installments are in alphabetical
     order of the journals covered; the install-
     ments for 1940 include The Colophon through
     London Quarterly Review. Brownell states
     (December, 3-4) that the coverage consists
     of known material contemporary with MT's
     early writing and, for more recent material,
     what he deems significant; he adds that
     coverage for the past ten years is incom-
     plete. This material has been incorporated
     in the present bibliography.

B11 ____. "The Chief Love and Delight of God,"
     Twainian, II (June), 1-2.
          Contains, with brief comment, the text of
     brief MT essay which appeared in Mark Twain
     in Eruption.

B12 ____. "Hannibal Honors Twain," Twainian, II
     (December), 5-6.
          On the observation of MT's 105th birthday
     anniversary in Hannibal; brief account,
     with lists of participants.

B13 ____. "Information Wanted," Twainian, II
     (February), 8.
          Reprints an MT letter from the Chicago
     Inter Ocean (December 15, 1875) on beautiful
     book illuminations produced by a girl in
     London whose vision failed just as she
     achieved recognition; may be a reprint from
     a Hartford paper.

B14 ____. "License Mystery Nears Solution,"
     Twainian, II (January), 2-3.
          On what appears to be the original pilot's
     license issued to MT, in Mariners' Museum,
     Newport News, Virginia; a news item from
     St. Louis Post-Dispatch (December 6, 1932)
     is reprinted. Earlier discussions appeared
     in Twainian, I (November, 1939), 1-3, 6, and
     (December, 1939), 1-2.

B15   ____. "Mark Twain on How Wars Start," Twainian, II (January), 3-4.
    Quotes a passage Brownell had been looking for, finally located in MS. Brownell's comments here are not of biographical or critical importance.

B16   ____. "Mark Twain on Photographs," Twainian, II (January), 6.
    Reprints, with brief comment, a portion of a letter from MT which Walter Francis Frear found in the Daily Hawaiian Herald for September 5, 1866.

B17   ____. "Mark Twain on 'Woman,'" Twainian, II (February), 4-5.
    Presents the text of MT speech "Woman: The Pride of the Professions and the Jewel of Ours," delivered before Correspondents' Club, Washington, January 11, 1868; also presents publication history of this speech and that of "Woman: God Bless Her," delivered before the New England Society of New York, December 22, 1882. Also see brief correction in March issue, p. 6, and brief note in Twainian, VI (November-December, 1947), 5.

B18   ____. "Mr. DeVoto Comes to Town," Twainian, II (April), 1-3.
    Summarizes a talk by DeVoto, "New Light on Mark Twain" (delivered March 5), attributing the falling-off of his creative powers by 1890 to business troubles and family tragedies. Describes meeting of DeVoto and Carl Sandburg, March 6. According to DeVoto, the MT papers are in a vast confusion, scattered through boxes and trunks, and achieving order will take a year or two.

B19   ____. "The Source of Mark Twain's Cigars?" Twainian, II (February), 7-8.
    Frank C. Willson has been searching for information on "Mark Twain Cigars" (a brand name), and on a "Mark Twain Waltz" published by Wm. Rohlfing & Co., Milwaukee; L. W. Herzog of that city is trying to locate a copy of the sheet music.

B20   ____. "The New Mark Twain Stamp," Twainian, II (March), 4-5.
    On the 10¢ commemorative, issued February 13.

B21   ____. "Twain on Democracy," Twainian, II (February), 3.
    Quotations from MT's works, submitted in a contest for MT fans.

B22   ____. "Who's Exaggerating Now?" Twainian, II (January), 7-8.
    Refuting Cyril Clemens's claim to have published the "first strictly accurate" account of MT's statement about exaggerated reports of his death, Brownell cites a halftone reproduction of MT's actual note appearing in Frank Marshall White's article in The Outlook for December 24, 1910, p. 965. There are details of the appearance of the words in The Journal, following White's cable from London.

B23   ____. [Brief item, describing motion picture of MT and his daughters at Stormfield, made by Edison in 1909.] Twainian, II (January), 1.

B24   ____. [Account of Captain Oberlin M. Carter's recollections of MT's visits to West Point in the 1870's, and a visit to the MT home in Hartford.] Twainian, II (February), 1-3.
    Also comments briefly on the publication of 1601 by the West Point print-shop, under Lieutenant Charles Erskine Scott Wood.

B25   ____. [Discussion of charges by Rep. Joseph B. Shannon of Missouri that MT was a coward and Confederate deserter.] Twainian, II (March), 1-3.
    Shannon's speech in Congress, January 25, called MT unworthy of being honored with a commemorative postage stamp. Brownell quotes Shannon and cites many persons defending MT; considers his "Private History of a Campaign that Failed" and the account by Absalom Grimes (1926) more reliable versions of MT's war experiences.

B26   ____. [Discussion of "To the Reading Public," ascribing it to MT.] Twainian, II (May), 1-2, 4-5.
    Text included. Appeared in first issue of Author's Sketch Book (November, 1870), apparently an American Publishing Company house organ to encourage the army of subscription agents. Also see Twainian for June, p. 4.

B27   ____. [On Franklin J. Meine's speculation that John A. Gray & Green (for whom MT worked as a compositor in 1853, in New York) might have been the printer for The Spirit of the Times.] Twainian, II (June), 1.
    No evidence is given.

B28   ____. [Discussion of articles in The American Publisher (Hartford: American Publishing Company, 1871-1872) by MT.] Twainian, II (October), 1-3.
    For 1871, lists "Old-Time Pony Express" (May); "A New Beecher Church" (July); "A Brace of Brief Lectures" (September); "A Brace of Brief Lectures" (concluded; October); "My First Lecture" (December); for 1872, January, "A Nabob's First Visit to New York."

B29   ____. [Anecdote, MT's reference to Bret Harte.] Twainian, II (November), 1-2.
    According to George Ade, at a Boston literary dinner attended by the great writers of the day, Howells as master of ceremonies and principal speaker reminisced about Bret Harte, then asked MT whether he knew him.

[BROWNELL, GEORGE HIRAM]
In reply, "Mark slowly rose to his feet, facing Howells. He bit off another inch of his cigar, spat venomously, and deliberately drawled, 'Yes, I knew the son-of-a-bitch.'"

B30 _____. [Discussion of Huckleberry Finn: first-issue points and the defacement of the illustration on p. 283.] Twainian, II (December), 1-3.
Based on discussion and comparison of copies of HF by members of the Mark Twain Society of Chicago at their November meeting; inconclusive.

B31 BURLINGAME, ROGER. Engines of Democracy: Inventions and Society in Mature America. New York and London: Charles Scribner's Sons, pp. 145-48.
A discussion of James W. Paige's typesetting machine and MT's financial backing; includes reproduction of a patent drawing.

B32 CLEMENS, CYRIL. "Mark Twain and St. Louis: Address at Unveiling of Mark Twain Fountain in Forest Park, July 23, 1940," Mark Twain Quarterly, IV (Summer), 15-16.
Text of the address, quoting statements by and about MT.

B33 _____, ed. "Republican Letters," Mark Twain Quarterly, IV (Fall-Winter), passim.
An unsigned introduction (pp. 1-2) says that the reprintings here include letters to the Chicago Republican in 1868, as well as "one of Clemens' first literary efforts from the 'Hannibal Journal' edited by his elder brother Orion, and an historically interesting contribution to the Washington 'Star.'" The reprinted material is as follows: "My Trip on the Henry Chauncey" (Republican, April 9, 1868), 3-5; "Captain Ned Wakeman" (n.d.), 6-7, 13; "My Return to Virginia City" (Republican, May 19, 1868), 8-9, 14; "One or Two California Items" (n.d.), 10-11; "A Railroad Mint" (n.d.), 12-13, 21; "Hartford" (n.d.), 13; "Up Among the Clouds" (n.d.), 14; "Novel Entertainment" (n.d.; on witnessing a public hanging), 15, 17; "A Recently Discovered Twain Letter" (Washington Star, December 16, 1867), 16-17; "Historical Exhibition--A No. 1 Ruse" (Hannibal Journal, September 16, 1852), 18-19, 24.

B34 _____. [Review: Edgar H. Hemminghaus, Mark Twain in Germany.] Commonweal, XXXI (March 1), 417-18.
Descriptive and laudatory. Cyril Clemens published a similar or identical review in Mark Twain Quarterly, III (Spring), 21.

B35 DEVOTO, BERNARD. "Calling All Twainians," Twainian, II (February), 6.
Letter to the editor, appealing for help in locating the autobiography of Orion Clemens, which was not in the papers turned over to DeVoto by the MT Estate.

B36 ESKEW, GARNETT LAIDLAW. "Mark Twain, Steamboat Pilot. He Was No Great Shakes at the Wheel, Say All the Rivermen--With One Exception," Coronet, VIII (May), 100-105.
Describes talking about MT with people who remembered him, or Captain Horace Bixby, or both of them; all but one remember MT as having only a superficial knowledge of the profession. "That one exception, however, Captain [sic] Walter Blair of Davenport, Iowa--says, and follows it with an exclamation point, that Mark Twain was a pilot and a damned fine one, and adduces irrefutable evidence to back up his statement." This "Captain Walter Blair" describes meeting MT and discussing piloting with him in Davenport in 1885.

B37 GABRIEL, RALPH HENRY. The Course of American Democratic Thought. New York: The Ronald Press (Revised edition, 1956).
Contains brief and rather minor references to MT's determinism, the distortion of his work by the materialism of the period he called the "Gilded Age," and the importance of literary nativism in his works.

B38 GARLAND, HAMLIN. "Twain's Social Conscience," Mark Twain Quarterly, IV (Summer), 8-9.
Garland says that in reviewing the CY he noted the dual satire, touching past and modern times. Dan Beard's part as illustrator brought him into disfavor with editors and made commissions hard to come by, according to his autobiography.

B39 GAY, ROBERT M. "The Two Mark Twains," Atlantic Monthly, CLXVI (December), 724-726.
"There were two Mark Twains: one, the man I have called the rhetorician, the other one whom we may call the poet.... Perhaps the showman was diffident about the poet." MT was an "intuitionalist," not an intellectual, and "his at times astonishing insight and wisdom were the fruit, not of philosophy, but of human sympathy. His illuminations came through his feelings." New material in Mark Twain in Eruption provides "no soul-shaking revelations." Reprinted in Kesterson (1973), pp. 51-53.

B40 HUTCHERSON, DUDLEY R. "Mark Twain as a Pilot," American Literature, XII (November), 353-55.
Based on an article in the Memphis Commercial Appeal (June 23, 1939) by Joe Curtis, the River Editor, and on letters received from Curtis and Captain Rees V. Downs (a friend of Captain Horace Bixby, who taught Clemens the river). The accounts agree that Clemens lacked confidence, and Bixby called him "a coward, a failure as a pilot."

B41 *KLETT, ADA M. 'Meisterschaft,' or the True State of Mark Twain's German," American-German Review, VII (December), 10-11.
[Source: MHRA Annual Bibliography (1940), No. 900; also listed in "Articles on American Literature Appearing in Current

(KLETT, ADA M.)
Periodicals," American Literature, XIII
(March, 1941), 101: "An examination of the
manuscript of 'Meisterschaft,' a comedy,
reveals Mark Twain's ignorance of correct
and idiomatic German."]

B42 LORCH, FRED W. "A Note on Tom Blankenship
(Huckleberry Finn)," American Literature,
XII (November), 351-3.
Quotes reports in the Hannibal Daily
Messenger in 1861 that Tom was sentenced to
thirty days in the county jail for stealing
turkeys (April 21) and suspected of stealing
onions (June 4), and two horses, a wash tub
of clothes, and a quantity of bacon, butter,
molasses, and sugar, in addition to robbing
a chicken house (June 12).

B43 MENCKEN, H. L. Happy Days, 1880-1892. New
York: Alfred A. Knopf, pp. 166-70.
As a boy, took HF off the shelf at home:
"I had not gone further than the first in-
comparable chapter before I realized, child
though I was, that I had entered a domain of
new and gorgeous wonders"; his father saw
what he was reading and reacted with "a kind
of shy rejoicing." Mencken continued to re-
read HF annually, "and only a few months ago
I hauled it out and read it once more--and
found it as magnificent as ever." He also
read the rest of the canon after HF, but
found it heavier going.

B44 ODELL, GEORGE C. D. Annals of the New York
Stage. New York: Columbia University Press,
Vol. XII (1882-1885), passim.
George Washington Cable was to have given
a reading at the Bedford Avenue Church on
February 6, 1884, but he was ill and remained at the MT home in Hartford (pp. 393-
94). On his readings with MT at Chickering
Hall, November 18, 19, 1884 (p. 544), and at
the Academy of Music, Brooklyn, November 22,
1884 and February 21, 1885 (pp. 571-72). MT
was listed among the authors to participate
at a reading in favor of international copyright at Madison Square Theatre, April 29,
1885 (pp. 427-28).

B45 OLIVER, ROBERT T. "Mark Twain's Views on Education," Education, LXI (October), 112-15.
MT was "an educational philosopher with remarkable insight," who "was before Dewey in
urging that the students be made partners in
the educational enterprise," although in part
his concern for education was the result of
"over-emphasizing the role of environment."

B46 PRICE, LAWRENCE M. [Review: Edgar H. Hemminghaus, Mark Twain in Germany (1939).]
Modern Language Quarterly, I (March),
119-20.
Hemminghaus has dealt with a "formidable"
amount of criticism in a "workmanlike" manner; the work was much needed.

B47 RICE, ALICE HEGAN. The Inky Way. New York,
London: D. Appleton-Century Company.
Quotes statements made to her by MT concerning Bret Harte, and Richard Watson Gilder's description of MT in a letter as "most
grim and unhappy but full of life and abound-
ing in scorn of a mismanaged universe." Includes facsimile of a note from MT, and a
sketch of him (pp. 77-80).

B48 RUFF, WILLIAM. "Mark Twain in the Sixties,"
Yale Review, XXX (1940), 423-25.
A review of Mark Twain's Travels with
Mr. Brown, "Worth reading for a sharp-tongued
humorist's account of American life in the
Sixties"; there is no comment on the editing.

B49 SCHRAMM, WILBUR L. [Review Article.] Philological Quarterly, XIX (July), 317-20.
Edgar Lee Masters, Mark Twain: A Portrait
(1938) is "a thin, irritating, disappointing
volume which does little credit to its distinguished author...contributes no new, and
misuses much old material. It is loaded
with errors," and apparently relies wholly
on Paine, Brooks, and Wagenknecht." Cyril
Clemens' My Cousin, Mark Twain (1939) "about
his very distant cousin is a completely unimportant volume...essentially a collection
of anecdotes and tributes. Most of them are
in Paine; most of the others are not very
interesting. None of them are documented."
Franklin Walker's The Washoe Giant in San
Francisco (1938) provides material of importance "beyond estimate" to scholars lacking access to files of the California papers.
Ivan Benson's Mark Twain's Western Years
(1938) is not stylistically graceful, but an
illuminating, solid contribution. The Ramsay and Emberson Mark Twain Lexicon (1938)
is the fullest available treatment of its
subject. "It is to be regretted that the
editors of the lexicon, having consulted so
many of Twain's works, did not consult all
of them. But what has been done has been
done well." Finally, the publication of the
material in G. Ezra Dane's edition of Letters
from the Sandwich Islands (1938) is extremely important to MT scholars.

B50 *SHANNON, REPRESENTATIVE, of Blue Springs,
Missouri. [Accuses MT of deserting the Confederate Army.] Congressional Record,
Washington, D.C. LXXXVI, Part 1.
Shannon's statement that MT "was not of
the same kidney as real Missourians" and attack on his "dismal failure as a belliger-
ent" are quoted by Fatout (1964), p. 64;
Fatout cites a reply by the New York Times
of February 7 (ibid., pp. 65-66).

B51 STROVEN, CARL. [Review: Letters from Honolulu Written for the "Sacramento Union," by
Mark Twain; introduction by John W. Vandercook (1939).] American Literature, XII
(November), 377-39.

1940 - Shorter Writings

(STROVEN, CARL)
Describes the four letters here which were omitted from Dane's edition of Mark Twain's Letters from the Sandwich Islands; praises the inclusion of these letters and the pleasing appearance of the book.

B52 VON HIBLER, LEO. "Mark Twain und die deutsche Sprache," Anglia: Zeitschrift für englische Philologie, LXV, 206-13.
On the gusto with which MT threw himself into the German language, his delight in the sound of the words and distress at its complexities, and his humorous discussion of the language. [In German.]

B53 WAGENKNECHT, EDWARD. "Mark Twain on Men and Events," New York Times Book Review (December 1), pp. 1, 38.
A long but chiefly descriptive review of Bernard DeVoto, ed., Mark Twain in Eruption.

B54 WERNER, M. R. "Mark Twain's Philosophy," New Republic, CIII (December 9), 805-806.
A review, chiefly descriptive, of Franklin Walker and G. Ezra Dane, eds., Mark Twain's Travels with Mr. Brown and Bernard DeVoto, ed., Mark Twain in Eruption.

1941 A BOOKS

A1 *CLARKE, NORMAN ELLSWORTH. Huckleberry Finn Again: A Bibliographical Study. Detroit.
[Source: Asselineau (1954), No. 904: "On the first edition of Huckleberry Finn" (14-page pamphlet).]

A2 CLEMENS, SAMUEL L. Republican Letters, ed. by Cyril Clemens, foreword by Hugh Walpole. Webster Groves, Missouri: International Mark Twain Society. "Number Ten of the Society's BIOGRAPHICAL SERIES."
Several letters by MT which appeared in the Chicago Republican (Spring, Summer, 1868), one from the Washington Star (December 16, 1867), and excerpts from his works. Facts of original publication not always given. Introduction thanks Walter Blair "for reading proofs, and for suggestions." Walpole's one-page foreword is a rather general appreciation, praising MT's timeless art. The editing has been severely criticized by reviewers. See 1942.B8, B41; 1943.B46; 1944.B39.

A3 HORNBERGER, THEODORE, ed. Mark Twain's Letters to Will Bowen, "My First, & Oldest & Dearest Friend." Austin: The University of Texas.
Hornberger's introduction gives background on Bowen and his friendship with MT, and notes give background on individual letters. The letter of August 31, 1876 is often quoted in studies of MT to illustrate his impatience with sentimentalism; it concludes: "Well, you must forgive me, but I

have not the slightest sympathy with what the world calls Sentiment--not the slightest." [34 page pamphlet.]

1941 B SHORTER WRITINGS

B1 ANDERSON, SHERWOOD. "Letters to Van Wyck Brooks" (with an introduction by Brooks), Story: The Magazine of the Short Story, XIX (September-October), 42-62.
Anderson comments frequently on MT in these letters, written 1918-1938, coming to his defence at the time Brooks was working on The Ordeal of Mark Twain: "Of course your book cannot be written in a cheerful spirit. In facing Twain's life you face a tragedy. How could the man mean what he does to us if it were not a tragedy. Had the man succeeded in breaking through he would not have been a part of us. Why can't you take it that way?" In his introduction to the letters Brooks says that when the book was published, Anderson "showed me clearly where my study had fallen short. I had failed to write the most important chapter, in which I should have praised Huckleberry Finn. I was too much concerned with the psychological problem, and the psychologist inhibited the poet in me. I regretted this as much as Sherwood, who loved Mark Twain above all writers."

B2 ANON. "The Art of Saying No: Mark Twain Refuses Permission to Dramatize 'Tom Sawyer,'" Reader's Digest, XXXVIII (March), 56.
The text of a letter, dated "Hartford, Sept. 8, '87," and never mailed. There is no editorial comment, but a note at the bottom of the page says the letter is from A Treasury of the World's Great Letters, ed. M. Lincoln Schuster, New York: Simon & Schuster, Inc., 1940.

B3 ANON. "Clemens, Samuel Langhorne," in James D. Hart, ed., The Oxford Companion to American Literature (London, New York, Toronto: Oxford University Press), pp. 139-41.
Includes a brief survey of MT's life and works, and the nature of his literary gift; he was "an artist of broad understanding and vital, though uneven and sometimes misdirected, achievement."

B4 ANON. "Huckleberry Finn in Public Domain," Publishers' Weekly, CXL (November 29), 2008.
Copyright has finally expired. A few brief comments on textual problems, but nothing not discussed elsewhere.

B5 BELLAMY, GLADYS CARMEN. "Mark Twain's Indebtedness to John Phoenix," American Literature, XIII (March), 29-43.
Shows parallels to published works of George Horatio Derby ("John Phoenix") in "Love's Bakery," "A Full and Reliable Account of the Extraordinary Meteoric Shower of Last Saturday Night," "Blanketing the

(BELLAMY, GLADYS CARMEN)
Admiral" (RI, II, Ch. XXI), "Some Learned
Fables for Good Old Boys and Girls" ("How
the Animals of the Wood Sent Out a Scientific Expedition"), "The Petrified Man," and
even the Whittier birthday dinner speech.
In this last, Miss Bellamy quotes the "John
Phoenix" treatment of Emerson's "Brahma" as
dealing with the game of euchre, with "the
red slayer" an allusion to the Right Bower.
There is a less persuasive case made that
the "solitary oesophagus" of "A Double-
Barrelled Detective Story" and Mark Twain's
dismissal of Jane Austen owe anything to
"John Phoenix."

B6   BENNETT, WHITMAN. A Practical Guide to Ameri-
can Book Collecting. New York: The Bennett
Book Studios, Inc.
Contains bibliographical descriptions of
Jumping Frog, IA, RI, TS, P&P, LOM, HF, CY,
JA, What Is Man? Captain Stormfield's Visit
to Heaven, MS, discussions of first editions
and issues, etc.

B7   BLAIR, WALTER. [Review: Edgar H. Hemminghaus, Mark Twain in Germany (1939).] American Literature, XIII (March), 87.
"The bibliography is excellent," but "Dr.
Hemminghaus has found little hitherto unknown German criticism which comments pene-
tratingly on the artistry or thought of
Twain."

B8   BLEARSIDES, OLIVER. "Mark Twain's Characters
Come From Real People," Mark Twain Quarter-
ly, IV (Summer-Fall), 16-19.
Anecdotal; contains no new information.

B9   [BROWNELL, GEORGE HIRAM.] Special issue of
Twainian, III (June).
On a meeting of MT enthusiasts planned at
George Ade's farm near Brook, Indiana,
planned for June 21. This is the only issue of the Twainian for 1941, and marks the
end of the old series. A new series begins
in 1942, and continues unbroken to the present.

B10   CLEMENS, CYRIL. "Twain and Libel," Saturday
Review of Literature, XXIV (August 30), 9.
A letter to the editor, citing a New York
Times interview (June 10, 1883) in which MT
accused C. C. Duncan (formerly captain of
the Quaker City) of fraud; in a letter MT
disavowed some of the language attributed
to him, and a news story of March 9, 1884
reports that Duncan sued MT and the Times
for damages; he was awarded six cents by
the court.

B11   _____. "Unpublished Recollections of Original Becky Thatcher," Mark Twain Quarterly,
IV (Summer-Fall), 20, 23.
Cyril Clemens "once had a long talk" with
Laura Hawkins Frazer, who passed on a number of reminiscences of MT as a boy; one of
them concerned his purchase of a copy of

Thomas Chandler Haliburton's "Sam Slick"
stories and his pleasure in the book.

B12   _____, ed. "Mark Twain's Unpublished Letters
to His English Publishers," Mark Twain Quarterly, IV (Summer-Fall), 1-2, 24.
When MT was offered either $10,000 or a
royalty for Innocents Abroad [in America]
he followed the advice of his friend A. D.
Richardson to take the royalty. The book
first appeared in England in a pirated edition published by John Camden Hotten, and
MT later arranged to have most of his works
published by Chatto & Windus; here are texts
of his letters to them October 7, 1881;
December 8, 1884; July 25, 1897; September
17, 1888; there are also two undated notes.

B13   DEVOTO, BERNARD (ed.). "Sam Clemens Tells a
Story: An Excerpt from the Recent Book,
Mark Twain in Eruption," Scholastic,
XXXVIII (February 10), 29-30.
On the telling of "His Grandfather's Old
Ram," with a brief note for high-school
students on DeVoto's editing of newly-pub-
lished material.

B14   EBY, E. H. [Review: Mark Twain in Eruption
(1940).] Modern Language Quarterly, II
(December), 654.
"These new portions of the autobiography
add nothing of vital importance to the data
already known.... Mr. DeVoto's editing
makes the material more understandable for
the general reader but makes no pretensions
to thoroughness."

B15   HORN, W. [Review: Robert L. Ramsay and Frances Guthrie Emberson, A Mark Twain Lexicon
(1938).] Archiv für das Studium der neueren
Sprachen, CLXXVIII, 57-58.
Descriptive. [In German.]

B16   JONES, HOWARD MUMFORD. [Review: Günther
Möhle, Das Europabild Mark Twains (1940),
and Bernard DeVoto, ed., Mark Twain in Eruption (1940).] Journal of English and Germanic Philology, XL (October), 448-49.
Möhle squanders eighty pages on background, leaving only fifty "to discuss a
rather intricate problem. The result is
naturally not illuminating." Moreover, the
proofreading is very poor. Mark Twain in
Eruption shows "an unfortunate monotony of
tone," because of DeVoto's choice of material to include, and biographers will still
need to go through the material that remains
unpublished. "Mr. DeVoto's introductory
analysis...is much more acute than anything
in Dr. Möhle's monograph."

B17   KRONENBERGER, LOUIS. "Now It Can Be Told,"
Nation, CLII (February 8), 161-62.
A review of Mark Twain in Eruption (1940),
previously unpublished material by MT "in
as effective a form as first-rate editing
can achieve."

1941 - Shorter Writings

B18   LORCH, FRED W. "Mark Twain and the 'Campaign that Failed,'" _American Literature_, XII (January), 454-70.
       Places in historical perspective MT's brief service as a Confederate irregular soldier: his conduct was fairly typical of the times. Extensively documented.

B19   McC., H. [Review: Bernard DeVoto, ed., _Mark Twain in Eruption_ (1940).] _More Books: The Bulletin of the Boston Public Library_, Sixth Series, XVI (January), 22-23.
       Brief review. "Mr. DeVoto has selected and printed the best of the unused papers... it is certainly...'Mark Twain in eruption,'" but it is also amusing: "There is stuff in 'Hannibal Days' as good as anything in _Tom Sawyer_."

B20   ORIANS, G. HARRISON. "Walter Scott, Mark Twain, and the Civil War," _South Atlantic Quarterly_, XL (October), 342-59.
       Comparatively little on MT, in a lengthy refutation of his charge in _LOM_ that Scott had filled Southern minds with romantic nonsense and thereby helped bring on the Civil War.

B21   PARRY, ALBERT. "Mark Twain in Russia," _Books Abroad_, XV (April), 168-75.
       A survey of changing Russian attitudes toward MT, who briefly visited and wrote about Russia and whose daughter married a Russian pianist. "In a period of three recent years Mark Twain's works sold over a million and a half copies printed in the various languages of Soviet peoples," leading all other American writers," and "his works were translated early and extensively." In translations of _IA_ before the Revolution his description of Odessa was softened to make it less offensive, while recent versions deliberately heighten his criticism. His satire is regarded as basically kindly, a fact that some critics praise and others deplore; he is not considered a forceful social critic.

B22   POCHMANN, HENRY A. [Review: _Mark Twain in Eruption_ (1940).] _American Literature_, XIII (May), 173-76.
       There is "little that is either genuinely novel or truly 'eruptive' in the book," and "like the _Autobiography_, of which this is properly a supplement, its chief interest lies in the inimitable witticisms and caustic comments which Mark Twain made upon men and events."

B23   PRITCHETT, V. S. "Books in General," _New Statesman and Nation_, CXIII (August 2), 113. Reprinted as "The American Puritan" in his _In My Good Books_ (London: Chatto & Windus), pp. 175-82.
       A review briefly discussing _PW_ but chiefly on _HF_: "although it is one of the funniest books in all literature and really astonishing in the variety of its farce and

character, we are more moved than we are amused by it" because "the particular character of American nostalgia is that it is not only harking back to something lost in the past, but suggests also the tragedy of a lost future." Reprinted, slightly abridged, as "_Huckleberry Finn_ and the Cruelty of American Humor" in Bradley (1962), pp. 305-309, and as "Cruelty in _The Adventures of Huckleberry Finn_' in Lettis (1962), pp. 317-20.

B24   SLADE, WILLIAM G. "Mark Twain's Educational Views," _Mark Twain Quarterly_, IV (Summer-Fall), 5-10.
       Lists his reading, interest in foreign languages, mnemonic games, comments on educational goals and methods. Despite MT's lack of formal education, "some of his observations are worthy of notice and the administrator and teacher alike can profit by this layman's opinions and criticisms."

B25   STEWART, GEORGE R. "Bret Harte upon Mark Twain in 1866," _American Literature_, XIII (November), 263-64.
       Harte's estimate of MT's October 2, 1866 lecture about the Sandwich Islands; final paragraph in one of a series of letters to the Springfield (Mass.) _Daily Republican_ (November 10, 1866). Harte criticized MT's coarsenesss but set his humor above Artemus Ward's and called him "a new star rising in this western horizon."

B26   TEMPLIN, E. H. "On Re-Reading Mark Twain," _Hispania_, XXIV (October), 269-76.
       With particular emphasis on _CY_, notes the influence of Cervantes and some parallels of Spanish works to those of MT; provides no new factual information.

B27   VON HIBLER, LEO. [Review: Ivan Benson, _Mark Twain's Western Years_ (1938).] _Englische Studien_, LXXIV (January), 250-53.
       Primarily an extensive summary of the book for German readers. [In German.]

B28   WALKER, STANLEY. "The Case of Mr. Whipple's Pants," _New Yorker_, XVII (September 27), 58-61.
       Bob Davis's column on the editorial page of the New York _Sun_ summarized an uncompleted MT story he had heard from Irving Bacheller, about middle-aged Henry Whipple, who returned to his old home town after an absence of many years and decided to go for a nude swim; while dressing, he heard a buggy approaching and leapt into his own buggy, and pulled a robe over his bare legs. In the other buggy were an old sweetheart and her father, who recognized him; when he hesitated to join them she climbed into his buggy and took the reins, and her father followed in the other buggy. Walker suggests several possible endings for the story.

B29   WECTER, DIXON. "Mark Twain as Translator from
       the German," American Literature, XIII
       (November), 257-63.
            In the winter of 1891 MT translated Dr.
       Heinrich Hoffman's Struwelpeter (1842);
       Harper & Brothers published the transla-
       tion as Slovenly Peter in 1935. Young
       readers still prefer the more conventional
       Winston translation.

B30   WOOLF, S. J. Here Am I. New York: Random
       House, passim.
            A more candid account of his visit to the
       Clemens home than in his 1910 Collier's ar-
       ticle. On visiting the New York apartment
       of Colonel Edward House, he saw that the
       portraits were of Woodrow Wilson, MT, Lin-
       coln, and Jackson (p. 132). Lithograph of
       MT in bed (facing p. 135; discussed
       pp. 135-36). Woolf visited President Masa-
       ryk in Prague; among the many books were
       some by MT, and Masaryk told him he had
       learned about the people of America in the
       Mississippi region from them.

1942 A BOOKS

A1   CLEMENS, CYRIL. Young Sam Clemens. Foreword
       by Hendrik Willem Van Loon and introduction
       by Grant Wood. Portland, Maine: Leon Teb-
       betts Editions.
            Biography for the general reader, enliv-
       ened by numerous anecdotes but undocumented.

A2   *CLEMENS, SAMUEL L. Adventures of Huckleberry
       Finn. New York: The Limited Editions Club,
       ed. and introduction by Bernard DeVoto.
       "The first edition in which an effort has
       been made to establish the text."
            [Source: Asselineau (1954), No. 929.]
       Introduction reprinted in Mark Twain at
       Work (1942.A4).

A3   _____. Mark Twain's Letters in the Muscatine
       Journal, ed. and introduction by Edgar M.
       Branch; foreword by George Hiram Brownell.
       Chicago: The Mark Twain Association of
       America.
            Texts of five letters, 1853-1855, to the
       newspaper of which MT's brother Orion was
       part-owner and an editor. Brownell discus-
       ses Orion Clemens, and Branch describes MT's
       early journalism before the move to Nevada.

A4   DEVOTO, BERNARD. Mark Twain at Work. Cam-
       bridge, Massachusetts: Harvard University
       Press; London: Humphrey Milford, Oxford
       University Press.
            Working from the manuscripts, DeVoto says
       "something about the actual writing" of TS
       and HF "for the first time by any critic.
       What is said...does outline the nature of
       his talent, its abundance, and its hia-
       tuses." A concluding essay, "The Symbols
       of Despair," is based "on a vast accumula-
       tion of data which Mr. Paine ignored and
       Mr. Brooks never heard about. The present

essay indicates the true ordeal of Mark
Twain. Anyone who is familiar with Mr.
Brooks's book will see at once that my interpretation of it differs altogether from
his" (pp. vii-ix). Contains text of "The
Great Dark" and early manuscript material
for TS and HF, including "Boy's Manuscript."
"The Symbols of Despair" is reprinted in
Smith (1963), pp. 140-58, and material on TS
in Scott (1955), pp. 259-71 and (1967),
pp. 244-56, and Marks (1959), pp. 28-43;
there is also an excerpt in Cardwell (1963),
pp. 46-50.

A5   MASON, MIRIAM E. Mark Twain: Boy of Old
       Missouri. Indianapolis, New York: The
       Bobbs-Merrill Company.
            A biography for younger readers, part of
       The Childhood of Famous Americans series.

A6   SHAFFER, ELLEN K., and LUCILLE S. J. HALL,
       comps. A Check List of the Mark Twain Col-
       lection Assembled by the Late Willard S.
       Morse of Santa Monica, California. Los
       Angeles, California: Dawson's Book Shop.
            Based on Morse's own "meticulous" cata-
       logue of the collection, which includes
       manuscripts, first editions, books that be-
       longed to MT, books and articles about him,
       newspaper material, as well as portraits,
       busts, etc. [The collection includes signi-
       ficant material not listed in the present
       bibliography; it is now at Yale.]

1942 B SHORTER WRITINGS

B1   ANON. "Quintus Curtius Snodgrass: His Final
       Letter in the New Orleans Crescent," Twain-
       ian, n.s., 1 (June), 1-3.
            Thomas Ewing Dabney found five more "Quin-
       tus Curtius Snodgrass" letters, in addition
       to the six discovered by Minnie M. Brashear
       and Ernest E. Leisy; the letter of
       March 30, 1861 is reprinted. Also see
       Twainian, V (September-October, 1946), 1-2.

B2   AUERNHEIMER, RAOUL. "Mark Twain and the Ges-
       tapo," Christian Science Monitor, XXXIV
       (October 10, Magazine Section), 6.
            Auernheimer's thoughts about MT; occasioned
       by applying for permission to emigrate at the
       Gestapo headquarters at the Hotel Metropole,
       Vienna, where MT wrote "The Man that Corrupt-
       ed Hadleyburg."

B3   BEARD, CHARLES A., and MARY R. BEARD. The
       American Spirit: A Study of the Idea of
       Civilization in the United States (Vol. IV
       in their The Rise of American Civilization).
       New York: The Macmillan Company.
            Contains little discussion of MT, quoting
       and citing him on the dubious blessings of
       civilization (pp. 49-51), on the pernicious
       influence of Sir Walter Scott on the South
       (pp. 295-96), and on American imperialism
       (pp. 589-91). There is little of interest
       here for the student of MT, with the excep-
       tion of extensive quotation from a reply to

(BEARD, CHARLES A., and MARY R. BEARD)
his criticism of Scott by Mrs. T. P. O'Connor in her My Beloved South (1913) on
pp. 396-97.

B4   BERNARD, HARRY. "Lettres Américaines. Filiation de Mark Twain," Revue de l'Université d'Ottawa, XII (Juillet-Septembre), 327-41.
MT's successors include Edgar Lee Masters (Mitch Miller), Alvin Johnson (Spring Storm), James Still (River of Earth), and Marjorie Kinnan Rawlings (The Yearling).

B5   BLAIR, WALTER. "Mark Twain, Hank, and Huck," in his Horse Sense in American Humor from Benjamin Franklin to Ogden Nash. (Chicago: The University of Chicago Press),
pp. 195-217, and passim.
On the alternation of the fool and the wise narrator, as Twain and Clemens. Hank Morgan is decent but an ignoramus, and CY attacks MT's America as well as Arthur's England. Tom Sawyer is the dupe of books and Huck and Jim follow him despite their common-sense reservations, both in HF and in TS Abroad, which contains "a whole series of dialogues which equal or surpass the dialogues in the earlier book" and a further probing of the mentality of St. Petersburg.

B6   _____. "The Methods of Mark Twain," Saturday Review of Literature, XXV (June 20), 11.
A review of Bernard DeVoto's Mark Twain at Work, chiefly descriptive, but praising DeVoto's scholarship and "skill comparable to that of a mystery novel writer."

B7   BLANCK, JACOB. "News from the Rare Book Sellers," Publishers' Weekly, CXLII (December 26), 3536-37.
An MT letter in the 1917 edition of his letters (pp. 182-85), which Paine says was addressed to Thomas Bailey Aldrich, previously appeared in part as "Concerning a Bear" in "The Pellet, an ephemeral newspaper" publicizing a hospital fund. The sketch tells of Bret Harte's adding railroad tracks in front of the snarling bear on the cover of the Overland, thereby providing an object for the picture.

B8   [BROWNELL, GEORGE HIRAM.] "Cyril Clemens has broken loose again," Twainian, n.s., I (February), 8.
Describes Republican Letters as "worth its price as a piece of Twain curiosa" which apparently follows a Pacific Coast newspaper reprinting of the 1868 MT letters to the Chicago Republican and is textually inaccurate.

B9   _____. "Did Mark also Invent this Children's Game?" Twainian, n.s., II (October), 5.
Frank C. Willson reports having purchased a game titled "Rambles through Our Country, an Instructive Geographical Game," published by The American Publishing Company in 1881. MT is not credited with the idea

for this game, which resembles one he used to teach history dates to his own children, but the illustrations include cuts from his books.

B10   _____. "Five New Letters by Sam Found in Muscatine Paper," Twainian, n.s., I (February), 7-8.
On Edgar M. Branch's discovery of five "Letters to the Editor" from Philadelphia, Washington, and St. Louis from late 1853 to March 5, 1855; the last of these is reproduced.

B11   _____. "Hannibal Honors 106th Birthday of Mark Twain," Twainian, n.s., I (January), 1-4.
Describes the ceremonies, names, speakers and guests.

B12   _____. "Mark Twain on Thanksgiving,' Twainian, n.s., II (December), 5-6.
Brief prefatory material on several topics unrelated to MT, and text of MT's article in Washington Times (November 27, 1905).

B13   _____. "Musical Melange," Twainian, n.s., II (November), 1-4.
Includes correspondence with Jerome Kern and others concerning his Mark Twain Symphony; a letter from Morris Anderson concerning the Orchestrelle from MT's home, and a number of the music rolls (MT's choices were primarily classical); the text of an MT letter about a benefit performance for the Legal Aid Society, published in a special booklet by the Metropolitan Opera Company, as quoted in the New York Evening Post (March 16, 1906); brief comment on a "Mark Twain Mazourka" and a "Mark Twain Waltz" discovered by Frank C. Willson.

B14   _____. "The Mystery of 'Jim Greeley,'" Twainian, n.s., II (December), 4-5.
The familiar "Jim Smiley" of "The Jumping Frog" became "Jim Greeley" in The Californian for December, 1865; there is a highly conjectural attempt to show possible connections to Horace Greeley. For further brief comment see note in Twainian, VI (May-June, 1947), 6; the question remains open.

B15   _____. "A Question as to the Origin of the Name, 'Mark Twain,'" Twainian, n.s., I (February), 4-7.
A cautious treatment of MT's account of the origin of his pen-name: the question is still open.

B16   _____. "Sam Clemens Roams Again," Twainian, n.s., II (November), 5.
During part of 1855 SLC left Keokuk and worked as a printer in Warsaw, Illinois.

B17   _____. "Thrilling Tale of a Tall Twain Tale," Twainian, n.s., I (April), 5-6.
On the tracing of "Millions in It," listed in Merle Johnson's 1935 Bibliography with a

[BROWNELL, GEORGE HIRAM]
cross-reference to "Mark Twain's Remarkable Gold Mine"; the tale of gold-bearing spring water first appeared as a letter to the New York *Evening Post* (September 16, 1880), and is here reprinted.

B18 _____. "Varied Comments on Origin of the Name: Mark Twain," *Twainian*, n.s. I (May), 3-6.
Cites Ernest E. Leisy's statement in *American Literature* (January) that a careful check of New Orleans papers for the period when SLC was a pilot revealed nothing signed "Mark Twain." A letter from Thomas Ewing Dabney argues that Captain Sellers was too illiterate to write a connected series of newspaper articles and too egotistical not to sign his own name. Quoting a letter from A. Lyle Mewhirter on a Nevada story with the pseudonym coming from SLC's habit of asking a brewery owner to "mark twain" for two beers on credit, Brownell says there were no breweries in Nevada at the time, and anyway SLC was accompanied by three friends on the occasion of the anecdote.

B19 _____. "Yale Gets Morse Twain," *Twainian*, n.s., II (November), 4-5.
On the purchase of the Samuel Willard Morse Collection of MT material by Judge Walter Francis Frear, who donated it to the Yale University Library.

B20 CARTER, PAUL. "Mark Twain and War," *Twainian*, n.s., I (March), 1-3, 7.
On the growth of MT's anti-war sentiments.

B21 CLEMENS, CYRIL. "DeVoto's *Mark Twain at Work*," *Mark Twain Quarterly*, V (Fall-Winter), 23.
Chiefly descriptive; questions an identification of "Truthful James" with Jim Gillis.

B22 _____. "Did Twain Know Whitman?" *Saturday Review of Literature*, XXV (September 26), 13.
A query in a letter to the editor, summarizing reasons why there ought to have been comment by one author on the other, including the fact that both were in Washington in 1868. [Answered by John G. Moore, October 31, 1942.B44.]

B23 _____, ed. "Washington in 1868," *Mark Twain Quarterly*, V (Summer), 1-3.
Introduction to a special issue, consisting of correspondence from MT in the Chicago *Republican* in 1868 (dates not given), as follows: "Congressional Poetry," pp. 3, 5; "Kalamazoo," pp. 4-7; "Defeat of the Impeachment Project," pp. 7, 24; "Senator Chandler's Party," pp. 8, 24; "St. Valentine's Day," pp. 9, 24; "Curious Legislation and Vinnie Ream," pp. 10-11; "The Illinois State Association," pp. 11-14; "A Sleeping Lion Aroused--Gideon Rampant," pp. 15-16.

B24 CLEMENS, SAMUEL L. "Letters to James Redpath," *Mark Twain Quarterly*, V (Winter-Spring), 19-21.
A series of letters from MT to the manager of the Redpath Lecture Bureau, 1870-1872, on current and projected lectures, and his reaction to Redpath's proposal that he write lectures for others to deliver: favorable, with a male lecturer, but "I question if a woman ever lived who could read a densely humorous passage as it should be read.... They *appreciate* and enjoy (you know I rely for my effects chiefly on simulated unconsciousness and intense absurdities) but they cannot render them effectively on the platform."

B25 _____. "Mark Twain on Rab," *Mark Twain Quarterly*, V (Fall-Winter), 19.
Letter to Fairchild, dated "Hartford, Sept. 22, 1882," on his dog Rab, who chases horses and street cars, and therefore can't be kept. "I am mighty sorry it has turned out so, for he is a noble dog."

B26 DABNEY, THOMAS EWING, and GEORGE HIRAM BROWNELL. "Mr. Dabney Reveals the Truth about Tangled 'Delta' Papers," *Twainian*, n.s., I (April), 7-8.
There was a New Orleans *True Delta*, but MT's burlesque of Captain Sellers (supposedly his source for the "Mark Twain" pseudonym) actually appeared in the New Orleans *Crescent*.

B27 DAVIDSON, WILLIAM EARL. "Mark Twain and Conscience," *Twainian*, n.s., I (April), 1-5. The "Conclusions" of Davidson's master's essay of the same title (University of Missouri).
A sense of honor and a sense of guilt influenced MT after his departure from traditional Christianity, and he retained the habit of "moral introspection." His pessimism grew in part from what he saw of man's self-deception and his own inability to find comfort in rationalization.

B28 DUFFY, CHARLES. "Three Essays on Mark Twain," *South Atlantic Quarterly*, XLI (October), 454.
A descriptive review of Bernard DeVoto, *Mark Twain at Work*, noting "this book is composed of three essays, each of which has previously been made public." *See* review by Haight, 1942.B36.

B29 FEINSTEIN, GEORGE W. "Vestigia in Pudd'nhead Wilson," *Twainian*, n.s., I (May), 1-3.
Cites a number of passages in *PW* which still reveal the original plan for Angelo and Luigi as Siamese twins.

B30 FERGUSON, DELANCEY. "Mark Twain's Comstock Duel: The Birth of a Legend," *American Literature*, XIV (March), 66-70.

1942 - Shorter Writings

(FERGUSON, DELANCEY)
MT's "How I Escaped Being Killed in a Duel," which appeared in Tom Hood's Comic Annual in 1873, is essentially just another good story of the sort the public expected from the author of RI, and in his further development of the anecdote in the Autobiography (North American Review, CLXXXIII [December 21, 1906], 1224 ff.) and the Paine biography (Mark Twain, I, p. 496) "he had honestly forgotten the original facts, and remembered only his fictional development of them."

B31   FISCHER, W.   [Review: Günther Möhle, Das Europabild Mark Twains (1940).] Anglia Beiblatt, LIII, 78-80.
Fischer says the book contains more than the title suggests, in placing MT's picture of Europe in the broader context of other American authors such as Irving and Hawthorne, and less than the title suggests, in that it restricts the discussion of MT's work to IA and CY.   [In German.]

B32   FLACK, FRANK MORGAN.   "Mark Twain and Music," Twainian, n.s., II (October), 1-4.
Introduction and "a group of outstanding paragraphs" from Flack's master's essay (State University of Iowa). Draws heavily on published discussions and concludes that MT originally lacked sympathy or appreciation for serious music, but gradually came to enjoy it and even used it as a literary device. What appears here is conventional and derivative.

B33   *____. "Mark Twain and Wagner," Opera (December 28) (not Opera News, which has been checked).
[Source: Twainian, II (April, 1943), 6.]

B34   FULLER, JOHN G.   "A Connecticut Yankee in King Arthur's Court: A New Dramatized Version of Mark Twain's Famous Novel," Scholastic, XL (March 9), 17-19.
A short adaptation for high-school students; Hank Bennett, the hero, is thrown back in time "when his hand touches the power tubes of his extra-voltage radio."

B35   GORDON, GEORGE STUART.   Anglo-American Literary Relations. London: Oxford University Press, pp. 108-109.
Notes with satisfaction that English readers recognized "this authentic man of genius" while Americans still saw only the clown.

B36   HAIGHT, GORDON S.   "Studies of Mark Twain's Papers," Yale Review, XXXII (Autumn), 176-78.
A review of DeVoto's Mark Twain at Work. "Strictly speaking, none of the three essays it contains is new; the first two were printed in the Tom Sawyer (1939) and Huckleberry Finn (1942) that Mr. DeVoto edited

for the Limited Editions Club; the third, outlined in Harper's Magazine for January, 1940, and again in the introduction to Mark Twain in Eruption, was a William Vaughan Moody lecture in the same year.... The most important new materials consist of a short preliminary study for Tom Sawyer and several pages of notes for Huckleberry Finn." "The third essay, 'The Symbols of Despair,' reiterates Mr. DeVoto's explanation" of MT's final pessimism through a tracing of three themes which led to MS. "One wishes Mr. DeVoto had published more of the manuscripts from which his explanation is deduced; the eight pages called 'The Great Dark'...hardly serve to substantiate it." Although "no fairer or more penetrating studies of Tom Sawyer and Huckleberry Finn have ever been written...Mr. DeVoto's work would lose none of its vigor if he were more generous towards his predecessors."

B37   JOHNSON, MERLE.   Merle Johnson's American First Editions, Fourth Edition. Revised and enlarged by Jacob Blanck. New York: R. R. Bowker Co., pp. 110-15.
Includes points for various states of first editions of MT's works; also lists a number of reprintings, etc., and several books of biographical interest (listed in this bibl.).

B38   KAZIN, ALFRED.   On Native Grounds; An Interpretation of Modern American Prose Literature. New York: Reynal & Hitchcock.
Discusses Brooks's The Ordeal of Mark Twain (pp. 280-85), now significant chiefly for "its effort to draw an analogy between the Gilded Age and the postwar scene; an analogy between the 'ordeal' of Mark Twain, which was dubious, and the self-consciousness of Brooks's literary generation, which was real enough."

B39   LEISY, ERNEST E.   "Mark Twain and Isaiah Sellers," American Literature, XIII (January) 398-405.
In his piloting days SLC parodied the river columns by Captain Sellers in the True Delta for March 22 and May 7, 1859; the parody appeared in the Daily Crescent for May 17, signed "Sergeant Fathom." Paine gives an exaggerated account of this, claiming that it "broke the literary heart" of Sellers (Mark Twain, I, 149-50). There is a fuller reprinting of the Sellers report here than in Paine (Mark Twain, III, 1593-96). Leisy sees no reason to suppose that SLC borrowed the pen-name "Mark Twain" from Sellers, as Paine suggests.

B40   LILLARD, RICHARD G.   "Hank Monk and Horace Greeley," American Literature, XIV (May), 126-34.
Documents the story in RI (I, Ch. 20) of Greeley's wild ride in a stage coach driven by Hank Monk.

B41 LORCH, FRED W. [Review: Cyril Clemens, ed., Republican Letters by Samuel L. Clemens (1941).] American Literature, XIII (January), 439-40.

A series of letters MT published in the Chicago Republican in the spring of 1868, describing his trip to San Francisco. Lorch says they actually come from some other source, probably a California paper which copied them. As they appeared in the Republican the letters are not MT's best work, but they are important to scholars. "It is regrettable, therefore, that Mr. Clemens did not present them as originally published and thus make them serviceable." Only three of the six letters in the Republican appear in the Cyril Clemens edition.

B42 "MALONE, TED" [pseud. FRANK ALDEN RUSSELL.] "Mark Twain," in his American Pilgrimage. New York: Dodd, Mead & Company, pp. 16-32 (also "Introduction," pp. xiii-xiv).

A general account of MT's life, containing no new information. One of a series of radio programs broadcast from the homes of American authors.

B43 MATTHIESSEN, F. O. "Twain into Clemens," New Republic, CVII (August 10), 179.

A review of DeVoto's Mark Twain at Work. "Bernard DeVoto continues to present his findings from the Mark Twain manuscripts. As usual he throws his weight around.... Despite all this pointless bluster and despite an equally unnecessary display of showy and rather amateur scholarship, the new material he offers us is of real interest. And...Mr. DeVoto's judgment has deepened since he wrote Mark Twain's America in 1932."

B44 MOORE, JOHN G. "Yes, Twain Knew Whitman," Saturday Review of Literature, XXV (October 31), 11.

A letter to the editor, answering a query of September 26 by Cyril Clemens, cites references in Traubel's and Frances Winwar's books on Whitman. Moreover, MT was a part owner of Charles L. Webster & Co., which in 1892 published Selected Poems by Whitman, with an unsigned preface of which Moore says that "the manner of its writing leads me to think that it might have been written by Mark Twain himself."

B45 ODELL, GEORGE C. D. Annals of the New York Stage. New York: Columbia University Press. Vol. XIII (1885-1888).

MT was a guest and made a speech at a "little supper" given by Augustin Daly after the hundredth performance of his production of The Taming of the Shrew, April 13, 1887 (p. 216). The American Claimant, or, Mulberry Sellers Ten Years Later had a "trial matinée" at the Lyceum Theatre, September 23, 1887, after earlier trials in New Brunswick, Rochester, and Syracuse; "Mark Twain was a great genius, but he simply could not write plays" (p. 426). MT was among the authors at a reading in aid of international copyright at Chickering Hall, November 28, 29, 1887 (p. 544).

B46 OLSON, JAMES C. "Mark Twain and the Department of Agriculture," American Literature, XIII (January), 408-10.

Correspondence with J. Sterling Morton, Secretary of Agriculture under Grover Cleveland, concerning MT's requests for free corn and watermelon seeds to plant for Livy in Florence (1893).

B47 POCHMANN, HENRY A. [Review: Theodore Hornberger, Mark Twain's Letters to Will Bowen: "My First, & Oldest & Dearest Friend" (1941).] American Literature, XIV (March), 94-95.

Sixteen letters over the period from May 7, 1866 to June 7, 1900, important biographically. "Professor Hornberger's notes ...are a model of good editing."

B48 POWELL, LAWRENCE CLARK. "An Unpublished Mark Twain Letter," American Literature, XIII (January), 405-407.

Letter to Sir John Adams (December 5, 1898) praising his book, The Herbartian Psychology Applied to Education (Boston, 1897). Text includes a passage deleted by MT (but legible under infrared light) expressing ideas central to his What Is Man?

B49 PROVENCAL, VALMORE. "Mark Twain as an Historian," Mark Twain Quarterly, V (Winter-Spring), 25.

A brief account of history-related writings, with praise for the "Winner of the 1941 Junior Prize."

B50 RICHARDSON, LYON N. "Men of Letters and the Hayes Administration," New England Quarterly, XV (March), 110-41.

On MT's changing view of Hayes, pp. 127-29; includes a letter from MT to Hayes (April 10, 1882), commenting on mental telegraphy and thanking him for a letter praising one of his books.

B51 ROBERTS, HAROLD: [INTRODUCTION BY THE REV. C. J. ARMSTRONG.] "Sam Clemens: Florida Days," Twainian, n.s. I (January), 7-8; (February), 1-3; (March), 4-7.

On MT's birthplace and early days, and the influence of John A. Quarles, who may have told him the "Jumping Frog" story. Insists the early influences were beneficial.

B52 TAYLOR, WALTER FULLER. "Mark Twain," in his The Economic Novel in America. Chapel Hill: The University of North Carolina Press, pp. 116-47; also passim.

"Mark Twain's, then, was a comparatively simple, coherent philosophy of acquisition, control of obvious abuses, and concern for the interests of the whole people. Within him satirist, capitalist, and democrat

(TAYLOR, WALTER FULLER)
worked toward the same object--that of enjoying the uses of the machine and lessening the abuses" (p. 146). His achievement
is valuable, despite his limited grasp of
economics and lack of discipline. Notes
that the capitalism in GA "is curiously
pre-machine" (p. 124), and ranks CY as "the
supreme work" among the economic novels of
its time, despite its flaws, because it has
abundant vitality (p. 321).

B53   TIDWELL, JAMES NATHAN. "Mark Twain's Representation of Negro Speech," American Speech,
XVII (October), 174-76.
Analysis of the pronunciations in HF reveals "honest and sincere" representation:
"His failure to systematize his spelling
allowed him to write each word as it would
sound in a given sentence, and thus he
could represent in full detail the nuances
of Jim's pronunciation."

B54   VOGELBACK, ARTHUR LAWRENCE. "The Prince and
the Pauper: A Study in Critical Standards,"
American Literature, XIV (March), 48-54.
"Critics approved of The Prince and the
Pauper because, more than any other of Mark
Twain's books up to that time, it complied
with conventional literary ideals" (p. 54).
Among the qualities praised were construction of plot, depiction of character, and
the author's capacity to deal with a serious theme. Vogelback quotes reviews in
Atlantic Monthly, Boston Transcript, Century, Critic, Harper's Monthly, and New York
Tribune, as well as the New York Herald
as quoted by Paine.

B55   WAGENKNECHT, EDWARD. "Mark Twain as He Wrote
in His Years of Trouble," New York Times
Book Review (July 5), p. 3.
A review of Bernard DeVoto's Mark Twain
at Work, "the fullest report we have yet
had concerning the unpublished Mark Twain
Papers now in Mr. DeVoto's care, and some
of the best Mark Twain criticism that has
been written" on the meaning of TS and HF,
and on MT's struggle against despair in
his late writings.

B56   *WINTERICH, JOHN T. [Foreword.] A Connecti-
cut Yankee at King Arthur's Court. New
York: The Heritage Press.
[Source: Asselineau (1954), No. 930.]

B57   WOOD, GRANT. "Letter from Grant Wood," Saturday Review of Literature, XXV
(February 28), 11.
From a letter in which Wood tells Cyril
Clemens that reading Huck's description of
Emmeline Grangerford's unfinished drawing
of a young woman about to leap from a
bridge gave him his "first intimation that
there was anything ridiculous about sentimentality." Apparently part of the letter,
not printed, praises TS.

1943 A BOOKS

A1   *CLEMENS, SAMUEL L. Las Aventuras de Huck,
traducción del inglés y prólogo por Carlos
Pereyra. Buenos Aires: Editorial Losada.
[Source: Asselineau (1954), No. 964.]

A2   CLEMENS, SAMUEL L. Washington in 1868, ed.
with an introduction and notes by Cyril
Clemens. Foreword by W. W. Jacobs. Webster Groves, Missouri: International Mark
Twain Society; London: T. Werner Laurie.
MT letters from Washington, published in
the Chicago Republican. February 8-March 1,
1868. See reviews for the severe criticism
of the editing.

A3   FERGUSON, DELANCEY. Mark Twain: Man and
Legend. Indianapolis: The Bobbs-Merrill
Company. [Also issued as a Charter Books
paperback by Bobbs-Merrill in 1963.]
A sound general study, well received by
many reviewers as one of the best works on
MT of its time and reflecting all the schol-
arship then available. The portion on the
significance of the river is reprinted in
Schmitter (1974), pp. 77-83.

A4   *VON BRANDT, RALPH VAN KIRK. Mark Twain.
Trenton: Privately Printed.
[Source: Asselineau (1954), No. 962:
"Imaginary Letters to and from Mark Twain."]

1943 B SHORTER WRITINGS

B1   ANON. "Clemens Before Twain: Prentice Steps
in Buffoonery," Times Literary Supplement
(April 24), p. 202.
A review of Cyril Clemens, Young Sam
Clemens (1942), a book which provides little
new information of interest to any but the
most dedicated students of MT; however, it
shows that even in the early period there
is evidence of the deliberate care with
which MT achieved his effects.

B2   ANON. "Mark Twain's First Curtain Speech,"
Mark Twain Quarterly, VI (Summer-Fall),
5.
Apparently a newspaper clipping, carries
the date August 2, 1877; the text of a
brief address to the audience on the New
York opening of MT's and Bret Harte's play,
Ah Sin.

B3   ANON. "Resuming the List of Writings about
Twain in Periodicals," Twainian, n.s., II.
A continuation of the bibliography begun
in The Twainian when it was published under
the auspices of the Mark Twain Society of
Chicago. Coverage is as follows:
February, 6, McClure's Magazine through
Musical Courier; March, 5, The Nation through
North American Review; April, 6, The Occi-
dent through Overland Magazine; May, 6,
Pacific Monthly through New Amstel Magazine;
June, 6, St. Nicholas through World's Work.

(ANON.)
This material has been included in the present bibliography.

B4   BENET, STEPHEN VINCENT. [Holograph tribute to MT.] Mark Twain Quarterly, VI (Winter-Spring), cover.
Benet has been reading MT since age nine or ten, and regards him as "our great novelist."

B5   BLAIR, WALTER. [Review: Bernard DeVoto, Mark Twain at Work (1942).] American Literature, XIV (January), 447-49.
The essays and documents concerned with the writing of TS, HF, and MS "will be important for future students of Twain...partly because, like Mr. DeVoto's earlier Mark Twain's America, they challenge previous scholarship when it seems vulnerable." "Some critics...may find Mr. DeVoto's treatment of fiction as mythology less illuminating than he feels it is, and there may be disagreements with his conclusions about structure." Praises "the meticulous study and the valuable data here available."

B6   [BROWNELL, GEORGE HIRAM.] "Billy Phelps Joins the Innumberable Caravan," Twainian, n.x., III (October), 1-4.
Reminiscenses about Phelps, who died in August, and his appreciation of the Twainian; repeats several MT anecdotes from the Phelps Autobiography with Letters (1939).

B7   _____. "Dan Beard Tells about those 'Yankee' Pictures," Twainian, n.s., III (October), 4-5.
The text of Dan Beard's marginal notations in a copy of CY Frank C. Willson saw at a Boston book sale; comments on models, costumes; confirms Merlin's features (p. 279) as based on Tennyson's.

B8   _____. "From 'Hospital Days,'" Twainian, n.s., II (March), 1-5; (April), 4-6.
On a brief passage attributed to MT in the first state of his Sketches New and Old (Hartford, 1875, p. 299, here reprinted), along with an erratum slip indicating that in fact he was not the author. The passage appeared in Hospital Days, the anonymous work of Jane Stuart Woolsey (1868), but Brownell argues that MT wrote and gave her the passage.

B9   _____. "Here's Another of those New-Found Mercury Tales," Twainian, n.s., III (December), 4-5.
Includes the text of MT's "Private Theatricals" ("A Curtain Lecture Concerning Skating"), one of five MT writings discovered in the New York Mercury (see November Twainian for details).

B10 _____. "The Home of the Prodigal Son," Twainian, II (April), 1-3.

On a passage in a Holy Land letter in the Alta California (February 8, 1868) omitted from IA, although the illustration to accompany it was retained; text here reprinted, pp. 2-3.

B11 _____. "An Important Question Settled," Twainian, n.s., II (February), 1-5.
On MT's newspaper comments on "Rock Me to Sleep" poem; located by Willard S. Morse in Cincinnati Evening Chronicle (March 9, 1868) and later by Brownell in Chicago Republican (March 15); also see "Rock Me to Sleep," Twainian, March. Also on "Sociable Jimmy," attributed to MT in an unidentified clipping in a scrapbook purchased by Irving S. Underhill; see Twainian, April, "The Home of the Prodigal Son," on the difficulty of attribution. "An Important Question Settled" and "Sociable Jimmy" are both reprinted here.

B12 _____. "I Shall Probably See Stormfield But Seldom Hereafter," Twainian, II (May), 4-6.
Text of a letter from MT in Bermuda to Paine, Feb. 5-7, 1910, on various household arrangements; Brownell sees evidence here that MT "remained calm, patient, and kindly in his relations with others."

B13 _____. [Introduction.] "Mark Twain's Eulogy on the Reliable Contraband," Twainian, n.s., II (June), 1-3.
Reprints one of three MT contributions to the short-lived Packard's Monthly in 1869 (the others were his "Open Letter to Commodore Vanderbilt" and "Personal Habits of the Siamese Twins"). A brief note in Twainian, n.s., III (March, 1944), 6 reports that the "Reliable Contraband" story also appeared in Greenwich Village, II, No. 1 (June 23, 1915), with an introductory note by Guido Bruno, the editor.

B14 _____. "Mark Twain's Memory Builder," Twainian, n.s., III (December), 1-4.
A cache of 300 copies of the game MT patented in 1885 was recently discovered in Brooklyn; bibliographic description provided.

B15 _____. "Mark Twain's Tribute to Francis Lightfoot Lee," Twainian, n.s., III (November), 1-3.
On MT's tribute (here reprinted, pp. 2-3) in The Pennsylvania Magazine of History and Biography, I, No. 3 (1877), 343. Brownell states (p. 2) that he prepared the checklist index at the back of Merle Johnson's 1935 Bibliography.

B16 _____. "New Twain Tale Found in Oxford Magazine," Twainian, n.s., II (January), 3-5.
On the discovery of "Magdalen Tower" in the undergraduate publication, The Shotover Papers, Or, Echoes from Oxford, I (October 17, 1874); MT's text is reproduced, pp. 4-5.

1943 - Shorter Writings

B17   [BROWNELL, GEORGE HIRAM]. "Remarks on the Script of 'Mark Twain in Hawaii,'" Twainian, n.s., III (October), 5-6.
Brownell has been looking over Judge Frear's book in manuscript, and testifies to its accuracy and value; wartime conditions may make it difficult to find a publisher.

B18   _____. "Rock Me to Sleep," Twainian, n.s., II (March), 6.
On the authorship and original publication of the poem discussed by MT in "An Important Question Settled," Twainian, 1943.B11.

B19   _____. "Seven New Twain Tales Discovered by Chance," Twainian, n.s., III (November), 3-6.
Recent searches have turned up two MT writings in the Washington Weekly Chronicle for 1867: "A Humorist's Eloquence" (January 12, a reprint of his "Announcement to Highwaymen" in the Territorial Enterprise of November 11, 1866) and "Mr. Seward's Real Estate Transactions" (December 28). Five were discovered in the New York Sunday Mercury of 1867: "The Brand-New Yankee Gentleman" (March 3; appeared in May Twainian as "The Winner of the Medal"); "Private Theatricals" ("A Curtain Lecture Concerning Skating," March 17; reprinted in December Twainian); "Barbarous" (March 24--reprint promised, but December issue, p. 4 says it is not worth printing); "Regulation Regimen" ("Official Physic," April 21; reprinted following the present article); "Though Dead, yet Speaketh" (July 7; commonly known as "First Interview with Artemus Ward"). For further discussion see Twainian 1943.B9.

B20   _____. "Twain's Version of Hamlet," Twainian, n.s., II (June), 4-6.
Reprints MT's parody; source was a four-page typescript from Irving S. Underhill, taken from an unidentified newspaper clipping.

B21   _____. "The Winner of the Medal," Twainian, n.s., II (May), 1-4.
Discusses the original publication of this MT item in The American Union, A Fireside Journal (Boston: XXXVIII, May 18, 1867). Topic was an endowment of $5,000 in stocks to provide an annual medal to the "first gentleman" of each Princton graduating class (the medal was never awarded, and the funds were returned in 1873 to the donor, Leonard Jerome--whose daughter Jennie later became Lady Randolph Churchill and mother of Winston Churchill). MT text pp. 2-3.

B22   _____. [Announcement that Franklin J. Meine is at work on a collection of stories about MT, apparently by people who knew him.] Twainian, n.s., II (January), 6.

B23   _____. [Brief Item.] Twainian, n.s., II (March), 5.
In full: "On page 272 of 'Mark Twain's Notebook,' (Harper 1935) Mark states that he met a 'Mr. Gandhi' who showed him the Jain Temple. Paine comments that this man is our 'good Mahatma of later years.' Not so; Twain's Gandhi was an Indian nabob--not the hunger-striker of recent newspaper fame."

B24   CHUBB, PERCIVAL. "Mark Twain at Sundown," Mark Twain Quarterly, V (Spring), 15-16, 18.
At a small dinner party in MT's later years Chubb found him "genial and communicative, but...subdued in a way that surprised me" until he learned of MT's late change "from the mood of comedy to that of tragedy."

B25   CLEMENS, CYRIL. "'The Birth of a Legend' Again," American Literature, XV (March), 64-65.
Claims that MT's account of his duel with James L. Laird (Autobiography, I, 350-61) is correct in its details--including the marksmanship of Steve Gillis. As evidence Clemens cites conversations with persons who knew MT and other individuals involved. A reply to DeLancey Ferguson (1942.B30).

B26   _____. "A Letter to the Editors," American Literature, XIV (January), 430-31.
Takes exception to the accusation by Fred W. Lorch (1942.B41) that he did not use the Chicago Tribune publication of the letters for his Republican Letters (1941) but rather, apparently, a reprinting from a western paper. Only three of the six letters were reprinted, to be sure, but the others were witheld for separate publication [Washington in 1868, ed. with an introduction and notes by Cyril Clemens, 1943.A2.]

B27   _____. [Review: Theodore Hornberger, ed. Mark Twain's Letters to Will Bowen (1941).] Mark Twain Quarterly, VI (Winter-Spring), 23.
Consists chiefly of the reprinting of an anecdote from the first of these "delightful and informative letters" (Maui, May 7, 1866).

B28   _____. "Twainiana," Hobbies--The Magazine for Collectors, XLIV (October), 96-97.
Anecdotes about MT's clothing purchases from Rogers Peet in New York; includes text of a letter from him ("Onteora, New York, August 15, 1900"), ordering what Cyril Clemens says was the first of his white suits.

B29   COWLEY, MALCOLM. "Mencken and Mark Twain," New Republic, CVIII (March 8) 321-22.
A review of H. L. Mencken's Heathen Days: 1890-1936, noting his tribute there to MT and commenting briefly on his earlier Happy Days: 1880-1892 (1940) and Newspaper Days: 1899-1906 (1940). "After reading his three books of memoirs, you feel that Mark Twain

(COWLEY, MALCOLM)
must have been the decisive influence in forming both his style and his picture of himself.... All his life he has been re-phrasing and modernizing the rather inno-cent bitterness of Twain's later years." MT surpasses Mencken chiefly in imagina-tion.

B30 FARRELL, JAMES T. "Twain's Huckleberry Finn and the Era He Lived In," New York Times Book Review (December 12), pp. 6, 37.
"Mark Twain was both a democrat and a cynic"; he was disillusioned, but "through his two unspoiled boys Twain forcefully em-phasized his own attitudes and values.... Tom and Huck are symbols of the possibili-ties in human beings."

B31 FERGUSON, DELANCEY. "Mark Twain's Lost Cur-tain Speeches on the Plays Gilded Age and Ah Sin," South Atlantic Quarterly, XLII (July), 262-69.
Reprints the texts of these speeches from New York papers and quotes reviews. In his speech given on the hundredth performance of the Gilded Age, MT said that the star, John T. Raymond, had shown the humor of Colonel Sellers but not the pathos.

B32 GALLAGHER, CHARLES J. [Review: DeLancey Ferguson, Mark Twain: Man and Legend.] Thought (Fordham University), XVIII (September), 534-35.
Ferguson wished "to separate his subject's life into its literary and non-literary elements; but the formula by which this is done is not apparent. It would have helped the reader somewhat had the author indicat-ed what he considered of real value in the writings of Mark Twain--an immense amount of which is pure balderdash; but from first to last there is no effort at selection." MT's "boisterous egotism was merely the intellectual superiority of the ignorant. Being a blatant atheist, he could pronounce infallibly on every subject which came his way."

B33 HEDGES, ISAAC A. "Carroll Beckwith and Mark Twain," Mark Twain Quarterly, VI (Summer-Fall), 4.
Notes two paintings and a black and white sketch of MT by Beckwith; a Mr. William L. Huse owned one of the boats on which MT was a cub pilot, and was later acquainted with him in Onteora, N.Y.

B34 JONES, HOWARD MUMFORD. [Review: DeLancey Ferguson, Mark Twain: Man and Legend.] American Speech, XVIII (December), 286-87.
Crediting journalism and the lecture platform for shaping MT "is an attractive theory, because of its simplicity, but Mr. Ferguson, in turn, becomes hobby-horsical" in that he overlooks "an art of literature, a technique, a quality of architecture that

Twain has laboriously learned"; apart from over-simplification, the book is "reliable, clear, sympathetic, and just."

B35 LILLARD, RICHARD G. "Evolution of the 'Wa-shoe Zephyr,'" American Speech, XVIII (December), 257-60.
Traces the development of tall tales about the violent desert wind to the time when MT described it in RI.

B36 *MORLEY, CHRISTOPHER. [Introduction.] Tom Sawyer and Huckleberry Finn. London: J. M. Dent & Sons (Everyman's Library). [Source: Asselineau (1954), No. 965.]

B37 PHELPS, WILLIAM LYON. "Billy Phelps Speaking," Rotarian, LXIII (July), 40.
Reviews DeLancey Ferguson, Mark Twain: Man and Legend (which he commends for its emphasis on the literary side of MT's life) and also "a little book of 119 pages, Anglo-American Literary Relations, by the late George Stewart Gordon, president of Magdalen College, Oxford, whom he quotes as regret-ting that MT was admitted "so late to his place on the summits of American literature" and calling him "this authentic man of ge-nius, the author of Huckleberry Finn--which I place, with Moby Dick, among the great books of the world, great by every test."

B38 SCHOEN, MAX. [Review: Bernard DeVoto, Mark Twain at Work (1942).] Journal of Aesthet-ics and Art Criticism, II (Fall), 97-98.
Brief, descriptive, and laudatory.

B39 SPILLER, ROBERT E. "The Phenomenon of Mark Twain," Saturday Review of Literature, XXVI (August 7), 15.
A review of DeLancey Ferguson, Mark Twain: Man and Legend, which shows a working out of the mysteries of Mark Twain's personality, a careful weighing of the evidence present-ed by Brooks and DeVoto, and an emphasis on MT's development as a writer; unfortunately, in his emphasis on this he has lost the col-or, and "the result is informative rather than entertaining or stimulating."

B40 *STOVALL, FLOYD. American Idealism. Norman: University of Oklahoma Press.
MT's youthfulness accounts for the charm of HF and the weakness of MS. [Source: Asselineau (1954), No. 967.]

B41 THOMAS, HENRY, and DANA LEE THOMAS. "Samuel Langhorne Clemens (Mark Twain), 1835-1910," in Living Biographies of Famous Novelists. Garden City, N.Y.: Garden City Publishing Co., Inc. [Reprinted Garden City, N.Y.: Halcyon House (1947).] Pp. 276-91.
Derivative and inaccurate: MT's "first child died soon after its birth. A second succumbed to pneumonia as a result of Mark Twain's absent-minded carelessness" (p. 279); "When the Civil War broke out, he enlisted in the federal army and served

1943 - Shorter Writings

(THOMAS, HENRY, and DANA LEE THOMAS)
until he was honorably discharged" (p. 285);
"He was anxious to show his father-in-law,
Mr. Rogers, that there was as much money in
writing books as there was in selling coal"
(p. 288). Critical judgments on MT's works
are less original or interesting.

B42 TROXELL, GILBERT McCOY. "Samuel Langhorne
Clemens, 1835-1910," Yale University Libra-
ry Gazette, XVIII (July), 1-5.
A description of the Willard Samuel Morse
collection of MT editions, manuscripts, and
Twainiana, presented to the Yale University
Library by Walter Francis Frear.

B43 VON HIBLER, LEO. [Review: Günther Möhle,
Das Europabild Mark Twains (1940).]
Englische Studien, LXXV (February), 259-62.
Only the final fifty pages of this 130-
page book concern the theme of the title,
and much of this concerns England and the
Middle Ages. There is much of interest,
such as the context provided by discussion
of Hawthorne and Irving, but this is not
the needed comprehensive study.

B44 WAGENKNECHT, EDWARD. "A New Biography of
Mark Twain," New York Times Book Review
(June 13), p. 8.
A review of DeLancey Ferguson's Mark
Twain: Man and Legend, which "sums up vir-
tually all that is known as of 1943," al-
though "the best criticism is still De-
Voto's." Describes Cyril Clemens's Young
Sam Clemens (1942) as "unpretentious...it
makes enjoyable reading."

B45 WILLSON, FRANK C. "That Gilded Age Again:
An Attempt to Unmuddle the Mystery of the
Fifty-seven Variants," Papers of the Bib-
liographical Society of America, XXXVII
(Second Quarter), 141-56.

B46 WILSON, EDMUND. The Shock of Recognition.
New York: Doubleday, Doran & Company, Inc.
Reprints MT's "Fenimore Cooper's Literary
Offences" (1895) and William Dean Howells's
My Mark Twain (1910), with headnotes by
Wilson, and letters from Sherwood Anderson
to Van Wyck Brooks (some on MT), with Wil-
son's headnote and "Introductory Note by
Van Wyck Brooks."

B47 WIMBERLY, LOWRY CHARLES. "Mark Twain and the
Tichenor Bonanza," Atlantic Monthly, CLXXII
(November), 117, 119. Condensed as "A Letter to the Editor" in Time, XLII
(November 1), 44-45.
Reprints with commentary a letter from
MT datelined "Hartford, Sept. 14, 1880" to
the New York Evening Post (n.d.), humorously commenting on a fraudulent scheme for
extracting gold from California spring
waters.

1944 A BOOKS

A1 *ANON. An Exhibition of the Works of Mark
Twain, including manuscripts, first editions
and association items, at the Main Public
Library, April 30 through May 31, 1944,
sponsored by the Friends of the Detroit Public Library, Detroit, Michigan.
[Source: Asselineau (1954), No. 989.]

A2 *DAVIS, SAMUEL P. The Typograhical Howitzer by
Sam Davis with a foreword by Thomas P. Brown.
Sacramento, California: The Meterorite
Press. Reprinted from his Short Stories
(San Francisco, 1886).
[Source: Asselineau (1954), No. 991.]

1944 B SHORTER WRITINGS

B1 ADAMS, J. DONALD. "Speaking of Books," New
York Times Book Review (April 30), p. 2.
"While Mr. DeVoto has nursed his private
feud with Van Wyck Brooks beyond the limits
of one's patience, and, equally, beyond the
pale of fair fighting...he has, nevertheless, made a definite contribution to American literary history." He errs in "his
growing conviction that the region beyond
the Mississippi is his private and untres-
passable domain." Ibid., May 14, p. 2,
continues a defence of Brooks, noting his
historical sense.

B2 *ALLEN, HERVEY. "A Great American," The Maga-
zine of Sigma Chi, George Ade Memorial Issue
(October-November), p. 12.
Stephen Crane's favorite MT book was LOM.
[Source: Bridgman (1966), p. 134.]

B3 ANON. "Mark Twain," Scholastic, XLIV
(April 17), 18-19.
Scenes from the Warner Brothers motion
picture on MT, starring Fredric March; the
script by Alan LeMay draws in part on the
stage play, Mark Twain, directed by Irving
Rapper.

B4 ANON. "Mark Twain: Despite the Reports of
His Death, He Lives All Over Again in New
Film," Life, XVI (May 8), 89-99.
On the Warner Brothers' film of his life,
starring Fredric March. Illustrated with
stills from the film, and with numerous
photographs of MT, his family and homes,
his grave at Elmira, etc.

B5 BLAIR, WALTER. [Review: DeLancey Ferguson,
Mark Twain: Man and Legend (1943).] American Literature, XVI (May), 143-45.
It is weak on MT's writings before 1875,
but good on later development, on "rehearsals and revisions," and correcting legendary aspects of the biography. The analyses
of individual works are rather brief. "A
book which deserves a place among the better
studies of Mark Twain."

B6 [BROWNELL, GEORGE HIRAM.] "About Mark Twain's Job on the San Francisco Call," Twainian, n.s., III (May), 4-6.
   Reprints several Virginia City items.

B7 ____. "About the Program of that 'Babies Banquet," Twainian, IV (November), 4-6.
   E. Earl Moore has acquired a copy of the printed program of the Chicago banquet (November 13, 1879), honoring General Ulysses S. Grant, at which MT delivered his famous speech on "The Babies." The text is reprinted, together with an MT letter. Also cites a report of the banquet in the Chicago Tribune.

B8 ____. "Baby vs. Burglar Alarm," Twainian, n.s., III (April), 6.
   Frank C. Willson has found in The Youth's Companion (May 18, 1882) a short MT letter, written in answer to a request for a gift tale for a fair raising money to aid abused children: "If you will start a society for the prevention of cruelty to fathers, I will write you a whole book."

B9 ____. "Concerning a Bear," Twainian, n.s., III (April), 3-4.
   On the use by Thomas Bailey Aldrich of part of an MT letter without permission in The Pellet, an ephemeral daily. The topic is Bret Harte's addition of railroad tracks in front of the snarling bear on the Overland cover. MT was not named, but the passage is in his Letters.

B10 ____. "Everybody's Friend," Twainian, n.s., III (February), 1-4.
   On the discovery by Frank C. Willson of an MT letter to Josh Billings in Street and Smith's New York Weekly (July 14, 1873) and reprinted by Billings in his book, Everybody's Friend. The item (appearing as a letter because publisher's contracts forbade MT contributing writings in other form) appears on p. 3; it teases Billings for his exaggerated misspellings.

B11 ____. "Hannibal Celebrates Twain's 108th Birthday," Twainian, n.s., III (February), 5-6.
   On the celebrations, a preview showing of the Warner Brothers film, The Adventures of Mark Twain, and dedication of the building in which MT's father had his office as justice of the peace.

B12 ____. "Index to The Twainian Now Being Prepared," Twainian, n.s., III (March), 6.
   The index was to cover the old and new series, from January, 1939 through June, 1944; the charge would be determined some time before June, by the Executive Committee. The June issue reports a delay until the October issue (Vol. IV), but there is no mention of the index in that issue and the matter appears to have been dropped.

B13 ____. "Mark Twain's Inventions," Twainian, n.s., III (January), 1-5.
   MT was granted three patents: on an adjustable vest-strap (1871), on a pre-gummed scrap-book (1873), and on a game for learning history dates (1885, described in Twainian, December, 1943). A Baltimore man applied for a patent on a vest-strap like MT's while the MT application was being considered, and MT enlisted his brother Orion's aid in establishing priority.

B14 ____. "Mark Twain's Love Song," Twainian, n.s., III (April), 5-6.
   On a comic lyric by MT, exalting the liver above the passions; first appeared in The Medical Fortnightly, May 15, 1892, and reprinted in I. E. (?) Booth, ed., The Medical Muse, Grave and Gay (New York, 1895).

B15 ____. "New First Issue Point in Life on the Mississippi," Twainian, IV (November), 1-3.
   The cut of MT in flames at the foot of p. 441 appeared in the first copies and was then deleted; now, Frank C. Willson reports a copy in which the cut on p. 443 is titled "St. Louis Hotel" rather than "St. Charles Hotel." Brownell suggests that "it would appear that the earliest copies of LOM sent to subscribers contained both the cut of the St. Louis hotel legend and the cut of Twain in flames." Also see brief note in December issue, p. 5, and Brownell's "That Picture of 'St. Louis Hotel' in Life on the Mississippi," Twainian, VI (September-October, 1947), 1-3.

B16 ____. "Rodman Gilder Writes of Twain and the Theatre," Twainian, n.s., III (March), 4-5.
   On Gilder's article, "Mark Twain Detested the Theatre," Theatre Arts, February (1944.B34).

B17 ____. "Twain Letter Tells of 'Francis Lightfoot Lee,'" Twainian, n.s., III (February), 4-5.
   John W. Wholihan has found a copy of Volume I of the Pennsylvania Magazine of History and Biography with a letter signed by MT inserted in front of the fly-leaf; Brownell finds it significant as "documentary evidence in Twain's own hand that I had erred in my judgment that Twain wrote his article [on Lee] without knowledge of the high-brow nature of the magazine."

B18 ____. "Twain Letters to Webster," Twainian, IV (October), 6.
   About Samuel Charles Webster's series of articles, containing letters from MT, appearing in The Atlantic Monthly; Brownell sees MT as almost impossible for a publisher to deal with, and largely to blame for the failure of the Charles L. Webster Company, but criticizes Webster as inexperienced and willing to be a yes-man.

1944 - Shorter Writings

B19   [BROWNELL, GEORGE HIRAM]. "An Unbiased Edi-
      torial," Twainian, n.s., III (April), 4-5.
         Reprints an MT item, "Inspired Humor,"
      from the Buffalo Express (August 19, 1869);
      the thesis is that it is a ghastly joke for
      an editorial to suggest that one political
      party can redeem the country from the cor-
      ruption of the other.

B20   _____. "'What Ought He to Have Done?' Some
      Remarks by Mark Twain on Child Management,"
      Twainian, n.s., III (May), 1-4.
         On a letter to the editor of Christian
      Union of July 16, 1885 (reprinted, pp. 2-3);
      See Paine biography, p. 280.

B21   _____. "When and Where Were These Twain Tales
      First Printed?" Twainian, IV (December),
      1-5.
         On two unidentified clippings, "The Re-
      vised Catechism" (on civic corruption) and
      "The Last Stamp" (probably apocryphal) in
      a collection bequeathed by Irving S. Under-
      hill. See Rodman Gilder's letter to the
      editor in the next issue (January, 1945,
      p. 4).

B22   _____. "Who was Frank Finlay?" Twainian, IV
      (October), 1-6.
         Contains text of five letters and a post-
      card from MT to Finlay, over the period
      1874-1900. They were acquired at an auction
      by Norman Bassett, without envelopes. In
      the attempt to identify Finlay, Bassett ac-
      quired the rare pamphlet, Who Was Sarah
      Findlay? By Mark Twain, with a Suggested
      Solution by J. M. Barrie. London: Clement
      K. Shorter, 1917. This pamphlet was pieced
      together by Shorter out of a preface he
      wrote, a brief article by Barrie, and an
      MT letter to the London Chronicle on copy-
      right and signed "An American." The name,
      "Sarah Findlay" (with the "d"), is ficti-
      tious, and similarity of names mere coinci-
      dence, but Bassett was able to identify
      Finlay through the British War Office and
      correspondence with Finlay's son. Dixon
      Wecter provided fuller details in his
      "Frank Finlay; Or, 'The Thameside Tenderfoot
      in the Wooly West.'" Twainian, VI (July-
      August, 1947), 1-4.

B23   _____. [Brief item.] Twainian, III (April),
      6.
         The "M'me Caprell [sic]" in the Paine
      biography (pp. 156-59) and MT's Letters
      (pp. 48-51) is mentioned in the New Orleans
      Crescent of February 18, 1861, with the
      spelling as MT gave it in a letter to his
      brother Orion.

B24   CLEMENS, CYRIL "Churchill and Twain," Satur-
      day Review of Literature, XXVII (January 8),
      13.
         A letter to the editor on the first meet-
      ing of MT and Churchill; includes text of
      a brief note from Churchill ("10 Downing
      Street, 25 October, 1943"), thanking Cyril

Clemens for the Gold Medal of the International Mark Twain Society.

B25   _____. "Contract for Roughing It," Mark Twain
      Quarterly, VI (Summer-Fall), 5.
         The text of an agreement dated July 15,
      1870 and signed by MT and E. Bliss, Jr.,
      concerning the book MT was to write for the
      American Publishing Company.

B26 * _____. "Mark Twain in St. Louis," Slant, I
      (October), 6, 16.
         [Source: Leary (1954), p. 47.]

B27 * _____. "Unique Origin of Mark Twain's Books,"
      Missouri School Journal, XL (January), 16,
      18-19.
         [Source: Asselineau (1954), No. 999.]

B28   _____. "Winston Churchill and Mark Twain,"
      Hobbies--The Magazine for Collectors, XLIV
      (April), 105-107.
         Anecdotes of meetings between MT and
      Churchill, first in 1897 at the London home
      of Sir John MacAllister and a few weeks la-
      ter at Sir Gilbert Parker's home. They met
      again in New York in 1900 and MT introduced
      Churchill at a Carnegie Hall lecture, and
      in 1907 once more in England, at another
      dinner given by Sir Gilbert Parker. This
      article was reprinted in Dalhousie Review,
      1945, with no indication of this publication
      in Hobbies.

B29   CLEMENS, KATHARINE. "Alice James, Neglected
      Sister," Mark Twain Quarterly, VI (Summer-
      Fall), 6-7.
         Alice James expressed dissatisfaction with
      the dullness and irreverence of an MT book,
      apparently CY, but also criticized the Hon.
      Reginald Brett for a column in Pall Mall
      Gazette taking MT "with solemnity."

B30   CLEMENS, SAMUEL L. "The Gorki Incident: An
      Unpublished Fragment," Slavonic and East
      European Review, XXI (American Series III,
      Part 2, August), 35-36.
         A little parable of "York Minster" from
      Tierra del Fuego, who created a sensation
      by appearing before the King of England in
      the national costume: nude. The moral is
      that one must conform to local customs when
      traveling abroad (as Gorki failed to do when
      he visited America with a mistress). The
      text is MT's, without added commentary.

B31   _____. "Mark Differs with Mrs. Astor," Mark
      Twain Quarterly, VI (Summer-Fall), 7, 24.
         The text of MT's defense of the social
      graces of the self-made man; dated March,
      1902, and possibly from a newspaper clip-
      ping.

B32 DUDGEON, L. W. "Twainiana," Hobbies--The
     Magazine for Collectors, XLIX (July), 98.
         "In my perusal of old family records...for
     data concerning the early history of Cane
     Valley, Ky., I find some interesting state-
     ments in the Hancock family concerning the
     grandparents of Mark Twain," Samuel Clemens
     and Pamelia [sic] Hancock.

B33 FARBER, MARJORIE. "Poisoned Pens," New York
     Times Book Review, (April 23), p. 5.
         A review of Bernard DeVoto's The Literary
     Fallacy; defends Van Wyck Brooks against
     attacks that began with DeVoto's Mark
     Twain's America.

B34 GILDER, RODMAN. "Mark Twain Detested the
     Theatre," Theatre Arts, XXVIII (February),
     109-16.
         After citing Howells on MT's expressions
     of distaste for the theater (and for lec-
     turing), traces his life-long involvement
     and concludes: "Did Mark Twain detest the
     theatre? I wonder." A popular account,
     illustrated with photographs of MT with
     actor John T. Raymond, and of Fredric March
     on the Warner Brothers' lot, made up for
     The Adventures of Mark Twain. See 1944.B16.

B35 GOHDES, CLARENCE. American Literature in
     Nineteenth Century England. New York:
     Columbia University Press, passim.
         Contains numerous references to MT's
     popularity in England, and editions of his
     works there. Notes that despite the criti-
     cism of CY as vulgar, the new Review of Re-
     views condensed it in the second issue,
     February, 1890.

B36 JONES, JOSEPH. [Introduction and postscript
     by George Hiram Brownell.] "More Twain
     Found in New York Weekly," Twainian, n.s.,
     III (March), 1-4.
         Five of MT's letters written for the Sac-
     ramento Union were reprinted, slightly
     abridged, in the New York Weekly, March-
     June, 1867. Jones and Brownell speculate
     that MT may have allowed this publication
     as a way to publicize his forthcoming
     Jumping Frog book and Cooper Union lecture.

B37 LILLARD, RICHARD G. "Contemporary Reaction
     to 'The Empire City Massacre,'" American
     Literature, XVI (November), 198-203.
         MT's hoax story in the October 28, 1863
     Territorial Enterprise described an imagi-
     nary mass-murder so vividly that readers
     failed to note the impossibility of the de-
     tails; the result was a chorus of indigna-
     tion. [For MT's version of the story see
     "My Bloody Massacre" in Sketches New and
     Old].

B38 LORCH, FRED,W. "Albert Bigelow Paine's Visit
     to Keokuk in 1910," Iowa Journal of History
     and Politics, XLII (April), 192-98.
         Shortly after MT's death, Paine went to
     Keokuk, Iowa to collect material for his
     biography. He knew of MT's brother Orion
     only from MT and from what he had seen of
     Orion's own autobiography, and because he
     did not know how highly Orion was esteemed
     in Keokuk, he provoked a lively controversy;
     the result was a tempering of his portrayal
     of Orion in the biography of MT.

B39 _____. "A Reply to Mr. Clemens," American
     Literature, XVI (March), 32-34.
         After comparing Cyril Clemens's edition of
     Republican Letters with photostats of the
     letters as they appeared in the Chicago Re-
     publican, Lorch says the book has only three
     of the original six and these suffer either
     from careless transcription or from altera-
     tion. "I am quite willing to accept Mr.
     Clemens's statement that he got his material
     'directly from the files of the Chicago Re-
     publican,' but his letters are not true
     copies of Mark Twain's letters; and by edit-
     ing them to the point of mutilation he has
     performed a distinct disservice."

B40 MacBRIDE, VAN DYK. "Captain Absalom Grimes--
     The Confederate Mail Carrier," The Stamp
     Specialist (New York), Maroon Book [the
     designation of the issue within a year],
     106-14.
         Describes James Bradley's The Confederate
     Mail Carrier (Mexico, Missouri: n.p.,
     1894), which gives a more flamboyant account
     of Grimes's adventures than appears in the
     1926 version edited by M. M. Quaife (See
     1944.B44); apparently the Bradley version
     does not mention MT's brief Civil War ser-
     vice. (Discussed by M. M. Quaife in "Mark
     Twain's Military Career," below.)

B41 MAYBERRY, GEORGE. "Reading and Writing,"
     New Republic, CX (May 1), 608.
         The language in the circus episode in HF
     typifies "a kind of writing no means exclu-
     sively American, but marked in modern Amer-
     ican writing at its best. Its apparent
     artlessness, emphasized by Huck's grammati-
     cal lapses and broad boy's dialect, conceals
     a structure that, if of a somewhat simpler
     order, is as consciously controlled as the
     grandiloquent prose architecture of the
     eighteenth century. It is prose that su-
     perbly fulfills its function." Hemingway
     and Sherwood Anderson have acknowledged
     their debt to MT, and the functional prose
     is also evident in Fitzgerald, Dos Passos,
     Faulkner, and Caldwell.

B42 ORCUTT, WILLIAM DANA. "From My Library
     Walls," Christian Science Monitor, XXXVI
     (November 17), 11.
         Contains an anecdote George Washington
     Cable told him about MT's response to noisy
     steam pipes while he was lecturing: "'Will
     someone in the audience,' he shouted, 'kind-
     ly go down in the basement and ask that jan-
     itor to stop gnashing his teeth?' From
     that moment, Cable concluded, Twain had the
     audience completely with him."

1944 - Shorter Writings

B43   QUAIFE, M. M. "George in Historyland," Twain-
    ian, n.s., III (January), 5-6.
        The "George" referred to is Brownell;
    Quaife questions his reference to The Penn-
    sylvania Magazine of History and Biography
    as an "obscure" publication in his article
    in the November, 1943 Twainian, "Mark
    Twain's Tribute to Francis Lightfoot Lee";
    Quaife gives no new information on MT here.
    In an introductory comment ("Dr. Quaife
    Corrects Our Remarks on Penn. Mag.")
    Brownell notes that "The Twainian has lat-
    terly become a one-man mouthpiece," as he
    recently said, with regret, in a letter to
    Quaife; this statement would support the
    attribution of unsigned material to Brown-
    ell in the present bibliography.

B44   _____. "Mark Twain's Military Career,"
    Twainian, n.s., III (June), 4-7.
        On the differing accounts in MT's "The
    Private History of a Campaign that Failed"
    and in Absalom Grimes, Confederate Mail
    Runner (Quaife, ed., 1926). Further doubt
    is cast on the Grimes account by the recent
    discovery of another treatment of his ad-
    ventures by James Bradley, in The Confeder-
    ate Mail Carrier, or, From Missouri to Ar-
    kansas, through Mississippi, Alabama,
    Georgia, and Tennessee. An Unwritten Leaf
    of the "Civil War." Being an account of
    the Battles, Marches, and Hardships of the
    First and Second Brigades, Mos. C. S. A.
    Together with the Thrilling Adventures and
    Narrow Escapes of Captain Grimes and his
    Fair Accomplice, who carried the Mail by
    "the Underground Route" from the Brigade to
    Missouri (Mexico, Missouri, 1894). Quaife
    indicates his debt to a discussion of the
    two books on Grimes in Van Dyk MacBride's
    "Absalom Grimes the Confederate Mail Carri-
    er," in The Stamp Specialist (See 1944.B40).

B45   RAYFORD, JULIAN LEE. "The Jumping Frog Jubi-
    lee," American Mercury, LIX (November),
    583-88.
        About the friendliness of the people at
    the 1929 jubilee at Angel's Camp; very
    little about MT.

B46   SHAW, BERNARD. "G. B. S.," Saturday Review
    of Literature, XXVII (August 12), 15.
        Excerpt from a letter to Cyril Clemens
    on meetings with MT.

B47   *WAGENKNECHT, EDWARD. [Introduction.] Life
    on the Mississippi, with...a number of pre-
    viously suppressed passages now printed for
    the first time, and with a note by Willis
    Wager. New York: The Limited Editions
    Club.
        [Source: Asselineau (1954), No. 990.]

B48   WEATHERLY, EDWARD H. "Beau Tibbs and Colonel
    Sellers," Modern Language Notes, LIX (May),
    310-13.

Beau Tibbs in Goldsmith's A Citizen of the
World and Colonel Sellers in The Gilded Age
show "striking parallelism...in scenes in
which each explains away an obviously cheap
and unappetizing dinner to which an unexpected guest has come."

B49   WEBSTER, SAMUEL CHARLES, ed. "Mark Twain,
    Business Man: Letters and Memoirs," Atlan-
    tic Monthly, CLXXIII (June), 37-46; CLXXIV
    (July), 72-80; (August), 71-77; (September),
    90-96; (October), 74-80; (November),
    100-106.
        Family and business correspondence, much
    of it to Charles L. Webster, who had married
    MT's niece, Annie Moffett; edited by Charles
    L. Webster's son. [Published as a book,
    1946.A6.]

B50   WEGELIN, CHRISTOF. [Review: Günter Möhle,
    Das Europabild Mark Twains (1940).] Ameri-
    can Literature, XVI (November), 255-56.
        "Dr. Möhle proposes to illustrate 'Ameri-
    can development and mentality' by comparing
    the attitudes toward England" of Irving,
    Hawthorne, and MT; the extent to which this
    is a study of the first two is unclear.
    Möhle has read comparatively little in his
    three authors: for MT, "The Innocents
    Abroad, A Connecticut Yankee, and a few
    passages from the letters and notebooks,"
    and he follows Turner to excess. "Möhle's
    contribution to scholarship is slight," but
    his book will give German readers a better
    understanding of MT and the American mind.

B51   WHITING, B. J. "Guyuscutus, Royal Nonesuch
    and Other Hoaxes," Southern Folklore Quar-
    terly, VIII (December), 251-75.
        A general discussion of practical jokes
    in the old Southwest, with some space de-
    voted to several "Guyuscutus" monster hoaxes
    and a brief discussion of the connection to
    HF.

1945 A BOOKS

A1   LILJEGREN, S[TEN] B[ODVAR]. The Revolt
    against Romanticism in American Literature
    as Evidenced in the Works of S. L. Clemens.
    Upsala: A. B. Lundequista Bokhandeln.
    [Also in Studia Neophilologica, XVII,
    207-58, according to Asselineau (1954),
    No. 1049; his No. 1094 lists a 1947 publi-
    cation, Upsala: Essays and Studies on Amer-
    ican Language and Literature. Publications
    of the American Institute of the University
    of Upsala, No. 1 (Confirmed in British Mu-
    seum Catalogue); also, reprinted, New York:
    Haskell House, 1964.]
        After a discussion of the neglect of Amer-
    ican literature by the European academic
    community, Liljegren defends MT as better
    read, more cultured and refined than his de-
    tractors will admit. As evidence of MT's
    attack on romanticism, cites his parodies of
    Gothic novels in the Weekly Occidental, and

(LILJEGREN, S[TEN] B[ODVAR])
of Longfellow's "Wreck of the Hesperus,"
Thomas Moore's "Those Evening Bells," etc.
Also briefly comments on MT's criticism of
Fenimore Cooper and Sir Walter Scott. [64-
page pamphlet, including the texts of some
of MT's parodies and the originals on which
they are based.]

A2 RODNEY, ROBERT M. Mark Twain in England: A
    Study of the English Criticism of and Atti-
    tude toward Mark Twain: 1867-1940.
        Unpublished Doctoral Dissertation, Uni-
    versity of Wisconsin. The evaluations and
    the bibliography in this dissertation have
    been of great value in tracing material for
    the present bibliography.

A3 *ROESSEL, JAMES. Mark Twain, en odölig humor-
    ist. Stockholm: Lindfors.
        [Source: Asselineau (1954), No. 1021.]

1945 B SHORTER WRITINGS

B1 A., P. B. "Clemens'...Huckleberry Finn," Ex-
    plicator, IV (November), Q. 7.
        In Mark Twain at Work, p. 54, DeVoto says
    MT disregards the fact that Jim could have
    reached free soil by crossing the river to
    Illinois; can any reader comment? [Answered
    by DeLancey Ferguson in April, 1946 Expli-
    cator.]

B2 ADAMS, J. DONALD. "Speaking of Books," New
    York Times Book Review.
        June 17, p. 2: On rereading IA, he finds
    the humor labored in the European portion,
    better in the part on the Holy Land because
    reading the Bible had made Palestine real
    to MT. June 24, p. 2: TA reflects "a
    much better adjustment to the European
    scene" than does IA, but "it was not as a
    writer of travel books that Mark Twain will
    be remembered," and FE "was not good."

B3 ANON. "Mark and Baseball," Mark Twain Quar-
    terly, VI (Winter-Spring), 12.
        Text of a "St. Louis Post-Dispatch spe-
    cial dispatch from Bermuda, dated March 8,
    1908," on MT at a baseball game.

B4 ARMSTRONG, C. J. "Sam Clemens Considered Be-
    coming a Preacher," Twainian, IV (May), 1.
    Reprinted from The Christian, June 13, 1931.
        Conventional speculations, based on a
    statement in the Paine biography that both
    Orion and Sam Clemens had considered enter-
    ing the ministry, and speculating on what
    sort of minister Sam would have made, with
    his lack of orthodoxy, but also with his
    courage, compassion, humor, and love of
    truth.

B5 BLANCK, JACOB. "News from the Rare Book
    Sellers," Publishers' Weekly, CXLVIII
    (August 18), 620-21.

On the recent publication by Manuscript
House of MT's A Murder, A Mystery, and A
Marriage in an edition limited to sixteen
copies, two of them deposited for copyright.

B6 [BROWNELL, GEORGE HIRAM.] "About the Origin
    of that 'Weather' Epigram," Twainian, IV
    (June), 4.
        Although it has been suggested that the
    famous saying may have originated in an
    editorial by Charles Dudley Warner, the
    editorial has not been found and thus the
    question of who said it remains open--but it
    is characteristically Twainian.

B7 _____. "Did Twain Write 'The Wrong Ashes?'"
    Twainian, IV (April), 2-4.
        Contains text of a macabre story in which
    a man kept an urn of ashes for several years
    before finding they were those of a mule,
    rather than of his wife.

B8 _____. "Here's Latest News about that Great
    Land-Slide Case," Twainian, IV (March),
    3-4.
        Corrects an erroneous statement in May,
    1944 Twainian, according to which an MT
    piece in the San Francisco Morning Call
    later showed up in TA: actually used in RI.
    Also quotes a letter from Frank C. Willson,
    who has found in Nevada Reports (1865) an
    account of an actual landslide case in which
    the Supreme Court upheld a lower court de-
    cision that the value of a buried piece of
    land was less than the cost of removing the
    transplanted earth which covered it. Oliver
    Barrett looked up the case and "found that
    the opinion related merely to the method of
    determining the amount of damages sustained
    (letter, "Why Mark Twain Registered His
    Name as a 'Trade Mark,'" Twainian, May, 3-4).
    Also see brief note in Twainian, IX
    (January-February, 1950), on a published ac-
    count of the landslide case in a book of
    humor in the legal profession, 1871.

B9 _____. "Mark Twain Launched the Chicago Press
    Club of which George Ade Later Became a
    Member," Twainian, IV (March), 1-2.
        Quotes an MT letter from William H. Free-
    man's The Press Club of Chicago (Chicago:
    The Press Club of Chicago, 1894), declining
    an invitation to visit the club (Hartford,
    December 29, 1880), and passage on MT's
    participation in the founding; brief adden-
    dum, p. 4.

B10 _____. "Mark Twain Tells of the Daring Deed
    of Professor Jenkins and His Velocipede,"
    Twainian, IV (February), 1-4.
        On a Canadian who crossed Niagara Falls.
    Includes the following, which appeared in
    the Buffalo Express, August 26 and
    September 9, 1869, attributed by Brownell to
    MT: "Prof. Jenkins," an unsigned news ac-
    count ("with a few excisions of unimportant

([BROWNELL, GEORGE HIRAM])
text"); "In Trouble," supposedly a telegram from an Express reporter named Michael J. Murphy who tried to follow Jenkins but ended up stuck on the middle of the rope; "Mark Twain in a Fix," attributing the Murphy telegram to MT (reprinted from Rochester Express by Buffalo Express; unsigned, but "thoroughly Twainesque in its style"). Also see "More of Prof. Jenkins and his Velocipede," March.

B11   ____. "More of Prof. Jenkins and his Velocipede," Twainian, IV (March), 4.
Thomas Ollive Mabbott reports Brownell guessed wrongly that there had never been a Rochester (N.Y.) Express in his article, "Mark Twain Tells of the Daring Deed of Professor Jenkins and His Velocipede," Twainian, February.

B12   ____. "No Mystery Now about 'A Mystery Cleared Up,'" Twainian, IV (May), 1-2.
The text of an interview with ex-Secretary Stanton and Secretary Fish on the most effective means for removing warts; attributed to MT in Wood's Household Magazine, October, 1869 (and listed in the 1935 Merle Johnson Bibliography of MT).

B13   ____. "A Tale of Twain's Shipboard Poem, 'Good-Bye' or 'The Parting of the Ships,'" Twainian, IV (June), 1-2.
On a poem MT wrote during the Quaker City voyage, with the encouragement of Mrs. Solon L. Severance; printed here with the title "Good Bye," but listed in the 1935 Merle Johnson Bibliography as "The Parting of the Ships." Brownell cites a first publication in the Cleveland Plain Dealer in 1910, and a partial reprinting in Current Literature (1935).

B14   ____. "That First Issue Point on Page 283 of 'Huck,'" Twainian, IV (May), 4.
A tipped-in p. 283 [replacing the mutilated "Who Do You Reckon It Is?" illustration--T.A.T.] has long been recognized as characterizing a first-issue copy; for a time it had been thought that this characterized the whole first edition of 30,000 copies.

B15   ____. "Twain Bibliography Owes Much to Rev. C. J. Armstrong," Twainian, IV (April), 4.
A tribute to Armstrong, who located early files of the Hannibal Journal containing contributions by young Sam Clemens; he also located a single copy of a St. Louis temperance periodical, The Saturday Evening Post; although this contains nothing by SLC and no other copies have been found, it ends speculation that his statement of publishing an article or two (circa 1851) refers to the Philadelphia journal.

B16   ____. "Twain Couldn't Take that Word 'Bogus,'" Twainian, IV (February), 4.
On the uncomplimentary connotations of the word, as MT would see it from a printer's view; this would explain the vindictive tone of his letter to Thomas B. Kirby reprinted in the January Twainian.

B17   ____. "Twain Writings Still Increase in Value," Twainian, IV (May), 2-3.
On recent Parke-Bernet auction prices of MT manuscripts and first editions: The Stolen White Elephant, $2,500; "On the Decay of the Art of Lying," $400; "The Regular Toast. Woman--God Bless Her" (delivered before the New England Society of New York, December 23, 1882), $375; "At the Shrine of St. Wagner," $850; "From the London 'Times' of 1904," $875; "The Invalid's Story," $575; "Legend of Sagenfeld, in Germany," $450; "A Murder, A Mystery, and A Marriage," $1250; three partial or complete chapters of A Tramp Abroad, $250, $225, $200; "The Death-Disk," $375; a freak copy of The Jumping Frog with p. 198 blank, $425 (another copy was offered by a dealer in 1932 for $25); a fine first-issue TS sold for $950, and a fine fine first-issue HF, with MT autograph to U. S. Grant, Jr. and with the latter's bookplate, $1050.

B18   ____. "Why Mark Twain Registered His Name as a 'Trade Mark,'" Twainian, IV (April), 3-4.
On MT's problems with pirates using his name, and his eventual solution; contains text of a letter from Oliver R. Barrett, who looked up details of "Clemens v. Belford, Clarke & Co.," 14 Federal Reporter 728 (1883).

B19   CESTRE, CHARLES. La Littérature Américaine. Paris: Librairie Armand Colin. There is now a third ed. (1957), apparently unrevised; pp. 103-106 on MT.
A short general study. The portion on MT is a biographical summary, followed by brief, conventional accounts of some of his books, pointing to TS as his great work and HF as comic and a valuable picture of its time. CY displeased some readers, but its criticism of the age is not unjustified and the anachronisms are amusing. Notes the serious side of MT beneath the humor.

B20   *CLEMENS, CYRIL. "An Incident in Mark Twain's Life," Slant, II (February), 7.
[Source: Leary (1954), p. 47.]

B21   ____. "F. D. Roosevelt and Mark Twain," Dalhousie Review, XXV (October), 339-41.
Describes a visit to the White House to present the Mark Twain Gold Medal to the President, who said that by 1900 he had read all of MT's works then in print, and that he took the phrase "New Deal" from CY.

B22 _____. "Mark Twain's Ancestry," Mark Twain Quarterly, VII (Winter-Spring), 8, 24.
On some of MT's remote ancestors and his more immediate ones, with sparse documentation.

B23 _____. "Mark Twain's Exaggerated Death," Rotarian, LXVII (August), 58-59.
Notes distorted accounts by Paine, Alexander Woolcott, and others. "Since so many different versions of the origin of this famous saying have appeared, it is high time to put on record the correct version"; a note MT wrote out for Frank Marshall White, London reporter for the New York Journal, is reproduced in facsimile.

B24 _____. "New Light on Mark Twain's Virginia Ancestors," Hobbies--The Magazine for Collectors, L (April), 104-105.
Quotes the marriage agreement of MT's grandparents, Pamelia [sic] Goggin and Samuel Clemens, and gives other details of family history.

B25 *_____. "They Knew Mark Twain," Hobbies, L (September), 106-108.
[Source: Asselineau (1954), No. 1035: "'They' i.e. Shaw, Helen Keller, etc."]

B26 _____. "Winston Churchill and Mark Twain," Dalhousie Review, XXIV (January), 402-405.
An article which appeared in Hobbies-- The Magazine for Collectors in 1944, with no indication of the earlier appearance.

B27 CLEMENS, SAMUEL L. "Mark on Boys," Mark Twain Quarterly, VI (Winter-Spring), 24.
A paragraph from "an unpublished letter written by Mark Twain" (n.d.) on his reluctance to drive away some neighborhood boys who have been a nuisance.

B28 _____. "Mark's Letter to Mrs. James Ross Clemens," Mark Twain Quarterly, VI (Winter-Spring), 12.
The text of a note from Olivia Clemens ("Hotel Krantz, Vienna, March 29, 1899") to Miss Boland, congratulating her on her engagement and adding that she considers "the marrying a Clemens the very best and happiest thing I ever did!" MT adds in a postscript that he has never married one himself, but "less particular people have taken the risk and found them well enough as a change.... I like my relative Jim very much, and as a Clemens he averages away up."

B29 _____. "Three Mark Twain Letters," Mark Twain Quarterly, VII (Summer-Fall), 24.
Notes to [R. U.] Johnson (Hartford, March 18, and Elmira, July 28, September 8, 1885) on "that war paper" for the Century War Series; the article is not going well. [Presumably, this was "The Private History of a Campaign That Failed"--T.A.T.]

B30 _____. "Twain is 'Out of Soap,'" Mark Twain Quarterly, VII (Summer-Fall), 14.
Text of an MT note ("Hartford, Jan. 25, 1887") to an unnamed recipient, in payment of two railroad fares from New York to Hartford.

B31 _____. "Twain to R. U. Johnson," Mark Twain Quarterly, VI (Winter-Spring), 23.
Text of a letter ("Elmira, N.Y., Aug. 15, 1889") on "the photograph matter" and "my war article" for the Century. [Presumably the "war article" was "The Private History of a Campaign that Failed"--T.A.T.]

B32 _____. "Unpublished Letters to Dan Beard," Mark Twain Quarterly, VII (Winter-Spring), 22.
The first, datelined "Elmira, N.Y., Aug. 28, '89," praises Beard's illustrations for A Connecticut Yankee, with particular attention to the King ("both face and figure are noble and gracious"), the "soft young grace and beauty" of Guinevere, and the Yankee himself. A letter dated December 20, 1889, to an unnamed person, expresses satisfaction with the illustrations and refers questions concerning them to Beard, who "illustrated the book throughout without requiring or needing anybody's suggestions... I merely approved of the pictures--and very heartily, too, the slave-driver along with the rest." [The slave-driver has the features of Jay Gould--T.A.T.] A letter to Beard datelined "Riverdale On The Hudson, Dec. 12, '02" agrees that "it is never too late to say the kindly word," adding that "you have done great work in great causes, and I have walked by your side."

B33 COWLEY, MALCOLM. "The Middle American Style: D. Crockett to E. Hemingway," New York Times Book Review (July 15), pp. 3, 14.
There is a new, distinctively American style, first used seriously and at length in HF, and thereafter by Hemingway, Gertrude Stein, John Hersey, and others. It is characterized by its repetitions, flat statements about emotional response, simple diction, loose sentence structure, use of intensifying adverbs, often an excessive use of present participles to give the effect of continuing action, and the avoidance of abstract nouns.

B34 DEVOTO, BERNARD. "Mr. DeVoto Explains as to Use of the Name 'Mark Twain,'" Twainian, IV (June), 2.
A letter from DeVoto explains that the pen-name has been registered as a protection against misuse of the name, and the Mark Twain Company regards even material on which copyright has expired as protected to the extent that it may be published with the name "Samuel L. Clemens" as author, but not "Mark Twain."

1945 - Shorter Writings

B35 FARRELL, JAMES T. "Mark Twain's Huckleberry Finn and Tom Sawyer," in his The League of Frightened Philistines and Other Papers (New York: The Vanguard Press), pp. 25-30.
MT has been misunderstood, particularly by Lewis Mumford (in The Golden Day) and Van Wyck Brooks. He had a healthy sense of justice despite his cynicism. Tom and Huck can rise above MT's discouragement because they are boys, and Huck is "an ideal expression of the positive side of Mark Twain." Today the boys "stand as a test not only of ourselves but of the whole of American society," asking why the promise has not been realized. Reprinted in Lettis (1962), pp. 321-25.

B36 FEINSTEIN, GEORGE. "Mark Twain's Regionalism in Fiction," Mark Twain Quarterly, VII (Winter-Spring), 7, 24.
On MT's insistence that a culture or a dialect cannot be accurately represented without intimate familiarity, and that the national culture is too diversified to be described in a single novel.

B37 GIBSON, CHARLES HAMMOND. "My Last Impression of Mark Twain," Mark Twain Quarterly, VII (Winter-Spring), 5-6.
On MT's address at the dedication of the Thomas Bailey Aldrich Memorial at Portsmouth, New Hampshire.

B38 GILDER, RODMAN. "Rodman Gilder Writes That One of Those Two Twain Tales is a Forgery," Twainian, IV (January), 4.
Of two tales attributed to MT in clippings of uncertain provenance, reprinted in Twainian, IV (December, 1944), 1-5; accepts "The Revised Catechism" as "entirely Twainesque," but "The Last Stamp" clipping indicates a date of composition (1872) when MT would not have had time for trivia.

B39 GRANGER, EUGENIE. "Mark Twain Versus Publicity," Mark Twain Quarterly, VII (Winter-Spring), 10.
Anecdotes told by Robert Sherwood, on MT criticized for smoking his pipe while lecturing before a university audience in New York and on his successful bid for publicity in London by appearing publicly in his bathrobe and boots, smoking a big cigar.

B40 GUEST, BOYD. "Twain's Concept of Woman's Sphere," Mark Twain Quarterly, VII (Winter-Spring), 1-4.
MT's works and public statements reflect his western chivalry and his belief in women's rights, including the right to vote.

B41 HALL, DON E. "A Mark Twain Sales Tip," Mark Twain Quarterly, VII (Winter-Spring), 9.
An anecdote, without corroboratory details, of MT's wearing out a book agent by inviting him to stay for dinner and for the night.

B42 HEMMINGHAUS, EDGAR H. "Mark Twain's German Provenience," Modern Language Quarterly, VI (December), 459-78.
"Mark Twain's approach to the Germans, their language, and their literature was unquestionably one of great amicability and affectionate admiration." Hemminghaus relies largely on American sources concerning MT; for German views of MT, see his 1939 book.

B43 HIFT, FRED W. "Radio in the Soviet," New York Times (September 2), p. 5.
Reports that the Russian radio features "whole evenings of readings from Mark Twain, de Maupassant, and Chekov. These are especially popular with Russian listeners because of the acute shortage of books."

B44 HORNBERGER, THEODORE. [Brief Review: Cyril Clemens, Young Sam Clemens.] American Literature, XVII (March), 102.
"It consists largely of a stream of stories and anecdotes about Mark Twain, picked up by Mr. Cyril Clemens in the course of his indefatigable pursuit of Mark Twain. Because Mr. Clemens has visited many of the places where Mark Twain lived, and talked with people who knew Mark Twain, his anecdotes are often fresh and amusing."

B45 KINNAIRD, CLARK. "Mark Twain's First Book," American Mercury, LX (January), 124.
A letter to the editor, giving a brief biographical sketch of Charles Henry Webb, "the man responsible for putting the Jumping Frog between book covers."

B46 LEDERER, MAX. "Mark Twain in Vienna," Mark Twain Quarterly, VII (Summer-Fall), 1-12.
An extensive account of MT's stay there, September, 1897-May, 1899, supported by references to local news stories.

B47 LORCH, FRED W. "Mark Twain's Early Views on Western Indians," Twainian, IV (April), 1-2.
The representation of the Goshoot Indians in RI reflects Nevada attitudes of the time, rather than careful observation or MT's later compassion for human suffering.

B48 O'LIAM, DUGAL. "They're Off at Angel's Camp," Collier's, CXV (May 5), 21, 41.
On the annual Jumping Frog Jubilee of Calaveras County, illustrated with a cartoon of the jubilee and two excellent photographs of modern frogs.

B49 STARRETT, VINCENT. "Some Anecdotes and Fair Words from an Old-time Well Wisher," Twainian, IV (January), 1-2.
Reprints two MT anecdotes from Lincoln Springfield's Some Piquant People (1924) and several reminiscences of MT in Douglas Sladen's Twenty Years of My Life (date unknown). Barr tells of MT expressing pleasure in "the fact that Darwin, for a year before

(STARRETT, VINCENT)

his death, read nothing but his works. Darwin's doctors, he added, had warned him he
would get softening of the brain if he read
anything but absolute drivel."

B50 WECTER, DIXON. "Mark Twain and the West,"
Huntington Library Quarterly, VIII (August),
359-77.
The text of "An address delivered at the
Huntington Library on Founder's Day,
February 26, 1945," this is a popular ac-
count, largely biographical, for a lay au-
dience.

B51 WILLSON, FRANK C. "Mark Twain on the Old-
Fashioned Spelling-Bee," Twainian, IV
(March), 2-3.
Includes the text of an MT speech which
Brownell found in The Trumpet, I (February,
1892) an obscure journal published in New
York by Albert S. King. George Hiram Brown-
ell confirms Willson's surmise that the
speech first appeared in a Hartford paper,
and lists other printings.

B52 _____. "Twain Spanks a Government Official
for Unofficial Impertinence," Twainian, IV
(January), 2-4.
Contains the text of a letter to MT and
two letters by him, a mock-serious dispute
with Thomas B. Kirby, Private Secretary to
the Postmaster General. Willson found the
letters in Gus Williams' World of Humor
(New York: The DeWitt Publishing Company,
1880, pp. 93-95), as reprinted from the
Hartford Courant, the last of them apparently in early December, 1879. There is further comment on the use by Kirby of the
word "Bogus," and MT's response, in the
February Twainian. The MT letter to the
Courant which began the controversy appears
in Twainian, IV (March-April, 1947), 3-4.

B53 _____. "Twain Tells How to Remove Warts and
Tattoo Marks," Twainian, IV (June), 3-4.
Text of a letter to the editor of the New
York Sun (date unknown); MT states that he
removed his warts with a heated needle, and
had an anchor and rope tattooed on the back
of his left hand when he was sixteen, but
removed it nine years later as he had removed the warts.

B54 WOOLF, S. J. "How S. J. Woolf Made His Two
Portraits of Twain," Twainian, IV (June),
4.
In the course of painting MT's portrait
in 1906, Woolf made a pencil sketch one day
and later used it as the basis for a litho-
graph in late 1919 or early 1920.

A1 *CLEMENS, SAMUEL L. ¿Qué es el Hombre? Con una
introducción de S. K. Ratcliffe. Barcelona:
Editorial Delfos.
[What Is Man? Source: Asselineau (1954),
No. 1062.]

A2 DEVOTO, BERNARD, ed. The Portable Mark Twain.
New York: The Viking Press.
An anthology including the complete texts
of HF and MS and judicious selections from
other works, as well as a number of MT's
letters, and a valuable 34-page introduction. Still in print. Pp. 33-34, on HF,
are reprinted in Gerber (1971), p. 42.

A3 *HARNSBERGER, CAROLINE THOMAS. Mark Twain at
Your Fingertips. Chicago: Cloud, Inc.
[Source: MHRA Annual Bibliography (1946),
No. 1800; this anticipates the more familiar
1948 publication, See 1948.A2.]

A4 LEISY, ERNEST E., ed. The Letters of Quintus
Curtius Snodgrass. Dallas: Southern Methodist University Press.
A series of ten letters in the New Orleans
Daily Crescent (January-March, 1861) attributed to MT by Leisy, who credits Minnie M.
Brashear with the discovery of the first
four, as noted in Mark Twain: Son of Missouri (1934). The attribution of the letters to MT is disputed by Brinegar
(1963.B11) and discredited by Bates
(1964.B13).

A5 PELLOWE, WILLIAM C. S. Mark Twain: Pilgrim
from Hannibal. New York: The Hobson Book
Press.
About MT's inner life, with emphasis on
religion. Concludes with "An Epilogue" by
Cyril Clemens, whom Pellowe thanks for help
which included "suggestions on arrangement
of manuscript" (p. 273).

A6 WEBSTER, SAMUEL CHARLES. Mark Twain, Business
Man. Boston: Little, Brown and Company.
An Atlantic Monthly Press Book.
In part this book represents a son's defence of his father, Charles L. Webster,
MT's associate in a publishing company which
ended in bankruptcy. Webster makes a good
case for his father, but documents carefully
and does not overstate his case. The result
is an important contribution to MT biography.
Includes many MT letters (some of which Webster published in Atlantic Monthly in 1944
(See 1944.B49).

B1 ADAMS, J. DONALD. "Speaking of Books," New
York Times Book Review (March 17), p. 2.

1946 - Shorter Writings

(ADAMS, J. DONALD)
Comments briefly on the charm of TS and HF, and notes with pleasure that in the preface to the Everyman's Library edition Christopher Morley tells of a 1938 visit to Hannibal, where he and some friends whitewashed Tom Sawyer's fence as an act of homage.

B2   ANON. "Dear Charley," Time, XLVII (February 11), 100-104.
A review of Samuel Charles Webster, Mark Twain, Business Man; largely descriptive, citing examples of MT's poor business judgment and quoting his unreasonable demands on the author's father, Charles L. Webster.

B3   BIDEWELL, GEORGE IVAN. "Mark Twain's Florida Years," Missouri Historical Review, XL (January), 159-73.
On the influence of life in Florida, Missouri, before the Clemens family moved to Hannibal and during the summers of 1840-1846 the boy spent there on the farm of his uncle John A. Quarles. Through parallel passages from the Paine biography and HF, argues that the Quarles farm was the model for the Silas Phelps farm in HF.

B4   BRANCH, EDGAR M. A Chronological Bibliography of the Writings of Samuel Clemens to June 8, 1867," American Literature, XVIII (May), 109-57.
"All entries are grouped chronologically, both under the year of writing and under seven divisions which correspond to the seven major regions of Clemens's literary and professional activity during this period: (1) Hannibal, (2) the East and Midwest, (3) the Mississippi River, (4) Washoe, (5) California, (6) the Sandwich Islands, and (7) New York City." "The check list records, so far as the facts are known to the compiler, four types of information: (1) the title of original publication, (2) relevant information supplied by the compiler, (3) the place and date of original publication, and (4) the most generally accessible reprint."

B5   [BROWNELL, GEORGE HIRAM.] "The After-Dinner Speaker's Best Friend: 'Mark Twain's Patent Adjustable Speech,'" Twainian, V (January-February), 1-3.
The text of "an address by Mark Twain on Forefathers' Day, Dec. 20, 1887, before the Boston Congregational Club," according to an unidentified clipping found by Frank C. Willson in a scrapbook.

B6   _____. "'Mark Twain, Business Man,'" Twainian, V (March-April), 4.
A favorable review of the book by Samuel Charles Webster.

B7   _____. "Maybe this Explains Why Mark Left Nevada," Twainian, V (September-October), 2-3.
Quotes an MT letter from Carson City in the San Francisco Morning Call (November 19, 1863): under the second article of the Nevada constitution, then being debated, former Confederate soldiers and civil officers would be disenfranchised. Brownell accepts the "Quintus Curtius Snodgrass" letters as genuine, and therefore as evidence that MT's Confederate service was more extensive than his brief period as an irregular in Missouri.

B8   _____. "Some Remarks on the 'Letter from the Recording Angel,'" Twainian, V (March-April), 3.
"He goes after Andrew so bitterly and minutely...that one is forced to the conclusion that the entire writing was a practice piece, the model from which he planned later to extract material for a writing of impersonal nature."

B9   _____. "Those 'Poems' by Twain in 'The Wasp' of San Francisco," Twainian, V (July-August), 3-4.
Contains "Ye Equinoctial Storm" and "Tropic Chidings," (airs of "Auld Lang Syne" and "Say Hast Thou No Feeling"), composed by MT on the Montana, when he sailed from San Francisco en route to New York (via Panama) in 1868. These poems were in the possession of Philip Shirley, published with his brief comment as "Some Verses by Mark Twain" in The Wasp (the first colored cartoon paper in America), January 19, 1884.

B10   _____. "Twain Refuses Offer of a Box of (Good) Cigars," Twainian, V (November-December), 3-4.
Contains text of an MT letter to the Rev. L. M. Powers (November 1, 1905), declining with thanks his offer of a box of cigars and stating a preference for cheap ones.

B11   _____. "Two Hitherto Unknown Twain Tales Found in New York Tribune," Twainian, V (November-December), 1-2.
Includes the texts of "Concerning General Grant's Intentions" (datelined Washington, December 8, 1868--a burlesque interview in which MT poses a series of unanswered questions) and "Information Wanted" (concerning MT's queries about George Francis Train; this appeared in the Tribune for January 22, 1868, and is not to be confused with a piece of the same title reprinted in Sketches, New and Old).

B12   _____. "What Do You Know about the Play Roughing It?" Twainian, V (May-June), 6.
On the play produced by Augustin Daly in 1873; full discussion in July-August issue, 1946.B27.

B13 _____. "Whence Came 'Well Done, Good and Faithful Servant,'" Twainian, V (January-February), 3-4.

On the concluding lines in "Riley--Newspaper Correspondent" (Buffalo Express, October 29, 1870; reprinted in Sketches New and Old, 1875); MT also used the joke in a letter from Hawaii to the Sacramento Union (September 6, 1866).

B14 _____. "Why Bibliographers are Just a Bit Daffy," Twainian, V (September-October), 3-4.

On the fruitless search for files of the Territorial Enterprise for the period when MT was connected with it. Apparently promising leads proved disappointing, but Brownell does list files for 1866, 1871, 1874-1892, and 1893-1912, scattered through several libraries.

B15 _____. "'Youths' Companion' Reveals Twain Tales and Advertisement of 'Huck Finn,'" Twainian, V (March-April), 1-3.

"How To Tell a Story" and portions of LOM. Frank C. Willson has found an advertisement for subscription agents for HF; the dates (November 20, 27, December 11, 1884) establish that the prospectus was ready by November 20. This information bears on the mutilation of the cut on p. 283, the discussion of which includes reprinted news stories from the November 29, 1884 New York Tribune ("Tampering with Mark Twain's Book") and Herald ("Mark Twain's Altered Book"); the latter quotes the caption as "What [sic] do you reckon it is?" Also see Twainian, May-June, p. 6.

B16 _____. [Brief Item: Frank C. Willson has acquired 1868-1869 volumes of the Portland (Maine) Transcript, containing a report of MT's Sandwich Islands lecture in Portland (December 30, 1869).] Twainian, V (January-February), 4.

B17 CARGILL, OSCAR. "The Ordeal of Van Wyck Brooks," College English, VIII (November), 55-61.

Only briefly mentions MT: the Brooks thesis concerning him is still not generally accepted.

B18 CASH, THELMA. "Mark Twain Goes West," Poet Lore, LII (Autumn), 256-60.

A short, vivid, popular account based on Roughing It, Paine, and DeVoto.

B19 CLEMENS, SAMUEL L. "Letter From the Recording Angel," Harper's, CXCII (February), 106-109.

Text of the previously unpublished sketch, with a headnote by Bernard DeVoto, who comments on the response to this sketch in "The Easy Chair," April, pp. 309-12 (1946.B20).

B20 DEVOTO, BERNARD. "The Easy Chair," Harper's, CXCII (April), 309-12.

MT's "intelligence was not analytical, it was intuitive," and his humor "was only the ambivalence we all share," a way of responding to inner conflict. Comments on "Letter from the Recording Angel."

B21 _____. "The Other Side of Some Mark Twain Stories: His Business Partner Was Also His Errand Boy, Broker, Detective and General Scapegoat," New York Herald Tribune Weekly Book Review (February 10), p. 3.

A review of Samuel Charles Webster, Mark Twain, Business Man, "a valuable addition to Mark Twain literature, vastly amusing to the general reader and indispensible to students," containing "the most detailed and by far the most convincing portrait of Jane Clemens ever written," with useful material on Orion Clemens and the full text of the Madame Caprell letter. The title is misleading, in that the book does not treat all of MT's business affairs but concentrates on publishing, in which MT was difficult to deal with and chiefly responsible for his own failures. Reprinted in Twainian, V (May-June), 3-5.

B22 _____. [Brief headnote to first publication of MT's "Fenimore Cooper's Further Literary Offenses."] New England Quarterly, XIX (September), 291-301.

Superseded in DeVoto, ed., Mark Twain's Letters from the Earth (1962), as "Cooper's Prose Style" (pp. 135-46).

B23 "THE EDITORS" [WALTER PILKINGTON and B. ASTER-LUND.] "Mark Twain's Introductory Remarks at the Time of Winston Churchill's First American Lecture," Notes and Queries (New York), V (January), 47-48.

Includes the text of MT's brief remarks as reported in the New York Tribune, December 13, 1900. "It differs measurably from that printed in the 1910 edition of Mark Twain's Speeches. It is not a complete transcript of the speech; the only full version can be found in the unpublished Mark Twain Papers. The New York Times account (December 13, 1900) quotes Clemens only indirectly, except for two lines," a direct quotation of the conclusion, which the Tribune apparently misquoted.

B24 FEINSTEIN, GEORGE. "Mark Twain's Idea of Story Structure," American Literature, XVIII (May), 160-63.

"A tale...must grow organically, from within, or the artificiality will show" (p. 160).

B25 FERGUSON, DELANCEY. "Clemens'...Huckleberry Finn," Explicator, IV (April), Item 42. A reply to P.B.A. in Explicator, IV (November, 1945), Q. 7.

(FERGUSON, DELANCEY)

Jim could not escape directly across the river into Illinois, because he would be quickly captured for a reward; his chances would be better if he entered free territory some distance from where he had escaped.

B26 _____. [Review: Samuel Charles Webster, ed., Mark Twain, Business Man.] American Literature, XVIII (May), 169-70.

Many letters are made public for the first time, and for others the text expurgated by Paine is restored. There is comparatively little new information about SLC's connection with the Webster Publishing Company, although the difficulty of working with Clemens is elaborated. "The real additions and corrections to the record come from the family correspondence, and from the reminiscences of the editor's mother, Annie Moffett Webster.... some of Paine's most romantic details of the humorist's youth suffer a deflation which extends to the conclusions drawn from them by the psychoanalytical critics."

B27 FLACK, FRANK MORGAN. "About the Play Roughing It as Produced by Augustin Daly," Twainian, V (July-August), 1-3.

Includes letters from MT and Howells to Daly, contemporary reviews from the New York Daily Tribune, but chiefly relies on known works on Daly and his theater; the synthesis is useful. The plot of the play "related the elopement of a rich man's daughter with a poor noodle, and the father's pursuit of these fugitives from the metropolis to Simpson's Bar. A few of its situations were seen to be ingeniously constructed, and parts of its texts were smartly written. Its intention appeared to be...farcical. Its attainment was utter puerility."

B28 FLAGG, JAMES MONTGOMERY. Roses and Buckshot. New York: G. P. Putnam's Sons. Anecdotes of MT, pp. 166-70.

On p. 169, tells of MT and Howells listening to Adelina Patti at the opera. "Howells noticed the wicked leer in Mark's eye and questioned him. Mark, heaving a big sigh, said in Howells' ear: 'I would rather sleep with that woman stark naked, than with General Grant in full uniform!'"

B29 FRIEDRICH, JOHN T. "Speaking of Books about Wm. Allen White and Mark Twain," Rotarian, LXVIII (April), 47-48.

On White's Autobiography, and "a very fine and important new book, Samuel Charles Webster's Mark Twain, Business Man," here summarized.

B30 GREEN, ROGER LANCELYN. Andrew Lang: A Critical Biography. With a Short-Title Bibliography of the Works of Andrew Lang. Leicester, England: Edmund Ward, p. 167.

Lang quoted: "I have tried in an ineffective but hearty manner, to praise Mark Twain as one of the greatest of living geniuses (perhaps it is not saying much), who now use the English language." This originally appeared in Lang's "International Girlishness" in Murray's Magazine, October, 1888.

B31 *HAINES, HAROLD H., ed. The Callaghan Mail, 1821-1859. Hannibal, Missouri: n.p.

[Source: Cited by Wecter (1952) on MT's strict father (p. 284, n. 4) and the partially respectable original of Injun Joe (pp. 151, 299).]

B32 HOBEN, JOHN B. "Mark Twain's A Connecticut Yankee: A Genetic Study," American Literature, XVIII (November), 197-218.

Thoroughly documented from published critical and biographical material, this is a substantial work often cited in CY criticism. The study of MT's growing anti-English feeling in the 1870's and 1880's is continued by McKeithan in "More about Mark Twain's War with English Critics of America" (1948).

B33 HOLLENBACH, JOHN W. "Mark Twain, Story-Teller, At Work," College English, VII (March), 303-12.

MT's skill as a raconteur and fondness for the oral form has been generally recognized "for the part it has played in developing the rhythm, vividness, and sense of immediacy of his prose style. Equal recognition should also be given this habit for the part it played in giving his short stories what unity and finish of structure they did have."

B34 HUVSTEDT, S. B. "The Preacher and the Gray Mare," California Folklore Quarterly, V (January), 109-10.

In Chapter XXV of LOM, MT quotes Uncle Mumford on a steamboat calamity resulting from carrying a preacher and a gray mare, and MT adds that he knew of another such case. Huvstedt links the preacher to the Jonah motif, adding that the connection with the gray mare is more difficult to follow and asking whether readers know of California parallels.

B35 *JOHNSON, E. C. [Review: Sten B. Liljegren, The Revolt Against Romanticism in American Literature as Evidenced in the Works of Samuel L. Clemens.] Studia Neophilologica, XIX, 184-87.

[Source: MHRA Annual Bibliography (1946), No. 1804.]

B36 JONES, JOSEPH. "The Duke's Tooth-Powder Racket: A Note on Huckleberry Finn," Modern Language Notes, LXI (November), 468-69.

According to a New York paper, there really were scoundrels who sold a dentrifice that removed the enamel with the tartar. (See HF, Chapter XIX).

B37 LEDERER, MAX. "Einige Bemerkungen zu Adolph Wilbrandts Der Meister von Palmyra," Modern Language Notes, LXI (December), 551-55.
Notes MT's interest in the play's themes of Faust and transmigration of souls, tracing them to What Is Man? and MS; cites an earlier discussion by Schönemann (1919.B19).

B38 LEISY, ERNEST E. "The Quintus Curtius Snodgrass Letters in the New Orleans Daily Crescent," Twainian, V (September-October), 1-2.
Contains the text of "Washington Artillery Ball," one of a series of ten letters attributed to MT and now published in book form as The Letters of Quintus Curtius Snodgrass. In a following note George Hiram Brownell chides Leisy for his modest failure to note that he edited the collection and his scholar's reluctance to state firmly that the letters are MT's work. The letter that concluded the series appeared in Twainian, n.s., I (June, 1942), 1-3. According to Brinegar (1963.B11) and Bates (1964.B13), the letters are not by MT.

B39 *LILJEGREN, STEN B. [Review: Bernard DeVoto, Mark Twain at Work (1942) and DeLancey Ferguson, Mark Twain: Man and Legend (1943).] Studia Neophilologica, XIX, 187-88.
[Source: MHRA Annual Bibliography (1946), No. 1796, 1798.]

B40 LOOMIS, C. GRANT. "Dan De Quille's Mark Twain," Pacific Historical Review, XV (September), 336-47.
Reprints articles and sketches by William Wright ("Dan De Quille") from the Golden Era and Territorial Enterprise on MT as a room-mate, on his wedding in the East, and on the story of a drunken river pilot who had been recommended by MT as competent--when sober.

B41 LORCH, FRED W. "Mark Twain's Philadelphia Letters in the Muscatine Journal," American Literature, XVII (January), 348-52.
These letters, written in December, 1853, owe much to R. A. Smith's Philadelphia As It Is in 1852, but to some extent MT avoided the triteness of Smith's style. Notes publication of these letters by Edgar M. Branch in 1942.

B42 MONKSWELL, LADY MARY. A Victorian Diarist: Later Extracts from the Journals of Mary, Lady Monkswell, 1895-1909. Edited by the Hon. E. C. F. Collier. London: John Murray.
The entry for Monday, February 15, 1897 describes MT's appearance when he visited her residence with the Poultney Bigelows (p. 23; quoted by Baetzhold [1970.A1], p. 197). A volume of extracts from her diaries for the years 1873-1895 (ed. by the Hon. E. C. F. Collier, London: John Murray, 1944), contains no reference to MT.

B43 NEWTON, JOSEPH FORT. River of Years: An Autobiography. Philadelphia, New York: J. B. Lippincott Company.
On pp. 89-90, describes MT at a St. Louis Press Club dinner, where he told a story of St. Francis concluding: "We have been happy in the love of God and the glory of His sunlight--that is our sermon for the day." The passage is reprinted in Mark Twain Journal, XV (Winter, 1970-1971), 6.

B44 RANDEL, WILLIAM PEIRCE. Edward Eggleston: Author of "The Hoosier School-Master." Morningside Heights, New York: King's Crown Press, passim.
Eggleston regarded MT primarily as a humorist (pp. 109, 184, 206). They met on several occasions, including Horace Greeley's sixty-fifth birthday party (p. 131) and in Washington in 1889, lobbying for changes in the copyright laws (p. 186). [Published doctoral dissertation, Columbia University.]

B45 TRILLING, LIONEL. "Mark Twain--A Dominant Genius," New York Times Book Review (February 3), pp. 1, 14.
A review of Samuel Charles Webster's Mark Twain, Business Man. Notes MT's bullying of Webster's father: "The evidence of the letters cannot prove that there was no reason for Mark Twain to dislike Webster, but only that he was unjust to a man he disliked." MT's business ventures, though disastrous financially, may have provided a diversion, a relaxation beneficial to his writing. Reprinted in Leary (1962), pp. 177-82.

B46 WHITE, BEATRICE. [Brief Review: S. B. Liljegren, The Revolt Against Romanticism in American Literature as Evidenced in the Works of Samuel L. Clemens.] Modern Language Review, XLI (January), 89.
"The treatment seems to be in part designed for the elementary reader," and the evidence "could, perhaps, have been more convincingly presented."

B47 WILLIAMS, STANLEY T. "Anecdotes About Mark Twain," Yale Review, n.s. XXXV (Summer), 758-60.
A review of Samuel Charles Webster, Mark Twain, Business Man.
The book is anecdotal, more valuable for casting light on those around MT than for clarifying his business troubles.

B48 WILLSON, FRANK C. "Twain's Tale, 'The Facts Concerning the Recent Important Resignation,'" Twainian, V (May-June), 1-3.
One of three MT letters discovered by Willson in the New York Tribune; in this one (datelined Washington, February 9, 1868) MT pretends to have joined a House debate as an ad interim member. In concluding remarks George Hiram Brownell promises publication of the other two letters in future issues.

B49 WOOD, JAMES PLAYSTEAD. "All Out of Step but Mark," Saturday Review of Literature, XXIX (March 2), 16-17.

A review of Samuel Charles Webster's Mark Twain, Business Man, which shows that MT was not justified in his accusations against Charles H. Webster, whom he burdened with tasks unrelated to the publishing company; MT was himself much to blame for the failure of the company. The editor shows "quiet but shrewd humor" in his "deft and nicely pointed insertions of additional information." Reprinted in Twainian, V (May-June), 5.

B50 WYMAN, MARY A. "A Note on Mark Twain," College English, VII (May), 438-43.

Edmund Aubrey, the Paladin in JA, and MT are alike "in their relationships to early companions who exploited their gifts and in their magnetism and success as public speakers." Similarities between them were noted in 1921 by Friedrich Schönemann, in "Mark Twains Weltanschauung."

1947 A BOOKS

A1 CARPENTER, EDWIN E., JR., comp.; introduction by Dixon Wecter. Mark Twain: An Exhibition Selected Mainly from the Papers Belonging to the Samuel L. Clemens Estate on Deposit in the Huntington Library. San Marino, California [Huntington Library].

A catalogue describing the contents of fourteen cases containing manuscripts, notebooks, books belonging to MT, etc.

A2 *CLEMENS, SAMUEL L. The Adventures of Tom Sawyer, Pagine scelte con note di Matilde Bargelli. Milan: C. Signorelli.
[Source: Asselineau (1954), No. 1097.]

A3 FREAR, WALTER FRANCIS. Mark Twain and Hawaii. Privately Printed. Chicago: The Lakeside Press.

A very thorough treatment of his four months spent in Hawaii in 1865; letters MT wrote for the Sacramento Union later were incorporated in RI (they are reprinted in an appendix). A valuable book.

A4 *LEMONNIER, LÉON. Mark Twain. Paris: A. Fayard.
[Source: Asselineau (1954), No. 1093, describing this as a psychological study of the man and works, following the Brooks interpretation.]

A5 MACK, EFFIE MONA. Mark Twain in Nevada. New York and London: Charles Scribner's Sons.

On MT in his formative years, 1861-1864, with samples of his writings and those of contemporaries in Nevada.

A6 WRIGHT, WILLIAM ("DAN DE QUILLE"). The Big Bonanza: An Authentic Account of the Discovery, History, and Working of the World-Renowned Comstock Lode of Nevada, Including the Present Condition of the Various Mines Situated Thereon--Sketches of the Prominent Men Interested in Them--Incidents and Adventures Connected with Mining, the Indians, and the Country--Amusing Stories, Experiences, Anecdotes, etc. and a Full Exposition of the Production of Pure Silver. Introduction by Oscar Lewis. New York: Alfred A. Knopf.

First published Hartford: American Publishing Company, 1876; provides useful background information on Nevada mining, but nothing directly on MT. Wright and MT worked together on the Territorial Enterprise in Virginia City, and the book incorporates suggestions by MT. The introduction by Oscar Lewis discusses MT's involvement and quotes several of his letters.

1947 B SHORTER WRITINGS

B1 ANON. "Much Fresh Mark Twain Material Will Be Made Available," Publishers' Weekly, CLI (May 10), 2433.

The Mark Twain Papers have recently been transferred from Harvard to the Henry E. Huntington Library in San Marino, California [and subsequently to the Bancroft Library at the University of California, Berkeley--T.A.T.]; Dixon Wecter will succeed Bernard DeVoto as literary editor of the MT estate.

B2 ANON. "Twain Suppressed, Russian Charges. Cites 'Anti-Imperialist' Essays--Editor Here Proves They Have Been Published," New York Times (July 28), p. 13.

On the charge by M. Mendelsohn (refuted by Bernard DeVoto and by Frederick L. Allen of Harper & Brothers) that "In Defense of General Funston" and "To the Person Sitting in Darkness" had been suppressed.

B3 *BECKER, MAY LAMBERTON. [Introduction.] The Adventures of Huckleberry Finn. Cleveland: World Publishing Company (Rainbow Classics).
[Source: Asselineau (1954), No. 1098.]

B4 BERGLER, EDMUND, M.D. "Exceptional Reaction to a Joke of Mark Twain," Mark Twain Quarterly, VIII (Winter), 11-12.

In his "Toast to the Babies" honoring General U. S. Grant (1879), "the object of attack was obviously hero-worship," as Bergler explains in Freudian terms; a "shuddering silence" then ensued, because MT was also touching on "the typical megalomania of the adult who conveniently forgets his original dependence in early childhood." [Bergler does not comment on the triumphant conclusion of the toast--T.A.T.]

B5 BLANCK, JACOB. "A Best Seller of the 70's," Publishers' Weekly, CLII (July 19), Section II, B37.
    A brief and partial summary of Dickinson's article on IA, (1947.B27).

B6 BOOTH, BRADFORD. "Mark Twain's Friendship with Emeline Beach," American Literature, XIX (November), 219-30.
    Emeline was the seventeen-year-old daughter of Moses Sperry Beach; the two were shipmates of MT on the Quaker City cruise. Booth gives us background, commentary, and a series of letters from MT to Miss Beach while he was writing IA and in later years.

B7 _____. "Mark Twain's Friendship with Emma Beach," Mark Twain Quarterly, VIII (Winter), 4-10.
    The same article as 1947.B6, with no indication of the fact.

B8 BROOKS, VAN WYCK. The Times of Melville and Whitman. New York: E. P. Dutton & Co., Inc., passim on MT (indexed).
    "Mark Twain in the West" (pp. 283-300) argues that "Mark Twain with his fathomless naivity prepared the ground, as Whitman did, for a new and unique American art of letters, in a negative way with The Innocents Abroad, in a positive way with the Western writings in which he contributed to establish and foster this art." TS, HF, and the first half of LOM "were germs of a new American literature with a broader base in the national mind than the writers of New England had possessed, fine as they were." On pp. 448-64, "Mark Twain in the East" shows MT as "the greatest American folkwriter of the time," who did not understand or respect his craft; thus, "He seemed all but indifferent to Huckleberry Finn when he was at work on this best of his best," and squandered his energies on ill-conceived projects; "Even Mark Twain's great books, with their brilliant beginnings, ended badly"; but some of his works "were destined to live with the best in America." Excerpted in Gerber (1971), pp. 29-32.

B9 [BROWNELL, GEORGE HIRAM.] "About that Heliotype Portrait of Mark Twain in 'Huck Finn,'" Twainian, VI (January-February), 1-2.
    Facing the frontispiece in first-edition copies of HF is a picture of the Karl Gerhardt bust of MT; the plates used in the heliotype process by which the picture was reproduced were good for an average of 300 impressions, so the process had to be repeated at least 100 times, introducing such variants as differing dimensions and the presence or absence of a table under the bust. In many copies the edge of the bust bears the words, "Karl Gerhardt, Sc.," apparently added on the negative, and Brownell is convinced that they cover an inscription chiseled on the bust itself, "To my Frent [sic] S. Clemens--Karl Gerdhardt."

In about half the copies Brownell has examined the inscription is simply blanked out. Also see "That Word 'Frent' on Gerhardt Bust of Twain" (May-June), 3-4: W. Allen DeLaney sent Brownell a list of page references to Gerhardt in books on MT and an encyclopedia sketch of his career; also included is the text of a letter from Gerhardt with the word "friend" spelled correctly.

B10 _____. "The First of Series II, American Travel Letters, in Alta California," Twainian, VI (May-June), 1-3.,
    The first of a series of fourteen letters by MT after his return from the Quaker City Tour; the series is reprinted in the Twainian through VIII (July-August, 1949). Franklin Walker had considered including these letters in his and G. Ezra Dane's Mark Twain's Travels with Mr. Brown (1940), but decided against doing so because Brown does not appear in these letters and the volume would become unwieldy. This first letter, datelined "New York, November 20th [1867]," covers the return of the Quaker City and a passenger list for MT's dream of "A Model Excursion."

B11 _____. "Second Letter of 'American Travel Letters, Series II,'" Twainian, VI (July-August), 4-6.
    Datelined "Washington, December 10th, 1867," contains MT's comments on the Hawaiian treaty; speculation by others about foul play in the deaths of presidents; the plague of office-seekers; and personal notes on individuals of interest to California readers.

B12 _____. "Third Letter of 'American Travel Letters, Series II,'" Twainian, VI (September-October), 3-4.
    Datelined "Washington, December 14, 1867," on government salaries, female clerks, assignment of clerkships, Seward's purchases of real estate, and Sutro's attempt to raise money for a tunnel to drain the Virginia City silver mines.

B13 _____. "Fourth Twain Letter in Alta First Printed in New York Citizen," Twainian, VI (November-December), 3-4.
    Datelined "Washington, D.C., Dec. 15th, 1867," a burlesque in which MT says he was appointed Senate doorkeeper: he tried to make a speech and was squelched, joined in a voice vote and was impeached.

B14 _____. "Mark Twain Orates on Death of Democratic Party in 1880(?)," Twainian, VI (January-February), 2-3.
    Reprint of a clipping from the Chicago Tribune, datelined, "Hartford, Conn., Nov. 3," reporting an MT oration at a Republican meeting the night before, and giving the text. It was not immediately clear that the speech was intended humorously, as it

1947 - Shorter Writings

([BROWNELL, GEORGE HIRAM])
followed an address by two clergymen and began with a reference to "occasions...so solemn, so weighted with the deep concerns of
life, that then even the licensed jester
must lay aside his cap and bells and remember that he is a man and mortal."

B15 ____. "Not So Good Is Mark's Effort to
Show He Can Pen a Poem Like the 'Raven' by
Poe," Twainian, VI (July-August), 3.
Contains the text of "The Mysterious Chinaman," written in Poe's style, "for
M. E. G.'s Album." Brownell places the
burlesque in MT's western period, and speculates that the "M. E. G." may have been a
relative of Steve Gillis.

B16 ____. "Some Figures on the 1st Edition of
'Tom Sawyer,'" Twainian, VI (March-April),
2.
On different accounts by Walter Bliss and
Merle Johnson as to the number of copies of
the first edition that were cloth-bound.
Based on Twainiana Notes from the Annotations of Walter Bliss, ed. Frances M. Edwards (1930).

B17 ____. "That Picture of 'St. Louis Hotel' in
'Life on the Mississippi,'" Twainian, VI
(September-October), 1-3.
On illustrations on pp. 441, 443 of LOM:
"In brief, the conclusion must be reached
that the correct first-state copies of LOM,
as long accepted, are those containing both
the St. Charles legend and the cut of Twain
in flames; that next in order of priority
are those copies containing the St. Louis
legend and cut of Twain; and that, third,
are the copies that contain the St. Charles
legend but lack the cut of Twain." There is
no record of a second edition published by
Osgood. A brief note in the November-December issue (p. 6) reports letters from New
York rare book dealers Gabriel Engel and
Howard S. Mott, both of whom contend that
the true first-state issue is the one with
the "St. Charles Hotel" legend on p. 443 and
MT in flames on p. 441. A letter from Mott
(Twainian, VII, January-February, 1948, 5)
corrects this statement: he had simply reported seeing a variant, making no claim
that it represented a true first state--al-
though logic would support an assumption
that it did.

B18 ____. "This German Biography Did Not Contain
Enough 'Frozen Truth' to Satisfy Twain,"
Twainian, VI (March-April), 1.
Robert Lutz in Stuttgart published a six-
volume edition of some of MT's works in
1892 and 1898; the 1898 edition included as
an appendix "Mark Twains Lebensgeschichte,"
an anonymous biography offensive to MT and
his wife. MT asked Lutz to suppress the
biography (which apparently was also issued
as a pamphlet), and offered to provide the
authorized Samuel E. Moffett biography

published first in McClure's Magazine
(October, 1899). Three MT letters to Lutz
(February 27, April 3, July 14, 1899) are
here reprinted from the January, 1947 issue
of More Books of the Boston Public Library,
1947.B21.

B19 ____. "Twain 'Ciphers' Loss from Postal De-
cree," Twainian, VI (March-April), 3-4.
Text of an MT letter to the Hartford Courant, complaining of the additional trouble
and expense of providing more complete addresses, as required by new regulations.
Also see Frank C. Willson's article on this,
with other letters, in Twainian, IV
(January, 1945), 2-4.

B20 ____. [Brief note on Clemens v. Belford
case, and the "Mark Twain" trade mark.]
Twainian, VI (March-April), 2.
Provides the legal citation: "14 Fed 728,
11 Biss 459, Table of 22 Decennial Digest
'06, p. 338, and...cited in 33 Century Digest Literary Property No. 34 and 46 Century
Digest Trade Marks No. 14." It was after
this case was decided that MT registered his
name as a trade mark in the Patent Office.

B21 C., T. "Mark Twain Protests About False German Biography," More Books: Bulletin of the
Boston Public Library, Sixth Series, XXII
(January), 30-31.
Contains three letters MT wrote in 1899
(February 27, April 3, and undated, early
summer) to Robert Lutz, the Stuttgart publisher of a six-volume collection of MT's
works, containing an introductory biography,
"Mark Twains Lebensgeschichte," of which MT
wrote: "Half of the history is true, and
the other half is not--& but little of it is
pleasant reading. According to the mainly
false 4th Chapter, my wife & I were mere
vulgar swine--& moreover that chapter is attributed to me! I never wrote a line of it."
MT asks that the offensive biography be replaced with an official one by Samuel E.
Moffett. [Letters reprinted 1947.B18.]

B22 CLEMENS, CYRIL. "Mark Twain's Southern Relative, Jeremiah Clemens," Mark Twain Quarterly, VII (Spring-Summer, "Combined with Summer, Fall, Winter, 1946"), 13; VIII (Winter),
15-17.
Only a passing reference to MT, who was
"proud to number as a relative" Jeremiah
Clemens," and "frequently referred" to him.
Born in Alabama in 1814, Jeremiah Clemens
became a member of the United States Senate,
where he spoke out in favor of slavery but
against secession. [The second installment
ended by announcing a continuation, which
finally appeared in VIII (Winter, 1950),
13-16, as "Jeremiah Clemens, Novelist and
Southern Supporter of Lincoln."]

B23 CLEMENS, SAMUEL L. "Unpublished Mark Twain
Letter," Mark Twain Quarterly, VII (Spring-
Summer, "Combined with Summer, Fall, Winter,
1946"), 19.

(CLEMENS, SAMUEL L.)

Datelined "Riverdale on the Hudson, June 17, 1902," thanks Henry Miller of the Burlington Railroad for naming a station near Hannibal, Missouri "Clemens" in his honor; unfortunately, no town materialized there.

B24 _____. [Holograph note on the report of his death as "an exaggeration."] Mark Twain Quarterly, VII (Spring-Summer, "Combined with Summer, Fall, Winter, 1946"), front cover.

This is the same note previously reproduced by Frank Marshall White in "Mark Twain as a Newspaper Reporter" (1910).

B25 COAD, ORAL S. "Mrs. Clemens Apologizes for Her Husband," Journal of the Rutgers University Library, XI (December), 30.

Text of a letter by Olivia Clemens (October 31, 1901, now in Stanton Memorial Collection, New Jersey College for Women) to Theodore Stanton, apologizing for MT's failure to offer him lunch: MT seldom ate lunch and forgot that others did.

B26 *DEVOTO, BERNARD. "Those Two Immortal Boys," Woman's Day (November), pp. 38-39, 131-34.

[Source: "Articles on American Literature Appearing in Current Periodicals," American Literature, XX (March, 1948), 98: "A critical analysis of The Adventures of Tom Sawyer and The Adventures of Huckleberry Finn, prompted by the author's hearing a 'cheap and vulgar' radio dramatization of the former."]

B27 DICKINSON, LEON T. "Marketing a Best Seller: Mark Twain's Innocents Abroad," Papers of the Bibliographical Society of America, XLI (First Quarter), 107-22.

On the subscription sale of MT's first major work. MT's publisher, Elisha Bliss, "took special pains to get out an attractive volume," and "promoted it vigorously." Describes details of this promotion. Article reprinted (without footnotes) in Twainian, X (March-April), 3-4; (May-June), 3-4.

B28 _____. "Mark Twain's Revisions in Writing The Innocents Abroad," American Literature, XIX (May), 139-157.

In 1867 MT contracted with the American Publishing Company of Hartford to make a book out of a series of some fifty travel letters he had written for the San Francisco Alta California. "Two factors--audience and form of publication--demanded that Clemens revise his travel letters. It is the purpose of this essay to show how the book differs from the letters and what exactly Clemens did to make it different. An exhibiting of these changes is instructive in revealing something of how Mark Twain operated as a writer." Reprinted (without the footnotes) in Twainian, X (January-February, 1961), 2-4; (March-April), 1-2.

B29 DONNER, STANLEY T. "Mark Twain as a Reader," Quarterly Journal of Speech, XXXIII (October), 308-11.

A general account of MT's very successful public readings from his works; documented from Paine, Howells, and other familiar sources.

B30 DUGAS, GAILE. "Mark Twain's Hannibal," Holiday, II (April), 102-107.

Hannibal, Missouri, and the Clemens house are described for the would-be tourist; there are many color photographs but no new information.

B31 FEINSTEIN, GEORGE W. "Mark Twain on the Immanence of Authors in Their Writing," Mark Twain Quarterly, VIII (Winter), 13-14.

"Twain often finds the show of personality more absorbing than the incidents."

B32 FREMERSDORFF, ELLEN H. "Mark Twain in Australia," Mark Twain Quarterly, VII (Spring-Summer, "Combined with Summer, Fall, Winter, 1946"), 20.

An anecdote concerning a visit by MT to an unnamed mining town (date not given), and his subsequent deflation of the pompous mayor.

B33 GIBSON, WILLIAM M. "Mark Twain and Howells: Anti-Imperialists," New England Quarterly, XX (December), 435-70.

On their response to the Boer War, the Boxer Rebellion, and the war in the Philippines.

B34 *GILMAN, STEPHEN. "Cervantes en la obra de Mark Twain," Cuadernos de Ínsula (Madrid), I, 202-22.

[Source: Listed in bibliography (p. 214) of Arturo Serrano-Plaja, "Magic" Realism in Cervantes: "Don Quixote" as Seen Through "Tom Sawyer" and "The Idiot." Berkeley, Los Angeles, London, 1970. (Trans. by Robert S. Rudder).]

B35 GRANT, RENA V. "The Word 'Pulu,'" American Speech, XXII (April), 150-51.

The word MT once applied to a Nevada tree in a letter to his mother (1861, in Letters, I, 54) actually is Hawaiian for a kind of silky vegetable wool; advertisements headed "PULU! PULU! PULU!" appeared regularly in the San Francisco Daily Bulletin between 1857 and 1861.

B36 HALL, FRED J. "Fred J. Hall Tells the Story of His Connection with Charles L. Webster & Co.," Twainian, VI (November-December), 1-3.

Hall succeeded Webster in managing the company, and was himself ruined in the company's bankruptcy. His letter of January 14, 1909 to Albert Bigelow Paine describes the financial over-extension, the hope placed in the Paige typesetting machine, his impression of Orion Clemens ("He seemed to have no sense of humor, and was the simplest, best natured,

1947 - Shorter Writings

(HALL, FRED J.)
most impractical and delightfully naive man
I ever met"), and a trip with MT which produced the sketch, "Traveling with a Reformer." George Hiram Brownell credits this
letter as "reproduced by courtesy of Mr.
Wesley A. DeLaney, of St. Louis, owner of
the papers left by Albert Bigelow Paine at
his death."

B37   HARRISON, JAMES G. "A Note on the Duke in
'Huck Finn': The Journeyman Printer as
Picaro," Mark Twain Quarterly, VIII (Winter), 1-2.
The Duke belongs to a literary type that
had appeared earlier in American literature, and MT referred elsewhere to the im-
providence and recklessness of journeyman
printers.

B38   HUTTON, GRAHAM. "Hawkeye, Huck Finn and an
English Boy. His Favorite Reading about a
Strange Land," Chicago Sun Book Week, V
(May 4), 2.
English boys and girls in the last centu-
ry read about the American West (very lit-
tle specifically on MT).

B39 * ____. [Introduction.] The Adventures of
Tom Sawyer. London: Paul Eleck.
[Source: Asselineau (1954), No. 1096.]

B40   LAVERTY, CARROLL D. "The Genesis of The Mysterious Stranger," Mark Twain Quarterly,
VII (Spring-Summer, "Combined with Summer,
Fall, Winter, 1946"), 15-19.
Suggests that MT's book may owe its theme
to a story by Jane Taylor, reprinted under
that title in McGuffey's Rhetorical Guide
and Fifth Reader and New Sixth Eclectic
Reader; another source may be Adolph Wilbrandt's The Master of Palmyra.

B41   LEARY, LEWIS. Articles on American Literature Appearing in Current Periodicals,
1920-1945. Durham, North Carolina: Duke
University Press.
Superseded by his 1954 edition, "a revision and an extension" of this one.

B42   *LE BRETON, MAURICE. [Review: Léon Lemonnier,
Mark Twain.] Langues Modernes, 51e année
(September-October), A 53-54.
[Source: Asselineau (1954), No. 1103:
"The reviewer considers it an excellent
synthesis."]

B43   LEWIS, OSCAR. Silver Kings: The Lives and
Times of Mackay, Fair, Flood, and O'Brien,
Lords of the Comstock Lode. New York:
Alfred A. Knopf.
On MT, pp. 31-32, 53, 68-69, 157, brief
mention. Old-timers supposedly recall MT
with far less than their admiration for his
friend William Wright ("Dan de Quille").

B44   LORCH, FRED W. "Mark Twain's Sandwich Islands Lectures at St. Louis," American
Literature, XVIII (January), 299-307.
Includes text of the lecture from the
Missouri Republican, a letter to the editor
of the Republican by MT, and a brief report
on the lecture.

B45   ____. [Review: Ernest E. Leisy, ed., The
Letters of Quintus Curtius Snodgrass
(1946).] American Literature, XIX (March),
93-95.
Leisy "has presented in the Preface, the
Introduction, and especially in the Notes
for each of the letters impressive evidence
which is also convincing to the reader" that
MT wrote these letters, showing that he was
in New Orleans while these letters were appearing in the Daily Crescent, that he had
used the pseudonym "Snodgrass" before [but
as "Thomas Jefferson Snodgrass"--T.A.T.],
that he later spoke of having written for
the Crescent, and that there are many parallels in theme and style. Lorch adds in support of the attribution his own observations
on the letter titled "Snodgrass Dines with
Old Abe," which he says appears to be based
on the efforts of Sam's brother Orion to
secure a consulship in Germany. This series
of letters is important biographically and
for what they reveal of MT's development as
a writer: there is a greater maturity than
in the earlier series of Snodgrass letters.

B46   LOVELL, CHARLES J. "The Background of Mark
Twain's Vocabulary," American Speech, XXII
(April), 88-98.
Although Ramsay and Emberson's Mark Twain
Lexicon (1938) lists over 600 words and
phrases for which MT's use antedates the
Oxford English Dictionary, the Dictionary
of American English cites use for many of
them before MT; further research might well
show that he originated very few, although
he gave them literary currency.

B47   LYDENBERG, JOHN. "A Frontier Product," New
York Times Book Review (May 25), pp. 5, 32.
A review of Effie Mona Mack, Mark Twain in
Nevada.
"It is impossible to see the creator of
Huck Finn in these early writings for the
Territorial Enterprise." They help explain
the lack of control in MT's later writing,
but "the sources of his superb diction and
of his subtle irony are in no way visible."

B48   PARSONS, COLEMAN O. "The Devil and Samuel
Clemens," Virginia Quarterly Review, XXIII
(Autumn), 582-606.
On "the source and mythology" of the
gloom of the Promethean Samuel Clemens, as
distinct from MT: "I cannot escape the
conviction that Samuel Clemens' guilt complex was rooted in his relations with Mother Jane and Brother Henry." Not documented;
apparently draws heavily on Paine's Biography and his edition of Mark Twain's Notebook. Reprinted in Leary (1962), 183-206.

B49 ROBINSON, MARIE J. "Mark Twain: Lecturer," Mark Twain Quarterly, VII (Spring-Summer, "Combined with Summer, Fall, Winter, 1946"), 1-12.

An extensive, general discussion, fully annotated, which shows how lecturing was sometimes a burden for MT, though profitable, but also that he sometimes wrote with pleasure of his triumphs. Included are accounts of his tours, the forms of his notes and his recorded statements on the art, and discussion of his style and topics.

B50 SAMPLEY, ARTHUR M. "New Letters of Mark Twain," Southwest Review, XXXII (Winter), 101-102.

A review of Ernest E. Leisy, ed., The Letters of Quintus Curtius Snodgrass (1946). "Professor Leisy does not state categorically that Snodgrass and Clemens are the same writer, but the evidence he produces...will convince most readers.... The editing of the letters is thorough, succinct, and meticulous, and the format of the book is pleasing."

B51 *SELLERS, J. L. [Review: Effie Mona Mack, Mark Twain in Nevada.] Nebraska History, XXX, 81-82.

[Source: MHRA Annual Bibliography (1949), No. 3968.]

B52 SNELL, GEORGE. "Mark Twain: Realism and the Frontier," in his The Shapers of American Fiction, 1798-1947 (New York: E. P. Dutton & Co.), pp. 211-22 and passim.

MT was "trimmed and tamed" by his wife and Howells. "Undoubtedly this repressive influence had a great deal to do with the truncation of a career that began with such fireworks and spluttered out so dismally toward its end." His reputation as a serious writer will rest on LOM and HF, in which language is "colloquial, natural, in harmony with its content, and by long odds the clearest, easiest prose to come from any native writer." On MT's influence on the style of Hemingway, pp. 160-161, 215.

B53 WAGNER, HETTIE DEVINNY. "A Glimpse of Mark Twain in 1880," Mark Twain Quarterly, VIII (Winter), 3.

One summer day, the author met MT at Elmira and talked about wild flowers with him.

B54 WALKER, FRANKLIN. [Review: Ernest E. Leisy, ed., The Letters of Quintus Curtius Snodgrass (1946).] Modern Language Notes, LXII (November), 503.

The evidence for attributing the letters to MT "though circumstantial, is impressive.... the sketches read something like Clemens' apprentice writing, but not enough to convince this reviewer that they are indisputably his."

B55 WECTER, DIXON. "Frank Finlay; Or, 'The Thameside Tenderfoot in the Wooly West,'" Twainian, VI (July-August), 1-4.

A brief introductory note, and the text of four letters from Finlay to MT. The letter of December 20, 1877 refers to "a well-meant but imperfect sketch of one Mark Twain" in the London World of that date; apparently the sketch is not listed in MT bibliographies. See also Brownell's "Who Was Frank Finlay?" in Twainian, IV (October, 1944), 1-6.

B56 _____. "Nuggets from Washoe," Saturday Review of Literature, XXX (July 12), 26.

A review of Effie Mona Mack, Mark Twain in Nevada. It gives useful background material on Orion Clemens and on Nevada people "thinly disguised in Roughing It," but the "captious" reader will find it rambling and repetitious, and sometimes lacking in realization of the central character himself."

B57 _____, ed. "The Love Letters of Mark Twain," Atlantic Monthly, CLXXX (November), 33-39; (December), 66-72 (series ends January, 1948).

Letters from MT to Olivia, beginning with their courtship; also includes a letter from MT, December 29, 1868 to his future father-in-law in response to a very plain-spoken letter: offers character references, concedes a rough life in the West but not a shameful one, and speaks of intention to live respectably. The letters appeared in book form in 1949.A2.

B58 _____, et al. "Dixon Wecter of Huntington Library Now Literary Editor of Clemens Estate," Twainian, VI (May-June), 4-5.

On the appointment of Wecter, the transfer of the Mark Twain collection from Harvard University to the Huntington Library, and brief discussion of the material; includes Wecter's appeal for the use of any MT letters or manuscripts readers may be able to provide.

B59 WILSON, EDMUND. [Review: Effie Mona Mack, Mark Twain in Nevada.] New Yorker, XXIII (June 7), 118.

Miss Mack has turned up a wealth of material to fill in "the rather sketchy picture" by MT of his life in Virginia City. "The weakest feature of Miss Mack's performance" is her inept paraphrasing of passages from RI, ruining their effect.

1948 A BOOKS

A1 *CLEMENS, SAMUEL L. Les Aventures d'Huckleberry Finn, traduit de l'américain par Suzanne Nétillard, préface de Jean Kanapa. Paris: Éditions d'Hier et d'Aujourd'hui.

(CLEMENS, SAMUEL L.)
[Source: Asselineau (1954), No. 1145, describing Kanapa's preface as "a communist interpretation of Mark Twain" which charges his bolder works are suppressed in America but that in Russia he is very popular and known for anti-imperialist views.]

A2   HARNSBERGER, CAROLINE THOMAS. Mark Twain at Your Fingertips. New York: Beechhurst Press.
Extracts from MT's published and unpublished writing, arranged alphabetically by topic from "Abroad to Ax" to "Yodeling to Youth," with a bibliography and indexes, and with a foreword by Clara Clemens. The MHRA Annual Bibliography (1946, No. 1800) cites a 1946 publication by Cloud, Inc., Chicago.

A3   SMALLEY, WEBSTER L. The Critical Reputation of Mark Twain in England: 1870-1910.
Unpublished Master's Thesis, Columbia University. The evaluations and the bibliography in this master's thesis have been of great value in locating material for the present bibliography.

A4   WECTER, DIXON, ed. Mark Twain in Three Moods: Three New Items of Twainiana. San Marino: Friends of the Huntington Library.
Previously unpublished material consisting of MT's description of Donner Lake and Lake Tahoe, his satiric description of a railroad subsidy for the Southern Pacific with the proviso that no Chinese labor be employed in the construction, and an account by Charles Erskine Scott Wood of MT's visiting and telling a story to explain why he hated babies; Wood was amused but his sister was not.

1948 B SHORTER WRITINGS

B1   ANON. "Twain Trustees Bring Suit to Halt Publication of Story," Publishers' Weekly, CLIII (January 17), 233.
A Murder, a Mystery, and a Marriage (1876) existed only as an unfinished manuscript, and "had never been intended for publication by Twain."

B2   ANON. "Owner of Mark Twain Manuscript Free to Publish Story," Publishers' Weekly, CLIII (January 24), 320.
"New York Supreme Court Justice Aron Steuer dismissed the suit brought by the trustees of the estate of Mark Twain to restrain publication of a hitherto unpublished story (Publishers' Weekly, January 17), the New York Times reported."

B3   *BECKER, MAY LAMBERTON. [Introduction.] The Prince and the Pauper. Cleveland: World Publishing Company.
[Source: Asselineau (1954), No. 1147; describes it as "a children's edition."]

B4   *BRODIN, PIERRE. Les Maîtres de la Littérature Américaine. Paris: Horizons de France.
[Source: Asselineau (1954), No. 1151: "On Mark Twain, pp. 267-306 and bibliography, pp. 472-480."]

B5   [BROWNELL, GEORGE HIRAM.] "'American Travel Letters, Series Two,' Fifth of Series in 'Alta California,'" Twainian, VII (January-February), 3-5.
The text of MT's letter dateline "Washington, Dec. 17th [1867]," on leaks of White House secrets to the press, and straight reporting of the doings of individuals of interest to western readers.

B6   _____ "'American Travel Letters, Series Two,' Sixth in Series in 'Alta California,'" Twainian, VII (March-April), 3-5.
Text of letter dateline "Washington, January 11th [1868]," describing a Dickens lecture in Steinway Hall, New York; MT found the delivery a disappointment. Brownell does not note the significance of MT's statement that "I am proud to observe that there was a beautiful young lady with me--a highly respectable young white woman"; this is Olivia Langdon, the future Mrs. Clemens, and apparently MT's first published mention of her.

B7   _____. "'American Travel Letters, Series Two,' Seventh in Series in 'Alta California,'" Twainian, VII (May-June), 3-5.
Dateline "Washington, January 16th [1868]," on Fernando Wood's speech in Congress, local gossip, and a reception by General Grant which MT later turned to comic account after Grant became President (See July-August, pp. 1-2).

B8   _____. "'American Travel Letters, Series Two,' Eighth in Series in 'Alta California,'" Twainian, VII (July-August), 3-4.
Dateline "Washington, January 12th, 1868," ordinary political and local reporting.

B9   _____. "'American Travel Letters, Series Two,' Ninth in Series in 'Alta California,'" Twainian, VII (September-October), 3-4.
Dateline "Washington, February 1st [1868]," describes girly shows on New York stage and a visit to Hartford.

B10   _____. "'American Travel Letters, Series Two,' Tenth In Series in 'Alta California,'" Twainian, VII (November-December), 5-7.
Dateline "Hartford, Conn., August, Recently, 1868," describes shipboard theatricals on a trip back east from California, praises Captain Ned Wakeman of the America, and gives a long and laudatory description of Hartford.

B11   _____. "Mark Found He Already Knew the Tricks of Professor Loisette's New Mnemonics," Twainian, VII (March-April), 1-3.

([BROWNELL, GEORGE HIRAM])

MT became so enthusiastic over a system for memorization that he wrote a testimonial, had it printed, and sent it to friends; Loisette used the testimonial in advertising until MT had second thoughts and suppressed it, and attempted to recall the copies he had mailed. The text is reproduced, together with that of a note to the Rev. John Davis, of Hannibal; at the end he expresses his regret over "that 'd'Unlap' cruelty" in "The Private History of a Campaign that Failed," adding, "I think John Robards deserved a lashing, but it should have come from an enemy, not a friend"; the statement refers to MT's ridicule of an imaginary Dunlap who changed his name to a more elegant form as Robards had to "Robards."

B12 _____. "Twain's Scrapbook Praised for Its Literary Excellence," Twainian, VII (July-August), 5-6.

Reprints "A New Book by Mark Twain," a tongue-in-cheek review of Mark Twain's Adhesive Scrap-Book in Scribner's Monthly for April, 1877; Brownell has found a statement by Robert Underwood Johnson in his Remembered Yesterdays (1923), confessing authorship of the review.

B13 _____. "Twain's Tale of the Washoe Miner at 'The Reception at the President's,'" Twainian, VII (July-August), 1-2.

A comic sketch, written for the Buffalo Express (October 1, 1870), and reprinted in the Galaxy of that month. See May-June, pp. 3-5.

B14 _____. "Unknown Twain Speech at Elmira in 1879," Twainian, VII (September-October), 5.

The text of MT's introduction of Gen. Joseph R. Hawley, who addressed a political rally in October; reprinted from an undated clipping from the Elmira Advertiser.

B15 _____. [Brief Note.] Twainian, VII (May-June), 6.

When MT's sketch, "Traveling with a Reformer," appeared in Cosmopolitan (December, 1893), an illustration by Dan Beard showed MT shaking hands with a man now identified as Fred J. Hall, who succeeded Webster as general manager of Charles L. Webster & Co.; his daughter owns the originals of this and the other Beard illustrations made for the tale.

B16 BRYNES, ASHER. "Boy-Men and Man-Boys," Yale Review, XXXVIII (Winter), 223-33.

On the accurate portrayal of boy-nature by MT and a few other American authors.

B17 CLEMENS, CYRIL. "Mark Twain's Story on the Siamese Twins,' Hobbies--the Magazine for Collectors, LIII (October), 139.

Anecdotal: "Some literalist" queried MT about the statement in Those Extraordinary Twins that "the ages of the Siamese Twins are respectively fifty-one and fifty-three years"; MT conceded that this statement was confusing and misleading: "What I meant to say was that the twins were born at the same time, but to different mothers."

B18 CLEMENS, SAMUEL L. "Ghost Life on the Mississippi: A Mark Twain Manuscript, with Foreword by Samuel C. Webster," Pacific Spectator, II (Autumn), 485-90.

The story of a steamboat taken through a difficult passage by the ghost of pilot William Jones; MT left it untitled. "The manuscript is in his handwriting and was probably left at the Moffett house when he went west to the territory of Nevada in 1861." Reprinted in Twainian, VIII (January-February, 1949), 1-2.

B19 _____. "Unpublished Twain Letter," Mark Twain Quarterly, VIII (Summer-Fall), 13.

Dated March 26, 1897, with a return address c/o Chatto and Windus in London, MT writes one "Frank" to introduce "My friend, Robert Chapin, late U. S. Consul at Johannesburg...a sterling man, but powerful quiet."

B20 COLEMAN, RUFUS A. "Trowbridge and Clemens," Modern Language Quarterly, IX (June), 216-23.

An anecdotal account of their meetings. Trowbridge, a popular poet in his time, "was critical of Clemens both as a speaker and as a writer, considering him diverting but prolix, and at times tiresome." Trowbridge was seated across the table from MT at the Whittier Birthday Dinner, but made no reference to MT's disastrous speech in his notebook, letters, or autobiography He also met MT at other public events.

B21 COWIE, ALEXANDER. "Mark Twain (1835-1910)," in his The Rise of the American Novel (New York: The American Book Company; reprinted 1951), pp. 599-652 (also, passim on MT; indexed).

A general study of MT's life and works, much of it descriptive, noting the critical fortunes of various books. Notes MT's active mind and lack of profundity, and stresses the value of his natural expression. Pp. 611-17 (on HF) reprinted in Lettis (1962), pp. 365-70.

B22 DELANEY, WESLEY A. "The Truth About That Humboldt Trip As Told by Gus Oliver to A. B. Paine," Twainian, VII (May-June), 1-3.

1948 - Shorter Writings

(DELANEY, WESLEY A.)
Judge A. W. Oliver, the "Oliphant" of RI and "The Uncomplaining Man" of IA (Ch. XXVII) adds another incident to the account in IA and describes MT, in a letter to Paine (April 24, 1910.)

B23 _____. "Twain's Last Visit to Bermuda Preceding the Final Days of His Life," Twainian, VII (January-February), 1-3.
On his visit to Bermuda in January, 1910, as a guest of Vice-Consul W. H. Allen; among the callers was Woodrow Wilson, with whom MT played miniature golf on the Allen lawn. Includes text of a letter to Allen from Paine (January 3, noting MT's mercurial temperament and the need to protect him) and extensive quotation from another (April 22, on MT's death and burial); also includes Joseph T. Goodman's letter to Paine (April 22) on hearing of MT's death.

B24 DUFFY, CHARLES. "Mark Twain Writes to Howells," Mark Twain Quarterly, VIII (Summer-Fall), 4.
Text of a letter from Hartford, February 27 (1874), on his distress over an inconvenient lecture engagement for March 5, in Boston.

B25 EIDSON, JOHN OLIN. "Innocents Abroad, Then and Now," Georgia Review, II (Summer), 186-92.
American soldiers in Europe ridicule what they cannot understand, just as MT did in Innocents Abroad.

B26 FEINSTEIN, GEORGE W. "Twain as Forerunner of Tooth-and-Claw Criticism," Modern Language Notes, LXIII (January), 49-50.
"Clearly Shaw, Mencken, DeVoto--Twainolaters all of them from their early formative years, by their own admission--and a horde of modern journalistic reviewers inherit, remotely or directly, something of Twain's flailing quality, his aggressive, epithetic line."

B27 FIEDLER, LESLIE. "Come Back to the Raft Ag'in, Huck Honey!" Partisan Review, XV (June), 664-71.
A general discussion of the Negro and homosexuality in American culture and literature, and only treating HF in passing; the title is not a quotation from HF. Reprinted in Fiedler's An End to Innocence (Boston: Beacon Press, 1952), pp. 142-51; The Collected Essays of Leslie Fiedler (New York: Stein and Day, 1971, 2 vols.), I, 142-51: Cardwell (1963), pp. 59-64.

B28 FLOWERS, FRANK C. "Mark Twain's Theories of Morality," Mark Twain Quarterly, VIII (Summer-Fall), 10.
Subtitled "Abstract," this appears to be the abstract of his 1941 doctoral dissertation for Louisiana State University, under the same title. What Is Man? illustrates

the principles and the didacticism prevalent in MT's works; but MT was not a pessimist.

B29 *GLOSTER, HUGH. Negro Voices in American Fiction, Chapel Hill, pp. 106-107.
[Source: Quoted in Gerald W. Haslam, "Huckleberry Finn: Why Read the Phelps Farm Episode?" Research Studies (Washington State University), XXXV (September), 191.] Gloster claims "that 'the foundations' of the present tendency to depict Negroes as human beings in literature 'were laid in the last quarter of the nineteenth century in the works of such writers as Albion Tourgee, G. W. Cable, and Mark Twain.'"

B30 HARNSBERGER, CAROLINE THOMAS. "Bernard Shaw Welcomes the Author of 'Mark Twain At Your Fingertips,'" Twainian, VII (November-December), 1-2.
Describes a trip to England, visit to Shaw, but says nothing interesting about MT except that his works were hard to find (as was all fiction, after the war).

B31 HART, JAMES D. [Review: Effie Mona Mack, Mark Twain in Nevada (1947).] American Literature, XIX (January), 379-80.
Dr. Mack is easily distracted from her subject and undiscriminating with sources. "Even when she senses a joke, she has an excruciating ability to ruin it. There is new information about MT and detailed social background material on RI, but "the picture that emerges is no different from that in Ivan Benson's crisper and more clearly conceived Mark Twain's Western Years."

B32 HOLLOWAY, T. E. "Mark Twain's Turning Point," Mark Twain Quarterly, VIII (Summer-Fall), 1-3.
Based on MT's own recollections, his book on Joan of Arc, and the Paine biography, discusses the Maid as his inspiration.

B33 HUTCHESON, AUSTIN E. "Twain Letter to Bob Howland Asks About Good Audience for Carson City Lecture," Twainian, VII (September-October), 1-2.
Contains the text of a brief note (October 29, 1866), as well as the text of MT's "Petrified Man" story, reprinted from George D. Lyman's The Saga of the Comstock Lode (1934).

B34 _____. "Twain Was 'News' to Other Newspapers While a Reporter on The 'Enterprise,'" Twainian, VII (November-December), 3-4.
On material relating to MT in Virginia City Evening Bulletin, still preserved in files at the University of Nevada (Reno) and elsewhere. Continued in Twainian, VIII (March-April, 1949), 2-3.

B35 HYMAN, STANLEY EDGAR. The Armed Vision: A Study in the Methods of Modern Literary Criticism. New York: Alfred A. Knopf, pp. 113-17, 123-25, and passim.

Discusses a number of major critics and their schools. Comments at some length on The Ordeal of Mark Twain, and accuses Brooks of overrating MT's potential and underestimating his achievements (pp. 57, 110, 113); nonetheless, it is in this work that Brooks is most successful in his biographical criticism. Notes many of the changes made in the revised edition after DeVoto's Mark Twain's America, which "itself is a stupid and ignorant book," but in regard to The Ordeal "more often right than wrong... an irritating but valuable corrective" (pp. 116-17). Hyman feels that Brooks's revisions showed "a new caution prepared to discard a good part of his thesis under attack. It is not a pretty picture" (p. 116).

B36 JACOBS, STANLEY S. "Mark Twain's Strangest Dream," Coronet, XXIV (June), 191.

Anecdote: premonition of his brother Henry's death in the explosion of the Pennsylvania.

B37 JONES, HOWARD MUMFORD. The Theory of American Literature. Ithaca, New York: Cornell University Press.

A collection of essays on literary history, with only passing references to MT-- generally in lists of authors discussed by literary historians.

B38 LEARY, LEWIS. "Doctoral Dissertations in American Literature, 1933-1948," American Literature, XX (May), 169-230.

Updates the Leisy and Hubbell listing in 1933.B21. For more recent dissertations, see the Selby listing and Dissertation Abstracts International.

B39 _____. [Review: Effie Mona Mack, Mark Twain in Nevada (1947).] South Atlantic Quarterly, XLVIII (April), 265-66.

Reflects careful scholarship and provides much useful background, but relies too heavily on Paine and RI and makes too little use of Ivan Benson's Mark Twain's Western Years. "Nevada is brilliantly there, but Mark Twain too often is not."

B40 _____. [Review: Dixon Wecter, ed., Mark Twain in Three Moods.] American Literature, XX (November), 362.

Descriptive and very brief.

B41 LILLARD, RICHARD D. [Review: Effie Mona Mack, Mark Twain in Nevada (1947).] Pacific Spectator, II (Autumn), 392.

Brief notice, merely that the book "uses Clemens' several years in Washoe as a frame for much background material."

B42 MANNING, CLARENCE A. [Review: M. Mendelson, Mark Twain (Moscow: Fskblksm Molodaya Gvardiya [Young Guard], 1939).] American Literature, XX (November), 358-59.

Lively and entertaining style, but a straight Marxist-Leninist approach; Mendelson sees MT censored by wife and friends, a serious critic of society treated as mere humorist.

B43 *MATTHEWS, BRANDER, and DIXON WECTER. [Introductions.] The Adventures of Huckleberry Finn. New York: Harper's.

[Source: Asselineau (1954), No. 1143; quotes Wecter's statement that "its real hero is Nigger Jim"--a striking realization for a later generation becoming aware of racial injustices.]

B44 McKEITHAN, DANIEL MORLEY. "A Letter from Mark Twain to Francis Henry Skrine in London," Modern Language Notes, LXIII (February), 134-35.

About Kipling's switch to approving conscription in the Boer War: "Why, why, why! has Kipling gone to satirizing Kipling?"

B45 _____. "More About Mark Twain's War With English Critics of America," Modern Language Notes, LXIII (April), 221-28.

Builds on Hoben's "superb article" on CY (1946), noting that MT had begun to show hostility toward British institutions in TA and P&P, as well as HF; agrees that "Hoben did well to point out that Twain was pro-English both at the beginning and at the end of his career." Reprinted in his Court Trials in Mark Twain and Other Essays (1958).

B46 _____. "The Occasion of Mark Twain's Speech 'On Foreign Critics,'" Philological Quarterly, XXVII (July), 276-79.

The immediate provocation was Matthew Arnold's essay, "Civilisation in the United States" (1888); MT mentioned by name Sir Henry Lepel Griffin, whose The Great Republic he may have read (Arnold's essay quoted some of its harsh words for America). Reprinted in his Court Trials in Mark Twain and Other Essays (1958).

B47 *MENDELSON, M. "Mark Twain Accuses," Soviet Literature, May, pp. 151-61. On MT's denunciation of American imperialism.

[Source: Asselineau (1954), No. 1183.]

B48 *NAOTARO, TATSUNOKUCHI. "Mark Twain's Views of American English," The Current English Press (November 1), p. 15.

[Source: MHRA Annual Bibliography (1948), No. 3421.]

B49 *RANKIN, J. W. [Introduction.] Life on the Mississippi. New York and London: Harper & Brothers (Harper's Modern Classics).

[Source: Asselineau (1954), No. 1146.]

1948 - Shorter Writings

B50 RUSSELL, LILLIS L. "Americanism as Typified
     by Mark Twain," Mark Twain Quarterly, VIII
     (Summer-Fall), 14.
          MT was truly American, and helped to shape
     and preserve our national character.

B51 SCHMITT, GLADYS. "Mark Twain Digs for Gold,"
     Scholastic, LII (May 10), 23-25.
          A radio play for high-school students;
     first appeared in Scholastic in 1937.

B52 SILLEN, SAMUEL. "Dooley, Twain and Imperial-
     ism," Masses & Mainstream, I (December),
     6-14.
          "It was the courage to oppose the aggres-
     sions of their own government that marked
     the anti-imperialist writers at the turn of
     the century, as it marked Thoreau and Emer-
     son in 1846, Randolph Bourne and John Reed
     in 1918."

B53 SPILLER, ROBERT, WILLARD THORP, THOMAS H.
     JOHNSON, and HENRY SEIDEL CANBY, eds.
     Literary History of the United States. New
     York: Macmillan.
          Now in revised edition combined in 1 vol-
     ume (1974), checked for present bibliogra-
     phy, containing Dixon Wecter, "Mark Twain"
     (pp. 917-39), a general biographical study;
     also, passim on MT (indexed). On
     pp. 1507-1508 there is "a reader's bibliog-
     raphy, and therefore highly selective." A
     separate bibliographical volume appeared in
     1963, containing primary and secondary MT
     bibliography pp. 446-50 and in a supple-
     ment, pp. 94-97. According to the "Preface
     to the Third Edition" (p.v.), "Except for
     a few corrections and the omission of the
     index, the 1948 volume is reprinted as it
     appeared originally. It is followed by the
     1959 Supplement, with its original Preface
     and no change in pagination," and a new,
     combined index. "Thomas H. Johnson under-
     took the principal work of compilation and
     editing of the original Bibliography and
     Richard M. Ludwig of the Supplement." Both
     the original bibliography and the supple-
     ment emphasize material available in the
     more familiar books and journals, and con-
     tain little or no secondary material not
     listed in the present bibliography; annota-
     tion is minimal.

B54 SQUIRES, J. RADCLIFFE. "Mark Twain," Accent,
     IX (Autumn) 32-3.
          A somewhat puzzling poem.

B55 *STONG, PHIL. "Mark Twain Cruise: Aboard a
     Modern River Boat, with Sam Clemens's
     Shade at the Wheel,"
          [Source: Asselineau (1954), No. 1187,
     listing publication as Holiday, V (April),
     56-62, 90, 92, 93, 95, 97. A check
     of Holiday reveals that Vol. V is 1949,
     and the article in question is not in the
     issue of April, 1948 or April, 1949--T.A.T.]

B56 TRILLING, LIONEL. "Introduction," The Adven-
     tures of Huckleberry Finn. New York: Rine-
     hart & Co., pp. v-xviii.
          "In form and style Huckleberry Finn is an
     almost perfect work"; even the ending,
     though weak and too long, is important as a
     way of returning Huck to his anonymity
     (pp. xv-xvi). Trilling takes from Eliot's
     "The Dry Salvages" (in Four Quartets) the
     notion of the river as a god, and "Huck
     himself is the servant of the river-god,"
     this "power which seems to have a mind and
     will of its own, and... appears to embody a
     great moral idea" (p. vii). Reprinted in
     Bradley (1962), pp. 310-20; Cardwell
     (1963), pp. 51-58; Lettis (1962), pp. 326-
     36; Marks (1959), pp. 44-52. Trilling pub-
     lished a somewhat revised version in The
     Liberal Imagination: Essays on Literature
     and Society (New York: The Viking Press,
     1950), pp. 104-17; reprinted in Scott (1955),
     pp. 272-78 and (1967), pp. 257-63.

B57 *VAN DOREN, CARL. [Introduction.] A Connecti-
     cut Yankee in King Arthur's Court. New
     York: Heritage Press.
          [Source: Asselineau (1954), No. 1148.]

B58 VOGELBACK, ARTHUR L. "Mark Twain: Newspaper
     Contributor," American Literature, XX (May),
     111-28.
          MT "was an incorrigible writer of letters
     to the press" on serious or trifling mat-
     ters. Letters to, and comments by the edi-
     tors of, a number of papers are discussed
     and quoted extensively.

B59 WEBSTER, SAMUEL MOFFETT. [Letter.] Twain-
     ian, VII (November-December), 4.
          MT felt he had slandered Injun Joe, who
     was liked, respected, and popular; also
     tells of MT's mother attending a play in
     St. Louis which had been declared immoral;
     she found it "all right, but not the sort
     of a play that a man should go to."

B60 WECTER, DIXON. "Clemens in the Ambrosial
     Isles," Saturday Review of Literature, XXXI
     (February 28), 18-19.
          A review of Frear, Mark Twain and Hawaii
     (1947). Wecter summarizes MT biographies,
     with passing reference to Paine's "four use-
     ful but sloppy volumes in 1912," Effie Mona
     Mack's "mediocre book on Mark Twain and Ne-
     vada," Webster's "delightful and documenta-
     ry" Mark Twain, Business Man, and DeVoto's
     "brilliant analysis of Mark Twain's devel-
     opment as an artist." The present monumen-
     tal study of a four-month period "makes
     most research in the field seem lax and un-
     critical by comparison," and is an "indis-
     pensable" addition to MT scholarship.

B61 _____, ed. "Mark Twain's Love Letters," At-
     lantic Monthly, CLXXXI (January), 83-88.

(WECTER, DIXON, ed.)
[Asselineau reports "excerpts to be found in Scholastic, vol. 51, 20, Jan. 19."] Letters from MT to his wife; completes a series beginning in 1947. They appeared in book form in 1949.A2.

B62 _____. "Mark Twain's River," Atlantic Monthly, CLXXXII (October), 45-47.
In 1947 Mr. and Mrs. Wecter went down the Mississippi on a tow-boat; passing references to MT.

B63 WEISINGER, MORT. "Listen! Mark Twain Speaking" (part of a weekly "Report to the Editors"), Saturday Evening Post, CCXX (July 3), 12.
On G. Robert Vincent's collection of recordings of famous individuals for "his unique Voice Library at Yale"; includes an MT recording, with "a voice curiously remindful of Jack Benny." [Twainian, VIII (March-April, 1949), 8, notes that the Edison film of MT and daughters at Stormfield is now at the MT Museum at Hannibal-- T.A.T.]

B64 *WILLIAMS, MENTOR L. "Mark Twain's Joan of Arc," Michigan Alumnus Quarterly Review, LIV (May 8), 243-50.
[Source: Asselineau (1954), No. 1193, MHRA Bibliography (1949), No. 3977; article reprinted in Twainian, IX (September-October, 1950), 1-4, 1950.B59.]

B65 *WILLIAMS, STANLEY T. Tres Escritores Clásicos de la Literatura de los Estados Unidos, translated by Filberto Gonzales. Mexico City: Instituto Mexicano-Norteamericano de Relaciones Culturales.
[Source: Asselineau (1954), No. 1156: "Contains the text of a lecture on Twain."]

B66 *WILSON, ROBERT H. "Malory in the Connecticut Yankee," Texas Studies in English, XXVII (June), 185-205.
On MT's faithful and clever use of the Morte d'Arthur in CY. [Source: Asselineau (1954), No. 1194; MHRA Annual Bibliography (1948), No. 330, 3429.]

B67 WORKMAN, MIMS THORNBURGH. "The Whitman-Twain Enigma," Mark Twain Quarterly, VIII (Summer-Fall), 12-13.
A search for references by Whitman to MT has been fruitless; possibly Whitman "was repelled by the genial cynicism."

1949 A BOOKS

A1 *CLEMENS, CYRIL. Mark Twain and Franklin D. Roosevelt. Webster Groves, Missouri: International Mark Twain Society.
A 20-page pamphlet, reprints the interview published in Tributes to Mark Twain (1930). [Source: Asselineau (1954), No. 1201.]

A2 CLEMENS, SAMUEL L. The Love Letters of Mark Twain, ed. Dixon Wecter. New York: Harper & Brothers.
MT's letters to Olivia, 1869-1903, supplemented by letters to other members of his family and to such friends as Joseph Twichell. In addition to being a tender record of his marriage, the letters cast important light on such topics as his writing and his lecturing. Includes a "List of Persons" to identify individuals mentioned in the text, and "Check List: Mark's Letters to Livy," including letters not printed here and providing synopses.

A3 _____. Mark Twain to Mrs. Fairbanks, ed. Dixon Wecter. San Marino, California: Huntington Library.
MT's letters to Mary Mason Fairbanks, whom he met on the Quaker City in 1867. She became his confidante and literary adviser [the extent to which he followed her advice has been questioned], and the letters are a source of information about his thoughts concerning IA, CY, and other works.

1949 B SHORTER WRITINGS

B1 ANON. "Pleasure Trip," Times Literary Supplement, November 18, p. 752.
A primarily descriptive review of Dixon Wecter, ed., Mark Twain to Mrs. Fairbanks. "These are charming letters, well arranged and lucidly annotated."

B2 ANON. "The Talk of the Town," New Yorker, XXIV (January 29), 15-16.
Regrets that the trustees of the MT estate have won a court order to prevent publication of "A Murder, a Mystery, and a Marriage"; speculation on a writer's motives in putting away a manuscript, coming to the conclusion that this one may be a poor thing but MT's "amiable, disappointed ghost" might have liked to see it published.

B3 ANON. "University of California to Get Mark Twain Papers," Publishers' Weekly, CLVI (December 3), 2281.
Brief announcement: the papers are being bequeathed to the University by Clara Clemens Samossoud.

B3A *BINGAY, MALCOLM W. Of Me I Sing. Indianapolis: Bobbs-Merrill.
[Source: Twainian, VIII (September-October, 1949), 5.] On friends at the Savage Club in London keeping a supply of bourbon for MT.

B4 BLANCK, JACOB. "More Shadowy Firsts," Antiquarian Bookman, IV (December 3), 1271-72.
On a newspaper said to have been published on the Quaker City and on MT's address to the Czar: it would be good to find copies of these.

1949 - Shorter Writings

B5   *BOMPIANI. Dizionario Bompiani delle Opere
e dei Personaggi di tutti tempi e di tutte
letterature. Milan: Bompiani.
        [Source: Asselineau (1954), No. 1207:
"Contains articles on Mark Twain's Works
in Vol. I, IV, VI, & VII."]

B6   [BROWNELL, GEORGE HIRAM.] "'American Travel
Letters Series Two,' Eleventh in Series in
Alta California," Twainian, VIII (January-
February), 3-6.
        Datelined "Hartford, October 22, 1868."

B7   _____. "'American Travel Letters Series Two,'
Twelfth in Series in Alta California,"
Twainian, VIII (March-April), 5-7.
        Datelined "Hartford, October 28th, 1868,"
mentions IA as "ready for the engravers and
electrotypers at last."

B8   _____. "'American Travel Letters Series Two,'
Thirteenth in Series in Alta California,"
Twainian, VIII (May-June), 3-6.
        Datelined "New York, July, 1869," on a
visit to Boston as guest of "Petroleum V.
Nasby" (David Ross Locke).

B9   _____. "'American Travel Letters Series Two,'
Final (14th) in Series in Alta California,"
Twainian, VIII (July-August), 3-6.
        Includes comments on the Overland Monthly
and speculation about aviation and space-
travel.

B10 _____. "Cyril Clemens Announces He'll Publish the 'Official Letters of Mark Twain,'"
Twainian, VIII (March-April), 3-5.
        Quotes correspondence in The Nation
(January 22, 26, February 19) and New York
Times (February 13, with a reply scheduled
for the New York Times Book Review of
March 20). Stating that "I am universally
considered the greatest living authority on
Mark Twain," Cyril Clemens requested copies
of Mark Twain letters for an official edition; Thomas G. Chamberlain, co-trustee of
the MT estate (with the Central Hanover
Bank and Trust Company of New York) replied
that no letters could be published without
the permission of MT's daughter, Mrs. Clara
Clemens Samossoud, asked that copies of
letters be sent to the Huntington Library
in California, and then sent a letter dated
March 21 "to every important daily newspaper throughout the country...as a means of
heading off further publication of the Cyril
letter." Brownell ridicules the claims by
Cyril Clemens, adding that "As a final instance of the ghastly and almost unbeliev-
able dearth of any sense of propriety with
which Cyril is endowed, I give you: In a
recent number of his publication, The Mark
Twain Quarterly, the name of 'Clara Clemens' appears on the list of 'Honorary Members' of the International Mark Twain Soci-
ety--and there's no law that will compel
Cyril to remove that name from the list."

The following issue (May-June, p. 6) cites
a clipping from the St. Louis Globe-Democrat
of April 26 reporting that the MT estate has
requested a restraining order against Cyril
Clemens.

B11 _____. "Much Mystery Still Surrounds Twain
Tale of 'Carson Footprints,'" Twainian,
VIII (May-June), 1-3.
        Speculation on MT's reasons for contribut-
ing the tale (here reprinted) in the Sacramento Record-Union of March 25, 1885.

B12 _____. "This Tale Looks Like a Sample of
Mark Twain's Work as His Own Press Agent,"
Twainian, VIII (September-October), 3-4.
        Text of a photostat of Harry Hazel's Yan-
kee Blade (week ending February 23, 1878),
sent by Frank C. Willson: an MT interview
(supposedly reprinted from New York Sun)
touches on the Whittier birthday dinner
speech and the patent scrap-book. Brownell
suggests the interview may be MT's own work.

B13 _____. "Twain's Letters in San Francisco Call
While a Reporter on the Enterprise," Twainian, VIII (September-October), 1-2.
        Datelined "Virginia City, N.T., July 5,
1863." On mines, shootings, politics;
twelve letters listed by dates. Fuller details on the content of one letter given in
the November-December issue, p. 6. Another
letter appears in Twainian, IX (March-April,
1950), 3-4.

B14 _____. "Twain's Tale in 'The Bazaar Record'
Based on Actual Heroic Rescue at Sea,"
Twainian, VIII (November-December), 1-5,
(6).
        Text of MT letter to the Royal Humane So-
ciety (November 19, 1872) and memorial to
Captain Mouland of the Cunard steamship
Batavia. See Storkan article (1949.B43) for
details of publication.

B15 _____. [Appeal for help in locating a brief
MT item, "Soundings," which appeared in
Chicago Republican (May 30, 1869).] Twain-
ian, VIII (September-October), 5.

B16 _____. [Introduction to a brief note from MT
to Adolph Sutro.] Twainian, VIII (March-
April), 8.

B17 CARPENTER, EDWIN H., JR. "Mining Methods in
Catgut Cãnon," Pacific Historical Review,
XVIII (February), 109-11. Reprints with
minimal comment two clippings from the New
York Evening Post of September 14, 17,
1880.
        The first, "Gold in Solution," is a news
story about one A. C. Tichenor, who supposedly developed a process for extracting gold
from the springs at a California health re-
sort; "Millions in It" follows, a comic letter by MT who claims to have owned the
springs in the past: "I should have held on

(CARPENTER, EDWIN H., JR.)
to those springs but for the badness of the roads and the difficulty of getting the gold to market."

B18   CHAMBERLAIN, THOMAS G. "Mark Twain's Trustees," Nation, CLXVIII (February 19), 224.
Calls the letter from Cyril Clemens in the January 22 issue "false and misleading in that the official collection of the Mark Twain letters is in the Huntington Library in San Marino, California" [later moved to Bancroft Library, University of California, Berkeley--T.A.T.]. He asks that any MT letters found be sent there, and not to Cyril Clemens.

B19   CLEMENS, CYRIL. "Harry S. Truman: Mark Twain Enthusiast," Dalhousie Review, XXIX (July), 198-99.
General statements on MT's wholesomeness and vigor by Truman, who said he had read all of MT's works he could find.

B20   _____. "Margaret Mitchell and Mark Twain," Hobbies--the Magazine for Collectors, LV (October), 140.
Chiefly on Margaret Mitchell, who died August 16; reprints a letter from her (June 23, 1942) to Cyril Clemens, declining his invitation to speak at the Mark Twain Birthday Banquet but praising the "very great American."

B21   _____. [Brief letter to editor.] Nation, CLXVIII (January 22), 113.
"I am editing the official collection of Mark Twain letters, and will be happy to hear from all who have Twain letters in their possession or know of their whereabouts."

B22   _____. "Mark Twain's Kinsman," Nation, CLXVIII (February 19), 224-25.
"I am universally considered the greatest living authority on Mark Twain.... I am editing the only official collection of Mark Twain's letters, and every important journal throughout the world is being officially notified. The response has been most gratifying."

B23   _____. "Mark Twain's Opinion of the Human Body," Hobbies--the Magazine for Collectors, LIV (April), 140.
A set of undocumented quotations from MT on inadequacies of the human body, printed without editorial comment.

B24   _____. "The President: Mark Twain Enthusiast," Hobbies--the Magazine for Collectors, LIV (May), 139.
Quotes Harry S. Truman's praise of MT in speeches and letters.

B25   CLEMENS, SAMUEL L. "My Methods of Writing," Mark Twain Quarterly, VIII (Winter-Spring), 1.
A letter to an unidentified clergyman, datelined "Hartford, Oct. 15, '88," comments on style, concluding: "Doubtless I have methods, but they beget themselves; in which case I am only their proprietor, not their father."

B26   DICKINSON, LEON T. "The Sources of The Prince and the Pauper," Modern Language Notes, LXIV (February), 103-106.
The sources include J. Hammond Trumbull's The True Blue Laws of Connecticut and Richard Head and Francis Kirkman's The English Rogue. MT was careful with his sources and documentation to make clear his serious purpose: "So anxious was he for the book to be taken seriously, that he considered publishing it anonymously."

B27   FERGUSON, DELANCEY. "'Mother' to Mark Twain," New York Herald Tribune Weekly Book Review, XXV (August 14), 11.
A review of Dixon Wecter, ed., Mark Twain to Mrs. Fairbanks. "With the exception of the correspondence with William Dean Howells, this is the most revealing series of letters to any one outside the humorist's own family which has yet been published.... To all this varied record Dixon Wecter has added commentary and elucidation which make the book a little masterpiece of humane scholarship."

B28   _____. [Review: Dixon Wecter, ed., The Love Letters of Mark Twain.] New York Herald Tribune Book Review, XXVI (November 27), 1, 25.
"The husband changed the wife far more than she changed him."

B29   HALSBAND, ROBERT. "Clemens and His 'Other Mother,'" Saturday Review of Literature, XXXII (October 22), 17.
A review of Dixon Wecter, ed., Mark Twain to Mrs. Fairbanks. MT's readiness to accept Mrs. Fairbanks' recommendations undercuts the contention by Brooks that censorship by Mrs. Clemens damaged MT's work. The letters reveal "how seriously he took the problems of his craft," and "Mr. Wecter's editing is in all ways a superb job."

B30   HINKLE, GEORGE, and BLISS HINKLE. Sierra Nevada Lakes. Indianapolis and New York: Bobbs-Merrill Company.
Passim on MT and his brother Orion ("Acting Governor" of Nevada Territory, pp. 208-209); indexed.

B31   HORNBERGER, THEODORE. [Review: Dixon Wecter, ed., Mark Twain to Mrs. Fairbanks.] American Quarterly, I (Winter), 378-80.

(HORNBERGER, THEODORE)
Although Wecter rightly points out that MT was his own censor, there is evidence between the lines to support the contention by Van Wyck Brooks that Olivia Clemens tamed and diminished him. These letters show much of MT's character, though not its full exuberance, and "Mr. Wecter's editing is painstaking but restrained."

B32 HUTCHESON, AUSTIN E. "Twain Was 'News' to Other Newspapers while a Reporter on the 'Enterprise,'" Twainian, VIII (March-April), 2-3.
Continues the reprinting of comments on MT from Nevada newspapers (See Twainian, VII, November-December, 1948, 3-4): the Virginia City Bulletin on MT's "first public lecture with charged admission" (delivered January 28, 1864, his address to the "Third House" of the territorial legislature); Gold Hill Daily News on Sanitary Fund controversy and MT hoaxes.

B33 *KANAPA, JEAN. "Mark Twain, Premier Classique de l'Amérique," Lettres Françaises, January 6.
[Source: Asselineau (1954), No. 1221.]

B34 KOHT, HALVDAN. The American Spirit in Europe: A Survey of Transatlantic Influences. Philadelphia: University of Pennsylvania Press, pp. 226-28.
Cursory and impressionistic, citing only Chesterton [who did not understand MT] and Howells. Conclusion: MT was popular in Europe and an influence for freedom.

B35 LEISY, ERNEST E. [Review: Walter Francis Frear, Mark Twain and Hawaii (1947).] American Literature, XXI (May), 251-52.
Primarily a description of the material, its publishing history, and biographical significance, noting that previous editions of MT's Sacramento Union letters were inadequate. "The late Governor Frear's legal training and bibliographic contacts enabled him to supply information not available to Paine...nor to Dane. He tells for the first time the complete story of Twain's visit to Hawaii. Particularly useful are the list of Mark's lectures on the Islands and the corrections of inadequate reporting."

B36 LONG, E. HUDSON. "Sut Lovingood and Mark Twain's Joan of Arc," Modern Language Notes, LXIV (January), 37-39.
On the story of a bull-ride in George Washington Harris's "Sicily Burns's Wedding" as a source for a similar incident in JA.

B37 LORCH, FRED W. "'Doesticks' and Innocents Abroad," American Literature, XX (January), 446-49.
Two letters to MT from Mortimer Neal Thomson, a popular humorous writer who used the pseudonym "Doesticks." The letters,

dated October 21 and November 5, 1870, "reveal that Mark Twain had conceived the idea of making a book of his Quaker City letters to the Alta California prior to his departure," and correct Paine's statement (Mark Twain, I, 349) that he "was not immediately interested in book publication."

B38 *McKEITHAN, DANIEL MORLEY. "Mark Twain's Tom Sawyer Abroad and Jules Verne's Five Weeks in a Balloon," Texas Studies in English, XXVIII, 257-70.
[Source: MHRA Annual Bibliography (1949), No. 337.] Reprinted in his Court Trials in Mark Twain and Other Essays (1958).

B39 ODELL, GEORGE C. D. Annals of the New York Stage. New York: Columbia University Press, Vol. XV (1891-1894).
The play based on TS was performed at the Harlem Theatre, February 22-27, 1892 (p. 83). February 26, 27 MT and James Whitcomb Riley read from their works at Madison Square Garden Concert Hall; Odell asks, "Why did Mark Twain thus occasionally exploit himself?" (p. 762).

B40 PETERSEN, SVEND. "Splendid Days and Fearsome Nights," Mark Twain Quarterly, VIII (Winter-Spring), 3-8, 15.
Following the mock-scholarship on the Sherlock Holmes stories, Petersen investigates MT's handling of "the details of time," to which his work is "amazingly faithful," despite a few errors. As an example of his dating, he shows that the murder of Muff Potter in Tom Sawyer is given as having happened on June 17 (Chapter XXIII), which fell on a Monday (Chapters VI-IX); thus, the story took place in 1839, 1844, or 1850, and other evidence of this sort reveals the year of the story as 1844.

B41 *POCHMANN, HENRY A., and GAY WILSON ALLEN. Masters of American Literature. New York: Macmillan. 2 vol.
[Source: Asselineau (1954), No. 1206, listing "in Vol. 2, pp. 436-441, an excellent introduction to Mark Twain and a selected bibliography," with extracts from his works, pp. 441-78.] Pochmann and Allen's introductions were reprinted separately in 1969 as Introduction to Masters of American Literature, See 1969.B58.

B42 SLATER, JOSEPH. "Music at Colonel Grangerford's: A Footnote to Huckleberry Finn," American Literature, XXI (March), 108-11.
Huck's reference in Chapter XVII to the piano "that had tin pans in it" is not comic exaggeration: there were such pianos at the time. "When the Last Link Is Broken" and "The Battle of Prague" would have been appropriate selections to play.

B43 STORKAN, CHARLES J. "That Tall Twain Tale, 'A Storm at Sea,' at Last Traced to It's [sic] Printed Origin," Twainian, VIII (July-August), 1-2.

(STORKAN, CHARLES J.)
Originally published in The Bazaar Record, an ephemeral Cleveland paper (January, 1876, contributed as a favor to Mary Mason Fairbanks); a postscript by George Hiram Brownell lists reprintings in the Troy (N.Y.) Budget, March 6, 1876, and the San Francisco Alta California, April 9, 1876. Also See Twainian for September-October, pp. 5, 6 for two notes: this account is related to the Batavia rescue; the manuscript was sold at auction in 1936. Also See Twainian, VIII (November December), 1-5 for the original on which this account is based.

B44 *THOMPSON, RALPH. "In and Out of Books" column, New York Times Book Review, n.d.
[Source: Quoted in Twainian, VIII (September-October), 5.] In their love for MT the Savage Club (London) imported six cases of Kentucky bourbon; years after his death, says Malcolm W. Bingay, the cases were still there, neatly labeled with his name.

B45 WALSH, ELIZABETH P. "A Connecticut Yankee of Our Lady's Court," Catholic World, CLXIX (May), 91-97.
This article, listed in a number of MT bibliographies, does not mention him. "This is an account of the life and work of William Thomas Walsh" (her father), whose writing appeared in Catholic World for twenty-three years.

B46 WEBSTER, ANNIE (MRS. CHARLES L.); dictated to Doris (Mrs. Samuel C.) Webster. "Recollections of the Clemens Family in St. Louis when Sam was a River Pilot," Twainian, VIII (March-April), 1-2.
These recollections by MT's niece (born 1852) deal mainly with St. Louis neighbors and mention MT only in passing.

B47 WEBSTER, SAMUEL C. "Unknown Ghost Story by Twain found by Samuel C. Webster in Old Family Papers," Twainian, VIII (January-February), 1-2.
The text of "Ghost Life on the Mississippi" (about the ghost of a pilot taking a steamboat through a difficult channel at night): the Webster introduction describes MT as a story-teller and notes the popularity of ghost stories in Missouri.

B48 WEST, RAY B., JR. "Mark Twain's Idyl of Frontier America," University of Kansas City Review, XV (Winter), 92-104.
Argues MT's enduring affection for the regions of his youth: "he could damn the whole human race in theoretical terms; but the background of the country and the life he had known as a boy was always treated with nostalgia and sympathy.... Life in the Mississippi River Valley and the Far West represented for him an idyllic existence which could be treated humorously, but not with personal rancour."

B49 WILLIAMSON, SAMUEL T. "Mark's Letters to His Livy," New York Times Book Review (November 13), p. 53.
A review of Dixon Wecter, ed., The Love Letters of Mark Twain, which are interesting in four ways: as love letters, as fuel for additional debate in the tradition of Brooks and DeVoto, as the portrait of a marriage, and for what they show of "the unrealness of a realistic writer' in his very ordinary, moving response to love, death, and grief.

1950 A BOOKS

A1 ADAMS, LUCILLE. "Huckleberry Finn": A Descriptive Bibliography of the Huckleberry Finn Collection at the Buffalo Public Library. Buffalo, N.Y.: Buffalo Public Library.
"Today the Buffalo Public Library has an unusual Collection. Aside from the Manuscript, a California Salesman's Prospectus, and several U. S. first editions revealing some of the variances in the printing, it contains a number of other editions, including editions in thirteen foreign languages. The related items range from a Metro-Goldwyn-Mayer movie script, three act plays, and music, to comic and paint books for the children. There is also critical and bibliographical material". (p. 5). [There is nothing previously unknown in this critical and bibliographical material-- T.A.T.]

A2 ANDREWS, KENNETH. Nook Farm: Mark Twain's Hartford Circle. Cambridge, Massachusetts: Harvard University Press.
A carefully documented description of the immediate community in which MT lived, showing the intellectual stimulation and also the soul-searchings.

A3 BELLAMY, GLADYS CARMEN. Mark Twain as a Literary Artist. Norman: University of Oklahoma Press.
Emphasizes MT's conscious craftsmanship: torn by mental conflict, he achieved artistic distance and control by use of the Huck Finn persona, placing satiric scenes far off in time or space, reducing the race to microscopic proportions, or regarding life as a dream. There is substantial discussion of the travel books. Pp. 25-40 reprinted in Leary (1962), pp. 207-24; pp. 335-47, on HF, reprinted in Lettis (1962), pp. 338-48.

A4 BRANCH, EDGAR MARQUESS. The Literary Apprenticeship of Mark Twain. With Selections from His Apprentice Writing. Urbana: University of Illinois Press.
Primarily concerned with MT's literary career from the beginnings to the Quaker City excursion (1867), but concluding with "Apprentice and Artist: Huckleberry Finn" (pp. 195-216). Accepts the "Quintus Curtius Snodgress" letters as MT's (pp. 47-56).

(BRANCH, EDGAR MARQUESS)
[Reprinted in facsimile with new title page, New York: Russell & Russell, 1966.]

A5   CLEMENS, CYRIL, ed. Mark Twain and Harry S. Truman, foreword by the Honorable Louis Johnson, Secretary of Defense. Webster Groves, Missouri: The International Mark Twain Society.
"Number eighteen of the society's biographical Series." Describes appreciation of MT by President Truman, who professes to have read the collected works by the age of twelve. (16-page pamphlet, containing brief notes from Truman).

A6   *EMRICH, DUNCAN. Comstock Bonanza: Rare Western Gallery of Mark Twain, Bret Harte, Sam Davis, James W. Gally, Dan de Quille, Joseph T. Goodman, J. Ross Browne, Fred Hart. New York: Vanguard Press.
[Source: Asselineau (1954), No. 1236; In card catalogue at Oakland (California) Public Library, but not on shelf.]

A7   *FAUST, CLARENCE L., ed. The Adventures of Huckleberry Finn. N.p.: Great Books Foundation.
[Source: Beebe and Feaster (1968), p. 113.]

A8   *HORNSTEIN, SIMON. Mark Twain: La Faillite d'un Idéal. Paris: Renée Lacoste & Cie.
[Source: Asselineau (1954), No. 1233.]
Following Brooks, an adequate, well-documented general study of MT's works, with an attempt to explain why he is not popular in France; includes bibliography of French translations and adaptations.

1950 B SHORTER WRITINGS

B1   ALTKUS, MARY. "Comet of Destiny," Coronet, XXVIII (August), 159.
Brief, popular account of MT's loss of his wife, and his belief that he could not join her until the return of Halley's Comet, which had been in the sky when he was born; his prediction was correct.

B2   ANON. "The Boy and the River," Times Literary Supplement, November 10, p. 708.
A review of the Cresset Press edition of HF with a ten-page introduction by T. S. Eliot. Sees Eliot as being at a disadvantage, having read TS and HF only as an adult and consequently unable to assess MT's achievements, including "his ability to write, simultaneously and in the same book, both as the boy of 30 or 40 years ago and as the mature man looking back on the same event." Questions the conventional account of the version of the origin of MT's pseudonym: "It is dubious as the word 'twain' was not used in counting at that time and place."

B3   ANON, as "Your Reviewer." "The Boy and the River," Times Literary Supplement, November 24, p. 747.
A letter to the editor, accepting one correction in Marcus Cunliffe's letter of November 17 (1950.B17) but holding his ground on three other points, including his statement that the leadsman's call "mark twain" was not in use when MT was a pilot. In another letter (December 8, p. 785), cites his own experience as a leadsman in European waters in support of his reservations about the assumption "that 'mark' meant a fathom, and that 'twain' meant two." [Also see Schofield letter, p. 785.]

B4   ANON. [Review: Edgar Marquess Branch, The Literary Apprenticeship of Mark Twain.] Nineteenth-Century Fiction, V (December), 247-48.
"The chief virtue of the compilation is the effective way in which the author has brought together the results of the many specialized regional studies of the past fifteen years," although "it is odd...that in the mountain of notes there should be no mention of Effie Mona Mack's Mark Twain in Nevada (1947)."

B5   ARMSTRONG, C. J. "Rev. Armstrong Reminisces on Twain's Loyalty to His Old Hannibal Friends," Twainian, IX (January-February), 1-2.
Anecdotes; asserts that John L. RoBards bore MT no ill-will for joking about his name in "The Private History of a Campaign that Failed."

B6   BLANCK, JACOB. "In Re Huckleberry Finn," New Colophon, III, pp. 153-59.
A collation of the first edition; praises Merle Johnson's "superb" description in his 1935 Bibliography of the Works of Mark Twain as "a brilliant beacon in a cloud of Underhillian fog"; Irving S. Underhill's "An Inquiry into Huckleberry Finn" (1931) and "The Haunted Book" (1935) should not have been accepted by the old Colophon: "the bibliographical problem of Huckleberry Finn was rendered an appalling disservice by their publication." Includes reproductions of "Original State of Cut on p. 283," "Corrected (Third) State of Cut," and of E. W. Kemble's note explaining the damage to Uncle Silas's trousers ("a bit of vulgarity inserted by an engraver") and "Handbill issued by Mark Twain's western agents."

B7   BOOTH, BRADFORD A. "Mark Twain's Comments on Holmes's Autocrat," American Literature, XXI (January), 456-63.
Contains 45 comments MT wrote in the margin for Livy to read while they were courting (pp. 459-63). MT liked Holmes and enjoyed his books, but Booth is cautious about suggesting the development of MT's style after Innocents Abroad could indicate influence.

B8   BRANCH, EDGAR M. "The Two Providences: Thematic Form in 'Huckleberry Finn,'" College
English, XI (January), 188-95.
     Miss Watson and the Widow Douglas offer
contrasting conceptions of heavenly providence. From these, there follows a choice
between conventional morality and humani-
tarian idealism; the duality is implicit in
the style of the novel, and provides thematic unity. Reprinted in Gerber (1971),
pp. 67-77.

B9   [BROWNELL, GEORGE HIRAM.] "Sam Webster Adds
to the Mystery of that Cut on Page 283 of
'Huck Finn,'" Twainian, IX (January-February), 2-3.
     Quotes a letter from Samuel Charles
Webster, who says he has a proof of p. 283
showing the indecent cut; also reprints the
text of a letter from MT to his brother
Orion on General Grant's confidence in
Charles L. Webster.

B10 ____. "Twain's Letter in San Francisco Call
while a Reporter on The Enterprise," Twainian, IX (March-April), 3-4.
     Datelined "Virginia City, N. T., July 12,
1863," miscellaneous local news on mines,
horse races, a petrified man hoax, and the
upcoming performance of "that sickest of
all sentimental dramas, 'East Lynne.'"
Another of these letters and a list of the
whole series appear in Twainian VIII
(November-December, 1949), 1-2.

B11 ____. "Who Knows about these Ghostly Twain
Firsts," Twainian, IX (January-February),
3-4.
     On Jacob Blanck's "More Shadowy Firsts,"
Antiquarian Bookman (December 3, 1949), inquiring about the newspaper supposedly published on board the Quaker City. Brownell
adds a query as to whether the text of
MT's address to the Russian Czar has been
preserved.

B12 *CAHEN, JACQUES FERNAND. [On MT., pp. 42-47]
in his La Littérature Américaine. Paris:
Presses Universitaires (Collection Que
Sais-Je?).
     [Source: Asselineau (1954), No. 1237.]
Condemns his tastelessness, praises him as
first American realist in LOM, TS, HF.

B13 CLEMENS, CYRIL. "Collecting Mark Twain,
Eugene Field, and Harry Truman," Hobbies--
the Magazine for Collectors, LV (November),
141.
     On his collection; MT material includes
letters from MT to Cyril Clemens's parents,
"part of the manuscript of The Gilded Age,"
"a group of twelve letters which he wrote
in 1886 to several young friends whom he
had met during a vacation," a letter in half
English, half German to the Austrian dramatist Schlesinger, and other letters and
documents pertaining to MT.

B14 ____. "Hervey Allen and Mark Twain," Hob-
bies--the Magazine for Collectors, LV
(April), 120.
     On the life and works of Hervey Allen,
who died December 28, 1949; notes his admiration of MT and quotes letters from him,
praising MT, declining an invitation to
speak, and thanking Cyril Clemens for election as a "Knight of Mark Twain."

B15 ____. "Recent Acquisitions of Mark Twain
Library," Mark Twain Quarterly, VIII (Win-
ter), 19.
     Included are three pages of manuscript of
The Gilded Age in MT's hand and eight in
Charles Dudley Warner's, a note from MT to
Warner, some copies of MT's works in Polish,
French, and Turkish, and a sheet describing
a mock trial of MT on a North German Lloyd
liner, with his inscription on the back:
"A true bill, Mark Twain."

B16 ____. "Shaw and Twain," Christian Science
Monitor, XLIII (December 5), 18.
     A letter to the editor, repeating what he
was said elsewhere about meetings of MT and
Shaw.

B17 CUNLIFFE, MARCUS. "The Boy and the River,"
Times Literary Supplement, November 17,
p. 727.
     A letter to the editor. The November 10
review of T. S. Eliot's introduction to HF
contains [minor] "slips and errors of emphasis" pertaining to MT's life and the
origin of his pseudonym. Defends his position concerning the pseudonym in another
letter, December 8, p. 785. [Also See
Schofield letter, p. 785 (1950.B47).]

B18 [DAVIS, CHESTER L.] "Mark Twain and President Hayes," Twainian, IX (November-December), 2-3.
     Letters from MT to Charles Warren Stoddard
(September 20, 1876) and William Dean Howells (February 22, 1877) mentioning Hayes,
and to Hayes (April 10, 1882), answering his
letter of April 6. Contains minimal editorial comment.

B19 ____. "Tom Sawyer Manuscript Purchased by
Missouri," Twainian, IX (July-August), 1-2.
     "The State of Missouri has recently com-
pleted a contract...for the purchase of the
manuscript from which the English edition of
Tom Sawyer was printed.... The main criticism of the manuscript is that it is not all
in the hand of Mark Twain, most of the pages
being in the hands of one or more copyists."

B20 ____. [Transitional Issue.] Twainian (May-
June).
     Announces the death of George Hiram Brown-
ell. Chester L. Davis, an attorney, is re-
placing Brownell as the Secretary of the Mark
Twain Research Association, thanks Clara
Clemens Samossoud for her financial support

([DAVIS, CHESTER L.])
of The Twainian, discusses future editorial
policy and promises confidentiality of the
files of correspondence. There is a brief,
descriptive notice of Gladys Carmen Bellamy's Mark Twain as a Literary Artist.

B21 DECAUNES, LUC. [Review: Un Yankee à la Cour
du Roi Arthur, traduction d'Odette Ferry
et J. de Plunkett. Paris, Bruxelles,
Éditions de la Paix, 332 pp.] Paru, No. 62
(Juillet), p. 68.
Calls the novel vulgar and boring.

B22 DICKINSON, LEON T. [Review: Dixon Wecter, ed.,
Mark Twain to Mrs. Fairbanks (1949).] American Literature, XXII (May), 202-203.
Praises Wecter's editing, and in particular his including letters by other people
as a supplement to MT's. The editing adds
to the biographical significance of this
book. "And although he does not care to re-
open the question of the female-dominated
Clemens, it is clear that he believes Mrs.
Fairbanks's influence to have been for the
best, as it probably was."

B23 EDWARDS, PETER G. "The Political Economy of
Mark Twain's 'Connecticut Yankee,'" Mark
Twain Quarterly, VIII (Winter), 2, 18.
Dowley, the blacksmith in Chapter XXXIII,
could not understand that an increase in income is valuable only if prices do not rise
correspondingly, and Americans today make
the same mistake. Edwards concludes by
grumbling that "right now I'm going to go
out and buy a steak for $1.10 that would
have cost 40 cents before the war."

B24 ELIOT, T. S. [Introduction.] The Adventures
of Huckleberry Finn. New York: Chanti-
cleer Press.
"In the writing of Huckleberry Finn Mark
Twain had two elements which, when treated
with his sensibility and his experience,
formed a great book: these two are the Boy
and the River.... We come to understand the
River by seeing it through the eyes of the
Boy; but the Boy is also the spirit of the
River." Also praises the colloquial ease of
Huck's diction. Reprinted in Bradley
(1962), pp. 320-27; in Simpson (1968, condensed), pp. 107-108; in Kesterson (1973),
pp. 62-69.

B25 *ENGLEKIRK, JOHN E. A Literatura Norteameri-
cano no Brasil. Privately printed in Mexico.
Distributed by Author (Tulane University).
[Source: Asselineau (1954), No. 1229*:
discusses Brazilian interest in MT, and
(presumably) lists translations of his works.]

B26 FATOUT, PAUL. "Mark Twain Lectures in Indiana," Indiana Magazine of History, XLVI
(December), 363-67.
On MT's lectures in Indianapolis and Lo-
gansport in January, 1872; documented from
contemporary newspaper accounts, some of them
unfavorable.

B27 FERGUSON, DELANCEY. [Review: Gladys Carmen
Bellamy, Mark Twain as a Literary Artist.]
New York Herald Tribune Book Review, XXVI
(August 13), 6.
Primarily descriptive, but says "Miss
Bellamy has not just written a new volume
about the humorist; she has done some new
thinking about him."

B28 _____. [Review: Edgar Marquess Branch, The
Literary Apprenticeship of Mark Twain.]
American Literature, XXII (November), 362-63.
More important as sound and detailed criticism than as biography, in which Branch is
too ready to accept Paine and the western
folklore about MT. "His criticism, which in
the major portion of the book seems too
detailed for the very slender merits of the
writing it is applied to, reaches a high
level in the closing section" with analysis
of the thematic structure of Huckleberry
Finn.

B29 _____. [Review: Dixon Wecter, ed., Mark
Twain to Mrs. Fairbanks (1949).] Modern
Language Notes, LXV (December), 568-69.
"Dixon Wecter is admirably carrying on the
work, begun by DeVoto, of bringing order out
of the chaos in which Albert Bigelow Paine
left the Mark Twain MSS, and of revealing
the biographical significance which Paine
was too indolent or too obtuse to understand."
The present volume is an indispensable companion to Mr. Wecter's edition of The Love
Letters of Mark Twain: "From now on, all
studies of Mark Twain's personality, and
therefore of his art and ideas, will have to
start from these two books."

B30 FRANCIS, RAYMOND L. "Mark Twain and H. L.
Mencken," Prairie Schooner, XXIV (Spring),
31-39.
As satirist and iconoclast, "Mencken is a
direct descendant of Mark Twain"; although
the two differed in their attitudes toward
democracy, they came from different directions
to a similar view of national institutions
and the ignorance of mobs. There are similarities in their targets and their forms of
statement.

B31 GEISMAR, MAXWELL. "High Thinking, Fine Living," New York Times Book Review, (October 8),
p. 5.
A review of Kenneth R. Andrews, Nook Farm:
Mark Twain's Hartford Circle as a good survey
of the community but "not highly successful...in telling of Mark Twain's connection
with the group" and tending to minimize his
tragedy by seeking purely psychological
causes for his bitterness.

B32 GOHDES, CLARENCE. [Review: Dixon Wecter, ed.,
Mark Twain to Mrs. Fairbanks (1949).] South
Atlantic Quarterly, XLIX (January), 118.
Although "the letters are of no importance
as literature or as humor," they add to and
correct MT biography. "The book is intended

(GOHDES, CLARENCE)
for the perusal of a Mark Twain specialist
or collector--and of its kind it is a
model."

B33   HART, JAMES D. The Popular Book: A History
       of America's Literary Taste. New York:
       Oxford University Press, passim.
          Includes information on sales of MT's
       books and a discussion of their appeal as
       part of a general study that concerns popu-
       lar tastes, subscription sale by book agents,
       etc. There is an extensive annotated "Bib-
       liographical Checklist" in place of notes
       (pp. 289-300).

B34   HOLMAN, C. HUGH. [Review: Dixon Wecter, ed.,
       Mark Twain to Mrs. Fairbanks (1949).] Mod-
       ern Language Review, XLV (October), 541-42.
          Wecter "has shown sound judgment, admira-
       ble thoroughness and knowledge, and wise
       discretion in annotating these letters,
       which are published without alteration."
       The non-specialist can consult DeLancey
       Ferguson's Mark Twain: Man and Legend,
       which draws on these letters, but for the
       MT specialist Wecter's edition is indispen-
       sable.

B35   JOHNSON, IRMIS. "Mark Twain's Only Love,"
       American Weekly (a Sunday supplement of the
       Hearst newspapers) (April 23), pp. 6-7.
          A popular account, following the familiar
       biographies.

B36   JONES, JOSEPH. "Utopia as Dirge," American
       Quarterly, II (Fall), 214-26.
          A comparison of MT's Connecticut Yankee
       with Aldous Huxley's Brave New World and
       George Orwell's Nineteen Eighty-Four, all
       of which reveal "antagonism to the super-
       organization--a protest against or a fear
       of the assault of institutions against the
       individual," and all three reveal "the loss
       of wonder, the loss of the past, the loss
       of humanitarian culture, and the loss of
       responsibility in the use of power." Jones
       regards Hank Morgan as a protagonist, his
       defeat as "a trick of fate."

B37   KAPLAN, ISRAEL. "Kipling's American Notes
       and Mark Twain Interview," Papers of the
       Bibliographical Society of America, XLIV
       (First Quarter), 69-73.
          Largely on the general question of Ameri-
       can publication of Kipling's travel letters.
       "The first complete Kipling letter to ap-
       pear in an American newspaper was his in-
       terview with Mark Twain, which the New York
       Herald printed on August 17, 1890," appar-
       ently without permission. "However, no
       earlier version of this letter is known,
       and the final paragraph, uncollected, is
       significant," a criticism of CY. "The
       paragraph in question now achieves its first
       American printing since August 17, 1890:
       'Later.-- Oh shame! Oh shock! Oh fie!
       I have been reading the new book which you

will also have read by this time--the book
about the Yankee animal in the court yard.
It's***but I don't believe he ever wrote
it; or, if he did, I am certain that if you
held it up to a looking glass or picked out
every third word or spelled it backward you
would find that it hid some crystal clean
tale as desirable as Huck Finn.'"

B38   KITZHABER, ALBERT. "Götterdämmerung in Topeka:
       The Downfall of Senator Pomeroy," Kansas His-
       torical Quarterly, XVIII (August), 243-78.
          Provides background for MT's treatment of
       the Senator's downfall in GA--here briefly
       noted; on p. 248, n. 8, Kitzhaber says he
       will discuss in detail MT's literary use of
       the case in a forthcoming issue of Modern
       Language Quarterly. (See 1954.B33.)

B39   LEISY, ERNEST E. "Mark Twain the Artist,"
       Southwest Review, XXXV (Autumn), 295-96. A
       review of Edgar Marquess Branch, The Liter-
       ary Apprenticeship of Mark Twain and Gladys
       Carmen Bellamy, Mark Twain as a Literary
       Artist.
          "Conscientious studies both, for which
       every reader of Mark Twain is the wiser.
       We have not heretofore had as thorough an
       analysis of Mark Twain's various styles as
       Mr. Branch offers us, and we have needed
       the many corrections of DeVoto's and Brooks's
       assumptions which Miss Bellamy brings out.
       Her discussion of the travel books breaks
       new ground." Leisy suggests, however, that
       there should be "a more rigid appraisal of
       Mark Twain," whose "craftsmanship is hardly
       that of the born writer.... Mark Twain was
       an anecdotist, who by sundry apprenticeships
       learned the art of occasionally striking
       out a memorable phrase, or even of making an
       episode convincing, if he had heard the yarn
       before or had personally known the charac-
       ters." Except for most of TS and HF, "and a
       few episodes in other books, he was not a
       great writer."

B40   LORCH, FRED W. "Mark Twain and the Pennsyl-
       vania Disaster," Twainian, IX (January-
       February), 2.
          On the death of Henry Clemens, scalded in
       a steamboat explosion; reprints a contem-
       porary account of SLC's grief on seeing Hen-
       ry in the hospital (St. Louis News and In-
       telligencer, June 19, 1858; reprinted from
       Memphis Eagle and Inquirer of June 16).

B41   _____. "Mark Twain's Lecture from Roughing
       It," American Literature, XXII (November),
       290-307.
          Includes the text as published in the
       Lansing (Michigan) State Republican,
       December 21, 1871. For Lorch's fully dev-
       eloped treatment of this and other MT lec-
       tures, see his The Trouble Begins at 8
       (1968.A2).

B42 MASTERS, EDGAR LEE. "The House Where Mark Twain Was Born, Florida, Missouri," Mark Twain Quarterly, VIII (Winter), 1.

A poem on the rural simplicity of the cottage.

B43 MECHLING, PHILIPP. "Mark Twain in Heidelberg," Twainian, IX (November-December), 3.

Reminiscences of MT by a guide who saw him on his visit there in 1896.

B44 MICHEL, ROBERT. "The Popularity of Mark Twain in Austria," Mark Twain Quarterly, VIII (Winter), 5-6, 19.

On MT's visits to Austria, and a meeting in his honor by the writers and journalists' club, Concordia, where a portrait of him by Gilbert Lehner was displayed; he was later received by the Emperor, Franz Joseph, and there was a great deal published by or about him in the Viennese papers.

B45 MOFFETT, WALLACE C. "Mark Twain's Lansing Lecture on Roughing It," Michigan History, XXXIV (June), 144-70.

After lecturing in Lansing in December, 1868, MT returned there in 1871, this time choosing his material to publicize his forthcoming RI. The text of his lecture is reprinted (pp. 153-70) from the Lansing State Republican (December 21, 1871), and a number of other contemporary accounts are quoted.

B46 REDDING, SAUNDERS. "Faith and Despair: The Alcotts and Mark Twain," American Scholar, XX (Winter), 112-22.

A review-article, discussing Gladys Carmen Bellamy's Mark Twain as a Literary Artist pp. 118-22. Her study falters in its attempt to demonstrate conscious artistry. She reveals MT's failure to achieve the artistic detachment needed for selection, simplification, and abstraction from the raw material of life. "This is Miss Bellamy's main thesis, and she expounds it sometimes brilliantly."

B47 SCHOFIELD, KENNETH B. "The Boy and the River," Times Literary Supplement, December 8, p. 785.

A letter to the editor, agreeing with Marcus Cunliffe in the controversy over the origin of MT's pseudonym.

B48 SMITH, HENRY NASH. "Origins of a Native American Literary Tradition," in Margaret Denny and William H. Gilman, eds., The American Writer and the European Tradition. Minneapolis: University of Minnesota Press (Reprinted: New York, Toronto, London: McGraw-Hill Book Company, 1964, paperbound, and New York: Haskell House Publishers Ltd., 1968. A comparison of indexes suggests that both of these are photographic reprints.), pp. 63-77; on MT, pp. 70-77.

On MT as influenced by southwestern humor, his repudiation of Europe, and America's literary debt to him.

B49 SPILLER, ROBERT E. "Mr. & Mrs. Clemens," Saturday Review of Literature, XXXIII (January 28), 17. A review of Dixon Wecter, ed., The Love Letters of Mark Twain (1949).

Wecter "supplies a calendar of all Mark's letters to Livy, but he wisely refrains from publishing them all; a man in love is likely to repeat himself." The book provides no new revelations, certainly no indication that Livy's censorship was stricter than MT's own.

B50 STEVENSON, ROBERT LOUIS. "Letter from Robert Louis Stevenson to Mark Twain," Twainian, IX (September-October), 1, 4.

Undated (Chester L. Davis assumes it was during the period 1888-1893), on the possibility of Charles L. Webster & Co. handling Stevenson's work.

B51 THOMPSON, LAWRANCE. "Twain's Prelude to Fame," New York Times Book Review (July 2), p. 4.

A review of Edgar Marquess Branch, The Literary Apprenticeship of Mark Twain, which fails in an attempt to reveal a "logic of development" in MT's work: even in the "superb" HF, "the formula, or informing artistic principle, is Twain's lifelong pet, improvisation. This time it was all he needed."

B52 THORP, WILLARD. "American Writers as Critics of Nineteenth-Century Society," in Denny and Gilman, The American Writer and the European Tradition (See Smith, Henry Nash, 1950.B48), pp. 90-105; on MT, pp. 103-104.

On MT as critic of American society, his failure to speak out as he might have, and his final despair.

B53 TROMMER, MARIE. "Mark Twain and the Missing Cat Chapter," Mark Twain Quarterly, VIII (Winter), 3-4.

When she was a child in Russia, the author read a copy of Tom Sawyer from which the chapter that accompanied a picture of a cat hanging above the schoolmaster had been cut out; years later, she was able to read a complete copy in New York.

B54 WALLACE, ELIZABETH. "The Beloved Jester's Many Moods," Saturday Review of Literature, XXXIII (September 23), 30.

A review of Gladys Carmen Bellamy, Mark Twain as a Literary Artist. After having presented moralism, determinism, pessimism, and patheticism as the bases of MT's mind, Miss Bellamy discusses "with skill and clarity" the way they conflict in MT's work as one or another becomes dominant. She writes clearly and convincingly, and also "delightfully and with vigorous freshness."

B55 WATTERS, R. E. [Review: Edgar Marquess Branch, The Literary Apprenticeship of Mark Twain.] Journal of Southern History, XVI (November), 555-57.

This is an "excellent study," and the reprinting of MT's early writings from original sources is so valuable that Watters wishes more space had been given to them, "even at the cost of curtailing the evaluations and analyses"; for example, "the sixteen-page thematic analysis of Huckleberry Finn (1884), excellent though it is, has little real connection with the rest of the book--so little, indeed that the author was able to publish a slightly abridged version of it separately in College English, XI (1950), 188-95."

B56 WEBSTER, SAMUEL C. "Here's Probably Twain's First Version of His Tale of 'Dick Baker's Cat,'" Twainian, IX (January-February), 3.

Reprints the text of an early MS story about the cat, Tom Quartz, who later appeared in RI.

B57 *WECTER, DIXON. [Introduction.] Life on the Mississippi. New York: Harper & Brothers. [Source: Asselineau (1954), No. 1235.]

B58 WHICHER, GEORGE F. "The Styles of Mark Twain," New York Times Book Review (August 13), p. 6.

A descriptive review of Gladys Carmen Bellamy's Mark Twain as a Literary Artist, which "fills a gap in the series of brilliantly able studies of Mark Twain that have been written during the past thirty years.... She has set the appropriate keystone on the arch of Mark Twain literary criticism."

B59 WILLIAMS, MENTOR L. "Mark Twain's Joan of Arc," Twainian, IX (September-October), 1-4.

On MT's long-enduring interest in the medieval world, where he sought "the ethical core of human society. He could not find it in the modern world." (Reprinted from Michigan Alumnus Quarterly Review for Spring, 1948).

B60 WILLIAMS, STANLEY T. "The Enigma of Mark Twain," Yale Review, XL (Winter), 340-43.

A review of Kenneth Andrews, Nook Farm: Mark Twain's Hartford Circle ("modern," in placing MT "in a pattern of American thought in a particular place at a particular time"); Gladys Carmen Bellamy, Mark Twain as a Literary Artist ("She assails the riddle of Mark Twain's mind; she tries to resolve the paradoxes.... Her theory is persuasive. It is...occasionally blurred by the manipulation of too many abstractions, as in her four 'bases' of Mark Twain's mind: moralism, pessimism, determinism, and--unhappy word--'patheticism'!"); Edgar Marquess Branch, The Literary Apprenticeship of Mark Twain ("biographically factual, rather than historical or critical").

B61 WILLSON, FRANK C. "Two Uncollected Twain Writings Found in British-Authored Books," Twainian, IX (March-April), 1-2.

The text of letters by MT on the use of tobacco and intoxicants, and on his unconscious of half-conscious method of composition; reprinted from A. Arthur Reade, ed., Study and Stimulants (Manchester, England, and Philadelphia, 1883) and George Bainton, ed., The Art of Authorship (New York and London: D. Appleton & Co., 1890).

B62 WINKLER, JOHN A. "Tom Sawyer's Town--A Sketch," Twainian, IX (May-June), 1, 4; (July-August), 3-4.

A popular account of MT's boyhood in Hannibal by the Chairman of the Mark Twain Municipal Board, following MT's Autobiography and adding little to this and other familiar sources.

B63 WINTERICH, JOHN T. "Clemens and Colony in the Hartford Days," Saturday Review of Literature, XXXIII (October 14), 26-27.

A review of Kenneth Andrews, Nook Farm: Mark Twain's Hartford Circle, "a contribution of major importance," marked by "depth, judgment, shrewd and accurate appraisal, and a scholarly detachment that still has room for humor, warmth, and sympathy." MT is not allowed to overshadow the other characters, particularly his wife Olivia and their pastor Joseph Twichell (whose twelve-volume diary, covering a period of fifty years, is in the library at Yale).

1951 A BOOKS

A1 *ANON. O'Connor Auction List, Mark Twain Library Auction, April 10th, 2005 Le Brea Ave., O'Connor Auction Studios, 7949 Sunset Boulevard, Hollywood 46, Calif. [Source: Asselineau (1954), No. 1269.]

A2 *ANON. Zeitlin and Ver Brugge List. Books from the Library of Mark Twain, also articles from his home purchased at the sale of the library of his daughter, Clara Clemens Samassoud, April 10-14, 1951, Zeitlin and Ver Brugge, Booksellers, 815 North Cienega, Los Angeles, Calif., List No. 132, May 1951. [Source: Asselineau (1954), No. 1270.]

A3 CANBY, HENRY SEIDEL. Turn West, Turn East: Mark Twain and Henry James. Boston: Houghton Mifflin Company.

Considers MT and James as representatives of their age. They are articulate, novelists of manners, come from the same moral climate, and "both are almost humorously exaggerated as representative of the Turn West and the Turn East American.... They belong, actually, in the same stream of pioneer American history, although Mark plunged in more thirstily than any of his contemporaries in literature, and Henry fought the current until he could scramble out" (p. xi). An

1951 - Books

(CANBY, HENRY SEIDEL)
extensive index includes major works and
characteristics of their writing.
Pp. 239-57 reprinted in Scott (1955),
pp. 279-85; (1967), pp. 264-70. Pp. 249-57
reprinted in Leary (1962), pp. 225-31.

A4 *GILKEY, ROBERT. Mark Twain Voyageur et Son
Image de l'Europe. Paris (a mimeographed
dissertation for the University of Paris).
[Source: Asselineau (1954), No. 1272.]

1951 B SHORTER WRITINGS

B1 ANON. "The Characters Mark Used in His Writings," Twainian, X (September-October), 4.
Reprints an undated clipping from the
newspaper, Grit, on Joe Douglas, supposedly
the original of "Injun Joe" in Tom Sawyer,
but a harmless, gentle friend of the boys
in Hannibal. This is listed as "The First
of a Series" in The Twainian, but the series
was not continued.

B2 ANON. "Mark Twain and Anthony Trollope,
Equestrians," Mark Twain Quarterly, IX
(Winter), 14-15.
At a dinner honoring Joaquin Miller,
Trollope tried unsuccessfully to draw MT
out on the subject of horses.

B3 *ANON. "Mark Twain, J. Swift e Alphonse Daudet Presentati ai Ragazzi," La Fiera Letteraria, No. 49 (December 10), p. 8.
[Source: Asselineau (1954), No. 1306.]

B4 ANON. "New & Notable: Mark Twain," Princeton
University Library Chronicle, XII (Summer),
217-18.
The library has acquired the Thomas L.
Leeming Collection, which includes first
American editions of most of MT's works,
"the nearly complete manuscript of "The
£1,000,000 Bank-Note," one of three copies
of The Suppressed Chapter of Following the
Equator (1928), and one of sixteen copies
of A Murder, a Mystery, and a Marriage
(1945).

B5 ANON. "New England Intellectuals," Times Literary Supplement, February 16, p. 97. A
review of Kenneth R. Andrews, Nook Farm:
Mark Twain's Hartford Circle (1950).
Impressively thorough but dry, "It is a
book for the student rather than for the
general reader. Even the student may think
it too intense a culture, unless he happens
to be digging the same ground."

B6 ANON. [Brief Review: Kenneth R. Andrews,
Nook Farm: Mark Twain's Hartford Circle.]
Nineteenth-Century Fiction, V (March),
334-35.
Brief and descriptive, noting that Andrews
has shown "patience and intelligence" in
sifting the mass of material, adding to our
understanding of American thought and MT's
growing concern for values.

B7 ARNAVON, CYRILLE. "Les Humoristes: Mark
Twain," in his Les Lettres Américaines devant
la Critique Française (Paris: Société d'Édi-
tion les Belles Lettres), pp. 71-80.
Traces French criticism of MT, concluding:
"Mark Twain n'aura substantiellement enrichi
ou approfondi notre vision des Américains."

B8 BARSAMIAN, KENNETH J. "Mark Twain's Mudhen
Victory," Mark Twain Quarterly, IX (Winter),
12-13.
On the abortive duel with James Laird
which supposedly led to MT's leaving Nevada
for California; apparently based entirely on
the Paine biography.

B9 BLAIR, WALTER [Review: Kenneth R. Andrews,
Nook Farm: Mark Twain's Hartford Circle
(1950).] American Literature, XXIII (May),
258-59.
"Professor Andrews has drawn upon an impressive array of previously unused primary
sources--diaries, private papers, Hartford
newspapers, books by seventeen Hartford
writers--to learn about the Nook Farm community." The book is useful on the thought of
the time and place, but more could have been
done toward showing how they influenced The
Gilded Age and A Connecticut Yankee in King
Arthur's Court; nonetheless, the book provides "many insights and a great deal of
valuable information."

B10 _____. [Review: Gladys Carmen Bellamy, Mark
Twain as a Literary Artist (1950).] American
Literature, XXII (January), 521-24.
Provides a useful summary of Miss Bellamy's
book and her approach; notes more emphasis
on MT's ideas than on his method. Concludes:
"It is a through study of the tone of Clemens's works and of the patterns of his
thinking. It throws a great deal of light
on the content--if not, perhaps, the form--
of a great artist's writings."

B11 BLUMFIELD, RALPH D. "Twain Note," Hobbies--
the Magazine for Collectors, LVI (December),
152.
Extract from a letter to Cyril Clemens,
briefly recalling several meetings with MT.

B12 BURNAM, TOM. "Mark Twain and the Paige Typesetter: A Background for Despair," Western
Humanities Review, VI (Winter), 29-36.
To MT the typesetter was not only an in-
vestment but also a work of the imagination,
and in its failure it became a "dream" of
rational, mechanical perfection.

B13 BURNET, RUTH A. "Mark Twain in the Northwest,
1895," Pacific Northwest Quarterly, XLII
(July), 187-202.
On MT's two weeks in Washington, Oregon,
and British Columbia on his round-the-world
lecture tour to pay off his debts. A number
of contemporary newspaper accounts are cited
and quoted.

B14 CANBY, HENRY SEIDEL. "Hero of the Great Know-How: Mark Twain's Machine-Age Yankee," Saturday Review of Literature, XXXIV (October 20), 7-8, 40-41.
 Excerpted from his Turn West, Turn East ("to be published next month"). "Mark Twain had no idea whatsoever of the inner ideals or the outer responsibilities of feudalism" and the book contains some of his worst writing, but Canby's generation read CY "with passionate delight" because in Hank Morgan they saw how "the kind of fellow we see every day became the Boss by using just the kind of science we were being taught in school."

B15 CARDWELL, GUY A. "Mark Twain's Hadleyburg," Ohio State Archaeological and Historical Quarterly [now Ohio History], LX (July), 257-64.
 A detailed refutation of the suggestion by Russel B. Nye (1938) that Oberlin, Ohio was the model for Hadleyburg.

B16 CARTER, PAUL J., JR. [Review: Gladys Carmen Bellamy, Mark Twain as a Literary Artist.] Western Humanities Review, VI (Winter), 75-77.
 The analysis of MT's internal conflict "is an original and stimulating contribution to the study of Twain," though less successful when Miss Bellamy argues that with a balanced view of the duality of life MT might have been a "great" artist: "To affirm that the artist must effect some synthesis between good and evil, must achieve an inner serenity, is to ignore the experience of too many artists, who derive power and direction from their inner conflicts."

B17 CHESTER, GIRAUD. Embattled Maiden: The Life of Anna Dickinson. New York: G. P. Putman's Sons.
 On MT's advice concerning subscription publication of books (p. 131) and his letters to her (p. 156); apparently this material is now in the Anna E. Dickinson Papers in the Manuscript Division of the Library of Congress.

B18 CLEMENS, CYRIL. "Bernard Shaw and Mark Twain," Notes and Queries (London), CXCVI (March 3), 104.
 "Your readers may be interested in what Bernard Shaw wrote me on 1st April, 1937, of his meetings with Mark Twain"; reproduces without further comment the text of the note, which Cyril Clemens has also published elsewhere.

B19 _____. "Mark Twain and His Corncob," Hobbies--the Magazine for Collectors, LVI (June), 160.
 Anecdote: MT dined with Sir Bruce and Lady Seton in England, 1907; afterward, offered a cigar, he said he preferred his pipe.

B20 _____. "Mark Twain Is Entertained by Edward 7th," Hobbies--the Magazine for Collectors, LVI (March) 138-39.
 On MT's attendance at a large garden party at Windsor Castle, June 28, 1907; not documented.

B21 _____. "The Missing Mark Twain Manuscript," Hobbies--The Magazine for Collectors, LVI (May), 136. Also in Mark Twain Quarterly, IX (Winter), 13.
 The locations of most MT manuscripts are known, but "All lovers of American literature await with high anticipation the discovery of the manuscript of The Prince and the Pauper."

B22 COLLINS, CARVEL. [Review: Kenneth R. Andrews, Nook Farm: Mark Twain's Hartford Circle (1950) and Gladys Carmen Bellamy, Mark Twain as a Literary Artist (1950).] New England Quarterly, XXIV (December), 540-42.
 Although his "well-documented chapters give the reader an excellent picture of many of the influences to which Mark Twain was exposed" and Andrews "presents many new insights" into the way they acted on MT, he is less successful in "separating these influences from earlier ones and from contemporary ones not originating in the Nook Farm community." Miss Bellamy's book is confused in purpose, and "never really deals meaningfully with the over-all form of any of Twain's works, good or bad. And nowhere does a well developed aesthetic theory appear." It provides evidence of MT's craftsmanship, but "the trouble is that the book does not adequately examine that craftsmanship."

B23 COLLINS, LOUISE. "Post Cards of Mark Twain and Tom Sawyer," Hobbies--the Magazine for Collectors, LVI (November), 150-52.
 The outlook is that of a collector, not a student of MT: "At one point in Mark Twain's life he went West, and while there he wrote several interesting stories." Describes a number of post cards showing MT and places where he lived.

B24 COMMAGER, HENRY STEELE. "The Golden West," Scholastic, LVII (January 3), 10-11.
 An account for high-school students of MT's picture of the West in RI.

B25 [DAVIS, CHESTER L.] "Mark's Marginal Notes on Macaulay," Twainian, X (July-August), 1-2; (September-October), 1-4; (November-December), 3.
 On underscorings and marginal notations in MT's copy of G. Otto Trevelyan's Macaulay's Life and Letters (New York: Harper & Brothers, 1876, copyright 1875).

B26 _____. "More Background on Innocents," Twainian, X (May-June), 3.

([DAVIS, CHESTER L.])
Three letters from MT to Elisha Bliss
(April 12, "April Something," and April 29,
1869) on the illustrations to IA, with
minimal editorial comment.

B27   . "The Prince and the Pauper," Twainian,
X (July-August), 3.
On unusual issues of P&P; contains MT
letters (August 31, 1880 and February 23,
1882) on the writing and sales of the book.

B28   . "Revising the Revisor," Twainian,
X (January-February), 1.
Brief comment on IA and a letter by MT
to Elisha Bliss (April 20, 1869).

B29   . "Who Is Your Secretary?" Twainian, X
(November-December), 4.
Biographical information provided by
Chester Davis, an electrical engineer and
later a patent lawyer, editing The Twainian
by request (and as a hobby, with remuner-
ation).

B30   DICKINSON, LEON T. [Review: Dixon Wecter,
ed., The Love Letters of Mark Twain
(1949).] American Literature, XXII
(January), 524-25.
Notes that Wecter did not include the
letters to Livy published in Paine's biography and Clara's My Father Mark Twain,
"and others of apparently slight interest."
The editing provides a context even for
readers unfamiliar with MT's life, but
the letters add little to the existing
picture of MT: "It seems more and more
likely that most of the evidence on Clemens
is in. Further biographical studies will
do well if, as this volume has done, they
manage to enrich the story of Mark Twain's
life."

B31   DOUGHTY, HOWARD, JR. [Review: Henry Seidel
Canby, Turn West, Turn East: Mark Twain
and Henry James.] Nation (New York),
CLXXIII (December 8), 505.
The contrast is a useful device, but
"the tensions of the question...are not
altogether resolved."

B32   DOUGLAS, ROBERT. "The Pessimism of Mark
Twain," Mark Twain Quarterly, IX (Winter),
1-4.
MT's pessimism sees man engaged in two
different struggles: "against a control-
lable society" and "against a mechanistic
and determined universe."

B33   EDEL, LEON. "Two Innocents at Home," New
York Times Book Review (November 11), p. 8.
A review of Henry Seidel Canby's Turn
West, Turn East: Mark Twain and Henry
James, which reflects sympathy for MT but
does injustice to James. "The blemishes
of too-casual scholarship...are all the
more regrettable in a book ingenious in
conception," blessed with a warm and lucid
prose, and "as mellow as it is worldly wise."

B34   EKSTRÖM, KJELL. "Extracts from a Diary Kept
by Ozias W. Pond During the Clemens-Cable
Tour of Readings in 1885," Archiv für das
Studium der neueren Sprachen, CLXXXVIII
(May), 109-13.
Comments by their manager on the audiences, weather, a train derailment, an interview in the Davenport (Iowa) Democrat
(quoted). MT, who was reading Malory's
Morte D'Arthur on the tour, gave Pond the
title "Sir Sagramore, Knight of the Lake,"
and he went by that title for the rest of
the tour.

B35   *ELIOT, T. S. "Huckleberry Finn," Bonniers
Litterära Magasin (Sweden), XX (December),
751-56.
[Source: Asselineau (1954), No. 1293.]

B36   FLACK, FRANK M. "Patent Adjustable Speech,"
Twainian, X (November-December), 1-2.
On a proof-sheet, signed by MT, of the
speech before he delivered it at the New
England Dinner, Boston, December 20, 1887
(text of this version is reprinted).

B37   *FRANCIOSA, MASSIMO. "I Meriti Nacosti di Mark
Twain Narratore," La Fiera Letteraria
(Italy), No. 25 (June 24), pp. 4, 7.
[Source: Listed by Asselineau (No. 1294)
and in "Articles on American Literature Ap-
pearing in Current Periodicals," American
Literature, XXIV (March, 1952), 130. Assel-
ineau's annotation reads: "On Mark Twain's
consummate skill as a storyteller." Ameri-
can Literature annotation: "Apropos of an
Italian translation of Tom Sawyer and
Huckleberry Finn published by Einaudi in
Turin, it is observed that Mark Twain is
not greatly appreciated in America."]

B38   GOHDES, CLARENCE. "Mirth for the Million,"
in Arthur Hobson Quinn, ed., The Literature
of the American People: An Historical and
Critical Survey (New York: Appleton-Century Crofts), pp. 701-20.
On MT, pp. 708-20, noting his mixture of
"instinctive barbarism" with an intellectual
humor and a feeling for literature. "Like
Emerson and Whitman, he seems to reflect
the qualities of his country with unusual
fullness."

B39   . [Review Article.] South Atlantic
Quarterly, L (July), 437-39.
Summarizes the Brooks-DeVoto controversy,
with eventual dominance of DeVoto's view of
the importance of the frontier. Edgar Marquess Branch, The Literary Apprenticeship
of Mark Twain (1950) "is a culmination of
much work along this line, though it is by
no means theory-ridden. In fact it delivers a severe blow to the frontier adherents."
Gladys Carmen Bellamy, Mark Twain as a Literary Artist "begins where Mr. Branch leaves
off. It uses as grist just about everything,
good and bad, that has been written about
Mark Twain.... Nevertheless, she has some

(GOHDES, CLARENCE)
very sensible opinions on her subject." Kenneth Andrews, Nook Farm: Mark Twain's Hartford Circle (1950) "is far more important than a mere background of Mark Twain and stands on its own feet as an exhaustive account of the ideas and mores prevailing in an American community during an era most apt to be misunderstood today."

B40   GRAY, JAMES. "Interpreting Genius," Saturday Review of Literature, XXXIV (December 1), 27.
A review of Henry Seidel Canby, Turn West, Turn East: Mark Twain and Henry James. This study of two lives in the Plutarchan manner is a fortunate use of Canby's gifts, as he achieves "that spontaneous identification with his material which...is the ally of moving and creative analysis." [Canby was a founder and chairman of the editorial board of this magazine--T.A.T.]

B41   HERZL, THEODOR. "Mark Twain in Paris" ["Translated by Alexander Behr, from Dr. Herzl's Feuilletons"], Mark Twain Quarterly, IX (Winter), 16-20.
Describes a reading by MT before a group of English schoolgirls at the British Embassy; followed by a burlesque account attributed to "Hesperus M. Dark, correspondent of the Minneapolis Bluffs."

B42   HILTON, EARL. "Mark Twain's Theory of History," Papers of the Michigan Academy of Science, Arts, and Letters, XXXVII, 445-53.
MT did not share his day's nostalgia for the Middle Ages or hold an evolutionary view of history. He inherited an eighteenth-century view of which the central concepts were "progress" and a universal "nature" of man which made it possible. "In the years between 1895 and 1900 Twain had come to see external nature as malicious, and human nature he doubted more and more. Now he had arrived at a complete reversal of his earlier position [as revealed, for example, in HF]. Now it was not 'nature,' but the cumulative human experience crystallized in institutions, which he urged men to follow."

B43   HORNBERGER, THEODORE. [Review: Kenneth Andrews, Nook Farm: Mark Twain's Hartford Circle (1950).] American Quarterly, III (Summer), 188-91.
Andrews depicts the neighborhood as self-contained and homogeneous, with standards that influenced the writers living there. A major source of material has been unpublished family papers, yielding considerable color. The generalizations seem more persuasive when applied to MT and Charles Dudley Warner than when applied to the community as a whole, and there are verbal infelicities and passages of fictionalized biography that seem inappropriate, but these are

minor flaws in a study that "is extraordinarily interesting and contains much that is new."

B44   HUTCHESON, AUSTIN E. "More Tales about Twain in Nevada, as Told by His Fellow Newspapermen," Twainian, X (September-October), 3-4.
Excerpts from the Gold Hill News and the Virginia City Territorial Enterprise (1865, 1866), chiefly on MT's lectures.

B45   IRVING, LAURENCE. Henry Irving: The Actor and His World. London: Faber and Faber, p. 454.
Mentions MT's presence at a public banquet honoring Irving, April 6, 1885; no details are given.

B46   JOHNSON, MERLE. "Merle Johnson's Letters," Twainian, X (July-August), 3-4.
An assortment of letters in one of which (December 23, 1924) he identified the author of The Literary Guillotine as William Wallace Whitelock.

B47   JONES, ALEXANDER E. "Heterodox Thought in Mark Twain's Hannibal," Arkansas Historical Quarterly, X (Autumn, 1951), 244-57.
Although MT's boyhood environment was "primarily...one of Calvinistic Presbyterianism...there were also underlying currents of liberal and unorthodox doctrine which could have reached the boy from his uncle, his father, his mother, and even from the church ritual itself...an investigation of the other members of Twain's immediate family reveals a significant fact: of those persons who lived beyond this early Hannibal period, not one remained orthodox in his religion." "All members...of Sam's immediate family underwent a process of religious development which curiously paralleled his own."

B48   McELDERRY, B. R., JR. [Review: Kenneth R. Andrews, Nook Farm: Mark Twain's Hartford Circle (1950).] Personalist, XXXII (Autumn), 442-43.
Thoughtfully descriptive, noting the book's interest as cultural history; Clemens could have chosen worse places than Hartford to live in the years 1871-1891. The portrayal of MT's friend Joseph Twichell is of much interest.

B49   _____. [Review: Edgar Marquess Branch, The Literary Apprenticeship of Mark Twain (1950).] Personalist, XXXII (Summer), 300-301.
Chiefly descriptive, but noting the presence of "fifteen pages of really perceptive criticism of Huckleberry Finn," although "not sufficiently linked to what has gone before." The twenty selections from MT's apprentice writing are not powerful evidence of its importance, and the space they take might better have been used for a revised and

1951 - Shorter Writings

(McELDERRY, B. R., JR.)
enlarged reprinting of his bibliography of
the early writings which appeared in American Literature in 1946.

B50 McGOWAN, GAULT. "Mark Twain and Heidelberg,"
Mark Twain Quarterly, IX (Winter), 30.
A miscellany about the Neckar, the University, and Nazi officers, but nothing of
interest on MT.

B51 PARSONS, COLEMAN O. "Mark Twain--Conscious or
Unconscious?" Virginia Quarterly Review,
XXVII (Winter), 142-47.
A review of Kenneth R. Andrews, Nook Farm:
Mark Twain's Hartford Circle (the environment was far from stultifying, but it en-
couraged MT to be "a professional writer
rather than a deliberate artist"); Gladys
Carmen Bellamy, Mark Twain as a Literary
Artist (1950; generally sound, but sometimes ignores evidence contrary to the point
being argued); and Edgar Marquess Branch,
The Literary Apprenticeship of Mark Twain
(1950; "Authoritative in all areas but one,
the book throws only a fitful light on the
maturing process," showing a clearer and
more logical pattern than in fact existed).

B52 *RICE, HOWARD C. Kipling in New England (revised edition). Brattleboro, Vermont:
n.p., p. 9. Kipling refers to MT as "the
master of us all."
[Source: Quoted by Baetzhold (1970),
pp. 195, 359, n. 38.]

B53 SHAW, G. BERNARD. "Mark Twain and Bernard
Shaw," Mark Twain Quarterly, IX (Winter),
30.
On his meetings in London with MT, who
visited his flat, lunched with him, told
stories, and gave him an autographed book.

B54 STONE, EDWARD. [Review: Henry Seidel Canby,
Turn West, Turn East: Mark Twain and Henry
James (1950).] South Atlantic Quarterly,
LI (July), 468-69.
The "juxtaposition...furnishes the reader
a fresh and provocative perspective," but
says little that is new: "to the James-
Twain initiate...Mr. Canby's prodigious
labor will seem to a great extent supere-
rogatory."

B55 STRONG, LEAH A. "Mark Twain on Spelling,"
American Literature, XXIII (November),
357-59.
Text of an introductory speech by MT at
a spelling-bee; reprinted from Hartford
Courant, May 13, 1875.

B56 TIGERT, JOHN. "Mark Twain, Man of the People,
Amidst Pomp and Circumstance at Oxford University," Mark Twain Quarterly, IX (Winter),
10-11.
On his 1907 trip to receive an honorary
degree; not documented and not going beyond
the familiar accounts.

B57 TRAINOR, JULIETTE A. "Symbolism in A Connecticut Yankee in King Arthur's Court," Modern
Language Notes, LXVI (June), 382-85.
Equates MT with Launcelot, who with his
sword ("Irreverence") assailed two giants
representing monarchy and the Catholic
Church. "Launcelot, in the opening Malory
episode, killed his two giants, but the ending of the Yankee is inconclusive."

B58 WAGENKNECHT, EDWARD. "Twain--A Literary Lincoln," Saturday Review of Literature, XXXIV
(January 20), 25-26.
MT is "still read more, I suppose, than
any other standard American author," yet as
one of "those who have created literature by
dramatizing their own lives" he is thought
of first as a personage, "the mightiest figure in the American literary mythology."

B59 WHICHER, GEORGE F. "Mark Twain, Henry James,"
New York Herald Tribune Book Review, XXVIII
(December 2), 4.
A review of Henry Seidel Canby, Turn West,
Turn East: Mark Twain and Henry James.
Canby has brought "fresh insight" and writ-
ten "a suggestive study," although at times
he "is betrayed into laboring a trivial
point."

B60 WIGGINS, ROBERT A. "The Original of Mark
Twain's Those Extraordinary Twins," American
Literature, XXIII (November), 355-57.
An article in the December, 1891 issue of
Scientific American may have inspired MT;
an account (quoted) of the different person-
alities of the Tocci twins resembles his
description.

B61 *WILLIAMS, CECIL B. "Mark Twain, American
Paradox," Bulletin of Oklahoma Agricultural
and Mechanical College, XLVIII
(September 30), 14-20.
[Source: Asselineau (1954), No. 1303.]

1952 A BOOKS

A1 CLEMENS, SAMUEL L. Report from Paradise.
New York: Harper & Brothers Publishers.
Contains the texts of Captain Stormfield's
Visit to Heaven and "Letter from the Recording Angel," together with a thorough discussion of the backgrounds in a fifteen-page
introduction by Dixon Wecter.

A2 WECTER, DIXON. Sam Clemens of Hannibal. Boston: Houghton Mifflin Company.
A thorough, scholarly study of MT's early
years, this is the beginning of what would
have been the definitive biography of MT,
but for Wecter's death. Chapter V reprinted
in Cardwell (1963), pp. 65-71.

1952 B SHORTER WRITINGS

B1 *ANON. "The Mark Twain House. Clemens and
His Fifth Avenue Years Are Recalled," New
York Herald Tribune, February 16.
[Source: Reprinted Twainian, XIII
(March-April, 1954), 3-4.]

B2 ANON. "Mark Twain's Cousin, His Favorite,
Tabitha Quarles," Twainian, XI (July-
August), 1-2.
A reprinting of a newspaper feature story
of "some 35 years ago," apparently in a
Missouri paper, containing recollections of
MT's boyhood--many of which appear to be
derived from the Autobiography and Paine
biography.

B3 ANON. "Origin of Mark Twain in Flames?"
Twainian, XI (July-August), 2.
Text of a clipping reading "Flag of Our
Union, July 4?? 1870." Page 448. Column
entitled "Humors of the Day," without other
identification; on MT as a Sunday-School
teacher.

B4 ANON. [Brief Review: Henry Seidel Canby,
Turn West, Turn East: Mark Twain and Henry
James (1951).] Nineteenth-Century Fiction,
VII (September), 146.
No new information on MT and James for
the serious student, who "will often quarrel with Canby on matters of fact and opinion," but there is "usefulness" in a book
that points up a significant contrast between two American attitudes toward culture."

B5 ANON. [Brief Review: Dixon Wecter, Sam
Clemens of Hannibal (1950).] Nineteenth-
Century Fiction, VII (December), 235.
"So powerful is its combination of dramatic intensity and scholarly thoroughness
that every reader will regret again that
its talented author did not live to carry
his work further." Fortunately, this
treatment of the first years is the most
important part, because it was the formative period and Paine had covered it inadequately.

B6 BLAIR, WALTER. "Last of the Jongleurs," Saturday Review of Literature, XXXV (August 30),
9-10.
A review of Dixon Wecter's Sam Clemens of
Hannibal, an "extensive study...justified by
the close relationship between the man's
early life and his best work." It is vastly
superior to Paine's study of the same period
because Wecter had a better understanding of
MT's work, was "a trained, experienced historian," had access to material discovered
since Paine wrote his biography, and "mastered his facts and molded them into an
orderly and readable narrative."

B7 BROOKS, VAN WYCK. The Confident Years: 1895-
1915. New York: E. P. Dutton & Co.
Mentions MT's name passim, but without new
critical statements on him.

B8 BURTIS, MARY ELIZABETH. Moncure Conway, 1832-
1907. New Brunswick, New Jersey: Rutgers
University Press. Passim on MT (indexed).
Conway was MT's agent for the English
publication of TS (pp. 158-59) and TA
(pp. 181-82).

B9 BUTTERFIELD, ROGER. "Roger Butterfield Forwards Enterprise Mark Twain Item Unknown to
Experts," Virginia City Territorial Enterprise, August 1, p. 1.
Reprints the text of an MT endorsement
(datelined Hartford, March 3, 1873) for
White's Patent Fly and Mosquito Net Frames:
"A fly will stand off and curse this invention till language utterly fails him. I
have seen them do it hundreds of times";
when the family uses it while dining on the
porch "the flies have to wait for the second
table."

B10 CARDWELL, GUY A. "Mark Twain's 'Row' with
George Cable," Modern Language Quarterly,
XIII (December), 363-71.
On MT's impatience with Cable during the
closeness of their 1884-1885 lecture tour;
extensively quotes newspaper commentary, as
well as MT letters, of which some are critical and some friendly toward Cable. Differences in temperament and philosophy explain
why there was little contact between the
two after their tour, as does MT's generally
bristly relation with business associates;
it was an achievement for Cable "to have
traveled for four months with Mark and to
have suffered nothing worse than half-intend-
ed, half-regretted verbal assaults."

B11 CARTER, EVERETT. "The Meaning of, and in,
Realism," Antioch Review, XII (March), 78-94.
"There never was a less metaphysical man,
at least before the hopelessness of determinism closed down upon him," and "his aim
was to be authentic, and...to find his re-
wards in the market-place." Huckleberry
Finn is significant for its sustained irony,
but it was written before 1890, when a realist could still write for Americans who believed in a happy ending.

B12 CLEMENS, CYRIL. "Sam Clemens into Mark Twain,"
Virginia City Territorial Enterprise,
XCVIII (May 2), 6.
Recollections of MT as told by Bill Gillis
to Cyril Clemens (here incorrectly identified
as "a direct descendant of Mark Twain").

B13 CLEMENS, SAMUEL L. [Reprint of MT letter in
New York World.] Twainian, XI (July-August),
3-4.

197

(CLEMENS, SAMUEL L.)
MT's letter to the editor (February 18, 1877) describes Captain Duncan of the Quaker City as the "head-waiter" of the Innocents Abroad cruise; he was without other authority, and, as subsequently revealed, without integrity. Includes a clipping from the New York Times (undated) on "The Ship-Owners and Mr. Duncan," and an unidentified "What an Old Shipmaster Thinks of the 'Head-Waiter.'"

B14   CUFF, ROGER PENN. "Mark Twain's Use of California Folklore in His Jumping Frog Story," Journal of American Folklore, LXV (April-June), 155-58.
Discusses previous printed versions of the story, with which he may have been familiar, as well as oral versions he heard; but the success of his story lay in the originality of his presentation.

B15   DAVIDSON, LEVETTE J. [Review: Duncan Emrich, ed., Comstock Bonanza (1950).] American Literature, XXIV (March), 107-109.
Emrich deserves thanks for this adequately annotated collection of humorous writings by MT and seven other Virginia City journalists of the boom period. Interesting in its own right, "this anthology further illustrates the contributions of 'the laughter of the West' to Mark Twain's literary development" (p. 108). The review is primarily descriptive.

B16   [DAVIS, CHESTER L.]. "First Editions--Collectors & Dealers," Twainian, XI (September-October), 1-3.
On Willard S. Morse, Irving S. Underhill, and Merle Johnson, with passages from their letters on collecting MT first editions and letters.

B17   _____. "Mark's Letters to San Francisco Call, from Virginia City, Nevada Territory, July 9th to November 19th, 1863," Twainian, XI (January-February), 1-4; (March-April), 1-4; (May-June), 1-4.
The text of the letters, prefaced by very brief editorial comment: "(Photostats from the paper itself were supplied by Dr. Austin E. Hutcheson.... We have made no corrections whatsoever, several errors in spelling being obviously overlooked by the proof-reader in the original printing)," (January-February, 1).

B18   _____. "Turn West, Turn East (A New Book)," Twainian, XI (March-April), 4.
Praises Henry Seidel Canby's 1951 book but makes no critical comment.

B19   _____. [Review: Dixon Wecter, Sam Clemens of Hannibal.] Twainian, XI (September-October), 4.
Appreciative, and concerned with Wecter as a friend and visitor to the Mark Twain

Research Foundation; says little of critical importance on the book.

B20   DEVOTO, BERNARD. "Boyhood Years that Shaped Mark Twain's Great Art," New York Herald Tribune Book Review, XXIX (August 31), 1, 9.
A review of Dixon Wecter, Sam Clemens of Hannibal. Paine was unqualified to write the story of MT's life, but Wecter "was the right man for Mark's biography: tough-minded but intuitive, a literary scholar who was also a man of letters, a brilliant historian, a first-rate writer." His new book "erases Paine. No one need ever write about the formative years again, the years on which everything in Mark Twain's books depends."

B21   FERGUSON, DELANCEY. "Mark Twain's Heaven," New York Times Book Review (September 7), p. 12.
A descriptive review of MT's Report from Paradise: "It is first-rate Mark Twain."

B22   _____. "When Mark Twain Was Young," New York Times Book Review (August 31), p. 3.
A descriptive review of Dixon Wecter's Sam Clemens of Hannibal, "which takes the humorist only to the age of 18, [but] renders obsolete all previous accounts of his formative years."

B23   FUSSELL, E. S. "The Structural Problem of The Mysterious Stranger," Studies in Philology, XLIX (January), 95-104.
"The Mysterious Stranger...was started and laid aside several times before it was finally abandoned. What is undoubtedly the final chapter was found in Twain's papers by Albert B. Paine, and attached to the uncompleted story when it was posthumously published in 1916. Because the tale was never formally completed, one cannot properly speak of Twain's formal achievement; but the very fact that Twain, even though he left the story unfinished, was able to construct the conclusion corroborates our impression that The Mysterious Stranger is somewhat unique in Twain's writings in its coherence of theme and in its adjustment of technique to the realization of that theme" (p. 95). "The solipsistic conclusion towards which Twain was apparently working is a theme embedded in the whole story, and Twain has liberally posted signs to indicate its presence."

B24   GIBSON, WILLIAM M. [Review: Henry Seidel Canby, Turn West, Turn East: Mark Twain and Henry James (1951).] American Literature, XXIV (May), 253-54.
Canby's thesis "does not sufficiently allow for Mark Twain's reputation and effect as American ambassador to the world, or the breadth of his views on race, or his late wildly bitter despair for democracy...he gives us a fresh view of Mark Twain as an

(GIBSON, WILLIAM M.)
uneasy composite of Huck and Tom. But he
takes a view of the creation of living
character which is too biographical and
too static." Canby convincingly argues
parallels in concern with independence and
freedom as topics, and treatment of American innocence. Gibson credits Canby with
the discovery that in The Princess Casa-
massima James anticipated MT's use of the
term "a new deal," and Canby "has made a
shrewd guess as to how Clemens got it from
James."

B25 *HARDING, WALTER. "A Note on the Binding of
the First Edition of Huckleberry Finn,"
Bibliographical Society of Virginia News
Sheet, No. 20 (March), pp. 1-2.
[Source: Asselineau (1954), No. 1323.]

B26 HINZ, JOHN. "Huck and Pluck: 'Bad' Boys in
American Fiction," South Atlantic Quarterly,
LI (January), 120-29.
Tom and Huck belong to a literary tradition reacting against the "model" boy; unfortunately, because of pressure for adjustment and conformity, "perhaps the real
boy is lost forever."

B27 JOHNSON, BURGES. "A Ghost for Mark Twain,"
Atlantic Monthly, CLXXXIX (May), 65-66.
As a Harper's junior editor, Johnson
selected materials for a revised ed. of
Mark Twain's Library of Humor. Although
he received no credit on the title page or
payment beyond his regular salary, Mr.
Duneka told him to include some of his own
work in the anthology. Later, at a dinner
of newspaper cartoonists, MT was guest of
honor; he was fatigued and tired of a line
of autograph-seekers when Johnson introduced himself, and cursed Johnson roundly,
then gained control and apologized. [A revised version of Johnson's "When Mark Twain
Cursed Me" (1937.B20).]

B28 LEAVIS, F. R. "The Americanness of American
Literature: A British Demurrer to Van Wyck
Brooks," Commentary, XIV (November), 466-74.
On MT, pp. 471-72: "It wasn't Huck who
wrote Huckleberry Finn; the mind that conceived him was mature, subtle, and sophisticated." MT, "though so unmistakably and profoundly American, writes out of a full continuity with the European past," as we also
see in PW, "an ironical masterpiece" in
which MT "adopts a style and a convention
of sophisticated literary tradition, and
handles them with the supreme skill of a
writer perfectly at home with them."

B29 _____. "Introduction," in Marius Bewley's
The Complex Fate: Hawthorne, Henry James,
and Some other American Writers (London:
Chatto & Windus; repr. New York: Gordian
Press, 1967), pp. vii-xv; on MT, pp. ix-xii.

Leavis argues that the idea of a "frontier
tradition" as a source of great American
literature "derives an illicit respectability from the aura of Mark Twain," who belongs
to "a too European past, along with Cooper,
Hawthorne, Melville and James," rather than
with Whitman, Dreiser, Scott Fitzgerald, and
Hemingway (pp. ix-x). Compared with Hemingway's idiom, "Huck's language...is Shake-
spearean in its range and subtlety," despite
its colloquial naturalness (p. xi).

B30 LEISY, ERNEST E. "Contrasting Craftsmen,"
Southwest Review, XXXVII (Winter), 80-81.
A review of Henry Seidel Canby, Turn West,
Turn East: Mark Twain and Henry James.
"Twain's best books have values; James's are
studies about values. Canby's approach to
the opposite techniques employed by his subjects is marked by rich insight and tolerance" in this Plutarchan comparison, informed by his familiarity with the writing
of both men.

B31 _____. [Review: Mark Twain to Mrs. Fairbanks
(1949).] Modern Language Quarterly, XIII
(March), 108-109.
"This excellently printed book is an indispensable contribution to Twainiana."

B32 LORCH, FRED W. "Cable and His Reading Tour
with Mark Twain in 1884-1885," American Literature, XXIII (January), 471-86.
Includes a picture of the friction between
the two, and contemporary reviews. For a
fuller account of this and other MT lecturing, See Lorch, 1968.A2.

B33 _____. "Mark Twain's 'Artemus Ward' Lecture
on the Tour of 1871-1872," New England Quarterly, XXV (September), 327-43.
"Since relatively little is known about
the Artemus Ward lecture, the purpose of
this article is to show first how it was received by the public, and second to repro-
duce as much of it as possible by piecing
together such parts of it as were found in
the newspapers of the localities where Mark
Twain lectured. The discussion will reveal
some of the causes which operated to make
the Artemus Ward lecture only moderately
successful and which may have contributed to
its abandonment at mid-tour. It will also
supply a few glimpses of Mark Twain's estimate of his celebrated fellow humorist." A
large number of contemporary newspaper accounts are quoted or cited.

B34 _____. "A Note on Mark Twain's Lecture on
the Far West," American Literature, XXIV
(November), 377-79.
Asserts the lecture fragment Wecter printed
in Mark Twain in Three Moods (1948.A4) probably belongs to a lecture on "Curiosities of
California," which he prepared in the summer
or fall of 1869 but abandoned.

1952 - Shorter Writings

B35 McELDERRY, B. R., JR. [Review: Gladys Carmen Bellamy, Mark Twain as a Literary Artist
(1950).] Personalist, XXXIII (Winter), 78.
Miss Bellamy's attribution of the mediocrity of much of MT's work to his alternately raging at the damned human race and the
imponderable force that damned it "is
worked out with commendable thoroughness,
a reasoned moderation, and even freshness
of approach to an almost hackneyed subject," but she treats style mechanically,
her treatments of structure in the several
books are not brought together, and she has
no answer for her question, "Why could Mark
Twain accept human nature only in boy nature?" Her approach through "moralism,
determinism, pessimism, and 'patheticism'"
provides an illuminating view of Tom Sawyer
and Huckleberry Finn.

B36 McKEITHAN, D[ANIEL] M[ORLEY]. "Mark Twain's
Story of the Bull and the Bees," Tennessee
Historical Quarterly, XI (September),
246-53.
Traces old Laxart's story of a bull-ride
in JA, II, Chapter XXXVI to "Sicily Burns's
Wedding," by George Washington Harris. MT
had originally written his version as "The
Whipping Boy's Story" for P&P, but dropped
it because Howells said it impeded the action of the story. Reprinted in his Court
Trials in Mark Twain and Other Essays
(1958.A5).

B37 NATHAN, MONIQUE. [Review: Robert Gilkey,
Mark Twain Voyageur et Son Image de l'Eu-
rope (1951).]
Critique, VIII (October), 893-94.

B38 REYNOLDS, HORACE. "Mark Twain's Queer Newspaper," Christian Science Monitor,
July 29, p. 9.
On MT's unsigned "To the Reading Public"
in the recently discovered first issue of
Author's Sketch Book (a small newspaper),
here partially reproduced in facsimile and
also described and quoted. [Article reprinted in Twainian, XIV (November-December, 1955), 1-2.]

B39 ROADES, SISTER MARIA TERESA. "Was Mark
Twain Influenced by the Prolog to Don
Quixote?" Mark Twain Quarterly, IX (Winter), 4-6, 24.
There may be reason to think that MT's
use of quotations from various languages
as chapter-headings in The Gilded Age and
his rejection of the excuses made in a
former age for having published a book may
have their origin in Cervantes, whose work
was familiar to him.

B40 SANDBURG, CARL. Always the Young Strangers.
New York: Harcourt, Brace and Company,
p. 117.
On the books he and his friends read in
their youth: "We read Huckleberry Finn and

Tom Sawyer by Mark Twain but they didn't
get the hold on us then that other books
did. They seemed to be for a later time.
It was the same way with the novels of
Charles Dickens."

B41 SANTAYANA, GEORGE. "Tom Sawyer and Don Quixote," Mark Twain Quarterly, IX (Winter),
1-3.
An impressionistic reaction to reading a
copy of Huckleberry Finn given him by Cyril
Clemens: both Tom and Huck show as their
deepest sentiment "kindness, humanity,
readiness to lend a helping hand to anyone
in trouble, no matter how degraded the creature may be. This is particularly clear in
Huck...a little ragamuffin... No wonder
that he should have no scruples about the
company he keeps and the means he resorts
to in his difficulties." "In the case of
Tom, the victory of pure kindness is more
difficult. Love of forms, of rules, of
making a sensation, has to be subordinated,"
although he is not mad like Don Quixote.

B42 SCHWARTZ, EDWARD. "Huckleberry Finn: The
Inward Thoughts of a Generation," Mark Twain
Quarterly, IX (Winter), 11-16, 23-24.
A general critical article, conventionally
documented, on Huckleberry Finn as "a concrete expression of the life and values of
the people of the Mississippi Valley of
pre-Civil War days," and the frontier and
institutional moralities.

B43 SMITH, H[ENRY] N[ASH]. [Review: Dixon Wecter, Sam Clemens of Hannibal.] Nation,
CLXXV (September 27), 274-75.
"We are not likely to find out much more
about Sam Clemens's first seventeen years
than is set forth in the present volume."

B44 *TRIPP, FRANK. "Tripp Recalls Mark Twain In-
terview. Twain's Kindly Rebuff," Port
Chester (N.Y.) Daily Item, February 27.
As a cub reporter, met MT in a railroad
station and said his editor had said to go
to see him; reported back: "The old crab
just grunted, 'That's nice of your editor.
Run along and tell him that you did.'"
[Source: Reprinted in Twainian, XIV
(January-February, 3.]

B45 VAN DOREN, MARK. "Two Items for Mark Twain
Collectors," New York Herald Tribune Book
Review, XXIX (September 7), p. 4.
A review of Dixon Wecter, ed., Report from
Paradise. Captain Stormfield's Visit to
Heaven is "vigorous," only mildly amusing,
and somewhat forced; "Letter from the Re-
cording Angel" is "more successful, being
more limited in its aim; and still it will
never be one of the immortal works."

B46 WAGENKNECHT, EDWARD. "'The Lincoln of Our Literature,'" in his The Cavalcade of the American Novel (New York: Henry Holt and Company), pp. 109-26.

  A general study of MT, his work, and his ideas; part of this chapter has appeared in Wagenknecht's Mark Twain: The Man and His Work (1935); there is an annotated bibliography, pp. 516-20 (superseded by later bibliographies, including those in later editions of Mark Twain: The Man and His Work). Pp. 114-16, classifying MT's work into the groups of "Fiction of the Contemporary Scene" (GA and AC); "Fiction out of Hannibal" (TS, HF, TS Abroad, TS Detective, PW); "History and Legend" (P&P, CY, JA, MS) reprinted in Kesterson (1973), pp. 60-61.

B47 WILSON, EDMUND. By the Shores of Light: A Literary Chronicle of the Twenties and Thirties. New York: Farrar, Straus and Young, Inc. Passim. [A collection of essays by Wilson in the twenties and thirties; most appeared in the New Republic.]

  On the Brooks Ordeal of Mark Twain in "The Delegate from Great Neck" (April 30, 1924; pp. 145-47); "The Pilgrimage of Henry James" (May 6, 1925; pp. 226-27). On DeVoto and the controversy with Brooks in "Bernard DeVoto" (February 3, 1937; pp. 650-57). In "The All-Star Literary Vaudeville" (June 30, 1926) he says Sherwood Anderson, Hemingway, Gertrude Stein and Ring Lardner have each "developed what seems only a special branch of the same colloquial language, based directly on the vocabulary and rhythm of ordinary American speech," in "a genre that has already produced one masterpiece in Mark Twain's Huckleberry Finn, a work to which Anderson, Hemingway and Lardner are probably all indebted" (p. 234). In "Talking United States" (New Yorker, date not given) Wilson contends that "Relatively uneducated writers like Ring Lardner and Mark Twain have had so poor a literary vocabulary that they were likely to seem bald or thin when they attempted straight English prose, and they could only express themselves adequately by having their story told by a character who spoke some form of illiterate dialect or special slang" (p. 638).

B48 YOUNG, JAMES HARVEY. "Anna Dickinson, Mark Twain and Bret Harte," Pennsylvania Magazine of History and Biography, LXXVI (January), 39-46.

  The "queen of the lyceum" was a Quaker girl born in Philadelphia, emancipated in many respects but bearing a genteel antipathy toward MT. A friend of the Langdon family, she wrote in 1873: "I have a fresh wonder how the flower of their house, Olivia, as frail in body as she is clear of mind & lovely of soul ever married the vulgar boor to whom she gave herself. -- I hear of him all about the country at wine suppers, & late orgies, -- dirty, smoking,

drinking--with brains no doubt, but--" On her request MT once spent an entire day writing letters of introduction to his acquaintances in England before she went there on a lecture tour, but when she asked him to do so a second time he refused; the words "Good God!" in his letter to her are imperfectly crossed out. Not blind to Bret Harte's failings, she esteemed him above MT, whom she blamed for a "brutal" review of one of his books in a New York paper in 1876. Young shows points of similarity between Anna Dickinson and Charles Dudley Warner's character Ruth Bolton in GA; MT's Laura Hawkins has something of her temperament.

B49 YOUNG, PHILIP. "Adventures of Huckleberry Finn," Chapter VI in his Ernest Hemingway (New York, Toronto: Rinehart & Company, Inc.), pp. 181-212.

  Compares Huck with Nick Adams, another outsider who cannot accept the values the world has presented him; both are honest and sensitive, lacking in humor and intensely serious (p. 202). Hemingway grew up as a young Huck Finn. Unfortunately, Young draws somewhat trustingly on MT's Autobiography as a source of much of his biographical information.

1953 A BOOKS

A1 CARDWELL, GUY ADAMS. Twins of Genius. East Lansing: Michigan State College Press.

  On the 1884-1885 tour of public readings by MT and George Washington Cable; includes press notices and previously unpublished letters (1881-1906), 18 by MT and 20 by Cable.

A2 CLEMENS, CYRIL. Mark Twain and Dwight D. Eisenhower. Foreword by Winston S. Churchill, Knight of Mark Twain; Mark Twain Gold Medal, 1943. Webster Groves, Missouri: International Mark Twain Society.

  Cyril Clemens's account of Eisenhower's enjoyment of Mark Twain, together with letters from Eisenhower and Mrs. Eisenhower. Two of these letters (typed) are reproduced in facsimile, together with generally accurate transcripts. "The Mark Twain Quarterly, Winter, 1953 (Volume IX, No. 3) pages 1-4, contained some of the material published in this book." [26-page pamphlet.]

A3 CLEMENS, SAMUEL L. Mark Twain's First Story, ed. Franklin J. Meine. N.p.: Prairie Press, n.d.

  Text of "The Dandy Frightening the Squatter," with a foreword by Meine dated October 15, 1952; an order slip in the copy in the Mark Twain Papers gives the year of publication as 1953.

1953 - Books

A4 ENGLISH, THOMAS, ed. Mark Twain to Uncle Re-
mus, 1881-1885. Atlanta: The Library,
Emory University. (Emory University Publi-
cations: Sources & Reprints, Series VII,
No. 3).
Letters from MT to Joel Chandler Harris.
Discusses the way "De Woman wid de Gold'n
Arm" ought to be read. Also includes a re-
view of The Prince and the Pauper reprinted
from the Atlanta Constitution of
December 25, 1881, p. 11 (pp. 21-22).

A5 KRUMPELMANN, JOHN T. Mark Twain and the German Language. (Louisiana State University
Studies, Humanities Series, No. 3). Baton
Rouge: Louisiana State University Press.
A general study of MT's amateurish interest in the language (21-page pamphlet, documented almost entirely from MT's own published writings).

1953 B SHORTER WRITINGS

B1 ANDERSON, SHERWOOD. Letters of Sherwood Anderson, ed. Howard Mumford Jones and Walter
B. Rideout. Boston: Little, Brown and Company.
Passim (indexed), with Anderson expressing
profound admiration for MT in letters to a
number of persons, among them Waldo Frank
before the publication of Our America
(1919.B12) and Van Wyck Brooks before the
publication of The Ordeal of Mark Twain
(1922). Several of the letters to Brooks
are reprinted in Edmund Wilson, ed., The
Shock of Recognition, with an introduction
by Brooks (1943, pp. 1256-90).

B2 *ANON. "Dan DeQuille's Papers Given Bancroft
Library. Rare Collection Bares Data on
Famous Comstock Editor," Oakland Tribune,
November 22, 1953.
[Source: Reprinted in Twainian, XIII
(March-April, 1954), 3.]

B3 AUDEN, W. H. "Huck and Oliver," Listener, L
(October 1), 540-41.
Contrasts attitudes toward nature in HF
and Oliver Twist; observes Huck's stoicism
and calls his decision to free Jim "an act
of moral improvisation." There is in the
book "a kind of sadness, as if freedom and
love were incompatible." (From a BBC Third
Programme broadcast.) Reprinted in Smith
(1963), pp. 112-16.

B4 BEEBE, LUCIUS. "Territorial Enterprise,"
American Heritage, IV (Spring), 20-23,
67-68.
A popular history of the old and the
resurrected Enterprise by the modern publisher.

B5 BLASSINGAME, WYATT. "The Use of the Lie in
'Huckleberry Finn' as a Technical Device,"
Mark Twain Quarterly, IX (Winter), 11-12.
There are twenty-nine lies told by seven
liars before Tom shows up at his Aunt Sal-
ly's, with little artistic justification.

B6 BUDD, LOUIS J. [Review: Dixon Wecter, Sam
Clemens of Hannibal (1952).] American
Literature, XXV (May), 249-50.
"Mr. Wecter's well-written, richly documented chronicle of Clemens's boyhood is in
its tentative form better than most mortals'
final copy" (p. 250), and it is our loss
that Wecter did not live to carry his study
beyond 1853.

B7 CARROLL, LEWIS. The Diaries of Lewis Carroll.
Now First Edited and Supplemented by Roger
Lancelyn Green. London: Cassell & Company
Ltd. 2 vols. II, p. 382 (entry of July 26,
1879).
Lewis Carroll's only comment on MT is "Met
Mr. Clemens (Mark Twain), with whom I was
pleased and interested." The editor supple-
ments this with MT's reaction as it appeared
in the Autobiography.

B8 CARTER, PAUL J., JR. "The Influence of William
Dean Howells upon Mark Twain's Social Satire," University of Colorado Studies, Series
in Language and Literature, No. 4,
pp. 93-100.
Far from having weakened MT's development
as a social critic, Howells was himself ac-
tively interested in sociological theories,
a reader of Tolstoy, and well aware of the
crimes of the capitalist order. In 1887 he
wrote a letter to the New York Tribune, criticizing the conviction of eight labor leaders for murder in the Haymarket Riot; although he and his wife believed that he was
risking his career, she supported him. Howells took a strong interest in the American
labor movement, and saw more deeply into
national and world issues than MT did. The
two were independent in their thinking, but
any influence of Howells on MT "should have
proved a stimulus rather than a hindrance."

B9 CLEMENS, CYRIL. "Mark Twain and Dwight D.
Eisenhower," Mark Twain Quarterly, IX (Winter), 1-4.
On Eisenhower's admiration of MT; contains
notes to Cyril Clemens from Eisenhower,
thanking him for books, for being made a
Knight of Mark Twain, etc., and from Mamie
Doud Eisenhower thanking him for the honor
of having been "unanimously elected a Daughter of Mark Twain."

B10 CLEMENS, SAMUEL L. Letter to Livingston
Wright. Twainian, XII (May-June), 4.
Dated April 17, 1903, discusses an MS by
Wright arguing that Mary Baker Eddy could
not have written Science and Health. ["Reprinted from the New York World. (Contains
an affadavit dated Boston, Oct. 31, 1906.)"]

B11 _____. "Mark Twain and the Reporter," Twainian, XII (September-October), 1-3.
Comic, rambling interview which appeared
in the Buffalo Express, April 1, 1894; a
long introductory letter from Frank C. Willson speculates that it might be reprinted

(CLEMENS, SAMUEL L.)
from a New York paper, or could be MT's own work. [The date may be significant--T.A.T.]

B12 COLEMAN, RUFUS A. "Mark Twain in Montana, 1895," Montana Magazine of History, III (Spring), 9-17.
On MT's visit there while lecturing, July 31-August 5; documented from Major James B. Pond, Eccentricities of Genius (1900, using the 1901 London ed.) and contemporary newspaper accounts.

B13 _____. "Mark Twain's Jumping Frog: Another Version of the Famed Story," Montana Magazine of History, III (Summer), 29-30.
Introduction and reprinted newspaper interview (Anaconda Standard, April 24, 1910) of William ("Doc") Paulding, who told an apocryphal story of a time when he and MT tricked a man with a bet on a frog they had loaded with shot.

B14 *COX, JAMES M. "Treasure Island and Tom Sawyer," Folio, XVIII (February), 7-21.
[Source: Leary (1970), p. 61.]

B15 [DAVIS, CHESTER L.] "Known and Unknown," Twainian, XII (July-August), 1-3.
An MT letter and some excerpts from his works, reprinted in American Union (Boston), Portland Transcript, Buffalo Express, and elsewhere, here reprinted without significant commentary.

B16 _____. "Mark Twain in London," Twainian, XII (September-October), 4; (November-December), 3-4; concluded XIII (January-February, 1954), 2-4.
Chiefly based on MT's copy (with his annotations) of Moncure Daniel Conway's Autobiography, Memories, and Experiences (Houghton, Mifflin & Co., 1904). Includes reprint of the chapter on "Mark Twain in London" in 1872.

B17 _____. "Research Goes On," Twainian, XII (May-June), 3-4.
Without editorial comment, reproduces the text of correspondence between George Hiram Brownell and The Kablegram (publication of Kable Brothers, printers) and the Merganthaler Linotype Company, concerning the Paige typesetting machine.

B18 _____. "Studies, Research and Books on Mark Twain," Twainian, XII (May-June), 1-2.
On the problems encountered in answering large numbers of queries concerning MT.

B19 _____. "The Typesetting Machine and Mark's Inventions," Twainian, XIII (July-August), 4.
"We have evidence now that the Merganthaler Company acquired the patents and Paige machines in the year 1897"; mostly speculation on the terms of acquisition, with little information.

B20 ELIOT, THOMAS STEARNS. American Literature and the American Language. An Address delivered at Washington University on June 9, 1953. Washington University Studies. New Series. Language and Literature, No. 23.
[Source: letter and photocopy from Frances Pfaff, Reference Librarian, Washington University Library, September 22, 1975.]
In HF, MT "reveals himself to be one of those writers, of whom there are not a great many in any literature, who have discovered a new way of writing, valid not only for themselves but for others. I should place him, in this respect, even with Dryden and Swift, as one of those rare writers who have brought their language up to date, and in so doing, 'purified the dialect of the tribe.' In this respect I should put him above Hawthorne: though no finer a stylist, and in obvious ways a less profound explorer of the soul." MT's Mississippi is "the universal river of human life--more universal, indeed, than the Congo of Joseph Conrad.... There is in Twain, I think, a great unconscious depth, which gives to Huckleberry Finn this symbolic value: a symbolism all the more powerful for being uncalculated and unconscious" (pp. 16-17). Reprinted 1966.B42.

B21 GOHDES, CLARENCE. [Review: Dixon Wecter, Sam Clemens of Hannibal (1952).] South Atlantic Quarterly, LII (April), 309-10.
This book "adds more details or removes credibility from more erroneous assertions than all its competitors," although "no startling new disclosures turn up.... Mr. Wecter was always an entertaining writer as well as an industrious scholar. His last book is delightful to read."

B22 LENNON, E. JAMES. "Mark Twain Abroad," Quarterly Journal of Speech, XXXIX (April), 197-200.
On MT's world lecture tour of 1895-1896 his audiences were impressed by the apparent spontaneity of his speeches. It is widely but mistakenly assumed that his performances consisted of readings from his works; in fact there were numerous local and topical references.

B23 LORCH, FRED W. "Mark Twain's 'Sandwich Islands' Lecture and the Failure at Jamestown, New York, in 1869," American Literature, XXV (November), 314-25.
Presents the contemporary reaction, considers what it reveals of popular attitudes concerning humorous lectures; it offers "at least a partial explanation of his fear of being considered a mere 'funny' man, a mere buffoon on the platform." Includes contemporary accounts. For fuller treatment of MT's lecturing and contemporary reactions to it see Lorch's The Trouble Begins at Eight (1968); in connection with one reaction at the time, See Alexander E. Jones, (1954.B32), pp. 421-25.

B24 McCLOSKEY, JOHN C. "Mark Twain as Critic in The Innocents Abroad," American Literature, XXV (May), 139-51.

"The Innocents Abroad is not mere ridicule, not the naïve pointing of the finger of scorn at whatever the unlettered man from the backwoods does not understand.... It is satire, the product of an alert, informed, and sophisticated mind, well aware of values and ready to acknowledge them, yet complicated by prejudices and by an awareness of its professional duties as a journalistic humorist with commitments to the Alta California."

B25 McKEITHAN, D. M. "Bull Rides Described by 'Scroggins,' G. W. Harris, and Mark Twain," Southern Folklore Quarterly, XXVII (December), 241-43.

Uncle Laxart's bull-ride story in JA (II, Chapter XXXVI), originally intended for P&P, probably came from "Sicily Burns's Wedding" in Sut Lovingood's Yarns by George Washington Harris. In a letter to McKeithan, Walter Blair suggests another possible source in "Scroggins's" "Deacon Smith's Bull, or Mike Fink in a Tight Place," which MT may also have known. Reprinted in his Court Trials in Mark Twain, and Other Essays (1958).

B26 _____. "Mark Twain's Letters of Thomas Jefferson Snodgrass," Philological Quarterly, XXXII (October), 353-65.

Traces parallels between William Tappan Thompson's Major Jones's Sketches of Travel (1847) and three letters of "Thomas Jefferson Snodgrass" MT wrote for the Keokuk Saturday Post (November 1, 1856) and Daily Post (November 29, 1856 and April 10, 1857); the "Major Jones" and "Snodgrass" material is quoted at length. After having established MT's familiarity with Thompson's "Major Jones" material, McKeithan suggests that parallels in Innocents Abroad and Roughing It may also be derivations; he is more cautious about a possible derivation in A Tramp Abroad. Reprinted in his Court Trials in Mark Twain and Other Essays (1958).

B27 *_____. "Mark Twain's Tom Sawyer, Detective," Studia Neophilologica, XXV, 161-79.

[Source: MHRA Annual Bibliography (1953-1954), No. 6567.] Reprinted in his Court Trials in Mark Twain and Other Essays (1958).

B28 MARBERRY, M. M. Splendid Poseur: Joaquin Miller--American Poet. New York: Thomas Y. Crowell Company. Passim on MT (indexed).

On Miller introducing MT to Richard Monckton Milnes (Lord Houghton), pp. 114-15; Charles Warren Stoddard introduced MT and Ambrose Bierce in 1873 (p. 134).

B29 MARX, LEO. "Mr. Eliot, Mr. Trilling, and Huckleberry Finn," American Scholar, XXII (Autumn), 423-40.

Replying to their defense of the ending, Marx argues that "it jeopardizes the significance of the entire novel. To take seriously what happens at the Phelps farm is to take lightly the entire downstream journey." When Huck says to Jim on Jackson's Island "They're after us!" he identifies himself with Jim's flight from slavery; yet in the end, although Jim is free, it was not the journey that took him to freedom. The symmetry of structure that some critics see is imposed on the novel from outside; in fact, the journey was doomed to failure, but "Clemens did not acknowledge the truth his novel contained," the inevitability of a partial defeat. Reprinted in Marks (1959), pp. 53-64; Bradley (1962), pp. 328-41; Lettis (1962), pp. 350-64; Cardwell (1963), pp. 72-81; Simpson (1968), pp. 26-40.

B30 MEYER, GEORGE W. "Days of Innocence," American Scholar, XXII (Winter), 112-14.

A review of Dixon Wecter's Sam Clemens of Hannibal (1952), "a monumental work of scholarship whose every page will be read with delight."

B31 PARSONS, COLEMAN O. "Sam Clemens in Mythland," Virginia Quarterly Review, XXIX (Winter), 152-55.

A review of Dixon Wecter, Sam Clemens of Hannibal (1952); discusses MT's youth and his temperament, making little evaluation of the book.

B32 PARTRIDGE, HENRY M. "Was Sam Clemens 'Lewis Carroll'?" Mark Twain Quarterly, IX (Winter), 19-20.

MT's fondness for hoaxes suggests that "he must have sought secret outlets for his overproduction" under several pseudonyms; moreover, "he was intrigued by acrostics and ciphers and was a master of the Morse code. His enthusiasm for short-hand led him to suggest the use of the short-hand alphabet in place of the Latin. He was proficient in the use of sign-language and dactylology, adept at making up anagrams and writing backwards, 'mirror writing.'" There is no documentation of these statements, which will surprise students of MT, nor is reason given for identifying MT as author of "Lewis Carroll's" works. A parenthetical note says that this was "Written in 1936," seventy years before the year 2006 [sic], and a promise at the end, "To be continued," was not kept--perhaps fortunately.

B33 SCHMIDT, PAUL. "Mark Twain's Satire on Republicanism," American Quarterly, V (Winter), 344-56.

(SCHMIDT, PAUL)
MT ridicules Eastern political orthodoxy and the eighteenth-century republicanism on which it is based, together with its characteristic emphasis on ideals of Individualism, Freedom, and Progress; his response to genteel charges of Western savagery and "loutish stupidity" is to burlesque them. His depiction of politics in the mining-camps, his sometimes approving accounts of irregular justice, and his portrayal in RI of the outlaw Slade neither glamorized nor condemned (but seen through the admiring eyes of a tenderfoot) are at odds with Eastern gentility.

B34 SCOTT, ARTHUR L. "The Innocents Abroad Revaluated," Western Humanities Review, VII (Summer), 215-23.
"It cannot be denied that Mark Twain wrote of Europe from the viewpoint of an American Westerner who was ignorant of many cultural values. He did not, however, lack the humility of his ignorance, as most critics would have us believe." A number of such critics are listed (without facts of publication and generally without titles of their studies); to balance their portrait of MT Scott cites examples of appreciation and sensitivity in IA. Article reprinted in Kesterson (1973), pp. 117-25.

B35 ____. "Mark Twain Looks at Europe," South Atlantic Quarterly, LII (July), 399-413.
MT's attitude matured after IA, though even there he betrayed "a deep romantic vein." MT represented "national culture in human terms.... As other writers had drawn America closer to Europe, Mark Twain drew Europe closer to America."

B36 ____. "Mark Twain's Revisions of The Innocents Abroad for the British Edition of 1872," American Literature, XXV (March), 43-61.
More than four hundred revisions produced a work more literary, more conventional in style, less positive in its judgment of things foreign. "The English edition is less wordy, less free in its comic spirit, less outrageous in its buffoonery, and less fun to read--at least for the average American."

B37 STEPHENS, H. B. "Mark Twain's 'Dorg,'" Twainian, XII (July-August), 3.
A mildly humorous account of MT's dog "Burns," with a note from MT and a few doggerel lines; reprinted from Every Other Saturday, I (December 20, 1884), 457-58.

B38 TRAUBEL, HORACE. With Walt Whitman in Camden, January 21 to April 7, 1889, ed. Sculley Bradley. Philadelphia: University of Pennsylvania Press.
Traubel quotes Whitman on MT: "I think he mostly misses fire: I think his life misses fire: he might have been something:

he comes near to being something: but he never arrives" (p. 208). "I have always regarded him as friendly, but not warm: not exactly against me: not for me either." Letters from Rudolph Schmidt to Whitman in 1874, 1875 are less gentle: "As representants for mental power and intellectual vigor such people as Bret Harte and Mark Twain are fading away into ridiculousness" (p. 337); "But your humorists of the day I don't like. Mark Twain has been translated into Danish this year. He is a detestable fool" (p. 464).

B39 "TWARK MAIN," "Archimedes," Twainian, XII (November-December), 2-3.
Contains the text of thoughts on land monopoly which could well have come from MT himself. An introductory note credits Caroline Harnsberger with having helped find the essay, and asks whether MT and Henry George were friends; the answer is not conclusive.

B40 WIGGINS, ROBERT A. "Mark Twain and the Drama," American Literature, XXV (November), 279-86.
MT was exposed to the theater even in his youth, later wrote reviews, had a kind of theatrical experience in his lecturing, appeared in private theatricals, and made attempts at writing for the stage. "The form of Twain's fiction recalls his practice in playwriting of concentrating on the scene or episode as his chief structural element" (p. 282).

B41 WILLIAMS, STANLEY T. [Review: Dixon Wecter, Sam Clemens of Hannibal (1952).] Yale Review, XLII (March), 475-78.
The details make the book heavy going, but "we must, however, admire both his tireless investigation and his courage in making his account so complete."

B42 WULIGER, ROBERT. "Mark Twain on King Leopold's Soliloquy," American Literature, XXV (May), 234-37.
Describes one letter and contains text of three others from MT to officials of the Congo Reform Association: October 15, 1904 (described), April 11, 1905, and (circa) January 12, 1906 to E. D. Morel; to Thomas S. Barbour, January 8, 1906. Adds no new information.

1954 A BOOKS

A1 ALLEN, JERRY. The Adventures of Mark Twain. Boston: Little, Brown and Company.
"Although he never completed his biography, the story of his life was written, and by him. He gave it in snatches, sometimes in the guise of fiction, sometimes in the guarded privacy of his notes and letters.... The clues he furnished to his fiction have been traced back to parent facts, and the people, the places, the incidents, have here been taken out of the fictional dress he

(ALLEN, JERRY)
gave them and put back into the life he
lived" (p. ix).

A2   ASSELINEAU, ROGER. The Literary Reputation of
Mark Twain from 1910 to 1950: A Critical
Essay and a Bibliography. Paris: Marcel
Didier.
Consists of an introductory critical essay
on the growth of MT criticism in the United
States and an annotated bibliography of secondary material on MT for this period, as
well as a few items for 1951-1952 and for
the years before 1910. The introductory
essay is a sound and valuable survey of
criticism for the years 1910-1950. The bibliography, including a number of items by
foreign critics, has been of great assistance in the compilation of the present bibliography, for some items in which it is
the only source.

A3   PEARE, CATHERINE O. Mark Twain: His Life.
New York: The Junior Literary Guild and
Henry Holt and Company.
A biography for young readers, based pri-
marily on Paine.

A4   STONG, PHIL. Mississippi Pilot: With Mark
Twain on the Great River. Garden City,
N.Y.: Doubleday & Company.
A work of fiction for young readers, in
which MT is a character.

1954 B SHORTER WRITINGS

B1   ANON. "Expressive Voices: The Emergence of
a National Style," Times Literary Supplement, September 17, pp. xii-xiii.
Passim on MT, praising the "instinctive
casualness and realism" of his colloquial
style and citing him as an examplar of the
emerging American style.

B2   ANON. "University Gets Mark Twain Items,"
New York Times, September 19, p. 120.
Reports the acquisition by the University
of California (Berkeley) of "about 1600
family letters," 134 of them signed by MT,
from the estate of his grandniece Anita
Moffett; also briefly describes other MT
acquisitions by the university.

B3   ANON. [Brief Review: Roger Asselineau, The
Literary Reputation of Mark Twain from 1910
to 1950.] Times Literary Supplement,
September 24, p. 614.
Asselineau deserves the gratitude of scholars who "will henceforth be saved the trouble of searching through library catalogues
and indexes of periodicals."

B4   APPEL, JOHN J. "Mark Twain's View of Jews,"
Congress Weekly (December 6), pp. 16-18.
A popular account, describing MT's com-
ments on the Jews in IA, his notebooks, and
"Concerning the Jews"; concludes that he was
sympathetic and tolerant, and "seems to have

understood the historical necessity behind
such a movement as Zionism," but was essentially superficial in his outlook.

B5   BAETZHOLD, HOWARD G. "Mark Twain's 'The Prince
and the Pauper,'" Notes and Queries (London), CXCIX, n.s. I (September), 401-403.
Although Paine gives Charlotte M. Yonge's
The Prince and the Page as inspiration for
The Prince and the Pauper, "the story and
characters...bear no resemblance whatever."
Her The Little Duke may be another matter,
since MT's book "contains parallels...which
must be more than coincidental" in characters, relationships, and situations.

B6   BOOTH, BRADFORD A. "Mark Twain's Comments on
Bret Harte's Stories," American Literature,
XXV (January), 492-95.
Consists primarily of 435 words of manuscript marginalia by MT in his copy of The
Luck of Roaring Camp, and Other Sketches
(1870). "Though he is always alert to
Harte's carelessness and inattention, particularly in the dialogue, he has a lively
sense of his friend's merits as a writer of
vigorous and colorful narrative"
(pp. 492-93).

B7   BROOKS, VAN WYCK. Scenes and Portraits: Memories of Childhood and Youth. New York:
E. P. Dutton & Co., Inc.
Describes seeing MT for the first and only
time--lying in his coffin at the Fifth Avenue church (p. 158 in the reprint of the
book as the first section of Van Wyck Brooks:
An Autobiography, 1965).

B8   BROWN, GLENORA W., and DEMING B. BROWN. A
Guide to Soviet Russian Translations of
American Literature. New York: King's
Crown Press, Columbia University.
Lists translations of MT's works, Nos.
1540-1632 (pp. 199-208).

B9   BURNHAM, TOM. "Mark Twain and the Austrian
Edison," American Quarterly, VI (Winter),
364-72.
On Jan Szczepanik and MT's interest in
him as reflected in "The Austrian Edison
Keeping School Again" and "From the 'London
Times' of 1904," both of which appeared in
Century Magazine (October, November, 1898).

B10   CARTER, EVERETT. Howells and the Age of Realism. Philadelphia and New York: J. B. Lippincott Company, passim.
Many references to MT's writing and specific works.

B11   *CLEMENS, CYRIL. "Mark Twain and Eugene Field,"
Hobbies--The Magazine for Collectors, LVIII
(April), 128.
[Source: Leary (1970), p. 60.]

B12   CLEMENS, SAMUEL L.   "Mark Twain's War Experiences: His Graphic Recital of them at the Dinner to the Boston Ancient and Honorable Artillery Company," Twainian, XIII (March-April), 1-2.
      Reprint of a clipping sent by Caroline Thomas Harnsberger from the New York Times, October 7, 1877; MT is quoted in an account of the Civil War experiences which he described elsewhere in "The Private History of a Campaign that Failed."

B13   _____. "Rev. Charles Kingsley and 'Mark Twain,'" Twainian, XIII (January-February), 1.
      Text of an MT address in Boston, 1874, apparently following an introduction by Charles Kingsley. A brief headnote by Chester L. Davis says this appeared in The Commonwealth, Boston, February 28, 1874, p. 4; he adds: "Johnson's Bibliography reports 'Introducing Charles Kingsley--Speech, Boston, February 17, 1874: 'Modern Eloquence 2, 1901.'" (sic). Caroline Thomas Harnsberger corrects this with a copy of Modern Eloquence with the relevant material reprinted in the following issue (March-April), 2.

B14   COX, JAMES M. "Remarks on the Sad Initiation of Huckleberry Finn," Sewanee Review, LXII (July-September), 389-405.
      On Tom and Huck and their antithetical values, and MT's fascination with Tom. Reprinted in Marks (1959), pp. 65-74.

B15   *CUNLIFFE, MARCUS. "American Humour and the Rise of the West: Mark Twain," in his The Literature of the United States (London: Penguin Books), pp. 149-69.
      [Source: Beebe and Feaster (1968), p. 98. Also in 1964.B32 revised ed., pp. 149-69.]

B16   [DAVIS, CHESTER L.] "The Anita Moffet[t] Collection of Mark Twain Materials," Twainian, XIII (November-December), 1.
      A brief description of the collection of letters by MT and relatives, and ten scrapbooks of clippings, recently acquired by the University of California, Berkeley.

B17   _____. "Dogberry," Twainian, XIII (July-August), 1-4.
      "From our correspondence files your Secretary has found four newspaper stories by "Dogberry," The Golden Era's Distressed Novelist, together with correspondence by and between Morse and Brownell which in the opinion of your Secretary most likely establishes the fact that they were written by Mark Twain." The texts from The Golden Era (December 17, 1865-January 14, 1866) follow, with a conclusion in the following issue of the Twainian (September-October).

B18   _____. "Johnson's Bibliography," Twainian, XIII (September-October), 2.
      On the Merle Johnson bibliography of MT's works and its continuation by various editors after his death.

B19   _____. "Life as I Find It," Twainian, XIII (September-October), 2.
      A sketch in Agricultural Almanac attributed to MT; place is either New York or Lancaster, Pennsylvania, and date appears to be 1874.

B20   _____. "Mark Twain in London," Twainian, XIII (January-February), 2-4.
      Conclusion of extracts from MT's own annotated copy of Moncure Daniel Conway's autobiography; for beginning of series see Twainian, 1953.

B21   _____. "Mark Twain's 'Author's Sketch Book,'" Twainian, XIII (November-December), 2-4.
      On a four-page newspaper published in Hartford in November, 1870; reprints much of the contents, attributing to MT material which may or may not be his. (Continued in the next issue of Twainian, January-February, 1955, but with nothing more relating to MT).

B22   _____. "Orion Clemens and the American Publisher," Twainian, XIII (September-October), 3-4.
      "The issue of May 1871 contains what appears to be pages 70-72 of the book 'Roughing It' but under the title 'The Old-Time Pony Express of the Great Plains, ['] by Mark Twain, and an editorial which bears the handwritten legend on the photostat we have 'By Orion Clemens, Editor.'" This turns out to be a veiled advertisement for a seed company in the text, which is reproduced.

B23   _____. "A Woman's Part in a Revolution, By Mrs. John Hays Hammond," Twainian, XIII (May-June), 1-2.
      On MT's marginal comments in his copy of that book about the Boer War. "Some of the words written by Mark as notations, especially concerning the brutalities, is better left out of this printing.... Your Secretary cannot see the necessity of printing in bold type any obscene words in the Twainian, the circulation being as general as it has become."

B24   _____. [Review: Roger Asselineau, The Literary Reputation of Mark Twain from 1910 to 1950: A Critical Essay and a Bibliography.] Twainian, XIII (September-October), 3.
      Uncritical, consisting chiefly of a lengthy quotation from the portions of Asselineau's "Foreword" which describe the plan of the bibliography and extend thanks for grants, the assistance of libraries, etc.

1954 - Shorter Writings

B25   FERGUSON, DELANCEY. "Mark Twain, Impresario," New York Times Book Review (February 7), p. 4.

        A descriptive review of Guy A. Cardwell, Twins of Genius (1953) as thorough, "informative," and "valuable and pleasant reading."

B26   FUSSELL, EDWIN. "Hemingway and Mark Twain," Accent, XIV (Summer), 199-206.

        Noting Philip Young's essay in comparative biography and psychology in the "Adventures of Huckleberry Finn" chapter of his Ernest Hemingway (1952), Fussell says that "Young's view of the Mark Twain-Hemingway connection and mine are not really contradictory; they are more like Marvell's lovers, so parallel they never meet." Fussell discusses the treatment of emotional, imaginative, and literary integrity in Huckleberry Finn, and Hemingway's concern with these matters in In Our Time, The Sun Also Rises, and other works.

B27   GERBER, HELMUT E. "Twain's Huckleberry Finn," Explicator, XII (March), Item 28.

        There is geographical, chronological, and thematic unity, and also a five-part "structural unity based on the pattern or rhythm of the alternating settings," but "organically asymmetrical or irregular." Huck has solved a problem and is changed by it.

B28   GOOLD, EDGAR H., JR. "Mark Twain on the Writing of Fiction," American Literature, XXVI (May), 141-53.

        Cites MT's observations on the work of other writers to illustrate the importance to him of realism, probability, concrete details, and suitable motivation and consistency on the part of the characters; notes a decorum that puts him in the company of Howells and Thackeray, rather than Thomas Hardy or George Moore.

B29   HENDERSON, ARCHIBALD. "Mark Twain and Bernard Shaw," Mark Twain Journal, IX (Summer), 1-3.

        On his appreciation of both MT and Shaw, whom he introduced to each other at St. Pancras Station in London, and of whom he wrote biographies.

B30   HOELTJE, HUBERT H. "When Mark Twain Spoke in Portland," Oregon Historical Quarterly, LV (March), 73-81.

        On MT's 1895 visit, during his world lecture tour. The cordial newspaper reception is summarized, and the interview in the Sunday Oregonian reprinted. In it, MT speaks favorably of governmental monopolies he has seen in Europe, reveals his plans for casual assembling of impressions for his next book (FE), and discusses the naming of Tom Sawyer and Huckleberry Finn; he denies the claim in recent San Francisco papers that a bartender named Tom Sawyer was his inspiration, and is reported as saying that "Finn was the name of the other boy, but I

tacked on the 'Huckleberry'"; Hoeltje points out that in the Autobiography MT said Tom Blankenship was the model for Huck. [In the North American Review serialization, August or September, 1907, MT said Huck was based on Frank Finn, son of Jimmy Finn (Source: Summary in Review of Reviews, London, XXXVI, September, 1907, 288)--T.A.T.]

B31   JONES, ALEXANDER E. "Mark Twain and Freemasonry," American Literature, XXVI (November), 363-73.

        MT became a Mason in 1861, a Master Mason on July 26; his interest lapsed when he went west, but he was reinstated before the Quaker City tour and "it is not surprising that Twain's renewed preoccupation with Masonic lore is reflected in The Innocents Abroad" (p. 365). Moreover, some of his philosophical views have Masonic parallels.

B32   _____. "Mark Twain and the 'Many Citizens' Letter," American Literature, XXVI (November), 421-25.

        Points out that a letter supposedly attacking MT's "Sandwich Islands" lecture in Jamestown, New York is in reality "not a serious attack but an example of tongue-in-cheek humor," the ostensible work of "a person who was often pompous, ordinarily gullible, and invariably ready to take a determined stand on an indefensible position." For the text of this letter and the circumstances surrounding it, see Lorch (1954.B40), pp. 314-25.

B33   KITZHABER, ALBERT R. "Mark Twain's Use of the Pomeroy Case in The Gilded Age," Modern Language Quarterly, XV (March), 42-56.

        Traces the parallel scandals of Senator Dilworthy in GA and Samuel Clarke Pomeroy, Republican Senator from Kansas: in addition to an absence of scruples, Pomeroy displayed "a convenient flair for prayer meetings and temperance movements...Twain's account in The Gilded Age, far from being overdrawn, is a surprisingly exact copy."

B34   KRUTCH, JOSEPH WOOD. "Speaking of Books," New York Times Book Review (May 23), p. 2.

        HF "conclusively...proves that a great work of fiction does not need to be what is called a 'good novel' or, indeed, a merely 'good' anything else." It is melodramatic and badly structured, "a botched job," but "uniquely delightful" in the same way as is the last quarter of LOM. HF has epic "largeness of plan...and there are ways in which an epic is better than even a 'good' novel." Reprinted in Bradley (1962.A2), pp. 362-63.

B35   LEARY, LEWIS. Articles on American Literature, 1900-1950. Durham, North Carolina: Duke University Press.

        Lists articles on MT, pp. 43-55; it has been a valuable source of information for the present bibliography; and all entries have been checked or listed as "not seen."

B36 _____. "Tom and Huck: Innocence on Trial," Virginia Quarterly Review, XXX (Summer), 417-30.
The structure and theme of TS express "a deeply underlying principle which haunted Mark Twain." In three sections, TS shows that adventure "leads innocently to knowledge of evil...wins out over prosaic adult methods of doing things," and, "compounded in part of the spirit of make-believe, imagination, illusion--that adventure, not common sense, leads to the wiping out of evil." In HF, Huck's response to evil was fear, repulsion, a desire to escape, but Tom's imaginative actions at the end, like Huck's attempt to flee, fail to end the evil. In sum, HF is the finer book, and "the contrived innocence of Tom fails," while "the questing spirit of Huck, who would be impatient at our even raising the spirit of innocence, lives on."

B37 LEASE, BENJAMIN. "Mark Twain and the Publication of Life on the Mississippi: An Unpublished Letter," American Literature, XXVI (May), 248-50.
Contains the text of a letter (January 6, 1883) to Osgood and Company about the plates and the proof-reading; adds little to the existing picture of MT.

B38 LENNON, E. JAMES [Review: Guy A. Cardwell, Twins of Genius (1953).] Quarterly Journal of Speech, XL (October), 339.
Descriptive and uncritical.

B39 LORCH, FRED W. "Mark Twain's 'Morals' Lecture during the American Phase of His World Tour in 1895-1896," American Literature, XXVI (March), 52-66.
Includes "as complete a text of the lecture as can be constructed from newspapers which reported it," quotations of contemporary reactions, and remarks by MT in interviews. For more about MT's lecturing, see Lorch's The Trouble Begins at Eight (1968.A2).

B40 _____. "Reply to Mr. Jones," American Literature, XXVI (November), 426-27.
Lorch says he himself considered the possibility that the "Many Citizens" letter was not a serious attack, but there is nothing else in the Jamestown Journal, apart from Coleman Bishop's article, which could have called forth MT's angry response. Lorch's main objection, however, is to a misinterpretation of his article by Jones: he did not assert that the attack contributed to a decision by MT to quit the lecture platform.

B41 McKEITHAN, D. M. "A Conjecture: Mark Twain and Winston Churchill," Notes and Queries (London), CXCIX, n.s. I (January), 39.
The words "blood and sweat and poverty" appear in Chapter X of The American Claimant, and in his essay "My Boyhood Dreams"

MT speaks of "blood and tears"; could these words have inspired Churchill's famous "blood, sweat, and tears"?

B42 P., L. [Brief Review: John T. Krumpelmann, Mark Twain and the German Language (1953).] English Studies (Amsterdam), XXXV (1954), 46.
"Mark Twain's peculiar brand of humor" may console "those who have no talent for foreign languages," but it seems unnecessary to "publish in a scientific and elaborate study every particular step on a road leading to...next to nothing."

B43 SHAW, BERNARD. "My Encounters with Mark Twain," Mark Twain Journal, IX (Summer), 24.
A reprinting, not indicated as such, of "Mark Twain and Bernard Shaw" in Mark Twain Quarterly, IX (Winter, 1951), 30.

B44 STALLMAN, ROBERT WOOSTER. "Come Back to the Raft!" Sewanee Review, LXII (July-September), 441-42.
A poem on the cleverness of Huck and the wisdom of the river.

B45 *SÜHNEL, RUDOLPH. "Huckleberry Finn," in Karl Brunner, ed., Anglo-Americana: Festschrift für Leo von Hibler (Wiener Beiträge zur engl. Philologie, LXII), pp. 150-56.
[Source: MHRA Annual Bibliography (1954), Nos. 658, 6572.]

B46 TURNER, ARLIN. "Notes on Mark Twain in New Orleans," McNeese Review, VI (Spring), 10-22.
On MT in New Orleans in 1861 in his river-piloting days, and in 1882 while gathering material for LOM. Quotes an interview with Horace E. Bixby (who taught MT piloting) in the Times-Democrat, May 7, 1882.

B47 _____. [Review: Guy A. Cardwell, Twins of Genius (1953).] American Literature, XXVI (May), 266-67.
Chiefly descriptive rather than evaluative. The book "parallels and supplements" Fred W. Lorch in American Literature for January (1952.B32). Lorch and Cardwell have examined newspaper reports "and have reached much the same conclusions: that preferences among reporters and audiences were about even; that Mark Twain made better copy for the newspapers but often Cable's stories and his rendering of them received the higher praise; that Cable's literary reputation was as great as Mark Twain's before they went on the road and was enhanced by the publication of another novel, Dr. Sevier, on the eve of the tour and his highly controversial article on Negro rights midway of the tour. Huckleberry Finn was not off the press until the tour was nearly over."

B48 VOGELBACK, ARTHUR L. "Mark Twain and the Fight for Control of the Tribune," American Literature, XXVI (November), 374-83.
Not primarily about MT, but includes the

(VOGELBACK, ARTHUR L.)
text of his "New Cock Robin," which appeared in the Hartford Evening Post and Chicago Tribune (January 2, 1873).

B49 WAGENKNECHT, EDWARD. "World of Huck's Dad," Saturday Review of Literature, XXXVII (May 29), 15.
A review of Jerry Allen, The Adventures of Mark Twain. "Though it is absorbingly interesting throughout, it is not all of a piece." There is heavy use of secondary material, using paraphrase legitimately but relying perhaps too much on what she considers autobiographical in MT's own writing. There is something of a novelist's license in this, "one of the most readable books about Mark Twain."

B50 WECTER, DIXON. [Untitled: Excerpts from MT's correspondence of 1867-1868, concerning his relations with the New York Herald and New York Tribune.] Twainian, XIII (March-April), 4.

1955 A BOOKS

A1 SCOTT, ARTHUR L., ed. Mark Twain: Selected Criticism. Dallas: Southern Methodist University Press.
Reprints a number of useful critical articles and excerpts from books, 1867-1951; a revised edition appeared in 1967. The material reprinted is listed in the present bibliography and cross-referenced.

1955 B SHORTER WRITINGS

B1 *ADERMAN, RALPH M. "When Mark Twain Came to Town," Historical Messenger (Milwaukee), XI (December), 2-5.
[Source: Beebe and Feaster (1968), p. 93.]

B2 *ANICETTI, M. "Mark Twain a Venezia," Ateneo Veneto, CXXXIX (July-December), 97-111.
[Source: MHRA Annual Bibliography (1955), No. 8006.]

B3 ANON. "'Mark Twain's Quest' (A Rare Book)," Twainian, XIV (March-April), 1-2.
Reprint of an undated Hartford Courant article on MT's unsuccessful attempt to obtain a copy of The Enemy Conquered; or, Love Triumphant, and a letter to the editor of The Palladium giving further details (signed Thomas H. Pease, New Haven, April 23, 1884).

B4 *BAETZHOLD, HOWARD G. "Mark Twain's 'First Date' with Olivia Langdon," Missouri Historical Society Bulletin [formerly Glimpses of the Past], XI (January), 155-57.
[Source: Beebe and Feaster (1968), p. 94.]

B5 BAILIN, GEORGE. "Tom Sawyer: In Memoriam," Colorado Quarterly, III (Winter), 288-90.
A poem on Tom and his boyhood world.

B6 BALDANZA, FRANK. "The Structure of Huckleberry Finn," American Literature, XXVII (November), 347-55.
"I propose to show that without advanced planning, and spurred by momentary impulses--in all probability unconsciously--Mark Twain constructed whole passages of Huckleberry Finn on an aesthetic principle of repetition and variation." Reprinted in Marks (1959), pp. 75-81; in Lettis (1962), pp. 371-79.

B7 BELL, ROBERT E. "How Mark Twain Comments on Society Through Use of Folklore," Mark Twain Journal, X (Summer), 1-8, 24-25.
MT preserved folk histories and dialect, and represented the flavor of a region in his work; he was close to his materials, and in his work showed "what I consider the three central patterns of Mississippi Valley folklore.... 1. the folk-hero pattern; 2. the tall-tale pattern, and 3. the supernatural pattern."

B8 BLAIR, WALTER. [Review: Jerry Allen, The Adventures of Mark Twain (1954).] American Literature, XXVII (March), 124-25.
Calls Miss Allen "credulous" in trusting MT for biographical details, and the book "unsatisfactory" as an account of his life.

B9 BLANCK, JACOB. "'Hospital Days' in 'Sketches Old and New,'" Twainian, XIV (March-April), 4.
On p. 299 of the first edition of Sketches Old and New (1875) appears a paragraph headed "From 'Hospital Days'"; there is also an erratum slip indicating that the sketch should not have been included, and bibliographers have long argued the source. Blanck points to a recently discovered copy of Jane Stuart Woolsey's Hospital Days, privately and anonymously published New York, 1868, and suggests that the passage is part of an MT book review accidentally included; Blanck also cites another passage from the Woolsey book which turned up in Following the Equator. Reprinted from Publishers' Weekly, October 30, 1937; ends with note: "To Be Continued"--but there was no continuation.

B10 *BROOKS, CLEANTH. "Teaching the Novel: Huckleberry Finn," Proceedings of the First Yale Conference on the Teaching of English.
[Source: cited by Edward J. Gordon, in "What's Happened to Humor?" (1958.B34).]

B11 BROWNELL, FRANCES V. "The Role of Jim in Huckleberry Finn," Boston University Studies in English, I (Spring-Summer), 74-83.

(BROWNELL, FRANCES V.)

Jim is passive or absent in most of the episodes involving physical action, and his main role is that of "moral catalyst...it is my thesis that Jim's primary function is to further the characterization of Huckleberry Finn: by his presence, his personality, his actions, his words, to call forth from Huckleberry Finn a depth of tenderness and moral strength that could not otherwise have been fully and convincingly revealed to the reader."

B12 BRUNEAU, JEAN. [Review: Roger Asselineau, The Literary Reputation of Mark Twain from 1900 to 1950 (1954).] Revue de Littérature Comparée, XXIX, No. 1, 136-37.

"Il est peut-être regrettable que l'auteur n'ait cru devoir inclure les editions et traductions des oeuvres de Mark Twain ne comportant ni introduction, ni préface,' and more might have been done with MT's critical fortunes in France since 1917 (Cyrille Arnavon had covered the earlier period in Les lettres américaines devant la critique française [1888-1917], Paris: Les Belles-Lettres, 1952), but "le livre de M. Asselineau, qui se termine par un excellent Index, constitue donc une mine des documents très précieuse pour la littérature comparée."

B13 CLEMENS, CYRIL. "The Model for Huckleberry Finn," Hobbies--the Magazine for Collectors, LIX (February), 106-109.

"Not long before his death," Courtland P. Morris told Cyril Clemens about posing as model for all the characters in HF in the illustrations by Edward Windsor Kemble.

B14 COWLEY, MALCOLM. "Introduction," in Van Wyck Brooks, The Ordeal of Mark Twain. New York: Meridian Books (paperbound).

A balanced description of the background of Brooks's book and the debate with Bernard DeVoto, whose Mark Twain's America (1932) was less temperate than his later writing; the two critics gained from their confrontation. Brooks had produced a seminal book, whose first appearance in 1920 "is one of the true events in American literature, comparable with the publication of Emerson's The American Scholar, which announced and helped to produce the renaissance of the 1850's."

B15 CUNLIFFE, MARCUS. [Brief Review: Nils Erik Envist, American Humor in England before Mark Twain (Abo: Acta Academiae Aboensis. Humaniora, XXI, 1953).] Modern Language Review, L (July), 364.

"An excellent scholarly investigation of British responses to American humor as represented by such writers as 'Sam Slick,' Oliver Wendell Holmes, J. R. Lowell (in The Bigelow Papers), Artemus Ward, and Charles Godfrey Leland ('Hans Breitmann')." [As the title suggests, the book is not about

MT; the book itself has been examined, but is not listed in the present bibliography --T.A.T.]

B16 [DAVIS, CHESTER L.] "Background on Autobiography. Valuable Letters to Paine," Twainian, XIV (September-October), 1.

The Mark Twain Research Foundation has acquired "more than 200 letters which were sent to Albert Bigelow Paine during the last few years of Mark Twain's life and for several years afterwards." Paine has been criticized for suppressing information available to him; some of these letters may be published in future issues of the Twainian.

B17 _____. "Mark Twain Manuscript," Twainian, XIV (January-February), 1-3.

On the exhibit at the Pierpont Morgan Library, New York, November 19, 1954- February 28, 1955; the Huckleberry Finn MS was included, on loan. Quotes Antiquarian Bookman account of the event (date of the issue not given).

B18 _____. "Mark Twain's Religious Beliefs, as Indicated by Notations in His Books," Twainian, XIV (May-June), 1-4; (July-August), 1-4; (September-October), 1-4; (November-December), 3-4.

On MT's personal copy of William Edward Hartpole Lecky's History of European Morals (New York: D. Appleton & Company, 1879). Includes long quotations of Lecky's text and MT's marginal comments, interspersed with comments by Chester Davis.

B19 _____. "Steve Gillis Letter to Albert Bigelow Paine (Background on 'Biography')," Twainian, XIV (November-December), 1.

Text of the letter, merely appreciative.

B20 FADIMAN, CLIFTON. "A Note on Huckleberry Finn," in his Party of One: The Selected Writings of Clifton Fadiman (Cleveland and New York: The World Publishing Company), pp. 129-31.

HF is our national epic, important for the language, the rebellion against civilization. (Originally written as the introduction to a 1940 Heritage Press edition of HF).

B21 FIEDLER, LESLIE A. "'As Free as Any Cretur...," New Republic, CXXXIII (August 15), 17-18; (August 22), 16-18.

"Pudd'nhead Wilson is, after all, a fantastically good book, better than Mark Twain knew or his critics have deserved. Morally, it is one of the most honest books, in our literature, superior in this one respect to Huckleberry Finn; for here Twain permits himself no sentimental relenting, but accepts for once the logic of his own premises." When the real Tom Driscoll is freed at the end there is an ironic echo of Tom Sawyer's declaration that Nigger Jim was "as free as any cretur that walks this earth," and the

1955 - Shorter Writings

(FIEDLER, LESLIE A.)
indictment of the community's racism becomes "a local instance of some universal
guilt and doom." Reprinted in Smith
(1963.A5), pp. 130-39.

B22 FORD, THOMAS W. "The Miscegenation Theme in
Pudd'nhead Wilson," Mark Twain Journal, X
(Summer), 13-14.
Through "skillful handling of the subject" and a refusal to "condemn or condone"
miscegenation," MT escaped public criticism, even though Ford says the theme "was
totally avoided in nineteen-century American literature."

323 GERBER, JOHN. "Mark Twain's 'Private Campaign,'" Civil War History, I (March),
37-60.
MT's "The Private History of a Campaign
that Failed" (here reprinted, pp. 45-60)
"is primarily a literary rather than an
historical document," entertaining to read
but inconsistent with MT's brief service in
the "Marion Rangers." There is an account
of this service, based on the available
data. Gerber also reproduces from the Congressional Record an attack on MT on
January 25, 1940, by Congressman Joseph B.
Shannon of Missouri for his unheroic service, and a reply in a New York Times editorial of February 7.

4 G[OHDES], C[LARENCE]. [Very brief mention of
Roger Asselineau, The Literary Reputation
of Mark Twain from 1910 to 1950: A Criti-
cal Essay and a Bibliography (Paris: Marcel
Didier, 1954).] American Literature, XXVII
(May), 290-91.

*HAMADA, MASAJIRO. Mark Twain: His Character
and Works. Tokyo: Kenkyusha.
[Source: Facts of Publication from MHRA
Annual Bibliography (1955), No. 8028; sub-
title from Shunsuke Kamei, "Mark Twain in
Japan" (1963).]

HERRICK, GEORGE H. "Mark Twain, Reader and
Critic of Travel Literature," Mark Twain
Journal, X (Summer), 9-10, 22-23.
MT was familiar with travel books, and
his own standards called for accuracy,
brevity, and literary artistry.

HEUER, HERMANN. [Review: John T. Krumpelmann, Mark Twain and the German Language
(1953).] Archiv für das Studium der neueren
Sprachen, CXCII (June), 71-72.
Brief and descriptive, noting MT's residence in German-speaking countries and his
comic way of describing the language. [In
German.]

IGNATIEFF, LEONID. "American Literature in
the Soviet Union," Dalhousie Review, XXXV
(Spring), 55-66.
"10,000,000 copies of the works of Jack
London and 3,000,000 copies of the works of

Mark Twain circulated in the USSR between
the early twenties and 1940, these two authors being consistently the favourite American writers in that country." Although
Soviet critics have tried to exploit the
social criticism of these authors, "Jack
London...was too inconsistent to be of much
help. Mark Twain offered greater promise....
Unfortunately for them, it was not the later
works at all, but Tom Sawyer, The Prince and
the Pauper, and Huckleberry Finn that interested the Soviet public."

B29 LANE, LAURIAT, JR. "Why Huckleberry Finn is
a Great World Novel," College English, XVII
(October), 1-5.
It is authentic, with real human figures,
a real society, genuine moral and ethical
problems, with a generally direct and realistic treatment; it transcends national
limitations, it is epical in form, and contains the allegory of Huck's journey
"through the world of spirit, ever working
out a pattern of increasing involvement with
the world of reality and with his own self,
both cast aside at the beginning of the
journey." Reprinted in Marks (1959.A5),
95-100; in Bradley, et al. (1962.A2),
364-71.

B30 LONG, E. HUDSON. [Review: Roger Asselineau,
The Literary Reputation of Mark Twain from
1910 to 1950]. Études Anglaises, VIII
(October-December), 369-70.
The result of "a comprehensive investigation of criticism devoted to Twain," the
book contains "a sound appraisal" of the
Brooks-DeVoto controversy and "a perceptive
study" of MT's literary reputation.

B31 LORCH, FRED W. "Mark Twain's Lecture Tour of
1868-1869: 'The American Vandal Abroad,'"
American Literature, XXVI (January), 515-27.
Liberally documented with quotations
from contemporary newspaper accounts. For
further treatment of MT's lecturing, see
Lorch's The Trouble Begins at Eight (1968.A2).

B32 O'CONNOR, WILLIAM VAN. "Why Huckleberry Finn
Is Not the Great American Novel," College
English, XVII (October), 6-10.
"The critical acumen of Eliot and Trilling
notwithstanding, there are a number of flaws
in Huckleberry Finn, some of them attributable to Twain's refusal to respect the 'work
of art' and others attributable to his imperfect sense of tone." Twain is hardly
the "Lincoln of our literature" that Howells
called him: "If Lincoln had written novels,
he would, without doubt, have been a greater
novelist than Twain. His virtues include
Twain's and surpass them." Huck's appeal is
through an immature sort of innocence, and
thus of limited usefulness as a symbol; "If
we refuse to over-value him as a symbol, we
may be less inclined to over-value the novel,
or to over-value the language in which it is
written." Reprinted in Marks (1959.A5),

212

(O'CONNOR, WILLIAM VAN)
100-106; Bradley, et al. (1962.A2), 371-78; Lettis, et al. (1962.A11), 379-83.

B33 RAVITZ, ABE C., and NORRIS YATES. "Mark Twain, Cable, and the Philistine," Mark Twain Journal, X (Summer), 14, 23.
A reprinting of a story from Elbert Hubbard's The Philistine ("Heart to Heart Talks with Philistines by the Pastor of His Flock," XII [April, 1901], 146-49), about an explosion on a lecture tour when George Washington Cable implored MT to give up smoking, drinking, and swearing, and was told to mind his own affairs; Ravitz and Yates add that the story "cannot be dismissed as completely incredible," although much of it is obviously fabricated.

B34 REMES, CAROL. "The Heart of Huckleberry Finn," Masses & Mainstream, VIII (November), 8-16.
A popular account, not obtrusively Marxist. "One does not think of Huck as a boy. He seems to be the embodiment of the conscience of a decent humanity confronted with the evils in society and wanting to right them."

B35 REYNOLDS, HORACE. "Author's Sketch Book," Twainian, XIV (November-December), 1-2.
A reprinting from the Christian Science Monitor of July 29, 1955 [misprinted as 1952] of reaction to "Author's Sketch Book" in Twainian for November-December, 1955; chiefly descriptive, adding little to material in that issue of Twainian.

B36 *RICHIE, DONALD. "Mark Twain," Study of Current English (Tokyo), X (September), 33-40.
[Source: Leary (1970), p. 72.]

B37 *SCHONFELDER, KARL-HEINZ. [Review: Roger Asselineau, The Literary Reputation of Mark Twain (1954). Zeitschrift für Anglistik und Amerikanistik, III, 212-14.
[Source: MHRA Annual Bibliography (1955-1956), No. 8007.]

B38 SCHORER, C. E. "Mark Twain's Criticism of The Story of a Country Town," American Literature, XXVII (March), 109-112.
The text of a letter from MT to E. W. Howe, February 13, 1884.

B39 SCOTT, ARTHUR L. "The Century Magazine Edits Huckleberry Finn, 1884-1885," American Literature, XXVII (November), 356-62.
Describes alterations made in the interest of genteel taste by Richard Watson Gilder in publishing more than a quarter of the novel in the Century.

B40 _____. "Mark Twain: Critic of Conquest," Dalhousie Review, XXXV (Spring), 45-53.
A heated response to the Communist charge (summarized in New York Times, July 28,

1947, p. 13) that America has suppressed MT's attacks on imperialism. Summarizes his anti-imperialist statements, noting his shift to an attack on American expansionism. Extensively researched, but based on familiar material and thinly documented, without facts of publication.

B41 _____. "Mark Twain Revises Old Times on the Mississippi, 1875-1883," Journal of English and Germanic Philology, LIV (October), 634-38.
When the seven installments which had appeared in the Atlantic in 1875 were incorporated as Chapters IV-XVII of Life on the Mississippi, a number of purely mechanical changes were made, of the sort "which might be the work of a conscientious proofreader." In addition, there were 45 changes involving style or facts--but MT's dislike of the chore of revision is evident.

B42 SHAIN, CHARLES E. "The Journal of the Quaker City Captain," New England Quarterly, XXVIII (September), 388-94.
The Patten Free Library of Bath, Maine recently acquired the journal of the captain of the ship which took MT on the tour described in Innocents Abroad. Included are "121 pages of almost daily entries, followed by 24 newspaper clippings, some of which draw on the captain's notes, which were evidently written for the New York Sun by Moses S. Beach." "Clemens evidently saw something of Captain and Mrs. Duncan in New York, and he soon became an intimate in the Beecher circle to which the Duncans belonged." MT and Duncan later quarreled, publicly and bitterly.

B43 SMITH, HENRY NASH. "'That Hideous Mistake of Poor Clemens's,'" Harvard Library Bulletin, IX (Spring), 145-80.
A thorough account of MT's speech at the 1877 dinner given by the publishers of the Atlantic Monthly in honor of John Greenleaf Whittier's seventieth birthday. MT and Howells mistakenly considered the speech a disaster, but only because they "churned themselves into a state of mind which bore little relation to external reality at the time and distorted their memories of what happened." In fact, the reception when the speech was delivered was mixed rather than entirely cold, and there was favorable comment in Boston papers the next day, although there were later second thoughts and there were hostile comments from papers in Springfield, Chicago, and elsewhere; a survey of newspaper comment "suggests that indignation over Mark Twain's speech was greater in upcountry Massachusetts and in the Middle West than in Boston." There is extensive documentation from newspapers, and published reminiscences and correspondence of several persons involved, and several documents are reproduced, including part of the holograph manuscript, MT's letter of apology to his

(SMITH, HENRY NASH)
victims, and a seating plan for the dinner autographed by those present. [Much of the material cited is not included in the present bibliography.]

B44 _____. [Review: Roger Asselineau, The Literary Reputation of Mark Twain from 1910 to 1950.] Modern Language Notes, LXX (May), 383-85.
"Belongs to a very useful genre and is excellent of its kind," with a bibliography in which "the list is selective rather than complete, but the selection is intelligently made, and in reading it through I have not been reminded of any important items that are omitted." The introductory essay provides a survey of MT's reputation which "neatly analyzes the issues raised by Bernard DeVoto's attack on Brooks in Mark Twain's America (1932) and describes with restrained amusement the sectional pieties" that led scholars to claim him for various regions. "Scholars interested in Mark Twain will long be grateful for this admirable manual."

B45 SPILLER, ROBERT. The Cycle of American Literature: An Essay in Historical Criticism. New York: The Macmillan Company.
Contains a perceptive general discussion of MT and his works, pp. 150-62; also frequent brief comments on him, passim.

B46 STONE, ALBERT E., JR. "The Twichell Papers and Mark Twain's A Tramp Abroad," Yale University Library Gazette, XXIX (April), 151-64.
The Yale library has been given the papers of the Reverend Joseph Hopkins Twichell by the Twichell family. In the collection are inscribed books and 67 letters from MT, and two notebooks he kept during the travels on which A Tramp Abroad was based and later presented to his friend, on whom the character "Harris" in that book is based. There are also ten volumes of Twichell's private journal, including the period of his travels with MT.

B47 TRIPP, FRANK. "Tripp Recalls Mark Twain Interview," Twainian, XIV (January-February), 3.
Reprinted from Port Chester (New York) Daily Item, February 27, 1952 (1952.B44).

B48 TURNER, ARLIN. "James Lampton, Mark Twain's Model for Colonel Sellers," Modern Language Notes, LXX (December), 592-94.
The character in GA was based on a cousin of MT's mother.

B49 _____. "Mark Twain, Cable, and 'A Professional Newspaper Liar,'" New England Quarterly, XXVIII (March), 18-33.
During the joint lecture tour of 1884-1885, MT's patience wore thin, partly because of fatigue and partly from occasional

chagrin at seeing Cable's readings better received. His feelings were expressed in letters to his wife, Olivia, and apparently in a letter which fell into the hands of a correspondent for the Boston Herald: on May 7, 1885 the "New York Literature" column detailed complaints, chiefly involving pettiness in financial matters. Cable demanded and received a published retraction, while MT took the lofty view that "the slander of a professional newspaper liar" was beneath the dignity of notice. There was a temporary coolness but no estrangement between the two, and Cable thereafter had nothing but kind words for MT.

B50 VOGELBACK, ARTHUR L. "Mark Twain and the Tammany Ring," Publications of the Modern Language Association, LXX (March), 69-77.
Provides a brief history of the Tammany Ring and its downfall, together with an annotated text of MT's "The Revised Catechism" (reprinted from New York Tribune, September 27, 1871), an indictment of municipal corruption, based on the form of the Westminster Catechism.

B51 WARREN, WILLIAM G., M.D. "On the Naming of Tom Sawyer," Psychoanalytic Quarterly, XXIV (July), 424-36.
The wood-sawyer was proverbially independent, and sawing is considered as a way to freedom in the escapes with which HF begins and ends. Sawing and cutting are further significant in that "Twain's works are rich in sadistic fantasies of death and mutilation." The name "Tom" is significant in that its derivatives "describe: 1, maleness; 2, the common man, in a derogatory sense; 3, foolishness (amateur and professional!), nonsense, stupidity and madness; 4, smallness; 5, untruthfulness; 6, the quality of being typical." Moreover, the term "Peeping Tom" suggests MT's exhibitionism. There are other significant Toms in P&P and PW, works involving twinship. "It would be interesting to know whether Clemens was familiar with the derivation of the name 'Tom' from the Aramaic, meaning 'twin.'.... The selection of the name 'Tom Sawyer'...springs from deep sources basic to the lifelong psychic conflicts of the author, Mark Twain."

B52 WELLAND, DENNIS S. R. "Mark Twain the Great Victorian." Chicago Review, IX (Fall), 101-109.
"In Huckleberry Finn Mark Twain did something that Arnold never achieved with equal success: he fused, for once, art and morality in such a way that the morality is the inevitable outcome of the characters and situations of the story." Also treats CY, IA, and MT's views of the Byron scandal.

B53 WILLIAMS, STANLEY T. The Spanish Background of American Literature. New Haven: Yale University Press; reprinted "in an unaltered

(WILLIAMS, STANLEY T.)
and unabridged edition" by Archon Books
(n.p.), 1968. 2 Vol.
Contains a number of brief references to
MT, passim.

B54 _____. [Review: Roger Asselineau, The Literary Reputation of Mark Twain (1954).]
Books Abroad, XXIX (Spring), 223.
Brief and descriptive: it "will be very
useful."

B55 WILLSON, FRANK C. "Mark Twain and the Foster
Murder Case," Twainian, XIV (March-April),
2-3.
Presents a summary of the murder case as
introduction to an MT letter to the editor
of the New York Tribune of March 10, 1873;
a reply by one H.K. criticizes his "ghastly
flippancy."

B56 WRIGHT, WALDO CARLTON. "The Mark Twain I Remember," American Mercury, LXXX (February),
123-25.
Recollections by the son of an Elmira,
New York contractor, not named, "as told to
Waldo Carlton Wright"; anecdotal and somewhat inaccurate.

1956 A BOOKS

A1 *CLEMENS, CLARA. Awake to Tomorrow. New York:
Harper and Row.
[Source: Thomas J. Smith, "Mark Twain's
Last Years at Redding," Yankee, XXXI
(June, 1967), 139.]

A2 *CLEMENS, SAMUEL L. Life on the Mississippi.
Mit Einleitung, Bibliographie und Kommentar
von Karl-Heinz Schönfelder (Englisch-
Amerikanische Bibliothek Band·VII). Halle
(Saale): VEB Max Niemeyer Verlag.
[Source: MHRA Annual Bibliography (1959),
No. 4578.]

1956 B SHORTER WRITINGS

B1 ADAMS, RICHARD P. "The Unity and Coherence
of Huckleberry Finn," Tulane Studies in
English, VI, 87-103.
After summarizing much of the debate over
the structure of HF, concentrates on Huck's
moral growth in a context of the evil of
slavery itself, of "the pseudo-aristocratic
society which fosters and depends on slavery," and "the sentimental culture veneer
with which that society conceals that evil
from itself, if not from others." A happy
ending in which Huck is reconciled to the
values of his society is clearly impossible,
but in terms of Huck's maturation and of
the portrayal of a society there is "a remarkably high degree of consistency, coherence, and unity." Reprinted in Marks
(1959.A5), pp. 82-94; Bradley (1962.A2),
pp. 342-57; Lettis (1962.A11), pp. 384-400;
Simpson (1968.A5), pp. 41-53.

B2 ALLEN, JERRY. "Tom Sawyer's Town," National
Geographic, CX (July), 120-40.
On present-day Hannibal, Missouri; with
map and 22 illustrations.

B3 BAETZHOLD, HOWARD G. "Mark Twain: England's
Advocate, American Literature, XXVIII
(November), 328-46.
A Connecticut Yankee represents views
quite different from those MT held in the
1870's, when he visited England twice and
so admired the English government that he
favored adopting some of its features in
the United States. Baetzhold traces MT's
admiration through the early period.

B4 BERGMAN, HERBERT. "The Whitman-Twain Enigma
Again," Mark Twain Journal, X (Winter),
22-23.
Referring back to Mims Thornburgh Workman's
"The Whitman-Twain Enigma" (1948) on the lack
of references by the two to each other, suggests that MT's "distaste for poetry and possible dislike of Whitman's frankness regarding sex and the body" and his flippancy and
lack of spirituality and optimism that were
important to Whitman would have kept the two
apart--although statements by the two are
quoted, showing they were at least well disposed toward each other. [Continued in
1957.]

B5 BLAIR, WALTER. "Why Huck and Jim Went Downstream," College English, XVIII (November),
106-107.
William Van O'Connor has criticized as a
flaw the trip on the raft, since free territory lay across the river in Illinois; the
objection has been made before, by DeVoto
and by Dixon Wecter, but takes no account of
the activity of slave-catchers there, or the
fact that Huck's father had got money from
Judge Thatcher "to hunt for the nigger all
over Illinois with."

B6 BUDD, LOUIS J. [Review: Arthur L. Scott, ed.,
Mark Twain: Selected Criticism (1955).]
South Atlantic Quarterly, LV (July), 390-91.
"The essays...are soundly and fairly chosen.... For anyone who knows current commentary well enough, the most interesting
evaluations are those written between 1890
and 1920, between the first rush of serious
respect for Twain and the first outbreak
of active controversy."

B7 CARTER, PAUL. [Review: Arthur L. Scott, ed.,
Mark Twain: Selected Criticism (1955).]
American Quarterly, VIII (Winter), 388-89.
"Criticism before 1900 is well represented
in thirteen of the selections, which remind
us that Twain's contemporaries had a keen
appreciation of his literary skill and significance. Haweis, Lang, and Howells are
especially perceptive and their critical
judgments have held up well." The value of
such a collection is doubtful, since the
scholar knows the material and can find it

1956 – Shorter Writings

(CARTER, PAUL)
in any good library, while the general reader will find the material confusing, even
dull.

B8   CLARK, GEORGE PEIRCE. "The Devil that Corrupted Hadleyburg," Mark Twain Journal, X
(Winter), 1-4.
"'The Man that Corrupted Hadleyburg'...be-
longs to those years when Mark Twain increasingly was turning his mind to the problem of the demonic in the nature of things,"
during the period when he was writing The
Mysterious Stranger. In each story a bag
of money is a danger to an honest poor man,
and there is serious or humorous reference
to casual killing. The stranger in Hadleyburg at one point is referred to as a "poor
devil." The theme of an untested virtue as
unreliable may be traced to Milton's Areopagitica.

B9   CLARK, HARRY HAYDEN. "Mark Twain," in Floyd
Stovall, ed., Eight American Authors: A
Review of Research and Criticism (New York:
Modern Language Association).
[Source: Reprinted 1963, New York: W. W.
Norton & Company, Inc., 319-63. Superseded
by 1971 revised edition (1971.B11).] A substantial bibliography of writings by and
about MT, with some annotation. Not systematically checked for the present bibliography.

B10   CLEMENS, CLARA. Awake to a Perfect Day: My
Experience with Christian Science. New
York: Citadel Press. Briefly mentions her
father passim.
"Had my father lived longer and witnessed
the phenomenal spread of Christian Science
and its benefactions throughout the world,"
he would have thought more highly of Mary
Baker Eddy.

B11   CLEMENS, CYRIL. "The True Account of Mark
Twain's Exaggerated Death," Virginia City
Territorial Enterprise, November 16,
pp. 9-10.
"It is high time to put the correct version on record." The report grew out of
the illness of James Ross Clemens, father
of Cyril Clemens.

B12   COYKENDALL, JAMES B., with JACK DENTON SCOTT.
"My Friend Mark Twain," American Mercury,
LXXXIII (August), 103-109.
A 94-year-old man reminisces. Coykendall
says he was a friend of Frank Beecher,
adopted son of Henry Ward Beecher, and was
present when Kipling visited MT "one bleak
winter day in 1889"; he also remembers that
Olivia Clemens was a great comfort to her
husband when their daughter Jean died. At
MT's funeral the undertaker "was openly
crying."

B13   COYLE, LEO P. "Mark Twain and William Dean
Howells," Georgia Review, X (Fall), 302-11.
Chiefly a repetition of material available
in Paine and other familiar sources. Suggests that friendship may have influenced
Howells's reviews of some of MT's works. His
influence on MT's writing was "considerable,"
but "that it was profound is less certain."

B14   CRANE, SUSAN. "Letters from Susan Crane,"
Twainian, XV (September-October), 1-4;
(November December), 3-4.
Reminiscences by MT's sister-in-law in
letters to Paine, 1906-1913. There are
touching recollections of the death of Jean
Clemens. On Olivia, she says that "Livy's
letters always make her so alive--her life
and her loving so worth while. It is no
wonder that Mr. Clemens was so crushed, so
changed by her going away from us all.
Whatever her own estimates of herself may
have been at times, she was very great..."
In 1911 Susan Crane asked Paine for an MT
autograph to give to a friend: I could
find nothing among my letters, as they were
never signed in full. Samuel S. [sic],
'S. L. C.' or 'Holy Samuel.' I asked Mr.
Langdon, but he was situated as I am--no
letters are signed." A concluding note by
Chester L. Davis observes that the Twainian
"reaches many different readers, including
many school children. We have no secrets
from our members, however we must use dis-
cretion as to what appears in our publication.... In the Susan Crane correspondence
we have not published all of it, likely we
never will, but it is available for inspection by our members."

B15   NO ENTRY

B16   [DAVIS, CHESTER L.] "The 'Mock Robbery' of
Mark Twain,'" Twainian, XV (January-February),
2-4.
Based on letters to Paine from Mrs. Alf
Doten (quoting her late husband's diary) and
Steve Gillis, on the mock robbery of MT on
the road between Virginia City and Gold Hill,
Nevada, in 1868.

B17   _____. [Review: Clara Clemens, Awake to a
Perfect Day.] Twainian, XV (November-December), 2-3.
Contains extensive quotation and praises,
but scant critical discussion.

B18   FATOUT, PAUL. "Mark Twain's First Lecture:
A Parallel," Pacific Historical Review, XXV
(November), 347-54.
MT's story of his San Francisco lecture
debut (October 2, 1866) in RI does not agree
with contemporary newspaper accounts, and
similarities to Washington Irving's description of the opening of She Stoops to Conquer

(FATOUT, PAUL)
in his Life of Goldsmith (New York, 1881, pp. 315-16) suggest that MT's source was literary rather than experience.

B19 FRANTZ, RAY W., JR. "The Role of Folklore in Huckleberry Finn," American Literature, XXVIII (November), 314-27.
For Huck, folklore is the equivalent of a religion governing his actions, values and virtues; in the book folklore supports much of the thematic development and serves as a device for foreshadowing events.

B20 FULLER, FRANK. "Letters from Frank Fuller," Twainian, XV (July-August), 1-3; (September-October), 4.
To Paine, answering queries in connection with the biography; provides very little information, but mentions the American Grocer, which supposedly printed MT's first speech; of an occasion when Governor James W. Nye was to introduce MT to a lecture audience but failed to appear, Fuller reports hearing him say twenty years later, "I never intended to introduce him. He is nothing but a damned Secessionist anyway."

B21 GILLIS, STEVEN E. "Jumping Frog Story; Gillis on Bret Harte; The Great Oak Plan," Twainian, XV (March-April), 1-4.
Letters to Paine in 1907, providing material for the biography. Gillis denies that Bret Harte had any part in editing the "Jumping Frog" story, reproduces a letter from MT recalling the time they first heard of it (and comments on "The Burning Shame," which was to become "The Royal Nonesuch" of HF, and also on his imminent marriage). Another letter comments on MT's gifted profanity, and jokes about a scheme to become rich selling acorns from the live oak tree that sheltered MT on Jackass Hill.

B22 GOODMAN, JOSEPH T. "Joseph Goodman's Assistance on the 'Biography,'" Twainian, XV (May-June), 2-4; (July-August), 3-4.
Letters to Paine, 1907-1911. Mentions enclosing some reminiscences not here reproduced: "The only justification I can offer for talking about him so freely is that the 'News' pays me $15.00 a column for anything I may write, and the struggle for maintenance has got down to a groundhog case with me" (May-June, 3; city not given for the News).

B23 _____. [Letter to Albert Bigelow Paine, March 13, 1908.] Twainian, XV (January-February), 1.
Takes issue with a statement by MT that his copies of Territorial Enterprise material were destroyed and suggests a careful search for them; also, describes MT saying grace at table while living in Buffalo.

B24 _____. "Letters from Joseph T. Goodman," Twainian, XV (March-April), 4.
To Paine, providing material for the biography. A letter of December 7, 1911 shares MT's cavalier attitude toward mere facts and criticizes Paine's choice of words as stilted and vague; a letter of December 17 comments on his description: "I recall but one thing in your portraiture of Mark that seems to me incorrect. You repeatedly insist on endowing him with physical vigor and activity. To my notion, he never had either. It was always a source of wonder and admiration to me, the contrast between his bodily helplessness, so to speak, and his mental power. But perhaps it would have been impossible to picture him that way without conveying the idea that he was a weakling-- which he wasn't--and so, probably you have chosen the better parts."

B25 HEADRICK, MRS. C. L. "Mining Days Sweetheart of Mark Twain," Twainian, XV (May-June), 1-2.
As a little girl she was Carrie Pixley, a friend of MT in Nevada (reminiscences sent to Paine for the biography).

B26 HOBEN, JOHN B. "Mark Twain: On the Writer's Use of Language," American Speech, XXXI (October), 163-71.
Although not a professional linguistic scholar, MT had a good ear and "put his language theory to practice in a cadence passionate and alive"; he contributed greatly to "making the vernacular a respected and appropriate medium for literary expression."

B27 HOELTJE, HUBERT L. [Review: Arthur L. Scott, ed., Mark Twain: Selected Criticism (1955).] Oregon Historical Quarterly, LVII (December), 357-58.
Questions the value of some of the essays, such as those by V. F. Calverton and Lionel Trilling, which he quotes, "the one being a foolish judgment and the other a cliquish one indeed." There are also some more interesting selections, such as Bret Harte's review of IA and an appraisal of MT by Gamaliel Bradford. The extract from Van Wyck Brooks's psychological interpretation represents "an effort which once created a sensation but which must now seem strange even to Mr. Brooks."

B28 JELLIFFE, ROBERT A., ed. Faulkner at Nagano. Tokyo: Kenkyusha Ltd., p. 88.
"In my opinion Mark Twain was the first truly American writer and all of us since are his heirs, we descended from him...Whitman was an experimenter with the notion that there could be an American literature. Twain was the first that grew up in the belief that there is an American literature and he found himself producing it. So I call him the father of American literature, though he is not the first one." Reprinted in Meriwether and Millgate (1968.B78), p. 137.

1956 - Shorter Writings

B29 JONES, ALEXANDER E. "Mark Twain and Sexuality," Publications of the Modern Language Association, LXXI (September), 595-616.
There may be a sexual element in MT's feelings of guilt. Youthful indiscretions, though unprovable, must not be ruled out; certainly, MT felt strongly about feminine purity but also believed in a double standard. He was more reticent in print than most authors, and his HF represents a sexless, masculine Eden "until the King and the Duke dash panting into the story, bringing to Eden a hint of the Fall with their presentation of that phallic beast-- the Royal Nonesuch." Reprinted in Leary (1962.A10), pp. 232-56, followed by a reprinting of Allen (1957.B1), who disagrees with Jones.

B30 KAPLAN, CHARLES. "Holden and Huck: The Odysseys of Youth," College English, XVIII (November), 76-80.
"In addition to being comic masterpieces and superb portrayals of perplexed, sensitive adolescence," The Catcher in the Rye and Huckleberry Finn "deal obliquely and poetically with a major theme in American life, past and present--the right of the nonconformist to assert his nonconformity." In a concluding note, Kaplan says that his article was accepted for publication before the appearance of Arthur Heiserman and James E. Miller, Jr., "Some Crazy Cliff," in Western Humanities Review, (Spring, 1955), 129-137, and "the numerous parallels between the two can be attributed only to coincidental simultaneous generation."

B31 KERR, AGNES ROGERS. "Happy Hours with Mark Twain," Mark Twain Journal, X (Winter), 11-13, 24.
Childhood memories of reading MT's books, naming a kitten after him, whitewashing a fence, and playing with a raft.

B32 KESTEN, HERMANN. "Der Humorist und die Gesellschaft: Das gross Gelächter des Mr. Samuel Langhorne Clemens," Akzente: Zeitschrift für Dichtung, III (October), 467-79.
Notes MT's role as moralist and satirist.

B33 LANE, LAURIAT, JR. "Letters to the Editor," College English, XVIII (November), 108-109.
A reply to Gilbert M. Rubenstein's criticism of his article on Huckleberry Finn; Lane calls Rubenstein's approach "both 'moral' in the wrong sense and unduly sentimental," and briefly answers his objections. There are also a letter by William Van O'Connor (1956.B42), and a concluding word by the editor.

B34 LEAVER, FLORENCE B. "Mark Twain's Pudd'nhead Wilson," Mark Twain Journal, X (Winter), 14-20.
A general study, noting the bitterness, the treatment of slavery, the village, human cruelty, the structural defects, and the style.

B35 LEAVIS, F. R. "Mark Twain's Neglected Classic: The Moral Astringency of Pudd'nhead Wilson," Commentary, XXI (February), 128-36.
"The present essay appears as an introduction to a new edition of Pudd'nhead Wilson that Grove Press is bringing out this month" (editor's note, p. 128). "A classic in its own right...for all the unlikeness, it bears a very close relation to Huckleberry Finn; a relation of such a kind that to appreciate the lesser work is to have a surer perception of the workings of the greater." There is power in the central irony of the exchange of the babies and their lives, although the book is not faultless. Article reprinted in Cardwell (1963.A3), pp. 82-91, and in Kesterson (1973), pp. 108-12. Excerpt from the 1955 printing as introduction to PW (London: Chatto & Windus, Ltd.) in Simpson (1968.A5), pp. 109-11 (noting that the article was also reprinted in Leavis, Anna Karenina and Other Essays, London: Chatto & Windus, 1967).

B36 LEISY, ERNEST E. "Mark Twain Seminar," Southwest Review, XLI (Spring), ix-x, 203. A review of Arthur L. Scott, Mark Twain: Selected Criticism (1955).
"One of the more useful undertakings in the field of criticism in recent years has been the assembling on one volume of articles that represent divergent points of view in regard to an author.... herewith is a good one for the most popular of American writers." Leisy summarizes some of the views toward MT represented in this volume.

B37 *LORCH, FRED W. "Julia Newell and Mark Twain on the Quaker City Holy Land Excursion," Rock County Chronicle, II (June), 15-25.
[Source: "Current Bibliography," American Literature, XXX (March, 1958), 152; on glimpses of MT in her letters to the Janesville (Wisconsin) Gazette.]

B38 MARX, LEO. "The Pilot and the Passenger: Landscape Conventions and the Style of Huckleberry Finn," American Literature, XXVIII (May), 129-46.
As in Tom Sawyer and Life on the Mississippi, MT uses landscape as "a primary source of unity and meaning." The superiority of Huckleberry Finn lies in its style, and "the distinguishing mark of style is language." It is in Huck that MT can strike a balance between the extremes of elevated description common in travel literature, on the one hand, and too harsh a reality on the other: "It does not occur to Huck to choose between beauty and utility." Reprinted in Smith (1963.A5), pp. 47-63.

B39   McKEITHAN, D[ANIEL] M[ORLEY]. [Review: Ar-
       thur L. Scott, Mark Twain: Selected Criti-
       cism (1955).] American Literature, XXVIII
       (May), 243-44.
          Scott has achieved a balance of early and
       late criticism, favorable and unfavorable,
       general and specific, with emphasis on MT.
       "This excellent volume concludes with a
       useful four-page annotated guide to the
       best bibliographies of writings by and about
       Mark Twain."

B40   MOSTECKY, VACLAV. "The Library Under Commu-
       nism: Czechoslovak Libraries from 1948 to
       1954," Library Quarterly, XXVI (April),
       105-17.
          On pp. 114-15, reproduces annotation on a
       catalog card distributed by the National
       and University Library, Prague: "CLEMENS,
       SAMUEL LANGHORNE. Adventures of Huckleberry
       Finn.--Mark Twain, the well-known American
       humorist, rejected in this work the false
       romanticism of worthless murder stories and
       sharply criticized American racism and the
       excesses of Puritan morality."

B41   O'BRIEN, DEAN. "Tom Sawyer in Maturity,"
       Mark Twain Journal, X (Winter), 9-10, 24.
          Working from Philip Young's suggestion
       that Huck Finn is the prototype of Heming-
       way, O'Brien adds that F. Scott Fitzgerald
       was Tom Sawyer: "Denial of Free Will pro-
       duces a Hemingway, a Huck Finn, who tries
       to act as best he can in the face of a pre-
       determined future. Emphatic acceptance of
       Free Will creates the romantic, Fitzgerald,
       Tom Sawyer, who is convinced that he is
       master of his fate."

B42   O'CONNOR, WILLIAM VAN. "Letters to the Edi-
       tor," College English, XVIII (November),
       108.
          Stands firmly on the ground he took when
       he "tried to relate the Huck cult to our
       American desire to live in a state of inno-
       cence," and adds as a postscript: "I have
       discovered that criticizing Twain is ap-
       parently as irreverent and sacrilegious as
       criticizing Mother's Day." The letter is in
       answer to the strictures of Gilbert M.
       Rubenstein (1956.B44) and Walter Blair
       (1956.B5), and is followed by a letter by
       Lauriat Lane, Jr. in answer to Rubenstein,
       and concluding remarks by the editor con-
       cerning the flight down the river.

B43   PERCY, WALKER. "The Man on the Train: Three
       Existential Modes," Partisan Review, XXIII
       (Fall), 478-94.
          On alienation in literature, with passing
       reference to Huck, Jim, and Tom (pp. 478,
       484-85).

B44   RUBENSTEIN, GILBERT M. "The Moral Structure
       of Huckleberry Finn," College English,
       XVIII (November), 72-76.
          Lauriat Lane, Jr. and William Van O'Connor
       (in the October, 1955 College English) ob-

scure or deny the greatness of the book;
Lane extends the moral realism "into fantastic patterns of allegory and symbolism" and
O'Connor "commits the graver fault of misreading the realities of the book entirely."
What the book is actually about is "nothing
that the ordinary reader--not given to su-
persubtle speculations and distortions, but
possessed only of common sense and a responsive heart--would fail to understand and appreciate": clear, direct insight, and "the
humorous but sharp exposure of human failings on the one hand and the warm faith in
human goodness and equality on the other."
Reprinted in Bradley (1962.A2), 378-84;
Simpson (1968.A5), 54-60.

B45   SCHMIDT, PAUL. "The Deadpan on Simon Wheeler,"
       Southwest Review, XLI (Summer), 270-77.
          In "The Jumping Frog," Simon Wheeler is
       not a comic butt as the narrator believes:
       "He is relaxed and friendly, in contrast to
       the efforts of his visitor to be imposing
       and superior.... Wheeler polarizes the val-
       ues generated by community as against the
       inept and grotesque isolation of individual-
       ism. What the genteel 'Mark Twain' careless-
       ly dismisses in the last lines is fraternity.
       He rudely walks out..."

B46   SCHÖNEMANN, FRIEDRICH. "Mark Twains "Huckle-
       berry Finn' (Zum 70. Geburtstag, 1885-1955),"
       Archiv für das Studium der neueren Sprachen,
       CXCII, 273-89.
          Discusses the book's realism, structure,
       and portrayal of character; the secondary
       sources cited are chiefly book-length gener-
       al studies of MT. [In German.]

B47   *SCHÖNFELDER, KARL-HEINZ. "Mark Twain und die
       Indianer," Zeitschrift für Anglistik und
       Amerikanistik, IV, 88-101.
          [Source: MHRA Annual Bibliography
       (1955-1956), No. 8043.]

B48   STEIN, JEAN. "The Art of Fiction XII: Wil-
       liam Faulkner," Paris Review, XII (Spring),
       28-52.
          An interview: "This conversation took
       place in New York City, mid-winter, early
       1956." On Sherwood Anderson, p. 46: "He
       was the father of my generation of American
       writers and the tradition of American writ-
       ing which our successors will carry on....
       Dreiser is his older brother and Mark Twain
       the father of them both." On favorite char-
       acters in literature (p. 47): "Huck Finn,
       of course, and Jim. Tom Sawyer I never
       liked much--an awful prig."

B49   TORCHIANA, DONALD T. "Will Huck Hang? The
       Individual and Society in Huckleberry Finn,"
       Mark Twain Journal, X (Winter), 5-8.
          After examining the hairball oracle, Jim
       warns Huck to avoid water and all risks,
       "'kase it's down in de bills dat you's gwyne
       to git hung," and MT "seldom fails to ex-
       ploit a lie, a sign, or a conversation as a

(TORCHIANA, DONALD T.)
means of shepherding his flow of narrative."
Huck avoids neither water nor other risks,
and a possible death by hanging is consistent with the book's theme of death and
violence. His evasion of social rules and
his plans to "light out for the territory"
may make him a victim of "the lynch law of
the West."

B50   TURNER, ARLIN. George W. Cable: A Biography.
Durham, North Carolina: Duke University
Press, passim.
Cable went on lecture tour with MT, and it
was in part his introducing MT to Malory's
Morte D'Arthur that led to CY. There are
many page-references to MT in the index.

B51   WALKER, PHILLIP. "Mark Twain, Playwright,"
Educational Theatre Journal, VIII (October),
185-93.
A factual history of MT's partially successful attempts to write for the stage;
providing no new information or interpretations, this is a useful summary of known
material.

B52   WOLFE, THOMAS. The Letters of Thomas Wolfe.
Collected and Edited, with an Introduction
and Explanatory Text, by Elizabeth Nowell.
New York: Charles Scribner's Sons, p. 656.
In a letter to Sherwood Anderson
(September 22, 1937): "I think of you with
Whitman and Twain--that is, with men who
have seen America with a poet's vision, and
with a poetic vision of life--which to my
mind is the only way it actually can be
seen."

B53   WOODFIELD, DENIS. "The 'Fake' Title-Page of
The Gilded Age: A Solution." Papers of
the Bibliographical Society of America, L
(Third Quarter), 292-6.
A variant title-page tipped in to some
copies of The Gilded Age may indicate that
Elisha Bliss, Jr. and his son Frank Bliss
misrepresented sales figures in their reports to MT and Warner.

B54   WOUK, HERMAN. "America's Voice Is Mark
Twain's," San Francisco Chronicle, August 5,
"This World" section, p. 20.
On MT as "the archetype of American writers," an exact observer whose novels are
"extravagant romances." In HF he "established at a stroke the colloquial style
which has swept American literature, and
indeed spilled over into world literature."
HF is "a jerky, uneven, patchwork tale...
jerry-built...yet it is the crown of our
literature." The modern writers "are hardly
conceivable except coming after Twain."

1957 A BOOKS

A1   CLEMENS, CYRIL, ed. Mark Twain Jest Book.
With an introduction by Carl Sandburg. Kirkwood, Missouri: Mark Twain Journal.
Consists of a number of anecdotes; the 94-
word introduction by Sandburg praises MT as
philosopher and storyteller. In the same
year there was a second edition titled Mark
Twain's Jest Book, containing a few more
stories and in facsimile, MT's note in which
he first said "the report of my death is an
exaggeration" (facing p. 1). [32 and 27-
page pamphlets, respectively.]

A2   CLEMENS, SAMUEL L. The Complete Short Stories
of Mark Twain. Now Collected for the First
Time. Edited with an introduction by Charles
Neider. Garden City, N.Y.: Hanover House.
Sixty stories, of which five are extracts
from RI, two from TA, three from LOM, and
three from FE; includes texts of "The Man
that Corrupted Hadleyburg" and MS. In his
introduction Neider says that MT buried fictional sketches in longer works, was aware
of the formlesness of his writings, and
"rarely bothered about the niceties of fiction."

A3   LONG, E. HUDSON. Mark Twain Handbook, New
York: Hendricks House.
An extensive and valuable survey of biographical and critical works, with a good summary of MT's life, thought, and works, and
annotated bibliography of books and articles
about him. [Not cross-checked for the present bibliography.]

A4   MIERS, EARL SCHENCK. Mark Twain on the Mississippi. New York: World Publishing Company; reprinted New York: Collier Books,
1963.
A fictionalized biography for young readers.

A5   SMITH, HENRY NASH, and FREDERICK ANDERSON, eds.
Mark Twain of the "Enterprise": Newspaper
Articles & Other Documents 1862-1864.
Berkeley and Los Angeles: University of
California Press.
Texts of MT's newspaper correspondence, as
well as some personal letters and texts of
writings by other parties in newspaper controversies, as in the dispute over the Sanitary Fund which resulted in MT's leaving
Nevada for California. This book is meticulously edited, with useful introductory
material and with a "Biographical Directory"
briefly describing forty individuals prominent in MT's correspondence (pp. 225-31).

1957 - Shorter Writings

B1   ALLEN, CHARLES A.   "Mark Twain and Conscience,"
       Literature and Psychology, VII (May), 17-21.
          "In this essay I will examine Twain's
       struggle against the orthodox conscience,
       speculate on the motives for the struggle,
       and suggest that the conflict helps account
       for both the strength and weakness of the
       fiction."   Allen attacks Alexander E.
       Jones's "Mark Twain and Sexuality"
       (1956.B29) as "warping the central insight
       of depth psychology."   Reprinted in Leary
       (1962.A10), pp. 257-68, immediately after
       the reprinted Jones essay.

B2   ANON.   "Mark Twain Toasts the Scotch," Twain-
       ian, XVI (November-December), 4.
          Reprint of a clipping provided by Paul
       Fatout from the Lafayette (Indiana) Daily
       Courier of January 14, 1874, giving MT's
       toast at a dinner of the St. Andrews Socie-
       ty in London, November 29, 1873.

B3   ANON.   "Mark Twain's Courtship" and "Mark
       Twain's Brother," Twainian, XVI (November-
       December), 4.
          Clippings provided by George H. Town from
       the Utica (N.Y.) Saturday Globe of Septem-
       ber 26, 1891 and May 21, 1892 containing
       anecdotes; neither contains important in-
       formation, and the first refers to Olivia
       Langdon as "Miss Lizzie" and her father as
       a judge.   MT's daughter Clara disputed the
       first of these in a letter to Chester Davis
       reprinted in "Clara, a Great Person in Her
       Own Right," Twainian, XXII (January-Febru-
       ary, 1963), 1-2.

B4   *ANON.   "Mark Twain's Piloting," Missouri His-
       torical Society Bulletin, XIII (July),
       403-405.
          [Source: Beebe and Feaster (1968),
       p. 94; a note received from Missouri His-
       torical Society adds: "From the St. Louis
       Republican, June 13, 1875."]

B5   *ANON.   [Editorial criticizing the dropping of
       HF from the approved reading lists in New
       York City public schools.]   Christian Sci-
       ence Monitor, September 14.
          [Source: Reprinted in Twainian, XVI
       (September-October), 1.]

B6   ANON.   [Review: Charles Neider, ed., The
       Complete Short Stories of Mark Twain.]   New
       York Herald Tribune Book Review, XXXIII
       (February 17), 13.
          One paragraph, descriptive and non-criti-
       cal.

B7   ANON.   [Review: Henry Nash Smith and Frede-
       rick Anderson, eds.   Mark Twain of the "En-
       terprise".]   New York Herald Tribune Book
       Review, XXXIII (July 7), 9.
          Short paragraph, descriptive rather than
       critical and with no evaluation.

B8   *BAETZHOLD, H. G.   "The Encaenia of 1907,"
       Oxford Magazine, LXXV (February 28), 322.
          [Source: Leary (1970.B51), p. 57.]

B9   BERGMAN, HERBERT.   "The Whitman-Twain Enigma
       Again," Mark Twain Journal, X (Fall-Winter),
       3-9.
          Summarizes critical discussions that may
       bear on the scant interest of the two in
       each other and notes that there are now
       three statements by each to consider.   [Con-
       tinues a discussion Bergman began in 1956.]

B10   BLAIR, WALTER.   "The French Revolution and
       Huckleberry Finn," Modern Philology, LV
       (August), 21-35.
          In addition to A Tale of Two Cities, of
       which the influence on Huckleberry Finn has
       been previously noted (and is here dis-
       cussed), MT was familiar with a number of
       other books dealing with the French Revolu-
       tion; of these, Thomas Carlyle's seems par-
       ticularly influential, not only for its de-
       piction of royalty and as a source for ele-
       ments of the burlesque escape of Jim, but
       also for its portrait of the cruelty and
       the cowardice of mobs.

B11   BLANCK, JACOB.   "Samuel Langhorne Clemens
       (Mark Twain), 1835-1910," in Bibliography of
       American Literature, Compiled by Jacob
       Blanck for the Bibliographical Society of
       America (New Haven: Yale University Press,
       and London: Oxford University Press), II,
       173-254.
          "It has been thought useful to present
       this list in three sections as follows:
       Section One: Primary books; and books by
       authors other than Clemens but containing
       first edition material by him.   Section Two:
       Collections of reprinted material issued
       under the Clemens name or pseudonym; sepa-
       rate editions (i.e., books reprinted from
       one of Clemens's books and issued in sepa-
       rate form); undated reprints; and ana.
       Section Three: Books by authors other than
       Clemens which contain material reprinted
       from Clemens's earlier books.   Books con-
       taining letters by Clemens are not listed.
       Books containing letters written for publi-
       cation are listed.   Formal collections of
       letters are listed in Section One.   Letters
       published in separate form which may be
       properly described as first book publication
       are listed in Section One."   [Not cross-
       checked for the present bibliography.]

B12   BRANCH, EDGAR.   "Mark Twain and J. D. Salin-
       ger: A Study in Literary Continuity,"
       American Quarterly, IX (Summer), 144-58.
          Without attempting to show influence or
       "to compare the 'then' and 'now' of American
       society through the illustrative use" of
       Huckleberry Finn and The Catcher in the Rye,
       Branch reveals parallels in "narrative pat-
       tern and style, characterization and criti-
       cal import....   Independently and in his own
       right each author has probed beneath surface

1957 - Shorter Writings

(BRANCH, EDGAR)
facts--so dramatically contrasted in Huck's
and Holden's environments--to the experien-
tial continuity of American life."

B13   BROOKS, VAN WYCK. Days of the Phoenix: The
Nineteen-Twenties I Remember. New York:
E. P. Dutton and Company, Inc., pp. 104,
170-74, 188-89 (also minor, passing references to MT on pp. 108, 111, 119, 125, 138,
193, 166).
        While writing The Ordeal of Mark Twain
Brooks felt emotionally that America had
long been "a kind of limbo" for the writer,
and he allowed psychology to crowd out literary and human appreciation. Sherwood
Anderson tried to show him where he had
fallen short: "I should have sung the
praises of Huckleberry Finn." Brooks stands
by his book, conceding it reveals "perhaps
only half of the real Mark Twain, but certainly much, if not the whole, of a well-
known abstract character, the typical American author as we knew him at the moment"
(pp. 170-74). Later, during "a season in
hell" of mental illness a doctor disagreed
with Brooks on whether "reason" or "emotion"
had been more influential in his writing;
in time, Brooks came to understand that he
generally "felt things out" rather than
thinking them out, and wrote intuitively
(pp. 188-89). The revised edition of The
Ordeal of Mark Twain (1933) came out after
this period, and, while it takes account of
the factual information on the West provided
by DeVoto in Mark Twain's America (1932),
the basic argument in the book remains substantially as before. Days of the Phoenix
also appears as the central section of Van
Wyck Brooks: an Autobiography (New York:
E. P. Dutton, Inc., 1965), 249-445, but the
index to the volume is sharply reduced.

B14   [BROWNELL, GEORGE HIRAM?] "Sam Slick, The
Connecticut Clockmaker, Original of Uncle
Sam and Source of Inspiration for Dickens,
Mark Twain, and Other Humorists," Twainian,
XVI (March-April), 3-4; (May-June), 4.
        Reprinted from Dearborn Independent, XXV
(October 10, 1925.B11)

B15   BUDD, LOUIS J. "Mark Twain Plays the Bache-
or," Western Humanities Review, XI (Spring),
157-67.
        The conventional view that MT was inhibit-
ed in treating sex in his writing is more
valid for the time after he met Olivia Langdon than for the preceding years; a different picture emerges from the earlier work,
"particularly the newspaper letters and columns in which from 1864 to 1868 he played
the manly bachelor."

B16   *CADY, EDWIN S. [On Huckleberry Finn],
pp. 8-10 in Richard S. Kennedy, Edwin S.
Cady, Stewart C. Dodge, and Perry D. Westbrook, "The Theme of the Quest," English
Record, VIII (Winter), 2-17.

[Source: Leary (1970), p. 60; AES, II
(1959), Item 169: Huck seeks his moral identity, learning that the morality of his society is false and corrupt.]

B17   CARTER, PAUL J., JR. "Mark Twain and the
American Labor Movement," New England Quarterly, XXX (September), 382-88. [Reprinted
in Twainian, XIX (September-October, 1960),
1-4.
        MT's championship of organized labor in
Connecticut Yankee is also reflected in
"The New Dynasty," an article he read to the
Monday Evening Club in Hartford on March 22,
1886, here published for the first time.

B18   _____. "Mark Twain Describes a San Francisco
Earthquake," Publications of the Modern Language Association, LXXII (December),
997-1004.
        MT's "The Great Earthquake in San Francis-
co" (here reprinted, pp. 999-1004), not listed by his bibliographers, appeared in the
New York Weekly Review November 25, 1865--
a week after the New York Saturday Press
published his "Jim Smiley and His Jumping
Frog." It shows his growing reputation in
the East, and is a kind of writing he considered superior to the "Jumping Frog" story; he introduced burlesque when reworking
it for Roughing It (Vol. II, Chapter XVII).
Abstract in AES, I (1958), 209.

B19   _____. "Mark Twain: 'Moralist in Disguise,'"
University of Colorado Studies, Series in
Language and Literature, No. 6, pp. 65-78.
        "Twain's morality, like Huck's, was emo-
tive, intuitive, and uncertain. It was a
morality which could be both militant and
tolerant. It prompted his sharpest satiric
judgments and his most trivial diatribes....
he could seldom see life without raging or
moralizing, and the detachment necessary to
art was lost.... This innate conflict was
the price he paid for his sensitivity."

B20   CHASE, RICHARD. "Mark Twain and the Novel,"
in his The American Novel and Its Tradition.
Garden City, New York: Doubleday Anchor
Books, pp. 139-56.
        On HF (pp. 139-49), praises the language,
Huck's clear vision, notes the mythic quality previously mentioned by DeVoto--it takes
the forms of initiation and the ritual of
exorcism; discusses the attack on romantic
falsifications. On PW (pp. 149-56). Only
in HF and first part of LOM is there anything really first rate by MT, and Fiedler
and Leavis over-praise PW. "But what keeps
this book from being a great novel is that
the characters and their relationships are
not adequate to the moral action." Pp. 138-
49 (on HF) reprinted in Lettis (1962.A11),
pp. 401-409; pp. 144-45 reprinted in Simpson
(1968.A5), pp. 111-12.

B21 *CLEMENS, CYRIL. "Mark Twain at Oxford," Hobbies, LII (May), 108.
[Source: Leary (1970), p. 60; volume and year seem inconsistent.]

B22 CLEMENS, KATHARINE (Mother of Cyril Clemens). "I Knew Mark Twain," Mark Twain Journal, X (Fall-Winter), 15-16.
On dining with MT in London and New York, and visiting him at his "Stormfield" home in Redding, Connecticut; includes the text of a note to her from MT in Bermuda, March 24, 1910.

B23 CLEMENS, SAMUEL L. "Samuel L. Clemens on 'Die Lorelei,'" Georgia Review, XI (Spring), 50-52.
An excerpt from TA, with no commentary or indication of the source.

B24 _____. "Two Civil War Letters," American Heritage, VIII (October), 62-64.
Texts of letters by MT and Walt Whitman on the prospects for survival of the Union. MT, writing his friend Billy Claggett on September 9, 1862, was pessimistic following the second battle of Bull Run.

B25 CUMMINGS, SHERWOOD. "Mark Twain's Social Darwinism," Huntington Library Quarterly, XX (February), 163-75.
"Thirty years of reading in current science" bore fruit in MT's later years when, crushed by business reverses and the loss of those he loved, he turned to a view of man as a Darwinian animal driven by nature's law to eat or be eaten.

B26 DA PONTE, DURANT. "Some Evasions of Censorship in Following the Equator," American Literature, XXIX (March), 92-95.
"While following the equator, Clemens found an Oriental word with which to strengthen the English language: lingam, the Hindu word for phallus. The term appears ten times within the space of thirty-nine pages in the second volume of his travel book.... Some of the references are clearly humorous; others seem to border upon the downright prurient, as though the author, relatively secure in the knowledge that the meaning of the word in question would be likely to escape most readers, were taking obvious delight in seeing how far he could go."

B27 [DAVIS, CHESTER L.] "American Bar Association Recognizes Mark Twain's Contribution to Our Copyright Laws," Twainian, XVI (July-August), 1.
On the passage of a resolution to that effect introduced by Chester L. Davis at the Annual Meeting in New York City. There is further commentary on p. 4 under "Mark Twain's Letters to Sylvester Baxter of the Boston Herald."

B28 _____. "Biography [sic] of American Literature, Released," Twainian, XVI (November-December), 1.
A review of the second volume of Jacob Blanck's monumental work; descriptive and laudatory.

B29 _____. "Mark Twain's Burglar," Twainian, XVI (January-February), 1-2.
Extensively quotes two letters from Henry Williams, one of two men convicted of breaking into MT's "Stormfield" home. Williams claims a previous connection with MT in having "worked for a certain company in which he was a stockholder," and Davis suggests he may have illustrated some of MT's books.

B30 _____. "Mark Twain's Copyright Lobbying," Twainian, XVI (July-August), 1-3.
Chiefly on MT in Washington in 1906; little more than extensive quotation from the Paine biography.

B31 _____. "Mark Twain's Letters to Sylvester Baxter of the Boston Herald," Twainian, XVI (July-August), 4.
On tottering thrones in Brazil and Portugal, and his CY; apparently these letters of late 1889 were not for publication.

B32 _____. "New York City Schools 'Banning' Huck Finn! Mark Twain and the Negro Race. Champion for Organized Labor," Twainian, XVI (September-October), 1-4.
A defense of MT, consisting chiefly of various reprints: Associated Press dispatch on the dropping of HF from approved reading lists in New York; a Christian Science Monitor editorial (September 14, as reprinted in the Hannibal Courier-Post of September 17); an MT letter from Paine's 1917 edition; William Dean Howells's My Mark Twain.

B33 _____. "Original Preface for 'Yankee' in 1889 Mentions 'Twin Civilizations of Hell and Russia'; Soviet Using Mark Twain's 'Yankee' for Satellite Propaganda; Mark Twain and Atomic Energy," Twainian, XVI (May-June), 1-4.
A lengthy, rambling answer to a recent paperbound edition of CY published in Leipzig: Davis reprints the original preface to CY from the 1912 Paine biography (Vol. III, Appendix S) and the Leipzig preface (noting such factual errors as MT's place of birth and which of his books was his first). Davis then quotes extensively from CY passages in Caroline Thomas Harnsberger's Mark Twain at Your Fingertips, and concludes with vague references to "Sold to Satan" in Europe and Elsewhere (Satan is made of radium). The article is of scant critical or biographical interest.

1957 - Shorter Writings

B34 [DAVIS, CHESTER L.] [Review: Henry Nash Smith, Mark Twain of the "Enterprise."] Twainian, XVI (March-April), 1-3.
Laudatory, but with no specific, critical discussion; chiefly descriptive, with a list of the contents.

B35 EDWARDS, OLIVER. "Hilarious Days,' The Times (London), September 19, p. 13.
On MT in Nevada; a popular account, providing no new information or interpretation.

B36 ELCONIN, VICTOR A. [Review: Arthur L. Scott, ed., Mark Twain: Selected Criticism. (1955).] Books Abroad, XXXI (Winter), 83.
Brief and descriptive.

B37 FATOUT, PAUL. "The Twain-Cable Readings in Indiana," Indiana Magazine of History, LIII (March), 19-28.
On the lecture tour of 1884-1885, documented from contemporary New York and Indiana newspaper accounts; Indiana papers regarded MT the more highly of the two, both in genius and in versatility.

B38 FEDERICO, P. J. "Mark Twain's Inventions and Patents," Twainian, XVI (November-December), 1-4.
Federico was an official in the Patent Office, and apparently used material in the files as well as biographical information from Paine. Reprints MT correspondence and quotes patent applications. [Originally appeared in Journal of the Patent Office Society, March, 1939, with illustrations not here reproduced.]

B39 FERGUSON, DELANCEY. "Sam Clemens Was the By-Line," New York Times Book Review (May 5), p. 10.
A brief, descriptive review of Henry Nash Smith and Frederick Anderson, eds., Mark Twain of the "Enterprise." MT's early writing printed there is "apprentice work," in which the good "lines are far between. Perhaps it is just as well that the Enterprise files are lost."

B40 _____. [Review: Henry Nash Smith and Frederick Anderson, eds., Mark Twain of the "Enterprise."] American Scholar, XXVI (Autumn), 515-16.
Makes no complaint about the editing, but "no other of our major writers, not even Walt Whitman, had to cleanse himself of more trash before achieving artistic maturity. It is unlikely that any masterpieces perished with the Enterprise files."

B41 GOODMAN, JOSEPH T. "Goodman O.K.'s Paine Inaccuracies," Twainian, XVI (January-February), 2 (incorrectly marked "Page Four").
Two letters to Paine, of which the first (December 7, 1911) had already appeared in Twainian, XV (March-April, 1956) and apparently printed again through carelessness;

the second (December 25, 1909) sends condolences on the death of Jean Clemens.

B42 GULLASON, THOMAS ARTHUR. "The 'Fatal' Ending of Huckleberry Finn," American Literature, XXIX (March), 86-91.
The concluding episode, "based on Tom's lie, cannot be considered fatal because Huck settles conflicts presented earlier in the novel. Important themes, which are repeated and varied, furnish the key." In the last chapters Huck rejects "Tom's romantic irresponsibility...and society's cruel nature... understands Jim's true worth"; and Huck's honest and humble facing and resolving of the conflicts shows his developing strength of character (p. 91). Reprinted in Bradley (1962.A2), pp. 357-61.

B43 JONES, ALEXANDER E. "Mark Twain and the Determinism of What Is Man?" American Literature, XXIX (March), 1-17.
This is not a pessimistic tract in the vein of The Mysterious Stranger; MT had been pondering determinism since 1880, and indeed had encountered it during his piloting days. "What Is Man? is not, then, a mere cry of despair. True, it does represent Twain's attempt to smother a burning sense of guilt; but it is even more important as an attack upon human pride."

B44 KEATING, L. CLARK. "Mark Twain and Paul Bourget," French Review, XXX (April), 342-49.
In a discussion of their depiction of each other's countries, considers the background, development, and attitudes of the two. There are persistent, minor errors of detail by Clark concerning MT; for example, he is said to have written "The Jumping Frog" while a reporter for the "Virginia City Gazette," and he is misquoted as having said that in France "adultery is the rule. Frenchmen do not seek to know their grandfather." Abstract in AES, XIV (1970-1971), 2840; reprinted in Twainian, XXXI (March-April, 1972).

B45 *KLAUS, ROSMARIE. "Mark Twain und die Negerfrage: Huckleberry Finn," Zeitschrift für Anglistik und Amerikanistik, V, 166-81.
[Source: MHRA Annual Bibliography (1959), No. 4560.]

B46 KOHN, JOHN S. VAN E. "Mark Twain's 1601," Princeton University Library Chronicle, XVIII (Winter), 49-54.
Provides a brief history of the writing and publication of the work. John Hay wrote three letters about the book to his friend Alexander Gunn (the one of June 24, 1880 is here reproduced in facsimile). "The holograph originals of these letters form a portion of a collection of letters and documents pertaining to Mark Twain's 1601 assembled by the late Frank H. Ginn of Cleveland that has recently been presented to the

(KOHN, JOHN S. VAN E.)
Library by Mr. Ginn's children....". There are also notes from MT in the collection.

B47 LEISY, ERNEST E. "Mark Twain in Nevada, 1862-1864," Southwest Review, XLII (Summer), 247-48.
A review of Henry Nash Smith and Frederick Anderson, eds., Mark Twain of the "Enterprise," which is "carefully edited.... It contains thirty newly discovered letters and dispatches plus background material, and it makes numerous corrections in the record."

B48 LORCH, FRED W. "Mark Twain's Public Lectures in England in 1873," American Literature, XXIX (November), 297-304.
"The purpose of this article is to offer a complete schedule of dates for Mark Twain's lecture engagements in England and to give a more detailed report of the reception which his lectures received there than Paine has given" (p. 297). MT was generally well received as a droll lecturer, but not taken as seriously as he would have wished. As always, Lorch documents liberally with citations from the contemporary press. For further treatment of MT's lecturing by Lorch, see his The Trouble Begins at Eight (1968). Abstract in AES, I (1958), 8.

B49 MERIWETHER, LEE. "Me and Mark Twain," Mark Twain Journal, X (Fall-Winter), 17-19.
Anecdotes of a visit to the MT home in Hartford in 1875, a jumping frog contest there in 1955 [sic], MT and an effusive drunk at a St. Louis luncheon in 1902.

B50 _____. "Our Struggle with the Internal Revenue Bureau," Mark Twain Journal, X (Fall-Winter), 1-2, 9.
A member of the Mark Twain Memorial Association, Harry Williams, without authorization "prepared a letterhead bearing the names of seven presidents of the United States, several Justices of the U.S. Supreme Court; Winston Churchill and Sir Anthony Eden, Britain's Prime Ministers; Attaturk, President of Turkey and a score of other world famous people.... That letterhead was used by Williams in soliciting contributions from lovers of Mark Twain in all parts of the world except St. Louis, Missouri, and near-by states. They were excluded in order to prevent the Society's members and friends from learning what he was doing." He deposited $31,000 in the bank in the name of the Society, and at the time of his death had withdrawn all but $11,000; when the facts became known "the Internal Revenue Bureau claimed the Mark Twain Society owed $11,309.96 income taxes and to secure that claim it seized all of the Mark Twain's assets [sic], $8,765.00," of which it later returned $4,427.

B51 _____. "A Short History of the Mark Twain Memorial Association," Mark Twain Journal, X (Fall-Winter), 10-11, 19.
Chiefly on the celebrities whose names have been associated with the organization (and Benito Mussolini's contribution of $250 toward a bust of MT in St. Louis), Cyril Clemens's relation to MT, and his successful suit against Harper & Brothers, resulting in an out-of-court settlement in which they paid him $1250 after having called him a "Faker and a liar" and having denied that he was related to MT.

B52 MILLER, WILLIAM C. "Mark Twain at the Sanitary Ball--and Elsewhere?" California Historical Society Bulletin, XXXVI (March), 35-40.
The text of "The Sanitary Ball," reprinted from the Territorial Enterprise of January 10, 1863, and here attributed to MT.

B53 PAUL, RODMAN WILSON. [Review: Henry Nash Smith and Frederick Anderson, eds., Mark Twain of the "Enterprise."] Mississippi Valley Historical Review, XLIV (September), 368-69.
Chiefly descriptive, noting that "the bulk of the present volume" consists of "thirty letters and dispatches to the Enterprise" from a scrapbook of clippings. Lacking the art of Roughing It, "these articles are samples of a man's day-to-day journalistic output." Smith's introduction is "excellent," and he "has added a twenty-page section that prints all known correspondence dealing with the question of whether Mark Twain had to leave Virginia City in order to avoid having to fight a duel."

B54 REINFIELD, GEORGE. "Huckleberry Finn, Candidate for Greatness," Mark Twain Journal, X (Fall-Winter), 12-14.
The book is a great novel, which reveals "the barefaced duplicity of fortune tellers," the cowardice of lynch mobs, and "the growth of character of Huck and Jim as they entrust each other with their freedom and form a fast friendship"; in the portrayal of the King and Duke "royalty comes in for a sound thrashing."

B55 ROGERS, FRANKLIN R. "Washoe's First Literary Journal," California Historical Society Quarterly, XXXVI (December), 365-70.
On the Weekly Occidental (described in RI), the first literary paper in Nevada; it died after four issues, a victim of insufficient audience, insufficient time on the part of the staff, and competition from the influential Golden Era.

B56 RUBIN, LOUIS D., JR. "Tom Sawyer and the Use of Novels," American Quarterly, IX (Summer), 209-16.
The book is important, not as a document that describes its times, but as a novel which helps explain them. Tom has won

1957 - Shorter Writings

(RUBIN, LOUIS D., JR.)
success, wealth, and fame, at the cost of
"something impractical and spiritual....
It took a Mark Twain to show us how the
meaning of success, and of loss, lies at
the heart of American experience" (p. 216).
Reprinted in Hennig Cohen, ed. The American
Experience: Approaches to the Study of the
United States (Boston: Houghton Mifflin
Company, 1968), 106-14. In an "Afternote"
to the reprinted article (p. 114) Rubin says
that he would have "written the essay very
differently" if he had had the benefit of
Henry Nash Smith's Mark Twain: The Development of a Writer (1962), "a superb demonstration of just how the work of a major
writer may profitably be used to interpret
a culture."

B57 *SCHÖNFELDER, KARL-HEINZ. "Kriege im Leben
und Werk von Mark Twain," Zeitschrift für
Anglistik und Amerikanistik, V, 414-32.
[Source: MHRA Annual Bibliography (1959),
No. 4574.]

B58 SMITH, HENRY NASH. "Mark Twain as an Interpretor of the Far West: The Structure of
Roughing It," in Walker D. Wyman and Clifton
B. Kroeber, eds., The Frontier in Perspective. Madison: The University of Wisconsin
Press (paperback ed., 1967), pp. 205-28.
(Also quotation from LOM and extensive quotation from RI on pp. 201-203 of Frederic G.
Cassidy, "Language on the American Frontier," pp. 185-204).
The first half of the book recounts the
gradual development of the tenderfoot narrator (p. 210), and in the second half,
"structurally distinct...the narrative
scheme is loosely autobiographical, and the
narrative is merely a framework within which
more or less fully developed anecdotes are
placed. The second half, that is, answers
closely to the description of the entire
work given by Mr. Fried and other critics"
(p. 224). Also treats MT's turn to Eastern
gentility though affirming frontier comrade-
ship and freedom, influence of vernacular on
style, and narration by a tenderfoot. The
West had considerable influence on American
literary development, if not on our democracy (editors' headnote, pp. 205-206).

B59 STALLMAN, R. W. "Huck Finn Again," College
English, XVIII (May), 425-26.
"Everything in the novel goes by pairs.
Doubleness is the dominant leitmotif, nota-
bly in the two Hucks," torn between conscience and conformity. "The structure of
Huckleberry Finn, as I see it, consists of
a recurrent counterpointing of the real or
true event with the juxtaposed parody of it.
Nothing is not parodied." The journey
southward on the raft, masking the true intention to go northward, is "justifiable
both at the literal and the thematic level.... Everything in the novel goes masked,
even Moses in the bullrushes; that's what

saved him." The article is followed by:
"Note: This letter ends the discussion of
Huckleberry Finn begun by Professor O'Connor's attack two years ago.--Ed." Reprinted
as "Reality and Parody in Huckleberry Finn,"
in Bradley (1962.A2), 384-87.

B60 STEGNER, WALLACE. "Yarn-Spinner in the American Vein," New York Times Book Review (February 10), pp. 1, 25.
A review of Charles Neider, ed., The Complete Short Stories of Mark Twain, "an entertaining volume," but much of its content
can be called short stories "only by stretching definition to its elastic limits....
Mark Twain is less a short-story writer than
a fabulist, satirist, parodist," although
his fables and yarns reveal artistic intelligence and sensibility.

B61 TOWN, GEORGE H. [Letter to Chester L. Davis.]
Twainian, XVI (January-February), 4.
Cites an article in the Utica (New York)
Saturday Globe of February 11, 1899, accord-
ing to which the original of Colonel Sellers
(in The Gilded Age) was one James W. Wardner.

B62 WASIOLEK, EDWARD. "The Structure of Make-Believe: Huckleberry Finn," University of
Kansas City Review, XXIII (October), 97-101.
"The river, and life on the river, is
fluid, sinuous, unpredictable. The shore,
and life on the shore, is still rigid, and
predictable," as in the Arkansas crowd's
watching the daily spectacle of Boggs's
drunkenness and in the feud whose origins
are forgotten and which has become ritual;
Huck can predict Tom Sawyer's actions and
feelings because "Tom's behavior is a regu-
lated show." The controversial ending is
consistent with his world and one of grown-
ups: "Both worlds are indifferent to real
human situations; both entranced with the
rules of their play-acting."

B63 WHITE, WILLIAM. "One Man's Meat: Societies
and Journals Devoted to a Single Author,"
American Book Collector, VIII (November),
22-24.
Lists Mark Twain Journal and Twainian,
with addresses and names of editors, but
provides no other information on MT. Abstract in AES, I (1958), 235.

B64 WIGGER, ANNE P. "The Composition of Mark
Twain's Pudd'nhead Wilson and Those Extraordinary Twins: Chronology and Development,"
Modern Philology, LV (November), 93-102.
The manuscript in the Morgan Library and
materials in the Mark Twain Papers reveal
"a remarkable literary metamorphosis" during
the composition of the book; they reveal
MT's intentions, "particularly in the characterization of Tom Driscoll, which becomes
rather obscured through the revisions," and
originally was a much more dramatic treatment of the effects of inherited training
and particularly of the legacy of slavery.
Abstract in AES, I (1958), 93.

B65 _____. "The Source of Fingerprint Material in Mark Twain's Pudd'nhead Wilson and Those Extraordinary Twins." American Literature, XXVIII (January), 517-20.

    The evidence indicates that MT's source was Sir Francis Galton's Finger Prints (London), a copy of which Chatto & Windus apparently sent him. Disputes the claim by Louis Hamon (a palmist who used the pseudonym "Cheiro") to have provided MT with the interest in fingerprinting.

B66 WILLSON, FRANK C. "Hartford 'Tom Sawyer' Club," Twainian, XVI (January-February), 4.

    On the formation of the club by respectable Hartford citizens in 1881; prints an MT letter of February 11, 1882 declining an invitation to their first annual dinner.

B67 WINTERICH, JOHN T. "Mark Twain, Reporter," Saturday Review, XL (July 27), 26.

    A brief, favorable review of Henry Nash Smith and Frederick Anderson, eds., Mark Twain of the "Enterprise" as "this colorful material, here admirably presented and annotated."

1958 A BOOKS

A1 CLEMENS, SAMUEL L. Traveling with the Innocents Abroad: Mark Twain's Original Reports from Europe and the Holy Land, ed. Daniel Morley McKeithan. Norman: University of Oklahoma Press.

    The texts of MT's newspaper letters to the San Francisco Daily Alta California and the New York Herald and Tribune, which formed the basis for Innocents Abroad. This picks up the correspondence where Franklin Walker and G. Ezra Dane stopped in Mark Twain's Travels with Mr. Brown (1940); parts of two letters in that volume also found their way into Innocents Abroad. McKeithan's editing is careful and thorough, not only in showing backgrounds for MT's writing but also in showing some of the changes the material underwent for Innocents Abroad.

A2 DARBEE, HENRY, ed. Mark Twain in Hartford. Hartford: The Mark Twain Library and Memorial Commission.

    A pamphlet including Hartford scenes, pictures and floor-plans of MT's home, and excerpts from published sources (not all cited in the present bibliography) bearing on MT in Hartford.

A3 EATON, JEANETTE. America's Own Mark Twain. New York: William Morrow and Company. Biography of MT for young readers.

A4 FONER, PHILIP S. Mark Twain: Social Critic. New York: International Publishers.

    A Marxist interpretation, carefully documented and supported by liberal quotation from MT to an extent that makes it a useful source of materials elsewhere unpublished or difficult of access.

A5 McKEITHAN, DANIEL M[ORLEY]. Court Trials in Mark Twain and Other Essays. 'S-Gravenhage [The Hague]: Martinus Nijhoff.

    "The major section of this volume, dealing with court trials in Mark Twain, is here published for the first time with the exception of the discussion of the trial of Silas Phelps. The account of this trial and the essay entitled 'The Origin of Mark Twain's Tom Sawyer, Detective' were originally published together as 'Mark Twain's Tom Sawyer, Detective' in Studia Neophilologica in 1953 (XXV, 161-179). In this section I have tried to retain at least a little of the quality of Twain in retelling the stories and on this basis alone it should be judged. The other essays appeared, respectively, in the Philological Quarterly for October, 1953 (XXXII, 353-365), the Tennessee Historical Quarterly for September, 1952 (XI, 246-253), the Southern Folklore Quarterly for December, 1953 (XVII, 241-243), the Philological Quarterly for July, 1948 (XXVII, 276-279), Modern Language Notes for April, 1948 (LXIII, 221-228), and the University of Texas Studies in English for 1949 (XXVIII, 257-270).... The major themes here dealt with are Twain's interest in the administration of justice in the United States, his use of court trials as elements in his plots, his debt to frontier American literature, his reply to foreign critics of America, and his ability to use foreign sources for details of plot while remaining thoroughly American in style, spirit, and point of view" (pp. ix-x). For commentary on the previously published materials see the years of original publication.

A6 SMITH, HENRY NASH, ed. Adventures of Huckleberry Finn. Boston: Houghton Mifflin Company.

    Appendices give the text of the "Raft Passage" from LOM and examples of MT's revisions of the text of HF. In his introduction Smith discusses the importance of language in HF, the use of Huck as innocent narrator, the gain and the loss in MT's rejection of cultural tradition, and structural questions in the flight downstream (Jim's escape is not always a central concern) and culminating at the Phelps farm. Smith disputes the notion, increasingly popular among critics, that Huck learns to see the evils of slavery or the society that condones it: "When Huck says he means to set out ahead of the others, there is nothing in the text to indicate that his intention is more serious than Tom's."

1958 B SHORTER WRITINGS

B1 ANON. [Miscellaneous material from December Harper's Magazine]. Twainian, XVII (November-December), 1-4.

(ANON.)
Statement by Charles Neider on MT's autobiography, followed by statements by MT on
various topics. Quoted in Twainian, XXXII
(November-December, 1973), 4.

B2   ASSELINEAU, ROGER. [Review: Arthur L. Scott,
Mark Twain: Selected Criticism (1955) and
Huckleberry Finns Abenteuer, translated into German by Barbara Cramer-Nauhaus, and
with an afterword by F. W. Schulze (1956).]
Etudes Anglaises, VIII (April-June),
183-84.
Scott's great fault is giving undue space
to the favorable notices MT received in his
lifetime, many of them superficial, with
the result that the book is more interesting as history than as criticism. It would
have been more useful to present texts
clarifying a certain number of important
points, such as the Brooks-DeVoto controversy, or the discussions of HF by Lionel
Trilling, T. S. Eliot, and Leo Marx. F. W.
Schulze's afterword to the German translation of HF provides an excellent analysis
of the characters of Tom, Huck, and, especially, Jim; it is unfortunate that, probably for want of space, he did not attempt
to define the particular flavor of MT's
humor in this book. [In French.]

B3   BARROWS, HERBERT. [Review: Daniel Morley
McKeithan, ed., Traveling with the Innocents Abroad.] Antioch Review, XVIII (Winter), 515-22.
No comment on the editing, but calls this
"just possibly a better book than The Innocents Abroad," revealing the "ebullient
spirit" of the letters before they were
toned down "into a self-conscious literary
production."

B4   BECK, WARREN. "Huck Finn at Phelps Farm: An
Essay in Defense of the Form of Mark Twain's
Novel," Archives des Lettres Modernes,
Nos. 13-15 (Juin-Septembre), pp. 1-31.
"What makes the Phelps farm episode conclusively relevant, therefore, in spite of
its juvenile flavor, is the constant presence of the realistic and increasingly responsible Huck, and his repeated interpola-
tions as the half-detached and more than
half-skeptical foil to Tom's fancifulness
and enslavement to tradition" (p. 22).
[32-page pamphlet, with an abstract in
French on p. 32.]

B5   BERRY, MABEL F. E. "Mark Twain in Hartford,"
Mark Twain Journal, X (Spring-Summer), 16.
She saw MT in church there and once de-
livered stationery to his house by bicycle.

B6   BLAIR, WALTER. "When Was Huckleberry Finn
Written?" American Literature, XXX (March),
1-25.
Contends that Paine is nearer the truth
in giving periods of composition as 1876,
1880, and 1883 than is DeVoto in giving

only 1876 and 1883. "Furthermore, I believe
that both, with most other students of
Twain, overestimate the influence of Clemens's Mississippi River trip of 1882 on the
novel. If my beliefs prove to be well
founded, significant revisions of the story
of the genesis of the book will be necessary." The evidence includes letters and recorded conversations, MT's notes, notebooks,
and the surviving MS material. Most of the
evidence not available to DeVoto is in Webster's Mark Twain, Business Man or in transcripts in the Mark Twain Papers in Berkeley. Abstract in AES, I (1958), 546.

B7   BOOMKAMP, LEEUWEN. "A Dutch Admirer Meets
Mark Twain," Mark Twain Journal, X (Spring-
Summer), 8.
In the summer of 1900, he was reading and
laughing over TS on a New York bus, and got
into "quite a pleasant argument, pro and
contra," with a man who called it "kid
stuff"; Boomkamp eventually recognized the
man as MT.

B8   BUDD, LOUIS J. [Review: Henry Nash Smith and
Frederick Anderson, eds., Mark Twain of the
"Enterprise."] South Atlantic Bulletin,
LVII (Winter), 145-46.
Thirty newspaper letters and dispatches
from scrapbooks recently added to the Mark
Twain Papers at Berkeley, "definitively
edited, handsomely printed...it is a valu-
able as well as an interesting book," both
for the MT scholar and for the "absorbing
Americana" it contains.

B9   CARTER, PAUL J. "Mark Twain Material in the
New York Weekly Review," Papers of the Bibliographical Society of America, LII (First
Quarter), 56-62.
Reveals eight MT items appearing there,
one of them (on a San Francisco earthquake)
previously unknown.

B10   _____. "Olivia Clemens Edits Following the
Equator," American Literature XXX (May),
194-209.
Consists primarily of the text of Livy's
comments and MT's responses, as preserved
in the Mark Twain Papers. She did urge some
changes for the sake of propriety, but her
main role was that of skilful proofreader;
MT appreciated her suggestions, but did not
accept them all. [See Da Ponte, 1957.] Abstract in AES, I (1958), 762.

B11   CLARK, GEORGE PEIRCE. "Mark Twain and Bret
Harte," Mark Twain Journal, X (Spring-Summer), 12-13.
Reprints the text of MT's comments to Howells in letters of April 15, 1879 and December 4, 1903; "neither of these letters is
printed in full, but nothing pertaining to
Harte is omitted from them." See 1958.B12.

B12   ____. "Mark Twain on Bret Harte: Selections from Two Unpublished Letters," Journal of English and Germanic Philology, LVII (April), 208-10.
        Letters from Paris (April 15, 1879) and Florence (December 4, 1903), attacking Harte as a man of no integrity and an author whose latest book MT read "through tears of rage over the fellow's inborn hypocrisy & snobbishness, his apprentice-art, his artificialities, his mannerisms, his pet phrases...his laboriously acquired ignorance, & his jejeune anxiety to display it. O my God!" Abstract in AES, III I (1960), 1453; reprinted in Twainian, XIX (November-December, 1960).

B13   CLEMENS, CYRIL. "Sir Max Beerbohm and Mark Twain," Hobbies--the Magazine for Collectors, LXIII (November), 110.
        Prints several notes from Beerbohm, one of them (February 14, 1953) recalling a luncheon with MT at Bernard Shaw's home: "He was then very old, but very beautiful to look at, and to listen to. A lovely voice, lovely manners, and, among other attributes, wonderfully eloquent hands."

B14   COCTEAU, JEAN. Sketch (not resembling MT), bearing the legend: "Mark Twain n'est pas un humoriste c'est un poète et je l'aime Jean Cocteau* 1958." Mark Twain Journal, X (Spring-Summer), front cover.

B15   CONSIGLIO, CARLA. "La Fortuna di Mark Twain in Italia: Nota Bibliografica di Carla Consiglio." Studi Americani, IV, 198-208.
        An annotated bibliography of translations and criticism, 1891-1957.

B16   ____. "La Prosa di Mark Twain e i Suoi Influssi" ["Mark Twain's Prose and Its Influences"], Studi Americani, IV, 175-97.
        A detailed examination of MT's influence on Gertrude Stein, Sherwood Anderson, and Ernest Hemingway. In his "superb adaptation of the vernacular to the purposes of art" MT "has forged a classic prose that moves according to the canons of simplicity, grace, and limpidness." Gertrude Stein knew his works, and "it would be interesting...to know if Stein was completely conscious of the affinity of her prose with that of Mark Twain." In turn, she helped shape Hemingway and Anderson. "All that Anderson and Hemingway proposed to say was similar to that which Mark Twain had said"; they shared his interest in the life of the common people, aversion to formal education, and, especially, a wish to depict reality objectively and without distortion.

B17   COOPER, M. LOVINA. "I Remember Mark Twain," Mark Twain Journal, X (Spring-Summer), 5.
        Recollection of MT's appearance when he spoke at the University of Minnesota. "We listened with wrapped [sic] attention while the famous Mark Twain talked. No, I can't tell you what he said."

B18   COSBEY, ROBERT C. "Letter to the Editor," College English, XIX (April), 320.
        Tom Sawyer's fence has horizontal boards, as described in Tyrus Hillway's note in the January issue (1958.B35), but Tom is described as easily scrambling over it; the extremely high fence "is the creation of impressionistic humor, not of carpenters."

B19   *CUMMINGS, SHERWOOD. "Memories of Mark Twain," North Dakota Quarterly, XXXVI (Spring), 65-66.
        [Source: Leary (1970), p. 62.]

B20   ____. "Science and Mark Twain's Theory of Fiction," Philological Quarterly, XXXVII (January), 26-33.
        "The idea of scientific determinism was...implicit in Mark Twain's earliest reading and thinking"; the influence of Darwin and Taine is evident. MT's theory applies in TS and HF, where "the power of place...is at once pervasive and unobtrusive" and in PW, where "the exposition of environmental influence upon Tom Driscoll and Chambers is worked out with the neatness of a sociologist's case history." Abstract in AES, I (1958), 1048.

B21   CURRIE, H. MacL. "Aristophanes and Mark Twain," Notes and Queries (London), CCIII, n.s. V (April), 165-68.
        Compares the attitude of the two as revealed in the latter part of the Thesmophoriazusae and in chapters XXXVI-XXXIX of Huckleberry Finn. They were "not dissimilar in spirit," and if there is no evidence that MT had read Aristophanes, he did read widely and the plays were readily available in the Bohn classical series. Abstract in AES, I (1958), 890.

B22   [DAVIS, CHESTER L.]. "Mark's Copy 'Origin of Religions-Aryan Sun-Myths,'" Twainian, XVII (September-October), 1-3.
        "Mr. Victor Jacobs...has sent us photostatic copies of certain pages from the above book, pages having marginal notations in the handwriting of Mark Twain, the book being one which was in the last public dispersal of Mark's library." Reproduces passages from the book with some of MT's comments (author of book not named). Quoted in Twainian, XXXII (November-December, 1973.B15), 4.

B23   ____. "Mark Twain and John Hays Hammond," Twainian (January-February), 1-3.
        On MT's marginalia in his copy of Mrs. John Hays Hammond's A Woman's Part in a Revolution (New York and Bombay: Longmans, Green & Co., 1897); Mrs. Hammond describes MT's visit to the prisoners at Pretoria on p. 152 of her book. Quoted in Twainian, XXXII (November-December, 1973.B15), 1.

1958 - Shorter Writings

B24 [DAVIS, CHESTER L.] "Mark Twain and Space
Travel," Twainian, pp. 3-4.
Quotations from his published works with
no new information.

B25 _____. "Mark Twain Coinage of Words," Twainian, p. 4.
On Robert L. Ramsay and Frances Guthrie
Emberson's A Mark Twain Lexicon (1938):
excerpts, with no new information or useful
comment. Quoted in Twainian, XXXII (November-December, 1973.B15), 1-2.

B26 _____. "Mark Twain Memorial--Future Home of
Twainian," Twainian, (May-June), 1-4.
On the plans for the building, to be
erected at Florida, Missouri, and on the
Mark Twain Research Foundation and its pre-
decessors. Quoted in Twainian, XXXII
(November-December, 1973.B15), 2-3.

B27 _____. "Mark Twain's Personal Library to Be
Collected and Contained in Mark Twain Memorial to Be Erected at His Birthplace in
Florida, Missouri," Twainian, (July-August),
2-4; (September-October), 3-4.
Lists titles of books containing MT's
marginalia; "Those which we do not have or
which we have not located approximates
about half of the total items listed."
Quoted in Twainian, XXXII (November-December, 1973.B15), 3-4.

B28 _____. "A Visit to Florida in the Year Paine
Published the 'Biography' 1912," Twainian,
(March-April), 1-4.
Headnote to reprint of T. V. Bodine,
"Birthplace of Mark Twain. The Story of
the Great Humorist and Philosopher and His
Equally Whimsical Uncle--Judge John S.
Quarles," in Kansas City Star, May 19, 1912:
"(The following article is not generally
available and has been referred to by many
writers. Repeated inquiries justify the
republication of the article almost in it's
entirety. Parts which are not reprinted
herein have definitely been of little value
to later writers and historians, parts
largely speculative and not proven, or better treated by later writers such as Paine,
DeVoto and Wecter.)" Quoted in Twainian,
XXXII (November-December, 1973.B15), 2.

B29 _____. [Review: E. Hudson Long's Mark Twain
Handbook (1958),] Twainian, (November-Decem-
ber), 1.
Descriptive and laudatory.

B30 ELLIOTT, GEORGE P. "Wonder for Huckleberry
Finn," in George P. Shipiro, ed., Twelve
Original Essays on Great American Novels.
(Detroit: Wayne State University Press),
pp. 69-95.
A general study of MT and his book; notes
the entertainment value of MT's books, his
sensitivity to words and their sound and
arrangement, his poor critical judgment of

his own work, and "his acceptance of standards of value--moral, social, literary--
which in his heart he disbelieved in." It
is our good fortune that he came to write
HF as he did.

B30A ELLISON, RALPH. "Change the Joke and Slip
the Yoke," Partisan Review, XXV (Spring),
212-22; reprinted in his Shadow and Act
(1964), pp. 45-59.
An answer to an essay by Stanley Edgar
Hyman on Negro American literature and
folklore (immediately preceding). On HF,
Ellison argues that "Twain fitted Jim into
the outlines of the minstrel tradition, and
it is from behind this stereotype mask that
we see Jim's dignity and human capacity--
and Twain's complexity--emerge." MT was
still too close to the Reconstruction to
escape "the white dictum that Negro males
must be treated either as boys or 'uncles'--
never as men. Jim's friendship for Huck
comes across as that of a boy for another
boy rather than as the friendship of an
adult for a junior; thus there is implicit
in it not only a violation of the manners
sanctioned by society for relations between
Negroes and whites, there is a violation of
our concept of adult maleness." Ellison
suggests that it was concern over this question that led Leslie Fiedler to argue a
homosexual relationship in "Come Back to the
Raft Ag'in, Huck Honey!" Fiedler was "so
profoundly disturbed by the manner in which
the deep dichotomies symbolized by blackness
and whiteness are resolved that, forgetting
to look at the specific form of the novel,
he leaped squarely into the middle of that
tangle of symbolism which he is dedicated
to unsnarling and yelled out his most terrifying name for chaos."

B31 FIEDLER, LESLIE A. "Boys Will be Boys!" New
Leader, XLI (April 28), 23-26.
HF conformed to the 19th century taboo on
any intimations of sex in books about children, although MT faced violence frankly;
however, in TS Tom takes both the punishment
and the blame for Becky's damaging the
schoolmaster's book: "It is as necessary to
him that Becky retain her mythical Goodness
as it is for her that he retain his equally
mythical Badness." Reprinted in his No! In
Thunder (1960), and The Collected Essays of
Leslie Fiedler (1971.B22).

B32 _____. "Good Good Girl and Good Bad Boy,"
New Leader, XLI (April 14), 22-25.
On the literary Cult of the Child: the
portrayal of the boy must reject the aristocratic "little gentleman," like Sid Sawyer.
HF exists on a superficially comic and deeper tragic level; it is "an astonishingly
complicated novel, containing not one image
of the boy-child as a symbol of the good life
of impulse, but a series of interlocking
ones: boys within boys." Reprinted in his

(FIEDLER, LESLIE A.)
No! In Thunder (1960) and The Collected Essays of Leslie Fiedler (1971.B22). Abstract in AES, I (1958), 1800.

B33 GERBER, JOHN C. "The Relation between Point of View and Style in the Works of Mark Twain," in Style in Prose Fiction, English Institute Essays, 1958; New York: Columbia University Press (1959), pp. 142-71.
"Twain's style is so intimately dependent upon his point of view that it flourishes only to the extent that the point of view is detached and sharply restricted," providing psychological distance and "forcing him to focus upon a specific and concrete situation" (p. 143). This accounts for the superiority of HF to TS and CY. In IA MT is more detached as storyteller than as observer or satirist, and as a result "The details are more specific and the incidents far better shaped for climax" (p. 149). Abstract in AES, VIII (1965), 2571; reprinted in Twainian, XXV (January-February, 1966). Article reprinted in Lettis (1962. A11), pp. 410-18.

B34 GORDON, EDWARD J. "What's Happened to Humor?" English Journal, XLVII (March), 127-33.
Huck Finn sees through the self-deceptions of others; he is contrasted with John Marquand's character George Apley, who deceives himself.

B35 HILLWAY, TYRUS. "Tom Sawyer's Fence," College English, XIX (January), 165-66.
The planks were horizontal, rather than vertical; moreover, it was a nine-foot fence, "an unusually high one, unless Mark Twain was intentionally exaggerating." Abstract in AES, I (1958), 271. For further commentary see Robert C. Cosbey (April), B. R. McElderry, Jr. (May), and Robert H. Woodward (October, with another letter by Hillway).

B36 _____, and Robert H. Woodward. "Rebuttal: Tom Sawyer's Fence," College English, XX (October), 32.
Hillway replies to Robert C. Cosbey's note in April (1958.B18) that climbing a nine-foot fence is no great feat, particularly with a toehold on horizontal boards. The Woodward letter notes an illustration "in The Book of Knowledge (1953 ed., VI, 2132), which pictures exactly the style of fence described in the novel"; he does not describe this illustration, but argues that the boards are vertical on the basis of a photograph taken in 1902, showing MT at the house; moreover, a guidebook on sale at Hannibal describes the fence as "just like" the original. [A photograph accompanying Henry M. Wharton's "The Boyhood Home of Mark Twain" in Century, LXIV (September, 1902), 674, shows the house with a fence on the right of a viewer facing toward the

house from the street, which slopes downhill to the right; the fence appears to be almost six feet high, with vertical boards. To the left, less than three feet from the house, appears a substantial brick building. According to the caption, "There was a high board fence on the left, for the whitewashing of which he sold privileges to one or more of his youthful companions, somewhat as related in 'Tom Sawyer.'"--ed.]

B37 HINZ, JOHN. "A No. 1 Ruse," Mark Twain Journal, X (Spring-Summer), 14.
Disputes the statement by Edgar M. Branch that this early sketch is "disappointing," merely "a long diffuse tale."

B38 HUNTING, ROBERT. "Mark Twain's Arkansaw Yahoos," Modern Language Notes, LXXIII (April), 264-68.
Chapters XXI-XXII ("An Arkansaw Difficulty" and "Why the Lynching Bee Failed") "in point of view and in tone...stand apart from the rest of the novel.... the mask slips and...the reporter in these two chapters looks suspiciously like Mark Twain himself," lacking in Huck's compassion. (See reply by E. Arthur Robinson, 1960.B95.) Abstract in AES, I (1958), 867.

B39 KELLER, HELEN. "My Friend Mark Twain," Mark Twain Journal, X (Spring-Summer), 1.
On her admiration and affection for MT, whom she first met when she was fourteen; "It seemed to me that his pessimism was rather superficial. I thought he enjoyed exercising his wonderful gift of making sardonic aphorisms," although they were incisive and arrested attention.

B40 LAING, DILYS. "His Own Bowdler," Nation, CLXXXVII (July 19), 37-38.
A review of Daniel Morley McKeithan, ed., Traveling with the Innocents Abroad. MT toned the letters down for the book.

B41 LORCH, FRED W. "Hawaiian Feudalism and Mark Twain's A Connecticut Yankee in King Arthur's Court," American Literature, XXX (March), 50-66.
Suggests supplementing John B. Hoben's "genetic study" (1946) with a "pre-genetic study": it was in Hawaii that MT first encountered the remnants of a feudal society, and his reading about the islands supplemented his vivid personal impressions. There is particularly clear evidence of the influence of James Jackson Jarves's History of the Sandwich Islands (Honolulu, 1847), with which MT was familiar and which anticipates the Yankee not only in the broad picture of the society, but also in such details as the interdict (Jarves describes the effects of taboo, and draws attention to its similarity to the interdict of the Roman Church). Abstract in AES, I (1958), 549.

B42   LORCH, FRED W. [Review: Henry Nash Smith and
       Frederick Anderson, ed., Mark Twain of the
       "Enterprise" (1957).] American Literature,
       XXX (March), pp. 125-27.
          The two great contributions to MT scholar-
       ship are the clear detailing of MT's kinds of
       reporting for the Enterprise (straight re-
       porting signed "Sam" or "SLC" and humorous
       material signed "Mark Twain"), and the docu-
       mented explanation of why MT suddenly left
       Nevada--not to avoid arrest for violation of
       the dueling laws, but because of his taste-
       less assertion that money being collected for
       the Sanitary Fund was being sent to support
       miscegenation societies. There are no seri-
       ous inaccuracies evident, and Smith provides
       valuable supplementary data in the headnotes.

B43   LOWENHERZ, ROBERT J. "Mark Twain Laughs at
       Death," Mark Twain Journal, X (Spring-Sum-
       mer), 2-5, 16.
          On comic treatments of death in MT's
       works; reprints the text of a burlesque
       obituary he wrote for the "Contributors'
       Club" of the Atlantic Monthly (November,
       1884).

B44   _____. "Mark Twain on Usage," American
       Speech, XXXIII (February), 70-72.
          A brief introductory note by Lowenherz
       precedes an abridged reprinting of MT's
       unsigned reply to "A Boston Girl" in "The
       Contributors' Club" of Atlantic, XLV
       (June, 1880), 849-60; MT's topics are gram-
       mar and the accurate rendering of speech.

B45   LUNDY, ROBERT W. "Mark Twain and Italy."
       Studi Americani, IV, 135-49.
          "His two travel books which include sec-
       tions on Italy confirm the impression that
       he learned little about or from it"
       (p. 137), because he had no real interest
       in the country or its history.

B46   LYNN, KENNETH S. "Huck and Jim," Yale Review,
       XLVII (March), 421-31.
          MT's early interest in Joan of Arc grew
       from reading about her in her prison cell,
       and "in a sense Twain spent all his life-
       time writing about Joan; the tension be-
       tween the nightmare of being locked up and
       forgotten and the dream of liberation is
       in all his best work." In HF there is a
       succession of Biblical themes, especially
       that of Moses--and a parallel in that when
       Moses led the Israelites toward freedom he
       moved toward death, and the movement carry-
       ing Jim to freedom will separate the two
       friends. Huck undergoes rebirths in a cy-
       cle of initiations culminating in deaths,
       and Jim passes through successive bondages.
       Abstract in AES, I (1958), 755. Article
       reprinted in Kaplan (1967), pp. 123-33.

B47   McELDERRY, B. R., JR. "Tom Sawyer's Fence--
       Original Illustrations," College English,
       XIX (May), 370.

          In answer to the note by Tyrus Hillway in
       the January issue and the letter by Robert
       C. Cosbey in May, calls attention to the
       illustrations in the first edition by True
       Williams, presumably with MT's approval:
       "Three illustrations (pp. 17, 28, 30) show
       a fence along the street, made of four wide
       boards, well spaced, and nailed horizontal-
       ly to square posts set six or eight feet apart.
       The height of the fence is about four
       feet.... the fence is shown extending to
       the left of the house. The fence shown in
       Hannibal today as a 'replica' stands about
       fifteen feet to the right of the house, and
       is, as Mr. Hillway remarks, a solid board
       fence about six feet high, the boards nailed
       vertically."

B48   McGRAW, WILLIAM CORBIN. "Polyanna Rides
       Again," Saturday Review, XLI (March 22),
       37-38.
          Illustrates the thesis that censorship by
       children's librarians stultifies the writing
       of children's books with a skit, "If Sam
       Clemens Had Been Born Sixty Years too Late
       (A Near-Tragedy in One Act)," with dialogue
       between MT and "Cordelia Minor, juvenile
       editor, harassed and fiftyish," who explains
       why HF cannot be published. This is fol-
       lowed by "An Answer to Mr. McGraw," by
       Frances Lander Spain, Coordinator, Chil-
       dren's Services, New York Public Library,
       who points out that HF did encounter censor-
       ship when it was new, and the taboos McGraw
       cites are those of society and not only of
       libraries; moreover, if authors and editors
       seek advice from librarians before publica-
       tion they share the guilt of "emasculating a
       manuscript."

B49   *MACK, EFFIE [MONA]. "Mark Twain in Nevada. A
       Leaf from the Civil War Story," Oakland
       (California) Tribune, November 16.
          [Source: Reprinted in Twainian, XIX
       (March-April), 4.] On the glorious sight of
       the flag on Mt. Davidson on the day Vicks-
       burg fell to Union forces; adds little to
       the account in RI.

B50   MESERVE, WALTER J. "Colonel Sellers as a Sci-
       entist: A Play by S. L. Clemens and W. D.
       Howells," Modern Drama, I (December),
       151-56.
          On the collaboration of MT and Howells,
       and later use of portions of the play in
       The American Claimant. Abstract in AES, II
       (1959), 288.

B51   MILLER, JAMES E., JR. [Brief review: Charles
       Neider, ed., The Complete Short Stories of
       Mark Twain.] Prairie Schooner, XXXII
       (June), 88.
          "Mr. Neider's collection not only makes
       pleasurable reading but also calls signifi-
       cant attention to Twain's mastery of the art
       of the short fictional form."

B52 MIRIZZI, PIERO. "Il Mondo di Mark Twain" ["The World of Mark Twain"], Studi Americani, IV, 151-74.
A general and somewhat derivative portrayal of MT's life and works, noting the influences by which he was shaped, his attitudes, and the quality of his authorship.

B53 MONTGOMERY, MARION. "The Old Romantic vs. the New: Mark Twain's Dilemma in Life on the Mississippi," Mississippi Quarterly, XI (Spring), 79-82.
MT's attack on the romanticism of Sir Walter Scott contrasts with his own portrait in LOM of the romance of a pilot's life twenty years earlier, "and, more exasperating, his mystical glorification of the industrial life of the late nineteenth century." Abstract in AES, I (1958), 1461. Article reprinted in Kesterson (1973), pp. 113-16.

B54 MORRIS, WRIGHT. "The Available Past: Mark Twain," in his The Territory Ahead: Critical Interpretations of American Literature. (New York: Harcourt, Brace & World), pp. 79-90.
[Source: 1963 paperback reprinting, New York: Athenaeum; the pagination is the same as that reported in Beebe and Feaster (1968), p. 106, where the year of publication is given as 1958.] Contrasts MT and Hemingway in their treatment of innocence and "the corruption and abuse of America's green promise," and MT and Henry James as "the supremely unconscious natural talent" and "the supremely self-conscious artist." "Hemingway's exile is a judgment on things as they are" in a spoiled America, that of Henry James is an attempt to re-possess his inheritance and share its culture with the new world, but MT was simply an innocent abroad who resisted foreign culture. His preference for facts over ideas left him at the end with "staleness and disenchantment.... And what was he? Stripped of his imagination, Henry James could have told him, he was not much." Reprinted in Leary (1962), pp. 269-76.

B55 *MUELLER, HAROLD L., ed. "Mark Twain Library Golden Anniversary" special edition of Redding (Connecticut) Times, December 4.
Includes article apparently by Mueller on history of the library, with a speech by MT at the dedication of the library at its first, temporary quarters. [Source: Reprinted in Twainian, XVIII (January-February, 1959), 1-3.]

B56 NEIDER, CHARLES, ed. "Mark Twain Speaks Out," Harper's, CCXVII (December), 36-41.
Previously unpublished writings by MT on the freedom of writing as from the grave, honorary degrees, amateur writing, and humor; from dictations of 1906-1907. Abstract in AES, II (1959), 171.

B57 OLIVER, EGBERT S. "The Pig-Tailed China Boys Out West," Western Humanities Review, XII (Spring), 159-78.
On the mistreatment of Chinese immigrants in the West; on pp. 174-77, describes the insight and sympathy with which they are portrayed by MT and Bret Harte.

B58 PAINE, ALBERT BIGELOW. "Mark Twain at Eighty-Eight," Redding (Connecticut) Times, December 4, pp. 14-15, 23.
Written in Chinon, France, according to a headnote by his daughter, Louise Paine Moore. On MT's birthdays, his billiard-playing, and his international popularity.

B59 PELLEGRINI, ALMA. "Mark Twain alla Scoperta dell'Europa: The Innocents Abroad" ["Mark Twain on the Discovery of Europe: The Innocents Abroad"], Studi Americani, IV, 109-33.
A general discussion of MT's perspective in IA and attitudes toward his material. From a position of practical, independent common sense he sometimes used the mask of the fool, sometimes turned to burlesque, and sometimes understated; he often took a moralist's view of the follies and vices of the Old World. His was almost a dual personality, and his inner defects sometimes appear in his works as well as determining the structure and defects of the self. Only in HF does he achieve "an almost perfect equilibrium of his expressive means"; in this aspect IA "is in essence an uneven book which lacks an intimate core that can assure continuity of tone and results, and furnish Twain a valid perspective in which to frame Europe."

B60 SANFORD, CHARLES. "Classics of American Reform Literature," American Quarterly, X (Fall), 295-311.
Includes a discussion of Connecticut Yankee (302-305) as MT's "symbolic attempt to persuade himself that all was right in the American garden after all," although suggesting that "the industrial order lacks the symbols to captivate the imagination and that the new American may have lost the sense of heart which characterized the simpler, agrarian past." Abstract in AES, II (1959), 129.

B61 SMITH, HENRY NASH. "Mark Twain's Image of Hannibal: From St. Petersburg to Eseldorf," Texas Studies in English, XXXVII, 3-23.
"Villagers of 1840-3," part of MT's memories which Smith collectively terms the "Matter of Hannibal," "embraced the glory of boyhood but it also embraced the terror and the guilt." From the idyllic portrayal of the small town in TS there is a decline in the image through HF, CY, PW and other works. "Mark Twain came nearer registering in fiction the death of nineteenth-century culture than did such contemporaries as Howells...or James." Unable from the 1890's to ignore his insights into the corruption of democracy

1958 - Shorter Writings

(SMITH, HENRY NASH)
by money and into war as a natural human
condition, he was also unable to embody
them successfully into his work. Nonetheless, "as we have slowly become aware, the
development of twentieth-century American
literature, its dominant themes and above
all its language, began on the day in 1876
when Mark Twain conceived the idea of treating the Matter of Hannibal from the viewpoint of the outcast, Huckleberry Finn."
Abstract in AES, II (1959), 1556; reprinted in Twainian, XIX (January-February,
1960). Article reprinted in Bradley
(1962), pp. 410-21; in Cardwell (1963),
pp. 92-103.

B62 *STARTSEV, A. "Something New about Young
Twain," Inostrannaja Literatura [Foreign
Literature], IV, 261-263.
A review of Mark Twain of the "Enterprise" (1957); Startsev notes the "abundant
historical commentary as well as interesting details describing an important period
in Twain's literary work." Source: Abstract in AES, I (1958), 1263.

B63 STEWART, RANDALL. "Dreiser and the Naturalistic Heresy," Virginia Quarterly Review,
XXXIV (Winter), 100-116.
On HF: despite What Is Man? MT does not
belong among the naturalists, "if for no
other reason than the fact that Huck Finn
is one of the most responsible of fictional
mortals." Reprinted in his American Literature & Christian Doctrine (1958),
pp. 120-21. Abstract in AES, I (1958), 233.

B64 WILKINS, THURMAN. Clarence King: A Biography. New York: The Macmillan Company.
Brief references to MT passim (indexed),
but no useful information.

1959 A BOOKS

A1 BRASHEAR, MINNIE M., and ROBERT M. RODNEY,
eds., The Art, Humor and Humanity of Mark
Twain. Norman: University of Oklahoma
Press.
An anthology of extracts from MT's published works, with commentary and notes,
in three parts: "Mark Twain, Master Story-
teller and Descriptive Artist"; Mark Twain,
Missouri Humorist"; "Mark Twain, Epigrammat-
ist." Includes an introduction by Edward
Wagenknecht, "an extensive "Chronology of
Mark Twain's Life and Literary Career,"
and a useful "Selected Bibliography."

A2 CLEMENS, SAMUEL L. Concerning Cats: Two
Tales by Mark Twain. With an Introduction
by Frederick Anderson. San Francisco: The
Book Club of California.
The texts of "A Cat Tale" and "The Autobiography of Belshazzar," with a generous
introduction on the Clemens family's

affection for cats and a discussion of the
care expended on these unfinished manuscripts, which he apparently considered
publishing. "The Autobiography of Belshazzar" is of interest as a portrait of the
Clemens family at Quarry Farm, and in MT's
self-description (later struck out): "He
was a kind of author, and made books, but
was afraid to print them in his own name,
for they were mainly nonsense and the rest
was lies. It was his idea that if he
changed his name he would not be found out,
and some innocent person would get the
blame; for he was of a malicious disposition
and had not much sense."

A3 *____. Mark Twain Tonight! An Actor's Por-
trait: Selections from Mark Twain. Edited,
Adapted, and Arranged with a Prologue, by
Hal Holbrook. New York: Ives, Washburn.
[Source: "Brief Mention," American Lit-
erature, XXXII (May), 227.]

A4 LYNN, KENNETH S. Mark Twain and Southwestern
Humor. Boston and Toronto: Little, Brown
and Company.
Many readers have misunderstood MT's mask
of innocence, and more have confused the
Southwestern humorists with the backwoods
mind they described. "My belief, however,
is that Mark Twain was a conscious and deliberate creator, and one of the purposes of
this book is to treat him as such.... As
with Mark Twain, my primary assumption about
the humorous tradition behind him is that it
is a self-conscious art, and not an expression of American mindlessness." Chapter IX,
Sections iii, vii, and viii are reprinted in
Bradley (1962), pp. 421-36. A part of Chapter V, dealing with RI, is reprinted in
Smith (1963), pp. 40-46. The portion dealing with "The Jumping Frog," pp. 144-48, is
reprinted in Cardwell (1963), pp. 113-15.

A5 MARKS, BARRY R. Mark Twain's Huckleberry Finn
(Problems in American Civilization). Boston: D. C. Heath and Company.
A collection of critical essays on HF, all
of which are listed in the present bibliography, cross-referenced to this collection.

A6 NEIDER, CHARLES, ed. The Autobiography of
Mark Twain, Including Chapters Now Published
for the First Time. New York: Harper &
Brothers, Publishers.
Material left by MT at his death, here for
the first time arranged in chronological order. "For the first time the whole manuscript is being used as the source, not
parts or selections of it. Also, the present volume contains from 30,000 to 40,000
words which have never before seen print."
Also available in paperback, New York:
Washington Square Press, 1961.

1959 B SHORTER WRITINGS

B1 ALTENBERND, LYNN. "Huck Finn, Emancipator,"
Criticism, I (Fall), 298-307.
"The purpose of this article is to show
that the final episode is the thematic climax of the novel because the rescue of Jim
from the cabin is an allegory representing
the Civil War": although the South could
have freed the slaves voluntarily, romantic
nonsense (represented by that of Tom Sawyer) interfered. "What actually frees Jim,
and what will actually free the nominally
emancipated slave, is a voluntary act of
human love," first from Huck, then from
Miss Watson, who gives him his freedom in
her will. Abstract in AES, IX (1966),
1584; reprinted in Twainian, XXVI (January-
February, 1967).

B2 ANDERSON, DAVID. "Twain Estate Up $65,000 in
Year. Accounting in Connecticut Discloses
$22,000 Came from Royalties," New York
Times, April 18, p. 25.
A half-column description of the annual
accounting.

B3 ANDERSON, FREDERICK. "Twain Papers a Fount
of Biographical Studies," Manuscripts, XI
(Fall), 14-15.
Describes the Mark Twain Papers in the
University of California Library at Berkeley, the materials that have been published,
and plans for further publication. Followed by "A Note on Copyrights," explaining
that "The Trustees of the Mark Twain Estate
control the right to publish any previously
unpublished writing by Mark Twain whether
the manuscript is in the possession of the
Estate or not (according to common-law
copyright)." [Permissions to publish are
now arranged through Frederick Anderson,
Editor, The Mark Twain Papers, The University of California Library, Berkeley, California 94720--T.A.T.]

B4 *ANON. "De Tom Sawyer à Mark Twain," Informa-
tions et Documents, No. 113 (November 15),
pp. 31-35.
[Source: Leary (1954), p. 56.]

B5 ANON. "Mark Twain in Tarrytown," The Chronicle of the Historical Society of the Tarry-
towns, Inc., No. 4 (September), pp. 3-4.
Quotes at length from a letter from Mrs.
Samuel C. Webster and records in the files
of Ernest F. Griffin on his purchase of a
property at Tarrytown, later sold after a
successful suit to have the tax assessment
reduced.

B6 ANON. "Two Letters Solve a Bitter Dispute,"
Manuscripts, XI (Fall), 13.
As Walter Blair points out in Mark Twain &
Huck Finn, soon to be published, letters to
MT from Charles L. Webster show that HF was
sold in England and Canada before it was

sold in the U.S., but copies existed in the
U.S. first. The letters, of March 16 and 18,
1885, are in the Mark Twain Papers in Berkeley.

B7 BAENDER, PAUL. "Mark Twain and the Byron
Scandal," American Literature, XXX (January),
467-85.
Includes the text of six unsigned editori-
als in the Buffalo Express in August and
September, 1869, attributed by Baender to
MT, discussing them in the light they cast
on MT's thought. Abstract in AES, II
(1959), 389.

B8 BERTHOFF, WERNER. "The Country of Jewett's
Pointed Firs," New England Quarterly, XXXII
(March), 31-53.
Only brief mention of MT: quotes Willa
Cather's grouping of HF with The Scarlet
Letter and The Country of the Pointed Firs
as the "three American books which have the
possibility of a long life" and suggests
that Miss Jewett came around to a narrative
technique more Twainian than Jamesian or
Flaubertian. Abstract in AES, II (1959),
1255; reprinted in Twainian, XIX (January-
February, 1960).

B9 *BRUNNER, KARL. "Dickens und Mark Twain in
Italien," in Festschrift für Walter Fischer,
Heidelberg, pp. 112-16.
[Other details not available. Source:
MHRA Annual Bibliography (1959), Nos. 3930,
4552.]

B10 BUDD, LOUIS J. "Southward Currents under Huck
Finn's Raft," Mississippi Valley Historical
Review, XLVI (September), 222-37.
"Perhaps no analysis of Huckleberry Finn
can fix its proportions of escape, abstract
moralizing, basic human warmth, nostalgia,
clowning, and social commentary. The debate
over the course of the New South, however,
was an important factor in the novel's genesis," and it "was revised and finished between 1880 and 1883, when Twain was an active
and sometimes angry commentator on the
southerner's way of life and his peculiar
institutions." Abstract in AES, VIII (1965),
2995; reprinted in Twainian, XXV (March-
April, 1966).

B11 _____. "Twain, Howells, and the Boston Nihil-
ists," New England Quarterly, XXXII (September), 351-71.
While Howells was reading Tolstoy, MT was
profoundly impressed by George Kennan's accounts of conditions in Siberia. Both were
sympathetic toward the efforts of Sergei
Kravchinski, who, as "Sergius Stepniak," organized the Society of American Friends of
Russian Freedom, with headquarters in Boston;
MT was one of the original members, and more
of a firebrand than Howells. Later, when
Gorky's mission to America was compromised
by the disclosure that the woman with whom
he was traveling was not his wife, Howells
withdrew partly because his support had been

(BUDD, LOUIS J.)
lukewarm from the outset; "as for Twain, his retreat was more grudging and orderly than anyone has granted." Abstract in AES, III (1960), 94; reprinted in Twainian, XIX (January-February, 1960).

B12 CARDWELL, GUY A. "Mark Twain's Failures in Comedy and The Enemy Conquered," Georgia Review, XIII (Winter), 424-36.
Traces MT.'s reading of the thin, sentimental story published in 1845 by Samuel Watson Royston. MT's attack on it in "A Cure for the Blues" (1893) "betrays characteristic excess," but "it was his allegorizing habit to look through the immediate offence to the universal unreason behind it and in this instance he moved into the genre of satiric allegory, as Dryden did in Mac Flecknoe." MT failed to equal Dryden's achievement because of "technical inexpertness" and failure to limit his scope to the reasonable. His humor fails when his anger and pessimism exceed reasonable bounds, or conversely, when he lapses into sentimentalism, as in P&P; HF succeeds because it is controlled: "the edge of MT's satiric contempt for man's feeble mind and corrupt heart is softened by pity." Abstract in AES, III (1960), 1216; reprinted in Twainian, XIX (November-December, 1960). Article reprinted in Cardwell (1963), pp. 104-12.

B13 *CARTER, PAUL J., JR. "The Influence of the Nevada Frontier on Mark Twain," Western Humanities Review, XIII (Winter), 61-70. [Source: Abstract in AES, II (1959), 991; reprinted in Twainian, XIX (January-February, 1960).]
Although Hannibal and Virginia City were not really frontier settlements, the frontier humor and burlesque tradition in journalism helped shape MT's writing--generally to its detriment, both in taste and form and, more seriously, in diverting MT's attention away from genuinely important topics.

B14 CLARK, HARRY HAYDEN. [Review: E. Hudson Long, Mark Twain Handbook (1958).] American Literature XXX (January), 543-44.
"On the whole...granting the lack of use of dissertations and the lack of full-length analysis of individual major books by Twain, and the omission of a few pertinent studies, this Handbook provides a wealth of information conveyed in a pleasing and even-tempered manner."

B15 CLEMENS, CYRIL. "Mark Twain's Mother," Hobbies--The Magazine for Collectors, LXIV (March), 107-109, 120-21.
A popular account, not documented but drawn in part from MT's published reminiscences; describes the misunderstanding that led MT's mother to marry John Marshall Clemens rather than young Dr. Barrett.

B16 COSBEY, ROBERT C. "Mark Twain's Joan of Arc--Not So Anonymous," Mark Twain Journal, XI (Summer), 10, 14, 16.
The scholarly tradition that MT successfully concealed his authorship when Joan of Arc appeared serially in Harper's is undercut by a teasing announcement in the March, 1895 issue that the next issue will begin the serial "by one of the most successful among America's writers of fiction," and by the recognizable style. The serialization ended in April, 1896, and in May MT's friend Joseph Twichell included it in a list of MT's works; the first edition in book form appeared the same month, with MT's name omitted from the title page but boldly stamped on the front cover and spine. Abstract in AES, III (1960), 353.

B17 COX, JAMES M. "Pudd'nhead Wilson: The End of Mark Twain's American Dream," South Atlantic Quarterly, LVIII (Summer), 351-63.
This is MT's "last American novel," foreshadowing "the corrosive disillusion so apparent in his late work"; it "precariously holds together...neither cynical nor sentimental." "Because miscegenation could culminate in the problem of mistaken identity, his arbitrary fictional device was justified and became the organic means of dramatizing the last phase of a society trapped by its secret history." Roxana, "one of Twain's greatest creations," has the strength, passion, and fertility lacking in the fragile white women.

B18 DA PONTE, DURANT. "Life Reviews Huckleberry Finn," American Literature, XXXI (March), 78-81.
The unsigned review, "Mark Twain's Blood-Curdling Humor," appeared in the old comic magazine, Life, V (February 26, 1885), 119; it was probably written by Robert Bridges, and one month later Life expressed satisfaction at the news that the Concord (Massachusetts) Library Committee had banned the book. The mention of "a polite version of the 'Gyascutus'" story indicates that an analogue of "The Royal Nonesuch" was familiar to Bridges and some of his readers. Abstract in AES, II (1959), 1376, reprinted in Twainian, XIX (January-February, 1960), 3. Life review reprinted in Anderson (1971), pp. 126-27.

B19 DARBEE, HENRY (ed.) "Mark Twain in Hartford: The Happy Years," American Heritage, XI (December), 65-80.
"This is the story of twenty happy and productive years in the life of Mark Twain, told by the author himself and by those who knew him. Portions of it were published earlier as a guide to the Mark Twain Memorial, the house now being restored in Hartford..." Contains photographs and extensive excerpts from various sources about MT in Hartford.

B20 [DAVIS, CHESTER L.] "General Grant and the National Publishing Company: Imitation of Mark Twain's 'Innocents Abroad,'" Twainian, XVIII (September-October), 1-4.

Passages from a travel book copyrighted by a subscription publishing company in 1879, credited to a General Grant (no first name given), "but in fact...mostly a series of letters by Mr. John Russell Young of the New York Herald. We also find many items of one Mr. Smalley of the New York Tribune." Abstract in AES, III (1960), 450.

B21 _____. "Jumping Frog and N.Y. Saturday Press; Boston and the N.Y. Bohemians; W. D. Howells and 'Literary Friends,'" Twainian, XVIII (March-April), 1-4.

On the New York Saturday Press, which first published MT's "Jumping Frog" about November 18, 1865; the greater part of this issue is devoted to quotation from William Dean Howells's Literary Friends and Acquaintance [sic], partly on a visit to the Saturday Press but chiefly on topics with no relation to MT. Abstract in AES, III (1960), 446.

B22 _____. "Mark Twain's Copy 'Life of Pasteur'; Background on 'What Is Man?' and 'The Adventures of a Microbe - - - By a Microbe'; Mark's Writing, Machinery Hiding Secret," Twainian, XVIII (November-December), 1-4.

On MT's personal copy of R. Vallery-Radot's 2-volume work, with marginal comments; Davis apparently means that this could have influenced the works named, and he quotes a marginal note in which MT comments on his view of authorship while praising Vallery-Radot: "A past-master of the pathetic, this author; he keeps one's tears near the surface all the time, yet hides his machinery so well that he never seems to be trying to do it."

B23 _____. "Mark Twain's Personal Marked Copy of John Bunyan's 'Pilgrim's Progress'; Value of First Editions," Twainian, XVIII (May-June), 1-4.

Contains MT letter of April 20, 1869 reprinted from Paine's 1912 biography, and criticizes Paine for saying in the 1917 edition of the Letters after a letter of February 27, 1869 that "No further letters have been preserved until June." Davis is chiefly concerned with description of MT's copy of a facsimile edition, and quotation from it, with almost nothing on MT. Abstract in AES, III (1960), 447.

B24 _____. "Mark Twain's 'Things Not Generally Known' as Background for His Writings," Twainian, XVIII (July-August), 1-4.

Quotes long passages and some of MT's marginal annotations from the book of scientific miscellany edited by John Timbs (London: Lockwood & Co., 1867), suggesting that it may have helped form his ideas. Abstract in AES, III (1960), 448.

B25 DONNER, STANLEY T. [Review: Philip S. Foner, Mark Twain: Social Critic.] Quarterly Journal of Speech, XLV (February), 95.

A brief review, calling the opening portrait "one of the best short biographies of Mark Twain ever written." The book shows "comprehensive scholarship" and insight; it is "easily readable...a useful as well as delightful volume."

B26 DREISER, THEODORE. Letters of Theodore Dreiser: A Selection. Ed. with Preface and Notes by Robert H. Elias. Philadelphia: University of Pennsylvania Press. 3 vols. Passim.

TS and HF were among the few American books Dreiser cared for (I: 121). Both appealed to him "immensely, especially Huckleberry Finn. I never believed of Twain, however, that he gave forth in philosophic form his inmost convictions. His country overawed him I think" (June 17, 1918, to Frank Harris; I: 253). There is also a letter to Mencken (December 2, 1920) in which Dreiser says he was introduced to MT by Henry M. Alden some time in 1905-1907. Later, he encountered MT in the back of a saloon, "lit up--and alone." In the conversation that ensued he said that he was unhappy in his marriage, as most men are, but had to keep up appearances (pp. 305-306).. See 1935.B33.

B27 EATON, VINCENT L. "Mark Twain, Washington Correspondent," Manuscripts, XI (Fall), 16-26.

On MT's stay in Washington, November, 1867-March, 1868, with a lengthy passage quoted from the Reminiscences of Senator William M. Stewart on MT as the despair of his landlady. Describes MT's somewhat informal correspondence for several newspapers.

B28 FATOUT, PAUL. "Mark Twain: Litigant," American Literature, XXXI (March), 30-45.

On the lawsuit brought against MT and others by Edward House, who claimed an agreement gave him rights to produce a dramatization of The Prince and the Pauper; the resulting legal maneuverings reflect little credit on either party. Liberally documented with citations from New York newspapers of 1890. Abstract in AES, II (1959), 1371; reprinted in Twainian, XIX (January-February, 1960), 3. The article is reprinted as "Daniel Frohman Production of 'Prince and the Pauper'" in Twainian, XXII (September-October, 1963), 1-4; (November-December), 3-4, without footnotes.

B29 FERGUSON, DELANCEY. "Some Nuggets from Tailings Left Behind," New York Times Book Review (February 8), p. 5.

A review of Charles Neider, ed., The Autobiography of Mark Twain. The scholar would appreciate an appendix listing sources, and "even for the general reader Mr. Neider has not always met his full editorial responsibilities," as in his acceptance of texts bowdlerized by Albert Bigelow Paine rather

(FERGUSON, DELANCEY)
than the versions in the North American Review, "chosen, proofread, and passed for press by Mark Twain himself." Moreover, Neider ought to have annotated MT's inaccurate and sometimes unjust statements, such as his accusations against Charles L. Webster.

B30 FIEDLER, LESLIE A. "Love Letter from the Grave," New Republic, CXL (May 18), 18-19.
A review of Charles Neider, ed., The Autobiography of Mark Twain. MT's clowning was part of a concealment of his inner beliefs, and "it is his hopeless submission... his conviction (half-wish, perhaps) that all men submit as he which make the Autobiography one of the saddest books ever written, a book terrible in a way possible only in America." Death is a recurring theme, and after the death of Jean "Twain's lover-letter is finally readdressed, directed no longer to his dead, but to Death itself."

B31 FRIEDRICH, OTTO. "Mark Twain and the Nature of Humor," Discourse: A Review of the Liberal Arts, II (April), 67-86.
Preceded by "Editor's Note: This article is based on a longer essay concerning Mark Twain, and his concept and use of humor. Mr. Friedrich's study of Twain is part of a projected book, The Dark Tradition, an analysis and re-evaluation of American literature from Jonathan Edwards to William Faulkner, based on the particular writer's recognition of evil in the universe and his efforts to come to grips with it. Mark Twain, who seems to see this evil as a kind of absurdity, chooses humor as his weapon and defense against fears of the utter void." Abstract in AES, II (1959), 679; reprinted in Twainian, XIX (January-February, 1960).

B32 GORDAN, JOHN D. "New in the Berg Collection: 1957-1958," Bulletin of the New York Public Library, LXIII (April), 205-15.
On p. 214, describes copies of The Gilded Age, Tom Sawyer, 1601 (West Point Edition), and a copy of Sir Granville George Greenwood's Shakespeare Problem Restated (London and New York: John Lane, 1908), with heavy annotations by MT. Abstract in AES, II (1959), 1608; reprinted in Twainian, XIX (January-February, 1960).

B33 GROSS, SEYMOUR L. "Mark Twain and Catholicism," Critic (Chicago), XVII (April-May), 9, 12, 88-91.
Although MT included the Catholic Church in his attack on formal religion, criticizing what he viewed as superstition and oppression, he was not a bigot and he did not ridicule the sacraments; he praised Catholic acts of courage and self-sacrifice. Abstract in AES, II (1959), 1408.

B34 _____. "Mark Twain on the Serenity of Unbelief: An Unpublished Letter to Charles Warren Stoddard," Huntington Library Quarterly, XXII (May), 260-62.
A warm, gentle letter ("Hartford June 1/85," here reproduced) which MT wrote after reading A Broken Heart (1885), a spiritual autobiography in which Stoddard describes his conversion to Roman Catholicism; MT says he went through similar soul-searchings before settling down to his own disbelief: "Both of us are certain now; & in certainty there is rest. Let us be content. May your belief & my unbelief never more be shaken in this life!" Abstract in AES, VI (1963), 1653; reprinted in Twainian, XXIII (January-February, 1964).

B35 *HALL, ROBERT A. "Cultural Symbolism in Mark Twain's Connecticut Yankee," Annali dell' Istituto Orientale di Napoli, Sezione Germanica, II, 127-40.
[Source: Leary (1970), p. 64.]

B36 HERZL, THEODOR. "Mark Twain and the British Ladies: A Feuilleton," trans. by Alfred Werner, Commentary, XXVIII (September), 243-45.
From the second volume of Herzl's Feuilletons (Berlin, 1903), an account written in 1894 of a reading by MT before an audience of English schoolgirls at the British Embassy in Paris; his appearance and reading style are described. Abstract in AES, II (1959), 1618; reprinted in Twainian, XIX (January-February, 1960). See 1951.B41.

B37 HICKS, GRANVILLE. "Mark Twain's Self-Portrait," Saturday Review, XLII (February 7), 16.
A review of Charles Neider's version of The Autobiography of Mark Twain, which has the advantage over Paine's version in that "it consistently holds the attention," and over DeVoto's in that "it tells the story of Twain's life." Chiefly descriptive, contending that "the best of the book is to be found at the beginning and in the end." Abstract in AES, II (1959), 802; reprinted in Twainian, XIX (January-February, 1960).

B38 HUDSON, RUTH. "A Literary 'Area of Freedom' Between Irving and Twain," Western Humanities Review, XIII (Winter), 47-60.
[Source: Abstract in AES, II (1959), 990; reprinted in Twainian, XIX (January-February, 1960).] Apparently places emphasis on twenty-five minor writers on the West between 1834 and 1862; they worked in a genre which began with Washington Irving's Tour on the Prairies and ended in the burlesque exemplified by RI.

B39 JOHNSON, JAMES WILLIAM. "The Adolescent Hero: A Trend in Modern Fiction," Twentieth Century Literature, V (April), 3-11.

(JOHNSON, JAMES WILLIAM)

Compares Huckleberry Finn and Catcher in the Rye (p. 5) as illustrating "the difference between the nineteenth- and twentieth-century use of the adolescent," in that Huckleberry Finn is external in its emphasis: Huck looks at the world and it is Huck's world that Twain is concerned with." Moreover, Huck's choices are determined by his character, which shows compassion, candor, honesty, and humor from the first: "His is an adult intelligence masquerading as an adolescent."

B40 KENNY, HERBERT A. [Review: Charles Neider, The Autobiography of Mark Twain.] Critic (Chicago), XVII (April-May, 12, 68.

Neither Paine nor DeVoto "set the material in chronological order which Neider has done here and which should have been done in the first place. The book is in general first-rate Twain and consequently first-rate reading."

B41 KLINGELHOFER, HERBERT E. "Mark Twain, Edited and Bowdlerized," Manuscripts, XI (Fall), 2-12.

On the correspondence between MT and T. Douglas Murray over "Saint Joan of Arc," which MT wrote by Murray's request as an introduction to a book on her, then withdrew when Murray tampered with the text (MT did change one minor word, on Murray's suggestion).

B42 *KLOTZ, GÜNTHER. [Review: Karl-Heinz Schönfelder, intro., bibliography, and notes, Life on the Mississippi (1956).] Zeitschrift für Anglistik und Amerikanistik, V, 222-24.

[Source: MHRA Annual Bibliography (1959), No. 4578.]

B43 KLOTZ, MARVIN. "Mark Twain and Socratic Dialogue," Mark Twain Journal, XI (Summer), 1-3.

"An April 10, 1951 auction sale checklist of books from Mark Twain's library lists 'Dialogues of Plato, by B. Jowett, 4 vols'"; although a lack of marginalia makes it uncertain whether MT read them, the device of Socratic dialogue appears in his works, particularly in Huckleberry Finn, Joan of Arc, and What Is Man? Abstract in AES, III (1960), 349.

B44 KNOX, GEORGE. "The Mysterious Stranger: Mark Twain's Last Laugh?" Mark Twain Journal, XI (Summer), 11-12.

The story may be "a kind of intellectual practical joke," in which "the humor is double-edged...because Twain is not only castigating the reader who swallows the 'philosophy' of the story but is lashing himself for being intellectually committed against his emotional sympathies." Abstract in AES, III (1960), 354.

B45 KOMROFF, MANUEL. "How I Shook Hands with Mark Twain," Mark Twain Journal, XI (Summer), 4-5.

As a boy, Komroff had a minor part in an amateur performance of the P&P play; afterward, MT autographed his program and shook his hand. Abstract in AES, II (1960), 350.

B46 KRAUSE, SYDNEY J. "Twain's Method and Theory of Composition," Modern Philology, LVI (February), 167-77.

"Although Twain minimized conscious craftsmanship in theory, he was in practice a most avid reviser." "He discovered his subject not before, but as he wrote." Abstract in AES, II (1959), 736; reprinted in Twainian, XIX (January-February, 1960).

B47 KRUMPELMANN, JOHN T. "Schiller's Rehabilitation of Jeanne d'Arc," American-German Review, XXVI (December, 1959-January, 1960), 8-9, 38.

Devotes some space to the impression Joan of Arc made on MT and the possibility that Schiller's Jungfrau von Orleans may have influenced his book on her. Abstract in AES, III (1960), 2560.

B48 LA COUR, TAGE (trans. by Poul Ib Liebe). "The Scandinavian Crime-Detective Story," American Book Collector, IX (May), 22-23.

Tom Sawyer, Detective shows points of similarity in plot to Praesten i Vejlby (The Vicar of Vejlby, 1829) by the Danish novelist, Steen Steensen Blicher, but in a letter to a Danish reviewer who noted the resemblance, MT's secretary, I. V. Lyon, denied that MT had read the earlier work. Abstract in AES, II (1959), 1365; reprinted in Twainian, XIX (January February, 1960).

B49 LYNN, KENNETH S. "The Actor Who Made Mark Twain Live Again on the Stage and in Our Minds," New York Herald Tribune Book Review, XXXVI (December 20), p. 5.

A review of Hal Holbrook's book, Mark Twain Tonight! "The reason his pastiche of Twain's work is so effective--both on the stage and within hard covers--is that he knows Marks Twain's books backwards and forwards...he is familiar with the whole range of critical and biographical works about Twain, which is considerable."

B50 _____. "Mark Twain Miscellany," New York Herald Tribune Book Review, XXXVI (September 27), 13. A review of Minnie M. Brashear and Robert M. Rodney, eds., The Art, Humor and Humanity of Mark Twain.

Miss Brashear's Mark Twain, Son of Missouri (1934) was "a reliable study," but the reliability of the present work is closer to that of Charles Neider: names and dates are rendered inaccurately, and the editors mistake MT's fiction for autobiography. They have rendered a service in making some of MT's neglected short pieces more widely available, but when they condensed CY and MS "the decision...was a miserable one."

B51 McKEITHAN, DANIEL MORLEY. "Madame Laszowska Meets Mark Twain," Texas Studies in Literature and Language, I (Spring), 62-65.
The text of three letters from Jean Emily (Gerard) de Laszowska and one from MT (October-November, 1897) to William Blackwood, whose note of introduction made possible a meeting in Vienna. She was impressed by MT as "at first an excessively serious almost solemn person," by Olivia Clemens as "also very intelligent and charming in manner but looks delicate," and by the two daughters as "pretty--the eldest one [Clara] remarkably so in a dark Creole style"; the family were still in mourning for Susan Clemens. Abstract in AES, II (1959), 1952; reprinted in Twainian, XIX (January-February, 1960).

B52 McINTOSH, BERYL HOBSON. "A Seamstress Remembers Mark Twain," Mark Twain Journal, XI (Summer), 7, 16.
Recollections by Annie Courtney, who worked in the MT house in Hartford when she was eighteen. Abstract in AES, III (1960), 351.

B53 MARKS, BARRY A. "Mark Twain's Hymn of Praise, English Journal, XLVIII (November), 443-48.
On meaning and structure in TS, in which the action is "a series of withdrawals and returns," by which Tom matures from sentimental individualism (self-love) to the joy of other-love. The first half of the book satirizes "both the romanticism of childhood and the conventionality of adulthood," followed by a growth in "the town's ability to experience joy and love simultaneously." Abstract in AES, III (1960), 758; reprinted in Twainian, XIX (November-December, 1960).

B54 MARX, LEO. "Two Kingdoms of Force," Massachusetts Review, I (October), 62-95.
On HF and the destruction of the raft, pp. 69-71. "Clemens provides his hero with an Arcadian landscape, a profound sense of unity with nature, and then he causes the sudden, menacing intrusion of the machine." [Revised, this essay became a part of Marx's The Machine in the Garden (1964).]

B55 MENDELSON, M. "'Novaya Dynastiya' Marka Tvena [Mark Twain's 'New Dynasty']," Voprosy Literatury, No. 7 (July), pp. 156-67.
MT's support for the American working class is revealed in his 1886 address by this title. Abstract in AES, III (1960), 2548; reprinted in Twainian, XIX (November-December, 1960).

B56 *MITCHELL, JOHN. [Review: A Connecticut Yankee in King Arthur's Court. Leipzig: Paul List Verlag, 1956--an East German edition.] Zeitschrift für Anglistik und Amerikanistik, VI, 203-207.
[Source: MHRA Annual Bibliography (1959), No. 4577.]

B57 MOORE, LOUISE PAINE. "Mark Twain as I Knew Him," Twainian, XVIII (January-February), 3-4.
Reminiscences by the daughter of Albert Bigelow Paine, one of the young girls MT called his "Angel-Fish"; includes an MT letter on the death of his cat Tammany, naming her survivors: "two children by her first marriage--Billiards and Babylon; and three grandchildren by her second--Amanda, Annanci and Sindbad." Abstract in AES, III (1960), 445.

B58 MOSES, W. R. "The Pattern of Evil in Adventures of Huckleberry Finn," Georgia Review, XIII (Summer), 161-66.
There is a progression of types of evil, similar to that of Dante's Inferno, from Pap's incontinence to the violence of the feuding Shepherdsons, and finally to the fraud of the King and Duke. A comic ending is needed because MT could not leave Huck in Hell or raise him to a Purgatory (unless one chooses so to interpret Aunt Sally's threat to adopt and civilize him). Abstract in AES, II (1959), 1644; reprinted in Twainian, XIX (January-February, 1960). Article reprinted in Bradley (1962), pp. 387-92.

B59 MUELLER, HAROLD L. "Redding [sic] Connecticut [sic] Mark Twain Library Observes 50th Birthday," Twainian, XVIII (January-February), 1-3.
Reprinted from Redding Times, December 4, 1958 (1958.B55). Abstract in AES, III (1960), 444.

B60 NEWARK, F. H. [Review: Daniel Morley McKeithan, Court Trials in Mark Twain, and Other Essays.] Modern Language Review, LIV (July), 423-4.
"This collection of essays, which have previously appeared in periodicals, is not, it must be confessed, very weighty. The pattern of each essay is the same--a long résumé of the plot with extracts from the work to illustrate the more exciting parts, and in conclusion a brief--very brief--attempt at a critical appreciation." However, McKeithan has made a solid contribution in showing the probable influence of Jules Verne's Five Weeks in a Balloon on Tom Sawyer Abroad.

B61 ORNSTEIN, ROBERT. "The Ending of Huckleberry Finn," Modern Language Notes, LXXIV (December), 698-702.
Miss Watson's freeing of Jim in her will is not a sacrifice, but "perhaps the crowning act of selfishness and pious greed: the desire to make the best of all possible worlds." Tom's childish intervention can be explained in personal terms: he could free a slave, as MT could attack slavery, when it had become safe to do so. Abstract in AES, V (1962), 2627.

B62   PODHORETZ, NORMAN. "The Literary Adventures
      of Huck Finn," New York Times Book Review
      (December 6), pp. 5, 34.
          Seventy-five years after the publication
      of HF, surveys its reputation among critics
      and argues that MT "was asserting through
      the image of life on the raft that the State
      of Nature is a reality, and he was asserting
      through the character of Huck that the dis-
      tinction between the individual and society
      is a true distinction and a necessary one."
      Abstract in AES, III (1960), No. 585; re-
      printed in Twainian, XIX (November-December,
      1960).

B63   REXROTH, KENNETH. "Humor in a Tough Age,"
      Nation (New York), CLXXXVIII (March 7),
      211-13. A review of Charles Neider, ed.,
      The Autobiography of Mark Twain.
          "Mark Twain was just a very wise nine-
      teenth-century man," and "an eminently nor-
      mal man." The Neider edition of MT's auto-
      biography is more coherent than those edited
      by Paine and DeVoto, but omits important
      political and social criticism that DeVoto
      included. [Reprinted in Rexroth's Assays
      (New York: New Directions, 1962),
      pp. 95-98.]

B64   *SARUKHANYAN, A. "Mark Twain in the Soviet
      Union," Redding (Connecticut) Times,
      June 18. Source: Reprinted, Twainian,
      XVIII (July-August), 4; (September-October),
      4.
          On MT's great popularity in the Soviet
      Union. Lists some Russian editions of his
      works and notes his personal acquaintance
      with I. S. Turgenev, S. M. Stepnyak-Krav-
      chinsky, and Maxim Gorky; quotes Corky's
      description of MT and mention of his visit
      to Russia in 1867 on the Quaker City, "and
      the name of Samuel Langhorne Clemens in
      the list of passengers of that American ship
      was published in the 'Odessky Vestnik.'"
      Notes considerable publication of MT's works
      and notes about him, and quotes an obituary
      of him by A. I. Kuprin. More recently, "A
      Mark Twain Memorial Meeting was held at Mos-
      cow's Central Writers' Club, on April 26,
      1950. A report on the work of Mark Twain
      was delivered by the Soviet writer Valentin
      Katayev. It is noteworthy that the materi-
      als published for the 120th anniversary of
      Mark Twain's birth [sic] marked by a special
      literary evening included [a] bibliographi-
      cal reference book covering the Russian
      translations of his productions." The ar-
      ticle is introduced by two letters to the
      editor of the Redding Times by A. Kuznetsov,
      Vice Chairman of the Committee for Cultural
      Relations with Foreign Countries. Abstract
      in AES, III (1960), 449, 451.

B65   *SCHÖNFELDER, KARL-HEINZ. [Review: Charles
      Neider, ed., The Complete Short Stories of
      Mark Twain (1957).] Zeitschrift für Angli-
      stik und Amerikanistik, VI, 98-100.
          [Source: MHRA Annual Bibliography (1959),
      No. 4570.]

B66   SCOTT, WINFIELD TOWNLEY. "A New Editor Brings
      Order to Mark Twain's Chaotic 'Autobiogra-
      phy,'" New York Herald Tribune Book Review,
      XXXV (February 8), 3.
          A review of Charles Neider, ed., The Auto-
      biography of Mark Twain. "The best ordered
      ...far and away the most important and most
      satisfactory text of the 'Autobiography' we
      have; and yet there are reasons for believ-
      ing that it is not--it cannot be--the final
      text." Neider has made "a valiant, mostly
      intelligent, largely successful attempt to
      shape this material to the greatness which
      is in it."

B67   SPACKS, BARRY B. "The Thematic Function of
      the 'Rescue' in Huckleberry Finn," Mark
      Twain Journal, XI (Summer), 8-9.
          Unlike Odysseus, Huck is alienated, flee-
      ing from home. The ending represents a se-
      duction back to "Tom's frame of reference,
      into the culture of Miss Watson and Aunt
      Sally," but despite the fraud "Huck emerges
      from it still resisting the false gods of
      sentiment and complacency." Abstract in
      AES, III (1960), 352.

B68   STONE, ALBERT E., JR. "Mark Twain's Joan of
      Arc: The Child as Goddess," American Liter-
      ature, XXXI (March), 1-20.
          "At a particular moment in his life Twain
      found that the Maid of Orleans gave him a
      means of dramatizing his own, and his age's,
      spiritual dilemma without the embarrassing
      obligation to solve the dilemma.... To the
      aging man who was both a realist and roman-
      tic in his writing, a determinist and a mor-
      alist in his thinking, an agnostic and yet
      a deist in his worship, Joan of Arc provided
      a temporary haven....in the timeless past
      of childhood" (pp. 19-30). Abstract in AES,
      II (1959), 1369; reprinted in Twainian, XIX
      (January-February, 1960), 3. The article
      later became a part of his The Innocent Eye:
      Childhood in Mark Twain's Imagination (1961).

B69   STRONG, LEAH A. [Review: Philip S. Foner,
      Mark Twain: Social Critic.] Books Abroad,
      XXXIII (Spring), 217.
          Brief, says the third and longest section
      "is a real contribution to the ever-growing
      body of Twainiana."

B70   ____. [Review: Daniel Morley McKeithan,
      Court Trials in Mark Twain, and Other Es-
      says.] Books Abroad, XXXIII (Autumn), 467.
          "A gallimaufry of plot summary and sketchy
      discussion."

B71   *VITZ, CARL. "J. B. Pond and Two Servants,"
      Historical and Philosophical Society of Ohio
      Bulletin, XVII (October), 277-84.
          During their 1884-1885 reading tour, MT
      and G. W. Cable concealed their names when
      they registered at the St. Nicholas Hotel,
      Cincinnatti, January 2, 1885. [Source: Ab-
      stract in AES, XI (1968), 3214; reprinted
      in Twainian, XXVIII (January-February, 1969).]

B72 WALDHORN, ARTHUR. "Twain: The Adventures of Huckleberry Finn," in J. Sherwood Weber, Jules Alan Wein, Arthur Waldhorn, and Arthur Zeiger, eds., From Homer to Joyce: A Study Guide to Thirty-Six Great Books (New York: Holt, Rinehart and Winston, Inc.), pp. 244-52.

Includes a survey of the book's critical reputation, "Questions for Study and Discussion," and a short annotated bibliography of critical discussions of MT.

B73 WALSH, WILLIAM. The Use of Imagination: Educational Thought and the Literary Mind. London: Chatto & Windus. "Huck in Huckleberry Finn" (pp. 139-48) in "The Writer and the Child: Mark Twain, Henry James, D. H. Lawrence and Walter de la Mare" (pp. 137-182); also, passim on MT.

Huck is a voice of sanity and integrity, in contrast to Tom Sawyer and to the people he meets along the river; the river "represents life unconstrained by artifice, and value uncomplicated by pretence" (p. 145).

B74 WEBER, CARL J. The Rise and Fall of James Ripley Osgood: A Biography. Waterville, Maine: Colby College Press.

Passim on MT's business relations with Osgood, the publisher (indexed); there is an extensive list of acknowledgements but scanty documentation.

B75 *WIRZBERGER, KARL-HEINZ. [Review: Henry Nash Smith and Frederick Anderson, eds., Mark Twain of the "Enterprise" (1957).] Zietschrift für Anglistik und Amerikanistik, VI, 317-18.
[Source: MHRA Annual Bibliography (1959), No. 8224.]

1960 A BOOKS

A1 BLAIR, WALTER. Mark Twain & Huck Finn. Berkeley and Los Angeles: University of California Press.

Blair calls this his "attempt to define the forces which gave Adventures of Huckleberry Finn its substance and its form." While considering the importance of MT's boyhood and piloting on the river, he feels that the way they were transmuted into fiction is more important; "therefore I discuss in greater detail the forces shaping such modifications--the man's life, his reading, his thinking, and his writing between 1874 and 1884" (p. vii). This definitive study concludes with a discussion of HF's popularity abroad in translation, and there is an appendix titled "First New York Edition, First Issue," discussing the bibliographical points and the damaged plate on p. 283 (pp. 385-87). Chapter V ("Tom and Huck"), pp. 71-76 is reprinted in Bradley (1962), pp. 392-96; pp. 131, 134-44 are reprinted in Simpson (1968), pp. 61-70; the

portion dealing with TS in Smith (1963), pp. 64-82; "Raft and Shore: Wish and Belief," pp. 334-46 in Gerber (1971), pp. 90-101.

A2 DOUBLEDAY, NEAL FRANK, ed. Mark Twain's Picture of His America: Selected Source Materials for College Research Papers. Boston: D. C. Heath and Company.

Selections from MT's works, with brief introductions, and with an eight-page introduction of suggestions on writing research papers.

A3 FATOUT, PAUL. Mark Twain on the Lecture Circuit. Bloomington: Indiana University Press (as reprinted, Gloucester, Massachusetts: Peter Smith, 1966).

"This book attempts to view, chiefly, his platform performances and to glance, though less intensely, at his dinner speaking." Traces his life-long career as speaker, arguing that his oral gifts rivaled his talents as a writer. Cites numerous contemporary newspaper reviews.

A4 *GIBSON, WILLIAM M., ed. A Connecticut Yankee in King Arthur's Court. New York: Harper.
[Source: MHRA Annual Bibliography (1960), No. 4794.]

A5 HARNSBERGER, CAROLINE THOMAS. Mark Twain: Family Man. New York: The Citadel Press.

An enthusiast's account of MT's family life, enlivened by profuse quotation; the quotation includes "20,000 words heretofore unpublished," according to the front flap of the dust jacket. The author joined the Mark Twain Association while working on her "Twain reference book, Mark Twain at Your Fingertips," and through this connection met Clara Clemens, whom she visited in her Hollywood home and came to know as a friend (pp. 9-10). There is much charm in the book, but the scholar may want to confirm statements of fact from other evidence.

A6 LEARY, LEWIS. Mark Twain. Minneapolis: University of Minnesota Press (University of Minnesota Pamphlets on American Writers, No. 5); also London: Oxford University Press. Reprinted in Richard Foster, ed., Six American Novelists of the Nineteenth Century: An Introduction, Minneapolis: University of Minnesota Press, 1968, pp. 118-54. Condensed as "Mark Twain and the Comic Spirit" in Leary's Southern Excursions: Essays on Mark Twain and Others (1971), pp. 3-41.

In a general study of his life and works Leary notes the importance of recognizing "Mark Twain" as a mask for Clemens. He was not a buffoon, but "a comic realist," in the end pessimistic because he was tired.

A7 *LONG, E. HUDSON, ed. A Connecticut Yankee in King Arthur's Court. New York: Dodd, Mead.
   [Source: Beebe and Feaster (1968), p. 124.]

A8 MELTZER, MILTON. Mark Twain Himself: A Pictorial Biography. New York: Thomas Y. Crowell.
   Over 600 contemporary photographs and drawings of MT and his surroundings, intelligently chosen and with a judicious text. More than a coffee-table ornament, this is of real interest to the student of MT; a Bonanza Books reprinting is frequently offered for sale at approximately six dollars by such remainder dealers as Marboro Books and Publishers Clearing House.

A9 *MINTON, HAROLD, ed. The Adventures of Huckleberry Finn. New York: Washington Square Press.
   [Source: Beebe and Feaster (1968), p. 113.]

A10 NEIDER, CHARLES Mark Twain and the Russians: An Exchange of Views. New York: Hill and Wang; London: Paterson.
   "This exchange of letters between the distinguished American critic Charles Neider and Y. Bereznitsky, editor of the official Soviet publication Literary Gazette, constitutes a fascinating official discussion of Mark Twain" (p. 3). It consists of a charge in Literaturnaya Gazeta that Neider's edition of The Autobiography of Mark Twain (1959) represents an official censorship of MT's social criticism, Neider's somewhat intemperate response, a reply to Neider in Literaturnaya Gazeta, and a last word by Neider which the Russian journal declined to publish. [29-page pamphlet.]

A11 PETERSON, SVEND (comp.). Mark Twain and the Government. Caldwell, Idaho: Caxton Printers, Ltd.
   An anthology of remarks by MT on topics ranging from "Americanism" (p. 13) to "World Power, America as a" (p. 138). Cross-referenced. Contains no significant commentary or new information.

A12 ROGERS, FRANKLIN R. Mark Twain's Burlesque Patterns as Seen in the Novels and Narratives 1855-1885. Dallas: Southern Methodist University Press.
   "The focus of the study is Twain's structural patterns derived from burlesque"; as a general principle, the term is restricted in this study to "literary burlesque, a humorous imitation and exaggeration of the conventions in plot, characterization, and style peculiar to a literary type, the works of a certain author, or a particular book, short story, play, or poem" (p. v).

A13 SMITH, HENRY NASH, and WILLIAM M. GIBSON, eds., Mark Twain-Howells Letters: The Correspondence of Samuel L. Clemens and William D. Howells, 1872-1910. Cambridge, Massachusetts: The Belknap Press of Harvard University Press. 2 Vols.
   The correspondence, meticulously edited and annotated, casting significant light on the personal and professional friendship of the two. [The dust jacket gives the years of correspondence as 1869-1910, but the first letter is dated January 7, 1872.]

A14 *STEGNER, WALLACE, ed. The Adventures of Huckleberry Finn. New York: Dell.
   [Source: MHRA Bibliography (1960), No. 4832.]

A15 TURNER, ARLIN, ed. Mark Twain and George W. Cable: The Record of a Literary Friendship. [East Lansing]: Michigan State University Press.
   Consists chiefly of letters by Cable and some by MT during their lecture tour of 1884-1885, excluding materials already in print. Reprints texts of Cable's column on MT and Josh Billings in the New Orleans Picayune (1870.B5) and a sketch of MT in The Letter of February 1, 1896, and Cable's speeches honoring MT at the Seventieth Birthday Dinner and the memorial service in New York on November 30, 1910.

1960 B SHORTER WRITINGS

B1 ADAMS, J. DONALD. "Speaking of Books," New York Times Book Review (May 29), p. 2.
   Describes the controversy between Charles Neider and Y. Bereznitsky of the Literary Gazette [Printed in Neider's pamphlet, 1960.A10] as "a tempest in a teapot": although the Russians now portray MT as a critic of America, he was popular with them before the Revolution. "Russian humor is not far removed from our own, and Russians could also understand a boyhood like Mark Twain's"; but they err in regarding him as a thinker.

B2 American Book Collector, X (June). Special Mark Twain Number.
   Also available as Twainian, stamped: "THIS SPECIAL ISSUE OF THE AMERICAN BOOK COLLECTOR HAS BEEN PROCURED BY US, IS AVAILABLE ONLY TO MEMBERS WHO HAVE PAID MEMBERSHIP DUES, AND CONSTITUTES THE ISSUE OF 'THE TWAINIAN' FOR JULY-AUGUST, 1960, NINETEENTH YEAR, NO. 4. THE MARK TWAIN RESEARCH FOUNDATION. PERRY, MO."

B3 ANON. "The Artist's Mind in Action," Times Literary Supplement, October 28, p. 686.
   A review of Charles Neider, ed., The Autobiography of Mark Twain (1959), criticizing the imposition of chronological order on the material. "Furthermore, in his pursuit of order Mr. Neider has not hesitated to alter the text in ways which will not commend his work to readers who respect an author's

(ANON.)

right to speak in his own voice. He has inserted his own sentences or has transferred
words from other Twain writings to fill in
the cracks in his structure; he has omitted
passages without indicating where he has
done so; he has dropped the titles and dates
of composition which Twain attached to his
sections; and he has improved Twain's punctuation."

B4   ANON. "Innocence and Experience," Times Literary Supplement, August 12, p. 512.
A review-article on Henry Nash Smith and
William M. Gibson, eds., Mark Twain-Howells
Letters (praising the editing); Walter
Blair, Mark Twain and Huck Finn (HF is "an
open book...much of Professor Blair's devoted scholarship is simply supererogatory");
and Kenneth S. Lynn, Mark Twain and Southwestern Humor (the part on MT is "instructive and compelling reading," but the section on minor humorous writers "is virtually a separate book, and a far less interesting one"). There is also a general discussion of MT, who "is not taken seriously
enough outside the academies," but within
them "is perhaps taken a bit too seriously."
On HF, suggests that Huck's journey is "a
process of self-discovery through experience...the Huck who emerges at the end
realizes that he cannot return to the Tom
Sawyer world of innocence and romantic
games." Cf. reply by Donald MacRae
(1960.B76).

B5   ANON. "Magazine Articles about Mark Twain
During Past Year," Twainian, XIX (January-
February), 1-4; continued as "Articles Published Elsewhere during Past Year about
Mark Twain" (November-December), 1-3.
Abstracts of material on MT from Abstracts
of English Studies, II (1959), III (1960).
This reprinting is continued as an annual
feature of the Twainian hereafter, and may
be used with much confidence since individual abstracts are reprinted with very few
errors and in full (including the original
AES numbering). Unfortunately, some of the
reprinted abstracts are of peripheral interest, with only passing reference to MT,
and not all AES abstracts are reprinted;
for example, abstracts of Twainian articles
are not always reprinted, and Mark Twain
Journal material is always excluded. The
present bibliography notes these and other
abstracts in the annotation of entries describing books and articles on MT.

B6   ANON. "Mark Twain," Look (May 10), pp. 40-51.
A popular, general account, illustrated.
"The pictures and Twain's words are taken
from Mark Twain Himself, by Milton Meltzer,
to be published in October by Thomas Y.
Crowell Company." Notes an NBC television
production of RI, starring Hal Holbrook,
scheduled for May 13.

B7   ANON. "Mark Twain Birthplace Shrine Dedication," Twainian, XIX (May-June), 1-4.
Consists of the news story reprinted from
the Perry (Missouri) Enterprise of June 9,
1960, with added photographs; the dedication
took place June 5, with a crowd of 7,000
persons. Abstract in AES, IV (1961), 676.

B8   ANON. "A Soviet View of Six Great Americans,"
American Heritage, XI (October), 64-74.
The article, "Twain, Mark," is "translated
in full from the current Large Soviet Encyclopedia" and followed by a discussion by
Henry Nash Smith, who describes the article
as determinedly fitting all "the facts of
history into a neat pattern.... of the class
struggle." MT's work in some ways invites
such interpretation because "he often invites the reader to adopt the viewpoint of a
low or humble character who is at odds with
the mores and conventions of society," but
the encyclopedia article "overinterprets
this recurrent theme" and ignores contrary
evidence.

B9   ANON. [Review: Henry Nash Smith and William
M. Gibson, eds., Mark Twain-Howells Letters.]
New Mexico Quarterly, XXX (Winter), 422.
Brief and descriptive.

B10   BAENDER, PAUL. [Review: Kenneth S. Lynn,
Mark Twain and Southwestern Humor.] Modern
Philology, LVII (May), 285-86.
Lynn fails to prove his "neat" but "too
categorical" thesis that the humorists wrote
in a declining Whig tradition, from which MT
departed by turning the Clown into a vernacular spokesman, without adopting his coarseness. "Lynn's indifference to probabilities
is especially evident from his analyses of
texts, which are usually sophistical except
when he paraphrases the work of other men....
The chapters on Clemens are the most defective," either oversimplified, glib, or unoriginal. The book may be well received by
newspapers and may awaken student interest
in its field, but it "has little other than
cautionary value for the professional scholar and critic."

B11   *BAY, ANDRÉ. "Voici Mark Twain, Père de la
Littérature Américaine," Figaro Littéraire,
No. 731 (April 23), p. 4.
[Source: Leary (1970), p. 58.]

B12   BEHRMAN, S. N. Conversations with Max. London:
Hamish Hamilton, pp. 19-20.
On Bernard Shaw's rudeness: he had invited Sir J. M. Barrie, Max Beerbohm, and
others to lunch to meet MT, but after lunch
he rushed off to a dentist appointment,
leaving his guests at a loss.

B13   BLAIR, WALTER. "A Long Friendship Filled With
Light and Laughter," New York Herald Tribune
Book Review (May 8), p. 1.
A review of Henry Nash Smith and William

(BLAIR, WALTER)
M. Gibson, eds., Mark Twain-Howells Letters. Praises the editing and describes the letters, more from MT in the early years and later more from Howells. The editors are probably too optimistic in hoping to "complete the destruction" of outmoded views of the MT-Howells relationship, as in Brooks's The Ordeal of Mark Twain, long disproved but still accepted by some critics. Abstract in AES, XI (1968), 2970; reprinted in Twainian, XXVIII (March-April, 1969).

B14 BOLOGNA, SANDO. "Marked for Twain," Travel, CXIII (May), 48-50.
On MT shrines and memorabilia in Hannibal and Florida, Missouri; Virginia City, Nevada; Hartford, Connecticut; and Elmira, New York. The emphasis is on hours and admission charges for the benfit of those planning pilgrimages on the 125th anniversary of MT's birth.

B15 BRIDGMAN, RICHARD. [Review: Walter Blair, Mark Twain & Huck Finn.] Moderna Språk, LIV (September), 305-306.
"Mr. Blair has examined Twain's various literary projects, his reading, social life, business problems, travels, family affairs, and general state of mind throughout the decade 1874-1884, so that we might observe Huckleberry Finn growing into the misshapen giant we know today," and he has reviewed its present reputation and the criticism and censorship over the years. "Of central interest in Mr. Blair's study is that he has discovered or collected hundreds of sources, relationships, similarities, coincidences, and even instances of plagiarism with a bearing upon Huckleberry Finn.... Always alert, patient, and knowledgeable," Blair sometimes guesses (as he admits), even "stretches his material precariously thin. On the other hand, the very inclusiveness of his work makes one aware of the variety of impulses that acted upon the conception of Huckleberry Finn."

B16 BROWNELL, GEORGE HIRAM. "Reprinting of George Hiram Brownell's First Issue--January 1939," Twainian, XIX (January-February), 4.
Material from the first issue of the original series of the Twainian.

B17 BUDD, LOUIS J. [Review: Kenneth S. Lynn, Mark Twain and Southwestern Humor.] South Atlantic Quarterly, LIX (Autumn), 580-81.
Like MT's own work, this is "uneven but always interesting, boldly venturesome rather than deliberate, more persuasive in snatches than in total effect, challenging but also vulnerable." Beginning with William Byrd of Westover, Lynn makes a useful point of showing antebellum humorists and Whig political tradition. Unfortunately, he sometimes stretches the texts to fit

his argument, and neglects some of the relevant scholarship.

B18 CAMBON, GLAUCO. "What Maisie and Huck Knew." Studi Americani, VI, 203-20.
MT and James both faced problems of showing reality through the eyes of a child, although Maisie's world is that of society while for Huck freedom can only be achieved by escape; yet both characters are saved by experience rather than coarsened by it. In a postscript Cambon points out that MT's "imaginative withdrawal is a simpler solution than James's."

B19 CARDWELL, GUY A. [Review: Walter Blair, Mark Twain and Huck Finn.] American Quarterly, XII (Fall), 428-29.
"The intention here is 'to define the forces which gave Adventures of Huckleberry Finn its substance and form,' but this intention is pursued in a conventional and, it must be confessed, at times a rather exhausting manner." Although there is useful information on the chronology of composition and the circumstances surrounding it, "Mr. Blair works with his eye perhaps excessively close to the object" and he fails to "settle Mark Twain largely and firmly in his times, which surely were the great 'influence' on him." Review listed in AES, IV (1961), 225, with brief comment.

B20 CARPENTER, FRANK G. Carp's Washington, Arranged and Edited by Frances Carpenter. New York: McGraw-Hill Book Company, Inc.
Washington newspaper correspondence in the Cleveland Leader; on pp. 130-32, an undated column describes MT lecturing with George Washington Cable.

B21 CARTER, PAUL J., JR. "Mark Twain and the American Labor Movement," Twainian, XIX (September-October), 1-4. Reprinted from New England Quarterly (1957.B17). Abstract in AES, III (1964), 1570.

B22 CLEMENS, CYRIL. "Mark Twain and the Man from Maine," Mark Twain Journal, XI (Summer), 17.
A brief review of Carl J. Weber, The Rise and Fall of James Ripley Osgood (Waterville, Maine: Colby College Press, 1959). "In this book Mark Twain's association with James R. Osgood is given careful treatment, with a special chapter about Life on the Mississippi and about Osgood's trip down the river with Mark Twain a year before the publication of the famous book"; a trip to Montreal, other meetings and trips, and Osgood's literary advice are also described. Abstract in AES, IV (1961), 515.

B23 COHEN, MORTON N. "Mark Twain and the Philippines: Containing an Unpublished Letter." Journal of the Central Mississippi Valley American Studies Association, I (Fall), 25-31; also, inside back cover.
About MT's anti-imperialism. Contains

(COHEN, MORTON N.)
facsimiles of holograph letters: MT's "A salutation-speech from the Nineteenth Century to the Twentieth," first published in the New York Herald, December 30, 1900 (reproduced on inside back cover), a letter of December 30, 1900 to MT from Abner C. Goodell, and MT's reply of December 31 (pp. 26-27).

B24 COVICI, PASCAL, JR. (ed.). "'Dear Master Wattie': The Mark Twain-David Watt Bowser Letters," Southwest Review, XLV (Spring), 104-21.
The texts of MT's correspondence (1880-1882) with a Texas schoolboy. The letters, some here reproduced in facsimile, are "destined for eventual deposit in the manuscript archives of the University of Texas"; they cast light on MT's views of writing, piloting, the river, and boyhood at a time halfway between the publication of TS and HF. Abstract in AES, III (1960), 2059; reprinted in Twainian, XIX (November-December, 1960).

B25 COX, JAMES M. "A Connecticut Yankee in King Arthur's Court: The Machinery of Self-Preservation," Yale Review, L (Autumn), 89-102.
"The Yankee, Pudd'nhead, and Philip Traum all insist that man is a machine who must obey the laws of his 'make,' that he cannot fully create anything." CY represents MT's "turning away from business and machinery, and Hank Morgan is perhaps the unmasked genius of Twain's comic art"; his death is thus a personal statement. Abstract in AES, X (1967), 752; reprinted in Twainian, XXVII (January-February, 1968). Article reprinted in Smith (1963), pp. 117-29, with a revised final paragraph.

B26 CUMMINGS, SHERWOOD. "Mark Twain and the Sirens of Progress." Journal of the Central Mississippi Valley American Studies Association, I (Fall), 17-24.
"Up to 1898 he gloried in the material progress of the nineteenth century," then "suffered a dramatic change of mind. From then on material progress seemed to him futile and meaningless inasmuch as man himself had not improved. But even to the end of his life...he was capable of marveling at its material achievements."

B27 CUNLIFFE, MARCUS. "A Lost American Masterpiece?" Encounter, XV (October), 71-74.
On MT's autobiographical writings, as edited by Paine, DeVoto, and, now, by Charles Neider (1959), whose version "has the distinct merit of arranging the material in a rough chronological sequence," although "a less casual editor" might have taken the trouble to distinguish between the factual and the fictious portions--"to distinguish, that is, between Mark Twain and Samuel L. Clemens." These writings are

not an MT masterpiece, because they lack the detachment with which he used autobiographical material in his best works, such as HF and parts of LOM, as well as in IA and RI. Abstract in AES, IV (1961), 1793; reprinted in Twainian, XXI (January-February, 1962, incorrectly attributing the review to Durham University Journal).

B28 DAICHES, DAVID. [Review: Charles Neider, ed., The Autobiography of Mark Twain (1959).] Listener, LXIV (December 15), 1111-12.
Questions Neider's use of a chronological order. "The crudities, sentimentalities, preposterousnesses in this book...stand beside the humour, the moralizing, the savagery, the thrashings at the limitations imposed by respectability, to reveal one of the most remarkable Americans of his time."

B29 [DAVIS, CHESTER L.] "Manuscript Transferred," Twainian, XIX (March-April), 2. On the acquisition of the manuscript for the English edition of TS.
"The manuscript--654 handwritten pages--is mainly in the script of several secretaries of the author. Mark Twain, however, wrote the preface, conclusion and 300 corrections. This manuscript was used to set type for the first printing of 'The Adventures of Tom Sawyer' in London in 1876," and is being placed in the Mark Twain Birthplace Memorial Shrine at Florida, Missouri.

B30 _____. "Personal Memoirs of U. S. Grant," Twainian, XIX (November-December), 3-4.
Quotes from MT's copy of the Grant memoirs on service in Missouri (I, 246 ff.), apparently with the implication that "The Private History of a Campaign that Failed" was written with Grant in mind.

B31 DRAKE, ROBERT Y., JR. "Huck Among the Doctors," National Review, IX (November 19), 320-22.
Critics have often misread HF, either because of Freudian preconceptions (as in the case of Leslie Fiedler) or through an inability to understand the Southwestern "intuitive apprehension that paradox inevitably lies at the heart of reality," as in the "paradox of slavery in the midst of a people so historically committed to the quest for freedom." Huck himself is always concerned "with the individual...never with society and institutions, which, all too often degenerate into a mob. (Unlike the sociologist or the 'enlightened' legislator, he is not concerned with class or race as such.)" Abstract in AES, IV (1961), 92; reprinted in Twainian, XXI (January-February, 1962).

B32 DUROCHER, AURELE A. "Mark Twain and the Roman Catholic Church." Journal of the Central Mississippi Valley American Studies Association, I (Fall), 32-43.
Throughout his life MT consistently "saw the Church as a very human institution which

(DUROCHER, AURELE A.)
had made many grave mistakes but had also
several redeeming features--both of which
he referred to in his writings."

B33 EASTMAN, MAX. "Mark Twain: Representative
American," New Leader, XLIII (September 26),
18-21.
An "amplification" of his keynote speech
at the opening banquet of the MT festival
in Elmira, New York (September, 1954). MT
was indeed a humorist, and in America "humor stands more on a level with serious art
and mixes more naturally with serious thinking" than in other countries. Eastman,
formerly from Elmira, tells of his own acquaintance with MT, describes MT's courtship
of Olivia Langdon, and argues that her influence benefited him; local accounts are
cited, among them that of Jervis Langdon,
son of Olivia's brother Charles. Abstract
in AES, IV (1961), 98; reprinted in Twainian, XXI (January-February, 1962).

B34 EBY, CECIL D., JR. "Mark Twain's 'Plug' and
'Chaw': An Anecdotal Parallel," Mark Twain
Journal, XI (Summer), 11, 25.
The joke by an Arkansas loafer "was in
circulation in the mining camps of Colorado
(and perhaps Nevada) for at least twelve
years before it was printed in The Adventures of Huckleberry Finn (1885)," as is
attested in an unpublished journal of David
Hunter Strother, who "was a noted raconteur," and could have told MT the story in
Philadelphia, in 1876. Abstract in AES, IV
(1961), 512.

B35 FATOUT, PAUL. "Mark Twain: A Footnote,"
Columbia University Forum, III (Fall),
51-52.
On Jap Herron: A Novel Written from the
Ouija Board (New York: Mitchell Kennerley,
1917). "In a long introduction, Mrs. Emily
Grant Hutchings of Hannibal, Missouri explains that the novel was written in 1915 by
the other-wordly essence of the humorist."
Fatout summarizes the story of Jasper (Jap)
Herron, adding: "Full of a lamentable mor-
tality, continual agonizing over coffins,
and people as wooden as puppets, the book
is alien to the robust manner of the living
Mark Twain. Snuffling and sobbing drench
the pages, so much tearful sobbing that, to
echo Huck Finn, the story is 'that damp I
never see anything like it.' Reviewers, to
a man, condemned." Legal action to halt
publication or suppress the book ended when
the New York Supreme Court refused to hear
the case. Abstract in AES, IV (1961), 36;
reprinted in Twainian, XXI (January-February,
1962).

B36 FEINSTEIN, HERBERT. "Mark Twain at the Bar,"
Journal of the State Bar of California,
XXXV (March-April), 192-96.
A review of D. M. McKeithan's Court Trials
in Mark Twain and Other Essays (1958).

Largely descriptive. "Mr. McKeithan is a
first-rate court reporter in relating six
trials by Mark Twain in that many novels."

B37 _____. "Two Pair of Gloves: Mark Twain and
Henry James," American Imago, XVII (Winter),
349-87.
On phallic and other symbolism of gloves
in The Turn of the Screw and the incident at
Gibraltar in IA. Abstract in AES, V (1962),
1811; reprinted in Twainian, XXII (January-
February, 1963).

B38 FERGUSON, DELANCEY. "How Sam Clemens Grew
into Mark Twain," New York Herald Tribune
Book Review, XXXVI (January 24), 5.
A review of Kenneth S. Lynn, Mark Twain
and Southwestern Humor, which points out
political backgrounds, clash of the Whigs
on the seaboard and Jacksonian democracy on
the frontier, and the literary consequences.

B39 _____. "The Legacy of Letters," American
Scholar, XXIX (Summer), 406-18.
A review-article, discussing the Mark
Twain-Howells Letters pp. 410, 412, 414; the
rest of the review article concerns the cor-
respondence of Swinburne, Melville, and
Stephen Crane.

B40 _____. "Many Faces of a Photogenic Man," New
York Times Book Review (November 20), p. 43.
A review of Milton Meltzer, Mark Twain
Himself. "This book would have delighted
Mark Twain." The many pictures of him and
his world are valuable, and the text is "no
perfunctory job. Mr. Meltzer has drawn
widely from contemporary newspapers and from
uncollected items in the files of long-for-
gotten magazines, as well as from volumes of
scholarly research."

B41 FIEDLER, LESLIE A. "Duplicitious Mark Twain,"
Commentary, XXIX (March), 239-48.
"Love and Death in the American Novel,
from which this essay has been adapted, will
be published this month." "The persona
called Mark Twain...is, first of all, a funny man, but more particularly, one who is
funny at the expense of culture: an anti-
literary writer, whose best books are trav-
esties of others." Nevertheless, "he is
not an open rebel," but "at worst a genteel
Noble Savage, the friend of enlightened
clergymen." "He was a man fitfully intelligent when he did not know he was thinking, a
spottily skillful stylist when he was not
aware he was writing artistically." "To
make of Twain a cult or a case...is...to lose
the sense of him as a poet, the possessor of
deep and special mythopoetic power, whose
childhood was contemporaneous with a nation's." If we consider TS and HF "not as
sequels but as alternative versions of the
same themes, these themes will reveal themselves in their mythic significance...dreamed
twice over, the second time as nightmare."
Abstract in AES, III (1960), 1871; reprinted

(FIEDLER, LESLIE A.)
in Twainian, XIX (November-December, 1960).
Article reprinted in Kaplan (1967),
pp. 134-51; in revised form in Fiedler's
Love and Death in the American Novel
(1960.B42).

B42   *____. Love and Death in the American Novel.
New York: Criterion Books.
[Source: 1966 revised edition, New York:
Stein and Day.] On MT, pp. 269-90, 402-408,
456-68, and passim (partly accessible
through the index). Places heavy emphasis
on HF and PW, on themes of the child, sexuality, race, and Gothic traditions. Includes material which appeared as "Duplici-
tous Mark Twain" in Commentary (1960.B41).
Pp. 553-74 of the 1960 edition reprinted
in Leary (1962), pp. 277-300 as "Faust in
The Eden of Childhood." "Accommodation and
Transcendence" (pp. 575-91, on HF) reprinted
in Gerber (1971), pp. 78-90.

B43   ____. "Travels with a Literary Source-Hunt-
er," New York Times Book Review (April 3),
p. 10.
A review of Walter Blair, Mark Twain &
Huck Finn. "There is no really satisfactory book-length study of Mark Twain," although the texts and criticism are now
available. As a history of HF Blair's
study is "clearly reasonable, reasonably
clear," but as criticism it is weakened by
Blair's "desire to avoid risky speculation
in favor of safe facts" of dates of editions, possible sources, etc.

B44   *FRAIBERG, LOUIS. "Van Wyck Brooks versus
Mark Twain versus Samuel Clemens," in his
Psychoanalysis and American Literary Criti-
cism (Detroit: Wayne State University
Press), pp. 120-33.
[Source: Beebe and Feaster (1968),
p. 100; also, cited in James R. Vitelli,
Van Wyck Brooks (New York: Twaine Publish-
ers, Inc., 1969), p. 171, n. 3.]

B45   FRENCH, BRYANT MOREY. "The Gilded Age Manuscript," Yale University Library Gazette,
XXXV (July), 35-41.
About one-fifth of the manuscript, 284
pages, survives, the greater part of it at
Yale University. "Not only is the extant
manuscript representative, but fortunately
for students of Mark Twain's writing methods it is highly revealing in its interpola-
tions, additions, deletions, and renumber-
ings of pages and chapters." Marginal annotations reveal "a greater interweaving of
the collaborators' work than would appear
from the basic assignment of chapters," and
concessions to gentility by both MT and
Charles Dudley Warner. Article reprinted
in Twainian, XX (March-April, 1961), 1-3,
and reprinting abstracted in AES, VII
(1964), 1571.

B46   FRIEDRICH, GERHARD. "Erosion of Values in
Mark Twain's Humor," CEA Critic, XXII (September), 1, 7-8.
MT's development from humorist to pessimist may be explained in other than Freudian
terms, in his technique of sententious
buildup followed by deflation. Ultimately,
"Twain's technique of humor became a cancer-
ous habit of laughing any and all values to
pieces," and "left him at last with nothing
but debris--cosmic debris." Abstract in
AES, VIII (1965), 1899; reprinted in Twainian, XXV (January-February, 1966).

B47   GARGANO, JAMES W. "Disguises in Huckleberry
Finn," University of Kansas City Review,
XXVI (March), 175-78.
"The 'disguises' in Huckleberry Finn...are
the vehicle of Twain's indictment of human
dissimulation and gullibility," but Huck and
Jim use disguises as protection, the King
and Duke as "predator's tools in their cease-
less battle to gull and exploit mankind."
"Perhaps it is as a disguise that the author's much-discussed prefatory 'notice' can
best be understood. Only too aware of the
Swiftian implications of Huckleberry Finn,
he attempted to disarm his readers by insist-
ing that his literary intentions were altogether innocent." Abstract in AES, III
(1960), 1353; reprinted in Twainian, XIX
(November-December, 1960).

B48   GERSTENBERGER, DONNA. "Huckleberry Finn and
the World's Illusions," Western Humanities
Review, XIV (Autumn), 401-406.
The consistent metaphor of disguise and
pretense may reveal "a significance for the
novel not unlike that which an examination
of the dramatic metaphor in Hamlet has provided." Huck (who can join society only
through one disguise or another, but never
as himself) gradually learns that "it is the
elaborate illusion that the world insists is
reality which causes man's moral confusion."
Abstract in AES, IV (1961), 2786; reprinted
in Twainian, XXI (January-February, 1962).

B49   GIBB, CARSON. "The Best Authorities," College
English, XXII (December), 178-83.
Tom and Huck "believe niggers and people
are two different things," but MT is not
ending HF "with a burst of spleen" aimed at
"two likable youngsters"; his target is the
culture which has shaped their attitudes.
Abstract in AES, IV (1961), 248; reprinted
in Twainian, XXII (January-February, 1962).
Article reprinted in Lettis (1962),
pp. 429-37.

B50   GRENANDER, M. E. "Ambrose Bierce and Charles
Warren Stoddard: Some Unpublished Correspondence," Huntington Library Quarterly,
XXIII (May), 261-92.
Contains several references to MT, including the account of a meeting in early September, 1872 between John Camden Hotten and MT,

(GRENANDER, M. E.)
whom Tom Hood the Younger introduced as "Mr. Bryce"; Hotten was not deceived, and both he and Hood told the story to Bierce. Abstract in AES, VI (1963), 1665; reprinted in Twainian, XXIII (January-February, 1964).

B51 GROSS, SEYMOUR L. "Sherwood Anderson's Debt to Huckleberry Finn," Mark Twain Journal, XI (Summer), 3-5, 24.
Places particular emphasis on "I Want to Know Why," which Anderson said was popular because it was "a story of immaturity... much like Mark Twain at his best." Gross adds that "both boys are morally finer than the adult world which they are describing," but distrust their own judgments. There are similarities in irony, criticism of society, and use of the Negro as "a kind of moral center." Abstract in AES, IV (1961), 509.

B52 *GUIDI, AUGUSTO. "L'Italia di Mark Twain," Revista di Letterature Moderne e Comparante (Firenze), XIII (December), 284-89.
[Source: MHRA Annual Bibliography (1960), No. 4796.]

B53 GULYEV, LEONID, and NELLI GULYEV. "Mark Twain about Russia," USSR Illustrated Monthly, No. 12 (December), pp. 50-51.
A popular account, noting his observations on the Quaker City tour, his praise of revolution in CY, "The Czar's Soliloquy," his [initial] cordiality to Maxim Gorky, etc. This is competent work for its purpose but provides no new information or insight.

B54 GUTTMAN, ALLEN. "Mark Twain's Connecticut Yankee: Affirmation of the Vernacular Tradition?" New England Quarterly, XXXIII (June), 232-37.
Arguing that "most critics...have seen the novel as a fierce attack upon Arthurian England and a thorough-going affirmation of nineteenth-century America (and of New England's technological triumphs)," Guttman warns that MT himself described Hank Morgan as "an ignoramus" and portrayed him in the book, not like Huck, but "more and more like an enlarged version of Colonel Sherburn." His conduct is increasingly dictatorial and ultimately destructive. Abstract in AES, III (1960), 1967; reprinted in Twainian, XIX (November-December, 1960). Article reprinted in Kesterson (1973), pp. 103-107.

B55 HANSER, RICHARD. "Mark Twain's America." Coronet, XLVIII (May), 111-45.
A minimal amount of text accompanies contemporary photographs illustrating the age, with no particular emphasis on what MT saw and described.

B56 HICKS, GRANVILLE. "The Mail of Two Men of Letters," Saturday Review, XLIII (April 23), 20.
A review of Henry Nash Smith and William M. Gibson, eds., The Mark Twain-Howells Letters. The "superlative job" of editing unobtrusively gives the reader "all he needs to know" without "fussiness over trivialities"; the correspondence reveals Howells as the better critic, with "everything but genius." Abstract in AES, III (1960), 2481; reprinted in Twainian, XIX (November-December, 1960).

B57 *HOBBIE, DIANA POTEAT. "Mark Twain's Letter to the Texas Schoolboy," Houston Post, February 7.
[Source: Reprinted in Twainian, XIX (March-April), 2-4.] With explanatory comments, provides the text of a letter from MT to young Watt Bowser of Dallas, March 20, 1880. MT comments on piloting, unwillingness to be a boy again, report cards, and the value of "plain, simple language, short words, and brief sentences." Abstract in AES, III (1960), 1614.

B58 HOFFMAN, DANIEL G. "Jim's Magic: Black or White?" American Literature, XXXII (March), 47-54.
Jim's "superstitions are used structurally to indicate his slavery while a slave and his spiritual freedom with Huck"; freed from credulity with his escape from bondage, "he becomes a magician able to read the mysterious signs of nature." Abstract in AES, III (1960), 1620; reprinted in Twainian, XIX (November-December, 1960), 3. Hoffman substantially rewrote this article for the chapter, "Black Magic--and White--in Huckleberry Finn," in his Form and Fable in American Fiction (1961.B39).

B59 JACOBSON, DAN. "Devilishness," Spectator, CCV (November 25), 846, 848.
A review of Charles Neider, ed., The Autobiography of Mark Twain (1959). Although "much of the book is banal and conventional," there are "spasmodic but unmistakable irruptions of his genius."

B60 _____. "Mark Twain and the Calm Squatter," Spectator, CCV (August 5), 219-20.
A review-article on Kenneth S. Lynn's Mark Twain and Southwestern Humor and Henry Nash Smith and William M. Gibson, eds., Mark Twain-Howells Letters, neither of which is discussed critically. Adopting the vernacular of his society was not a surrender by MT, but "the condition of his freedom from either shame or boastfulness in writing about it"; nonetheless, he blundered in his life and work, "was at once a vulgarian and the victim of the worst gentilities of his time...debased his own gifts for the sake of money and applause...was a clown, a show-off and a coward," as he sadly admitted. His

(JACOBSON, DAN)
highest aspirations produced "an unreadable book like The Personal Recollections of Joan of Arc," but there is evidence of his "prodigious talent" in several of his works, and sustainedly in Huckleberry Finn, where Huck and Jim show a degree of civilization uncommon elsewhere because "it demands mutual responsibility, self-abnegation, and moral choice." Abstract in AES, III (1960), 2502; reprinted in Twainian, XIX (November-December, 1960).

B61 JEFFERIES, WILLIAM B. "The Montesquiou Murder Case: A Possible Source For Some Incidents in Pudd'nhead Wilson," American Literature, XXXI (January), 488-90.
A murder in St. Louis in 1849 involving two French brothers parallels the murder in Pudd'nhead Wilson; accounts in the St. Louis papers (cited) were available to MT in his youth. Abstract in AES, III (1960), 703, reprinted in Twainian, XIX (November-December, 1960), 1-3.

B62 JONES, LLEWELLYN. "Mark Twain--a Humanist Too," Humanist, XX (November-December), 365-67.
A review-article, somewhat impressionistic and descriptive, of Minnie M. Brashear and Robert M. Rodney, eds., The Art, Humor, and Humanity of Mark Twain; The Adventures of Huckleberry Finn, with an Afterword by George Elliott, who discusses the "moral grandeur" of Huck's character (A Signet Classic: New York, The New American Library); The Adventures of Tom Sawyer, with an Afterword by George Elliott (A Signet Classic: New York, The New American Library); A Connecticut Yankee in King Arthur's Court, Introduction by Charles Neider, who "tells us that the book was read by Mark Twain's wife Libby who did a little editing in the interests of propriety of speech" (New York: Hill & Wang); Charles Neider, Mark Twain and the Russians: an Exchange of Views (New York: Hill & Wang).

B63 KARL, FREDERICK R. "Joseph Conrad and Huckleberry Finn," Mark Twain Journal, XI (Summer), 21-22.
MT matured between Tom Sawyer and Huckleberry Finn as Conrad did between Youth and Heart of Darkness; there are similar treatments of river and shore in the two mature works, which "as studies in human degradation surrounded by the possibilities of regeneration...symbolize an era." Abstract in AES, IV (1961), 517.

B64 KLOTZ, MARVIN. "Goethe and Mark Twain," Notes and Queries (London), CCV, n.s. VII (April), 150-151.
The possibility that the equating of madness with lasting happiness at the end of The Mysterious Stranger is derived from The Sorrows of Young Werther adds "to the overwhelming evidence that Mark Twain was not a genius-in-the-rough, but a well-read and erudite author." Abstract in AES, III (1960), 1761; reprinted in Twainian, XIX (November-December, 1960).

B65 *KOSTER, DONALD N. "Mark Twain, Mysterious Stranger," Adelphi Quarterly, III (Summer), 16-26.
[Source: Beebe and Feaster (1968), p. 103.]

B66 KRISTOL, IRVING. "D-a-v-y Da-vy Crockett," Commentary, XXIX (February), 169-71. A review of Kenneth S. Lynn, Mark Twain and Southwestern Humor.
The importance of MT's almost-forgotten predecessors lies "in their eventual radical impact on serious American writing and in their status as witnesses to a transformation of the democratic idea in America." "The triumph of the vernacular over the trans-Atlantic rhetoric of the genteel tradition was a momentous event in American letters, American politics, American culture. It meant the victory of the masculine tone in the novel, hitherto regarded as a feminine entertainment--the way was open for Stephen Crane, Dreiser, Sherwood Anderson." Abstract in AES, III (1960), 963; reprinted in Twainian, XIX (November-December, 1960).

B67 KRUTCH, JOSEPH WOOD. "The Kremlin Claims Mark Twain," New York Times Magazine Section (March 6), pp. 16, 68-69.
The official Russian critical view misrepresents American criticism in assuming that here, too, there is an "official line" and that it attempts to suppress MT's social criticism. The error of this view is revealed by disagreement among American critics. The Russians err, too, in the "tacit assumption that...he might have turned his bitterness into faith in a People's Democracy." However, it is also reported that Russian children (and probably adults as well) read TS and HF "simply as the delightful tales they have always seemed to English-speaking children."

B68 LAING, NITA. "The Later Satire of Mark Twain," Midwest Quarterly, II (October), 35-48.
On the devastating influence of MT's despair on his later work, which, however, shows traces of his old brilliance; based on the familiar scholarship, to which the debt is acknowledged. Abstract in AES, VIII (1965), 1663; reprinted in Twainian, XXV (January-February, 1966).

B69 LOOMIS, C. C., JR. "Twain's Huckleberry Finn," Explicator, XVIII (January), Item 27.
Tom Sawyer "lacks Huck's realism, toughness, and moral sensitivity," but his romanticism offers a means of seeing the often brutal world as adventure. Abstract in AES, III (1960), 778; reprinted in Twainian, XIX (November-December, 1960).

B70 *LOOMIS, EDWARD W. "Three Notes on Plot," Spectrum, IV (Spring-Summer), 94-99.
   The absurd ending of HF follows the absurdity of the novel's prose. (Also on plot in James Gould Cozzens and as described in The Notebooks of Henry James.) [Source: AES, III (1960), 1610; reprinted in Twainian, XIX (November-December, 1960).]

B71 LONG, E. HUDSON. [Review: Charles Neider, ed., The Autobiography of Mark Twain.] American Literature, XXXI (January), 494-95.
   Neider's organization adds to the entertainment value at the expense of the insights provided by the editing of Paine and DeVoto. The general reader will enjoy the great passages by MT, but "there is still the need for a complete scholarly edition of Mark Twain's autobiographical writings which Mr. Neider's popular, abbreviated version does not fill."

B72 LYNN, KENNETH S. "Case History of Huckleberry Finn," New York Herald Tribune Book Review, (May 22), p. 8.
   A review of Walter Blair, Mark Twain & Huck Finn, which clears up the chronology of the book's composition and shows that MT was not henpecked by his wife. The book "pathetically fails," however, in its objective of illuminating MT's life and times, and the quality of HF, because Blair does not know how to use the material he has unearthed, is "abjectly dependent on the insights of other critics," and "draws parallels by the hundreds, but he cannot connect."

B73 MACDONALD, DWIGHT. "Mark Twain: An Unsentimental Journey." New Yorker, XXXVI (April 9), 160-96. Reprinted as "Mark Twain" in his Against the American Grain (New York: Random House, 1962), 80-122 (incorrectly giving the date of publication in the New Yorker as April 2); also reprinted in part in Kaplan (1967), 91-122, and in Cardwell (1963), pp. 116-30.
   A thoughtful and informed discussion of MT, his works, and the editors and critics. The occasion is the recent publication of The Autobiography of Mark Twain, assembled by "Charles Neider, a literary Jack-of-all-trades whose interests have ranged from Kafka to the diaries of Mrs. Robert Louis Stevenson.... One's first reaction is: why?... If there is any need for a new edition, it is for a complete one, edited by a specialist in Mark Twain," (p. 160). Macdonald discusses the editing of MT biographical material by Paine and DeVoto, the controversy between DeVoto and Brooks (in which he takes the side of Brooks as the more perceptive, but notes that in later years the two practically exchanged positions), and summarizes some of the important scholarship. In his own discussion of MT, Macdonald admits that for him "the great bulk of Mark Twain's work is no longer

readable"-- IA, CY, JA, and much of the trivia. TS is important as a forerunner of HF: Tom became the matrix of a stereotype and "his rebellion is phony...while Tom is a sentimental abstraction, Huck is Huck" (p. 173). The autobiographical ramblings are less revealing than MT thought, "the tone is that of the public performer" (p. 181), and "the tragedy of Mark Twain, I think, is this peculiar inability to speak in his own voice" (p. 183).

B74 MACK, EFFIE [MONA]. "Mark Twain in Nevada. A Leaf from the Civil War Story." Twainian, XIX (March-April), 4; reprinted from Oakland (California) Tribune, November 16 (1958.B49).
   Describes the flag on Mt. Davidson. (See RI, II, Ch. XIV.) Abstract in AES, III (1960), 1615.

B75 McKEE, JOHN DEWITT. "A Connecticut Yankee as a Revolutionary Document," Mark Twain Journal, XI (Summer), 18-20, 24.
   On the book's attack on institutions. Abstract in AES, IV (1961), 516.

B76 MacRAE, DONALD. "Huck and Experience," Times Literary Supplement, August 26, p. 545.
   A letter to the editor, arguing that Huck "learns nothing whatever from his experience" because, contrary to what he thinks, he was indeed "started right" and is spontaneously right in the crucial points in the book. [A reply to a statement in the anonymous "Innocence and Experience," (August 12), p. 512, 1960.B4.]

B77 *MALONE, DAVID H. "Analysis of Mark Twain's Novel Life on the Mississippi," in Hans Galinsky, ed., The Frontier in American History and Literature (Frankfurt a/M [Diesterweg, Beiheft 7 of N.S.?]), pp. 80-93.
   [Source: Beebe and Feaster (1968), p. 132.]

B78 *____. "Mark Twain and the Literature of the Frontier," ibid., pp. 65-79.
   [Source: MHRA Annual Bibliography (1961), 5292.]

B79 MAYFIELD, JOHN S. [Review: Svend Petersen, Mark Twain and the Government.] American Book Collector, X (June), 3-4.
   [Also available as Twainian, XIX (July-August).] Chiefly descriptive, favorable.

B80 MEINE, FRANKLIN J. "Some Notes on the First Editions of 'Huck Finn,'" American Book Collector, X (June), 31-34 [Also available as Twainian, XIX (July-August)].
   Chiefly concerned with the mutilation of the cut on p. 283; six illustrations on pp. 32-33 show various states of the cut, before and after the picture was defaced. The documentation is based on Walter Blair's Mark Twain & Huck Finn. Abstract in AES, III (1960), 1856.

B81   MESERVE, WALTER J., ed., The Complete Plays
       of William Dean Howells. New York: New
       York University Press, pp. 205-41 and
       passim.
          Contains the text of Colonel Sellers as a
       Scientist, by MT and Howells (not previous-
       ly published), with an introduction
       (pp. 205-208) discussing their collabora-
       tion.

B82   MILLER, WILLIAM C. "Mark Twain's Source for
       'The Latest Sensation' Hoax?" American
       Literature, XXXII (March), 75-78.
          On MT's "Dutch Nick Massacre" story: "A
       Twain item copied from the columns of the
       Virginia City Territorial Enterprise for
       'July 22d' (1863) and unnoticed until now,
       appears to be the source for the famous
       hoax"; the story, apparently factual, is
       here reproduced from a reprinting in the
       Sacramento Daily Union of July 24, 1863.
       Abstract in AES, III (1960), 1622, re-
       printed in Twainian, XIX (November-December,
       1960), 3.

B83   MOYNE, ERNEST J. "Mark Twain Meets a Lady
       from Finland," Mark Twain Journal, XI
       (Summer), 9-10, 25.
          On MT's meetings with Baroness Alexandra
       Gripenberg. An expanded version of this
       article appeared in American Literature as
       "Mark Twain and Baroness Alexandra Gripen-
       berg" (1973.B43). Abstract in AES, XI
       (Summer, 1960), 511.

B84   PARKE, RICHARD H. "Soviet Edition of Mark
       Twain Given to Connecticut Library," New
       York Times, (December 11), p. 88.
          Datelined "Reddington [sic: presumably
       Redding], Conn., Dec. 10" reports that "a
       resident of this town who has been exchang-
       ing books by and about Mark Twain with a
       Soviet library gave a Russian book to the
       Mark Twain Library here today"; it is titled
       Mark Twain Collections.

B85   PARSONS, COLEMAN O. "The Background of The
       Mysterious Stranger," American Literature,
       XXXII (March), 55-74.
          On the originals for setting and some of
       the characters, and on literary sources
       and analogues,; "These background materials
       will be grouped under five headings: Title,
       Setting, Characters, Plot, and Ideas." Ab-
       stract in AES, III (1960), 1621, reprinted
       in Twainian, XIX (November-December, 1960),
       3.

B86   PEARSON, NORMAN HOLMES. "Mark Twain--Genius
       or Jokesmith? Fifty Years After His Death,
       the Critics Are Still Bemused," Saturday
       Review, XLIII (June 25), 24-25.
          A review-article, summarizing Charles
       Neider's Mark Twain and the Russians, Svend
       Petersen's Mark Twain and the Government,
       Kenneth S. Lynn's Mark Twain and Southwest-
       ern Humor, and Walter Blair's Mark Twain &

Huck Finn ("a brilliant parallel to J. L.
Lowes's 'The Road to Xanadu' in reconstruct-
ing the road from Hannibal").

B87   _____. "The Mark Twain Memorial in Hartford,
       Connecticut." Journal of the Central Mis-
       sissippi Valley American Studies Association,
       I (Fall), 10-16.
          Describes the house as "a document," trac-
       ing its ownership since MT's death and de-
       scribing in some detail the restoration.
       Among resources being collected for scholars
       are a facsimile of his library, a log of his
       Hartford years (based in part on "a combing
       of Hartford newspapers"), and as complete a
       collection as possible of "all known photo-
       graphs of Mark Twain," in addition to manu-
       script material.

B88   PIPER, HENRY DAN. "Fitzgerald, Mark Twain and
       Thomas Hardy," Fitzgerald Newsletter, No. 8
       (Winter), pp. 1-2.
          Fitzgerald admired MT, and called the
       Paine biography "excellent." A member of
       the International Mark Twain Society, he
       sent a note to the 1935 banquet: "Huckle-
       berry Finn took the first journey back. He
       was the first to look back at the republic
       from the perspective of the West. His eyes
       were the first eyes that ever looked at us
       objectively that were not eyes from over-
       seas." (Hardy is not mentioned in connec-
       tion with MT; in a letter he expressed ad-
       miration for Fitzgerald.) Abstract in AES,
       IV (1961), 1830. Fitzgerald's tribute is
       reprinted in Simpson (1968), p. 107.

B89   POCHMANN, HENRY A. Introduction to "Mark
       Twain Anniversary Number," Journal of the
       Central Mississippi Valley American Studies
       Association, I (Fall), 1.
          MT's reputation is secure in 1960, the
       125th anniversary of his birth and the 50th
       of his death; he is commemorated by a dozen
       convocations and conferences, and a number
       of magazines and learned journals honor him
       with special issues.

B90   PRATT, WILLIS C. (as told to Grace Valliere
       King). "The Last Time I Saw Mark Twain,"
       Mark Twain Journal, XI (Summer), 6-8, 23.
          Pratt interviewed MT at his Fifth Avenue
       home for the New York Herald. MT was in
       bed, recovering from bronchitis, but he
       spoke at length on political bossism, reveal-
       ing considerable knowledge of Richard Croker,
       and he complained of a humorist's difficulty
       in being taken seriously. Abstract in AES,
       IV (1961), 510.

B91   PRITCHETT, V. S. "First Person Singular,"
       New Statesman, LX (November 26), 848-49.
       Includes a review of Charles Neider, ed.,
       The Autobiography of Mark Twain.
          The material MT left is "a huge and disas-
       trous ragbag of shaggy anecdotes. Mr. Neid-
       er is the latest editor to attempt an

(PRITCHETT, V. S.)
arrangement of it. Twain set out to tell
the whole truth and we can certainly deduce
his inner terror and insecurity from it,
but characteristically his notion of telling the truth was simply never to stop
talking."

B92 RANDOLPH, VANCE. "A Treasury to Draw Upon,"
New York Times Book Review (February 28),
pp. 6, 42.
A descriptive review of Kenneth S. Lynn's
Mark Twain and Southwestern Humor, a book
"full of splendid stuff."

B93 RAYFORD, JULIAN LEE. "The Mississippi River
Leadline Chant," American Book Collector, X
(June), 6-10 [also available as Twainian,
XIX (July-August)].
The chant as Rayford heard it on a towboat
in 1946; not directly related to MT.

B94 REED, JOHN Q. "Mark Twain: West Coast Journalist," Midwest Quarterly, I (January),
141-61.
A critical survey of MT's journalistic
writings, 1861-1866, based on familiar, published material. Although his writing for
the Territorial Enterprise "displays course
[sic] humor, ineffective satire, florid
style, and chaotic form, it also shows a
steady advance in quality," which continued
in his later Western writings; nonetheless,
"when he left the West in 1866 he was still
a journalist and not a literary artist."
Abstract in AES, VIII (1965), 1660; reprinted in Twainian, XXV (January-February,
1966).

B95 ROBINSON, E. ARTHUR. "The Two 'Voices' in
Huckleberry Finn," Modern Language Notes,
LXXV (March), 204-208.
The authorial intrusion in HF is not limited to Chapters XXI-XXII (discussed by
Robert Hunting, 1958.B38); rather, "not in-
frequently, Huck seems oblivious of implications which are clear to the reader," as in
the passage where Jim talks of stealing his
wife and children out of slavery: "the
thoughts are Huckleberry Finn's, but the
significance is Mark Twain's." As Huck
matures, he becomes more able to carry the
irony himself. Abstract in AES, X (1967),
3063; reprinted in Twainian, XXVII (January-
February, 1968).

B96 ROPER, GORDON. "Mark Twain and His Canadian
Publishers," American Book Collector, X
(June), 13-29 [also available as Twainian,
XIX (July-August)].
A detailed account of authorized and pi-
rated editions of MT's works in Canada; con-
cludes with "Check List of Canadian Editions
of Mark Twain's Work" (pp. 28-29). Abstract
in AES, III (1960), 1855. Also see Roper's
"Mark Twain and His Canadian Publishers: A
Second Look" (1966.B92).

B97 RYAN, PAT M., JR. "Mark Twain: Frontier
Theatre Critic," Arizona Quarterly, XVI
(Autumn), 197-209.
"Though ready enough to present himself to
his public as a fairly unsophisticated chap
capable of immense enjoyment at the theatre,
Twain was also a critic, in the true sense,
of American culture." Examples of his theater criticism in California papers are quoted, as are passages from his later books,
indicating that his interest in the theater
was life-long. Abstract in AES, IV (1961),
1296; reprinted in Twainian, XXI (January-
February, 1962).

B98 SCHMIDT, PAUL. "River vs. Town: Mark Twain's
Old Times on the Mississippi," Nineteenth-
Century Fiction, XV (September), 95-111.
"Speaks eloquently and often of a tragic
split in life and mind. The bleached life-
lessness of the town and the dark dramatic
color of the river and the boat spell out
Clemens's version of this conflict. At the
heart of his best work lies a rich registra-
tion of this conflict and his solid conviction that in the steamboat and what it represents lies its creative resolution." Abstract in AES, IV (1961), 1655; reprinted in
Twainian, XXI (January-February, 1962).

B99 SCOTT, ARTHUR L. "Mark Twain Today." Journal
of the Central Mississippi Valley American
Studies Association, I (Fall), 2-10.
Portions of a talk delivered in Hannibal
on October 15. Scott briefly lists recent
books on MT; describes holdings in the Mark
Twain Papers at the University of California
in Berkeley, and comments on other significant collections of MT material in this country: the Berg Collection in the New York
Public Library, Buffalo Public Library (most
of the Huckleberry Finn manuscript), Houghton
Library at Harvard, Huntington Library at San
Marino, California, Lilly Collection at the
University of Indiana, the private collections
of C. Walter Barrett and Samuel Charles Webster, and the Hartford Memorial Library and
the Mark Twain Research Foundation. Concludes
by discussing current popularity of MT's works,
and their translations and film adaptations.

B100 SCOTT, WINFIELD TOWNLEY. "Hannibal and the
Bones of Art," New Mexico Quarterly, XXX
(Winter), 339-46.
On a two-day visit to the town of MT's boyhood Scott saw houses and memorabilia, but
"I was not as moved as I expected to be....
I had been closer when I was not here." The
town is more vivid in MT's books than in its
present-day actuality. Abstract in AES, IV
(1961), 2416. Article reprinted in Kaplan
(1967), pp. 152-60.

B101 SHOCKLEY, MARTIN STAPLES. "The Structure of
Huckleberry Finn," South-Central Bulletin,
XX (Winter), 3-10.
"I propose that Huckleberry Finn is the-
matically coherent and structurally unified.

(SHOCKLEY, MARTIN STAPLES)
I propose a logical, ordered, five-part structure, with introduction, rising action, climax, falling action, conclusion. I propose proportion and balance among these parts, achieving a total aesthetic harmony." Thus, the Phelps farm chapters, though unsatisfactory as a conclusion, may be interpreted as falling action; the true conclusion is the brief "Chapter the Last: Nothing More to Write," in which Huck, having repudiated the civilization he has seen, "is ready to live by innate morality, a free man." Abstract in AES, IV (1961), 1272; reprinted in Twainian, XXI (January-February, 1962). Article reprinted in Kesterson (1973), pp. 70-81.

B102 SMITH, HENRY NASH. "Mark Twain's World Restored in Words and Pictures," New York Herald Tribune Book Review, XXXVII (November 6), 1. A review of Milton Meltzer, Mark Twain Himself.
"Mr. Meltzer has done his work well"--but, paradoxically, the accumulation of pictorial data adds to our sense of the remoteness of MT's time from our own.

B103 _____. "Old Mark Loved an Audience," New York Herald Tribune Book Review, XXXVII (December 18), 36. A review of Paul Fatout, Mark Twain on the Lecture Circuit.
Fatout "has found an abundance of material and put it together in a clear, workmanlike narrative"; he "has dug out hundreds of reviews of Mark Twain's lectures in newspapers all over the world."

B104 SOLOMON, ERIC. "Huckleberry Finn Once More," College English, XXII (December), 172-78.
Both critics and defenders of the thematic unity of HF assume that MT's intention "was either to show Huck's growth to maturity, to hail the joys of freedom on the river, or to depict the escape from civilization and slavery." Judged under this assumption, the ending is a failure; but the book may also be viewed in terms of the major theme of a search for security, as exemplified by Huck's invention of various family patterns for himself. Abstract in AES, IV (1961), 247; reprinted in Twainian, XXI (January-February, 1962). Article reprinted in Bradley (1962), pp. 436-43; in Lettis (1962), pp. 420-28.

B105 STARRETT, VINCENT. "Shaking Hands with Immortality," American Book Collector, X (June), 9-12. [Also available as Twainian, XIX (July-August).]
On the discovery in Rome of a statuette of MT from the studio of Luigi Amici; the statuette (illustrated) and a medallion portrait (apparently lost) were described to Starrett as "both taken from life," but he notes problems with provenance and documentation. Abstract in AES, III (1960), 1854.

B106 _____. [Review: Walter Blair, Mark Twain & Huck Finn.] American Book Collector, X (June), 3. [Also available as Twainian, XIX (July-August).]
"Literary detection at its liveliest and best," reflecting thorough familiarity with the book and its genesis, and the influence of MT's life and reading.

B107 TEITELBAUM, HAROLD. "Samuel Langhorne Clemens (Mark Twain)," Book Bulletin of the Chicago Public Library, XLII (September), 123-26.
A very brief estimate of MT, followed by summaries and estimates of major books by and about him; introductory.

B108 VITELLI, J. R. "The Innocence of Mark Twain," Bucknell Review, IX (December), 187-98.
A conscious craftsman and stylist, MT created an American Innocent as "a composite--as all such images are--of two character-types of the Innocent: the Innocent as complacent fool, and the Innocent as wise-seeker, both merged by and with the informing presence of their creator, that is, the personality of Mark Twain."

B109 VITTORINI, ELIO. "An Outline of American Literature (1941)," Sewanee Review, LXVIII (July), 423-37.
MT was "the chief and most typical" of the authors who created "an American legend of the son of the West, the symbol of the new man." Abstract in AES, XIV (1970-1971), 1609; reprinted in Twainian, XXXI (January-February, 1972).

B110 VON KREBS, MARIA. "'Rache' Is the German for 'Revenge,'" Baker Street Journal, X, n.s. (January), 12-14.
Six years before A Study in Scarlet, MT in TA commented on the inscription Rache in a cell at the college prison at Heidelberg University; "It is clear that Doyle, like Twain, recognized the inherent dramatic possibilities of the scrawled word on the wall, and...incorporated his famous story around it." Both books contain illustrations (here reproduced) of walls with the inscription. Abstract in AES, III (1960), 1163.

B111 WEBB, HOWARD W., JR. "Mark Twain and Ring Lardner," Mark Twain Journal, XI (Summer) 13-15.
A comparison between the two, showing no evidence of influence or other contact except for Lardner's statement in the New York Times Magazine (March 25, 1917, p. 44) that he felt George Ade had superceded MT as our national humorist and Booth Tarkington's Penrod had replaced Huckleberry Finn: "I've known Booth Tarkington's boys, and I've not known those of Mark Twain. Mark Twain's boys are tough and poverty-stricken and they belong to a period very different from that of our own boys." Abstract in AES, IV (1961), 514.

B112 WELLS, ARVIN R. "Huck Finn and Holden Caulfield: The Situation of the Hero," Ohio
University Review, II, 31-42.
Examines in the books by MT and Salinger
"the marked dissimilarities as contributory
to the ultimately very different effects
produced by these two novels," to reveal
"the essential qualities and fundamental attitudes found in each" and emphasize "the
fact that these novels are, after all, the
products of two unique creative imaginations
responding to quite different milieux."
Abstract in AES, IV (1961), 578; reprinted
in Twainian, XXI (January-February, 1962).

B113 YATES, NORRIS W. "The 'Counter-Conversion'
of Huckleberry Finn," American Literature,
XXXII (March), 1-10.
On the phenomenon of conversion to and
away from religion--in Huck's case to "wickedness" as an alternative to betrayal of
Jim. Abstract in AES, III (1960), 1616; reprinted in Twainian, XIX (November-December,
1960), 3.

1961 A BOOKS

A1 BALDANZA, FRANK. Mark Twain: An Introduction
and Interpretation. New York: Barnes &
Noble, Inc.; London: Constable.
"This study of the life and works of Mark
Twain is intended for both the general
reader and the student. The aim has been
to take into account all the biographical
research that has been done since A. B.
Paine's monumental authorized biography."
The chapters on MT's works "have been organized in a unique manner, treating the
autobiographical, the travel, the historical, the juvenile, the American, and the
polemical writings as units in themselves,"
in order to concentrate on "fresh insights
to be drawn from the inter-relations of the
work themselves" (p. v.). The portion on
CY is reprinted in Schmitter (1974),
pp. 117-21.

A2 *BRADLEY, SCULLEY, RICHMOND CROOM BEATTY, and
E. HUDSON LONG, eds. Samuel Langhorne
Clemens: Adventures of Huckleberry Finn:
An Annotated Text. Backgrounds and Sources,
Essays in Criticism. New York: W. W. Norton & Company, Inc.
A standard casebook for classroom use; it
was copyrighted in 1961 and reviewed at
least once (in Twainian), but the copies
now available also carry a 1962 copyright
date and the present bibliography lists the
volume under both years to prevent possible
loss of material cross-referenced to this
important reprinting.

A3 CLEMENS, SAMUEL L. Contributions to "The
Galaxy" 1868-1871 by Mark Twain (Samuel
Langhorne Clemens). Facsimile Reproductions,
Edited with an Introduction and Notes by
Bruce R. McElderry, Jr., Gainesville, Flori-
da: Scholars' Facsimiles & Reprints.

In a "Bibliographical Note" (p. xxi)
McElderry points out that "Only a few of
Twain's Galaxy sketches have never appeared
elsewhere, and these uncollected items are
chiefly brief paragraphs." Nonetheless,
McElderry's careful editing and the bibliographical data he provides make this an extremely useful source for students of this
period in MT's life.

A4 _____. "My Dear Bro": A Letter from Samuel
Clemens to His Brother Orion, Foreword by
Frederick Anderson. Berkeley, California:
The Berkeley Albion.
"In this previously unpublished letter
[San Francisco, October 19, 1865] sent to
his brother, Orion, and Orion's wife, Mol-
lie, Samuel Clemens expresses the ambiguous
attitude toward his view of himself as a
writer that would trouble him throughout his
life.... it was not until the fall of 1865,
when he was nearly thirty, that Mark Twain
concluded he must commit himself to a literary career, and even then his decision was
reluctant." He hesitated to become a professional humorist.

A5 _____, and BRET HARTE. "Ah Sin," a Dramatic
Work by Mark Twain and Bret Harte, ed.
Frederick Anderson. San Francisco: The
Book Club of California.
Anderson's preface describes the growth
and decline of the two men's friendship and
traces the fortunes of the play, of which
"much, perhaps most, of the initial material...came from Bret Harte," while MT's contribution lay in turning Harte's stilted
dialogue to "the rhythms and vocabulary of
actual speech." The play was a failure and
has since received little critical attention, "since while Ah Sin is not the poorest work by either man, it is not far from
it."

A6 FONER, PHILIP. Mark Tven-Socialny Kritik.
Moskva: Izdatelstvo Inostrannoi Literatur.
A Russian translation of Foner's Mark
Twain: Social Critic (1958).

A7 FRIED, M[ARTIN] B. Mark Twain on the Art of
Writing. Buffalo [N.Y.]: The Salisbury
Club.
A brief foreword gives the background for
MT's "Report to the Buffalo Female Academy"
(Buffalo Express, June 18, 1870), "A General
Reply" (Buffalo Express, November 12, 1870,
and Galaxy, X [November, 1870], 732-34), and
"A Good Letter: Mark Twain's Idea of It"
(Buffalo Express, November 10, 1869). [41
page pamphlet.]

A8 HARNSBERGER, CAROLINE THOMAS. Mark Twain's
Views of Religion. Evanston, Illinois:
The Schori Press.
A general study, annotated from MT's pub-
lished and unpublished writings. In 1906
Rufus K. Noyes gave him a copy of his Views
of Religion. "Mark Twain did not agree

(HARNSBERGER, CAROLINE THOMAS)
with every doctrine expressed in the volume. His extensive marginal notes, printed here for the first time, are the inspiration for this résumé of his views of religion." His extensive annotations of Jonathan Edwards' Freedom of the Will are noted in passing but not quoted.

A9   LEARY, LEWIS, ed. Mark Twain's Letters to Mary. New York: Columbia University Press.
      The text of MT's letters to Mary Benjamin Rogers, the wife of Henry Huttleston Rogers, Jr. Leary's account is a useful contribution to MT biography for the years 1900-1910.

A10   McKEITHAN, DANIEL MORLEY. The Morgan Manuscript of Mark Twain's "Pudd'nhead Wilson." Uppsala: A.-B. Lundequistska Bokhandeln (Essays and Studies on American Language and Literature, 12).
      "In 1909 the manuscript was purchased by J. Pierpont Morgan [from MT]. I shall describe the manuscript, call attention to the revisions in it, and point out the differences between it and the book" (p. 14); there is also a general discussion of PW, with attention to the racial theme.

A11   *NEIDER, CHARLES, ed. The Complete Humorous Sketches and Tales of Mark Twain. Garden City, New York: Hanover House.
      [Source: MHRA Annual Bibliography (1961), No. 5302.]

A12   ____, ed. Life as I Find It: Essays, Sketches, Tales, and Other Material, the Majority of Which is Now Published in Book Form for the First Time. Garden City, New York: Hanover House.

A13   ____, ed. The Travels of Mark Twain. New York: Coward-McCann, Inc.
      Excerpts from MT's travel books with an introduction (largely biographical, and useful only to the general reader) and a few background footnotes by Neider.

A14   QUICK, DOROTHY. Enchantment: A Little Girl's Friendship with Mark Twain. Norman: University of Oklahoma Press.
      Dorothy Quick was almost eleven years old in 1907 when she met MT, a lonely old man who missed his family of young daughters. This book is the record of the friendship of the two, and is interesting for the record of MT by one of his "Angel-Fishes" and for his advice to a very young writer. A number of letters from MT are included, with four photographs of him in the text and another on the dust-jacket.

A15   ROGERS, FRANKLIN R., ed. The Pattern for Mark Twain's "Roughing It": Letters from Nevada by Samuel and Orion Clemens 1861-1862. Berkeley and Los Angeles: University of California Press.

Correspondence published in the Keokuk (Iowa) Gate City and St. Louis Missouri Democrat, valuable as background for RI and interesting as early writing by MT. Rogers questions Ernest E. Leisy's attribution of the Quintus Curtius Snodgrass letters to MT.

A16   SALOMON, ROGER B. Twain and the Image of History. New Haven: Yale University Press (Yale Studies in English, 150).
      "Twain's images of history reflect the interaction of a writer's private insights with a major facet of his cultural tradition, an interaction that was to have a radical influence on the form and content of most of his work." Commonly, "behind the ambiguity, the divided intentions, the stylistic lapses of even his best books lies a confused and bitter conflict between his conception of history and his conception of human nature; behind them also lies a passionate desire to escape the moral and aesthetic implications of both through some sort of transcendent dream" (p. 4).

A17   SCHÖNFELDER, KARL-HEINZ. Mark Twain: Leben, Persönlicheit und Werk. Halle (Saale): VEB Verlag Sprache und Literatur.
      A brief, general study with a section on his life followed by chapters titled "Humor und Satire," "Gesellschaftskritik," "Pessimismus," "Lokalkolorit," and a concluding "Mark Twain in Spiegel der Kritik," which summarizes the criticism of MT.

A18   STONE, ALBERT E., JR. The Innocent Eye: Childhood in Mark Twain's Imagination. New Haven: Yale University Press.
      [Source: 1970 reprinting "in an unaltered and unabridged edition," Hamden, Connecticut: Archon Books.] Placing MT in a context of the developing interest in childhood as a theme after the Civil War, reveals his fascination with immaturity. Treats the portrayal of childhood in TS, HF, JA, and other works, distinguishing in the discussion of CY between the kind of innocence that is laudable and the kind that is merely a limitation. Pp. 153-58, dealing with HF, reprinted in Bradley (1962), pp. 444-48.

A19   WAGENKNECHT, EDWARD. Mark Twain: The Man and His Work. Norman: University of Oklahoma Press.
      "A completely new and revised edition" of the 1935 book, with a new bibliography dropping entries which may readily be found in LHUS and elsewhere, but also with some not listed in the present bibliography. Pp. 164-73 are reprinted as "Literature and Love" in Leary (1962), pp. 301-310.

1961 B SHORTER WRITINGS

B1 ANDERSON, DAVID D. "Melville and Mark Twain in Rebellion," Mark Twain Journal, XI (Fall), 8-9.
On parallels between The Mysterious Stranger and The Confidence Man. Abstract in AES, V (1962), 1277.

B2 ANON. [Review: Gladys Brooks, Gramercy Park: Memories of a New York Girlhood (Dent).]. Times Literary Supplement, January 27, p. 54.
Book not seen. Reviewer notes that MT was a friend of the Brooks family [unrelated to Van Wyck Brooks]: "As the children ate their corned beef hash and codfish cakes he would prowl round the table talking on and on."

B3 ASSELINEAU, ROGER. [Review: E. Hudson Long, Mark Twain Handbook (1957), and Lewis Leary, Mark Twain 1960).] Études Anglaises, XIV (January-March), 83-84.
The full and accurate bibliographies following the chapters constitute an unequaled and valuable documentation, and the Handbook is marked by good sense and objectivity. Despite a greater emphasis on the biographical part of MT studies than is perhaps justified, the book gives a judicious choice of the superabundant literature on MT and it will be indispensable for the student of MT; its inadequacies are the inadequacies of the existing criticism itself. Lewis Leary gives a very good description of the work of MT and sensibly refuses to see a great thinker in him. [In French.]

B4 BABCOCK, C. MERTON. "Mark Twain: A Heretic in Heaven," ETC: A Review of General Semantics, XVIII (July), 189-96.
On "Mark Twain's concern for facts and judgments, and for the tendency of people to confuse the two"; notes MT's own "semantic sophistication." Abstract in AES, V (1962), 744; reprinted in Twainian, XXII (January-February, 1963).

B5 BAETZHOLD, HOWARD G. "'The Autobiography of Sir Robert Smith of Camelot': Mark Twain's Original Plan for A Connecticut Yankee," American Literature, XXXII (January), 456-61.
Reprints accounts from New York newspapers of MT's reading an early version of the first three chapters before the Military Service Institute, November 11, 1886; the conception of the book changed sharply thereafter, and the discovery of this early fragment supports the conjecture by John B. Hoben in 1946 that MT broke off his composition at this point. Abstract in AES, IV (1961), 709; reprinted in Twainian, XXI (January-February, 1962).

B6 _____. "The Course of Composition of A Connecticut Yankee: A Reinterpretation," American Literature, XXXIII (May), 195-214.
John B. Hoben (1946) and Fred W. Lorch (1958) "have contributed important insights into the genesis of A Connecticut Yankee. But new evidence--unpublished materials in the Mark Twain Papers and in the Berg Collection of the New York Public Library...suggests a reassessment of the shaping forces" and chronology; Baetzhold lists a number of literary sources apparently not previously noted. Abstract in AES, V (1962), 1824; reprinted in Twainian, XXII (January-February, 1963).

B7 *BARUCCA, PRIMO. "Mark Twain e l'Italia," La Fiera Letteraria, XVI (May 21), 4.
[Source: AES, IV (1961), 1828; reprinted in Twainian, XXI (January-February, 1962).] Cites Agostino Lombardo's comment on IA as a pessimistic contrast to The Marble Faun: MT sees tradition, conformity, and the past as destructive.

B8 BELL, NEIL. "Mark Twain's Joan of Arc," Mark Twain Journal, XI (Fall), 4-6.
Personal response to MT's treatment of the story. Abstract in AES, V (1962), 1274.

B9 BOOTH, WAYNE C. The Rhetoric of Fiction. Chicago and London: The University of Chicago Press.
Very brief comments on Huck Finn as a narrator, passim (indexed).

B10 BOWDEN, EDWIN T. The Dungeon of the Heart: Human Isolation and the American Novel. New York: The Macmillan Company, pp. 30-43 and passim.
Huck is detached, but sympathetic, and has a deep sense of ethics (p. 35). He gradually comes to form a commitment to Jim.

B11 BRITTAIN, SIR HARRY. "My Friend Mark Twain," Mark Twain Journal, XI (Fall), 1-3.
On MT's 1907 visit to England. Abstract in AES, V (1962), 1273.

B12 BROWNE, RAY B. "Mark Twain and Captain Wakeman," American Literature, XXXIII (November), 320-29.
On Edgar ("Ned") Wakeman, whom MT first met in 1866 and who served as a model for the hero in Captain Stormfield's Visit to Heaven and less familiar works by MT; based in part on 1878 California newspaper material and on The Log of an Ancient Mariner, Being the Life and Adventures of Captain Edgar Wakeman, Written by Himself and Edited by His Daughter [Minnie Wakeman-Curtis], (San Francisco, 1878). Abstract in AES, V (1962), 1831, reprinted in Twainian, XXII (January-February, 1963).

1961 - Shorter Writings

B13 *BURHANS, CLINTON S., JR. "Mark Twain's View
       of History," Papers of the Michigan Academy
       of Science, Arts and Letters, XLVI, 617-27.
          On the conflict between his belief in
       progress and his view of history as repeti-
       tious and decadent. [Source: MHRA Annual
       Bibliography (1961), No. 5268, and abstract
       in AES, IV (1961), 2712; reprinted in Twain-
       ian, XXI (January-February, 1962).]

B14 CARPENTER, KENNETH E. "An Unrecorded Mark
       Twain," Papers of the Bibliographical Soci-
       ety of America, LV (Third Quarter), 236-39;
       reprinted Twainian, XXI (January-February,
       1962), 3-4.
          The first appearance of "The Czar's Solil-
       oquy" in book form was an eight-page pam-
       phlet, in Russian translation, published
       in Geneva by the Socialist Revolutionary
       Party, 1905. Abstract in AES, V (1962),
       843; reprinted in Twainian, XXII (January-
       February, 1963).

B15 CARSTENSEN, BRODER. "The Adventures of Huckle-
       berry Finn: Die Problematik des Schlusses,"
       Neueren Sprachen, XII (December), 541-51.
          Explains the weak ending of HF in terms of
       MT's use of his unfinished novel, The Mys-
       terious Chamber, also dealing with a prisoner.
       [In German]. Abstract in AES, V (1962),
       1105; reprinted in Twainian, XXII (January-
       February, 1963); article reprinted in
       1968.B19.

B16 CLEMENS, SAMUEL L. "A Boston Girl," Harper's,
       CCXXII (June), 52-53.
          Text of an MT reply to a letter criticiz-
       ing his grammar. Followed by a brief note
       by Charles Neider: "This article was pub-
       lished anonymously in the June, 1880 issue
       of The Atlantic Monthly.... The article,
       which is slightly cut here, will be pub-
       lished next fall in my new collection,
       Life as I Find It." Abstract in AES, VIII
       (1965), 2004; reprinted in Twainian, XXV
       (January-February, 1966).

B17 COLTON, HAROLD S[ELLERS]. "Mark Twain's Lit-
       erary Dilemma and Its Sequel," Arizona
       Quarterly, XVII (Autumn), 229-32.
          The author's great-uncle, George Escol
       Sellers, was a businessman and mechanical
       engineer; an attempt to raise money in
       Philadelphia to build up a coal industry at
       Sellers Landing, Illinois was unsuccessful
       because people thought he was the prototype
       for the impractical Colonel Escol Sellers
       of The Gilded Age. He was said to have re-
       ceived the middle name "Escol" because on
       the night he was born, his father dreamed
       of four men carrying a large bunch of
       grapes, recalling the brook of Eschol (Num-
       bers XIII:23). Abstract in AES, V (1962),
       4; reprinted in Twainian, XXII (January-
       February, 1963).

B18 COX, JAMES M. "Walt Whitman, Mark Twain, and
       the Civil War," Sewanee Review, LXIX (Spring),
       185-204.
          "Mark Twain's Civil War was never the his-
       torical Civil War but an emotional equivalent
       of that war in which Mark Twain was perpetu-
       ally involved as he created for himself and
       for his nation an image of the past which
       could contain the war instead of being de-
       stroyed by it," but for MT the cost "was ul-
       timately to be overtaken by the chaos of the
       inner war that all the stratagems and eva-
       sions of humor, burlesque, and parody could
       not resolve." He was the novelist--or poet--
       of Reconstruction, "for in Huckleberry Finn
       he brought not the old south but an entirely
       new south back into the Union." Abstract in
       AES, XI (1968), 1563; reprinted in Twainian,
       XXVIII (January-February, 1969).

B19 CUMMINGS, SHERWOOD. "What's in Huckleberry
       Finn?" English Journal, L (January), 1-8.
          An analysis geared to teaching in high
       school. Students are accustomed to tele-
       vision dramas in which the moral values are
       clear and nothing is left to inference; but
       MT tells the story through Huck, who himself
       is unaware of what MT is implying. The two
       major themes are Huck's rejection of society
       and his struggle with his conscience. Ab-
       stract in AES, V (1962), 1479; reprinted in
       Twainian, XXII (January-February, 1963).

B20 DAHL, CURTIS. "Mark Twain and the Moving Pano-
       ramas," American Quarterly, XIII (Spring),
       20-32.
          MT must have seen the moving panoramas in
       his youth; he had "a primarily visual imagi-
       nation...absorbed much of their technique
       into his writing," and the fact helps ex-
       plain both the defective structure of his
       works and their vitality. There were pano-
       ramas of the Mississippi, and of journeys to
       the West and to Europe and the Near East,
       with subclasses depicting the Gold Rush,
       Classical antiquity, and the Holy Land, all
       of which have parallels in MT's writings.
       In such set-pieces as the description of Lake
       Tahoe in Chapter XXIII of Roughing It "one
       can practically see the changing diorama and
       hear the lecturer's spiel." Abstract in AES,
       V (1962), 1173.

B21 [DAVIS, CHESTER L.] "The Adventures of Huck-
       leberry Finn (annotated)," Twainian, XX
       (September-October), 3-4.
          Praises the footnotes of the edition of HF
       incorporated in the current The American
       Tradition in Literature edited by Sculley
       Bradley, Richard Croome Beatty, and E. Hudson
       Long (New York: W. W. Norton).

B22 _____. "Twentieth Year of 'The Twainian' Be-
       gins: Review of Shrine accomplishment,"
       Twainian, XX (January-February), 1-4.

258

([DAVIS, CHESTER L.])

A chatty reminiscence of the Mark Twain Research Foundation and the Shrine at MT's birthplace in Florida, Missouri. Reproduces text of a feature story by Jack Rice in the St. Louis Post-Dispatch of May 22, drawing heavily on an interview with Davis on the same topic and quoting him on the policy concerning use of unpublished material: "I don't show notes that haven't been printed in the Twainian, Keeps up the interest." Also reprints article by Davis in the Perry (Missouri) Enterprise on the Foundation and Memorial Park (June 23, apparently paid for as an advertisement).

B23　DICKINSON, LEON T. [Review: Daniel Morley McKeithan, Court Trials in Mark Twain, and Other Essays (1958).] English Studies (Amsterdam), XLII, 325-27.

A disappointing treatment of a promising topic, this consists mostly of summaries with little analysis or commentary. The other essays in the book, reprinted from journals, "pinpoint specific borrowings" from various sources, but might be enriched if the critical comment were more extensive.

B24　DYSON, A. E. "Huckleberry Finn and the Whole Truth," Critical Quarterly, III (Spring), 29-40; reprinted in his The Crazy Fabric: Exercises in Irony (New York: St. Martin's Press, 1965), pp. 96-111.

Argues against simplistic readings: for example, there is not a simple contrast between corrupt society and virtuous outsiders, since "the Duke, the King, and Huck's father...are all far further away from the 'respectable' folk than Huck himself is," and they "are all failures, who stand outside society...simply because they are lazy, vicious, and by nature parasitic." In contrast, the respectable people do not wholly lack the virtues embodied in Huck and Jim. The disputed ending of the story is consistent with "the logic and texture of the whole book," in that "actual human progress does come about...through muddled insights, muddled kindliness, muddled actions as much as from the straightforward vindication of ideals." Abstract in AES, V (1962), 1443; reprinted in Twainian, XXII (January-February, 1963). Article reprinted from the 1965 book in Schmitter (1974), pp. 95-107.

B25　EASTMAN, MAX. "Mark Twain and Socialism," National Review, X (March 11), 154-55.

MT's "feelings toward the underprivileged and the working class were not sharply different from those of the socialists," but his "casual observation and shrewd common sense" kept him from embracing socialist doctrine. Abstract in AES, IV (1961), 1628; reprinted in Twainian, XXI (January-February, 1962).

B26　FERGUSON, DELANCEY. "Honorary Grandfather," New York Times Book Review (October 8), p. 22.

A review of Dorothy Quick's Enchantment: A Little Girl's Friendship with Mark Twain. The letters from MT make the book essential for every MT collector, and "it has genuine charm as a record of a friendship. But its essentials could have been conveyed in fewer pages."

B27　*FIGUERA, ANGELA. Tres Escritores Norteamericanos: Mark Twain, Henry James, Thomas Wolfe. Madrid: Gredos.

[Source: MHRA Annual Bibliography (1962), Nos. 5108, 5668.

B28　FLANAGAN, JOHN T. [Review: Henry Nash Smith and William M. Gibson, eds., The Mark Twain-Howells Letters (1960).] Journal of English and Germanic Philology, LX (April), 342-44.

The 680 surviving letters, written over 41 years, cover the range of literary, business, and personal matters. "Twain's letters, as might be expected, are more charged with spirit and show the wider emotional range." The editing is impeccable, but not obtrusive, making this a book for the scholar and the general reader.

B29　FRIEDMAN, ROBERT P. [Review: Paul Fatout, Mark Twain on the Lecture Circuit (1960).] Quarterly Journal of Speech, XLVII (April), 206-207.

A product of "diligent research and able writing," this book "corrects mistaken ideas and clarifies hazy aspects of Twain's lecture career"; it is "a genuine contribution."

B30　FRIEDRICH, GERHARD. [Brief Review: Brashear and Rodney, eds., The Art, Humor, and Humanity of Mark Twain (1959).] Books Abroad, XXXV (Autumn), 389.

"An entertaining assortment."

B31　GERBER, JOHN C. [Review: Franklin R. Rogers, Mark Twain's Burlesque Patterns.] Modern Language Notes, LXXVI (December), 902-904.

"Unfortunately, while this is a helpful work, it is not a great one. And in some respects it is not even a very good one." There are "oversimplifications," "strained connections," "an oppressive over-use of awkward terms," and "unconvincing conclusions." "More fundamentally, the book is weakened by a procedure that hardens into a routine and by a conclusion that comes much too soon."

B32　HAMBLEN, ABIGAIL ANN. "Uncle Tom and 'Nigger Jim': A Study in Contrasts and Similarities," Mark Twain Journal, XI (Fall), 13-17.

"Because of lack of opportunity for development, Jim's mentality and his moral nature cannot be matched with those of Uncle Tom," but the two slaves are similar in loyalty and in the loyalty and love they inspire in the white people around them. Abstract in AES, V (1962), 1279.

B33   HEYM, STEFAN. [Introduction.] King Leopold's
       Soliloquy, New York: International Pub-
       lishers, and Berlin (D.D.R), Seven Seas
       Books, pp. 11-26.
            The booklet is an East German reprinting
       of the 1906 edition of the pamphlet MT
       wrote for the Congo Reform Association;
       the contemporary illustrations are supple-
       mented by nine pages of photographs showing
       Patrice Lumumba, the United Nations debate
       on the Congo, a shooting in Leopoldville,
       a school and shanties in the Congo, etc.
       Heym's introduction emphasizes MT's social
       criticism, his understanding of imperialism
       based on what he had seen, since although
       "he knew Gorki...he did not know Lenin or
       Lenin's thoughts on the subject." In his
       pamphlet MT shows his customary discipline
       in his craft, even though he feels strong-
       ly: "Mark Twain the artist remains an
       artist even when a propagandist."

B34   HIGHFILL, PHILIP H., JR. "Incident in Huck-
       leberry Finn," Mark Twain Journal, XI
       (Fall), 6.
            When Huck was revealed as a boy in girl's
       clothes when he clapped his knees together
       to catch a lump of lead (Chapter XI), MT
       could have been following an English source
       "in the grab-bag of scholarly argument, ana,
       and country custom called Literary Anec-
       dotes...Of Professor Porson and Others;
       from the Manuscript Papers of the Late E.
       H. Barker...London, 1852 (Anecdote No.
       CCXXXIV The Two Thieves, p. 282)." Abstract
       in AES, V (1962), 1276.

B35   HILL, HAMLIN. "The Composition and Structure
       of Tom Sawyer," American Literature, XXXII
       (January), 379-92. Reprinted in Twainian,
       XX (May-June), 1-4.
            After briefly summarizing the views of
       Blair, Wecter, Gladys Bellamy, E. H. Long,
       Ferguson, Cowie, and Asselineau, cites the
       manuscript at Georgetown University, as
       "convincing evidence to corroborate Blair's
       interpretation of the book" as a structured
       account of a boy's maturation. Abstract in
       AES, IV (1961), 702.

B36   _____. "Mark Twain's Book Sales, 1869-1879,"
       Bulletin of the New York Public Library,
       LXV (June), 371-89.
            Elisha Bliss published MT's works through
       the American Publishing Company during this
       period. His shrewd (and occasionally un-
       scrupulous) promotion of MT's books, sold
       by subscription, contributed to the sale of
       337,902 volumes in the 1870's; MT's books
       continued to sell over the years, in con-
       trast with most subscription books, which
       became unmarketable after a year. Sales of
       Sketches New and Old were disappointing,
       and sales of TS still more so; TA was more
       successful, but MT switched to a new pub-
       lisher, James R. Osgood, who had no experi-
       ence in subscription publishing and botched
       the sales of P&P and LOM. Abstract in AES,

       VI (1964), 718; reprinted in Twainian, XXIII
       (January-February, 1964).

B37   _____. "Mark Twain's 'Brace of Brief Lectures
       on Science,'" New England Quarterly, XXXIV
       (June), 228-39.
            Reprints for the first time the text of
       MT's "A Brace of Brief Lectures on Science,"
       which appeared in The American Publisher
       (edited by his brother, Orion) in September
       and October, 1971 as "I. Paleontology" and
       "II. Paleontology Concluded--Primeval Man."
       They reveal a shifting tone: "How is it pos-
       sible to explain the somewhat forced and
       repetitious irony of the first half, the rol-
       licking burlesque of the second half, and the
       apologia in the last paragraph?" The answer
       may lie in a "conflict between propriety and
       personal opinion, which caused both the un-
       usual attitude toward science and the mix-
       ture of comic techniques." Abstract in AES,
       IV (1961) 1944; reprinted in Twainian, XXI
       (January-February, 1962).

B38   _____. [Review: Franklin R. Rogers, Mark
       Twain's Burlesque Patterns as Seen in the
       Novels and Narratives 1855-1885 (1960.]
       Prairie Schooner, XXXV (March), 8-9.
            "In spite of minor points of argument, I
       think Mr. Rogers' skillful tracing of the
       dominent structural patterns in Twain's ma-
       jor works from Innocents Abroad through
       Huckleberry Finn, benefitted by the examina-
       tion of hitherto unpublished Twain materi-
       als, is a major achievement and a cohesive
       analysis that cannot be ignored by future
       Twain scholars."

B39   HOFFMAN, DANIEL. "Mark Twain," in his Form
       and Fable in American Fiction (London and
       New York: Oxford University Press).
            On pp. 317-42, "Black Magic--and White--
       in Huckleberry Finn," showing three attitudes
       toward life, indicated in supernatural terms:
       both "the conventional piety of the villag-
       ers" and "the irrelevant escape of the roman-
       tic imagination" are "morally inadequate,"
       but "the third--which pays homage to the
       river god--gives dignity to human life"
       through the world of supernatural omens un-
       derstood by Jim; Jim, too, undergoes growth
       in the story. This article is a complete
       revision of "Jim's Magic: Black or White?"
       (1960.B58). This 1961 revision is reprinted
       in part in Bradley (1962), pp. 396-409; Leary
       (1962), pp. 311-334; Smith (1963), pp. 101-11.
       On pp. 343-50, "Huckleberry Finn: His Mas-
       querade," on his disguises, his several iden-
       tities, and his problem of preserving his
       essential self. In the end, as in the begin-
       ning, his only safety lies in flight.

B40   HOWARD, ROBERT WEST. "The Mark Twain Story,"
       Twainian, XX (July-August), 1-4.
            A popular account of MT's life, reprinted
       from the house organ (name not given) of the
       Inland Steel Company (Summer, 1961); empha-
       sizes the significance of the Middle West in

(HOWARD, ROBERT WEST)
shaping him. Abstract in AES, VII (1964), 1573.

B41 *KAMEI, SHUNSUKE. "On Interpretations of The Adventures of Huckleberry Finn," Comparative Literature and Comparative Culture (1961).
[Source: Kamei, Shunsuke, "Mark Twain in Japan," Mark Twain Journal, XII (Spring), 20.]

B42 KENDALL, LYLE H., JR. "The Walter Scott Episode in Huckleberry Finn," Nineteenth-Century Fiction, XVI (December), 279-81.
The organization of Huckleberry Finn is based on "Huck's emancipation, from Pap Finn, from the King and the Duke, and from Tom Sawyer's darkly humorous influence." In the cabin Pap had called Huck the "Angel of Death," and this is "precisely what Huck becomes on board the Walter Scott six chapters later." Kendall identifies Pap Finn with "Old Hatfield," murdered by Jim Turner, and "ironically, Pap Finn's evil existence is to be closed out by Huck's exacting retribution for his father's murder" as Huck strands the robbers on the wrecked steamboat. Abstract in AES, V (1962), 818; reprinted in Twainian, XXII (January-February, 1963).

B43 LAKIN, R. D. "Mark Twain and the Cold War," Midwest Quarterly, II (January), 159-67.
Summarizes the debate between Charles Neider and Yan Bereznitsky, of the Russian Literary Gazette, as published in Neider's Mark Twain and the Russians (1960); both reflect the conventional thinking of their societies, and MT himself would feel out of place in either camp. Abstract in AES, VIII (1965), 1665; reprinted in Twainian, XXV (January-February, 1966).

B44 LAVIGNE, GARY W. "The Day Mark Twain Came to Geneseo, New York," Twainian, XX (November-December), 1-4.
MT was originally scheduled to give his "American Vandals in the Old World" lecture on February 18, 1869, but an error in booking caused a delay until March 1. LaVigne's account draws partly on local sources and partly on such familiar material as letters to Livy and to Mrs. Fairbanks. Abstract in AES, VII (1964), 1577.

B45 LEARY, LEWIS. "Mark Twain at Barnard College." Columbia Library Columns, X (May), 12-17.
About MT as "the belle of New York," speaking before women's college groups in the spring of 1906. According to an editor's note the article is an expansion of material collected by Leary for his edition of Mark Twain's Letters to Mary.

B46 LONG, E. HUDSON. "Tom Sawyer's 'Pitchiola,'" Twainian, XX (September-October), 4.
When the captive Jim was urged in Chapter XXXVII of HF to raise a flower, MT's source was Picciola, the Prisoner of Fenestrella, or Captivity Captive, by Joseph Xavier Saintine (pseudonym for Boniface), 1798-1865.

B47 ____. [Review: Walter Blair, Mark Twain & Huck Finn (1960.] American Literature, XXXII (January), 467-68.
Blair "has apparently neglected nothing in the way of published material, and the minute notes testify that he has been equally thorough in using available manuscripts. His book is a storehouse of information, all of it based on sound, documented evidence," and "furnishes a perceptive account of Samuel Clemens the creative artist from 1876 through 1883"; it is a "major contribution to our knowledge of Mark Twain as a man and writer."

B48 ____. [Review: Milton Meltzer, Mark Twain Himself (1960).] American Quarterly, XIII (Fall), 438-39.
This is "an informative pictorial biography of Samuel Clemens" and of his times, 1835-1910, in which Meltzer lets MT tell his own story, setting the record straight where necessary. The information is accurate, and "the more than six hundred illustrations will attract anyone interested in photography."

B49 LORCH, FRED W. [Review: Henry Nash Smith and William M. Gibson, eds., Mark Twain-Howells Letters (1960).] American Literature, XXXIII (March), 78-80.
This is "a superb job of editing" 681 notes and letters, 385 of them previously unpublished.

B50 LOWE, WILLIAM J. "The Mountain Shakes," College English, XXIII (October), 62-63.
Eric Solomon (1960.B104) and Carson Gibb (1960.B49) in their investigations of HF "are trying to bolster the weak ending of a fine novel with materials drawn from today's frame of reference"--MT was tired when he wrote it, and modern psychology and portraits of Tom as a modern playboy are inappropriate to a novel of an earlier age. In a brief rebuttal, Carson Gibb says that Lowe's premise would reduce literature of the past to mere relics. Abstract in AES, V (1962), 731; reprinted in Twainian, XXII (January-February, 1963).

B51 *LYDENBERG, JOHN. "American Novelists in Search of a Lost World," Revue des Langues Vivantes, XXVII, 306-21.
MT is one of a number of American authors discussed in an essay dealing with the theme of loss, betrayal, and vain searching. [Source: Abstract in AES, IX (1966), 2407; reprinted in Twainian, XXVI (January-February, 1967).]

B52 LYNN, KENNETH S. [Review: Franklin R. Rogers, Mark Twain's Burlesque Patterns: As Seen in the Novels and Narratives 1855-1885 (1960).] American Literature, XXXIII (November), 384-86.

A witty review, depicting contemporary criticism of MT as "that age-old American struggle between the Dandies and the Squatters" [the terms are taken from an 1852 sketch by MT]; the former show imagination but "a tendency to be carried away by their theories, especially the psychological variety," and the latter work hard but launch few speculative flights with their ideas. The Rogers book reflects patient research but "considerable faults," including a "failure to deal with A Connecticut Yankee, surely the most interesting of Twain's major works from the point of view of burlesque. But its main flaw is its Squatterishness.... The best one can say for Mark Twain's Burlesque Patterns is that it may well prove useful to more imaginative critics."

B53 McELDERRY, B[RUCE] R., JR. "Who Was Sarah Findlay?" Twainian, XX (September-October), 3.

On a rare pamphlet by that title, "By Mark Twain, with a Suggested Solution of the Mystery by J. M. Barrie. London: Privately Printed by Clement Shorter, April 1917." Contains an MT letter to the London Daily Chronicle (written November 18, 1896, but not printed) chiding Barrie for failure to protect his books by copyright in America; the "Sarah Findlay" name was invented by Barrie to substitute for a real one in an MT inscription quoted from a copy of HF.

B54 McKEITHAN, D. M. "The Morgan Manuscript of The Man that Corrupted Hadleyburg," Texas Studies in Literature and Language, II (Winter), 476-80.

The autograph MS in the Pierpont Morgan Library in New York reveals that at the outset MT was uncertain concerning his trap to catch the leading citizens; "The fact that nearly all the revisions concerned details of plot points to one other conclusion: that whenever Twain had clearly in mind what he wanted to say, the style and diction in the first draft were so excellent that few changes were necessary." Abstract in AES, VII (1964), 1240.

B55 MALIN, IRVING. "Mark Twain: The Boy as Artist," Literature and Psychology, XI (Summer), 78-84.

MT's "fiction is boyish and incomplete" because "he does not face squarely the emotional patterns which are involved" in his treatment of "authoritarianism and rebellion in the family and outside." Bixby and Brown in LOM, and Jim and Pap in HF, represent good and bad fathers, and an ambivalent view on MT's part. In CY, the Boss is "a good, powerful father-image for the dark ages." PW, like CY, "is a cruel book written by an immature author," and in Hadleyburg and MS "we enter a new world, where we meet the triumphant bad father." As Americans we have made MT, with his hatred and love of power, "a national father after all. Perhaps some day we will grow up." Abstract in AES, V (1962), 1978; reprinted in Twainian, XXII (January-February, 1963).

B56 MENDELSON, M. O. "Mark Twain's Unpublished Literary Heritage," Soviet Review: A Journal of Translations, II (September), 33-53.

"An authority on Mark Twain takes his literary executors to task for allowing a significant part of Twain's literary heritage to remain unpublished. Izvestia Akademii Nauk SSR, Otdeleniye Literatury i Yazyka (Bulletin of the USSR Academy of Sciences, Literature and Languages Section), 1961, Vol. XX, No. 1." Abstract in AES, V (1962), 872; reprinted in Twainian, XXII (January-February, 1963).

B57 MICHAELSON, L. W. "Four Emmeline Grangerfords," Mark Twain Journal, XI (Fall), 10-12.

Possible literary models for the "Ode to Stephen Dowling Bots, Dec'd" In Chapter XVII of Huckleberry Finn are in the poetry of Julia A. Moore, Bloodgood H. Cutter, William McGonagall (1830-189?), and Seba Smith. Abstract in AES, V (1962), 1278.

B58 MILLGATE, MICHAEL. [Review: Lewis Leary, Mark Twain (1960) and Henry Nash Smith and William M. Gibson, eds., Mark Twain-Howells Letters (1960).] Modern Language Review, LVI (July), 417-18.

Leary's University of Minnesota pamphlet is "a pleasant introduction to Mark Twain's work." The MT-Howells letters are well-edited, not all of them important in their own right but valuable as a collection that adds to our understanding of the men and their times; their publication enhances the stature of Howells as friend and critic, although MT's letters are the more lively.

B59 MILLER, WALLACE C. "Mark Twain's Account of the Goodman-Fitch Duel," Twainian, XX (September-October), 1-2; reprinted from Nevada Historical Society Quarterly, II, No. 3, "The Back Number" (unexplained, and year, pp. not given).

MT's account of the duel between Joseph T. Goodman and Thomas S. Fitch is given as reprinted in Myron Angel, ed., History of Nevada (Oakland: Thompson and West, 1881) and in a fuller reprint from the Sacramento Union, "probably copied word for word from the Enterprise." Abstract in AES, VII (1964), 1574.

B60 MONTIERO, GEORGE. "A Note on the Mark Twain-
Whitelaw Reid Relationship," Emerson Society
Quarterly, XIX (Second Quarter, 1960), 20-21.
    MT dropped his plans to write a hostile
biography of Reid after deciding he had
erred in thinking that the New York Tribune
had been campaigning against him in late
1881; moreover, the Tribune had printed a
long, enthusiastic review by Howells of The
Prince and the Pauper on October 25, 1881.
MT's hostility toward Reid would not have
cooled if he had known that the editorial
decision to print the Howells review was
made independently by John Hay, despite a
letter from Reid expressing disapproval on
the ground that "it isn't good journalism
to let a warm personal friend & in some
matters literary partner, write a review of
him in a paper wh. [sic] has good reason
to think little of his delicacy and highly
of his greed." Abstract in AES, IV (1960),
2610; reprinted in Twainian, XXI (January-
February, 1962).

B61 MOSER, CHARLES A. "A Nihilist's Career:
S. M. Kravchinskij," American Slavic and
East European Review, XX (February), 56-71.
    Contains a brief reference to MT's sup-
port for an appeal expressing sympathy with
the cause of a Russian revolution
(pp. 68-69).

B62 MUELLER, HAROLD L. "Mark Twain's Stormfield
Days" [title appears as "The Stormfield-
Redding Library" on p. 1], Twainian, XX
(March-April), 3-4.
    On MT's pleasure in the Redding, Connec-
ticut home where he passed his last years,
and the part he played in founding a town
library. As the Mark Twain Library, the
institution now houses a rich collection of
portraits and memorabilia. "Among the
2,000-odd books that Twain gave are hundreds
that are autographed. Some are distinguished with marginal markings and notations, underlinings, exclamation points,
question marks, and pages turned-down at
the corners. In some are bits of tobacco
spilled from the pipe he smoked as he read
them at Stormfield or elsewhere." Abstract
in AES, VII (1964), 1572.

B63 PARSONS, COLEMAN O. "Mark Twain in Australia,"
Antioch Review, XXI (Winter), 455-68.
    Traces the itinerary of MT's lecture tour
from September 16, 1895-January 4, 1896,
and quotes speeches and interviews (without
dates) in which MT commented in general
terms on his works, criticized prohibition
and Bret Harte, and praised Australia for
having the modern conveniences. Abstract
in AES, VIII (1965), 602; reprinted in
Twainian, XXV (January-February, 1966).

B64 PICKETT, CALDER M. "Mark Twain as Journalist
and Literary Man: A Contrast," Journalism
Quarterly, XXXVIII (Winter), 59-66.

"A comparison of Samuel Clemens' Holy Land
letters for newspaper publication and The
Innocents Abroad shows a transition from
journalist to literary writer, and recognition of his larger and differing audience"
(headnote). Shows a number of the changes
made, and notes that IA reveals not only
more restraint, but also an increase in the
amount and the sophistication of the humor.

B65 PIZER, DONALD. "Late Nineteenth-Century Real-
ism: An Essay in Definition," Nineteenth-
Century Fiction, XVI (December), 263-69.
    The realism discussed is diverse in sub-
ject matter and "ethically idealistic.
Three texts will illustrate my thesis:
Howells' The Rise of Silas Lapham (1885),
Twain's Adventures of Huckleberry Finn
(1884), and James's What Maisie Knew (1897)."
In the first two books "the social world is
the embodiment of evil," and the latter two
"juxtapose a child and an evil world....
The three writers...dramatize a vision of
experience in which individuals achieve that
which is still a goal for mankind at large."
Abstract in AES, V (1962), 815.

B66 POCHMANN, HENRY A. [Review: Caroline Thomas
Harnsberger, Mark Twain: Family Man (1960).]
American Literature, XXXIII (March), 86-87.
    The 20,000 words of previously unpublished
material will give this book "a place of
modest importance among students of Mark
Twain," but "the documentation is inadequate"
and "the author's too feminine and domestic
point of view" is irritating. Because MT's
daughter Clara was a prime source of information she tends to become a major concern
of the book, but her "reminiscences...are
germane and of prime importance. Herein lies
the book's essential worth."

B67 _____. [Review: Arlin Turner, Mark Twain and
George W. Cable: The Record of a Literary
Friendship (1960).] American Literature,
XXXIII (May), 233-34.
    Turner's editing of these MT-Cable letters
"is faultless. The interchapters and notes,
supplying relevant facts and continuity,
make an interesting and complete chapter in
the lives of both men" and commentary on the
audience.

B68 POLI, BERNARD. [Review: Blair, Mark Twain &
Huck Finn (1960) and Rogers, Mark Twain's
Burlesque Patterns (1960).] Étude Anglaises,
XIV (April-June), 175-76.
    Blair's is a basic book for the special-
ist, written with the inflexible objectivity of the historian; but, although we
doubtless know MT better after this "gi-
gantesque autopsie d'un chef-d'oeuvre," we
may not always be sufficiently aware of
the distance Huck always kept between himself and "Mr. Mark Twain." The "excellent
study of literary technique" by Franklin
Rogers might nonetheless take more note of
the part improvisation and fantasy played
in MT's art. [In French.]

B69 POWER, WILLIAM. "Huck Finn's Father," University of Kansas City Review, XXVIII (Winter), 83-94.

"Mark Twain minimizes, even conceals, the force of Huck's animus against his father," who "is responsible for Huck's moral development"; "Huck's strength, finally, is Finn's." Abstract in AES, V (1962), 446; reprinted in Twainian, XXII (January-February, 1963).

B70 REYES, PEDRO A., JR. "A Difference of Grammar," Diliman Review (University of the Philippines, Quezon City), IX (January), 117-23.

Comparing HF with Joyce's A Portrait of the Artist as a Young Man, finds "the statement of revolt in different grammars," with Huck's "WE" contrasted to Stephen's inward-turning "I."

B71 RUBIN, LOUIS D., JR., and JOHN REES MOORE, eds. The Idea of an American Novel. New York: Thomas Y. Crowell Company.

Passim on MT (indexed); on pp. 258-72, reprints statements on him by Howells, Sherwood Anderson, Van Wyck Brooks, Henry Nash Smith, and Lionel Trilling; these are extracts from material generally available in the original publications (listed in the present bibliography), and for this reason they are not here cross-referenced.

B72 SALOMON, ROGER R. "Escape from History: Mark Twain's Joan of Arc," Philological Quarterly, XL (January), 77-90.

Like others of the eighteenth and nineteenth centuries, MT substituted faith in history for faith in God, but what he saw of man and "the oligarchic and imperialistic drift of America" made his "a tenuous faith--tormented by a dream of freedom and innocence outside the grip of time." For this reason, A Connecticut Yankee is "ultimately an artistic failure because of its ambivalence," and "Joan of Arc can be most fruitfully examined as a final, desperate attempt to establish values apart from the futile treadmill of sin and suffering which was the life of man on earth." Although MT took essentially a Catholic view of Joan, he wrote "a deeply pessimistic book. If it is an affirmation of the existence and power of innocence, it is also a scathing record of its betrayal." Abstract in AES, IV (1961), 1944; reprinted in Twainian, XXI (January-February, 1962).

B73 SCHULMAN, IVAN A. "José Martí and Mark Twain: A Study of Literary Sponsorship," Symposium: A Quarterly Journal in Modern Literatures, XV (Summer), 105-13.

The Cuban poet of the modernista period "first popularized the literary productions of Samuel L. Clemens throughout the Spanish-speaking world. There is even evidence to believe that Martí may have been the first

to disseminate the popular humorist's name in Spanish literary circles." He admired MT as stylist and satirist, and praised a number of his books, among them A Connecticut Yankee, which he compared to Don Quixote. In a footnote (p. 112, n. 5) Schulman reports that "Our investigations failed to uncover a single study on Twain by outstanding Spanish American writers who might conceivably have been acquainted with his work, either because they lived in the United States for a period of time or because they were familiar with our culture and literature" during this period. Schulman lists a few articles on MT, including one by the poet Rubén Darío, who commented on the limited awareness of MT in the Spanish-speaking world. Abstract in AES, V (1962), 2144; reprinted in Twainian, XXII (January-February, 1963).

B74 SCOTT, WINFIELD TOWNLEY. "Mark Twain Revisited," New York Times Book Review (December 3), p. 48.

A review of Lewis Leary, ed., Mark Twain's Letters to Mary (the letters are of minor importance, but "Leary has surrounded them with a knowledgeable account of the last of Mark Twain's decades") and Albert E. Stone, Jr.'s The Innocent Eye: Childhood in Mark Twain's Imagination ("a model of what such academic work should be...its subject is of genuine importance, it is analyzed with great intelligence," Stone has done extensive research, "and--Heaven be praised--he writes well").

B75 SMITH, HENRY NASH. "The Backwoods Bull in the Boston China Shop," American Heritage, XII (August), 32-33, 108-12.

A popular account of MT's disastrous Whittier Birthday Dinner speech of December 17, 1877; illustrated with a full-page color reproduction of the Carroll Beckwith portrait of MT, now in the Hartford house. The text of MT's speech introducing Winston Churchill to an audience at the Waldorf Astoria, December 12, 1900 is printed for the first time.

B76 _____. "Mark Twain on Tour," New York Herald Tribune Book Review, XXXVII (April 23), 32.

A review of Charles Neider, ed., The Travels of Mark Twain. "Given the inexorable limitations of space, the selections are sensible enough."

B77 _____. "Mr. Clemens to 'Niece,'" New York Herald Tribune Book Review, XXXVII (May 21), 27.

A review of Lewis Leary, ed., Mark Twain's Letters to Mary. "The letters to Mary Rogers hold little interest for the student of his literary career. But the biographical interest is high."

B78   STEWART, PAUL R. [Review: Kenneth S. Lynn, ed., "Huckleberry Finn": Text, Sources, and Criticism]. College English, XXIII (October), 70.
      A brief, harsh notice: there is little justification for the book, and "the collateral materials are too thin and spotty."

B79   STONE, ALBERT E., JR. "Mark Twain and the Story of the Hornet," Yale University Library Gazette, XXXV (April), 141-57.
      While traveling in the Sandwich Islands as a correspondent for the Sacramento Union, MT had the opportunity to interview the survivors of the clipper ship Hornet, which had burned at sea; he later rewrote the story for Harper's, and in 1899 published the account and described his own involvement in "My Debut as a Literary Person." In the writing he drew on the journals of the ship's captain, and accounts by two passengers, Samuel and Henry Ferguson. These journals, privately printed, have been given to the Yale Library, together with correspondence, including four unpublished letters from MT. Ferguson criticized MT for not having allowed him to edit the journal material before it appeared in Harper's: "What was published did do harm, I am informed, to one man of the party & caused great grief to another," and he asked that names be changed or deleted before the account was given the permanence of publication in a book.

B80   TANNER, TONY. "The Literary Children of James and Clemens," Nineteenth-Century Fiction, XVI (December), 205-18.
      MT used a boy, a first-person vernacular narrator, whose own bewilderedness produced moral clarity, but James used girls as protagonists, maintained his omniscience and ironic detachment, and "worked out a literary style...as far removed from the vernacular as possible"; there is "an increasing moral ambiguity in his work." James found innocence endearing, but to be outgrown, while MT "saw no dividend in the exchange of innocence for maturity." Abstract in AES, V (1962), 810; reprinted in Twainian, XXII (January-February, 1963).

B81   ____. "The Lost America--the Despair of Henry Adams and Mark Twain," Modern Age, V (Summer), 299-310.
      Their growing move toward despair "argues concurrence rather than coincidence.... this despair is in a slow process of incubation from their earliest work, and...it is finally hatched by the growing discords, conflicts, and problems of the age. It is not a despair of personal bereavement but of country--ultimately of man." Abstract in AES, IV (1961), 2387. Article reprinted in Smith (1963), pp. 159-74.

B82   ____. [Review: Charles Neider, ed., The Autobiography of Mark Twain (1960).] Critical Quarterly, III (Autumn), 284-85.
      Contains an appreciation of MT and concludes by thanking Neider "for bringing this work to the attention of the general reader in a form which will attract him," but criticizing "Neider's scissors and paste method which has wrenched the material into a pseudo-chronological sequence it was never intended to have in the first place."

B83   WALDRON, ELI. "Mark Twain: The World He Left Behind. Hannibal, Missouri Keeps the Great Writer's Reputation Alive, in Ways both Lovable and Weird," Holiday, XXX (July), 54-55, 72-75, 97-99.
      A popular account of a visit to Hannibal, Missouri; provides no new information, but is enlivened by sketches by Ronald Searle, two depicting MT.

B84   WALLACE, ROBERT D. "Mark Twain on the Great Lakes," Inland Seas, XVII (Fall), 181-86.
      On MT's lecturing in 1895 in Cleveland, Sault St. Marie, Mackinac, Petosky, and Duluth; documented from contemporary newspapers and Major J. B. Pond's Eccentricities of Genius (1900.B33). Abstract in AES, IX (1966), 792; reprinted in Twainian, XXVI (January-February, 1967).

B85   WARREN, LUCIAN C. "Mark Twain on the Income Tax," New York Times Magazine Section, (April 9), pp. 16, 69.
      A brief headnote on the history of the income tax, as introduction to a reprinting of MT's "A Mysterious Visit" from Sketches New and Old.

B86   WHITE, WILLIAM. "Mark Twain to the President of Indiana University," American Literature, XXXII (January), 460-63.
      Contains the text of a letter from William L. Bryan, asking whether a loved and admired author may "somehow sense the innumerable friendships which he has made?" MT's reply ("Mar 29/07," apparently not mailed) follows, speaking of the comfort of receiving such letters in his lonely old age. Abstract in AES, IV (1961), 710; reprinted in Twainian, XXI (January-February, 1962).

B87   *WIRZBERGER, KARL-HEINZ. [Review: Henry Nash Smith and William M. Gibson, eds., Mark Twain-Howells Letters (1960.] Zeitschrift für Anglistik und Amerikanistik, IX, 431-33.
      [Source: MHRA Annual Bibliography (1961), No. 4729.]

B88   WOUK, HERMAN. "Huck Finn Pumped Vigor into American Literature," Twainian, XX (November-December), 4; XXI (January-February, 1962), 4.

1961 - Shorter Writings

(WOUK, HERMAN)
Described by Chester Davis as "written as a special feature for the Associated Press. It appeared in the 'Sacramento Union,' issue of August 5, 1956." A general discussion, noting MT's chaotic structure and underlying strength. Abstract in AES, VII (1964), 1578.

1962 A BOOKS

A1   BLAIR, WALTER, ed. Selected Shorter Writings of Mark Twain. Boston: Houghton Mifflin Company (Riverside Editions.)
A comprehensive anthology, from the early writings to The Man that Corrupted Hadleyburg and The Mysterious Stranger. Blair's introduction is a substantial treatment of MT's literary career, the forces that shaped it, and the style and perspective he developed.

A2   BRADLEY, SCULLEY, RICHMOND CROOM BEATTY, and E. HUDSON LONG, eds. Samuel Langhorne Clemens, Adventures of Huckleberry Finn. An Annotated Text   Backgrounds and Sources. Essays in Criticism. New York: W. W. Norton & Company, Inc. (also copyrighted 1961).
A classroom casebook, with text of HF (including the "Raft Passage" from LOM), plus significant background and source material and excerpts from MT's autobiography, the Paine biography, etc. Also contains a valuable set of reprinted critical essays from periodicals and excerpted from books, all of which are listed in the present bibliography with cross-references to the reprinting here. The bibliography of primary and secondary material at the end is intelligently selective (it does not contain material not listed in the present bibliography).

A3   BUDD, LOUIS J. Mark Twain, Social Philosopher. Bloomington: Indiana University Press.
Approaches MT's social attitudes through his habit of taking interest in topical matters and personalities; emerges with view of him as essentially allied in politics with the business community and, more broadly, with nineteenth-century Liberalism and its commitment to rationalism and the doctrine of progress though he could sincerely appeal to romantic democracy; reviewers handled the book respectfully though several held it understated his ambivalences and his sympathies for the underdog.

A4   CLEMENS, CYRIL. Mark Twain and John F. Kennedy. Kirkwood, Missouri: Mark Twain Journal.
Consists of several letters from John F. Kennedy as Senator and later as President, thanking Cyril Clemens for honorary membership in the International Mark Twain Society, a complimentary life subscription to the Mark Twain Journal, and the gift of

Mark Twain and Dwight D. Eisenhower. There are also tributes to MT by Kennedy, Eisenhower, William Howard Taft, Herbert Hoover, and Harry S. Truman (previously published, for the most part). [4-page pamphlet.]

A5   CLEMENS, SAMUEL L. The Adventures of Tom Sawyer. Boston: Houghton Mifflin Company (Riverside Literature Series).
Includes a scholarly introduction by Walter Blair well directed toward younger readers, and stimulating "Suggestions for Reading and Discussion" by Frank Townsend.

A6   _____. Letters from the Earth, ed. Bernard DeVoto, with a Preface by Henry Nash Smith. New York and Evanston: Harper & Row, Publishers.
Consists of a section of writings on Biblical themes and a section of shorter pieces and The Great Dark. This book was edited by DeVoto in 1939, but MT's daughter Clara witheld permission to publish it until recently.

A7   COVICI, PASCAL, JR. Mark Twain's Humor: The Image of a World. Dallas: Southern Methodist University Press.
"My concern is primarily with the use of humor in what Twain wrote.... That Twain's attempts to perform a multiple function through his humor did not always succeed will be obvious to the reader: 'One can deliver a satire with telling force through the insidious medium of a travesty,' Twain warned, 'if he is careful not to overwhelm the satire with the extraneous interest of the travesty.' Twain's attacks on the spirit of his times are often obscured by his delight in 'travesty.'" This book is an attempt to "show what Twain was attempting, to suggest its importance, and to re-examine a few of his works in the light of the artistry organized and given meaning by the humor" (Preface, p. ix).

A8   GRANT, DOUGLAS. Mark Twain. Edinburgh, Scotland: Oliver and Bond, Ltd. and New York: Grove Press, Inc.
A good introduction for the general reader. The portion on IA is reprinted in Schmitter (1974), pp. 71-76.

A9   HILL, HAMLIN, and WALTER BLAIR, eds. The Art of Huckleberry Finn: Text, Sources, Criticisms. San Francisco: The Chandler Publishing Company.
The text is a facsimile of the first edition, and the biographical and literary source material includes excerpts from writings by Dixon Wecter, John Marshall Clemens, (MT's father), William Wright, Charles Dickens, Thomas Carlyle, Julia A. Moore, Johnston J. Hooper, Richard M. Johnston, and W. E. H. Lecky; the criticism is less extensive, consisting of the 1885 Brander Matthews review, Lionel Trilling's introduction to the 1948 Rinehart edition, and 1955 articles by

(HILL, HAMLIN, and WALTER BLAIR, eds.)
William Van O'Connor and Frank Baldanza
(these criticisms are listed in the present
bibliography, but are not cross-referenced
to this collection, and the source materials are not listed). There is also useful
classroom material on the writing of HF,
with suggestions for use of sources and
criticisms, and a short bibliography; this
is an excellent teaching text.

A10 LEARY, LEWIS. A Casebook on Mark Twain's
Wound. New York: Thomas Y. Crowell Company
A collection of critical essays from periodicals and excerpted from books, tracing
the Brooks-DeVoto controversy and the response of other critics. These essays and
excerpts are listed in the present bibliography, with cross-references to the reprintings here. Leary opens with a summary of
the debate in an essay, "Standing with Reluctant Feet," pp. 3-32; reprinted in his
Southern Excursions: Essays on Mark Twain
and Others (1971), pp. 42-74.

A11 LETTIS, RICHARD, ROBERT F. McDONNELL, and
WILLIAM E. MORRIS. Huck Finn and His Critics. New York: The Macmillan Company.
A casebook for students, consisting of
the text of HF (including the "Raftsmen
Passage" published in LOM), a generous assortment of critical articles from periodicals and excerpted from books (all of
which are cross-referenced in the present
bibliography, with the exception of a brief
passage from the Paine biography). Includes
questions for students, topics and suggestions for research, "Notes on the Critics,"
and a bibliography which lists a number of
studies of J. D. Salinger's The Catcher in
the Rye but nothing on MT not listed in
the present bibliography.

A12 McNEER, MAY. America's Mark Twain. Boston:
Houghton Mifflin Company.
A juvenile biography, apparently based on
Paine and on MT's works. "Previews" of
his works appear in the order of composition
as an encouragement to young readers, and
there are attractive illustrations by Lynd
Ward (1953 winner of the Caldecott Award for
The Biggest Bear) which reflect an intelligent familiarity with the times and with
existing photographs.

A13 SCHOLES, JAMES B. (ed. by Walter Harding).
Samuel L. Clemens "The Adventures of Huckleberry Finn." A Study Guide. Bound Brook,
New Jersey: Shelley Publishing Company.
This is similar to the guides currently
on the market, but differs from others in
asking the student to do more of the work
of interpretation for himself.

A14 SIOUI, TAK. "Huckleberry Finn": More Mole-
cules. N.p.: privately printed. [Copyright
by John Hakac.]
Attributes the mutilation of the illustration on p. 283 of the first ed. of Huckleberry Finn to E. W. Kemble, the illustrator.
Two states of the offending engraving are reproduced, with the portrayal of Uncle Silas
(saying, "Who do you reckon it is?") made
more clearly indecent after a first altera-
tion which could have been considered innocent. It is also argued that the illustration on p. 290 ("A Pretty Long Blessing") is
also indecent: "If one is hesitant about deciding on the artist's intention, he should
try blotting out the false leg-line in the
table cloth with a finger in order to simpli-
fy the view" (p. 25). MLA Bibliography (1964)
No. 6286, gives place as Tucson, Arizona.

A15 SMITH, HENRY NASH. Mark Twain: The Development
of a Writer. Cambridge, Massachusetts: The
Belknap Press of Harvard University Press.
"This book considers first the problems of
style and structure Mark Twain faced at the
outset of his career, and then traces his
handling of these problems in nine of his
principal works [TS, HF, CY, IA, LOM, Hadleyburg, MS, PW, RI]. Since questions of
technique necessarily involve questions of
meaning, I have dealt also with his ethical
ideas. The inquiry leads ultimately to the
consideration of how his writing reveals a
conflict between the dominant culture of
his day and an emergent attitude associated
with the vernacular language of the native
American humorists." The concluding chapter
previously appeared in Massachusetts Review
(1962.B68). The chapter titled "A Sound
Heart and a Deformed Conscience" is reprinted, more or less completely, in Smith (1963),
pp. 83-100; Simpson (1968), pp. 71-81;
Gerber (1971), pp. 43-67; Kesterson (1973),
pp. 82-86. The section on TS is reprinted
in Schmitter (1974), pp. 85-94.

A16 SMITH, JANET, ed. and introduction. Mark
Twain on the Damned Human Race. Preface by
Maxwell Geismar. New York: Hill and Wang.
A popular anthology excerpted from MT's
published writing on such topics as war,
race, imperialism, national vanity, and
religion. A good introduction to MT as satirist and advocate.

1962 B SHORTER WRITINGS

B1 ANON. "Digest of Mark Twain Items Published
Elsewhere," Twainian, XXI (January-February),
1-3.
A reprinting of abstracts from Abstracts
of English Studies, IV (1961). The reprinting is accurate, except for the omission
(in this one year) of the AES abstract numbers, but a number of abstracts (including
those involving Mark Twain Journal) are silently omitted.

1962 - Shorter Writings

B2   ANON. "Double Bill," <u>Times Literary Supplement</u>, May 18, p. 358.
      A short review of Guy A. Cardwell's <u>Twins of Genius</u>, which provides little new information. The MT-George Washington Cable letters of 1881-1906 "are not many in number or particularly interesting, as Twain's correspondence goes, but Mr. Cardwell manages to compensate for their weakness by his ample introduction and commentary."

B3   ANON. [Brief Review: Harold Beaver, ed., <u>Life on the Mississippi</u>. London: Oxford University Press; World's Classics Series.] <u>Times Literary Supplement</u>, October 5, p. 782.
      Praises Beaver's introduction to <u>LOM</u>, "one of Mark Twain's most important books" despite its dull parts.

B4   ANON. [Review: Bernard DeVoto, ed., <u>Letters from the Earth</u>.] <u>Time</u>, LXXX (September 21), 91.
      Descriptive, emphasizing MT's despair as here revealed.

B5   ANON. [Review: Charles Neider, ed., <u>Mark Twain: Life as I Find It</u> (1961).] <u>Missouri Historical Review</u>, LVII (October), 116-17.
      "Charles Neider is a well-known authority on Mark Twain," and in collecting the sketches (of varying quality) in this volume he "has done a service to those who appreciate the literary efforts of Mark Twain whatever his mood."

B6   ASHMEAD, JOHN. "A Possible Hannibal Source for Mark Twain's Dauphin," <u>American Literature</u>, XXXIV (March), 105-107.
      Reprints "A Visit from Our Bourbon" from the Hannibal <u>Journal</u> for May 12, 1853; this hard-drinking pretender visiting a newspaper office may explain why MT's notes describe the Duke and Dauphin in <u>HF</u> as "printers." Abstract in <u>AES</u>, VI (1963), 1957; reprinted in <u>Twainian</u>, XXIII (March-April, 1964), 3.

B7   ASPIZ, HAROLD. "Lecky's Influence on Mark Twain," <u>Science & Society</u>, XXVI (Winter), 15-25.
      In writing <u>CY</u>, MT used William E. H. Lecky's <u>History of European Morals from Augustus to Charlemagne</u> (1869) for three purposes: "as a source, conscious or otherwise, of characters, incidents, and bits of 'local color'"; for the novel's unifying "theme of training and of those dedicated souls who attempt to raise the level of humanity and the mass of men unwilling to think for themselves. Finally, Mark Twain translated the thematic concepts developed with Lecky's help into the fictional framework of the novel," thus achieving "a well-defined theme and a large measure of artistic unity." Abstract in <u>AES</u>, XII (1969), 1328; reprinted in <u>Twainian</u>, XXIX (January-February, 1970).

B8   BABCOCK, C. MERTON. "Mark Twain and the Freedom to Tell a Lie," <u>Texas Quarterly</u>, V (Autumn), 155-60.
      On MT's interest in the lie--in the unconscious lie, and in the willful lie as a topic and as a literary device. Abstract in <u>AES</u>, VI (1963), 1906; reprinted in <u>Twainian</u>, XXIII (March-April, 1964).

B9   BAKER, CARLOS. "Two Rivers: Mark Twain and Hemingway," <u>Mark Twain Journal</u>, XI (Summer), 2.
      Shows similarities in descriptions of rivers by Huck (Chapter XIX) and by Frederick Henry in <u>A Farewell to Arms</u> (Chapter XXXI); many more such parallels could be drawn, though not as evidence of direct influence; the two writers share a directness and appearance of simplicity. Abstract in <u>AES</u>, VIII (1965), 1052.

B10   BLAIR, WALTER. [Review: Albert E. Stone, Jr., <u>The Innocent Eye: Childhood in Mark Twain's Imagination</u> (1961).] <u>American Literature</u>, XXXIV (May), 296-97.
      Stone provides valuable background in American writing about children as he defines MT's achievements, and "he is particularly enlightening when he relates Twain's concept of youthful innocence to portrayals of the protagonists in <u>Huckleberry Finn</u> and <u>Joan of Arc</u>." His discussions of <u>Huck Finn and Tom Sawyer among the Indians</u>, <u>Tom Sawyer's Conspiracy</u>, and the Hannibal version of <u>MS</u> "add important biographical data and round out Mr. Stone's valuable survey."

B11   BROOKS, ROGER L. "A Second Possible Source for Mark Twain's 'The Aged Pilot Man,'" <u>Revue de Littérature Comparée</u>, XXXVI (July-September), 451-53.
      Although MT said in <u>Roughing It</u> that the poem was probably suggested by an old song, 'The Raging Canal,' it more closely resembles Coleridge's <u>The Rime of the Ancient Mariner</u> in language and structure, and "there are over thirty similarities" in rhymes. [In English]. Abstract in <u>AES</u>, VIII (1965), 1189.

B12   BROWN, DEMING. <u>Soviet Attitudes toward American Writing</u>. Princeton, N.J.: Princeton University Press.
      This is a general study in which most of the references to MT are in lists of American authors long popular with Russian readers. There is an account of more interest describing Communist reaction when <u>HF</u> was removed from New York City schools in 1958, after Negro protests. Clearly, said <u>Inostrannaya Literatura</u>, in this day of Little Rock and McCarthy MT was removed because he fought for racial equality (p. 197). Yel. Romanovna was even more misled in describing the Mark Twain Society, which had long operated "under the aegis of Truman, Churchill, and DeGaulle"--and now there were plans for an affiliate of the society in Western Germany, with a membership of 50,000! (p. 165).

B13   BROWNELL, GEORGE HIRAM. "Shrine Builders," Twainian, XXI (May-June), 3-4.
    Text of a letter (June 21, 1931) to Willard S. Morse and apparently also intended for Franklin J. Meine and Merle Johnson, concerning bibliography of material by and about MT (title apparently provided by Chester L. Davis).

B14   BRUMM, URSULA. [Review: Roger B. Salomon, Twain and the Image of History (1961).] Archiv für das Studium der neuren Sprachen und Literaturen, CXCIX, 197-98.
    Surveys the scholarship on the topic, noting that Salomon is one of Henry Nash Smith's students. "Das schmale Buch von Roger B. Salomon ist insofern ein Ereignis, als hier zum erstenmal konsequent und mit weiter gestecktem Blickfeld die Ungereimtheiten, Brüch und Widersprüche in Mark Twains Werk nicht primär psychologisch sondern geistesgeschichtlich durchleuchtet werden."

B15   BUDD, LOUIS J. [Review: Roger B. Salomon, Twain and the Image of History (1961) and Albert E. Stone, Jr., The Innocent Eye: Childhood in Mark Twain's Imagination (1961).] South Atlantic Quarterly, LXI (Winter), 109-10.
    Both books "trace a theme or value that doubled as a narrative device in Mark Twain's writing. Stone exaggerates the technique and intellectual depth in TS, "achieves an original analysis of both the sources and the emotional patterns behind The Prince and the Pauper," makes JA more interesting than MT did, and "superbly lights up the nightmare world of The Mysterious Stranger." Salomon's book is "first-rate" on broad perspective, very good on P&P and JA, but less helpful on GA and CY.

B16   BURHANS, CLINTON S., JR. "The Sober Affirmation of Mark Twain's Hadleyburg," American Literature, XXXIV (November), 375-84.
    Affirmation of a virtue tested by temptation "places Twain within a great and positive tradition." Abstract in AES, VI (1963), 1972, reprinted in Twainian, XXIII (March-April, 1964), 3-4.

B17   CADY, EDWIN H. "Howells and Twain: The World in Midwestern Eyes," Ball State Teachers College Forum, III (Winter), 3-8.
    The two were alike in their Ohio and Missouri backgrounds and outlooks. "The realism and penetration of Twain and Howells sprang from their sense of strangeness, of isolation, of cultural relativity between the middle West and the otherwise civilized world. That coincidence of view was a source of strength and renewal in their friendship as it was of significance in their work." Abstract in AES, VI (1963), 2404; reprinted in Twainian, XXIII (March-April, 1964).

B18   CAMBON, GLAUCO. "Mark Twain and Charlie Chaplin as Heroes of Popular Culture," Minnesota Review, III (Fall), 77-82.
    Both dramatized "the tramp as mythical figure.... And, certainly, both Twain's and Chaplin's late productions are attempts to get behind their respective mythical masks, to converse with them, to explain or reform them...whatever the results." Both maintained their artistic standards while reaching "the largest audience an artist can get," but "our two pilgrims' progress from humor to disenchantment and horror is similar, and testifies to their basically naive thinking." Abstract in AES, IX (1966), 1739; reprinted in Twainian, XXVI (January-February, 1967).

B19   CLEMENS, CYRIL. "Mark Twain's Impressions of the Play 'Palmyra,'" Hobbies--The Magazine for Collectors, LXVII (August), 124.
    Reprints from "an old newspaper that I recently came across" MT's praise of Adolph Wilbrandt's play, The Master of Palmyra.

B20   COFFEE, JESSIE A. "Mark Twain's Use of 'Hain't' in Huckleberry Finn," American Speech, XXXVII (October), 234-36.
    The form ain't, used 305 times, commonly represents the present am not, is not, and are not; the form hain't is used 74 times, where the word have or has is indicated, as in the present perfect, or in the expression he has not got.

B21   *COHEN, HENNIG. "Mark Twain's Sut Lovingood," in Ben Harris McClary, ed. The Lovingood Papers, 1962 (Athens, Tenn.: The Sut Society; 1962.) [1st vol. of an annual.]
    [Source: MLA Bibliography (1962), No. 5199.]

B22   CROWE, CHARLES. "Mark Twain's Huckleberry Finn and the American Journey," Archiv für das Studium der neuren Sprachen und Literaturen, CXCIX, 145-58.
    Summarizes critical views of the book; argues that it must be recognized as "a great comic novel and a boy's tale," with Huck as "the single authentic American folk hero and...the voyage down the river as a mythic representation of the fundamental national experience." Abstract in AES, VIII (1965), 2804; reprinted in Twainian, XXV (January-February, 1966).

B23   CUMMINGS, SHERWOOD. "Mark Twain's Acceptance of Science," Centennial Review, VI (Spring), 245-61.
    MT read Darwin and often treated science favorably, using its findings to attack religion, but he also played several roles as detractor of science, as "Swiftian satirist" and "common sense 'common man,'" and "twice he wrote in a white heat of moral indignation against what he thought were abominations and frauds of science" (in "A Dog's Tale" and in a letter to Twichell, condemning physicians and surgeons as "shams and humbugs"). Abstract in AES, VI (1963), 240; reprinted in Twainian, XXIII (January-February, 1964).

1962 - Shorter Writings

B24 [DAVIS, CHESTER L.]. "Foundation Receives Gift from Julian and Helene Sprague Foundation. Shrine Builders Brownell, Ade, Cities of Denver and Elmira," Twainian, XXI (March-April), 1-4.

Publishes correspondence of George Hiram Brownell and Anna B. Morse, 1935-1938 concerning the Willard S. Morse Collection; the MT material went to the library at Elmira, New York. Abstract in AES, VIII (1965), 1843; reprinted in Twainian, XXV (January-February, 1966). The following issue of Twainian begins with a correction: the Morse collection went to Yale, not to the Elmira library.

B24A *DEVOTO, BERNARD. "Introduction to Mark Twain," in Literature in America: An Anthology of Literary Criticism, selected and introduced by Philip Rahv. New York: World Publishing Company. Copyright 1957.

[Source: Cited by D. E. S. Maxwell (1965), p. 219; full title and facts of publication are from LC-NUC Author Lists, 1942-1962.]

B25 EBY, E. H. "Mark Twain's Testament," Modern Language Quarterly, XXIII (September), 254-62.

In MS, only the "presumed final chapter" creates the solecism and places the story in a dream-frame; in other respects the story is implicitly and explicitly "a testament to man's imagination as a creator." Satan personifies the artist, and "can free man from the bonds of necessity"; man may be saved through imagination. Abstract in AES, VII (1964), 850.

B26 _____. [Review: Henry Nash Smith and William M. Gibson, eds., Mark Twain-Howells Letters.] Modern Language Quarterly, XXIII (March), 90-91.

Well edited, "a valuable reference work for almost any study of Howells or Mark Twain" in the organization of data, but "the letters themselves are disappointing.... One can see that the most meaningful exchanges came not in their letters but in their face-to-face talks."

B27 EDEL, LEON. Henry James: The Conquest of London, 1870-1883. London: Rupert Hart-Davis, p. 186.

James in 1875 "had clearly been reading Mark Twain's Mississippi installments in the Atlantic, for he on one occasion observes that 'in the day of Mark Twain there may be no harm in being reminded that the absence of drollery may, at a stretch, be compensated by the presence of sublimity.'"

B28 ESS, KARL. "Shooting Pool with Mark Twain. Billiards Was More than a Game to the Great Humorist--It Was the Obsession of His Later Years," Sports Illustrated, XVI (February 26), 57-58.

Presents no new information, but blends such sources as Paine, Willie Hoppe, and Katy Leary to produce a readable and accurate popular account.

B29 FATOUT, PAUL. "Mark Twain's Nom de Plume," American Literature, XXXIV (March), 1-7.

According to western newspapers, the "Mark Twain" pseudonym was derived from Clemens's custom of chalking up drinks in local saloons. Abstract in AES, VI (1963), 1947; reprinted in Twainian, XXIII (March-April, 1964), 3; article reprinted (without footnotes) in Twainian, XXV (September-October, 1966), 2-4; also (with footnotes) in Kaplan (1967), 161-68.

B30 FEINSTEIN, HERBERT. "Mark Twain & the Pirates," Harvard Law School Bulletin, XIII (April), 6-18.

Reprinted as "Mark Twain and the Copyright Pirates," Twainian, XXI (May-June), 1-3; (July-August), 1-4; (September-October), 1-4; (November-December), 3-4. On MT's extensive litigation to prevent unauthorized publication of his works, use of his name with the works of others, and re-sale in stores of his works sold by subscription; also treats his efforts to promote more favorable copyright legislation and to prolong copyright of his collected works by leaving material in manuscript to be released over a period of years. Abstract in AES, VIII (1965), 1844-1847, reprinted in Twainian, XXV (January-February, 1966); not noted in the abstracts are details of MT's resentment of John Wanamaker's actions in sales of his subscription books, but later kind words in connection with reform in the Congo. Contains quotations from Philadelphia Press (May 15, August 4, 1886), Philadelphia Times (July 28, August 3, 1886), New York Herald (November 12, 1905).

B31 FRANTZ, RAY W., JR. "Sam Clemens's Belt," Twainian, XXI (July-August), 1.

The picture of Sam Clemens at age fifteen in Wecter's Sam Clemens of Hannibal and, more recently, in Meltzer's Mark Twain Himself shows what appears to be a belt-buckle; closer inspection reveals a compositor's stick with "SAM" in type.

B32 GANZEL, DEWEY. "Samuel Clemens and Captain Marryat," Anglia (Tübingen), LXXX, No. 4, 405-16.

MT used Marryat's A Diary in America in LOM; moreover, his descriptions in HF of a camp meeting and the moral cowardice condemned by Colonel Sherburn also suggest Marryat's influence. Abstract in AES, VIII (1965), 942.

B33 _____. "Twain, Travel Books, and Life on the Mississippi," American Literature, XXXIV (March), 40-55.

(GANZEL, DEWEY)

On MT's extensive use of earlier travelers' accounts for information, direct quotation, and for indirect use (here shown through parallel passages). Significantly, MT's apparent use in HF of notes taken in 1882 for LOM supports DeVoto's dating of the composition of parts of HF later than the 1880 date given by Blair. Abstract in AES, VI (1963), 1950; reprinted in Twainian, XXIII (March-April, 1964), 3.

B34 GELB, ARTHUR. "Witheld Work by Twain is Due," New York Times (August 24), p. 23.

On the forthcoming publication of MT's Letters from the Earth (ed. Bernard DeVoto). Describes attempts by Charles Neider to obtain permission from MT's daughter Clara to publish five chapters by MT on religion in his edition of the Autobiography; permission was finally granted, although "two magazines have already rejected the chapters as being 'too inflammatory.'" [They eventually appeared both in Hudson Review (1963.B64) and in Letters from the Earth (1962.A6).]

B35 GERBER, JOHN C. "Mark Twain's Use of the Comic Pose," Publications of the Modern Language Association, LXXVII (June), 297-304.

"Mark Twain" is not a consistent persona employed by Samuel Clemens: the pseudonym is not used with consistency. The point of view taken may be MT's own, a pose, or an alternation between the two. The pose was aesthetically useful, though seldom used "to give a work tonal and structural unity"; it was personally useful to Clemens "because its restricted point of view simplified life and made it more tolerable." Abstract in AES, VIII (1965), 2336; reprinted in Twainian, XXV (January-February, 1966). Article reprinted in Scott (1967), pp. 271-85.

B36 HIGGINS, WILLIAM. "I Try to Do It Another Way and Am Sorry," Ball State Teachers College Forum, III (Winter), 13-14.

In the manner of Chapter XIV of HF, a dialogue in which Huck tries to explain symbolism, myth, and structure in the book to Jim, but fails in the attempt: "I never saw a nigger so down on critics. Anyway, maybe Jim was right and they are all like that fellow Percrusty Aunt Polly told me about.... But making a book over is harder than the first time, so I guess I won't tackle it."

B37 HILL, HAMLIN. "Eschol Sellers from Uncharted Space: A Footnote to The Gilded Age," American Literature, XXXIV (March), 107-113.

Publishes correspondence of Charles Dudley Warner with one George Escol Sellers (with whom he was acquainted through a friend) on use of his name in GA; the facts given here refute three incorrect versions

related by MT. Abstract in AES, VI (1963), 1958; reprinted in Twainian, XXIII (March-April, 1964), 3.

B38 _____. "Mark Twain's Quarrels with Elisha Bliss," American Literature, XXXIII (January), 442-56.

"The purpose of this study is to reconstruct the most serious altercations between Bliss and Twain...to show that Twain's statements about Bliss in Mark Twain in Eruption were surprisingly accurate, and to estimate ...Twain's actual loss on his American Publishing Company books." Subscription publication was profitable, both to Bliss and to MT, but Bliss misrepresented costs, as when he concealed the fact that he used the same (or slightly modified) engravings for MT's and other books he published. There are also details of the involvement of Bliss and MT's brother Orion in the short-lived journal, The American Publisher. Abstract in AES, V (1962), 1838; reprinted in Twainian, XXII (January-February, 1963).

B39 HINER, JAMES. [Review: Charles Neider, Mark Twain and the Russians (1960).] American Quarterly, XIV (Summer), 217.

This series of letters between Neider and Y. Bereznitsky of the Literary Gazette about Neider's edition of The Autobiography of Mark Twain now has an added introduction "reviewing the facts of the exchange and justifying the present publication." The debate is ideological, with Neider taking a somewhat dogmatically liberal stand, and "the editors of the Literary Gazette were correct in punctuating the exchange when they did."

B40 HOLMES, CHARLES S. "A Connecticut Yankee in King Arthur's Court: Mark Twain's Fable of Uncertainty," South Atlantic Quarterly, LXI (Autumn), 462-72.

"Ultimately destructive of all value," the book expresses MT's "deep contraditions in his feelings about his own career, about American culture, and, finally, about life itself." Hank Morgan's character is ambiguous, and the dream-framework of the book undercuts the values of both the earlier time and the bustling nineteenth century. Abstract in AES, VI (1963), 658; reprinted in Twainian, XXIII (January-February, 1964).

B41 HOLTZMAN, FILIA. "A Mission that Failed: Gor'kij in America," Slavic and East European Journal, VI (Fall), 227-35.

On the 1906 visit of Gorki to the United States to raise money for the Bolshevik Party; he spoke at the "A Club," and a photograph of Gorki seated beside MT is preserved. Unfortunately, a newspaper released the news that the woman traveling with him was not his legal wife, and MT, Howells, and others withdrew their support.

1962 - Shorter Writings

B42   JONES, HOWARD MUMFORD. "The Other Face of the Humorist," New York Times Book Review (September 23), pp. 7, 53.
A review of Letters from the Earth (ed. DeVoto) as "the most impressive contribution to books by Mark Twain since The Mysterious Stranger of 1916, the imaginative grandeur of which it shares."

B42A   KAZIN, ALFRED. "Almost Perfect," Library Journal, LXXXVII (November 15), 4243-45 (also numbered as Children's Section, 23-25).
Although HF deteriorates in the horseplay of the last chapters, the ending is a way of returning the action to TS, where it began. Modern critics are more conscious of such blemishes than was MT, who did not necessarily notice--or care: HF "is the product of a mind whose lapses were virtually necessary to his imaginative strength. For he had above all to feel easy to write at all, and if he had had to check himself every time he was in danger of displeasing the unnaturally severe taste of our time he wouldn't have found himself in the unexpected depths of Huckleberry Finn." Abstract in AES, XVII (1973-1974), 853; reprinted in Twainian, XXXIV (March-April, 1975).

B43   LORCH, FRED W. [Review: Paul Fatout, Mark Twain on the Lecture Circuit (1960).] American Literature, XXXIII (January), 540-541.
The chronological organization of the book is at the expense of "comprehensive, unified discussion" of MT's platform art, his theory of lecturing and reading, and significant criticism; comments on these matters are scattered and hard to find, and source references are inadequate. Fatout writes vigorously, "with here and there a tendency toward exaggeration for the sake of effect," and he "is no inordinate admirer of Mark Twain." [Note: Lorch had already published a number of articles on MT as a lecturer, and in 1968 published his own book on the subject, The Trouble Begins at Eight--T.A.T.]

B44   LYNN, KENNETH S. [Review: Henry Nash Smith and William M. Gibson, eds., Mark Twain-Howells Letters (1961).] New England Quarterly, XXXV (March), 110-11.
"The most spectacular exhibition afforded by these volumes is that of Mark Twain blowing his top," but we also see "how Mark Twain's feeling for the American language gradually has become a literary style. In this epochal development--from the colloquial flair of the early stories to the vernacular perfection of Huckleberry Finn to the breakdown of narrative tone in A Connecticut Yankee--Twain was enormously aided by the advice and encouragement of Howells." The editing is superb, both in accuracy and in thoroughness, dating letters, identifying references, and the notes are "often capsule essays which set Twain's friendship with Howells in the broader perspective of his total career."

B45   McALEER, JOHN J. "Noble Innocence in Huckleberry Finn," Ball State Teachers College Forum, III (Winter), 9-12.
On the use of nakedness to reveal both innocence and a gross exploitation of it, taking examples from MT, Sherwood Anderson, Hemingway, and Swift; also shows parallels between Anderson and MT in depicting the destructive power of the machine. Abstract in AES, VI (1963), 2405; reprinted in Twainian, XXIII (March-April, 1964).

B46   MACKANESS, GEORGE. "Mark Twain's Visit to Australia," American Book Collector, XII (May), 6-10.
A popular account of MT's 1895 visit, quoting his reactions to what he saw (but only vaguely documented); also quotes anecdotes in an article [title not given] by Roy Chase in Australian National Review, May, 1939. Illustrations: photo of MT and facsimiles of title pages of first Australian editions of IA and Jumping Frog books. Abstract in AES, V (1962), 1399; reprinted in Twainian, XXII (January-February, 1963).

B47   McKEITHAN, D. M. [Review: Frank Baldanza, Mark Twain: An Introduction and Interpretation (1961).] American Literature, XXXIV (November), 424-25.
Largely descriptive; questions some of Baldanza's interpretations but notes his familiarity with his subject and enthusiastic writing, "and his study is interesting and at times quite stimulating."

B48   MESERVE, WALTER J. [Review: Roger B. Salomon, Twain and the Image of History (1961) and Albert E. Stone, Jr., The Innocent Eye: Childhood in Mark Twain's Imagination (1961).] American Quarterly, XIV (Spring), 100-101.
An uncritical summary of the two books.

B49   MILLGATE, MICHAEL. [Review: Franklin R. Rogers, ed., The Pattern for Mark Twain's Roughing It" (1961).] Modern Language Review, LVII (January), 147.
"The intrinsic interest of the letters is not great," but the commentary is useful and the "effect of the volume is...to reinforce the work of other recent critics who have increasingly challenged the view, particularly associated with the late Bernard DeVoto, that Twain, far from being a craftsman, was essentially a natural and instinctive writer."

B50   MILNE, W. GORDON. [Brief review: Roger B. Salomon, Twain and the Image of History (1961).] Books Abroad, XXXVI (Winter), 76-77.
"Carefully balanced...perceptive."

B51 MONTEIRO, GEORGE. "Publication of Mark Twain in Canada," American Notes and Queries, I (October), 20-21.

To the list of unauthorized publications of MT's works may be added translations of his sketches, "Running for Governor" and "About Barbers," which appeared in L'Opinion Publique, Montreal, as "Une Candidature" (October 20, 1881) and "Les Barbiers" (January 26, 1882). Abstract in AES, VI (1963), 2002; reprinted in Twainian, XXIII (March-April, 1964).

B52 *MORIOKA, SAKAE. "Huckleberry Finn and A Farewell to Arms." Kyusha American Literature, No. 5 (April), pp. 27-35.

[Source: MHRA Annual Bibliography (1962), No. 5689.]

B53 * ___. "Pudd'nhead Wilson and the Racial Problem," Studies in English Language and Literature (Kyushu University), No. 12, pp. 1-11.

[Source: MHRA Annual Bibliography (1962), No. 5688.]

B54 MUNFORD, HOWARD. [Review: Roger B. Salomon, Twain and the Image of History (1961).] Mississippi Valley Historical Review, XLIX (September), 360-61.

"In this reworking of a dissertation done under Henry Nash Smith, the student does credit to his mentor." Salomon shows how MT came to anticipate twentieth-century thinking as a result of the conflict between his inherited assumptions and his intuitive sense of American life; Salomon's failure to consider scientific thinking of the age is not a defect, because the subject has been treated elsewhere.

B55 MURADIAN, THADDEUS. "Huckleberry Finn: an Approach to Literature in the High School," The Independent School Bulletin (National Association of Independent Schools, Boston). Series of 62-63 (November), pp. 6-9.

On the successful teaching of HF, the questions raised, and the ways of discussing it in relation to other books. Considers the question of censorship at some length. "This article won the 1961-62 prize for the best article in a specific subject field."

B56 *NARAIN, S. K. "Mark Twain: A Consideration of His Realism," Literary Criterion (Mysore, India), V, 66-71.

[Source: MHRA Annual Bibliography (1963), No. 4737.]

B57 *OBA, HIROYOSHI. "An Essay on Mark Twain," Kamereon, No. 5 (August), pp. 50-63.

[Source: Leary (1970), p. 71.]

B58 O'CONNOR, WILLIAM VAN. "Huckleberry Finn and the Great American Novel," in his The Grotesque: An American Genre (Carbondale: Southern Illinois University Press), pp. 109-18.

This appears to be essentially the same text as appears in O'Connor's "Why Huckleberry Finn Is Not the Great American Novel" (1955; reprinted in Bradley, 1962).

B59 *OKAMOTO, KATSUMI. "The Tragedy of Mark Twain, the Man and Artist," Geibun (Kinki University), III (August), 1-32.

[Source: Leary (1970), p. 71.]

B60 PARSONS, COLEMAN O. "Mark Twain in New Zealand," South Atlantic Quarterly, LXI (Winter), 51-76.

On the 38 days MT spent there in November-December, 1895, his itinerary, his lectures, and his reception; abundantly documented from the New Zealand press. Abstract in AES, V (1962), 1156; reprinted in Twainian, XXII (January-February, 1963).

B61 POCHMANN, HENRY A. [Review: Karl-Heinz Schönfelder, Mark Twain: Leben, Persönlichkeit und Werk (1961).] American Literature, XXXIII (January), 541-42.

In four times the length of one of the University of Minnesota Pamphlets, this East German booklet does half as well: there are significant inaccuracies, and MT's attacks on capitalism are overemphasized, everything he said taken "with heavy-handed seriousness."

B62 *POIRIER, RICHARD. "Huckleberry Finn: Attitudes Toward Tricks and Adventure," Exercise Exchange, X (November), 23-34.

[Source: Beebe and Feaster (1968), p. 119.]

B63 ___. "Mark Twain, Jane Austen, and the Imagination of Society," in Reuben A. Brower and Richard Poirier, eds., In Defence of Reading: A Reader's Approach to Literary Criticism (New York: E. P. Dutton & Co., Inc.), pp. 282-309.

Criticisms of Jane Austen by Emerson, Henry James, and MT "reveal a significantly American dissatisfaction with the novel of manners." MT's fantasy in PW and MS moves "toward a saturnalia of repudiation," but HF, "more complicated than anything in James before The Bostonians," has MT's "affection for a character whose longings are a curious and inseparable blend of Isabel Archer's dream of 'freedom' with some of Mark Twain's own nostalgic desire for community." [According to Leo Marx's "Selected Bibliography" in the Bobbs-Merrill ed. of HF, this article was revised as Chapter IV of Poirier's A World Elsewhere: The Place of Style in American Literature (1966).]

B64 POMMER, HENRY F. "Mark Twain's 'Commissioner of the United States,'" American Literature, XXXIV (November), 385-92.

Pommer describes William Gibson, M.D., the original of this character, as "a pompous windbag" and publishes some of Gibson's scientific correspondence and MT's descriptions

1962 - Shorter Writings

(POMMER, HENRY F.)
of him in letters to show why his satire took the form it did. Abstract in AES, VI (1963), 1973 (item number incorrectly given as 1873 in the volume index); reprinted in Twainian, XXIII (March-April, 1964), 4.

B65 *RICE, JACK. [Article on MT's Letters from The Earth and his marginal notations in W. E. H. Lecky's History of European Morals, with passing comment on Chester L. Davis and the Twainian.] St. Louis Post-Dispatch, October 14.
[Source: Reprinted in Twainian, XXI (November-December), 1-3.]

B66 *ROBERTS, THOMAS. "Huckleberry Finn: Understanding Comic Devices," Exercise Exchange, X (November), 22-23.
[Source: Beebe and Feaster (1968), p. 120.]

B66A ROSS, JOHN F. [Review: Salomon, Twain and the Image of History; Stone, The Innocent Eye (both 1961).] Nineteenth-Century Fiction, XVI (March), 366-69.
Salomon provides "a valuable account" of what history meant to MT, but may overestimate his later disillusionment with it. Ross praises CY, questions whether structure or unity of tone are essential, and criticizes Stone's view that it is a falling-off after HF and his picture of Hank Morgan.

B67 SCOTT, ARTHUR L. "'Review of Holiday Literature,'" College English, XXIII (February), 385-87.
A spoof under this title in the Buffalo Express of Christmas Eve, 1870, signed "Carl Byng" (here reprinted) may be by MT; it anticipates the New Criticism "with its detailed textual analysis, its admiration for subtlety, imagination, audacity, ambiguity, conceits, and allegory." Also comments on MT's sending twenty dollars to Walt Whitman, but no evidence of familiarity with his work. Abstract in AES, V (1962), 2577.

B68 SMITH, HENRY NASH. "Pudd'nhead Wilson and After," Massachusetts Review, III (Winter), 233-53.
"This essay is the last chapter of a book to be called Mark Twain the Writer: A Study in Method and Meaning [Mark Twain: The Development of a Writer], to be published in the autumn of 1962." Abstract in AES, V (1962), 2300; reprinted in Twainian, XXII (January-February, 1963).

B69 STARTSEV, A. "Problema Pozdnego Tvena [The Problem of the Later Twain]," Voprosy Literatury, VI:11 (November), 138-59.
In the pessimism of his late years MT mistook the defects of American society for universal attributes of the human condition. Abstract in AES, VI (1963), 1207; reprinted in Twainian, XXIII (January-February, 1964).

B70 TANNER, TONY. "Samuel Clemens and the Progress of a Stylistic Rebel," Bulletin of the British Association for American Studies, n.s., No. 3 (December, 1961), pp. 31-42.
On MT's vernacular style, used successfully in HF, but not in TS Abroad and TS Detective, where his use of Huck as narrator "never escapes the trivial because the naive vernacular style is not being applied to anything calculated to call its deepest ironic potentialities into play."

B71 _____. [Review: Henry Nash Smith, Mark Twain: The Development of a Writer, and Bernard DeVoto, ed., Letters from the Earth.] Critical Quarterly, IV (Winter), 380-83.
With "an extensive knowledge of nineteenth-century American culture as well as an unparalleled intimacy with Twain's work," Smith has confronted questions of the relation of language and style to vision. There is a "really masterly chapter on Innocents Abroad," and "Smith's book is indispensable and will remain so for a long while." In Letters from the Earth "there is nothing childish in a man agonising over the sufferings of mankind. This is not great literature, but it is a remarkable example of the anguished turbulence of the late nineteenth-century mind--crucified on a childhood of Calvinism and an adulthood of Darwinism, collapsing under the weight of a Determinism which argued either an atrociously cruel God or a terrifyingly meaningless universe."

B72 THORP, WILLARD. "A Bittersweet Treasury of Posthumous Twain," New York Herald Tribune Book Review, XXXIX (September 30), 4, 15.
A review of Letters from the Earth, ed. Bernard DeVoto: a description, with commentary, of the selections.

B73 VAN WHY, JOSEPH S. "Nook Farm," The Stowe, Beecher, Hooker, Seymour, Day Foundation Bulletin for 1962, I, i-iii, 1-36.
On MT's Hartford neighborhood and neighbors, with map and key (pp. ii-iii), table of "Nook Farm Residents and their Relationships" (p. 34), and photographs of MT's and other houses (pp. 35-36). Includes the text of MT's humorous sketch, "Fearful Calamity in Forest St.," which first appeared as a letter to the editor of the Hartford Courant (March 31, 1871; not previously reprinted).

B74 WELSH, DONALD H. "Sam Clemens' Hannibal: 1836-1838 [sic]," Midcontinent American Studies Journal, III (Spring), 28-43.
On the town as described by local newspapers, 1846-1848 [sic]; describes business activity, public health, patent-medicine advertising, problems with vice and dogs, and resentment over the presence of free Negroes. This town, "which in some ways demonstrated its Southern heritage and in others seemed to be a child of New England," gave MT "many

(WELSH, DONALD H.)
impressions from which he drew in later
years." Abstract in AES, VI (1963), 345;
reprinted in Twainian, XXIII (January-
February, 1964).

B75 *ZAPULLA, GIUSEPPE. "Gli Inediti di Mark
Twain," La Fiera Letteraria, XVII (October
14).
[Source: Leary (1970), p. 77.]

1963 A BOOKS

A1 CAMP, JAMES E., and X. J. KENNEDY. Mark
Twain's Frontier: A Textbook of Primary
Source Materials for Student Research and
Writing. New York: Holt, Rinehart and
Winston, Inc.
A generous selection from MT's writings
about Nevada, together with "Memoirs and
Tales by Twain's Contemporaries," selec-
tions from Brooks and DeVoto, a brief bib-
liography, and suggested topics for short
and long papers.

A2 CARDWELL, GUY A. Discussions of Mark Twain.
Boston: D. C. Heath and Company.
A collection of critical essays, from
periodicals and excerpted from books; all
are cross-referenced in the present bibliography.

A3 DUSKIS, HENRY, ed. The Forgotten Writings of
Mark Twain. New York: Philosophical Library; paperbound edition by The Citadel
Press. London: Peter Owen.
Reprinted material from the Buffalo Express 1869-71, signed by MT or attributed
to him by Duskis. Unfortunately, this material consists of excerpts rather than
complete texts, dates are given vaguely or
not at all, and many of the attributions
to MT are questionable.

A4 ROGERS, FRANKLIN R., ed. and introduction.
Simon Wheeler, Detective. New York: The
New York Public Library.
Makes an interesting MT piece more ac-
cessible and provides background through a
lengthy introduction.

A5 SMITH, HENRY NASH, ed. Mark Twain: A Collection of Critical Essays. Englewood
Cliffs, New Jersey: Prentice-Hall, Inc.
Contains essays by critics over a period
of years, from periodicals and excerpted
from books, dealing broadly with MT's life
and several of his works; all of these essays are cross-referenced in the present
bibliography.

A6 *STARTSEV, A. Mark Tven i Amerika [Mark
Twain and America], Moskva: Sovietskii
Pisatel.
[Source: MHRA Annual Bibliography, 1963,
No. 4751, and review by A. Elistratova,
1963.B27.]

A7 STOUTENBURG, ADRIEN, and LAURA NELSON BAKER.
Dear, Dear Livy: The Story of Mark Twain's
Wife. New York: Charles Scribner's Sons.
Written as a story for the general reader,
drawing on primary sources for details.

A8 TAPER, BERNARD, ed. Mark Twain's San Francisco. New York, Toronto, London: McGraw-
Hill Book Company, Inc.
A collection of MT's writings which appeared in the Nevada and California papers,
1863-66. There are a good introduction and
introductory head-notes, both directed primarily toward the general reader. The introduction also appears in American Heritage 1963.B82 and Twainian 1963.B83.

A9 TUCKEY, JOHN S. Mark Twain and Little Satan:
The Writing of "The Mysterious Stranger."
West Lafayette, Indiana: Purdue University
Studies.
Establishes time of composition of several
versions from 1897 to 1908, with "the actual
order...very nearly the reverse of the one
that was assumed by DeVoto" (pp. 76-77); the
conflation of the different versions has
been a source of confusion to scholars. An
extensive portion of this book is reprinted
in Tuckey's Mark Twain's "The Mysterious
Stranger" and the Critics (1968),
pp. 127-54.

1963 B SHORTER WRITINGS

B1 ABEL, DARREL. "Mark Twain," in his Master-
works of American Realism: Twain, Howells,
James (vol. III in his American Literature).
Great Neck, New York: Barron's Educational
Series. Pp. 10-121.
A general work for school use, this consists primarily of biography and plot summaries; there is very little of critical
significance.

B2 *ANDERSSON, THOMAS. "Mark Twain's Views on
Politics, Religion and Morals," Moderna
Språk, LVII (September), 283-89.
[Source: MHRA Annual Bibliography (1963),
No. 4703; abstract in AES, VIII (1964),
1098.]

B3 ANON. "Articles Published Elsewhere During
Past Year," Twainian, XXII (January-February), 2-4.
Reprints a number of abstracts from Abstracts of English Studies, V (1962).

B4 ANON. "The Bear and Huckleberry Finn: Heroic
Quests for Moral Liberation," Mark Twain
Journal, XII (Spring), 12-13, 21.
Ike McCaslin and Huck lack parents and
find substitute fathers in older Negroes;
they undergo initiations in isolation, and
both novels end on an affirmative note:
"Both boys have transformed their knowledge
and ability into charity and humility, and
both are now guided by a moral vision."
Abstract in AES, VIII (1965), 1059.

B5   ANON. "Collections," Mark Twain Journal, XII
     (Spring), back cover.
       "As founder of the Mark Twain Society and
     Editor of the Mark Twain Journal since
     1936, Cyril Clemens has had occasion to
     correspond with literary figures of note.
     His correspondence has been acquired by the
     following libraries: George Santayana--
     Duke University Library, Durham, N.C.;
     John Cowper Powys--Northwestern University
     Library, Evanston, Ill.; George Bernard
     Shaw--University of North Carolina Library,
     Chapel Hill; Robert Frost--Boston Public
     Library; Edgar Lee Masters--Berg Collection,
     New York Public Library; Margaret Mitchell--
     University of Georgia Library, Athens;
     George Ade--University of Indiana Library,
     Bloomington; Wendell Willkie--University of
     Indiana Library, Bloomington; H. L. Menck-
     en--University of Pennsylvania Library,
     Philadelphia; James Branch Cabell-Universi-
     ty of Pennsylvania Library, Philadelphia;
     Sinclair Lewis--University of Minnesota
     Library, Minneapolis; Willa Cather--Willa
     Cather Memorial, Red Cloud, Nebraska; Ezra
     Pound--Hamilton College Library, Clinton,
     N.Y.; Arthur Machen--Houghton Library,
     Harvard University; Will and Wallace Irwin--
     Stanford University, California; Walter de
     la Mare--Gordon T. Banks, Esq., Boston;
     Albert Einstein--George T. Goodspeed, Esq.,
     Boston."

B6   ANON. "Missouri Boy," Times Literary Supple-
     ment, January 4, p. 5.
       A review of Douglas Grant's Mark Twain,
     praising the concise biography, good use of
     Charles Neider's edition of the Autobiogra-
     phy, and a course steered with "dexterity
     and fairness" between Brooks and DeVoto.

B7   AUSTIN, JAMES C. "Artemus Ward, Mark Twain,
     and the Limburger Cheese," Midcontinent
     American Studies Journal, IV (Fall), 70-73.
       MT's friend anticipated "The Invalid's
     Story" with an earlier tale of the odor of
     Limburger cheese in a baggage-car being
     mistaken for that of a corpse. The differ-
     ence between the two versions "illustrates
     brilliantly the difference between the
     Southwestern yarn and the Yankee anecdote,
     and it also shows Twain's manner of develop-
     ing a story." Abstract in AES, VII (1964),
     1416.

B8   BABCOCK, C. MERTON. "Mark Twain's Seven
     Lively Sins," Texas Quarterly, VI (Autumn),
     92-97.
       On MT's accounts of his stealing, gam-
     bling, laziness, smoking, drinking, swear-
     ing, and lying: "When one considers the
     consecration and devotion with which he
     pursued his lively vices, it is quite ap-
     parent that he had a 'damned good moral
     character.'" Abstract in AES, VIII (1965),
     2401; reprinted in Twainian, XXV (January-
     February, 1966).

B9   BAENDER, PAUL. "The 'Jumping Frog' as a Come-
     dian's First Virtue," Modern Philology, LX
     (February), 192-200.
       "The critical tradition has sometimes gone
     astray" concerning MT, as is the case when
     "The Jumping Frog" is used in portraying
     him as a frontiersman; the southwestern
     frame-story on which such interpretations
     are based was declining in popularity, and
     MT's intention is revealed in what he said
     ironically of an inept tragic actor who had
     "the first virtue of a comedian, which is
     to do funny things with grave decorum and
     without seeeming to know that they are fun-
     ny." Abstract in AES, VI (1963), 2512;
     reprinted in Twainian, XXIII (March-April,
     1964).

B10 BLAIR, WALTER. [Review: Roger B. Salomon,
     Twain and the Image of History (1961).]
     American Literature, XXXIV (January),
     578-80.
       "Mr. Salomon sees Clemens's faith in prog-
     ress foredoomed by disillusionment about
     human nature...wavering between a belief
     that progress was at best temporary and a
     belief that it was merely an illusion."
     Salomon's "over-all history of Twain's
     shifting ideas is accurate, sufficiently
     complex, and convincingly documented," and
     his insights are "both sensible and sensi-
     tive."

B11 BRINEGAR, CLAUDE S. "Mark Twain and the
     Quintus Curtius Snodgrass Letters: A Sta-
     tistical Test of Authorship," Journal of
     the American Statistical Association, LVIII
     (March), 85-96.
       Ten letters in the New Orleans Daily
     Crescent in 1861, often attributed to MT,
     have been interpreted as casting light on
     his service in the Civil War; "this study
     applies an old, though little used statis-
     tical test of authorship--a word-frequency
     test--to show that Twain almost certainly
     did not write these 10 letters." Reprinted
     in Twainian, XXIII (July-August, 1964),
     1-2; (September-October, 1964), 4. An un-
     signed headnote by Chester L. Davis notes
     "some necessary cutting...most of the text
     minus the charts, tables, graphs and foot-
     notes follows," but "for those who want the
     complete scientific story the original arti-
     cle should be consulted and studied." Ab-
     stract in AES (1965), 1855; reprinted in
     Twainian, XXV (January-February, 1966), 3.

B12 BUCCO, MARTIN. "Mark Twain to the Editor of
     the Columbia Missouri Herald," Missouri
     Historical Review, LVII (July), 398-99.
       Text of a letter to Walter Williams
     (March 4, 1894), declining what is apparent-
     ly an invitation to speak in Columbia.

B13 BUDD, LOUIS J. "Twain Could Mark the Beat,"
     Midcontinent American Studies Journal, IV
     (Spring), 39-44.

(BUDD, LOUIS J.)

Biographical accounts, letters, and passages in his works reveal that MT "found a deep release in dancing that comes only to the enthusiast, and never felt the need to justify it." Abstract in AES, VI (1963), 2490; reprinted in Twainian, XXIII (March-April, 1964).

B14 _____. [Review: Pascal Covici, Mark Twain's Humor: The Image of a World (1962).] American Literature, XXXIV (January), 581-82.

Covici is "better on Twain's artistry than ideas," and "the force of [his] book is cumulative. Its sum is greater than its parts, and it builds steadily toward a major insight."

B15 CARDWELL, GUY A. [Review: Louis J. Budd, Mark Twain: Social Philosopher (1962).] Nineteenth-Century Fiction, XVIII (September), 197-200.

"So far as large social matters are concerned, Budd's evidence makes incidentally plain that Mark Twain had a frowsy, superficial mind. He expressed muddled opinions on such matters as determinism, the capacities of the Negro, and social Darwinism." Compared to Philip S. Foner's Mark Twain: Social Critic (1958), Budd's book reflects a "more objective, better informed, and more critical" view, and familiarity with recent criticism, but the chapters often become chaotic because of various interests of MT's in the material under discussion. This is one of the better recent studies of MT, and will be valuable to future scholars.

B16 CARTER, PAUL J. [Review: Henry Nash Smith, Mark Twain: The Development of a Writer (1962).] American Literature, XXXV (May), 248-50.

Notes Smith's treatment of MT's efforts to develop "a consistent fictional persona which would allow him to evade the cult of gentility while defining his own role in society," and praises this "major contribution to scholarship," which "focuses attention upon style, upon the role of language in the writer's achievement."

B17 CHAPIN, HENRY B. "Twain's Pudd'nhead Wilson, Chapter VI," Explicator, XXI (April), Item 61.

"The Italian twins' reception in Dawson's Landing is...an essential element of the novel's exploration of the relativity of good and evil": the citizens readily submit to their spell but in turn the twins become the property of the widow Cooper and of Rowena. Abstract in AES, VI (1963), 2085; reprinted in Twainian, XXIII (March-April, 1964).

B18 _____. [Review: Charles Neider, ed., The Complete Essays of Mark Twain (1963).] New Mexico Quarterly, XXXIII (Winter), 474.

"Nieder [sic] has six books to his credit--all of them written by Twain. This one does not contain Twain's complete essays contrary to the title...it omits all essays not collected in Twain's lifetime and in that of his chief literary executor, Albert Bigelow Paine. Twain's papers have been ignored completely. Of the essays that have been included, the notes are scanty and erratic.... Some more-revealing notes begin 'Paine says ...' which is Nieder's [sic] way of borrowing not only the author's work but his editor's as well."

B19 CLEMENS, SAMUEL L. "A Twain Letter," Southwest Review, XLVIII (Autumn), 348.

Dated "Farmington Avenue, Hartford. Dec. 21," to Howells, explaining that he didn't invite Thomas Bailey Aldrich to stay with him because he thought he was living in town. The letter is reproduced in facsimile on the front cover; the original is in the Ferguson collection of the Bridwell Library, Southern Methodist University.

B20 COHEN, HENNIG. "Twain's Jumping Frog: Folktale to Literature to Folktale," Western Folklore, XXII (January), 17-18.

The story of a frog filled with shot was common in oral tradition and had appeared in newspapers several times before MT wrote his famous sketch. The account of a gamecock filled with rifle balls (here reprinted from the San Francisco Evening Bulletin of December 11, 1867, with credit to the Territorial Enterprise) conjectures that the trickster got his idea from MT, but the story may well have existed independently as a folk tale. Abstract in AES, VI (1963), 2674; reprinted in Twainian, XXIII (March-April, 1964).

B21 COX, JAMES M. "The Muse of Samuel Clemens," Massachusetts Review, V (Autumn), 127-41.

MT made his wife Olivia his editor, "defining the much deeper role her image played in his creative memory. She was, by virtue of his imagination, part of his identity as a man and as a writer." Abstract in AES, VIII (1965), 101; reprinted in Twainian, XXV (January-February, 1966).

B22 COYLE, WILLIAM. "Never the Twain," CEA Critic, XXVI (November), 1, 3.

On school adaptations of HF, some American and some British, which he saw on sale in Brazil when he was a Fulbright lecturer there. Simplified classics have their value to foreign students, but HF is a poor choice, with the language destroyed and with it the characterization. "Little remains but the plot, which some have defended but few have praised." Abstract in AES, XI (1968), 2794; reprinted in Twainian, XXVIII (March-April, 1968).

B23 [DAVIS, CHESTER L.] "Clara, a Great Person in Her Own Right," Twainian, XXII (January-February), 1-2.

On MT's daughter, who died November 19, 1962, and her assistance to the Mark Twain

1963 - Shorter Writings

([DAVIS, CHESTER L.])
Research Foundation, while declining to
act as censor; "The files, [sic] of your
Foundation, [sic] must necessarily be made
public solely in the manner and to the extent that your Secretary believes it in
the furtherance of scholarship relating to
the life and writings of Mark Twain. It
can now be said that at no time during the
past 20 years had Clara given to your foundation any substantial money to defray expenses of operation, she very early taking
the position that to do so during her lifetime would be improper." Quotes a letter
from Clara dated January 8, 1958, denying
"so palpably false an untruth as that described in the Utica Globe" (reprinted
as "Mark Twain's Courtship" in Twainian,
XVI, November-December, 1957, 4, 1957.B28).

B24   _____. "Edward H. House Correspondence.
'Prince and the Pauper' Dramatization,"
Twainian, XXII (March-April), 1-3; (May-
June), 2-4.
Letters by MT and others on a variety of
topics, including the participation of
House in a stage version of The Prince and
the Pauper. There is a letter from MT to
his sister Pamela touching this topic, and
other letters include one from M. E. (Mary
Elenor?) Clemens, concerning Pamela's ill-
ness in her later years. MT letters to
House concern The Prince and the Pauper,
Colonel Mulberry Sellers in Age, the publication of Grant's Memoirs, "An Imaginary
Conversation between Mr. & Mrs. Clemens"
(delightfully profane), the Paige type-setting machine, and the text of "S'klk!
G'lang!," a 25-line poem by MT "apparently
unpublished." Abstract in AES, VIII (1965),
1849, 1851; reprinted in Twainian, XXV
(January-February, 1966), 3.

B25   DUNNE, FINLEY PETER. "On Mark Twain," in his
Mr. Dooley Remembers, ed. Peter Dunne (Boston: Little, Brown and Company),
pp. 239-68.
Dunne's comments on MT in December, 1935,
praising him, recalling personal acquaintance, and recounting anecdotes. On p. 242,
tells of MT dining in London with Edwin Abbey and repeating his talk originally given
in Paris before the Stomach Club [text in
Playboy, 1974.B11]. Some time later, on Abbey's urging, MT repeated it before a larger
audience at a dinner given at the Lyceum by
Henry Irving; the response was one of general embarrassment. Also tells of the time
when "Henry James, the flawless, the sedate,
the impeccable Henry asked him, 'Do you know
Bret Harte?' 'Yes,' Mark replied readily,
'I know the son of a bitch.'" [Excerpts are
reprinted as "Mr. Dooley's Friends: Teddy
Roosevelt and Mark Twain," in Atlantic
Monthly, CCVII (September), 78-80, 88-99 and
abstracted in AES, X (1967), No. 1592; reprinted in Twainian, XXVII (January-February,
1968).]

B26   DURHAM, PHILIP. [Brief review: Pascal Covici, Mark Twain's Humor: the Image of a
World (1962).] Western Folklore, XXII
(July), 217.
"Such an ambitious project must lose direction at times and become thin on occasion, but the result is a fairly sensible
interpretation," much preferable to "those
recently coming from prominent academic
psychologists."

B27   ELISTRATOVA, A. "Mark Tven--Nepoiukhshii
Vulkan [Mark Twain--an Unextinguished Vol-
cano]," Voprosy Literatury, VII (August),
224-28.
A review of A. Startsev, Mark Tven i Amerika [Mark Twain and America]. Contemporary
American biographers describe MT's life as
a triumph of individualism in a land of
equal opportunity; this is "using the name
and fame of a great writer to promote American capitalism," in the opinion of A. Startsev, who tries to present the writer's life
as an American tragedy and stresses his passionate hostility toward capitalist America.
[In Russian.]

B28   *FAIRLEY, BARKER. "Raabe and Mark Twain: A
Point of Contact," Jahrbuch der Raabe-
Gesellschaft, nv: 76-77.
[Source: Leary (1970), p. 63.]

B29   FEUCHTWANGER, LION. The House of Desdemona;
or, the Laurels and Limitations of Historical Fiction, Detroit: Wayne State University Press. On MT and his historical fiction
(CY, GA, HF, Hadleyburg, MS, JA, P&P),
pp. 97-108.
"The greatest of American poets, Samuel
Langhorne Clemens...is scarcely less bitter
at heart than Herman Melville. But for most
of his life he bound his bitterness up in
his breast." He is a romantic, moved by
human suffering, but a good reporter and
"thoroughly and completely honest."

B30   FITZGERALD, F. SCOTT. The Letters of F. Scott
Fitzgerald, ed. Andrew Turnbull. New York:
Charles Scribner's Sons.
On p. 593, acknowledges his debt to "the
great central parts of Huckleberry Finn" in
a letter to Morton Kroll (August 9, 1939).

B31   GALE, ROBERT L. "The Prince and the Pauper
and King Lear," Mark Twain Journal, XII
(Spring), 14-17.
MT read widely in preparation for writing
P&P; among his sources may have been Shake-
speare, whom he had occasionally mentioned.
Several parallels to Lear are noted, includ-
ing speeches on mercy by the boy-king and by
Lear. Abstract in AES, VIII (1961), 1060.

B32   GERBER, JOHN C. "Mark Twain," in James Wood-
ress, ed., American Literary Scholarship:
An Annual/1963 (Durham, North Carolina:
Duke University Press, 1965), pp. 53-63.

(GERBER, JOHN C.)

The first of what has become an annual survey of MT scholarship (and as the first, covering some material earlier than 1963). Contents: "i. Texts and Editions"; "ii. Biography"; "iii. Criticism." Although Gerber does not list everything written about MT in 1963, he provides extremely valuable brief descriptions and frank estimates of a number of items he lists. [Contents have not been cross-checked for this and succeeding years, but most of the material appears also to be incorporated in the present bibliography. The chief value of Gerber's survey lies in the annotations, which are important individually and for placing many items within a broader context of Mark Twain scholarship; the survey may also prove useful as an independent check of published material, and, in case of error, on facts of publication. This has been responsible and thoughtful work from the first, and, if anything, has shown a steady growth in sophistication with passing years. It was the work of John Gerber through the coverage for 1968 (published in 1970), and since then it has been the very able work of Hamlin Hill; both are known MT scholars and familiar with trends in their field of study.]

B33   GIBSON, WILLIAM M. [Review: Louis J. Budd, Mark Twain: Social Philosopher (1962).] American Literature, XXXV (May), 250-51.

"Adds much new evidence for the understanding of Clemens's social commitments and political forays." "If the tenor of Mr. Budd's book occasionally seems restrictively modern, the analysis...is new and authentic."

B34   GILENSON, BORIS. "Mark Twain--An Accuser," Soviet Literature, XII, 152-56.

Surveys Russian editions and criticisms of MT, who is very popular in Russia. Principal emphasis is on Abel Startsev's Mark Twain and America, which emphasizes the relation of the writer and his society, and is supported by new data made available in recent years. Also observes that Van Wyck Brooks's The Ordeal of Mark Twain, "despite its obviously mistaken, Freudian treatment of Mark Twain as an individual, presented the fruitful thesis of the hostility of American society to the full creative development of the writer." Abstract in AES, VII (1964), 1523.

B35   GIPSON, LAWRENCE H. "Reminiscences of a Rhodes Scholar at Oxford in the Edwardian Era," The American Oxonian, L (April), 64-72.

On pp. 70-72, describes MT receiving his Oxford degree in 1907 and his solemn disregard of the friendly comments by students in the galleries.

B36   GREEN, MARTIN. "Twain and Whitman: the Problem of 'American' Literature," in his Re-Appraisals: Some Commonsense Readings in American Literature (London: Hugh Evelyn).

Considers MT as an entertainer and Huckleberry Finn "a charming children's book, with some beautiful passages," but not a major novel (pp. 142-43). However, "in ways that transcend the limits of humour, Twain was a fine lyric poet, a master of spoken language in print, and a beautiful ironist. The first two talents are best exemplified in Huckleberry Finn, but the third becomes major in A Connecticut Yankee; and this book represents Twain's true achievement perhaps better than the more famous one.... The important part of the book is the friendly, uncritical but lively irony it directs at the Yankee himself and what he stands for."

B37   GRUNDY, J. OWEN. "R. L. S. in Greenwich Village," Bulletin of the New York Public Library, LXVII (March), 152-54.

When Stevenson came to America in 1887 he and MT "spent several restful hours together" in Washington Square Park; a watercolor of them by Luis Mora, National Arts Club, 15 Gramercy Park is reproduced in black-and-white, facing p. 154. Abstract in AES, VI (1963), 1567; reprinted in Twainian, XXIII (January-February, 1964).

B38   GUIDO, JOHN FOOTE. "King Leopold's Soliloquy," Papers of the Bibliographical Society of America, LVII (Third Quarter), 351-52.

The Bibliography of American Literature (II, No. 3485) describes a copy in the New York Public Library as intermediate between the first two issues of the first edition. "I have recently come upon what is apparently another intermediate in the Cornell University Library. This copy is identical to that described in the BAL, with the exception that page 32 is in the early state, that is, consistent with the first, second, and third issues of the first published edition." Abstract in AES, VII (1964), 197; reprinted in Twainian, XXIV (January-February, 1965).

B39   HANSEN, CHADWICK. "The Character of Jim and the Ending of Huckleberry Finn," Massachusetts Review, V (Autumn), 45-66.

Jim was Huck's "moral burden," in that "by his constant presence, and his constant decency, and his constant humanity he forces Huck to do something more than drift with the river. He forces Huck to come to grips with that part of himself which belongs to society"; in the ending Huck and Jim both allow themselves to be drawn into Tom's romantic schemes, but not without reservations. The closing sentences represent "for Huck an emotional, if not an intellectual rejection of civilization," and an escape both for Huck and for Jim. Abstract in AES, VIII (1965), 100; reprinted in Twainian, XXV (January-February, 1966).

1963 - Shorter Writings

B40 *HAYASHI, TETSUMARO. "Mark Twain's The Adventures of Huckleberry Finn: Hope for Mankind," Lumina, No. 3 (1960).
     [Source: Kamei, Shunsuke, "Mark Twain in
Japan," Mark Twain Journal, XII (Spring,
1963), 20.]

B41 HAYS, JOHN Q. "Twainiana: Two Studies of
Mark Twain's Art," Southwest Review, XLVIII
(Summer), iv-v, 296-300.
     A review article on Pascal Covici, Mark
Twain's Humor: The Image of a World and
Henry Nash Smith, Mark Twain: The Develop-
ment of a Writer. The approach is chiefly
descriptive, summarizing and comparing the
intentions and conclusions in the two books.

B42 *HIETSCH, OTTO. "Mark Twain and Johann
Strauss," Jahrbuch für Amerikastudien,
VIII, 210-11.
     A letter from MT to Strauss's widow in
the Vienna City Library shows that MT visit-
ed him May 26, 1899. [Source: MHRA Annual
Bibliography (1963), No. 4723, and abstract
in AES, VIII (1965), No. 1397, reprinted in
Twainian, XXV (January-February, 1966).]

B43 HILL, HAMLIN. "Mark Twain: Audience and
Artistry," American Quarterly, XV (Spring),
25-40.
     On the influence of subscription publica-
tion on MT's writing, and particularly on
his padding, sensationalsim, and moralizing.
Abstract in AES, VI (1963), 1552; reprinted
in Twainian, XXIII (January-February, 1964).
Article reprinted in Scott (1967),
pp. 286-302. Reprinted without footnotes as
"The Business and Social Influence of The
Subscription Book," Twainian, XXII (May-
June).

B44 HOFSTADTER, RICHARD. Anti-Intellectualism in
American Life. New York: Alfred A. Knopf,
pp. 241-44.
     Van Wyck Brooks is right to consider MT's
enthusiasm for machinery over-done, but MT
"was too much a moralist and a pessimist to
imagine that mechanical progress was an all-
sufficient end." Even in CY, MT recognized
Hank Morgan's limitations. With other Americans, MT ambivalently shared "a robust
faith in the patent office and the future"
and a regard for genteel Eastern culture.

B45 HUNTER, JIM. "Mark Twain and the Boy-Book
in 19th-Century America," College English,
XXIV (March), 430-38.
     This genre consists of works "composed
about children for the amusement of adults,"
but MT's writing overlaps with the genre of
children's tales. "The moral impulse in
Twain's books is toward maturity," but he
remained "intensely nostalgic for his own
childhood."

B46 JACOBS, ROBERT D. [Review: Louis J. Budd,
Mark Twain: Social Philosopher (1962).]
Journal of Southern History, XXIX (August),
410-12.
     Praises the examination of neglected ma-
terial to demonstrate that MT never became
a liberal democrat.

B47 KAMEI, SHUNSUKE. "Mark Twain in Japan," Mark
Twain Journal, XII (Spring), 10-11, 20.
     On MT's reputation in Japan, and transla-
tions of his works. His reputation as a
funny man, and the Japanese emphasis on
British culture and lack of a frontier tradition have reduced his literary influence,
despite his wide popularity. Cites Masajiro
Hamada's Mark Twain: His Character and
Works (1955) as the only "notable book on
Mark Twain" he knows, "and of recent works
on Twain I can cite only two articles:
Tetsumaro Hayashi's 'Mark Twain's The Adventures of Huckleberry Finn: Hope for Mankind' in Lumina No. 3 (1960) and Shunsuke
Kamei's 'On Interpretations of The Adventures
of Huckleberry Finn' in Comparative Literature and Comparative Culture (1961)." Abstract in AES, VIII (1965), 1058.

B48 KANELLAKOU, CHRIS. "Mark Twain and the Chinese," Mark Twain Journal, XII (Spring),
7-9, 20.
     Chiefly on his reaction to mistreatment of
the Chinese in the West, and his respect for
their honest, orderly conduct. Abstract in
AES, VIII (1965), 1057.

B49 KAUFFMANN, STANLEY. "Mark Twain from Under
Ground," New Republic, CXLVIII (April 6),
20-22. A review of Bernard DeVoto, ed.,
Letters from the Earth (1962).
     The fact that MT did not publish freely in
his own time shows that he "was an artistic
genius but morally an average man," although
"he told as much truth as any American writer of his generation, more than most." Abstract in AES, VII (1964), 2726; reprinted
in Twainian, XXIV (January-February, 1965).

B50 KAUL, A. N. "Huckleberry Finn: A Southwestern Statement," in his The American Vision:
Actual and Ideal Society in Nineteenth-Century American Fiction. New Haven and London: Yale University Press, pp. 280-304.
     On the community of the raft.

B51 *KLOTZ, GÜNTHER. [Review: Bernard DeVoto, ed.,
Letters from the Earth (1962).] Zeitschrift
für Anglistik und Amerikanistik, XI (July),
281-87.
     [Source: Abstract in AES, IX (1966), 342;
reprinted in Twainian, XXVI (January-February, 1967).]

B52   LEARY, LOUIS. "On Diminishing Mark Twain," Virginia Quarterly Review, XXXIX (Spring), 334-39.

A review-article covering Janet Smith's Mark Twain on the Damned Human Race (with remarks by MT which "can be as arresting today as they must have been fifty years ago"); DeVoto's Letters from the Earth ("much of Mark Twain's fulmination is dull indeed"); Budd's Mark Twain: Social Philosopher ("a hard-headed, informed, and reliable study," showing, in Budd's words that despite MT's "outrageous irony and his impulses toward nonconformity he was usually, at heart, in tune with his times"); and Henry Nash Smith's "carefully wrought Mark Twain: The Development of a Writer, which goes over much of the same ground, but draws less generously on topical writings." The collections of MT's later writings will give pleasure, but they diminish MT by diverting attention from a great artist to an ordinary thinker.

B53   LITTLE, GAIL B. "Three Novels for Comparative Study in the Twelfth Grade," English Journal, LII (October), 501-505.

On examining narrative technique, the three protagonists, and literary achievement in HF, The Catcher in the Rye, and Intruder in the Dust.

B54   LONG, E. HUDSON. "Mark Twain's Ordeal in Retrospect," Southwest Review, XLVIII (Autumn), 338-48.

Brooks undertook his study in order to show that MT was defeated by his environment, but more recent studies vitiate many of his arguments. MT's pessimism may best be explained, not as a consequence of an artist's surrender to materialism, but of personal tragedy; "moreover, there were national and international events in the making that a person of Twain's prescience could not face with optimism. Once he warned of the possibility of 'an inundation of Russian and German political degradations which would envelop the globe and steep it in a sort of Middle-Age night and slavery which would last till Christ comes again." Abstract in AES, VII (1964), 591; reprinted in Twainian, XXIV (January-February, 1965). The article is reprinted in Twainian, XXIII (May-June, 1964), 3-4; (July-August), 2-4.

B55   LOWENHERZ, ROBERT J. "The Beginning of Huckleberry Finn," American Speech, XXXVIII (October), 196-201.

In the opening 108 words, "Mark Twain firmly establishes the vernacular speech of his narrator, Huck, characterizes him, enunciates one of the major themes of the story [truth and falsehood], provides a frame of reference for the action, and even works in some free advertisement [sic] for his earlier novel The Adventures of Tom Sawyer." Here, as in the rest of HF, MT used

phonetic spelling of dialect "sparingly" and "functionally." Abstract in AES, VIII (1964), 1290.

B56   LYDENBERG, JOHN. [Review: Louis J. Budd, Mark Twain: Social Philosopher (1962) and Henry Nash Smith, Mark Twain: The Development of A Writer (1962).] American Quarterly, XV (Spring), 101-103.

In these "more stately and sophisticated structures...Henry Nash Smith shows the ordeal of Mark Twain to be more complex than Van Wyck Brooks had thought, and Louis Budd makes clear that Mark Twain's vision of America was more complicated than Bernard DeVoto had imagined." These new books present "almost diametrically opposed views of the same man," where Budd's emphasis on what MT said about particular social questions reveals "a comparatively simple man" and Smith "tells us more about Twain's underlying social philosophy."

B57   LYON, PETER. Success Story: The Life and Times of S. S. McClure. New York: Charles Scribner's Sons.

Mentions MT passim (indexed); on the abortive plan to have him edit a new magazine, pp. 180-86.

B58   McCLARY, BEN HARRIS. "Melville, Twain, and the Legendary 'Tennessee Poet,'" Tennessee Folklore Society Bulletin, XXIX (September), 63-64.

"The poor poet of Tennessee" in Moby Dick (Chapter I) has not been identified, but in Captain Stormfield's Visit to Heaven MT describes "that tailor Billings, from Tennessee, [who] wrote poetry that Homer or Shakespeare couldn't begin to come up to; but nobody would print it"; Billings cannot be traced. Abstract in AES, VII (1964), 1564.

B59   McCURDY, FRANCES L. [Review: Pascal Covici, Mark Twain's Humor: The Image of a World (1962).] Quarterly Journal of Speech, XLIX (February), 92-93.

"An occasional symbolic interpretation is strained and unconvincing, and psychological insights generally associated only with trained psychiatrists are ascribed to Clemens, but the writer's thesis is, on the whole, interestingly supported by illustrations and quotations."

B60   MACINNES, COLIN. "Everything on Our Raft," New Statesman, LXV (June 21), 933-34.

Notes MT's portrayal of his times, and his language and his controlled balance of the tragic and the idyllic. "Huckleberry Finn is one of those stories, rare even among masterpieces, on which grace has descended absolutely; and this is because the narrative, so charming and arresting in itself, is constantly and effortlessly sustained by underlying theme and symbol." For example, "the raft is a birth-life symbol, and therein lies its fascination." Abstract in AES, VII (1964), 1109.

1963 - Shorter Writings

B61 McNAMARA, EUGENE. "A Note on 'My Platonic Sweetheart,'" Mark Twain Journal, XII (Spring), 18-19, 21.
"The cohesion of the dream-world and the child-world is most clearly seen" in this sketch of a recurring dream; dreams offered a means of escape to child-like innocence after failures in the adult world. Abstract in AES, VIII (1965), 1061.

B62 MAXWELL, D. E. S. "Twain as Satirist," in his American Literature: The Intellectual Background. London: Routledge & Kegan Paul, pp. 192-235.
Traces MT's satire through his various works, relating it to other traditions of satire. On pp. 292-93, praises the colloquial language of HF as well as MT's more formal prose, "capable...of a piercing simplicity."

B63 MILNE, W. GORDON. [Review: Bernard DeVoto, ed., Letters from the Earth (1962).] Books Abroad, XXXVII (Summer), 336-37.
Brief and primarily descriptive. The average reader "will appreciate the opportunity to read some vintage Twain."

B64 NEIDER, CHARLES, ed. "Mark Twain: 'Reflections on Religion.'" Hudson Review, XVI (Autumn), 329-52.
The text of previously unpublished material, now released by MT's daughter Mrs. Clara Clemens Samossoud, with brief introduction and notes by Neider. Abstract in AES, VII (1964), 355; reprinted in Twainian, XXIV (January-February, 1965), 3.

B65 O'CONNOR, WILLIAM VAN. [Review: Henry Nash Smith, Mark Twain, The Development of a Writer (1962).] Nineteenth-Century Fiction, XVIII (December), 291-95.
"For a long time now, Twain scholars have been a strange breed in the study of literature, American or otherwise. They direct their concern less at the work than at the man.... It is everywhere evident in Smith's work that he is very knowledgeable about Mark Twain. I am critical of Mark Twain, The Development of a Writer only because it seems representative of the whole Twain mystique." O'Connor devotes over a page to the imperfections of Pudd'nhead Wilson and concludes: "My main point ought to be perfectly clear. Twain--a very imperfect writer--was no true novelist, and we ought to quit saying or implying that he was." Abstract in AES, VIII (1964), 2235; reprinted in Twainian, XXIV (January-February, 1965).

B66 OLAN, LEVI A. "The Voice of the Lonesome: Alienation from Huck Finn to Holden Caulfield," Southwest Review, XLVIII (Spring), 143-50.
Begins with the Brooks thesis, chiefly on the destructive influence of surroundings on MT, though warning that his "posing and childish self-adulation" and the probability

that "the major part of his literary productivity is of a low grade" should not blind the reader to the merits of Huckleberry Finn, in which "he responded to the human situation as a total being, an artist who apprehends by a mysterious talent and creates uninhibited by either logic or purpose," anticipating the theme of alienation in modern literature. Abstract in AES, VII (1964); reprinted in Twainian, XXIV (January-February).

B67 PARSONS, COLEMAN O. "Mark Twain in Ceylon," Twainian, XXII (January-February), 4; (March-April), 3-4.
On MT's 1896 visit during the lecture tour described in Following the Equator. Concludes: "My materials are chiefly drawn from the great newspaper collection of the British Museum: The Times of Ceylon, Columbo, January 16, 22, and April 1, 9, 1896; The Ceylon Observer, Columbo, January 16, April 1, 9, 1896; and The Ceylon Examiner, Columbo, April 2, 4, 6, 1896" (liberally quoted, together with other local material). Abstracts in AES, VIII (1965), 1848, 1850; reprinted in Twainian, XXV (January-February, 1966), 3.

B68 _____. "Mark Twain: Sightseer in India," Mississippi Quarterly, XVI (Spring, 1963), 76-93.
A detailed account of MT's 1896 visit to India while on the world lecture tour that was the basis for FE; documented from contemporary Indian newspapers, published works by and about MT, and MT's unpublished papers. Abstract in AES, VII (1964), 844.

B69 PEARCE, ROY HARVEY. "'The End. Yours Truly, Huck Finn': Postscript," Modern Language Quarterly, XXIV (September), 253-56.
The territory for which Huck was going to "light out" was Indian Territory (now Oklahoma); although he sought to escape civilization, he would be only "one step ahead of the rest: boomers, dukes and dauphins, Aunt Sallies, Colonel Sherburns, and Wilkses-- civilizers all." Abstract in AES, VII (1964), 1795; reprinted in Twainian, XXIV (January-February, 1965).

B70 *RIZZARDI, A. "Anglo-American Literature," Convivium (Bologna?), XXX (May-June), 370-71.
A review of DeVoto, ed., Letters from the Earth. [Source: Abstract in AES, VII (1964), 727.]

B71 ROGERS, FRANKLIN R. "The Road to Reality: Burlesque Travel Literature and Roughing It," Bulletin of the New York Public Library, LXVII (March), 155-68.
After tracing the tradition from William Combe's The Tour of Dr. Syntax in Search of the Picturesque (which began appearing serially in 1809), with the development of a companion who "constantly reminds the reader

(ROGERS, FRANKLIN R.)
and the traveler himself of those unpicturesque elements of the actuality which the traveler has chosen to ignore," Rogers shows MT's experiments with point of view. From using the imaginary companion "Mr. Brown" in his travel letters in California papers, MT went on to the portrayal of a narrator in Roughing It who links the old-timer and the tenderfoot. Abstract in AES, VI (1963), 1568; reprinted in Twainian, XXIII (January-February, 1964).

B72 ROVIT, EARL. [Review: Pascal Covici, Mark Twain's Humor: The Image of a World (1962).] Books Abroad, XXXVII (Summer), 333-34.
"In a sense, an extension of Kenneth Lynn's argument in Mark Twain and Southwestern Humor." The argument for conscious artistry in the ending of HF is "ingenious, but to me unconvincing." Despite "the intrusive clumsiness of Covici's thesis-machinery, there is much perception on Twain and his organic relation to the American tradition."

B73 RUBIN, LOUIS D., JR. "Mark Twain and the Language of Experience," Sewanee Review: LXXI (Autumn), 664-73.
A review of Henry Nash Smith's Mark Twain: The Development of a Writer (1962), which applies to Huckleberry Finn the critical approach suggested by Erich Auerbach in Mimesis: The Representation of Reality in Western Literature (1946). "One great merit of Henry Nash Smith's study is its demonstration of the way in which for Twain the problem of idea and image, of form and meaning, is always one of fictional technique. The successes and failures of Huckleberry Finn clearly and matchlessly reflect its author's struggle to give meaning to his experience."

B74 SCHROEDER, FRED. "America's First Literary Realist: Horatio Alger, Jr.," Western Humanities Review, XVII (Spring), 129-37.
Includes comparisons of Alger's books to Huckleberry Finn. Abstract in AES, VII (1964) 691; reprinted in Twainian, XXIV (January-February, 1965).

B75 SCOTT, ARTHUR L. "The Innocents Adrift Edited by Mark Twain's Official Biographer," Publications of the Modern Language Association, LXXVIII (June), 230-37.
What was originally the beginning of a book was trimmed by Paine to produce "Down the Rhône" for Europe and Elsewhere; what disappeared was a wealth of anecdote and digression, four companions, and MT's spelling and punctuation. The irresponsible editing is of the sort also to be found in Paine's version of MS, which, with other posthumously published manuscripts, has "given us an exaggerated picture of Mark Twain's bitterness and pessimism at the turn of the century." Abstract in AES, VIII (1965), 1497; reprinted in Twainian, XXV (January-February, 1966).

B76 SMITH, BRADFORD. "Mark Twain and the Mystery of Identity," College English, XXIV (March), 425-30.
"The key to Mark Twain's mind is the concept of identity": MT focuses on the identity of the individual, and "nearly everybody in Mark Twain's books, consciously or unconsciously, is playing a part." There is a consistent pattern in which the hero solves or attempts to solve problems involving choices "by a change of identity and a change of place."

B77 SPILLER, ROBERT E. "Columnist's Chats," Saturday Review of Literature, XLVI (April 27), 39, 44.
A review of Charles Neider, ed., The Complete Essays of Mark Twain. "These pieces in Mr. Neider's latest collection are neither 'essays,' nor is the book 'complete'; they are simply some more miscellaneous writings that deserve republication and that didn't get into the two earlier volumes... Mr. Neider's books are well-printed, well-bound, and well-indexed, and they fill in the gaps for the Mark Twain enthusiast... even though there are annoying elements of misrepresentation."

B78 STARTSEV, A. "Mark Tven i Russkie [Mark Twain and the Russians]," Voprosy Literatury, VII (December), 116-21.
American publishers suppress MT's criticism of the political, religious, and moral views of the American capitalist society. The protests of Soviet literary critics and their discussion with Charles Neider have led to improvement, as has the publication in the Soviet Union of a complete edition of MT's works in Russian translation, with none of his anti-American writings omitted. [In Russian.]

B79 STEWART, D. H. "Myth and Truth in Criticism," Minnesota Review, III (Summer), 452-60.
Condemns "the critics' pilfering of modern anthropological and psychological apparatus," and makes only passing mention of HF criticism: "A critic who tells me I am somehow rehearsing a bear-myth or making sacrifice to a River God when I read Huckleberry Finn forfeits my trust immediately." Abstract in AES, IX (1966), 1742; reprinted in Twainian, XXVI (January-February, 1967).

B80 STRONKS, JAMES B. "Mark Twain's Stage Debut as Seen by Hamlin Garland," New England Quarterly, XXXVI (March), 85-6.
Garland heard MT and George Washington Cable lecture in Boston, either November 13 or 15, 1884, and recorded his impressions in a notebook which has not been published; his comments appear here for the first time, describing MT's voice as "flexible and with a

(STRONKS, JAMES B.)
fine compass. Running to very fine deep notes easily. He hits off his most delicious things with a raspy, dry 'rosen' voice" and he never smiles. Abstract in AES, VI (1963), 2530; reprinted in Twainian, XXIII (March-April, 1964).

B81　TANNER, TONY. "Mark Twain and Wattie Bowser," Mark Twain Journal, XII (Spring), 1-6.
MT's letter of March 20, 1880, in answer to a Dallas schoolboy who had asked him whether he would be a boy again if he could. MT's comments on boyhood are interesting in view of the problems he was currently having with HF; there is also commentary on style, and a discussion by Tanner of the question of youth for MT and his reaction to Howells's Indian Summer. Abstract in AES, VIII (1965), 1056.

B82　TAPER, BERNARD. "Mark Twain's San Francisco," American Heritage, XIV (August), 50-53, 93-94.
A brief popular account consisting largely of familiar biographical material. "A revised version of 'Mark Twain's San Francisco' will serve as the introduction to his edition of Twain's San Francisco journalism to be published by McGraw-Hill this fall under the same title." Abstract in AES, VI (1963), 2388; reprinted in Twainian, XXIII (March-April, 1964). Article reprinted in Twainian, 1963.B83.

B83　_____. "Mark Twain's San Francisco, Introduction by Taper," Twainian, XXII (November-December), 1-3 (concluded in the following issue).
Reprinting of the introduction to Taper's new book, a description of the city and its literati in the 1860's.

B84　TAYLOR, NANCY DEW. "The River of Faulkner and Mark Twain," Mississippi Quarterly, XVI (Fall), 191-99.
Parallels in character suggest that Faulkner had HF in mind as he wrote The Old Man, and his tall convict may be "a composite of the outstanding characteristics of Huck, Jim, and Tom." There are also parallels in theme and in symbolic use of the river. Abstract in AES, VIII (1965), 2642; reprinted in Twainian, XXV (January-February, 1966).

B85　Van Der BEETS, RICHARD. "A Note on Henry James' 'Western Barbarian,'" Western Humanities Review, XVII (Spring), 175-78.
There is evidence of a possible influence in "some rather curious parallels of both incident and phrase that exist between the characterization of The American's central figure, Christopher Newman, and the early persona, or projected image, of Mark Twain as revealed primarily in his early writings and The Innocents Abroad (1869)," providing "characterization, details, and background"

not available from James's personal experience. Abstract in AES, VII (1964), 695; reprinted in Twainian, XXIV (January-February, 1965).

B86　WAGENKNECHT, EDWARD. [Review: Louis J. Budd, Mark Twain: Social Philosopher (1962) and Henry Nash Smith, Mark Twain: The Development of a Writer (1962).] English Language Notes, I (September), 75-77.
Budd lets his materials take him where their own logic leads, and shows MT as "essentially a good, intelligent Republican"; this portrait contrasts with Philip Foner's depiction of MT as rather more radical, although Foner has not distorted his materials. Smith "studies primarily his author's style but he studies it not in isolation but rather in full consciousness that 'questions of meaning' and 'ethical ideas' are involved." Smith's approach is essentially sound, although his contention that Huck is "a mask for the writer, not a fully developed character...is valid only if one believes the reactions and judgments of Huck himself unconvincing"; Smith overstates the matter when he says that MT's Whittier Birthday Speech manifests in MT "a latent hostility" toward the New England writers he burlesqued.

B87　WERMUTH, PAUL C. "Santayana and Huckleberry Finn," New England Quarterly, XXXVI (March), 79-82.
Summarizes Santayana's "Tom Sawyer and Don Quixote" (Mark Twain Quarterly, IX [Winter, 1952], 1-3; 1952.B41), observing that from all other evidence "Santayana seems to have been monumentally uninterested in Twain." Having been given a copy of Huckleberry Finn by Cyril Clemens, he dutifully read it; but "in his wonderfully polite and subtle way," Santayana seems to be saying between the lines: "Well, here I am, an old man; I have taken my precious time to read this man's books because everybody said I should; and all I found was that I was right in the first place not to have read them years ago."

B88　WHITFORD, KATHRYN. "Rough Spots in 'Roughing It,'" Mississippi Quarterly, XVI (Spring), 94-96.
A hoax article, citing inconsistent details [in Chapters XXXII-XXXIII] as evidence that "Mark Twain is a hoax--any work composed after Roughing It cannot be other than the work of an imposter, for young Samuel Clemens died one night in a snowstorm on the Nevada desert." Abstract in AES, VII (1964), 845.

B89　WIGGINS, ROBERT A. "Pudd'nhead Wilson: A Literary Caesarian Operation," College English, XXV (December), 182-86.
Disagreeing with recent praise of the book, follows the contention by Richard

(WIGGINS, ROBERT A.)
Chase that "the characters and their relationships are not adequate to the moral
action"; even Chase might have made more of
the flawed structure of the work. Abstract
in AES, VII (1964), 299; reprinted in
Twainian, XXIV (January-February, 1965).

B90 WINTEROWD, W. ROSS. [Review: Pascal Covici,
Jr., Mark Twain's Humor: The Image of a
World (1962).] Western Humanities Review,
XVII (Spring), 194.
"Covici's work does not constitute an informing theory, but rather an extended ex-
plication, and in most instances a good
one," revealing the transformation of humor
from an end in itself to a tool of the artist. There is a weakness in Covici's shifting view of the hoax from a stylistic device
to one of plot, but the book contains "insight and sound judgment...above all, a
fresh and usually acute look at several of
Mark Twain's most provocative works."

1964 A BOOKS

A1 CLEMENS, SAMUEL L. Pudd'nhead Wilson. New
York: New American Library (A Signet Classic).
Includes a brief foreword by Wright Morris, dealing sensibly with MT's life but
not examining PW in depth. There is a
"Selected Bibliography" in which the section
devoted to "Other Works by Mark Twain" emphasizes Signet editions and the "Selected
Biography and Criticism" stresses well-known
books without consideration of their avail-
ability, relevance, or value; it lists no
articles in journals, and gives no indication of where a reader might find material
dealing specifically with PW.

A2 DUCKETT, MARGARET. Mark Twain and Bret Harte.
Norman: University of Oklahoma Press.
An attempt to put the relationship of the
two in perspective: "though the break in
the friendship has frequently been alluded
to by critics hostile to Harte, there is
another side of the story which has never
been told" (p. viii). Notes that Bret
Harte's diary, 1881-1888, is now in the New
York Public Library. (p. ix).

A3 FATOUT, PAUL. Mark Twain in Virginia City.
Bloomington: Indiana University Press.
A valuable work on this formative period
in MT's life. Fatout has found previously
unknown writing by MT; cites contemporary
newspaper material about MT not listed in
the present bibliography.

A4 HILL, HAMLIN. Mark Twain and Elisha Bliss.
Columbia: University of Missouri Press.
"The present volume concentrates on
Twain's business relationship with Bliss and
the American Publishing Company. The decade
during which Twain was Bliss's most important

author was germinal, I think, to Twain's
later career as a publisher and businessman
and significant, in ways that have never
been fully explored, to his aims, techniques, and development in writing" (p. vii).

A5 SMITH, HENRY NASH. Mark Twain's Fable of
Progress: Political and Economic Ideas in
"A Connecticut Yankee." New Brunswick, N.J.:
Rutgers University Press.
Places MT's book in context by comparing
it to Charles Dudley Warner's A Little Journey in the World and William Dean Howells's
A Hazard of New Fortunes as contemporary
portrayals of industrialism, then traces the
development of the novel and concludes with
a treatment of ideas in the book, including
MT's growing distaste for the human costs of
the machine. Meticulously documented.

A6 VARBLE, RACHEL M. Jane Clemens: The Story of
Mark Twain's Mother. Garden City, N.Y.:
Doubleday & Company, Inc.
Written as a popular account, without spe-
cific documentation for individual state-
ments of fact.

A7 WIGGINS, ROBERT A. Mark Twain: Jackleg Novelist. Seattle: University of Washington
Press.
Begins with the disastrous Whittier Birthday Dinner speech of 1877 as "traumatic for
Twain's literary psyche," revealing "his
deep-seated insecurity as a writer and...
especially relevant to his career as a novelist." Wiggins argues that "limited understanding of realism and humor," together
with effective technical equipment, helped
shape MT's personal approach to writing, and
that "his difficulties as a novelist began
when he became self-conscious about the novel." He traces the twelve novels, from GA
through MS, explaining their success or relative failure in terms of MT's fidelity to
a realistic approach. Wiggins argues that
MT's popularity grew in part from "a strong
and pervasive American folk tradition," and
in him "the public was approving an image of
itself."

1964 B SHORTER WRITINGS

B1 ALTER, ROBERT. Rogue's Progress: Studies in
the Picaresque Novel. Cambridge, Massachusetts: Harvard University Press. Pp. 117-21.
Places Huck in a tradition of picaroons,
with compassion but a sufficiently "thick
skin to prevent experience from paralyzing
him or torturing him excessively," while rejecting society's hypocrisies. HF is superior to the traditional picaresque novels in
its language, which reflects Huck's moral
position.

B2 ANDERSON, JAMES BRUCE. "Mark Twain in Shawneetown, Illinois, Home of Tom Sawyer and Colonel Sellers," Charlatan (Iowa City, Iowa),
No. 2, [pp. 1-8].

(ANDERSON, JAMES BRUCE)
Although TS is generally thought to be based on memories of Hannibal, Missouri, a case may be made that MT's more immediate source was Shawneetown; he was acquainted with one Thomas Sawyer Spivey of that city. The Eschol Sellers who threatened suit over use of his name in GA is probably the individual of that name from Bowlesville, Illinois, three miles from Shawneetown. Among sources cited on the acquaintance of MT and Thomas Sawyer Spivey are a Spivey family history and Geo. P. Dent, ed., Four Score and More (n.p., n.d.; Chapter VII, "Looking Backward," is here extensively quoted). MT may have found inspiration not only for locale, but also for such incidents as being lost in a cave. Abstract in AES, IX (1966), 2870.

B3 ANON. "Juvenilia," Times Literary Supplement, January 16, p. 41. Includes a review of Henry Duskis, The Forgotten Writings of Mark Twain (1963).
This material from the Buffalo Express is not MT's best work, and the material is fragmentary and inconvenient to read.

B4 ANON. "Mark Twain Items Published Elsewhere from 'Abstracts of English Studies, Vol. 6,'" Twainian, XXIII (January-February), 3-4; (March-April), 3-4.
Reprints all the abstracts of articles pertaining to MT from Abstracts of English Studies, VI (1963), accurately and with AES numbering.

B5 ANON. "Mark Twain Letter Found," Mark Twain Journal, XII (Winter), 15.
While the library of the late Walter Williams was being catalogued at the University of Missouri, a letter from MT was found (March 4, 1894, here reprinted), declining an unspecified invitation from Williams, then editor of the Columbia Herald and later founder and dean of the School of Journalism, and finally president of the University of Missouri.

B6 ANON. "Twain Goes West," Times Literary Supplement, November 19, p. 1041.
A review article, covering Robert A. Wiggins, Mark Twain: Jackleg Novelist; Henry Nash Smith, Mark Twain's Fable of Progress; Paul Fatout, Mark Twain in Virginia City. Descriptive and laudatory.

B7 *ARIKAWA, SHOJI. "Mark Twain's Sense of Equilibrium in The Prince and the Pauper," Kyusha American Literature, No. 7, pp. 13-20.
[Source: MHRA Annual Bibliography (1965), No. 6957.]

B8 BABCOCK, C. MERTON. "Mark Twain, Mencken and 'The Higher Goofyism,'" American Quarterly, XVI (Winter), 587-94.
Compares the satire of these two moralists and gifted users of the language.

B9 _____. "Mark Twain's Map of Paris," Texas Quarterly, VII (Autumn), 92-97.
On MT's 1870 map of Paris as a mirror-image: "The trouble with a great many readers of Mark Twain is that they forget to read him backwards. They might as well try to find their way about the city of Paris with the author's Map--but no mirror. Like Swift, Mark Twain employed irony so masterfully in his writings as, frequently, to defeat his own purposes." Abstract in AES, VIII (1965), 2413; reprinted in Twainian, XXV (January-February, 1966).

B10 BAENDER, PAUL. "The Date of Mark Twain's 'The Lowest Animal,'" American Literature, XXXVI (May), 174-79.
MT apparently began the essay "around August 13, 1896, shortly before Susy's death on the 18th," rather than in 1897 or 1905, as DeVoto speculates; "What helped Twain complete 'The Lowest Animal' in those heavy days was his familiarity with its opinions, not an infatuation with them because of the circumstances." Abstract in AES, VIII (1965), 5; reprinted in Twainian, XXV (January-February, 1966).

B11 _____, and FREDERICK ANDERSON. "Twain in Progress: Two Projects," American Quarterly, XVI (Winter), 621-23.
Baender briefly describes the forthcoming edition of MT's previously published works and lists the editors, and Anderson describes plans for the materials previously unpublished or only "published in such inadequately prepared editions as to be unacceptable by contemporary scholars."

B12 BASSAN, MAURICE. "The Poetaster and the Horse-Doctors," Midcontinent American Studies Journal, V (Spring), 55-59.
"Will Carleton is one of the more deservedly obscure of our nineteenth-century poetasters"; as a member of the Authors' Club in New York, MT was dragged into the controversy over Carleton's election to membership, and subsequently resigned. Abstract in AES, VII (1964), 2183; reprinted in Twainian, XXIV (January-February, 1965).

B13 BATES, ALLAN. "The Quintus Curtius Snodgrass Letters: A Clarification of the Mark Twain Canon," American Literature, XXXVI (March), 31-37.
A series of travel letters published in the New Orleans Daily Crescent in 1861 have been tentatively attributed to MT. Minnie M. Brashear published four of these letters in Mark Twain, Son of Missouri (1934), and Ernest E. Leisy and Thomas Ewing Dabney published these and six more letters in The Letters of Quintus Curtius Snodgrass (1946). These letters cannot be the work of MT, because they involve a running exchange with another reporter and discuss events in Louisiana at a time when MT was in St. Louis.

(BATES, ALLAN)
Abstract in AES, VII (1964), 1993; reprinted in Twainian, XXIV (January-February, 1965), 4.

B14 BAUMRIND, SHELDON, D.D.S. "Mark Twain Visits the Dentist," Journal of the California Dental Association, December.
[Source: reprint in Mark Twain Papers.]
On MT's unfinished and unpublished "Happy Memories of the Dental Chair," which described his lengthy and painful treatment of Riggs' Disease by Dr. John M. Riggs of Hartford, Connecticut.

B15 BAYLEN, JOSEPH O. "Mark Twain, W. T. Stead, and 'The Tell-Tale Hands,'" American Quarterly, XVI (Winter), 606-12.
On MT's interest in palmistry, and Stead's publication of pictures of his hands, together with palmists' readings of them in Borderland, 1894.B2, 1895.B2.

B16 *BENNETT, JAMES R. "The Thematic Importance of Chapter One of Huckleberry Finn," Exercise Exchange, XII (November), 23-25.
[Source: Beebe and Feaster (1968), p. 112.]

B17 BIGNAMI, MARIALUISA. "La Letteratura Americana in Italia," Studi Americani, X, 443-95.
On pp. 454-55 there is a brief list of Italian translations of MT's works and secondary material about him; the secondary material is listed in the present bibliography.

B18 BOGGAN, J. R. "That Slap, Huck, Did It Hurt?" English Language Notes, I (March), 212-15.
Huck's concern over "the plain hand of Providence slapping me in the face and letting me know my wickedness was being watched all the while from up there in heaven" has been exaggerated by the critics: his statements elsewhere show that "hell has no emotional meaning for Huck...the force of his exclamation is much diminished...Twain's attempt to win an added Christian sympathy for his good 'bad boy' is unconvincing." Abstract in AES, VIII (1965), 1279; reprinted in Twainian, XXV (January-February, 1966).

B19 BORST, CHARLES V. S. [Introduction.] Mark Twain's A Cure for the Blues. With "The Enemy Conquered; or, Love Triumphant" by G. Ragsdale McClintock. Rutland, Vermont: Charles E. Tuttle Co.
Borst's introduction is primarily factual, following Paine. He identifies the author of The Enemy Conquered as Samuel Watson Royston, a native of Cumming, Georgia, who was graduated from the Yale Law School in 1845.

B20 BRATCHER, JAMES T. "Twain's Tom Sawyer," Explicator, XXII (January), Item 40.
Although MT sometimes used the generic noun sawyer to denote independence, the term

was also used on the river to denote drifting trees--a hazard of which the ex-pilot was fully aware; hence, the name has a dual significance. Abstract in AES, VII (1964), 1369.

B21 BRIDGMAN, RICHARD. [Brief Review: Henry Duskis, ed., The Forgotten Writings of Mark Twain (1963).] Western Folklore, XXIII (October), 276-77.
The material reprinted from the Buffalo Express is fragmentary, and there is inadequate basis for attribution of some of it to MT. "It could contribute to our understanding of Twain, except that, to be of value, the editorial work would have to be done afresh. This edition has effectively lessened the chance of that happening for some time."

B22 BROWN, CLARENCE A. "Huckleberry Finn: A Study in Structure and Point of View," Mark Twain Journal, XII (Spring), 10-15, 5.
The novel "must be read as a 'pastoral,' albeit one on which a nightmare world of human injustice and brutality constantly impinges"; thus, "the concluding episode in the novel is simply Huck's return to the world of Tom Sawyer." The core of the narrative is not Jim's flight to freedom, "but, quite simply, the adventures of Huckleberry Finn," and too much can be made of his moral growth--at the Phelps farm he returns to the world from which he set out. "While Huck functions as a sensitive center of consciousness, he does not function as a direct voice for Twain," and MT's style, though unlike that of Henry James, is equally effective in conveying to the reader the consciousness of the central character. Abstract in AES, VIII (1965), 1066.

B23 BUDD, LOUIS J. "Mark Twain on Joseph the Patriarch," American Quarterly, XVI (Winter), 577-86.
On MT's comic portrayal of Joseph in IA and later treatment of him as an embodiment of the laissez-faire capitalist with a corner in the grain market.

B24 ____. [Review: Henry Nash Smith, Mark Twain's Fable of Progress.] Nineteenth-Century Fiction, XIX (December), 304-306.
Smith's "thesis is that A Connecticut Yankee in King Arthur's Court signaled 'something like a negative conversion' for Twain which 'all but paralyzed his powers of imagination and condemned him to the relative sterility of his last twenty years.'" "Mark Twain and Smith make a very rewarding pair, all the more because their minds are so dissimilar"; that readers may disagree in part with Smith's argument seems likely, because of the book's originality and because he "evades no challenges."

287

1964 - Shorter Writings

B25   CALDWELL, DOROTHY. [Review: Paul Fatout, Mark Twain in Virginia City.] Missouri Historical Review, LVIII (July), 541-43.
     An extensive but uncritical summary of the book, which reflects extensive research and the discovery of much new material.

B26   _____. [Review: Albert E. Stone, Jr., The Innocent Eye (1961); Roger B. Salomon, Twain and the Image of History (1961); Louis J. Budd, Mark Twain: Social Philosopher (1962).] Missouri Historical Review, LVIII (April), 398-401.
     Chiefly descriptive, praising the scholarly thoroughness of the three works.

B27   CARSTENSEN, VERNON. "The West Mark Twain Did Not See," Pacific Northwest Quarterly, LV (October), 170-76.
     On the early days of Washington and Oregon: "It is a pity that Mark Twain did not see the Pacific Northwest in the third quarter of the last century." [This article has been listed in other bibliographies of MT, but does not concern him.]

B28   CHARBONNEL, AVIS BLIVEN. "My Friend Clara Clemens," Mark Twain Journal, XII (Spring), 16-17.
     The author knew MT's daughter when they both studied piano in Vienna under Theodor Leschetizky; here she recalls anecdotes about Clara and Ossip Gabrilowitsch.

B29   CHARD, LESLIE F., II. "Mark Twain's 'Hadleyburg' and Fredonia, New York," American Quarterly, XVI (Winter), 595-601
     Unpleasant experiences turned MT's early favorable view of the town to a hostility which may have led him to pillory Fredonia in "The Man that Corrupted Hadleyburg"; "Even today it is commonly supposed in Fredonia that the community was the original for Hadleyburg and that many of the characters in the story were based on prominent Fredonians of the past."

B30   CLEMENS, CYRIL. "Mark Twain and Lyndon B. Johnson," Hobbies--The Magazine for Collectors, LXIX (April), 112, 122, 126.
     Quotes the praise of several presidents for MT, in conversation with Cyril Clemens or in letters to him.

B31   CUMMINGS, SHERWOOD. "What is Man?: The Scientific Sources," in Sydney J. Krause, ed., Essays on Determinism in American Literature. (Kent, Ohio: Kent State University Press), pp. 108-16.
     What Is Man? has been treated as a curiosity, and comments on it have been casual and impressionistic, but "the formation of Mark Twain's deterministic ideas, far from being peculiar, was in the classical pattern." MT read widely, and in particular he was influenced by Holmes, Darwin, Lecky, Lubbock, and Huxley. MT "swam during his whole career in the mainstream of ideas that produced the naturalistic writers." He did not join their number partly because determinism did not dominate his thinking until the later years and partly because his best writing was unconscious rather than doctrinal; in any case there is an influence of environment in P&P, CY, and PW.

B32   CUNLIFFE, MARCUS. "American Humour and the Rise of the West (Mark Twain)," in his The Literature of the United States (Harmondsworth and Baltimore: Penguin Books), pp. 157-78.
     This book is described as a revised edition, with original publication in 1954, and the bibliography lists a number of more recent studies of MT. Cunliffe's discussion is for the general reader, beginning with treatment of western humor and showing how MT transcended it though not entirely escaping it. Cunliffe notes unevenness in CY, which is weakened by burlesque. "At moments, instead of indicting King Arthur's England, he speaks of it nostalgically in much the same terms as when he recalls the Missouri of his boyhood.... At other times, perhaps unwittingly, he implies that the industrial order is cruel, greedy, and destructive." Posterity will remember MT for "Tom Sawyer, Life on the Mississippi,--and, above all-- Huckleberry Finn. In them he wrote with warmth and accuracy of the life he most vividly knew."

B33   DAICHES, DAVID. "Mark Twain as Hamlet," Encounter, XXII (February), 70-76.
     A review-article, with passing reference to Douglas Grant's Mark Twain as "a useful little book" and dismissing Caroline Thomas Harnsberger's Mark Twain's Views of Religion (1961) as "a rather scrappy little book...in which a somewhat perfunctory introduction is followed by a collection of extracts from Mark Twain's notebooks, marginal notes in books, essays, letters, and the autobiography." There is extensive and laudatory discussion of Henry Nash Smith's Mark Twain: The Development of a Writer. Daiches calls HF MT's "greatest work," but CY "in some respects his most interesting one...because in the latter we see him trapped in the ambiguous implications of modern industrial civilisation in a way that illuminates a whole area of modern history, British as well as American." The mask of humor is a necessary defense: MT "is not like the traditional comedian who longs to play Hamlet; he is rather Hamlet who puts on an antic disposition in order to save his reason." Abstract in AES, VII (1964), 1341.

B34   [DAVIS, CHESTER L.] "'Mark Twain and Longfellow' in 'Life' Magazine," Twainian, XXIII (September-October), 2-4.
     Reprints Dora Jane Hamblin's "Mark (Ye) (the) Twain" from Life (July 10), p. 13; in

([DAVIS, CHESTER L.])

an unsigned headnote Chester L. Davis says the story is reprinted "only to let our members see how utterly ridiculous it is. If it were a light sort of thing, some story in a magazine of small circulation, we likely would let it pass. Things being as they are we are reprinting it as a far-fetched assertion, a speculation by one who should have checked the facts (and thus killed the story before it was ever written), but how else can a million or so readers be enlightened except through our serious student members saying 'maybe so', but 'highly unlikely'." Abstract in AES, VIII (1965), 1855, reprinted in Twainian, XXV (January-February, 1966), 3. The following issue acknowledges a letter from the editors of Life "with an explanation as useless and futile as that given by Orson Wells [sic] for his 'Invasion from Mars' program, never to be forgotten, but only because it too was a 'Special Report,' without warning."

B35 ____. "'Simon Wheeler, Detective' Published," Twainian, XXIII (March-April), 1-3.
On the MT manuscript recently published by the New York Public Library: discusses significance of the Missouri milieu and reprints the first pages of Chapter I. Abstract in AES, VIII (1965), 1852; reprinted in Twainian, XXV (January-February, 1966).

B36 ____. "Writings on Mark Twain, Average in Top Ten," Twainian, XXIII (May-June), 2.
"For the past three years we have been publishing annually, usually with the January-February 'Twainian', [sic] an abstract of all articles which have been published during the past year or so relating to the life and writings of Mark Twain"; the source of these abstracts is Abstracts of English Studies, a study of which reveals that MT is among the leaders in the number of articles published about him. [The opening statement must be qualified: not everything written about MT is abstracted in AES, and Twainian does not reprint all the AES abstracts (abstracts of material from Mark Twain Journal, for example, are silently passed over)--T.A.T.] Abstract in AES, VIII (1965), 1853; reprinted in Twainian, XXV (January-February, 1966).

B37 ____. [Review: Bradley, Beatty, Long, eds., The Adventures of Huckleberry Finn (Norton Critical Edition, 1962).] Twainian, XXIII (November-December).
Laudatory; describes contents, then quotes extensively from the introduction.

B38 ____. [Review: Hamlin Hill, Mark Twain and Elisha Bliss.] Twainian, XXIII (September-October), 1.
Descriptive and laudatory.

B39 ____. [Review: Rachel M. Varble, Jane Clemens: The Story of Mark Twain's Mother.] Twainian, XXIII (November-December), 1-3.
Laudatory, more analytical than usual in Twainian reviews; contains much quotation.

B40 ____. [Statement on Mark Twain Research Foundation.] Twainian, XXIII (March-April), 1.
"We have had and now have quantities of material including intimate letters which we believe good taste justified witholding from publication. We will continue to publish what we believe to be in the interest of research into the life and writings of Mark Twain, and this statement must stand as the sole reply to the many letters of inquiry which are continually received and seldom answered by us. Again we believe we are reacting as Mark himself would have done and we like to think, as he would have expected of us."

B41 DEKKER, GEORGE. "Lilies that Fester: The Last of the Mohicans and The Woman that Rode Away," New Left Review, No. 28 (November-December), pp. 75-84.
On p. 79, contrasts Cooper's Leatherstocking Tales with "two of the central masterpieces of American fiction. Although Moby Dick and The Adventures of Huckleberry Finn are concerned with racial relations, they do not invite us to ask: what will become of the white, red, and black races in North America--what in fact will become of North America? In Cooper's Leatherstocking Tales these questions are almost automatically raised..." and D. H. Lawrence's novel brings them up to date. Abstract in AES, VIII (1965), 2656; reprinted in Twainian, XXV (January-February, 1966).

B42 DILLINGHAM, WILLIAM B. "Setting and Theme in Tom Sawyer," Mark Twain Journal, XII (Spring), 6-8.
"The principal tensions in Tom's growth are those between freedom and involvement, illusion and reality," as represented by Jackson's Island and St. Petersburg, Cardiff Hill and the cave. Tom's "'salvation' and new growth, even though represented in terms of Christian rebirth [three days and nights in an underworld] are in Twain's view no cause for jubilation," since they cost him his boyish illusion. Abstract in AES, VIII (1965), 1064. Article reprinted in Kesterson (1974), pp. 87-91.

B43 DUFFY, MYRTLE M. "Twain in Howells' A Modern Instance," American Quarterly, XVI (Winter), 612-14.
Squire Gaylord resisted his wife's efforts to change his agnosticism, and eventually her own faith declined; Howells had seen the same thing happen in the Clemens family, and described it in his My Mark Twain (1910) and "Editor's Easy Chair" (Harper's Monthly, CXXXVI [March, 1918], 603).

B44 ELLISON, RALPH. Shadow and Act. New York: Random House.

Includes "The Seer and the Seen" (1946; published in Confluence, December, 1953), pp. 24-44; "Change the Joke and Slip the Yoke" (Partisan Review, Spring, 1958), pp. 45-59; "The Art of Fiction: An Interview" (Paris Review, Spring, 1955), pp. 167-83; "Some Questions and Some Answers" (Preuves, May, 1958), pp. 261-72. On Huck who, "like Prometheus...embraces the evil implicit in his act in order to affirm his belief in humanity," and the recognition of Jim's humanity (and on "Hemingway's blindness to the moral values of Huckleberry Finn despite his sensitivity to it technical aspects"), pp. 29-36. On MT's failure to represent Jim as an adult, pp. 50-51; again on the central moral question in HF, pp. 182-83. On language, Ellison speaks of "having inherited the language of Shakespeare and Melville, Mark Twain and Lincoln and no other," although American Negro speech has been important to our language (pp. 266-67). Pp. 58-59, on Ellison's own use of folklore, and his ability to imagine himself as Huck Finn more readily than as Jim, reprinted in Simpson (1968), pp. 112-13.

B45 FLORY, CLAUDE R. "Huck, Sam and the Small-Pox," Mark Twain Journal, XII (Winter), 1-2, 8.

MT was well acquainted with Harriet Beecher Stowe, and--as Walter Blair has pointed out--there are parallels between Uncle Tom's Cabin and Huckleberry Finn. There is a further parallel in Mrs. Stowe's Sam Lawson's Oldtown Fireside Stories (1871), in which pretended smallpox is used to frighten away a man who came to collect a debt, just as Huck evaded the slave-catchers in Chapter XVI. Abstract in AES, VIII (1965), 1067.

B46 FRENCH, BRYANT MOREY. "Mark Twain, Laura D. Fair, and the New York Criminal Courts," American Quarterly, XVI (Winter), 545-61.

"That the trial and acquittal of Laura Hawkins [in GA] was intended by Mark Twain primarily as an exposé of the American jury system and only secondarily as a parody of the Fair case is made abundantly clear by the play he based on the novel." Describes the trial and the climax of the play, and praises Franklin Walker's "well-documented pioneering article" (1936) on MT's use of the trial.

B47 FRENCH, WARREN. [Review: Simon Wheeler, Detective, ed. Franklin R. Rogers (1963).] American Notes and Queries, III (September), 14-15.

This is very poor MT stuff, and the interests of scholars and collectors might better have been served by simply reproducing the manuscript in facsimile. The editing, introduction, and printing are admirable, but was it worth the time and expense?

B48 GANZEL, DEWEY. "Samuel Clemens, Sub Rosa Correspondent," English Language Notes, I (June), 270-73.

The greater part of MT's correspondence from the Quaker City tour has been collected in Daniel Morley McKeithan's Traveling with the Innocents Abroad (1958); to these Ganzel adds two brief dispatches from Naples (here reprinted) and a longer one probably from Constantinople (summarized) to the New York Herald. These are unsigned, because MT was under contract to the Tribune. He also notes a dispatch in the Herald from Captain Duncan and an unsigned letter by Dr. Abraham Reeves Jackson. Abstract in AES, VIII (1965), 1954; reprinted in Twainian, XXV (January-February).

B49 *GARVENKO, F. (ed.). Vēstules No Zemes: Antireliǧisku Rakstu Krājums. Trans. by I. Melnbrade. Riga: Latvijas Valsts Izdevniecība. [Letters from the Earth.]
[Source: MHRA Annual Bibliography (1965), No. 6978.]

B50 GERBER, JOHN C. "Mark Twain," in James Woodress, ed., American Literary Scholarship: An Annual/1964 (Durham, North Carolina: Duke University Press, 1966), pp. 50-61.

The second annual survey of MT scholarship; See 1963 entry for coverage.

B51 _____. "The Mark Twain Edition," Books at Iowa (October), pp. 15-17.

On the need for an accurate edition of MT, because "there is not a single major work of Mark Twain's in print that is as he wrote it. There has never been a complete and correct edition of his works, or of any one of his major works. Minor errors have crept into the works through printers' errors and major errors through the ill-advised activity of his editors. Sometimes the changes seem almost incredible," as in MS. Describes plans for a new, authoritative edition to be edited by scholars at several major universities, with Gerber as Chairman of the Editorial Board.

B52 _____. [Review: Bernard DeVoto, ed., Letters from the Earth, by Mark Twain, with a Preface by Henry Nash Smith (1962).] American Literature, XXXVI (May), 220-22.

"The first half of the book, containing 'Letters from the Earth' and 'Papers of the Adam Family,' is by far the more interesting part," with the vigor of MT's journalism of the sixties, but also with its unevenness and occasional coarseness. Paul Baender, currently working on some of this material, "tells me that Bernard DeVoto's editing is quite careless," with "misreadings of the manuscript" as a result of DeVoto's apparently having allowed a typist to establish text.

B53 HAGOPIAN, JOHN V., and MARTIN DOLCH, with the assistance of W. Gordon Cunliffe and Arvin Wells. Insight I: Analyses of American Literature. Frankfurt am Main: Hirschgraben-Verlag.

The second edition of a 1952 text for German schools. On pp. 248-53 contains a brief account of MT's life and works, and summaries of "The Jumping Frog" and "Traveling with a Reformer," with questions for students.

B54 HAMBLEN, ABIGAIL ANN. "The American Scene: Dickens and Mark Twain," Mark Twain Journal, XII (Winter), 9-11, 16.

A comparison of Martin Chuzzlewit and GA as portraits of the vulgarity and corruption in American life. Abstract in AES, VIII (1965), 1070.

B55 HAMBLIN, DORA JANE. "Mark (Ye) (the) Twain," Life, LVII (July 10), 13.

A spoof, attributing the authorship of MT's works to Henry Wadsworth Longfellow: the July 31 issue contains letters to the editors (p. 12) from deceived readers seeking to refute her argument and by Sherwood Cummings, Paul Fatout, and Henry Morgan, who enjoyed the joke. Article reprinted with comment in Twainian, XXIII (September-October), 2-4, 1964.B34.

B56 HAVARD, WILLIAM C. "Mark Twain and the Political Ambivalence of Southwestern Humor," Mississippi Quarterly, XVII (Spring), 95-106.

On MT's treatment of man and society in GA, HF, and CY, tracing his thought from early days as a frontier humorist to the despair of later years. Abstract in AES, VIII (1965), 2993; reprinted in Twainian, XXV (January-February, 1966).

B57 HEMINGWAY, LEICESTER. "Ernest Hemingway's Boyhood Reading," Mark Twain Journal, XII (Spring), 4-5.

The author heard from his mother that his much older brother, years ago, "said Mark Twain had the real stuff." What he learned from MT is uncertain, "but it must have been plenty." Abstract in AES, VIII (1965), 1063.

B58 HENDERSON, ROSWELL P., and RALPH GREGORY. "Judge John Marshall Clemens," Missouri Historical Society Bulletin, XXI (October).

[Source: Missouri Historical Society price list of publications.]

B59 HILL, HAMLIN. "Barnum, Bridgeport and The Connecticut Yankee," American Quarterly, XVI (Winter), 615-16.

Hank Morgan's references in Chapter I to Bridgeport and circuses, and his casual acceptance of a knight and a turreted fortress, may be explained simply: P. T. Barnum had his headquarters in Bridgeport, Connecticut, and he built a series of "castles" there.

B60 HINCHCLIFFE, ARNOLD P. [Review: Douglas Grant, Mark Twain (1962).] Critical Quarterly, VI (Winter), 376-77.

This is a corrective to "Van Wyck Brooks' unfortunate volume The Ordeal of Mark Twain." Grant does not resolve the contradictions in MT's psyche and art, but "the puzzle...is at least given a comprehensible and sane form."

B61 HINER, JAMES. "Mark Twain: Ambivalence Not Disjunction," American Quarterly, XVI (Winter), 620-21.

The conflicts in HF between raft and shore, the real and the romantic have been misread by critics who seek in MT an allegiance to either side. "Head and heart are not merely opposed...but self contradictory. The heart goes toward suicide, and the head to madness. Those are the ultimate conditions of each drive."

B62 HOUGH, ROBERT L. [Review: John S. Tuckey, Mark Twain and Little Satan (1963).] College English, XXV (January), 310.

"An important study," containing "convincing evidence to overthrow the established assumptions concerning the dates and order of the three versions of The Mysterious Stranger" and "some indication of the editorial tinkering done by Albert Paine and Frederick Duneka."

B63 JENSEN, FRANKLIN L. "Mark Twain's Comments on Books and Authors," Emporia State Research Studies, XII (June), 5-53.

"This study originated as a Master's thesis at Kansas State Teachers College of Emporia"; based on published material generally available and familiar. Abstract in AES, VIII (1965), 341; reprinted in Twainian, XXV (January-February, 1966).

B64 KAPLAN, JUSTIN. [Introduction.] The Gilded Age: A Tale of Today. New York: Trident Press. pp. v-xxiv.

Considers MT's own views toward money and power after settling into Eastern respectability. The book reflects "a casual attitude toward the power of fiction to digest an immense amount of raw topical material and still have the wholeness of fiction." In this first sustained fiction, MT "found a matrix for the materials of his past" which would characterize all of his major books.

B65 KAZIN, ALFRED. "The Scholar Cornered: A Progression of Children" [From A Critic's Notebook], American Scholar, XXXII (Spring), 171-83.

On TS and HF, pp. 176-77, 180-81; notes "the indulgent, arch, patronizing tone that Mark Twain adopts in Tom Sawyer" as typical of boy stories until Crane's Whilomville Stories of 1900 and Tarkington's Penrod of 1914. "Only once, actually, did Mark Twain break through this all-too-twinkly, chuckly

1964 - Shorter Writings

(KAZIN, ALFRED)
softness," in HF, where the boy's "experience is not middle-class, not comfortable, not an exclusive concern with fun and games." Abstract in AES, VII (1964), 2003; reprinted in Twainian, XXIV (January-February, 1965).

B66 KOMPASS, ARTHUR M. "Twain's Use of Music: a Note on Life on the Mississippi," American Quarterly, XVI (Winter), 616-19.
Gives the text of the hymn, "Last Beam," a line of which the pilot Bixby sang in the chapter "A Cub-Pilot's Experience" in LOM; dealing with fears of the dark, it is an effective device for mocking both the cub and the genteel culture.

B67 KRAUSE, S. J. "The Art and Satire of Twain's 'Jumping Frog' Story," American Quarterly, XVI (Winter), 562-76.
Although recent studies have emphasized evidence the story provides of conflict between genteel, civilized values of the East and those of the western frontier, the question of form has been neglected. In eight levels of point of view MT "employs an order of increasing detail and of ascending absurdity and fantasy," and "the structure of the Jim Smiley story is that of a moral satire in the classical mold."

B68 LEVY, LEO B. "Society and Conscience in Huckleberry Finn," Nineteenth-Century Fiction, XVIII (March), 383-91.
The critical view that equates what Huck calls "conscience" with the views of the society in which he lives are basically correct, but "criticism of the novel has suffered from too much insistence upon its schematic or doctrinal aspects. "Natural man is not necessarily innocent--vide the degraded Pap--and the growing closeness of Huck and Jim is "the recognition and fulfillment of mutual needs so strong that they can transcend racial barriers"; hence, Huck's decision to help Jim escape may be, not "rebellious and isolating," but "a socializing decision through which he begins to discover a deeper bond with society than any he has known." Abstract in AES, VII (1964), 2240; reprinted in Twainian, XXIV (January-February, 1965).

B69 *LONG, E. HUDSON. [Introduction.] Pudd'nhead Wilson and The Man that Corrupted Hadleyburg. New York: Harper & Row
Provides useful biographical, textual, and critical background. [Source: Extensively quoted in Twainian, XXIV (May-June, 1965), 4.]

B70 LYDENBERG, JOHN. "New Books on Twain," American Quarterly, XVI (Winter), 624-28.
A review of Bernard Taper, ed., Mark Twain's San Francisco (1963; only moderately amusing, and inadequate for the serious scholar); Hamlin Hill, Mark Twain and Elisha

Bliss (meticulously detailed, "a scholarly contribution of the most orthodox and approved variety"); Henry Nash Smith, Mark Twain's Fable of Progress ("this one I confess to finding slender in substance as well as in form"); and Robert A. Wiggins, Mark Twain, Jackleg Novelist (Wiggins forgets his title and concentrates instead on MT's concentration on a single story, that of the folk hero).

B71 McELDERRY, BRUCE R., JR. "Wolfe and Twain," in his Thomas Wolfe (New York: Twayne Publishers), pp. 64-66.
Compares Wolfe's autobiographical method to that of MT, who, however, did little with "the painful years of adolescence"; Wolfe shows "a serious treatment of intimate personal relationships he never attempted in his successful books."

B72 McNULTY, JOHN BARD. Older than the Nation: The Story of the Hartford "Courant." Stonington, Connecticut: The Pequot Press, Inc.
On MT's friendship with Charles Dudley Warner, rivalry over pay rates, sorrow at Warner's death, pp. 104-106, 143; also includes MT's comments when his telephone was being installed ("The voice carries too far as it is. If Bell had invented a muffler or a gag, he would have done a real service") and his introductory remarks at an 1875 spelling-bee (pp. 104-106).

B73 MANIERRE, WILLIAM R. "'No Money for to Buy the Outfit': Huckleberry Finn Again," Modern Fiction Studies, X (Winter), 341-48.
The pragmatic Huck is "a natural born joiner. He 'joins' Tom's gang; he 'joins' Jim; later, he 'joins' the Grangerfords; later still he 'joins' Mary Jane Wilks and her cause; finally, he 'joins' society, presumably for good.... Huck's 'moral growth' has, I believe, been vastly overestimated." Abstract in AES, IX (1966), 1748; reprinted in Twainian, XXVI (January-February, 1967).

B74 MARX, LEO. The Machine in the Garden: Technology and the Pastoral Ideal in America. New York: Oxford University Press, pp. 319-40 and passim.
In HF the pastoral mode "for the first time...is wholly assimilated to a native idiom." The motif of the intruding machine "has as much to do with the defects as with the merits of the work," and MT's "ingenious efforts to contrive an affirmation virtually break his masterpiece in two" (p. 319). In between the perspective of the innocent traveler who sees only beauty and that of the pilot to whom lovely details stand for hidden dangers stands Huck, with a "willingness to accept the world as he finds it, without anxiously forcing meanings on it" (p. 334).

B75 *MENDELSON, M. Mark Tven (new issue). Moskva: Molodaja Gvardija.
[Source: MHRA Annual Bibliography (1964), No. 6569.]

B76 METZGER, CHARLES R. "The Adventures of Huckleberry Finn as Picaresque," Midwest Quarterly, V (April), 249-56.
Unlike the romantic Tom Sawyer, "Huck... is doomed to play the picaresque role, as are possibly all pícaros, because he is an essentially honest person living in a dishonest world." MT knew the literary character Gil Blas de Santillana, and Huck embodies attributes of the pícaro. Abstract in AES, IX (1966), 2321; reprinted in Twainian, XXVI (January-February, 1967).

B77 MILLGATE, MICHAEL. [Review: Henry Nash Smith, Mark Twain: The Development of a Writer (1962).] Modern Language Review, LIX (July), 469-70.
"Professor Smith, in this admirable study, has come as close as anyone to a succesful penetration of Mark Twain's intricate mechanisms of defence," through close familiarity with his subject, "the nice management of differing critical strategies," and a "strict critical scrupolosity" which has confined his claims to what can be fully sustained.

B78 MILLS, BARRISS. "Old Times on the Mississippi as an Initiation Story," College English, XXV (January), 283-89.
Here, for once, MT found unity in his story, by using "the motif...of the initiation story--the account of a boy's becoming a man as he moves from innocence and ignorance, through the difficult process of acquiring knowledge of the world, to the practical but somewhat disillusioning wisdom of adulthood." MT "characteristically" destroyed the unity when he padded out the shorter work to make LOM. Abstract in AES, VII (1964), 974.

B79 MOBLEY, LAWRENCE E. "Mark Twain and the Golden Era," Papers of the Bibliographical Society of America, LVIII (First Quarter), 8-23.
Includes an annotated list of sixty contributions by MT up to April 17, 1868, and reprints several of them. Abstract in AES, VII (1964), 1843; reprinted in Twainian, XXIV (January-February, 1965).

B80 PARSONS, COLEMAN O. [Review: John S. Tuckey, Mark Twain and Little Satan: The Writing of "The Mysterious Stranger" (1963).] American Literature, XXXVI (March), 92.
Tuckey has reversed DeVoto's chronology, convincingly, but he conspicuously qualifies his statements and might better have waited until material in the Mark Twain Papers at the University of California (Berkeley) is made available.

B81 PERKINS, GEORGE. "Death by Spontaneous Combustion in Marryat, Melville, Dickens, Zola, and Others," Dickensian, LX (Winter), 57-63.
MT's reference in LOM to the death of Jimmy Finn "of a combination of delirium tremens and spontaneous combustion" [Author's National Edition, n.d., p. 453] follows a long-standing literary tradition of a grisly death of drunkards. Abstract in AES, VIII (1965), 1915; reprinted in Twainian, XXV (January-February, 1966).

B82 RATNER, MARC L. "Two Letters of Mark Twain," Mark Twain Journal, XII (Spring), 9, 17.
Contains texts of two previously unpublished letters from the Boyesen Collection, Columbia University Library (April 23, 1880 and January 11, 1882) to Hjalmar Hjorth Boyesen, the Norwegian-American writer and teacher, reflecting their personal friendship and MT's current involvement with TA and P&P; MT mentions having read from TA one evening in Twichell's "chapel." Abstract in AES, VIII (1965), 1065.

B83 RODNON, STEWART. "Mark Twain's Get-Rich-Quick Schemes: A Balance Sheet," Mark Twain Journal, XII (Winter), 3-5.
Although early poverty and his latent romanticism led MT into schemes in which he lost money, his "use of get-rich-quick projects in his novels was consistently successful." In addition to his portrayal of Colonel Sellers, MT "employed the easy-money motif in three general ways: occasionally money is passively received, sometimes it is gained through a quirk of fate and manipulated to extend the luck, and often it is won by chicanery." Abstract in AES, VIII (1965), 1068.

B84 ROGERS, FRANKLIN R. "Mark Twain and Daudet: A Tramp Abroad and Tartarin sur les Alpes," Comparative Literature, XVI (Summer), 254-63.
Suggests "a substantial debt on Daudet's part to Mark Twain": his itinerary follows the travels in TA rather than those of Daudet himself--but Daudet's treatment shows originality and we should not be too quick to join those who dismiss him as a mere plagiarizer from MT--as well as from Chateaubriand, Balzac, Flaubert, Zola, Goncourt, and Charles Dickens. Abstract in AES, IX (1966), 1095; reprinted in Twainian, XXVI (January-February, 1967).

B85 SALOMON, ROGER B. "Realism as Disinheritance: Twain, Howells, and James," American Quarterly, XVI (Winter), 531-44.
A foe of romance, MT was intellectually a realist; yet such works as CY and even IA reflect a longing for the past. "Twain alternately fondled and violated the past depending on the mode that was uppermost at any given time. Only occasionally--the great

293

(SALOMON, ROGER B.)
example is, of course, Huckleberry Finn--
did the modes come into any kind of fruitful equilibrium."

B86　SAMUELS, THOMAS CHARLES. "Mr. Trilling, Mr.
Warren, and An American Tragedy," Yale Review, LIII (Summer).
Pp. 637-39 concern Leo Marx and the debate over HF: "Since he had demonstrated
that the ending is a cruel travesty of the
book's human, un-illusioned attack on hypocrisy and discrimination, Marx neatly
proves that Trilling and Eliot had stressed
form and ignored morality. He then shrewd-
ly speculates that so egregious a blunder
in critics so eminent could only result
from an indifference to the book's moral
point." Abstract in AES, XIII (1969-1970),
672; reprinted in Twainian, XXIX (January-
February, 1970).

B87　SCHELL, EDGAR T. "'Pears' and 'Is' in Pudd'n-
head Wilson," Mark Twain Journal, XII (Winter), 12-15.
Two major characters "stand outside the
world of Dawson's Landing: Roxy because
she is a Negro and a slave, Pudd'nhead because he is an outsider and apparently a
fool. In a sense they frame that world.
Roxy is a focus for all the attitudes, good
and bad, of the Southern past, Pudd'nhead
represents the Northern future; Roxy acts,
Pudd'nhead observes; Roxy obscures reality,
Pudd'nhead uncovers it. Their association
with opposing attitudes and values is reflected in their rolls [sic] as principal
antagonists." The book "is a far more unified, more balanced novel than many of its
critics have been willing to grant...an exposition of the extremely fine line between
appearance and reality." Abstract in AES,
VIII (1965), 1071.

B88　SCOTT, ARTHUR L. "Letters from Mark Twain to
William Walter Phelps, 1891-1893," Hunting-
ton Library Quarterly, XXVII (August),
375-81.
Describes and quotes from six letters to
Phelps, American minister in Berlin, and one
to his daughter Marian; their light-hearted
tone gives no hint of his fears and anxie-
ties of the time. "These letters are part
(HM 27353-59) of the William Walter Phelps
Correspondence, a recent acquisiton of the
Huntington Library." Abstract in AES, VIII
(1965), 1378; reprinted in Twainian, XXV
(January-February, 1966).

B89　SHARP, EUGENE. [Review: Paul Fatout, Mark
Twain in Virginia City.] Journalism Quarterly, XLI (Summer), 446-47.
Brief and descriptive: journalists will
be interested to see the picture of their
profession in Nevada.

B90　SMITH, HENRY NASH. "The Search for a Capitalist Hero: Businessmen in American Fiction,"
in Earl F. Cheit, ed., The Business Establishment (New York: John Wiley & Sons,
Inc.), pp. 77-112.
Passim on GA and CY (indexed).

B91　SMITH, PAUL. "The Infernal Reminiscence:
Mythic Patterns in Mark Twain's 'The Celebrated Jumping Frog of Calaveras County,'"
Satire Newsletter, I (Spring), 41-44.
A critical spoof: "In this dark and nearly tragic story...Mark Twain seems to have
first become aware of the archetypal and
mythic, the deeply autochthonic qualities of
his fictional material."

B92　SORIA, REGINA. "Mark Twain and Vedder's Medusa," American Quarterly, XVI (Winter),
602-606.
Chiefly on the artist Elihu Vedder, whose
picture of Medusa MT bought at his studio in
Rome in 1878.

B93　TAPER, BERNARD. "Mark Twain's San Francisco,
Introduction by Taper," Twainian, XXIII
(January-February), 1-3.
The second of two installments reprinting
the introduction to Taper's book.

B94　*TIRUMALAI, C. K. "Father-Son Relationships in
Huckleberry Finn," Exercise Exchange, XII
(November), 22-23.
[Source: Beebe and Feaster (1968),
p. 121.]

B95　TRILLING, DIANA. "Tom Sawyer, Delinquent, in
her Claremont Essays (New York: Harcourt,
Brace & World, Inc.), pp. 143-52.
The book is a celebration of boyhood by an
author who had small use for the adult
world. And yet, after all, Tom makes compro-
mises Huck does not; this is "a town book,"
and the world of the Mississippi still lies
ahead. (This first appeared in 1962 as the
introduction to the Crowell-Collier Publishing Company ed. of TS.)

B96　*TUTTLETON, JAMES W. "Twain's Use of Theatrical Traditions in the Old Southwest," College Language Association Journal, VIII
(December), 190-97.
On the dramatic declaration and the camp
meeting, as seen in HF. [Source: MHRA Annual Bibliography (1964), No. 6589; Abstract
in AES, X (1967), 416, and reprinted in
Twainian, XXVII (January-February, 1968).]

B97　*VAGTS, ALFRED. "Mark Twain at the Courts of
the Emperors" [Also listed as "Mark Twain at
the Courts of Europe"], Jahrbuch für Amerikastudien, IX, 149-51.
On MT's visits to Czar Alexander II and
Emperor Wilhelm II; passages on the meeting
with Alexander II at Yalta were censored
before and after the Revolution in Russian
editions of IA, first for flippancy and then
for too friendly a portrayal. [Source:

(VAGTS, ALFRED)
MHRA Annual Bibliography (1964), No. 6590;
Abstract in AES, VIII (1965); 1402, and
reprinted in Twainian, XXV (January-February, 1966).]

B98　WILLIAMS, JAMES D. "Revision and Intention
in Mark Twain's A Connecticut Yankee,"
American Literature, XXXVI (November),
288-97.

"The notebook entries, the manuscript,
and the published novel do not support the
thesis that A Connecticut Yankee began simply as a humorous contrast and then--be-
cause of a conscious change in intention--
became at a specific point an 'inverted
satire.'" MT had been thinking about "chivalry, slavery, and progress" for twenty
years, but "his Anglophobia...had shallow
roots and was poor in associations." Abstract in AES, VIII (1965), 1555, reprinted
in Twainian, XXV (January-February, 1966).

1965 A BOOKS

A1　CLEMENS, SAMUEL L. The Adventures of Colonel
Sellers. Being Mark Twain's Share of "The
Gilded Age," a Novel which He Wrote with
Charles Dudley Warner. Now Published Sepa-
rately for the First Time and Comprising,
in Effect, a New Work. Ed. Charles Neider.
Garden City, N.Y.: Doubleday.

The introduction includes a useful account of the reception of GA, quoting a
number of reviews (many of them English)
not listed in the present bibliography.
Neider argues that "It was an error for
Mark Twain to seek Warner's help.... As it
happens, his share of The Gilded Age is
the central share and the text is cohesive
and extensive enough to be printed separately if certain sections by Warner are synop-
sized to carry the story along" (p. xiii).

A2　FRENCH, BRYANT MOREY. Mark Twain and "The
Gilded Age": The Book that Named an Era.
Dallas: Southern University Press.

On the backgrounds of the novel, models on
whom characters are based, with discussion
of the play Colonel Sellers and appendices
on copyright and details of publication,
Colonel Sellers' Railroad Map, and the chapter mottoes. Extensively documented.

A3　GREGORY, RALPH. Mark Twain's First America:
Florida, Missouri, 1835-1840. Florida,
Missouri: Friends of Florida.

A brief history of the town and the connection of the Clemens family with it;
documentation includes local accounts (34-
page pamphlet).

A4　McKEITHAN, DANIEL MORLEY. A Mark Twain Notebook for 1892. Uppsala: A.-B. Lundquista
Bokhandeln. (Essays and Studies on American Language and Literature, XVII.)

On a notebook kept by MT, mainly in Florence and Bad Nauheim; quotes passages of the
text, which is in the Miriam Lutcher Stark
Library, University of Texas.

A5　MIRIZZI, PIERO. Mark Twain. (Biblioteca di
Studi Americani, 10). Rome: Edizioni di
Storia e Letteratura.

A general study, attempting to strike a
balance between the "admiring critics" and
the "dissenting critics." Contains a brief
survey of Italian criticism (pp. 302-303).
[In Italian.]

A6　PFLUG, RAYMOND J. The Adventures of Huckleberry Finn: The Evolution of a Classic.
Boston: Ginn and Company.

A school "Casebook for Objective Writing."

A7　POLI, BERNARD. Mark Twain: Écrivain de
l'Ouest. Régionalisme et Humour. Paris:
Presses Universitaires de France.

A major study by one of the few French
scholars currently concerned with MT as an
important author. [In French.]

A8　SALSBURY, EDITH COLGATE, ed. Susy and Mark
Twain: Family Dialogues. New York: Harper
& Row, Publishers.

"The family, their friends, and their servants tell the story of Susy Clemens and her
father, Mark Twain.... In some cases I have
combined two versions of the same story...In
a few cases anecdotes have been shifted
chronologically." Mrs. Salsbury tells the
story by editing the actual words of MT,
Susy, Olivia Clemens, Howells, and others,
and as "Narrator" provides the needed commentary.

A9　STEARNS, MONROE. Mark Twain. New York:
Franklin Watts, Inc.

A biography for young readers, with full
index and a bibliography; carefully researched and generally reliable, though
sometimes perhaps too trusting of sources.

1965 B SHORTER WRITINGS

B1　ANDERSON, FREDERICK. [Review: Bryant Morey
French, Mark Twain and "The Gilded Age."]
Nineteenth-Century Fiction, XXI (June),
106-108.

French has made a valuable contribution
in tracing background material, identifying
figures portrayed, and assessing the respec-
tive contributions made by MT and Charles
Dudley Warner, but the book should have been
"edited so that the valid points made by its
author would appear with greater economy and
force"; the failure by the Southern University Press to provide such help "does little
credit to the author it publishes or to the
reputation of the publisher."

1965 - Shorter Writings

B2   ANON. "The Cow Tracks Stop at the Tree,"
      Times Literary Supplement (May 6), p. 344.
          A review of MT's Simon Wheeler, Detective
      (1964), a poor specimen of his writing
      somewhat redeemed by "the handsome produc-
      tion and impeccable editing." The reviewer
      adds his own interesting comments on PW, in n
      which the fact that he was dealing with
      Negro characters allowed MT to master some
      of his literary taboos, among them the fact
      "that a mother may be hated by her son."

B3   ANON. "Mark Twain Items Appearing Elsewhere,"
      Twainian, XXIV (January-February), 3-4.
          Reprints several abstracts from AES, VII
      (1964).

B4   ANON. "Mark Twain's First 'Literary Ven-
      ture,'" Missouri Historical Review, LX
      (October), 75-76.
          Reprints without editorial comment MT's
      letter signed "A Dog-Bedevilled Citizen"
      from the Hannibal Journal of September 16,
      1852, followed by his comment on it in "My
      First Literary Venture" (Sketches New and
      Old).

B5   ANON. [Review: Charles Neider, ed., The Ad-
      ventures of Colonel Sellers.] Choice, II
      (June), 225.
          "Warner has suffered enough among critics
      for daring to collaborate with the master
      humorist, but this is literary snobbery
      and opportunistic publishing at its worst."

B6   ANON. [Brief Review: Edith Colgate Sals-
      bury, Susy and Mark Twain: Family Dia-
      logues.] Choice, II (December), 685.
          "The reader's interest lags, as each
      chapter...becomes bogged down in insignifi-
      cant and often very personal details of
      family life."

B7   *ARIKAWA, SHOJI. "Huck and Death," Kyusha
      American Literature, No. 8, pp. 19-24.
          [Source: MHRA Annual Bibliography (1965),
      No. 6956.]

B8   BABCOCK, C. MERTON. "Mark Twain and Mencken:
      A Literary Kinship," Menckeniana, XIV (Sum-
      mer), 4-5.
          Menken began reading MT's writings at the
      age of nine, came to develop an outlook
      like MT's, and was unmistakably influenced
      by him, although there is no evidence that
      they ever met. Menken's "A Prayer for Puri-
      tans" (Smart Set, XLV, March, 1915, p. 228,
      here quoted at length) is strikingly simi-
      lar to MT's "The War Prayer"--which, how-
      ever, was first published in Europe and
      Elsewhere in 1923. Abstract in AES, XII
      (1969), 462; reprinted in Twainian, XXIX
      (January-February, 1970).

B9   BALDANZA, FRANK. [Review: Robert A. Wiggins,
      Mark Twain: Jackleg Novelist (1964.]
      American Literature, XXXVI (January), 535.
          The approach with little note of other

critics is "refreshing," as Wiggins depicts
in MT "a man who dreams of, and succeeds in,
performing an action which will embody values and aspirations of the primitive folk
mind. Huckleberry Finn is the unquestioned
masterpiece of this genre," but MT's later
"pessimistic determinism jarred disastrously
against the folk values and the realistic
and colloquial style" and resulted in an
artistic decline. Wiggins makes "a reasoned
and--within the confines of his thesis--
sympathetic assessment," and one may hope it
will not stir bitter controversy.

B10   BARNES, DANIEL R. "Twain's The Adventures of
      Huckleberry Finn, Chapter I," Explicator,
      XXIII (April), Item 62.
          Biblical prototypes cast light on the por-
      trayal of the lives of the major characters,
      as in the parallel between Huck and Moses
      in the "bullrushers." Abstract in AES, IX
      (1966), 2605.

B11   BERTHOFF, WARNER. The Ferment of Realism:
      American Literature 1884-1919. New York:
      The Free Press, and London: Collier-Macmil-
      lan Ltd.
          MT's art was that of the performer, and
      his "great influence on subsequent American
      writing has been in the main a technical and
      not an imaginative influence." Like Poe,
      also schooled as a journalist, "Twain con-
      ceived of the writer's work as pre-eminently
      a manipulation of responses, a staging of
      irresistible effects"; this resulted in an
      art which was often mechanical, but both
      writers also achieved "a trance-like direct-
      ness and integrity of enacted vision that
      comes upon us with the force of unarguable
      revelation," with an effect "that compels us
      to rank both men among the few original
      masters of our literature." In the effort
      to explain their artistry, criticism of both
      authors is inclined to turn to psychoanaly-
      sis which, however, is adequate only with
      their less successful works (p. 63).

B12   BOESER, LINDA. "Two Comstock Journalists:
      Samuel L. Clemens and William L. Wright,"
      Missouri Historical Review, LIX (July),
      428-38.
          On MT and his friend (who used the pseudo-
      nym "Dan De Quille") and their work on the
      Territorial Enterprise; Wright, born a Quak-
      er, was quieter and more retiring than MT,
      and less successful; "Apparently the very
      conservatism and high regard for facts which
      made De Quille such an able reporter, also
      ironically worked against him as an author."

B13   BOOTH, BRADFORD A. [Review: Margaret Duckett,
      Mark Twain and Bret Harte (1964).] Nine-
      teenth-Century Fiction, XX (June), 101-102.
          The evidence that has become available,
      revealing MT's "egregious slanders" of
      Harte, "has been sifted by Margaret Duckett
      with painstaking thoroughness, ingenuity,
      and skill," and we now see Harte "as an

(BOOTH, BRADFORD A.)
essentially honorable, if sometimes thought-
less man, often calumniated and much misunderstood." This book "admirably" refutes
the slanders, and impartial critics will
appreciate "its informed scholarship and
its essential objectivity in the face of
controversial material."

B14   BROOKS, VAN WYCK. Van Wyck Brooks: An Autobiography. Foreword by John Hall Wheelock;
Intro. by Malcolm Cowley. New York: E. P.
Dutton & Co., Inc.
Consists of Scenes and Portraits (1954),
Days of the Phoenix, and From the Shadow of
the Mountain (1961); the indexes of those
works are less extensive than in their original publication.

B15   BROWNE, RAY B. "Huck's Final Triumph," Ball
State Teachers College Forum, VI (Winter),
3-12.
After summarizing the debate over the
ending of HF, argues that the book's theme
is "Huck's search for personal liberation,"
for the maturity that will allow him to
proclaim that he is his own master. The
novel's theme develops in three strands as
Huck outgrows Tom, Jim and Pap, and in the
end he can be true to himself rather than
to society. Abstract in AES, IX (1966),
715; reprinted in Twainian, XXVI (January-
February, 1967).

B16   *BUTCHER, PHILIP. "Mark Twain Sells Roxy Down
the River," College Language Association
Journal, VIII (March), 225-33.
The portrait of the slave-woman in PW is
a caricature, reflecting "popular notions
about the Negro's emotional instability and
lack of profound feeling." [Source: MHRA
Annual Bibliography (1965), No. 6963; Abstract in AES, X (1967), 417, and reprinted
in Twainian, XXVII (January-February,
1968).]

B17   CALLAN, RICHARD J. "The Burden of Innocence
in Melville and Twain," Renascence, XVII
(Summer), 191-94.
A comparison of Billy Budd and Huckleberry
Finn, whose authors were skeptics about man
and "in the matter of religiosity...shook
and shocked us into attention. Finally, the
leading characters of those fictions and
some of their predicaments have a surprising
similarity." Abstract in AES, VIII (1965),
3077; reprinted in Twainian, XXV (March-
April, 1966).

B18   CARTER, PAUL J. [Review: Robert A. Wiggins,
Mark Twain: Jackleg Novelist (1964).]
Western Humanities Review, XIX (Summer),
277-78.
Wiggins contends that uneasiness in his
role as novelist led MT to reliance primarily on instinct rather than conscious craftsmanship, to an emphasis on realism, and to
an overestimation of the potentialities of

humor to allow him to write almost anything,
so long as it was entertaining. Application
of this thesis to MT's novels illustrates
it but adds little knowledge or critical insight.

B19   CHAPUT, DONALD. "Mark Twain: Copied Originality," Mark Twain Journal, XII (Summer),
20-21.
"Twain's debt to others is enormous. Almost every important work or character by
Twain had been suggested by someone he knew
or something he read"; for example, Huck
Finn is merely Tom Blankenship renamed, Jim
is Uncle Dan'l, and Sid is MT's brother
Henry. "Twain was ready for the ideas. He
was ready to write." Abstract in AES, IX
(1966), 2656.

B20   CLARK, WILLIAM G. "Mark Twain's Visual and
Aural Descriptions," Mark Twain Journal, XII
(Summer), 1-9, 16.
MT's ear was better than his eye: descriptions of what he has seen read like derivative set-pieces, but his "aural descriptions
...usually seem to represent a real understanding of the person, place or event being
described." Abstract in AES, IX (1966),
2652.

B21   COX, JAMES M. [Review: Henry Nash Smith,
Mark Twain's Fable of Progress (1964).]
American Literature, XXXVII (March), 81-82.
Smith includes "a fine analysis of Charles
Dudley Warner's A Little Journey in the World
and William Dean Howells' A Hazard of New
Fortunes" to provide context; his "argument
is persuasive, yet one wonders whether it is
not a more heroic effort to come to terms
with the novel than the novel was to create
a capitalist hero."

B22   [DAVIS, CHESTER L.] "The Adventures of Colonel Sellers, by Neider," Twainian, XXIV
(March-April), 1-4.
A "review," consisting of introductory
comments on the theory of patents and copyright, an estimate of Twainian readership at
30,000 (for 300 members of the Mark Twain
Research Foundation), and description of
Neider's edition of MT's part of The Gilded
Age as "a fine contribution of lasting merit...something new and useful.... We now
reprint from the book what would normally be
the introduction, which Neider calls 'A Novelists's Debut,' a great part of it, and a
short sketch from the 'Sellers' story to remind our readers how fine it is." Reprint
follows, pp. 2-4, extensively citing contemporary newspaper reviews.

B23   _____. "Contemporary Newspaper Accounts of
Mark Twain's Lectures," Twainian, XXIV
(November-December), 1-3.
Reprints accounts of MT lectures in Keokuk
(Iowa) Gate City and Paris Kentuckian
(1885.B8, B10). This is followed by a list
of "the worthwhile collection of complete

1965 - Shorter Writings

([DAVIS, CHESTER L.])
newspaper accounts now in the possession of one of our members," for some of which information is apparently lacking, but which appears to represent a valuable contribution to MT secondary bibliography. Chester Davis writes of acting as a clearing-house for further information of this sort, but cautions that its value is uneven: "We know of one report which is hardly worth reprinting in our publication, because it is so prejudiced against the man and so contrary to the facts." Abstract in AES, XI (1968), 1728; reprinted in Twainian, XXVIII (January-February, 1969).

B24　＿＿＿. "Hannibal Boy-hood Home, Mahan Correspondence with Albert Bigelow Paine," Twainian, XXIV (September-October), 1-3.
One letter to F. A. Duneka of Harper's (September 16, 1911) and six to Paine (October 18, 1911-July 13, 1916) from George A. Mahan, a Hannibal attorney, on purchase of the MT home as a memorial; notes accounts in St. Louis Republic and New York Herald of September 2, 1911. Abstract in AES, XI (1968), 1726; reprinted in Twainian, XXVIII (January-February, 1969).

B25　＿＿＿. "Jervis Langdon and Other Correspondence with Paine on 'Biography,'" Twainian, XXIV (July-August), 1-4.
A miscellany of letters, 1910-1912, on topics relating to business affairs rather than the Paine biography of MT. Includes letters by Charles T. Lark on the estate of Jean L. Clemens, and Jervis Langdon on funeral expenses, pictures, bequests by MT, sale of "Stormfield" and the billiard table there, etc. Abstract in AES, XI (1968), 1724, reprinted in Twainian, XXVIII (January-February, 1969).

B26　＿＿＿. [Review: Edith Colgate Salsbury, Susy and Mark Twain.] Twainian, XXIV (November-December), 1.
Fitting together the actual words of MT, Susy, and others "in an interesting and novel manner," the editor has produced "a very scholarly work," although the readability could be improved.

B27　DICKINSON, LEON T. [Review: Hamlin Hill, Mark Twain and Elisha Bliss (1964).] American Literature, XXXVII (November), 334-35.
Recapitulates the history of the business raltionship and observes that "Mr. Hill tells his story well. He presents much new evidence--letters, sales figures, publishing records--to support his contention that for twelve years Elisah Bliss exerted a great influence in determining the direction of Mark Twain's literary development."

B28　DIXON, ELIZABETH WHITE. "Mark Twain Dresses Up," Mark Twain Journal, XIII (Winter), 17-20.
Loosely and confusedly biographical. MT's love of fine clothing is a compensation for a childhood in which his parents could not "afford to buy toys like those of other children.... to provide for his own amusement during his formidable years [sic], he was forced to hold the world up by the tail, so to speak, and laugh at it."

B29　EDISON, THOMAS A. [Letter to Cyril Clemens, dated "Orange, N. J., January 12, 1927"; signed typescript, here reproduced in facsimile.] Mark Twain Journal, XIII (Winter), front cover.
Describes a visit to the Edison Laboratory by MT, who made a recording (destroyed in a fire in 1914).

B30　EMBERSON, FRANCES GUTHRIE, and ROBERT L. RAMSAY. A Mark Twain Lexicon (1938), partially reprinted in Twainian, XXIV (May-June), 1-4; (July-August), 4; (September-October), 3-4; (November-December), 3-4.
A headnote by Chester L. Davis expresses the wish that it were possible to reprint the entire book, but "we must content ourselves, at least at the start of this series, with only a part of the some 500 pages." Abstracts in AES, XI (1968), 1723, 1725, 1727, 1729; reprinted in Twainian, XXVIII (January-February, 1969).

B31　FALK, ROBERT. "Mark Twain and the Earlier Realism," in his The Victorian Mode in American Fiction, 1865-1885. (East Lansing: Michigan State University Press), pp. 157-66.
Although MT was both a realist and a Victorian, he lies outside the mainstream. His contributions lay in his attack on romanticism and insistence on the authentic. "The association of realism with local color and especially with the western story was Twain's one positive contribution to theoretical criticism of the novel" (p. 163).

B32　GAINES, ERVIN J. [Review: Margaret Duckett, Mark Twain and Bret Harte (1964).] Library Journal, XC (January 1), 123.
The book fails to answer the central question of what caused the fatal rupture between the two men. "Facts are loosely interpreted throughout, and the expository skills demanded by an undertaking like this are unfortunately absent."

B33　GANZEL, DEWEY. "Clemens, Mrs. Fairbanks, and Innocents Abroad," Modern Philology, LXIII (November), 128-140.
Scholarly legend exaggerates the influence Mary Mason Fairbanks exerted on MT while he was touring Europe and the Holy Land on the Quaker City and writing newspaper correspondence. She was a good friend, but not a mentor, and she was helpful chiefly in proofreading and in reminding him of topics--particularly after MT discovered fourteen of his letters had been lost in the mails. Abstract in AES, IX (1966), 2672.

B34 GANZEL, DEWEY. "Samuel Clemens and John Camden Hotten," The Library, Fifth Series, XX (September), 230–42.

Although MT reviled Hotten for publishing his books without permission and without paying royalties, Hotten was a strong advocate of better international copyright and had in fact written MT to ask permission to reprint Innocents Abroad but received no answer; he did pay Bret Harte and Artemus Ward for works of theirs he reprinted, and presumably would have been willing, as he claimed, to pay MT. Abstract in AES, XI (1968), 495; reprinted in Twainian, XXVIII (January–February, 1969).

B35 _____. "Samuel Clemens, Guidebooks, and Innocents Abroad," Anglia (Tübingen), LXXXIII, No. 1, pp. 78–88.

MT used several familiar guidebooks not only for information but also for some of his organization and perspectives. Abstract in AES, X (1967), 827; reprinted in Twainian, XXVII (January–February, 1968).

B36 GERBER, JOHN C. "Mark Twain," in James Woodress, ed., American Literary Scholarship: An Annual/1965. (Durham, North Carolina: Duke University Press, 1967), pp. 57–68.

A survey of MT scholarship for the year; See 1963.B32. Contents: "i. Texts and Editions"; "ii. Biography"; "iii. Criticism"; "iv. Innocents Abroad"; "v. The Gilded Age"; "vi. Tom Sawyer"; "vii. Huckleberry Finn"; "viii. A Connecticut Yankee"; "ix. Short Selections."

B37 GOODER, R. D. "One of Today's Best Little Writers?" Cambridge Quarterly, I (Winter), 81–90.

On J. D. Salinger; contrasts Catcher in the Rye and Huckleberry Finn, observing that Holden "calls the tune, and proves himself morally and spiritually superior to everyone except his little sister...Holden judges all, but is not judged.... Where do we ever find Holden in a position of admitted moral inferiority, as we find Huck when he admits he has played a mean trick on Jim? Where does Holden have to make the difficult choice between what he has been taught and what he knows in himself is right, as Huck has to do when he decides to shield Jim?" Abstract in AES, XV (1971–1972), 1248.

B38 GORDAN, JOHN D. "An Anniversary Exhibition. The Henry W. and Albert A. Berg Collection 1940–1965," Bulletin of the New York Public Library, LXIX (December), 665–677.

Concludes a three-part series. On pp. 675–76, describes a dedication copy of P&P presented to Susie Clemens and notes the rich holdings in the Berg Collection of MT material, including the manuscript of CY, the corrected typescript of FE, and almost four hundred letters. The remainder of the installment and the series does not concern MT. Abstract in AES, IX (1966), 2851; reprinted in Twainian, XXVI (January–February, 1967).

B39 _____. "Novels in Manuscript: An Exhibition from the Berg Collection," Bulletin of the New York Public Library, LXIX (May), 317–29.

On p. 325, briefly summarizes MT's career and notes: "The manuscript of A Connecticut Yankee, here displayed, is over nine hundred pages long. These pages show considerable correction, from the very first line..." A continuation of this article in the following issue contains nothing further on MT. Abstract in AES, IX (1966), 45; reprinted in Twainian, XXVI (January–February, 1967).

B40 *GORDON, JOSEPH T. "The Gilded Age and Democracy: A Literary View of Post-Civil War America," Forum (Houston), VI (Winter-Spring), 4–9.

[Source: AES, X (1967), 2695, reprinted in Twainian, XXVII, January–February, 1968; facts of publication confirmed by note from Forum.] AES abstract notes the satire of the corruption of the day in the novels of MT and Warner, and by Henry Adams.

B41 GREENLEAF, RICHARD. "Mark Twain and the Bishop of Woolwich," Religion in Life: A Christian Quarterly of Opinion and Discussion (Nashville: Abington Press), XXXV (Winter).

[Source: unpaged offprint in Mark Twain Papers]. Arranged as a dialogue, consisting of quotations from MT's "Reflections on Religion" (edited by Charles Neider in Hudson Review, 1963) and Honest to God by John A. T. Robinson, Bishop of Woolwich; concludes that most atheists are opposed merely to false images of God, "a way of conceiving him which has become an idol."

B42 HALVERSON, JOHN. "Patristic Exegesis: A Medieval Tom Sawyer," College English, XXVII (October), 50–55.

When Tom is slighted by Becky and broods in the woods (Chapter VIII) he follows the example of The Man in Black in Chaucer's The Book of the Duchess, which MT probably "knew and understood" (Halverson's italics). The underlying doctrine is Augustinian, and in TS "underneath the apparently frivolous cortex of this extraordinary work there is a profound condemnation of the foolishness and vice to which unbridled concupiscence leads."

B43 HARDING, WALTER. "Mark Twain's Blue Jays and the Red-Headed Woodpeckers," Twainian, XXIV (January–February), 1.

Compares Jim Baker's story in TA of a blue jay attempting to fill a knot-hole in a cabin roof to a similar account in Arthur Cleveland Bent's Life History of North American Woodpeckers (Smithsonian Institution, U. S. National Museum Bulletin 174, 1939, pp. 202–203) of a woodpecker poking acorns in a hole extending through a telephone pole:

1965 - Shorter Writings

(HARDING, WALTER)
"On the ground under the pole was about a double handful of acorns that had fallen out." Contains no information on MT.

B44 *HENDERSON, ROSWELL P. "Judge John Marshall Clemens," Bulletin of the Missouri Historical Society, XXI (October), 25-30.
Reveals a more impressive figure than depicted by his son, MT. [Source: Abstract in AES, XI (1968), 1842; Leary (1970), p. 65 lists this for 1964.]

B45 HILL, HAMLIN. "Toward a Critical Text of The Gilded Age," Papers of the Bibliographical Society of America, LIX (Second Quarter, 1965), 142-49.
"Over 170 variants, then, belong by best judgment in the copy-text which represents the closest version to Mark Twain's intended one, almost half of them substantive readings. And derived texts of The Gilded Age almost without exception corrupt the text further." Abstract in AES, IX (1966), 924; reprinted in Twainian, XXVI (January-February, 1967).

B46 _____. "Two Mark Twain Heresies," Modern Language Quarterly, XXVI (June), 327-32.
A review article. Margaret Duckett's Mark Twain and Bret Harte (1964) is too long. "Duckett demonstrates admirably that Bret Harte was an extremely important influence on the early Mark Twain," but later she "becomes an apologist for Harte; and on several occasions the defense is inadequate." Robert A. Wiggins's Mark Twain: Jackleg Novelist (1964) "would have been immeasurably more useful if it had assimilated some of the critical and scholarly studies written during the past decade and a half."

B47 HOROWITZ, FLOYD R. "Mark Twain's Belle Lettre in 'The Loves of Alonzo Fitz Clarence and Rosannah Ethelton,'" Mark Twain Journal, XIII (Winter), 16.
This story, written in 1878, accurately represents the first commercial model of the telephone (1877). Abstract in AES, XI (1968), 2263.

B48 JAUCH, CLEVELAND E., JR. "The Huckleberry Finn Exhibition," Grosvenor Society Occasional Papers, I (January), 27-35.
An appreciative discussion of HF and the manuscript of it exhibited by the Buffalo and Erie County Public Library, October 12-17 [1964?]; for the general reader.

B49 JOHNSON, ROBERT L. "The Road Out in Australian and American Fiction: a Study of Four Spokesmen," Southern Review: An Australian Journal of Literary Studies (University of Adelaide), I:3, pp. 20-31.
Uses HF and Cooper's Leatherstocking Tales as a basis of comparison for the discussion of Australian authors Joseph Furphy and Henry Lawson. Abstract in AES, X (1967), 3158; reprinted in Twainian, XXVII (January-February, 1968).

B50 JORDAN, PHILIP D. [Review: Margaret Duckett, Mark Twain and Bret Harte (1964).] American Notes and Queries, IV (October), 29.
Miss Duckett provides a useful record of the relationship of the two men but fails to explain the break in their friendship: "She records symptoms, but ignores causes.... It might have been profitable had Miss Duckett shown her manuscript to a psychiatrist." Nonetheless, "the volume as it stands is sound and will no doubt become the definitive work on a pair of talented but abnormal men of letters."

B51 KAHN, SHOLOM J. "Mark Twain's Final Phase." Studi Americani, XI, 143-62.
The last twenty years of MT's literary career constitute a phase of his development which has been somewhat neglected and perhaps misunderstood: after FE in 1897 he was no longer pressed by financial obligations and he turned his attention increasingly to commenting on man, religion, and society, and recording his own past.

B52 KEELEY, MARY PAXTON. [Review: Rachel M. Varble, Jane Clemens: The Story of Mark Twain's Mother (1964).] Missouri Historical Review, LX (October), 120-21.
Chiefly descriptive; praises the book as "delightful...well documented; some of the material, such as family letters, is new," presenting "a more realistic and less eulogistic picture of Mark Twain" than most books on him.

B53 KELLY, JAMES J. "They're Trying to Kill Huckleberry Finn," Mark Twain Journal, XIII (Winter), 13-14.
On the removal of HF from New York schools as racially offensive, and (briefly) on past bannings of the book. Kelly defends the portrayal of Jim and the representation of Negro speech, adding: "For any individual or organization to deny the fact that the American Negro generally, and with the exception of a small minority, speaks a limited and lower-vulgate English is ridiculous.... It is hardly the fault of Samuel Clemens if the average American Negro remains inarticulate in English after being in this country for three-hundred years."

B54 KRAUSE, SYDNEY J. "Cooper's Literary Offences: Mark Twain in Wonderland," New England Quarterly, XXXVIII (September), 291-311.
The assault on Cooper is delivered by a literary persona, rather than the responsible Samuel Clemens. "Actually, he is an unabashable hack and in his baccanal of sophistry latches on to just enough fact to silence doubt. Thus, over the long haul,

(KRAUSE, SYDNEY J.)
what this creature has gotten away with on the basis of gall alone is literary mayhem pure and simple" in his successful misrepresentation of Cooper, as may be seen by returning to what Cooper actually said; for example, MT's "account of the ambush is almost a complete canard." Abstract in AES, IX (1966), 2675.

B55 ____. "Huck's First Moral Crisis," Mississippi Quarterly, XVIII (Spring), 69-73.
Huck's moral awareness of Jim does not come in the fog episode in Chapter XV (as Lionel Trilling suggests), since his reponse there is psychological rather than moral; apologizing to Jim and recognizing him as a person prepares Huck for the following chapters, in which he "saves Jim by dint of courage and wit" from slave hunters. Abstract in AES (1966), 2328; reprinted in Twainian, XXVI (January-February, 1967).

B56 ____. "Twain and Scott: Experience versus Adventures," Modern Philology, LXII (February), 227-36.
MT "felt that unsound social views yielded an unsound literature and that bad writing sprang from a stultification of experience. Both situations he regarded as excesses of romanticism, and he tried to combat them by injecting critical analogues of romantic fiction into his books. In Adventures of Huckleberry Finn there is a group of such analogues that implicate Sir Walter Scott's representation of history as adventures." Abstract in AES, IX (1966), 399; reprinted in Twainian, XXVI (January-February, 1967).

B57 KUBICEK, EARL C. "Becky Thatcher Grants an Interview," American Book Collector, XV (Summer), 37-38.
Recollections of Sam Clemmens [sic] by Laura Hawkins Frazer, whom Kubicek visited in 1928; she conversed politely and told him nothing she had not told other interviewers. Abstract in AES, IX (1966), 12; reprinted in Twainian, XXVI (January-February, 1967).

B58 LAWRENCE, MARY MARGARET. "A Low Comedian," North American Review, n.s. II (May), 14-15.
"Low comedian" is MT's term for the Indian crow, the subject of this article. There is nothing of critical or biographical interest on MT, although Following the Equator (II, Ch. II) is quoted extensively.

B59 LEITER, LOUIS H. "Dawson's Landing: Thematic Cityscape in Twain's Pudd'nhead Wilson," Mark Twain Journal, XIII (Winter), 8-11.
Although Dawson's Landing is superficially a typical American small town, it is symbolically given greater significance through references to other cities and countries (suggesting that it is a microcosm), to "one- and two-storey frame dwellings" (like there

may have "more than one 'story,' more than one meaning"), and "climbing tangles of rose-vines, honeysuckles, and morning glories" (implying complication, concealment, and "the rosy view, the honeyed view, the glorious view of existence--the superficial, communal view of the status quo"). "Twain exposes theme by forcing descriptions of houses to suggest ethical attitudes (superficial) and species of plants (old-fashioned) to suggest traditional beliefs." Abstract in AES, XI (1968), 2261.

B60 LEWIS, R. W. [Review: Hamlin Hill, Mark Twain and Elisha Bliss (1964).] College English, XXVI (March), 492.
Brief; chiefly descriptive. "Thoroughly researched and carefully documented, the book still reads easily and it makes a convincing case for Bliss's indirect influence."

B61 LILLARD, RICHARD G. [Review: Paul Fatout, Mark Twain in Virginia City (1964).] Journal of American History, LI (December), 511-12.
"The author presents here a long article's worth of new material in a book that reorganizes much that historians already have access to. ...the approach is descriptive rather than analytical," giving a full and accurate picture of MT's twenty months with the Enterprise.

B62 LINNEMAN, WILLIAM R. "Punch and Huckleberry Finn," English Language Notes, II (June), 293-94.
The weekly "Roundabout Readings" column for January 4, 1896 tells of the author's eleven year old nephew's "keen and appreciative enjoyment" of Huckleberry Finn and adds his own praise of "this Homeric book--for Homeric it is in the true sense, as no other English book is, that I know of." Abstract in AES, X (1967), 1199; reprinted in Twainian, XXVII (January-February, 1968).

B63 LYDENBERG, JOHN. [Review: Bryant Morey French, Mark Twain and "The Gilded Age."] American Quarterly, XVII (Winter), 768.
"Mr. French has assiduously collected almost all the facts about The Gilded Age that one could conceivably find, or want to find," and although he "tells us little that is new," he makes a good case for the political criticism and gives persuasive evidence that the sentimentalism and melodrama "are in large part intentional...as burlesques of the popular fiction of the time."

B64 McKEE, JOHN DeWITT. "Three Uses of the Arming Scene," Mark Twain Journal, XII (Summer), 18-19, 21.
MT's description of the dressing of a knight [Chapter XI: "The Yankee in Search of Adventures"] has no counterpart in Malory's "Le Mort D'Arthur"; it is here compared to an account in Chaucer's "Sir Thopas," and to one in Sir Gawain and the Green Knight, which

1965 - Shorter Writings

(McKEE, JOHN DeWITT)
"could have served as sources for both Chaucer and Twain." Abstract in AES, IX (1966), 2655.

B65   MANN, CHARLES W. [Review: Charles Neider, ed., The Adventures of Colonel Sellers.] Library Journal, XC (March 1), 1120-21.
The book is "a bibliographical curiosity. ...Twain and Warner, whatever their differences in temper and genius, did it their way, not Mr. Neider's."

B66   MANSFIELD, LILLIAN M. "Early Members, Parishioners, and Mark Twain," in her The History of Asylum Hill Congregational Church, Hartford, Connecticut (Hartford: Asylum Hill Congregational Church), pp. 12-22.
Passim on MT, his friendship for the pastor Joseph Twichell, and his renting a pew at the church although he and his wife did not become members officially; elsewhere, notes the church was more liberal than it had been in former times.

B67   MAXWELL, D. E. S. "Twain as Satirist," in his American Fiction: The Intellectual Background (New York: Columbia University Press; London: Routledge and Kegan Paul), pp. 192-235; also, p. 292 on HF.
A major study, beginning with eighteenth-century conceptions of satire, then treating MT's satire as an assault on the failure of institutions as seen in HF and other works.

B68   MILLER, F. DeWOLFE. "Whitman Bibliography in Russia," Walt Whitman Review, XI (September), 77-79.
MT receives more space than any other American author in a bibliography of Russian criticism of American writers in G. P. Zlobin, ed., "Studies in American Literature (more literally, Problems in the History of the Literature of the U.S.A.)," Moscow: Izdatelstvo "Hayka" (n.d.).

B69   MORGAN, H. WAYNE. "Mark Twain: The Optimist as Pessimist," in his American Writers in Rebellion from Mark Twain to Dreiser (New York: Hill and Wang), pp. 1-36.
Begins with a long biographical summary, using the Paine biography rather trustingly and MT's own accounts more cautiously. Without dismissing MT's pessimism and determinism, Morgan argues that "their hidden purpose weakened them; it was always that of the humanist, to lift, to cleanse, and to create as well as to criticize.... the shock of his losses late in life did not make him a pessimist"; rather, the outlook of his last years was the result of youthful freethinking and the "profound social changes of his lifetime."

B70   MORRIS, WRIGHT. "The Lunatic, the Lover, and the Poet," Kenyon Review, XXVII (Autumn), 727-37.
On the element of the grotesque in American literature, noting that "neither Mark Twain nor the times was ripe for the gallow's [sic] humor beneath his smiling platform manner, but he was too much of an artist, and he suffered too deeply, to conceal his feelings completely. The story of Pudd'nhead Wilson charts this personal crisis," although MT abandoned his original topic of Siamese twins (pp. 732-33). Abstract in AES, IX (1966), 2968; reprinted in Twainian, XXVI (January-February, 1967).

B71   PEDERSON, LEE A. "Negro Speech in The Adventures of Huckleberry Finn," Mark Twain Journal, XIII (Winter), 1-4.
An expanded version of a paper read to the American Dialect Society at the 1964 meeting of the Modern Language Association, this "preliminary report on a projected study of all the literary dialects in the novel" is a "brief account...limited to phonology," revealing close correspondence between the speech in HF and that still in use. Abstract in AES, XI (1968), 2260.

B72   *POWERS, RICHARD H. "To Mark Twain's Missionary Defenders," Forum (Houston), VI (Winter-Spring), 10-16.
[Source: AES, X (1967), 2696; reprinted in Twainian, XXVII, January-February, 1968; facts of publication confirmed by note from Forum. AES abstract notes that MT was restricted by his lack of formal education, although he learned of the human problem and the difficulty of its solution.]

B73   REGAN, ROBERT. [Review: Edith Colgate Salsbury, Susy and Mark Twain: Family Dialogues.] Library Journal, XC (September 15), 3605.
Brief review: Making a book of excerpts from books, journals, and letters, allowing people to speak for themselves, still tells us "nothing very interesting" about MT's books, "but for that shortcoming and others, Mrs. Salsbury's book compensates abundantly by conveying the reality of Mark Twain's family life with remarkable immediacy."

B74   RIDLAND, J. M. "Huck, Pip, and Plot," Nineteenth-Century Fiction, XX (December), 286-90.
Huck struggles with his conscience, and his decision to help Jim parallels that of Pip in Great Expectations to help the escaped convict Magwitch; Pip has learned morality from a "tall and bony" older sister comparable to Miss Watson, and in each book there is a collision with a steamboat on a river. Abstract in AES, XI (1968), 2329.

B75 ROGERS, FRANKLIN R. [Review: Paul Fatout, Mark Twain in Virginia City (1964).] American Literature, XXXVI (January), 534.

Because of a too-severe limitation in the scope of the book, Fatout "is unable to add anything to our understanding of the author's development as a writer"; moreover, he misrepresents MT as "a flamboyant feature writer who expended his major effort on hoaxes and humorous squibs"; and, finally, he has paid insufficient attention to original sources or the scholarship concerning them.

B76 _____. [Review: Robert A. Wiggins, Mark Twain: Jackleg Novelist (1964.] Nineteenth-Century Fiction, XIX (March), 412-13.

This brief book "deserves and will reward the reader's careful attention" as it follows "Twain's development from a humorist thoroughly untutored in the art of the novel to the novelist who wrote Huckleberry Finn and struggled with the complexities inherent in later conceptions." Wiggins finds MT's strength as located in the folk mind, which he later partially deserted, to his cost, since there was not an offsetting in sophisticated self-control. Although Wiggins does not come to grips with contrary critical opinions he is aware of them, and his own thesis is "worth considering"; he has written "a quite refreshing book."

B77 ROSSKY, WILLIAM. "The Reivers and Huckleberry Finn: Faulkner and Twain," Huntington Library Quarterly, XXVIII (August), 373-87.

As a young man Faulkner once disparaged MT, but he later praised his work and influence. The two humorous boys' books here discussed are alike in relations of boys to companions, their protective attitude toward young women, struggles with conscience, a revolt against conventional morality leading to higher morality, and "similar use of the tramp pattern with its variations." Abstract in AES, IX (1966), 1691; reprinted in Twainian, XXVI (January-February, 1967).

B78 *SCANLON, LAWRENCE E. "Unheroic Huck," East-West Review, II (Winter, 1965-1966), 99-114.

A passive character, Huck is further alienated from society by events beyond his control. [Source: Abstract in AES, XI (1968), 1219.]

B79 SMITH, HENRY NASH. "Mark Twain, The Adventures of Huckleberry Finn," in Wallace Stegner, ed., The American Novel from James Fenimore Cooper to William Faulkner (New York, London: Basic Books, Inc.), pp. 61-72.

"Huck's habit of moral improvisation, his antinominian attitude toward established authorities and institutions, his tolerance of a wide disparity between theory and practice" stem from what MT called his "sound heart and a deformed conscience." The book's structure reveals basic American attitudes, from near farce at the start to a growing richness in the quest for freedom, and then a "tragic realization that freedom cannot be attained in this or any world," and MT apparently "taking refuge from tragedy in a joke."

B80 _____. [Review: Hamlin Hill, Mark Twain and Elisha Bliss (1964).] Nineteenth-Century Fiction, XX (June), 96-98.

Hill has supported his "modest but clear thesis" that MT was shaped as a writer by the demands of subscription publication. Hill furnishes "a number of fresh insights into how Mark Twain's imagination functioned," and the book should be "permanently useful."

B81 SMITH, J. HAROLD. "Mark Twain's Basic Political Concepts: Men, Parties, Democracy," Missouri Historical Review, LIX (April), 349-54.

MT's generally derogatory portrait of political life derived both from a bitterness growing out of personal sorrows and from disillusionment founded on his own observations of a corrupt age.

B82 SMITHLINE, ARNOLD. [Review: Bryant Morey French, Mark Twain and "The Gilded Age."] Library Journal, XC (September 15), 3604.

"Rather clumsy and pedantic," but useful in showing the degree of collaboration between MT and Warner.

B83 *STEWART, VINCENT. "Out of the Looking Glass: Illusion and Reality in Tom Sawyer," Missouri English Bulletin, XXII (January), 1-8.

[Source: Beebe and Feaster (1968), p. 123; Leary (1970), p. 74; MHRA Annual Bibliography (1969), No. 7988.]

B84 SWAN, JON. "Innocents at Home," American Heritage, XVI (February), 58-61, 97-101.

On the 1906 visit of Maxim Gorky to New York, raising funds for a Russian revolution. MT and Howells lent enthusiastic support but withdrew upon public revelation that the woman traveling with Gorky was not his wife. A photograph shows MT with Gorky and others at a banquet at Club A in Manhattan. Abstract in AES, VIII (1965), 2181; reprinted in Twainian, XXV (January-February, 1966).

B85 TANNER, TONY. "Mark Twain" in his The Reign of Wonder: Naivety and Reality in American Literature (Cambridge: Cambridge University Press). pp. 97-183.

Beginning with the Simon Suggs and Sut Lovingood perspective, Tanner examines "the way in which the vernacular supplanted the official rhetoric in Clemens's writing," then turns to "examine some of the details

(TANNER, TONY)
of this important stylistic shift" (p. 127). In MT's inversion of oratory and of the pastoral situation, "the low uneducated figure is in fact wiser than the educated tourist, and he speaks more tellingly." His early works show him looking for appropriate speakers (p. 129). He found such a speaker in Huck Finn, and "The young vernacular rebel is alone with his wonder, his candour, and his sound heart" (p. 154); he stands in contrast to Tom Sawyer, who accepts the rules and outlook of society (Ch. X, passim). "The Pond of Youth" is reprinted in Schmitter (1974), pp. 29-39.

B86 _____. "Versions of Pastoral," Encounter, XXIV (June), 59-62.
A review-article, chiefly concerned with Leo Marx, The Machine in the Garden; a briefer account of Henry Nash Smith's Mark Twain's Fable of Progress accepts and describes the detailed exploration of "one of the most important early attempts to celebrate the technological age positively," only to culminate in "an orgy of embittered destruction."

B87 TAYLOR, J. GOLDEN. [Introduction.] "The Celebrated Jumping Frog of Calaveras County," American West, II (Fall), 73-76.
Provides the general reader an account of the first publication of the sketch (here reprinted, pp. 76-79) and the part it played in MT's development as vernacular stylist. "The literary significance...lies in the authenticity and artistry with which a humorous incident in an early western mining-camp is made to yield fable-like insights into certain universal traits in human nature." Abstract in AES, XIV (1970-1971), 2541 ("adapted from 'Abstracts of Folklore Studies' [Canada], 8:1, Sp., 1970, 13"); reprinted in Twainian, XXXI (January-February, 1972).

B88 TEDESCHINI LALLI, BIANCA MARIA. "Il Piccolo Satana di Mark Twain" [Mark Twain's Little Satan], Studi Americani, XI, 163-80.
On The Mysterious Stranger, taking into account current American scholarship. Concludes that the Stranger is imperfectly delineated, representing an anti-God, involuntary cruelties, a symbol of sorrow but at the same time creator of joy: "He made birds out of clay and he set them free, and they flew away singing" (p. 180).

B89 TODD, WILLIAM B. "Problems in Editing Mark Twain," Books at Iowa (April), 3-8.
A paper read at the meeting of the Modern Language Association in New York, December 27, 1964, on textual difficulties created by variants and by MT's carelessness and his readiness to allow friends to make textual decisions for him.

B90 *TOEBASCH, WIM. "Der Neger in de Amerikaanse Literatuur" [The Negro in American Literature], Vlaamse Gids, XLIX (September), 602-15.
[Source: Abstract in AES (1965), 2825.] Notes the important character Jim in HF. [In Flemish.]

B91 TULIP, JAMES. "Huck Finn--The Picaresque Saint," Balcony/The Sydney Review, No. 2 (Winter), pp. 13-18.
[Source: photocopy provided by kindness of Professor Stephen Knight, University of Sydney.] A broad and provocative criticism of HF. "I been there before," the concluding sentence, dramatically involves both Huck and MT, whose "deepest response is, then to the past even at the moment when he appears to be sending his hero off into a hopeful future.... Huck's run for the future is really a race from the past," and his "most vital image" is the lies he tells. They "have a saving effect, but their cause and their content imply a world that is damned: his family are dead, the farm has been sold up, there's smallpox on the raft." It is "the effervescence of the picaresque" that "establishes a moral order in the narrative," but one "which in its very quality of continual moments of release from the past is in no sense a triumph over that past." MT's "imagination is reaching out to a reality far beyond the capacity of Huck's imagination," and "the most dramatic writing in the book is to be found in those passages where Twain 'takes over' from Huck the role of hero-cum-narrator." Abstract in AES, XVII (1973-74), 2836.

B92 TURNER, MARTHA ANNE. "Mark Twain's '1601' Through Fifty Editions," Mark Twain Journal, XII (Summer), 10-15, 21.
A discussion for the general reader, with data culled from familiar sources. Abstract in AES, IX (1966), 2653.

B93 TWICHELL, JOSEPH H. Letter to Albert Bigelow Paine (June 1, 1911), Twainian, XXIV (May-June), 1.
According to F. E. Bliss, Charles Dudley Warner received no share in the profits from the Gilded Age play, and there was consequent ill-feeling between Warner and MT. In a headnote Chester Davis comments on policy of the Mark Twain Research Foundation: "We often are blamed for not permitting the general public to inspect and make copies of material in our Foundation files, which material we have not yet published in The Twainian. As such material is published by us, the original material is then available and not before." Abstract in AES, XI (1968), 1722; reprinted in Twainian, XXVIII (January-February, 1969).

B94 WARNER, DEANE M. "Huck and Holden," CEA Critic, XXVII (March), 4a-4b.
"I propose to show, through a discussion of Huckleberry Finn, The Red Badge of Courage, and The Catcher in the Rye, the evolution of American reaction to initiation, and how the perspective of pre-initiation innocence is an indication, and even an indictment, of contemporary attitudes." Abstract in AES, XIII (1969-1970), 1754; reprinted in Twainian, XXX (January-February, 1971).

B95 WEISHERT, JOHN J. "Once Again: Mark Twain and German," Mark Twain Journal, XII (Summer), 16.
First reprinting of an MT letter dated "Hotel Metropole, Wien, March 15, 1898," from the Louisville Anzeiger (May 1, 1910); contains an amusing mixture of German and English, tells of distant past when he used to trade a German-language weekly received in the exchange "to our German baker every week for a slab of gingerbread as big as a flagstone," and concludes by mentioning his prized acquaintance with Carl Schurz.

B96 WELLAND, DENNIS. "Mark Twain's Last Travel Book," Bulletin of the New York Public Library, LXIX (January), 31-48.
On the publication of the book in America as Following the Equator and in England as More Tramps Abroad. Andrew Chatto, the English publisher, took considerable pains with the book; by contrast, the American publisher, Frank Bliss "seems to have made so many textual changes on his own authority that it might not be unreasonable to see More Tramps Abroad as the editio princeps, and to describe Following the Equator as an abridged variant of it." The differences in chapter division are tabulated, and there is a list of maxims not used in the English edition, together with the texts of those used only there. Abstract in AES, IX (1966), 30; reprinted in Twainian, XXVI (January-February, 1967).

B97 WERGE, THOMAS. "Huck, Jim and Forty Dollars," Mark Twain Journal, XIII (Winter), 15-16.
The generosity of the slave-hunters who give Huck forty dollars, which he promptly shares with Jim (Chapter XVI) underscores Huck's sense of guilt in not betraying Jim; it contrasts with the action of the King, who sells Jim for forty dollars and keeps the money for himself. The concluding episode repeats the theme, when Tom Sawyer gives Jim forty dollars for his trouble as a prisoner. "This forty dollars is freely given and freely accepted, and this act of generosity recalls and reaffirms Huck's values while denying those predatory hunters whose lust for money is surpassed only by their absolute moral corruption." Abstract in AES, XI (1968), 2262.

B98 WHITE, WILLIAM. "Teaching Huck Finn in Korea," Mark Twain Journal, XIII (Winter), 5-7.
As a visiting professor under a Fulbright grant, White found his students at three different colleges unprepared for college-level work in English.

B99 WILLIAMS, JAMES D. "The Use of History in Mark Twain's A Connecticut Yankee," Publications of the Modern Language Association, LXXX (March), 102-10.
MT learned of medieval life chiefly from secondary sources, among them Lecky and Carlyle, but drew more heavily on post-Renaissance history; "Since for the most part he was collecting examples of misery and injustice the modernity of his material implied increasingly narrow chronological limits for his theme of social and moral progress." Abstract in AES, IX (1966), 525; reprinted in Twainian, XXVI (January-February, 1967).

B100 *WILSON, COLIN. "Madach's Tragedy of Man and Mark Twain's Mysterious Stranger," in his Eagle and Earwig (London: John Baker), pp. 162-70.
[Source: Beebe and Feaster (1968), p. 133.]

B101 WINKELMAN, DONALD A. "Goodman Brown, Tom Sawyer and Oral Tradition," Keystone Folklore Quarterly, X (Spring), 43-48.
An early member of the American Folklore Society, MT uses folklore "as a series of psycho-physical functions which often motivate and always affect the actions of Tom and Huck," but he does not allow it to interrupt a mood, such as that established with Tom and Becky in the cave. "This paper was read at a meeting of the American Folklore Society in Washington, D.C., December, 1963."

B102 ____. "Three American Authors as Semi-Folk Artists," Journal of American Folklore, LXXVIII (April-June), 130-35.
On folklore in the works of MT, Charles W. Chesnutt, and Manley Wade Welman. MT's folklore, centered around a locale, lets him "demonstrate that a man can interpret but never control nature"; but MT "used folklore chiefly as a device for portraying local color or setting the stage for future action." Abstract in AES, IX (1966), 1880 ["Reprinted from Abstracts of Folklore Studies, III:4 (December, 1965)"]; reprinted in Twainian, XXVI (January-February, 1967).

B103 WOODWARD, ROBERT W. "'Personating Mark Twain': a Folk Story," Mark Twain Journal, XIII (Winter), 12, 20.
Reprints an anecdote by this title from The Californian: A Western Monthly Magazine; IV (July, 1881), about a temperance lecturer who took the stage when MT failed to appear for a lecture; the audience was unaware of the substitution and laughed at every word.

1966 A BOOKS

A1 BRASHEAR, MINNIE M., and ROBERT M. RODNEY,
    eds. The Birds and Beasts of Mark Twain.
    Norman: University of Oklahoma Press.
    An anthology of anecdotes and descrip-
    tions of animals from MT's works.

A2 COX, JAMES M. Mark Twain: The Fate of Hu-
    mor. Princeton, New Jersey: Princeton
    University Press.
    On the role of humor in shaping MT's lit-
    erary identity as it appears in his major
    works. "Southwestern Vernacular"
    (pp. 167-84, on HF) reprinted in Simpson
    (1968), pp. 82-94.

A3 DAY, A. GROVE, ed. Mark Twain's Letters from
    Hawaii. New York: Appleton-Century.
    VAluable chiefly for putting a complete
    text of Mark Twain's letters to the Sacra-
    mento Union in 1866 back in print. Con-
    tains a sensible introduction explaining
    the circumstances under which the letters
    were written, but no notes or introductions
    to the individual letters.

A4 GORDON, EDWIN. Mark Twain. New York: Crow-
    ell-Collier Press.
    Popular biography for teenage readers.

A5 KANE, HARNETT T. Young Mark Twain and the
    Mississippi. New York: Random House.
    A reliable biography for young readers.

A6 KAPLAN, JUSTIN. Mr. Clemens and Mark Twain:
    A Biography. New York: Simon and Schus-
    ter.
    Covering the period from 1866, when MT
    left the West, emphasizes his inner ten-
    sions as exemplified in a dual nature.
    Incorporating previously unpublished mate-
    rials, Kaplan's book is dramatically pre-
    sented and was enthusiastically greeted by
    many reviewers, though more temperately in
    some academic journals. It received the
    National Book Award and Pulitzer Prize for
    Biography in 1967. The reviews by Day,
    DeMott, Blair, and Krause (1966-1967) are
    summarized by Robert H. Woodward in ALA, I
    (December, 1967), 125-26.

A7 NEIDER, CHARLES, ed. The Complete Travel
    Books of Mark Twain. The Early Works:
    "The Innocents Abroad" and "Roughing It."
    Garden City, N.Y.: Doubleday & Company, Inc.
    Consists of the two books, introduced by
    "Mark Twain's Travels" by Charles Neider
    (pp. vii-xxix), which includes a letter
    MT wrote the night before the Quaker City
    sailed but is otherwise of interest only
    as background for the general reader.
    Does not contain editorial matter or notes,
    except for "A Note on the Text," which
    states that the text is that of the first
    American edition, with only minor changes
    and with the chapter numbers changed from
    Roman to Arabic (p. xxxi).

A8 REGAN, ROBERT. Unpromising Heroes: Mark
    Twain and His Characters. Berkeley and Los
    Angeles: University of California Press.
    Takes the theme of the Unpromising Hero
    from folklore (though not dealing with spe-
    cific folktales). "Tom Sawyer, little
    Prince Edward and his pauper double, the
    Connecticut Yankee, and Pudd'nhead Wilson
    are among the many characters in Mark
    Twain's books who are significantly related
    to this familiar figure of folk literature,"
    as is the character of "Mark Twain"
    (pp. viii-ix).

A9 SCOTT, ARTHUR L. On the Poetry of Mark Twain.
    With Selections from His Verse. Urbana and
    London: University of Illinois Press.
    "Let no one mistake this book as an effort
    to establish a reputation for Mark Twain in
    the realm of poetry. It is no such thing.
    Nor is it a critical study of Mark Twain's
    poetry. It is, rather, a survey of the
    life-long interest of Mark Twain in poetry--
    a form of writing which almost everyone
    thinks he detested" (p. vii). Includes
    poetry previously published, as well as
    some from the Mark Twain Papers. There is
    a 39-page discussion of MT's poetry, and
    there are bibliographical and other comments
    on the poems.

A10 SPENGEMANN, WILLIAM C. Mark Twain and the
    Backwoods Angel: The Matter of Innocence in
    the Works of Samuel L. Clemens. Kent, Ohio:
    The Kent State University Press.
    "As Clemens presents it, the myth of Amer-
    ican innocence entails three distinguishable
    but obviously related problems": "the moral
    drama" of the innocent hero confronting
    evil; "the conflict between agrarian and
    urban, industrial values"; and an examina-
    tion of the reliability of MT's faith "by
    putting it to the imaginative test of set-
    ting, character, and action.... This ten-
    sion between faith and fact engenders the
    conflict which makes his best work more
    than a mere reflection of popular sentiment
    and raises Huckleberry Finn to the level of
    prophecy" (pp. xi-xii). Among the works
    treated are the travels with Brown and IA;
    RI and Captain Stormfield's Visit to Heaven;
    GA and TS; Old Times on the Mississippi;
    P&P and "A Campaign that Failed"; HF; CY;
    JA, and MS.

A11 STRONG, LEAH A. Joseph Hopkins Twichell:
    Mark Twain's Friend and Pastor. Athens:
    University of Georgia Press.
    The friendship of "Joe" Twichell and MT
    extended from their meeting in the winter
    of 1867-1868 until MT's death in 1910, and
    in warmth is comparable to that of MT and
    Howells. Twichell was MT's traveling com-
    panion on trips to Bermuda and to Europe
    (where he was the original of "Harris" in
    A Tramp Abroad), and the broadly tolerant
    friend for whom MT wrote the naughty 1601
    (Dr. Strong also recounts MT's disastrous

(STRONG, LEAH A.)
miscalculation in reading it years later before Twichell's wife, Harmony, and the next
day to a literary club consisting of some
of the grandes dames of Hartford
[pp. 138-39]). The book begins with a biography of Twichell revealing him as an interesting man in his own right, but major
emphasis is on his friendship with MT and
his influence on MT's thought and writing.
Reviews by Mann (1966) and Branch (1967)
are summarized by Robert B. Hausmann in ALA,
I (December, 1967), 132-33.

1966 B SHORTER WRITINGS

B1   ADE, GEORGE. "One Afternoon with Mark Twain,"
     Twainian, XXV (July-August), 1-4.
        Reprint of a pamphlet which appeared in
     1939 under this title, 1939.A1. Abstract in
     AES, XI (1968), 1735; reprinted in Twainian,
     XXVIII (January-February, 1969).

B2   ALLEN, GERALD. "Mark Twain's Yankee," New
     England Quarterly, XXXIX (December),
     435-46.
        "In its ragged but surprisingly complete
     way, CY expresses more consistently and en-
     gagingly than any other work the seminal
     attitude of American writers between 1870
     and 1910. In a time when the old ideals of
     progress were being subjected to the ex-
     periences of the Civil War, political cor-
     ruption, and massive industrialization,
     Twain is completely in tune." The artistic
     failure and indication "that Twain is con-
     fused and unsure of this thesis" is valu-
     able, because "successes put forth answers,
     while failures define the questions more
     precisely." Abstract in AES, X (1967),
     2027; reprinted in Twainian, XXVII (January-
     February, 1968).

B3   ALLISON, JOHN M. "Victorian View of Honolu-
     lu," Saturday Review, XLIX (March 19), 33.
        A review, largely descriptive, of A.
     Grove Day (ed.), Mark Twain's Letters from
     Hawaii.

B4   ALTER, ROBERT. "The Apocalyptic Temper,"
     Commentary, XLI (June), 61-66.
        Includes passing mention of MS in a tra-
     dition beginning with Melville's The Con-
     fidence-Man--a tradition that R. W. B.
     Lewis calls "savagely comical apocalypse."

B5   ALTIERI, JOANNE. "The Structure of 'The
     Private History of a Campaign That Failed,'"
     Mark Twain Journal, XIII (Winter), 2-5.
        Behind the apparent rambling and digres-
     sion lies "a relatively tight structure
     which achieves simultaneously a narrative
     crisis and affective climax, unobtrusively,
     with seeming ease." A better case may be
     made for the architectonics in MT's short
     works than in his long ones. Abstract in
     AES, XII (1969), 1234.

B6   ANON. "Gutting the Gilded Age," Times Liter-
     ary Supplement, June 16, p. 539.
        A review of Charles Neider, ed., The Ad-
     ventures of Colonel Sellers (1965), MT's
     share of GA with the contributions by
     Charles Dudley Warner omitted. "There is
     something to be said for this rather ruth-
     less act of salvage," but it might have been
     better to reprint the entire novel. "But
     the most notable thing is Mark Twain's com-
     pulsive interest in voices. He never analy-
     ses characters--he imitates them speaking."

B7   ANON. "Innocent Abroad," Time, LXXXVII
     (March 18), 114, 116.
        A descriptive review of A. Grove Day, ed.,
     Mark Twain's Letters from Hawaii.

B8   ANON. "Mark Twain Items Published Elsewhere,"
     Twainian, XXV (January-February), 1-4;
     (March-April), 4.
        Reprints most of the abstracts of material
     relating to MT from AES, VIII (1965). Ab-
     stract in AES, XI (1968), 1730, 1732; re-
     printed in Twainian, XXVIII (January-Februa-
     ry, 1969).

B9   ANON. [Review: Peter Coveney, ed. and intro-
     duction, The Adventures of Huckleberry Finn,
     1966.B31).] Times Literary Supplement,
     September 29, p. 901.
        Criticizes Coveney's heavy-handed inter-
     pretation and excessive annotation of the
     obvious. Coveney's "Suggestions for Further
     Reading" following the introduction "Sur-
     prisingly...does not include Lionel Tril-
     ling's essay on Huckleberry Finn. Especial-
     ly surprising, because Mr. Coveney's essay
     is at times so similar to Mr. Trilling's."
        On November 17 (p. 1052) Coveney defends
     himself in a letter to the editor: his sug-
     gested reading list included Barry Marks's
     Mark Twain's Huckleberry Finn: Problems in
     American Civilization, which contains the
     Trilling essay. In a reply that follows,
     the reviewer points to close verbal paral-
     lels between the texts of Coveney and Tril-
     ling. "Surely when Mr. Coveney is in such
     substantial and detailed agreement with Mr.
     Trilling's essay it deserved mention in its
     own right by name, rather than silently as
     part of a collection of articles," especial-
     ly since The Liberal Imagination is far more
     generally available than the Marks anthology.

B10 ANON. [Review: Justin Kaplan, Mr. Clemens
     and Mark Twain.] Time, LXXXVII (June 24),
     108, 110.
        Descriptive and approving, emphasizing
     MT's pessimism.

B11 ANON. [Brief review: Edith Colgate Salsbury,
     Susy and Mark Twain (1965).] Times Literary
     Supplement, July 28, p. 692.
        Criticizes the format but notes interest-
     ing family details and "some enchanting pho-
     tographs"; Mrs. Salsbury has handled her ma-
     terial (some of it previously unpublished)
     "with respect."

B12 ARVIN, NEWTON. American Pantheon, ed. Daniel
Aaron and Sylvan Schendler. New York:
Delacorte Press.
Contains "Mark Twain Simplified" (1932.B4)
and "The Friend of Caesar" (1933.B6).

B13 BABCOCK, C. MERTON. "Mark Twain and the Dictionary," Word Study (G. & C. Merriam Co.),
XLII (October), 1-6.
On MT's painstaking choice of words; includes facsimile reproduction of an MT letter (Hartford, March, 1891) to G. & C. Merriam & Co., praising their dictionary and
thanking them for the copy they sent him.

B14 _____. "Mark Twain's Religious Creed,"
Southern California Quarterly, XLVIII
(June), 169-74.
On MT's comments on theology and organ-
ized religion, as revealed in his Notebook
(1935, ed. Paine) and Letters from the
Earth (1962, ed. DeVoto). Abstract in AES,
X (1967), 490; reprinted in Twainian, XXVII
(January-February, 1968).

B15 BAENDER, PAUL. "Alias Macfarlane: A Revision of Mark Twain Biography," American
Literature, XXXVIII (May), 187-97.
Passages in Paine's 1912 Biography (I,
115) and 1924 ed. of the Autobiography
(I, 143-47) have been taken as evidence
that MT acquired his pessimistic doctrine
in 1856-1857 from a laboring man and self-
taught philosopher named Macfarlane; a more
convincing case can be made that Macfarlane
is a character, like the "Mr. Brown" of
MT's early travel sketches, used to deflate
pretension; "but by the 1890's Mark Twain
was most concerned with the premises of
societies, not their manners." Abstract in
AES, X (1967), 790; reprinted in Twainian,
XXVII (January-February, 1968).

B16 BARCHILON, JOSE, and JOEL S. KOVEL. "Huckleberry Finn: A Psychoanalytic Study," Journal of the American Psychoanalytic Association, XIV (October), 775-814.
Deliberately limited to evidence in HF,
excluding biographical data and evidence
from MT's other works. "The essential
feature of the method is that we treat the
novels as if they were the life histories
of real people." Sub-sections are "The
Structure of Huck's Personality"; "The
Wish to be Dead: Reunion with the Dead
Mother"; "The Wish to Kill the Mother and
Its Resolution through Passivity"; "The
Theme of Moses and the Wish to Live: The
Nile and the Mississippi"; "Jim's Charac-
ter"; "Sexuality In Huckleberry Finn"; "Tom
Sawyer's Character"; "Huck's Growth through
the Relationship with Jim"; "Children's
Games: The Three Orphans Reborn as Sib-
lings"; "The Wish to Have a Negro Mother?"
"The Relationship of the Moses' Myth to the
Story of Huck"; "A Wanderer on the American
Frontier"; and a "Postcript" on "Method"

and "Goals." Reprinted (in part:
pp. 799-808) in Gerber (1971), pp. 113-21.

B17 BEWLEY, MARIUS. "Split in Twain," New York
Review of Books, VII (September 8), 19-22.
Reprinted in Bewley's Masks & Mirrors: Essays in Criticism (New York: Athenaeum,
1970), pp. 180-90.
A review of Justin Kaplan, Mr. Clemens
and Mark Twain: "The best life of Twain
that we possess...in his treatment of Twain's
work Kaplan shows himself to be a thoroughly
reliable and astute critic."

B18 BRANCH, EDGAR M. [Review: Leah A. Strong,
Joseph Hopkins Twichell: Mark Twain's Friend
and Pastor (1966).] American Literature,
XXXIX (May, 1967), 228-30.
Summarizes the book, which would benefit
from fuller use of the Mark Twain Papers,
and which "in effect demonstrates the unim-
portance of Twichell's influence upon
Twain's writing."

B19 BRIDGMAN, RICHARD. "Henry James and Mark
Twain," in his The Colloquial Style in America. New York: Oxford University Press,
pp. 78-130; also passim.
The chief difference between the two is in
subject-matter: "Huck and the other characters in his book talk about things, whereas
the Jamesian characters discuss states of being" (p. 78). Quotes Alice B. Toklas as saying that MT was Gertrude Stein's favorite
American writer--whom "she was continuously
reading," but recognizes possible hyperbole,
since this was in a letter to MT's biographer
Miss Jerry Allen, and transcribed in a copy
of her book given to Miss Isabel Lyon
(pp. 166-7, and 243 n. 8).

B20 *BROWN, MAURICE. "Mark Twain as Proteus:
Ironic Form and Fictive Integrity," Papers
of the Michigan Academy of Science, Arts
and Letters, LI, 515-27.
[Source: MHRA Annual Bibliography (1967),
No. 7098.]

B21 *BRUNVAND, JAN HAROLD. "The Western Folk Humor in Roughing It," The Western Folklore
Conference: Selected Papers (ed. by Austin
E. Fife and J. Golden Taylor. Monograph
Series, IX, iii). Logan: Utah State University Press, 1964, pp. 53-65.
[Source: Beebe and Feaster (1968),
p. 137; additional details from MLA Bibliography (1966), Nos. 14, 8028.]

B22 BUDD, LOUIS J. "Camaraderie," South Atlantic
Bulletin, XXXII (March), 21-22.
A review of Leah A. Strong's Joseph Hop-
kinds Twichell: Mark Twain's Friend and
Pastor, in which she draws heavily on Twichell's fourteen volumes of scrapbooks on his
church but passes over The Mark Twain-Howells Letters (1960). She trusts some reminiscences too much, but makes a good case
for the steadying influence of Twichell.

B23   . "Mark Twain and the Upward Mobility of Taste," in Ray B. Browne, Donald M. Winkelman, and Allen Hayman, eds., New Voices in American Studies (West Lafayette, Indiana: Purdue University Studies, pp. 21-34.

    After the iconoclasm of IA, MT showed a growing interest in the arts. He bought paintings, took painting lessons, and subsidized the study abroad of sculptor Karl Gerhardt, but "he pondered dismayingly little about art in any form as making a unique kind of discourse and, most of his life, shied away from conceiving of his writing in such terms."

B24 BURGESS, ANTHONY. "Mark Twain and James Joyce," Mark Twain Journal, XIII (Winter), 1-2.

    Although James Joyce "did not read either Tom Sawyer or Huckleberry Finn very thoroughly, if at all," in Finnegans Wake he punningly links MT with Arthurian legend through King Mark of Cornwall, Tom with peeping Tom ("Tom saw-yer"), and Huck with the revived Finnegan, "Finn again." Abstract in AES, XII (1969), 1233.

B25 NO ENTRY

B26 *CLEMENS, CYRIL. "A Chat with Joseph Conrad," Hobbies (January), pp. 85, 88, 92. [Source: Reprinted in Conradiana, II (Winter, 1969-1970), 97-103.]

    In the course of the interview, Conrad mentions his pleasure in reading Life on the Mississippi and his thoughts about MT while piloting a steamboat on the Congo. The Conradiana reprint is abstracted in AES, XIV (1970), 2140.

B27 CLEMENS, SAMUEL L. "Mark Twain's Last Letter, Written the Editor's Mother, Mrs. James Ross Clemens," Mark Twain Journal, XIII (Winter), front cover.

    From Bermuda, March 24, 1910 (reproduced in facsimile), on his loss of Jean, Livy, and Susy; expresses his heavy sorrow but says he would not bring them back if he could: "Death is the most precious of all the gifts this life has for us."

B28   . [Letter to Governor David R. Francis of Missouri.] Mark Twain Journal, XIII (Winter), 21.

    Publishes without comment MT's letter from Florence (May 26, 1904), expressing regret that circumstances do not allow him "to exhibit myself at the great St. Louis Fair and get a prize."

B29 CLOUGH, WILSON O. [Review: Margaret Duckett, Mark Twain and Bret Harte (1964).] American Literature, XXXVII (January), 491-92.

    "Less a literary evaluation than a study in divergent characters.... while not denying Harte's limitations as man and artist, and while not greatly shifting critical verdicts on either man, does round out the portrait of Harte more conformably to fact." MT's bitterness and perhaps "a sense of guilt, remains the enigma still, a part of the more complex of the two characters."

B30 COCKERILL, DONALD J. [Review: Henry Duskis, ed., The Forgotten Writings of Mark Twain (1963).] Denver Quarterly, I (Summer), 128-29.

    Duskis "edits the wildly impromptu melange of comment (often silly or saccharine) on woman's suffrage, gold mine exploiters, etc., plus all the contemporary trivia a journalist can contrive, into snippets bridged by synopses and running commentary. The result is not unlike gargling bourbon instead of drinking it." The material is "essentially third-rate Twain," and "the lack of an index makes the book a major publishing disaster for the scholar since Duskis' technique favors simple chronology."

B31 COVENEY, PETER. [Introduction.] The Adventures of Huckleberry Finn. Harmondsworth, Middlesex, England: Penguin Books, pp. 9-41.

    Provides an over-view of the book and summary of the published criticism, but no new insights. See 1966.B9.

B32 [DAVIS, CHESTER L.] "Mark Twain's Marginal Notes on 'The Queen's English,'" Twainian, XXV (March-April), 1-4.

    Extensively discusses and quotes G. Washington Moon's Learned Men's English: The Grammarians (London, 1867; revised ed. London: George Routledge & Sons, 1892), and reproduces some of MT's marginal notations in a copy he gave his daughter Clara; the comments reveal MT's views of the English language and of Moon. In a concluding note Chester L. Davis announces that the copy annotated by MT may be examined by members of the Mark Twain Research Foundation: "It is only after we have printed the material in The Twainian that it is released and is then generally available. Our planning of future issues is often governed by such requests for information.... We welcome inquiries from authors while they are working on articles or on entire books...such inquiries might cause us to publish items which otherwise might be released years later. Certainly there is no desire to deprive the world of any material in our files which rightfully adds to enrichment of literature, however we alone must be the judge of what we do release, and once again, only after publication in The Twainian, later the same material and perhaps some related material we decided not to use, is open for examination in our offices." Among such material Davis is prepared to publish in part and then release are letters by Laura Frazer (the original for Becky Thatcher)

([DAVIS, CHESTER L.])
and letters to Albert Bigelow Paine. "There are some definite restrictions however. Inquiries for information and the release of material which could serve no worthwhile purpose, get no attention from us. An example would be what our files contain relating to Nina, the granddaughter of Mark Twain having recently died. We do not propose to ever release any material concerning Nina, no member should ever ask for it." Incorrectly attributed to James B. Stronks in MHRA Annual Bibliography (1966), No. 7046; Abstract in AES, XI (1968), 1731; reprinted in Twainian, XXVIII (January-February, 1969).

B33 _____. "New Edition of Mark Twain Books," Twainian, XXV (September-October), 2.
Begins: "Many of the serious students of Mark Twain have known for the past several years that a group of capable authors are getting together a new set of Mark Twain books for the publishing firm Harper & Row;" mentions having been written or visited by some of the editors, and readiness "to cooperate and permit the use in our office of the valuable card-index compiled by George Hiram Brownell." Davis urges readers with useful material to send it to the Foundation or to the editors themselves. There follows a list of the editors and the works for which they are responsible [this seems to be essentially the same as the edition being published by the University of California Press in cooperation with the Center for Editions of American Authors--T.A.T.]. Abstract in AES, XI (1968), 1737; reprinted in Twainian, XXVIII (January-February, 1969).

B34 _____. "The Transition from Wisconsin to Missouri in 1950," Twainian, XXV (November-December), 3-4.
On the transfer of the files of the Mark Twain Research Foundation from Elkhorn, Wisconsin to Perry, Missouri.

B35 _____. "'Twainian' First Published in 1939-- Regular Series Began in 1941. 'Our Silver Anniversary'--An Appraisal and Review," Twainian, XXV (November-December), 2-3.
Highlights of the history of the Mark Twain Research Foundation and of some of the 1939 issues.

B36 _____. "Why 'Research' Is in Our Corporate Name," Twainian, XXV (May-June), 1-2.
On MT material filed at the Mark Twain Research Foundation, and the continuing search for first publication of his writings, etc. Abstracted in AES, XI (1968), 1733; reprinted in Twainian, XXVIII (January-February, 1969).

B37 DAY, A GROVE. "He Was His Own Best Character," Saturday Review, XLIX (June 18), 31-33.
A review of Mr. Clemens and Mark Twain: A Biography, by Justin Kaplan, who "has read all the books and articles, all the letters and notes. He has sifted all the biographical grains and blown away the chaff of legends and lies. He has listened to all the theories but has swallowed none." The book "supersedes previous accounts of its subject's later years.... It is the book that Dixon Wecter, had he lived, could have written."

B38 DEMOTT, BENJAMIN. "In the American Vein," New York Times Book Review (July 3), pp. 1, 16-17.
A review of Justin Kaplan's Mr. Clemens and Mark Twain as "the closest biographical approach yet made to the writer," revealing MT's limitations in temperament, taste, and ideas in "a book of dignity, evenhandedness and grace."

B39 *DE SCHWEINITZ, GEORGE W. "Huck and Holden," Proceedings of Conference of College Teachers of English at Texas, XXXI (September), 27-28.
[Source: MHRA Annual Bibliography (1967), No. 7102, with annotation: "(Abstract)."]

B40 DICKINSON, LEON T. [Review: Arthur L. Scott, On the Poetry of Mark Twain.] English Studies (Amsterdam), LII (1971), 82-83.
This is verse, rather than poetry, and "the serious pieces are interesting and moving, though more, one feels, because one knows the circumstances that prompted them than for the power of the verse itself"; this is interesting only because it is by MT. Scott's editing has included meticulous proof-reading, but for some of the selections better copy-texts could have been used, as for "Good-Bye."

B41 _____. [Review: Henry Nash Smith, Mark Twain's Fable of Progress (1964).] English Language Notes, III (March), 234-37.
With a lengthy summary, declares "this short study...is truly admirable in its multiple approach to the study and evaluation of a puzzling work, and the clarity with which it sorts out and yet relates the various strands of a complex literary problem." Says Smith "dates Mark Twain's decline as a writer from the composition of this fable."

B42 ELIOT, T. S. "American Literature and the American Language," Sewanee Review, LXXIV (January-March), 1-20. See 1953.B20.
On pp. 11-13, links MT with Poe and Whitman as one of his "landmarks I have chosen for the identification of American literature"; in HF, MT "reveals himself to be one

(ELIOT, T. S.)
of those writers, of whom there are not a
great many in any literature, who have discovered a new way of writing, valid not
only for themselves but for others. I
should place him, in this respect, even with
Dryden and Swift, as one of those rare writers who have brought their language up to
date, and in so doing, 'purified the dialect
of the tribe.'" Abstract in AES, IX (1966),
2434; reprinted in Twainian, XXVI (January-
February, 1967); annotation: "(reprinted
from To Criticize the Critic, 1965)."

B43 FATOUT, PAUL. "Mark Twain's Nom de Plume,"
Twainian, XXV (September-October), 2-4.
Reprinted from American Literature, XXXIV
(March, 1962), 1-7.
Prefaced by Chester L. Davis: "Again we
regret that it is difficult for us to reprint reference characters and notes. This
article is well documented and the original
publication should be studied for details."
Abstract in AES, XI (1968), 1738; reprinted
in Twainian, XXVIII (January-February,
1969).

B44 _____. [Review: Edith Colgate Salsbury,
Susy and Mark Twain: Family Dialogues
(1965).] American Literature, XXXVIII
(May), 251-52.
"The record sharpens general impressions
of the life of Mark Twain," and "the materials of this book are copious and authentic, but the method of using them causes
distracting incoherence and a failure to
follow through."

B45 FIEDLER, LESLIE A. "An American Abroad,"
Partisan Review, XXXIII (Winter), 77-91.
On IA, in which MT to some extent embodied
the limitations of his time but also recognized and satirized them. "Yet, over and
over, he was to return to the themes of The
Innocents Abroad: not only in other self-
declared travel books like A Tramp Abroad or
Following the Equator," but also in P&P, CY,
JA, TS Abroad, MS, and even in HF. Abstract
in AES, X (1967), 241; reprinted (incorrectly attributed to Notes and Queries) in
Twainian, XXVII (January-February, 1968).

B46 * _____. "Toward a Centennial: Notes on Innocents Abroad," New American Review (as reprinted in The Collected Essays of Leslie
Fiedler, 1971, 2 vols., II, 296-311).
Notes MT's inability to throw away conventional outlooks entirely, despite his
professed irreverence under the protection
of an assumed boyishness.

B47 FOX, MAYNARD. "Two Primitives: Huck Finn
and Tom Outland," Western American Literature, I (Spring), 26-33.
The character in Willa Cather's The Professor's House (1925) followed Huck in a
tradition in which nature is not necessarily benevolent; but both boys "found

independence, spontaneity, freedom, and an
energizing vitality in their retreats from
the center of population." Abstract in AES,
XI (1968), 2772; reprinted in Twainian,
XXVIII (January-February, 1969).

B48 FRANKLIN, H. BRUCE. "Mark Twain and Science
Fiction," in his Future Perfect: American
Science Fiction of the Nineteenth Century.
New York: Oxford University Press,
pp. 374-79.
An anthology, with critical introductions.
Franklin briefly discusses several of MT's
imaginative works, among them CY and The
Great Dark, and reprints his "From the 'Lon-
don Times' of 1904" (pp. 380-90; this first
appeared in The Century Magazine, 1898).

B49 FRIEDRICH, GERHARD. [Review: Bryant Morey
French, Mark Twain and "The Gilded Age"
(1965).] Books Abroad, XL (Spring), 205.
More abstract than review; uncritical.

B50 GAFFNEY, W. G. "Mark Twain's 'Duke' and
'Dauphin,'" Names: Journal of the American
Dialect Society, XIV (September), 175-78.
After the embarrassment over having used
the name of a real Eschol Sellers in GA, MT
was careful in naming characters; he could
call a rascal in HF the Duke of Bridgewater
because the actual Dukedom was extinct;
moreover, Francis Egerton, third Duke of
Bridgewater, had been one of the wealthiest
men in the world, and his son, from whom
MT's character claimed descent, died a bachelor and without issue. The Dauphin could
not claim descent from the English or other
active European thrones, because they were
well occupied; "Literally the only way to
outrank the Duke of Bridgewater was to be
the (equally disinherited) rightful King of
France."

B51 GERBER, JOHN C. "Mark Twain," in James Wood-
ress, ed., American Literary Scholarship:
An Annual/1966 (Durham, North Carolina:
Duke University Press, 1968), pp. 48-64.
A survey of MT scholarship for the year;
See 1963.B32. Contents: "i. Texts and
Editions"; "ii. Biography"; "iii. Criti-
cism"; "iv. Travel Books"; "v. Tom Sawyer
and Tom Sawyer Abroad"; "vi. Huckleberry
Finn"; "vii. A Connecticut Yankee"; "viii.
Pudd'nhead Wilson"; "ix. Miscellaneous."

B52 GILHOOLEY, LEONARD. [Review: Justin Kaplan,
Mr. Clemens and Mark Twain.] America, CXV
(July 16), 71-72.
Kaplan explores MT's duality "with such
depth and force and grace that Clemens/Twain
emerges in whole and in part as he has
from no other biography." The book is "a
product of intense and scrupulous research,"
and Kaplan does not allow personal feelings
to distort it.

1966 - Shorter Writings

B53 GILL, BRENDAN. "The Confidence Man," New Yorker, XLII (September 3), 114-17.
A review of Justin Kaplan's Mr. Clemens and Mark Twain, in which Kaplan "has proved in every respect worthy of his great subject. It must be a very pleasant feeling to begin one's career as a biographer with a work that is sure to be read as long as Twain is read." Abstract in AES, XII (1969), 975.

B54 *GOWDA, H. H. ANNIAH. "Mark Twain in India," Literary Half-Yearly, July, 17-23.
[Source: Abstract in AES, XII (1969), 928; reprinted in Twainian, XXIX (January-February, 1970), with author's name spelled "Gooda" and title of journal given as "Library Half-Yearly."]

B55 GRAUMAN, LAWRENCE, JR. "Mark Twain Beside Himself," New Republic, CLV (July 16), 31-34.
A review of Justin Kaplan, Mr. Clemens and Mark Twain, a book which "represents a prodigious accumulation of data, selected and shaped from both a biographical and a critical perspective, and presented without much style," or rather in a style which attempts to be both popular and scholarly.

B56 GURIAN, JAY. "Literary Convention and the Mining Romance," Journal of the West, V (January), 106-14.
Our picture of the West is colored by literary conventions. For example, MT's description of the Comstock was meant to entertain, and "the purposes of DeVoto and Mack are to instruct, yet their use of literary conventions prevents them from doing so.... The problem is that the Comstock's historians and Twain's critics have tacitly accepted the burlesque as reality, the caricature as character."

B57 HAMBLEN, ABIGAIL ANN. "The Best-Known Teenager: Huck Finn," Mark Twain Journal, XIII (Winter), 15-19.
"Huck Finn's is a sensitive imaginative mind," though practical rather than philosophical; he matures in the book but still cannot accept the shackles of civilization.

B58 *HARPER, MARION. "The West of Twain and Cather," Diliman Review, XIV (January), 60-80.
MT's West is masculine, Cather's feminine; contrasts their tone and values, and the names of characters. [Source: Abstract in AES, XIV (1970-1971), 584; reprinted in Twainian, XXXI (January-February, 1972).]

B59 HILL, HAMLIN. [Review: Bryant Morey French, Mark Twain and "The Gilded Age" (1965).] American Literature, XXXVIII (March), 134-35.
"In effect a comprehensive handbook to Mark Twain and Charles Dudley Warner's novel...explores more thoroughly than anyone else previously the transformation of raw material and biographical data into a novel--or something deceptively similar to a novel, at any rate."

B60 HOROWITZ, FLOYD R. "'The Invalid's Story': an Early Mark Twain Commentary on Institutional Christianity," Midcontinent American Studies Journal, VII (Spring), 37-44.
In his story of the exchange of a box of rifles and a Limburger cheese sandwich for a coffin in an express car MT satirizes institutional religion: "Center of the structure, then, is a Christ-like body which is actually no body, but guns and odiferous [sic] cheese hidden from sight." Abstract in AES, X (1967), 507; reprinted in Twainian, XXVII (January-February, 1968).

B61 HOWELL, ELMO. "Mark Twain, William Faulkner, and the First Families of Virginia," Mark Twain Journal, XIII (Summer), 1-3, 19.
Although MT's PW lacks Faulkner's reverence toward Virginia and the South, both authors abhor "the violence and the injustice inherent in the social system of the South" but respect the tranquility, courage, and integrity of the Southern gentleman. Abstract in AES, XI (1968), 2264.

B62 *HUDON, EDWARD. "Mark Twain and the Copyright Dilemma," American Bar Association Journal, LII (January), 56-60.
An account of MT's troubles with British and Canadian pirate publishers, and his efforts to promote copyright legislation more favorable to authors. [Source: Reprinted in Twainian, XXV (May-June), 2-4; (July-August), 4; a headnote by Chester L. Davis adds: "It is with regret that our form of publication makes it difficult to print reference notes, the article being well supplied with authoritative references."] Abstracts in AES, XI (1968), 1734, 1736; reprinted in Twainian, XXVIII (January-February, 1969).

B63 JONES, HOWARD MUMFORD. "James, Howells, Mark Twain," in his Jeffersonianism and the American Novel. New York: Teachers College Press, Teachers College, Columbia University, pp. 35-47.
Only the last section of the chapter (pp. 44-47) concerns MT who, despite his humanitarianism and anti-imperialism, distrusted the common man: see Colonel Sherburn face down the mob in HF, and note Hank Morgan as enlightened despot in CY; note also MT's attack on the Moral Sense, and his deterministic philosophy. Thus, MT may be considered anti-Jeffersonian.

B64 KOHN, JOHN S. VAN E. "The Doubly Suppressed Chapter of Following the Equator," Princeton University Library Chronicle, XXVII (Spring), 156-58.

The copy of this rarity acquired by the library from the collection of Thomas F. Leeming contains a statement by Jacob Blanck (December, 1939) that made it possible to describe it as one of three extant copies, although in the Bibliography of American Literature, II (1959) Blanck had described the publication under BAL 3546: "Privately Printed for Merle Johnson. Not published. The entire edition, save for two copies preserved for the printer, destroyed by Jacob Blanck by order of Merle Johnson." Olivia Clemens had originally asked that the chapter be dropped because of indelicacy; it was suppressed the second time because of serious typographical errors in the printed copy.

B65 KRUSE, HORST. "Die Literaturkritischen Elementen in Mark Twains Life on the Mississippi," Neueren Sprachen, XV (July), 297-309; (August), 355-63.

On MT's conception of a writer's social responsibility, and his duty to avoid bias or mere tradition, as revealed in his literary criticism in LOM. Abstract in AES, X (1967), 184, 186; reprinted in Twainian, XXVII (January-February, 1968).

B66 LAHOOD, MARVIN I. "Huck Finn's Search for Identity," Mark Twain Journal, XIII (Winter), 11-14.

"Huck Finn is one of a handful of classic American frontier heroes...who are able to find their identity only in opposition to the society that threatens their freedom. All are essentially anarchic, and must 'light out for the territory ahead of the rest.'" Huck sees through the hypocrisy of those around him, including Tom and the Phelpses, and he seeks "a society with a heart as good as his." Abstract in AES, XII (1969), 1236.

B67 LEE, ROBERT EDSON. "From West to East: Mark Twain," in his From West to East: Studies in the Literature of the American West (Urbana and London: University of Illinois Press), pp. 82-111.

Argues that MT's backgrounds were basically of the East rather than the West, and traces his development through IA and RI. "The East seemed determined that the West should be romantic, and Twain concurred, and romantic it therefore was."

B68 "Letters to Paine--Early Days of 'The Mark Twain Company,'" Twainian, XXV (September-October), 4; (November-December), 1.

Letters from E. E. Loomis, Charles T. Lark, and Jervis Langdon on business matters and the forthcoming Mark Twain and the Happy Island (1913) by Elizabeth Wallace.

Abstract in AES, XI (1968), 1739, 1741; reprinted in Twainian, XXVIII (1969).

B69 LEWIS, MERRILL. [Review: Margaret Duckett, Mark Twain and Bret Harte (1964).] Western Humanities Review, XX (Winter), 85-86.

Professor Duckett is admittedly partisan, and her attribution of MT's hostility toward Harte to professional jealousy and later feelings of guilt is "intriguing but not very well supported." Moreover, "emphasis as well as thesis seem to me to distort the personalities and literary stature of both men." In any case, not all the stories about Harte began with MT.

B70 McNAMARA, EUGENE. "Huck Lights Out for the Territory: Mark Twain's Unpublished Sequel," University of Windsor Review, II (Fall), 68-74.

Huck's concluding statement has received undue attention from critics who ignore Tom Sawyer's suggestion, noted "a scant nine paragraphs before it," that the boys go off for adventures in the territory among the Indians; MT's intention was simply to leave the way open for a sequel, such as the unfinished Huck Finn and Tom Sawyer Among the Indians, here discussed. Abstract in AES, X (1967), 3250; reprinted in Twainian, XXVII (January-February, 1968).

B71 MALE, ROY R. "The Story of the Mysterious Stranger in American Fiction," Criticism, III (Fall), 281-94.

A study of examples from MT, Hawthorne, Melville, Harte, Howells, and others, in which "the settings are...isolated in place, time, or both. And they are circumscribed." "The problem of the ending results chiefly from the character of the stranger." Abstract in AES, IX (1966), 2523.

B72 MATTHEWS, JACK. "Mark Twain, 'Cartographer,'" ETC: A Journal of General Semantics, XXIII (December), 479-84.

On the contrast between Tom's abstract thinking and the literal-mindedness of Huck and Jim, who cannot understand why the countries over which they pass are not the colors by which they are represented on maps. Abstract in AES, X (1967), 1243; reprinted in Twainian, XXVII (January-February, 1968).

B73 MEINE, FRANKLIN J. [Review: Arthur L. Scott, On the Poetry of Mark Twain.] American Book Collector, XVI (Summer), 5.

"A sensitive and competent account" of MT's poems, more than 120 of which Scott has located, giving texts of 65 of them. "Twain's poetry gives the reader and the Twain collector an entirely different feeling and insight into this complex personality."

B74   MILLER, JIM WAYNE. "Pudd'nhead Wilson's Cal-
      endar," Mark Twain Journal, XIII (Winter),
      8-10.
         Refuting the contention by Richard Chase
      (in The American Novel and Its Tradition)
      that the aphorisms are inappropriate to
      Wilson's character, shows that they fall
      into four groups: "1) Death 2) Religion
      3) The Fall 4) Pessimistic View of Man,"
      and argues that they add to the portrait of
      Wilson's character either directly or by re-
      flecting the contradictions inherent in his
      position as an outsider. Abstract in AES,
      XII (1969), 1235.

B75   MILNE, GORDON. "Expertise: Twain, De Forest,
      and Adams," in his The American Political
      Novel (Norman: University of Oklahoma
      Press), pp. 40-64; pp. 40-45 on MT.
         Notes the unevenness of GA, the indictment
      of corruption, lively portrayal of the leg-
      islative sessions, and some well-drawn char-
      acters; J. W. De Forest covers some of the
      ground, "and, on the whole, more penetrat-
      ingly" (p. 46).

B76   MOERS, ELLEN. "The 'Truth' of Mark Twain,"
      New York Review of Books, V (January 20),
      10-15.
         Begins as a review article, covering
      Edith Colgate Salsbury, Susy and Mark Twain:
      Family Dialogues (1965: "the best possible
      memorial to the improbable Clemens estab-
      lishment"); Margaret Duckett, Mark Twain and
      Bret Harte (1964: "a rougher, nastier Mark
      Twain"); Robert A. Wiggins, Mark Twain:
      Jackleg Novelist (1964, briefly dismissed);
      and Bryant Morey French, Mark Twain and
      "The Gilded Age": The Book that Named an
      Era (1965: "a more useful approach to the
      assessment of Twain as a spokesman for Amer-
      ican values and delineator of the American
      character"). There follows a more general
      discussion of MT's work: on Tom and Huck
      as town boys, the justified stealing in HF
      as opposed to the corruption in GA, and MT's
      racial views.

B77   *MUGGERIDGE, MALCOLM. [Review: Charles Neid-
      er, ed. The Adventures of Colonel Sellers
      (1965).] Observer, August 14, p. 19.
         [Source: MHRA Annual Bibliography (1966),
      No. 7024.]

B78   *NIELSEN, VENETA. "The Savage Prophet; or,
      Who's Afraid of Samuel Twain?" Proceedings
      of the Utah Academy of Science, Arts, and
      Letters, XLIII, 1-7.
         [Source: Leary (1970), p. 71.]

B79   NYREN, DOROTHY, comp. "Twain, Mark (1835-
      1910)," in her A Library of Literary Criti-
      cism (Third Edition. New York: Frederick
      Ungar Publishing Co.), pp. 489-93.
         Excerpts from criticisms by Frank R. Stock-
      ton (1893), Henry Dwight Sedgwick (1908),

Stuart P. Sherman (1910), Brander Matthews
(1910), Hamlin Garland (1910), Henry M. Alden (1910), William Dean Howells (1910),
Edith Wyatt (1917), Van Wyck Brooks (1920),
Theodore Dreiser (1935), Henry Seidel Canby
(1951), Dixon Wecter (1952), Leslie A. Fiedler (1955), Kenneth S. Lynn (1958), and, on
HF, Edgar Marquess Branch (1950) and F. R.
Leavis (1956). Also, passim on HF, TS, PW,
LOM (as "autobiography"), and MS (as "short
story").

B80   O'CONNOR, RICHARD. Bret Harte: A Biography.
      Boston, Toronto: Little, Brown and Company,
      passim.
         The numerous references to MT are based on
      his own statements in his Autobiography and
      elsewhere, and on other material familiar to
      students of MT. There is no new light on
      the causes for the break in friendship be-
      tween MT and Harte.

B81   PECK, RICHARD E. "On Three Mark Twain Poems,"
      Mark Twain Journal, XIII (Winter), 10-11.
         The C. Walter Barrett Collection at the
      Alderman Library, University of Virginia has
      autograph manuscripts of three poems, of
      which two differ textually from the versions
      in Arthur L. Scott's On the Poetry of Mark
      Twain and one is not included there. One
      differs only in the spelling of a single
      word, and Peck gives the texts of "Be Good,
      Be Good. A Poem" and a short poem previous-
      ly unpublished.

B82   *PILKINGTON, JOHN. "About this Madman Stuff,"
      University of Mississippi Studies in English,
      VII, 65-75.
         Like Huck Finn, Holden Caulfield in Catcher
      in the Rye is sane, idealistic, individual-
      istic, and compassionate. [Source: MHRA
      Annual Bibliography (1966), No. 7027; ab-
      stract in AES, X (1967), 723; and reprinted
      in Twainian, XXVII (January-February,
      1968).]

B83   PIZER, DONALD. Realism and Naturalism in Nine-
      teenth-Century American Literature. Carbon-
      dale and Edwardsville: Southern Illinois
      Press; London and Amsterdam: Feffer & Si-
      mons, Inc., pp. 3-10, 134-35, 141.
         Uses HF, The Rise of Silas Lapham, and
      What Maisie Knew to illustrate his thesis
      that late nineteenth-century American real-
      ism does not always stress the representa-
      tive, and it is subjective and ethically
      idealistic (pp. 3-10); briefly comments on
      statements by Leo Marx on the destruction of
      the raft in HF as illustrating MT's hostility
      toward the coming of the machine, and W. F.
      Taylor on MT's stated approval of the machine.

B84   PLANTE, PATRICIA R. "Mark Twain, Ferber and
      the Mississippi," Mark Twain Journal, XIII
      (Summer), 8-10.

(PLANTE, PATRICIA R.)
Edna Ferber's Show Boat "reveals marked resemblances to both Twain's Life on the Mississippi and Huckleberry Finn," especially in the symbolic use of the river. Abstract in AES, XI (1968), 2267.

B85   POIRIER, RICHARD. "Transatlantic Configurations: Mark Twain and Jane Austen," in his A World Elsewhere: The Place of Style in American Literature. (New York: Oxford University Press. pp. 144-207; also passim on MT.
"An enlarged and considerably revised version of an essay first printed in In Defense of Reading" (p. x.). Pp. 183-95 reprinted, abridged as "Huck Finn and the Metaphors of Society," in Simpson (1968), pp. 95-101.

B86   PRICE, LAWRENCE MARSDEN. The Reception of United States Literature in Germany. Chapel Hill: The University of North Carolina Press.
On MT, pp. 11-19 and passim; a considerably more extensive treatment may be found in Hemminghaus, Mark Twain in Germany (1939), which Price cites, but there is also some material updating Hemminghaus.

B87   PRITCHETT, V. S. "Chicaneries," New Statesman, LXXII (July 8), 56. A review of Charles Neider, ed., The Adventures of Colonel Sellers (1965).
"Neither Mark Twain nor his collaborator, C. D. Warner, was capable of getting a real novel out of their material.... Twain was a cocky, peddling traveller and autobiographer who never saw below the surface of reality: his genius lay in his gift for escaping from it." Abstract in AES, X (1967), 1324; reprinted in Twainian, XXVII (January-February, 1968).

B88   *RODD, LEWIS CHARLES. The Bad Boy from the Mississippi: The Story of Mark Twain. Melbourne: Cheshire. (Know Your Author; 28-pp. pamphlet).
[Source: MHRA Annual Bibliography (1966), No. 7134.]

B89   ROGERS, FRANKLIN R. "Mark Twain's First Venture into Fiction," Southwest Review, LI (Winter), 97-98.
A review of Bryant Morey French, Mark Twain and "The Gilded Age" (1965) as "an exhaustive study...Mr. French discusses in an impressively detailed fashion the composition of the novel, the nature of the collaboration between the two authors, and the specific targets of the satire. He provides useful information on such matters as the play based on the novel, the manuscript, and copyright problems," and the scattered work by other scholars on GA. By astute detective work he has collected evidence supporting his claim that GA is a roman à clef.

Unfortunately, GA itself lacks "an artistic grace...a timelessness of theme or characterization," as is revealed by French's "attempt...to resurrect the satiric targets."

B90   ROLLINS, RONALD G. "Huckleberry Finn and Christie Mahon: The Playboy of the Western World," Mark Twain Journal, XIII (Summer), 16-19.
MT's novel and Synge's play show parallels in that the fathers are "cruel, arbitrary and despotic tyrants," and when Huck and Christy escape "both flights are similar in that they involve fake or symbolic murders," after which the boys hide their true identities or personalities and later are reborn to new maturity. Abstract in AES, XI (1968), 2269.

B91   ROOT, ROBERT. [Review: A. Grove Day, ed., Mark Twain's Letters from Hawaii.] Journalism Quarterly, XLIII (Winter), 793.
Brief and descriptive: "These are personal essays...will meet some needs of journalism students looking into the conjunction of literature and journalism."

B92   ROPER, GORDON. "Mark Twain and His Canadian Publishers: A Second Look," Papers of the Bibliographical Society of Canada, V, 30-89.
Supplements Jacob Blanck's Bibliography of American Literature on MT editions. "This essay is an expansion of an article entitled 'Mark Twain and His Canadian Publishers' in the 'Special Mark Twain Number' of The American Book Collector, X (June, 1960), pp. 13-29" (p. 84, n. 2). On MT's problems with Canadian pirates and eventual success in arranging for authorized publication. Includes "Check List of Canadian Editions of Mark Twain's Work," with references to Blanck and with 27 editions not listed in Blanck (pp. 82-84).

B93   ROSE, MARILYN GADDIS. "Pudd'nhead Wilson: A Contemporary Parable," Mark Twain Journal, XIII (Summer), 5-7.
The racial theme is still relevant: "In fact, Twain's fluctuating boundaries of Negro and white and master and slave are as intricate and relevant as, say, Jean Genet's in Les Negres (1962)." Wilson is "a Thoreau with practical ambitions" and, "incidentally, one year younger than Hawthorne" on his arrival at Dawson's Landing in 1830. Abstract in AES, XI (1968), 2266.

B94   ROSENTHAL, RAYMOND. "Bohemian from the Sage-Brush," New Leader, XLIX (July 18), 15-16. A review of Justin Kaplan's Mr. Clemens and Mark Twain.
MT's "influence on his wife and on Howells was much greater than theirs on him. He turned his wife Livy from a strait-laced Puritan into a tippler, an unbeliever and almost a cynic.... Kaplan's account is more subtle and more convincing than Brooks'.

1966 - Shorter Writings

(ROSENTHAL, RAYMOND)
Mark Twain was a forceful artist, a compelling personality, who carried his conflicts within him."

B95   NO ENTRY

B96   ROTHBERG, ABRAHAM. "The Flawed Dream: American Novels of Politics," London Magazine, VI (April), 17-33.
Briefly mentions GA as having anticipated the attitudes and approaches in political novels of the present day. Abstract in AES, IX (1966), 3004; reprinted in Twainian, XXVI (January-February, 1967).

B97   SABITH, BARNEY. "All Things to All Men," Chicago Tribune, "Books Today" (June 26), Section 9, p. 10.
A review of Justin Kaplan, Mr. Clemens and Mark Twain. Uncritical, basically a description of the book; but, "Kaplan's examination of Clemens's life is compelling. His sources include material made public only recently, as well as letters not previously used in analysis of Clemens' work and personality. Kaplan's special gift is his analysis of events and relationships."

B98   *SACHS, VIOLA. "Wedrujaca Granica a Literatura Amerykanska," Przeglad Humanistyczny, X, No. 1, 43-57.
[Source: AES, X (1967), 2861; reprinted in Twainian, XXVII (January-February, 1968).] Includes discussion of the character Jim in HF. [In Polish.]

B99   SAMOSSOUD, CLARA CLEMENS. "One of the Last Letters from Clara Samossoud to Our Foundation," Twainian, XXV (November-December), 1.
A letter of January 15, 1961, thanking Chester L. Davis for a copy of a letter sent to a person (not named) being considered as president of the Mark Twain Research Foundation, Inc.; this is of no biographical or critical interest. Abstract in AES, XI (1968), 1740; reprinted in Twainian, XXVIII (January-February, 1969).

B100 SAN JUAN, PASTORA. "A Source for Tom Sawyer," American Literature, XXXVIII (March), 101-102.
The Hartford Courant of April 21, 1873 contained a story of boys lost in a Hannibal cave; this "is probably Mark Twain's source for the episode in The Adventures of Tom Sawyer"; moreover, "the style of the news item is reminiscent of Twain," who may have written it. Abstract in AES, X (1967), 781; reprinted in Twainian, XXVII (January-February, 1968).

B101 *SAPOSHNIKOV, G. "Sholem Aleichem and Mark Twain," Zukunft, LXXI, 174-76.
[In Yiddish. Source: MLA Bibliography (1966), No. 15039.]

B102 SCANLON, LAWRENCE E. "'They're After Us' Again," Mark Twain Journal, XIII (Summer), 20-21.
In "Mr. Eliot, Mr. Trilling, and Huckleberry Finn," Leo Marx puts undue stress on Huck's words to Jim; in fact he is as much a fugitive as Jim is, but has not yet come to identify his own flight with Jim's. Abstract in AES, XI (1968), 2270.

B103 SCHLESINGER, ARTHUR, JR. "Mark Twain; or, the Ambiguities," Atlantic Monthly, CCXVIII (August), 61-64.
Based on Justin Kaplan's Mr. Clemens and Mark Twain, this is essentially a review and summary. Kaplan's "remarkable...book is nonportentous and nonideological, concerned with telling Clemens' story rather than with making points about America. He has mastered the Mark Twain scholarship (even if he is something less than generous in acknowledging debts to those who went before) but has moved beyond the familiar Mark Twain controversies." Schlesinger discusses MT's lifelong inner tensions, emphasizing the later years, and follows Kaplan's view of him as a divided personality. He takes exception to the Howells description of MT as "the Lincoln of our literature," comparing him, rather, to Grant: "Like Grant, Mark Twain was a flawed man who never composed his inner schisms, never purged himself of bitterness, never distilled serenity out of torment."

B104 SCOTT, WINFIELD TOWNLEY. "Combed All to Hell," Book Week (Washington Post), III (June 26), 4, 15.
A review of Justin Kaplan, Mr. Clemens and Mark Twain, "a brilliant biography." Kaplan's "vast research and his scholarly intelligence are impeccable but never heavy, for he writes extremely well--with verve, wit, penetration, compassion," and revealing MT's inner conflicts. "This is not a theory-ridden book," as are those by Brooks and DeVoto, and the criticism of MT's works is "superb."

B105 SMITH, HENRY NASH. [Review: Bernard Poli, Mark Twain, Écrivain de l'Ouest: Regionalisme et Humour (1965).] Études Anglaises, XIX, 457-58.
Meeting his responsibilities in this first full-length introduction of MT to French readers, Poli provides essays on MT as "béotien au royaume des lettres," his religious and moral thought, his humor, and his style, as well as "a discriminating guide to relevant American scholarship. The European reader may turn to this book with confidence. It is a thoroughly reliable introduction to its subject." It is also an interpretation "with a fresh and arresting thesis" that MT's West was his experiences and remembered past which he attempted to use through "a surrogate narrator capable of mediating between reality and fantasy in the author's reminiscences"; thus, the loss of his

(SMITH, HENRY NASH)
creative powers in the later years may be attributed to a solidification of thoughts and consequent loss of "the delicate ambiguities of statement made possible by the use of a fully dramatized narrator." [In English.]

B106 STEIN, RUTH. "The ABC's of Counterfeit Classics: Adapted, Bowdlerized, and Condensed," English Journal, LV (December), 1160-63.
Exemplified by HF, in classroom editions and other adaptations. Generally the book is cut to "the mere story of a runaway slave," language is changed, and descriptions are reduced. Great stories so distorted are of doubtful value, and "in the 'popular' editions school children may actually learn to tolerate mediocrity."

B107 STEPHENS, GEORGE D. "Huckleberry Finn as a Journey," Mark Twain Journal, XIII (Summer), 11-15.
MT himself was an inveterate traveler, and "at one time or another Twain read LeSage, Rabelais, Fielding, and Smollett. Don Quixote was an early and lasting favorite." He read and admired the work of Dickens." HF follows some of the traditions of the picaresque novel in the journey and adventures, and in the use of an anti-hero as the central character. Abstract in AES, XI (1968), 2268.

B108 STOWELL, ROBERT F. "Notes on Geography in Huckleberry Finn," Mark Twain Journal, XIII (Summer), front cover, 22.
Stowell's map on the front cover shows Huck and Jim's route, with state boundaries and approximate distances; in his "Notes" Stowell asks for any needed corrections, as the map is to be incorporated in an Atlas for American Literature being compiled.

B109 STRONKS, JAMES B. [Review: Hamlin Hill, Mark Twain and Elisha Bliss (1964).] Modern Philology, LXIII (May), 369-71.
The subscription publisher who helped MT achieve wide sales (but may have underpaid him by some $50,000 in royalties) influenced his form of writing for an uncritical market; but the book is not primarily about him: "What Hill has actually written is a step-by-step history of the composition and publication of the six books that Bliss marketed for Twain: The Innocents Abroad (1869), Roughing It (1872), The Gilded Age (with C. D. Warner, 1873), the Sketches, New and Old (1875), Tom Sawyer (1876), and A Tramp Abroad (1880). The approach is solidly factual, sometimes tediously so, and some of the ground has been covered before; "and if the present book is not invariably interesting or unified it is because the author, skirting the claims of these previous prospectors, often mines lower-grade ore in scattered pockets."

B110 TRILLING, LIONEL, RAY B. WEST, and LYMAN BRYSON. "Mark Twain: The Adventures of Huckleberry Finn," in George D. Crothers, ed., Invitation to Learning: English & American Novels. New York, London: Basic Books, pp. 242-51.
One of a series of radio conversations on great novels; laudatory and somewhat general. Notes the terror in the book, and the significance of Huck's Pap; four kinds of authority: convention, nature, the supernatural, and (what counts with Huck) affection. There is brief comment on the importance of the language, and a concluding word on Huck's rejection of both convention and of romance: Tom does his rebelling in conventional terms, Huck does not.

B111 VALES, ROBERT T. "Thief and Theft in Huckleberry Finn," American Literature, XXXVII (January), 420-29.
"Huck has decided to steal Jim, and it is theft and its related synonyms which united all aspects of the novel. It is also through theft that we learn about the nature of man and society." Abstract in AES, X (1967), 767; reprinted in Twainian, XXVII (January-February, 1968).

B112 WALCUTT, CHARLES CHILD. "Freedom Afloat--and Adrift," pp. 131-44 in his Man's Changing Mask: Modes and Methods of Characterization in Fiction. Minneapolis: University of Minnesota Press.
"There is no firm theme to be realized in the plot; hence the action must turn into melodrama and the characters, having no firm beginnings, do not develop in great problems and decisions but recede into deeper obscurity as the melodramatic conclusion takes over."

B113 *WILLIAMS, PHILIP. "Mark Twain and Social Darwinism," Essays and Studies in English Language and Literature (Tohoku Gakuin University Review, Sendai, Japan), No. 49-50, pp. 143-72.
[Source: MHRA Annual Bibliography (1966), No. 7057; Leary (1970), p. 77.]

B114 WOODWARD, ROBERT H. "More on Mark Twain and the Dictionary," Word Study (G. & C. Merriam Co.), XLII (December), 8.
Repeats "a story--probably apocryphal: such anecdotes generally are--that appeared in one of the early issues of Word Study and was reprinted in the Word Study deskside reader entitled Vocabulary Building, Bibliography, and Word Study (1937). Over the name of the contributor, George A. Posner, and under the title 'Plagiarism'" appeared the story of MT's telling a speaker that "I have a book at home (and a very old book) that contains every word of that speech you just delivered"--and sending him a dictionary.

1966 - Shorter Writings

B115 WOODWARD, ROBERT H. "Teaching Huckleberry Finn to Foreign Students," Mark Twain Journal, XIII (Winter), 5-7.
    Students from the Republic of Mali, West Africa responded well to selections from HF in a class at San Jose State College.

B116 *YOUNG, PHILIP. Ernest Hemingway: A Reconsideration. University Park, Pennsylvania: Pennsylvania State University Press.
    [Source: pp. 228-29, on HF, reprinted in Simpson (1968), pp. 113-14.] Describes Huck as hurt by his experiences, and not amused even by such nominally funny encounters as that with the Duke and Dauphin: "But Huck is not amused; they disgust him with mankind in general. He is wounded, and bitter, and suffering from both insomnia and nightmare, and he finally rebels." Faced with a decision on whether to betray Jim, "off on his own, and exposed to the violence and evil of society as a whole, he renounces it.... If it is good, he is wicked. And if it aims for heaven, he will go elsewhere."

B117 ZIFF, LARZER. "Literary Absenteeism: Henry James and Mark Twain," pp. 50-72 in his The American 1890s: Life and Times of a Lost Generation (New York: Viking).
    "The lessons that the nineties slowly and painfully brought home to Howells and James came on [MT] more swiftly, like a thunderclap. The decade...had battered Twain so severely that his art was never to recover."

1967 A BOOKS

  A1 ANDERSON, FREDERICK, WILLIAM M. GIBSON, and HENRY NASH SMITH, eds. Selected Mark Twain-Howells Letters, 1872-1910. Cambridge, Massachusetts: The Belknap Press of Harvard University Press.
    "The text of the letters we have included reproduces the text in the two-volume edition, except that we have omitted canceled words...and have condensed many letters by deleting passages having small interest or relevance for readers who are not specialists in American literature"; includes two additional letters from MT to Howells (p. v). The letters reveal the literary influence of Howells as beneficial (p. xii), and "help to clarify the outlines of a vernacular tradition in the Gilded Age, which has exerted a powerful influence on a number of the best writers of tales and novels in the twentieth century. Howells fostered the tradition," both through his editing of the Atlantic Monthly, and in his own writing (p. xiii).

  A2 ANON. Mark Twain in Romania: Bibliography of the Romanian Translations Published in Volume and in Magazines. Bucharest: Romanian Institute for Cultural Relations with Foreign Countries.

In English. Includes Introduction and Bibliographical Presentation by Dorothea Sasu-Timerman, bibliography (annotated briefly, and indexed), and "Number of Mark Twain's Works Editions Published in the Socialist Republic of Romania, 1949-1966," giving the number of copies in each edition. Introduction names several of "the foremost fifty translators attracted by Mark Twain's deep genuine creation," but notes the difficulty in dealing with his style. "That is why till 1944 translations have been made after French or German versions." More recent translations "have a high aesthetic value; those realized after the English original, are often accompanied by biographical presentations or studies, and bibliographical notes, which introduce the readers in the atmosphere and the social political events which generated a lot of incidents evoked with such a wit and irony in his books" (pp. 4-5). "The translations published in volumes and Romanian reviews, presented us the often dramatic action of his writings, the funny part and sharp irony covering his ideas as fighter against bondage, hypocrisy, superstition, lie and corruption, ever being in search for honesty, truth and justice. That is why Mark Twain is one of the most appreciated foreign writers in Romania" (p. 5).

  A3 BALDWIN, MARY AUSTIN, ed. William Dean Howells, My Mark Twain: Reminiscences and Criticisms. Baton Rouge: Louisiana State University Press.
    This reprint of the 1910 edition (1910.A3) contains a useful ten-page introduction, twenty pages of notes to the text, and an index. It should be the new standard edition of a work important for the critical judgment of the author and for his close friendship with MT. Available hardbound and in paperback.

  A4 CLEMENS, CYRIL. Mark Twain and Lyndon B. Johnson. Foreword by Adlai E. Stevenson. Kirkwood, Missouri: Mark Twain Journal.
    Consists of letters from Lyndon Johnson thanking Cyril Clemens for a newspaper clipping, an invitation to address the Mark Twain Birthday Banquet, etc., together with letters from Hubert Humphrey and Mrs. Johnson. The introduction by Adlai E. Stevenson does not mention this 23-page pamphlet, but tells of the time when MT wrote a bit of doggerel on the back of a menu for Stevenson's father, on the pronunciation of "Adlai" (p. 9).

  A5 CLEMENS, SAMUEL L. "A Curtain Lecture Concerning Skating"; Being an Unusual Example of Mark Twain's Early Journalistic Humor, Written Entirely in Dialogue, and Reprinted for the First Time in Book Form as it Originally Appeared in the New York Sunday Mercury of March 17, 1867; and, the Later, Unauthorized Revision, Mrs. Mark Twain's Shoe; Being a

(CLEMENS, SAMUEL L.)
Facsimile Taken from the Pages of Beadle's The Dime Dialogues No. 10: For Homes, Schools and Exhibitions. New York: Beadle and Company, Publishers, 98 William Street. First Published in April, 1871. Edited by Donald M. Kunde. Denver, Colorado: Privately Printed by Ralph Baldwin.

A contribution to a column titled "Table-Talk" in the Sunday Mercury. Unfamiliar with this early version, Merle Johnson dismissed the Beadle's distorted reprinting: "I cannot think Mark Twain wrote it."

A6 ____. Mark Twain's Letters to His Publishers, 1867-1894, ed. Hamlin Hill. Berkeley, Los Angeles, London: University of California Press.

A volume in the CEAA edition of the MT Papers. Texts of 290 letters, 28 of them reprinted from earlier book publications because the originals are no longer available. "A few letters not addressed to Mark Twain's official publishers--letters to Orion Clemens, Charles Dudley Warner, T. B. Pugh, Thomas Bailey Aldrich, and Moncure Conway, for example--are included because their major substance concerns publishing."

A7 ____. Mark Twain's Satires & Burlesques, ed. Franklin R. Rogers. Berkeley and Los Angeles: University of California Press.

A volume in the CEAA edition of the MT Papers. Includes the Simon Wheeler and Hellfire Hotchkiss sequences, the burlesque Hamlet, and other unpublished manuscript materials.

A8 ____. Mark Twain's "Which Was the Dream?" and Other Symbolic Writings of the Later Years, ed. John S. Tuckey. Berkeley and Los Angeles: University of California Press.

A volume in the CEAA edition of the MT Papers. "All of the selections in this volume were composed between 1896 and 1905," after the death of his daughter Susy and heavy financial disasters. "Their principal fable is that of a man who has been long favored by luck while pursuing a dream of success that seemed about to turn into reality." Following sudden reverses, he takes refuge in the thought that he may be living in a nightmare from which he will awaken; but his nightmares may be the actuality of his life.

A9 ____, and C. D. WARNER. The Gilded Age, ed. by Herbert Van Thal, with an introduction by Richard Church. London: Cassell. The First Novel Library.

Van Thal's introduction concerns novels in general, and Church's is biographical rather than critical.

A10 KAPLAN, JUSTIN, ed. and Introduction. Great Short Works of Mark Twain. New York: Harper & Row.

Kaplan's introduction gives brief biography and conventional description of MT as author.

A11 ____, ed. Mark Twain: A Profile. New York: Hill and Wang.

A collection of articles on MT (cross-referenced to this anthology in the present bibliography) and extracts from books (not cross-referenced where more readily available in their original form). Includes the account by Henry Nash Smith (from Mark Twain: The Development of a Writer) of the Whittier Birthday Dinner and its consequences, and Kaplan's own "The Yankee and the Machine: The Perfectable World" ("Adapted from Mr. Clemens and Mark Twain...1966").

A12 *KASYAN, A. K. Mark Tven v Rossii. (1872-1966). [Mark Twain in Russia]. Leningrad: Leningradskii Pedagogicheskii Institut Imeni A. I. Gertsena.
[Source: MHRA Annual Bibliography (1967), No. 7118.]

A13 KRAUSE, SYDNEY J. Mark Twain as Critic. Baltimore: Johns Hopkins Press.

Traces MT's critical approach from his early innocent mask of "Muggins" to the later, more worldly "Grumbler," noting his treatment of Goldsmith, Cooper, Scott, and Harte, and its relation to his anti-romanticism; also considers at length his appreciation of Macaulay, Howells, Howe, Zola, and Adolph Wilbrandt. MT was a sensitive reader and a serious student of his literary craft. Reviews by Wiggins, Budd, Gerber, Regan, Fatout, and an anonymous reviewer for Choice (1967-1968) are summarized by Warren B. Benson in ALA, II (June, 1969), 337-39.

A14 MARX, LEO., ed. Adventures of Huckleberry Finn. Indianapolis and New York: The Bobbs-Merrill Company, Inc.

Introduction describes MT's life, backgrounds and composition of HF, and summarizes the critical controversy. There are also aids to the student and an appendix of excerpts from LOM.

A15 NEIDER, CHARLES, ed. The Complete Travel Books of Mark Twain. The Later Works: "A Tramp Abroad," "Life on the Mississippi," "Following the Equator." Garden City, N.Y.: Doubleday & Company, Inc.

Consists of the three books, with no introduction, editorial matter, or notes, except for "A Note on the Text," which states that the texts are those of the first American editions of the books with only minor changes and with the chapter numbers changed from Roman to Arabic (p. ix).

319

A16   NEIDER, CHARLES. Mark Twain. New York:
       Horizon Press.
            According to a "Prefatory Note" (p. ix),
       "The majority of these chapters were pub-
       lished as introductions to volumes of Mark
       Twain's work. 'On Mark Twain Censorship'
       and 'The Notebooks' have not been published
       previously." The chapters on MT are "The
       Novels" (1964), "The Adventures of Colonel
       Sellers," (1964), "The Travel Books and
       Travels" (1966), "The Essays" (1962), "The
       Autobiography" (1958), "Mark Twain and the
       Russians" (1959), "On Mark Twain Censor-
       ship" (1966), "The Notebooks" (1966), "The
       Sketches" (1961), "The Stories" (1956), and
       "Life as I Find It" (1961). "Mark Twain
       and the Russians" is subtitled "An Exchange
       of Views," and consists of Neider's corres-
       pondence with Literaturnaya Gazeta (Mos-
       cow), concerning the Russian charges that
       Neider's edition of MT's autobiography
       represented deliberate suppression of at-
       tacks on the establishment of his day;
       Neider reports this exchange (originally
       published by Hill and Wang in 1959), was
       later included in the Washington Square
       Press edition of the Autobiography (p. v).

A17   SCOTT, ARTHUR L., ed. Mark Twain: Selected
       Criticism. Dallas: Southern Methodist
       University Press.
            A revised edition of a 1955 collection of
       critical articles and excerpts from books,
       1867-1963. The material reprinted is in-
       cluded in the present bibliography and
       noted in cross-references to both editions.

A18   SIMON, JOHN Y., ed. and introduction. "Gen-
       eral Grant" by Matthew Arnold, with a Re-
       joinder by Mark Twain. Carbondale and Ed-
       wardsville: Southern Illinois University
       Press (1966).
            Contains the text of Arnold's two-part
       essay on Grant originally published in
       Murray's Magazine (repr. 1887, 1888) and
       the reply by MT in a speech at the Annual
       Reunion of the Army and Navy Club of Con-
       necticut, April 27, 1887. Simon's intro-
       duction describes Arnold's article as "a
       graceful tribute" to Grant, intended "to
       strengthen trans-Atlantic good will" (p. 4).

A19   WAGENKNECHT, EDWARD. Mark Twain: The Man
       and His Work, Third Edition. Norman:
       University of Oklahoma Press.
            Essentially the same as the 1961 edition,
       with an added thirty-page "Commentary on
       Mark Twain Criticism and Scholarship Since
       1960" (not systematically incorporated in
       the present bibliography). Excerpt (bio-
       graphical summary) reprinted in Schmitter
       (1974), pp. 11-18.

B1   ANON. "German Reds Use Mark Twain Work. Play
       Makes the Connecticut Yankee G.I. Slain in
       [Vietnam] War." New York Times, February 26.
            The play by Claus Hemmel, a warning to
       those who advocate socialism as a middle
       way, made its premiere in Erfurt the previ-
       ous week. This article is based on a review
       in the national Communist party newspaper.
       "The Yankee's cardinal sin, according to
       Rainier Kerndl, the Neues Deutschland thea-
       ter critic, is that he 'ignores the obvious
       signs of class conflict and believes that
       the telephone, mirror, fire insurance and
       postal service can benefit everyone without
       affecting the relationships between the
       classes.'"

B2   ANON. "Mark Twain Items Published Elsewhere,"
       Twainian, XXVI (January-February), 1-4.
            Reprints a number of abstracts from AES,
       IX (1966) of material relating to MT; some
       involve only passing mention, and a number
       of abstracts in AES are not here reprinted.
       Abstract in AES, XII (1969); 674; reprinted
       in Twainian, XXIX (January-February, 1970).

B3   ATHERTON, JAMES S. "To Give Down the Banks
       and Hark from the Tomb!" James Joyce Quar-
       terly, IV (Winter), 75-83.
            On quotations from HF incorporated in
       Finnegans Wake.

B4   BABCOCK, C. MERTON. "Mark Twain and the
       Belles of San Francisco," San Francisco, IX
       (November), 38.
            A popular account, consisting chiefly of
       MT's comments on women in his days as a San
       Francisco newspaperman and in RI.

B5   BAILEY, ROGER B. "Twain's Huckleberry Finn,
       Chapters 1 and 2," Explicator, XXVI (Septem-
       ber), Item 2.
            The fact that Huck trips over a root but
       Tom Sawyer steps on and snaps a dry twig
       (like a Fenimore Cooper character) reveals
       the contrast between Huck's realism and
       Tom's romancing. Abstract in AES, XII
       (1969), 823; reprinted in Twainian, XXIX
       (January-February, 1970).

B6   BATES, ALLAN. "Sam Clemens, Pilot-Humorist
       of a Tramp Steamboat," American Literature,
       XXXIX (March), 102-109.
            Reprints the text of a burlesque river re-
       port from the Missouri Republican of August
       30, 1860, signed by MT and J. W. Hood; MT
       was pilot on the Arago July 28-September 9.
       Bates suggests that some of the references
       were bawdy, and MT was not taking his

(BATES, ALLAN)
profession seriously at the time. Extracts appeared in the New Orleans Daily Delta September 2, with credit and praise for MT as the author. Abstract in AES, X (1967), 2250; reprinted in Twainian, XXVII (January-February, 1968). Also abstracted in ALA, I (December, 1967), 43-44.

B7   BENJAMIN, WILLIAM EVARTS. "Letters from William Evarts Benjamin to Paine," Twainian, XXVI (November-December), 4.
Four letters of May-June, 1910; the first is interesting because it notes that Benjamin is sending Paine the texts of an MT speech at the opening of the Virginian Railway (n.d., paying tribute to Benjamin's father-in-law Henry H. Rogers) and "Mark Twain," an article by Charles Lancaster in the Liverpool Daily Post and Mercury, May 5, 1910. Abstract in AES, XIII (1969-1970), 1356; reprinted in Twainian, XXX (January-February, 1971).

B8   BENNETT, JAMES R. "The Adventures of Huck Finn in Chapter One," Iowa English Yearbook, XII, 68-72.
"The opening chapter suggests all the major motifs of the novel--freedom, the slave society, religion, money, illusion, the family, superstition, loneliness, death, and moral growth. Chapter One presents a series of concise scenes which epitomize the book." Abstract in AES, XI (1968), 470; reprinted in Twainian, XXVIII (January-February, 1969).

B9   BERTOLOTTI, D. S., JR. "Mark Twain Revisits the Tailor," Mark Twain Journal, XIII (Summer), 18-19.
MT's contention in CY that men are distinguished more by their clothes than by their characters may be derived from Carlyle's Sartor Resartus. There are "many philosophic parallels" between the two authors, although MT was never able to progress beyond Carlyle's "Everlasting No."

B10   _____. "Structural Unity in 'The Man that Corrupted Hadleyburg,'" Mark Twain Journal, XIV (Winter), 19-21.
The episodes are linked by the letters from Howard L. Stephenson, which comment ironically on the supposed integrity of the "holy nineteen" and initiate the action which follows. Abstract in ALA, I (June, 1968), 188-89.

B11   BLAIR, WALTER. "Mark Twain," American Book Collector (Chicago), XVIII (November), 7.
Announces that the University of California has begun publishing the Mark Twain Papers, and, probably joined by the University of Iowa, will publish definitive editions of his works.

B12   _____. [Review: Justin Kaplan, Mr. Clemens and Mark Twain (1966).] American Literature, XXXIX (May), 220-23.
Kaplan's book is titillating, rich in lurid or sexy quotations or bits of gossip, but inadequately documented and often inaccurate, and questionable in its interpretations; it is unworthy of the praise it has received.

B13   BOWEN, JAMES K., and RICHARD VanDerBEETS, eds., American Literature Abstracts, I (December), pp. 43-47, 125-26, 132-33.
Contains abstracts more extensive than those in the present bibliography, often prepared by the authors of the articles abstracted; however, these abstracts represent only part of a year's work and a large proportion of them are from journals such as American Literature, which are more readily available than the abstracts. A useful feature is the "Book Review Consensus," summarizing at some length the reviews of individual books; again, the emphasis is on major (and hence readily available) journals. The abstracts and book review summaries are noted in the present bibliography.

B14   BRANCH, EDGAR M. "Major Perry and the Monitor Camanche: An Early Mark Twain Speech," American Literature, XXXIX (May), 170-79.
Reprints from the San Francisco Alta California of June 13, 1864 the text of MT's second earliest extant speech: "It honored Major Edward C. Perry, who had helped to raise the ship Aquila and its cargo, the dismantled monitor Camanche, from the floor of the San Francisco harbor," and shows MT's growing skill and reputation as a popular lecturer. Abstract in AES, X (1967), 2255; reprinted in Twainian, XXVII (January-February, 1968). Also abstracted in ALA, I (December, 1967), 44-45.

B15   _____. "'My Voice Is Still for Setchell': A Background Study of 'Jim Smiley and His Jumping Frog,'" Publications of the Modern Language Association, LXXXII (December), 591-601.
Some of the episodes, characters, and names may be traced to MT's experiences, as shown in his 1864-1865 journalism; it was probably written in the period October 16-25, 1865. Branch relates the tale's "compelling appeal and its poetic unity" to MT's development as a writer. Abstract in AES, XI (1968), 646; reprinted in Twainian, XXVIII (January-February, 1969). Also abstracted in ALA, I (June, 1968), 189.

B16   _____. "Samuel Clemens and the Copperheads of 1864," Mad River Review (Wright State Campus, Dayton, Ohio), II (Winter-Spring), 3-20.

1967 - Shorter Writings

(BRANCH, EDGAR M.)

In his four months with the San Francisco Morning Call MT wrote hundreds of unsigned items, from brief notices to long articles on local events. "Among these, in my opinion, were several political meetings held that summer in San Francisco during the Lincoln-McClellan election campaigns. This article reprints three of these reports, all unsigned but all bearing distinctive marks of Clemens' authorship. They help us to gauge Clemens' political feelings in 1864, and they preface the more active interest he took in politics in later times." Abstract in AES, X (1967), 3301; reprinted in Twainian, XXVIII (March-April, 1969).

B17   BROWN, SPENCER. "Huckleberry Finn for Our Time: A Re-Reading of the Concluding Chapters," Michigan Quarterly Review, VI (Winter), 41-46.

The "uneasy amusement" and "irritation" intelligent readers feel over the ending are "the reactions Mark Twain deliberately provoked" in an attack on slavery through showing its effect on ordinary, kind people, and most of all, its effect on Huck and Jim: "Thus slavery has corrupted and rendered selfish the best character in the novel" and reduced the manly Jim to a clown. Abstract in AES, X (1967), 1999; reprinted in Twainian, XXVII (January-February, 1968).

B18   BUDD, LOUIS J. [Review: Hamlin Hill, ed., Mark Twain's Letters to His Publishers, 1867-1894; Franklin R. Rogers, ed., Mark Twain's Satires & Burlesques; John S. Tuckey, ed., Mark Twain's "Which was the Dream?" and Other Symbolic Writings.] New England Quarterly, XL (December), 583-86.

The editing of these volumes should "satisfy the needs of all but those who would have gone to the original manuscripts in any case," and "the Mark Twain Papers are off to the glittering start that Samuel Langhorne Clemens craved for any of his enterprises." Hill's edition of the letters shows MT's wholehearted dedication to making money from his books, but there is comfort in the evidence that he "was mostly right about the incompetence of Charles Webster. Among some "richly suggestive passages" is one in 1881 beginning "Howells don't have no taste." Mark Twain's Satires & Burlesques "run the gamut of quality with fewer of his total misfires than usual," although they will not raise MT's stature: "No matter how important burlesque was to his creative circuits, it is usually tedious unless muted or integrated with other purposes. On the contrary Mark Twain's "Which Was the Dream?" and Other Symbolic Writings of the Later Years prints items of major interest and appeal, at present anyway," revealing humor and playfulness rather

than unrelieved gloom; Tuckey assumes that MT's darkening outlook was a result of his personal tragedies and reverses.

B19   _____. [Review: James M. Cox, Mark Twain: The Fate of Humor (1966).] Modern Philology, LXV, 420-21.

"Cox is continually lucid, incisive, fresh, and persuasive and has come closer than anyone else to explicating Twain within his own frame of mind. I feel major qualms only when Cox reproves Twain for not keeping a total commitment to humor and thus letting all good causes slide."

B20   CARDWELL, GUY A. [Review: Richard Bridgman, The Colloquial Style in America (1966).] American Literature, XXXIX (March), 124-25.

"Mr. Bridgman's chief contribution...is perhaps his view of the stylistic relationships" of MT (with the boy-narrator), James, Hemingway, and Gertrude Stein.

B21   CARTER, EVERETT. [Review: Bernard Poli, Mark Twain, Écrivain de l'Ouest: Régionalisme et Humour (1965).] Criticism, IX (Winter), 98-100.

MT "has found a commonsensical, shrewd cultural historian in Bernard Poli, who has presented this most representative of American writers to his countrymen with sympathy and understanding," presenting a judicious synthesis of MT's work and the criticisms it.

B22   CASEY, DANIEL J. "Universality in Huckleberry Finn: A Comparison of Twain and Kivi," Mark Twain Journal, XIV (Winter), 13-18.

Argues the case for the book's universal appeal by comparing it to Aleksis Kivi's Seven Brothers, which portrays the Finnish national character; does not suggest influence. Abstract in ALA, I (June, 1968), 189-90. See 1968.B20.

B23   CHRISTIAN, SHELDON. "The Day the Hornet Burned," Yankee XXXI (May), 74-5, 118-23.

Adds little or nothing to MT's account in the Sacramento Union, which it credits.

B24   COYNE, BERNARD V. "Mark Twain and the Transatlantic Mail," New Mexico Philatelist (Official Organ of the New Mexico Philatelic Association), XX (October-November), 1, 4-5.

An attempt to calculate the speed of surface mail, based on MT's correspondence of 1892-93.

B25   CRANE, SUSAN. "Letters from Susan Crane to Albert Bigelow Paine," Twainian, XXVI (July-August), 3-4.

Seven 1912 letters from Olivia Langdon Clemens's sister, chiefly interesting for their mention of family matters, including letters from Olivia, hostility toward MT's secretary Isobel Lyon ("how sure she was, how wiley [sic], and how she hastened the

(CRANE, SUSAN)
good man out of this life!"), and praise for Paine's work as official biographer. Brief abstract in AES, XII (1969), 687.

B26 CUMMINGS, SHERWOOD. [Review: Justin Kaplan ed., Mark Twain: A Profile.] American Literary Realism, I (Summer), 69-70.
Many of the essays in Kaplan's collection are a joy to read, but they do not bear on MT's realism and they have appeared in print before.

B27 [DAVIS, CHESTER L.]. "'All Right!' from 'The Carpet-Bag'--Possibly Twain?" Twainian, XXVI (November-December), 1-2.
This sketch from The Carpet-Bag (Boston, June 14, 1851) antedates MT's first known published story, "The Dandy Frightening the Squatter," which appeared there May 1, 1852; it is on file at the Mark Twain Research Foundation as part of "a large accumulation of material the identification of which was in dispute between Morse, Underhill, Johnson and others at the time your secretary took over the duties of Brownell." Abstract in AES, XIII (1969-1970), 1335.

B28 _____. [Comment on holdings of Mark Twain Research Foundation and policy concerning their disclosure.] Twainian, XXVI (July-August), 1.
The Foundation "has many unpublished letters, some of which would undoubtedly have been of some value to the authors of those books [reviewed in the March-April Twainian]. Certainly we would not throw open our files to permit the indiscriminate selection and publication of material which we ourselves would refuse to publish. We have often thought that perhaps what we consider should not be published, should be destroyed, yet we are not 'book burners' nor are we unofficial protectors of anyone, past or present, whether an unknown or a famous personality. It is hard to draw the line, but in the opinion of your Secretary certain things have been published by others, often out of context, and to say the least, add little or nothing to our knowledge of Mark Twain and quite often merely disclosing the exercise of bad taste." Pays tribute to Paine for his monumental achievement, and recognizes his situation, his love for MT and the difficulty in dealing with a mass of contradictory material.

B29 _____. "Identification of Mark Twain Material," Twainian, XXVI (September-October), 4.
General comments on the problems involved with passages vaguely remembered, oddities such as part of a letter by Olivia but in MT's hand (apparently copied by him for Paine's use in the biography), and material collected by Paine but not used. Brief abstract in AES, XIII (1969-1970), 1347.

B30 _____. "1838 Letter from Florida, Missouri Found," Twainian, XXVI (November-December), 2-3.
Text of a letter from MT's uncle John A. Quarles to another uncle, James T. Quarles; adds to family history. Abstract in AES, XIII (1969-1970), 1355; reprinted in Twainian, XXX (January-February, 1971).

B31 _____. "Mark Twain on Lynching," Twainian, XXVI (November-December), 3.
On MT's visit to Paris, Missouri, June 3, 1902, a speech he made there, and his condemnation of lynching on being told of the recent hanging of Abe Witherup there; apparently this article is based on a contemporary account, but the source is not given. Abstract in AES, XIII (1969-1970), 1343.

B32 _____. "Mark Twain's Room-Mate in St. Louis--Burrough," Twainian, XXVI (May-June), 1.
A letter to Paine from "Ida Burrough Coil (Coit?)" and one from Mary Burrough, establishing that MT's room-mate in St. Louis (as listed in Paine's biography, p. 103) was not Frank E. Burrough, but his father, Jacob Hutchinson Burrough. Abstract in AES, XII (1969), 680; reprinted in Twainian, XXIX (January-February, 1970).

B33 _____. "Progress in the Mark Twain Region," Twainian, XXVI (September-October), 1.
On the improvements made to Mark Twain shrines in Missouri in recent years. Abstract in AES, XIII (1969-1970), 1358; reprinted in Twainian, XXX (January-February, 1971).

B34 _____. "Three New Books Released Under Direction of 'Mark Twain Papers,'" Twainian, XXVI (March-April), 1-2.
Review article, briefly commenting on Mark Twain's Letters to His Publishers, ed. Hamlin Hill; Mark Twain's "Which Was the Dream?" ed. John S. Tuckey; Mark Twain's Satires & Burlesques, ed. Franklin R. Rogers. The comments by Davis note the value of indexes and appendixes and quote extensively from the books, but are not a detailed critical commentary.

B35 DAVIS, SAM. "Letter from Sam Davis to Paine," Twainian, XXVI (July-August), 2.
Expresses regret for the financial losses of MT, Joseph T. Goodman, and others. Abstract in AES (1969), 685.

B36 DENNIS, LARRY R. "Mark Twain and the Dark Angel," Midwest Quarterly, VIII (January), 181-97.
On the varied perspectives toward death in HF; they are all denied to Edwards in The Great Dark. Abstract in AES, XI (1968), 1477; reprinted in Twainian, XXVIII (January-February, 1969).

B37 DIAS, EARL J. "Mark Twain in Fairhaven," Mark Twain Journal, XIII (Summer), 11-15.
On MT's visit there as guest of Henry Rogers, and his address at the dedication of the new town hall on February 22, 1894. The text of the address and an MT letter to the officials of the Millicent Library are printed here, from manuscripts in the library collection.

B38 DUNLAP, JOSEPH R. "Future Times," Independent Shavian, V (Spring), 44.
Both MT (in "From the London Times of 1904") and Shaw published satiric sketches supposedly from the London Times of later dates. Abstract in AES, X (1967), 3295; reprinted in Twainian, XXVIII (March-April, 1969).

B39 ENSOR, ALLISON. "Twain's The Adventures of Huckleberry Finn, Chapter 37," Explicator, XXVI (November), Item 20.
MT had already quoted in IA from Acts XVII, and would have known Paul's statement that God "hath made of one blood all nations of men for to dwell on all the face of the earth"; thus, the fact that Uncle Silas Phelps was preparing next week's sermon from the same chapter may be an ironic thrust at his dual role as minister and slave-owner. Abstract in AES, XII (1969), 840 (incorrectly attributing the passage to Acts XXVII), also abstracted in ALA, I (June, 1968), 190.

B40 EXMAN, EUGENE. The House of Harper: One Hundred and Fifty Years of Publishing. New York, Evanston, London: Harper & Row, Publishers, passim.
Contains brief references to MT and his relations with his publishers, but very little not already in print elsewhere.

B41 FATOUT, PAUL. [Review: Sydney J. Krause, Mark Twain as Critic.] Journal of American History, LIV (December), 689-90.
The book is heavily researched and useful, but ponderous and verbose: "compression could have made room for criticism of writers not discussed--Cable, Harris, Riley, Holmes, Ward, and so forth," and the topic of public speaking.

B42 FEINBERG, LEONARD. Introduction to Satire. Ames: The University of Iowa Press, passim.
MT is among the authors noted as examples in a study of the nature, material, technique, and results of satire.

B43 FIFIELD, WILLIAM. "Joyce's Brother, Lawrence's Wife, Wolfe's Mother, Twain's Daughter," Texas Quarterly, X (Spring), 69-87.
On great writers as described in books by relatives; describes Clara Clemens Gabrilowitsch as having had "something too sweet about her overrefined," and tells of a visit to her California home. Fifield finds "Twain, a conscious artist, linked more really to Joyce than to Wolfe."

B44 FRASER, JOHN. "In Defence of Culture: Huckleberry Finn," Oxford Review, No. 6 (Michaelmas), pp. 5-22.
Summarizing and answering a number of critics' statements on HF, argues that in many ways the book is "soothing," and "Huck's progress through the ostensible dangers of the trip downstream is largely that of the kind of superboy of Tom Sawyer's imaginings." The depiction of slavery is not a central theme, but consists of set-pieces; in general the treatment of the Negro is validated rather than attacked. Huck is not a coherent and developing character, just as Gulliver is not, because, like Swift, MT was concentrating on the local and the immediate. Abstract in AES, XI (1968), 2024; reprinted in Twainian, XXVIII (January-February, 1969).

B45 GALE, ROBERT L. [Review: Justin Kaplan, Mr. Clemens and Mark Twain (1966).] Books Abroad, XLI (Autumn), 472-73.
"A study that should prove to be a major contribution to American literary scholarship and biography.... Kaplan rides hard his thesis that Clemens was self-divided, and he neglects no opportunity to make full use of all evidence supporting Mark Twain's doubts, rages and disappointments. The book is...incidentally packed with casual aesthetic insights of the most provocative sort."

B46 _____. [Review: Edward Wagenknecht, Mark Twain: The Man and His Work.] Studies in Short Fiction, V (Summer), 399.
This is "one of the finest general, introductory volumes on Twain," but "the only thing new about the third edition...is the bibliographical essay." The book "remains what it was in 1961, that is, a sane, balanced biographical but not literary study, organized by psychographic topics but not chronologically."

B47 GANZEL, DEWEY. "Samuel Clemens' Correspondence in the St. Louis Missouri Republican," Anglia (Tübingen), LXXXV, 390-403.
Supports John Camden Hotten's biographical sketch of MT in The Choice Humorous Works of Mark Twain (London, [1872]), which contains verifiable data apparently approved by MT himself. Ganzel reprints with commentary the texts of river correspondence which suggest MT's expertise as a pilot, reveal his membership in the Western Boatmen's Benevolent Association, and cast light on his movements during the piloting years, but give no hint of his future career as a writer.

B48 GERBER, JOHN C. "Mark Twain," in James Woodress, ed., American Literary Scholarship: An Annual/1967 (Durham, North Carolina: Duke University Press, 1969), pp. 56-72.

A survey of MT scholarship for the year; See 1963.B32. Contents: "i. Texts and Editions"; "ii. Biography"; "iii. General Criticism"; "iv. Earlier Works"; "v. Huckleberry Finn"; "vi. Later Works."

B49 GIBSON, WILLIAM M. [Review: Robert Regan, Unpromising Heroes: Mark Twain and His Characters (1966) and James M. Cox, Mark Twain: The Fate of Humor (1966).] American Literature, XXXIX (November), 412-14.

Regan proposes to examine the "psychological imperatives" of the folklore type important in MT's works, buttressing his case by showing MT's portrayal of real heroes such as General Grant and Anson Burlingame; fortunately, "he employs his thesis only where it works." Cox's book contains a few oversights and factual errors, but "easily overrides all such flaws. It brings Clemens's humor into sharp focus and will remain a powerful study of his imagination."

B50 GILMORE, T. B. "Critic of What?" North American Review, n.s., V (September), 39-40.

A review of Sydney J. Krause, Mark Twain as Critic, which devotes too much space to MT's criticism of Sir Walter Scott and Bret Harte, but provides a clear, readable, thorough treatment of its subject for those already familiar with MT's work--as Krause obviously is.

B51 GOODMAN, JOSEPH T. "Letters from Joe Goodman," Twainian, XXVI (May-June), 3-4.

Three letters to Paine from MT's editor on the Territorial Enterprise; one indicates that Goodman was checking text of biographical material for Paine, and another comments on Howard Taylor, once a printer on the Enterprise, who secured MT's permission to dramatize CY--but the language was hopelessly bad--and now Taylor writes Goodman that he has prepared a book of recollections concerning MT and hopes [in vain--T.A.T.] to have it published. The remaining material in the letters chiefly concerns Goodman himself, and his declining health. Appended is what Chester Davis describes as the full text of the review of MT's professional lecture debut with his Sandwich Islands address, copied by Goodman from the Daily Alta California, April 3, 1866. Abstract in AES, XII (1969), 682; reprinted in Twainian, XXIX (January-February, 1970).

B52 GRIMM, CLYDE L. "The American Claimant: Reclamation of a Farce," American Quarterly, XIX (Spring), 86-103.

This novel, though hastily and crudely written, is interesting for what it shows of "Twain's imaginative conversion of pointless humor into meaningful satire" and because the political and social themes reflect a mature statement of views MT had long held. The increasingly sympathetic portrait of Colonel Sellers reflects MT's understanding of "the American disparity between noble motives and opportunities for their fulfillment." Abstract in ALA, I (December, 1967), 45.

B53 HALL, FRED J. "Letters from Fred J. Hall to Paine," Twainian, XXVI (July-August), 2.

Hall, who took over the management of Webster and Company, owns several letters from MT and Olivia, speaks of her loyal and generous attitude, and says MT made the final decisions as to what books should be published after Hall took charge of the company; thanks Paine for describing the Webster & Company failure "skilfully, justly, and honestly." Abstract in AES, XII (1969), 686.

B54 HALL, ROBERT A. "The Innocents Abroad a Hundred Years Later," Annali dell'Istituto Orientale di Napoli, Sezione Germanica, X 217-32.

[Source: Reprint in Mark Twain Papers.] A general criticism; IA is still significant, both as a picture of its time and because it treats the relation between European and American culture.

B55 HARDING, DOROTHY STURGIS. "Mark Twain Lands an Angel-Fish," Columbia Library Columns, XVI (February), 2-12.

The friendship of a little girl with MT, whom she met on the S.S. Bermudian in 1908; tells of having done the lettering of MT's "Notice. To the Next Burglar" (reproduced in Meltzer, Mark Twain Himself, 1960, p. 283). Reprints the story of a joke played on MT at the Tavern Club (January 15, 1901), from club records. Photographs of MT, pp. 2, 5. Abstract in AES, XII (1969), 64; reprinted in Twainian, XXIX (January-February, 1970).

B56 HASLAM, GERALD W. "Huckleberry Finn: Why Read the Phelps Farm Episode?" Research Studies (Washington State University), XXXV (September), 189-97.

Although the ending of HF is weakened by stylistic excesses, and defenses based on form are unsatisfactory, it can be justified "as a logical extension of the often-emphasized moral texture of the novel...the dissonance one senses in the final episodes of the novel is largely a product of Twain's fictional projection of the seminal moral dilemma of a slave-holding society: human beings viewed as commodity." Abstract in AES, XII (1969), 1310; also abstracted in ALA, I (June, 1968), 190-91.

1967 - Shorter Writings

B57 HILL, JOHN S. "Huck Finn's Reaffirmation of
     Rejection," Mark Twain Journal, XIII (Sum-
     mer), 16-17.
        The concluding episode exploits both Jim
     and Huck, reflecting "the view that a white
     person of a lower class may also be duped,
     be used for sport." Huck has already gone
     through successive stages under the rule of
     the South, as a rebel, and again under the
     rule of the South, and in the end he rebels
     once more against the old order and Tom
     Sawyer, its symbol. Abstract in AES, XII
     (1960), 1238.

B58 HOLLAND, LAURENCE B. [Review: Richard Bridg-
     man, The Colloquial Style in America
     (1966).] Yale Review, LVI (Spring), 438-42.
        Notes "Huckleberry Finn's central posi-
     tion in advancing 'the movement toward an Ameri-
     can prose.'"

B59 HOWE, IRVING. "Anarchy and Authority in
     American Literature," Denver Quarterly, II
     (Autumn), 5-30.
        On HF (pp. 22-25): on the raft, "itself
     so wonderful a symbol of the isolation,
     purity and helplessness on which the an-
     archist vision rests," Huck and Jim "create
     a community of equals," but the idyllic
     existence is constantly threatened by the
     world and it cannot last. Abstract in AES,
     XI (1968), 1882; reprinted in Twainian,
     XXVIII (January-February, 1969).

B60 INGLIS, K. S. "Mark Twain and The Gilded Age:
     Some Suggestions for Comparative Study,"
     Australian Economic History, VII (March),
     19-37.
        On MT's portrayal of the brutality and
     corruption of his time, with particular
     attention to his symbolic use of the rail-
     roads.

B61 IRWIN, ROBERT. "The Failure of Tom Sawyer
     and Huckleberry Finn on Film," Mark Twain
     Journal, XIII (Summer), 9-11.
        The reluctance of producers to give of-
     fence has resulted in false interpretations,
     despite pains taken to achieve authenticity
     in casting, costumes, and scenery. A num-
     ber of film versions are discussed, and
     there is a bibliography of reviews.

B62 JONES, HOWARD MUMFORD. "The Pessimism of
     Mark Twain," in his Belief and Disbelief in
     American Literature. Chicago & London:
     The University of Chicago Press; Toronto:
     The University of Toronto Press, pp. 94-115.
        MT's pessimism was philosophical and
     temperamental, a blend of eighteenth-cen-
     tury rationalism and romantic sensibility.
     In his works "some human beings totally es-
     cape the inglorious human predicament....
     In fact it would be easy to go through his
     writings and cull out instance after in-
     stance of human generosity, saintliness,

self-sacrifice, and humility that totally
contradict his officially cynical attitude
toward altruism.... He judged Christianity
not by its performance but by its principle.
He appealed from Christian fact to Christian
idealism" (p. 110). Reprinted in Schmitter
(1974), pp. 41-56.

B63 JORDAN-SMITH, PAUL. "Mark Twain of Nevada,"
     American Book Collector (Chicago), XVII
     (March), 7.
        A review of James M. Cox's Mark Twain:
     the Fate of Humor (1966) as a "scholarly-
     entertaining study of the greatest American
     humorist.... In a brief review of this
     scholarly work it is not needful to point
     out all the by-paths followed by its author,"
     but the book takes the reader on "a joyous
     journey."

B64 *KASYAN, A. K. "Iz Istorii Perevodov Marka
     Tvena v Rossii" ["The History of Transla-
     tions of Mark Twain in Russia"], Irkutskii
     Pedagogicheskii Institut, Irkutsk, XXVI,
     185-97.
        [Source: MHRA Annual Bibliography (1967),
     No. 7117.]

B65 *_____. "Mark Twain v Rossii (1917-1965 gg.)"
     ["Mark Twain in Russia"], Irkutskii Peda-
     gogicheskii Institut, Irkutsk, XXVI, 162-85.
        [Source: MHRA Annual Bibliography (1967),
     No. 7119.]

B66 KRAUS, W. KEITH. "Huckleberry Finn: A Final
     Irony," Mark Twain Journal, XIV (Winter),
     18-19.
        The supposedly genuine Wilks heirs are a
     second set of frauds, who probably "met the
     same young man, or someone as equally well
     informed about the Wilks' family, as the
     King and Duke." The "lost" luggage and
     William's broken arm are clever ruses, but
     suspicion is raised by their lack of grief
     at Peter's death, by Harvey's "poor grammar
     and lapses into colloquial speech," and by
     the vagueness of his description of the
     tattoo on Peter's chest. Abstract in ALA,
     I (June, 1968), 191.

B67 KRAUSE, SYDNEY J. "Olivia Clemens's 'Editing'
     Reviewed," American Literature, XXXIX
     (November), 325-51.
        MT respected his wife's suggestions, of
     which some were innocuous and others useful,
     but he did not always follow her advice, as
     is revealed in the manuscript of More Tramps
     Abroad (the British edition of Following the
     Equator). Not only did some indecorous and
     irreverent material slip by, but MT added
     still more, as in his account of the phallic
     worship in Benares (a city he referred to
     as "Lingamburg"). The editorial suggestions
     by Olivia Clemens are listed and classified.
     Abstract in AES, XI (1968), 1789; reprinted
     in Twainian, XXVIII (January-February,
     1969). Also abstracted in ALA, I (June,
     1968), 191-92.

B68 ____. [Review: Justin Kaplan: Mr. Clemens and Mark Twain (1966) and James M. Cox, Mark Twain: The Fate of Humor (1966).] New England Quarterly, XL (September), 441-45.

Agreeing that Cox may be right in calling Kaplan's book "the decisive work on Mark Twain in our time," Krause praises it as "eminently readable," though exaggerated in some of its interpretations. The portrait of MT is painful, emphasizing his obsession with money, his vanity, his "incurably selfish motives" and "unfounded paranoia." Cox has written "a book that is at once wholly basic and wholly new," with the thesis that Clemens discovered his artistic imagination when he discovered Mark Twain, was effective when he followed the strategies of humor, but failed when he tried to be serious; however, some passages which have been interpreted in that light are actually instances where MT appropriated the conventions he parodied--but many readers will find such an interpretation difficult to accept.

B69 KRUSE, HORST H. "Annie and Huck: A Note on The Adventures of Huckleberry Finn," American Literature, XXXIX (May), 207-14.

MT's "A Complaint About Correspondents" (written in late 1865 or early 1866) contains what purports to be a letter from his niece Annie. "It is...safe to conclude that in writing Annie's letter Mark Twain realized what could be done with the combination of the first-person narrator and the child perspective," a forerunner of Huck, who is "perfectly suited for his purposes both as a humorist and as a social and moral critic." Abstract in AES, X (1967), 2261; reprinted in Twainian, XXVI (January-February, 1968). Also abstracted in ALA, I (December, 1967), 45-46.

B70 LEE, CHARLOTTE I. [Review: Hamlin Hill, ed., Mark Twain's Letters to His Publishers, 1867-1894; Franklin S. Rogers, ed., Mark Twain's Satires and Burlesques; John S. Tuckey, ed., Mark Twain's "Which Was the Dream?"] Quarterly Journal of Speech, LII (December), 390-91.

Chiefly descriptive, praising the scholarship but noting that there is little here of great interest to members of the speech profession.

B71 "Letters from Susan Crane, Skrine, Webb, Goodman," Twainian, XXVI (September-October), 1-4.

For the most part this is correspondence concerning the transmission of material to Paine for his biography of MT, and contains very little biographical information of interest. The letter from Elizabeth Webb, abstracted in AES, XIII (1969-1970), 1336, mentions her possession of various photographs and correspondence of her father, C. H. Webb, publisher of The Celebrated Jumping Frog of Calaveras County; among the material is a play based on this MT story, and an incomplete article about MT in San Francisco by her father. Abstracts of the remaining material in AES, XIII (1969-1970), 1352, 1353, 1354, and reprinted in Twainian, XXX (January-February, 1971).

B72 LANGDON, CHARLES J. "Letters to Paine from Charles J. Langdon," Twainian, XXVI (July-August), 1-2.

On the day his sister Olivia married MT, Charles Langdon was in Calcutta on his world tour. Abstract in AES, XII (1969), 684.

B73 *LONG, ELEANOR. "Superstitious Belief in Huckleberry Finn," Northern California Folklore Society, II (July), 51-55.

[Source: Leary (1970), p. 68.]

B74 MacALISTER, J. Y. W. "Letters from J. Y. W. MacAlister to Paine," Twainian, XXVI (May-June), 4.

MacAlister says he has "something like 200 letters, of all kinds,--many of them of too intimate and personal a nature to print," but others which he may copy and send; also tells of MT receiving two letters, addressed "Mark Twain--God knows where" and "Mark Twain--devil knows where." Abstract in AES, XII (1969), 683.

B75 MANIERRE, WILLIAM R. "Parallel Scenes in Tom Sawyer and Huck Finn," CEA Critic, XXX (November), 1, 4, 6-7.

Carries further Walter Blair's discussion in Mark Twain & Huck Finn (Chapter V), to show that TS contains "rehearsals" of three scenes in HF dealing with Huck's inner debate (documented from the Riverside Edition of HF and the Signet Classic ed. of TS). Abstract in ALA, I (June, 1968), 192.

B76 MARTIN, JAY. "Adding up the Double," Nation, CCV (July 3), 24-26.

A review of Justin Kaplan, Mr. Clemens and Mark Twain (1966). Generally favorable: although the book "should be supplemented by those of Walter Blair, Henry Nash Smith, and James Cox, still it provides a rich understanding of Twain's life that none of these can give."

B77 ____. "Mark Twain: The Dream of Drift and the Dream of Delight," in his Harvests of Change: American Literature 1865-1914. Englewood Cliffs, N.J.: Prentice-Hall, Inc., pp. 165-201.

Presents an extensive discussion of MT's gauging of the popular taste, his treatment of foreign travel, and his use of history. "Emphasizing the true importance of creation above memory" in the apparent formlessness of his Autobiography, "Twain reasserted his potency as an artist to the last. His revelation of creativity preserved the man--perhaps from the madness that in the late 1890s Twain hovered near.... he made his drift a dream of delight."

B78 MENCKEN, H[ENRY] L[OUIS]. A Mencken Chresto-
     mathy. Edited and Annotated by the Author.
     New York: Alfred A. Knopf.
         On pp. 485-89, reprints the texts of Menck-
     en's "Credo" (1913.B12) and "The Man Within"
     (1919.B17) from Smart Set, for which Mencken
     was the book reviewer.

B79 MIZENER, ARTHUR. "Mark Twain: Huckleberry
     Finn," in his Twelve Great American Novels
     (New York: The New American Library),
     pp. 37-48.
         Mizener's preface describes his book as
     being intended "for the reader who...does
     not feel entirely at home with novels when
     he tries to read them seriously" (p. x).
     The discussion of HF is sensible but breaks
     no new ground.

B80 *NASU, YORIMASA. "Mark Twain's 'Horseshoe
     Pattern' and Huckleberry Finn," Jimbungaku,
     XLIII (January), 70-84.
         [Source: Leary, 1970), p. 71.]

B81 NEIDER, CHARLES. "Major Author in a Minor
     Key," Saturday Review of Literature, L
     (March 25), 34-35.
         A review-article, chiefly descriptive
     (but deriding excessive scholarly serious-
     ness in the editors) of John S. Tuckey,
     ed., Mark Twain's "Which Was the Dream?"
     and Other Symbolic Writings of the Later
     Years; Hamlin Hill, ed., Mark Twain's Let-
     ters to His Publishers, 1867-1894; and
     Franklin R. Rogers, ed., Mark Twain's Sat-
     ires and Burlesques.

B82 OLIVER, A. W. "Letter from Judge A. W.
     ('Gus') Oliver," Twainian, XXVI (January-
     February), 4.
         Letter to Albert Bigelow Paine, April 24,
     1910, recalling incidents in RI by a friend
     MT recorded there as "Oliphant." Abstract
     in AES, XII (1969), 675; reprinted in
     Twainian, XXIX (January-February, 1970).

B83 PICKERING, JAMES H. [Review: Hamlin Hill,
     ed., Mark Twain's Letters to His Publish-
     ers.] New York History, XLVIII (October),
     399-400.
         An "impeccable job of editing and anno-
     tating," reveals MT's growing involvement
     in the publishing business and the impos-
     sible demands he made on his publishers.

B84 POCHMANN, HENRY A. [Review: Hamlin Hill,
     ed., Mark Twain's Letters to His Publish-
     ers; Franklin R. Rogers, ed., Mark Twain's
     Satires and Burlesques; John S. Tuckey,
     ed., Mark Twain's "Which Was the Dream?"]
     American Literature, XXXIX (November),
     397-400.
         Hill's edition of the letters "provides
     altogether engaging reading" and gives
     evidence for choosing between MT's portrait
     of himself as victim and the less flatter-
     ing one drawn by S. C. Webster. "There

is as yet no agreement with Mr. Rogers that
burlesque was the chief vehicle by which
Mark Twain learned the art of authorship."
Pochmann notes the bitterness and sense of
personal failure in MT's late writings edited by Tuckey, but they "may be regarded as
steps in the process of literary self-heal-
ing by which he achieved a dramatic recovery
of his literary powers near the end." There
is also evidence of an interest on MT's part
in "the implications of depth psychology,
especially with respect to the role and function of the unconscious for the creative
literary artist."

B85 PRITCHETT, V. S. "Twainship and Twinship,"
     New Statesman, LXXIII (June 23), 876. A
     review-article, describing Justin Kaplan,
     Mr. Clemens and Mark Twain (1966); A. Grove
     Day, Mark Twain's Letters from Hawaii (1966);
     John S. Tuckey, ed., Mark Twain's "Which Was
     the Dream?"; Hamlin Hill, ed., Mark Twain's
     Letters to His Publishers; and Franklin R.
     Rogers, ed., Mark Twain's Satires and Bur-
     lesques.
         The more valuable part is a probing dis-
     cussion of MT and his works, emphasizing his
     Ego, foundation in myth, and idealist's jeer-
     ing at both raw experience and bland hypo-
     crisy. Abstract in AES, XI (1968), 3291.

B86 REGAN, ROBERT. "Mark Twain's 'Unfinished
     Properties,'" Virginia Quarterly Review,"
     XLIII (Summer), 494-99.
         A review-article, praising the editing of
     the previously unpublished, fragmented ma-
     terial in Hamlin Hill, ed., Mark Twain's
     Letters to His Publishers, 1867-1894;
     Franklin R. Rogers, ed., Mark Twain's Sat-
     ires and Burlesques; John S. Tuckey, ed.,
     Mark Twain's "Which Was the Dream?" and Oth-
     er Symbolic Writings of the Later Period.

B87 _____. [Review: James M. Cox, Mark Twain:
     The Fate of Humor (1966).] South Atlantic
     Quarterly, LXVI (Summer), 473-74.
         "On the identity of 'Mark Twain' and on
     other matters of primarily biographical in-
     terpretation, few scholars have been so il-
     luminating.... Cox demonstrates, for ex-
     ample, that Olivia Clemens served not only
     as censor but also as muse for her husband
     and that she contributed positively in both
     capacities to his artistic success." Cox
     is more successful in discussing MT's pure-
     ly humorous works than those which, like
     HF and CY, "combine humorous and satiric
     modes."

B88 REINITZ, NEALE. "'Mark Twain Tonight,'"
     Colarado Quarterly, XVI (Summer), 71-80.
         As a Fulbright lecturer in Jyväskylä,
     Finland, Reinitz made the arrangements for
     publicity and for the properties and stage-
     lighting for a performance of Hal Holbrook's
     "Mark Twain Tonight" program in Jyväskylä.
     After lecturing to a small audience at

(REINITZ, NEALE)
Turku, Holbrook was concerned about the inadequate lighting and difficulties with the
Finnish workmen, but here the audience was
far larger than expected. Holbrook found
them unresponsive and later said the preparation had been inadequate; Reinitz says in
rebuttal that "The applause was not tumultu-
ous, but it was warm enough. The show was
a success." A Finnish senior colleague who
had earlier argued against bringing Holbrook
to the small, provincial city later conceded, "I was entirely wrong. It was a
great day for Finnish-American relations."
Abstract in AES, XVI (1972-1973), 2937.

B89   REXROTH, KENNETH. "Classics Revisited--
XLVI: Huckleberry Finn," Saturday Review,
L (May 13), 14-15.
An anti-Odyssey: "It would have been
quite impossible for Mark Twain not to have
had Homer constantly in mind, as he must
also have had Robinson Crusoe, the travels
of Peter and Paul, Pilgrim's Progress, and
dozens of others, not the least Marco Polo.
He carefully contradicts them all." The
raft carries Huck and Jim "through a universe of moral chaos," but in the controversial ending "the social lie wins again
against the brotherhood of man." Abstract
in AES, X (1967), 3141; reprinted in Twainian, XXVII (January-February, 1968).

B90   ROBINSON, TRACY. "Letter from Tracy Robinson," Twainian, XXVI (January-February), 4;
(March-April), 4.
To Paine, dated February 10, 1912; remembers meeting MT in Aspinwall, Panama in
1869, and the pleasure with which he read
MT's books. Abstract in AES, XII (1969),
676, 679; reprinted in Twainian, XXIX
(January-February, 1970).

B91   ROTH, MARTIN. [Review: Bernard Poli, Mark
Twain: Écrivain de l'Ouest (1965).]
Modern Philology, LXV (November), 171-72.
An exhaustive study which, unfortunately,
distorts the picture of MT. There are
valuable synthetic chapters throughout the
book for the benefit of French readers.
"The first chapter is a cogent discussion
of the American West. One of the final
chapters admirably sorts out the various
metaphors used by Twain to define his art."

B92   RUBIN, LOUIS D., JR. "Mark Twain Tonight,"
in his The Teller in the Tale (Seattle,
London: University of Washington Press),
pp. 52-82; also, in "Concerning Cide Hamete
Benengeli and Others," pp. 17-21 on HF.
The book is concerned with the authorial
presence in the novel. Rubin notes different uses of MT's presence when Huck decides
to risk his soul for Jim and later on, at
Phelps Farm (pp. 17-21), and takes up the
matter at greater length in "Mark Twain
Tonight" (which is not a review of Hal Holbrook's stage impersonation of MT).

B93   _____. "Tom Sawyer and the Use of Novels,"
in his The Curious Death of the Novel: Essays in American Literature (Baton Rouge:
Louisiana State University Press), pp. 88-99.
"It took a Mark Twain to show us how the
meaning of success, and of loss, lies at
the heart of American experience.... Documentation can tell us what, but fiction
tells us why."

B94   RULAND, RICHARD. The Rediscovery of American
Literature: Premises of Critical Taste,
1900-1940. Cambridge, Massachusetts: Harvard University Press, pp. 129-31 and passim.
Passing references to the consideration
given MT by such critics as Brooks, Sherman,
Matthiessen, and others. There is a useful
summary of Mencken's views of MT (pp. 129-
31): MT was a Philistine, insensitive to
art and afraid of public opinion, but one
of "the five first-rate artists that America has produced," in the company of Emerson, Hawthorne, Poe, and Whitman.

B95   RULON, CURT M. "Geographical Limitation of
the Dialect Areas in The Adventures of Huckleberry Finn," Mark Twain Journal, XIV
(Winter), 9-12.
Internal evidence suggests that "the
Phelps farm is probably located well south
of Memphis rather than above Memphis as
Stowell would have it but still in southern
Arkansas rather than in northern Louisiana
as Marx maintains." "What is important for
the linguistic geographer is that the general location is in the proximity of the
Mississippi River below Cairo, Illinois,
which point is the heel of an overturned
boot configuration delimiting known contemporary dialect areas: Midland and Southern,
respectively." Abstract in ALA, I (June,
1968), 192-93.

B96   SALOMON, ROGER B. "Mark Twain and Victorian
Nostalgia," in Marston LaFrance, ed., Patterns of Commitment in American Literature.
Published in Association with Carleton
University by University of Toronto Press.
Sees in MT a "double vision" which "manifests itself in the differing points of view
of the invader and the worlds he invades,"
and "involves an ambivalent relation between
the author and even his most sympathetic
characters" (p. 74).

B97   SIDNELL, M. J. "Huck Finn and Jim: Their
Abortive Freedom Ride," Cambridge Quarterly,
II (Summer), 203-11.
MT was more perceptive than his critics
who view the ending of HF as flawed: "Life
on the raft has offered a beautiful vision
of what might be the relationship of negro
and white, but the vision is not, and cannot be, a representation of America as it
really is." Huck "must return to the triv-
ially vicious world of Tom Sawyer's America," at the end "utterly changed not in
itself but in our perception of it."

1967 - Shorter Writings

(SIDNELL, M. J.)
Abstract in AES, XV (1971-1972), 1496; reprinted in Twainian, XXXII (January-February, 1973). Also abstracted in ALA, I (December, 1967), 46-47.

B98 SIMMS, HENRY H. [Review: John Y. Simon, "General Grant" by Matthew Arnold, with A Rejoinder by Mark Twain (1966).] Ohio History, LXXV, 178-79.
Descriptive and mildly favorable.

B99 SKLAR, ROBERT. F. Scott Fitzgerald: The Last Laocoön. New York: Oxford University Press.
Passim on Fitzgerald's interest in MT and familiarity with his works (indexed).

B100 SMITH, H. ALLEN. "Humorous Critic of the Human Race," Saturday Review of Literature, L (February 11), 37.
A descriptive, appreciative review of Charles Neider's Mark Twain, complaining only of the price.

B101 SMITH, THOMAS J. "Mark Twain's Last Years at Redding," Yankee, XXXI (June), 68-73, 128-39.
A popular account providing no new information or insights.

B102 STANCHFIELD, CLARA. "Letters from Clara Stanchfield," Twainian, XXVI (May-June), 1-3.
Two letters to Paine from "the 'Clara Spaulding', close friend of Olivia, after whom Clara Clemens was named," about traveling in Europe twice with MT and Olivia (1873 and a second time for which the year is not given). Unfortunately, Clara Stanchfield destroyed her diaries of the tours, but she remembers being present at meetings of MT with Robert Browning, Turgenev, Sir Charles Dilke, Henry Stanley, Lord Houghton, Sir John Millais, "the artists Abbey and Frank Millet, whose wedding we afterwards attended in Paris," Joaquin Miller, Charles Kingsley ("I remember a delightful luncheon he gave for Mr. Clemens"), and "Lord Dunraven who brought Mr. Hume, the medium with him for an evening with Mr. Clemens." There is also a brief note from John Brown (the son of the author of Rab and His Friends) testifying to MT's "honest manliness" and "warm heartedness." Abstract in AES, XII (1969), 681; reprinted in Twainian, XXIX (January-February, 1970).

B103 STONE, ALBERT E., JR. "Later, Lesser Twain," New York Times Book Review, (July 30), p. 8.
A review of Hamlin Hill, ed., Mark Twain's Letters to His Publishers, 1867-1894; Franklin R. Rogers, ed., Mark Twain's Satires and Burlesques; and John S. Tuckey, ed., Mark Twain's "Which Was the Dream?"

And Other Symbolic Writings of the Later Years ("the most interesting of these three volumes, for it reveals the most about the myth of Mark Twain").

B104 ____. [Review: James M. Cox, Mark Twain: The Fate of Humor (1966).] Nineteenth-Century Fiction, XXII (December), 304-307.
"A model of literary criticism: sensitive, judicious, beautifully written. Wiser than anyone who has yet tackled this thorny subject, Cox...joins that small group of writers--Paine, Brooks, DeVoto, Smith, Andrews, Blair, Kaplan--who have contributed most to our understanding of Mark Twain."

B105 ____. [Review: Robert Regan, Unpromising Heroes (1966).] Nineteenth-Century Fiction, XXII (December), 304-307.
"Regan's study, at times illuminating and original, remains at bottom partial because its thesis does not sufficiently acknowledge the sovereignty of character (not plot) and style (not belief) in the work of Mark Twain." The characters are fit "too exclusively into the pattern of an archetypal plot."

B106 STRONG, LEAH A. "Mark Twain and Frontier Folklore," Pacific Northwest Quarterly, LVIII (July), 113-18.
MT incorporated themes from the folklore of the past (as in the chapter from HF transferred to LOM, incorporating "the tall tale, the exaggeration, the gigantic lie, the anticlimactic ending...the contest, the defeat of the bully..."), and he used superstition as a device in HF.

B107 STUBBLEFIELD, CHARLES. "Mark Twain's Unpublished Works," Denver Quarterly, II (Autumn), 113-17.
A review of Franklin R. Rogers, ed., Mark Twain's Satires and Burlesques; Hamlin Hill, ed., Mark Twain's Letters to His Publishers; John S. Tuckey, ed., Mark Twain's "Which Was the Dream?" Praises the editing, but adds: "These volumes are not disappointing; it is just that they contain nothing very interesting....they contain little that is not already known."

B108 STURDEVANT, JAMES R. "Mark Twain's Unpublished Letter to Tom Taylor--an Enigma," Mark Twain Journal, XIV (Winter), 8-9.
An MT letter acquired by Sturdevant (January 5, 1874, here printed for the first time) refers to Taylor as "the author of the only play I ever appeared in on any stage." Taylor (1817-1880) became editor of Punch shortly after MT ended his 1874 trip to England, and remained in that post until 1880; he also wrote almost one hundred plays, among them Our American Cousin, the play Abraham Lincoln was watching when he was assassinated. Abstract in ALA, I (June, 1968), 193-94.

B109 SYKES, ROBERT H. "A Source for Mark Twain's Feud," West Virginia History, XXVIII (April), 191-98.
The Shepherdson-Grangerford feud in HF is probably not based on a Darnell-Watson feud (described in LOM but not mentioned elsewhere); however, there are "ten significant points of similarity" to the actual feud of the Hatfields and McCoys. Abstract in AES, X (1967), 3614; reprinted in Twainian, XXVIII (March-April, 1969).

B110 TANNER, TONY. "Two Men at War in a Great Writer," Sunday Times (London), February 5, p. 48.
A review of Justin Kaplan, Mr. Clemens and Mark Twain (1966). "It is an excellent biography. The clarity and intelligence it brings to bear on this most fascinating American writer make it immediately indispensible, even though it avails itself of the crucial pioneer work of such people as Albert Bigelow Paine, Bernard DeVoto, Henry Nash Smith, and others. (Kaplan is very thin on acknowledging his indebtedness to secondary sources)."

B111 THAYER, EMMA B., and SEVERANCE, S. L. "Letters from Emma B. Thayer and S. L. Severance," Twainian, XXVI (March-April), 2-3.
Three letters from companions on the Quaker City tour which MT recorded in IA. Emma B. Thayer's letter (June 22, 1907) remembers the influence of Mary Mason Fairbanks on MT's newspaper letters written on the trip, his taking the side of young Charles Langdon when the boy was teased by other passengers, and MT's asking her (then only 17) to sit up with him under the stars: "He would call my attention to the beauty of Curtis' language in The Howaji in Syria, reading passages aloud." S. B. Severance comments on MT's "intense likes and dislikes" in his letter of November 23, 1911, and his letter of March 13, 1912 passes on a number of details: "the talk on shipboard ran to the effect that Dan Leary was going to try to sell the ship to the Khedive of Egypt and we all wished that he could do so," because the food was becoming uninteresting on board; a letter from a friend named Fairbanks says his mother [presumably Mary Mason Fairbanks--T.A.T.] received a letter from MT before publication of Innocents Abroad, listing possible titles, and Fairbanks says the book was written, not in Washington, but in Elmira and Hartford [this is only partially correct: by the time MT was visiting in Elmira the book had reached the proofreading stage--T.A.T.]. Severance also notes an issue of the Portland Sunday Oregonian of July 3, 1910 containing "some very good pictures." Abstract in AES, XII (1969); reprinted in Twainian, XIX (January-February, 1970).

B112 THURMOND, MARGARET E. [Review: Franklin R. Rogers, ed., Mark Twain's Satires and Burlesques.] Journal of the West, VI (April), 341-42.
Roger's "Introduction, Editor's Notes, and annotations may well be the most valuable parts of the entire book," and he makes an important point in showing the hard work and trial and error in MT's creative process.

B113 _____. [Review: John S. Tuckey, ed., Mark Twain's "Which Was the Dream?" and Other Symbolic Writings of the Later Years.] Journal of the West, VI (April), 342-43.
"Professor Tuckey has met this challenge gracefully and well," and the book will be of interest both to the specialist and to the general reader.

B114 _____. [Review: Hamlin Hill, ed., Mark Twain's Letters to His Publishers.] Journal of the West, VI (April), 343-44.
"Hamlin Hill, who...is well-versed in Twainiana, does a truly James Bondsmanlike piece of detective work with his precise and painstaking footnoting following immediately upon the printing of each letter." The letters show MT's financial motivation, and the general reader will enjoy his explosions at publishers.

B115 VOLLMER, JOHN P. "Letter from John P. Vollmer," Twainian, XXVI (March-April), 3-4.
The letter, to Albert Bigelow Paine (December 26, 1911), tells of MT playing "Seven Up" with a card-shark on shipboard in 1868 on the way to San Francisco; earlier on the same trip he saw MT as one of a party who had chosen to make part of the trip across the Isthmus carried by porters--but the breech-clout of MT's porter had slipped, making a spectacular picture: "There he was perched in a chair on the back of his human ship of the Isthmus, his legs dangling in unison with each step of his carrier. As his position was such that he could look only backwards, he was unaware of the scene in front." Brief abstract in AES, XII (1969), 678; reprinted in Twainian, XXIX (January-February, 1970).

B116 WELLAND, DENNIS. "A Note on Some Early Reviews of Tom Sawyer," Journal of American Studies, I (April), 99-103.
Moncure Daniel Conway took the manuscript of TS to England, negotiated its publication, and apparently wrote the lengthy favorable unsigned review in the Examiner (here summarized, together with a patronizing review in the Athenaeum). Welland shows points of similarity between the Examiner review and one Conway wrote for the Cincinatti Commercial when TS appeared in America six months later; other newspapers drew on this for their own reviews of TS. Abstract in AES, XI (1968), 2216; reprinted in Twainian, XXVIII (January-February, 1969).

1967 - Shorter Writings

B117   WHITE, WILLIAM. "Roger Butterfield and the
        Earliest Mark Twain," Mark Twain Journal,
        XIII (Summer), 20.
            "In an attractive folio, privately print-
        ed for the 18th annual meeting of the Anti-
        quarian Booksellers' Association of America,
        Roger Butterfield tells the story of 'Sam
        Clemens and the American Courier,'" in
        which an MT sketch appeared; however, the
        issue bears two dates, May 1 and May 8,
        1852, so priority for MT's first publication
        remains with "The Dandy Frightening the
        Squatter" in The Carpet-Bag.

B118   WIGGINS, ROBERT A. [Review: Sydney J.
        Krause, Mark Twain as Critic.] New England
        Quarterly, XL (December), 609-11.
            "Probably the most original and creative
        contribution to Twain scholarship in the
        past decade.... This is a good book. It
        might have been a better book." Still
        needed is a treatment of MT as self-critic,
        although Krause has done admirably in col-
        lecting MT's critical statements from vari-
        ous sources. Wiggins agrees that "there is
        more critical substance in him than has
        generally been recognized," but insists
        that "Mark Twain was not a literary critic
        in the usual meaning of the term."

B119   WYATT, BRYANT N. "Huckleberry Finn and the
        Art of Ernest Hemingway," Mark Twain Jour-
        nal, XIII (Summer), 1-8.
            "Aside from the purely stylistic affini-
        ties between Finn and the writings of Hem-
        ingway, there are certain affinities of
        subject-matter," among them the opposition
        of reality and illusion, the loss of illu-
        sion, the use of superstition, the symbolic
        use of rivers, and self-realization through
        experience. Abstract in AES, XII (1969),
        1237.

B120   *YU, BEONGCHEON. "The Ending of the Adven-
        tures of Huckleberry Finn," Phoenix (Seoul),
        II (Spring), 23-30.
            [Source: Leary (1970), p. 77.]

B121   _____. "The Immortal Twins: An Aspect of
        Mark Twain," The English Language and Lit-
        erature (The English Literary Society of
        Korea), XXIII (Summer), 48-77.
            [Source: Photocopy in Mark Twain Pa-
        pers.] "There is singular persistence in
        Mark Twain's interest in identical twins,
        changelings, impostors, and claimants--
        something we cannot dismiss as symptoms of
        his weakness for burlesque and melodrama.
        These motifs and devices are there where
        apparently uncalled for, and are often cen-
        tral in many of his works." Tracing MT's
        treatment of doubles through three succes-
        sive periods shows "his central concern
        progressing from the moral-psychological
        to the metaphysical to the psychical direc-
        tion, and, likewise, his art developing
        from the realistic to the allegorical to

the symbolic realm. On the whole, his is a
drama unfolding an artist's quest for identity in terms of duality--beyond appearance
and reality--at each of three levels with
deepening implications."

1968 A BOOKS

A1   GANZEL, DEWEY. Mark Twain Abroad: The Cruise
        of the "Quaker City." Chicago and London:
        The University of Chicago Press.
            A detailed study of the 1867 tour of Eu-
        rope and the Holy Land described by MT in IA.
        Documentation includes the log of Captain
        Duncan of the Quaker City (in the Patten
        Free Library, Bath, Maine) and published ac-
        counts of the trip by Mary Mason Fairbanks
        (1892), Mrs. Stephen Griswold (1871), and
        Emily Severance (1938), as well as The Long
        Island Farmer's Poems (n.d.) by Bloodgood
        Cutter (the "Poet Lariat" of the party), and
        a number of newspaper letters, not listed in
        the present bibliography, by other passen-
        gers.

A2   LORCH, FRED W. The Trouble Begins at Eight:
        Mark Twain's Lecture Tours. Ames: Iowa
        State Universtty Press.
            Traces MT's lifetime career as a lecturer,
        with a discussion of his manners and tech-
        niques, audiences and reception, and prof-
        its; includes "Texts of Tour Lectures," from
        manuscript and newspaper sources; some are
        composites from several sources.

A3   RABAN, JONATHAN. Mark Twain: "Huckleberry
        Finn," London: Edward Arnold. Studies in
        English Literature No. 36.
            One of a series of studies intended for
        "the advanced sixth-former and the universi-
        ty student" (p. 5). The study concludes:
        "Huckleberry Finn is a masterpiece of equi-
        vocation: its humour suddenly switches into
        tragic realism; its two languages, vernacu-
        lar and rhetoric, are perpetually opposed;
        its situations are largely unresolved; its
        characters, so important for brief periods,
        fade into the passing blur of the crowd.
        It tells two truths, and they will not be
        reconciled" (pp. 59-60).

A4   ROSA-COLT, PAOLA. L"Angoscia di Mark Twain
        [The Anguish of Mark Twain]. Milan: M.
        Ursia & Co.
            Sections titled "La Crisi Ideologica"
        ("The Ideological Crisis," emphasizing CY);
        "Fra Realismo E Simbolismo" ("Between Real-
        ism and Symbolism"); "Verso Il Racconto
        Filosofico" ("Toward Philosophical Narra-
        tion"); "La Fase Finale" ("The Final Phase,"
        on MS, CS, Captain Stormfield's Visit to
        Heaven, etc.); "Conclusione: Opera Aperta"
        ("Conclusion: Unfinished Work"). [In Ital-
        ian.]

A5 SIMPSON, CLAUDE M., ed. Twentieth Century Interpretations of "Adventures of Huckleberry Finn": A Collection of Critical Essays. Englewood Cliffs, N.J.: Prentice-Hall, Inc.

Includes discussions of HF by major authors and critics; contains some articles not readily obtained elsewhere. All of this material is listed in the present bibliography and cross-referenced to Simpson's reprinting.

A6 TUCKEY, JOHN S. Mark Twain's "The Mysterious Stranger" and the Critics. Belmont, California: Wadsworth Publishing Company.

The text of MS, followed by a selection of critical discussions reprinted from books and scholarly journals. These reprintings are not cross-referenced in the present bibliography because their original printings are generally accessible, although Professor Tuckey has done the student a service in bringing them together here. Also included are Tuckey's "The Mysterious Stranger: Mark Twain's Texts and the Paine-Duneka Edition," here published for the first time (pp. 85-89) and "Mark Twain and Little Satan: The Writing of The Mysterious Stranger" (pp. 126-54), an extensive excerpt from his Mark Twain and Little Satan (1963). "It is now clear that Albert Bigelow Paine and Frederick A. Duneka, who edited the story as it was published six years after Mark Twain's death, actually wrote into the tale a character--the astrologer –who did not appear at all in the manuscript as Mark Twain had written it; they also deleted thousands of Mark Twain's own words.... For the text of The Mysterious Stranger I have followed the 1916 edition of Paine and Duneka. I have, however, corrected an obvious misprint.... I have also annotated the text to give some indication of the ways in which the 1916 edition differs from the manuscript on which it is based" (Preface, p. v).

A7 WILSON, EDMUND. The Fruits of the MLA. New York: A New York Review Book.

A reprinting of material which previously appeared in the New York Review of Books; Part II, pp. 21-35 is the part on MT (1968. B116).

A8 WOOD, JAMES PLAYSTED. Spunkwater, Spunkwater! A Life of Mark Twain. Illustrated with Photographs. New York: Pantheon Books.

A biography for teenage readers; accurate and interesting.

1968 B SHORTER WRITINGS

B1 American Literature Abstracts, I (June); II (December).

Contains a number of abstracts of articles on MT; many are by the authors of the articles abstracted, and all are longer than abstracts in the present bibliography; however, in many cases the journal articles are more readily available than the abstracts, and coverage for the year's scholarship is not complete.

B2 ANON. "Grumblings," Times Literary Supplement, March 28, p. 311.

A review of Sydney J. Krause, Mark Twain as Critic (1967), chiefly descriptive. MT "really cannot be considered seriously as a critic. Mr. Krause is a good scholar and a discriminating one and cannot be held responsible for the sorry stuff [MT] turned out under this title."

B3 ANON. "Mark Twain Items from 'Abstracts of English Studies' in 1967," Twainian, XXVII (January-February), 1-4.

Most of the abstracts related to MT from AES, X (1967), plus one entry from AES, IX (1966), 3352; Items 3295, 3301, and 3614 from AES, X appear in Twainian, XXVIII (March-April, 1969). Abstract in AES, XIII (1969-1970), 1360; reprinted in Twainian, XXX (January-February, 1971).

B4 BAENDER, PAUL. "Review Article: Two Books on Mark Twain," Philological Quarterly, XLVII (January), 117-35. On Justin Kaplan, Mr. Clemens and Mark Twain and James M. Cox, Mark Twain: The Fate of Humor (both 1966).

Kaplan has done extensive research, has avoided "the sentimental nostalgia that has stultified so many of the accounts since Paine," and successfully "conveys Clemens's sense that the past, present and future were all unsure," but he rides too hard his thesis that explains MT as a parvenu, confused and unstable. Many of Kaplan's contentions are merely "slipshod, smarty, unimaginative," there are annoying inaccuracies of fact, and Kaplan frequently quotes "misleading extracts designed to prove what they do not prove when read in context." Cox seeks in MT a "depth and consistency of intention he did not have," through two main points: "that 'Mark Twain' served Samuel L. Clemens as a means of emotional economy and pleasure" and that the Freudian process may be reconstituted as an ideological struggle. Unfortunately, Cox has taken a rigid approach which leads to some serious misinterpretations of MT's work.

B5 BANTA, MARTHA. "Escape and Entry in Huckleberry Finn," Modern Fiction Studies, XIV (Spring), 79-91.

Huck's flight to the river and his failure to escape thereby from society must be explained, not by the reader's moral preconceptions, but by Huck's "loose-hung code that is beholden only to what provides the free, the easy, and the comfortable." Huck's experiences reflect MT's own discovery that there can be no escape from the

(BANTA, MARTHA)
consequences of heredity and environment: novelty may offer man a free choice of new routes, "or may simply show him driven by yet one more compulsive thrust into predetermined paths of action." Abstract in AES, XII (1969), 1263; reprinted in Twainian, XXIX (January-February, 1970). Abstracted by Martha Banta in ALA, II (December), 47.

B6   BEEBE, MAURICE, and JOHN FEASTER. "Criticism of Mark Twain: A Selected Checklist, "Modern Fiction Studies, XIV (Spring), 93-139.
"Part I consists of general studies of Twain's life and work. Part II lists discussions of his individual works in the following order--(A) editions of the works containing some kind of critical apparatus, Introductions, Afterwords, etc., (B) an index to the general studies listed in Part I, and (C) special studies not previously listed.... we have listed in Part II only the better known works, thus omitting many short topical pieces and his lesser works of non-fiction.... As usual, we have omitted foreign criticism, unpublished theses or dissertations, and routine discussions in encyclopedias, handbooks, and histories of literature." This is a valuable and responsible piece of work, of which one especially useful feature is the lists of page references showing where particular works by MT are treated in the longer studies of his thought and writing; these lists of page references have not been transferred to the present bibliography. The compilers have also found a number of articles in books, material not readily to be found through bibliographies which emphasize periodical articles and books devoted entirely to MT. Comparatively few errors in other bibliographies are here repeated. This checklist has been invaluable as a finding-list for the present bibliography, which incorporates the major part of its listings (but not the indexes to general studies). Listed in AES, XII (1969), 1264, and in Twainian, XXIX (January-February, 1970).

B7   BEIDLER, PETER G. "The Raft Episode in Huckleberry Finn," Modern Fiction Studies, XIV (Spring), 11-20.
MT dropped the episode, which had already appeared in LOM, on the advice of his publisher, Charles Webster; the intention was to make the book shorter, as a companion volume to TS. In the excision MT lost a passage important technically as the explanation of how Huck learned that the raft had passed Cairo, and psychologically for revealing his "generally morbid outlook on life, his repeated identification with dead and suffering human beings." Huck's lies add to the psychological portrait, since

"in many of them Huck casts himself in the role of a boy who is alone in the world and whose family is dead, sick, or in grave danger." Abstract in AES, XII (1969), 1256; reprinted in Twainian, XXIX (January-February, 1970). Abstracted by Beidler in ALA, II (December), 47-48. Article reprinted in Gerber (1971), pp. 101-12.

B8   BENARDETE, JANE JOHNSON. "Huckleberry Finn and the Nature of Fiction," Massachusetts Review, IX (Spring), 209-26.
"It is the thesis of this essay that Huckleberry Finn is a book about the nature of fiction (which epitomizes the deceptive power of language, for fiction is told or written and heard or read although it is known to be untrue): that each episode illustrates some quality of fiction; that the major theme of Huck's development is his increasing preference for fiction over fact; and that the novel itself is deliberately devised to exemplify fiction's power to distort life."

B9   BERCOVITCH, SACVAN. "Huckleberry Bumppo: A Comparison of Tom Sawyer and The Pioneers," Mark Twain Journal, XIV (Summer), 1-4.
Despite MT's ridicule of Cooper, the two books are similar in structure and such characters as the town patriarchs Judge Thatcher and Judge Temple, who stand at opposite poles from Huck and Natty; other parallels are evident as well, but there are also significant differences in the treatment of the frontier myth and the Indian. Abstract in ALA, II (December), 48.

B10   BERGMANN, FRANK. "Mark Twain and the Literary Misfortunes of John William DeForest," Jahrbuch für Amerikastudien (Heidelberg), XIII, 249-52.
Text of a letter to MT (July 31, 1874), in which DeForest asks, "Could we not publish a conjoint volume by subscription" of their short stories; the letter appears to be the first contact between the two, and nothing came of the proposal. Abstract in AES, XII (1969), 1551; reprinted in Twainian, XXIX (January-February, 1970).

B11   *BERKOVE, LAWRENCE I. "The 'Poor Players' of Huckleberry Finn," Papers of the Michigan Academy of Science, Arts and Letters, LIII, 291-310.
[Source: MHRA Annual Bibliography (1968), No. 7709.]

B12   BIER, JESSE. The Rise and Fall of American Humor. New York: Holt, Rinehart and Winston.
On MT, pp. 117-61, with a valuable discussion of HF and the reasons why it is "inaccessible" to foreigners.

B13   BLANCK, JACOB. "BAL Addendum 3479: Twain's 'A Dog's Tale,'" Papers of the Bibliographical Society of America, Vol. LXII (Fourth Quarter), 617.
    Reports 3,000 copies of the pamphlet were were printed by Harper and Brothers, New York for use by the National Anti-Vivesectionist Society, London: the order to print was issued January 26, 1904. Abstract in AES (1969), 2041; reprinted in Twainian, XXIX (January-February, 1970).

B14   BLUES, THOMAS. "The Strategy of Compromise in Mark Twain's 'Boy Books,'" Modern Fiction Studies, XIV (Spring), 21-31.
    "The heroes of Tom Sawyer, The Prince and the Pauper, and Huckleberry Finn harbor aggressive designs against the community," but each hero achieved his victory in a way that left the community's stability intact, through "a compromise solution that had the important value of permitting triumph without isolation." Abstract in AES, XII (1969), 1257; reprinted in Twainian, XXIX (January-February, 1970). Abstract in ALA, II (December), 48-49.

B15   BOLAND, SALLY. "The Seven Dialects in Huckleberry Finn," North Dakota Quarterly, XXXVI (Summer), 30-40.
    MT's use of dialect is not an end in itself, but a literary tool to delineate characters. The speech of the Negro and backwoodsman is represented phonetically, in a conspicuous "eye-dialect," but there is no such representation of the pronunciation of more educated persons. The dialects are used to represent regional and social differences in the characters, and there is also "a childhood lingo that cuts across all other distinctions." "The study was limited to the text of the novel...no conclusions were drawn as to the relation of the novel to linguistic realities."

B16   BROWN, CLARENCE A. [Review: Sydney J. Krause, Mark Twain as Critic (1967).] Thought, XLIII (Autumn), 445-46.
    "In spite of the magnitude of its achievement, this book is weakened somewhat by its failure to develop in sufficient detail Twain's theoretical statements concerning literature...the treatment of Twain's criticism would have been enhanced by a concluding chapter in which some formulation and evaluation of Twain's theory and criticism was attempted."

B17   BUDD, LOUIS J. "Mark Twain and the Quaker City," Southern Literary Journal, I (Autumn), 112-16.
    A review of Mark Twain Abroad: The Cruise of the "Quaker City," by Dewey Ganzel, who "has gone just about as far as possible in nailing down the facts...he wavers between scholarliness and gusto, between cross-examination and joining the laughter....whenever possible, Ganzel pushes on to Twain's development as an artist."

B18   _____. [Review: Sydney J. Krause, Mark Twain as Critic (1967).] South Atlantic Quarterly, LXVII (Winter), 184-85.
    Worth the money but perhaps not worth the time, this book "sometimes deals with minor or worn items" and most readers should "let the specialists isolate and subsume the many useful insights of this book."

B19   CARSTENSEN, BRODER. "The Adventures of Huckleberry Finn: Die Problematik des Schlusses," in Franz H. Link, ed., Amerika, Vision und Wirklichkeit: Beiträge deutscher Forschung zur amerikanischen Literaturgeschichte. Frankfurt am Main, Bonn: Athenäum Verlag, pp. 199-210. First appeared in Neueren Sprachen (1961.B15).
    Finds the last fifth of HF inappropriate to the rest of the book. Concludes: "Huckleberry Finn is no Ulysses, Faust, Don Quixote, Don Juan and no Hamlet, and Huckleberry Finn does not belong in the library of great books of world literature." [In German.]

B20   CASEY, DANIEL J. "Huckleberry in Finland: A Comparison of Twain and Kivi," Moderna Språk, LXII (December), 385-94.
    MT's universal appeal is attested by the ease with which Casey has been able to introduce HF to students in the United States, Italy, and Finland; moreover, HF is much like the book portraying the Finnish national character, Kivi's Seven Brothers, in that both books concern the independence, self-reliance, and compassion of outcast characters. Abstract in AES, XIV (1970-1971), 583; reprinted in Twainian, XXXI (January-February, 1972). See 1967.B22.

B21   CLERC, CHARLES. "Sunrise on the River: The 'Whole World' of Huckleberry Finn," Modern Fiction Studies, XIV (Spring), 67-78.
    A rhetorical analysis of a 400-word paragraph at the beginning of Chapter XIX. Its strength lies not in mere accurate imitation of an uneducated boy's speech, but in a sophisticated art: "Any suggestion of sloppiness in the passage may be dispelled...by a consideration of the wide variety of rhetorical forms and grammatical techniques used to achieve vividness and vivacity." Abstract in AES, XII (1969), 1262; reprinted in Twainian, XXIX (January-February, 1970). Abstract by Clerc in ALA, II (December), 49.

B22   COARD, ROBERT L. "The Dictionary and Mark Twain," Word Study (G. & C. Merriam Co.), XLIII (February), 1-4.
    "On the basis of the numerous and frequently specific references to dictionaries in his works, one must conclude that Mark Twain, like so many other authors, was something of a dictionary buff."

B23 COX, JAMES M. "The Approved Mark Twain: The Beginning of the End," Southern Review, n.s. IV (April), 542-50.

A review-article on the first three volumes of the Mark Twain Papers: Rogers's Mark Twain's Satires and Burlesques, Hill's Mark Twain's Letters to His Publishers, 1867-1894, and Tuckey's Mark Twain's "Which Was the Dream?" and Other Symbolic Writings of the Later Years. Though ably edited, the newly published writings "reveal how little of value remains among the unpublished papers." There is some question of whether the editors should "continue publishing the letters by category rather than chronology," since the effect is misleading.

B24 CUMMINGS, SHERWOOD. [Review: Sydney J. Krause, Mark Twain as Critic (1967).] Western Humanities Review, XXII (Summer), 272-73.

Krause divides MT's critical approach into three periods, in which he successively posed as "muggins," as "grumbler," and, finally, spoke without a mask. The analysis of examples of MT's criticism generally leads to "an informative study which produces a steady sparkling of illuminations," but some topics are so limited that the method becomes tedious. The chapters on Macaulay, Howells, Howe, and Zola are "pithier and more convincing" than the chapter on Harte, and Macaulay's influence on Twain's theory of realism is "important news."

B25 [DAVIS, CHESTER L.] "'Life as I Find It' or 'Poor Little Stephen Girard,'" Twainian, XXVII (July-August), 1.

On the confusion concerning early publication of this story by MT, here reprinted from the Boston Evening Transcript, "Magazine Section," April 27, 1935. Abstract in AES, XIII (1969-1970), 1341.

B26 _____. "Mark Twain's Marginal Notations on 'Life, Letters and Journals of George Ticknor,'" Twainian, XXVII (July-August), 4; (September-October), 1-4; (November-December), 1-4.

On George S. Hillard (?), comp., The Life, Letters, and Journals of George Ticknor, Boston: James R. Osgood and Company, 1876, 2 vols. Follows the copy from MT's personal library, liberally quoting the text of the book, with MT's underlinings and notations. The series continues in Twainian through XXIX (March-April, 1970); the first installment noted that the second volume was unavailable, but it was found and reported in XXVIII (November-December, 1969), 1, and reprinting continued through this volume. The series is significant for what it reveals of MT's interests in a variety of topics. Abstracts in AES, XIII (1969-1970), 1350 (not reprinted in

Twainian; 1351, reprinted in Twainian, XXX (January-February, 1971); in AES, XIV (1970-1971), 585, reprinted in Twainian, XXXI (January-February, 1972).

B27 _____. "Mark Twain's Marginal Notes on Girard College," Twainian, XXVII (May-June), 1-4; (July-August), 2-4.

On MT's personal copy of Richard B. Westbrook, Girard's Will and Girard College Theology (Philadelphia, 1888). Reprints passages concerning Girard's desire that the students not be exposed to warring orthodox theologies, and the failure of the officers to follow his wishes; many of MT's underscorings are noted and marginal comments reproduced. Abstract in AES, XIII (1969-1970), 1348, 1349.

B28 _____. "Modern Language Association Center for Editions of American Authors, Works on Mark Twain," Twainian, XXVII (March-April), 2-4.

Provides a brief description and history of the CEAA, followed by "some random quotations especially significant in Mark Twain work" from the CEAA Statement of Editorial Principles: A Working Manual for Editing Nineteenth Century American Texts (1967). Abstract in AES, XIII (January-February), 1359; reprinted in Twainian, XXX (January-February, 1971).

B29 _____. "University of California Collection--Howe 'Story of a Country Town,'" Twainian, XXVII (January-February), 4; (March-April), 1-2.

On a visit by Davis to the Mark Twain collection at the University of California, Berkeley. The March-April installment reprints the text of MT's letter of February 12, 1884 to Edgar Watson Howe on his The Story of a Country Town. Abstract in AES, XIII (1969-1970), 1357; reprinted in Twainian, XXX (January-February, 1971).

B30 DOYNO, VICTOR A. "Over Twain's Shoulder: The Composition and Structure of Huckleberry Finn," Modern Fiction Studies, XIV (Spring), 3-9.

"Twain created in Huckleberry Finn three parallel sequential patterns of action. Each pattern involves first the meeting of Huck with someone who thinks him dead, the formation or renewal of a partnership to free the slave which ends in failure, and finally, the exchange of forty dollars." This pattern extends through "the natural world [of] the Mississippi...the picaresque adventures and deceptions of the King and Duke; and, finally, the burlesque romanticism of Tom's plot on the Phelps's farm. This pattern, and the ultimate impossibility of winning the slave's freedom," become increasingly evident: "for Huck freedom exists, if at all, in the process of seeking freedom." The disputed ending is an

(DOYNO, VICTOR A.)
appropriate framing element. Abstract in
AES, XII (1969), 1255; reprinted in Twainian, XXIX (January-February, 1970). Abstract by Doyno in ALA, II (December),
49-50.

B31 EBY, E. H. "Gold in the Slag Heap: More
Mark Twain Material," Pacific Northwest
Quarterly, LIX (January), 45-47.
A review of Hamlin Hill, ed., Mark Twain's
Letters to His Publishers, 1867-1894; Frank-
lin R. Rogers, ed., Mark Twain's Satires and
Burlesques; John S. Tuckey, ed., Mark Twain's
"Which Was the Dream?" and Other Symbolic
Writings of the Later Years (all 1967).
These books are not for the general reader,
but for the scholar they are "indispensable.
Here is a rich and enormously complex store
of material ably edited both as to text and
essential background." The greater part of
the review is on MT as revealed in these
volumes of his unpublished writings; the
approach is more descriptive than critical.

B32 ELLIS, HELEN E. "Mark Twain: The Influence
of Europe," Mark Twain Journal, XIV (Winter), 12-18.
Although MT spent more than ten years
abroad, he was never out of America longer
than eighteen months and he developed a
perspective for judging Europe and America
in terms of each other, a broader understanding of Man, and view of the world's
future; "In consequence of his expanding
vision, Twain altered from a young, naive
and proud young American to an old, embittered and disillusioned man." Abstract by
Ellis in ALA, II (June, 1969), 250-51.

B33 ENSOR, ALLISON. "The Contributions of Charles
Webster and Albert Bigelow Paine to Huckleberry Finn," American Literature, XL
(May), 222-27.
The captions for the illustrations and
the titles of the chapters in the original
Huckleberry Finn are the work of Charles L.
Webster, and somewhat inconsistent with the
narrative voice of Huck. Chapter titles
introduced in 1912 in the Author's National
Edition have been attributed by Charles
Neider to Albert Bigelow Paine; they "offer
no striking divergence from the tone and
point of view of the work itself." Abstract
in AES, XIII (1969-1970), 1339. Abstract
by Ensor in ALA, II (December), 50.

B34 _____. "The 'Opposition Line' to The King
and The Duke in Huckleberry Finn," Mark
Twain Journal, XIV (Winter), 6-7.
Answering W. Keith Kraus, "Huckleberry
Finn: A Final Irony" (1967), points out
that the language of the second set of
brothers appears only as reported by Huck,
their lack of visible grief may be the result of shock at having their identity
disputed, the point of the tattoo was not

worth making unless some benefit might come
of it, and the broken arm could be a device
of the author, rather than the character;
in sum: the second set of brothers are not
proven to be frauds. Abstract by Ensor in
ALA, II (June, 1969), 251.

B35 *ERICKSON, MILDRED. "Our Paths Have Crossed,"
University College Quarterly, XIII (January),
17-23.
A list of miscellaneous information concerning Hannibal, Missouri, circa 1820-1850,
may illuminate MT's boyhood. [Source: Abstract in AES, XI (1968), 2424.]

B36 *FILCEV, PETAR. "Princat i Prosekat" ["The
Prince and the Pauper"], Narodna Kultura
(Sofia), No. 4 (January), p. 24.
[Source: MHRA Annual Bibliography (1968),
No. 7727.]

B37 FOSTER, EDWARD F. "A Connecticut Yankee Anticipated: Max Adeler's Fortunate Island,"
Ball State University Forum, IX (Autumn),
73-76.
The 1881 novel by "Max Adeler" (Charles
Heber Clark) "contains an identical theme
and numerous parallels" in the story of a
sociology professor and his daughter ship-
wrecked on a floating island that had broken
loose from Arthurian England; after a stun-
ning blow on the head the hero awoke to find
the experience had been a dream. There is
no evidence that MT had read the book, although in 1915 Adeler felt it necessary to
point out that his book appeared before CY.
Abstract in AES, XIV (1970-1971), 2838; reprinted in Twainian, XXXI (March-April,
1972).

B38 FREIMARCK, JOHN. "Pudd'nhead Wilson: A Tale
of Blood and Brotherhood," University Review
(Kansas City), XXXIV (Summer), 303-306.
Ranks the book with HF in importance,
above it in "unity of theme and general or-
ganization," though "at times mechanical."
The most important criticisms are by Leslie
Fiedler (1955) and F. R. Leavis (1956).
"Richard Chase soon followed with the cau-
tion that these were extravagant estimates,
The American Novel and Its Tradition (New
York, 1957)." Both Tom Driscoll and Valet
de Chambre are victims of society; they have
their counterpart in the more harmonious
Italian twins, with circumstances and con-
duct serving as a contrast. Abstract in
AES, XIII (1969-70), 3090.

B39 GANZEL, DEWEY. [Review: Franklin R. Rogers,
ed., Mark Twain's Satires & Burlesques
(1967); John S. Tuckey, ed., Mark Twain's
"Which Was the Dream?" and Other Symbolic
Writings of the Later Years (1967); Hamlin
Hill, ed., Mark Twain's Letters to His Publishers, 1867-1894 (1967).] Modern Philology, LXVI (August), 83-87.

(GANZEL, DEWEY)

In a detailed discussion, notes the value of primary materials such as these to scholarship increasingly concerned with MT's aesthetic and his mode of composition. "Both the specialist and the non-specialist will find much to interest them in Clemens' correspondence; the manuscripts, on the other hand, will be of interest chiefly to the scholar." Unfortunately, the editing of the manuscript material to produce "readable text" for a general reader (who will find the abortive attempts disappointing) has produced "not the manuscript transcriptions one might have hoped them to be, but, rather, edited versions of those manuscripts." Hill's edition of MT's letters contains much of value, though Ganzel criticizes the selection.

B40　GARDNER, JOSEPH H. "Gaffer Hexam and Huck Finn," Modern Philology, LXVI (November), 155-56.

Although A Tale of Two Cities has often been suggested as a source for Pap's attack on Huck for learning to read and write, there is a closer analogue in Our Mutual Friend; Gardner documents MT's familiarity with Dickens' work. Abstract in AES, XII (1969), 1280; reprinted in Twainian, XXIX (January-February, 1970).

B41　GARLAND, HAMLIN. Hamlin Garland's Diaries, ed. by Donald Pizer. San Marino, California: The Huntington Library, passim.

At a memorial meeting to MT, April 30, 1910, among the old guard, one intoxicated and "Opie Read purple-visaged walking sedately and talking a lot of 'guff'" (p. 17). Dined with Clarence Darrow (November 4, 1920), who "particularly dwelt upon Mark Twain and his savage attacks on the Christian religion. It was all rather wearisome to me" (p. 123). Says Howells inspired MT with reform ideas, and P&P and CY "were due to Howells almost directly" (p. 152). Went to see Will Rogers on the film set for CY (December 28, 1930; pp. 181-82). Describes MT at a dinner honoring Henry James (December 9, 1904): "When Mark Twain's humor vanishes he is tragic. His wife is dead, one daughter is dead, another is in a sanitarium" (p. 191). At a lunch with Colonel Harvey (March 13, 1906) "Twain looked old and sluggish and congested, his purplish face and bushy yellow-white hair making him a picturesque figure. He drank more than he should and ate more than he should. He is old and his work is nearly done" (pp. 191-92). On MT's friendship for Howells and the differences between them, MT's coarse anecdotes-- "His profanity was oriental in its richness and power" (pp. 192-93).

B42　GEISMAR, MAXWELL. "Mark Twain on U. S. Imperialism, Racism & Other Enduring Characteristics of the Republic," Ramparts, VI (May), 64-71.

Defends the late writings of social protest as part of MT's most important work and far from an artistic failure. According to an editorial headnote, "Maxwell Geismar, the distinguished literary critic and historian, is presently at work on a study of Mark Twain [Mark Twain: An American Prophet (1970)]. This essay is excerpted from his chapter on the political radicalism of Twain's later writings." The front cover of this issue shows the American flag as MT suggested it might be remade, with black stripes and with skulls and crossbones instead of stars. Abstract in AES, XI (1968), 2642; reprinted in Twainian, XXVIII (March-April, 1969).

B43　GERBER, JOHN C. "Mark Twain," in J. Albert Robbins, ed., American Literary Scholarship: An Annual/1968 (Durham, North Carolina: Duke University Press, 1970), pp. 66-83.

A survey of MT scholarship for the year; See 1963.B32. Contents: "i. Textual and Bibliographical Matters"; "ii. Biography"; "iii. General Criticism"; "iv. Earlier Works"; "v. Huckleberry Finn"; "vi. Later Works."

B44　_____. [Review: Sydney J. Krause, Mark Twain as Critic (1967).] American Literature, XL (November), 408-409.

"The book is divided into three parts: Twain's Early Criticism: The Critic as Muggins, Twain's Later Criticism: The Critic as Grumbler, and Twain's Appreciative Criticism: From History into Life. As these titles reveal, there is an over-neatness about the division between the first two, and a confusion about the relation of the third to the other two. These difficulties are at the heart of the troubles that beset what could have been an important work." The third section of the book represents an improvement, and the section on Macaulay is particularly good.

B45　GIBSON, DONALD B. "Mark Twain's Jim in the Classroom," English Journal, LVII (February), 196-99, 202.

On the twentieth-century problems arising from the stereotyped portrayal of Jim in HF, and from MT's ambivalent attitude toward him.

B46　GIBSON, WILLIAM M. "Mark Twain's Mysterious Stranger Manuscripts: Some Questions for Textual Critics," Bulletin of the Rocky Mountain Modern Language Association, XXII (December), 183-91.

(GIBSON, WILLIAM M.)

"The following paper was delivered at the annual meeting of the RMMLA in October 1968 at Colorado Springs. It is an abbreviation of a paper given at the Dublin meeting of the International Association of University Professors of English." A description of the three texts cobbled together by Paine and Duneka as MS; Paine "secretly tried to fill Mark Twain's shoes, and he tampered with the faith of Mark Twain's readers." Gibson discusses "the scholarly, esthetic, and moral questions" he has had to face in his turn.

B47 GRAVES, WALLACE. "Mark Twain's 'Burning Shame,'" Nineteenth-Century Fiction, XXIII (June), 93-98.

The "Royal Nonesuch" of HF appears in the typescript as "The Burning Shame." Graves repeats a Swedish version as he heard it told in the thirties. "Interesting for its sustained drama as well as its obscenity," the story involves two destitute actors who performed for an audience from which women and children were excluded. One actor appeared on hands and knees, naked, while his partner introduced the act: "'And now, gentlemen, you are about to see The Tragedy of the Burning Shame.' He inserted a candle in the naked man's posterior, and lit it. When nothing further happened, the audience shouted for something more; the man said the performance was over...'have you ever seen a better example of a "Burning Shame"?'" And the actors fled with the receipts. Abstract by Graves in ALA, II (December), 50-51.

B48 HART, JOHN E. "Heroes and Houses: The Progress of Huck Finn," Modern Fiction Studies, XIV (Spring), 39-46.

Identifies the term "house" broadly, to include "sheds and rafts, huts and mansions," and even steamboats. A view of Huck's journey as a progression from house to house gives the story unity; "in one way or another, the house stands for civilization, a container of ambiguities: of freedom and bondage, of mystery and insight, of good and evil, of life and death." Abstract in AES, XII (1969), 1259; reprinted in Twainian, XXIX (January-February, 1970). Abstract by Hart in ALA, II (December), 51.

B49 HILL, HAMLIN. "Mark Twain and His Enemies," Southern Review, n.s. IV (April), 520-29.

"Towering rages" were "quite possibly an ingredient in the essential Mark Twain." Often, what he attacked in his enemies were aspects of himself: "His bitterness and vitriol were, then, as often touchstones to Mark Twain's self-doubts, recriminations, and inadequacies as to his enmities." He was motivated chiefly by fear--of failure, of success, of offending, of being laughed at. "He was a man most flawed by his fear of revealing his flaws."

B50 _____. [Review: Sydney J. Krause, Mark Twain as Critic (1967).] Modern Language Quarterly, XXIX (June), 236-38.

"Twain was a literary cat toying with pathetically unimportant mice. Mark Twain as Critic will impress any reader with the scope and the range of its subject's critical writings--which are all the more impressive because they lacked a solid basis or a theoretical depth."

B51 HOUGH, ROBERT L. "Mark Twain as Traveler," Prairie Schooner, XLII (Winter), 360-61.

A review of Dewey Ganzel, Mark Twain Abroad, which he praises for showing the effect which the pressure of time and lost letters had on the correspondence making up the latter half of Innocents Abroad, for showing that the influence of Mrs. Fairbanks on MT has been exaggerated, and for the portrayal of the other passengers on the Quaker City. Although "Ganzel sometimes pushes his evidence too far," the "lapses...are minor and do not seriously impair the informational or critical insights of the book."

B52 _____. "Twain's Double-Dating in 'A Connecticut Yankee,'" Notes and Queries, CCXIII, n.s. XV (November), 424-25.

MT uses two sets of dates for Hank Morgan's scheduled execution and his exploitation of the solar eclipse: that of Sir Kay and the mistaken dating of Clarence; Hank's first full day in prison is the 21st, so Clarence's advancing the date of execution to the 20th is impossible. Abstract in AES, XII (1969), 1998; reprinted in Twainian, XXIX (January-February, 1970).

B53 HOWELL, ELMO. "Huckleberry Finn in Mississippi," Louisiana Studies, VII (Summer), 167-72.

On the locations in Mississippi of some of the incidents in HF, in which MT's "purpose is to give a kindly rendering of a country and a civilization" he loved. Abstract in AES, XII (1969), 936; reprinted in Twainian, XXIX (January-February, 1970).

B54 _____. "Uncle John Quarles' Watermelon Patch," Midwest Quarterly, IX (April), 271-82.

On the tender recollections in HF of MT's own boyhood days on his uncle's farm: "He had been in Eden and he knew whereof he spoke." (Documentation is from familiar works on MT). Lengthy abstract by Howell in ALA, II (December), 52.

B55 _____. "Uncle Silas Phelps: A Note on Mark Twain's Characterization," Mark Twain Journal, XIV (Summer), 8-12.

"Mark Twain was a friend of the Negro... and he never failed to speak out against the injustice he suffered, particularly in the South," but he "also loved those Valley people who enslaved Jim.... Thus Huckleberry Finn is built around a paradox," the Phelps

1968 - Shorter Writings

(HOWELL, ELMO)
family "are among Mark Twain's favorite people, and Uncle Silas Phelps is his finest portrait of a good man," kindly and decent rather than clever. Lengthy abstract by Howell in ALA, II (December), 52-53.

B56 *IVANOVA, ELKA. "Mǎdǎr Urok. Piesata 'Princǎt i Prosekǎt v Nar. teatar za mladežta" ["A Good Lesson. 'The Prince and the Pauper' as Staged by the Nat. Theatre of Youth"], Teatǎr (Sophia), XXI, No. 3, 40-41.
      [Source: MHRA Annual Bibliography (1968), No. 7745.]

B57 JONES, JOSEPH. "Mark Twain's Connecticut Yankee and Australian Nationalism," American Literature, XL (May), 227-31.
      Although the book met a hostile reception from English reviewers, Australians found it attuned to their own sentiments. Among Australian reviews quoted is one from the Sydney Bulletin (March 8, 1890), titled "Mark Twain's New Book. A Crusher for Royalty." Abstract in AES, XIII (1969-1970), 1337. Also abstracted in ALA, II (December), 53.

B58 KAPLAN, JUSTIN. "What Really Happened to the Innocents Abroad," Chicago Tribune, "Book World," II (October 6), 5.
      A review of Dewey Ganzel's Mark Twain Abroad; primarily descriptive, with limited evaluation: "In trying to set the record straight to tell what actually happened, Ganzel has taken on a thankless task. He is up against a brilliant entertainer. Ganzel's synoptic version may be 'truer' than Mark Twain's, more historical and evenhanded, but it is inevitably drabber and less acute."

B59 KIMBALL, WILLIAM J. "Samuel Clemens as a Confederate Soldier: Some Observations About 'The Private History of a Campaign That Failed,'" Studies in Short Fiction, V (Summer), 382-84.
      MT's account of his brief service in an irregular Confederate unit is not wholly accurate. Abstract in AES, XII (1969), 1404; reprinted in Twainian, XXIX (January-February, 1970). Abstract by Kimball in ALA, II (December), 54.

B60 *KOHLI, RAJ K. "Huck Finn and Isabel Archer: Two Responses to the Fruit of Knowledge," in Banasthali Patrika (Rajasthan), XI (July), 73-82. Special Number on American Literature, ed. by Rameshwar Gupta. [Proceedings of the Seminar on American Literature, 2-3 March 1968 at Banasthali Vidyapath.]
      [Source: MLA Bibliography (1968), Nos. 78, 10284.]

B61 *LAIDLAW, R. P. "More Huck Finn in Finnegans Wake," A Wake Newsletter, V (October), 71-73.
      On references to HF not listed in Atherton's The Books at the Wake (1960), Hosty, introduced on p. 40, is described as, like Huck, having "no slouch of a name." [Source: Abstract in AES, XIII (1969-1970), 577; reprinted in Twainian, XXIX (January-February, 1970).]

B62 LEARY, LEWIS. "The Bankruptcy of Mark Twain," The Carrell: Journal of the Friends of the University of Miami Library, IX (June), 13-20.
      Describes MT's failure in publishing, and his friendship with Henry Rogers, who put MT's business affairs in order and retrieved his fortune. Also, describes use of the MT mask to conceal inner weakness. As a writer "he had great successes and horrible failures--how marvelous he can be at his best... but how jejeune and embarrassing he can be at his worst, when he becomes serious or tries to think." It is "our brother, Mark Twain, who speaks for us because he is human and fallible," but he fails to go beyond "to something we had not thought to say. And that which he nor we do not say defines the artist."

B63 _____. "On Writing about Writers: Mark Twain and Howells," Southern Review, n.s. IV (April), 551-57.
      A review article; the portion on MT deals with James M. Cox, Mark Twain: The Fate of Humor (1966), on "Mark Twain" as a creation of Samuel Clemens, and the achievement of Cox in distinguishing between the two. When "Mark Twain" fails it is because Samuel Clemens intrudes, and "the fate of humor is that it becomes platitude...becomes serious at last." An aging, bitter Clemens "allowed Mark Twain to speak as an agent rather than a catalyst."

B64 LEHAN, RICHARD. [Review: Edward Wagenknecht, Mark Twain: The Man and His Work (revised ed., 1967).] Nineteenth-Century Fiction, XXIII (June), 133-24.
      "Much of this book is trivial and irrelevant." MT's views on religion, politics, love, and "preoccupation with nakedness-- are important subjects superficially treated," but Wagenknecht is "disarmingly honest" about the limits of the book as it originally appeared, and he now "makes at times excellent use of recent criticism... and appends a superb 'Commentary on Mark Twain Criticism and Scholarship Since 1960.'"

B65 LEVIN, DAVID. "Mark Twain and Samuel L. Clemens," Yale Review, LVII (Spring), 434-37.
      A review of James M. Cox, Mark Twain: The Fate of Humor (1966). Cox begs a few questions, but the book "gives great pleasure along with serious instruction" and reveals "a shrewd use of scholarship...a scrupulous respect for the complexity of unpublished texts...and an admirable combination of biographical and literary intelligence."

B66 McDERMOTT, JOHN FRANCIS. "Mark Twain and the Bible," Papers on Language and Literature (Journal of the Midwest Modern Language Association for Scholars and Critics of Language and Literature), IV (Spring), 195-98.

Contains the text of a letter to MT from C. F. Davis, of Keokuk, Iowa (May, 1882) asking for reminiscences, reminding him of the time as a child when he was accidentally left behind when the Clemenses moved from Florida, Missouri, to Hannibal (and was found asleep in a flour barrel), and inquiring about "your familiar quotations from the Bible, when you were never known to read that book." MT's reply on July 8 enclosed a "manuscript scrap" (here printed), confessing that "I did manufacture a lot of bogus biblical 'quotations' & play them off on Patterson & the others, knowing that they would not be able to detect the swindle." McDermott concludes the article with a list of the books in the estate of John Marshall Clemens on his death in 1847. Abstract in ALA, II (December), 55.

B67 McINTYRE, JAMES P. "Three Practical Jokes: A Key to Huck's Changing Attitude Toward Jim," Modern Fiction Studies, XIV (Spring), 33-37.

Beginning with Chadwick Hansen's 1963 study, traces Huck's growing awareness of Jim's humanity: first Tom hung Jim's hat on a tree, then Huck nearly killled him in a joke involving a rattlesnake skin, but it was only through offending Jim's human dignity in the "trash" episode that Huck fully recognized his companion as an individual rather than a type. McIntyre's interpretation contrasts with Hansen's picture of Jim as developing from a minor figure to a symbol of man. Abstract in AES, XII (1969), 1258; abstract by McIntyre in ALA, II (December), 55.

B68 McMILLAN, DOUGLAS J. [Brief Review: Robert Regan, Unpromising Heroes: Mark Twain and His Characters (1966).] Western Folklore, XXVII (July), 223.

"The psychological interpretation (interwoven with the folkloristic, but not so detailed) of Twain's view of himself--as an unpromising hero mirrored in his fictional alter egos--is convincingly and entertainingly presented, provided one accepts its Freudian bases."

B69 *MALHOTRA, M. L. "The Question of Unity in Huckleberry Finn," The Banasthali Patrika (Rajasthan), No. 11 (July), pp. 69-72.
[Source: MHRA Annual Bibliography (1968), 7753. Additional publication facts in MLA Bibliography (1969), Nos. 78, 10288.]

B70 MANIEERE, WILLIAM R. "Huck Finn, Empiricist Member of Society," Modern Fiction Studies, XIV (Spring), 57-66.

The opening chapters do not represent Tom's point of view, or that of society; rather, the first three prepare for the story and define "the moral standards which give it meaning. The values of St. Petersburg--money, church, 'aristocracy,' to name only the most important--are equated with untruth, Tom Sawyer's 'lies,' and, for the moment at least, are rejected"; the fourth chapter introduces Pap and gives portents of future troubles. These first four chapters juxtapose opposing concepts, and Huck pragmatically tests and either accepts or rejects various ways of dealing with experience; but in the end his pragmatism has become "merely verbal." Abstract in AES, XII (1969), 1261; reprinted in Twainian, XXIX (January-February, 1970). Also abstracted in ALA, II (December), 54.

B71 ____. "On Keeping the Raftsmen's Passage in Huckleberry Finn," English Language Notes, VI (December), 118-22.

Removal of the passage to serve as padding for LOM damages HF structurally by obscuring Huck's responses to Jim's imminent freedom; the passage should be restored. Abstract in AES, XIV (1970-1971), 1542; reprinted in Twainian, XXXI (January-February, 1972). Abstract by Manierre in ALA, II (July, 1969), 252.

B72 MANN, CAROLYN. "Innocence in Pudd'nhead Wilson," Mark Twain Journal, XIV (Winter), 18-21, 11.

The influence of temperament and environment is stressed as a means of absolving characters of responsibility for their conduct, and in the end Wilson is not embittered. The author's "sympathy with those of his characters in Pudd'nhead Wilson who mean no harm is...proof that Mark Twain's nature profoundly desired innocence in man, or that he was willing to forgive man wherever possible."

B73 MATTSON, J. STANLEY. "Mark Twain on War and Peace: the Missouri Rebel and 'The Campaign that Failed,'" American Quarterly, XX (Winter), 783-94.

In October, 1884 the Century Magazine began a three-year series of "Battles and Leaders of the Civil War," the major part of which was written by celebrated leaders from both sides; their approach was serious, though not sentimental. In contrast to the general picture of the war as rational and important is MT's "The Private History of a Campaign that Failed" (Century, XXXI [December, 1885], 255-82), which portrays both the war and his own participation as inglorious. "In all, Mark Twain left to posterity no less than four major and five minor disparate versions of his career with the Confederate Army" (here listed). Mattson describes MT's anti-war sentiments and notes his correspondence with Robert Underwood Johnson, co-editor of the series.

B74 MATTSON, J. STANLEY. "Twain's Last Months
     on the Mississippi," Missouri Historical
     Review, LXII (July), 398-409.
        Tracing MT's movements in 1861, concludes
     that "both Twain and Paine were considerably
     more careful of the facts than we have here-
     tofore been led to believe."

B75 MAYBERRY, GEORGE. "Huckleberry Finn Enriched,"
     Nation, CCVII (August 26), 154-57.
        Discusses in some detail several of the
     more than twenty paperbound editions of HF
     intended for classroom use; most of those
     here considered contain useful introduc-
     tions, and several include biographical
     summaries, critical essays, and, in some
     cases, materials for class study. The Nor-
     ton Critical Edition and the Harbrace
     Sourcebook contain a wealth of supplementary
     material, as does The Art of Huckleberry
     Finn (Chandler), in which the text is a fac-
     simile of the first American edition, with
     the original Kemble illustrations. The Vik-
     ing, Bobbs-Merrill, Riverside, and Rinehart
     editions range from good to superb, and a
     simple Chandler edition using a facsimile
     of the first edition (with the Kemble il-
     lustrations) and an introduction and bib-
     liography by Hamlin Hill is "my favorite
     among paperback editions and...possibly the
     'best buy.'" Editions published by Pocket
     Books, Bantam, Dell, and Signet reveal
     small concern by their editors for MT's
     text and vary in the quality of the added
     material. The poorest of these is the
     Reader's Enrichment edition (Pocket Books:
     Washington Square Press), in which the back-
     ground material is "barely adequate" and
     "the sections on writing skills, vocabulary
     development and spelling include the fasci-
     nating suggestion to study such words as
     'ingots,' 'nabob,' and 'reticule,' 'because
     they are popular with good writers and
     speakers.'" The Bantam, Dell, and Signet
     editions are considerably better, and some
     of the supplementary material is quite
     good. Very brief abstract in AES, XII
     (1969), 1955; reprinted in Twainian, XXIX
     (January-February, 1970).

B76 MAYNARD, REID. "Mark Twain's Ambivalent Yan-
     kee," Mark Twain Journal, XIV (Winter), 1-5.
        Summarizes the "one-sided" interpreta-
     tions of the book, in which "the Yankee's
     overt attitude and actions are taken at
     face value while his moments of admiration
     for certain elements in Arthur's kingdom are
     either overlooked or conveniently neglect-
     ed." After summarizing various other criti-
     cal views, Maynard concludes that the book
     is "a thematically uneven novel" in which
     various aspects of MT's "damned human race,"
     past and present, "are satirized intention-
     ally and unintentionally." Abstract by
     Maynard in ALA, II (June, 1969), 252-53.

B77 *MELNIKOV, I. "Raskoldovannoe Leto" ["Disen-
     chanted Summer"; on HF.] Detskaya Litera-
     tura, VII, 41-43.
        [Source: MHRA Bibliography (1968), No.
     7760.]

B78 MERIWETHER, JAMES B., and MICHAEL MILLGATE,
     eds. Lion in the Garden: Interviews with
     William Faulkner. New York: Random House.
     Passim on MT (indexed).
        HF is "too loose" to be called a novel,
     "just a series of events" (p. 56); Hawthorne
     and James were not strictly American authors
     as MT, Whitman, and Sandburg were
     (pp. 167-68). The passage in Faulkner at
     Nagano (1956.B28) appears on p. 137.

B79 MILLER, J. HILLIS. "Three Problems of Fiction-
     al Form: First-Person Narration in David
     Copperfield and Huckleberry Finn," in Roy
     Harvey Pearce, ed., Experience in the Novel:
     Selected Papers from the English Institute
     (New York and London: Columbia University
     Press), pp. 21-48.

B80 MORRISON, CLAUDIA C. "Van Wyck Brooks's Analy-
     sis of Mark Twain," in her Freud and the
     Critic: The Early Use of Depth Psychology
     in Literary Criticism (Chapel Hill: The
     University of North Carolina Press).
        Traces Brooks's argument, frequently tak-
     ing issue with him; nonetheless, The Ordeal
     of Mark Twain, despite the thesis ridden
     too hard and the occasionally false psycholo-
     gizing, "is a provocative and, in its broad
     outlines at least, an essentially sound in-
     terpretation of Mark Twain's character"
     (p. 189). Brooks's success can be attribut-
     ed to his intelligence and critical sophisti-
     cation (p. 191). Suggests (pp. 112-13) that
     a more rounded psychological portrait may be
     found in O'Higgins and Reede: The American
     Mind in Action (1924.B25).

B81 MURRAY, DONALD. "Hong Kong Letter: Bombs,
     Books, and Hemingway," American Book Col-
     lector (Chicago), XVIII (March), 16-21.
        In a Mandarin Chinese translation, Huck
     Finn's language is stiff and formal. "I
     haven't yet found out about the 'complete
     edition' of Mark Twain, with propaganda
     prefaces, reportedly published on the Main-
     land." Abstract in AES, XI (1968), 2449;
     reprinted in Twainian, XXVIII (January-
     February, 1969).

B82 MYERS, MARGARET. "Mark Twain and Melville,"
     Mark Twain Journal, XIV (Summer), 5-8.
        "In thematic development, Melville seems
     to begin where Twain left off": MT goes
     from the "fond nostalgia" of HF to the bit-
     ter disillusionment of MS, while "Melville
     seems to seize Twain's disenchantment for
     the source of Ahab's defiance in Moby-Dick,
     then renounces the struggle in the submis-
     sion of Billy Budd." Lengthy abstract by
     Myers in ALA, II (December), 55-56.

B83 NOBLE, DAVID W. "The Realists: Mark Twain, William Dean Howells, Henry James," in his The Eternal Adam in the New World Garden: The Central Myth in the American Novel Since 1830. (New York: George Braziller), pp. 49-98; on MT, pp. 51-67.
On the decline of MT's optimistic belief in New World innocence and the possibility of progress: "It is man who imposes evil upon his social environment rather than the other way around" (p. 66).

B84 PECK, RICHARD E. "A Mark Twain 'Literary Offence,'" Mark Twain Journal, XIV (Winter), 7-9.
In HF, MT commits literary offences of which he accused Fenimore Cooper, particularly in violation of rules on the relevancy of incidents to the development of the plot, and on the use of language appropriate to the characters.

B85 *PETROVA, E. N. "Bor'ba Vokrug Tvorcheskogo Naslediya Marka Tvena v Literaturnoi Kritike Ameriki 1910-1920 Godov" ["The Controversy Surrounding the Creative Legacy of Mark Twain in the Literary Criticism of 1910-1920"], Leningradskii Pedagogicheskii Institut Imeni A. I. Gertsena (Leningrad) CCCXVI, 29-45.
[Source: MHRA Annual Bibliography (1970), No. 8271.]

B86 PICKETT, CALDER M. Ed Howe: Country Town Philosopher. Lawrence and London: University Press of Kansas, pp. 75-77 and passim.
Contains the text of MT's letter of February 13, 1884 to Howe about The Story of a Country Town, which MT and Cable liked; the letter is in two parts, the first to be made public if Howe chose and the second making some pointed suggestions for improvement (pp. 75-77). Also, quotes Howe in the Atchinson Globe of June 2, 1902 (1902. B18; quoted p. 123).

B87 RAVITZ, ABE C. [Review: Sydney J. Krause, Mark Twain as Critic (1967).] Mississippi Quarterly, XXI (Spring), 160-63.
Praises Krause's "gracefully-written, thoroughly-searched study," with the reservation that he does not adequately reveal the haste and shallowness of MT's judgments; however, his book is significant in showing that MT approached criticism "with wit and sensitivity," and "It is Twain's standard for Twain that one can now evaluate with keener understanding."

B88 REES, ROBERT A. "Mark Twain and Lucius Fairchild," Wisconsin Academy Review, XV (Spring), 8-9.
On the friendship of "Wisconsin's famous Civil War hero and ex-governor" and "the Twains," who missed an opportunity for a joint balloon ascension in Paris in 1879. Notes further meetings and a performance of Die Meisterschaft by the German Conversation Club of Madison. Documented from the Fairchild Papers at the Wisconsin Historical Society, Madison, and other sources; quotes MT correspondence.

B89 _____. [Review article.] Nineteenth-Century Fiction, XXIII (June), 113-16.
John S. Tuckey, ed., Mark Twain's "Which Was the Dream?" (1966) is "interesting from a biographical-critical viewpoint." MT withheld these pieces, not because they were bad work, but because "his soul is here laid so bare"; Hamlin Hill, ed., Mark Twain's Letters to His Publishers (1967) is 290 letters which "in their totality give a rare and candid view of one of the more complex personalities in American letters," and "Hill's excellent introduction and notes unify the narrative." In Mark Twain's Satires and Burlesques Franklin R. Rogers "continues his excellent work on Twain's burlesque patterns with the eight pieces he edits with introductions...while these pieces tend to be uneven and unfinished, there is an occasional flash of Twainian brilliance, as in the burlesque of Victor Hugo's Les Travailleurs de la Mer."

B90 REEVES, PASCHAL, et al. "A Checklist of Scholarship for 1968." Mississippi Quarterly, XXII (Spring, 1969); on MT, pp. 160-62.
The first appearance of what has become an annual checklist. This is considerably less extensive than the annual bibliographies published by the MLA and MHRA, but has the advantage of appearing at least two years earlier.

B91 RICKELS, MILTON. "Samuel Clemens and the Conscience of Comedy," Southern Review, n.s. IV (April), 558-68.
A review-article on Fatout's Mark Twain in Virginia City, Hill's Mark Twain and Elisha Bliss, Wiggins's Mark Twain: Jackleg Novelist, and Smith's Mark Twain's Fable of Progress (all 1964). Rickles praises Fatout's and Hill's "careful research," adding that "by doing only the most modest violence to their authors' intentions it is possible to examine elements of the developing conscience of Samuel Clemens," which he then traces. Wiggins's depiction of MT as improviser is weak in the portrayal of the moral basis of MT's art and in support through analysis of a charge that MT did not understand the nature of humor. Finally, Smith's book is rich in insights and critical implications, showing that "subtle analysis of characterization, form, style, and humorous technique reveal how Mark Twain's imagination confronted profound ethical questions."

B92 RUST, RICHARD DILWORTH. "Americanisms in A Connecticut Yankee," South Atlantic Bulletin, XXXIII (May), 11-13.
The language is used partly to amuse, and partly to characterize Hank Morgan; there is

1968 - Shorter Writings

(RUST, RICHARD DILWORTH)
ambivalence in such terms as "The Boss" and "Yankee," and Hank's drawing the majority of his Americanisms from baseball, the stock market, and poker shows his limitations. In the end, the failure of his technology is marked by "his breakdown in communication and his ultimate reliance on the language he originally ridiculed." Abstract in AES, XII (1969-1970), 1338; reprinted in Twainian, XXX (January-February, 1961).

B93   SALOMON, ROGER B. "Mark Twain Today," Case Western Reserve University Magazine: A Quarterly Publication for Alumni and Other Friends, I (Winter), 7-11.
Surveys his current status and the criticism; for the general reader.

B94   SCHONHORN, MANUEL. "Mark Twain's Jim: Solomon on the Mississippi," Mark Twain Journal, XIV (Winter), 9-11.
Defending the portrayal of Jim in Chapter XIV against the contention of Daniel Hoffman (Form and Fable in American Fiction, 1951, p. 321) and Chadwick Hansen ("The Character of Jim and the Ending of Huckleberry Finn," 1963), that he is shown as a minstrel-show comic, argues that in the passage discussing Solomon's wisdom Jim and Huck are taking the roles previously given to Huck and the romantic Tom Sawyer; subsequently, when the lost raft is found by the Grangerford slaves, Jim amicably settles the question of its ownership with an ease and grace that contrast with the bloody feud over a trifling lawsuit thirty years in the past.

B95   SHARMA, MOHAN LAL. "Mark Twain's Passage to India," Mark Twain Journal, XIV (Summer), 12-14.
On his visit there in 1896, as reflected in Following the Equator, his notebooks, and "old press clippings of the period" (quoted, but naming only the Bombay Gazette and giving no dates). Lengthy abstract by Sharma in ALA, II (December), 56-57.

B96   SIMPSON, LOUIS P. "Mark Twain: Critical Perspectives," Southern Review, n.s. IV (April), 491-92.
Introduces a section of this issue collecting essays and review-essays by Arlin Turner, Hamlin Hill, Robert Tracy, James M. Cox, Lewis Leary, and Milton Rickels. The question of the Clemens-Mark Twain identity "involves the identity of us all," as people and as a nation. "By virtue of his Southern environment, Mark Twain had the most fertile education nineteenth-century America afforded in the dilemma of being an American."

B97   SOLOMON, JACK. "Huckleberry Finn and the Tradition of the Odyssey," South Atlantic Bulletin, XXXIII (March), 11-13.
In the debated ending of HF, Tom's and Huck's use of disguises is in the tradition of the homecoming of Odysseus; there are other parallels, among them the journey, Huck's imprisonment in the hut, the destruction of the raft, and even--in Huck's faking his own death and later hiding gold in a coffin--a sort of descent into a world of the dead. Abstract in AES, XIII (1969-1970), 1340.

B98   SPENGEMANN, WILLIAM C. [Review: Sydney J. Krause, Mark Twain as Critic (1967).] Criticism, X (Spring) 166-68.
"The first book to present Clemens' critical theories in a way which might help us to fix his position on a line stretching from the Romantic subjectivism of Emerson to the Romantic objectivism of Eliot." Krause's effect is occasionally vitiated by a tendency "to emphasize the object Clemens criticized instead of the mind of Clemens the critic," but the book "will prove a rich source of information and inspiration to American scholars."

B99   STEWART, GEORGE R. "Travelers by 'Overland': Stagecoaching on the Central Route, 1859-1865," American West, V (July), 4-12.
On the journeys by Horace Greeley (1859), Richard Burton (1860), MT (1861), and Samuel Bowles and Schuyler Colfax (1865). With a map on pp. 8-9 showing the various routes, this is interesting chiefly as general background, but has little direct interest for the study of MT.

B100   STOEHR, TAYLOR. "Tone and Voice," College English, XXX (November), 150-61.
On pp. 157-61, "Sam Clemens and Mark Twain: Finding a Voice," discusses his gradual development of a persona, most successfully in HF.

B101   TANSELLE, G. THOMAS. "Anderson, Annotated by Brooks," Notes and Queries (London), CCXIII, n.s. XV (February), 60-61.
A copy of A Story Teller's Story in Tanselle's possession carries the marginal notation by Brooks: "Paul R. [Rosenfeld] thought I was a traitor attacking artists Mark Twain etc." Tanselle also notes Brooks's statement on Anderson's admiration of MT in Story magazine (1941.B1). Abstract in AES, XI (1968), 61; reprinted in Twainian, XXVIII (January-February, 1969).

B102   TATE, ALLEN. "Faulkner's Sanctuary and the Southern Myth," Virginia Quarterly Review, XLIV (Summer), 418-27.
(Apparently this was the introduction to an edition of Sanctuary). Links HF with Augustus Baldwin Longstreet's Georgia Scenes as "a second crucial novel"; it is "the first Southern novel in which the action is generated inside the characters. It is not perhaps the masterpiece that the academic Mark Twain 'industry' has made it out to be; yet for the reason I have indicated, it is a work of great originality and historical

(TATE, ALLEN)
importance. These two works are the beginning of modern Southern literature; they are also important for American literature as a whole."

B103 _____. "A Southern Mode of the Imagination," in his Essays of Four Decades (Chicago: The Swallow Press, Inc.), pp. 577-92.
On HF, pp. 591-92; calls this "the first modern novel by a Southerner," with the mode of progression no longer that of rhetoric but with the action "generated inside the characters...Mark Twain seems not to have been wholly conscious of what he had done; for he never did it again." He was "a forerunner who set an example which was not necessarily an influence," and "the shift from the rhetorical mode to the dialectical mode had to be rediscovered by the twentieth-century novelists of the South." (The date "1959" appears at the end, but there is no indication of where this was previously published.)

B104 TATHAM, CAMPBELL. "'Dismal and Lonesome' A New Look at Huckleberry Finn," Modern Fiction Studies, XIV (Spring), 47-55.
"The Huck Finn who takes part in the events at the Phelps farm is a logical projection of the Huck Finn who at three crucial moments based his actions on his pathological fear of loneliness and his personal need for acceptance and comfort. The book ends where it began because that is what the book is all about. Twain simply did not have the confidence in man's ability to effect a moral progression to pose Huck as a conventional hero"; this reflects the outlook MT expressed in What Is Man? Abstract in AES, XII (1969), 1260; reprinted in Twainian, XXIX (January-February, 1970). Abstract by Tatham in ALA, II (December), 57-58.

B105 TIECK, WILLIAM A. Riverdale, Kingsbridge, Spuyten Duyvil: A Historical Epitome of the Northwest Bronx. Old Tappan, New Jersey: Fleming H. Revell Company.
On "Wave Hill," the Riverdale house MT rented, with photograph of the house, pp. 53-54.

B106 TRACY, ROBERT. "Myth and Reality in The Adventures of Tom Sawyer," Southern Review, n.s. IV (April), 530-41.
In TS "Mark Twain attempts a subtle interplay of reality, bookish romance, and myth in order to express an ambiguous attitude to both American civilization and the savage American wilderness." Tom expresses both freedom and conformity, and MT conceals the evasion through melodrama.

B107 TURNER, ARLIN. "Mark Twain and the South: An Affair of Love and Anger," Southern Review, n.s. IV (April), 493-519.

MT criticized in the South what he saw in mankind, but more severely because the blame lay nearer himself. There is extensive discussion of MT's maturing views on race, the influence of Cable, and the treatment of Southern themes in MT's works, especially in PW. The part on PW is reprinted in Schmitter (1974), pp. 123-32.

B108 _____. [Review article.] South Atlantic Quarterly, LXVII (Summer), 566-67.
John S. Tuckey, Mark Twain's "Which Was the Dream?" And Other Symbolic Writings of the Later Years (1966) shows the editor's conviction that MT retained his creative powers; Franklin R. Rogers, ed., Mark Twain's Satires and Burlesques (1967) shows MT's fondness for the mode and insists perhaps too emphatically on the influence of burlesque in shaping his satire; Hamlin Hill, ed., Mark Twain's Letters to His Publishers, 1867-1894 (1967) "provides sounder bases than we have ever had for judging the wrath Mark Twain poured upon his publishers."

B109 *TURNER, MARTHA ANNE. "Was Frank Dobie a Throwback to Mark Twain?" Western Review, V (Winter), 3-12.
[Source: MHRA Annual Bibliography (1968), No. 7776.]

B110 VANDERSEE, CHARLES. "The Mutual Awareness of Mark Twain and Henry Adams," English Language Notes, V (June), 285-92.
Joseph Gilder's "Glimpses of John Hay" (Critic, XLVII [September, 1905], 248) records a meeting in January, 1886 between Adams (then depressed over his wife's recent suicide) and MT; although a closer acquaintance failed to develop, references by the two to each other are favorable and Gilder's recollection "does seem to establish that the two were more at ease than 'at odds' with each other. And the clear awareness that each man had of the other forms a more solid basis on which to study further the analogies in their thought and art." Abstract in AES, XII (1969), 1518; reprinted in Twainian, XXIX (January-February, 1970). Abstract by Vandersee in ALA, II (December), 58.

B111 WAGER, WILLIS. "Mainly the Novel, Amateur to Professional: Twain to James," in his American Literature: A World View (New York: New York University Press, and London: University of London Press, Limited), pp. 129-84 (On MT, pp. 131-39).
A solid general study, providing no new information or interpretation.

B112 WALKER, I. M. [Review: James M. Cox, Mark Twain: The Fate of Humor (1966).] Review of English Studies, n.s., XIX (August), 331-32.
"It is the development and final betrayal of Mark Twain's identity as a humorous writer that Professor James Cox argues in this

(WALKER, I. M.)
stimulating and often persuasive book....
It is...in his discussion of Twain's satire
that Mr. Cox is least satisfactory," and
the fact explains "his failure fully to
come to terms with Huckleberry Finn, for
the novel involves satiric dimensions
which he virtually ignores. Nevertheless
he has written a valuable and suggestive
study which deserves careful reading."

B113 WARD, HARRY M. [Review: Edward Wagenknecht,
Mark Twain: The Man and His Work (1967).]
Journal of the West, VII (October), 573.
Chiefly descriptive. "If the author
might have given more weight to the Gilded
Age and the travel books as self-revealing
of the man, he has, nevertheless, given us
a sharper glance of Twain through his
dichotomous character."

B114 WEEKS, LEWIS E., JR. "Mark Twain and Hemingway: 'A Catastrophe' and 'A Natural History of the Dead,'" Mark Twain Journal,
XIV (Summer), 15-17.
The descriptions of makeshift hospitals
by MT in LOM and by Hemingway are similar
in circumstances but different in that MT
is merely reporting, without advancing a
thesis.... "In some ways, too, Twain's writing in this chapter is ironically similar
to the very style and treatment that Hemingway is satirizing."

B115 WELSH, JOHN R. [Review: Sydney J. Krause,
Mark Twain as Critic.] Georgia Review,
XXIII (Summer), 244-45.
Chiefly descriptive, but suggests the
book "could stand some tightening up, for
it occasionally borders on the tedious";
by undue emphasis on the critic as "muggins" and "grumbler," Krause fails to show
how these masks related to the unmasked
critic.

B116 WILSON, EDMUND. "The Fruits of the MLA: II.
Mark Twain," New York Review of Books, XI
(October 10), 6-14.
On the University of California edition
of the MT Papers and works, which are useful to the biographer; but the vastness of
the project is essentially "boondoggling."
In passing, notes "the serious shortcomings" of Justin Kaplan's Mr. Clemens and
Mark Twain," which "rather indecently" ignores the work of Brooks, Dixon Wecter, and
Effie Mona Mack. For what made MT attractive to his public "we are obliged to go
back to Albert Payson Terhune's [sic] old
biography, written in the spirit of the
period."

B117 WINTERICH, JOHN T. "Missouri Yankee: Mark
Twain," in his Writers in America 1842-
1967: An Informal Glance at Some of the
Authors Who Have Flourished Since the Establishment of the Davey Company One Hundred
and Twenty-Five Years Ago (Jersey City,
N.J.: The Davey Company), pp. 55-59.
A general discussion to entertain the general reader. The book is a gift volume to
celebrate the 125th anniversary of a firm
manufacturing binder's board for the book
industry.

B118 WYSONG, JACK P. "Samuel Clemens' Attitude
Toward the Negro as Demonstrated in Pudd'n-
head Wilson and A Connecticut Yankee in
King Arthur's Court," Xavier University
Studies, VII (July), 41-57.
The difference in the portrayal of slaves
in the two books lies in the fact that in
CY they are white, and they show courage and
the ability to benefit from education. "In
Pudd'nhead Wilson we see that all Negroes
steal and are humble.... All whites are in-
herently noble and magnanimous," and even
Tom and Chambers, though exchanged, act ac-
cording to their race. The contrast with
CY strengthens the evidence that MT retained
the racial attitudes of his youth.

1969 A BOOKS

A1 CLEMENS, SAMUEL L. Clemens of the "Call":
Mark Twain in San Francisco, ed. Edgar M.
Branch. Berkeley and Los Angeles: University of California Press.
A selection of 200 contributions by MT
during his four months' employment on the
San Francisco Daily Morning Call in 1864;
arranged topically rather than chronologically.

A2 _____. Mark Twain's Correspondence with Henry
Huttleston Rogers, 1893-1909, ed. Lewis
Leary. Berkeley and Los Angeles: University
of California Press.
A volume in the CEAA edition of the MT
Papers. Continues the account of MT's business affairs from where Hamlin Hill left it
in Mark Twain's Letters to His Publishers,
1867-1894 (1967), and also "illuminates a
friendship which Clemens came to value
above all others, and...suggests a profound
change in his patterns of living," from that
of family man to a life more like that of
the California and Nevada days, as "a man
among sporting men."

A3 _____. Mark Twain's Hannibal, Huck & Tom,
ed. Walter Blair. Berkeley and Los Angeles:
University of California Press.
A volume in the CEAA edition of the MT
Papers, consisting of unpublished material
on Hannibal and the villagers, and manu-
script material dealing with Huck and Tom;
includes the texts of Huck Finn and Tom
Sawyer Among the Indians, and Tom Sawyer:
A Play.

A4 _____. Mark Twain's Mysterious Stranger Manuscripts, ed. William M. Gibson. Berkeley and Los Angeles: University of California Press.

A volume in the CEAA edition of the MT Papers. Presents, meticulously edited, the texts of the manuscript material from which Albert Bigelow Paine and Frederick A. Duneka assembled their "editorial fraud," the 1916 edition of MS.

A5 ENSOR, ALLISON. Mark Twain and the Bible. Lexington: University of Kentucky Press.

MT knew the Bible well, "raged against it as wicked, obscene, and damnatory; but he could never ignore it.... It has often been recognized that Twain was more influenced by the Bible than by any other book and that he drew upon it uniquely for ideas, subjects, and imagery.... During two periods of his life he made extensive use of it: in his Quaker City excursion to the Holy Land and his courtship of Olivia Langdon, roughly 1867-1870, and in the final years of his life, roughly 1893-1909, when biblical fantasies and criticism flowed freely from his pen" (pp. 1-2). Reviews are summarized by Elmer F. Suderman in ALA, IV (June, 1971), 117-18.

A6 SCOTT, ARTHUR L. Mark Twain at Large. Chicago: Henry Regnery Company.

"This book is about Mark Twain's travels and his opinions concerning the entire foreign scene. The fun-loving Westerner of 1867 slowly grew into the international personage of 1897.... He had not become global in his fame without becoming global in his thinking as well. And because Mark Twain symbolized the American spirit to millions of people the world over, his voice seemed truly to be that of an unofficial Ambassador.... How Mark Twain became such an Ambassador-at-Large and finally a kind of oracle and how he served in these capacities are the subjects of the present study" (Preface, vii).

A7 SELBY, P. O. Chronology of the Life of Mark Twain. Kirksville: Missouriana Library, Northeast Missouri State College.

Lists a number of events in MT's life and publications of works, by dates. The sources are in a list at the end, and include familiar works on MT, but sources for individual dates are not given. [Mimeographed 67-page pamphlet.]

A8 _____. Mark Twain Namesakes and Memorials. Kirksville: Missouriana Library, Northeast Missouri State College.

A letter received from Dr. Selby explains the method of compilation: "To make a list of Mark Twain's namesakes and memorials, I wrote to superintendents of public instruction in the various states to get information about schools named for Mark Twain.

I examined city directories in a hundred cities to see where the name Mark Twain was being used. And I have visited Hannibal, Hartford, Redding, Elmira, and Jackass Hill, where he lived." [Mimeographed 5-page pamphlet.]

A9 WALKER, FRANKLIN. San Francisco's Literary Frontier. Seattle and London: University of Washington Press.

The 1939 edition, with corrections and a new introduction by the author. On MT in California and Nevada, his travels, and his later writings, passim (indexed).

A10 WILSON, WILLARD. Mark Twain Returns to Hawaii. Honolulu: University of Hawaii Press.

Contains facsimile reproductions of MT letters to Gilder (July 8, 1900) and to Frank E. Bliss (February 2, 1900, about the forthcoming uniform edition of his works, and the importance of having Brander Matthews do the "re-arranging"). The "return" consisted of the acquisition of these two letters and a first edition of TS. [15-page pamphlet.]

1969 B SHORTER WRITINGS

B1 ALLEN, WALTER. The Urgent West: The American Dream and Modern Man. New York: E. P. Dutton & Co., Inc., pp. 168-79 and passim.

MT brought native American speech to literature, preparing the way for writers who have followed. He was influenced by Calvinism, his mother, and his wife (whose literary influence was negative), but in HF he wrote "the classic of boyhood everywhere. It dramatises every man's dream of freedom" (p. 172). "Huck's sweetness of mind and common sense, which is the product of seeing truly, irradiate the book. He is, in fact, that rarest of characters in fiction, the human being who convinces us as being positively good" (p. 177).

B2 ANDERSON, KENNETH. "The Ending of Mark Twain's A Connecticut Yankee in King Arthur's Court," Mark Twain Journal, XIV (Summer), 21.

As a metaphor, the ending can be taken as a statement of "an unknown character (fate, determinism, or something in human nature) which works against human aspirations and thereby corrupts and destroys them." "On an artistic level, the melodramatic ending ...fails to provide the reader with the author's ultimate judgment of Hank Morgan," who appears as both liberator and dictator, the dichotomy making him an ultimately tragic figure, "but the nature and intensity of that tragedy are never defined."

B3 ANON. "Clemens, S. L.," in American Literature Abstracts, II (June), 250-53 (also includes a survey by Warren B. Benson of reviews of Krause, Mark Twain as Critic [1967], 337-39); III (December), 21-23.

(ANON.)
Abstracts of several journal articles on
MT; the abstracts are longer than in the
present bibliography and a number of them
are by the authors themselves.

B4   ANON. "'Huck Finn' Banned from Reading List,"
Philadelphia Evening Bulletin, January 15,
p. 12.
An Associated Press dispatch on the dropping of HF from the required reading list
at Miami Dade Junior College, Florida because of complaints by Black students.

B5   ANON. "Mark Twain Items Published Elsewhere,"
Twainian, XXVIII (January-February), 1-4;
(March-April), 4.
Reprints a number of abstracts of material about MT or mentioning him in passing,
from AES, XI (1968) and three from AES, X
(1967). Abstracts in AES, XIV (1970-1971),
593, 594.

B6   ANON. "Samuel L(anghorne) Clemens (1835-
1910), (Mark Twain)," in The American Writer
in England: An Exhibition Arranged in Honor
of the Sesquicentennial of the University of
Virginia, with a Foreword by Gordon N. Ray
and an Introduction by C. Waller Barrett
(Charlottesville: The University Press of
Virginia), pp. 69-75.
A list of some first editions, inscrip-
tions, text of a previously unpublished
letter inviting Charles Kingsley and his
family for a visit (February 13, 1874), and
reproductions of a caricature of MT by
"Fudge" and an oil portrait of him in his
Oxford robe by Mrs. Edward A. Ward.

B7   BABCOCK, C. MERTON. "'Dusting Off' Mark
Twain, the Incorrigible," New England Galaxy (Old Sturbridge, Inc., Sturbridge,
Massachusetts), XXX (Winter), 3-8.
A popular account of MT's courting Olivia
Langdon, and her later trials with his profanity and her editing of his manuscripts;
undocumented, this adds nothing to material
available from familiar sources.

B8   BANTA, MARTHA. "Rebirth or Revenge: The End-
ings of Huckleberry Finn and The American,"
Modern Fiction Studies, XV (Summer),
191-207.
"Huck Finn and Christopher Newman meet
head-on with the forces of conscience well
past mid-way in their quests," and neither
heaven nor Claire de Cintré is a real loss;
both heroes make the decisions that result
in personal satisfaction. Abstract in AES,
XIII (1969-70), 2075; reprinted in Twainian,
XXX (January-February, 1971). Abstract by
Banta in ALA, III (December), 21.

B9   BARSNESS, JOHN A. "Platform Manner in the
Novel: A View from the Pit," Midcontinent
American Studies Journal, X (Fall), 49-56.
MT's early works reveal the style of the

platform, often with "scarcely any change
from the lecture to the printed page"; consciousness of the created persona continues
in HF, CY, MS, and other works. Abstract
by Barsness in ALA, IV (December, 1970), 22.

B10   BIRCHFIELD, JAMES. "Jim's Coat of Arms,"
Mark Twain Journal, XIV (Summer), 15-16.
MT's criticism of romantic foolishness appears often in HF, where the wrecked steamboat is named the Walter Scott, and Tom and
Huck both display "unlikely bits of historical and antiquarian book learning." Tom
Sawyer's confused description of a coat of
arms shows him "possessed by the aristocratic delusions which infect the South...fasci-
nated by the ceremony, the trappings and ex-
ternalities of the chivalric code"; Huck,
on the other hand, thinks of the old nobility as "regular rapscallions."

B11   BRADBURY, MALCOLM. "Mark Twain in the Gilded
Age," Critical Quarterly, XI (Spring),
65-73.
Surveys recent criticism of MT and takes
issue with the excessive emphasis on psychology; describes MT as "very much at the
centre of the Gilded Age, in all its ener-
gies and contradictions, and he is surely
very much made by the literary and professional opportunities it threw up--for, like
Dickens, Twain very much created himself
against a newly emerging audience." Abstract in AES, XIII (1969-1970), 1024; reprinted in Twainian, XIX (January-February,
1970). Abstract by Bradbury in ALA, III
(December), 21-22.

B12   BRANCH, EDGAR M. "Mark Twain Reports the
Races in Sacramento," Huntington Library
Quarterly, XXXII (February), 179-86.
On MT's attendance at the Thirteenth Annual Fair of the California State Agricultural Society, with reprinted passages from
the Sacramento Daily Union of September 13
and 14, 1866; though unsigned, they "have
the familiar ring of Mark Twain's early manner and the stamp of his imagination."

B13   BUNGERT, HANS. [Review: Bernard Poli, Mark
Twain, Écrivain de l'Ouest: Régionalisme
et Humour (1965).] Archiv für das Studium
der neuren Sprachen und Literatur, CCV,
405-407.
Notes Poli's contention that Hannibal,
Virginia City, and the Mississippi are central to MT's best work, and that it was between 1870 and 1885 that his great work was
possible. [In German.]

B14   *BUTCHER, PHILIP. "'The God-fathership' of A
Connecticut Yankee," College Language Asso-
ciation Journal, XII (March), 189-98.
[Source: MHRA Annual Bibliography (1969),
Nos. 6358, 7929.
A lengthy abstract by Butcher in ALA, III
(December), 22 says that the inspiration was

(BUTCHER, PHILIP)
considerably broader than George Washington Cable's giving him a copy of Malory's Morte D'Arthur, as Cable claimed after MT's death (later supported by Paine). Citing notebook entries, Butcher concedes that MT indeed drew on Malory, but also on "articles on contemporary Russia and a book on slavery in the United States.... So conscious was he of the multitude of influences that helped to shape his book and so disenchanted did he become with Cable that he refrained from conferring on him in public the honor of 'the godfathership.'"] Also abstracted in AES, XIX (1975-1976), 236.

B15 _____. "Mark Twain's Installment on the National Debt," Southern Literary Journal, I (Spring), 48-55.
On MT's concern over the injustice done Negroes by slavery and racism; traces the career of Warner Thornton McGuinn, whose expenses he paid at Yale Law School.

B16 CARSON, HERBERT L. "Mark Twain's Misanthropy," Cresset, XXXIII (December), 13-15.
"According to Twain, all of mankind is sick, and that sickness is his normal condition." MT had something of Huck's sensitivity, but the sheltered world of the raft could not last.

B17 CECIL, L. MOFFITT. "Tom Sawyer: Missouri Robin Hood," Western American Literature, IV (Summer), 125-31.
Like Robin Hood, Tom successfully stands against the establishment (p. 130). "Tom Sawyer is a better book, a truer book, than The Mysterious Stranger. It is Mark Twain's happiest and most hopeful novel" (p. 131). Abstract in AES, XV (1971-1972), 536; reprinted in Twainian, XXXII (January-February, 1973). Abstract by Cecil in ALA, III (June, 1970), 113-14.

B18 CHELLIS, BARBARA A. "Those Extraordinary Twins: Negroes and Whites," American Quarterly, XXI (Spring), 100-12.
On racial themes in Pudd'nhead Wilson: the real Tom Driscoll, though completely white, acquired all the characteristics of a slave from his twenty-three years of slavery, while Valet de Chambers, taking his place, learned hatred of the Negro. Roxy, though a slave, has learned the values of the community and she largely accepts them. Abstract by Chellis in ALA, III (December), 22.

B19 COARD, ROBERT L. "Huck Finn and Mr. Mark Twain Rhyme," Midwest Quarterly, X (July), 317-29.
"A study of Huck Finn's rhymes, placed in the larger context of Mark Twain's rhymes in his other prose, should shed considerable light on the exuberant word-play that, perhaps as much as any unified theme,

helped to shape an American masterpiece." Abstract by Coard in ALA, III (June, 1970), 114.

B20 [DAVIS, CHESTER L.] "Life, Letters and Journals of George Ticknor," Twainian, XXVIII (January-February), 4; (March-April), 1-4; (May-June), 1-4; (July-August), 1-4; (September-October), 1-4; (November-December), 1-4.
Continues a series of MT's underlinings and marginal annotations in this two-volume work; series begins July-August, 1968. Abstracts in AES, XIV (1970-1971), 586-592; reprinted in Twainian, XXXI (January-February, 1972).

B21 DUCKETT, MARGARET. [Review: Fred W. Lorch, The Trouble Begins at Eight (1868).] Western Humanities Review, XXIII (Summer), 175-76.
Lorch is justified in asserting that MT was one of the most successful of American lecturers and that he owed his fame more to his lectures than to his writing. Although this book covers much the same ground as Fatout's Mark Twain on the Lecture Circuit (1960), uses the same sources, and reaches similar conclusions, the focus here is on "physical appearance, mannerisms, voice inflection, and carefully calculated emphases and pauses." Structural weaknesses in the book lead to repetitiousness, but the reworking of old ground has produced "valuable nuggets."

B22 ENSOR, ALLISON R. "The Birthplace of Samuel Clemens: A New Mark Twain Letter," Tennessee Studies in Literature, XIV, 31-34.
Text of MT's note to George H. Morgan (December 16, 1882), correcting the story told in Tennessee that he was born in either Gainesboro or Jamestown, Tennessee, rather than Florida, Missouri; MT enclosed a reprint of a biographical sketch from the British reference work, The Men of the Time. Abstract by Ensor in MLA Abstracts (1970), 6774.

B23 _____. "The Location of the Phelps Farm in Huckleberry Finn," South Atlantic Bulletin, XXXIV (May), 7.
After summarizing guesses by various scholars, concludes "that Pikesville and the Phelps farm are located in the extreme southeastern part of Arkansas," citing MT's Autobiography and TS, Detective. Abstract in AES, XV (1971-1972), 3022; reprinted in Twainian, XXXII (January-February, 1973).

B24 FREDERICK, JOHN T. "Mark Twain," in his The Darkened Sky: Nineteenth-Century American Novelists and Religion (Notre Dame, London: University of Notre Dame Press), pp. 123-76.
"Closely examined...the evidence fails to support the legend that Calvinism had a traumatic impact on Mark Twain in childhood" (p. 129).

B25   GARDNER, JOSEPH H. "Mark Twain and Dickens,"
      Publications of the Modern Language Associ-
      ation, LXXXIV (January), 90-101.
            Traces a thorough familiarity with Dick-
      ens from MT's youth; fear of him as a rival
      made MT reluctant to praise Dickens or ex-
      press critical judgments. Abstract in AES,
      XIII (1969-70), 229 (condensed from Gard-
      ner's own abstract on contents page); re-
      printed in Twainian, XXIX (January-February,
      1970).

B26   GIBSON, WILLIAM M. [Review: Fred W. Lorch,
      The Trouble Begins at Eight: Mark Twain's
      Lecture Tours (1968).] American Litera-
      ture, XLI (November), 440-41.
            Lorch wrote this book independently of
      Fatout's Mark Twain on the Lecture Circuit
      (1960), "a more truly critical work"; but
      the two books are complementary. "Lorch
      is interesting...for a group of analytic
      concluding chapters on platform manners
      and techniques, the vexed question of sub-
      stance versus manner, good and bad audi-
      ences, and profits," and he has reconstruct-
      ed texts of tour lectures from various news-
      paper sources.

B27   GLICK, WENDELL. "The Epistomelogical Theme
      of The Mysterious Stranger," in Ray B.
      Browne and Donald Pizer, eds. Themes and
      Directions in American Literature (West
      Lafayette, Indiana: Purdue University
      Studies), pp. 130-47.
            "The bitterness...derives, not so much
      from Twain's conviction that man is irra-
      tional, as from Twain's impatience with
      man's presumption that he is not" (p. 130).
      "To argue as this paper does that Twain's
      theme is the ubiquitous twentieth century
      idea of the breakdown of epistomelogical
      certainty is to argue for a continuity in
      Twain's thought between The Adventures of
      Huckleberry Finn and The Mysterious Strang-
      er and for the emergence of similar episto-
      melogical themes in the two works" (p. 131).

B28   GREENAGEL, FRANK J. [Review: Dewey Ganzel,
      Mark Twain Abroad: The Cruise of the
      "Quaker City."] Quarterly Journal of
      Speech, LV (April), 204.
            "The reconstruction of the journey is
      thorough, and only occasionally tedious,"
      although MT never comes to life. The in-
      fluence of Mary Mason Fairbanks is treated
      with unusual perception, and there is good
      analysis of MT's use of guidebooks, "al-
      though Ganzel curiously omitted any dis-
      cussion of two apparent sources [not here
      identified] of Twain's often-quoted descrip-
      tion of the Sphinx."

B29   *GREGORY, RALPH. "John A. Quarles: Mark
      Twain's Ideal Man," Missouri Historical
      Society Bulletin, XXV (April), 229-35.
            On the influence of the uncle with whom
      MT spent two or three months a year, as a
      boy. Quarles was known for his freethink-

ing and story-telling, and may even have
been a source for the "Jumping Frog."
[Source: Abstract in AES, XVI (1972-1973),
1773; reprinted in Twainian, XXXIII (January-February, 1974.)]

B30   HARWOOD, C. EDWIN. "Twain's Huckleberry Finn,
      Chapter XIV," Explicator, XXVIII (December),
      Item 36.
            The debate between Huck and Jim on why a
      Frenchman speaks French is "no digression
      at all but an ingenious statement of a main
      theme of the book...the brotherhood of man."
      The insight revealing the point was that of
      Miss Laura Helton, while writing an examina-
      tion.

B31   HILFER, ANTHONY CHANNELL. "Mark Twain: The
      Southwest and the Satirist," in his The
      Revolt from the Village 1915-1930 (Chapel
      Hill: The University of North Carolina
      Press), pp. 64-83.
            "Twain's conception is that what holds
      the small town together is communal fear....
      No later writer surpassed the ferocity of
      Twain's assault on the conformist mass
      mind" (p. 83). Hilfer shows complete fam-
      iliarity with the work of Neider, Brooks,
      DeVoto, Kaplan, and other students of Mark
      Twain, but adds comparatively little to
      this secondary material.

B32   HILL, HAMLIN. "Mark Twain," in J. Albert
      Robbins, ed., American Literary Scholarship:
      An Annual/1969 (Durham, North Carolina:
      Duke University Press, 1971), pp. 77-88.
            A survey of MT scholarship for the year,
      begun by John C. Gerber in 1963.B32 and con-
      tinued by him through coverage for 1968.
      Contents: "i. Textual and Bibliographical";
      "ii. Biography"; "iii. General Criticism";
      "iv. Earlier Works"; "v. Huckleberry Finn";
      "vi. Later Works." [Contains material not
      listed in the present bibliography.]

B33   _____. [Review: Leah A. Strong, Joseph Hop-
      kins Twichell: Mark Twain's Friend and
      Pastor (1967).] American Literary Realism,
      1867-1910, I (Spring), 97-98.
            "Miss Strong's bibliographical record is
      scanty. She ignores a multitude of histori-
      cal information published since she first
      explored this topic in her 1953 doctoral
      dissertation. No use whatsoever is made of
      the Mark Twain-Howells Letters, for example,
      nor of the unpublished storehouse in the
      Mark Twain Papers at Berkeley. Although
      the Yale University holdings of Twichell
      papers (which includes seventy letters from
      Twain to Twichell) are included in the bib-
      liography, no quotation, paraphrase, or
      reference is made based upon them." The
      evidence that Twichell influenced MT's
      writing is tenuous at best, and in any case
      "if the friendship between Twain and Twich-
      ell deserves study, it is for biographical
      and psychological reasons, not literary
      ones."

B34 HOFFMANN, MICHAEL J. "Huck's Ironic Circle," Georgia Review, XXIII (Fall), 307-22.
    HF "is not a novel about a boy's moral awakening, nor a polemic against slavery, nor a book about how good instincts are stronger than an evil society. We have always overestimated Huck Finn and have likewise underestimated his creator.... The dynamic theme that runs throughout Huckleberry Finn is an unresolved dialectic between the moral responsibility of the individual and the morality of the society in which he moves and against which he must function." Huck does not share the perceptiveness of MT and the reader; he never truly learns to regard Jim as an equal, but believes in property rights and the institution of slavery, and he follows the leadership of Tom Sawyer. The ending is consistent with this unimaginative Huck: "The irony of the book has now come full circle in that Huck has not rejected society's standards at all. He just feels personally inconvenienced by things like school, and clothes. But he still believes just as strongly that society is right."

B35 JAMES, STUART B. "The Politics of Personal Salvation: The American Literary Record," Denver Quarterly, IV (Autumn), 19-45.
    On Huck Finn as "another Tocquevillean democrat...yet another American fictional character at odds with and fleeing from the culture in which he grew up. But when we ask the question, What are his responsibilities to this culture, we hit a snag," because of its nature as a brutalizing, slave-holding society. There is a danger however, that such portraits of society by MT and others will breed in the young contempt for all laws and encourage the "very idealistic and self-righteous role of the Holy Revolutionary"; Huck's answer was to escape, deserting Jim (pp. 34-39). Abstract in AES, XIII (1969-1970), 2734; reprinted in Twainian, XXX (January-February, 1971).

B36 KAHN, SHOLOM J. "The Real Mark Twain: School of Tuckey," Jahrbuch für Amerikastudien, XIV, 301-307.
    A review-article, on Hamlin Hill, ed., Mark Twain's Letters to His Publishers, 1867-1894 (1967); Franklin A. Rogers, ed., Mark Twain's Satires and Burlesques (1967); John S. Tuckey, ed., Mark Twain's "Which Was the Dream?" (1967). Contains comparatively little on the editing and criticism, though hailing Tuckey's volume as the most important of the three: "What not enough of the Mark Twain scholars seem to realize is that Tuckey's findings render obsolete most of the earlier criticisms of The Mysterious Stranger and other later writings." Kahn's main emphasis is on MT's works, as here revealed and as seen by the critics; publication of full and reliable editions of MT will force reassessment, and Tuckey does much to point the way.

B37 KAPLAN, JUSTIN. "Never Quite Sane in the Night," Psychoanalytic Review, LVI (Spring), 113-27.
    On MT's self-castigation, given focus by the death of his daughter Susan. [From Chapter XVI of the 1968 Pocket Book edition of Mr. Clemens and Mark Twain, pp. 396-412.]

B38 KIRKHAM, E. BRUCE. "Huck and Hamlet: An Examination of Twain's Use of Shakespeare," Mark Twain Journal, XIV (Summer), 17-19.
    The Duke's speech in Chapter XXI combines garbled lines from Hamlet and Macbeth, in which "indecision...prevents Hamlet from acting when he should and keeps Macbeth from acting when he shouldn't," and from Richard III, in which Richard acts without regard for moral questions. As a confidence man, the Duke "is required to have the ability to shift ground on a moment's notice and channel his activities in another vein," and he is a man of action, in contrast to the passive Huck. "It is ironic that a man with his moral character on the raft should give the very moral advice that Huck, the innocent aboard, most needs," but "after Huck has heard and memorized the speech on action from 'Hamlet,' after he has seen the Duke operate on the Wilkses and Jim sold into slavery again, he...rebels against his environment...and says he will 'go to work and steal Jim out of slavery again.'"

B39 KOLB, HAROLD H., JR. The Illusion of Life: American Realism as a Literary Form. Charlottesville: The University Press of Virginia, passim.
    On realism in the works of MT, Howells, and Henry James. The extensive listing of MT in the index includes such topics as point of view, author-narrator, complexity, ambiguity, morality, and Huck's pragmatism and his freedom.

B40 KRUSE, HORST H. "'Gatsby' and 'Gadsby,'" Modern Fiction Studies, XV (Winter), 539-41.
    The name "Gatsby" may derive from a Washington, D.C. hotel-owner named "Gadsby" in TA; "Although there is no direct evidence that Fitzgerald read A Tramp Abroad," he is known to have been "a lifelong admirer of Mark Twain."

B41 LEHAN, RICHARD. [Review: Dewey Ganzel, Mark Twain Abroad (1968); Sydney J. Krause, Mark Twain as Critic (1967); and Fred W. Lorch, The Trouble Begins at Eight (1968).] Nineteenth-Century Fiction, XXIV (December), 377.
    Brief and descriptive, with a short commendation of the usefulness of each book.

B42 LONG, ROBERT EMMET. [Review: Lewis Leary, ed., Mark Twain's Correspondence with Henry Huttleston Rogers; Walter Blair, ed., Mark Twain's Hannibal, Huck & Tom; William M. Gibson, ed., Mark Twain's Mysterious Stranger Manuscripts.] Saturday Review, LII (June 21), 49-50.

(LONG, ROBERT EMMET)
"One has the impression...that this edition answers a need for enlarged information about its subject, but that there is nothing about it to suggest an urgency such as to pre-empt the editions of American authors proposed by Edmund Wilson." [See Wilson's "The Fruits of the MLA," 1968.] The three volumes are described, favorably, but "the scholarship that went into them is far more impressive than the revelations they contain."

B43 M McELDERRY, BRUCE R., JR. [Review: James Playstead Wood, Spunkwater, Spunkwater! A Life of Mark Twain (1968).] Modern Fiction Studies, XV (Winter), 554.
"A commendable simplification...as the younger reader proceeds to a mature interest in the author, there is little that he will have to unlearn. In fact, the scholar may spend a pleasant hour with this volume."

B44 MARTIN, JAY. "Mark Twain: The Fate of Primitivity," Southern Literary Journal, II (Fall), 123-37.
A review article, covering Walter Blair, ed., Mark Twain's Hannibal, Huck & Tom (briefly described); William M. Gibson, ed., Mark Twain's Mysterious Stranger Manuscripts (briefly described); Allison R. Ensor, Mark Twain and the Bible ("Ensor writes well and almost entirely avoids the pedantry which such studies threaten," but he misunderstands MT's awareness that unorthodoxy was a saleable commodity); Lewis Leary, ed., Mark Twain's Correspondence with Henry Huttleston Rogers (described); and Arthur L. Scott, Mark Twain at Large ("A remarkably detailed account not only of Twain's travel writing but also of the special place which the non-American scene occupied in his imagination." Unfortunately, Scott over-simplifies, and "there is reason to suspect that he has not kept pace with the recent Mark Twain studies-- his notes refer to few works published after 1960--which have made his simple view an old-fashioned one.")

B45 MASEFIELD, JOHN. [Holograph note reproduced in facsimile.] Mark Twain Journal, XIV (Summer), front cover.
On his delight in HF, which he has read at least once a year since he was fourteen.

B46 MEWS, SIEGFRIED. "German Reception of American Writers in the Nineteenth Century," South Atlantic Bulletin, XXXIV (March), 7-9.
Notes MT's great popularity in Germany, chiefly as a humorist rather than as a serious writer; not documented (pp. 8-9). Abstract in AES, XV (1971-1972), 3015; reprinted in Twainian, XXXII (January-February, 1973).

B47 MILLER, HENRY. The Books in My Life. New York: New Directions, pp. 41, 318.
Lists TS and HF among books he read as a boy and longs to re-read--along with Rider Haggard, G. A. Henty, Fenimore Cooper. [An earlier ed., undated, is mentioned by Walter Blair in Mark Twain and Huck Finn (1960), pp. 7, 390.]

B48 MORSBERGER, ROBERT E. "Pap Finn and the Bishop's Candlesticks: Victor Hugo in Hannibal," CEA Critic, XXXI (April), 17.
Jim's elaborate escape at the end of HF includes several elements borrowed from Dumas: from The Man in the Iron Mask, The Count of Monte Cristo, and Twenty Years After. Less evident is the conversion and downfall of Pap Finn, patterned on the conversion of Jean Valjean in Les Miserables. These incidents in HF parody their romantic models.

B49 *NAGEL, JAMES. "Huck Finn and The Bear: The Wilderness and Moral Freedom," English Studies in Africa, XII (March), 59-63.
Each work pairs an adult male with a young white boy, but Faulkner is less optimistic because the frontier has diminished. [Source: Abstract in AES, XIV (1970-1971), No. 1543; reprinted in Twainian, XXXI (January-February, 1972.)]

B50 ORTH, MICHAEL. "Pudd'nhead Wilson Reconsidered; or, The Octoroon in the Villa Viviani," Mark Twain Journal, XIV (Summer), 11-15.
There are numerous parallels to the octoroon fiction from before the Civil War; even the device of the fingerprints is anticipated by the use of photography in Mayne Reid's The Quadroon (1856), and its dramatization by Dion Boucicault as The Octoroon (1859), and "in both cases the accidental discovery of the true identity of a murderer comes through the novel and scientific-gadgeteering hobby of a fool Yankee, who rights all wrongs by defending the innocent in a climactic trial at the end of the story." The novel has been overpraised, but it deserves critical attention for what it shows of MT's mind and art. Abstract by Orth in ALA, III (June, 1970), 114.

B51 PARSONS, COLEMAN O. "Down the Mighty River with Mark Twain," Mississippi Quarterly, XXII (Winter), 1-18.
On MT's 1882 trip to gather material for LOM. Abstract by Parsons in ALA, III (December), 22-23.

B52 PATRICK, WALTON R. [Review: Edward Wagenknecht, Mark Twain: The Man and His Work (Third Edition, 1967), and James M. Cox, Mark Twain: The Fate of Humor (1966).] Southern Humanities Review, III (Summer), 293-95.

(PATRICK, WALTON R.)

Wagenknecht's 1935 study, "substantially revised in 1960, has already won its place among reputable commentaries on Mark Twain," and this third edition is new chiefly in the updating of its "excellent bibliography." Cox, arguing that the "Mark Twain" pseudonym exposed and freed the writer in Clemens, passes too lightly over the fact that even some of MT's humorous works are poorly written; moreover, there is insufficient evidence to support the contention that MT's humor was frequently a compensation for his failings. It often appears "that any resemblance between the Mark Twain of Mr. Cox's book and the real Mark Twain is purely coincidental."

B53   PEDERSON, LEE A. "Mark Twain's Missouri Dialects: Marion County Phonemics," American Speech, XLII (December, 1967), 261-78.

A study based on tape-recorded interviews with six Caucasian and six Negro informants in 1964, using "more than 1,300 specific items, to which I added almost 300 words and phrases from the novel" (HF); the emphasis is on description of current speech rather than with MT's representation in HF. Abstract in AES, XIV (1970-71), 1544; reprinted in Twainian, XXXI (January-February, 1972).

B54   PETERSON, CLARENCE. [Brief Review: Justin Kaplan, Mr. Clemens and Mark Twain (1968).] Book World (Chicago Tribune), I (May 12), 19.

"Justin Kaplan's great biography...is available in paperback at last.... The book is so deeply researched and so intelligent that it stands as the definitive Clemens biography and it is almost as rich and readable as Twain himself."

B55   PICKETT, CALDER M. [Review: Edgar M. Branch, Clemens of the "Call."] Journalism Quarterly, XLVII (Summer), 383-84.

Descriptive and uncritical, except for observing that "It is a valuable compilation, even though it is something rather dull and a bit inconsequential"; this is not MT's best work and Branch's language is sometimes pedantic.

B56   _____. [Review: Justin Kaplan, ed., Mark Twain: a Profile (1968) and Dewey Ganzel, Mark Twain Abroad (1968).] Journalism Quarterly, XLVI (Summer), 385-86.

"Ganzel's book is always fun, but it's not Mark Twain.... this new book becomes mere recitation of what the travelers were doing and where they were at certain times," and shows that MT wrote differently, and for a wider audience, when he revised his travel letters into IA. Kaplan's collection of essays runs from the "slashing iconoclasm" of Dwight MacDonald to the "treacly" sentimentalism of Howells. "Most

of the essays are good," especially Kaplan's at the end, but they add little to our understanding of MT.

B57   _____. [Review: Arthur L. Scott, Mark Twain at Large.] Journalism Quarterly, XLVI (Autumn), 628-29.

Brief summary. "Much has been done in recent years...on Mark Twain as world traveler-commentator. Here is one of the better books."

B58   POCHMANN, HENRY A., and GAY WILSON ALLEN. "Samuel L. Clemens (Mark Twain) (1835-1910)," in their Introduction to Masters of American Literature. Carbondale and Edwardsville: Southern Illinois University Press; London and Amsterdam: Feffer & Simons, Inc. [Copyright 1949 under the title Masters of American Literature.]

This book consists of the introductions in the two-volume anthology of 1949. The treatment of MT is a sound general discussion, and the titles of his works discussed are listed by page number in the index on p. 155.

B59   *POPA, IOAN. "Opera Nepublicată a lui Mark Twain" ["Mark Twain's Unpublished Works"], Familia, No. 5 (March), p. 15.

[Source: MHRA Annual Bibliography (1969), No. 7976.]

B60   REES, ROBERT A., and RICHARD DILWORTH RUST. "Mark Twain's 'The Turning Point of My Life,'" American Literature, XL (January), 524-35.

On MT's last work written for publication; traces the extensive revisions after MT's daughter Jean and biographer Paine gave the first version a chilly reception which "brought Twain's acute self-criticism into play and caused him to discard a mediocre piece of writing and to turn out something fine instead." As published in Harper's Bazaar it incorporated changes apparently made by editor Elizabeth Jordan to improve MT--as she did for letters of Henry James in the Bazaar. Abstract in AES, XIII (1969-1970), 1342; reprinted in Twainian, XXX (January-February, 1971).

B61   REEVES, PASCHAL, et al. "A Checklist of Scholarship on Southern Literature for 1969," Mississippi Quarterly, XXIII (Spring, 1970); on MT, pp. 189-93.

Annotated.

B62   REXROTH, KENNETH. "Mark Twain, Huckleberry Finn," in his Classics Revisited (New York: Avon Books), pp. 280-85.

"Mark Twain's judgment of that life [on shore] is very different from Homer's, and not unlike that of Saint Paul in the Book of the Acts of the Apostles--if Saint Paul had been an atheist."

B63　RUBIN, LOUIS D., JR. "Mark Twain: The Adventures of Tom Sawyer," in Hennig Cohen, ed., Landmarks of American Writing (New York, London: Basic Books, Inc.), pp. 157-71. ["These essays were originally prepared for the Voice of America for presentation as lectures to audiences abroad through its Forum series" (p. x).]

TS would have made MT a reputation even without HF, which overshadows it. The presence of the adult storyteller in TS deprives us of Huck's voice but allows MT to provide a sense of time and its passage (p. 165).

B64　RULE, HENRY B. "The Role of Satan in The Man that Corrupted Hadleyburg," Studies in Short Fiction, VI (Fall), 619-29.

Traces MT's interest in Satan, then shows Satanic parallels to the stranger in Hadleyburg "(Hadesburg?)" and possible allegorical significance of the names of characters. Ultimately, "Satan is Hadleyburg's greatest benefactor," purging the town of hypocrisy. Abstract in AES, XIV (1970-1971), 1835; reprinted in Twainian, XXXI (January-February, 1972).

B65　SCOTT, ARTHUR L. [Review: Dewey Ganzel, Mark Twain Abroad: The Cruise of the "Quaker City" (1968).] American Literature, XLI (March), 124-25.

"A charming, informative volume, carefully researched and presented in an easy descriptive manner," useful both as an account of the trip and the passengers and for correcting misconceptions in the Paine biography and in studies of IA.

B66　SEELYE, JOHN. "'De Ole True Huck': An Introduction," Tri-Quarterly, XVI (Autumn), 5-19.

The introduction and the final chapters of Seelye's The True Adventures of Huckleberry Finn (1970). In the introduction Seelye summarizes objections to MT's HF by librarians, pressure groups, and critics; this version will retell the story as the "crickits" would have it. Abstract in AES, XV (1971-72), 2144.

B67　SPANGLER, GEORGE M. "Locating Hadleyburg," Mark Twain Journal, XIV (Summer), 20.

The theme of the story is not a Miltonic echo that untried virtue is meaningless; rather, "the tale demonstrates the distressingly crude proposition that all men have their price," and the real target is Gilded Age America. Abstract by Spangler in ALA, III (June, 1970), 114-15.

B68　SPENCER, BENJAMIN T. "Sherwood Anderson: American Mythopoetist," American Literature, XLI (March), 1-18.

Passing references to MT, pp. 4-6, noting the statements in Dark Laughter of regret that MT's America stunted his literary development and that his moving to the genteel East was an acquiescence. Abstract in AES,

XIII (1969-1970), 1365; reprinted in Twainian, XXX (January-February, 1971).

B69　STANDART, PHOEBE. "Introduction," in Your Personal Mark Twain: In Which the Great American Ventures an Opinion on Ladies, Language, Liberty, Literature, Liquor, Love, and Other Controversial Subjects (New York: International Publishers, and Berlin (D.D.R.): Seven Seas Books), pp. 9-14.

An East German anthology of short pieces by MT and selections from his works, very few of them with any political overtones whatever and none of them especially startling. Phoebe Standart's introduction stresses his personal humor and warmth, commenting only in passing on his social criticism. [In English.]

B70　*STARTSEV, A. [Introductory article to Russian translation of "The United Lynching States" ("The United States of Lyncherdom").] Moscow: Khudozhestvennaya Literatura.

[Source: MHRA Annual Bibliography (1970), No. 8284.]

B71　STERN, MADELEINE B. "Mark Twain Had His Head Examined," American Literature, XLI (May), 207-18.

On a phrenological examination of MT in 1901, probably by Dr. Edgar C. Beall, described in the Phrenological Journal and Science of Health, CXI (April, 1901), 103-106; following MT's death the Phrenological Journal paid tribute to his character as revealed in "the organs of Mirthfulness, Comparison, Combativeness, Benevolence, and Human Nature" [CXXIII (June, 1910), 190]. Both articles are here reprinted. Abstract in AES, XIII (1969-1970), 1345; reprinted in Twainian, XXX (January-February, 1971. Abstract by Stern in ALA, III (December), 23.

B72　STESSIN, LAWRENCE. "The Businessman in Fiction," Literary Review (Fairleigh Dickinson University), XII (Spring), 281-89.

A Professor of Management, Stessin complains against frequently unsympathetic portrayals and praises CY as an exception, "an imaginative chronicle in which the glorified days of knight errantry are exposed as a form of childish barbarism. Beneath a layer of wonderful wit, Twain defends the cause that a society which is not business and technology oriented leaves its people abused and impoverished.... Using the 4-M's of management--money, men, materials, and motivation--his protagonist, Hank Morgan, galvanizes the backward nation into a beehive of builders, whose collective handiwork appreciably raises the standard of living.... Hank Morgan anticipates the rise of the new professional manager who takes textbook examples of good management--direction, coordination, delegation, staffing, and control--and unifies them to bring both material and social wealth to society." Abstract in AES, XV (1971-72), 2243; reprinted in Twainian, XXXII (January-February, 1973).

B73 *SYKES, MADELENE McEUEN. "Mark Twain's Atti-
tudes Toward Women as Revealed Through His
Writings," Missouri English Bulletin, XXII
(May), 1-9.
[Source: MHRA Annual Bibliography
(1969), No. 7991.]

B74 TUCKEY, JOHN S. [Review: Fred W. Lorch, The
Trouble Begins at Eight (1968).] Journal
of Popular Culture, III (Summer), 172-74.
Compares Lorch's book with Paul Fatout's
Mark Twain on the Lecture Circuit. Lorch
provides the "comprehensive, unified discussion of the celebrated humorist's platform art, his theory of the humorous lecture, his theory and practice of the art of
reading, [and] the major critical apprais-
als of Mark Twain's lectures" which his review in American Literature (1962) accused
Fatout of neglecting. Tuckey notes the
value of this material, but also praises
"Mr. Fatout's more chronological and better
integrated narrative presentation." This
new book "does not supersede it," although
it "comes off very well as what it was intended to be, Fred Lorch's major contribution." Tuckey observes that Lorch mentions
Fatout's works in the bibliography but not
in his notes.

B75 *VĂLČEV, TODOR. [Introduction.] "Neugasnal
Vulkan" ["An Inextinct Volcano"], in Mark
Tven, Avtobiografija [Mark Twain's Auto-
biography]. Sofia: Narodna Mladež,
pp. 5-10.
[Source: MHRA Annual Bibliography
(1969), No. 7994.]

B76 VITELLI, JAMES R. Van Wyck Brooks. New
York: Twayne Publishers, Inc., pp. 38,
87-95, 113, and passim.
Mentions the attempt by Randolph Bourne
to persuade Brooks to revise his view of
American writers, and of MT in particular
(p. 38). On The Ordeal of Mark Twain,
pp. 87-95.

B77 WHITE, RAY LEWIS, ed. Sherwood Anderson's
Memoirs: A Critical Edition. Chapel Hill:
The University of North Carolina Press.
Passim on MT (indexed), whom Anderson
admired; on p. 342, describes HF as "that
amazingly beautiful book," but notes MT's
reticence concerning sex in his books.

B78 WILLIAMSON, JERRY M. "Winslow Homer and Mark
Twain," Mark Twain Journal, XIV (Summer),
2-7.
Compares them as local colorists, in attitudes toward the Negro, and in their
artistic careers, but gives no indication
they were aware of each other.

B79 ZARASPE, RAQUEL SIMS. "The Picaresque Tradition in Mark Twain," Diliman Review (University of the Philippines, Quezon City),
XVII (July), 218-43.

"The intention of this paper is to trace
the development of the picaresque hero in
Mark Twain." Contrasts Huck Finn with Hank
Morgan, who lacks Huck's ability to form
"a more vital and enduring fraternity with
Jim and the river." Shows parallels of
Spanish character types, values, and conditions in Lazarillo de Tormes and in TS, HF,
and CY. Abstract in AES, XIV (1970-1971),
2139; reprinted in Twainian, XXXI (March-
April, 1972).

B80 *ZIL'BERBROD, B. A. "Oblichenie Monarkhii
Dollara v Publitsistike Marka Tvena. (An
accusation of a dollar monarchy in the
journalistic writings of Mark Twain.)"
Vestnik Khar'kovskogo Universiteta, 1969
[Seriya Inostrannykh Yazykov] (2), pp. 26-30.
[Source: MHRA Annual Bibliography (1970),
No. 8295.]

1970 A BOOKS

A1 BAETZHOLD, HOWARD G. Mark Twain and John Bull:
The British Connection. Bloomington and
London: Indiana University Press.
Discusses MT's many visits to England, his
popular lectures there, the influence on him
of British thought and writing, and the
shifts in the warmth of his feelings toward
things British.

A2 BLUES, THOMAS. Mark Twain & the Community.
Lexington: The University Press of Kentucky.
In GA, TS, P&P, and HF the protagonists
are committed to the community although MT
repudiates its values and stability; he was
"deeply distrustful of the character and
fearful for the fate of the individual who
attempts to triumph over the community."
CY fails because MT could no longer use this
commitment as a structural device. In developing Hank Morgan, MT "faced the fact that
the individual is in no sense the superior
of the community he triumphs over," but the
community "is in no sense a worthy refuge
for the individual" (pp. x-xi).

A3 BROWNE, RAY B., ed. and introduction. Mark
Twain's Quarrel with Heaven: "Captain
Stormfield's Visit to Heaven and other
Sketches." New Haven: College & University
Press.
An unpretentious and attractive edition
for the general reader. Also contains texts
of "The Late Reverend Sam Jones's Reception
in Heaven," "Mental Telegraphy?" "Appendix
A: Old Abe's 'Slap' at Chicago [Lincoln,
from a popular humorous collection published in 1864]": "Appendix B: Alternate
Passage [by MT, but alternate to "Stormfield," rather than to Appendix A]." There
is a good introduction (pp. 11-32) for the
reader encountering this aspect of MT's
thought for the first time.

A4   CLEMENS, SAMUEL L. Mark Twain's Letters to the Rogers Family (The Millicent Library Collection). Edited with Notes and an Introduction by Earl J. Dias. New Bedford, Massachusetts: Reynolds-DeWalt Printing, Inc.

Forty letters from MT and Olivia Clemens, plus background information on the individuals involved and the friendship of MT and Henry Rogers, and a chapter on "Mark Twain and the Millicent Library" (in Fairhaven, Massachusetts; named for the deceased daughter of Henry Rogers).

A5   GEISMAR, MAXWELL. Mark Twain: An American Prophet. Boston: Houghton Mifflin Company.

MT had "the double soul of a great artist" rather than a split personality, and he was not destroyed by materialism or censorship (pp. 4-5). "A whole area of Twain's social criticism of the United States has been repressed or avoided by Twain scholars precisely because it is so bold, so brilliant, satirical, and prophetic. He was one of the most mature American artists precisely because he had, so to speak, such a long, deep childhood" (p. 6). See Index for numerous reviews of this book, most of them hostile.

A6   GROVER, GURU DAYAL. Mark Twain: The Adventures of Huckleberry Finn (A Critical Study). Delhi, Doaba House.

A very general treatment, with no specifically Indian perspectives. "My method has been to arrive at an eclectic synthesis of several approaches to the novel, and to concentrate on a close reading of the text, and to assess whatever contributions the text itself demands from folklore, myth, ritual, biographical, and literary antecedents."

A7   *KRUSE, HORST H. Mark Twains "Life on the Mississippi": Eine Entstehungs- und Quellengeschichtliche Untersuching zu Mark Twains "Standard Work." Kieler Beiträge zur Anglistik und Amerikanistik, VIII. Neumünster: Karl Wachholz.

[Source: MLA Bibliography (1971), No. 6987 and Eichelberger review (1972.B39).]

A8   *MENDELSOHN M. Mark Tven. Erevan: Aiastan. (In Armenian,; biography for children.)

[Source: MHRA Annual Bibliography (1971), No. 8859.]

A9   SEELYE, JOHN. The True Adventures of Huckleberry Finn. Evanston, Illinois: Northwestern University Press.

A retelling of HF as the critics would like to have it, with the sex and profanity put in and a more acceptable ending provided; an amusing tour de force.

A10 *TUCKEY, JOHN S., ed. Mark Twain's "The Mysterious Stranger" and the Critics. Belmont, California: Wadsworth.

[Source: MHRA Annual Bibliography (1970), No. 8886.]

A11 WALKER, I[AN] M[ALCOLM]. Mark Twain. London: Routledge & Kegan Paul.

Extracts from MT's work, intended to introduce him to the general reader. Contains brief introduction and commentary, emphasizing his humor.

1970 B SHORTER WRITINGS

B1   ANDERSON, KENNETH. "Mark Twain, W. D. Howells, and Henry James: Three Agnostics in Search of Salvation," Mark Twain Journal, XV (Winter), 13-16.

All three believed that heaven was dubious and looked for salvation on earth; CY, A Hazard of New Fortunes, and The Ambassadors "provide three different conclusions to this quest for salvation." Abstract in AES, XIII (1969-70), 3088.

B2   ANON. "Huckleberry Jam," Time, XCV (March 2), 80.

A review of John Seelye, The True Adventures of Huckleberry Finn as "one of the best literary stunts in a long while."

B3   ANON. "Mark Twain Items Published Elsewhere," Twainian, XXIX (January-February), 1-4.

Contains a number of abstracts from AES, XII (1969) and a few from AES, XIII (1969-1970). Abstract in AES, XIV (1970-1971), 1840.

B4   *BABCOCK, C. MERTON. "Mark Twain as 'A Majority of One,'" University College Quarterly, XV (May), 3-7.

On his attitudes toward moral courage, and toward brutality and violence. [Source: Abstract in AES, XIV (1970-1971), No. 1272; reprinted in Twainian, XXXI (January-February, 1972).]

B5   _____. "Mark Twain's Chuck-Wagon Specialties," Western American Literature, V (Summer), 147-51.

MT appreciated good food, but described unappetizing concoctions in his Notebook, the Buffalo Express, TA, and "A Majestic Literary Fossil." Abstract by Babcock in ALA, IV (June, 1971), 91.

B6   BELSON, JOEL JAY. "The Nature and Consequences of the Loneliness of Huckleberry Finn," Arizona Quarterly, XXVI (Autumn), 243-48.

Huck is an outcast from a society which "by denying the rightness of every truly humane impulse he seeks to express...by convincing him of his own intellectual and moral inadequacy and by providing no approval or positive satisfactions...isolates him finally and absolutely as nature, as Twain presents it, does not do." He is a fugitive, victim, and observer, and his chief protection is concealment from an unintelligible and hostile world. Abstract

(BELSON, JOEL JAY)
in AES, XVI (1972-1973), 2053. Abstract by Belson in MLA Abstracts (1970), 6754; in ALA, IV (June, 1971), 92.

B7   BICKLEY, R. BRUCE, JR. "Humorous Portraiture in Twain's News Writing," American Literary Realism, III (Fall), 395-98.
      After listing Nevada and California papers for which MT wrote, and his varied subject matter, gives examples of portraiture in legislative and local reporting as anticipating the depiction of character in his later work. Abstract in AES, XVIII (1974-1975), 2589, with name listed as "Beckley."

B8   BOWEN, JAMES K., and RICHARD VAN DER BEETS, eds. American Literature Abstracts, III (June), 113-15; IV (December), 22-25.
      Contains sixteen abstracts by the authors of articles on MT.

B9   BUDD, LOUIS J. [Very brief, descriptive review: Lewis Leary, ed., Mark Twain's Correspondence with Henry Huttleston Rogers, 1893-1909; William M. Gibson, ed., Mark Twain's "Mysterious Stranger" Manuscripts; Walter Blair, ed., Mark Twain's Hannibal, Huck & Tom (all 1969).] South Atlantic Quarterly, LXIX (Winter), 164-65.

B10   BURNS, STUART R. "St. Petersburg Re-Visited: Helen Eustis and Mark Twain," Western American Literature, V (Summer), 99-112.
      The Fool Killer (1954) is a deliberate imitation of TS and HF. "Perhaps because she had the advantage of retrospect, Helen Eustis faces squarely the fact that Mark Twain hinted at but backed away from: that there can be no escape from society" (p. 111). Abstract in AES, XVII.(1973-1974), 2106; reprinted in Twainian, XXXIV (March-April, 1975).

B11   CARTER, PAUL J. [Review-Article: Lewis Leary, ed., Mark Twain's Correspondence with Henry Huttleston Rogers (1969); Walter Blair, ed., Mark Twain's Hannibal, Huck & Tom (1969); William M. Gibson, ed., Mark Twain's "Mysterious Stranger" Manuscripts (1969).] American Literature, XLII (March), 105-107.
      In the letters to Rogers, "unfortunately, the one-sided correspondence is dull reading," dealing largely with business matters, including "the rectification of Clemens's repeated idiocies. He is a pathetic figure" as his dreams fail "and his family life shatters; the letters are full of his illnesses, despair, and self-pity. But there are occasional bits of humor and of good companionship." "Walter Blair shows us Mark Twain struggling to exploit the 'Matter of Hannibal'.... These are flawed pieces, interesting primarily as illustrations of the author's personality and method

of composition, although they do serve to refute the view that Clemens in this period was interested only in sales." Gibson's edition of the MS material "reveals glaringly the extent of the bowdlerization of the edition put together by Albert B. Paine and Frederick A. Duneka," who, nonetheless, "did make use of the best material in the manuscripts, including the only ending.... The student will have rich hunting in the fragments."

B12   CHAMBLISS, AMY. "The Friendship of Helen Keller and Mark Twain," Georgia Review, XXIV (Fall), 305-10.
      When Helen Keller met MT she was 14, the age of Jean Clemens. MT admired her character and talents, and persuaded Henry Rogers to sponsor her. Their friendship and correspondence are heart-warming. Abstract in AES, XIV (1970-1971), 3162; reprinted in Twainian, XXXI (March-April, 1972). Abstract by Chambliss in MLA Abstracts (1970), 6764.

B13   COBURN, MARK D. "'Training is Everything': Communal Opinion and the Individual in Pudd'nhead Wilson," Modern Language Quarterly, XXXI (June), 209-19.
      Wilson shares the town's views on "the rightness of slavery, the supremacy of white men, and the glory of the code duello," and "his desire to be a 'person of consequence' in the town is as strong as that of any other character"; conditioned by the same antebellum society that formed his neighbors, he sees truths of his own only in the calendar entries. Abstract in AES, XVI (1972-73), 536; reprinted in Twainian, XXXIII (January-February, 1974). Abstract by Coburn in MLA Abstracts (1970), 6768.

B14   COOK, DORIS E. Sherlock Holmes and Much More; or, Some of the Facts about William Gillette. Hartford: The Connecticut Historical Society.
      On Gillette in the GA play, pp. 12-13; on MT's part in bringing the play, The Professor, to the New York stage, pp. 19-20; living at Nook Farm in Hartford, p. 32; rejecting MT sketches as material for a radio series in 1935, pp. 87-88.

B15   COPLIN, KEITH. "John and Sam Clemens: A Father's Influence," Mark Twain Journal, XV (Winter), 1-6.
      The father-figures in MT's major novels are almost all failures, either weak and ineffectual or tyrannical and overpowering (the discussion emphasizes TS and HF). The reasons can be traced back to MT's own cold, austere father, whose integrity and authority he respected but toward whom he felt basically hostile. This essay is heavily indebted to secondary material. Abstract in AES, XIII (1969-1970), 3089.

B16 COX, JAMES M. "Mark Twain's Mysterious Stranger," Virginia Quarterly Review, XLVI (Winter), 144-50.

A review-article on Walter Blair, ed., Mark Twain's Hannibal, Huck & Tom; William M. Gibson, ed., Mark Twain's "Mysterious Stranger" Manuscripts; Lewis Leary, ed., Mark Twain's Correspondence with Henry Huttleston Rogers (all 1969). After praising the editing of all three, Cox goes on to a discussion of the periods they cover in MT's life.

B17 ____. "Toward Vernacular Humor," Virginia Quarterly Review, XLVI (Spring), 311-330.

A discussion chiefly in terms of MT's HF, and Ring Lardner and J. D. Salinger. Extensive abstract in AES, XIV (1970-1971), 2611; reprinted in Twainian, XXXI (March-April, 1972).

B18 DAVIS, CHESTER L. "'Harper's New Monthly Magazine,' May, 1896, No. 552 (Article by Joseph H. Twichell)," Twainian, XXIX (September-October), 1-4; November-December), 1-3.

Describes the issue of Harper's, with comments on advertisements, other articles, etc., and quotes long passages from Twichell's article (1896.B13). Abstracts in AES, XV (1971-1972), 1509, 1510; reprinted in Twainian, XXXII (January-February, 1973).

B19 ____. "Life, Letters and Journals of George Ticknor," Twainian, XXIX (January-February), 4; (March-April), 1-4.

Concludes a series of MT's underlinings and marginal annotations in this two-volume work; series begins July-August, 1968.B25. Abstracts in AES, XIV (1970-1971), 1836, 1837; reprinted in Twainian, XXXI (January-February, 1972).

B20 ____. "Mark Twain and Dan Beard and Boy Scouts of America (Illustrations and Philosophies as Revealed in 'Connecticut Yankee', 'American Claimant', Etc.)," Twainian, XXIX (May-June), 1-4; "(Illustrations and Philosophies as Revealed in 'American Claimant', 'Tom Sawyer Abroad' and 'Following the Equator')" (July-August), 1-4.

Dan Beard, one of the founders of the Boy Scouts of America, illustrated these books in whole or in part, as well as The Million-Pound Bank-Note; a number of his illustrations incorporate the fleur-de-lis or the scroll now familiar as Boy Scout insignia. Davis discusses the Scouts, merit badges, and Scout principles at some length; he argues that MT's works reveal a number of these principles, and that MT and Beard had similar philosophies: "disgust with sham and hypocrisy, with insincerity, with slavery and lack of care for the downtrodden"; he is also at pains to argue that MT "was not anti-religious, he was anti-doctrine or

anti-dogma perhaps, but he did believe in God as a divine being." Abstracts in AES, XIV (1970-1971), 1838; reprinted in Twainian, XXXI (January-February, 1972); AES, XV (1971-1972), 1505; reprinted in Twainian, XXXII (January-February, 1973).

B21 ____. "Review of Foundation Activities During Past Twenty Years," Twainian, XXIX (May-June), 1.

Contains no new critical or biographical material on MT. Abstract in AES, XIV (1970-1971), 1839; reprinted in Twainian, XXXI (January-February, 1972).

B22 DEMOTT, BENJAMIN. "Maxwell Geismar in Eruption," New York Times Book Review, (November 8), pp. 4-5, 47.

A review of Maxwell Geismar's Mark Twain: An American Prophet. "Likable traits of earnestness and embattled forthrightness do appear at moments.... But for most of its length it is too disheveled, self-righteous and simplistic to secure sympathetic hearing of its (to this reviewer) doubtful cause."

B23 DICKINSON, LEON T. [Review: Dewey Ganzel, Mark Twain Abroad: The Cruise of the "Quaker City" (1968).] Modern Philology, LXVIII (August), 117-19.

"Ganzel has done a good job of historical recovery. His book is lively, well written, and essentially accurate. It is well indexed." Dickinson argues, however, that Ganzel states inferences as though they were facts, and is "misleading" in his representation of some of the persons on the tour, incidents in which they are involved, and MT's relation to them; in particular, he underestimates the influence on MT's writing of Mary Mason Fairbanks, who indeed persuaded him to tone down some of his statements. In support, Dickinson here prints for the first time a letter to John Russell Young of the New York Tribune (November 22, 1867; it is in the Young Correspondence in the Library of Congress), in which MT mentions "some twenty letters, which have survived the examination of a most fastidious censor on shipboard." Dickinson concludes his review by suggesting that Ganzel's study provides a "detailed and convincing account of MT's writing of his letters en route...it will be a useful companion" to IA.

B24 DOYLE, PAUL A. "Henry Harper's Telling of a Mark Twain Anecdote," Mark Twain Journal, XV (Summer), 13.

"In a recently discovered letter of Henry Harper's, written to the journalist and author Edward Sandford Martin" (May 20, 1895--location not given), Harper repeats MT's account of an Australian impostor who profitably impersonated him on stage. When the impostor died a friend of MT's served as pallbearer and sent Mrs. Clemens his condolences--which MT read. Abstract in AES, XIV (1970-71), 912.

B25 DUSKIS, HENRY A. "Serious Wilkins in Boston: A Previously Unpublished Manuscript by Mark Twain," Yankee, XXXIV (June), 78-79, 179-83.
  The text of a piece attributed to MT by Duskis, here printed with minimal editorial comment; includes photograph of MT by George Kendall Warren.

B26 EARNEST, ERNEST. The Single Vision: The Alienation of American Intellectuals. New York: New York University Press; London: London University Press, pp. 14-20.
  On Brooks' The Ordeal of Mark Twain (chiefly summary, with objections) and the prudery of William Dean Howells. Provides no new material on MT.

B27 ELSBREE, LANGDON. "Huck Finn on the Nile," South Atlantic Quarterly, LXIX (Autumn), 504-10.
  On his experiences and observations as a Fulbright teacher of American literature in Cairo, 1966-67. He felt that although the Nile was not the Mississippi, Huck "might have stopped earlier and hoped to grow up in a community that was not too far from home." Abstract in AES, XV (1971-72), 1205; reprinted in Twainian, XXXII (January-February, 1973). Abstract by Elsbree in ALA, IV (June, 1971), 92.

B28 ENSOR, ALLISON. "A Clergyman Recalls Hearing Mark Twain," Mark Twain Journal, XV (Winter), 6.
  Reprints the account of an MT talk at a St. Louis Press Club dinner in his honor from River of Years, the autobiography of Joseph Fort Newton (1946.B43). Abstract in AES, XV (1971-72), 270. Abstract by Ensor in ALA, IV (June, 1971), 92.

B29 _____. "Mark Twain's 'The War Prayer': Its Ties to Howells and to Hymnology," Modern Fiction Studies, XVI (Winter), 535-39.
  Shows a number of parallels to Howells' "Editha," and argues that MT's choice of hymn reveals an ironic contrast in that "it does not fit the mood of the service Twain describes." Abstract by Ensor in ALA, IV (June, 1971), 93; in MLA Abstracts (1971), 7970.

B30 _____. "The 'Tennessee Land' of The Gilded Age: Fiction and Reality," Tennessee Studies in Literature, XV, 15-23.
  Si Hawkins in GA dreamed that his thousands of acres would make his children rich, but schemes failed and offers were refused and the land was finally sold for taxes. Ensor discusses the acquisition of 75,000-100,000 acres over a period of years by MT's father, John Marshall Clemens: "The total price was apparently $400-$500." Like Hawkins, MT's brother Orion turned down better offers and the land eventually brought "ten to fifty cents an acre--much more than John Clemens had paid for it, but far short of his

expectations." Abstract in AES, XIV (1970-1971), 3138; reprinted in Twainian, XXXI (March-April, 1972). Abstract by Ensor in MLA Abstracts (1970), 6776.

B31 FATOUT, PAUL. [Review: Allison Ensor, Mark Twain and the Bible (1969).] Indiana Magazine of History, LXVI (March), 89-90.
  Ensor is zealous, but solemn, and might have probed more deeply ("An unexplored topic is [MT's] appreciation of the sound and rhythm of biblical language"). The book is "a scholarly exposition of the shifting emotions, gentle and explosive of a paradoxical genius who could neither take the Bible nor let it alone."

B32 GEISMAR, MAXWELL. "Mark Twain and the Robber Barons," Scanlan's Monthly, I (March), 32-36.
  On MT's criticism of Gould, Rockefeller, et al., with an attack on other scholars for slighting his social commentary.

B33 *GERVAIS, RONALD J. "The Mysterious Stranger: The Fall as Salvation," Pacific Coast Philology, V (April), 24-33.
  [Source: Data provided by letter from R. S. Meyerstein, Secretary-Treasurer, Pacific Coast Philology.]

B34 GRIMES, GEOFFREY ALLEN. "Vagrancy, Vagabondage, and Vigilance: Periods of Vice in the Style of Mark Twain," Journal of the American Studies Association of Texas, I (June), 34-42.
  Emphasizes topic rather than style: "Samuel Clemens was severely criticized throughout his literary career for sins against good taste, for his inability to discern the dust and chaff in his works, and for his usual habit of flaunting much well intended and often well deserved criticism, which he considered superfluous and an imposition on his genius as an artist." His early journalism often exploited "sordid, squeamish, or risque matters," and "In spite of much high-minded criticism, Mark Twain continued to employ throughout his lifetime the trademarks of his western brand of humor."

B35 HAKAC, JOHN. "Huckleberry Finn: a Copy Inscribed in 1903," American Book Collector (Chicago), XX (January), 7-9.
  A copy at the University of Texas is inscribed: "None genuine without this label/ on the bottle Mark Twain/ Oct 23/03." Abstract in AES, XV (1971-72), 1494; reprinted in Twainian, XXXII (January-February, 1973).

B36 *HAMSUN, KNUT, ed. and translated by Barbara Morgridge. The Cultural Life of Modern America. Cambridge, Massachusetts: Harvard University Press.
  [Source: Anon. review, "Thirty Years Before Main Street," Book World (Chicago Tribune), June 7, p. 17, which states that

1970 - Shorter Writings

(HAMSUN, KNUT)
"He correctly described Mark Twain as no
creative artist, but a 'wily wag who gets
the world to laugh while he himself sits
sobbing.'"]

B37   HARKEY, JOSEPH H. "When Huck Finn Smouched
that Spoon," Mark Twain Journal, XV (Summer), 14.
      About a class discussion of the word
"smouch," which a freshman looked up in
the O.E.D.; with some amusement at the
discomfiture of a Jewish friend sitting
next to him, he reported meanings of "Jew"
and "filch." There is no evidence that
MT's use of the term was anti-Semitic. Abstract in AES, XIV (1970-71), 909.

B38   HILL, HAMLIN. "Mark Twain," in J. Albert
Robbins, ed., American Literary Scholarship: An Annual/1970 (Durham, North Carolina: Duke University Press, 1972),
pp. 77-89.
      A survey of MT scholarship for the year,
begun by John C. Gerber in 1963.B32 and
continued by him through 1968. Contents;
"i. Textual and Bibliographical"; "ii. Biography"; "iii. General Criticism"; "iv.
Earlier Works"; "v. Huckleberry Finn";
"vi. Later Works."

B39   _____. [Review: Allison Ensor, Mark Twain
and the Bible (1969).] American Literary
Realism, 1870-1910, III (Winter), 83-85.
      A brief but thorough analysis of the
book, which might have been more effective
had Ensor either confined himself more
rigorously to his central thesis or else
followed up references for a fuller consideration of What Is Man?, JA, and Hadleyburg. "There is too much attention to
mechanical borrowings from the Bible and
not enough to the possibility of Biblical
influence on the cadence, tone, and rhythm
of Mark Twain's prose style. The attempt
to correlate the humorist's attitude toward
the Bible with a dominant culture vs. vernacular value dichotomy seems to me unconvincing. In short, Mark Twain and the
Bible is synopsis and prolegomenon only."

B40   *HOOK, ANDREW. "Huckleberry Finn and Scotland," English Record, XXI (December),
8-14.
      Scots respond to Huck's religion and
language. [Source: MHRA Annual Bibliography (1970), No. 8254. Abstract in AES,
XIV (1970-1971), 2542; reprinted in Twainian, XXXI (January-February, 1972).]

B41   HOWELL, ELMO. "In Defense of Tom Sawyer,"
Mark Twain Journal, XV (Winter), 17-19.
      On Tom as a representative of those as-
pects of the aristocratic Old South which
MT admired and expressed through such
characters as Colonel Driscoll in PW.
Huck Finn, by contrast, is "the mouthpiece

of Twain's views...not easy to envision,
since his role is essentially passive."
Abstract in AES, XIII (1969-70), 3091. Abstract by Howell in ALA, III (June), 114.

B42   _____. "Mark Twain's Arkansas," Arkansas Historical Quarterly, XXIX (Autumn), 195-208.
      "Although he falls into the easy manner
of his time of using Arkansas to suggest
frontier raucousness, his generalizations
belie his treatment of Arkansas people,
which is uniformly kind."

B43   *JANKOVIĆ, MIRA. "Formativna Funkcija Sitnog
Oblika Književnosti" [About Mark Twain's
Short Stories.] Umjetnostrijeci (Zagreb),
XIV, 1-2, 107-13.
      [Source: MHRA Annual Bibliography (1970),
No. 8256.]

B44   JOHNSON, ELLWOOD. "Mark Twain's Dream Self
in the Nightmare of History," Mark Twain
Journal, XV (Winter), 6-12.
      A discussion of MS as illustrating a dou-
ble consciousness MT shared with Emerson,
of seeing the world in terms of freedom and
fate. The central figure in MT's later
works is "the 'dream self' in the prison of
history." Abstract in AES, XIII (1969-70),
3092. Abstract by Johnson in ALA, IV
(December), 23.

B45   *KAPOOR, S. D. "Tradition and Innovation in
Huckleberry Finn," Modern Review, No. 762
(June), pp. 409-13.
      [Source: Abstract in AES, XVII (1973-
1974), 1806; reprinted in Twainian, XXXIV
(March-April, 1975).] Treats American identity, confrontation with reality, and
speech, as revealed in MT's portrayal of
social reality against a historical background.

B46   KEGEL, PAUL. "Henry Adams and Mark Twain:
Two Views of Medievalism," Mark Twain Journal, XV (Winter), 11-21.
      A comparison of Mont Saint-Michel and
Chartres with CY and P&P: "Adams extolls
the beautiful while ignoring the unpleasant;
Twain flails away at all he finds wrong with
medievalism while ignoring the positive aspects." Abstracts in AES, XV (1971-72),
156.

B47   KIRALIS, KARL. "Two Recently Discovered Letters by Mark Twain," Mark Twain Journal,
XV (Winter), 1-5.
      Letters to Jerome B. Stillson (January 19,
25, 1875, here printed for the first time)
charge that a statement in the New York
Tribune praising the performance of Kate
Field in the Gilded Age play are an edited
and distorted version of comments in a private letter and published without his consent; moreover, his remarks were based only
on hearsay evidence, since "in truth I never
have seen the lady play at all." Abstract
in AES, XV (1971-72), 271.

B48 KOLIN, PHILIP. "Mark Twain, Aristotle, and Pudd'nhead Wilson," Mark Twain Journal, XV (Summer), 1-4.
   The tragic success of PW can be explained in terms of Aristotle's Poetics, which MT may have known either directly or through literary histories; a number of his statements on drama and books parallel Aristotle. Abstract in AES, XIV (1970-71), 911. Abstract by Kolin in ALA, IV (December), 23.

B49 *LANINA, T. [Afterword to Lettish translation of P&P.] Riga: Liesma.
   [Source: MHRA Annual Bibliography (1970), No. 8260.]

B50 *____. [Afterword to Russian translation of P&P.] Moscow: Detskaya Literatura.
   [Source: MHRA Annual Bibliography (1970), No. 8261.]

B51 LEARY, LEWIS. Articles on American Literature, 1950-1967. Durham, North Carolina: Duke University Press.
   Lists articles on MT, pp. 56-77; this material has been included in the present bibliography.

B52 ____. "More Letters from the Quaker City," American Literature, XLII (May), 197-202.
   Three letters written on the 1867 tour by one of the owners, Daniel Leary, who describes the passengers as "nothing but a common lot of western people" and mentions plans to sell the ship, if possible. Abstract in AES, XIV (1970-1971), 1547; reprinted in Twainian, XXXI (January-February, 1972). Abstract by Leary in ALA, IV (December), 23; in MLA Abstracts (1970), 6790.

B53 LEGATE, DAVID M. Stephen Leacock: A Biography. Toronto: Doubleday Canada Limited, and Garden City, New York: Doubleday & Company, Inc., passim.
   Leacock "never cared for" TS (p. 13). His Mark Twain (1932) is described as "in the main a succession of endearing generalities," and inadequately researched (p. 180).

B54 LEWIS, STUART A. "Pudd'nhead Wilson's Election," Mark Twain Journal, XV (Winter), 21.
   Wilson's election as mayor in PW suggests only that the office was "so unrewarding and trivial that only the town fool was fit for it," but the abortive Those Extraordinary Twins from which PW was derived shows him taking the office in triumph when the Whigs had no candidate strong enough to run against him; "thus Wilson's election, which makes little sense in the final version, can be seen as an example of Twain's carelessness in matters of detail, and should not be taken as an example of genuine Missouri political life." Abstract in AES, XIII (1969-70), 3093.

B55 LOWERY, CAPTAIN ROBERT E. "The Grangerford-Shepherdson Episode: Another of Mark Twain's Indictments of the Damned Human Race," Mark Twain Journal, XV (Winter), 19-21.
   The names of the feuding families in HF allegorically represent the roots of the conflict: grange suggests a farmer, "particularly a gentlemen farmer with large holdings," and a "'ford'--a river crossing or a port--implies settlement, stability, and permanence in a specific area." The Shepherdsons, by contrast, represent nomads, and, significantly, "are always on horseback." Other details, such as the artificial fruit with which the Grangerfords decorate their home, reveal them as "only imitations of the noble and cultured society which established itself in the South." Abstract in AES, XIII (Winter), 3094.

B56 McCARTHY, HAROLD T. "Mark Twain's Pilgrim's Progress: The Innocents Abroad," Arizona Quarterly, XXVI (Autumn), 249-58.
   When MT wrote about Nevada, California, and the Sandwich Islands there was some serious social criticism; "but his criticism applied to local ills and often to specific personalities and did not pretend to have touched upon any fundamental disorder in American society." The Quaker City tour of 1867 gave him a chance to observe the educated, respectable and devout, and in the Holy Land to see their inability to distinguish between reality and their preconceptions; moreover, the biblical precepts to which they assented verbally were not evident in their personal conduct. Abstract in AES, XVI (1972-1973), 2054. Abstract by McCarthy in MLA Abstracts (1970), 6795; in ALA, IV (June, 1971), 93.

B57 McKEE, JOHN DEWITT. "Roughing It as Retrospective Reporting," Western American Literature, V (Summer), 113-19.
   MT caught the spirit of the flush times in Virginia City because "he was more than an observer. He was a participant" (p. 118). Abstract in AES, XVII (1973-1974), 2087; reprinted in Twainian, XXXIV (March-April, 1975). Abstract by McKee in ALA, IV (June, 1971), 94.

B58 McKEITHAN, D. M. [Review: Allison Ensor, Mark Twain and the Bible (1969).] American Literature, XLII (November), 410-11.
   Summarizes MT's attitudes, calls Ensor's book "a useful, fascinating, and thorough survey of the subject."

B59 MENDELSOHN M. "Strannaia Sud'ba 'Tainstvennogo Neznakomtsa' [The Strange Fate of The Mysterious Stranger]," Voprosy Literatury, XIV (September), 158-64.
   The publication of MS six years after MT's death came as a shock to American readers, most of whom knew him as a joker and

(MENDELSOHN, M.)
author of popular books for children. In the mid-sixties the University of California began publishing a complete edition of MT's letters and unpublished writings; one volume is W. M. Gibson, ed., Mark Twain's "Mysterious Stranger" Manuscripts, which Mendelsohn discusses in great detail. MS is a "creation of a writer who until his last minute of life continued to scourge cruelty, exploitation and false inventions of priests."

B60 *MILLER, RUTH. "But Laugh or Die: The Mysterious Stranger and Billy Budd," Literary Half-Yearly, XI:1.
[Source: Abstract in AES, XV (1971-1972), 250; reprinted in Twainian, XXXII (January-February, 1973). MLA Bibliography (1970), No. 6798 gives Mysore as place of publication.]

B61 MILLS, NICOLAUS C. "Prison and Society in Nineteenth-Century American Fiction," Western Humanities Review, XXIV (Autumn), 325-31.
On Cooper, Hawthorne, Melville, and MT, all of whom found the structure of society imprisoning. "Throughout Huckleberry Finn slavery is seen imprisoning whites as well as blacks," and CY shows that MT "saw exploitation characteristic of society as a whole, not merely the antebellum South." Abstract in AES, XIV (1971-1972), 1450.

B62 _____. "Social and Moral Vision in Great Expectations and Huckleberry Finn," Journal of American Studies, IV (July), 61-72.
A meticulously detailed and documented comparison of the two books, noting the boys' "outward allegiance to a society whose values they instinctively oppose," in which home is dominated by women, the values are those of an oppressive economic and legal system, and religion has been reduced to a defence of the corrupted society. The boys face similar psychological and moral decisions, and there is even a parallel in final betrayal by the River: "At the moment when it should lead to freedom it leads to the capture of Magwitch and Jim." Abstract in AES, XV (1971-1972), 1089; reprinted in Twainian, XXXII (January-February, 1973).

B63 MORROW, PATRICK. [Review: Edgar M. Branch, Clemens of the "Call" (1969).] Western American Literature, V (Summer), 155-56.
"Branch's book, quite simply, is a beautiful job. He took the fifty-four hundred or so local items printed in the Call during Clemens's tenure there, and...selected the best two hundred that can reasonably be attributed to Clemens." Their value lies in what they show of 19th-century attitudes and in particular of MT's views concerning race, although they lack any great literary merit.

B64 MOTT, BERTRAM, JR. "Twain's Joan: A Divine Anomaly," Études Anglaises, XXIII (July-September), 246-55.
After comparing portrayals of Joan by Shaw and Anouilh, treats MT's Joan of Arc in terms of Calvinist views on the nature of God, divine grace, and private interpretation of the Bible. His Joan is like the Calvinists' Christ, saving the predestined elect, but she does not transform men. If in Joan MT "was seeking a model, a Christ, salvation from the Calvinist limitations of depravity and predestination, he failed...he could not respond to the divine half of the elusive Maid of Orleans.... She is a divine anomaly; and mortal man is still both willless and depraved."

B65 PARKER, GAIL. "Mary Baker Eddy and Sentimental Womanhood," New England Quarterly, XLIII (March), 3-18.
Frequent, passing reference to MT, who attacked Christian Science, "was outspoken in his repugnance for sentimentalism in all its forms, and felt particularly uncomfortable about the notion that women were the conscience of the nation." Mrs. Eddy was not a "monster of American success"; to the contrary, she failed, because "the combination pope and holy mother of Christian Science consolidated an empire and healed thousands without ever really integrating her own conflicted personality."

B66 PAVESE, CESARE. American Literature: Essays and Opinions. Translated by Edwin Fussell. Berkeley, Los Angeles, London: University of California Press, pp. 28, 83, 147-48.
Pavese gradually came to appreciate MT's use of the American idiom, regarding it first only as local color (p. 28), or a concession to his public (p. 83), then recognizing the poetry and original language in HF (pp. 147-48). The essays involved first appeared in 1930, 1932, and 1934.

B67 PETTIT, ARTHUR GORDON. "Mark Twain, Unreconstructed Southerner, and His View of the Negro, 1835-1860," Rocky Mountain Social Science Journal, VII (April), 17-27.
"The experiences of his first twenty-five years were responsible in large part for the fact that neither Clemens, the private man, nor Mark Twain, the writer of Huckleberry Finn and of Pudd'nhead Wilson, ever completely outlived his earliest impressions of the Negro."

B68 _____. "Mark Twain's Attitude Toward the Negro in the West," Western Historical Quarterly, I (January), 51-62.
MT's expressed views in his formative years and during the time when he lived in the West were consistently racist, and he often joked about the inferiority of the Negro. His outlook on racial matters was

(PETTIT, ARTHUR GORDON)
not modified significantly by a shift in
his political allegiance from South to
North, but when he moved to the East,
worked to establish himself as a national
writer, and married the daughter of "a
leading conductor on the New York under-
ground railway before the war," his views
began to change. He "left most (not all,
but most) of his more violent prejudice
behind him in the West."

B69 REED, KENNETH T. "Mirth and Misquotation:
Mark Twain in Petosky, Michigan," Mark
Twain Journal, XV (Summer), 19-20.
Supplements the sparse details in Fred
W. Lorch's The Trouble Begins at Eight
(1968) of MT's lecture delivered July 20,
1895 in Petosky. When the Daily Resorter
[sic] attributed to him statements bearing
on its feud with a "volunteer newspaper"
sponsored by a Dr. Hall of a local summer
school, MT denied them in a note published
in the Petosky Record: "I don't like being used as a waste-pipe for the delivery
of another man's bile." Abstract in AES,
XIV (1970-71), 913.

B70 REES, ROBERT A. "Captain Stormfield's Visit
to Heaven and The Gates Ajar," English Language Notes, VII (March), 197-202.
Elizabeth Stuart Phelps's The Gates Ajar
(1868) anticipates Captain Stormfield in
suggesting that halos, wings, and a life
of singing and prayers may be unsatisfactory; that in Heaven a person can follow what
career he chooses, with increased intellect, and with a recognition of abilities
that may have been denied in his earthly
life; and that in a vast Heaven the celebrities may find it an imposition to greet
everybody who has been looking forward to
meeting them. Although, as Franklin Rogers points out, MT was not burlesquing The
Gates Ajar in Captain Stormfield, he did
so in "The Story of Mamie Grant, the Child
Missionary." Rees also quotes "an unpublished fragment entitled 'Captain Stormfield Resumes,'" which mentions The Gates
Ajar.

B71 REEVES, PASCHAL, et al. "A Checklist of
Scholarship on Southern Literature for
1970," Mississippi Quarterly, XXIV (Spring,
1971), 175-222; on MT, pp. 186-89.

B72 RODNON, STEWART. "The Adventures of Huckleberry Finn and Invisible Man: Thematic
and Structural Comparisons," Negro American
Literature Forum, IV (July), 45-51.
There are similarities in "the journey
concept, the education motif, and the essential theme," as well as something deeper
than "a satiric examination of...American
society" and a "basic-goodness-of-the-heart
theme," and "the novels are stylistically
alike in at least four areas: language,

folklore, humor, and narrator point-of-view."
In Shadow and Act (1964), Ellison has commented on Jim's role as a symbol of humanity
for Huck, whose decision to help him escape
represents MT's acceptance of a personal responsibility.

B73 RUBIN, LOUIS D. "Southern Local Color and the
Black Man," Southern Review, n.s. VI (October), 1011-30; on HF, 1026-30.
Huck provides a voice, and Jim a basis for
evaluating "the moral worth of the town and
the countryside along the river." MT may
not have recognized the importance of his
theme of Jim's yearning for freedom; Ralph
Ellison has argued that Jim's character
could be more fully rounded, though he is a
triumph of characterization and understanding, a symbol of humanity. Abstract in AES,
XIV (1970-1971), 3140; reprinted in Twainian, XXXI (March-April, 1972).

B74 _____. "Three Installments of Mark Twain,"
Sewanee Review, LXXVIII (August), 678-84.
A review article covering three volumes
of the MT papers published in 1969 by the
University of California Press, Berkeley:
Walter Blair, ed., Mark Twain's Hannibal,
Huck & Tom ("The most interesting document
is... 'Villagers of 1840-3,'" with MT's
1897 recollections of Hannibal people);
William M. Gibson, ed., Mark Twain's "Mys-
terious Stranger" Manuscripts (this shows
what Paine did in splicing together dispar-
ate material to make a book, and destroys
DeVoto's argument that MT came back from
the edge of insanity to a restoration of
his creative powers); Lewis Leary, ed., Mark
Twain's Correspondence with Henry Huttleston
Rogers, 1893-1909 ("The truly interesting
book of the three volumes," revealing that
MT was less noble than he has been depicted
in his settlement of his financial affairs).
The effect of publishing MT's papers is to
support his portrait by Van Wyck Brooks.
Abstract in AES, XIV (1970-1971), 1548; reprinted in Twainian, XXXI (January-February,
1972).

B75 SAPPER, NEIL G. "'I Been There Before':
Huck Finn as Tocquevillian Individual,"
Mississippi Quarterly, XXIV (Winter),
35-45.
Tocqueville used the terms of individualism and conformity to denote prevalent American qualities. Huck had a strong sense of
the community of the raft, but he rejected
the civilization on shore and thereby "demonstrated finally and conclusively that he
was a Tocquevillian individual. Perhaps he
was the only one that we have had." Abstract in AES, XVII (1973-1974), 2408; reprinted in Twainian, XXXIV (March-April,
1975). Abstract by Sapper in MLA Abstracts
(1971), 8007.

B76 SEELYE, JOHN. "Mark Twain as Grumbler," New Republic, CLXIII (November 28), 21-24.
A review of Maxwell Geismar, Mark Twain: An American Prophet. The book is enlivened by extensive quotation from MT. "Geismar's method is to slap down a few choice paragraphs, applaud, slap down some more, applaud, and then slap down a page and a half for emphasis, boot Justin Kaplan with a footnote, and burst into cheers. Well, it's lots of fun, and though Maxwell Geismar may be full of prunes, his book is full of plums--mostly Mark Twain's."

B77 SERRANO-PLAJA, ARTURO. "Magic" Realism in Cervantes: "Don Quixote" as Seen Through "Tom Sawyer" and "The Idiot." Translated by Robert S. Rudder. Berkeley, Los Angeles, London: University of California Press.
Also treats HF, passim, although the emphasis is on Cervantes. Serrano-Plaja says he did not read MT until he was in his thirties. One afternoon during the Civil War in Spain, in a cafe with Hemingway, "I learned about two things from the Anglo-Saxon world: whiskey and the importance of Mark Twain.... Hemingway told me it was absolutely impossible to understand anything about the United States without knowing Mark Twain in depth; and he, Hemingway, considered him the most important writer of his country" (pp. 2, 3). [MLA Bibliography (1968), No. 16226 lists the Spanish publication as: "Realismo 'magoci' en Cervantes: 'Don Quixote' dese 'Tom Sawyer' y 'El Idiota.' Madrid: Gredos, 1967."]

B78 SHRELL, DARWIN H. "Twain's Owl and His Bluejays," in Thomas Austin Kirby and William John Olive, eds., Essays in Honor of Esmond Linworth Marilla (Baton Rouge: Louisiana State University Press), pp. 283-90.
MT was still distressed and puzzled over the apparent failure of his Whittier Birthday Dinner speech when he was writing TA, and "Jim Baker's Bluejay Yarn" in Chapter III parallels the address in that "the settings for both stories are in a California mining camp, and each story is told by a California miner. In both there are clearly polarized and contrasting cultural standards reflecting eastern and western attitudes or values. In each story the easterners are on a pilgrimage to Yosemite. The literary methods in each story are essentially the same: the use of learned and vernacular language for humorous effect; the use of quasi-dramatic form to illustrate a point." Moreover, "the ambitious intentions and comic frustrations of the first jay are in no small way similar to [MT's] own motives and reactions at that famous Atlantic dinner," while the humorless owl allows MT "to re-create--with artistic detachment--another situation in which grotesque or audacious western humor failed to be understood."

B79 SIMONSON, HAROLD R. "Huckleberry Finn as Tragedy," Yale Review, LIX (Summer), 532-48; reprinted (revised) in his The Closed Frontier: Studies in American Literary Tragedy. New York: Holt, Rinehart and Winston, pp. 57-76; also, pp. 129-33 on Connecticut Yankee.
The concluding section is "a dramatic travesty of this rebirth, of Huck's becoming Tom. The tragedy rests in the irony that only as Tom can Huck survive" (p. 60). On the CY, 129-33: "Culminating in an Armageddon...does not concern the triumph of modern technology over medieval feudalism as much as it damns this same technology." Article abstracted by Simonson in ALA, IV (December), 23.

B80 SKOW, JOHN. "Quarter Twain," Time, XCVI (November 30), 80, 82.
A review of Maxwell Geismar's Mark Twain: An American Prophet. "This latest critical appreciation of Mark Twain is not without blemish, being sloppy, narrow, quarrelsome, doctrinaire, vague, repetitive," but it is redeemed by Geismar's love for MT and frequent quotations from him and by the "modest patches of solid ground" in the criticism.

B81 *SOLOMON, PETRE. "Verva Postumă a lui Mark Twain" ["Mark Twain's Posthumous Verve"], Romănia Litară (Bucharest), III (April), 21.
[Source: MHRA Annual Bibliography (1970), 8281.]

B82 SPANGLER, GEORGE M. "Pudd'nhead Wilson: A Parable of Property," American Literature, XLII (March), 28-37.
Traditional interpretations in terms of racial themes and environmental determinism do not reflect the unity that may be found in a view of the book as illustrating "the perils of an obsession with property to the exclusion of all other human values and needs." Abstract in AES, XIV (1970), 1546; reprinted in Twainian, XXXI (January-February, 1972). Abstract by Spangler in ALA, IV (December), 24; in MLA Abstracts (1970), 6807.

B83 SPILLER, ROBERT E., ed. The Van Wyck Brooks-Louis Mumford Letters: The Record of a Literary Friendship, 1921-1963. New York: E. P. Dutton & Co., Inc., pp. 84-87, 218-19.
Letters between Mumford and Brooks discussing DeVoto as a fool and his Mark Twain's America as providing little information of value (December 27, 30, 1932; pp. 84-87); letter from Mumford to John Chamberlain commenting on The Golden Day, Waldo Frank's Our America, and about DeVoto on MT's reticence concerning sex (August 6, 1942; pp. 218-19).

B84 SPOFFORD, WILLIAM K. "Mark Twain's Connecticut Yankee: An Ignoramus Nevertheless," Mark Twain Journal, XV (Summer), 15-18.
MT "never intended the revolution to succeed," as he shows through "Hank's 'practical' and insensitive character and by endowing the Boss with a warped notion of democracy, and an incomplete comprehension of the significance of training. Throughout the novel Twain thus implicitly and explicitly undermines the Yankee's goal." Abstract in AES, XIV (1970-71), 908. Abstract by Spofford in ALA, IV (December), 24.

B85 STEVENSON, ADLAI E. [Typed, signed letter of November 20, 1951 to Cyril Clemens, reproduced in facsimile.] Mark Twain Journal, XV (Summer), back cover.
Declines with thanks and regrets an invitation to address the Mark Twain Birthday Banquet, and recalls doggerel by MT on the pronunciation of "Adlai."

B86 *STRELNIKOV, BORIS, and ILYA SHATUNOVSKII. "V Avtomobile po Amerike [O poeshchenii g. Hannibala--rodiny M. Tvena: Iz putevogo dnevnika]." "[Through America by Car (a visit to Hannibal--the birthplace of M. Twain: a diary).]" Zhurnalist, I, 71-73.
[Source: MHRA Annual Bibliography (1970), No. 8285.]

B87 *TOLCHARD, CLIFFORD. "Mark Twain's Australia," Walkabout, XXXVI (July), 52-55.
[Source: MHRA Annual Bibliography (1970), No. 8286.]

B88 TRACHTENBERG, ALAN. "The Form of Freedom in Adventures of Huckleberry Finn," Southern Review, n.s. VI (October), 954-71.
"Huckleberry Finn became a cultural object of special intensity" as a view of freedom, "the precise negation of all the forces felt as oppressive in the 1950s.... Huck's freedom...requires that he achieve a conscious moral identity," but his role as narrator helps to define him, and in any case MT "seriously doubted the possibilities of personal freedom within a social setting." The cost of Huck's freedom and survival is high: "he pays with his chance to grow up." Abstract in AES, XIV (1970-1971), 3137; reprinted in Twainian, XXXI (March-April, 1972).

B89 TUCKEY, JOHN S. "Hannibal, Weggis, and Mark Twain's Eseldorf," American Literature, XLII (May), 235-40.
Examination of MT's notebook shows that "in The Mysterious Stranger his first portrayal of village boys...reflects his recent observations of Weggis [near Lake Lucerne, in Switzerland] more directly and immediately than it evidently does any recollection of Hannibal in the 1840's," as DeVoto had asserted. Abstract by Tuckey in ALA, IV (December), 24; in MLA Abstracts (1970), 6810.

B90 ____. "Mark Twain's Later Dialogue: The 'Me' and the Machine," American Literature, XLI (January), 532-42.
The frequent despair of MT's last years was leavened by "expressions of faith and hope" which "were something more than occasional and random." Even in Three Thousand Years Among the Microbes, MS, and What Is Man? there are indications of a readiness to believe in an immortal self. Abstract in AES, XIV (1970-1971), 1549; reprinted in Twainian, XXXI (January-February, 1972). Abstract by Tuckey in ALA, III (June), 115; in MLA Abstracts (1970), 6811. Article reprinted in Schmitter (1974), pp. 57-67.

B91 ____. [Review: Arthur L. Scott, Mark Twain at Large (1969) and Allison Ensor, Mark Twain and the Bible (1969).] Modern Fiction Studies, XVI (Autumn), 214-17.
Scott's book is solidly founded in the MT papers and available scholarship, and "careful and modest, perhaps even stinted, in its conclusions," since there is evidence here that MT's "marked shift in tone and treatment" may be the result of a loss of contrasts as the freshness of experiences wore off. Mark Twain and the Bible, treating "the theme of a lost Eden as it applies to Twain's works," is "a good beginning," but the subject requires a bigger book; however, Chapter III provides a valuable treatment of MT's use of the Biblical images of the Prodigal Son; Adam, Eve, and the fall; and Noah and the flood.

B92 TWICHELL, JOSEPH H. "Letters from Twichell to Paine," Twainian, XXIX (September-October), 4; (November-December), 3-4.
Ten letters, 1908-1911, chiefly concerning the transmission of material pertinent to the forthcoming Biography; Twichell relies on Paine's judgment in guarding MT's privacy while discussing MT letters, some of which should not be preserved. There is also mention of Twichell letters written during the tour with MT which led to TA, a series of photographs of MT in the Hartford Courant (apparently either taken in Dublin, N.H., or annotated there), and a talk and a Harper's article on MT by Twichell; Twichell also comments on MT's wedding, and his "deep humilities." There is a final installment of these letters in the next issue of Twainian (January-February, 1971). Abstracts in AES, XV (1971-1972), 1506, 1507; reprinted in Twainian, XXXII (January-February, 1973).

B93 WAGENKNECHT, EDWARD. "Huckleberry Finn as the Devil's Disciple," Boston University Studies, XVIII (Spring), 20-24.
On Huck's decision to go to Hell for Jim's freedom: "What he knows as God is only a cruel caricature of God. If this were what God is like, He would deserve no obedience," and religious history is filled with examples of defiance of church and state by

(WAGENKNECHT, EDWARD)
"those who truly love God...The Devil's
Disciple becomes God's own child" (p. 23).

B94   _____. [Review: William M. Gibson, ed.,
Mark Twain's "Mysterious Stranger" Manuscripts; Walter Blair, ed., Mark Twain's
Hannibal, Huck & Tom; Lewis Leary, ed.,
Mark Twain's Correspondence with Henry Huttleston Rogers (all 1969).] Studies in the
Novel, II (Spring), 88-95.
    Includes not only a useful, general dis-
cussion of the materials, but also a summary of the history of the unpublished papers of Mark Twain, commenting on Paine's
trusteeship and his editing of The Mysterious Stranger; he observes in passing that
the new knowledge about the composition
"makes it necessary to scrap Bernard De-
Voto's brilliant essay, 'The Symbols of
Despair' (Mark Twain at Work), which is
probably the most moving thing that has
ever been written about Mark Twain....
Chronology can be very cruel to literary
theories." Abstract in AES, XIV (1970-
1971), 1273; reprinted in Twainian, XXXI
(January-February, 1972).

B95   WERGE, THOMAS. "Mark Twain and the Fall of
Adam," Mark Twain Journal, XV (Summer),
5-13.
    On MT's continuing use of Adam to repre-
sent child-like innocence and yielding to
temptation, whether through direct portrayal or allusion. "Twain measures Adam's
significance for his own time not by his
pre-lapsarian goodness, but by his fallen
state, which is, finally, the state of all
men." Abstract in AES, XIV (1970-71),
910. Abstract by Werge in ALA, IV (December), 24.

B96   WHEELOCK, C. WEBSTER. "The Point of Pudd'n-
head's Half-a-Dog Joke," American Notes and
Queries, VIII (July), 150-51.
    When Wilson expressed the wish that he
owned half of a barking dog so he could
kill his half, he was considered a fool in
the small Southern community. There is a
major satiric point here, in that a white
person cannot be enslaved, but a person
with some Negro blood and a preponderance
of white blood can be, as were Roxy and her
natural son Valet de Chambers: "Men who
are aghast at the prospect of the newcomer's killing a creature that may be only
partially his--a moral and legal crime,
clearly--are daily accustomed to dealing
with their own species on precisely the
same terms."

1971 A BOOKS

A1   ANDERSON, FREDERICK, ed. With the assistance
of Kenneth M. Sanderson. Mark Twain: The
Critical Heritage. London: Routledge &
Kegan Paul, and New York: Barnes & Noble.

Reprints reviews of MT's books and evaluations of his writing, in his lifetime and
for the period immediately after his death,
in chronological order, with an extensive
introduction (pp. 1-19); an MT letter to
Andrew Lang and a previously unpublished
letter to Andrew Chatto (16 July 1889) are
also included. The present bibliography indicates reprintings of listed material in
this book.

A2   ANON. Hartford as a Publishing Center in the
Nineteenth Century. Hartford: Stowe-Day
Foundation.
    A pamphlet issued for an exhibit, listing
works by MT, contracts, salesman's prospectuses, etc.

A3   GERBER, JOHN C., ed. Studies in "Huckleberry
Finn." Columbus, Ohio: Charles E. Merrill
Publishing Company.
    Contains early reviews, excerpts from var-
ious sources concerning "The Fracas Created
by the Concord Public Library" in 1885, and
articles and excerpts from books by nine
critics since MT's death. All of this material is listed in the present bibliography, with cross-references to Gerber's reprintings.

A4   LEARY, LEWIS. Southern Excursions: Essays
on Mark Twain and Others. Baton Rouge:
Louisiana State University Press. On MT,
pp. 3-110.
    Contains the following essays on MT, with
previous publication as indicated: "Mark
Twain and the Comic Spirit" (pp. 3-41), a
slightly shortened version of his Mark
Twain pamphlet (1960); "Mark Twain's Wound:
Standing with Reluctant Feet" (pp. 42-74),
reduced from the introduction to his A Casebook on Mark Twain's Wound (1960); "The
Bankruptcy of Mark Twain" (pp. 75-86) in
Carrell (1968) and as "Mark Twain among the
Malefactors" in Brom Weber's Sense and Sensibility in Twentieth-Century Writing
(1970), with other material derived from
Leary's ed. of Mark Twain's Correspondence
with Henry Huttleston Rogers (1969); "On
Writing about Writers: Especially Mark
Twain" (pp. 87-95), in Southern Review
(1968); "Tom and Huck: Innocence on Trial"
(pp. 96-110), in Virginia Quarterly Review
(1954). For details, see the original publication of this material.

A5   ROWLETTE, ROBERT. Mark Twain's "Pudd'nhead
Wilson": The Development and Design. Bowling Green, Ohio: Bowling Green University
Popular Press.
    "The present study will examine the form
and substance of Pudd'nhead Wilson. In
particular it will examine what I consider
to be Twain's structural achievement of
integrating the novel's three apparently
disparate themes and the plots that dramatize them: slavery, detection, and twin-
hood" (p. ix).

1971 B SHORTER WRITINGS

B1 ALLEN, MARTHA. "Train Travel in the Mississippi West, 1869-1900 as Seen by Travelers," Journal of the American Studies Association of Texas, II, 5-14.
    On p. 8, briefly cites MT's complaint about railroad-station dining, with little time to consume the "Bare Stake and Dear Meet" (from San Francisco Daily Examiner, May 25, 1869).

B2 ANDERSEN, DAVID M. "Basque Wine, Arkansas Chawin' Tobacco: Landscape, and Ritual in Ernest Hemingway and Mark Twain," Mark Twain Journal, XVI (Winter), 3-7.
    The social ritual at Berguete of sharing wine, described in The Sun Also Rises, has its parallel in the dispute over chewing tobacco in HF: "Reciprocity, beginning even with such material symbols as wine and tobacco, is not just essential to civilization, it is civilization." Abstract in AES, XVI (1972-1973), 1768.

B3 ANON. "Mark Twain Items Published Elsewhere During Past Year," Twainian, XXX (January-February), 1-3.
    Reprints a number of abstracts from AES, XIII (1969-1970). Abstract in AES, XV (1971-1972), 1512; reprinted in Twainian, XXXII (January-February, 1973).

B4 *ARIKAWA, SHOJI. "Huckleberry Finn in Japan," English Record (Japan), XXI (February), 20-26.
    Japanese students respond to Huck's American character and status as fugitive, and gain insight into American racial problems through his book. [Source: MHRA Annual Bibliography (1971), No. 8815, and abstract in AES, XIV (1970-1971), 2839; reprinted in Twainian, XXXI (March-April, 1972).]

B5 *BOBROVA, M. [Afterword to Moldavian translation (from Russian) of Connecticut Yankee.] Kishinev: Kartya Moldovenyaskè.
    [Source: MHRA Annual Bibliography (1971), No. 8820.]

B6 BOWEN, JAMES K., and RICHARD VAN DER BEETS, eds. American Literature Abstracts, IV (June), 91-94, 117-18; V (December), 135.
    Contains eleven abstracts by the authors of articles on MT, and (June, 117-18) Elmer F. Suderman's summary of reviews of Allison Ensor's Mark Twain and the Bible (1969.A5).

B7 BUGLIARI, JEANNE. "The Picaresque as a Flaw in Mark Twain's Novels," Mark Twain Journal, XV (Summer), 10-12.
    P&P, RI, LOM, TS, and CY "are diminished as serious literary efforts because either their characters are more or less flat, static, and insufficiently drawn or because their themes are not purposefully directed";

HF suffers from its "curious admixture of style and content," but gains stature in departing from the picaresque mode. Abstract in AES, XV (1971-72), 1498.

B8 BYERS, JOHN R., JR. "Miss Emmeline Grangerford's Hymn Book," American Literature, XLIII (May), 259-63.
    The "Ode to Stephen Dowling Bots, Dec'd" from HF and Isaac Watts's "Alas! and did my Saviour Bleed!" are printed in parallel columns to show a possible derivation; particularly significant are parallels in the first and second lines, the common bathos, and similar structure of questions and answers concerning death. Abstract in AES, XVI (1972-1973), 1121; reprinted in Twainian, XXXIII (January-February, 1974). Brief abstract by Byers in ALA, V (December), 135; in MLA Abstracts (1971), 7963.

B9 CADY, EDWIN H. "Huckleberry Finn by Common Day," in his The Light of Common Day: Realism in American Fiction. Bloomington, London: Indiana University Press, pp. 88-119; also, pp. 36-39 on "A True Story," pp. 79-84 on IA, and passim on MT.
    In HF morality is based on the value of the individual (p. 32); notes an element of the mock-heroic (pp. 65-66). On HF as picaresque and anti-romantic, pp. 88-119. "A True Story" summarized and praised for its language and the vivid portrayal of Aunt Rachel (pp. 36-39). IA treated as an assault on romantic, dishonest perceptions by travel writers (pp. 79-84).

B10 CAMPBELL, FRANK, and INA CAMPBELL. "Mark Twain's Florentine Villas in 1964-1965," Mark Twain Journal, XV (Summer), 12-14.
    Describes the Villa Quarto and Villa Viviani, which have been changed but resemble MT's descriptions of them; a search for the "Villa Paulhof" summer home in Kaltenleutgeben was unsuccessful. Abstract in AES, XV (1971-72), 1502.

B11 CLARK, HARRY HAYDEN. "Mark Twain" (with corrections and additions by Howard G. Baetzhold), in James B. Woodress, ed., Eight American Authors: A Review of Research and Criticism (New York: W. W. Norton & Company, Inc.), pp. 273-320.
    A revised edition of the bibliography originally published by the Modern Language Association in 1956 and reprinted by Norton in 1963. Contents: "Bibliography," "Editions and Texts," "Biographies," "Criticism"; annotated. [Not systematically checked for the present bibliography.]

B12 CLEMENS, CYRIL. "Bernard Shaw Meets Mark Twain," Mark Twain Journal, XVI (Winter), back cover.
    Facsimile of a typed, signed letter (London, n.d., text previously published) from Shaw to Cyril Clemens on two meetings with MT in London; in a note below, Cyril Clemens

1971 - Shorter Writings

(CLEMENS, CYRIL)
quotes Shaw's gracious refusal of permission to dedicate a book to him. Briefly described in AES, XVI (1972-1973), 1746.

B13 COLWELL, JAMES L. "Huckleberries and Humans: on the Naming of Huckleberry Finn," Publications of the Modern Language Association, LXXXVI (January), 70-76.
MT did not see huckleberries until he went to Hartford in 1868; the name suggests rusticity and wildness. "Finn" came from a Hannibal drunkard, like the father of Tom Blankenship, the boy on whom Huck was modeled. Moreover, "To the nonpsychologically trained ear, 'Huck' is to 'Mark' about as 'Finn' is to 'Twain,' and the resemblance seems both striking and deliberate." Abstract (condensed from Colwell's own abstract) in AES, XV (1971-1972), 269; reprinted in Twainian, XXXII (January-February, 1973). Abstract by Colwell in ALA, IV (June), 92; in MLA Abstracts (1971), 7965.

B14 CRACROFT, RICHARD H. "The Gentle Blasphemer: Mark Twain, Holy Scripture, and the Book of Mormon," Brigham Young University Studies, XI (Winter), 119-40.
Although MT "obviously" had not read the Book of Mormon, he ridiculed it, as he ridiculed the Bible, Mary Baker Eddy's Science and Health, and the religious practices of Moslems and Hindus; but he did so without malice. "On reading Mark Twain's gentle blasphemies, whether concerning the Almighty or His foible-prone creatures, everybody, including the victim, has a good time." Abstract in AES, XV (1971-1972), 2143. Abstract by Cracroft in MLA Abstracts (1971), 7967.

B15 CRONIN, FRANK C. "The Ultimate Perspective in Pudd'nhead Wilson," Mark Twain Journal, XVI (Winter), 14-16.
"The moral center...is the omniscient narrator who...unfolds before the reader some of the darker ironies of life to which Pudd'nhead is tragically blind." The real subject is "the terrifying discrepancy between appearance and 'reality' which reveals the ultimate uncertainty of man's identity." Abstract in AES, XVI (1972-1973), 1771.

B16 [DAVIS, CHESTER L.] "Paine, Book Publishing, Dispersal of Mark Twain Manuscripts," Twainian, XXX (March-April), 4; (May-June), 1-4, with added sub-title, "Letters from Langdon, Laura Frazer (Becky Thatcher) and (July-August), 1-4, as "Letters from Laura Frazer (Becky Thatcher) to Paine, 1907-1912"; (September-October), 1-4, as "Letters from Laura Frazer (Becky Thatcher), Helen K. Garth, Fee, Fuller, RoBards and Mahan."

This series, with varying titles, reprints correspondence received by Paine while he was working on his biography of MT. Abstracts in AES, XV (1971-1972), 1511, reprinted in Twainian, XXXII (January-February, 1973); AES, XVI (1972-1973), 788, 789, 790, reprinted in Twainian, XXXIII (January-February, 1974).

B17 ____. "Walter F. Frear, Willard S. Morse, Yale University Collection. M. T. Bibliographies Started 'Foundation' and 'Mark Twain and Hawaii,'" Twainian, XXX (November-December), 1-4.
A general discussion of the Mark Twain Research Foundation, and Mark Twain collecting, bibliography, and scholarship. Contains the text of an address given by Frear before The Social Science Association of Honolulu, October 6, 1947, on MT's visit to Hawaii in 1866. Abstract in AES, XVI (1972-1973), 791; reprinted in Twainian, XXX (January-February, 1974). A confusing entry in the 1971 MHRA Annual Bibliography, No. 8833, lists this as "Mark Twain in Hawaii. Twainian (6), 1-4."

B18 DENTON, LYNN W. "Mark Twain and the American Indian," Mark Twain Journal, XVI (Winter), 1-3.
MT's early prejudice against the Indian "eventually changed to toleration and then finally to idealism." Although MT's views of other national and racial groups are well known, "Maxwell Geismar, in Mark Twain, an American Prophet, is one of the very few critics to even mark Twain's attitudes toward the Indian." Abstract in AES, XVI (1972-1973), 1772.

B19 DONALDSON, SCOTT. "Pap Finn's Boy," South Atlantic Bulletin, XXXVI (May), 32-37.
Although Huck matures, he remains a loner, like his Pap, though rejecting society rather than being rejected by it. In matters of religion, as in those of race, Huck maintains a view like his father's--little more than a set of superstitions.

B19A *DURAM, JAMES C. "Mark Twain and the Middle Ages," Wichita State University Bulletin, University Studies. XLVII (August), 1-16.
[Source: Abstract in AES, XVIII (1974-1975), 591.] JA, CY, P&P, and MS criticized and accurately represented the Middle ages, and embody MT's view that Church and feudalism dehumanize man; gradually, however, MT turned from his belief in progress to a cyclic view of history, with institutions rooted in human nature.

B20 EBÓN, MARTIN. "Mark Twain's 'Mental Telegraphy,'" in his They Knew the Unknown, New York: The World Publishing Company, pp. 79-87.

(EBON, MARTIN)
A summary of MT's psychic experiences, drawn from the autobiographical material, the Paine Biography, and other familiar sources.

B21 FETTERLEY, JUDITH. "The Sanctioned Rebel," Studies in the Novel, III (Fall), 293-304.
Tom Sawyer's escapades break the tedium of life in St. Petersburg for the adults, who in turn furnish prohibitions against which to rebel. MT was exposing the hypocrisy of the Bad Boy fiction of his day, in which the Bad Boy is just the Good Boy in disguise, in the same category with the adults Tom Sawyer exposes. Basically, the tone of TS is positive and the focus is on the benefits of the symbiotic relationship between Tom and the adults. Abstract in AES, XVI (1972-1973), 245; reprinted in Twainian, XXXIII (January-February, 1974). Article reprinted in Kesterson (1973), 92-102.

B22 FIEDLER, LESLIE. The Collected Essays of Leslie Fiedler. New York: Stein and Day. 2 vols., passim.
There are frequent insights into MT in essays not specifically about him, as in the observation that he represents a Folk, rather than Pop tradition, and thus "has become ever more remote from an urban, industrialized world" (II, 470), and in the sadness in IA (I, 91-92). Among the essays dealing extensively with MT are "Come Back to the Raft Ag'in, Huck Honey!" (I, 142-51, originally in Partisan Review, June, 1948); a lengthy treatment of the "Good Good Girl and Good Bad Boy" and "Boys Will Be Boys!" (I, 481-94, passim on MT; originally in The New Leader, April 14, 28, 1958); and "Toward a Centennial: Notes on Innocents Abroad" (I, 296-311, originally in New American Review, 1966). The two volumes are well indexed.

B23 FLECK, RICHARD L. "Mark Twain in the American Wilderness," Nature Study: A Journal of Environmental Education and Interpretation (Verbank, New York), XXV (Summer), 12-14; (Autumn), 10-11.
On RI, noting MT's spirit of freedom in his writings, his growing love for the West, and his portrayal of Hawaii. "While the landscape passages are not, by any means, the whole of Roughing It, they must be considered as a significant element in that they not only illustrate Twain's techniques in language, but they also serve as a subtle barometer of his varying emotional attitudes toward the land."

B24 _____. "Mark Twain's Social Criticism in The Innocents Abroad," Bulletin of the Rocky Mountain Modern Language Association, XXV (June, 1971), 39-48.
"Twain had to swallow his national pride when it came to judging the welfare of the common man." After tracing the social criticism in IA and recent criticism of the book, concludes by noting the awareness MT had gained of social injustices throughout the world. Regardless of what social system might be at fault, foreign or American, "the effects were always the same--the loss of human dignity.... that man should be reduced to the animal state was for Mark Twain insufferable."

B25 FORTENBERRY, GEORGE. "The Unnamed Critic in William Dean Howells' Heroines of Fiction," Mark Twain Journal, XVI (Winter), 7-8.
In the chapter "Scott's Jeanie Deans and Cooper's Lack of Heroines," when discussing Cooper Howells says he "turned to a literary friend who had made rather a special study of him"; Howells's "use of the word 'females' and his reference to The Last of the Mohicans almost makes it a certainty that his critic is Mark Twain." Abstract in AES, XVI (1972-1973), 1763.

B25A FRENCH, BRYANT MOREY. "James Hammond Trumbull's Alternative Chapter Headings for The Gilded Age," Philological Quarterly, L (April), 271-80.
The mottoes chosen by Trumbull parodied the contemporary over-use of chapter mottoes and added satirical running commentary on the plot. Trumbull also furnished alternative mottoes (here printed) which "vie in cleverness with and sometimes exceed" the mottoes used in GA. Abstract by French in MLA Abstracts (1971), 7974.

B26 GERBER, JOHN C. [Review: Maxwell Geismar, Mark Twain: An American Prophet (1970).] American Literature, XLIII (May), 296-98.
"A long, repetitious, highly personal biography that creates a Mark Twain most of us do not recognize...something of a corrective for many of the mucky analyses" of MT in recent years, "yet the fact remains that this is an inept work. Its facts are not always correct, its organization is confusing, its style is irritating, and its thesis is at times absurd." Nonetheless, Gerber agrees with Geismar's view that the last two decades were not a time when MT, on the verge of psychic collapse, wrote works of unrelieved gloom.

B27 GIBSON, WILLIAM M. [Review: Thomas Blues, Mark Twain & the Community (1970).] American Literary Realism, 1870-1910, IV (Summer), 291-92.
"Professor Blues concerns himself...with the subject...how is the individual to fulfill himself in a democracy, by resistance or accommodation, withdrawal or leadership? Unhappily his treatment of this great topic is mostly inadequate" because he tries to cover too much and because his rejection of old views and quest for new ones lead him astray.

B28   GOAD, MARY ELLEN. "The Image and the Woman in the Life and Writings of Mark Twain," _Emporia State Research Studies_, XIX (March), 5-70.

Traces the influence of MT's wife, his mother, and Mary Mason Fairbanks, among others, with particular emphasis on the question of whether he made serious concessions to propriety because of them. "This study originated as a partial fulfillment of the requirements for the degree Master of Arts, Kansas State Teachers College, Emporia, Kansas." Based on familiar, published sources. Abstract in _AES_, XV (1971-1972), 537; reprinted in _Twainian_, XXXII (January-February, 1973).

B29   GOLDSTIEN, NEAL L. "Mark Twain's Money Problem," _Bucknell Review_, XIX (Spring), 36-54.

"Twain thought of things in terms of money and profit," and "the confusion over money which permeates his books is the result, not the cause, of his lack of art." _RI_ and _CY_ furnish useful examples, because "the dominant tones of each are those which rule the author as well," and because the seventeen years between their publication shows a ubiquitous money theme which "almost suggests...an outpouring, an unburdening, and a confession." Abstract in _AES_, XV (1971-1972), 1207; reprinted in _Twainian_, XXXII (January-February, 1973). Abstract by Goldstien in _MLA Abstracts_ (1971), 7976.

B30   GOODYEAR, RUSSELL H. "Huck Finn's Anachronistic Double Eagles," _American Notes and Queries_, X (November), 39.

Although the book was published in 1885 and the preface says "Time: forty to fifty years ago," Chapters XVI and XXII mention twenty-dollar gold pieces--which were first minted in 1849.

B31   GRIMM, CLYDE L., JR. [Review: Howard G. Baetzhold, _Mark Twain and John Bull: The British Connection_ (1970) and Maxwell Geismar, _Mark Twain: an American Prophet_ (1970).] _Studies in the Novel_, III (Spring), 118-21.

Baetzhold's book reflects long and close familiarity with MT, "so much so, indeed, that Baetzhold has had some difficulty in bringing his material into steady focus"; a number of connections are explored, and "in summary, Professor Baetzhold has provided a comprehensive and detailed account of a shaping force on the works of Mark Twain at least as significant as the Missouri frontier or the frontier humorists." The first seventy pages of Geismar's book were enough for Grimm, who tired of the factual inaccuracies, awkward phrasing, amateur psychology, and "distortions of Clemens' social and political views," and refused to read further.

B32   HILL, HAMLIN. "Mark Twain," in J. Albert Robbins, ed., _American Literary Scholarship: An Annual/1971_ (Durham, North Carolina: Duke University Press, 1973), pp. 75-85.

A survey of MT scholarship for the year (See 1963.B32). Contents: "i. Textual and Bibliographical"; "ii. Biographical"; "iii. General Criticism"; "iv. Earlier Works"; "v. _Huckleberry Finn_"; "vi. Later Works."

B33   HOUSMAN, A[LFRED] E[DWARD]. _The Letters of A. E. Housman_. Cambridge, Massachusetts: Harvard University Press, pp. 246-47, 277, 388-89.

Contains the texts of three notes from Housman to Cyril Clemens. He declines the office of honorary Vice-President in the Mark Twain Society, and refers to the elegy on Stephen Dowling Bots in _HF_ as "one of the poems I know by heart" (2 February 1927, pp. 246-47), and permits him to reprint his words about _HF_ although he does not remember what he said (16 February 1929, p. 277). He declines with thanks the Silver Medal of the Mark Twain Society, adding that he has also declined honors offered by two Universities and by the King (2 March 1936), pp. 388-89).

B34   HOWELL, ELMO. "Mark Twain's Indiantown," _Mark Twain Journal_, XV (Summer), 16-19.

The village of a short sketch and the longer _Which Was It?_ appears to be based on Napoleon, Arkansas; the nostalgic excursion is evidence that MT "always felt at home only in the deep South." Abstract in _AES_, XV (1971-72), 1497.

B35   KING, BRUCE. "Huckleberry Finn," _Ariel: A Review of International English Literature_ (University of Calgary), II (October), 69-77.

The "absolute internalization of moral values is peculiarly American," and "_Huckleberry Finn_ is a spiritual autobiography. Its main themes are the development of Huck's acceptance of Jim as an equal...and his willingness to be rejected by society and risk damnation so that Jim may escape." The trip down the river has as its archetype "the traditional allegory of the soul's pilgrimage through this world." It is a radical book, though not in the sense that it would substitute populism: _vide_ Pap Finn. "Huck, isolated, uncorrupted, true to himself, could never be assimilated into any society." Reprinted in Schmitter (1974), pp. 109-16.

B36   KOLIN, PHILIP C. "Mark Twain's Pudd'nhead Wilson: A Selected Checklist," _Bulletin of Bibliography_, XXVIII (April-June), 58-59.

In preparing this checklist of criticism, "I have used the resources of the bibliographies found in _PMLA_ and _American Literature_ as well as such useful tools as

(KOLIN, PHILIP C.)
Dissertation Abstracts and Stovall's guide to research in Eight American Authors. I have excluded earlier, incorrect readings of the novel that don't even follow the plot and I have concentrated on those studies which stay well within the mainstream of useful criticism."

B37 LEARY, LEWIS. [Review: Howard G. Baetzhold, Mark Twain and John Bull: The British Connection (1970) and Thomas Blues, Mark Twain and The Community (1970).] Modern Fiction Studies, XVII (Summer), 276-78.
"Mr. Baetzhold has told just about everything that there is to tell about Clemens and his relations with and attitudes toward Britain," in a book of lasting value for its revelation of how the "readings, reflections, prejudices, and long-toed resentments" of Clemens became the pronouncements of the persona MT. Thomas Blues leaves the term community somewhat unclear, and his book is annoying and puzzling, but the more stimulating of the two, demanding that the reader return to MT with a fresh vision; and for this Blues deserves gratitude.

B38 LEHAN, RICHARD. [Review: William M. Gibson, ed., Mark Twain: "The Mysterious Stranger" Manuscripts (1969) and John S. Tuckey, ed., Mark Twain's "The Mysterious Stranger" and the Critics (1970).] Nineteenth-Century Fiction, XXV (March), 502-508.
The two complementary books "in some ways are central to all Twain criticism." There is an important theme in MT's work of a physical and a spiritual self, an "essential self" and an alter ego, and the topic needs further exploration.

B39 _____. [Review: Arthur L. Scott, Mark Twain at Large (1969), and Howard G. Baetzhold, Mark Twain and John Bull: The British Connection (1970).] Nineteenth-Century Fiction, XXVI (September), 248-50.
Chiefly descriptive, praising both books as well written and valuable additions to MT scholarship.

B40 LONG, E. HUDSON. [Review: Howard G. Baetzhold, Mark Twain and John Bull (1970).] American Literature, XLII (January), 579-81.
A thorough investigation and full documentation make this "a significant contribution to scholarship"; moreover, there are "careful analyses" of a number of MT's works and his mind, which was "free and flexible," though impulsive. There is a useful discussion of the influence on MT of English writers, especially W. E. H. Lecky.

B41 McCULLOUGH, JOSEPH B. "Mark Twain and Journalistic Humor Today," English Journal, LX (May), 591-95.
Iconoclasm is characteristic of American literature, particularly of humor. It is not uncommon for one of our outstanding humorists to end in despair, no longer "able to cope with those aspects of melancholy, terror, violence, and death that he at one time found fit to deal with comically." Abstract in AES, XVI (1972-1973), 870; reprinted in Twainian, XXXIII (January-February, 1974).

B42 _____. "Mark Twain and the Hy Slocum-Carl Byng Controversy," American Literature, XLIII (March), 42-59.
Comic sketches in the Buffalo Express, 1868-1871 under the pseudonyms "Carl Byng" and "Hy Slocum" have been linked to MT. In The Forgotten Writings of Mark Twain (1963) Henry Duskis identifies this and other material as the work of MT, but "his reasons for attribution are usually tenuous and conjectural, and he offers little evidence to support his contentions"; moreover, he does not reprint material in its original form, and misses some sketches, making identification difficult. It appears that MT wrote the sketches signed "Byng" but not those signed "Slocum." Abstract in AES, XV (1971-1972), 1208; reprinted in Twainian, XXXII (January-February). Abstract by McCullough in ALA, IV (June), 93; in MLA Abstracts (1971), 7990.

B43 McMAHAN, ELIZABETH E. "The Money Motif: Economic Implications in Huckleberry Finn," Mark Twain Journal, XV (Summer), 5-10.
Money provides plot motivation and is a means of characterization; it also "serves to focus the reader's attention on the central theme: the indictment of human greed and hypocrisy in a corrupt, profit-oriented society." Abstract in AES, XV (1971-72), 1495.

B44 MALHOTRA, M. L. Bridges of Literature: 23 Critical Essays in Literature. Mayur Colony, Ajmer (India): Sunanda Publications, pp. 25-36, 45-54.
"Notes on Mark Twain's Humour" (pp. 25-37) considers MT as frontiersman and newspaperman, primarily a humorist, though conceding that he was more. In HF emphasizes the humorous aspects of Pap, and the King and Duke. The essay ends by noting that Hal Holbrook, "who physically resembles him a great deal in every detail," has shown the durability of MT's humor by "making huge money" out of stage appearances. ["Read at the All-Rajasthan Universities Seminar on American Literature, sponsored by the USEFI, at Government College, AJMER (1968)."]

(MALHOTRA, M. L.)
"Is Huckleberry Finn a Flawed Work?"
(pp. 45-54) argues that "the book fails to
tell how [Huck's] non-conformism is a pragmatic approach to life"; Huck's decision to
run away at the end and the "evasion of the
issues" illustrate this failure. The book
survives because of its vitality and humor
(pp. 52-53). ["Read at the Regional Seminar on American Literature held at Nainital
(1969)."]

B45   MATTHEWS, BRANDER. "The Penalty of Humor,"
Twainian, XXX (March-April), 1-4, reprinted
from Harper's, May, 1896 (1896.B10). Abstract in AES, XV (1971-1972), 1504; reprinted in Twainian, XXXII (January-February, 1973).

B46   MAY, JOHN R. "The Gospel According to Philip
Traum: Structural Unity in The Mysterious
Stranger," Studies in Short Fiction, VIII
(Summer), 411-22. Reprinted in his Toward
a New Earth: Apocalypse in the American
Novel. Notre Dame, London: University of
Notre Dame Press, 1972, pp. 74-91.
"The structural unity of The Mysterious
Stranger develops out of Philip Traum's
mission of salvation to Theodor Fischer."
Abstract by May in ALA, V (December), 135.
Reprinted in Schmitter (1974), pp. 133-43.

B47   *MENDELSOHN, M. [Introduction to Russian edition of TS and HF.] Moscow: Khudozhestvennaya Literatura.
[Source: MHRA Annual Bibliography
(1971), No. 8858.]

B48   MILLER, BRUCE E. "Huckleberry Finn: the
Kierkegaardian Dimension," Illinois Quarterly, XXXIV (September), 55-64.
In TS, MT portrays boyish egotism and
pursuit of excitement and pleasure. "In
Huckleberry Finn he examines another side--
the tentative reaching towards companionship, the sorting out of responsibilities,
and the troubled investigation of oneself
and one's surroundings," and "Huck's final
move to the Indian Territory, like Abraham's pilgrimage to Mount Moriah in Soren
Kierkegaard's account expresses a unique
spiritual adjustment which replaces the
norms of social intercourse with a tran-
scedent and terrifyingly immediate acquaintance with supernatural force." Abstract
in AES, XV (1971-1972), 2692; reprinted in
Twainian, XXXII (January-February, 1973).

B49   MILLICHAP, JOSEPH R. "Calvinistic Attitudes
and Pauline Imagery in The Adventures of
Huckleberry Finn," Mark Twain Journal, XVI
(Winter), 8-10.
Presbyterianism has been predominant as
subject matter and ideological influence
in Southern literature (although Baptist
and Methodist churches are more common),
because it insists on human limitations.

St. Paul's influence on the thinking of John
Calvin is reflected in HF, especially in the
treatment of Huck's father, a figure of the
"fallen Adam in the New World." This role
is underscored by Huck's references to him
as "the old man," who became drunk and
"raised Cain...A body would a thought he
was Adam--he was just all mud," and by the
illusory snakes and devils of his delirium
tremens. Abstract in AES, XIV (1972-1973),
1769.

B50   NEBEKKER, HELEN E. "The Great Corrupter or
Satan Rehabilitated," Studies in Short Fiction, VIII (Fall), 635-36.
Henry B. Rule's argument in "The Role of
Satan in 'The Man That Corrupted Hadleyburg'" (1969) can be further strengthened
if we remember that the town had already
feared burglars before Satan arrived; in the
"Calvinist ethos which Twain both knew and
detested," man is already corrupt and the
stranger therefore no corrupter.

B51   PEARCE, ROY HARVEY. "Huck Finn in His History," Études Anglaises, XXIV (July-September), 283-91.
Hawthorne's Hester Prynne and Melville's
Ishmael will ultimately come to terms with
their society, but Huck by his nature cannot:
"His function, it turns out, is to demonstrate the absolute incompatability of the
sort of self he is and the sort of world in
which he tries so hard to live. He gains no
sense of his own history and has no future.... He exists not to judge his world
but to furnish us the means of judging it--
and also our own world as it develops out of
his."

B52   PETTIT, ARTHUR G. "Mark Twain and the Negro,
1867-1869," Journal of Negro History, LVI
(April), 88-96.
On MT's ambivalent attitudes. In the
West he learned that he could be both pro-
Northern and anti-Negro, and for a long
time he was prone to make jokes about such
topics as the odor of sweating Negroes; but
by 1867 he was attacking the dead issue of
slavery and reconciled to the idea of Negro
citizenship. He later condemned lynching,
and eventually learned the need to depict
Black men and women "with certain emotional
and intellectual attributes long denied the
Negro in American literature." The change
in his attitudes was partly the result of
environment--Nevada was pro-Union and his
father-in-law Jervis Langdon was pro-aboli-
tion--but MT also was becoming more liberal
in his outlook with greater experience of
the world.

B53   _____. "Mark Twain, the Blood-Feud, and the
South," Southern Literary Journal, IV (Fall),
20-32.
MT's published works and late, unpublished
manuscripts reveal "that there were clearly

(PETTIT, ARTHUR G.)
two Souths in Mark Twain's literary imagi-
nation--one of nostalgia, the other of
nausea and nightmare...the unfallen Eden
of his boyhood" and "a Waste Land of murder, miscegenation, blood-feuding, dueling,
smalltown depravity, lynching, and white
race guilt." He became disenchanted with
the South because he changed, but he "remained a Southerner to the end." Abstract
in AES, XVI (1972-1973), 246; reprinted in
Twainian, XXXIII (January-February, 1974).
Abstract by Pettit in MLA Abstracts (1971),
7999.

B54   PICKETT, CALDER M. [Review: Maxwell Geismar,
Mark Twain: An American Prophet (1970) and
Howard G. Baetzhold, Mark Twain and John
Bull (1970).] Journalism Quarterly,
XLVIII (Summer), 355-56.
Geismar's "long and curious work which is
not really a biography" follows the pattern
of his Henry James and the Jacobites, "a
brutal commentary not only of [sic] Henry
James but on all his admirers." Geismar
devotes less than half of his book to what
have been considered the major works, emphasizing instead "the diatribes, the dis-
quisitions, the criticisms of contemporary
affairs"; nonetheless, it is refreshing to
see the attention given to the Autobiography
(seen as one of the major works) and FE.
Baetzhold's book is briefly described, with
the comment that "it is pure scholarship,
and it is not as much fun to read as angry
old Geismar, but it is a much better book."

B55   RACKHAM, JEFF. "The Mysterious Stranger in
'The Campaign that Failed,' Southern Humanities Review, V (Winter), 63-67.
"A mysterious stranger murdered at night
by arcadian boys playing soldier is an
imaginative creation inserted into what
otherwise would have been only a humorous
recollection," indicting war not only for
its destruction of human life but also because it turns innocent boys into killers.
Abstract in AES, XV (1971-1972), 535; reprinted in Twainian, XXXII (January-February, 1973).

B56   *RAKNEM, INGVALD. Joan of Arc in History,
Legend and Literature. Oslo: Universi-
tetsforlaget.
[Source: MHRA Annual Bibliography
(1971), 2004, 8869; other details not giv-
en.]

B57   REEVES, PASCHAL, et al. "A Checklist of
Scholarship on Southern Literature for
1971," Mississippi Quarterly, XXV (Spring,
1972), 199-246. On MT, pp. 209-13.

B58   RITUNNANO, JEANNE. "Mark Twain vs. Arthur
Conan Doyle on Detective Fiction," Mark
Twain Journal, XVI (Winter), 10-14.
A Double-Barreled Detective Story burlesques A Study in Scarlet, a similar story
of revenge, which it follows in plot and
several details; however, they differ in
that Doyle leads through a series of ordered
events to a triumph of justice, while MT's
chaotic story "makes no effort to balance
the scales of justice." Abstract in AES,
XVI (1972-1973), 1767.

B59   ROWLETTE, ROBERT. "Mark Twain's Barren Tree
in The Mysterious Stranger: Two Biblical
Parallels," Mark Twain Journal, XVI (Winter),
19-20.
Satan's creating and blighting of a tree
in Chapter X is a "blending of two of
Christ's miracles--the feeding of the five
thousand and the cursing of the fig tree";
previously in MS Satan merely pointed to
man's shabby nature, but "here, he is shifted from observer to participant, with the
result that the scene grows taut with dramatic interest." Abstract in AES, XVI (1972-
1973), 1770.

B60   RUBIN, LOUIS D., JR. "How Mark Twain Threw
off His Inhibitions and Discovered the Vitality of Formless Form," Sewanee Review,
LXXIX (July-September), 426-33.
A review of Maxwell Geismar's Mark Twain:
An American Prophet, hostile, and in its
vigor reminiscent of some of MT's own criticisms. Geismar, who "frequently can't tell
the difference between a novel and a political pamphlet," is mainly interested in
MT's anti-imperialism, and distorts his subject to emphasize this point. In this
opinionated book, "the list of Mr. Geismar's
dislikes constitutes almost a Who's Who of
intellectual distinction in our time. Name
a good mind, and the chances are that Mr.
Geismar dislikes him. Name a good book, and
the chances are that Mr. Geismar dislikes
it." ("This review is an expanded version
of one which originally appeared in the
Washington Star.")

B61   SCHIECK, WILLIAM J. "The Spunk of a Rabbit:
An Allusion in Huckleberry Finn," Mark
Twain Journal, XV (Summer), 14-16.
Shortly before saving Jim from the slave-
hunters, Huck wrote, he couldn't speak up
because he lacked courage, "the spunk of a
rabbit"; but he drove them away by pleading
with them to come on the raft to help his
father, ill with small-pox. Asking for the
opposite of what he wants repeats a device
in Uncle Remus, His Songs and Sayings
(1880), where Brer Rabbit begs Brer Fox not
to throw him in the briar patch. Abstract
in AES, XV (1971-72), 1499.

B62   SCHMITZ, NEIL. "The Paradox of Liberation in
Huckleberry Finn," Texas Studies in Literature and Language, XIII (Spring), 125-36.
"The freedom Huck strives to attain is
his right to be a child, not an impertinent
manikin like Tom Sawyer, but the unregener-
ate poetic child alive in his body and sensitive to the mystery of being in the world."

(SCHMITZ, NEIL)
For Jim, however, the question is one of his manly independence, and he shows his recognition of a slave's position in his attack on Solomon's proposal to divide the child--he has seen "black families dismembered on the [auction] block." The ending throws away the character, Jim "after he has served as a 'moral burden.'" The emancipations of Huck and Jim were different and conflicting in nature. Abstract by Schmitz in MLA Abstracts (1971), 8009.

B63   ____. "Twain, Huckleberry Finn, and the Reconstruction," American Studies (Kansas; formerly Midcontinent American Studies Journal), XII (Spring), 59-67.
"Jim's situation at the end of Huckleberry Finn reflects that of the Negro in the Reconstruction, free at last and thoroughly impotent, the object of devious schemes and a hapless victim of constant brutality." Abstract by Schmitz in MLA Abstracts (1971), 8010.

B64   SKINNER, OTIS. "Mark Twain at the Players' Club," Mark Twain Journal, XV (Summer), back cover.
Facsimile reproduction of a signed typescript; Skinner briefly recalls MT in rather general and conventional terms. Abstract in AES, XV (1971-72), 1501.

B65   SMITH, LUCIAN R. "Sam Clemens: Pilot," Mark Twain Journal, XV (Summer), 1-5.
From MT's published statements and discussions by Paine, DeLancey Ferguson, Dudley R. Hutcherson, and others, concludes that MT "did not enjoy piloting nearly as much as he said he did. From the outset it has been apparent that piloting was not an end in itself, but merely a means to another end: wealth and prestige." Abstract in AES, XV (1971-72), 1500.

B66   STEIN, ALLEN F. "Return to Phelps Farm: Huckleberry Finn and the Old Southwestern Framing Device," Mississippi Quarterly, XXIV (Spring), 111-16.
"The events at Phelps Farm combine with the opening of the novel at St. Petersburg to enclose the account of the trip down the river in a frame which works in much the same way as did the framing device traditionally used by writers in this school of humor," but MT "subtly adds to the functions of the frame, thus enhancing the effectiveness of the novel." Abstract by Stein in MLA Abstracts (1971), 8014; in ALA, V (June, 1972), 183.

B67   STEIN, GERTRUDE. "Unique Tribute to Mark Twain from the Inimitable Gertrude Stein," Mark Twain Journal, XV (Summer), front cover.
Facsimile reproduction of a hand-written note comparing MT to the Mississippi River, with the signature of Alice Toklas in the margin. "Written for her fellow members of the Mark Twain Society when she visited St. Louis and now published for the first time." Abstract in AES, XV (1971-1972), 1503.

B68   STERN, MADELEINE B. Heads & Headlines: The Phrenological Fowlers. Norman: University of Oklahoma Press.
On the family of phrenologists. Passim on MT, with an account of Jessie Fowler's phrenograph of MT (pp. 253-54; reprinted from Phrenological Journal of April, 1901).

B69   STONE, ALBERT E. [Review: Arthur L. Scott, Mark Twain at Large (1969).] American Literature, XLIII (November), 459-60.
"This is a brisk, informative, but not very profound survey of Twain's career from 1866, when he sailed to Hawaii, to 1910, when he returned from Bermuda to die.... Scott offers no radically new interpretation of the man, the career, the work"; he "jousts with writers of a bygone day...on points no longer moot," but might have made fuller use of recent scholarship.

B70   TWICHELL, JOSEPH H. "Twichell's Letters to Paine," Twainian, XXX (January-February), 3-4.
Twelve letters, 1911-1913, concerning the Paine biography of MT, currently appearing serially in Harper's, making a minor correction and commenting on notebooks, letters, etc. Concludes a series beginning in 1970, (1970.B92). Abstract in AES, XV (1971-1972), 1508; reprinted in Twainian, XXXII (January-February, 1973).

B71   VORPAHL, BEN M. "'Very Much Like a Fire-Cracker': Owen Wister on Mark Twain," Western American Literature, VI (Summer), 83-98.
Based on Wister's "In Homage to Mark Twain," which appeared in Harper's in 1935, summarizes Wister's comments and gives background on Wister and his slight acquaintance with MT. Abstract in AES, XVII (1973-1974), 2151; reprinted in Twainian, XXXIV (March-April, 1975).

B72   WEBER, BROM. [Review: Maxwell Geismar, Mark Twain: An American Prophet (1970).] Saturday Review, LIV (February 27), 27-28.
"Shrouded in a paranoid fog that blurs the book's positive contributions." [Saturday Review editor's note: "Brom Weber has praised Mark Twain's social criticism in The Art of American Humor (1962, 1970) and reprinted it in American Literature: Tradition and Innovation (1969)."]

B73   ZWAHLEN, CHRISTINE. "Of Hell or Hannibal?" American Literature, XLII (January), 562-63.
The title of MT's juvenile poem, "Love Concealed: to Miss Katie of H--L" (Hannibal

(ZWAHLEN, CHRISTINE)
Journal, May 6, 1853) represents a deliberate ambiguity for humorous effect and not
an abbreviation to fit a limited space;
a photostat of the Journal shows room to
write out "Hannibal" in full. MT later
asked his brother about events in "H--L,"
and recalled the reaction to this poem with
amusement. Abstract in AES, XV (1971-1972),
1206; reprinted in Twainian, XXXII (January-
February, 1973). Christine M. Zwahlen's abstract in ALA, V (December), 135, reads in
full: "A pica count of the headline, 'To
Miss Katie of H...L,' suggests that Mark
Twain intended an ambiguous reading"; identical text of this abstract is in MLA Abstracts (1971), 8017.

1972 A BOOKS

A1   CLEMENS, SAMUEL L. The Adventures of Tom Saw-
      yer. New York: Washington Square Press.
      Enriched Classics Edition.
         A "Reader's Supplement" in the center (as
      in other books in this series) includes bio-
      graphical data and study aids, among them
      brief extracts from published criticism.
      Contains fifteen stills from the 1938 film
      of the novel by Selznick International Pic-
      tures, released through United Artists,
      with Tommy Kelly as Tom. [A paperbound
      popular edition.]

A2   _____. Fables of Man, ed. John S. Tuckey.
      Berkeley, Los Angeles, London: University
      of California Press.
         A volume in the CEAA edition of the MT
      Papers. "This collection offers Mark
      Twain's pieces on such large topics as God,
      providence, Christianity, and human nature,
      gathered from the unpublished writings in
      the Mark Twain Papers. Although Albert
      Bigelow Paine and Bernard DeVoto printed
      some of the works included here and various
      scholars have quoted extracts in support
      of their arguments, none of these texts
      has ever appeared in an authoritative print-
      ing and few are currently accessible."

A3   _____. The Great Landslide Case: Three Ver-
      sions, With Editorial Comment by Frederick
      Anderson and Edgar M. Branch. Berkeley:
      Friends of the Bancroft Library, University
      of California.
         On the lawsuit described in RI, Chapter
      XXXIV. Includes a tipped-in full-size re-
      production of the San Francisco Daily Morn-
      ing Call, August 20, 1863, p. 1.

A4   _____, ed. Frederick Anderson. A Pen Warmed-
      Up in Hell: Mark Twain in Protest. New
      York, London: Harper & Row, Publishers,
      Toronto: Fitzhenry & Whiteside, Ltd.
         An anthology of MT's anger, in published
      writings and in material from the Mark Twain
      Papers. An introduction (pp. x-xviii) de-
      scribes MT's "bitterness about the terrors

imposed by useless war, the squalor of racial injustice, the fraudulent distribution
of wealth, and the exploitation of their
citizens by indifferent governments."

A5   _____, and CHARLES DUDLEY WARNER, ed. Bryant
      Morey French. The Gilded Age: A Tale of
      To-Day. Indianapolis and New York: The
      Bobbs-Merrill Company, Inc.
         Introduction gives MT and Warner biography,
      and background, composition, and criticism
      of GA. Appendixes include "Author's Preface
      to the London Edition"; "The British Copy-
      right"; "Colonel Sellers's Improvised 'Rail-
      road Map'"; "The Given Name of Colonel Sell-
      ers"; a discussion of the chapter-head mot-
      toes.

A6   HARNSBERGER, CAROLINE THOMAS, ed. Everyone's
      Mark Twain. South Brunswick and New York:
      A. S. Barnes and Company; London: Thomas
      Yoseloff Ltd.
         Like her Mark Twain at Your Fingertips
      (1948), this is a collection of quotations
      from MT's published works with a small amount
      of material published for the first time.
      Arranged alphabetically by categories from
      "ABROAD See also ASS, FORGETFULNESS, OPINION"
      to "ZEAL See RELIGION," with an extensive
      bibliography (pp. 686-92) and a "Correlated
      Subjects Index" (pp. 693-703). "Foreword"
      by Clara Clemens (pp. 7-8).

A7   SMITH, JANET, ed. Mark Twain on Man and Beast.
      New York, Westport: Lawrence Hill & Co.
         "What we have here are forty-four of Mark
      Twain's highly emotional comments on life,
      distinguished from his other comments only
      because in each of them birds or beasts or
      fish or insects play a part. And so do peo-
      ple," and his animals are often human types,
      though true to nature (p. 13). The standard
      of selection was the editor's taste, and
      "Out of all the Mark Twain that could, by
      any definition, be called an animal story,
      I discarded nine because they seemed to me
      inferior. I made no effort to concentrate
      on the obscure, although eleven of these
      selections are not in print elsewhere"
      (p. 14).

A8   *YOSHIDA, HIROSHIGE. Mark Twain Kenkyu--Shiso
      to Gengo no Tenkai [Study of Mark Twain--
      Development of Thought and Language]. Tokyo:
      Nanundo.
         [Source MLA International Bibliography
      (1972), 8804.]

1972 B SHORTER WRITINGS

B1   ALSEN, EBERHARD. "Pudd'nhead Wilson's Fight
      for Popularity and Power," Western American
      Literature, VII, 135-43.
         Wilson pretends to support the aristocrat-
      ic code "because he knows that this will
      help his career" (p. 140). The themes of
      power and property, evolving out of the

1972 - Shorter Writings

(ALSEN, EBERHARD)
stories of the protagonist and antagonist help create a "structural and thematic symmetry" which makes PW "Mark Twain's most tightly constructed novel" (p. 143).

B2 ANAND, SHALINE. "Huckleberry Finn and the Hemingway Hero," in C. D. Narasimhaiah, ed., Student's Handbook of American Literature. Ludhiana, India: Kalyani Publishers. [Papers presented at the All India Postgraduate Student Seminar in American Literature held at Mysore University in December, 1968; organized by the U. S. Educational Foundation in India.]
A comparison of Huck Finn and Nick Adams; this is based on Philip Young and Sheridan Baker, according to the bibliography, and reflects their thinking.

B3 ANDERSON, FREDERICK, and HAMLIN HILL. "How Samuel Clemens Became Mark Twain's Publisher: A Study of the James R. Osgood Contracts," Proof, II, 117-43.
A discussion of the terms under which MT's books were published with Osgood, and facsimile reproductions of actual contracts. Abstract by Anderson and Hill in MLA Abstracts (1972), 8742.

B4 ANDERSON, SHERWOOD. "Four American Impressions," in Horace Gregory, ed., The Portable Sherwood Anderson (rev. ed.). New York: The Viking Press, pp. 428-33.
("These sketches were written in 1919 and published in The New Republic.") Compares Ring Lardner to MT, pp. 430-31.

B5 ANON. "Mark Twain Items Published Elsewhere," Twainian, XXXI (January-February), 1-4; (March-April), 3-4.
Reprints a number of abstracts from AES, XIV (1970-1971).

B6 ANON. "More Mark Twain," Bancroftiana (Bancroft Library, University of California, Berkeley), No. 52 (April), p. 7.
New acquisitions by the Mark Twain Papers include manuscript of a chapter in TA and two leaves of GA, prospectuses of four books, and an annotated copy of CY showing passages MT omitted in readings.

B7 ARNER, ROBERT D. "Acts Seventeen and Huckleberry Finn," A Note on Silas Phelps' Sermon," Mark Twain Journal, XVI (Summer), 12.
Allison Ensor's note on Chapter XXXVII of HF in Explicator (1967) should be expanded: not only does the Biblical chapter refer to the brotherhood of all men in verse 26, but in verse 29 it cautions against the worship of Mammon, "the chief reason the Southerners...continue to hold slaves"; moreover, "the fact that one of the preachers mentioned in Acts Seventeen, the man who accompanies Paul to Athens, is named Silas seems further evidence that this is no

casual allusion on Twain's part." Abstract in AES, XVI (1972-1973), 2364.

B8 ASPIZ, HAROLD. "Mark Twain and 'Doctor' Newton," American Literature, XLIV (March), 130-36.
On James Rogers Newton, the faith doctor who successfully treated Olivia Langdon (future wife of MT) for a partial paralysis. Abstract in AES, XVIII (1974-1975), 1904. Abstract by Aspiz in ALA, V (June), 182; in MLA Abstracts (1972), 8745.

B9 BAETZHOLD, HOWARD G. "Found: Mark Twain's 'Lost Sweetheart,'" American Literature, XLIV (November), 414-29.
The short story "My Platonic Sweetheart" (1898), originally titled "My Lost Sweetheart," is based on MT's fond memories of Laura M. Wright (not to be confused with Laura Frazer, the original of Becky Thatcher); she was the subject of a recurring dream by MT, and the dream of a lost sweetheart recurs in his works. Abstract by Baetzhold in MLA Abstracts (1972), 8746.

B10 BARNES, BARBARA LAMKIN. "Mark Twain's Family Christmas," Yankee, XXXVI (December), 106-109, 136-41.
Based in part on material in the Mark Twain Papers; includes a description of the Clemens home in Hartford, with two color photographs by Willis L. Lamkin.

B11 BARTON, MARION. "Shavian Mirth Recalled. Shaw and Mark Twain in 1907 Laughed in House of Commons," Independent Shavian, X (Spring), 48.
A letter to the editor of the New York Times (New York, April 19, 1933; appeared in issue of April 24, p. 14, column 7). A very brief comment on seeing MT and Shaw at a distance. Abstract in AES, XVI (1972-1973), 742; reprinted in Twainian, XXXIII (January-February, 1974).

B12 BELLAMY, JOE D. "Two Eras, Two Epitaphs: Steamboating Life in the Works of Mark Twain and Richard Bissell," Ball State University Forum, XIII (Autumn), 48-52.
MT portrayed the grandeur of the age of steamboating he had known; Bissell writes with similar love about the decline of another age of steamboating.

B13 BIE, WENDY A. "Mark Twain's Bitter Duality," Mark Twain Journal, XVI (1972-1973), 14-16.
"Many critics have dealt with duality in Twain's works as the psychological expression of Clemens/Twain or the Polemicist/Humorist schizophrenia, or as a narrative device which Twain very nearly overworked"; in fact it is an expression of the duality MT recognized in human nature, the product of "the disparity between man's 'low' impulses, drives, and instincts and his 'high' social and moral code." Abstract in AES, XVI (1972-1973), 2367.

B14   BONAZZI, ROBERT. [Review: Maxwell Geismar, Mark Twain: An American Prophet (1970).] New Orleans Review, III, 95-97.
Discusses Geismar's debates with other critics, among them Brooks, DeVoto, Leavis, and biographers and editors Paine, Neider, Kaplan. Praises the "very intelligently detailed appraisal of Twain's work," and finds the book "well detailed and gracefully written," though thin on the early period and too detailed on Christian Science and MT's speeches.

B15   BOWEN, JAMES K., and RICHARD VAN DER BEETS, eds. American Literature Abstracts, V (June), 183.
Contains four abstracts by the authors of articles on MT. Discontinued publication with this issue; superseded by MLA Abstracts.

B16   BRACK, O. M., JR. "Mark Twain in Knee Pants: The Expurgation of Tom Sawyer Abroad," Proof, II, 145-51.
This book first appeared serially in St. Nicholas: An Illustrated Magazine for Young Folks, edited by Mrs. Mary Elizabeth Mapes Dodge (author of Hans Brinker; or, The Silver Skates), who made extensive changes to make Huck's dialect more genteel and to soften or remove references to sweating and other bodily functions, to alcohol, to death, and to Negroes and to religious groups in terms which might offend. For book publication in America the expurgated text from St. Nicholas was used for the first two-thirds and the authoritative typescript for the remainder; the English edition published by Chatto & Windus is closer to MT's intentions, apparently set from a carbon copy of the original typescript.

B17   BRAND, JOHN M. "The Incipient Wilderness: A Study of Pudd'nhead Wilson," Western American Literature, VII, 125-34.
A way of entering the setting of PW is through Cooper's The Prairie, which has a "zest and flair" MT's book lacks (p. 125); in both works "existing law proves insufficient to reorder a threatened society" (p. 126), and even if there were a Divine Law which could change the laws of society, "it is doubtful that even Wilson, the best in his community, would have eyes to see and the will to apply it" (p. 134).

B18   BRODWIN, STANLEY. "The Humor of the Absurd: Mark Twain's Adamic Diaries," Criticism, XIV (Winter), 49-64.
"For Twain, humor ultimately derives from contradiction, absurdity and incongruity, the principle of irony triumphant; it functions as a theological sign of man's fall but at the same time enables him to deal with that pathetic state.... Twain's perception of the nature and role of humor in relation to his theological determinism has not been delineated.... I propose to confront this problem in theological-literary terms," showing how MT's diaries of Adam, Eve, and Satan reflect "a variety of ideas illuminating one central concept: that humor is a theological element that binds God's creation to man's fall." Abstract by Brodwin in MLA Abstracts (1972), 8750.

B19   BROGUNIER, JOSEPH. "An Incident in The Great Gatsby and Huckleberry Finn," Mark Twain Journal, XVI (Summer), 1-3.
Compares the killings of Myrtle Wilson and Boggs, with the reactions by Nick and Huck and by the morbidly curious neighbors. Fitzgerald admired MT and expressed his indebtedness to the influence of HF in a letter of August 9, 1939. Abstract in AES, XVI (1972-1973), 2386.

B20   BRONSON, DANIEL ROSS. [Review: Frederick Anderson, ed., Mark Twain: The Critical Heritage (1971).] American Literary Realism, V (Summer), 323-25.
"As a scholarly tool...cannot be faulted.... The selection of criticisms is ample, representative, and without a hint of manipulation for the sake of argument.... For the student just approaching Twain seriously this book is a valuable guidepoint; for the Twain scholar it is a handy reference and a source of continuing conjecture." Anderson makes it clear that the reviews influenced later criticism more than they influenced MT's writing.

B21   *BRUMM, URSULA. "Amerikanische Dichter und europäische Geschichte: Nathaniel Hawthorne und Mark Twain," in Alfred Weber and Harmut Grandel, eds. Geschichte und Fiktion: Amerikanische Prosa im 19 Jahrhundert/History and Fiction: American Prose in the 19th Century (Göttingen: Vanderhoeck & Ruprecht), pp. 85-108.
[Source: MLA Bibliography (1972), Nos. 117, 8236.]

B22   BUDD, LOUIS J. "Did Mark Twain Write 'Impersonally' for the New York Herald?" Library Notes (Duke University Library), No. 43 (November), pp. 5-9.
"Gossip at the National Capital" (February 3, 1868) and two "Washington Gossip" letters (February 10, p. 8 and February 18, p. 3) are unsigned and "do not sound all that much like Mark Twain.... the problem is to judge how Mark Twain would sound when he was trying not to project his breezy, raucous, and witty persona."

B23   BURNS, GRAHAM. "Time and Pastoral: The Adventures of Huckleberry Finn," Critical Review (Melbourne), No. 15, pp. 52-63.
Extends the approach of Leo Marx in The Machine in the Garden (1964); but where Marx "concentrates almost exclusively on

377

(BURNS, GRAHAM)
the technological subversion of the pastoral ideal.... I want to argue, myself, that the lyrical river journey in Huckleberry Finn, while splendidly realized as a naturalistic re-creation, it is also felt, as we experience it, as a kind of analogue for life itself; and that the characteristic pacing of Twain's writing in the central lyrical episodes creates a sense of timelessness central to its pastoral qualities." Abstract in AES, XVI (1972-1973), 2935.

B24 BUSH, ROBERT. "Grace King and Mark Twain," American Literature, XLIV (March), 31-51.
On the New Orleans author (1851-1932), who visited the Clemenses repeatedly in Hartford (after meeting them there in 1887), and was their guest in Florence in 1892. In addition to her reminiscences of MT in Memories of a Southern Woman of Letters (1932), there are "impressions" of MT and impressions about the Clemens family in her notebooks and letters (here liberally quoted, by permission of Mr. John M. Coxe and the Department of Archives, Louisiana State University, Baton Rouge). Three MT letters are here published, and one appeared in her 1932 Memories. Abstract in AES, XVIII (1974-1975), 1903. Abstract by Bush in ALA, V (June), 182.

B25 CHRISTOPHER, J. R. "On the Adventures of Huckleberry Finn As a Comic Myth," Cimarron Review, No. 18 (January), pp. 18-27 ["This paper was read at a meeting of the South Central Modern Language Association in Memphis, Tennessee, on October 30, 1970."]
Northrop Frye's Anatomy of Criticism (1957) mentions HF three times; "The purpose of this essay is simply to investigate the ways in which Northrop Frye's Theory of Myths is applicable to this Twain fiction."

B26 CLEMENS, OLIVIA and SAMUEL L. CLEMENS. [Facsimile reproduction of joint letter by Olivia Clemens and MT.] Mark Twain Journal, XVI (Winter), front cover.
To the mother of Cyril Clemens, expressing good wishes on her engagement to James Ross Clemens.

B27 COARD, ROBERT L. "Mark Twain's The Gilded Age and Sinclair Lewis's Babbitt," Midwest Quarterly, XIII (April), 319-33.
"Although there seems to be no question of any specific indebtedness of the latter book to the earlier, a comparison...may illuminate the satirical techniques of the two celebrated practitioners and say something about the continuity of American satirical tradition." (Based on texts of the Signet Classic Edition for the two works). Abstract in AES, XVI (1972-1973), 787; reprinted in Twainian, XXXIII (January-February, 1974).

B28 CROWLEY, JOHN W. "A Note on The Gilded Age," English Language Notes, X (December), 116-18.
"A recently discovered Charles Dudley Warner letter" about GA "indicates that the book was completed more quickly than generally supposed" and "supports B. M. French's contention that Warner and Mark Twain were reacting to specific Washington scandals such as the Credit Mobilier affair." The letter (here reprinted) is to Edward Burlingame, who had reviewed the book in Appleton's Journal, XI (January 10, 1874), 59. Abstract in AES, XVII (1973-1974), 1808; reprinted in Twainian, XXXIV (March-April, 1975).

B29 D'AVANZO, MARIO L. "In the Name of Pudd'nhead," Mark Twain Journal, XVI (Summer), 13-14.
The name may be traceable to the reward, the "solid Pudding," which Benjamin Franklin said he received for Poor Richard's Almanac --to which the aphorisms of "Pudd'nhead Wilson's New Calendar" have been compared. Abstract in AES, XVI (1972-1973), 2365.

B30 [DAVIS, CHESTER L.] "Annie Moffett Webster and Charles Noel Flagg Letters to Paine (Pictorial Mark Twain)," Twainian, XXXI (March-April), 1-3.
Chiefly concerned with paintings of MT; Davis speaks of "our promise to print substantially all of the letters written to Paine." Abstract in AES, XVII (1973-1974), 2089; reprinted in Twainian, XXXIV (March-April, 1975).

B31 _____. "Financial Support for Worthy Studies and Publications Supplied by Private, Foundation and Government Sources (Writing and Publication of 'Mark Twain and Hawaii')," Twainian, XXXI (July-August), 1-4; (September-October), 1-4.
A general discussion of the collecting of Twainiana and the contributions made by various individuals; reprints correspondence between Walter Francis Frear and George Hiram Brownell. Abstract in AES, XVII (1973-1974), 2091; reprinted in Twainian, XXXIV (March-April, 1975). The abstract of the September-October installment, "Frear's 'Mark Twain and Hawaii,'" in AES, XVII (1973-1974), 2282 is not yet reprinted in Twainian; see later issues.

B32 _____. "Francis D. Millet, James Montgomery Flagg and Spiridon Portraits (pictorial Mark Twain)," Twainian, XXXI (May-June), 1-4.
On paintings of MT; factual, chiefly indebted to published material. Abstract in AES, XVII (1973-1974), 2090; reprinted in Twainian, XXXIV (March-April, 1975).

B33 _____. "'The Letters of Madame de Sevigne' (17th Century History); (Mark Twain's Marked Copy)," Twainian, XXXI (November-December), 1-4.

([DAVIS, CHESTER L.])

On MT's personal copy of The Letters of Madame de Sevigne to Her Daughter and Friends, Edited by Mrs. Hale...(Revised Edition, Boston: Roberts Brothers, 1878). Begins a series of extensive reprinting of the text of the book (both letters and editorial background), with underscorings and comments by MT; this series in Twainian continues into 1974. Abstract in AES, XVIII (1974-1975), 2274.

B34   ____. [Editor's comment on holdings.] Twainian, XXXI (May-June), 1.

"Many of our members have asked us to give them some idea as a rough estimate how much UNPUBLISHED material we have in our files and our reply is that we have enough, or enough available on call, to fill our four-page 'Twainian' every two months for the NEXT FIFTY YEARS. Some arrangement may be worked out to permit a more rapid use of this material, yet as new material comes to us or the several other depositories in the United States and abroad, we are quite certain that our subtitle 'Mark Twain--Yesterday and Today' was wisely chosen."

B35   ____. [Review: Franklin R. Rogers, ed., Roughing It.] Twainian, XXXI (September-October), 3-4.

Provides useful description of book and editing.

B36   ____. [Review: John S. Tuckey, ed., Fables of Man.] Twainian, XXXI (September-October), 4.

Provides useful description of book and editing.

B37   DINAN, JOHN S. "Hank Morgan: Artist Run Amuck," Massachusetts Studies in English, III (Spring), 72-77.

"The Arthurian world is cruel and unacceptable," but "Hank's art does not illumine, it mystifies. It does nothing to purge his audience of the characteristics that make them slaves.... Without his being aware of it, Hank's Great Artifact, his New World, is but a change in form, not spirit." Abstract in AES, XVIII (1974-1975), 244.

B38   [EICHELBERGER, CLAYTON L.] [Review: Samuel L. Clemens, The Great Landslide Case: Three Versions, ed. Frederick Anderson and Edgar M. Branch.] American Literary Realism, V (Fall), 497.

Brief notice of "an impressively designed and printed publication which reproduces Twain's three versions of a single episode, accompanied by well-documented historical background and comment."

B39   ____. [Review: Horst H. Kruse, Mark Twains "Life on the Mississippi": Eine Entstehungs- und Quellengeschichtliche Untersuchung zu Mark Twains "Standard Work" (1970).] American Literary Realism, V (Spring), 179.

A brief description of this "detailed examination" of the chapters added in 1882.

B40   FETTERLEY, JUDITH. "Disenchantment: Tom Sawyer in Huckleberry Finn," Publications of the Modern Language Association, LXXXVII (January), 69-74.

In TS Tom was a leader, but in HF he has nothing to offer, is pointlessly cruel in his jokes, and becomes a minor tyrant. He has counterparts throughout HF, as in his sharing with Miss Watson "the syndrome of moralism, aggression, and hypocrisy"; the Grangerford-Shepherdson feud reveals a false code of honor when "Southern chivalry is exposed as sneaking up behind a couple of kids and shooting them in the back. But the exposure of that cruelty is not so important as the exposure of the connection between that cruelty and the language of honor. What Mark Twain is recording in Huckleberry Finn, through the Grangerfords, through Miss Watson, and through Tom Sawyer, is his sense of the inevitable connection between moralism, the language of right and wrong with its inevitable concomitant of self-righteousness, and the fact, the act, of aggression." Abstract in AES, XV (1971-1972), 2455 [condensed from Judith Fetterley's own abstract on contents page (p. 5)]; reprinted in Twainian, XXXII (January-February, 1973). Abstract by Judith Fetterley in ALA, V (June), 182; in MLA Abstracts (1972), 8760. [See reply by Anna Mary Wells, 1972.B84.]

B41   NO ENTRY

B42   FISHER, MARVIN, and MICHAEL ELLIOTT. "Pudd'nhead Wilson: Half a Dog is Worse than None," Southern Review, n.x., VIII (July), 533-47.

Wilson is not the hero of the story or "a largely sympathetic character reflecting the author's own feelings"; although an underdog, "he is essentially unfeeling and only superficially perceptive." In a sense a slave's "more than spectral fear of being sold down the river, the precarious condition of a dog's life, and Wilson's fateful remark solving the problem of a barking dog by killing half are symbolic equivalents." Dogs take on a new symbolic value in this book, chiefly as victims. Abstract by Fisher and Elliott in MLA Abstracts (1972), 8762.

B43   GASSAWAY, BOB M. "Tom Sawyer is Back on the River," Contempora (Atlanta, Georgia), II (August-December), 36-40.

(GASSAWAY, BOB M.)

An illustrated account of the filming of TS by APJAC Productions in Arrow Rock, Missouri, noting the expense and logistical complexity: "Mark Twain would have liked it."

B44 GERBER, JOHN C. "Practical Editions: Mark Twain's The Adventures of Tom Sawyer and The Adventures of Huckleberry Finn," Proof, II, 285-92.

MT's concern with precise degrees of emphasis in his writing is revealed by his attention to both conventional punctuation and liberal use of dashes, parentheses, brackets, italics, and exclamation points, and his linking by hyphens words not customarily joined; "as a result, the exact accidental in one of his novels can be almost as crucial for meaning as the right word." Unfortunately, there is no single text of TS that can be used as printer's copy for a new edition, and even HF presents problems because the manuscript used by the printer is lost. School and college texts of both books introduce large numbers of variants and "are unsatisfactory, in some instances dramatically so. At best, our students are reading approximations of what Mark Twain wanted them to read." Abstract by Gerber in MLA Abstracts (1972), 8765.

B45 GOTTFRIED, LEON. "The Odyssean Form: An Exploratory Essay," in Peter Uwe Hohendahl, Herbert Lindenberger, and Egon Schwarz, eds., Essays on European Literature in Honor of Liselotte Dieckmann (St. Louis: Washington University Press), pp. 19-43, passim.

On the Odyssey, Don Quixote, Joseph Andrews, and Huckleberry Finn. In each there is a contrast of "home" and "road," with problems in the final homecoming (p. 29), "pattern of flight and return," and "a symbolic death" for the hero; and "at some point he is rescued naked or nearly so from pit, ditch, river, or sea. In each work, finally, there is an initiation, that is, a significant transmission of values from an older, wiser, or higher ranking central figure to his junior" (p. 33). HF "is the least hopeful" of the four books, because MT "found (or presented) no social reality of any sort that he could affirm as being worthy of his heroes."

B46 GRIBBEN, ALAN. "Mark Twain, Phrenology and the 'Temperaments': A Study of Pseudoscientific Influence," American Quarterly, XXIV (March), 44-68.

"In the following essay I wish to demonstrate that his fascination with this pseudoscience actually had begun by the time he was nineteen years old; that he made use of its terminology and tenets in a minor but persistent manner in his literature; that while he scorned its practitioners, he displayed a lifelong uncertainty about the soundness of its theories; and that one of the fundamental doctrines which he absorbed from his early study of phrenology--the notion of 'temperaments'--not only shaped his self-concept, but also influenced his choice of language in expressions of his later deterministic philosophy." Abstract by Gribben in MLA Abstracts (1972), 8766.

B47 HARRELL, DON W. "A Chaser of Phantoms: Mark Twain and Romanticism," Midwest Quarterly, XIII (January), 201-12.

MT's dream fragments "The Enchanted Sea Wilderness," "An Adventure in Remote Seas," and The Great Dark "employ identical protagonists and frame stories, and they echo strangely the best of Twain's earlier writing" such as RI and HF; parallels may be traced back as far as his newspaper correspondence from the Sandwich Islands. Abstract in AES, XV (1971-1972), 3023; reprinted in Twainian, XXXII (January-February, 1973). Abstract by Harrell in MLA Abstracts (1972), 8767.

B48 HARRISON, STANLEY R. "Mark Twain's Requiem for the Past," Mark Twain Journal, XVI (Summer), 3-10.

Explanations of MT's early optimism and late cynicism in terms of his personal experiences tend to overlook the obvious fact that his life paralleled that of his country: the growth of a more sober, disillusioned national outlook is reflected in his works. Abstract in AES, XVI (1972-1973), 2368.

B49 HILL, HAMLIN. "Mark Twain," in J. Albert Robbins, ed., American Literary Scholarship: An Annual/1972.

A survey of MT scholarship for the year (See Gerber 1963.B32). Contents: "i. Textual and Bibliographical"; "ii. Biographical"; "iii. General Criticism"; "iv. Earlier Works"; "v. Huckleberry Finn"; "vi. Later Works."

B50 HOWELL, ELMO. "Mark Twain and the Civil War," Ball State University Forum, XIII (Autumn), 53-61.

On MT's slight involvement in the War, the importance of the South in his writings, and, as exemplified in his river piloting, his self-doubts.

B51 _____. "Tom Sawyer's Mock Funeral: A Note on Mark Twain's Religion," Mark Twain Journal, XVI (Winter), 15-16.

MT "seemed emancipated, but the best of his work reflects the spirit of Missouri fundamentalist faith," as in the emotional scene in the church: "In his most moving moments Mark Twain turned instinctively to the values derived from religious faith."

B52 HUBBELL, JAY B. Who Are the Major American Writers?: A Study of the Changing Literary Canon. Durham, North Carolina: Duke University Press, pp. 135-44 and passim.
     Traces the growth of MT's reputation in an extended study ("Mark Twain," pp. 135-44), with a number of significant comments on him elsewhere in the volume, as in references to him in literary histories and the standing he achieved in various polls to determine who were the nation's major writers. Includes references to anthologies and critical surveys which are not listed in the present bibliography. Article reprinted in Schmitter (1972), pp. 19-28.

B53 KAPLAN, HAROLD. "Huckleberry Finn: What It Means to Be Civilized," in his Democratic Humanism and American Literature (Chicago and London: University of Chicago Press), pp. 225-52.
     "Huck is demonstrably a frontier Thoreau, who has a ritualistic need for isolation, and whose escape from his social role is dramatized by his false death and funeral" (p. 237); but "for Huck this isolation won't sustain itself" and he needs Jim (p. 238). Huck and Jim continually face the community on shore, and thereby discover the primary values that might redeem its existence" (p. 242). As in Melville's The Confidence Man, "the issue...remains the question of whom to trust" (p. 251); in the end Huck has been civilized: he "lives in the civilized imagination of his society."

B54 KERR, HOWARD. "'Sperits Couldn't A Done Better': Mark Twain and Spiritualism," in his Mediums, and Spirit-Rappers, and Roaring Radicals: Spiritualism in American Literature, 1850-1900 (Urbana, Chicago, London: University of Illinois Press), pp. 155-89.
     A thorough treatment of spiritualism in MT's life and works. Includes his visits to mediums in San Francisco, seances in the Nook Farm colony, and visiting mediums in London with Olivia after Susan's death--although he was not a believer. Kerr relies principally on the familiar published material about MT, but has discovered interesting parallels between the tricks of Tom and Huck at the Phelps farm and the activities of a spirit at the home of the Reverend Eliakim Phelps in 1850: in each case there were straw-stuffed dummies, anonymous letters, mysterious writings in unknown symbols, and wandering sheets, spoons, nails, and candlesticks; and details of the Eliakim Phelps haunting were available to MT (pp. 173-80).

B55 KIM, YONG-KWON. "Teaching and Survey of American Literature in Korea: A Survey," in C. D. Narasimhaiah, ed., Asian Responses to American Literature (Delhi, London: Vikas Publications), pp. 395-98.
     The Periodical Index published by the Republic of Korea National Assembly Library in 1970 lists eight articles on MT out of 101 on American literature for the period 1963-1969 (p. 397), and five master's theses were written on MT in Korean universities between 1945 and 1968.

B56 KRAUS, W. KEITH. "Mark Twain's 'A Double-Barreled Detective Story': A Source for the Solitary Oesophagus," Mark Twain Journal, XVI (Summer), 10-12.
     Compares the famous passage to a descriptive passage in Conan Doyle's A Study in Scarlet, of which MT's story is a parody and to which he appears to have referred previously, in "Hadleyburg," Abstract in AES, XVI (1972-1973), 2363.

B57 "Letters to Paine from Samuel E. Moffett, S. L. Severance and Annie M. Webster in Years 1906-1917," Twainian, XXXI (May-June), 4.
     Contain little information directly pertaining to MT. Abstract in AES, XVII (1973-1974), 2088; reprinted in Twainian, XXXIV (March-April, 1975).

B58 LEWIS, STUART. "Twain's Huckleberry Finn, Chapter XIV," Explicator, XXX (March), Item 61.
     While Huck takes the traditional view of Solomon's wisdom in proposing to divide a baby, "Jim realizes the terror of one man's holding absolute power over another.... The test is too close for comfort." Abstract by Lewis in MLA Abstracts (1972), 8776.

B59 *LLOYD, JAMES B. "The Nature of Twain's Attack on Sentimentality in The Adventures of Huckleberry Finn," University of Mississippi Studies in English, XIII, 59-63.
     Characters cry a total of 71 times in HF, for the right reason, or sentimentally, or hypocritically; this crying is one of MT's ways of demonstrating a proper balance of head and heart. [Source: Abstract by Lloyd in MLA Abstracts (1973), 8876.]

B60 LYCETTE, RONALD. "Mark Twain Mapping His Territory," ETC: A Review of General Semantics, XXIX (June), 155-64.
     MT's "works reveal a persistent effort to understand the process that enables a man to grow emotionally and intellectually," as is revealed in Old Times on the Mississippi and HF.

B61 McCULLOUGH, JOSEPH B. "A Listing of Mark Twain's Contributions to the Buffalo Express, 1869-1871," American Literary Realism, 1870-1910, V (Winter), 61-70.
     Lists a total of 134 items, grouped as "Sketches," "Sketches and Poems Signed Carl Byng," "Editorials," "People and Things," and "Miscellaneous."

B62　*MELLARD, JAMES. "Prolegomena to a Study of the Popular Mode in Narrative," Journal of Popular Culture, VI (Summer), 1-19. [Source: Abstract in AES, XVIII (1974-1975), 2512.

As part of a broader study, treats MT's assimilation of formulaic material from the "folk."

B63　MEYER, HORST E. "An Unnoticed Twain Letter," Mark Twain Journal, XVI (Winter), back cover.

To Christian Bernard, first Baron Tauchnitz (September 14, 1876), on the German publication of Tom Sawyer; MT had learned through "my friend, Bret Harte" that Tauchnitz was interested in the book.

B64　MILLER, LEO. "Huckleberries and Humans," Publications of the Modern Language Association, LXXXVII (March), 314, (letter).

MT's choice of the Christian name "Eschol" for his Colonel Sellers in GA may be significant, referring to the Hebrew word for "a bunch of grapes" and to an incident in Numbers XIII, 23-24; it could have been suggested by MT's friend, the Reverend Joseph Twichell.. See 1961.B17; 1962.B37.

B65　MURRAY, DONALD, CHAN WAI-HUENG, and SAMUEL HUANG. "A Checklist of American Books in Chinese Translation," American Book Collector (Chicago), XXII (March-April), 15-37.

On pp. 28-29, lists 37 books by MT, most of them published in the '30's and '40's, or in Hong Kong or on Taiwan.

B66　OSTROM, ALAN. "Huck Finn and the Modern Ethos," Centennial Review, XVI (Spring), 162-79.

It is a misreading to see HF in terms of our day, as "a socially liberal/radical Bildungsroman": the novel's structure reveals a denial of the perfectability of man, and Huck, no Noble Savage, is merely "trying his best, a man of good will trapped in a world he never made." Abstract in AES, XVI (1972-1973), 2936.

B67　REEVES, PASCHAL, et al., comps. "A Checklist of Scholarship on Southern Literature for 1972," Mississippi Quarterly, XXVI (Spring 1973), 201-203 (portion on MT.)

Fifth annual checklist, including about two dozen books and articles on MT published in 1972; annotated. Generally duplicates other standard bibliographies.

B68　*ROBINSON, FRED C. "Appropriate Naming in English Literature," Names, XX (June), 131-37. [Source: Abstract in AES, XVIII (1974-1975), 1013.] As part of a broader study, discusses the names of Tom Sawyer and Huck Finn.

B69　ROWLETTE, ROBERT. "Mark Twain, Sarah Grand, and The Heavenly Twins," Mark Twain Journal, XVI (Summer), 17-18.

"Hundreds of notations" in MT's copy of Sarah Grand's popular novel, shows his interest in a book burdened, like his own Those Extraordinary Twins, with "a sub-plot featuring twins...who interfered with the main line of action." MT's harsh judgments, as he must have recognized, "were apropos not only of her book but essentially of the uncut version of his," which he revised into PW. "Internal evidence indicates that he revised his book before reading hers," although it is still possible that he was already familiar with Sarah Grand's book and influenced by it. Abstract in AES, XVI (1972-1973), 2366.

B70　ROYOT, DANIEL. "Éléments Phonologiques du Dialect Noir dans ' Huckleberry Finn,'" Langues Modernes, LXVI, No. 1, 79-83.

This examination of Negro dialect in Huckleberry Finn consists chiefly of three lists: "Graphonologie: Système Vocalique" (on the pronunciation of specific phonemes); "Phonétique et Morphologie" (on the structure of words, as in the adding or dropping of sounds); "Valeur de la Transcription" (notes that Jim's speech is a synthesis of "Low Colloquial," "Southern Speech," and Negro dialect).

B71　RUBIN, LOUIS D., JR. "Mark Twain and the Post-War Scene," in his The Writer in the South: Studies in a Literary Community. Athens: University of Georgia Press. Mercer University Lamar Memorial Lectures, No. 15.

Only MT and George W. Cable "were able to escape the trauma of the Lost Cause," and Cable did so only through lifetime struggle against it; "Thus it is Mark Twain, and Mark Twain alone, whose imagination was sufficiently free to look within himself" (p. 48), but he never fully broke away. "It seems to me that in A Connecticut Yankee the whole ambivalent love-hate relationship of Sam Clemens with the South is dramatized and laid out plainly. That the Arthurian England which Hank Morgan, master mechanic from Connecticut, sets out to reform is in effect the South of Clemens's youth, is clear from the very outset" (p. 69).

B72　SACKETT, S. J. E. W. Howe. New York: Twayne Publishers, Inc., passim.

Contains numerous quotations from correspondence between MT and Howe, little of it particularly revealing. Quotes Howe's estimate in 1881 that MT's literary career was almost over (Atchinson Globe, December 31, p. 3, 1881.B6; quoted p. 74).

B73　SCHERTING, JACK. "Poe's 'The Cask of Amontillado': A Source for Twain's 'The Man That Corrupted Hadleyburg,'" Mark Twain Journal, XVI (Summer), 18-19.

(SCHERTING, JACK)

Although the story's theme is that of Milton's Areopagitica, which "cannot praise a fugitive and cloistered virtue...that never sallies out and sees her adversary," the structural parallels are closer to Poe's story of a delayed revenge for an unspecified offence; moreover, both Montresor and Stephenson "exploit human vanity by challenging the reputation of their victims." Although MT probably did not deliberately pattern his story on Poe's, he was sometimes unconsciously influenced by his reading; "In this connection it is also worth noting that Poe's story 'William Wilson' may have provided Twain with some of the ingredients for his novel with a similar title, Pudd'nhead Wilson." Abstract in AES, XVI (1972-1973), 2357.

B74 SHETTY, NALINI V. "A Case for the Study of Twain's Pudd'nhead Wilson," in C. D. Narasimhaiah, ed., Asian Response to American Literature (Delhi and London: Vikas Publications), pp. 207-14.

Expresses surprise that there is so little interest displayed in PW, important for its treatment of the Negro and the theme of miscegenation; this is especially relevant to India, with its phenomenon of the Anglo-Indian.

B75 SIMPSON, LOUIS P. "Mark Twain and the Pathos of Regeneration: A Second Look at Geismar's Mark Twain" Southern Literary Journal, IV (Spring), 93-106.

Defends Maxwell Geismar's Mark Twain: An American Prophet (1970) against the charge by Brom Weber (Saturday Review, February 27, 1971) that it is merely a continuation of Geismar's "ugly political attack" against "American literary intellectuals." In reply, Simpson calls it a "big, ill-organized, clumsily written--but in its way important--book," in which Geismar appeals less to our view of MT as radical than "to the image of an aged prophet speaking to us out of the depths of the Old Republic about an American pastoral destiny that could never be." Abstract in AES, XVI (1972-1973), 1447; reprinted in Twainian, XXXIII (January-February, 1974). Article reprinted in Simpson's The Man of Letters in New England and the South: Essays on the History of the Literary Vocation in America (1973), pp. 150-66.

B76 SKERRY, PHILIP J. "The Adventures of Huckleberry Finn and Intruder in the Dust: Two Conflicting Myths of the American Experience," Ball State University Forum, XIII (Winter), 4-13.

Compares MT's and Faulkner's novels on "the basic narrative level, the psychological level, the sociological level, and the symbolic level," with opposing interpretations of the American experience and the American hero.

B77 SOLOMON, ANDREW. "Jim and Huck: Magnificent Misfits," Mark Twain Journal, XVI (Winter), 17-24.

Despite the damage done to the ending by MT's amateurishness, HF is "a brilliantly warm and comic portrait of two human beings, one white and one black, who fall outside of and above their society." Abstract by Solomon in MLA Abstracts (1972), 8792.

B78 TARIQ, AZIZUDDIN. "Mark Twain and the Damned Human Race," in C. D. Narasimhaiah, ed., Asian Response to American Literature (Delhi and London: Vikas Publications), pp. 20 pp. 201-207.

Beneath the scathing commentator there was a man of great warmth. "No American writer has been more dedicated, to the welfare of mankind, and at the same time, more grievously wounded by its follies" (p. 206).

B79 TAYLOR, ROBERT, JR. "Sounding the Trumpets of Defiance: Mark Twain and Norman Mailer," Mark Twain Journal, XVI (Winter), 1-14.

On their social criticism and questioning of the American myth.

B80 VANDERBILT, KERMIT. "Mark Twain Writes to Poet Longfellow," Mark Twain Journal, XVI (Summer), front cover.

Facsimile reproduction of MT letter (June 4, 1877), asking Longfellow's support (together with that of Lowell, Whittier, and Holmes) in urging President Hayes to appoint William Dean Howells to a government mission in Switzerland. Abstract in AES, XVI (1972-1973), 2369.

B81 _____. "Correction and Further Note on Mark Twain and Longfellow," Mark Twain Journal, XVI (Winter), 24.

MT's letter to Longfellow reproduced on the front cover of the preceding issue helps reveal his inner conflict in viewing the Eastern literary establishment a few months before the Whittier Birthday Dinner speech in Boston. The date of a Howells letter, misprinted in the preceding issue, is here corrected.

B82 WALTERS, THOMAS N. "Twain's Finn and Alger's Gilman: Picaresque Counter-Directions," Markham Review, III (May), 53-58.

"Whereas Huck struggles with questions of what morality is, Jed [in Horatio Alger, Jr.'s Jed, The Poorhouse Boy, 1900] conforms to the morality of the society he wishes to join," and is a less successful, imaginative creation than Huck. Abstract in AES, XVIII (1974-1975), 1546.

B83 WARREN, ROBERT PENN. "Mark Twain," Southern Review, n.s. VIII (July), 459-92.

A study of MT's incoherent character and his major works, with particular emphasis on HF.

1972 - Shorter Writings

B84   WELLS, ANNA MARY. "Huck Finn, Tom Sawyer, and Samuel Clemens," Publications of the Modern Language Association, LXXXVII (October), 1130-31.

A reply to Judith Fetterley's article in the January PMLA: Huck Finn is not Mark Twain or Samuel Clemens; what he "finally sees in Tom is unendurable, and if the function of art is to make us endure the unendurable, it is still hard to do it in a book for boys." Huck's decision to abandon civilization was not that of Clemens, who in his letters to Howells "was clearly identifying with Tom."

B85   WELSH, JOHN R. [Review: Lewis Leary, Southern Excursions: Essays on Mark Twain and Others (1971).] Southern Literary Journal, IV (Spring), 128-32.

MT isn't really a Southerner, and perhaps the book's title is misleading: "Southern Excursions is really a book about the national literature, and a very good one."

B86   WHITE, RAY LEWIS. Sherwood Anderson/Gertrude Stein: Correspondence and Personal Essays. Chapel Hill: University of North Carolina Press, pp. 45, 73, 97, 104.

Contains brief, laudatory comments on MT by Gertrude Stein.

B87   YOUNG, PHILIP. "Huckleberry Finn: The Little Lower Layer," in his Three Bags Full: Essays in American Fiction (New York: Harcourt Brace Jovanovich, Inc.), pp. 136-53.

HF represents a national dream of escape, but Huck is wounded by his experiences on shore and has grown up out of MT's control; it is for this reason that the story is turned over to Tom Sawyer. The date "1952" appears at the end of the essay, but there is no indication that this is from Young's book on Ernest Hemingway of that year. Young also discusses the wounded Huck in his Ernest Hemingway: A Reconsideration (1966).

1973 A BOOKS

A1   BISSELL, RICHARD. My Life on the Mississippi; or, Why I am Not Mark Twain. Boston: Little, Brown and Company.

Bissell, who was formerly a Mississippi River pilot and still holds a license, had been reading and thinking for years about MT and brings a professional's interest to speculations about him as a pilot, describes MT as "a nut," but respects his strengths.

A2   CLEMENS, SAMUEL L., ed. Paul Baender. The Works of Mark Twain: "What is Man?" And Other Philosophical Writings. Berkeley, Los Angeles, London: Published for the Iowa Center for Textual Studies by the University of California Press.

A volume in the standard edition of MT's works: "An Approved Text, Center for Editions of American Authors, Modern Language Association of America."

A3   GALE, ROBERT L. Plots and Characters in the Works of Mark Twain. With a foreword by Frederick Anderson. Hamden, Connecticut: Archon Books, 1973. 2 vol.

Vol. I summarizes book and "notebook material, autobiographical dictation (including Mark Twain in Eruption), and collected letters." Vol. II alphabetically lists "all fictional characters and all real-life people as well, provided they move, speak, or otherwise have a part in action which Twain vivifies (except where indicated in footnotes after certain titles). Well over seven thousand characters are collected from Twain's works and identified here..." (I, xi). Meticulously prepared and invaluable to students of MT.

A4   GEISMAR, MAXWELL, ed. and introduction. Mark Twain and the Three R's: Race, Religion, Revolution--and Related Matters. Indianapolis and New York: The Bobbs-Merrill Company, Inc.

"This is an anthology of Mark Twain's radical social commentary," from 1869. "I claim that, far from being the embittered old man of the scholarly legend, Twain was a revolutionary temperament from the very beginning of his literary career (or his life) to the end. Indeed, it is true that his best polemics and social satires were written after 1900, in the closing decade of his life" (p. xv). "In this book I have tried to keep editorial comment to a minimum. As usual Mark Twain speaks for himself better than anybody can speak for him, and that is what he is doing in these pages" (p. xxvi). This is not new material, and it overlaps Foner's Mark Twain: Social Critic (1958) and Janet Smith's Mark Twain on the Damned Human Race (1962), but the selections are intelligently made and the introduction is an interesting portrayal of MT as a man of his time.

A5   HILL, HAMLIN. Mark Twain: God's Fool. New York: Harper & Row, Publishers.

A meticulously documented picture of the tragic last ten years of MT's life, based on original material, most of it unpublished, in the Mark Twain Papers and other collections. Hill reveals the disintegration of a family, struggles for the favor of "The King," and rages and alienations, and he suggests that these years were the culmination of a life of guilt and uncertainty: "Fear had been the controlling interest of his life: fear of poverty, fear of offending and alienating his family and friends, fear of being mistaken by his audience. He moved insecurely in all the worlds he inhabited, much like the mysterious stranger in a dream world who obsessed him in his fiction" (p. 269).

A6   KESTERSON, DAVID B. Critics on Mark Twain: Readings in Literary Criticism. Coral Gables, Florida: University of Miami Press.
      "Critics on Mark Twain: 1882-1940" (pp. 13-36) and "Critics on Mark Twain Since 1940" (pp. 37-50) consist largely of very brief excerpts from 31 sources; because of their brevity and the ease with which they may be found elsewhere most of these are not cross-referenced in the present bibliography. There are also longer or complete reprintings of critical material, in the remainder of the book, and in most cases these are cross-referenced in the present bibliography.

A7   SMITH, J. HAROLD. Mark Twain: Rebel Pilgrim. New York: Heath Cote Publishing Corp.
      A study of MT's skepticism and his search for understanding. "The aim of this analysis of Mark Twain's life and thought is two-fold: (1) to provide a human-interest account of the events and experiences in the life of a fascinating man. (2) To illuminate the thought of the author by arranging his views, attitudes, and concepts under distinctive topical areas of consideration." Two appendixes tabulate his references to God, Jesus Christ, and Heaven, and "Subject-Areas of Major Writings in Relation to Time-Pattern of Publication."

A8   _____. Women in Mark Twain's World. New York: Carlton Press, Inc.
      On women in MT's domestic, social, romantic, love, literary, and political worlds, including extensive quotation from his works in the text of 23 pages.

1973 B SHORTER WRITINGS

B1   ANON. "Mark Twain Items Published Elsewhere," Twainian, XXXII (January-February), 1-4. Reprints a number of abstracts from AES, XV (1971-1972).
      "Actually our reprinting each year starts with the issue of A.E.S. last carried by us, not necessarily opening and closing the calendar year but only from such issues as have been received by us before going to press for this issue. Attention is also called to the fact that many of the items appeared in their original printing much earlier than the past year however they had not been abstracted and available to us. We make no attempt to read or reprint everything mentioning Mark Twain" (unsigned headnote by Chester L. Davis). Of the 29 abstracts, nine concern material in past issues of Twainian, a few involve only passing mention of MT, and (following what appears to be an unstated Twainian policy) abstracts of material from Mark Twain Journal are silently passed over. Abstract in AES, XVIII (1974-1975), 2283.

B2   ARMS, GEORGE. [Review: John S. Tuckey, ed., Mark Twain's Fables of Man, (1972).] American Literature, XLV (March), 122.
      "Mr. Tuckey has perceptively observed th three major motifs in his collection and grouped the manuscripts accordingly.... 'The Myth of Providence'... 'The Dream of Providence'... 'The Nightmare of History.'" They include some of MT's better work, and the editing (with full textual apparatus) is excellent.

B3   *BRODWIN, STANLEY. "Blackness and the Adamic Myth in Mark Twain's Pudd'nhead Wilson," Texas Studies in Literature and Language, XV, 167-76.
      On the two "falls" in PW: that of America, as exemplified by slavery, and the fall of Roxana and her son Tom; Wilson links the falls and provides revelation through his fingerprinting. [Source: Abstract by Brodwin in MLA Abstracts (1973), 8837.]

B4   _____. "Mark Twain's Masks of Satan: The Final Phase, American Literature, XLV (May), 206-27.
      MT cast Satan in four basic roles: "the conventional tempter and 'Father of Lies,'" "a sympathetic commentator on the tragedy of man's fall," "a mischievous, sarcastic questioner of God's ways," and "a force of spiritual though amoral 'innocence' charged with divine-like creative power"; he ultimately came "to the 'position' that salvation lay outside of man, in the inevitable triumph of Satan." Abstract by Brodwin in MLA Abstracts (1973), 8838.

B5   BYERS, JOHN R., JR. "Mark Twain's Mary Jane Wilks: Shamed or Shammed?" Mark Twain Journal, XVII (Winter), 13-14.
      Huck writes in Chapter XXVII of "them devils laying right there under her own roof, shaming her and robbing her"; the word "shaming" is probably misspelled. Abstract in AES, XVIII (1974-1975), 2932.

B6   CARDWELL, GUY A. "Life on the Mississippi: Vulgar Facts and Learned Errors," ESQ: A Journal of the American Renaissance, XIX (4th Quarter), 283-93.
      Discusses a number of factual errors in accounts of the inception, writing, and publication of LOM. Abstract by Cardwell in MLA Abstracts (1973), 8840.

B7   CARY, RICHARD. "In Further Defence of Harriet Shelley: Two Unpublished Letters by Mark Twain," Mark Twain Journal, XVI (Summer), 13-15.
      Texts of two MT letters (July 17, 30, 1901, from Ampersand, near Lower Saranac Lake, N.Y.) to Elizabeth Akers Allen (author of the sentimental song, "Rock Me to Sleep, Mother"), responding to letters in which she defended Percy Shelley's conduct. Abstract in AES, XVIII (1974-1975), 595. Abstract by Cary in MLA Abstracts (1973), 8842.

B8   CATHER, WILLA. "Willa Cather's Tribute to
      Mark Twain," Mark Twain Journal, XVII (Win-
      ter), back cover.
          Facsimile of a signed typescript with her
      corrections (n.d.), here published for the
      first time, relating how a Russian violin-
      ist enjoyed HF in translation. Asking how
      this is possible, with MT's virtually un-
      translatable language, she concludes: "The
      only answer seems to be that if a book has
      vitality enough, it can live through even
      the brutalities of translators." Abstract
      in AES, XVIII (1974-1975), 2937.

B9   CLEMENS, SAMUEL L. "Complete Text of Letter
      to Mark Twain's Kinsman, Dr. James Ross
      Clemens, the Editor's Father, Whom the Hu-
      morist Nicknamed 'Doctor Jim,'" Mark Twain
      Journal, XVI (Summer), front cover.
          Facsimile reproduction of letter from
      Hotel Krantz, Vienna (March 5, 1899) on
      various family matters; urges him to keep
      his moustache. Abstract in AES, XVIII
      (1974-1975), 597.

B10   CLOUTIER, ARTHUR C. "'Dear Mr. Seelye...Yours
      Truly, Tom Sawyer,'" College English, XXXIV
      (March), 849-53.
          A reply to Seelye's The True Adventures of
      Huckleberry Finn (1970); written in boy-
      dialect by Tom Sawyer, who discusses ques-
      tions of style, the debated ending of HF,
      and his own place in the novel. Abstract by
      Cloutier in MLA Abstracts (1973), 8844.

B11   CLYMER, KENTON J. "John Hay and Mark Twain,"
      Missouri Historical Review, LXVII (April),
      397-406.
          On their personal and literary friendship
      of 38 years. MT never criticized Secretary
      of State Hay, although sharing with Howells
      a disagreement with Hay's social and politi-
      cal philosophy, and opposition to his for-
      eign policy. It was John Hay who assented
      to a proposal by Howells to review P&P in
      the New York Tribune, supporting him in the
      face of Whitelaw Reid's objections to the
      ethics of allowing "a warm personal friend
      & in some matters literary partner, write a
      critical review of him in a paper."

B12   COX, JAMES M. "Mark Twain, the Height of Hu-
      mor," in Louis D. Rubin, Jr., ed., The Comic
      Imagination in American Literature (New
      Brunswick, New Jersey: Rutgers University
      Press), pp. 139-48 (also passim on MT; in-
      dexed).
          A rebel against the Union and a deserter
      from Confederate forces, MT remained a
      troublemaker when he went to Nevada. As a
      humorist he dealt with a less reputable
      genre, but learned a balance between affront
      to his audience and a bland predictability;
      thus, we can laugh at the townspeople duped
      by the "Royal Nonesuch" in HF, where "the
      image of a naked King which reduces us to a
      wail of pain in King Lear, finally reduces
      us to helpless laughter."

B13   ____. "Mark Twain: The Triumph of Humor,"
      in Matthew J. Bruccoli, ed., The Chief Glory
      of Every People (Carbondale and Edwardsville:
      Southern Illinois University Press; London
      and Amsterdam: Feffer & Simmons, Inc.),
      pp. 211-30.
          Past criticism has dismissed MT as a "mere"
      humorist or praised him for being something
      more; Cox argues in favor of the importance
      of the humor itself. He also sees in MT's
      Civil War experiences "treason" in joining
      Confederate forces and "desertion" in leav-
      ing them: "He had in the space of a month
      committed two capital crimes," and there was
      a streak of the outlaw in the man and his
      humor (p. 215).

B14   [DAVIS, CHESTER L.] "The Letters of Madame de
      Sevigne," Twainian, XXXII (January-February),
      1; (March-April), 3-4; (May-June), 1-4;
      (July-August), 1-4; (September-October), 1-4;
      (November-December), 4.
          Continues a series begun in 1972 and con-
      tinuing into 1974, extensively reprinting
      the text of this book from MT's library with
      his annotations and underlinings. Abstracts
      through July-August in AES, XVIII (1974-
      1975), 2275-2278.

B15   ____. "Mark Twain's Reading, His Library and
      Our Foundation," Twainian, XXXII (July-Au-
      gust), 4; (September-October), 1-2; (Novem-
      ber-December), 1-3.
          On the disposition of MT's estate through
      various heirs; eventually, after the death
      of his daughter Clara and her daughter Nina,
      the assets of more than one million dollars
      were divided between Yale University and The
      American Red Cross; the latter "has refused
      our request to earmark their bequest for the
      furtherance of Mark Twain knowledge, saying
      that there was no restriction." Various
      trusts were also created by Clara, one of
      them establishing a Mark Twain Foundation
      apparently distinct from the Mark Twain Re-
      search Foundation although Davis says that
      "Clara had our Foundation in mind at the
      time." There is also discussion of MT mate-
      rials but little specifically relating to
      his reading and his library, as mentioned in
      the title. The third issue in this series
      consists of extensive quotations from the
      six 1958 issues of Twainian. Abstract of
      July-August installment in AES, XVIII (1974-
      1975), 2281.

B16   THE EDITORS. "Here Comes Tom Sawyer!" Read-
      er's Digest, CIII (July), 16-22.
          About the making of a film version by the
      Reader's Digest. Laudatory.

B17   THE EDITORS, comp. "The Many Sides of Mark
      Twain," Reader's Digest, CIII (August),
      191-205, 210-31.
          Brief excerpts from MT's published works
      and familiar works written about him, com-
      piled for a popular audience.

B18   EMBLEN, D. L. "Mark Twain Alive and Well--
       Very Well Indeed--in Sweden," Mark Twain
       Journal, XVI (Summer), 16-18.
          MT's works have been in print and popular
       in Sweden since their first appearance; the
       major libraries also have his works in Eng-
       lish, together with some of the major sec-
       ondary material about him. There is a list
       of recent publications of translations of
       his works. Abstract in AES, XVIII (1974-
       1975), 592.

B19   ESCHOLZ, PAUL A. "Mark Twain and the Lan-
       guage of Gesture," Mark Twain Journal, XVII
       (Winter), 5-8.
          On non-verbal communication, some of it
       unconscious, in CY, TA, HF, and PW. Ab-
       stract in AES, XVIII (1974-1975), 2935.

B20   ____. "Twain's The Tragedy of Pudd'nhead
       Wilson," Explicator, XXXI (April), Item 67.
          The tragedy of Wilson is revealed in the
       ironic conclusion, in which he becomes a
       member of the Dawson's Landing community
       which had ridiculed him: he is no longer
       the independent person he had once been.
       Abstract by Escholtz in MLA Abstracts
       (1973), 8871.

B21   FETTERLEY, JUDITH. "Yankee Showman and Re-
       former: The Character of Mark Twain's
       Hank Morgan," Texas Studies in Literature
       and Language, XIV (Winter), 667-79.
          A Connecticut Yankee "offered Mark Twain
       the opportunity of indulging in a fantasy
       of omnipotence," but "Hank as a character
       is ambiguous," because his power can be
       creative or destructive. Much of his at-
       titude is aggressive, even in his humor,
       and in the end his betrayal "is ultimately
       a self-betrayal"; he has been a violent
       man who entered Arthurian England as a re-
       sult of a blow suffered in a fight, and
       there he felt insufficiently appreciated.
       Abstract by Fetterley in MLA Abstracts
       (1972 [sic]), 8761.

B22   FULLER, DANIEL J. "Mark Twain and Hamlin Gar-
       land: Contrarieties in Regionalism," Mark
       Twain Journal, XVII (Winter), 14-18.
          "Both of them were influenced by the dic-
       tates of Hippolyte Taine, and he helped
       them gain the spirit to portray common and
       familiar scenes as settings for their nov-
       els and stories." HF and PW reveal a con-
       trast between MT's social criticism and his
       portrayal of a region. Concluding Note:
       "From the Editor, We regret that the foot-
       notes for this article have been misplaced.
       If you desire any reference information,
       please write the author." Abstract in AES,
       XVIII (1974-1975), 2936.

B23   GOGOL, J. M. "Nikolai Aseev and Mark Twain,"
       Mark Twain Journal, XVI (Summer), 15-16.
          A brief biography of the Russian Futurist
       poet, with the text of his 1949 poem, "Mark
       Twain" (translated by J. M. Gogol). Ab-
       stract in AES, XVIII (1974-1975), 594.

B24   *GORDON, CAROLINE. "The Shape of the River,"
       Michigan Quarterly Review, XII (Winter),
       1-10.
          Notes the role of the central intelligence
       as protagonist and narrator in LOM. [Source:
       Abstract in AES, XVIII (1974-1975), 1028;
       part of a general study and perhaps dealing
       only tangentially with LOM.]

B25   GOUDIE, ANDREA. "'What Fools These Mortals
       Be!' A Puckish Interpretation of Mark
       Twain's Narrative Stance," Kansas Quarterly,
       V (Fall), 19-31.
          "Both Twain and Puck are keenly perceptive
       auditors, actors too when they see cause,"
       "and humor for both Twain and Puck is fre-
       quently an involuntary response" (p. 20).
       Abstract in AES, XIX (1975-1976), 237. Ab-
       stract by Goudie in MLA Abstracts (1973),
       8857.

B26   HAMILTON, MAXWELL. "'Tom Sawyer' Lives Again.
       Filmed on Location in the Missouri Country-
       side, the New Musical, 'Tom Sawyer,' Prom-
       ises Warm Authenticity," Holiday Inn Inter-
       national Magazine, July/August, pp. 48-50.
          Adds no information to the Reader's Digest
       account of the film (1973.B16), but provides
       an additional nine stills of the film (five
       in color).

B27   HANSEN, CHADWICK. "The Once and Future Boss:
       Mark Twain's Yankee," Nineteenth-Century
       Fiction, XXVIII (June), 62-73.
          In CY, the Yankee anticipates the 20th-
       century dictator with his love of mob scenes,
       his mixture of sentimentality and insensitiv-
       ity, and his destructiveness on an apocalyp-
       tic scale. "We have all seen him. But it
       was Mark Twain, in this brilliant nightmare
       of a novel, who saw him first." Abstract by
       Hansen in MLA Abstracts (1973), 8858.

B28   HANSON, R. GALEN. "Bluejays and Man: Twain's
       Exercise in Understanding," Mark Twain Jour-
       nal, XVII (Winter), 18-19.
          Summarizes the bluejay yarn in RI, in
       which MT "makes light of human collective
       behavior, of human deceptions, of the range
       of ways that are human ways." Abstract in
       AES, XVIII (1974-1975), 2934.

B29   KAHN, SHOLOM J. "Mark Twain as American Rabel-
       ais," Hebrew University Studies in Litera-
       ture, No. 1 (Spring), pp. 47-75.

(KAHN, SHOLOM J.)
Provides several definitions of "Rabelaisianism" in the sense of indelicacy, satire, in a literary world that is "not only anatomical and geographical...but also historical, folkloristic, legendary, and ultimately metaphysical." Draws on Rabelais scholarship, and suggests that "to be an 'American Rabelais' implies performing a satiric, or more broadly literary, function for the United States comparable, or parallel, to that of Rabelais in sixteenth-century France." Abstract by Kahn in MLA Abstracts (1973), 8866.

B30 *KARPOWITZ, STEVEN. "Tom Sawyer and Mark Twain: Fictional Women and Real in the Play of Conscience with the Imagination," Literature and Psychology, XXIII, No. 1, 5-12.
[Source: Abstract in AES, XVIII (1974-1975), 1554.] Because of the women in MT's life, his thought often linked thoughts of fame and death with woman's suffering, in his Nevada writing and in TS where the humor masks murderous wishes; Tom's fantasies blend sadism and fame.

B31 KETTERER, DAVID. "Epoch-Eclipse and Apocalypse: Special 'Effects' in A Connecticut Yankee," Publications of the Modern Language Association, LXXXVIII (October), 1104-14.
Hank Morgan is defective in his perception of reality, unaware of symbolism and imagery; he does not see, as the reader does, the nature of MT's statement on Arthurian England and nineteenth-century America through the eclipse, and succeeding episodes involving solar images, leading to the concluding battle of the sand-belt. Abstract in AES, XVIII (1974-1975), 1274. Abstract by Ketterer in MLA Abstracts (1973), 8870.

B32 KINGHORN, NORTON D. "E. W. Kemble's Misplaced Modifier: A Note on the Illustrations for Huckleberry Finn," Mark Twain Journal, XVI (Summer), 9-11.
On MT's reactions to the HF illustrations by Kemble. On p. 322 his illustration of Uncle Silas Phelps with a brass warming pan that "belonged to one of his ancestors with a long wooden handle" showed a wooden handle on the pan and on the ancestor, a wooden leg--which might have been called a "handle" in contemporary slang. Abstract in AES, XVIII (1974-1975), 588.

B33 KIRALIS, KARL "Two More Recently Discovered Letters by S. L. Clemens," Mark Twain Journal, XVI (Summer), 18-20.
Contains background data and texts of two brief notes. The first, to the Clover Club (January 2, 1891) declines with thanks a dinner invitation, and the second (May 8, 1894) asks Fred J. Hall (general manager

and part-owner of the defunct Webster and Company) to speak to Mr. Rogers about an unnamed project. Abstract in AES, XVIII (1974-1975), 596. Abstract by Kiralis in MLA Abstracts (1973), 8872.

B34 KRAUSE, SYDNEY J. "Steinbeck and Mark Twain," Steinbeck Quarterly, VI (Fall), 104-11.
Although there is no external evidence as to whether Steinbeck read MT "with the kind of attention that would have invited borrowing," there are parallels in thinking--especially in The Pearl and "Hadleyburg" (which Krause proposes to treat in a sequel to this article). Abstract in AES, XVIII (1974-1975), 1966.

B35 *LANGLEY, DOROTHY. Tom Sawyer Comes Home. Chicago: The Traumwald Press.
[Source: Advertisement in Mark Twain Journal, XVI (Summer), back cover.] "Stemming not only from the Tom Sawyer-Huck Finn series but particularly from The Mysterious Stranger, the book takes Tom, Huck and Jim on a ride through history on Satan's ticket, and brings them back to Missouri around 1950."

B36 LINDBORG, HENRY J. "A Cosmic Tramp: Samuel Clemens's Three Thousand Years Among the Microbes," American Literature, XLIV (January), 652-57.
In this rambling novel which personifies the universe as the body of the tramp Blitzowski, MT reveals a dual view of a God of "unthinkable grandeur and majesty," but indifferent to man. Notes possible sources and influences in W. H. Conn's The Life of the Germ (1897) and C. W. Saleeby's The Cycle of Life According to Modern Science (1904). Abstract by Lindborg in MLA Abstracts (1973), 8875.

B37 *MAURANGES, J.-P. "Aliénation et Châtiment chez Mark Twain et Heinrich Böll," Revue des Langues Vivantes, XXXIX, No. 2, 131-36.
[Source: Abstract in AES, XVII (1973-1974), 1807; reprinted in Twainian, XXXIV (March-April, 1975).]
In Böll's Der Bahnhof von Zimpren, as in "Hadleyburg," a small town is duped by the promise of easy riches, those in power perpetuate the swindle, and the society disintegrates in fear and distrust. Although MT is the more pessimistic, there remains hope for Hadleyburg. [In French.]

B38 MENDELSOHN, EDWARD. "Mark Twain Confronts the Shakespeareans," Mark Twain Journal, XVII (Winter), 20-21.
MT ridicules cultural pretension in his "Is Shakespeare Dead?" and shows Shakespeare's name cheapened by grasping impostors in HF. Though no scholar, MT put first emphasis on the works; he also observed that his society regarded Shakespeare as a symbolic fetish, as it regarded Satan as a symbolic bugbear. Abstract in AES, XVIII (1974-1975), 2933.

B39 MILLER, WILLIAM C. "Samuel L. and Orion Clemens vs. Mark Twain and His Biographers (1861-1862)," Mark Twain Journal, XVI (Summer), 1-9.

On the early days of the two Clemens brothers in Nevada Territory, the regulations governing the duties of Orion as Secretary, his employment of Samuel for sixty days as an assistant, and Samuel's early newspaper work: he was the Aurora correspondent for the Carson City Silver Age and tried to obtain the same post with the Sacramento Union, in the time before he joined the Territorial Enterprise; an item from the Silver Age, possibly by MT, was copied by the San Francisco Daily Alta California (here reprinted). There is also a discussion of MT's contributions to the Enterprise over the pseudonym "Josh." It would appear that Orion Clemens "may have been in large part responsible for Samuel Clemens' becoming Mark Twain"--far more than MT or his biographers acknowledge. Abstract in AES, XVIII (1974-1975), 593.

B40 MILLS, NICOLAUS. "Charles Dickens and Mark Twain," in his American and English Fiction in the Nineteenth Century: An Antigenre Critique and Comparison. Bloomington and London: Indiana University Press.

Compares Great Expectations and HF in their division into three sections dealing with childhood and the home, with society as a whole, and with psychological and moral decisions. [Incorporates parts of "Social and Moral Vision in Great Expectations and Huckleberry Finn," Journal of American Studies, July, 1970.]

B41 *MIXON, WAYNE. "Mark Twain, The Gilded Age, and the New South Movement" Southern Humanities Review, VII, 403-409.

In 1873 MT could see the beginning of the movement which would become evident in the next decade, to make the South like the industrial North; although MT believed in such progress he condemned the means used to achieve it. [Source: Abstract by Mixon in MLA Abstracts (1973), 8880.]

B42 MONTEIRO, GEORGE. "'Such as Mother Used to Make': An Addition to the Mark Twain Canon," Papers of the Bibliographical Society of America, LXVII (Fourth Quarter), 450-52.

Reprints a sketch by this title in the "Contributors' Club" in the Atlantic Monthly for January, 1903. Abstracted by Monteiro in MLA Abstracts (1973), 8881. Also abstracted in AES, XVIII (1974-1975), 2279.

B43 MOYNE, ERNEST J. "Mark Twain and Baroness Alexandra Gripenberg," American Literature, XLV (November), 370-78.

On MT's meeting and subsequent correspondence with the Finnish author and leader in Finnish woman suffrage and temperance movements; she recorded the meeting and a dialect story he told in her A Half Year in the New World: Miscellaneous Sketches of Travel in the United States (trans. and ed. Ernest J. Moyne, Newark, Delaware, 1954) and in articles for the Scandinavian press. A letter to the editor of the Stockholm Nya Dagligt Allehanda accused MT of plagiarism from Boccaccio's Decameron, and MT wrote the Baroness a letter of explanation: his own source had been Hopkinson Smith's "Ginger and the Goose" in Harper's Monthly, LXIV (March, 1882), 138-40. Moyne includes the text of two MT letters and cites pertinent material in Finnish and Swedish newspapers of 1888-1889, as well as Alexandra Gripenberg's diary and letters. [This is a re-written and expanded version of Moyne's "Mark Twain Meets a Lady from Finland," which appeared in Mark Twain Journal in 1960.B84.] Abstract by Moyne in MLA Abstracts (1973), 8882.

B44 NIBBELINK, HERMAN. "Mark Twain and the Mormons," Mark Twain Journal, XVII (Winter), 1-5.

Contrasts their portrayal in RI with accounts by other writers of the time. Abstract in AES, XVIII (1973-1975), 2937. Abstract by Nibbelink in MLA Abstracts (1974), 9635.

B45 *PARK, MARTHA M. "Mark Twain's Hadleyburg: A House Built on Sand," College Language Association Journal, XVI, 508-13.

MT may have had in mind the New Testament parable of the two houses, one built on rock and one on sand, when he wrote the story, in which there are frequent references to crumbling foundations. [Source: Abstract by Park in MLA Abstracts (1973), 8884.]

B46 PAULY, THOMAS H. "Directed Readings: The Contents Tables in Huckleberry Finn," Proof, III, 63-68.

Critical discussions of Huckleberry Finn have often quoted and been influenced by one of two tables of contents; they are presumably the work of Charles L. Webster and Albert Bigelow Paine, but in any event are not by MT. Abstract by Pauly in MLA Abstracts (1973), 8885.

B47 POCHMANN, HENRY A. [Review: Franklin R. Rogers and Paul Baender, eds., Roughing It (1972).] American Literature, XLIV (January), 687-89.

Includes a lengthy discussion of editorial principles involved in the Center for Editions of American Authors publications, with praise for the introduction by Franklin R. Rogers as "superb" and his Explanatory Notes as "especially full, as they need to be for a book like Roughing It." Paul Baender's textual notes are "succinct but adequate," though they might well have been expanded to cover MT's idiosyncratic spellings and unusual words.

B48   *POWERS, LYALL H.   "The Sweet Success of
      Twain's Tom," Dalhousie Review, LIII,
      310-24.
         The popularity of TS derives from its
      structure and narrative development of
      the themes of death, treasure-hunting, and
      romantic adventure, with growing serious-
      ness and respectability; MT skilfully un-
      derscores his theme by his management of
      time. [Source: Abstract by Powers in
      MLA Abstracts (1973), 8886.]

B49   REGAN, ROBERT. [Review: John S. Tuckey, ed.,
      Mark Twain's Fables of Man (1972) and
      Franklin R. Rogers, ed., Roughing It
      (1972).] American Literary Realism, 1870-
      1910, VI (Winter), 82-84.
         The introductions and textual apparatus
      of the two volumes are quite different, be-
      cause one consists of previously unpub-
      lished material, left in manuscript, call-
      ing for considerable analysis, and the oth-
      is a book which was never revised and for
      which no manuscript survives. There is a
      marked disparity of the promise in RI and
      "the literary ruins of his declining
      years" in Fables of Man: "The Mark Twain
      of Roughing It had--rightly or wrongly--
      respected himself and respected his audi-
      ence; the Mark Twain of Fables of Man had
      come to despise both." There is an exten-
      sive and valuable discussion of the Iowa-
      California edition of MT's published and
      previously unpublished writing.

B50   REEVES, PASCHAL, et al., comps. "A Checklist
      of Scholarship on Southern Literature for
      1973," Mississippi Quarterly, XXVII
      (Spring, 1974), 235-39 (portion on MT).
         Sixth annual checklist, including about
      three dozen books and articles on MT pub-
      lished in 1973; annotated. Generally
      duplicates other standard bibliographies.

B51   RODGERS, PAUL C., JR. "Artemus Ward and Mark
      Twain's 'Jumping Frog,'" Nineteenth-Century
      Fiction, XXVIII (December), 273-86.
         MT's use of the frame structure and dead-
      pan narrator are a result of his desire to
      employ Ward's lecture technique in a story,
      or a need to make the story conform to the
      context of Ward's Travels (1865), of which
      it was originally intended to be a part. Ab-
      stract by Rodgers in MLA Abstracts (1973),
      8887.

B52   ROGERS, RODNEY O. "Twain, Taine, and Lecky:
      The Genesis of a Passage in A Connecticut
      Yankee," Modern Language Quarterly, XXXIV
      (December), 436-47.
         On a passage MT originally wrote for TA
      after reading Taine's L'Ancien Régime; he
      did not use the passage there, but later
      revised it for CY under the influence of
      Lecky's History of European Morals. Ab-
      stract by Rogers in MLA Abstracts (1973),
      8888.

B53   *ROSS, MICHAEL. "Mark Twain's Pudd'nhead Wil-
      son: Dawson's Landing and the Ladder of
      Nobility," Novel, VI (Spring), 244-56.
         On MT's indictment of mankind, here shown
      in a feudal society. [Source: Abstract in
      AES, XVIII (1974-1975), 928.]

B54   ROWLETTE, ROBERT. "'Mark Ward on Artemis
      Twain': Twain's Literary Debt to Ward," Amer-
      ican Literary Realism, VI (Winter), 13-25.
         Quotes passages revealing a number of
      parallels, some fairly persuasively indicat-
      ing "that Twain borrowed considerably from
      Ward, far more than DeVoto would allow.
      Mostly he borrowed the staples of the comic-
      writers' trade--jokes, anecdotes, catch-
      phrases, snappers, one-liners--for use in
      his Sandwich Islands letters, The Innocents
      Abroad, Life on the Mississippi, and several
      sketches," as well as ideas for the form of
      RI. "After Roughing It, except for striking
      correspondences in Life on the Mississippi,
      it virtually ceased." Abstract by Rowlette
      in MLA Abstracts (1973), 8890.

B55   SEARS, ROBERT R. "Episodic Analysis of Nov-
      els," Journal of Psychology, LXXXV, 267-76.
         [Source: Offprint in Mark Twain Papers.]
      Among the novels analyzed are Captain Storm-
      field's Visit to Heaven, TS, HF, CY, PW,
      MS, IA, and P&P. Episodes are used as a
      basis for investigation of the growth of
      MT's personality.

B56   SIMPSON, LOUIS P. "Mark Twain: The Pathos
      of Regeneration," in his The Man of Letters
      in New England and the South: Essays on
      the History of the Literary Vocation in
      America. Baton Rouge: Louisiana State Uni-
      versity Press, pp. 150-66. Reprinted from
      Southern Literary Journal, 1972.B75.

B57   STOWELL, ROBERT F. "River Guide Books and
      Mark Twain's Life on the Mississippi," Mark
      Twain Journal, XVI (Summer), 21.
         LOM makes no mention of a number of guide-
      books useful both to the apprentice learning
      the river and to the working steamboat pilot.
      With the maps available, "there was no neces-
      sity for him to attempt to keep the multi-
      tude of details of eleven hundred miles of
      river constantly in mind when he could readi-
      ly turn to such books as The Western Pilot."
      Abstract in AES, XVIII (1974-1975), 589.

B58   TRUMAN, HARRY S. [Letter to Chester L. Davis
      (July 30, 1957), expressing admiration for
      MT: "He has quite a record; in fact, I be-
      lieve he was the first newspaper columnist
      to be run out of Washington. His Civil War
      record is also highly interesting."] Twain-
      ian, XXXII (March-April), 1-2. Abstract in
      AES, XVIII (1974-1975), 2280.

B59 WEXMAN, VIRGINIA. "The Role of Structure in Tom Sawyer and Huckleberry Finn," American Literary Realism, 1870-1910, VI (Winter), 1-11.
In the dual world of TS, comic incidents involving boyish innocence prepare the way for incidents of a more somber kind, as in Tom's playing Robin Hood with Joe Harper before the murder of Dr. Robinson by Injun Joe, the search for treasure by Tom and Huck in a haunted house soon found by Injun Joe and a companion, and Huck's following the two villains through a maze of streets reminiscent of the cave in which the village children had been playing. The alternation of light and dark scenes "helps to preserve our sense of the comic in this book" and permits a conclusion which, "in true comic spirit, reaffirms social unity." HF takes a different course, as Huck's imagination is educated by experience, and his "creativity cannot be harmless as Tom's had been, for he finds himself in a world where innocence is immoral rather than merely premoral." Again, MT parallels incidents from the dark and light worlds, but here the effect is to heighten the portraits of human depravity. Abstract by Wexman in MLA Abstracts (1973), 8896.

B60 WILSON, JAMES D. "Hank Morgan, Philip Traum, and Milton's Satan," Mark Twain Journal, XVI (Summer), 20-21.
CY and MS bear out Milton's prediction of increasingly deadly machines of war. Abstract by Wilson in MLA Abstracts (1973), 8897.

1974 A BOOKS

A1 ANON. Nook Farm Genealogy. [Hartford, Connecticut]: Stowe-Day Foundation.
Part I: "Alphabetical Listing of Nook Farm residents, a partial listing of their ancestors and descendants, and a cross-section of their contemporaries as they pertain to Library materials"; Part II: "ADDENDA. Chronological listing of major Nook Farm families." Provides useful data on MT's neighbors, but no new material on his own family. (Typescript).

A2 KAPLAN, JUSTIN. Mark Twain and His World. New York: Simon and Schuster.
A life of MT for the general reader, attractively illustrated with color prints revealing the man and his age.

A3 PETTIT, ARTHUR G. Mark Twain & the South. Lexington: University Press of Kentucky.
Describes MT's evolving racial and regional views, the mingled love and loathing he felt for the South. MT "reflected and expressed some of the most advanced thoughts and entrenched prejudices of his time,"

mirroring the changing national attitudes; he "came to look upon his personal lot and that of the country, especially that of the South, as similar and tragic."

A4 SCHMITTER, DEAN MORGAN, ed. Mark Twain: A Collection of Critical Essays. New York: McGraw-Hill Book Company.
Essays from journals and excerpted from books; all are listed in the present bibliography, with cross-references to Schmitter's reprintings. The material is in two sections, the first on MT's life, literary career, and the themes of humor and pessimism, and the second devoted to criticism of major works. There is a bibliography (with brief annotations) of books about MT.

A5 WALKER, FRANKLIN. Irreverent Pilgrims: Melville, Browne, and Mark Twain in the Holy Land. Seattle and London: University of Washington Press.
Traces the 1851 travels of John Ross Browne as recorded in his Yusef; or, the Journey of the Frangi (New York, 1853), Melville's 1857 visit as described in Clarel (1876), and the 1867 tour MT portrayed in newspaper letters and IA.

A6 WATKINS, T. H. Mark Twain's Mississippi. Also Selected Excerpts from Mark Twain's "Life on the Mississippi." Palo Alto, California: American West Publishing Company.
Consists of appropriate material from LOM and many contemporary and modern pictures of the river and the scenes MT described.

1974 B SHORTER WRITINGS

B1 ALSEN, EBERHARD. "The Futile Pursuit of Truth in Twain's What Is Man? and Anderson's 'The Book of the Grotesque,'" Mark Twain Journal, XVII (Winter), 12-14.
Sherwood Anderson's correspondence with Van Wyck Brooks in 1918-1919 shows that he often thought of MT while writing Winesburg, Ohio. "The introductory sketch, 'The Book of the Grotesque,' revolves around a conception of truth which is very similar to the one developed in 'What Is Man?'" and in A Story Teller's Story (New York, 1924, p. 189) Anderson shows familiarity with this late work. Derivation is suggested by the self-portrait in the "old man" and the conception that there are no absolute truths and that pursuit of a single idea can turn a man into a grotesque.

B2 BAUM, JOAN. "Mark Twain on the Congo," Mark Twain Journal, XVII (Summer), 7-9.
Describes MT's 1905 pamphlet, King Leopold's Soliloquy, recently reissued by International Publications (New York) and Seven Seas Press (East Berlin). Abstract by Baum in MLA Abstracts (1974), 9589.

B3   BEBB, BRUCE. [Review: Paul Baender, ed., "What Is Man?" and Other Philosophical Writings (1973).] American Literary Realism 1870-1910, VII (Summer), 283-86.
      "It is a big, solid, handsome book, and should be a source of pride to the many people associated with its production. Most of the more than two dozen pieces of Mark Twain's writings that make up this volume have appeared in print before, though at...diverse times and places.... They are a heterogeneous lot." Bebb criticizes the editing; in particular "the textual notes are next to impossible to work with." However, "What is Man? is done right, basically," avoiding some of the errors in the editing of RI, the first volume in this edition, and "Paul Baender's introduction is a thoughtful and lucid guide to the development of Mark Twain's ideas."

B4   BERGER, SIDNEY. "New Mark Twain Items," Papers of the Bibliographical Society of America, LXVIII (Third Quarter), 331-35.
      Chatto & Windus used the best copy-text available for the English editions of TS Abroad and PW; for the latter they apparently were forced to use the Century serialization, but for TS Abroad they had a carbon copy of the typescript sent to St. Nicholas and hence had a text free of emendations by Mary Mapes Dodge. Quotes letters from Chatto & Windus to MT (August 15, 1893) and to Frederick Hall of Charles L. Webster & Company (January 16, 1894). Abstract by Berger in MLA Abstracts (1974), 9591.

B5   BLEI, NORBERT. "Marking Twain in Hannibal-- a Trip to Missouri to Learn What Influence Mark Twain has Had upon His Boyhood Home," American Libraries, V (March), 128-34.
      On the town of Hannibal, memorials, use of the MT name for local businesses; photographs.

B6   BRIDEN, E. F. "Samuel L. Clemens and Elizabeth Jordan: An Unpublished Letter," Mark Twain Journal, XVII (Summer), 11-13.
      Text of a letter (December 4, 1908) in which MT declines to write something for Miss Jordan because he lacks interest and would do it badly, and "The Harpers would flay me for destroying my commercial value." Also quotes from her autobiography, Three Rousing Cheers (New York and London: D. Appleton-Century, 1934) a letter of August 4, 1906 in which MT declines to contribute a chapter to a composite novel, The Whole Family, which failed despite the contributions by Howells, Henry James, Mary E. Wilkins Freeman, and others. Briden also quotes Miss Jordan's autobiography on meetings with MT at the Harpers' offices in New York, and breakfasts with him during visits to Colonel George Harvey's summer home, "Jorjalma," at Deal Beach, New Jersey.

B7   *BRUNVAND, JAN HAROLD. "Western Folk Humor in Roughing It," The Western Folklore Conference: Selected Papers, Utah University Press Monograph Series, XI, ed. Austin Fife and J. Golden Taylor (June), 53-65.
      [Source: Citation provided by kindness of D. K. Wilgus, Folklore and Mythology Group, U.C.L.A., adding that it is cited by Barrick (1975.B3).]

B8   BUDD, LOUIS J. "Mark Twain Talks Mostly about Humor and Humorists," Studies in American Humor, I (April), 4-22.
      MT's theoretical statements about humor, liberally documented both from the familiar published works and from newspaper interviews. Includes the texts of interviews in the New York Sun (January 27, 1895), Sydney (Australia) Morning Herald (September 17, 1895), and Auckland New Zealand Herald (November 21, 1895).

B9   CHURCH, SAMUEL HARDEN. [Facsimile reproduction of letter to Cyril Clemens, February 19, 1942, on three meetings with MT at the home of Andrew Carnegie.] Mark Twain Journal, XVII (Winter), back cover.
      Mentions having written MT to ask about his statement that the Siamese Twains were of different ages; in reply MT wrote that the statement was "an egregious blunder... What I meant to say was that the twins were born at the same time but of different mothers."

B10   CLEMENS, SAMUEL L. "Mark Twain Approves the Staging of Huckleberry Finn," Mark Twain Journal, XVII (Winter), front cover.
      Facsimile reproduction, without comment, of an MT letter on hotel stationery of Marshall House, York Harbor, Maine (the printed year is "190_," with the last figure not filled in) to Klaw & Erlanger; he is completely satisfied with the stage adaptation by Lee Arthur.

B11   _____. "Some Thoughts on the Science of Onanism," Playboy, XXI (September), 157.
      The text of a humorous talk delivered by MT before the Stomach Club, in Paris, 1879.

B12   CRACROFT, RICHARD H. "Distorting Polygamy for Fun and Profit: Artemus Ward and Mark Twain among the Mormons," Brigham Young University Studies, XIV (Winter), 272-88.
      "Twain's was the greater fictional imagination," but in portraying the Mormons he was "the lesser artist of the two" (p. 287). Both knowingly perpetuated falsehoods about the Mormons for humorous effect.

B13   DENTON, L. W. "Mark Twain on Patriotism, Treason, and War," Mark Twain Journal, XVII (Summer, 4-7.
      Undated quotations from various published writings by MT, on a citizen's responsibility to oppose his country's policies when they are wrong.

B14 ENSOR, ALLISON. "The Downfall of Poor Rich-
     ard: Benjamin Franklin as Seen by Haw-
     thorne, Melville, and Mark Twain," Mark
     Twain Journal, XVII (Winter), 14-18.
        Like most writers of the nineteenth cen-
     tury MT--somewhat unjustly--criticized
     Franklin's sententiousness in his epigrams
     on industry and frugality.

B14A HILL, HAMLIN. "Mark Twain," in James Wood-
     ress, ed., American Literary Scholarship:
     An Annual/1974. Durham, North Carolina:
     Duke University Press, 1976, pp. 75-85.
        The annual survey of MT scholarship (be-
     gun by John Gerber in 1963.B32). Includes
     material not listed in the present bibliog-
     raphy. Contents: "i. Textual and Bibliog-
     raphical"; "ii. Biographical"; "iii. Gener-
     al Criticism"; "iv. Earlier Works";
     "v. Huckleberry Finn"; "vi. Later Works."

B15 ____. "Who Killed Mark Twain?" American
     Literary Realism, 1870-1910, VII (Spring),
     119-24.
        "The major problem with the current state
     of Mark Twain studies is that most of it is
     written by humorless, dull pedants whose
     prose style alone would be enough to petri-
     fy an unwary reader as comprehensively as
     Ice-9." They occupy themselves with triv-
     ia, and some of the work done is perfunctory
     and careless: "It somehow does not inspire
     confidence in a scholar's own estimate of
     the importance of his research to see him
     cite a Dell paperback as his documentation."
     It is time to revive MT with a new assess-
     ment, and the publication of his previously
     unpublished writings by the University of
     California Press will provide the opportuni-
     ty. Hill points to some of the new insights
     made possible; for example, "there is evi-
     dence that he terrorized most of the people
     who knew him well, that he was if not impo-
     tent at least unable to satisfy his wife
     Olivia sexually, and that much of their ten-
     sion and her frustration arose from his ob-
     sessive absences from her bed. There is
     evidence that his fixation on teen-age girls
     in his last years was the result of a love
     affair with Laura Wright when he was twenty-
     one and she was fifteen." Some of the use-
     ful criticism of recent years is described,
     and there are suggestions of fruitful topics
     for investigation. Abstract by Hill in MLA
     Abstracts (1974), 9614.

B16 HOOD, ROBERT E. "Mark Twain's Huck Finn,"
     Scouting (published eight times a year by
     Boy Scouts of America for adult leaders),
     LXII (March-April), 28-31, 68.
        A popular account, largely descriptive,
     praising the book for its humor. Illustrat-
     ed by Mary Ellen Mark's color photographs
     during the filming of the current musical
     treatment (the cover illustration is also
     from the filming).

B17 HYDE, JAMES H. (told to Cyril Clemens).
     "Mark Twain and Colonel George Harvey,"
     Mark Twain Journal, XVII (Winter), 21.
        Brief and superficial. "The first time
     I met Mark Twain was at a dinner given at
     the Metropolitan Club shortly after 1900
     by Colonel George Harvey" in honor of Admi-
     ral Lord Charles Beresford, who dined too
     well and fell asleep under a table. MT
     spoke after dinner on his bad investments
     and the help he had received from Henry
     Rogers in putting his affairs in order.
     Hyde later invited MT to a large dinner and
     found him "perfectly charming."

B18 ILLIANO, ANTONIO. "'Italian Without a Master':
     A Note for the Appreciation of Mark Twain's
     Undictionarial Translation as Exercise in
     Humor," Mark Twain Journal, XVII (Summer),
     17-20.
        Reprints the Italian passages and MT's
     comic translations, together with literal
     translations.

B19 JAGER, RONALD B. "Mark Twain and the Robber
     Barons: A View of the Gilded Age Business-
     man," Mark Twain Journal, XVII (Winter),
     8-12.
        Personally inept in business, MT admired
     the productive genius of Andrew Carnegie and
     his friend Henry Rogers, but could not "dis-
     associate personal moral integrity from the
     more impersonal, corporate standards that
     were coming to apply in this new age of in-
     dustrialization." He deplored the money-
     grubbing of Jay Gould and his kind.

B20 KIBLER, JAMES, et al. "A Checklist of Schol-
     arship on Southern Literature for 1974,"
     Mississippi Quarterly, XXVIII (Spring, 1975),
     228-32 (portion on MT).
        Seventh annual checklist, including about
     three dozen books and articles on MT pub-
     lished in 1974; annotated. Generally dupli-
     cates other standard bibliographies.

B21 LEARY, LEWIS. "Mark Twain Did Not Sleep Here:
     Tarrytown, 1902-1904," Mark Twain Journal,
     XVII (Summer), 13-15.
        A meticulously detailed account of Olivia
     Clemens's purchase of a house and nineteen
     acres in Tarrytown, New York after the
     death of Susan, when the family could no
     longer bear to live in the Hartford house;
     problems over the tax assessment were set-
     tled, but repairs were needed, the family
     went to Florence (where Mrs. Clemens died),
     and MT apparently visited the place but
     never lived there; he leased it in May, 1903,
     and sold it in January, 1905. Abstract by
     Leary in MLA Abstracts (1974), 9622.

B21A ____. "Troubles with Mark Twain: Some Con-
     siderations on Consistency," Studies in
     American Fiction, II, 89-103.
        Briefly discusses the pitfalls of enumera-
     tive bibliography, but is primarily concerned

(LEARY, LEWIS)
with the textual problems of IA and the raft passage MT removed from HF to pad LOM: the difficulties are compounded by the fact that MT was not always a sound critic of his own work or uniformly conscientious in decisions concerning his text.

B22 LIGHT, MARTIN. "Sweeping out Chivalric Silliness: The Example of Huck Finn and The Sun Also Rises," Mark Twain Journal, XVII (Winter), 18-20.

Tom Sawyer and Robert Cohn are romantic and Quixotic, and Huck Finn and Jake Barnes, "linked by their adherence to common sense and the lessons of experience, bear a likeness to Sancho Panza." Hemingway follows MT in the attack on romantic folly once swept away by Cervantes but restored by Sir Walter Scott.

B23 LONG, TIMOTHY. "Mark Twain's Speeches on Billiards," Mark Twain Journal, XVII (Summer), 1-3.

On MT's speech, delivered when he visited a tournament in 1906, describing his defeat by a left-handed player. Paine gives different texts in the 1912 biography and 1929 edition of the speeches; Willie Hoppe's Thirty Years of Billiards (1925, quoted in "Mark Twain as a Billiard Fan," Literary Digest, July 25, 1925, p. 55) quotes verbatim the version in the biography. Long also cites accounts in the New York Times of April 10, 12, 18, 20, 23, and 25, 1906, as well as Newsweek (February 24, 1941, p. 56), Time (November 20, 1937, p. 50), and New Yorker (November 16, 1940, pp. 27-28), in which Hoppe quotes MT. Abstract by Long in MLA Abstracts (1974), 9626.

B24 *McELRATH, JOSEPH R., JR. "Mark Twain's America and the Protestant Work Ethic," CEA Critic, XXXVI (March), 42-43.

[Source: Abstract in AES, XVIII (1974-1975), 2588.] In CY, Hank Morgan harnesses a bowing pillar saint to a sewing machine; thereby he demonstrates attitudes of MT's bourgeois, Protestant America.

B25 MONTEIRO, GEORGE. "New Mark Twain Letters," Mark Twain Journal, XVII (Summer), 9-10.

Three brief notes to Atlantic Monthly (January 5, 6, 1875, and February 12, year not given) from the Houghton Library, Harvard University; MT asks that the Atlantic be sent to his brother Orion and sends his check, thanks them for a complimentary subscription, and declines with thanks a suggestion of theirs (not described) which he likes but thinks would not be profitable.

B26 PRINCE, GILBERT. "Mark Twain's 'A Fable': The Teacher as Jackass," Mark Twain Journal, XVII (Winter), 7-8.

On MT's short tale as an attack on the long-established notion that it is a teacher's function to interpret a subject for his students; as a consequence they tell him what he wants to hear and they fail to experience for themselves.

B27 RACHAL, JOHN. "Scotty Briggs and the Minister: An Idea from Hooper's Simon Suggs?" Mark Twain Journal, XVII (Summer), 10-11.

In HF, MT drew on Hooper's "Simon Attends a Camp-Meeting," which also anticipates the passage in RI in which a clergyman is puzzled by card-game lingo.

B28 REQUA, KENNETH A. "Counterfeit Currency and Character in Mark Twain's Which Was It?" Mark Twain Journal, XVII (Winter), 1-6.

On his unfinished novel, with its "variations on important themes found in other late works of Mark Twain: money as the irresistible temptation, hypocrisy, and existence as a dream." Despite flaws of structure and tone, "Mark Twain had found a center for his novel: the idea of counterfeits, through which he brought together action, method, character, preaching, and had he gone further, he could also have successfully integrated the dream-frame of the novel."

B29 SIMPSON, LEWIS P. [Review: Paul Baender, ed., "What Is Man?" And Other Philosophical Writings (1973).] American Literature, XLV (January), 617-18.

"Reservations about some aspects of selection and methodology...can only be incidental in the face of yet another demonstration by the Iowa-California edition of the sophistication and maturity Mark Twain scholarship has attained." Baender's Introduction is "carefully constructed, well-written, and thoughtful," though prone to find "more structure or pattern" in MT's philosophical inquiries than is truly present; Baender rightly takes issue with reviewers who criticized "Letters from the Earth" in the light of the present-day assumption that Christian literalism is of no significance," rather than as a fiction "which presents the story of the modern fall from faith in reason."

B30 TUCKEY, JOHN S. [Review: Hamlin Hill, Mark Twain: God's Fool (1973).] American Literature, XLVI (March), 116-18.

Chiefly following the journal of Isabel V. Lyon, MT's secretary (1902-1909), but also other unpublished material, including the Ashcroft-Lyon MS, Hill "sees Clemens in the classic role of the domestic tyrant, self-centered and vindictive, who makes psychological cripples of his wife and children." Here, as in Hill's argument that MT was unjustified in dismissing Miss Lyon and his financial secretary Roger Ashcroft, Tuckey disagrees with Hill.

B31 TUCKEY, JOHN S. [Review: Hamlin Hill, Mark Twain: God's Fool (1973).] American Literary Realism, 1870-1900, VII (Spring), 175-77.

Tuckey appears reluctant to accept a portrait of MT as domestic tyrant in his last decade, noting that Hill also gives evidence to show Olivia as "all-dominating mother," leaving the reader to reconcile the two diagnoses. "In his previous works Mr. Hill has abundantly demonstrated that he is capable of the most rigorous scholarship and critical analysis." Hill's "searching look at, mainly, the domestic Clemens of the final decade" draws on "the splendid resources of the Mark Twain Papers collection and especially the diary of Isabel V. Lyon, Clemens' secretary from November 1902 until the spring of 1909," and breaks new ground.

B32 WEAVER, WILLIAM. "Mark Twain and Kate Field Differ on Constitutional Rights," Mark Twain Journal, XVII (Summer), 16-17.

Reproduces from Lilian Whiting, Kate Field: A Record (Boston, 1899) an MT letter of March 8, 1886, apparently declining to publish one of her books; MT shares her antipathy toward Mormonism, and he "would like to see it extirpated, but always by fair means" and not by oppressive laws, "by arguments and facts, not brute force."

B33 _____. "Samuel Clemens Lectures in Kentucky," Mark Twain Journal, XVII (Summer), 20-21.

On MT's lecture in Paris, Kentucky and two lectures on Louisville during his 1884-1885 tour with George Washington Cable; based chiefly on familiar studies but also quoting reports from contemporary newspapers. Abstract by BLW in MLA Abstracts (1974), 9646.

B34 WILSON, MARK K. "Mr. Clemens and Madame Blanc: Mark Twain's First French Critic," American Literature, XLV (January), 537-56.

MT's hostility toward the French may be attributed in part to "snide" and "condescending" statements about the man and his books by Marie-Thérèse Blanc (writing as "Th. Bentzon") in "Les Humoristes américains" and "L'Âge doré en Amérique," which appeared in the Revue des Deux Mondes July 15, 1872 and July 15, 1875. Madame Blanc, who translated "The Jumping Frog" and included it as a part of the first article, confused the poses MT assumed with his own attitudes; her estimates are not always perceptive or just. The first article treats IA in some detail and RI in passing, and the second devotes considerable space to a plot-summary of GA, a lesser amount of space to a critique (unsympathetic to the structure and to the portrait of Colonel Sellers); these were the first French criticisms of MT and have affected subsequent estimates of his work. The Clemenses met Madame Blanc in Paris in 1879. Abstract by Wilson in MLA Abstracts (1974), 9648.

1975 A BOOKS - NONE

1975 B SHORTER WRITINGS

B1 ANDREWS, WILLIAM L. "The Source of Mark Twain's 'The War Prayer,'" Mark Twain Journal, XVII (Summer), 8-9.

On Henry Clay Dean (portrayed in LOM, Chapter LVII) as the original of the stranger who took the pulpit.

B2 ASPIZ, HAROLD. "The Other Half of Pudd'nhead Wilson's Dog," Mark Twain Journal, XVII (Summer), 10-11.

Reveals a possible source in The Life of P. T. Barnum, Written by Himself (New York: Redfield, 1854), describing a dispute between two owners of an elephant and the threat of one to kill his half.

B3 *BARRICK, Mac E. "The Hat Ranch: Fact, Fiction or Folklore?" Western Folklore, XXXIV (April), 149-53.

[Source: Citation provided by kindness of D. K. Wilgus, Folklore and Mythology Group, U.C.L.A., with the annotation: "Discusses use of the story (X1611.1) by Peter B. Kyne, Earl Stanley Gardner, Dan De Quille, and Mark Twain."]

B4 BRANCH, EDGAR M. "Samuel Clemens: Learning to Venture a Miracle," American Literary Realism, 1870-1910, VIII (Spring), 91-99.

["This essay, appearing here in slightly revised form, was read at the 89th annual convention of the Modern Language Association, December 1974."] MT attacked romance in Scott and Cooper, satirized other popular romance in his apprentice writing, but submitted experience to a literary ordering of his own. "In Clemens's fiction, Huck's realistic language is the medium that best realizes the romantic ideal seeking to unify subject and object while it simultaneously and faithfully presents each, sacrificing neighter one to the other--but that is another and a better known story of Clemens's later years."

B5 DITSKY, JOHN M. "Mark Twain and 'The Great Dark': Religion in Letters from the Earth," Mark Twain Journal, XVII (Summer), 12-19.

On conceptions of the Moral Sense and the Deity, and the relevance of "The Great Dark" to conclusions made possible by other portions of the volume.

B6 GERBER, JOHN C. [Review: Franklin Walker, Irreverent Pilgrims: Melville, Browne, and Mark Twain in the Holy Land (1974).] American Literary Realism, VIII (Spring), 173-75.

"Specialists in American literature may find the Browne chapters in Irreverent Pilgrims mildly interesting because Browne's life and works are relatively unknown. But they will find nothing new in the accounts of Melville and Mark Twain: the facts recorded in them have been recorded elsewhere,

1975 - Shorter Writings

(GERBER, JOHN C.))
and Mr. Walker seems disinclined to specu-
late freshly or even to draw the comparisons
that the material constantly invites. As in
all his works, Mr. Walker's style here is
clear and easy to read," but the parts dealing with Melville and MT "can be read most
profitably by those relatively unfamiliar
with both authors.

B7   GRANANDER, M.E. "Mark Twain's English Lectures and George Routledge & Sons," Mark
Twain Journal, XVII (Summer), 1-4.
Contains texts of two receipts for pay-
ments from Routledge (July 10, 1872 for IA
and November 10, 1875 for GA), and a brief
note (July 10, 1872) on writing a preface
for IA; also describes MT's arranging for
GA copyrights when he was in London.

B8   GROVE, NOEL. "Mark Twain: Mirror of America,"
National Geographic, CXLVIII (September),
300-37.
A popular account, but following modern
scholarship in giving a balanced view that
includes MT's fears and despair as well as
the humor and local color in his works.
Illustrated with modern photographs of Hannibal and other river towns, Virginia City,
and the MT house in Hartford, by James L.
Stanfield, and by contemporary photographs,
including a color photograph of MT in his
Oxford gown, here published for the first
time.

B9   HARRIS, HELEN L. "Mark Twain's Response to
the Native American," American Literature,
XLVI (January), 495-505.
MT described the Indian unsympathetically
in his early writings, later recognized
both "the American treachery toward the Indian" and his own guilt in having helped
to shape attitudes; "in his silence then he
gave consent to that injustice."

B10 SCHINTO, JEANNE M. "The Autobiographies of
Mark Twain and Henry Adams: Life Studies
in Despair," Mark Twain Journal, XVII (Summer), 5-7.
They regretted the loss of a simpler age
of the past and condemned materialism.

B11 SCRIVNER, BUFORD, JR. "The Mysterious
Stranger: Mark Twain's New Myth of the
Fall," Mark Twain Journal, XVII (Summer),
20-21.
"The Mysterious Stranger is the working-
out of a kind of restoration, or anti-fall,
which reverses the baneful consequences of
the fall of man by negating altogether the
Christian world view which established and
sustains such a belief."

B12 WARREN, ROBERT PENN. "Bearers of Bad Tidings:
Writers and the American Dream," New York
Review of Books, XXII (March 20), 12-19.
On pp. 12-14 discusses MT's deep embodi-
ment of the tensions of his age and his
pessimistic ambivalences, as revealed in
HF, CY, and elsewhere.

Addenda

No Date

FITZROY, SIR ALMERIC. Memoirs. London: Hutchinson & Co., 2 vols., I, 236.
"July 6th [1907].--We dined with the Clintons last night, and went to Lady Portsmouth's party, at which 'Mark Twain' was a prominent figure."

RIDGE, W. PETT. A Story Teller: Forty Years in London. London: Hodder and Stoughton, pp. 43-44.
Tells story of being introduced to MT as "the Mark Twain of London" [also in 1910.B99]. At dinners only two days apart, MT delivered the same speech, with the story about a watermelon-- but Ridge says "economy is permissible when a man is called on to speak frequently," and gives examples of English speakers who do the same.

1939

*HOLTHAUSEN, F. [Review: Frances Guthrie Emberson, Mark Twain's Vocabulary: A General Survey (1935.A8) and Robert L. Ramsay and Frances Guthrie Emberson, A Mark Twain Lexicon (1938.A8).] Anglia Beiblatt, L, 91-95.
[Source: MHRA Annual Bibliography (1939), Nos. 4395, 4406.]

1948

*WEST, VICTOR ROYCE. "Mark Twain's Idyl of Frontier America," University of Kansas City Review, XV, 92-104.
[Source: MLA Bibliography (1948), p. 52.]

1949

*SAINT-PIERRE, MARCEL. "Mark Twain," Action Universitaire, XV (July), 42-51.
[Source: MHRA Annual Bibliography (1949), No. 3972.]

1950

*FERGUSON, DELANCEY. [Review: Kenneth R. Andrews, Nook Farm: Mark Twain's Hartford Circle (1950.A2).] New York Herald Tribune Book Review (December 31), p. 5.]
[Source: MHRA Annual Bibliography (1950-1952), No. 9381.]

1952

FELHEIM, MARVIN. [Incorrect attribution.] 1952.B33 is correctly attributed in the present bibliography to Fred W. Lorch. The 1952 MLA Bibliography incorrectly attributes it to Marvin Felheim, author of an article which immediately precedes the Lorch article in New England Quarterly, XXV (September, 1952). The incorrect attribution is also in Beebe and Feaster (1968), p. 100.

1953

PAUL, RODMAN. "Introduction," Roughing It. New York: Rinehart, pp. iii-xvi.
[Source: Tenth Printing, 1966.] A biographical and critical account of the background and perspective shaping RI. "This text omits the last eighteen chapters and the three appendixes of the original edition.... The omitted chapters and appendixes occupy 147 of the original 591 pages."

1955

*ASSELINEAU, ROGER. [Review: Jerry Allen, The Adventures of Mark Twain (1954.A1).] Études Anglaises, IX, 281.
[Source: MHRA Annual Bibliography (1955-1956), No. 8005.]

*SCHÖNFELDER, KARL-HEINZ. [Review: Jerry Allen, The Adventures of Mark Twain (1954.A1).] Zeitschrift für Anglistik und Amerikanistik, III, 490-91.
[Source: MHRA Annual Bibliography (1955-1956), No. 8005.]

1956

*CADY, E. H., FREDERICK J. HOFFMAN, and ROY HARVEY PEARCE. "Notes on Reading Huckleberry Finn, in The Growth of American Literature (New York), I, 856-58. [Publisher not named in source.]
[Source: Blair (1960.A1), p. 425.]

*JONES, HOWARD MUMFORD. The Frontier in American Fiction: Four Lectures on the Relationship of Landscape to Literature. Jerusalem: Magness Press. [On Cooper, MT, Cather.]
[Source: MLA Bibliography (1957), No. 4137.]

*ROMM, A. C. Rannie Iumoristitseskie Raskazi Marka Tvena (K Voprosyo Iumore Tvena.) Utsenie Zapiku Leningradskogo Pedagogitseskogo Instituta, m. 18: Fakultet Iazika i Literatury, 1956, vp. 5, str. 125-39. [Various Humorous Short Stories by Mark Twain (About Problems of Twain's Humor). Scholarly Publications of the Leningrad Pedagogical Institute, Vol. XVIII: Department of Language and Literature, 1956, No. 5, pp. 125-39.]
[Source: MHRA Annual Bibliography (1955-1956), No. 8039.]

1957

*CAMPBELL, WALTER STANLEY, ed. Life on the Mississippi. With Introduction. New York: Sagamore Press.
[Source: MLA Bibliography (1957), No. 4590.]

NEVIUS, BLAKE. [Review: Henry Nash Smith and Frederick Anderson, eds., Mark Twain of the "Enterprise" (1957.A5).] Nineteenth-Century Fiction, XII (September), 164-66.
Most of this newspaper material is of little value, although the compilation is useful for showing the difference between "Sam. L. Clemens," the political reporter, and "Mark Twain," and for casting light on MT's sudden departure from Nevada in May, 1864. "For the most part the humor has evaporated, along with the personalities and conditions at which it was aimed. What remains, happily, is the local color, admittedly less distinct than in Roughing It, but also less subject to embroidery."

1958

*FREDDI, GIOVANNI. Mark Twain. Brescia: La Scuola.
[Source: MLA Bibliography (1959), No. 4953.]

*MARX, LEO. "The Vernacular Tradition in American Literature: Walt Whitman and Mark Twain," Die neueren Sprachen, pp. 46-57.
[Source: MLA Bibliography (1959), No. 5150.]

1959

*EGRI, PÉTER. "Mark Twain ifjusági regenyei." [Mark Twain's Novels for Young People.] Filológia Közlöny, V, 198-208.
[Source: MHRA Annual Bibliography (1962), No. 5664.]

ELLIOTT, GEORGE P. "Afterword: A Game of Truth," in The Adventures of Huckleberry Finn. New York: New American Library (A Signet Classic), pp. 284-88.
Like TS, HF is "a game," but motives are different: the questions are serious ones, and, as in the "trash" episode in Chapter XV, Huck learns human truths.

_____. "Afterword: Vacation into Boyhood," The Adventures of Tom Sawyer. New York: New American Library (A Signet Classic), pp. 220-24.
Treats TS as a vacation escape from sex, work, tedium, and money, and an escape to MT's style and unpretentiousness. [The text has been silently altered, beginning on the first page, where Aunt Polly asks, "What's wrong with that boy, I wonder?"]

*FRIED, MARTIN B. "Mark Twain in Buffalo," Niagara Frontier, V (Winter), 89-110.
[Source: MLA Bibliography (1959), No. 4954.]

*HAMSUN, KNUT Drei Amerikaner: Mark Twain, Ralph Waldo Emerson, Walt Whitman--Essays. München: Albert Langen, Georg Müller. [German translation of an essay on MT published in a Norwegian periodical in 1885; the other two were in Hamsun's first book, 1888.]
[Source: MLA Bibliography (1961), No. 5190.]

HUGHES, LANGSTON. [Introduction.] Pudd'nhead Wilson. New York: Bantam Books.
"In this book the basic theme is slavery, seriously treated, and its main thread concerns the absurdity of man-made differentials, whether of caste or 'race.' The word race might properly be placed in quotes for both of Twain's central Negroes are largely white in blood and physiognomy, slaves only by circumstance..." but "Mark Twain, in his presentation of Negroes as human beings, stands head and shoulders above the other Southern writers of his times, even such distinguished ones as Joel Chandler Harris, F. Hopkins Smith [sic], and Thomas Nelson Page."

*SCHMIDT-HIDDING, WOLFGANG. Sieben Meister des literarischen Humors in England und Amerika. Heidelberg: Quelle und Meyer. [Chaucer, Shakespeare, Fielding, Sterne, Lamb, Dickens, MT.]
[Source: MLA Bibliography (1961), No. 2371.]

*SMITH, HENRY NASH, ed. Roughing It. With Introduction. New York: Harper.
[Source: MLA Bibliography (1959), No. 4976.]

1960

*DAVIS, CURTIS CARROLL. "His Name Was Diomed," Virginia Cavalcade, X, ii (1960), 42-47.
[Source: MLA Bibliography (1960), No. 5430.]

*MARX, LEO. "The Vernacular Tradition in American Literature," Die neueren Sprachen, Beiheft 3, n.d. 46-57. Reviewed by *HANS BUNGERT in Archiv für d. Studien der neueren Sprachen (Herrig), CXCVI, 342.
[Source: MHRA Annual Bibliography (1960), Nos. 1318, 4811.]

NEIDER, CHARLES. "Introduction," A Connecticut
Yankee in King Arthur's Court. New York: Hill
and Wang, pp. ix-xii.
    Neider's brief introduction notes MT's "humani-
tarianism and savage satire."

1961

BRANCH, EDGAR M. [Review: Walter Blair, Mark
Twain & Huck Finn (1960.A1).] Modern Language
Notes, LXXVI (June), 562-64.
    Blair provides a useful record of influences on
the writing of HF (including MT's personal life
at the time), but "the accumulation of sources
cannot replace the insight essential to a genuine
synthesis of meaning."

*HOWARD, LEON. [Review: Walter Blair, Mark Twain &
Huck Finn (1960.A1).] Western Folklore, XX,
136-37.
    [Source: MHRA Annual Bibliography (1961),
No. 5262.]

KRIEGEL, LEONARD. "Afterword," Life on the Mississippi. New York: New American Library (A Signet
Classic), pp. 375-81.
    Kriegel ranks LOM with TS and HF "as one of the
indisputably great works in the Twain canon"; the
lack of structure is part of the appeal.

*LYNN, KENNETH S., ed. "Huckleberry Finn": Text,
Sources, and Criticism. New York: Harcourt,
Brace & World.
    [Source: MHRA Annual Bibliography (1961),
No. 5921.]

TANNER, TONY. "Samuel Clemens and the Progress of
a Stylistic Rebel," See 1962.B70.

*VANČURA, Z. [Review: Walter Blair, Mark Twain &
Huck Finn (1960.A1).] Časopis pro Moderní Filogii,
XLIII, 180.
    [Source: MHRA Annual Bibliography (1961),
No. 5262.]

1962

*ARVIN, NEWTON. [Introduction.] Adventures of
Huckleberry Finn. New York: Collier Books.
    [Source: MLA Bibliography (1962), No. 5468.]

*BEAVER, HAROLD. [Introduction.] Life on the Mis-
sissippi. London: Oxford University Press.
    [Source: MLA Bibliography (1962), No. 5471;
for review See 1963.B3.]

CLEMENS, SAMUEL L. Adventures of Huckleberry Finn:
A Facsmile of the First Edition. Introduction by
Hamlin Hill. San Francisco: Chandler Publishing
Company.
    With the original illustrations, this is an at-
tractive reading edition of HF. Hill's introduction provides a sound foundation for the reader
unfamiliar with HF; among the topics considered
are the course of composition, reputation, themes,
and structure of the book, and the character of
Huck in his role as narrator. Hill provides a
carefully-selected bibliography of books and articles for further reading; it is classified,

annotated where necessary, and far more useful
than the lists in many popular editions of HF.

*MARSHALL, PERCY. Masters of the English Novel.
London: Dennis Dobson. [Section on MT.]
    [Source: MLA Bibliography (1963), No. 2674.]

*REISS, EDMUND. [Foreword.] "The Mysterious
Stranger" and Other Stories. New York: New American Library.
    [Source: MLA Bibliography (1962), No. 5472.]

RUBIN, LOUIS. "The South and the Faraway Country,"
Virginia Quarterly Review, XXXVIII (Summer),
444-59.
    Treats MT in passing as "the prototype of the
Southern writers of our own time. Like them he
grew up in a tranquil, contained community, and
like them he was propelled by his art and his
times far beyond that community." Like MT, the
modern Southern writers symbolize the disintegration of the smalltown life before the forces of
the twentieth century.

*WAGENKNECHT, EDWARD. [Introduction.] The Innocents
Abroad. New York: Heritage Press.
    [Source: MLA Bibliography (1963), No. 5501.]

1963

*BUNGERT, HANS. [Review: Kenneth S. Lynn, Mark
Twain and Southwestern Humor (1959.A4).] Archiv
für d. Studium d. neueren Sprachen (Herrig), CC,
466-68.
    [Source: MHRA Annual Bibliography (1963),
No. 4734.]

CLEMENS, SAMUEL L. A Connecticut Yankee in King
Arthur's Court: A Facsimile of the First Edition.
San Francisco: Chandler Publishing Company. "Introduction," "A Note on the Text," and "Bibliography" by Hamlin Hill.
    This is the most interesting of the Chandler Fac-
simile Editions of MT's books, because of Dan
Beard's added satiric comments through his illustrations [and the likenesses of Sarah Bernhardt
(p. 38), Tennyson (pp. 41, 279), Edward, Prince of
Wales and the Emperor of Germany (p. 297), and Jay
Gould (p. 465).] Hill's bibliography is well selected and annotated to lead the student into a
fruitful investigation of the background and critical problems. His introduction gives the general
reader a good foundation for understanding the intentions, confusions, and achievements of MT in
this remarkable book.

*NEIDER, CHARLES, ed. The Complete Essays of Mark
Twain. With Introduction. Garden City, New York:
Doubleday.
    [Source: MLA Bibliography (1963), No. 5524.]

REISS, EDMUND. "Afterword," in A Connecticut Yankee
in King Arthur's Court. New York: New American
Library (A Signet Classic), pp. 321-31.
    In a sound discussion for the general reader
Reiss follows the major criticism, recognizing the
ambiguous nature of Hank Morgan and of the modern
benefits he brought to Arthurian England. "The
ambiguous presentation of good and evil leads to

(REISS, EDMUND)
Twain's major difficulty in the book," and, faced
with man's dual nature, "Twain never decides anything."

1964

*ARNOLD, ARMIN. "Friedrich Dürrenmatt und Mark
Twain: Zur Methode der vergleichenden Inter-
pretationen," in Jost, François, ed., Proceedings
of the IVth Congress of the International Comparative Literature Association, 1964. 2 vols. (The
Hague: Mouton), II: 1097-1104.
[Source: MLA Bibliography (1967), Nos. 64,
17544.]

1965

ANON. [Contemporary Newspaper Accounts.] Twainian, XXIV (January-February), 1-3.
Reprints 1895.B6 and 1895.B13, on MT lecturing
in Washington.

*ANON. [Review: Ralph Gregory, Mark Twain's First
America: Florida, Missouri, 1835-1840
(1965.A3).] Missouri Historical Review, LIX, 523.
[Source: MHRA Annual Bibliography (1965),
No. 6982.]

COHEN, RALPH, ed. The Adventures of Huckleberry
Finn. New York: Bantam Books.
Added matter for the student includes a critical discussion, "Games and Growing Up: a Key to
understanding Huckleberry Finn"; "Is Huckleberry
Finn a Great Novel? Opinions, Reviews, and Comments (reprints excerpts from 1939.B61; 1955.B29,
32); "Huckleberry Finn and The Catcher in the Rye
(reprints part of 1956.B30); "Mark Twain: A Biographical Sketch."

WILLOUGHBY, JOHN, ed. Life on the Mississippi.
New York: Airmont Publishing Company.
Willoughby's brief introduction is descriptive
and appreciative.

1966

ANON. [Brief Review: A. Grove Day, ed., Mark
Twain's Letters from Hawaii (1966.A3).] Nineteenth-Century Fiction, XXI (December), 302.
Brief description: Day's "editing" consists of
"an introduction rehearsing the contents of the
letters"; there are no notes or index.

*ANON. [Review: John Y. Simon, ed., "General Grant"
by Matthew Arnold, with a Rejoinder by Mark Twain
(1967.A18).] Lincoln Herald, LXVIII, 54.
[Source: MHRA Annual Bibliography (1966),
Nos. 5432, 7039.]

*ASPIZ, HAROLD. [Review: Robert Regan, Unpromising
Heroes: Mark Twain and His Characters (1966.A8);
Justin Kaplan, Mr. Clemens and Mark Twain
(1966.A6).] Studies in Scottish Literature, IV,
241-42.

[Source: MHRA Annual Bibliography (1967),
Nos. 7116, 7131. This review could not be located
in the copy of Studies in Scottish Literature, IV,
examined at Sir George Williams University.]

CLEMENS, SAMUEL L. The Adventures of Tom Sawyer,
ed. Robert D. Spector. New York: Bantam.
"The World of Tom Sawyer" (pp. 221-27) follows
the familiar critics, describing Tom as symbolic
of all boys, but individual and complex; follows
Blair's interpretation of the structure (1939.B7).
"The Making of Tom Sawyer" (pp. 228-36) includes
passages from MT's Autobiography and "Boy's Manuscript." "Tom's Readers and Critics" (pp. 238-42)
includes excerpts from Howells (1876.B6) and Kipling (1899.B19). "Islands of Good and Evil: Tom
Sawyer and Lord of the Flies" (pp. 243-45) contrasts idyllic and frightening views of nature.
"Mark Twain: A Biographical Sketch" (pp. 246-49)
is conventional, helpful to the reader unfamiliar
with MT, but very brief.

*ELLIS, ALLAN B., and F. ANDRÉ FAVAT. "From Computer
to Criticism: An Application of Automatic Content
Analysis to Literature, pp. 628-38 in The General
Inquirer: A Computer Approach to Content Analy-
sis, eds. Philip J. Stone, Dexter C. Dunphy, Mar-
shall S. Smith, and Daniel M. Ogilvie (Cambridge,
Mass.: MIT).
[Source: MLA Bibliography (1966), No. 4678.]

FIEDLER, LESLIE A. "Afterword," The Innocents
Abroad. New York: New American Library (A Signet
Classic), pp. 477-92.
Provides a context for IA through an extensive
and perceptive examination of popular travel writing of the nineteenth century, with attention to
the interests and prejudices of the travelers,
most of them Anglo-Saxon Protestants; also, considers the use of travel in developing perspective
toward one's own country.

*WAGENKNECHT, EDWARD. [Introduction.] A Tramp
Abroad. New York: Heritage.
[Source: MLA Bibliography (1967), No. 9389.]

1967

BABCOCK, C. MERTON. "Mark Twain's Adventures in
Art," Art in America, LV (March-April), 66-71.
For the general reader, a summary of MT's comments on art, with a mock-serious discussion of
his sketches, which, "clearly in a class by themselves, had the power of soliciting comments previously unheard in temples of art." Illustrated
with 21 drawings by MT.

*DURAM, JOHN M., Jr. "Mark Twain Comments on Reli-
gious Hypocrisy," Revista de Letras da Faculdade
de Filosofia Ciencias e Letras de Assis, X, 60-75.
[Source: MLA Bibliography (1970), No. 6772.]

*KAPLAN, JUSTIN. [Review: Hamlin Hill, ed., Mark
Twain's Letters to His Publishers (1967.A6);
Franklin R. Rogers, ed., Mark Twain's Satires &
Burlesques (1967.A7).] Book Week/World, March 5,
p. 4.

(*KAPLAN, JUSTIN)
[Source: MHRA Annual Bibliography (1967), Nos. 7112, 7135. The attribution is unclear, but is probably to the Washington Post Book World, in which Kaplan published another review in 1973 (See p. 405, below.]

*LEFCOURT, CHARLES R. "Dürrenmatt's Güllen and Twain's Hadleyburg: The Corruption of Two Towns," Revue des Langues Vivantes (Bruxelles), XXXIII, 303-308.
[Source: MHRA Annual Bibliography (1967), No. 7123; MLA Bibliography (1967), No. 17549.]

*SMITH, HENRY NASH. "The Morals of Power: Business Enterprise as a Theme in Mid-Nineteenth-Century American Fiction," in Clarence Gohdes, ed., Essays on American Literature in Honor of Jay B. Hubbell (Durham, N.C.: Duke University Press), pp. 90-107. [On GA and The House of the Seven Gables.]
[Source: MLA Bibliography (1967), Nos. 105, 9052.]

*WILLIAMS, PHILIP. "Huckleberry Finn and the Dialectic of History," Essays and Studies in English Language and Literature (Tohoku Gakuin University, Sendai, Japan), 51-52, pp. 59-98.
[Source: MLA Bibliography (1971), No. 8016.]

1968

*ANDERSON, FREDERICK. "Hazards of Photographic Sources," Center for Editions of American Authors Newsletter (MLA), I, 5.
[Source: MLA Bibliography (1968), No. 10260.]

* ____. "Overlapping Texts," Center for Editions of American Authors Newsletter (MLA), I, 6-7.
[On MS. Source: MLA Bibliography (1968), No. 10261.]

*BAETZHOLD, HOWARD. "An Emendation in A Connecticut Yankee," Center for Editions of American Authors Newsletter (MLA), I, 10.
[Source: MLA Bibliography (1968), No. 10263.]

*BURRISON, JOHN A. "The Golden Arm": The Folk Tale and Its Literary Use by Mark Twain and Joel C. Harris. (Research Paper 19). Atlanta: Georgia State University.
[Source: MLA Bibliography (1970), No. 6763.]

*CLEMENS, SAMUEL L. "An Unpublished Letter: Mark Twain to Chatto & Windus, 25 July 1897," Center for Editions of American Authors Newsletter (MLA), I, 1.
[Source: MLA Bibliography (1968), No. 10305. See Hart, James D., 1969, p. 402, below.]

____. Pudd'nhead Wilson and Those Extraordinary Twins, Facsimile of the First Edition, with Introduction, Note on Text, and Bibliography by Frederick Anderson. San Francisco: Chandler Publishing Company.
Drawing on his close familiarity with the scholarship and on the rich resources of the Mark Twain Papers, Anderson describes the backgrounds and composition of GA and the associated Those Extraordinary Twins, and the critical reception they

received; he discusses their relation to MT's concern with the problem of identity and his conflicting attitudes toward the South. The brief bibliography is annotated and chosen for its appropriateness to this particular book. The reader will appreciate the clear type and illustrations of the original edition.

* ____. Tom Sawyer and Huckleberry Finn. Introduction by Andrew Sinclair and Notes by Michael Lerner. London: Pan. (Best-Sellers of Literature).
[Source: MHRA Annual Bibliography (1968), No. 7777.]

*CRIŞAN, CONSTANTIN. [Introduction.] "Viaţa lui Mark Twain" [The Life of Mark Twain], in Mark Twain, Aventurile lui Tom Sawyer [The Adventures of Tom Sawyer]. Bucuresti: Editura timeretuli, pp. 5-15.
[Source: MHRA Annual Bibliography (1968), No. 7718.]

*DAVIDSON, LOREN K. "The Darnell-Watson Feud," Duquesne Review, XIII, 76-95.
[Source: MLA Bibliography (1969), No. 6462.]

LINDEMAN, JACK, ed. The Conflict of Convictions: American Writers Report the Civil War. A Selection and Arrangement from the Journals, Correspondence and Articles of the Major Men and Women of Letters Who Lived through the War. Philadelphia: Chilton.
Listed in one of the major bibliographies, this is simply an anthology containing MT's "The Private History of a Campaign that Failed."

*REST, JAIME. "Huckleberry Finn como Innovación en la Técnica Narrativa," in Actas de las Terceras Jornadas de Investigación de la Historia y Literatura Rioplatense y de los Estados Unidos. Mendoza (Argentina): Universidad Nacional de Cuyo, pp. 257-62.
[Source: MLA Bibliography (1971), No. 8003.]

*YOSHIDA, HIROSHIGE. "Huckleberry Finn ko," Eigo Seinen [The Rising Generation] (Tokyo), CXIV, 84-86.
[Source: MLA Bibliography (1970), No. 6816.]

1969

*ANDERSON, FREDERICK. "Team Proofreading: Some Problems," Center for Editions of American Authors Newsletter (MLA), II, 15. [On MT Papers.]
[Source: MLA Bibliography (1969), No. 6448.]

ANON. [Review: Justin Kaplan, ed., Mark Twain: A Profile (1967.A12).] Civil War History, XV, 86. Only a brief mention.

*DMITRIEV, V. G. Pod Chuzim Imenem (Under Another's Name). Moscow: Nauka.
[Source: MHRA Annual Bibliography (1969), No. 7939.]

*DOUGHTY, NANELIA S. "Realistic Characterization in Postbellum Fiction," Negro American Literature Forum, III, 57-62, 68.
[Source: MLA Bibliography (1969), No. 6418.]

FELHEIM, MARVIN. "Introduction," The Gilded Age. New York: New American Library (A Signet Classic), pp. vii-xviii.

A sound general discussion of the backgrounds of MT's and Warner's composition of GA, and their satiric portrait of the age.

GERBER, JOHN C. "Mark Twain's Search for Identity," in Max F. Schulz, William D. Templeman, and Charles R. Metzger, eds., Essays in American and English Literature. Presented to Bruce Robert McElderry, Jr. (Athens, Ohio: Ohio University Press), pp. 27-47.

MT's inner contradictions are revealed in the variety of forms in which he signed his name, in his dress, in his cheerfulness and melancholy; he was torn by an ambivalence of decorum and rebellion, of admiration for the rich and great, and his native democracy. "On reflection it almost seems as though there were two consciousnesses at work in Twain, one constantly sensing personal opportunity, the other constantly sensing human need and aspiration. Ultimately, however, MT's "search for identity was the search of every thoughtful man, and his failures were the failures of his age--and ours."

*GOTO, AKIO. "Seijuku no Kyozetsu--M. Twain no Amerikateki Seikaku," Eigo Seinen [The Rising Generation] (Tokyo), CXV, 286-87. [Rejection of Maturity--MT's American character.]

[Source: MLA Bibliography (1970), No. 6783.]

*HART, JAMES D. "On an 'Unpublished Letter' by Mark Twain," Center for Editions of American Authors Newsletter (MLA), II, 15.

[Source: MLA Bibliography (1969), No. 6475; reference is to an entry for 1968 (See p. 401, above).]

KOHLI, RAJ K. "Isabel Archer and Huck Finn": Two Responses to the Fruit of Knowledge," in Sujit Mukherjee and D. V. K. Raghavacharyulu, eds., Indian Essays in American Literature: Papers in Honour of Robert E. Spiller (Bombay: Popular Prakashan), pp. 167-78.

[Source: MLA International Bibliography (1969), Nos. 82, 6666.] See 1968.B60.

*ODESSKY, MARJORY H. "The Impartial Friend: The Death of Mark Twain," Journal of Historical Studies, II, 159-60.

[Source: MLA Bibliography (1969), No. 6484.]

*PLESSNER, MONIKA. "Huckleberry Finns wirkliches Ende," Frankfurter Hefte, XXIV, 441-46.

[Source: MLA Bibliography (1969), No. 6486.]

SELBY, PAUL OWEN. Theses on Mark Twain, 1910-1967. Kirksville, Missouri: Missouriana Library, Northeast Missouri State College.

A letter from Dr. Selby says this is based on the replies to his requests for data from the graduate institutions where the theses were written.

*TALBOTT, LINDA H. "Huck Finn: Mark Twain at Midstream," Nassau Review (Nassau Community College), I, v, 44-60.

[Source: MLA Bibliography (1969), No. 6496.]

1970

*ANON. "A Certain Private Letter--Author's Reading," Yankee (November), pp. 126-31.

[Source: Quoted by Charles R. Duke (1974); See p. 406, below.] An 1887 letter from a young man to his fiancée describes MT at a reading with Hale, Aldrich, Howells, Higginson, Holmes, and Longfellow.

*BOWEN, JAMES K., and RICHARD VAN DER BEETS, eds. Adventures of Huckleberry Finn. Glenview, Illinois: Scott, Foresman. [Includes Edgar M. Branch, "Mark Twain Scholarship: Two Decades."]

[Source: MLA Bibliography (1970), No. 6759.]

*BUDD, LOUIS J. "Baxter's Hog: The Right Mascot for an Editor (with CEAA Standards) of Mark Twain's Political and Social Writings," Center for Editions of American Authors Newsletter (MLA), III, 3-10.

[Source: MLA Bibliography (1970), No. 6762.]

_____. [Review: Walter Blair, ed., Mark Twain's Hannibal, Huck & Tom (1969.A3); William M. Gibson, ed., Mark Twain's "Mysterious Stranger" Manuscripts (1969.A4); Lewis Leary, ed., Mark Twain's Correspondence with Henry Huttleston Rogers (1969.A2).] South Atlantic Quarterly, LXIX (Winter), 164-65.

A brief review, describing the books and praising the editing.

*CLEMENS, SAMUEL L. "Mark Twain to Chatto & Windus: Two Unpublished Letters," Center for Editions of American Authors Newsletter (MLA), III, 1-2.

[Source: MLA Bibliography (1970), No. 6794.]

*ENGLISH TEACHERS' ASSOCIATION OF NEW SOUTH WALES. Reading and Teaching the Novel. Ashfield, New South Wales: English Teachers' Association of New South Wales.

[Source: MHRA Annual Bibliography (1970), Nos. 2502, 8239.]

*LEARY, LEWIS. "Mark Twain among the Malefactors," in Brom Weber, ed., Sense and Sensibility in Twentieth-Century Writing: A Gathering in Memory of William Van O'Connor (Carbondale and Edwardsville: Southern Illinois University Press; London: Feffer & Simons), pp. 109-17.

Extensively revised from 1968.B62. On MT in his last years, enjoying the luxuries of a millionaire in the company of Henry H. Rogers and Andrew Carnegie; in turn, being seen with MT improved their public image. The Brooks "reasoned explanation of what Clemens had allowed to be done to the genius of Mark Twain...has needed only small revision in the almost fifty years since it was first made. Like many of his countrymen, before or since, Clemens did sell out."

*RAO, B. RAMACHANDRA. "Structural Devices in The Adventures of Huckleberry Finn," Banasthali Patrika, XIV, 23-29.

[Source: MLA Bibliography (1971), No. 8001.]

*SHEPPERSON, WILBUR S. Restless Strangers: Nevada's Immigrants and Their Interpretors. Reno: Nevada University Press.
[Source: MHRA Annual Bibliography (1972), Nos. 6425, 8745.]

*SHULTS, DONALD. "On The Gilded Age," Kyushu American Literature (Fukuoka, Japan), XII, 1-13.
[Source: MLA Bibliography (1970), No. 6805.]

*TOWERS, TOM H. "Mark Twain's Connecticut Yankee: The Trouble in Camelot," in Ray B. Browne, Larry N. Landrum, and William K. Bottorff, eds., Challenges in American Culture. (Bowling Green, Ohio: Bowling Green University Popular Press), pp. 190-98.
[Source: MLA Bibliography (1971), Nos. 58, 8015.]

1971

*ATCHITY, KENNETH JOHN. [Review: Arturo Serrano-Plaja, "Magic" Realism in Cervantes (1970.B77).] Western Humanities Review, XXV, 182-83.
[Source: MHRA Annual Bibliography (1971), No. 8881.]

BAETZHOLD, HOWARD. [Review Article.] Modern Fiction Studies, XVII (Winter), 645-49.
Maxwell Geismar's Mark Twain: An American Prophet (1970.A5) providing some insights, is marred by misstatements and the caustic tone. Mary Ellen Goad's The Image and the Woman in the Life of Mark Twain (1971.B28) needs modification in some specific arguments, but provides the foundation for "a much more accurate assessment of the role of women in Mark Twain's life and works than we heretofore have had." Lewis Leary's Southern Excursions (1971.A4) is a pleasure to read for the style alone, and "Mark Twain and the Comic Spirit" is "still one of the best brief introductions to Mark Twain. 'Mark Twain's Wound: Standing with Reluctant Feet' is also an exceptionally good summary of the Van Wyck Brooks-Bernard DeVoto controversy."

*BONAZZI, ROBERT. [Review: Maxwell Geismar, Mark Twain: An American Prophet (1970.A5).] Southwest Review, LVI, 202-206.
[Source: MHRA Annual Bibliography (1971), No. 8840.]

COX, JOHN F. "On the Naming of Huckleberry Finn," Publications of the Modern Language Association, LXXXVI (October), 1038.
A brief letter to the editor in response to Colwell (1971.B13): "The boy was a 'hick' who loved to have 'fun,' or a 'fun hick.' The transposition of letters would not have been all that difficult."

DETWEILER, ROBERT. "Articulate Scholarship," South Atlantic Bulletin, XXXVI (March), 60-62.
A review, primarily descriptive, of Allison Ensor's Mark Twain and the Bible (1969.A5), as "well-structured and clearly written.... The subject of Twain and the Bible is worth precisely the size and kind of book that Ensor has provided."

*DURAM, JAMES C. "Mark Twain and the Middle Ages," Wichita State University Bulletin, XLVII, iii, 3-16.
[Source: MLA Bibliography (1974), No. 9603.]

EBY, E. H. [Review: Howard G. Baetzhold, Mark Twain and John Bull: The British Connection (1970.A1).] Pacific Northwest Quarterly, LXII, 156-57.
[Source: MHRA Annual Bibliography (1972), No. 8687.]

*HAUCK, RICHARD BOYD. "The Prisoner at the Window: Mark Twain," in his A Cheerful Nihilism: Confidence and "The Absurd" in American Humorous Fiction (Bloomington, London: Indiana University Press), pp. 133-66.
Treats ambiguity of meaning in CY (MT's "masterpiece of the absurd"), IA, RI, HF, and shows that the late works demonstrate a belief "that the imagination to create meaning in a meaningless universe was not one of man's gifts"; certainly, it had not been a gift of Huck Finn or Hank Morgan. In CY, MT used the satirist's shifting points of view, but he also satirized the perception process that makes satire possible--thereby experimenting in the comedy of the absurd. "The process is emblemized by Hank Morgan's analysis of his conscience."

*JUSTUS, JAMES H. [Review: Thomas Blues, Mark Twain & The Community (1970.A2).] Indiana Magazine of History, LXVII, 84-85.
[Source: MHRA Annual Bibliography (1971), No. 8819.]

*LANINA, T. [Afterword to Russian translation of TS and HF.] Moscow: Detskaya Literatura.
[Source: MHRA Annual Bibliography (1971), No. 8850.

*LO-JOHANSSON, IVAR. "Mark Twains Resa i Sverige" [Mark Twain's Swedish Journey]. Böckernas Värld, VI, No. 5, 49-54.
[Source: MHRA Annual Bibliography (1971), No. 8852.]

*RIGAUX, JACQUES. Ces Écrivains-Vagabonds: Borrow, Twain, Kipling, London, Cendrars, Stevenson, Conan Doyle, Hemingway, Leurs Vies, Leurs Oeuvres. Liège: Editions Jalis.
[Source: MHRA Annual Bibliography (1971), Nos. 6746, 8872.]

*ROBINSON, VIRGINIA P. "The Double Soul: Mark Twain and Otto Rank," Journal of the Otto Rank Association, VI, 32-53.
[Source: MLA Bibliography (1971), No. 8005.]

*SAWEY, ORLAN. "The Consistency of the Character of Nigger Jim in Huckleberry Finn," TAIUS (Texas A&I), IV, 35-41.
[Source: MLA Bibliography (1974), No. 9641.]

*TOMISCH, JOHN. A Genteel Endeavor: American Culture and Politics in the Gilded Age. Palo Alto, California: Stanford University Press.
[Source: MHRA Annual Bibliography (1971), No. 6481; (1972, with name spelled "Tomsich"), Nos. 6450, 8749.]

*WILCOX, EARL. "Jake and Bob and Huck and Tom: Hemingway's Use of Huck Finn," in Matthew J. Bruccoli and C. E. Frazer Clark, eds., Fitzgerald/ Hemingway Annual, 1971 (Washington, D.C.: NCR Microcard Editions), pp. 322-24.

In Chapter II of The Sun Also Rises, Jake Barnes and Robert Cohn are juxtaposed as realist and romantic, like Huck and Tom; Barnes observes that Cohn believes too much in the books he has read. There is a verbal parallel to Huck's opening statement on TS in Barnes's comment on Cohn's reading of a W. H. Hudson book: "You understand me, he made some reservations, but on the whole the book to him was sound." Hemingway's chapter reflects both a major theme in HF and his own respect for MT.

1972

BABCOCK, C. MERTON. [Review: John S. Tuckey, ed., Mark Twain's "Which Was the Dream?" and Other Symbolic Writings of the Later Years (1967.A8).] Etc.: A Review of General Semantics, XXIX (March), 101-103.

Largely descriptive; praises the editing.

BAZERMAN, CHARLES. "Toward the End, an Effete Snob," Nation, CCXV (September 18), 215-16.

A review, chiefly descriptive, of Frederick Anderson, ed., A Pen Warmed-Up in Hell: Mark Twain in Protest (1972.A4); defends the polemics of the late years: "Directness and clarity are achievements, whether or not we are pleased with our portraits."

BLUEFARB, SAM. "Huckleberry Finn: Escape from Conscience and the Discovery of the Heart," in his The Escape Motif in the American Novel: Mark Twain to Richard Wright (Columbus: Ohio State University Press), pp. 12-24.

HF is "the first modern American novel in which the theme is dominant," anticipating later novels is the genre in "violence, the difference between the uses of rhetoric and the contrasting realities, conscious and unconscious hypocrisy, gratuitous cruelty...but in amounts that may seem immodest or overplayed when we compare the work with the novels that follow it."

*CHELIDZE, V. [Introductory article to Georgian translation of TS and HF.] Tbilisi: Sabchota Sakartvelo.

[Source: MHRA Annual Bibliography (1972), No. 8697.]

CLEMENS, SAMUEL L. Roughing It. With an Introduction and Explanatory Notes by Franklin R. Rogers. Text Established and Textual Notes by Paul Baender. Berkeley, Los Angeles, London. Published for the Iowa Center for Textual Studies by the University of California Press. A CEAA approved text.

*COLEMAN, ALEXANDER. "Notes on Borges and American Literature," Tri-Quarterly, XXV, 356-77.

[Source: MHRA Annual Bibliography (1973), Nos. 2260, 8700.]

*GIDNEY, JAMES B. [Review: Maxwell Geismar, Mark Twain: An American Prophet (1970.A5).] Ohioana Quarterly, XV:1, 29-31.

[Source: MHRA Annual Bibliography (1972), No. 8712.]

*JEFFERSON, DOUGLAS W. "Mark Twain: Adventures of Huckleberry Finn," in Hans-Joachim Lang, ed., Der amerikanische Roman: Von den Anfang bis zur Gegenwart (Düsseldorf: August Bagel), pp. 142-67.

[Source: MLA Bibliography (1973), Nos. 132, 8864.]

*LIBMAN, Z. [Introductory article to Ukrainian translation of stories and pamphlets.] Kiev: Dnipro.

[Source: MHRA Annual Bibliography (1972), No. 8729.]

McCARRY, CHARLES, and DAVID L. ARNOLD. "Yesterday Lingers along the Connecticut," National Geographic, CXLII (September), 334-68.

Includes a photograph of MT's Hartford home, p. 366.

*MOORE, RAYBURN S. [Review: Lewis Leary, Southern Excursions (1971.A4).] Georgia Review, XXVI (Summer), 237-40.

The essays on MT "offer considerable information in compact form...gracefully marshal materials on important topics [and] provide valuable critical insights into problems old and new." Leary "has provided information, insight, and understanding sufficient to satisfy the interest he has aroused."

*ORLOVA, R. [Afterword to Kornei Chukovsky's translation of TS.] Kaliningrad: Knizhnoe Izdatel'stvo.

[Source: MHRA Annual Bibliography (1972), No. 8736.]

*OVERLAND, ORM. [Review: Walter Blair, ed., Mark Twain's Hannibal, Huck & Tom (1969.A3); William M. Gibson, ed., Mark Twain's "Mysterious Stranger" Manuscripts (1969.A4); Lewis Leary, ed., Mark Twain's Correspondence with Henry Huttleston Rogers (1969.A2).] English Studies (Amsterdam), LIII, 372-74.

[Source: MHRA Annual Bibliography (1972), Nos. 8690, 8714, 8726.]

TERRY, CLIFFORD. [Review: Frederick Anderson, ed., A Pen Warmed-Up in Hell: Mark Twain in Protest (1972.A4).] Book World (Chicago Tribune), June 4, p. 8.

[Source: MHRA Annual Bibliography (1972), No. 8682.]

1973

*AGRAWAL, I. N. "Mark Twain's Visit to Allahabad," Indian Journal of American Studies, III, i, 104-108.

[Source: MLA Bibliography (1974), No. 9587. Abstract in 1974 MLA Abstracts.]

*ANON. "Mark Twain's Last Manuscript," Bancroftiana (Berkeley), LV (June), 9.

[Source: MLA Bibliography (1973), No. 8877.]

CARDWELL, GUY A. "Mark Twain, James R. Osgood, and Those 'Suppressed' Passages," New England Quarterly, XLVI (June), 163-88.

(CARDWELL, GUY A.)

Chapter XLVIII of LOM was not dropped out of consideration for Southern readers, as has been suggested, but because the book was becoming too long. That this and some of the other portions removed are more interesting than some that remained "is almost surely indicative of nothing more than slapdash editing."

*CATE, HOLLIS L. "Two American Bumpkins," Research Studies (Washington State University), XLI, 61-63.
[Source: MLA Bibliography (1973), No. 8911.]

*COHEN, EDWARD H. "The Return to St. Petersburg," Iowa English Bulletin: Yearbook, XXIII, 50-55.
[Source: MLA Bibliography (1973), No. 8845.]

*ENANG, S. D. "The Deceptive Simplicity of Mark Twain's Novels," Horizon (Ibadan), IX, 55-61.
[Source: MLA Bibliography (1973), No. 8850.]

*FREESE, PETER. "Adventures of Huckleberry Finn und The Catcher in the Rye: exemplarischen Deutung der Romananfänge," Die Neueren Sprachen (LLBA), XXII, 658-68.
[Source: MLA Bibliography (1974), No. 9606.]

GASTON, GEORG MERI-AKRI. "The Function of Tom Sawyer in Huckleberry Finn," Mississippi Quarterly, XXVII (Winter), 33-39.
"Tom, a true child of his society, is capable of terrible selfishness and cruelty," and serves as a foil in the portrayal of Huck's moral development. Abstract by Gaston in 1974 MLA Abstracts, No. 9608.

*GEISMAR, MAXWELL. Mark Twain: An American Prophet. New York: McGraw-Hill.
Geismar's own abridgement of 1970.A5. Source: MLA Bibliography (1974), No. 9609.

*HANSEN, CHADWICK. "There Warn't No Home Like a Raft Floating Down the Mississippi, or Like a Raft Floating Down the Neckar, or Like a Balloon Ballooning Across the Sahara: Mark Twain as Improviser," in Stanley Weintraub and Philip Young, eds., Directions in Literary Criticism: Contemporary Approaches to Literature. Festschrift for Henry W. Sams (University Park and London: Pennsylvania State University Press), pp. 160-67.
[Source: MLA Bibliography (1973), Nos. 64, 8859.]

*KAPLAN, JUSTIN. "Never the Twain," Washington Post Book World (July 29), pp. 2-3.
[Source: Bray, 1974; See p. 405, below.] A review of Hamlin Hill, Mark Twain: God's Fool (1973.A5), which Kaplan calls "moralistic and even hostile," too "preoccupied with the obvious aspects of aging--escalating narcissism coupled with physical and psychic degeneration."

*KARITA, MOTOJI. "Mark Twain Mikan no Isaku," Eigo Seinen [The Rising Generation] (Tokyo), CXIX, 462-64. [MT's Unfinished Piece.]
[Source: MLA Bibliography (1973), No. 8867.]

*LANG, H. JACK. "Mark Twain A.L.S. More Valuable than Lincoln," Manuscripts, XXV, 187-91.
[Source: MLA Bibliography (1973), No. 8874.]

*MAURANGES, J.-P. "Aliénation et Châtiment chez Mark Twain et Heinrich Böll," Revue des Langues Vivantes (Bruxelles), XXXIX, 131-36.
[Source: MLA Bibliography (1974), No. 9630.]

ROEMER, KENNETH M. "The Yankee(s) in Noahville," American Literature, XLV (November), 434-37.
Franklin H. North's The Awakening of Noahville (1898) is "an obvious attempt to rewrite" CY, which it resembles not only in plot and characters, but even in specific illustrations. North's Yankees show his awareness of "the ingenuity, the power, the cruelty, and the ridiculousness of Twain's hero." Abstract by Roemer in 1973 MLA Abstracts, No. 9145.

*SCHÄFER, JÜRGEN. "Huckleberry, U.S.," English Studies, LIV, 334-35.
[Source: MLA Bibliography (1973), No. 8891.]

*SMITH, LAURA. "Fictive Names in Mark Twain's Pudd'nhead Wilson," pp. 91-94 in Fred Tarpley, ed., Love and Wrestling, Butch and O.K. (So. Central Names Inst. Pub. 2.) Commerce, Texas: Names Inst. P. [Order from ed. Dept. of Lit. and Lang., E. T. Station, Commerce, Texas 75428.]
[Source: MLA Bibliography (1973), Nos. 171, 8893.]

1974

*ANON. "The Appert Collection of Mark Twain," Bancroftiana (University of California, Berkeley), LVII (January), 5-6.
[Source: MLA Bibliography (1974), No. 9643. On new acquisition of letters, clippings, etc.]

*BANKS, R. JEFF. "Mark Twain: Detective Story Writer. An Appreciation," Armchair Detective, VII, 176-77.
[Source: MLA Bibliography (1974), No. 9588.]

BEAVER, HAROLD. "Run, Nigger, Run: Adventures of Huckleberry Finn as a Fugitive Slave Narrative," Journal of American Studies, VIII (December), 339-61.
Jim is an adult and a slave, and his situation is not Huck's: "If young Huck is taken in by that river-born camaraderie between black and white on a Mississippi raft, it does not follow that his friend (and victim) was equally taken in."

BERGER, SIDNEY. "New Mark Twain Items," Papers of the Bibliographical Society of America, LXVIII (July-September), 331-35.
Chatto & Windus correspondence reveals that the first English edition of PW was based on serial publication in the Century Magazine; "The variants in it, then, have no authority--a fact which greatly reduces my work" [as editor of the CEAA edition of PW]. Abstract by Berger in 1974 MLA Abstracts, No. 9591.

BRAY, ROBERT. "Mark Twain Biography: Entering a New Phase," Midwest Quarterly, XV (Spring), 286-301.
On the depiction of MT by Paine, Brooks, DeVoto, Howells, more recently by Justin Kaplan, and now

(BRAY, ROBERT)
by Hamlin Hill; who has "superbly" corrected the portrayal of MT's last years fabricated by Paine and Clara Clemens. The debunking is well documented and prepares the way for a new interpretation of MT and his works. Lengthy abstract in AES, XVIII (June, 1975), 3294.

*BROGAN, HOWARD O. "Early Experience and Scientific Determinism in Twain and Hardy," Mosaic: A Journal for the Comparative Study of Literature and Ideas, VII, iii, 99-105.
  [Source: MLA Bibliography (1974), No. 9595. Abstract by Brogan in 1974 MLA Abstracts, No. 9595.]

BURG, DAVID F. "Another View of Huckleberry Finn," Nineteenth-Century Fiction, XXIX (December), 299-319.
  The ending of HF is not the failure described in "largely moralistic interpretations which argue its shortcomings"; on the contrary, "it constitutes both a valid formal completion of the novel and an emphatic declaration of the author's metaphysics." HF "is, in fact, a revolutionary novel. It dispels the conventional morality and the conventional wisdom of its own time and ours. And in its joining of a vision of life's absurdity with a circular structure, Huckleberry Finn comprehends and manifests the essence of literary modernity." Huck "is the first absurd hero in our literature, and his story is the prototype of the American novel of black humor." Abstract by Burg in 1974 MLA Abstracts, No. 9597.

CROWLEY, JOHN W. "The Sacerdotal Cult and the Sealskin Coat: W. D. Howells in My Mark Twain," English Language Notes, XI (June), 287-92.
  "All of My Mark Twain may be regarded as a tale in the Southwestern humor tradition in which the antics of a 'vernacular hero' (Mark Twain) are related by a self-consciously distanced 'genteel narrator' (Howells).... Howells as narrator betrays divided feelings toward his vernacular hero," and with his own Midwestern background was not wholly at ease in Boston. The disastrous Whittier Birthday Dinner address is discussed at length.

DAVID, BEVERLY R. "The Pictorial Huck Finn: Mark Twain and His Illustrator, E. W. Kemble," American Quarterly, XXVI (October), 331-51.
  Reprints 20 illustrations from HF, including the mutilated p. 283 cut and the replacement that was tipped in. Concerned with potential sales, MT was attentive to the book's illustration, making it "a tool that converted the cruelty and sexuality of the story into a series of boyish adventures." Abstract by David in 1974 MLA Abstracts, No. 9599.

*DELANEY, PAUL. "The Avatars of The Mysterious Stranger: Mark Twain's Images of Christ," Christianity and Literature, XXIV, i, 25-38.
  [Source: MLA Bibliography (1974), No. 9600.]

DUKE, CHARLES R. "Mark Twain: Speaker at Large," English Record (New York State English Council), XXV (Spring), 43-52.
  A general discussion of MT as lecturer, based largely on Paine, Lorch, and other familiar

sources; also, quotes the description of an 1887 MT reading in Boston from a private letter published in Yankee (November, 1970; See p. 402, above).

HENDERSON, HARRY B., III. "Twain: The Varieties of History and A Connecticut Yankee," in his Versions of the Past: The Historical Imagination in American Fiction (New York: Oxford University Press), pp. 175-97.
  CY is "perhaps the most magnificent failure of all American historical fiction," and "as a progressive historical novel...terribly divided against itself." Henderson attributes the confusion of CY to a lack of control by MT. There is also a briefer discussion of P&P and JA.

*HSU, C. Y. "Mark Twain and the Chinese," Asian Student, XVI (March), 6-7.
  [Source: MLA Bibliography (1974), No. 9615.]

*KAMEI, SHUNSUKE. "Mark Twain no Ie," [Mark Twain's House], Eigo Seinen [The Rising Generation] (Tokyo), CXIX, 738-39.
  [Source: MLA Bibliography (1974), No. 9617.]

KETTERER, DAVID. "Epoch-Eclipse and Apocalypse: 'Special Effects' in A Connecticut Yankee," Chapter IX (pp. 213-32) in his New Worlds for Old: The Apocalyptic Imagination, Science Fiction, and American Literature (Bloomington and London: Indiana University Press).
  This previously appeared in Publications of the Modern Language Association (1973.B31).

*KLASS, PHILIP. "An Innocent in Time: Mark Twain in King Arthur's Court," Extrapolation, XVI, 17-32.
  [Source: MLA Bibliography (1974), No. 9620.]

KRAUTH, LELAND. "Mark Twain: At Home in the Gilded Age," Georgia Review, XXVIII (Spring), 105-13.
  "Domesticity was the key to Twain's identity, and it became a touchstone within his fiction"; it is "the heart of The Gilded Age," where in effect corruption is sanctioned for the sake of home and family. Abstract by Krauth in 1974 MLA Abstracts, No. 9621.

*LEE, L. L. "Mark Twain's Assayer: Some Other Versions," Markham Review, IV, 47-48.
  [Source: MLA Bibliography (1974), No. 9624; abstract by Lee in 1974 MLA Abstracts.]

*LIVINGSTON, JAMES L. "Names in Mark Twain's The Mysterious Stranger," American Notes and Queries, XII, 108-109.
  [Source: MLA Bibliography (1974), No. 9625.]

McELRATH, JOSEPH R., Jr. "Mark Twain's America and the Protestant Work Ethic," CEA Critic, XXXVI (March), 42-43.
  In CY, Hank Morgan hitched the pillar saint, St. Simeon Stylites, to a sewing-machine; thus, MT reveals his view of the work ethic as part of the American national character.

*MANIERRE, WILLIAM R. "Contemporary Relevance of Huckleberry Finn," pp. 77-94 in Klaus Lanzinger, ed., Americana Austriaca: Beiträge zur Amerikakunde. Band 3. Wien und Stuttgart: Braumüller.
  [Source: MLA Bibliography (1974), Nos. 102, 9629.]

PAULY, THOMAS H. "'The Science of Piloting' in Twain's 'Old Times': The Cub's Lesson on Industrialization," Arizona Quarterly, XXX, 229-38.

On the increasingly complex understanding of the age of industrialization gained by MT's narrator. Abstract by Pauly in 1974 MLA Abstracts, No. 9636.

*ROHDE, REGITZE. "St. St. Blicher og Mark Twain," in Felix Nørgaard, ed., Omkring Blicher 1974. Copenhagen: Gylendal, pp. 58-66.

[Source: MLA Bibliography (1974), No. 9639.]

*SCHUBERT, KARL. "Mark Twain: Adventures of Huckleberry Finn," in Edgar Lohner, ed., Der amerikanische Roman im 19. und 20. Jahrhundert (Berlin: Erich Schmidt), pp. 70-91.

[Source: MLA Bibliography (1974), Nos. 103, 9642.]

*TOWERS, TOM H. "Hateful Reality: The Failure of the Territory in Roughing It," Western American Literature, IX, 3-15.

[Source: MLA Bibliography (1974), No. 9644.]

*WEINTRAUB, RODELLE, ed. "Mental Telegraphy?: Mark Twain on G. B. S.," Shaw Review, XVIII, 68-70.

[Source: MLA Bibliography (1974), No. 8419.]

*WILSON, JAMES D. "Adventures of Huckleberry Finn: From Abstraction to Humanity," Southern Review, X (January), 80-94.

"The pragmatic Huck encounters a series of ideal codes of behavior" of the Widow Douglas, Tom Sawyer, his father, the Grangerfords, and Sherburn, "before discovering each one inadequate to meet the demands of his intuitive moral nature, his environment, and his companions." Ironically, in his personal life MT could put abstract intellectual concepts ahead of human needs, as in the painful destruction of his wife's religious faith. Abstract by Wilson in 1974 MLA Abstracts, No. 9647.

1975

ANDERSON, DAVID M. "A Mark Twain Practical Joke: An Unpublished Anecdote," Mark Twain Journal, XVIII (Winter), 20-21.

An apocryphal tale about MT on a train, heard at third hand in Finland.

CLEMENS, CYRIL. "Tributes to Mark Twain, by Sax Rohmer, Will Rogers, and W. Somerset Maugham," Mark Twain Journal, XVIII (Winter), outside back cover.

Rohmer briefly remembers meeting MT in London; Rogers and Maugham express conventional appreciation.

CLEMENS, SAMUEL L. [Letters to James Ross Clemens.] Mark Twain Journal, XVIII (Winter), front cover.

Brief notes to James Ross Clemens, January 12, 1903 and June 25 [1897], reproduced in facsimile.

HOY, JAMES F. "The Grangerford-Shepherdson Feud in Huckleberry Finn," Mark Twain Journal, XVIII (Winter), 19-20.

Stresses the importance of the names, which represent "wandering herders versus settled gardeners."

KESTERSON, DAVID B. "The Mark Twain-Josh Billings Friendship," Mark Twain Journal, XVIII (Winter), 5-9.

Both lectured for Redpath's bureau, and there were similarities of temperament, but MT was less outgoing toward his friend and seldom mentioned him--possibly out of professional jealousy.

MARTIN, WILLARD E., Jr. "Letters and Remarks by Mark Twain from the Boston Daily Journal," Mark Twain Journal, XVIII (Winter), 1-5.

Reprints with explanatory footnotes the text of a long letter on "A Rescue at Sea" by the Cunard steamship Batavia (February 7, 1873), on the Jubilee Singers (March 13, 1875), his Civil War experiences (news report, October 3, 1877, on his remarks at a banquet); a letter on money for the preservation of battle-flags (September 12, 1879); and his remarks on introducing Henry M. Stanley, the explorer, to a lecture audience (December 10, 1886).

MOTT, BERTRAM. "The Turn-of-the-Century Mark Twain: A Revisit," Mark Twain Journal, XVIII (Winter), 13-16.

On the several versions of The Mysterious Stranger, and on "The Man that Corrupted Hadleyburg" and What Is Man? "Though it is easy to overstate the case, surely there is copious evidence that the pessimism of the turn-of-the-century Mark Twain...has been somewhat exaggerated."

WEEKS, ROBERT P. "The Captain, the Prophet, and the King: A Possible Source for Twain's Dauphin," Mark Twain Journal, XVIII (Winter), 9-12.

The character in HF may be modeled on George J. Adams, whom MT mentioned in IA; he and the King had more in common than their rascality. There is a survey of attempts by other scholars to suggest models for the character, but some of the documentation is inconsistent and hard to follow.

WERGE, THOMAS. "The Sin of Hypocrisy in 'The Man that Corrupted Hadleyburg' and Inferno XXIII," Mark Twain Journal, XVIII (Winter), 17-18.

MT and Dante treat hypocrisy as a sin of fraud and incontinence, and both use "gilded lead as an image of hypocrisy," and "a pervasive tone and imagery of weight, weariness, and oppressiveness to dramatize the external and inner life of the hypocrite."

1976

BERGER, ARTHUR ASA. "Huck Finn as an Existential Hero: Making Sense of Absurdity," Mark Twain Journal, XVIII (Summer), 12-17.

Central to our national literature for its humor and use of the vernacular, HF is marked by its realism and by "absurdity and alienation and other existential concerns."

CLEMENS, CYRIL. "Two Presidents and the Journal," Mark Twain Journal, XVIII (Summer), back cover.

Facsimile reproductions of brief notes by Lyndon B. Johnson and Gerald R. Ford thanking Cyril Clemens for sending them his publications; both were vice-presidents when they wrote.

CLEMENS, SAMUEL L. "The Mammoth Cod," and Address to The Stomach Club, with an Introduction by G. Legman. Milwaukee: Maledicta: 25 pages.

The text of a bawdy poem and letter, apparently written to be read aloud during a 1902 cruise on Henry Rogers's yacht, the Kanawha; also includes the text of MT's eight-line poem, "A Weaver's Beam" (about "the Penis mightier than the Sword," now stilled by the impotence of old age) and "Some Remarks [sic] on the Science of Onanism" (See 1974.B11). The greater part of this book consists of an introduction by Gershon Legman, who traces the surviving record of MT's bawdy writings, suggesting that "perhaps the impotence that tormented Twain for so many decades was only the physical counterpart of his self-achieved literary castration, like that of his penultimate image on the subject: the spoutless teapot." Legman argues, however, that "it may be suspected that Twain's much-lamented impotence was in part imaginary, as were some of the other masochistic and hypochondriacal complaints that made him take to his bed and wear only white daytime clothing." Legman's psychological discussion and bibliographical information will be of considerable interest to the students of this aspect of MT.

EVANS, ELIZABETH. "Thomas Wolfe: Some Echoes from Mark Twain," Mark Twain Journal, XVIII (Summer), 5-6.

Documents statements by Wolfe showing that he had read MT. "It is not unexpected then to find echoes from Mark Twain in Wolfe. Even though the proof of the echoes rests in similarities, those similarities are strong." The evidence here adduced is subjective.

FELLOWS, LAWRENCE. "Sketch of Huck Finn Returning to Twain's Home," New York Times (January 19).

The original E. W. Kemble drawing of Huck holding a dead rabbit has been donated to the Mark Twain Memorial in Hartford by Lessing Whitford Williams, whose sister had received it as a gift from MT when she was a baby.

GAYLIN, WILLARD. "Two Routes to Unselfish Behavior. From Twain to Freud: an Examination of Conscience," Hastings Center Report (Institute of Society, Ethics, and the Life Sciences), VI (August), 5-8.

Chiefly on the broader topic of conscience, but opens with an example from HF, when Huck sees the King and Duke ridden on a rail. "The words that Twain uses in an attempt to dissect the emotions of conscience are enormously sophisticated and not redundant. They are the words that only a student of conscience, or an intuitive genius,

would have used: 'ornery,' 'humble,' and 'to blame.'" ["Willard Gaylin, M.D., is President of the Institute, a practicing psychiatrist, and professor of psychiatry and law at Columbia University. This article is adapted from his book, Caring, to be published in October by Alfred A. Knopf, Inc."]

GREGORY, RALPH. "Joseph P. Ament--Master-Printer to Sam Clemens," Mark Twain Journal, XVIII (Summer), 1-4.

On the owner of the Hannibal Courier and for a time Samuel Clemens's employer; includes useful documentation.

ISLER, CARL. "Mark Twain's Style," Mark Twain Journal, XVIII (Summer), 18-19.

Primarily on TS Abroad and HF, briefly commenting on dialogue and contrasting personalities. In discussing point of view, states incorrectly that "Tom Sawyer is told by Tom."

KEETCH, BRENT. "Mark Twain's Literary Sport," Mark Twain Journal, XVIII (Summer), 7-10.

"The purpose of this paper is to advance the view that Huck Finn has a fully logical structure that enhances the theme of a boy's quest for freedom." The title of this essay is derived from a misreading of Henry Nash Smith (in p. 72 of 1965.B 1965.B79); Smith calls HF "a literary sport," in the sense that it does not belong to any literary tradition, has "no connections with the past, no history." Misunderstanding the sense in which Smith used the word, Keetch refers to "the literary sport played by Twain" (p. 7) and concludes: "Such sport as this evokes the laughter of the gods" (p. 10).

KRAVEC, MAUREEN T. "Huckleberry Finn's Aristocratic Ancestry," Mark Twain Journal, XVIII (Summer), 19-20.

"One of the most subtle instruments of semantic irony concern's Huck's surname," which may be linked with the Fin MacCool of James MacPherson's "Ossian" forgeries; the root "fiona" means "white" or "fair." MT has shown "the pernicious effect of a culturally-imposed notion of nobility upon natural mankind," though Pap is evidence that Huck's natural nobility was not hereditary; moreover, the Ossian poems were fabrications.

SHUTT, RANDALL, ed. "Of Mark Twain and Hannibal," Mark Twain Journal, XVIII (Summer), 21.

Excerpts from the unpublished memoirs of Wallace Bruce Amsbary, actor and Chautauqua lecturer; Amsbary remembered a world like that described in TS, but never met MT.

Index

A

B

Boer War, 1930.B5; 1948.B44
Boeser, Linda, 1965.B12
Boggan, J. R., 1964.B18
Bok, Edward, 1921.B3
Boland, Sally, 1968.B15
Böll, Heinrich, 1973.B37
Bologna, Sando, 1960.B14
Bolton, Sarah H., 1887.B2
Bombay Gazette, 1968.B95
Bompiani, 1949.B5
Bonazzi, Robert, 1972.B14
Book of Mormon, 1971.B14
Boomkamp, Leeuwen, 1958.B7
Booth, Bradford A., 1947.B6-7; 1950.B7; 1954.B6;
    1965.B13
Booth, Edwin, 1910.B135
Booth, Wayne C., 1961.B9
Borderland, 1964.B15
Borges, Jorge Luis, 1935.B18
Borrow, George, 1935.B69
Borst, Charles V. S., 1964.B19
Borzi, Professor, 1907.B31
Bosc, R., 1919.B6
Boston, 1949.B8
Boston Advertiser, 1949.B43
Boston Ancient and Honorable Artillery Company,
    1954.B12
Boston Congregational Club, 1946.B5
Boston Herald, 1955.B49; 1957.B31
Boston Transcript, 1873.B9; 1879.B3; 1909.B6;
    1949.B43; 1968.B25
Bostwick, Arthur E., 1939.B10
Boucicault, Dion, 1969.B50
Bourget, Paul, 1895.B3, B18; 1957.B44
Bourne, Randolph, 1969.B76
Bowden, Edwin T., 1961.B10
Bowen, Edwin W., 1916.B2
Bowen, William, 1938.A3; 1941.A3; 1943.B27
Bowser, David Watt, 1940.B4; 1960.B24, B57;
    1963.B81
Boyesen, Hjalmar Hjorth, 1881.B5; 1964.B82
Boynton, Henry Walcott, 1903.B11
Boynton, Percy H., 1919.B7; 1920.B10; 1924.B11;
    1932.B6; 1933.B8
Boy Scouts of America, 1970.B20
Brack, O. M., Jr., 1972.B16
Bradford, Gamaliel, 1920.B11; 1922.B10; 1924.B11;
    1933.B9
Bradbury, Malcolm, 1969.B11
Bradley, 1919.B15
Bradley, James, 1944.B40, B44
Bradley, Sculley, 1953.B38; 1961.A2, B21; 1962.A2;
    1964.B37
Bragman, Louis J., 1925.B9
Branch, Edgar Marquess, 1942.A3, B10; 1946.B4;
    1950.A4, B8; 1957.B12; 1958.B37; 1966.B18;
    1967.B14-16; 1969.A1, B12; 1972.A3; 1975.B4
    Works, Reviewed: The Literary Apprenticeship
    of Mark Twain (1950), 1950.B4, B28, B39, B51,
    B55, B60; 1951.B39, B49, B51
    Clemens of the "Call" (1969), 1969.B55;
    1970.B63
Brand, John M., 1972.B17
Brandl, Alois, 1925.B10
Brashear, Minnie M., 1929.B5; 1930.B3; 1934.A1;
    1936.B5; 1939.B11; 1959.A1; 1964.B13; 1966.A1
    Works, Reviewed: Mark Twain: Son of Missouri
    (1934), 1934.B5-6, B11, B16; 1935.B5, B53
    The Art, Humor and Humanity of Mark Twain (Ed.,
    with Robert M. Rodney, 1959), 1959.B50;
    1960.B62; 1961.B30

Bratcher, James T., 1964.B20
Brereton, Austin, 1908.B6
Brett, Reginald, 1944.B29
Briden, E. F., 1974.B6
Bridges, Horace James, 1919.B8; 1923.B7
Bridges, Robert, 1885.B15; 1959.B18
Bridgman, L. J., 1900.B20
Bridgman, Richard, 1960.B15; 1964.B21; 1966.B19
    Works, Reviewed: The Colloquial Style in
    America (1966), 1967.B20, B58
Briggs, John Ely, 1929.B6
Bright, John, 1934.B19
Brinegar, Claude S., 1963.B11
Brittain, Sir Harry, 1961.B11
Broadley, A. M., 1910.B72
Brodin, Pierre, 1948.B4
Brodwin, Stanley, 1972.B18; 1973.B3-4
Brogunier, Joseph, 1972.B19
Bronson, Daniel Ross, 1972.B20
Bronson, Walter C., 1900.B21
Brookings, Robert, 1937.B17
Brooklyn Public Library, 1935.B31
Brooks, Cleanth, 1955.B10
Brooks, Gladys, 1961.B2
Brooks, Noah, 1898.B19-20; 1899.B11
Brooks, Roger L., 1962.B11
Brooks, Sydney, 1907.B18-19; 1910.B71
Brooks, Van Wyck, 1919.B12; 1920.A1, B12-15, B21;
    1921.B17; 1923.B8, B12, B24, B32; 1924.B11,
    B32; 1925.B38; 1927.B8; 1929.B10, B38; 1930.B10;
    1932.A2, B4, B10, B15, B21, B34; 1933.A1, B17,
    B24, B28; 1935.B18, B20, B73; 1936.B47;
    1937.B19; 1938.B39; 1939.B16; 1940.B9; 1941.B1;
    1942.B38; 1943.B46; 1944.B1, B33; 1945.B35;
    1946.B17; 1947.B8; 1948.B35; 1949.B31; 1952.B7,
    B28, B47; 1954.B7; 1955.B14; 1957.B13; 1960.B13,
    B44, B73; 1963.B34, B54, B66; 1965.B14; 1968.B80,
    B101; 1969.B76; 1970.B26
    Works, Reviewed: The Ordeal of Mark Twain
    (1920; revised 1932), 1920.B2, B5, B7, B33;
    1921.B4; 1922.B2; 1923.B19; 1925.B25; 1933.B6,
    B22, B25; 1934.B4, B20
Brown, Clarence A., 1964.B22; 1968.B16
Brown, Deming B., 1954.B8; 1962.B12
Brown, George Rothwell, 1908.B11; 1930.B4
Brown, Glenora W., 1954.B8
Brown, John, 1967.B102
Brown, Maurice, 1966.B20
Brown, Robert, 1883.B7
Brown, Spencer, 1967.B17
Brown, Sterling, 1937.B7
Brown, Thomas P., 1944.A2
Browne, Charles Farrar. See "Artemus Ward"
Browne, John Ross, 1974.A5
Browne, Ray B., 1961.B12; 1965.B15; 1970.A3
Browne, Sir Thomas, 1910.B118
Brownell, Frances V., 1955.B11
Brownell, George Hiram (Unsigned material in
    Twainian is here attributed to him as Editor),
    1925.B11; 1932.B7; 1933.B10-13; 1934.B7;
    1936.A1; 1937.B8; 1939.B12-22; 1940.B10-30;
    1941.B9; 1942.A3, B8-19, B26; 1943.B6-23;
    1944.B6-23, B36, B43; 1945.B6-18, B51;
    1946.B5-16, B38; 1947.B9-20; 1948.B5-15;
    1949.B6-16, B43; 1950.B9-11, B20; 1953.B17;
    1954.B17; 1957.B14; 1960.B16; 1962.B13, B24;
    1972.B31
Browning, Robert, 1911.B5; 1934.A3; 1935.B67;
    1939.B54; 1967.B102
Brumm, Ursula, 1962.B14; 1972.B21
Bruneau, Jean, 1955.B12

Cather, Katherine Dunlap, 1925.B12
Cather, Willa, 1959.B8; 1963.B5; 1966.B47, B58;
  1973.B8
Cecil, L. Moffitt, 1969.B17
Century Company, 1923.B17
Century Magazine, 1912.B28; 1917.B1; 1945.B29, B31;
  1955.B39; 1968.B73
Cervantes, Miguel de, 1922.B25; 1932.B23; 1938.B35;
  1941.B26; 1947.B34; 1952.B39, B41; 1961.B73;
  1970.B77; 1972.B45
Cestre, Charles, 1926.B3; 1931.B9; 1945.B19
Ceylon Examiner, 1963.B67
Ceylon Observer, 1963.B67
Chamberlain, Thomas G., 1949.B10, B18, B22
Chambers, E. K., 1894.B6
Chambliss, Amy, 1970.B12
Chapin, Adèle le Bourgeois (Mrs. R. W. Chapin),
  1931.B10
Chapin, Christina, 1931.B10
Chapin, Henry B., 1963.B17-18
Chapin, Robert, 1948.B19
Chaplin, Charlie, 1962.B18
Chapman, Helen Post, 1928.B5
Chapman, John W., 1932.B12
Chaput, Donald, 1965.B19
Charbonnel, Avis Bliven, 1964.B28
Chard, Leslie F., II, 1964.B29
Charles, Ernest, 1910.B10
Charpentier, John, 1935.B21
Chase, Mary Ellen, 1933.B14
Chase, Richard, 1957.B20; 1963.B89; 1966.B74
Chase, Roy, 1939.B26; 1962.B46
Chatto and Windus, 1929.A1; 1939.B44; 1941.B12
Chaucer, Geoffrey, 1965.B42
Chellis, Barbara A., 1969.B18
Chenoweth, Mrs., 1917.B8; 1919.B14
Chester, Giraud, 1951.B17
Chesterton, Gilbert Keith, 1903.B7; 1910.B5, B77;
  1922.B24; 1930.A4; 1934.A2; 1949.B34
Chicago Daily News, 1939.B14, B20
Chicago Inter ocean, 1940.B13
Chicago Republican, 1940.B33; 1941.A2; 1942.B23;
  1943.A2, B11; 1949.B15
Chicago Tribune, 1875.B3; 1979.B3; 1944.B7;
  1947.B14
Childs, Marquis W., 1926.B4
Christian, Sheldon, 1967.B23
Christian, The, 1945.B4
Christian Science Monitor, 1955.B35; 1957.B32
Christian Union, 1944.B20
Christopher, J. R., 1972.B25
Chubb, Percival, 1910.A1; 1936.B10; 1943.B24
Chubb, Thomas Caldecott, 1936.B36
Church, Richard, 1967.A9
Church, Samuel Harden, 1974.B9
Churchill, Lady Randolph, 1943.B21
Churchill, Winston S., 1930.B5; 1944.B24, B28;
  1945.B26; 1946.B23; 1954.B41; 1961.B75
Cicero, 1924.B22
Cincinnati Commercial, 1876.B5
Cincinnati Evening Chronicle, 1943.B11
Claggett, Billy, 1957.B24
Clarion, The, 1921.B1
Clark, Champ, 1910.B32
Clark, Charles Heber (see "Adeler, Max")
Clark, Charles Hopkins, 1885.B16; 1938.B5
Clark, George Peirce, 1956.B8; 1958.B11-12
Clark, Harry Hayden, 1956.B9; 1959.B14; 1971.B11
Clark, William G., 1965.B20
Clarke, Edward J., 1936.B11
Clarke, Norman Ellsworth, 1941.A1

Clemens Family (General), 1888.B5; 1972.B24
Clemens, Clara, 1909.B3; 1910.B54; 1923.B9;
  1924.B14; 1926.A3; 1930.B6; 1931.A3, B11;
  1932.B19; 1936.B5; 1938.A3, B7; 1939.B47;
  1948.A2; 1949.B3, B10; 1950.B20; 1956.A1, B10,
  B17; 1959.B51; 1961.B66; 1962.B34; 1963.B23;
  1964.B28; 1966.B99; 1967.B43; 1973.B15
  Works, Reviewed: My Father, Mark Twain (1931),
  1931.B1, B24, B32; 1932.B2, B6, B17, B25
Clemens, Cyril, 1929.A1-2, B7-11, B16, B40;
  1930.B7; 1932.A1, B13; 1933.A2, B15; 1934.A2,
  B3, B8; 1935.A2-3, B11, B22-23, B48; 1936.B12;
  1937.B10; 1938.B8; 1939.A3, B8, B14, B27-28,
  B36-37; 1940.B22, B32-34; 1941.A2, B10-12;
  1942.A1, B8, B21-23, B44, B57; 1943.A2, B25,
  B27-28; 1944.B24-28, B46; 1945.B20-26; 1946.A5;
  1947.B22; 1948.B17; 1949.A1, B10, B18, B20-24;
  1950.A5, B13-16; 1951.B11, B18-21; 1952.B12;
  1953.A2, B9; 1954.B11; 1955.B13; 1956.B11;
  1957.A1, B21, B51; 1958.B13; 1959.B15;
  1960.B22; 1962.A4, B19; 1963.B5, B87; 1964.B30;
  1966.B26; 1967.A4; 1971.B12, B33; 1974.B17
  Works, Reviewed: Mark Twain The Letter Writer
  (1932), 1933.B5, B7
  Mark Twain Wit and Wisdom (1935), 1935.B3, B54,
  B56; 1937.B21
  My Cousin Mark Twain (1939), 1939.B1, B3, B11,
  B29, B37; 1940.B49
  Republican Letters (1941), 1942.B41; 1943.B26;
  1944.B39
  Young Sam Clemens (1942), 1943.B1, B44;
  1945.B44
Clemens, Florence, 1929.B21
Clemens, Henry, 1858.B1; 1889.B3; 1929.B32;
  1950.B40
Clemens, Dr. James Ross, 1929.B12-13; 1933.B16;
  1935.B11; 1938.B8; 1973.B9
Clemens, Jane, 1885.B7-8; 1925.B38; 1939.B16;
  1946.B21; 1948.B59; 1959.B15; 1964.A6, B39
Clemens, Jean, 1932.B19; 1936.B4; 1957.B41;
  1959.B51; 1965.B25; 1969.B60
Clemens, Jeremiah, 1947.B22
Clemens, John Marshall, 1946.B31; 1964.B58;
  1965.B44; 1968.B66; 1970.B15, B30
Clemens, Katharine, 1938.B8; 1944.B29; 1945.B28;
  1957.B22
Clemens, Langdon (photograph), 1936.B52
Clemens, M. E., 1963.B24
Clemens, Mildred Leo, 1917.B7
Clemens, Molly, 1917.B13; 1929.B27, B29, B32
Clemens, Olivia, 1897.B21; 1904.B7; 1918.B8;
  1919.B10; 1920.B1, B3, B16; 1922.B19; 1929.B10,
  B24; 1930.B20; 1932.B19, B21; 1933.B27;
  1935.A14, B19; 1936.B13; 1939.B32, B40;
  1945.B28; 1947.B25, B57; 1948.B6, B61; 1949.A2;
  1950.B35; 1952.B48; 1955.B4; 1956.B14; 1957.B26;
  1958.B10; 1959.B26, B51; 1960.B33; 1963.A7, B21,
  B24; 1967.B25, B29, B53, B67, B72, B87; 1969.B7;
  1970.A4; 1972.B8, B26; 1974.B21
Clemens, Orion, 1917.B2; 1928.A1; 1929.B6, B27-28,
  B30, B32-33, B40; 1940.B35; 1942.A3; 1944.B38;
  1946.B21; 1947.B36; 1949.B30; 1950.B9; 1954.B22;
  1961.A4, A15, B37; 1962.B38; 1970.B30; 1973.B39
Clemens, Pamela Goggin, 1935.B66; 1963.B24
  (also see Goggin, Pamelia [sic])
Clemens, Samuel L.
--Autographs, 1916.B8; 1956.B14; 1970.B35
--Birthday Dinners, 1902.B9; 1903.A1; 1922.B29;
  1925.B5; 1926.B17
--Birthplace, 1896.B1; 1919.B18; 1923.B2;
  1942.B51; 1960.B7

(Clemens, Samuel L.)
--(Works and Attributed Works)
 --(Poems)
   --"The Mysterious Chinaman," 1947.B15
   --"Ode To Stephen Dowling Botts," 1971.B33
   --"Tropic Chidings," 1884.B12; 1946.B9
   --"Ye Equinoctial Storm," 1884.B12; 1946.B9
 --The Prince and the Pauper, 1881.B3-5, B7;
    1882.B5-10; 1895.B9; 1898.B16; 1902.B14;
    1909.B8; 1910.A6, B46; 1913.B10; 1916.B9;
    1920.B28; 1925.B41; 1928.B14; 1935.B25;
    1938.A5; 1939.A6; 1941.B6; 1942.B54; 1948.B3,
    B45; 1949.B26; 1951.B21, B27; 1952.B36;
    1953.A4, B25; 1954.B5; 1955.B51; 1959.B12;
    1962.B15; 1963.B24, B29, B31; 1964.B7;
    1965.B38; 1966.A8, A10; 1968.B14, B36;
    1970.A2, B46, B49-50; 1971.B7, B19A; 1973.B11
    --Dramatization, 1890.B14; 1900.B34; 1911.B11;
      1925.B40; 1935.B39; 1937.B16, B24; 1938.B1;
      1959.B28; 1968.B56
 --"The Private History of a Campaign that Failed,"
    1926.B9; 1940.B25; 1941.B18; 1944.B44; 1945.B29,
    B31; 1948.B11; 1950.B5; 1954.B12; 1955.B23;
    1960.B30; 1966.B5; 1968.B59, B73; 1971.B55
 --"The Private History of the Jumping Frog Story,"
    1894.B7
 --"Private Theatricals." See "A Curtain Lecture
    Concerning Skating."
 --"Prof. Jenkins," 1945.B10-11
 --Pudd'nhead Wilson. See The Tragedy of
    Pudd'nhead Wilson.
 --"The Recent Carnival of Crime in Connecticut,"
    1882.B13
 --"The Reception at the President's," 1948.B13
 --"Reflections on Religion," 1963.B64; 1965.B41
 --"The Reliable Contraband," 1943.B13
 --"The Remarkable Sagacity of a Cat," 1950.B56
 --Republican Letters (Ed. Cyril Clemens),
    1942.B8; also see Clemens, Cyril, for reviews
 --"Review of Holiday Literature," 1962.B67
 --"The Revised Catechism," 1939.B18; 1944.B21;
    1945.B38; 1955.B50
 --"Riley - Newspaper Correspondent," 1946.B13
 --Roughing It, 1867.B2; 1872.B3-4, B13; 1893.B7,
    B10; 1901.B21; 1903.B9; 1915.B9; 1917.B7, B13;
    1927.B8; 1929.B14; 1937.A1; 1938.A2, B18, B28;
    1939.B51; 1941.B6; 1942.B40; 1943.B25, B35;
    1944.B25; 1945.B8, B47; 1947.A3, B44; 1948.B22,
    B31; 1950.B41, B45, B56; 1951.B24; 1953.B26;
    1954.B22; 1956.B18; 1957.B58; 1959.A4; 1960.A12,
    B6; 1961.A15, B20; 1962.A15, B11; 1963.B71, B88;
    1964.A3; 1966.B21, B67; 1967.B82; 1970.B57;
    1971.B7, B23, B29; 1972.A3; 1973.B39, B44;
    1974.B7, B27, B34; 1975.B3
 --"Running For Governor," 1962.B51
 --"Saint Joan of Arc," 1959.B41
 --[Sandwich Islands Letters], 1944.B36
 --"The Sanitary Ball," 1957.B52
 --[Savage Club, Description], 1925.B37
 --Screamers, 1872.B5, B8, B12
 --"Serious Wilkins" (Apocryphal), 1970.B25
 --Simon Wheeler, Detective, 1963.A4; 1964.B35,
    B47
 --"Sir Robert Smith of Camelot," 1886.B1-2;
    1961.B5
 --1601. See Conversation as it Was By the Social
    Fireside in the Time of the Tudors.
 --[Sketch in London World], 1877.B7; 1947.B55
 --Sketches, New and Old, 1875.B4; 1876.B1;
    1937.B6; 1943.B8; 1955.B9

--Slovenly Peter (Mark Twain's Translation of Dr.
   Heinrich Hoffman's Struwelpeter), 1935.A6,
   B13-14; 1936.B40; 1941.B29
--Snodgrass, Quintus Curtius. See Letters of
   Quintus Curtius Snodgrass (Apocryphal).
--Snodgrass, Thomas Jefferson. See Adventures of
   Thomas Jefferson Snodgrass.
--"Sociable Jimmy," 1943.B11
--"Some Rambling Notes of an Idle Excursion,"
   1910.B118
--"Some Thoughts on the Science of Onanism,"
   1936.B11; 1963.B25; 1974.B11
--"Soundings," 1949.B15
--The Stolen White Elephant, 1882.B10-15, B22;
   1899.B13; 1901.B10; 1945.B17
--Stomach Club Address. See "Some Thoughts on
   the Science of Onanism."
--"A Storm at Sea," 1949.B14, B43
--"Such as Mother Used to Make," 1973.B42
--The $30,000 Bequest, and Other Stories, 1907.B32
--Those Extraordinary Twins. (Also see The
   Tragedy of Pudd'nhead Wilson), 1942.B29;
   1948.B17; 1951.B60; 1970.B54; 1972.B69
--"3,000 Years Among the Microbes," 1918.B3;
   1970.B90; 1973.B36
--Tom Sawyer. See The Adventures of Tom Sawyer.
--Tom Sawyer Abroad, 1894.B3-6, B11; 1929.B3;
   1935.B45; 1942.B5; 1949.B38; 1966.B51, B72;
   1970.B20; 1972.B16; 1974.B4
--Tom Sawyer, Detective, 1897.B10-12; 1929.B4;
   1953.B27; 1959.B48
--"To the Person Sitting in Darkness," 1901.B2,
   B5, B9; 1947.B2
--"To the Reading Public," 1940.B26
--The Tragedy of Pudd'nhead Wilson (Also see
   Those Extraordinary Twins), 1894.B1-2, B9;
   1895.B10-12; 1902.B20; 1912.B11; 1936.B23;
   1941.B23; 1942.B29; 1952.B28; 1955.B21-22, B51;
   1956.B34-35; 1957.B20, B64-65; 1958.B20;
   1959.B17; 1960.B25, B42, B61; 1961.A10, B55;
   1962.A15, B53, B68; 1963.B17, B65, B89; 1964.A1,
   B31, B69, B87; 1965.B2, B16, B59, B70; 1966.A8,
   B51, B61, B74, B93; 1968.B38, B72, B107, B118;
   1969.B18, B50; 1970.B13, B48, B54, B82, B96;
   1971.A5, B15, B36; 1972.B1, B17, B29, B42, B69,
   B73-74; 1973.B3, B20, B22, B53; 1974.B4;
   1975.B2
--A Tramp Abroad, 1880.B3-7; 1883.B7; 1901.B23;
   1902.B15; 1903.B16; 1905.B14; 1922.B28; 1925.B41;
   1935.A11; 1945.B2, B17; 1952.B8; 1955.B46;
   1960.B110; 1964.B84; 1967.A15; 1969.B40;
   1970.B78, B92; 1973.B28, B52
--"Traveling with a Reformer," 1947.B36; 1948.B15
--"A True Story," 1971.B9
--"The Turning Point of My Life," 1969.B60
--"The United States of Lyncherdom," 1969.B70
--[Unsigned Newspaper Writing], 1972.B22
--"The War Prayer," 1965.B8; 1970.B29; 1975.B1
--"Washington Artillery Ball," 1946.B38
--"Weather" Epigram, 1939.B19; 1945.B6
--What Is Man? 1911.B1; 1913.B4-5; 1919.B2, B5,
   B7, B12, B17, B19; 1921.B15; 1934.B1; 1936.B39;
   1941.B6; 1942.B48; 1946.A1, B37; 1948.B28;
   1957.B43; 1959.B22; 1964.B31; 1968.B104;
   1970.B90; 1973.A2; 1974.B1
--"What Ought He to Have Done?" 1944.B20
--"Which Was the Dream?" 1967.A8
--Which Was It? 1971.B34; 1974.B28

Daily Hawaiian Herald, 1940.B16
Daily Resorter, 1970.B69
Daly, Augustin, 1942.B45; 1946.B12, B27
Dane, G. Ezra, 1937.A1; 1938.A2; 1940.A2
    Works, Reviewed: Letters From the Sandwich
    Islands (ed., 1937, 1938), 1938.B22; 1939.B24,
    B48, B52; 1940.B49
Danziger, Samuel, 1918.B6
Da Ponte, Durant, 1957.B26; 1959.B18
Darbee, Henry, 1958.A2; 1959.B19
Darió, Rubén, 1961.B73
Darrow, Clarence, 1968.B41
Darwin, Charles, 1899.B16; 1924.B36; 1933.B29;
    1945.B49; 1958.B20; 1962.B23; 1964.B31
Daudet, Alphonse, 1951.B3; 1964.B84
Daulton, Major Frank, 1917.B12
D'Avanzo, Mario L., 1972.B29
Davenport, Basil, 1939.B27, B34, B36, B43
Davidson, Levette J., 1952.B15
Davidson, Louis B., 1935.B27; 1936.B13
Davidson, William Earl, 1942.B27
Davis, Arthur Kyle, Jr., 1931.B12
Davis, Bob, 1941.B28
Davis, C. F., 1968.B66
Davis, Chester L. [Most of this material is un-
    signed, and here attributed to Davis as Editor
    of The Twainian], 1854.B19; 1899.B8; 1925.B11;
    1950.B18-20; 1951.B25-29; 1952.B16-19;
    1953.B15-19, B39; 1954.B13, B16-18, B20-24;
    1955.B16-19; 1956.B14, B16-17; 1957.B14,
    B27-34, B61; 1958.B22-29; 1959.B20-24;
    1960.B29-30; 1961.B21-23; 1962.B24, B30;
    1963.B11, B23-24; 1964.B34-40; 1965.B22-26,
    B93; 1966.B32-36, B99; 1967.B27-34, B71;
    1968.B25-29; 1969.B20; 1970.B18-21; 1971.B16-17;
    1972.B30-36; 1973.B1, B14-15, B58
Davis, Rev. John, 1948.B11
Davis, Sam, 1967.B35
Davis, Samuel P., 1944.A2
Day, A. Grove, 1966.A3, B37
    Works, Reviewed: Mark Twain's Letters From
    Hawaii (1966), 1966.B3, B7, B91; 1967.B85
Dean, Henry Clay, 1975.B1
Deane, The Rev. Canon Anthony, 1935.B28
Dearborn Independent, 1957.B14
DeCasseres, Benjamin, 1934.A3
Decaunes, Luc, 1950.B21
DeForest, John William, 1968.B10
Dekker, George, 1964.B41
de Laguna, Theodore, 1898.B21
de la Mare, Walter, 1929.B45; 1930.A4; 1963.B5
DeLaney, Wesley A., 1947.B9, B36; 1948.B22-23
De Leon, Daniel, 1905.B11
DeMott, Benjamin, 1966.B38; 1970.B22
Dennis, Larry R., 1967.B36
Denslow, Ray V., 1928.B1
Densmore, Gilbert S., 1923.B21
Denton, Lynn W., 1971.B18; 1974.B13
"De Quille, Dan" (pseud. Wright, William),
    1862.B1; 1880.B1; 1893.B8-10; 1910.B82;
    1911.B13; 1936.B17; 1946.B40; 1947.B43;
    1953.B2; 1965.B12
Derby, George Horatio: see "Phoenix, John"
De Schweinitz, George W., 1966.B39
De Voto, Bernard, 1929.B14; 1931.B13-15; 1932.A2,
    B15-17; 1933.A1, B2, B17, B25; 1935.B18,
    B29-30, B73; 1936.B14-16; 1937.B13; 1938.B9-10;
    1939.A7, B28, B33, B36-37; 1940.A1, B18, B35;
    1941.B13; 1942.A2, A4; 1944.B1, B33; 1945.B34;
    1946.A2, B19-22; 1947.B1-2, B26; 1948.B26, B35,
    B60; 1952.B20, B47; 1960.B27, B73; 1962.A6,

B24A, B33; 1964.B10; 1966.B56; 1970.B83, B89,
B94
    Works, Reviewed: Mark Twain's Letters From the
    Earth (Ed., 1962), 1962.B4, B71; 1963.B49, B52;
    1964.B52
    Mark Twain At Work (1942), 1942.B6, B21, B28,
    B36, B43, B55; 1943.B5, B38; 1946.B39
    Mark Twin in Eruption (Ed., 1940), 1940.B5, B39,
    B53-54; 1941.B14, B16-17, B19, B22
    Mark Twain's America (1932), 1932.B4, B10, B28,
    B33; 1933.B7-8, B14, B24, B28, B30; 1935.B16
Dias, Earl J., 1967.B37; 1970.A4
Dickens, Charles, 1934.B14; 1948.B6; 1953.B3;
    1957.B10; 1964.B54; 1965.B74; 1968.B40;
    1969.B25; 1970.B62; 1973.B40
Dickey, Marcus, 1922.B15
Dickie, J. F., 1910.B83
Dickinson, Anna, 1951.B17; 1952.B48
Dickinson, Asa Don, 1935.B31
Dickinson, Leon T., 1947.B5, B27-28; 1949.B26;
    1950.B22; 1951.B30; 1961.B23; 1965.B27;
    1966.B40-41; 1970.B23
Diederich, B., 1903.B8; 1905.B12; 1906.B8
Dilke, Sir Charles, 1967.B102
Dillingham, William R., 1964.B42
Dinan, John S., 1972.B37
Ditsky, John M., 1975.B5
Dixon, Elizabeth White, 1965.B28
Dobie, Frank, 1968.B109
Dodge, Mrs. Mary Elizabeth Mapes, 1972.B16
Dodge, Peter Mapes, 1897.B27
"Dogberry," 1954.B17
Dolch, Martin, 1964.B53
Donaldson, Scott, 1971.B19
Donner, Stanley T., 1947.B29; 1959.B25
Donovan, M. M., 1926.B5
Dos Passos, John, 1939.B38
Dostoyevsky, Fyodor, 1970.B77
Doten, Alf, 1899.B12; 1910.B51; 1956.B16
Doten, Mrs. Alf, 1956.B16
Doubleday, Neal Frank, 1960.A2
Doughty, Howard, Jr., 1951.B31
Douglas, Gilbert, 1934.B10
Douglas, Joe, 1951.B1
Douglas, Lloyd C., 1937.B14
Douglas, Robert, 1951.B32
Doumic, René, 1899.B13; 1901.B10
Doyle, Sir Arthur Conan, 1960.B110; 1971.B58;
    1972.B56
Doyle, Paul A., 1970.B24
Doyno, Victor A., 1968.B30
Drake, Eric, 1931.B16
Drake, Robert Y., Jr., 1960.B31
Dredd, Firmin, 1910.B84
Dreiser, Theodore, 1935.B32-33; 1956.B48; 1959.B26
Drew, John, 1922.B16
Drinkwater, John, 1934.A2
Drury, Wells, 1936.B17
Dryden, John, 1959.B12
Duckett, Margaret, 1964.A2; 1969.B21
    Works, Reviewed: Mark Twain and Bret Harte
    (1964), 1965.B13, B32, B46, B50; 1966.B29,
    B69, B76
Dudgeon, L. W., 1944.B32
Duffie, Myrtle M., 1964.B43
Duffy, Charles, 1942.B28; 1948.B24
Dugas, Gaile, 1947.B30
Dugmore, A. Radclyffe, 1909.B7
Duncan, Captain Charles, N.D.A3; 1867.B1; 1877.B1,
    B5; 1941.B10; 1952.B13; 1955.B42; 1964.B48
Duneka, Frederick A., 1952.B27; 1965.B24; 1968.A6

(Ferguson, DeLancey)
  1952.B21-22; 1954.B25; 1957.B39-40; 1959.B29;
  1960.B38-40; 1961.B26
    Works, Reviewed: Mark Twain: Man and Legend
    (1943), 1943.B32, B34, B37, B39, B44; 1944.B5;
    1946.B39
Ferris, George T., 1874.B8
Ferry, d'Odette, 1950.B21
Fetterley, Judith, 1971.B21; 1972.B40, B84;
  1973.B21
Feuchtwanger, Lion, 1963.B29
Field, Eugene, 1902.B8; 1954.B11
Field, Kate, 1900.B37; 1970.B47; 1974.B32
Fiedler, Leslie A., 1948.B27; 1955.B21; 1957.B20;
  1958.B30A-32; 1959.B30; 1960.B41-43; 1966.B45-46;
  1971.B22
Fielder, Elizabeth Davis, 1899.B14
Fielding, Henry, 1972.B45
Fields, Mrs. James T., 1904.B8; 1922.B18-19
Fifield, William, 1967.B43
Figaro, Le, 1895.B3
Figuera, Angela, 1961.B27
Filčev, Petăr, 1968.B36
Films on MT's Life and Works, 1930.B11;
  1940.B23; 1944.B4, B11; 1967.B61
Finger, Charles J., 1924.A3, B13; 1926.A3
Finlay, Frank, 1944.B22; 1947.B55
Finn, Frank, 1954.B30
Finnegans Wake, 1966.B24
Fischer, M., 1909.B9
Fischer, Walther, 1926.B6; 1935.B37; 1939.B42;
  1942.B31
Fishback, Margaret, 1936.B36
Fisher, Henry W., 1922.A2
    Works, Reviewed: Abroad with Mark Twain and
    Eugene Field (1922), 1922.B5-7, B26
Fisher, Marvin, 1972.B42
Fisher, Samuel J., 1923.B12
Fitch, George Hamlin, 1916.B3
Fitch, Thomas S., 1903.B9; 1919.B11; 1961.B59
Fitzgerald, F. Scott, 1923.B13; 1956.B41; 1960.B88;
  1963.B30; 1967.B99; 1969.B40; 1972.B19
Flack, Frank Morgan, 1942.B32-33; 1946.B27;
  1951.B36
Flagg, Charles Noël, 1897.B19; 1972.B30
Flagg, James Montgomery, 1946.B28; 1972.B32
Flanagan, John T., 1936.B21; 1961.B28
Fleck, Richard L., 1971.B23-24
Florence, Italy, 1932.B19; 1965.A4
Florida, Missouri, 1912.B19; 1919.B18; 1946.B3;
  1958.B28; 1965.A3
Flory, Claude R., 1964.B45
Flowers, Frank C., 1948.B28
Floyd, John B., 1931.B25
Flynt, Josiah, 1939.B47
"Folio, Tom," 1869.B5
Foner, Philip S., 1958.A4; 1961.A6; 1963.B15, B86
    Works, Reviewed: Mark Twain: Social Critic
    (1958), 1959.B25, B69
Foote, E. B., 1935.B38, B79
Foote, Mary Hallock, 1934.A3; 1935.B67; 1939.B54
Ford, James L., 1900.B25
Ford, Sewell, 1910.B121
Ford, Thomas W., 1955.B22
Forgues, Eugène, 1886.B3
Fortenberry, George, 1971.B25
Foss, Sam Walter, 1910.B129
Foster, Edward F., 1968.B37
Foster, William (Murder Case), 1873.B11; 1955.B55
Foulke, W. D., 1930.B19
Fraiberg, Louis, 1960.B44
France, Clemens J., 1901.B13

Franciosa, Massimo, 1951.B37
Francis, Raymond L., 1950.B30
Frank, Waldo, 1919.B12; 1933.B17; 1970.B83
Franklin, Benjamin, 1972.B29; 1974.B14
Franklin, H. Bruce, 1966.B48
Frantz, Ray W., Jr., 1956.B19; 1962.B31
Fraser, Horatio N., 1901.B11
Fraser, John, 1967.B44
Frazer, Laura Hawkins, 1899.B14; 1910.B81;
  1913.B1; 1918.B2; 1920.B4; 1925.B21; 1927.B15;
  1929.B2, B7; 1935.B25; 1965.B57; 1966.B32;
  1971.B16
Frear, Walter Francis, 1939.B13; 1940.B16;
  1942.B19; 1943.B17, B42; 1947.A3; 1971.B17;
  1972.B31
    Works, Reviewed: Mark Twain and Hawaii (1947),
    1948.B60; 1949.B35
Frederick, John T., 1969.B24
Fredonia, New York, 1964.B29
Freeman, Mary E. Wilkins, 1922.B24
Freeman, William H., 1894.B8; 1945.B9
Freimarck, John, 1968.B38
Fremersdorff, Ellen, 1947.B32
French, Bryant Morey, 1960.B45; 1964.B46; 1965.A2;
  1971.B25A; 1972.A5
    Works, Reviewed: Mark Twain and "The Gilded
    Age" (1965), 1965.B1, B63, B82; 1966.B49, B59,
    B76, B89
French, Mrs. Daniel Chester, 1928.B9
French, Warren, 1964.B47
Fried, Martin B., 1961.A7
Friedman, Robert P., 1961.B29
Friedrich, Gerhard, 1960.B46; 1961.B30; 1966.B49
Friedrich, John T., 1946.B29
Friedrich, Otto, 1959.B31
Frisbee, George S., 1934.B27
Frohman, Daniel, 1911.B7; 1935.B39; 1937.B16
Frost, Robert, 1963.B5
Frye, Northrop, 1972.B25
Fuller, Daniel J., 1973.B22
Fuller, Frank, 1956.B20; 1971.B16
Fuller, John G., 1942.B34
Fuller, Muriel, 1939.B43
Fuller, Thomas, 1892.B6
Fulton, Robert, 1914.B3
Fussell, E. S., 1952.B23; 1954.B26; 1970.B66

G

Gabriel, Ralph Henry, 1940.B37
Gabrilowitsch, Ossip, 1909.B3; 1938.B7; 1964.B28
Gaffney, W. G., 1966.B50
Gagnot, B., 1926.B3
Gaines, Clarence H., 1910.B88
Gaines, Ervin J., 1965.B32
Gaither, Rice, 1929.B18
Galaxy, 1870.B6; 1948.B13; 1961.A3
Gale, Robert L., 1963.B31; 1967.B45-46; 1973.A3
Gallagher, Charles J., 1943.B32
Galsworthy, John, 1930.A4; 1934.A2
Galton, Sir Francis, 1957.B65
Gandhi, 1943.B23
Gannon, William, 1932.B31
Ganzel, Dewey, 1962.B32-33; 1964.B48; 1965.B33-35;
  1967.B47; 1968.A1, B39
    Works, Reviewed: Mark Twain Abroad (1968),
    1968.B17, B51, B58; 1969.B28, B41, B56, B65;
    1970.B23

H

I

J

K

Kruse, Horst, 1966.B65; 1967.B69; 1969.B40;
    1970.A7; 1972.B39
Krutch, Joseph Wood, 1954.B34; 1960.B67
Kubicek, Earl C., 1965.B57
Kunde, Donald M., ed., 1967.A5
Kuprin, A. I., 1959.B64
Kuznetsov, A., 1959.B64
Kwest, Dr. Franz, 1922.B21
Kyne, Peter B., 1912.B23

L

Labadie-Lagrave, 1895.B3
Lacey, Alex, 1917.B12
LaCossitt, Henry, 1935.B46
La Cour, Tage, 1959.B48
Lafayette (Indiana) Daily Courier, 1957.B2
LaHood, Marvin I., 1966.B66
Laidlaw, R. P., 1968.B61
Laing, Dilys, 1958.B40
Laing, Nita, 1960.B68
Laird, James, 1951.B8
Lakin, R. D., 1961.B43
Lamond, Hammond, 1905.B18
Lampton, James, 1919.B22; 1955.B48
Lancaster, Charles, 1910.B102; 1967.B7
Landon, Melville D. ("Eli Perkins"), 1891.B10
Lane, Lauriat, Jr., 1955.B29; 1956.B33, B44
Lang, Andrew, 1885.B2; 1886.B4; 1888.B6; 1889.B4;
    1891.B11; 1907.B23-24; 1932.B22; 1946.B30
Langdon, Charles J., 1967.B72, B111; 1971.B16
Langdon, Jervis, 1892.B12; 1922.B8; 1935.A13;
    1938.A5, B11; 1947.B57; 1960.B33; 1965.B25;
    1966.B68
Langley, Dorothy, 1973.B35
Lanina, T., 1970.B49-50
Lans, Matthew Irving, 1900.B30
Lapidus, Deborah, 1973.B55
Lardner, Ring W., 1917.B4; 1960.B111; 1970.B17;
    1972.B4
Large Soviet Encyclopedia, 1960.B8
Lark, Charles T., 1965.B25; 1966.B68
Larom, Walter H., 1924.B15
Larowe, Nina, 1910.B48, B97
Laszowska, Jean Emily Gerard de, 1959.B5
Lautrec, Gabriel de, N.D.A4; 1900.A1, B13;
    1922.A3; 1935.B47
Laverty, Carroll D., 1947.B40
LaVigne, Gary W., 1961.B44
Law, Frederick Houk, 1926.B15
Lawrence, D. H., 1936.B24; 1964.B41
Lawrence, Mary Margaret, 1965.B58
Lawton, Mary, 1925.A2, B24; 1938.B29
    Works, Reviewed: A Lifetime With Mark Twain
    (1925), 1925.B4
Leacock, Stephen, 1922.B24; 1929.B45; 1932.A3;
    1933.B29; 1934.B14; 1935.A3, B48; 1936.B25;
    1970.B53
    Works, Reviewed: Mark Twain (1932), 1932.B3;
    1933.B6, B26
Leary, Daniel, 1970.B52
Leary, Katy, 1925.A2, B4, B24
Leary, Lewis, 1947.B41; 1948.B38-40; 1954.B35-36;
    1960.A6; 1961.A9, B45; 1962.A10; 1963.B52;
    1967.B111; 1968.B62-63; 1969.A2; 1970.B51-52;
    1971.A4, B37; 1974.B21, B21A
    Works, Reviewed: Mark Twain (1960), 1961.B3,
    B58

Mark Twain's Correspondence With Henry Huttleston
    Rogers (ed., 1969), 1969.B42, B44; 1970.B9, B11,
    B16, B74, B94
Mark Twain's Letters To Mary (ed., 1961),
    1961.B77
Southern Excursions (1971), 1972.B85
Lease, Benjamin, 1954.B37
Leathers, Jesse, 1932.B12
Leaver, Florence B., 1956.B34
Leavis, F. R., 1952.B28-29; 1956.B35; 1957.B20
Le Breton, Maurice, 1934.B15-16; 1935.B49; 1937.B22;
    1947.B42
Lecky, William Edward Hartpole, 1955.B18; 1962.B7,
    B65; 1964.B31; 1965.B99; 1973.B52
Lederer, Max, 1945.B46; 1946.B37
Lee, Alfred Pyle, 1938.A6
Lee, Charlotte I., 1967.B70
Lee, Francis Lightfoot, 1943.B15; 1944.B17, B43
Lee, Robert Edson, 1966.B67
Leeming, Thomas L., 1951.B4; 1966.B64
Legal Aid Society, 1942.B13
Le Gallienne, Richard, 1896.B9
Legate, David M., 1970.B53
Lehan, Richard, 1968.B64; 1969.B41; 1971.B38-39
Lehner, Gilbert, 1950.B44
Leisy, Ernest Edwin, 1924.B16; 1929.B26; 1933.B21;
    1937.B23; 1942.B18, B39; 1946.A4, B38; 1949.B35;
    1950.B39; 1952.B30-31; 1956.B36; 1957.B47;
    1961.A15; 1964.B13
    Works, Reviewed: The Letters of Quintus
    Curtius Snodgrass (Ed., 1946), 1947.B45, B50,
    B54
Leiter, Louis H., 1965.B59
LeMay, Alan, 1944.B3
Lemmon, Leonard, 1891.B9
Lemonnier, Léon, 1935.B50-52; 1937.A2; 1939.B50;
    1947.A4
    Works, Reviewed: La Jeunesse Aventureuse de
    Mark Twain (1937), 1937.B22
    Mark Twain (1947), 1947.B42
Lennon, E. James, 1953.B22; 1954.B38
Leslie, Elsie, 1890.B14; 1925.B40
Lessing, O. E., 1927.B9
Letter, The, 1960.A15
Lettis, Richard, 1962.A11
Leupp, Francis E., 1901.B20
Levering, Albert, 1903.B13
Levin, David, 1968.B65
Levy, Leo B., 1964.B68
Levy, M. S., 1899.B20
Lewis, C. B. ("M. Quad"), 1910.B121
Lewis, Dudley Payne, 1913.B17
Lewis, Merrill, 1966.B69
Lewis, Oscar, 1931.A4; 1947.A6, B43
Lewis, R. W., 1965.B60
Lewis, Sinclair, 1963.B5; 1972.B27
Lewis, Stuart, 1970.B54; 1972.B58
Lewisohn, Ludwig, 1932.B21
Light, Martin, 1974.B22
Likens, Mrs. J. W., 1874.B9
Liljegren, S[ten] B[odvar], 1945.A1; 1946.B39
    Works, Reviewed: The Revolt Against Romanticism
    in American Literature as Evidenced in the Works
    of Samuel L. Clemens (1945), 1946.B35, B46
Lillard, Richard S., 1942.B40; 1943.B35; 1944.B37;
    1948.B41; 1965.B61
Lindborg, Henry J., 1973.B36
Lindsay, Vachel, 1917.B9; 1935.B59
Linneman, William R., 1965.B62
Literary Guillotine, The, 1902.B27

M

N

O

P

Q

R

S

T

U

V

W

Y

Z